American Prisoners of War

Held at

Bermuda, Cape of Good Hope and Jamaica

During the War of 1812

Transcribed by
Harrison Scott Baker II

Society of the War of 1812
in the
State of Ohio

HERITAGE BOOKS
2007

HERITAGE BOOKS
AN IMPRINT OF HERITAGE BOOKS, INC.

Books, CDs, and more—Worldwide

For our listing of thousands of titles see our website
at
www.HeritageBooks.com

Published 2007 by
HERITAGE BOOKS, INC.
Publishing Division
65 East Main Street
Westminster, Maryland 21157-5026

Copyright © 2007 Society of the War of 1812 in the State of Ohio

Other Heritage Books by Harrison Scott Baker II:
American Prisoners of War Held at Halifax During the War of 1812, Volumes I and II
American Prisoners of War Held at Barbados, New Providence and Newfoundland During the War of 1812

All rights reserved. No part of this book may be reproduced or transmitted in any form or by any means, electronic or mechanical, including photocopying, recording or by any information storage and retrieval system without written permission from the author, except for the inclusion of brief quotations in a review.

International Standard Book Number: 978-0-7884-4499-9

- Table of Contents -

Introduction	ii
The Dead	v
Bermuda -	
Alphabetical listing of names	1
Numeric listing by prison number	143
Crew listing by ship	164
Americans on British ships	186
Service affiliation not known	187
United States Marines	188
Cape of Good Hope -	
Alphabetical listing of names	189
Numeric listing by prison number	205
Crew listing by ship	208
Americans on British ships	210
Service affiliation not known	211
United States Marines	212
Jamaica -	
Alphabetical listing of names	213
Numeric listing by prison number	295
Crew listing by ship	306
Americans on British ships	317
Service affiliation not known	318
United States Marines	320

Introduction

This is a transcription of prisoner of war records of American marines, merchantmen and sailors held at the internment facilities at Bermuda, Cape of Good Hope and Jamaica during the War of 1812 by the British Empire.

The list was compiled from microfilm copies of the original roster books of the British Admiralty made by the Public Record Office in London (ADM 103 / 26; ADM 103 / 27 ADM 103 / 47 and ADM 103 / 190).

The *General Entry Book* records are composed of bound volumes that were printed with lines for the recording of names of those incarcerated. The record of each prisoner is comprised of two facing pages. The clerk making the entries wrote page numbers on the upper right corner on each right side page of the book.

<u>The columns across the top on the left side:</u>
Current Number
By what Ship, or how Taken
Time when - Day, Month, Year
Place where
Name of prize
Whither Man of War, Privateer, or Merchant Vessel
Prisoners' Names

<u>The columns across the top on the right side:</u>
Quality - Navy, Army
Time when received into Custody - Day, Month, Year
From what Ship, or whence received
Exchanged, Discharged, Died, or Escaped
Time when - Day, Month, Year
Whither, and by what order, or Number of Re-entry

The volume for Bermuda has prisoner numbers 1 through 2875 in two books. Volume I has pages 1 through 97; Volume II starts over with page 1 and goes through page 19, with no index of captured ships. It was in operation from August 1812 to March 1815. On the right hand side of pages 1 through 7, St. Georges is crossed out and Bermuda written in. Lieutenant Edmund Bacon was Agent.

The volume for Cape of Good Hope has prisoner numbers 1 through 296 with a total of 19 pages, with an index of captured ships. It was in operation from January 1813 to April 1815. The index of ships has only a few entries and was not maintained. Lieutenant James Meres, RN was Agent.

The volume for Jamaica has prisoner numbers 1 through 1553 with a total of 65 pages, with no index of captured ships. It was in operation from July 1812 to April 1815. Captain J. Bosmer was Agent.

Bermuda has eight lines with no information being entered; the facility has seven duplicate records, most being recaptures of escapees who were issued new prison numbers. Cape of Good Hope has one duplicate record. Jamaica has one line with no information on it and seventeen duplicate records of new numbers being issued either to recaptured prisoners or through clerical error.

A problem is the ditto mark (both the symbol ' " ' and the letter 'd '); it is used on practically every page. Some records have information that over runs from the previous entries.

The photocopy and the handwriting varies from fair to good, except for Jamaica where the penmanship is poor. It appears that the spelling of non-familiar names was done phonically.

There are many Spanish and French names entered at Jamaica. Several were from ships out of Cartagena, Columbia in South America or from Spanish merchant ships recaptured from Cartagena privateers by the British navy. The clerk had some difficulty with the spelling of these names.

More than 100 from unnamed gunboats captured in early January 1815 from the American Naval Flotilla near New Orleans were incarcerated at Jamaica.

Twenty-two men escaped from Bermuda, while no escapes were recorded for Cape of Good Hope.

One hundred and four escaped from Jamaica. Nine escaped on December 30, 1814 and another six were 'Killed by the Guard' on the same date.

During the operation of the Bermuda prison camp: a total of 87 were sent to England and 429 to Halifax. Cape of Good Hope shows 85 being sent to England, many being transported on Indiamen or British whaling ships. Four were sent to England from Jamaica.

Thirty-eight were incarcerated for being American at Bermuda, eight at Cape of Good Hope and fifty-four at Jamaica. Apparently they were American citizens serving on British merchantmen and warships; some entries state the individual was 'impressed'.

Three slaves were claimed by owners: one from Jamaica: Jean Josef # 930 and two from Bermuda: Charles Johnson # 1611 and William Young # 1664.

Crews of United States naval vessels incarcerated at Bermuda include the frigate *USS President*, *Gunboat 160*, Schooner *USS Asp* and the Sloops *USS Viper* and *USS Wasp*. Naval personal imprisoned at Jamaica were from the Sloop *USS Vixen*. Cape of Good Hope had the crew from the Brig *USS Syren*.

The rosters for Bermuda indicate that 15 died as prisoners of war; 3 died at Cape of Good Hope; 32 deaths were recorded at Jamaica.

Any errors or omissions are regretted and are the fault of the transcriber.

Harrison Scott Baker II

President (1996 - 1999)
Society of the War of 1812 in the State of Ohio

- In memory of those who did not return -

- The Dead -

Ball, E	Jasser, Juan
Baptiste, John	Joseph, John
Boon, James	Joseph, Peter
Boyia, Thomas	Leof, Unis
Bunker, Frederick	Lopez, Francis
Burn, Peter	Moss, Elijah
Chripo	Moucrieff, James
Dale, Richard	Pane, Cheny
Darby, Joseph	Peek, Darius
Demers, William	Powell, Juan
Dennet, William	Reynolds, Christian
Devenero, Francis	Robien, John
Dexter, Charles	Rose, John
Dunton, Thomas	Ryan, Patrick
Flurit, Aman	Selby, Joseph
Gerin, Luis	Springer, William
Gerlock, Charles	Stanley, Simon
Gorman, Joseph	Stephens, John
Goss, John	Strong, Selvister
Grandy, Poll	Thompson, Philip
Hanson, Howe	Tieu, John
Harvey, Peter	Turk, Richard
Hendrick, Hugh	Vanwick, Thomas
Henry, Samuel	Wilson, James
Hudson, Joseph	Yohet, Pedro

- Those who die in service to the United States should not be forgotten -

American Prisoners of War Held at Bermuda During the War of 1812

---, Francisco   Prisoner 2716. Rank: Seaman, from: American Gun Boat, Not Recorded.
    Cap: 06 Feb 1815 off Charleston by Tonnant Int: 02 Mar 1815 Dis: 28 Mar 1815.
    Received from Armede. Clarendon Transport for U States. (Last name not recorded.)

---, George   Prisoner 1220. Rank: Seaman, from: Flavoriott, Merchant Schooner.
    Cap: Aug 1813 off Charlestown by HMS Calibri Int: 16 Nov 1813 Dis: 15 Apr 1814.
    Received from HMS Sceptre. Diana Transport for Halifax. (Last name not recorded.)

---, Hard Times   Prisoner 1899. Rank: Seaman, from: Emily, Merchant Vessel.
    Cap: 11 Aug 1814 Tapella Sound by Not Recorded Int: 09 Sep 1814 Dis: 28 Mar 1815.
    Received from Lacedaemonian. Clarendon Transport for U States. (Last name not recorded.)

---, Nathan   Prisoner 448. Rank: Boy, from: Adventure, Merchant Brig.
    Cap: 15 Dec 1812 off Bermuda by HM Sloop Childers Int: 17 Dec 1812 Dis: 27 Jan 1813.
    Received from HM Sloop Childers. Bostock Cartel for New York. (Last name not recorded.)

---, Paulsow   Prisoner 764. Rank: Seaman, from: Hazard, Merchant Brig.
    Cap: 28 Dec 1812 Lat 37.35, Long 70.10 by HM Sloop Sylph Int: 26 Jan 1813 Dis: 14 Jun 1813.
    Received from Sloop Sylph. Permitted to return to the United States in the Perseverance Cartel.
    (Last name not recorded.)

---, Pinkey   Prisoner 1901. Rank: Seaman, from: Dusty Miller, Merchant Vessel.
    Cap: 11 Aug 1814 Tapella Sound by Lacedaemonian Int: 09 Sep 1814 Escaped: 20 Sep 1814.
    Received from Lacedaemonian. Run from Prison Ship. (Last name not recorded.)

---, Poitless Moe   Prisoner 1163. Rank: Seaman, from: Caledonian, Merchant.
    Cap: 20 Jul 1813 at Sea by HM Ship Marlborough Int: 15 Aug 1813 Dis: 03 Oct 1813.
    Received from HM Ship Woolwich. Caledonian Order of Commodore Evans she being Liberated.
    (Last name not recorded.)

---, Sayler   Prisoner 1223. Rank: Seaman, from: Flavoriott, Merchant Schooner.
    Cap: Aug 1813 off Charlestown by HMS Calibri Int: 16 Nov 1813 Dis: 15 Apr 1814.
    Received from HMS Sceptre. Diana Transport for Halifax. (Last name not recorded.)

---, Tom   Prisoner 1224. Rank: Seaman, from: Flavoriott, Merchant Schooner.
    Cap: Aug 1813 off Charlestown by HMS Calibri Int: 16 Nov 1813 Dis: 15 Apr 1814.
    Received from HMS Sceptre. Diana Transport for Halifax. (Last name not recorded.)

Abbeson, John   Prisoner 243. Rank: Seaman, from: Wasp, Sloop of War.
    Cap: 18 Oct 1812 at Sea by HM Ship Poictiers Int: 26 Oct 1812 Dis: 05 Nov 1812.
    Received from HM Ship Poictiers. Brig Diamond on Parole to new London United States of America.

Abbot, George   Prisoner 424. Rank: 1 Mate, from: Eliza, Merchant Ship.
    Cap: 25 Nov 1812 Lat 37.00, Long 65.46 by HM Ship Tartarus Int: 03 Dec 1812 Dis: 27 Jan 1813.
    Received from HM Ship Tartarus. Bostock Cartel for New York.

Abrahams, G D   Prisoner 83. Rank: Supercargo, from: Ariel, Merchant Brig.
    Cap: 13 Aug 1812 of Bermuda by Goree Int: 28 Aug 1812 Dis: 06 Sep 1812.
    Received from HM Schooner Cuttle. Sloop Sally for New York.

Abreeve, Pirzanno   Prisoner 871. Rank: Seaman, from: Gustavas, Merchant Brig.
    Cap: 16 Mar 1813 Chesapeake by HM Ship Laurustinus Int: 23 Mar 1813 Dis: 24 Mar 1813.
    Received from Laurustinus. St. Michael per Order Adl Sir J B Warren.

Adams, Charles   Prisoner 2630. Rank: Seaman, from: Moreau, Merchant Vessel.
    Cap: 22 Nov 1814 off Delaware by Spencer Int: 06 Feb 1815 Dis: 28 Mar 1815.
    Received from HMS Telegraph. Clarendon Transport for U States.

Adams, Daniel   Prisoner 2656. Rank: Seaman, from: Falcon, Merchant Vessel.
    Cap: 22 Jan 1815 Delaware by Forth Int: 13 Feb 1815 Dis: 28 Mar 1815.
    Received from Goree. Clarendon Transport for U States.

Adams, Isaac   Prisoner 1715. Rank: Passenger, from: Olive Branch, Merchant Vessel.
    Cap: 16 Apr 1814 Chesapeake by Acasta Int: 26 May 1814 Dis:
    Received from Lacedaemonian. (Date of discharge not recorded.)

Adams, John   Prisoner 202. Rank: Seaman, from: Wasp, Sloop of War.
    Cap: 18 Oct 1812 at Sea by HMS Poictiers Int: 26 Oct 1812 Dis: 05 Nov 1812.
    Received from HM Ship Poictiers. Brig Diamond on Parole to new London America.

Adams, John   Prisoner 2183. Rank: Seaman, from: President, U States Frigate.
    Cap: 15 Jan 1815 Not Recorded by HMS Endymion Int: 30 Jan 1815 Dis: 28 Mar 1815.
    Received from Pomone. Mars Transport for U States.

Adams, William   Prisoner 2515. Rank: Seaman, from: President, U States Frigate.
    Cap: 15 Jan 1815 Not Recorded by Endymion Int: 04 Feb 1815 Dis: 28 Mar 1815.
    Received from HMS Endymion. Clarenden Transport for U States.

Adier, Simon   Prisoner 719. Rank: Seaman, from: High Flyer, Privateer.
    Cap: 09 Jan 1813 at Sea by HM Ship Acasta Int: 21 Jan 1813 Dis: 27 Jan 1813.
    Received from HMS Acasta. Bostock Cartel for New York.

American Prisoners of War Held at Bermuda During the War of 1812

Adrica, Peter   Prisoner 2390. Rank: Seaman, from: President, U States Frigate.
    Cap: 15 Jan 1815 Not Recorded by HM Ship Endymion Int: 04 Feb 1815 Dis: 28 Mar 1815.
    Received from Endymion. Mars Transport for U States.

Afferil, Charles   Prisoner 2043. Rank: Seaman, from: Rising Sun, Merchant Vessel.
    Cap: 20 Nov 1814 off Bermuda by Pandora Int: 28 Nov 1814 Dis: 28 Mar 1815.
    Recaptured. Received from HMS Goree. Clarendon Transport for U States.

Alcock, John   Prisoner 2590. Rank: Seaman, from: Lark, Merchant Vessel.
    Cap: 01 Dec 1814 off New York by HM Ship Majestic Int: 05 Feb 1815 Dis: 28 Mar 1815.
    Recaptured. York Privateer. Received from HMS Forth. Clarendon Transport for U States.

Alden, Benjamin   Prisoner 914. Rank: Master, from: Albert, Merchant Schooner.
    Cap: 05 Mar 1813 Chesapeake by HM Ship Marlborough Int: 23 Mar 1813 Escaped: 06 Apr 1813.
    Received from Laurustinus. Escaped.

Alderson, Jeremiah   Prisoner 2429. Rank: Seaman, from: President, U States Frigate.
    Cap: 15 Jan 1815 Not Recorded by HM Ship Endymion Int: 04 Feb 1815 Dis: 28 Mar 1815.
    Received from Endymion. Mars Transport for U States.

Alexand, John   Prisoner 1531. Rank: Seaman, from: Romp, Merchant Vessel.
    Cap: 02 Jan 1814 Latt 22.0 by Prometheus Int: 23 Jan 1814 Dis: 15 Apr 1814.
    Received from Prometheus. Diana for Halifax.

Alexander, Hector   Prisoner 1172. Rank: Seaman, from: Elizabeth, Merchant.
    Cap: 15 Jun 1813 at Sea by HM Ship Marlborough Int: 15 Aug 1813 Dis: 28 Oct 1813.
    Received from HM Ship Woolwich. Per order of Rear Adml Cockburn the vessel being Liberated.

Allen, David   Prisoner 36. Rank: Seaman, from: Laura, Merchant Sloop.
    Cap: 24 Jul 1812 of Bermuda by Cuttle Int: 28 Aug 1812 Dis: 18 Sep 1812.
    Received from HM Schooner Cuttle. Order of Commd Evans for England.

Allen, Duffy   Prisoner 2028. Rank: Seaman, from: Swiftsure, Merchant Vessel.
    Cap: 26 Oct 1814 off Halifax by Armide Int: 07 Nov 1814 Escaped: 07 Feb 1815.
    Recaptured. Received from HMS Armide. Run.

Allen, Henry   Prisoner 1183. Rank: Seaman, from: Caledonian, Merchant.
    Cap: 20 Jul 1813 at Sea by HM Ship Marlborough Int: 18 Aug 1813 Dis: 03 Oct 1813.
    Received from HM Ship Woolwich. Caledonian per Order of Commodore Evans she being Liberated.

Allen, John   Prisoner 1024. Rank: 2 Mate, from: Dart, Merchant Schooner.
    Cap: 17 Mar 1813 off the Chesapeake by HMS Statira Int: 06 Apr 1813 Dis: 24 Jun 1813.
    Received from HMS Junon. Magnet Cartel for New York.

Allen, Joseph   Prisoner 1535. Rank: Seaman, from: Surprize, Not Recorded.
    Cap: Not Recorded by Not Recorded Int: 23 Jan 1814 Dis: 15 Apr 1814.
    Received from Surprize. being an American. Diana for Halifax. (Date of capture not recorded.)

Allen, Peter   Prisoner 1948. Rank: Seaman, from: Pike, Privateer.
    Cap: 25 Aug 1814 off Savannah by Primrose Int: 09 Sep 1814 Dis: 10 Nov 1814.
    Received from Lacedaemonian. Joseph MV order Cockburn.

Allen, Richard   Prisoner 275. Rank: Seaman, from: Little William, Merchant Brig.
    Cap: 18 Oct 1812 at Sea by HM Ship Poictiers Int: 26 Oct 1812 Dis: 05 Nov 1812.
    Received from HM Ship Poictiers. Brig Diamond on Parole to new London United States of America.

Allen, Samuel   Prisoner 2447. Rank: Lieutenant Marines, from: President, U States Frigate.
    Cap: 15 Jan 1815 Not Recorded by Endymion Int: 04 Feb 1815 Dis: 28 Mar 1815.
    Received from Endymion. Clarenden Transport for U States.

Allen, Truman   Prisoner 1047. Rank: 1 Mate, from: General Knox, Merchant.
    Cap: 18 Mar 1813 Chesapeake by HM Ship Victorious Int: 06 Apr 1813 Dis:
    Received from HMS Junon. (Date of discharge not on roster.)

Allender, William   Prisoner 803. Rank: Seaman, from: Sheppard, Merchant Schooner.
    Cap: 04 Jan 1813 at Sea by Narcissus Int: 16 Feb 1813 Dis: 14 Jun 1813.
    Received from Narcissus. Permitted to return to the United States in the Perseverance Cartel.

Allison, B C   Prisoner 1370. Rank: Seaman, from: Rolla, Privateer.
    Cap: 10 Dec 1813 Block Island by Loire Int: 20 Dec 1813 Dis: 15 Apr 1814.
    Received from San Domingo. HMS Rammillies for Halifax.

Allison, William   Prisoner 1170. Rank: Seaman, from: Elizabeth, Merchant.
    Cap: 15 Jun 1813 at Sea by HM Ship Marlborough Int: 15 Aug 1813 Dis: 02 Sep 1813.
    Received from HM Ship Woolwich. Per order of Commodore Evans being liberated.

Alliston, John   Prisoner 528. Rank: Seaman, from: Herald, Letter of Marque Brig.
    Cap: 25 Dec 1812 at Sea by HMS Maidstone Int: 05 Jan 1813 Dis: 27 Jan 1813.
    Received from HM Ship Maidstone. Bostock Cartel for New York.

Allock, Elijah   Prisoner 1180. Rank: Seaman, from: Calmer, Merchant.
    Cap: 15 Jun 1813 at Sea by HM Ship Marlborough Int: 15 Aug 1813 Dis: 21 Aug 1813.
    Received from HM Ship Woolwich. Per Order Commodore Evans.

American Prisoners of War Held at Bermuda During the War of 1812

Ambruster, Peter   Prisoner 192. Rank: Marine, from: Wasp, Sloop of War.
    Cap: 18 Oct 1812 at Sea by HMS Poictiers Int: 26 Oct 1812 Dis: 05 Nov 1812.
    Received from HM Ship Poictiers. Brig Diamond on Parole to new London America.

Amos, Samuel   Prisoner 1619. Rank: Seaman, from: Brookhaven, Merchant Vessel.
    Cap: 09 Dec 1813 Block Island by Abion Int: 14 Feb 1814 Dis: 23 Apr 1814.
    Received from Sceptre. HMS Bulwark for Halifax.

Anderson, Andrew   Prisoner 1355. Rank: Seaman, from: Rolla, Privateer.
    Cap: 10 Dec 1813 Block Island by Loire Int: 20 Dec 1813 Dis: 15 Apr 1814.
    Received from San Domingo. HMS Rammillies for Halifax.

Anderson, Charles   Prisoner 2060. Rank: Mate, from: Mary, Merchant Schooner.
    Cap: 26 Nov 1814 off Cape Delaware by Telegraph Int: 11 Dec 1814 Dis: 25 Jan 1815.
    Received from HMS Goree. Bridges Transport being Subject to Friendly power Order Com Evans.

Anderson, Edward   Prisoner 1138. Rank: Seaman, from: Asp, Man of War Schooner.
    Cap: 20 Jul 1813 at Sea by HM Ship San Domingo Int: 13 Aug 1813 Dis: 13 Aug 1813.
    Received from HM Ship Woolwich. American Ship Rolla per Order Commr Evans.

Anderson, George   Prisoner 2373. Rank: Seaman, from: President, U States Frigate.
    Cap: 15 Jan 1815 Not Recorded by HMS Endymion Int: 04 Feb 1815 Dis: 28 Mar 1815.
    Received from Endymion. Mars Transport for U States.

Anderson, Jacob   Prisoner 915. Rank: Seaman, from: Albert, Merchant Schooner.
    Cap: 05 Mar 1813 Chesapeake by HM Ship Marlborough Int: 23 Mar 1813 Escaped: 21 Apr 1813.
    Received from Laurustinus. Escaped.

Anderson, John   Prisoner 889. Rank: Seaman, from: Hannah, Merchant Schooner.
    Cap: 24 Feb 1813 Chesapeake by HMS Marlborough Int: 23 Mar 1813 Dis: 21 May 1813.
    Received from HM Ship Laurustinus. Per Order Commodore Evans the Vessel being Liberated.

Anderson, Nathaniel   Prisoner 2637. Rank: Seaman, from: Superb, Merchant Vessel.
    Cap: 23 Nov 1814 off Delaware by Spencer Int: 06 Feb 1815 Dis: 28 Mar 1815.
    Received from HMS Telegraph. Clarendon Transport for U States.

Anderson, Peter   Prisoner 1080. Rank: Seaman, from: Not Recorded, Not Recorded.
    Cap: Not Recorded by Not Recorded Int: 24 Apr 1813 Dis: 24 Jun 1813.
    Received from HMS Barrosa. Surrendered them Selves as Prisoners of War. Magnet Cartel for New York. (Date of capture not recorded.)

Anderson, William   Prisoner 1147. Rank: Seaman, from: Acricoake, Merchant.
    Cap: 22 Jul 1813 at Sea by HM Sloop Conflict Int: 13 Aug 1813 Dis: 13 Aug 1813.
    Received from HM Ship Woolwich. American Ship Rolla per Order Governor Strong.

Anderson, William   Prisoner 2606. Rank: Seaman, from: Edward, Merchant Vessel.
    Cap: 30 Dec 1814 Sandy Hook by HM Ship Pomone Int: 05 Feb 1815 Dis: 28 Mar 1815.
    Received from HMS Forth. Clarendon Transport for U States.

Anderson, William   Prisoner 2867. Rank: Seaman, from: Limerick, Not Recorded.
    Cap: 06 Mar 1815 Not Recorded by Asia Int: 29 Mar 1815 Dis: 28 Mar 1815.
    From West Indies. Received from La Brune. Clarendon Transport for U States. (Date of discharge before date of internment.)

Andrews, A   Prisoner 2355. Rank: Seaman, from: President, U States Frigate.
    Cap: 15 Jan 1815 Not Recorded by HMS Endymion Int: 04 Feb 1815 Dis: 28 Mar 1815.
    Received from Endymion. Mars Transport for U States.

Andrews, Hercules   Prisoner 512. Rank: Seaman, from: St. Augustina, Merchant Brig.
    Cap: 19 Dec 1812 at Sea by HM Ship San Domingo Int: 29 Dec 1812 Dis: 27 Jan 1813.
    Received from HM Ship San Domingo. Bostock Cartel for New York.

Andrews, John   Prisoner 1862. Rank: Seaman, from: Sally, Merchant Vessel.
    Cap: Not Recorded by Not Recorded Int: Dis: 04 Sep 1814.
    as a Noncombatant. (Dates of capture and internment not recorded.)

Anthony, Joseph   Prisoner 2322. Rank: Seaman, from: President, U States Frigate.
    Cap: 15 Jan 1815 Not Recorded by Endymion Int: 04 Feb 1815 Dis: 28 Mar 1815.
    Received from Endymion. Mars Transport for U States.

Anthony, Joseph   Prisoner 2790. Rank: Seaman, from: Limerick, Not Recorded.
    Cap: 07 Mar 1815 Lat 30, Long 75.38 W by Asia Int: 25 Mar 1815 Dis:
    Received from Asia. (Date of discharge not recorded.)

Anthony, Peter   Prisoner 529. Rank: Seaman, from: Herald, Letter of Marque Brig.
    Cap: 25 Dec 1812 at Sea by HMS Maidstone Int: 05 Jan 1813 Dis: 27 Jan 1813.
    Received from HM Ship Maidstone. Bostock Cartel for New York.

Antonia, Joseph   Prisoner 117. Rank: Seaman, from: Lydia, Merchant.
    Cap: 03 Sep 1812 Near Bermuda by HMS Orpheus Int: 08 Sep 1812 Dis: 09 Sep 1812.
    Received from HMS Orpheus. Portuguese per Order of C. Evans.

American Prisoners of War Held at Bermuda During the War of 1812

Antonia, Peter   Prisoner 383. Rank: Seaman, from: Snapper, Privateer Schooner.
    Cap: 16 Nov 1812 at Sea by HM Ship Galus Int: 22 Nov 1812 Dis: 27 Jan 1813.
    Received from HM Ship Galus. Bostock Cartel for New York.

Antonio, John   Prisoner 2645. Rank: Seaman, from: Dash, Merchant Vessel.
    Cap: 19 Jan 1815 Bahamas by HMS Statira Int: 06 Feb 1815 Dis: 25 Feb 1815.
    Received from HMS Statira. Mars Transport per order of Commadore Evans.

Antonio, Manuel   Prisoner 2055. Rank: Seaman, from: Amy, Merchant Schooner.
    Cap: 26 Nov 1814 off Cape Delaware by Telegraph Int: 05 Dec 1814 Dis: 13 Dec 1814.
    Received from HMS Goree. Jublilee Transport Spanish Transport Order of Commadore Evans.

Antonis, Frederick   Prisoner 378. Rank: Seaman, from: Snapper, Privateer Schooner.
    Cap: 16 Nov 1812 at Sea by HM Ship Galus Int: 22 Nov 1812 Dis: 14 Dec 1812.
    Received from HM Ship Galus. per Order Commd Evans.

Apenny, William   Prisoner 1551. Rank: Pilot, from: Bordeaux Packet, Letter of Marque.
    Cap: 28 Jan 1814 off Cape Henry by Nieman Int: 12 Feb 1814 Dis: 15 Apr 1814.
    Received from Nieman. Rammilles for Halifax.

Appleton, John   Prisoner 1105. Rank: Seaman, from: Apollo, Merchant Vessel.
    Cap: 15 May 1813 at Sea by HM Ship Success Int: 27 May 1813 Dis: 24 Jun 1813.
    Received from HMS Success. Magnet Cartel for New York.

Appleton, John   Prisoner 1767. Rank: Seaman, from: Yankelass, Privateer.
    Cap: 01 May 1814 L 40-4N, Long 38-0W by Severn & Surprise Int: 07 Jun 1814 Dis: 28 Mar 1815.
    Received from Surprise. Mars Transport for U States.

Appleturit, Charles   Prisoner 869. Rank: Seaman, from: Gustavas, Merchant Brig.
    Cap: 16 Mar 1813 Chesapeake by HM Ship Laurustinus Int: 23 Mar 1813 Dis: 24 Apr 1813.
    Received from Laurustinus. Per Order Commodore Evans Vessel Liberated.

Apthy, Robert   Prisoner 279. Rank: Seaman, from: Little William, Merchant Brig.
    Cap: 18 Oct 1812 at Sea by HM Ship Poictiers Int: 26 Oct 1812 Dis: 05 Nov 1812.
    Received from HM Ship Poictiers. Brig Diamond on Parole to new London United States of America.

Archer, John   Prisoner 2697. Rank: Seaman, from: Speed, Merchant Vessel.
    Cap: 19 Jan 1815 off Nantucket by Pylades Int: 17 Feb 1815 Dis: 28 Mar 1815.
    Received from Majestic. Clarendon Transport for U States.

Archer, Thomas   Prisoner 1074. Rank: Boy, from: Ring Dove, Merchant.
    Cap: 31 Mar 1813 Chesapeake by HM Ship Junon Int: 06 Apr 1813 Dis: 17 Apr 1813.
    Received from HMS Junon. being Under Age per Order Commodore Evans.

Ardrey, Alexander   Prisoner 1248. Rank: Not Recorded, from: Eliza & Susan, Merchant Vessel.
    Cap: 08 Oct 1813 Chesapeake by Lacedaemonian Int: 02 Dec 1813 Dis: 15 Apr 1814.
    Received from HMS Sceptre. Diana Transport for Halifax.

Armstrong, James   Prisoner 2420. Rank: Seaman, from: President, U States Frigate.
    Cap: 15 Jan 1815 Not Recorded by HM Ship Endymion Int: 04 Feb 1815 Dis: 28 Mar 1815.
    Received from Endymion. Mars Transport for U States.

Armstrong, John   Prisoner 2416. Rank: Seaman, from: President, U States Frigate.
    Cap: 15 Jan 1815 Not Recorded by HM Ship Endymion Int: 04 Feb 1815 Dis: 28 Mar 1815.
    Received from Endymion. Mars Transport for U States.

Armstrong, Nicholas C   Prisoner 2051. Rank: Seaman, from: Mary, Merchant Schooner.
    Cap: 26 Nov 1814 off Cape Delaware by Telegraph Int: 05 Dec 1814 Dis: 28 Mar 1815.
    Received from HMS Goree. Clarendon Transport for U States.

Armstrong, William   Prisoner 2241. Rank: Seaman, from: President, U States Frigate.
    Cap: 15 Jan 1815 Not Recorded by Endymion Int: 30 Jan 1815 Dis: 28 Mar 1815.
    Received from Pomone. Mars Transport for U States.

Arnold, William   Prisoner 1263. Rank: Mate, from: Huntress, Merchant Vessel.
    Cap: 12 Nov 1813 Long Island by HM Brig Borer Int: 19 Dec 1813 Dis: 15 Apr 1814.
    Received from HMS Acasta. HMS Rammillies for Halifax.

Arnon, Peter   Prisoner 350. Rank: Seaman, from: Snapper, Privateer Schooner.
    Cap: 16 Nov 1812 at Sea by HMS Galus Int: 22 Nov 1812 Dis: 27 Jan 1813.
    Received from HM Ship Galus. Bostock Cartel for New York.

Ashbourn, Ralph   Prisoner 2552. Rank: Seaman, from: President, US Frigate.
    Cap: 15 Jan 1815 off N York by HMS Endymion Int: 05 Feb 1815 Dis: 28 Mar 1815.
    Received from President. Clarenden Transport for U States.

Ashcroft, Hugh   Prisoner 697. Rank: Seaman, from: High Flyer, Privateer.
    Cap: 09 Jan 1813 at Sea by HMS Acasta Int: 21 Jan 1813 Dis: 27 Jan 1813.
    Received from HMS Acasta. Bostock Cartel for New York.

Aspenell, Elijah   Prisoner 1786. Rank: Seaman, from: Yankelass, Privateer.
    Cap: 01 May 1814 Latt 40-4N, Long 38-0W by Severn & Surprise Int: 07 Jun 1814 Dis: 28 Mar 1815.
    Received from Surprise. Mars Transport for U States.

American Prisoners of War Held at Bermuda During the War of 1812

Astor, Doroty   Prisoner 1763. Rank: Seaman, from: Yankelass, Privateer.
    Cap: 01 May 1814 L 40-4N, Long 38-0W by Severn & Surprise Int: 06 Jun 1814 Dis: 28 Mar 1815.
    Received from Severn. Mars Transport for U States.

Atkins, George   Prisoner 2120. Rank: Seaman, from: Armistice, Merchant Vessel.
    Cap: 07 Dec 1814 off Delaware by Pictolus Int: 27 Jan 1815 Dis: 28 Mar 1815.
    Received from Pictolus. Clarendon Transport for U States.

Atkins, Lemuel   Prisoner 2762. Rank: Seaman, from: Maria, Not Recorded.
    Cap: 16 Feb 1815 St Augustine by Severn Int: 03 Mar 1815 Dis: 16 Mar 1815.
    Received from Hebrus. Merchant Service.

Atkinson, John   Prisoner 203. Rank: Seaman, from: Wasp, Sloop of War.
    Cap: 18 Oct 1812 at Sea by HM Ship Poictiers Int: 26 Oct 1812 Dis: 05 Nov 1812.
    Received from HM Ship Poictiers. Brig Diamond on Parole to new London United States of America.

Atwater, Levi   Prisoner 816. Rank: Seaman, from: Stockholm, Merchant Schooner.
    Cap: 18 Feb 1813 at Sea by HMS Statira Int: 01 Mar 1813 Dis: 14 Apr 1813.
    Received from HMS Statira. Per Order Commodore Evans Vessel Liberated.

Atwood, Isaac   Prisoner 1071. Rank: Master, from: Ring Dove, Merchant.
    Cap: 31 Mar 1813 Chesapeake by HMS Junon Int: 06 Apr 1813 Dis: 24 Jun 1813.
    Received from HMS Junon. Magnet Cartel for New York.

Augh, James Henry   Prisoner 1256. Rank: Captain, from: Hero, Merchant Schooner.
    Cap: 14 Nov 1813 Delaware by Belvidera Int: 06 Dec 1813 Dis: 15 Apr 1814.
    Received from HMS Sceptre. HMS Rammillies for Halifax. Or James Mervy Augh.

Austin, Joseph   Prisoner 691. Rank: Seaman, from: High Flyer, Privateer.
    Cap: 09 Jan 1813 at Sea by HMS Acasta Int: 21 Jan 1813 Dis: 27 Jan 1813.
    Received from HMS Acasta. Bostock Cartel for New York.

Avery, Daniel   Prisoner 1412. Rank: Passenger, from: Industry, Merchant Vessel.
    Cap: 08 Dec 1813 Lat 37.25 by Loire Int: 21 Dec 1813 Dis: 06 Feb 1814.
    Received from Romulus. Being a Non Combatant.

Awner, Charles   Prisoner 2469. Rank: Seaman, from: President, U States Frigate.
    Cap: 15 Jan 1815 Not Recorded by Endymion Int: 04 Feb 1815 Dis: 28 Mar 1815.
    Received from Endymion. Clarenden Transport for U States.

Axford, Thomas   Prisoner 2311. Rank: Seaman, from: President, U States Frigate.
    Cap: 15 Jan 1815 Not Recorded by Endymion Int: 04 Feb 1815 Dis: 28 Mar 1815.
    Received from Endymion. Mars Transport for U States.

Bablisto, John   Prisoner 1915. Rank: Seaman, from: Dolphin, Packet.
    Cap: 20 Aug 1814 St. Catherine by Lacedaemonian Int: 09 Sep 1814 Dis: 05 Nov 1814.
    Received from Lacedaemonian. Order Adml Cockburn.

Bacchus, A   Prisoner 1409. Rank: Seaman, from: John & James, Merchant Vessel.
    Cap: 07 Dec 1813 Lat 37 by Loire Int: 21 Dec 1813 Dis: 15 Apr 1814.
    Received from Romulus. Diana Transport for Halifax.

Bacon, Silvester   Prisoner 1264. Rank: Seaman, from: Huntress, Merchant Vessel.
    Cap: 12 Nov 1813 Long Island by HM Brig Borer Int: 19 Dec 1813 Dis: 15 Apr 1814.
    Received from HMS Acasta. Diana for Halifax.

Badger, Peter   Prisoner 586. Rank: Seaman, from: Lydia, Merchant Ship.
    Cap: 26 Dec 1812 at Sea by HM Ship Maidstone Int: 06 Jan 1813 Dis: 27 Jan 1813.
    Received from HM Ship Maidstone. Bostock Cartel for New York.

Bagley, Daniel   Prisoner 754. Rank: Seaman, from: Delaclea, Merchant Schooner.
    Cap: 17 Dec 1812 Lat 34.31 N, Long 74.44 W by HM Sloop Sylph Int: 26 Jan 1813 Dis: 14 Jun 1813.
    Received from Sloop Sylph. Permitted to return to the United States in Perseverance.

Bagnell, Joseph   Prisoner 766. Rank: Seaman, from: Lucy, Merchant Schooner.
    Cap: 28 Dec 1812 Lat 36.45, Long 73.18 by HM Sloop Sylph Int: 26 Jan 1813 Dis: 14 Jun 1813.
    Received from Sloop Sylph. Permitted to return to the United States in the Perseverance Cartel.

Bailey, Cyral   Prisoner 1261. Rank: Seaman, from: His Majesty's Schooner St. Lawrence, Not Recorded.
    Cap: Not Recorded by Not Recorded Int: 11 Dec 1813 Dis: 15 Apr 1814.
    Received from His Majesty's Schooner St. Lawrence. gave himself up as an American. Diana Transport for Halifax. (Date of capture not recorded.)

Bailie, Joseph   Prisoner 991. Rank: Seaman, from: Nancy, Merchant.
    Cap: 04 Mar 1813 Chesapeake by Narcissus Int: 23 Mar 1813 Dis: 24 Jun 1813.
    Received from HM Ship Laurustinus. Magnet Cartel for New York.

Bakeman, John   Prisoner 2. Rank: Mate, from: Symmetry, Merchant Ship.
    Cap: 05 Jul 1812 Not Recorded by Rattler Int: 28 Aug 1812 Dis: 10 Sep 1812.
    Received from HM Schooner Cuttle. Schooner Hero for N York per order Commd Evans.

American Prisoners of War Held at Bermuda During the War of 1812

Baker, George C   Prisoner 509. Rank: Master, from: Eagle, Merchant Schooner.
    Cap: 16 Dec 1812 at Sea by HMS Sophia Int: 28 Dec 1812 Dis: 27 Jan 1813.
    Received from the Prize Schooner Eagle. Bostock Cartel for New York.

Baker, John C   Prisoner 175. Rank: Midshipman, from: Wasp, Sloop of War.
    Cap: 18 Oct 1812 at Sea by HMS Poictiers Int: 26 Oct 1812 Dis: 05 Nov 1812.
    Received from HM Ship Poictiers. on Parole Brig Diamond to new London America.

Baker, Robert   Prisoner 1277. Rank: Corporal, from: Perry, Merchant Schooner.
    Cap: 03 Dec 1813 Long Island by Indemyion Int: 19 Dec 1813 Dis:
    Received from Sceptre. (Date of discharge not recorded.)

Baker, Samuel   Prisoner 1267. Rank: Seaman, from: United States, Merchant Vessel.
    Cap: 14 Nov 1813 Long Island by HM Brig Borer Int: 19 Dec 1813 Dis: 15 Apr 1814.
    Received from HMS Acasta. Diana for Halifax.

Baldis, Anthony   Prisoner 188. Rank: Seaman, from: Wasp, Sloop of War.
    Cap: 18 Oct 1812 at Sea by HMS Poictiers Int: 26 Oct 1812 Dis: 05 Nov 1812.
    Received from HM Ship Poictiers. Brig Diamond on Parole to new London America.

Ball, Isaac   Prisoner 834. Rank: Seaman, from: Portsmouth, Merchant Ship.
    Cap: 27 Feb 1813 off Bermuda by HM Sloop Martin Int: 09 Mar 1813 Dis: 27 Mar 1813.
    Received from Sloop Martin. Per Order Commodore Evans the Vessel being Liberated.

Ballast, Samuel   Prisoner 2869. Rank: Seaman, from: Limerick, Not Recorded.
    Cap: 06 Mar 1815 Not Recorded by Asia Int: 29 Mar 1815 Dis: 28 Mar 1815.
    From West Indies. Received from La Brune. Clarendon Transport for U States. (Date of discharge before date of internment.)

Banatt, John   Prisoner 2456. Rank: Seaman, from: President, U States Frigate.
    Cap: 15 Jan 1815 Not Recorded by Endymion Int: 04 Feb 1815 Dis: 28 Mar 1815.
    Received from Endymion. Clarenden Transport for U States.

Banks, James   Prisoner 2154. Rank: Boatswain, from: President, U States Frigate.
    Cap: 15 Jan 1815 Not Recorded by Endymion Int: 30 Jan 1815 Dis: 22 Mar 1815.
    Received from President. Merchant Vessel.

Bankson, W C   Prisoner 1440. Rank: Seaman, from: Nonsuch, Letter of Marque.
    Cap: 14 Dec 1813 Lat 32 by Doterel Int: 25 Dec 1813 Dis: 15 Apr 1814.
    Received from HM Brig Doterel. Diana Transport for Halifax.

Baptiste, John   Prisoner 2646. Rank: Seaman, from: Dash, Merchant Vessel.
    Cap: 19 Jan 1815 Bahamas by HMS Statira Int: 06 Feb 1815 Dis: 25 Feb 1815.
    Received from HMS Statira. Mars Transport per order of Commadore Evans. John Baptiste (1).

Baptiste, John   Prisoner 2664. Rank: Seaman, from: President, U States Frigate.
    Cap: 15 Jan 1815 off New York by Endymion Int: 14 Feb 1815 Died: 01 Mar 1815.
    Received from Goree. Died. Wounds. John Baptiste (2).

Baptiste, John   Prisoner 2672. Rank: Seaman, from: Gunboat 160, U States Man of War.
    Cap: 06 Sep 1814 off New York by Lacedaemonian Int: 14 Feb 1815 Dis: 28 Mar 1815.
    Gun Vessel. Received from Childers. Clarendon Transport for U States. John Baptiste (3).

Barber, George   Prisoner 621. Rank: Seaman, from: Enterprize, Merchant Schooner.
    Cap: 15 Dec 1812 at Sea by HMS Tartant Int: 12 Jan 1813 Dis: 27 Jan 1813.
    Received from Schooner Enterprize. Bostock Cartel for New York.

Barber, Henry   Prisoner 30. Rank: Seaman, from: Survanou, Merchant.
    Cap: 14 Jul 1812 at Bermuda by Recruit Int: 28 Aug 1812 Dis: 18 Sep 1812.
    Received from HM Schooner Cuttle. Order of Commd Evans for England.

Barber, Henry   Prisoner 2605. Rank: Seaman, from: Edward, Merchant Vessel.
    Cap: 30 Dec 1814 Sandy Hook by HM Ship Pomone Int: 05 Feb 1815 Dis: 16 Mar 1815.
    Received from HMS Forth. Merchant Service.

Barber, J H   Prisoner 1343. Rank: Seaman, from: Rolla, Privateer.
    Cap: 10 Dec 1813 Block Island by Loire Int: 20 Dec 1813 Dis: 15 Apr 1814.
    Received from HM Ship San Domingo. HMS Rammillies for Halifax.

Barber, John   Prisoner 259. Rank: Seaman, from: Wasp, Sloop of War.
    Cap: 18 Oct 1812 at Sea by HM Ship Poictiers Int: 26 Oct 1812 Dis: 05 Nov 1812.
    Received from HM Ship Poictiers. Brig Diamond on Parole to new London United States of America.

Barber, John   Prisoner 2563. Rank: Seaman, from: Funchall, Merchant Vessel.
    Cap: 15 Jan 1815 off New York by HMS Pomone Int: 05 Feb 1815 Dis: 16 Mar 1815.
    Received from HMS Forth. Merchant Service.

Barkam, Thomas   Prisoner 2119. Rank: Seaman, from: Armistice, Merchant Vessel.
    Cap: 07 Dec 1814 off Delaware by Pictolus Int: 27 Jan 1815 Dis: 13 Mar 1815.
    Received from Pictolus. Merchant Service.

American Prisoners of War Held at Bermuda During the War of 1812

Barker, A L   Prisoner 1669. Rank: 2 Lieutenant, from: Fieri Facias, Privateer.
    Cap: 26 Feb 1814 at Sea by Ramilies Int: 18 Mar 1814 Dis: 15 Apr 1814.
    Received from Ramilies. Rammilles for Halifax.

Barker, Benjamin   Prisoner 2638. Rank: Master, from: Platoff, Merchant Vessel.
    Cap: 16 Jan 1815 off New York by Spencer Int: 06 Feb 1815 Dis: 17 Mar 1815.
    Received from HMS Telegraph. Merchant Vessel.

Barker, Charles   Prisoner 421. Rank: Boy, from: Isabella, Merchant Brig.
    Cap: 15 Nov 1812 at Sea by HM Sloop Childers Int: 24 Nov 1812 Dis: 27 Jan 1813.
    Received from HM Ship Childers. Bostock Cartel for New York.

Barles, Frederick   Prisoner 1389. Rank: Seaman, from: Policy, Merchant Vessel.
    Cap: 04 Dec 1813 Not Recorded by Loire Int: 20 Dec 1813 Dis: 02 Jan 1814.
    Recaptured. Received from San Domingo. HMS Diadem for a Passage to England.

Barlie, Aron   Prisoner 555. Rank: Seaman, from: Herald, Letter of Marque Brig.
    Cap: 25 Dec 1812 at Sea by HM Ship Maidstone Int: 05 Jan 1813 Dis: 27 Jan 1813.
    Received from HM Ship Maidstone. Bostock Cartel for New York.

Barlow, Joseph   Prisoner 265. Rank: Seaman, from: Wasp, Sloop of War.
    Cap: 18 Oct 1812 at Sea by HM Ship Poictiers Int: 26 Oct 1812 Dis: 05 Nov 1812.
    Received from HM Ship Poictiers. Brig Diamond on Parole to new London United States of America.

Barlow, Rodney   Prisoner 2835. Rank: Seaman, from: Limerick, Not Recorded.
    Cap: 15 Mar 1815 Not Recorded by Asia Int: 25 Mar 1815 Dis:
    From Depot at Jamaica. Received from Asia. (Date of discharge not recorded.)

Barnes, Isaac   Prisoner 49. Rank: Seaman, from: Ariel, Merchant Brig.
    Cap: 28 Jul 1812 of Bermuda by Recruit Int: 28 Aug 1812 Dis: 18 Sep 1812.
    Received from HM Schooner Cuttle. Order Commd Evans for England.

Barnes, Nathaniel   Prisoner 2534. Rank: Seaman, from: President, U States Frigate.
    Cap: 15 Jan 1815 Not Recorded by HM Ship Endymion Int: 04 Feb 1815 Dis: 28 Mar 1815.
    Received from HMS Endymion. Clarenden Transport for U States.

Barnes, Timothy W   Prisoner 651. Rank: Seaman, from: Not Recorded, Not Recorded.
    Cap: Not Recorded by Not Recorded Int: 19 Jan 1813 Dis: 27 Jan 1813.
    Surrendered himself as an American. Bostock Cartel for New York. (Date of capture not recorded.)

Barnes, William   Prisoner 652. Rank: Seaman, from: Not Recorded, Not Recorded.
    Cap: Not Recorded by Not Recorded Int: 19 Jan 1813 Dis: 27 Jan 1813.
    Surrendered himself as an American. Bostock Cartel for New York. (Date of capture not recorded.)

Barnet, George   Prisoner 1617. Rank: Seaman, from: Monticello, Merchant Vessel.
    Cap: 09 Dec 1813 Block Island by Abion Int: 14 Feb 1814 Dis: 23 Apr 1814.
    Received from Sceptre. HMS Bulwark for Halifax.

Barnet, John   Prisoner 1244. Rank: Not Recorded, from: Julia, Schooner.
    Cap: 10 Aug 1813 Lake Ontario by Wolf Int: 30 Nov 1813 Dis: 15 Apr 1814.
    Received from HM Ship Goliah. Diana Transport for Halifax.

Barney, Olpha   Prisoner 2633. Rank: Seaman, from: Superb, Merchant Vessel.
    Cap: 23 Nov 1814 off Delaware by Spencer Int: 06 Feb 1815 Dis: 28 Mar 1815.
    Received from HMS Telegraph. Clarendon Transport for U States.

Barney, Samuel   Prisoner 675. Rank: Cook, from: High Flyer, Privateer.
    Cap: 09 Jan 1813 at Sea by HM Ship Acasta Int: 21 Jan 1813 Dis: 27 Jan 1813.
    Received from HMS Acasta. Bostock Cartel for New York.

Barns, James   Prisoner 994. Rank: Seaman, from: Jefferson, Merchant.
    Cap: 18 Mar 1813 at Sea by HMS Atalante Int: 30 Mar 1813 Dis: 24 Jun 1813.
    Received from HMS Atalante. Magnet Cartel for New York.

Barns, Lincoln   Prisoner 617. Rank: Mate, from: Morning Star, Merchant Schooner.
    Cap: 17 Dec 1812 at Sea by HM Ship Tartarus Int: 12 Jan 1813 Dis: 27 Jan 1813.
    Received from HMS Belvidera. Bostock Cartel for New York.

Barr, F M   Prisoner 2819. Rank: Seaman, from: Limerick, Not Recorded.
    Cap: 15 Mar 1815 Not Recorded by Asia Int: 25 Mar 1815 Dis:
    From Depot at Jamaica. Received from Asia. (Date of discharge not recorded.)

Barr, Robert   Prisoner 2025. Rank: Seaman, from: Swiftsure, Merchant Vessel.
    Cap: 26 Oct 1814 off Halifax by Armide Int: 07 Nov 1814 Dis: 28 Mar 1815.
    Recaptured. Received from HMS Armide. Clarendon Transport for U States.

Barret, Alexander   Prisoner 220. Rank: Seaman, from: Wasp, Sloop of War.
    Cap: 18 Oct 1812 at Sea by HM Ship Poictiers Int: 26 Oct 1812 Dis: 05 Nov 1812.
    Received from HM Ship Poictiers. Brig Diamond on Parole to new London United States of America.

Barret, Samuel   Prisoner 160. Rank: Seaman, from: Ranger, Merchant Ship.
    Cap: 02 Oct 1812 Lat 32, Long 65 W by HM Ship Goree Int: 13 Oct 1812 Dis: 24 Oct 1812.
    Received from HMS Goree. on Parole Brig Diamond to new London America.

American Prisoners of War Held at Bermuda During the War of 1812

Barrett, James   Prisoner 299. Rank: Seaman, from: Symmetry, Merchant Ship.
    Cap: 05 Jul 1812 at Sea by HM Ship Rattler Int: 02 Nov 1812 Dis: 04 Nov 1812.
    Received from HMS Poictiers. Brig Diamond on Parole to new London United States of America.

Barrett, Peter   Prisoner 2837. Rank: Seaman, from: Limerick, Not Recorded.
    Cap: 15 Mar 1815 Not Recorded by Asia Int: 25 Mar 1815 Dis:
    From Depot at Jamaica. Received from Asia. (Date of discharge not recorded.)

Barrett, Thomas   Prisoner 1659. Rank: Seaman, from: Flash, Letter of Marque.
    Cap: 11 Feb 1814 Off Block Island by Acasta Int: 13 Mar 1814 Dis: 23 Apr 1814.
    Received from Active. HMS Bulwark for Halifax.

Barrett, William S   Prisoner 1788. Rank: Prize Master, from: Yankelass, Privateer.
    Cap: 01 May 1814 Latt 40-4N, Long 38-0W by Severn & Surprise Int: 07 Jun 1814 Escaped: 23 Nov 1814. Received from Surprise. Run.

Barritt, William   Prisoner 2189. Rank: Seaman, from: President, U States Frigate.
    Cap: 15 Jan 1815 Not Recorded by HMS Endymion Int: 30 Jan 1815 Dis: 28 Mar 1815.
    Received from Pomone. Mars Transport for U States.

Barsabella, Julian   Prisoner 1986. Rank: Seaman, from: Eclipse, Merchant Vessel.
    Cap: 29 Sep 1814 Bermuda by Copark Int: 05 Oct 1814 Dis: 07 Nov 1814.
    Recaptured. Received from Goree. Diadem for a Passage to England.

Barthoff, Nicholas   Prisoner 2227. Rank: Seaman, from: President, U States Frigate.
    Cap: 15 Jan 1815 Not Recorded by Endymion Int: 30 Jan 1815 Dis: 28 Mar 1815.
    Received from Pomone. Lord Collingwood.

Bartholomew, Herain   Prisoner 906. Rank: Seaman, from: Elizabeth, Merchant Brig.
    Cap: 26 Feb 1813 Chesapeake by HMS Marlborough Int: 23 Mar 1813 Dis: 24 Apr 1813.
    Received from HM Ship Laurustinus. Vessel Liberated By Order Commodore Evans.

Bartholomew, Joseph   Prisoner 1667. Rank: Captain, from: Fieri Facias, Privateer.
    Cap: 26 Feb 1814 at Sea by Ramilies Int: 18 Mar 1814 Dis: 15 Apr 1814.
    Received from Ramilies. Rammilles for Halifax.

Bartlett, H G   Prisoner 2831. Rank: Seaman, from: Limerick, Not Recorded.
    Cap: 15 Mar 1815 Not Recorded by Asia Int: 25 Mar 1815 Dis:
    From Depot at Jamaica. Received from Asia. (Date of discharge not recorded.)

Barton, John   Prisoner 964. Rank: Mate, from: Janett, Merchant Brig.
    Cap: 25 Feb 1813 Chesapeake by HMS Junon Int: 23 Mar 1813 Dis: 24 May 1813.
    Received from Laurustinus. for a Passage to Halifax.

Barton, Lette   Prisoner 1794. Rank: 1 Mate, from: Yankelass, Privateer.
    Cap: 01 May 1814 Latt 40-4N, Long 38-0W by Severn & Surprise Int: 07 Jun 1814 Dis: 28 Mar 1815.
    Received from Surprise. Mars Transport for U States.

Barton, Samuel   Prisoner 1574. Rank: Seaman, from: Bordeaux Packet, Letter of Marque.
    Cap: 28 Jan 1814 off Cape Henry by Nieman Int: 12 Feb 1814 Dis: 15 Apr 1814.
    Received from Nieman. Diana Transport for Halifax.

Barton, William   Prisoner 1139. Rank: Seaman, from: Asp, Man of War Schooner.
    Cap: 20 Jul 1813 at Sea by HM Ship San Domingo Int: 13 Aug 1813 Dis: 13 Aug 1813.
    Received from HM Ship Woolwich. American Ship Rolla per Order Governor Strong.

Bartoph, Abber S   Prisoner 453. Rank: 3 Lieutenant, from: Teazer, Privateer Schooner.
    Cap: 16 Dec 1812 at Sea by HM Ship St. Domingo Int: 21 Dec 1812 Dis: 27 Jan 1813.
    Received from HM Ship St. Domingo. Bostock Cartel for New York.

Basden, John   Prisoner 74. Rank: Mate, from: White Oak, Merchant.
    Cap: 08 Aug 1812 of Bermuda by Recruit Int: 28 Aug 1812 Dis: 10 Sep 1812.
    Received from M Schooner Cuttle. Schooner Hero for New York.

Bashford, William   Prisoner 1710. Rank: Seaman, from: Grecian, Letter of Marque.
    Cap: 02 May 1814 Chesapeake by Jansur Int: 26 May 1814 Dis: 20 Mar 1815.
    Received from Lacedaemonian. Merchant Vessel.

Basler, Amos   Prisoner 808. Rank: Seaman, from: Elouisa, Merchant Schooner.
    Cap: 16 Feb 1813 at Sea by HM Sloop Morgiana Int: 25 Feb 1813 Dis: 14 Jun 1813.
    Received from Morgiana. Permitted to return to the United States in the Perseverance Cartel.

Basset, Samuel   Prisoner 1516. Rank: 1 Officer, from: Matchless, Merchant Vessel.
    Cap: 02 Jan 1814 Latt 22.0 by Prometheus Int: 22 Jan 1814 Dis: 15 Apr 1814.
    Received from Surprize. Rammilles for Halifax.

Bassett, Freeman C   Prisoner 411. Rank: Master, from: Isabella, Merchant Brig.
    Cap: 15 Nov 1812 at Sea by HM Sloop Childers Int: 24 Nov 1812 Dis: 27 Jan 1813.
    Received from HM Ship Childers. Bostock Cartel for New York.

Batis, John   Prisoner 1287. Rank: Seaman, from: Perry, Merchant Schooner.
    Cap: 03 Dec 1813 Long Island by Indemyion Int: 19 Dec 1813 Dis: 15 Apr 1814.
    Received from Sceptre. Diana Transport for Halifax. John Batis (1).

American Prisoners of War Held at Bermuda During the War of 1812

Batis, John   Prisoner 1318. Rank: Seaman, from: Rolla, Privateer.
     Cap: 10 Dec 1813 Block Island by Loire Int: 20 Dec 1813 Dis: 15 Apr 1814.
     Received from San Domingo. HMS Rammillies for Halifax. John Batis (2).

Batt, James   Prisoner 769. Rank: 1 Mate, from: Trinadada, Merchant Brig.
     Cap: 06 Jan 1813 Lat 37.20, Long 75.00 by HM Sloop Sylph Int: 26 Jan 1813 Dis: 24 Jun 1813.
     Received from Sloop Sylph. Magnet Cartel for New York.

Baty, William   Prisoner 655. Rank: Seaman, from: Not Recorded, Not Recorded.
     Cap: Not Recorded by Not Recorded Int: 21 Jan 1813 Dis: 27 Jan 1813.
     Received from HMS Ruby. Surrendered them selves as Prisoners of War.
     Bostock Cartel for New York.

Baxter, John   Prisoner 1108. Rank: Captains Mate, from: Revenge, Privateer Brig.
     Cap: 25 May 1813 at Sea by Narcissus Int: 27 May 1813 Dis: 24 Jun 1813.
     Received from HM Ship San Domingo. Magnet Cartel for New York.

Bayer, Abner   Prisoner 550. Rank: Seaman, from: Herald, Letter of Marque Brig.
     Cap: 25 Dec 1812 at Sea by HM Ship Maidstone Int: 05 Jan 1813 Dis: 27 Jan 1813.
     Received from HM Ship Maidstone. Bostock Cartel for New York.

Baylee, George   Prisoner 2029. Rank: Prize Master, from: Swiftsure, Merchant Vessel.
     Cap: 26 Oct 1814 off Halifax by Armide Int: 07 Nov 1814 Dis: 28 Mar 1815.
     Recaptured. Received from HMS Armide. Clarendon Transport for U States.

Bayley, Joseph   Prisoner 2075. Rank: Seaman, from: May Flower, Merchant Sloop.
     Cap: 22 Dec 1814 Grafy Bay Bermuda by Came in by Stress of Weather Int: 22 Dec 1814 Dis: 11 Jan 1815. Received from American Sloop May Flower. This Vessel was blown off the Coast of America & ran into Bermuda in Distress. To wait for a passage to the United States.

Bayley, Warren   Prisoner 1342. Rank: Seaman, from: Rolla, Privateer.
     Cap: 10 Dec 1813 Block Island by Loire Int: 20 Dec 1813 Dis: 15 Apr 1814.
     Received from HM Ship San Domingo. HMS Rammillies for Halifax.

Baymanth, Lander   Prisoner 2631. Rank: Boy, from: Moreau, Merchant Vessel.
     Cap: 22 Nov 1814 off Delaware by Spencer Int: 06 Feb 1815 Dis: 28 Mar 1815.
     Received from HMS Telegraph. Clarendon Transport for U States.

Bayton, John   Prisoner 390. Rank: Seaman, from: Snapper, Privateer Schooner.
     Cap: 16 Nov 1812 at Sea by HM Ship Galus Int: 22 Nov 1812 Dis: 27 Jan 1813.
     Received from HM Ship Galus. Bostock Cartel for New York.

Beach, John   Prisoner 837. Rank: Seaman, from: Portsmouth, Merchant Ship.
     Cap: 27 Feb 1813 off Bermuda by HM Sloop Martin Int: 09 Mar 1813 Dis: 27 Mar 1813.
     Received from HM Ship Martin. Per Order Commodore Evans the Vessel being Liberated.

Beach, John   Prisoner 1292. Rank: Passenger, from: Dolphin, Merchant Sloop.
     Cap: 03 Dec 1813 off Cape Henry by Lacedaemonian Int: 19 Dec 1813 Dis: 21 Jan 1814.
     Received from Sceptre. Without Exchange being a Noncombatant.

Bearans, George   Prisoner 700. Rank: Seaman, from: High Flyer, Privateer.
     Cap: 09 Jan 1813 at Sea by HMS Acasta Int: 21 Jan 1813 Dis: 27 Jan 1813.
     Received from HMS Acasta. Bostock Cartel for New York.

Beard, James   Prisoner 57. Rank: Seaman, from: Ariel, Merchant Brig.
     Cap: 28 Jul 1812 of Bermuda by Recruit Int: 28 Aug 1812 Dis: 18 Sep 1812.
     Received from M Schooner Cuttle. Order of Commd Evans for England.

Beard, James   Prisoner 1356. Rank: Seaman, from: Rolla, Privateer.
     Cap: 10 Dec 1813 Block Island by Loire Int: 20 Dec 1813 Dis: 15 Apr 1814.
     Received from San Domingo. HMS Rammillies for Halifax.

Beard, Martin   Prisoner 1357. Rank: Seaman, from: Rolla, Privateer.
     Cap: 10 Dec 1813 Block Island by Loire Int: 20 Dec 1813 Dis: 15 Apr 1814.
     Received from San Domingo. HMS Rammillies for Halifax.

Beatey, James   Prisoner 2063. Rank: Seaman, from: Industry, Merchant Vessel.
     Cap: 01 Dec 1814 off Cape Henry by HMS Niemen Int: 15 Dec 1814 Dis: 28 Mar 1815.
     Recaptured. Belong to Carolina Privateer. Received from HMS Niemen.
     Clarendon Transport for U States.

Beats, John   Prisoner 264. Rank: Seaman, from: Wasp, Sloop of War.
     Cap: 18 Oct 1812 at Sea by HM Ship Poictiers Int: 26 Oct 1812 Dis: 05 Nov 1812.
     Received from HM Ship Poictiers. Brig Diamond on Parole to new London United States of America.

Beatty, Henry   Prisoner 1978. Rank: Seaman, from: Antelope, Merchant Vessel.
     Cap: 21 Aug 1814 Western Island by Whiting Int: 17 Sep 1814 Dis: 28 Mar 1815.
     Recaptured. Received from Goree. Clarendon Transport for U States.

Beatty, Joshua   Prisoner 673. Rank: Ship Steward, from: High Flyer, Privateer.
     Cap: 09 Jan 1813 at Sea by HM Ship Acasta Int: 21 Jan 1813 Dis: 27 Jan 1813.
     Received from HMS Acasta. Bostock Cartel for New York.

American Prisoners of War Held at Bermuda During the War of 1812

Beckwith, Henry   Prisoner 2270. Rank: Seaman, from: President, U States Frigate.
    Cap: 15 Jan 1815 Not Recorded by Endymion Int: 30 Jan 1815 Dis: 28 Mar 1815.
    Received from Pomone. Mars Transport for U States.

Beeby, Joseph   Prisoner 185. Rank: Seaman, from: Wasp, Sloop of War.
    Cap: 18 Oct 1812 at Sea by HMS Poictiers Int: 26 Oct 1812 Dis: 05 Nov 1812.
    Received from HM Ship Poictiers. Brig Diamond on Parole to new London America.

Beek, James   Prisoner 2392. Rank: Seaman, from: President, U States Frigate.
    Cap: 15 Jan 1815 Not Recorded by HM Ship Endymion Int: 04 Feb 1815 Dis: 28 Mar 1815.
    Received from Endymion. Mars Transport for U States.

Beers, Oliver   Prisoner 868. Rank: Seaman, from: Gustavas, Merchant Brig.
    Cap: 16 Mar 1813 Chesapeake by HM Ship Laurustinus Int: 23 Mar 1813 Dis: 24 Apr 1813.
    Received from Laurustinus. Per Order Commodore Evans Vessel Liberated.

Belding, Emos   Prisoner 813. Rank: Seaman, from: Stockholm, Merchant Schooner.
    Cap: 18 Feb 1813 at Sea by HMS Statira Int: 01 Mar 1813 Dis: 14 Apr 1813.
    Received from HMS Statira. Per Order Commodore Evans Vessel Liberated.

Belfeur, James   Prisoner 1296. Rank: Seaman, from: Dragon, Not Recorded.
    Cap: Not Recorded by Not Recorded Int: 19 Dec 1813 Dis: 15 Apr 1814.
    Received from Sceptre. Gave himself up from the Dragon being an American. Diana Transport for Halifax. (Date of capture not recorded.)

Bell, David   Prisoner 2309. Rank: Seaman, from: President, U States Frigate.
    Cap: 15 Jan 1815 Not Recorded by Endymion Int: 04 Feb 1815 Dis: 28 Mar 1815.
    Received from Endymion. Mars Transport for U States.

Bell, George   Prisoner 2477. Rank: Seaman, from: President, U States Frigate.
    Cap: 15 Jan 1815 Not Recorded by Endymion Int: 04 Feb 1815 Dis: 28 Mar 1815.
    Received from Endymion. Clarenden Transport for U States.

Bell, James   Prisoner 1089. Rank: Seaman, from: Langdon Cheves, Merchant.
    Cap: 12 May 1813 at Sea by HM Sloop Atalante Int: 25 May 1813 Dis: 24 Jun 1813.
    Received from HMS Atalante. Magnet Cartel for New York.

Bell, Samuel   Prisoner 2153. Rank: Masters Mate, from: President, U States Frigate.
    Cap: 15 Jan 1815 Not Recorded by Endymion Int: 30 Jan 1815 Dis: 18 Mar 1815.
    Received from President. Merchant Vessel.

Bell, William   Prisoner 1813. Rank: Passenger, from: Not Recorded, Not Recorded.
    Cap: Not Recorded by Not Recorded Int: 14 Jun 1814 Dis: 15 Jun 1814.
    From St. Bartholomew in the Swedish Schooner Oscar. on Parole per Order Com in Chief to America. (Date of capture not recorded.)

Bella, John   Prisoner 1918. Rank: Seaman, from: Dolphin, Packet.
    Cap: 20 Aug 1814 St. Catherine by Lacedaemonian Int: 09 Sep 1814 Dis: 28 Mar 1815.
    Received from Lacedaemonian. Clarendon Transport for U States.

Bemous, Abraham   Prisoner 2502. Rank: Seaman, from: President, U States Frigate.
    Cap: 15 Jan 1815 Not Recorded by Endymion Int: 04 Feb 1815 Dis: 28 Mar 1815.
    Received from Endymion. Clarenden Transport for U States.

Benedick, John   Prisoner 1175. Rank: Seaman, from: Elizabeth, Merchant.
    Cap: 15 Jun 1813 at Sea by HM Ship Marlborough Int: 15 Aug 1813 Dis: 02 Sep 1813.
    Received from HM Ship Woolwich. Per order of Commodore Evans vessel being liberated.

Benitt, Juan   Prisoner 927. Rank: Seaman, from: Albert, Merchant Schooner.
    Cap: 05 Mar 1813 Chesapeake by HM Ship Marlborough Int: 23 Mar 1813 Dis: 24 Mar 1813.
    Received from Laurustinus. St. Michael per Order Adl Sir J B Warren.

Bennedick, George   Prisoner 222. Rank: Seaman, from: Wasp, Sloop of War.
    Cap: 18 Oct 1812 at Sea by HM Ship Poictiers Int: 26 Oct 1812 Dis: 05 Nov 1812.
    Received from HM Ship Poictiers. Brig Diamond on Parole to new London United States of America.

Bennet, Abua   Prisoner 1315. Rank: Seaman, from: Rolla, Privateer.
    Cap: 10 Dec 1813 Block Island by Loire Int: 20 Dec 1813 Dis: 15 Apr 1814.
    Received from San Domingo. HMS Rammillies for Halifax.

Bennett, Albeno   Prisoner 11. Rank: Seaman, from: General Blake, Merchant.
    Cap: 09 Jul 1812 near Bermuda by Recruit Int: 28 Aug 1812 Dis: 18 Sep 1812.
    Received from HM Schooner Cuttle. Order of Commd Evans for England.

Bennett, George   Prisoner 1011. Rank: Seaman, from: Nymble, Merchant.
    Cap: 19 Mar 1813 off the Chesapeake by HM Ship San Domingo Int: 06 Apr 1813 Dis: 24 Jun 1813.
    Received from HMS Junon. Magnet Cartel for New York.

Bennett, John   Prisoner 2177. Rank: Seaman, from: President, U States Frigate.
    Cap: 15 Jan 1815 Not Recorded by HMS Endymion Int: 30 Jan 1815 Dis: 28 Mar 1815.
    Received from Pomone. Mars Transport for U States.

American Prisoners of War Held at Bermuda During the War of 1812

Bennett, John   Prisoner 2212. Rank: Seaman, from: President, U States Frigate.
    Cap: 15 Jan 1815 Not Recorded by Endymion Int: 30 Jan 1815 Dis: 28 Mar 1815.
    Received from Pomone. Mars Transport for U States.

Bennett, Peley   Prisoner 1417. Rank: Seaman, from: Nonsuch, Letter of Marque.
    Cap: 14 Dec 1813 Lat 32 by Doterel Int: 25 Dec 1813 Dis:
    Received from HM Brig Doterel. (Date of discharge not recorded.)

Bennett, Peter   Prisoner 2439. Rank: Marine, from: President, U States Frigate.
    Cap: 15 Jan 1815 Not Recorded by Endymion Int: 04 Feb 1815 Dis: 28 Mar 1815.
    Received from Endymion. Clarenden Transport for U States.

Bennett, Thomas   Prisoner 1553. Rank: Seaman, from: Bordeaux Packet, Letter of Marque.
    Cap: 28 Jan 1814 off Cape Henry by Nieman Int: 12 Feb 1814 Dis: 15 Apr 1814.
    Received from Nieman. Diana Transport for Halifax.

Bennison, Lenord   Prisoner 858. Rank: Passenger, from: Bona, Letter of Marque Schooner.
    Cap: 12 Mar 1813 Chesapeake by HM Ship Laurustinus Int: 23 Mar 1813 Dis: 05 May 1813.
    Received from HM Ship Laurustinus. being a Swede.

Bensham, William   Prisoner 692. Rank: Seaman, from: High Flyer, Privateer.
    Cap: 09 Jan 1813 at Sea by HMS Acasta Int: 21 Jan 1813 Dis: 27 Jan 1813.
    Received from HMS Acasta. Bostock Cartel for New York.

Bensley, William   Prisoner 1042. Rank: Seaman, from: Revinue, Merchant Sloop.
    Cap: 19 Mar 1813 off the Chesapeake by HMS Statira Int: 06 Apr 1813 Dis: 24 Jun 1813.
    Received from HMS Junon. Magnet Cartel for New York.

Benson, George   Prisoner 2272. Rank: Seaman, from: President, U States Frigate.
    Cap: 15 Jan 1815 Not Recorded by Endymion Int: 30 Jan 1815 Dis: 28 Mar 1815.
    Received from Pomone. Mars Transport for U States.

Benson, Samuel   Prisoner 2609. Rank: Mate, from: Falcon, Merchant Vessel.
    Cap: 22 Jan 1815 Sandy Hook by HM Ship Pomone Int: 05 Feb 1815 Dis: 09 Mar 1815.
    Received from HMS Forth. Merchant Service.

Benson, William   Prisoner 2206. Rank: Seaman, from: President, U States Frigate.
    Cap: 15 Jan 1815 Not Recorded by Endymion Int: 30 Jan 1815 Dis: 28 Mar 1815.
    Received from Pomone. Mars Transport for U States.

Beont, John   Prisoner 2486. Rank: Seaman, from: President, U States Frigate.
    Cap: 15 Jan 1815 Not Recorded by Endymion Int: 04 Feb 1815 Dis: 28 Mar 1815.
    Received from Endymion. Clarenden Transport for U States.

Bernard, James   Prisoner 280. Rank: Seaman, from: Little William, Merchant Brig.
    Cap: 18 Oct 1812 at Sea by HM Ship Poictiers Int: 30 Oct 1812 Dis: 05 Nov 1812.
    Received from HM Ship Poictiers. Brig Diamond on Parole to new London United States of America.

Bernard, John   Prisoner 1187. Rank: Seaman, from: Caledonian, Merchant.
    Cap: 20 Jul 1813 at Sea by HM Ship Marlborough Int: 18 Aug 1813 Dis: 03 Oct 1813.
    Received from HM Ship Woolwich. Caledonian per Order of Commodore Evans she being Liberated.

Bernard, William   Prisoner 1511. Rank: 2 Mate, from: Nonsuch, Letter of Marque.
    Cap: 14 Dec 1813 Latt 38.0 by Doterel Int: 22 Jan 1814 Dis: 15 Apr 1814.
    Received from Surprize. Rammilles for Halifax.

Berris, John   Prisoner 255. Rank: Seaman, from: Wasp, Sloop of War.
    Cap: 18 Oct 1812 at Sea by HM Ship Poictiers Int: 26 Oct 1812 Dis: 05 Nov 1812.
    Received from HM Ship Poictiers. Brig Diamond on Parole to new London United States of America.

Berry, Daniel   Prisoner 600. Rank: Seaman, from: Windward Planter, Merchant Sloop.
    Cap: 22 Dec 1812 at Sea by HM Ship Belvidera Int: 10 Jan 1813 Dis: 27 Jan 1813.
    Received from HMS Belvidera. Bostock Cartel for New York.

Berry, Gordon   Prisoner 981. Rank: Mate, from: Mary, Merchant.
    Cap: 10 Mar 1813 Chesapeake by HMS Maidstone Int: 23 Mar 1813 Dis: 25 May 1813.
    Received from HM Ship Laurustinus. United States to Effect his Exchange.

Berry, Jessy   Prisoner 1280. Rank: Seaman, from: Perry, Merchant Schooner.
    Cap: 03 Dec 1813 Long Island by Indemyion Int: 19 Dec 1813 Dis: 23 Apr 1814.
    Received from Sceptre. HMS Bulwark for Halifax.

Berry, Lyman   Prisoner 942. Rank: Master, from: Mary, Merchant Schooner.
    Cap: 10 Mar 1813 Chesapeake by HMS Maidstone Int: 23 Mar 1813 Dis: 30 Apr 1813.
    Received from Laurustinus. United States to Effect his Exchange per Order C Evans.

Berryman, John   Prisoner 681. Rank: Seaman, from: High Flyer, Privateer.
    Cap: 09 Jan 1813 at Sea by HM Ship Acasta Int: 21 Jan 1813 Dis: 27 Jan 1813.
    Received from HMS Acasta. Bostock Cartel for New York.

Bert, Thomas   Prisoner 1346. Rank: Seaman, from: Rolla, Privateer.
    Cap: 10 Dec 1813 Block Island by Loire Int: 20 Dec 1813 Dis: 15 Apr 1814.
    Received from HM Ship San Domingo. HMS Rammillies for Halifax.

American Prisoners of War Held at Bermuda During the War of 1812

Bertram, John   Prisoner 1848. Rank: Seaman, from: Little Catherine, Merchant Vessel.
    Cap: Not Recorded by Not Recorded Int: Dis: 10 Nov 1814.
    Recaptured. Joseph MV Order Rear Adm Cockburn. (Dates of capture and internment not recorded.)

Besson, Joseph   Prisoner 2358. Rank: Seaman, from: President, U States Frigate.
    Cap: 15 Jan 1815 Not Recorded by HMS Endymion Int: 04 Feb 1815 Dis: 28 Mar 1815.
    Received from Endymion. Mars Transport for U States.

Best, Samuel   Prisoner 2728. Rank: Citizen, from: St Marys, Not Recorded.
    Cap: 18 Feb 1815 St Marys by Primrose Int: 03 Mar 1815 Dis: 28 Mar 1815.
    Received from Hebrus. Clarendon Transport for U States.

Bewditch, Thomas   Prisoner 2717. Rank: Prize Master, from: American Gun Boat, Not Recorded.
    Cap: 06 Feb 1815 off Charleston by Tonnant Int: 02 Mar 1815 Dis:
    Received from Armede. (Date of discharge not recorded.)

Biddle, James   Prisoner 165. Rank: 2 Lieutenant, from: Wasp, Sloop of War.
    Cap: 18 Oct 1812 at Sea by HMS Poictiers Int: 26 Oct 1812 Dis: 05 Nov 1812.
    Received from HM Ship Poictiers. on Parole Brig Diamond to new London America.

Binghouse, William   Prisoner 951. Rank: Seaman, from: Bona, Letter of Marque Schooner.
    Cap: 12 Mar 1813 Chesapeake by Laurustinus Int: 23 Mar 1813 Dis: 24 Jun 1813.
    Received from Laurustinus. Magnet Cartel for New York.

Bird, Henry   Prisoner 2242. Rank: Seaman, from: President, U States Frigate.
    Cap: 15 Jan 1815 Not Recorded by Endymion Int: 30 Jan 1815 Dis: 28 Mar 1815.
    Received from Pomone. Mars Transport for U States.

Black, David   Prisoner 797. Rank: Seaman, from: Not Recorded, Not Recorded.
    Cap: Not Recorded by Not Recorded Int: 14 Feb 1813 Dis: 24 Jun 1813.
    Received from Narcissus. Surrendered himself as a Prisoner of War. Magnet Cartel for New York.
    (Date of capture not recorded.)

Blackburn, William   Prisoner 14. Rank: Seaman, from: General Blake, Merchant.
    Cap: 09 Jul 1812 near Bermuda by Recruit Int: 28 Aug 1812 Dis: 18 Sep 1812.
    Received from HM Schooner Cuttle. Order of Commd Evans for England.

Blackler, Henry   Prisoner 1540. Rank: Mate, from: Defiance, Merchant Vessel.
    Cap: 05 Jan 1814 at Sea by Childers Int: 26 Jan 1814 Dis:
    Received from Childers. (Date of discharge not recorded.)

Blackwell, William   Prisoner 1491. Rank: Seaman, from: Maresoil, Merchant Brig.
    Cap: 25 Dec 1813 Latt 35.0 by HMS Fox Int: 09 Jan 1814 Dis: 15 Apr 1814.
    Received from Fox. Diana Transport for Halifax.

Bladen, Thomas   Prisoner 1251. Rank: Not Recorded, from: Dolphin, Merchant Schooner.
    Cap: 23 Oct 1813 Gulph of Florida by Conflict Int: 02 Dec 1813 Dis: 15 Apr 1814.
    Received from HMS Sceptre. HMS Rammillies for Halifax.

Blair, John R   Prisoner 1252. Rank: Not Recorded, from: Circe, Merchant Vessel.
    Cap: 23 Oct 1813 Cape Hatterus by Acteon Int: 02 Dec 1813 Dis: 24 Apr 1814.
    Received from HMS Sceptre. HMS Sceptre for England.

Blake, Perry   Prisoner 2482. Rank: Seaman, from: President, U States Frigate.
    Cap: 15 Jan 1815 Not Recorded by Endymion Int: 04 Feb 1815 Dis: 28 Mar 1815.
    Received from Endymion. Clarenden Transport for U States.

Blakely, M   Prisoner 1423. Rank: Seaman, from: Nonsuch, Letter of Marque.
    Cap: 14 Dec 1813 Lat 32 by Doterel Int: 25 Dec 1813 Dis: 15 Apr 1814.
    Received from HM Brig Doterel. Diana Transport for Halifax.

Blanchard, Ebenezer   Prisoner 2125. Rank: Seaman, from: Post Boy, Merchant Vessel.
    Cap: 09 Dec 1814 off Delaware by HMS Pictolus Int: 27 Jan 1815 Dis: 13 Mar 1815.
    Received from Pictolus. Merchant Service.

Blass, J G   Prisoner 1839. Rank: Seaman, from: Antelope, Merchant Sloop.
    Cap: 30 May 1814 between Cape Roman and Cape Fear by Doteral & Morgiana Int: 30 Jun 1814 Dis:
    Received from HMS Doterel. (Date of discharge not recorded.)

Blayer, Robert   Prisoner 949. Rank: Seaman, from: Bona, Letter of Marque Schooner.
    Cap: 12 Mar 1813 Chesapeake by Laurustinus Int: 23 Mar 1813 Dis: 24 Jun 1813.
    Received from Laurustinus. Magnet Cartel for New York.

Blether, Nathaniel   Prisoner 2652. Rank: Seaman, from: President, U States Frigate.
    Cap: 11 Feb 1815 off N York by Endymion Int: 11 Feb 1815 Dis: 28 Mar 1815.
    Received from President. Clarenden Transport for U States.
    (Date of capture should be January 15, 1815.)

Blocke, Edmond   Prisoner 1430. Rank: Seaman, from: Nonsuch, Letter of Marque.
    Cap: 14 Dec 1813 Lat 32 by Doterel Int: 25 Dec 1813 Dis: 15 Apr 1814.
    Received from HM Brig Doterel. Diana Transport for Halifax.

American Prisoners of War Held at Bermuda During the War of 1812

Bloom, John   Prisoner 1295. Rank: Seaman, from: Dolphin, Merchant Sloop.
    Cap: 03 Dec 1813 off Cape Henry by Lacedaemonian Int: 19 Dec 1813 Dis: 15 Apr 1814.
    Received from Sceptre. Diana Transport for Halifax.

Blosdale, Jacob   Prisoner 2407. Rank: Seaman, from: President, U States Frigate.
    Cap: 15 Jan 1815 Not Recorded by HM Ship Endymion Int: 04 Feb 1815 Dis: 28 Mar 1815.
    Received from Endymion. Mars Transport for U States.

Blosom, Joseph   Prisoner 2574. Rank: Seaman, from: John, Merchant Vessel.
    Cap: 30 Dec 1814 off New York by HMS Pomone Int: 05 Feb 1815 Dis: 16 Mar 1815.
    Received from HMS Forth. Merchant Service.

Bluck, B W   Prisoner 2846. Rank: Seaman, from: Limerick, Not Recorded.
    Cap: 15 Mar 1815 Not Recorded by Asia Int: 25 Mar 1815 Dis:
    From Depot at Jamaica. Received from Asia. (Date of discharge not recorded.)

Blue, George   Prisoner 581. Rank: Seaman, from: Lydia, Merchant Ship.
    Cap: 25 Dec 1812 at Sea by HM Ship Maidstone Int: 06 Jan 1813 Dis: 27 Jan 1813.
    Received from HM Ship Maidstone. Bostock Cartel for New York.

Blyden, John   Prisoner 1955. Rank: Seaman, from: Pike, Privateer.
    Cap: 25 Aug 1814 off Savannah by Primrose Int: 09 Sep 1814 Dis: 28 Mar 1815.
    Received from Lacedaemonian. Clarendon Transport for U States.

Bocock, Matthew   Prisoner 828. Rank: Seaman, from: Portsmouth, Merchant Ship.
    Cap: 27 Feb 1813 off Bermuda by HM Sloop Martin Int: 09 Mar 1813 Dis: 27 Mar 1813.
    Received from Sloop Martin. Per Order Commodore Evans the Vessel being Liberated.

Bogardus, J B   Prisoner 1291. Rank: Master, from: Dolphin, Merchant Sloop.
    Cap: 03 Dec 1813 off Cape Henry by Lacedaemonian Int: 19 Dec 1813 Dis: 15 Apr 1814.
    Received from Sceptre. HMS Rammillies for Halifax.

Bohom, John   Prisoner 2732. Rank: Master, from: True American, Not Recorded.
    Cap: 11 Nov 1814 Chesapeake by Dragon Int: 03 Mar 1815 Dis: 28 Mar 1815.
    Received from Hebrus. Clarendon Transport for U States.

Bohoni, Cazer   Prisoner 2749. Rank: Seaman, from: Fair American, Not Recorded.
    Cap: 10 Dec 1814 St Augustine by Dragon Int: 03 Mar 1815 Dis: 28 Mar 1815.
    Received from Hebrus. Clarendon Transport for U States.

Bolt, Charles   Prisoner 2629. Rank: Mate, from: Moreau, Merchant Vessel.
    Cap: 22 Nov 1814 off Delaware by Spencer Int: 06 Feb 1815 Dis: 28 Mar 1815.
    Received from HMS Telegraph. Clarendon Transport for U States.

Bolt, James   Prisoner 2451. Rank: Seaman, from: President, U States Frigate.
    Cap: 15 Jan 1815 Not Recorded by Endymion Int: 04 Feb 1815 Dis: 28 Mar 1815.
    Received from Endymion. Clarenden Transport for U States.

Bond, Robert   Prisoner 922. Rank: Seaman, from: Albert, Merchant Schooner.
    Cap: 05 Mar 1813 Chesapeake by HM Ship Marlborough Int: 23 Mar 1813 Escaped: 21 Apr 1813.
    Received from Laurustinus. Escaped.

Bond, Thomas   Prisoner 2823. Rank: Seaman, from: Limerick, Not Recorded.
    Cap: 15 Mar 1815 Not Recorded by Asia Int: 25 Mar 1815 Dis:
    From Depot at Jamaica. Received from Asia. (Date of discharge not recorded.)

Bondleau, Thomas   Prisoner 1873. Rank: Seaman, from: Lion, Merchant Vessel.
    Cap: Not Recorded by Not Recorded Int: Dis: 28 Mar 1815.
    Clarendon Transport for U States. (Dates of capture and internment not recorded.)

Bonker, Daniel   Prisoner 1397. Rank: Mate, from: John & James, Merchant Vessel.
    Cap: 07 Dec 1813 Lat 37 by Loire Int: 21 Dec 1813 Dis: 15 Apr 1814.
    Received from Romulus. Rammilles for Halifax.

Bonwell, Garland   Prisoner 1930. Rank: Lieutenant Marines, from: Pike, Privateer.
    Cap: 25 Aug 1814 off Savannah by Primrose Int: 09 Sep 1814 Dis: 28 Mar 1815.
    Received from Lacedaemonian. Clarendon Transport for U States.

Boon, James   Prisoner 1335. Rank: Seaman, from: Rolla, Privateer.
    Cap: 10 Dec 1813 Block Island by Loire Int: 20 Dec 1813 Died: 22 Mar 1814.
    Received from HM Ship San Domingo. Died. Pneumonia.

Booth, Benjamin W   Prisoner 166. Rank: Midshipman, from: Wasp, Sloop of War.
    Cap: 18 Oct 1812 at Sea by HMS Poictiers Int: 26 Oct 1812 Dis: 05 Nov 1812.
    Received from HM Ship Poictiers. on Parole Brig Diamond to new London America.

Boothe, Thomas   Prisoner 2845. Rank: Seaman, from: Limerick, Not Recorded.
    Cap: 15 Mar 1815 Not Recorded by Asia Int: 25 Mar 1815 Dis:
    From Depot at Jamaica. Received from Asia. (Date of discharge not recorded.)

Borrswell, Paul   Prisoner 1301. Rank: Lieutenant, from: Rolla, Privateer.
    Cap: 10 Dec 1813 Block Island by Loire Int: 20 Dec 1813 Dis: 15 Apr 1814.
    Received from San Domingo. HMS Rammillies for Halifax.

American Prisoners of War Held at Bermuda During the War of 1812

Bosman, Henry   Prisoner 638. Rank: Seaman, from: Crown Prince, Merchant Schooner.
    Cap: 19 Dec 1812 at Sea by HM Ship Galus Int: 17 Jan 1813 Dis: 27 Jan 1813.
    Received from HM Ship Galus. Bostock Cartel for New York.

Boss, Joseph   Prisoner 1305. Rank: Prize Master, from: Rolla, Privateer.
    Cap: 10 Dec 1813 Block Island by Loire Int: 20 Dec 1813 Dis: 15 Apr 1814.
    Received from San Domingo. HMS Rammillies for Halifax.

Boston, Daniel   Prisoner 445. Rank: Seaman, from: Adventure, Merchant Brig.
    Cap: 15 Dec 1812 off Bermuda by HM Sloop Childers Int: 17 Dec 1812 Dis: 27 Jan 1813.
    Received from HM Sloop Childers. Bostock Cartel for New York.

Bostwick, John   Prisoner 204. Rank: Marine, from: Wasp, Sloop of War.
    Cap: 18 Oct 1812 at Sea by HM Ship Poictiers Int: 26 Oct 1812 Dis: 05 Nov 1812.
    Received from HM Ship Poictiers. Brig Diamond on Parole to new London United States of America.

Bottings, Carter   Prisoner 969. Rank: Seaman, from: Janett, Merchant Brig.
    Cap: 25 Feb 1813 Chesapeake by HMS Junon Int: 23 Mar 1813 Dis: 24 Jun 1813.
    Received from HM Ship Laurustinus. Magnet Cartel for New York.

Bourne, Esra   Prisoner 1821. Rank: Passenger, from: Not Recorded, Not Recorded.
    Cap: Not Recorded by Not Recorded Int: 14 Jun 1814 Dis: 15 Jun 1814.
    From St. Bartholomew in the Swedish Schooner Oscar. on Parole per Order Com in Chief to America.
    (Date of capture not recorded.)

Boverham, Abraham   Prisoner 2730. Rank: Passenger, from: Kate, Not Recorded.
    Cap: 10 Nov 1814 Potomac by Dragon Int: 03 Mar 1815 Dis: 17 Mar 1815.
    Received from Hebrus. Merchant Vessel.

Bowdel, William   Prisoner 196. Rank: Marine, from: Wasp, Sloop of War.
    Cap: 18 Oct 1812 at Sea by HMS Poictiers Int: 26 Oct 1812 Dis: 05 Nov 1812.
    Received from HM Ship Poictiers. Brig Diamond on Parole to new London America.

Bowden, Stephen   Prisoner 2374. Rank: Seaman, from: President, U States Frigate.
    Cap: 15 Jan 1815 Not Recorded by HMS Endymion Int: 04 Feb 1815 Dis: 28 Mar 1815.
    Received from Endymion. Mars Transport for U States.

Bowden, Thomas   Prisoner 2680. Rank: Master, from: Ruby, Merchant Vessel.
    Cap: 28 Dec 1814 off New York by Lacedaemonian Int: 14 Feb 1815 Dis: 17 Mar 1815.
    Received from Childers. Merchant Vessel.

Bowditch, Joseph   Prisoner 423. Rank: Master, from: Eliza, Merchant Ship.
    Cap: 25 Nov 1812 Lat 37.00, Long 65.46 by HM Ship Tartarus Int: 03 Dec 1812 Dis: 12 Dec 1812.
    Received from HM Ship Tartarus. To the United States of America per Brig Diamond.

Bowen, Nathaniel   Prisoner 1775. Rank: 2 Mate, from: Yankelass, Privateer.
    Cap: 01 May 1814 Latt 40-4N, Long 38-0W by Severn & Surprise Int: 07 Jun 1814 Dis: 17 Dec 1814.
    Received from Surprise. Eolus Transport on Parole to United States Order Com Evans.

Bowling, Garrett   Prisoner 502. Rank: Seaman, from: Ann, Merchant Sloop.
    Cap: 19 Dec 1812 at Sea by HMS Sophia Int: 27 Dec 1812 Dis: 27 Jan 1813.
    Received from Sophia. Bostock Cartel for New York.

Bowman, Thaddus   Prisoner 1228. Rank: Not Recorded, from: HM Ship Cleopatra, Not Recorded.
    Cap: 21 Sep 1813 Not Recorded by Dragon Int: 16 Nov 1813 Dis: 15 Apr 1814.
    Received from HMS Sceptre. Surrendered himself. Diana Transport for Halifax.

Bowman, William   Prisoner 974. Rank: Seaman, from: Janett, Merchant Brig.
    Cap: 25 Feb 1813 Chesapeake by HMS Junon Int: 23 Mar 1813 Dis: 24 Jun 1813.
    Received from HM Ship Laurustinus. Magnet Cartel for New York.

Bowman, William   Prisoner 2271. Rank: Seaman, from: President, U States Frigate.
    Cap: 15 Jan 1815 Not Recorded by Endymion Int: 30 Jan 1815 Dis: 28 Mar 1815.
    Received from Pomone. Mars Transport for U States.

Bowmen, John   Prisoner 62. Rank: Seaman, from: Mary, Merchant Brig.
    Cap: 08 Aug 1812 of Bermuda by Cuttle Int: 28 Aug 1812 Dis: 18 Sep 1812.
    Received from M Schooner Cuttle. Order of Commd Evans for England.

Bowre, Henry   Prisoner 2163. Rank: School Master, from: President, U States Frigate.
    Cap: 15 Jan 1815 Not Recorded by Endymion Int: 30 Jan 1815 Dis: 18 Mar 1815.
    Received from President. Merchant Vessel.

Bowring, Jesse   Prisoner 207. Rank: Marine, from: Wasp, Sloop of War.
    Cap: 18 Oct 1812 at Sea by HM Ship Poictiers Int: 26 Oct 1812 Dis: 05 Nov 1812.
    Received from HM Ship Poictiers. Brig Diamond on Parole to new London United States of America.

Boyd, Thomas   Prisoner 374. Rank: Seaman, from: Snapper, Privateer Schooner.
    Cap: 16 Nov 1812 at Sea by HM Ship Galus Int: 22 Nov 1812 Dis: 27 Jan 1813.
    Received from HM Ship Galus. Bostock Cartel for New York.

American Prisoners of War Held at Bermuda During the War of 1812

Boyd, Thomas D   Prisoner 1233. Rank: Not Recorded, from: HM Ship Cleopatra, Not Recorded.
    Cap: 21 Sep 1813 Not Recorded by Dragon Int: 16 Nov 1813 Dis: 15 Apr 1814.
    Received from HMS Sceptre. Surrendered himself. Diana Transport for Halifax.

Boyen, James   Prisoner 556. Rank: Seaman, from: Herald, Letter of Marque Brig.
    Cap: 25 Dec 1812 at Sea by HM Ship Maidstone Int: 05 Jan 1813 Dis: 27 Jan 1813.
    Received from HM Ship Maidstone. Bostock Cartel for New York.

Boyles, Charles   Prisoner 2813. Rank: Mate, from: Limerick, Not Recorded.
    Cap: 04 Mar 1815 Not Recorded by Asia Int: 25 Mar 1815 Dis:
    From Depot at Jamaica. Received from Asia. (Date of discharge not recorded.)

Boyles, James   Prisoner 1497. Rank: Seaman, from: Santo Cateno Venturuso, Merchant.
    Cap: 28 Dec 1813 Latt 34.0 by HMS Fox Int: 09 Jan 1814 Dis: 15 Apr 1814.
    Received from HM Ship Fox. Diana Transport for Halifax.

Bradbury, George   Prisoner 645. Rank: Seaman, from: Dolphin, Merchant Brig.
    Cap: 30 Dec 1812 at Sea by HM Ship Galus Int: 17 Jan 1813 Dis: 27 Jan 1813.
    Received from HM Ship Galus. Bostock Cartel for New York.

Bradbury, John H   Prisoner 1260. Rank: Seaman, from: His Majesty's Schooner St. Lawrence, Not Recorded.
    Cap: Not Recorded by Not Recorded Int: 11 Dec 1813 Dis: 24 Apr 1814.
    Received from His Majesty's Schooner St. Lawrence. gave himself up as an American. HMS Sceptre for England. (Date of capture not recorded.)

Bradbury, Nathaniel   Prisoner 37. Rank: Seaman, from: Laura, Merchant Sloop.
    Cap: 24 Jul 1812 of Bermuda by Cuttle Int: 28 Aug 1812 Dis: 18 Sep 1812.
    Received from HM Schooner Cuttle. Order of Commd Evans for England.

Bradbury, William   Prisoner 2013. Rank: Seaman, from: Bridges, Merchant Vessel.
    Cap: 25 Oct 1814 off Halifax by Armide Int: 07 Nov 1814 Dis: 28 Mar 1815.
    Recaptured. Received from HMS Armide. Clarendon Transport for U States.

Bradford, Carn   Prisoner 2701. Rank: Seaman, from: Experiment, Merchant Vessel.
    Cap: 19 Jan 1815 off Block Island by Nimrod Int: 18 Feb 1815 Dis: 28 Mar 1815.
    Received from Nimrod. Clarendon Transport for U States.

Bradford, John   Prisoner 1210. Rank: Seaman, from: Ambition, Merchant Sloop.
    Cap: 26 Sep 1813 at Sea by HM Brig Acteon Int: 16 Nov 1813 Dis: 15 Apr 1814.
    Received from the Custody of Lieut Bacon. HMS Ramillies for Halifax.

Bradfort, Cuffy   Prisoner 2684. Rank: Seaman, from: Farmers Branch, Merchant Vessel.
    Cap: 06 Feb 1815 off Delaware by Lacedaemonian Int: 14 Feb 1815 Dis: 28 Mar 1815.
    Received from Childers. Clarendon Transport for U States.

Bradley, Philip   Prisoner 905. Rank: Seaman, from: Elizabeth, Merchant Brig.
    Cap: 26 Feb 1813 Chesapeake by HMS Marlborough Int: 23 Mar 1813 Dis: 24 Apr 1813.
    Received from HM Ship Laurustinus. Vessel Liberated By Order Commodore Evans.

Bradshaw, John   Prisoner 1879. Rank: Seaman, from: Levant, Merchant Vessel.
    Cap: Not Recorded by Not Recorded Int: Dis: 20 Mar 1815.
    Merchant Vessel. (Dates of capture and internment not recorded.)

Bradt, Francis   Prisoner 272. Rank: Marine, from: Wasp, Sloop of War.
    Cap: 18 Oct 1812 at Sea by HM Ship Poictiers Int: 26 Oct 1812 Dis: 05 Nov 1812.
    Received from HM Ship Poictiers. Brig Diamond on Parole to new London United States of America.

Bragdon, Joseph   Prisoner 2015. Rank: Seaman, from: Bridges, Merchant Vessel.
    Cap: 25 Oct 1814 off Halifax by Armide Int: 07 Nov 1814 Dis: 28 Mar 1815.
    Recaptured. Received from HMS Armide. Clarendon Transport for U States.

Brager, Abner K   Prisoner 454. Rank: Surgeon, from: Teazer, Privateer Schooner.
    Cap: 16 Dec 1812 at Sea by HM Ship St. Domingo Int: 21 Dec 1812 Dis: 27 Jan 1813.
    Received from HM Ship St. Domingo. Bostock Cartel for New York.

Brailey, Elisha   Prisoner 1620. Rank: Seaman, from: Perseferanda, Merchant Vessel.
    Cap: 03 Jan 1814 Block Island by Abion Int: 14 Feb 1814 Dis: 23 Apr 1814.
    Received from Sceptre. HMS Bulwark for Halifax.

Bramhold, Charles   Prisoner 2256. Rank: Seaman, from: President, U States Frigate.
    Cap: 15 Jan 1815 Not Recorded by Endymion Int: 30 Jan 1815 Dis: 28 Mar 1815.
    Received from Pomone. Mars Transport for U States.

Branch, Cyrus   Prisoner 276. Rank: Seaman, from: Little William, Merchant Brig.
    Cap: 18 Oct 1812 at Sea by HM Ship Poictiers Int: 26 Oct 1812 Dis: 05 Nov 1812.
    Received from HM Ship Poictiers. Brig Diamond on Parole to new London United States of America.

Brant, Solomon   Prisoner 2269. Rank: Seaman, from: President, U States Frigate.
    Cap: 15 Jan 1815 Not Recorded by Endymion Int: 30 Jan 1815 Dis: 28 Mar 1815.
    Received from Pomone. Mars Transport for U States.

American Prisoners of War Held at Bermuda During the War of 1812

Brashears, Richard   Prisoner 177. Rank: Midshipman, from: Wasp, Sloop of War.
    Cap: 18 Oct 1812 at Sea by HMS Poictiers Int: 26 Oct 1812 Dis: 05 Nov 1812.
    Received from HM Ship Poictiers. Brig Diamond on Parole to new London America.

Brauphau, Romain   Prisoner 525. Rank: Passenger, from: Herald, Letter of Marque Brig.
    Cap: 25 Dec 1812 at Sea by HMS Maidstone Int: 05 Jan 1813 Dis: 27 Jan 1813.
    Received from HM Ship Maidstone. Bostock Cartel for New York.

Bray, Henry   Prisoner 1031. Rank: Seaman, from: Dart, Merchant Schooner.
    Cap: 17 Mar 1813 off the Chesapeake by HMS Statira Int: 06 Apr 1813 Dis: 24 Jun 1813.
    Received from HMS Junon. Magnet Cartel for New York.

Bray, Josh E   Prisoner 2220. Rank: Seaman, from: President, U States Frigate.
    Cap: 15 Jan 1815 Not Recorded by Endymion Int: 30 Jan 1815 Dis: 28 Mar 1815.
    Received from Pomone. Mars Transport for U States.

Bray, Robert   Prisoner 1888. Rank: Passenger, from: Sally, Merchant Vessel.
    Cap: Not Recorded by Not Recorded Int: Dis: 28 Mar 1815.
    Clarendon Transport for U States. (Dates of capture and internment not recorded.)

Brazier, William   Prisoner 1871. Rank: Seaman, from: Lion, Merchant Vessel.
    Cap: Not Recorded by Not Recorded Int: Dis: 28 Mar 1815.
    Clarendon Transport for U States. (Dates of capture and internment not recorded.)

Brett, James   Prisoner 1232. Rank: Not Recorded, from: HM Ship Cleopatra, Not Recorded.
    Cap: 21 Sep 1813 Not Recorded by Dragon Int: 16 Nov 1813 Dis: 28 Mar 1815.
    Received from HMS Sceptre. Surrendered himself. Mars Transport for U States.

Brewster, Benjamin   Prisoner 2142. Rank: Midshipman, from: President, U States Frigate.
    Cap: 15 Jan 1815 Not Recorded by Endymion Int: 30 Jan 1815 Dis: 22 Mar 1815.
    Received from President. Merchant Vessel.

Brickman, John   Prisoner 2353. Rank: Seaman, from: President, U States Frigate.
    Cap: 15 Jan 1815 Not Recorded by HMS Endymion Int: 04 Feb 1815 Dis: 28 Mar 1815.
    Received from Endymion. Mars Transport for U States.

Briddon, Thomas   Prisoner 1561. Rank: Seaman, from: Bordeaux Packet, Letter of Marque.
    Cap: 28 Jan 1814 off Cape Henry by Nieman Int: 12 Feb 1814 Dis: 15 Apr 1814.
    Received from Nieman. Rammilles for Halifax.

Brigden, John   Prisoner 417. Rank: Seaman, from: Isabella, Merchant Brig.
    Cap: 15 Nov 1812 at Sea by HM Sloop Childers Int: 24 Nov 1812 Dis: 27 Jan 1813.
    Received from HM Ship Childers. Bostock Cartel for New York.

Briggs, B   Prisoner 1326. Rank: Seaman, from: Rolla, Privateer.
    Cap: 10 Dec 1813 Block Island by Loire Int: 20 Dec 1813 Dis: 15 Apr 1814.
    Received from HM Ship San Domingo. HMS Rammillies for Halifax.

Briggs, Barb   Prisoner 575. Rank: Seaman, from: Peakin, Merchant Ship.
    Cap: 17 Dec 1812 at Sea by HM Ship Acasta Int: 06 Jan 1813 Dis: 27 Jan 1813.
    Received from HM Ship Maidstone. Bostock Cartel for New York.

Briggs, John   Prisoner 289. Rank: Seaman, from: Wasp, Sloop of War.
    Cap: 18 Oct 1812 at Sea by HMS Poictiers Int: 02 Nov 1812 Dis: 04 Nov 1812.
    Received from HMS Poictiers. Brig Diamond on Parole to new London United States of America.

Briggs, Silvinus   Prisoner 1259. Rank: Seaman, from: Hero, Merchant Schooner.
    Cap: 14 Nov 1813 Delaware by Belvidera Int: 06 Dec 1813 Dis: 15 Apr 1814.
    Received from HMS Sceptre. Diana for Halifax.

Brill, Christopher   Prisoner 2002. Rank: Seaman, from: Dry Farbourn, Merchant Vessel.
    Cap: 21 Oct 1814 off Bermuda by Pandora Int: 27 Oct 1814 Dis: 10 Nov 1814.
    Dry Farborn. Recaptured. Received from Goree. Joseph MV order Adl Cockburn.

Bringham, John William   Prisoner 849. Rank: Master, from: Federal Jack, Merchant Schooner.
    Cap: 02 Mar 1813 off Charlestown by HMS Galus Int: 18 Mar 1813 Dis: 24 Jun 1813.
    Received from HMS Galus. Magnet Cartel for New York.

Britt, Thomas   Prisoner 510. Rank: Master, from: Crown Prince, Merchant Schooner.
    Cap: 19 Dec 1812 at Sea by HMS Galus Int: 28 Dec 1812 Dis: 27 Jan 1813.
    Received from Crown Prince. Bostock Cartel for New York.

Britt, William K   Prisoner 632. Rank: Mate, from: Crown Prince, Merchant Schooner.
    Cap: 19 Dec 1812 at Sea by Ship Galus Int: 14 Jan 1813 Dis: 27 Jan 1813.
    Received from Schooner Crown Prince. Bostock Cartel for New York.

Brock, Thomas   Prisoner 579. Rank: 2 Mate, from: Lydia, Merchant Ship.
    Cap: 25 Dec 1812 at Sea by HM Ship Maidstone Int: 06 Jan 1813 Dis: 27 Jan 1813.
    Received from HM Ship Maidstone. Bostock Cartel for New York.

American Prisoners of War Held at Bermuda During the War of 1812

Brockitt, William   Prisoner 1834. Rank: Passenger, from: Not Recorded, Not Recorded.
    Cap: Not Recorded by Not Recorded Int: 14 Jun 1814 Dis: 15 Jun 1814.
    From St. Bartholomew in the Swedish Schooner Oscar. on Parole per Order Com in Chief to America.
    (Date of capture not recorded.)

Brockway, John   Prisoner 978. Rank: Master, from: Betsy Ann, Merchant.
    Cap: 04 Mar 1813 Chesapeake by HM Ship Fantom Int: 23 Mar 1813 Dis: 19 May 1813.
    Received from HM Ship Laurustinus. United States to Effect their Exchange per Order Commd Evans.

Brook, Calvin   Prisoner 1928. Rank: Prize Master, from: Pike, Privateer.
    Cap: 25 Aug 1814 off Savannah by Primrose Int: 09 Sep 1814 Dis: 28 Mar 1815.
    Received from Lacedaemonian. Clarendon Transport for U States.

Brook, Peley   Prisoner 1398. Rank: Seaman, from: John & James, Merchant Vessel.
    Cap: 07 Dec 1813 Lat 37 by Loire Int: 21 Dec 1813 Dis: 15 Apr 1814.
    Received from Romulus. Rammilles for Halifax.

Brooking, John   Prisoner 2593. Rank: SM, from: Lark, Merchant Vessel.
    Cap: 01 Dec 1814 off New York by HM Ship Majestic Int: 05 Feb 1815 Dis: 28 Mar 1815.
    Recaptured. York Privateer. Received from HMS Forth. Clarendon Transport for U States.

Brooks, Edward   Prisoner 94. Rank: Seaman, from: Gossepuim, Merchant.
    Cap: 16 Aug 1812 of Bermuda by Goree Int: 28 Aug 1812 Dis: 18 Sep 1812.
    Received from HM Schooner Cuttle. Order of Commd Evans for England.

Brooks, George   Prisoner 130. Rank: Captain, from: James Maddison, Man of War.
    Cap: 22 Aug 1812 Lat 31 by HMS Barbados Int: 14 Sep 1812 Dis: 24 Oct 1812.
    Received from HMS Barbados. Brig Diamond on Parole to new London United States of America.

Brooks, Thomas   Prisoner 777. Rank: Seaman, from: Not Recorded, Not Recorded.
    Cap: Not Recorded by Not Recorded Int: 02 Feb 1813 Dis: 24 Jun 1813.
    Received from Sloop Sylph. Detained per Order of the Governor. Magnet Cartel for New York.
    (Date of capture not recorded.)

Brooks, Thomas   Prisoner 1469. Rank: Seaman, from: Vixen, Man of War.
    Cap: 25 Dec 1813 Lat 38.0 by Belvidera Int: 05 Jan 1814 Dis: 15 Apr 1814.
    U States Schooner. Received from HMS Belvidera. Diana Transport for Halifax.

Broughton, Elijah   Prisoner 1912. Rank: Seaman, from: Resolution, Merchant Vessel.
    Cap: 20 Aug 1814 St. Catherine by Lacedaemonian Int: 09 Sep 1814 Dis: 28 Mar 1815.
    Received from Lacedaemonian. Clarendon Transport for U States.

Broughton, Nicholas   Prisoner 1541. Rank: Part Owner, from: Defiance, Merchant Vessel.
    Cap: 05 Jan 1814 at Sea by Childers Int: 26 Jan 1814 Dis:
    Received from Childers. (Date of discharge not recorded.)

Browel, William   Prisoner 968. Rank: Seaman, from: Janett, Merchant Brig.
    Cap: 25 Feb 1813 Chesapeake by HMS Junon Int: 23 Mar 1813 Dis: 24 Jun 1813.
    Received from HM Ship Laurustinus. Magnet Cartel for New York.

Brown, Alexander   Prisoner 1142. Rank: Seaman, from: Asp, Man of War Schooner.
    Cap: 20 Jul 1813 at Sea by HM Ship San Domingo Int: 13 Aug 1813 Dis: 13 Aug 1813.
    Received from HM Ship Woolwich. American Ship Rolla per Order Commr Evans.

Brown, Charles   Prisoner 335. Rank: Seaman, from: Snapper, Privateer Schooner.
    Cap: 16 Nov 1812 at Sea by HMS Galus Int: 22 Nov 1812 Dis: 27 Jan 1813.
    Received from HM Ship Galus. Bostock Cartel for New York.

Brown, Daniel   Prisoner 893. Rank: Seaman, from: Hannah, Merchant Schooner.
    Cap: 24 Feb 1813 Chesapeake by HMS Marlborough Int: 23 Mar 1813 Dis: 24 Jun 1813.
    Received from HM Ship Laurustinus. Magnet Cartel for New York.

Brown, Francis   Prisoner 1396. Rank: Mate, from: Rising Sun, Merchant Vessel.
    Cap: 01 Dec 1813 Lat 40 by Loire Int: 21 Dec 1813 Dis: 15 Apr 1814.
    Received from Romulus. Rammilles for Halifax.

Brown, George   Prisoner 1327. Rank: Seaman, from: Rolla, Privateer.
    Cap: 10 Dec 1813 Block Island by Loire Int: 20 Dec 1813 Dis: 15 Apr 1814.
    Received from HM Ship San Domingo. HMS Rammillies for Halifax.

Brown, Hans   Prisoner 2058. Rank: Master, from: Amy, Merchant Schooner.
    Cap: 26 Nov 1814 off Cape Delaware by Telegraph Int: 11 Dec 1814 Dis: 21 Feb 1815.
    Received from HMS Goree. Paroled to the U States having served six months as Carpenter's Mate order of Adl Sir A Cockburn.

Brown, James   Prisoner 447. Rank: Seaman, from: Adventure, Merchant Brig.
    Cap: 15 Dec 1812 off Bermuda by HM Sloop Childers Int: 17 Dec 1812 Dis: 27 Jan 1813.
    Received from HM Sloop Childers. Bostock Cartel for New York.

Brown, James   Prisoner 1436. Rank: Seaman, from: Nonsuch, Letter of Marque.
    Cap: 14 Dec 1813 Lat 32 by Doterel Int: 25 Dec 1813 Dis: 15 Apr 1814.
    Received from HM Brig Doterel. Diana Transport for Halifax.

American Prisoners of War Held at Bermuda During the War of 1812

Brown, James   Prisoner 1749. Rank: Seaman, from: Yankelass, Privateer.
    Cap: 01 May 1814 L 40-4N, Long 38-0W by Severn & Surprise Int: 06 Jun 1814 Dis: 28 Mar 1815.
    Received from Severn. Mars Transport for U States.

Brown, James   Prisoner 2723. Rank: Seaman, from: American Gun Boat, Not Recorded.
    Cap: 06 Feb 1815 off Charleston by Tonnant Int: 02 Mar 1815 Dis:
    Received from Armede. (Date of discharge not recorded.)

Brown, John   Prisoner 193. Rank: Seaman, from: Wasp, Sloop of War.
    Cap: 18 Oct 1812 at Sea by HMS Poictiers Int: 26 Oct 1812 Dis: 05 Nov 1812.
    Received from HM Ship Poictiers. Brig Diamond on Parole to new London America.
    John Brown (1st).

Brown, John   Prisoner 253. Rank: Seaman, from: Wasp, Sloop of War.
    Cap: 18 Oct 1812 at Sea by HM Ship Poictiers Int: 26 Oct 1812 Dis: 05 Nov 1812.
    Received from HM Ship Poictiers. Brig Diamond on Parole to new London United States of America.
    John Brown (2).

Brown, John   Prisoner 391. Rank: Seaman, from: Snapper, Privateer Schooner.
    Cap: 16 Nov 1812 at Sea by HM Ship Galus Int: 22 Nov 1812 Dis: 27 Jan 1813.
    Received from HM Ship Galus. Bostock Cartel for New York.

Brown, John   Prisoner 690. Rank: Seaman, from: High Flyer, Privateer.
    Cap: 09 Jan 1813 at Sea by HMS Acasta Int: 21 Jan 1813 Dis: 27 Jan 1813.
    Received from HMS Acasta. Bostock Cartel for New York.

Brown, John   Prisoner 833. Rank: Seaman, from: Portsmouth, Merchant Ship.
    Cap: 27 Feb 1813 off Bermuda by HM Sloop Martin Int: 09 Mar 1813 Dis: 27 Mar 1813.
    Received from Sloop Martin. Per Order Commodore Evans the Vessel being Liberated.

Brown, John   Prisoner 913. Rank: Master, from: Harmony, Merchant Schooner.
    Cap: 05 Mar 1813 Chesapeake by HM Ship Laurustinus Int: 23 Mar 1813 Dis: 24 Jun 1813.
    Received from Laurustinus. Magnet Cartel for New York.

Brown, John L   Prisoner 1462. Rank: Seaman, from: Vixen, Man of War.
    Cap: 25 Dec 1813 Lat 38.0 by Belvidera Int: 05 Jan 1814 Dis: 15 Apr 1814.
    U States Schooner. Received from HMS Belvidera. Diana Transport for Halifax.

Brown, John F   Prisoner 1981. Rank: Seaman, from: Antelope, Merchant Vessel.
    Cap: 21 Aug 1814 Western Island by Whiting Int: 17 Sep 1814 Dis:
    Recaptured. Received from Goree. (Date of discharge not recorded.)

Brown, John   Prisoner 2266. Rank: Not Legible, from: President, U States Frigate.
    Cap: 15 Jan 1815 Not Recorded by Endymion Int: 30 Jan 1815 Dis: 28 Mar 1815.
    Received from Pomone. Mars Transport for U States.

Brown, John   Prisoner 2770. Rank: Seaman, from: Brant, Not Recorded.
    Cap: 05 Feb 1815 St Augustine by Severn Int: 03 Mar 1815 Dis: 28 Mar 1815.
    Received from Hebrus. Clarendon Transport for U States.

Brown, Jonas   Prisoner 867. Rank: Seaman, from: Gustavas, Merchant Brig.
    Cap: 16 Mar 1813 Chesapeake by HM Ship Laurustinus Int: 23 Mar 1813 Dis: 24 Apr 1813.
    Received from Laurustinus. Per Order Commodore Evans Vessel Liberated.

Brown, Joseph   Prisoner 2282. Rank: Seaman, from: President, U States Frigate.
    Cap: 15 Jan 1815 Not Recorded by Endymion Int: 30 Jan 1815 Dis: 28 Mar 1815.
    Received from Pomone. Mars Transport for U States.

Brown, Joshua   Prisoner 230. Rank: Seaman, from: Wasp, Sloop of War.
    Cap: 18 Oct 1812 at Sea by HM Ship Poictiers Int: 26 Oct 1812 Dis: 05 Nov 1812.
    Received from HM Ship Poictiers. Brig Diamond on Parole to new London United States of America.

Brown, Liberty   Prisoner 1129. Rank: Seaman, from: Mary, Merchant.
    Cap: 17 Apr 1813 at Sea by HM Ship Fox Int: 21 Jun 1813 Dis: 24 Jun 1813.
    Received from HM Ship Ruby. Magnet Cartel for New York.

Brown, P F   Prisoner 1628. Rank: Seaman, from: Perseferanda, Merchant Vessel.
    Cap: 03 Jan 1814 Block Island by Albion Int: 14 Feb 1814 Dis: 18 Dec 1814.
    Received from Sceptre. Ardente S L being British Subject.

Brown, Parker   Prisoner 989. Rank: Seaman, from: Nancy, Merchant.
    Cap: 04 Mar 1813 Chesapeake by Narcissus Int: 23 Mar 1813 Dis: 24 Jun 1813.
    Received from HM Ship Laurustinus. Magnet Cartel for New York.

Brown, Peter   Prisoner 2193. Rank: Seaman, from: President, U States Frigate.
    Cap: 15 Jan 1815 Not Recorded by HMS Endymion Int: 30 Jan 1815 Dis: 28 Mar 1815.
    Received from Pomone. Mars Transport for U States.

Brown, R   Prisoner 1866. Rank: Seaman, from: Viper, Merchant Vessel.
    Cap: Not Recorded by Not Recorded Int: Dis: 20 Mar 1815.
    Merchant Vessel. (Dates of capture and internment not recorded.)

American Prisoners of War Held at Bermuda During the War of 1812

Brown, Richard   Prisoner 1815. Rank: Passenger, from: Not Recorded, Not Recorded.
    Cap: Not Recorded by Not Recorded Int: 14 Jun 1814 Dis: 15 Jun 1814.
    From St. Bartholomew in the Swedish Schooner Oscar. on Parole per Order Com in Chief to America. (Date of capture not recorded.)

Brown, Samuel   Prisoner 2156. Rank: Carpenter, from: President, U States Frigate.
    Cap: 15 Jan 1815 Not Recorded by Endymion Int: 30 Jan 1815 Dis: 28 Mar 1815.
    Received from President. Mars Transport for U States.

Brown, Samuel   Prisoner 2274. Rank: Seaman, from: President, U States Frigate.
    Cap: 15 Jan 1815 Not Recorded by Endymion Int: 30 Jan 1815 Dis: 28 Mar 1815.
    Received from Pomone. Mars Transport for U States.

Brown, Soloman   Prisoner 822. Rank: Seaman, from: Elove & Unity, Merchant.
    Cap: 07 Mar 1813 at Bermuda by Sandimingo Int: 08 Mar 1813 Dis: 13 Jun 1813.
    Received from Sandimingo. Perseverance Cartel for the United States per Order Adm Sir J B Warren.

Brown, Stephen   Prisoner 986. Rank: Master, from: Nancy, Merchant.
    Cap: 04 Mar 1813 Chesapeake by Narcissus Int: 23 Mar 1813 Dis: 25 May 1813.
    Received from HM Ship Laurustinus. United States to Effect his Exchange.

Brown, Thomas   Prisoner 2388. Rank: Boatswains Mate, from: President, U States Frigate.
    Cap: 15 Jan 1815 Not Recorded by HM Ship Endymion Int: 04 Feb 1815 Dis: 28 Mar 1815.
    Received from Endymion. Mars Transport for U States.

Brown, Thomas   Prisoner 2492. Rank: Marine, from: President, U States Frigate.
    Cap: 15 Jan 1815 Not Recorded by Endymion Int: 04 Feb 1815 Dis: 28 Mar 1815.
    Received from Endymion. Clarenden Transport for U States.

Brown, Webster   Prisoner 1118. Rank: Master, from: Gold Coiner, Merchant.
    Cap: 24 Mar 1813 at Sea by HM Sloop Lyra Int: 21 Jun 1813 Dis: 24 Jun 1813.
    Received from HMS Ruby. Magnet Cartel for New York.

Brown, William   Prisoner 1943. Rank: Seaman, from: Pike, Privateer.
    Cap: 25 Aug 1814 off Savannah by Primrose Int: 09 Sep 1814 Dis: 10 Nov 1814.
    Received from Lacedaemonian. Joseph MV Order Adm Cockburn.

Brown, William   Prisoner 2179. Rank: Seaman, from: President, U States Frigate.
    Cap: 15 Jan 1815 Not Recorded by HMS Endymion Int: 30 Jan 1815 Dis: 28 Mar 1815.
    Received from Pomone. Mars Transport for U States.

Brown, William   Prisoner 2273. Rank: Seaman, from: President, U States Frigate.
    Cap: 15 Jan 1815 Not Recorded by Endymion Int: 30 Jan 1815 Dis: 28 Mar 1815.
    Received from Pomone. Mars Transport for U States.

Brown, Willliam   Prisoner 1368. Rank: Seaman, from: Rolla, Privateer.
    Cap: 10 Dec 1813 Block Island by Loire Int: 20 Dec 1813 Dis: 15 Apr 1814.
    Received from San Domingo. HMS Rammillies for Halifax.

Brown, Zacheus   Prisoner 2873. Rank: Seaman, from: Limerick, Not Recorded.
    Cap: 06 Mar 1815 Not Recorded by Asia Int: 29 Mar 1815 Dis: 28 Mar 1815.
    From West Indies. Received from La Brune. Clarendon Transport for U States. (Date of discharge before date of internment.)

Bruce, James   Prisoner 1055. Rank: Seaman, from: Massoil, Merchant.
    Cap: 18 Mar 1813 Chesapeake by HMS Dragon Int: 06 Apr 1813 Dis: 24 Jun 1813.
    Received from HMS Junon. Magnet Cartel for New York.

Bruce, Jonathan   Prisoner 1754. Rank: Seaman, from: Yankelass, Privateer.
    Cap: 01 May 1814 L 40-4N, Long 38-0W by Severn & Surprise Int: 06 Jun 1814 Dis: 28 Mar 1815.
    Received from Severn. Mars Transport for U States.

Bruster, William   Prisoner 367. Rank: Prize Master, from: Snapper, Privateer Schooner.
    Cap: 16 Nov 1812 at Sea by HM Ship Galus Int: 22 Nov 1812 Dis: 27 Jan 1813.
    Received from HM Ship Galus. Bostock Cartel for New York.

Bryan, Fagalte   Prisoner 1863. Rank: Seaman, from: Ann, Merchant Vessel.
    Cap: Not Recorded by Not Recorded Int: Dis: 20 Mar 1815.
    Merchant Vessel. (Dates of capture and internment not recorded.)

Bryant, James   Prisoner 2369. Rank: Seaman, from: President, U States Frigate.
    Cap: 15 Jan 1815 Not Recorded by HMS Endymion Int: 04 Feb 1815 Dis: 28 Mar 1815.
    Received from Endymion. Mars Transport for U States.

Buchan, Benjamin   Prisoner 1446. Rank: Seaman, from: Nonsuch, Letter of Marque.
    Cap: 14 Dec 1813 Lat 32 by Doterel Int: 25 Dec 1813 Dis: 15 Apr 1814.
    Received from Doterel. Diana Transport for Halifax.

Buckford, Andrew   Prisoner 1097. Rank: Mate, from: Apollo, Merchant Vessel.
    Cap: 15 May 1813 at Sea by Success Int: 27 May 1813 Dis: 24 Jun 1813.
    Received from HMS Atalante. Magnet Cartel for New York.

American Prisoners of War Held at Bermuda During the War of 1812

Buckin, Bartholomew   Prisoner 1002. Rank: Seaman, from: Jefferson, Merchant.
    Cap: 18 Mar 1813 at Sea by HM Sloop Atalante Int: 06 Apr 1813 Dis: 24 Jun 1813.
    Received from HMS Junon. Magnet Cartel for New York.

Buckland, John   Prisoner 744. Rank: Seaman, from: Savannah Packet, Merchant Brig.
    Cap: 05 Jan 1813 at Sea by HM Ship Poictiers Int: 21 Jan 1813 Dis: 27 Jan 1813.
    Received from HMS Poictiers. Bostock Cartel for New York.

Budgeron, William   Prisoner 2808. Rank: Seaman, from: Limerick, Not Recorded.
    Cap: 04 Mar 1815 Not Recorded by Asia Int: 25 Mar 1815 Dis:
    From Depot at Jamaica. Received from Asia. (Date of discharge not recorded.)

Bughton, James   Prisoner 1523. Rank: Seaman, from: Livce, Merchant Vessel.
    Cap: 27 Dec 1813 at Sea by Nieman Int: 22 Jan 1814 Dis: 15 Apr 1814.
    Received from Jaseur. Diana Transport for Halifax.

Bull, Francis   Prisoner 2318. Rank: Seaman, from: President, U States Frigate.
    Cap: 15 Jan 1815 Not Recorded by Endymion Int: 04 Feb 1815 Dis: 28 Mar 1815.
    Received from Endymion. Mars Transport for U States.

Bullock, Joseph   Prisoner 2589. Rank: Cook, from: Thestis, Merchant Vessel.
    Cap: 18 Nov 1814 off New York by HM Ship Majestic Int: 05 Feb 1815 Dis: 28 Mar 1815.
    Received from HMS Forth. Clarendon Transport for U States.

Bulter, Richard   Prisoner 1265. Rank: Seaman, from: Huntress, Merchant Vessel.
    Cap: 12 Nov 1813 Long Island by HM Brig Borer Int: 19 Dec 1813 Dis:
    Received from HMS Acasta. (Date of discharge not recorded.)

Bunkar, Isa   Prisoner 1623. Rank: Seaman, from: Perseferanda, Merchant Vessel.
    Cap: 03 Jan 1814 Block Island by Albion Int: 14 Feb 1814 Dis: 23 Apr 1814.
    Received from Sceptre. HMS Bulwark for Halifax.

Bunker, Nathaniel   Prisoner 582. Rank: Seaman, from: Lydia, Merchant Ship.
    Cap: 26 Dec 1812 at Sea by HM Ship Maidstone Int: 06 Jan 1813 Dis: 27 Jan 1813.
    Received from HM Ship Maidstone. Bostock Cartel for New York.

Bunquar, Obsolou   Prisoner 1486. Rank: Seaman, from: Luckey, Merchant Vessel.
    Cap: 19 Dec 1813 off the Delaware by Niemen Int: 07 Jan 1814 Dis: 15 Apr 1814.
    Received from HM Sloop Jaseur. Diana Transport for Halifax. (Name of capturing ship not legible, assume to be Nieman.)

Burch, Robert   Prisoner 380. Rank: Seaman, from: Snapper, Privateer Schooner.
    Cap: 16 Nov 1812 at Sea by HM Ship Galus Int: 22 Nov 1812 Dis: 27 Jan 1813.
    Received from HM Ship Galus. Bostock Cartel for New York.

Burding, Joseph   Prisoner 1773. Rank: Seaman, from: Yankelass, Privateer.
    Cap: 01 May 1814 Latt 40-4N, Long 38-0W by Severn & Surprise Int: 07 Jun 1814 Dis: 28 Mar 1815.
    Received from Surprise. Mars Transport for U States.

Burfield, Charles   Prisoner 2261. Rank: Marine, from: President, U States Frigate.
    Cap: 15 Jan 1815 Not Recorded by Endymion Int: 30 Jan 1815 Dis: 28 Mar 1815.
    Received from Pomone. Clarenden Transport for U States.

Burgess, Isaah   Prisoner 2703. Rank: Seaman, from: Sally, Merchant Vessel.
    Cap: 26 Jan 1815 off Block Island by Nimrod Int: 18 Feb 1815 Dis: 28 Mar 1815.
    Received from Nimrod. Clarendon Transport for U States.

Burgess, William   Prisoner 2313. Rank: Seaman, from: President, U States Frigate.
    Cap: 15 Jan 1815 Not Recorded by Endymion Int: 04 Feb 1815 Dis: 28 Mar 1815.
    Received from Endymion. Mars Transport for U States.

Burk, Greenbury   Prisoner 711. Rank: Seaman, from: High Flyer, Privateer.
    Cap: 09 Jan 1813 at Sea by HM Ship Acasta Int: 21 Jan 1813 Dis: 27 Jan 1813.
    Received from HMS Acasta. Bostock Cartel for New York.

Burke, Humphrey   Prisoner 1609. Rank: Seaman, from: Monticello, Merchant Vessel.
    Cap: 09 Dec 1813 Block Island by Albion Int: 14 Feb 1814 Dis: 23 Apr 1814.
    Received from Sceptre. HMS Bulwark for Halifax.

Burke, John   Prisoner 16. Rank: Seaman, from: Sally, Merchant Ship.
    Cap: 09 Jul 1812 near Bermuda by Recruit Int: 28 Aug 1812 Dis: 18 Sep 1812.
    Received from HM Schooner Cuttle. Order of Commd Evans for England.

Burke, Thomas   Prisoner 2655. Rank: Mate, from: Falcon, Merchant Vessel.
    Cap: 22 Jan 1815 Delaware by Forth Int: 13 Feb 1815 Dis: 17 Feb 1815.
    Received from Goree. Harriot M Vessel order of Commadore Evans.

Burn, Peter   Prisoner 308. Rank: Seaman, from: Wasp, Sloop of War.
    Cap: 18 Oct 1812 at Sea by HMS Poictiers Int: 05 Nov 1812 Died: 29 Dec 1812.
    Received from HM Ship Poictiers. Missing Supports to be drowned.

American Prisoners of War Held at Bermuda During the War of 1812

Burnam, Beasson   Prisoner 1573. Rank: Seaman, from: Bordeaux Packet, Letter of Marque.
    Cap: 28 Jan 1814 off Cape Henry by Nieman Int: 12 Feb 1814 Dis: 15 Apr 1814.
    Received from Nieman. Diana Transport for Halifax.

Burnell, Thomas   Prisoner 776. Rank: Resident of Bermuda, from: Not Recorded, Not Recorded.
    Cap: Not Recorded by Not Recorded Int: 02 Feb 1813 Dis: 24 Jun 1813.
    Received from Sloop Sylph. Detained per Order of the Governor. permitted to remain in the Colony.
    (Date of capture not recorded.)

Burns, Daniel   Prisoner 209. Rank: Marine, from: Wasp, Sloop of War.
    Cap: 18 Oct 1812 at Sea by HM Ship Poictiers Int: 26 Oct 1812 Dis: 05 Nov 1812.
    Received from HM Ship Poictiers. Brig Diamond on Parole to new London United States of America.

Burns, James   Prisoner 1325. Rank: Seaman, from: Rolla, Privateer.
    Cap: 10 Dec 1813 Block Island by Loire Int: 20 Dec 1813 Dis: 15 Apr 1814.
    Received from HM Ship San Domingo. HMS Rammillies for Halifax.

Burr, William   Prisoner 1795. Rank: Masters Mate, from: Yankelass, Privateer.
    Cap: 01 May 1814 Latt 40-4N, Long 38-0W by Severn & Surprise Int: 07 Jun 1814 Dis: 28 Mar 1815.
    Received from Surprise. Clarendon Transport for U States.

Burrett, John   Prisoner 213. Rank: Seaman, from: Wasp, Sloop of War.
    Cap: 18 Oct 1812 at Sea by HM Ship Poictiers Int: 26 Oct 1812 Dis: 05 Nov 1812.
    Received from HM Ship Poictiers. Brig Diamond on Parole to new London United States of America.

Burridge, James   Prisoner 465. Rank: Seaman, from: Teazer, Privateer Schooner.
    Cap: 16 Dec 1812 at Sea by HM Ship St. Domingo Int: 21 Dec 1812 Dis: 27 Jan 1813.
    Received from HM Ship St. Domingo. Bostock Cartel for New York.

Burrows, A H   Prisoner 1300. Rank: Sailing Master, from: Rolla, Privateer.
    Cap: 10 Dec 1813 Block Island by Loire Int: 20 Dec 1813 Dis: 15 Apr 1814.
    Received from San Domingo. HMS Rammillies for Halifax.

Bush, George   Prisoner 1434. Rank: Seaman, from: Nonsuch, Letter of Marque.
    Cap: 14 Dec 1813 Lat 32 by Doterel Int: 25 Dec 1813 Dis: 15 Apr 1814.
    Received from HM Brig Doterel. Diana Transport for Halifax.

Bushnam, James   Prisoner 1322. Rank: Seaman, from: Rolla, Privateer.
    Cap: 10 Dec 1813 Block Island by Loire Int: 20 Dec 1813 Dis: 15 Apr 1814.
    Received from San Domingo. HMS Rammillies for Halifax.

Bussell, William   Prisoner 603. Rank: Seaman, from: Noetoin, Packet Brig.
    Cap: 05 Jan 1813 at Sea by HM Ship Belvidera Int: 10 Jan 1813 Dis: 27 Jan 1813.
    Received from HMS Belvidera. Bostock Cartel for New York.

Butill, Dennis   Prisoner 1403. Rank: Seaman, from: John & James, Merchant Vessel.
    Cap: 07 Dec 1813 Lat 37 by Loire Int: 21 Dec 1813 Dis: 15 Apr 1814.
    Received from Romulus. Diana Transport for Halifax.

Butler, George   Prisoner 1817. Rank: Passenger, from: Not Recorded, Not Recorded.
    Cap: Not Recorded by Not Recorded Int: 14 Jun 1814 Dis: 15 Jun 1814.
    From St. Bartholomew in the Swedish Schooner Oscar. on Parole per Order Com in Chief to America.
    (Date of capture not recorded.)

Butler, George   Prisoner 2464. Rank: Seaman, from: President, U States Frigate.
    Cap: 15 Jan 1815 Not Recorded by Endymion Int: 04 Feb 1815 Dis: 28 Mar 1815.
    Received from Endymion. Clarenden Transport for U States.

Butler, John   Prisoner 120. Rank: Mate, from: William of Baltimore, Merchant.
    Cap: 31 Aug 1812 Lat 37 by HM Ship Recruit Int: 14 Sep 1812 Dis: 24 Oct 1812.
    Received from Recruit. on Parole to New London united States of America, Diamond Brig.

Butler, John   Prisoner 1473. Rank: 2 Mate, from: Rapid, Letter of Marque Schooner.
    Cap: 16 Dec 1813 off Sandy Rock by Plantagenet Int: 06 Jan 1814 Dis:
    Received from HM Ship Plantagenet. (Date of discharge not recorded.)

Butler, John   Prisoner 2010. Rank: Seaman, from: Bridges, Merchant Vessel.
    Cap: 25 Oct 1814 off Halifax by Armide Int: 07 Nov 1814 Dis: 28 Mar 1815.
    Recaptured. Received from HMS Armide. Clarendon Transport for U States.

Butler, John   Prisoner 2095. Rank: Seaman, from: Levant, Merchant Vessel.
    Cap: 04 Jan 1815 near New Providence by Forester Int: 19 Jan 1815 Dis: 28 Mar 1815.
    Received from HMS Peruvian. Clarendon Transport for U States.

Butler, John   Prisoner 2218. Rank: Seaman, from: President, U States Frigate.
    Cap: 15 Jan 1815 Not Recorded by Endymion Int: 30 Jan 1815 Dis: 28 Mar 1815.
    Received from Pomone. Mars Transport for U States.

Butler, Joseph   Prisoner 1684. Rank: Seaman, from: St. Joquin, Merchant Vessel.
    Cap: 26 Mar 1814 Chesapeake by Albion Int: 16 Apr 1814 Dis: 23 Apr 1814.
    Received from Canso. HMS Bulwark for Halifax Order Comm in Chief.

American Prisoners of War Held at Bermuda During the War of 1812

Butler, Joseph   Prisoner 2791. Rank: Seaman, from: Limerick, Not Recorded.
    Cap: 07 Mar 1815 Lat 30, Long 75.38 W by Asia Int: 25 Mar 1815 Dis:
    Received from Asia. (Date of discharge not recorded.)

Butler, Robert   Prisoner 1445. Rank: Seaman, from: Nonsuch, Letter of Marque.
    Cap: 14 Dec 1813 Lat 32 by Doterel Int: 25 Dec 1813 Dis: 15 Apr 1814.
    Received from Doterel. Diana Transport for Halifax.

Butler, Thomas   Prisoner 583. Rank: Seaman, from: Lydia, Merchant Ship.
    Cap: 26 Dec 1812 at Sea by HM Ship Maidstone Int: 06 Jan 1813 Dis: 27 Jan 1813.
    Received from HM Ship Maidstone. Bostock Cartel for New York.

Butterfield, Richard   Prisoner 2126. Rank: Seaman, from: Post Boy, Merchant Vessel.
    Cap: 09 Dec 1814 off Delaware by HMS Pictolus Int: 27 Jan 1815 Dis: 13 Mar 1815.
    Received from Pictolus. Merchant Service.

Butters, Benjamin   Prisoner 81. Rank: Captain, from: Ariel, Merchant Brig.
    Cap: 13 Aug 1812 of Bermuda by Goree Int: 28 Aug 1812 Dis: 10 Sep 1812.
    Received from HM Schooner Cuttle. Schooner Hero for New York.

Buttler, Lephnik   Prisoner 47. Rank: Captain, from: Ariel, Merchant Brig.
    Cap: 28 Jul 1812 of Bermuda by Recruit Int: 28 Aug 1812 Dis: 10 Sep 1812.
    Received from HM Schooner Cuttle. Schooner Hero for N Y.

Bythwood, John   Prisoner 1895. Rank: Mate, from: Eliza & Mary, Merchant Vessel.
    Cap: 13 Aug 1814 St. Catherine by Lacedaemonian Int: 02 Sep 1814 Dis: 17 Mar 1815.
    Received from Goree. Merchant Ship.

Caffsky, John   Prisoner 2070. Rank: Boy, from: Industry, Merchant Vessel.
    Cap: 01 Dec 1814 off Cape Henry by HMS Niemen Int: 15 Dec 1814 Dis: 28 Mar 1815.
    Recaptured. Belong to Carolina Privateer. Received from HMS Niemen.
    Clarendon Transport for U States.

Cairns, Thomas   Prisoner 271. Rank: Seaman, from: Wasp, Sloop of War.
    Cap: 18 Oct 1812 at Sea by HM Ship Poictiers Int: 26 Oct 1812 Dis: 05 Nov 1812.
    Received from HM Ship Poictiers. Brig Diamond on Parole to new London United States of America.

Calder, Thomas   Prisoner 161. Rank: Seaman, from: Ranger, Merchant Ship.
    Cap: 02 Oct 1812 Lat 32, Long 65 W by HM Ship Goree Int: 13 Oct 1812 Dis: 24 Oct 1812.
    Received from HMS Goree. on Parole Brig Diamond to new London America.

Callahan, Joshua   Prisoner 910. Rank: Seaman, from: Elizabeth, Merchant Brig.
    Cap: 26 Feb 1813 Chesapeake by HMS Marlborough Int: 23 Mar 1813 Dis: 24 Jun 1813.
    Received from HM Ship Laurustinus. Magnet Cartel for New York.

Callam, John   Prisoner 1235. Rank: Not Recorded, from: HM Ship Cleopatra, Not Recorded.
    Cap: 21 Sep 1813 Not Recorded by Dragon Int: 16 Nov 1813 Dis: 15 Apr 1814.
    Received from HMS Sceptre. Surrendered himself. Diana Transport for Halifax.

Callam, Theop   Prisoner 1238. Rank: Not Recorded, from: Farmer, Merchant Vessel.
    Cap: 23 Sep 1813 Chesapeake by Lacedaemonian Int: 16 Nov 1813 Dis: 15 Apr 1814.
    Received from HMS Sceptre. Diana Transport for Halifax.

Callow, Stephen   Prisoner 2468. Rank: Seaman, from: President, U States Frigate.
    Cap: 15 Jan 1815 Not Recorded by Endymion Int: 04 Feb 1815 Dis: 28 Mar 1815.
    Received from Endymion. Clarenden Transport for U States.

Campbell, Charles   Prisoner 1294. Rank: Seaman, from: Dolphin, Merchant Sloop.
    Cap: 03 Dec 1813 off Cape Henry by Lacedaemonian Int: 19 Dec 1813 Dis:
    Received from Sceptre. (Date of discharge not recorded.)

Campbell, Daniel   Prisoner 1897. Rank: Seaman, from: Emily, Merchant Vessel.
    Cap: 11 Aug 1814 Tapella Sound by Not Recorded Int: 09 Sep 1814 Dis:
    Received from Lacedaemonian. Alias Daniel Cameron. (Date of discharge not recorded.)

Campbell, John   Prisoner 1784. Rank: Boatswain, from: Yankelass, Privateer.
    Cap: 01 May 1814 Latt 40-4N, Long 38-0W by Severn & Surprise Int: 07 Jun 1814 Dis: 20 Mar 1815.
    Received from Surprise. Merchant Vessel.

Campbell, Thomas   Prisoner 2493. Rank: Seaman, from: President, U States Frigate.
    Cap: 15 Jan 1815 Not Recorded by Endymion Int: 04 Feb 1815 Dis: 28 Mar 1815.
    Received from Endymion. Clarenden Transport for U States.

Cane, James   Prisoner 796. Rank: Seaman, from: Not Recorded, Not Recorded.
    Cap: Not Recorded by Not Recorded Int: 14 Feb 1813 Dis: 24 Jun 1813.
    Received from Narcissus. Surrendered himself as a Prisoner of War. Magnet Cartel for New York.
    (Date of capture not recorded.)

Cankling, Thomas C   Prisoner 1725. Rank: Supercargo, from: Hound, Merchant Vessel.
    Cap: 09 May 1814 off the Delaware by Niemen Int: 30 May 1914 Dis: 14 Jun 1814.
    Received from Asia. United States for Parole.

American Prisoners of War Held at Bermuda During the War of 1812

Canshard, T R   Prisoner 1442. Rank: Seaman, from: Nonsuch, Letter of Marque.
    Cap: 14 Dec 1813 Lat 32 by Doterel Int: 25 Dec 1813 Dis: 15 Apr 1814.
    Received from HM Brig Doterel. Diana Transport for Halifax.

Card, John   Prisoner 2082. Rank: Seaman, from: Trim, Merchant Vessel.
    Cap: 28 Dec 1814 Lat 34, Long 68 by HMS Telegraph Int: 04 Jan 1815 Dis: 28 Mar 1815.
    Received from HMS Goree. Clarendon Transport for U States.

Carey, Allen   Prisoner 2801. Rank: Seaman, from: Limerick, Not Recorded.
    Cap: 04 Mar 1815 Not Recorded by Asia Int: 25 Mar 1815 Dis:
    From Depot at Jamaica. Received from Asia. (Date of discharge not recorded.)

Carland, Edward   Prisoner 59. Rank: Captain, from: Mary, Merchant Brig.
    Cap: 08 Aug 1812 of Bermuda by Cuttle Int: 28 Aug 1812 Dis: 06 Sep 1812.
    Received from M Schooner Cuttle. Sloop Sally for New York.

Carlisle, William   Prisoner 2009. Rank: Seaman, from: Bridges, Merchant Vessel.
    Cap: 25 Oct 1814 off Halifax by Armide Int: 07 Nov 1814 Dis: 28 Mar 1815.
    Recaptured. Received from HMS Armide. Clarendon Transport for U States.

Carnes, Charles   Prisoner 2412. Rank: Marine, from: President, U States Frigate.
    Cap: 15 Jan 1815 Not Recorded by HM Ship Endymion Int: 04 Feb 1815 Dis: 28 Mar 1815.
    Received from Endymion. Clarendon Transport for U States.

Carney, Charles   Prisoner 2443. Rank: Seaman, from: President, U States Frigate.
    Cap: 15 Jan 1815 Not Recorded by Endymion Int: 04 Feb 1815 Dis: 28 Mar 1815.
    Received from Endymion. Mars Transport for U States.

Carpenter, James   Prisoner 501. Rank: Seaman, from: Ann, Merchant Sloop.
    Cap: 19 Dec 1812 at Sea by HMS Sophia Int: 27 Dec 1812 Dis: 27 Jan 1813.
    Received from Sophia. Bostock Cartel for New York.

Carpenter, Joseph   Prisoner 2859. Rank: Seaman, from: Limerick, Not Recorded.
    Cap: 15 Mar 1815 Not Recorded by Asia Int: 25 Mar 1815 Dis:
    From Depot at Jamaica. Received from Asia. (Date of discharge not recorded.)

Carpenter, Nathaniel   Prisoner 1458. Rank: Seaman, from: Vixen, Man of War.
    Cap: 25 Dec 1813 Lat 38.0 by Belvidera Int: 05 Jan 1814 Dis: 15 Apr 1814.
    U States Schooner. Received from HMS Belvidera. Diana Transport for Halifax.

Carpenter, Vincent   Prisoner 1662. Rank: Seaman, from: Tram, Merchant Vessel.
    Cap: 20 Feb 1814 Chesapeake by Dragon Int: 13 Mar 1814 Dis: 23 Apr 1814.
    Received from Active. HMS Bulwark for Halifax.

Carrans, Joseph   Prisoner 2310. Rank: Seaman, from: President, U States Frigate.
    Cap: 15 Jan 1815 Not Recorded by Endymion Int: 04 Feb 1815 Dis: 28 Mar 1815.
    Received from Endymion. Mars Transport for U States.

Carrico, James   Prisoner 2616. Rank: Seaman, from: Falcon, Merchant Vessel.
    Cap: 22 Jan 1815 Sandy Hook by HM Ship Pomone Int: 05 Feb 1815 Dis: 28 Mar 1815.
    Received from HMS Forth. Clarendon Transport for U States.

Carrolan, James   Prisoner 2087. Rank: Seaman, from: Erin, Merchant Vessel.
    Cap: 20 Dec 1814 off Charleston by Portia Int: 06 Jan 1815 Dis: 24 Mar 1815.
    Received from HMS Portia. Merchant Vessel.

Carroll, Carn   Prisoner 2243. Rank: Seaman, from: President, U States Frigate.
    Cap: 15 Jan 1815 Not Recorded by Endymion Int: 30 Jan 1815 Dis: 28 Mar 1815.
    Received from Pomone. Mars Transport for U States.

Carroll, Michael   Prisoner 2398. Rank: Seaman, from: President, U States Frigate.
    Cap: 15 Jan 1815 Not Recorded by HM Ship Endymion Int: 04 Feb 1815 Dis: 28 Mar 1815.
    Received from Endymion. Mars Transport for U States.

Carroll, Thomas   Prisoner 2336. Rank: Seaman, from: President, U States Frigate.
    Cap: 15 Jan 1815 Not Recorded by Endymion Int: 04 Feb 1815 Dis: 28 Mar 1815.
    Received from Endymion. Mars Transport for U States.

Carsay, Richard   Prisoner 2175. Rank: Boy, from: President, U States Frigate.
    Cap: 15 Jan 1815 Not Recorded by HMS Endymion Int: 30 Jan 1815 Dis: 28 Mar 1815.
    Received from President. Mars Transport for U States.

Carson, John   Prisoner 657. Rank: Seaman, from: Not Recorded, Not Recorded.
    Cap: Not Recorded by Not Recorded Int: 21 Jan 1813 Dis: 27 Jan 1813.
    Received from HMS Ruby. Surrendered them selves as Prisoners of War.
    Bostock Cartel for New York.

Carter, Benjamin   Prisoner 727. Rank: Seaman, from: High Flyer, Privateer.
    Cap: 09 Jan 1813 at Sea by HM Ship Acasta Int: 21 Jan 1813 Dis: 27 Jan 1813.
    Received from HMS Acasta. Bostock Cartel for New York.

American Prisoners of War Held at Bermuda During the War of 1812

Carter, Benjamin   Prisoner 770. Rank: Seaman, from: Trinadada, Merchant Brig.
    Cap: 06 Jan 1813 Lat 37.20, Long 75.00 by HM Sloop Sylph   Int: 26 Jan 1813   Dis: 14 Mar 1813.
    Received from Sloop Sylph. Savannah Packet for New York per Order Adl Sir J B Warren.

Carter, John   Prisoner 2357. Rank: Seaman, from: President, U States Frigate.
    Cap: 15 Jan 1815 Not Recorded by HMS Endymion   Int: 04 Feb 1815   Dis: 28 Mar 1815.
    Received from Endymion. Mars Transport for U States.

Carter, Thomas   Prisoner 1706. Rank: Seaman, from: Grecian, Letter of Marque.
    Cap: 02 May 1814 Chesapeake by Jansur   Int: 26 May 1814   Dis: 17 Dec 1814.
    Received from Lacedaemonian. Eolus Transport on Parole to US.

Carter, William   Prisoner 376. Rank: Seaman, from: Snapper, Privateer Schooner.
    Cap: 16 Nov 1812 at Sea by HM Ship Galus   Int: 22 Nov 1812   Dis: 27 Jan 1813.
    Received from HM Ship Galus. Bostock Cartel for New York.

Carter, William   Prisoner 2238. Rank: Seaman, from: President, U States Frigate.
    Cap: 15 Jan 1815 Not Recorded by Endymion   Int: 30 Jan 1815   Dis: 28 Mar 1815.
    Received from Pomone. Mars Transport for U States.

Cartey, John   Prisoner 472. Rank: Seaman, from: Teazer, Privateer Schooner.
    Cap: 16 Dec 1812 at Sea by HM Ship St. Domingo   Int: 21 Dec 1812   Dis: 27 Jan 1813.
    Received from HM Ship St. Domingo. Bostock Cartel for New York.

Carton, Joseph   Prisoner 2298. Rank: Seaman, from: President, U States Frigate.
    Cap: 15 Jan 1815 Not Recorded by Endymion   Int: 04 Feb 1815   Dis: 28 Mar 1815.
    Received from Endymion. Mars Transport for U States.

Cartwright, Alexander   Prisoner 1085. Rank: Mate, from: Camelia, Merchant.
    Cap: 26 Apr 1813 off Block Island by Ramillies   Int: 07 May 1813   Dis: 08 Jun 1813.
    Received from Prize Camelia. Permitted to remain in the Colony order of Sir J B Warren.

Carven, Thomas   Prisoner 1258. Rank: Seaman, from: Hero, Merchant Schooner.
    Cap: 14 Nov 1813 Delaware by Belvidera   Int: 06 Dec 1813   Dis: 15 Apr 1814.
    Received from HMS Sceptre. Diana for Halifax.

Casey, Henry   Prisoner 658. Rank: Seaman, from: Not Recorded, Not Recorded.
    Cap: Not Recorded by Not Recorded   Int: 21 Jan 1813   Dis: 27 Jan 1813.
    Received from HMS Goree. Surrendered them selves as Prisoners of War.
    Bostock Cartel for New York.

Casora, Amanuel   Prisoner 365. Rank: Seaman, from: Snapper, Privateer Schooner.
    Cap: 16 Nov 1812 at Sea by HM Ship Galus   Int: 22 Nov 1812   Dis: 18 Jan 1813.
    Received from HM Ship Galus. being a Spaniard per Order of Adl Evans.

Casora, Samuel   Prisoner 410. Rank: Seaman, from: Snapper, Privateer Schooner.
    Cap: 16 Nov 1812 at Sea by HM Ship Galus   Int: 22 Nov 1812   Dis: 27 Jan 1813.
    Received from HM Ship Galus. Bostock Cartel for New York.

Cass, Caleb   Prisoner 2597. Rank: Seaman, from: John, Merchant Vessel.
    Cap: 18 Dec 1814 off New York by HMS Pomone   Int: 05 Feb 1815   Dis: 16 Mar 1815.
    Received from HMS Forth. Merchant Service.

Castaway, Antonia   Prisoner 236. Rank: Seaman, from: Wasp, Sloop of War.
    Cap: 18 Oct 1812 at Sea by HM Ship Poictiers   Int: 26 Oct 1812   Dis: 05 Nov 1812.
    Received from HM Ship Poictiers. Brig Diamond on Parole to new London United States of America.

Castignet, John   Prisoner 1348. Rank: Seaman, from: Rolla, Privateer.
    Cap: 10 Dec 1813 Block Island by Loire   Int: 20 Dec 1813   Dis: 15 Apr 1814.
    Received from HM Ship San Domingo. HMS Rammillies for Halifax.

Caston, John   Prisoner 46. Rank: Seaman, from: Trim, Merchant Schooner.
    Cap: 28 Jul 1812 of Bermuda by Cuttle   Int: 28 Aug 1812   Dis: 18 Sep 1812.
    Received from HM Schooner Cuttle. Order Commd Evans for England.

Caswell, Samuel   Prisoner 2475. Rank: Seaman, from: President, U States Frigate.
    Cap: 15 Jan 1815 Not Recorded by Endymion   Int: 04 Feb 1815   Dis: 28 Mar 1815.
    Received from Endymion. Clarenden Transport for U States.

Catan, William   Prisoner 1755. Rank: Seaman, from: Yankelass, Privateer.
    Cap: 01 May 1814 L 40-4N, Long 38-0W by Severn & Surprise   Int: 06 Jun 1814   Dis: 27 Mar 1815.
    Received from Severn. Merchant Vessel.

Catehard, Charles   Prisoner 1485. Rank: Seaman, from: Luckey, Merchant Vessel.
    Cap: 19 Dec 1813 off the Delaware by Niemen   Int: 07 Jan 1814   Dis: 15 Apr 1814.
    Received from HM Sloop Jaseur. Diana Transport for Halifax. (Name of capturing ship not legible, assume to be Nieman.)

Catehart, Robert   Prisoner 1522. Rank: Seaman, from: Lukey, Merchant Vessel.
    Cap: 19 Dec 1813 off the Delaware by Niemen   Int: 22 Jan 1814   Dis: 15 Apr 1814.
    Received from Jaseur. Diana Transport for Halifax.

American Prisoners of War Held at Bermuda During the War of 1812

Catley, William   Prisoner 199. Rank: Seaman, from: Wasp, Sloop of War.
    Cap: 18 Oct 1812 at Sea by HMS Poictiers Int: 26 Oct 1812 Dis: 05 Nov 1812.
    Received from HM Ship Poictiers. Brig Diamond on Parole to new London America.

Catlin, Othello   Prisoner 1826. Rank: Passenger, from: Not Recorded, Not Recorded.
    Cap: Not Recorded by Not Recorded Int: 14 Jun 1814 Dis: 15 Jun 1814.
    From St. Bartholomew in the Swedish Schooner Oscar. on Parole per Order Com in Chief to America.
    (Date of capture not recorded.)

Caton, Joseph   Prisoner 900. Rank: Seaman, from: Princessa, Merchant Brig.
    Cap: 07 Feb 1813 Chesapeake by HMS Marlborough Int: 23 Mar 1813 Dis: 24 Mar 1813.
    Received from HM Ship Laurustinus. St. Michael per Order Adl Sir J B Warren.

Caulson, Uriah   Prisoner 2229. Rank: Seaman, from: President, U States Frigate.
    Cap: 15 Jan 1815 Not Recorded by Endymion Int: 30 Jan 1815 Dis: 28 Mar 1815.
    Received from Pomone. Mars Transport for U States.

Caustin, Nicholas   Prisoner 2171. Rank: Seaman, from: President, U States Frigate.
    Cap: 15 Jan 1815 Not Recorded by Endymion Int: 30 Jan 1815 Dis: 28 Mar 1815.
    Received from President. Mars for United States.

Cavines, John   Prisoner 935. Rank: Seaman, from: Sidney, Letter of Marque Schooner.
    Cap: 09 Mar 1813 Chesapeake by Marlborough Int: 23 Mar 1813 Dis: 24 Jun 1813.
    Received from Laurustinus. Magnet Cartel for New York.

Cawdrick, Samuel   Prisoner 1960. Rank: Seaman, from: Pike, Privateer.
    Cap: 25 Aug 1814 off Savannah by Primrose Int: 09 Sep 1814 Dis: 28 Mar 1815.
    Received from Lacedaemonian. Clarendon Transport for U States.

Cayton, John   Prisoner 2324. Rank: Quartermaster, from: President, U States Frigate.
    Cap: 15 Jan 1815 Not Recorded by Endymion Int: 04 Feb 1815 Dis: 28 Mar 1815.
    Received from Endymion. Mars Transport for U States.

Cer, Levi   Prisoner 100. Rank: detained American, from: Gossepuim, Merchant.
    Cap: 16 Aug 1812 of Bermuda by Not Recorded Int: 31 Aug 1812 Dis: 18 Sep 1812.
    Received from HMS Ruby. detained per order of the Commodore.
    Order of Commd Evans for England.

Chan, Frederick   Prisoner 1401. Rank: Seaman, from: John & James, Merchant Vessel.
    Cap: 07 Dec 1813 Lat 37 by Loire Int: 21 Dec 1813 Dis: 15 Apr 1814.
    Received from Romulus. Diana Transport for Halifax.

Chase, Peter   Prisoner 150. Rank: Seaman, from: Ranger, Merchant Ship.
    Cap: 02 Oct 1812 Lat 32, Long 65 W by HMS Goree Int: 13 Oct 1812 Dis: 24 Oct 1812.
    Received from HMS Goree. Brig Diamond on Parole to new London United States of America.

Chavers, Sidney   Prisoner 2005. Rank: Boy, from: Dove, Merchant Vessel.
    Cap: 06 May 1814 from Halifax by Dolphin Int: 01 Nov 1814 Dis: 28 Mar 1815.
    Received from Dolphin. Clarendon Transport for U States.

Chaves, M   Prisoner 2669. Rank: Seaman, from: Enterprise, Merchant Vessel.
    Cap: 12 Aug 1814 off New York by Childers Int: 14 Feb 1815 Dis: 28 Mar 1815.
    from N. Providence. Received from Childers. Clarendon Transport for U States.

Cherriers, Beattie   Prisoner 2067. Rank: Seaman, from: Industry, Merchant Vessel.
    Cap: 01 Dec 1814 off Cape Henry by HMS Niemen Int: 15 Dec 1814 Dis: 25 Jan 1815.
    Recaptured. Belong to Carolina Privateer. Received from HMS Niemen. Bridges Transport being
    Subject to Friendly power Order Com Evans.

Chessnutt, Adam   Prisoner 2117. Rank: Seaman, from: Armistice, Merchant Vessel.
    Cap: 07 Dec 1814 off Delaware by Pictolus Int: 27 Jan 1815 Dis: 17 Feb 1815.
    Received from Pictolus. Harriot Merchant Vessel per order of Commadore Evans.

Chester, William   Prisoner 1621. Rank: Seaman, from: Perseferanda, Merchant Vessel.
    Cap: 03 Jan 1814 Block Island by Albion Int: 14 Feb 1814 Dis: 23 Apr 1814.
    Received from Sceptre. HMS Bulwark for Halifax.

Chester, William   Prisoner 1687. Rank: Seaman, from: Pacifiranda, Merchant Vessel.
    Cap: 03 Jan 1814 Block Island by Albion Int: 06 May 1814 Dis: 20 Mar 1815.
    Received from Hospital. Merchant Vessel.

Chew, Henry   Prisoner 2618. Rank: Seaman, from: Falcon, Merchant Vessel.
    Cap: 22 Jan 1815 Sandy Hook by HM Ship Pomone Int: 05 Feb 1815 Dis: 28 Mar 1815.
    Received from HMS Forth. Clarendon Transport for U States.

Chiddell, Daniel   Prisoner 2787. Rank: Seaman, from: Limerick, Not Recorded.
    Cap: 07 Mar 1815 Lat 30, Long 75.38 W by Asia Int: 25 Mar 1815 Dis:
    Received from Asia. (Date of discharge not recorded.)

Chidry, Abraham   Prisoner 1680. Rank: Seaman, from: St. Joquin, Merchant Vessel.
    Cap: 26 Mar 1814 Chesapeake by Albion Int: 16 Apr 1814 Dis: 23 Apr 1814.
    Received from Canso. HMS Bulwark for Halifax Order Comm in Chief.

American Prisoners of War Held at Bermuda During the War of 1812

Childs, Adam   Prisoner 1001. Rank: Seaman, from: Jefferson, Merchant.
    Cap: 18 Mar 1813 at Sea by HM Sloop Atalante Int: 06 Apr 1813 Dis: 24 Jun 1813.
    Received from HMS Junon. Magnet Cartel for New York.

Childs, Adam   Prisoner 1556. Rank: Seaman, from: Bordeaux Packet, Letter of Marque.
    Cap: 28 Jan 1814 off Cape Henry by Nieman Int: 12 Feb 1814 Dis: 15 Apr 1814.
    Received from Nieman. Diana Transport for Halifax.

Childsey, Abraham   Prisoner 123. Rank: Seaman, from: William of Baltimore, Merchant.
    Cap: 31 Aug 1812 Lat 37 by HM Ship Recruit Int: 14 Sep 1812 Dis: 18 Sep 1812.
    Received from Recruit. Order of Commd Evans for England.

Chinik, G   Prisoner 2767. Rank: Seaman, from: Maria, Not Recorded.
    Cap: 16 Feb 1815 St Augustine by Severn Int: 03 Mar 1815 Dis: 17 Mar 1815.
    Received from Hebrus. Merchant Vessel.

Chont, Robert   Prisoner 2531. Rank: Seaman, from: President, U States Frigate.
    Cap: 15 Jan 1815 Not Recorded by Endymion Int: 04 Feb 1815 Dis: 28 Mar 1815.
    Received from HMS Endymion. Clarenden Transport for U States.

Churchill, Benjamin   Prisoner 1726. Rank: Captain, from: Yankelass, Privateer.
    Cap: 01 May 1814 L 10-4N, L 33-0W by Severn & Surprise Int: 06 Jun 1814 Dis:
    Received from Severn. (Date of discharge not recorded.)

Chuseman, John   Prisoner 835. Rank: Seaman, from: Portsmouth, Merchant Ship.
    Cap: 27 Feb 1813 off Bermuda by HM Sloop Martin Int: 09 Mar 1813 Dis: 27 Mar 1813.
    Received from Sloop Martin. Per Order Commodore Evans the Vessel being Liberated.

Cill, John F   Prisoner 1211. Rank: Seaman, from: Ambition, Merchant Sloop.
    Cap: 26 Sep 1813 at Sea by HM Brig Acteon Int: 16 Nov 1813 Dis: 15 Apr 1814.
    Received from the Custody of Lieut Bacon. HMS Ramillies for Halifax.

Cilley, Cutting   Prisoner 811. Rank: Seaman, from: Elouisa, Merchant Schooner.
    Cap: 16 Feb 1813 at Sea by Morgiana Int: 25 Feb 1813 Dis: 14 Jun 1813.
    Received from HMS Morgiana. Permitted to return to the United States in the Perseverance Cartel.

Clarey, John   Prisoner 546. Rank: Seaman, from: Herald, Letter of Marque Brig.
    Cap: 25 Dec 1812 at Sea by HM Ship Maidstone Int: 05 Jan 1813 Dis: 27 Jan 1813.
    Received from HM Ship Maidstone. Bostock Cartel for New York.

Clark, Charles   Prisoner 865. Rank: Seaman, from: Alert, Merchant Sloop.
    Cap: 14 Mar 1813 Chesapeake by HM Ship Laurustinus Int: 23 Mar 1813 Dis: 13 Jun 1813.
    Received from Laurustinus. Perseverance Cartel for the United States per Order Adml Sir J B Warren.

Clark, Erren   Prisoner 114. Rank: Seaman, from: Lydia, Merchant.
    Cap: 03 Sep 1812 Near Bermuda by HMS Orpheus Int: 08 Sep 1812 Dis: 18 Sep 1812.
    Received from HMS Orpheus. Order of Commd Evans England.

Clark, James   Prisoner 1661. Rank: Seaman, from: Tram, Merchant Vessel.
    Cap: 20 Feb 1814 Chesapeake by Dragon Int: 13 Mar 1814 Dis: 23 Apr 1814.
    Received from Active. HMS Bulwark for Halifax.

Clark, John   Prisoner 26. Rank: Seaman, from: Hero, Merchant Schooner.
    Cap: 14 Jul 1812 at Bermuda by Schooner Cuttle Int: 28 Aug 1812 Dis: 18 Sep 1812.
    Received from HM Schooner Cuttle. Order of Commd Evans for England.

Clark, John   Prisoner 1366. Rank: Seaman, from: Rolla, Privateer.
    Cap: 10 Dec 1813 Block Island by Loire Int: 20 Dec 1813 Dis: 15 Apr 1814.
    Received from San Domingo. HMS Rammillies for Halifax.

Clark, John   Prisoner 2830. Rank: Seaman, from: Limerick, Not Recorded.
    Cap: 15 Mar 1815 Not Recorded by Asia Int: 25 Mar 1815 Dis:
    From Depot at Jamaica. Received from Asia. (Date of discharge not recorded.)

Clark, Obea   Prisoner 17. Rank: Captain, from: Sally, Merchant Ship.
    Cap: 09 Jul 1812 near Bermuda by Recruit Int: 28 Aug 1812 Dis: 06 Sep 1812.
    Received from HM Schooner Cuttle. Sloop Sally for N Y.

Clark, Peleg   Prisoner 1633. Rank: Seaman, from: Not Recorded, Not Recorded.
    Cap: 05 Feb 1814 Not Recorded by Sceptre Int: 14 Feb 1814 Dis: 15 Apr 1814.
    Received from Sceptre. Rammilles for Halifax.

Clark, Thomas   Prisoner 1932. Rank: Captain, from: Pike, Privateer.
    Cap: 25 Aug 1814 off Savannah by Primrose Int: 09 Sep 1814 Dis: 28 Mar 1815.
    Received from Lacedaemonian. Clarendon Transport for U States.

Clark, William   Prisoner 1196. Rank: Seaman, from: HM Sloop Rifleman, Not Recorded.
    Cap: Not Recorded by Not Recorded Int: 03 Sep 1813 Dis: 12 Sep 1813.
    Received from HM Sloop Rifleman. Discharged from HM Sloop Rifleman being an American. Per Order of Commodore Evans to the American Ship Georgiana restored.

American Prisoners of War Held at Bermuda During the War of 1812

Clarke, James   Prisoner 891. Rank: Seaman, from: Hannah, Merchant Schooner.
    Cap: 24 Feb 1813 Chesapeake by HMS Marlborough Int: 23 Mar 1813 Dis: 21 May 1813.
    Received from HM Ship Laurustinus. Per Order Commodore Evans the Vessel being Liberated.

Clarke, John   Prisoner 2330. Rank: Seaman, from: President, U States Frigate.
    Cap: 15 Jan 1815 Not Recorded by Endymion Int: 04 Feb 1815 Dis: 28 Mar 1815.
    Received from Endymion. Mars Transport for U States.

Clasker, C   Prisoner 1435. Rank: Seaman, from: Nonsuch, Letter of Marque.
    Cap: 14 Dec 1813 Lat 32 by Doterel Int: 25 Dec 1813 Dis: 15 Apr 1814.
    Received from HM Brig Doterel. Diana Transport for Halifax.

Clatt, George   Prisoner 548. Rank: Seaman, from: Herald, Letter of Marque Brig.
    Cap: 25 Dec 1812 at Sea by HM Ship Maidstone Int: 05 Jan 1813 Dis: 27 Jan 1813.
    Received from HM Ship Maidstone. Bostock Cartel for New York.

Claxton, Alexander   Prisoner 284. Rank: Midshipman, from: Wasp, Sloop of War.
    Cap: 18 Oct 1812 at Sea by HM Ship Poictiers Int: 01 Nov 1812 Dis: 04 Nov 1812.
    Received from HM Ship Poictiers. Brig Diamond on Parole to new London United States of America.

Claxton, Philip   Prisoner 790. Rank: Seaman, from: Resolution, Merchant Schooner.
    Cap: 26 Jan 1813 at Sea by HM Ship Victorious Int: 04 Feb 1813 Dis: 14 Jun 1813.
    Received from Victorious. Permitted to return to the United States in the Perseverance Cartel.

Claxton, Robert   Prisoner 818. Rank: Seaman, from: Resolution, Merchant Schooner.
    Cap: 26 Jan 1813 at Sea by HM Ship Victorious Int: 04 Mar 1813 Dis: 13 Jun 1813.
    Received from Victorious. Perseverance Cartel for the United States per Order Adm Sir J B Warren.

Cleareyd, James   Prisoner 1885. Rank: Seaman, from: Frolic, U States.
    Cap: Not Recorded by Not Recorded Int: Dis: 28 Mar 1815.
    Clarendon Transport for U States. (Dates of capture and internment not recorded.)

Cleary, William   Prisoner 613. Rank: Seaman, from: Noetoin, Packet Brig.
    Cap: 05 Jan 1813 at Sea by HMS Belvidera Int: 10 Jan 1813 Dis: 27 Jan 1813.
    Received from HMS Belvidera. Bostock Cartel for New York.

Clement, Joseph   Prisoner 1890. Rank: Mate, from: Achilles, Merchant Vessel.
    Cap: Not Recorded by Not Recorded Int: Dis: 28 Mar 1815.
    Clarendon Transport for U States. (Dates of capture and internment not recorded.)

Clemons, Henry   Prisoner 1104. Rank: Boy, from: Apollo, Merchant Vessel.
    Cap: 15 May 1813 at Sea by HM Ship Success Int: 27 May 1813 Dis: 24 Jun 1813.
    Received from HMS Success. Magnet Cartel for New York.

Clerk, Andrew   Prisoner 628. Rank: Master, from: Dolphin, Merchant Brig.
    Cap: 30 Dec 1812 at Sea by HM Ship Galus Int: 14 Jan 1813 Dis: 27 Jan 1813.
    Received from Prize Brig Dolphin. Bostock Cartel for New York.

Clerk, Perry   Prisoner 242. Rank: Seaman, from: Wasp, Sloop of War.
    Cap: 18 Oct 1812 at Sea by HM Ship Poictiers Int: 26 Oct 1812 Dis: 05 Nov 1812.
    Received from HM Ship Poictiers. Brig Diamond on Parole to new London United States of America.

Cleveland, H C   Prisoner 2807. Rank: Seaman, from: Limerick, Not Recorded.
    Cap: 04 Mar 1815 Not Recorded by Asia Int: 25 Mar 1815 Dis:
    From Depot at Jamaica. Received from Asia. (Date of discharge not recorded.)

Clicy, Peter   Prisoner 1969. Rank: Seaman, from: Pike, Privateer.
    Cap: 25 Aug 1814 off Savannah by Primrose Int: 09 Sep 1814 Dis: 05 Nov 1815.
    Received from Lacedaemonian. Order Adm Cockburn.

Clifton, Thomas   Prisoner 637. Rank: Mate, from: Crown Prince, Merchant Schooner.
    Cap: 19 Dec 1812 at Sea by HM Ship Galus Int: 17 Jan 1813 Dis: 27 Jan 1813.
    Received from HM Ship Galus. Bostock Cartel for New York.

Clinton, James   Prisoner 302. Rank: Seaman, from: Symmetry, Merchant Ship.
    Cap: 05 Jul 1812 at Sea by HM Ship Rattler Int: 02 Nov 1812 Dis: 04 Nov 1812.
    Received from HMS Poictiers. Brig Diamond on Parole to new London United States of America.

Cloeth, John   Prisoner 890. Rank: Seaman, from: Hannah, Merchant Schooner.
    Cap: 24 Feb 1813 Chesapeake by HMS Marlborough Int: 23 Mar 1813 Dis: 21 May 1813.
    Received from HM Ship Laurustinus. Per Order Commodore Evans the Vessel being Liberated.

Clop, Abner   Prisoner 547. Rank: Seaman, from: Herald, Letter of Marque Brig.
    Cap: 25 Dec 1812 at Sea by HM Ship Maidstone Int: 05 Jan 1813 Dis: 27 Jan 1813.
    Received from HM Ship Maidstone. Bostock Cartel for New York.

Closs, Peter   Prisoner 2252. Rank: Seaman, from: President, U States Frigate.
    Cap: 15 Jan 1815 Not Recorded by Endymion Int: 30 Jan 1815 Dis: 28 Mar 1815.
    Received from Pomone. Mars Transport for U States.

Clough, John   Prisoner 2711. Rank: Seaman, from: South Boston, Merchant Vessel.
    Cap: 13 Feb 1815 off Charleston by Pandora Int: 02 Mar 1815 Dis: 28 Mar 1815.
    Received from Pandora. Clarendon Transport for U States.

American Prisoners of War Held at Bermuda During the War of 1812

Clough, William   Prisoner 1393. Rank: Seaman, from: Scorpion, Merchant Vessel.
    Cap: 29 Nov 1813 Lat 39 by Loire Int: 21 Dec 1813 Dis: 15 Apr 1814.
    Received from Romulus. Diana for Halifax.

Cloutman, Abaneza   Prisoner 1903. Rank: Mate, from: Polly & Sally, Merchant Vessel.
    Cap: 13 Aug 1814 St. Catherine by Lacedaemonian Int: 09 Sep 1814 Dis: 28 Mar 1814.
    Received from Lacedaemonian. Clarendon Transport for U States.

Clyde, Bartin   Prisoner 504. Rank: Seaman, from: Teazer, Privateer Schooner.
    Cap: 16 Dec 1812 at Sea by HM Ship St. Domingo Int: 28 Dec 1812 Dis: 17 Jun 1813.
    Received from San. Domingo. Halifax Order of the Commander in Chief supports to be an Englishman.

Clyne, Lewis   Prisoner 1586. Rank: Seaman, from: Bordeaux Packet, Letter of Marque.
    Cap: 28 Jan 1814 off Cape Henry by Nieman Int: 12 Feb 1814 Dis: 15 Apr 1814.
    Received from Nieman. Diana Transport for Halifax.

Coalman, Joseph   Prisoner 1021. Rank: Seaman, from: Lusiana, Merchant.
    Cap: 20 Mar 1813 off the Chesapeake by HM Ship Rammillies Int: 06 Apr 1813 Dis: 20 May 1813.
    Received from HMS Junon. Vessel being Liberated per Order Commodore Evans.

Coats, Humphrey   Prisoner 2724. Rank: Seaman, from: American Gun Boat, Not Recorded.
    Cap: 06 Feb 1815 off Charleston by Tonnant Int: 02 Mar 1815 Dis:
    Received from Armede. (Date of discharge not recorded.)

Coffen, G B   Prisoner 1376. Rank: Prize Master, from: Policy, Merchant Vessel.
    Cap: 04 Dec 1813 Not Recorded by Loire Int: 20 Dec 1813 Dis: 15 Apr 1814.
    Recaptured. Received from San Domingo. HMS Rammillies for Halifax.

Coffin, Alexander   Prisoner 1603. Rank: Seaman, from: Monticello, Merchant Vessel.
    Cap: 09 Dec 1813 Block Island by Albion Int: 14 Feb 1814 Dis: 23 Apr 1814.
    Received from Sceptre. HMS Bulwark for Halifax.

Coffin, Barna   Prisoner 162. Rank: Seaman, from: Ranger, Merchant Ship.
    Cap: 02 Oct 1812 Lat 32, Long 65 W by HM Ship Goree Int: 13 Oct 1812 Dis: 24 Oct 1812.
    Received from HMS Goree. on Parole Brig Diamond to new London America.

Coffin, Edward   Prisoner 159. Rank: Seaman, from: Ranger, Merchant Ship.
    Cap: 02 Oct 1812 Lat 32, Long 65 W by HM Ship Goree Int: 13 Oct 1812 Dis: 24 Oct 1812.
    Received from HMS Goree. on Parole Brig Diamond to new London America.

Coffin, Linzey   Prisoner 1533. Rank: Seaman, from: Romp, Merchant Vessel.
    Cap: 02 Jan 1814 Latt 22.0 by Prometheus Int: 23 Jan 1814 Dis: 15 Apr 1814.
    Received from Prometheus. Diana for Halifax.

Coffin, Obediah   Prisoner 142. Rank: Mate, from: Ranger of Nantucket, Merchant Ship.
    Cap: 02 Oct 1812 Lat 32, Long 65 by HMS Goree Int: 11 Oct 1812 Dis: 24 Oct 1812.
    Received from HMS Goree. Brig Diamond on Parole to New London United States of America.

Coffin, Thaddias   Prisoner 86. Rank: Mate, from: Gossepuim, Merchant.
    Cap: 16 Aug 1812 of Bermuda by Goree Int: 28 Aug 1812 Dis: 10 Sep 1812.
    Received from HM Schooner Cuttle. Schooner Hero for New York.

Coffin, William   Prisoner 1484. Rank: Seaman, from: Luckey, Merchant Vessel.
    Cap: 19 Dec 1813 off the Delaware by Niemen Int: 07 Jan 1814 Dis: 05 Jun 1814.
    Received from HM Sloop Jaseur. United States on Parole. (Name of capturing ship not legible, assume to be Nieman.)

Coil, R M   Prisoner 1302. Rank: Lieutenant, from: Rolla, Privateer.
    Cap: 10 Dec 1813 Block Island by Loire Int: 20 Dec 1813 Dis: 15 Apr 1814.
    Received from San Domingo. HMS Rammillies for Halifax.

Cole, David   Prisoner 749. Rank: Seaman, from: Rhode, Merchant Schooner.
    Cap: 07 Jan 1813 at Sea by HM Ship Poictiers Int: 21 Jan 1813 Dis: 27 Jan 1813.
    Received from HMS Poictiers. Bostock Cartel for New York.

Cole, Edward   Prisoner 682. Rank: Seaman, from: High Flyer, Privateer.
    Cap: 09 Jan 1813 at Sea by HM Ship Acasta Int: 21 Jan 1813 Dis: 27 Jan 1813.
    Received from HMS Acasta. Bostock Cartel for New York.

Cole, H A   Prisoner 1615. Rank: Prize Master, from: Telamachur, Merchant Vessel.
    Cap: 26 Oct 1813 Latt 41.0 by Narcissus Int: 14 Feb 1814 Dis: 15 Apr 1814.
    Recaptured. Received from Sceptre. Rammilles for Halifax.

Cole, Henry   Prisoner 1058. Rank: Seaman, from: Amason, Merchant.
    Cap: 18 Mar 1813 Chesapeake by HM Ship Victorious Int: 06 Apr 1813 Dis: 24 Jun 1813.
    Received from HMS Junon. Magnet Cartel for New York.

Cole, John   Prisoner 3. Rank: Captain, from: Yorick, Merchant Ship.
    Cap: 09 Jul 1812 near Bermuda by Rattler Int: 28 Aug 1812 Dis: 06 Sep 1812.
    Received from HM Schooner Cuttle. Ship Sally for New York.

American Prisoners of War Held at Bermuda During the War of 1812

Cole, John   Prisoner 201. Rank: Seaman, from: Wasp, Sloop of War.
    Cap: 18 Oct 1812 at Sea by HMS Poictiers Int: 26 Oct 1812 Dis: 05 Nov 1812.
    Received from HM Ship Poictiers. Brig Diamond on Parole to new London America.

Cole, John   Prisoner 1407. Rank: Seaman, from: John & James, Merchant Vessel.
    Cap: 07 Dec 1813 Lat 37 by Loire Int: 21 Dec 1813 Dis: 15 Apr 1814.
    Received from Romulus. Diana Transport for Halifax.

Cole, Lutha   Prisoner 1779. Rank: Prize Master, from: Yankelass, Privateer.
    Cap: 01 May 1814 Latt 40-4N, Long 38-0W by Severn & Surprise Int: 07 Jun 1814 Dis: 21 Feb 1815.
    Received from Surprise. Paroled to the U States having served six months as Carpenter's Mate order of Adl Sir Alex Cockburn.

Cole, Nathaniel   Prisoner 710. Rank: Seaman, from: High Flyer, Privateer.
    Cap: 09 Jan 1813 at Sea by HM Ship Acasta Int: 21 Jan 1813 Dis: 27 Jan 1813.
    Received from HMS Acasta. Bostock Cartel for New York.

Cole, Nathaniel   Prisoner 1339. Rank: Seaman, from: Rolla, Privateer.
    Cap: 10 Dec 1813 Block Island by Loire Int: 20 Dec 1813 Dis: 15 Apr 1814.
    Received from HM Ship San Domingo. HMS Rammillies for Halifax.

Cole, Richard   Prisoner 132. Rank: 2 Lieutenant, from: James Maddison, Man of War.
    Cap: 22 Aug 1812 Lat 31 by HMS Barbados Int: 14 Sep 1812 Dis: 24 Oct 1812.
    Received from HMS Barbados. Brig Diamond on Parole to new London United States of America.

Coleman, B   Prisoner 2129. Rank: Seaman, from: New York, Merchant Vessel.
    Cap: 09 Jan 1815 off Delaware by Dispatch Int: 27 Jan 1815 Dis: 17 Feb 1815.
    Received from Pictolus. Harriot MV.

Coleman, George   Prisoner 2335. Rank: Seaman, from: President, U States Frigate.
    Cap: 15 Jan 1815 Not Recorded by Endymion Int: 04 Feb 1815 Dis: 28 Mar 1815.
    Received from Endymion. Mars Transport for U States.

Coleman, James   Prisoner 2224. Rank: Marine, from: President, U States Frigate.
    Cap: 15 Jan 1815 Not Recorded by Endymion Int: 30 Jan 1815 Dis: 28 Mar 1815.
    Received from Pomone. Clarenden Transport for U States.

Coleman, Robert   Prisoner 158. Rank: Seaman, from: Ranger, Merchant Ship.
    Cap: 02 Oct 1812 Lat 32, Long 65 W by HM Ship Goree Int: 13 Oct 1812 Dis: 24 Oct 1812.
    Received from HMS Goree. on Parole Brig Diamond to new London America.

Coleman, Samuel   Prisoner 190. Rank: Marine, from: Wasp, Sloop of War.
    Cap: 18 Oct 1812 at Sea by HMS Poictiers Int: 26 Oct 1812 Dis: 05 Nov 1812.
    Received from HM Ship Poictiers. Brig Diamond on Parole to new London America.

Coleman, William   Prisoner 1607. Rank: Seaman, from: Monticello, Merchant Vessel.
    Cap: 09 Dec 1813 Block Island by Albion Int: 14 Feb 1814 Dis: 23 Apr 1814.
    Received from Sceptre. HMS Bulwark for Halifax.

Coles, Charles   Prisoner 1427. Rank: Seaman, from: Nonsuch, Letter of Marque.
    Cap: 14 Dec 1813 Lat 32 by Doterel Int: 25 Dec 1813 Dis: 15 Apr 1814.
    Received from HM Brig Doterel. Diana Transport for Halifax.

Coles, Thomas   Prisoner 1454. Rank: Seaman, from: Vixen, Man of War.
    Cap: 25 Dec 1813 Lat 38.0 by Belvidera Int: 05 Jan 1814 Dis: 15 Apr 1814.
    U States Schooner. Received from HMS Belvidera. Diana Transport for Halifax.

Colgan, Christian   Prisoner 1648. Rank: Seaman, from: George, Merchant Vessel.
    Cap: 22 Dec 1813 Chesapeake by Dragon Int: 28 Feb 1814 Dis: 23 Apr 1814.
    Received from Active. HMS Bulwark for Halifax.

Collagon, John   Prisoner 1652. Rank: 1 Mate, from: Flash, Letter of Marque.
    Cap: 11 Feb 1814 Off Block Island by Acasta Int: 13 Mar 1814 Dis: 15 Apr 1814.
    Received from Active. Ramilles for Halifax.

Collet, Peter   Prisoner 497. Rank: Boy, from: Teazer, Privateer Schooner.
    Cap: 16 Dec 1812 at Sea by HM Ship St. Domingo Int: 21 Dec 1812 Dis: 21 Jan 1813.
    Received from HM Ship St. Domingo. French Prison Halifax per Order Commander in Chief.

Collins, James   Prisoner 1161. Rank: Seaman, from: Caledonian, Merchant.
    Cap: 20 Jul 1813 at Sea by HM Ship Marlborough Int: 15 Aug 1813 Dis: 03 Oct 1813.
    Received from HM Ship Woolwich. Caledonian Order of Commodore Evans she being Liberated.

Collins, John   Prisoner 459. Rank: Boatswain, from: Teazer, Privateer Schooner.
    Cap: 16 Dec 1812 at Sea by HM Ship St. Domingo Int: 21 Dec 1812 Dis: 27 Jan 1813.
    Received from HM Ship St. Domingo. Bostock Cartel for New York.

Collins, John   Prisoner 1100. Rank: Boy, from: Apollo, Merchant Vessel.
    Cap: 15 May 1813 at Sea by HM Ship Success Int: 27 May 1813 Dis: 24 Jun 1813.
    Received from HMS Success. Magnet Cartel for New York.

American Prisoners of War Held at Bermuda During the War of 1812

Collins, John   Prisoner 1384. Rank: Seaman, from: Policy, Merchant Vessel.
    Cap: 04 Dec 1813 Not Recorded by Loire Int: 20 Dec 1813 Dis: 15 Apr 1814.
    Recaptured. Received from San Domingo. Diana Transport for Halifax.

Collins, Samuel   Prisoner 1193. Rank: Seaman, from: Priscilla, Merchant Ship.
    Cap: 09 Aug 1813 at Sea by HM Sloop Forrester Int: 27 Aug 1813 Dis: 03 Sep 1813.
    Received from HM Sloop Forrester. to the American Ship Leander restored.

Collins, Thomas   Prisoner 1762. Rank: Seaman, from: Yankelass, Privateer.
    Cap: 01 May 1814 L 40-4N, Long 38-0W by Severn & Surprise Int: 06 Jun 1814 Dis: 28 Mar 1815.
    Received from Severn. Mars Transport for U States.

Colloden, Patrick   Prisoner 2540. Rank: Marine, from: President, U States Frigate.
    Cap: 15 Jan 1815 Not Recorded by HM Ship Endymion Int: 04 Feb 1815 Dis: 28 Mar 1815.
    Received from HMS Endymion. Clarenden Transport for U States.

Combes, Peter   Prisoner 48. Rank: Mate, from: Ariel, Merchant Brig.
    Cap: 28 Jul 1812 of Bermuda by Recruit Int: 28 Aug 1812 Dis: 10 Sep 1812.
    Received from HM Schooner Cuttle. Schooner Hero for N Y.

Coney, Thomas   Prisoner 2331. Rank: Seaman, from: President, U States Frigate.
    Cap: 15 Jan 1815 Not Recorded by Endymion Int: 04 Feb 1815 Dis: 28 Mar 1815.
    Received from Endymion. Mars Transport for U States.

Congdon, Henry   Prisoner 98. Rank: detained American, from: Gossepuim, Merchant.
    Cap: 16 Aug 1812 of Bermuda by Not Recorded Int: 31 Aug 1812 Dis: 18 Sep 1812.
    Received from HMS Ruby. detained per order of the Commodore.
    Order of Commd Evans for England.

Connell, G   Prisoner 2734. Rank: Seaman, from: Not Recorded, Not Recorded.
    Cap: 15 Feb 1815 St Marys by Dragon Int: 03 Mar 1815 Dis: 28 Mar 1815.
    by Kings Troops. Received from Hebrus. Clarendon Transport for U States.

Conner, James   Prisoner 170. Rank: Masters Mate, from: Wasp, Sloop of War.
    Cap: 18 Oct 1812 at Sea by HMS Poictiers Int: 26 Oct 1812 Dis: 05 Nov 1812.
    Received from HM Ship Poictiers. on Parole Brig Diamond to new London America.

Conner, John   Prisoner 309. Rank: Seaman, from: Wasp, Sloop of War.
    Cap: 18 Oct 1812 at Sea by HMS Poictiers Int: 05 Nov 1812 Dis: 17 Jun 1812.
    Received from HM Ship Poictiers. Order the Commd in Chief supports to be an Englishman.

Connor, Charles   Prisoner 782. Rank: Seaman, from: Governor Ankerheim, Merchant.
    Cap: 24 Jan 1813 at Sea by HM Ship Ramiles Int: 04 Feb 1813 Dis: 13 Mar 1813.
    Received from HMS Ramilies. Per Order Sir John Warren the Vessel being Liberated.

Connor, Edward   Prisoner 398. Rank: Seaman, from: Snapper, Privateer Schooner.
    Cap: 16 Nov 1812 at Sea by HM Ship Galus Int: 22 Nov 1812 Dis: 27 Jan 1813.
    Received from HM Ship Galus. Bostock Cartel for New York.

Connor, John   Prisoner 349. Rank: Seaman, from: Snapper, Privateer Schooner.
    Cap: 16 Nov 1812 at Sea by HMS Galus Int: 22 Nov 1812 Dis: 27 Jan 1813.
    Received from HM Ship Galus. Bostock Cartel for New York.

Connor, John   Prisoner 498. Rank: Seaman, from: Teazer, Privateer Schooner.
    Cap: 16 Dec 1812 at Sea by HM Ship St. Domingo Int: 21 Dec 1812 Dis: 17 Jun 1813.
    Received from HM Ship St. Domingo. Halifax Order of the Commander in Chief supports to be an Englishman.

Conover, Thomas A   Prisoner 615. Rank: Midshipman, from: Noetoin, Packet Brig.
    Cap: 05 Jan 1813 at Sea by HMS Belvidera Int: 11 Jan 1813 Dis: 27 Jan 1813.
    Received from HMS Belvidera. Bostock Cartel for New York.

Contee, Augustus   Prisoner 27. Rank: Captain, from: Survanou, Merchant.
    Cap: 14 Jul 1812 at Bermuda by Recruit Int: 28 Aug 1812 Dis: 06 Sep 1812.
    Received from HM Schooner Cuttle. Sloop Sally for N Y.

Cook, Alexander   Prisoner 1970. Rank: Seaman, from: Pike, Privateer.
    Cap: 25 Aug 1814 off Savannah by Primrose Int: 09 Sep 1814 Dis: 24 Mar 1815.
    Received from Lacedaemonian. Merchant Vessel. Or Alexander Caugor.

Cook, Dennis   Prisoner 1304. Rank: Surgeon, from: Rolla, Privateer.
    Cap: 10 Dec 1813 Block Island by Loire Int: 20 Dec 1813 Dis: 21 Jan 1814.
    Received from San Domingo. Without Exchange being an Noncombatant.

Cook, Dennis   Prisoner 1727. Rank: Surgeon, from: Yankelass, Privateer.
    Cap: 01 May 1814 L 10-4N, L 33-0W by Severn & Surprise Int: 06 Jun 1814 Dis: 20 Sep 1814.
    Received from Severn. Comm Evans Command.

Cook, Justice   Prisoner 462. Rank: Seaman, from: Teazer, Privateer Schooner.
    Cap: 16 Dec 1812 at Sea by HM Ship St. Domingo Int: 21 Dec 1812 Dis: 27 Jan 1813.
    Received from HM Ship St. Domingo. Bostock Cartel for New York.

American Prisoners of War Held at Bermuda During the War of 1812

Cook, Samuel   Prisoner 1896. Rank: Seaman, from: Emily, Merchant Vessel.
    Cap: 11 Aug 1814 Tapella Sound by Not Recorded Int: 09 Sep 1814 Dis: 28 Mar 1815.
    Received from Lacedaemonian. Clarendon Transport for U States.

Cook, W F   Prisoner 2737. Rank: Soldier, from: Not Recorded, Not Recorded.
    Cap: 13 Jan 1815 St Marys by Dragon Int: 03 Mar 1815 Dis: 28 Mar 1815.
    by Kings Troops. Received from Hebrus. Clarendon Transport for U States.

Coole, David   Prisoner 658. Rank: Seaman, from: Not Recorded, Not Recorded.
    Cap: Not Recorded by Not Recorded Int: 21 Jan 1813 Dis: 27 Jan 1813.
    Received from HMS Goree. Surrendered them selves as Prisoners of War.
    Bostock Cartel for New York.

Coole, Nathaniel   Prisoner 553. Rank: Seaman, from: Herald, Letter of Marque Brig.
    Cap: 25 Dec 1812 at Sea by HM Ship Maidstone Int: 05 Jan 1813 Dis: 27 Jan 1813.
    Received from HM Ship Maidstone. Bostock Cartel for New York.

Coone, William   Prisoner 1408. Rank: Seaman, from: John & James, Merchant Vessel.
    Cap: 07 Dec 1813 Lat 37 by Loire Int: 21 Dec 1813 Dis: 15 Apr 1814.
    Received from Romulus. Diana Transport for Halifax.

Cooper, James   Prisoner 1962. Rank: Seaman, from: Pike, Privateer.
    Cap: 25 Aug 1814 off Savannah by Primrose Int: 09 Sep 1814 Dis: 22 Mar 1815.
    Received from Lacedaemonian. Merchant Vessel.

Cooper, James   Prisoner 2576. Rank: Seaman, from: Recovery, Merchant Vessel.
    Cap: 20 Nov 1814 off New York by HMS Majestic Int: 05 Feb 1815 Dis: 28 Mar 1815.
    Received from HMS Forth. Clarendon Transport for U States.

Cooper, John   Prisoner 124. Rank: Seaman, from: William of Baltimore, Merchant.
    Cap: 31 Aug 1812 Lat 37 by HM Ship Recruit Int: 14 Sep 1812 Dis: 18 Sep 1812.
    Received from Recruit. Order of Commd Evans for England.

Cooper, John   Prisoner 1956. Rank: Seaman, from: Pike, Privateer.
    Cap: 25 Aug 1814 off Savannah by Primrose Int: 09 Sep 1814 Dis: 27 Mar 1815.
    Received from Lacedaemonian. Merchant Vessel.

Cooper, Lad   Prisoner 1337. Rank: Seaman, from: Rolla, Privateer.
    Cap: 10 Dec 1813 Block Island by Loire Int: 20 Dec 1813 Dis: 15 Apr 1814.
    Received from HM Ship San Domingo. HMS Rammillies for Halifax.

Cooper, Thomas   Prisoner 183. Rank: Seaman, from: Wasp, Sloop of War.
    Cap: 18 Oct 1812 at Sea by HMS Poictiers Int: 26 Oct 1812 Dis: 05 Nov 1812.
    Received from HM Ship Poictiers. Brig Diamond on Parole to new London America.

Coote, Thomas O   Prisoner 924. Rank: Seaman, from: Albert, Merchant Schooner.
    Cap: 05 Mar 1813 Chesapeake by HM Ship Marlborough Int: 23 Mar 1813 Dis: 24 Jun 1813.
    Received from Laurustinus. Magnet Cartel for New York.

Corbett, John   Prisoner 1125. Rank: Seaman, from: Mary, Merchant.
    Cap: 17 Apr 1813 at Sea by HM Ship Fox Int: 21 Jun 1813 Dis: 24 Jun 1813.
    Received from HM Ship Ruby. Magnet Cartel for New York.

Corie, John   Prisoner 1171. Rank: Seaman, from: Elizabeth, Merchant.
    Cap: 15 Jun 1813 at Sea by HM Ship Marlborough Int: 15 Aug 1813 Dis: 02 Sep 1813.
    Received from HM Ship Woolwich. Per order of Commodore Evans being liberated.

Corkes, Dan   Prisoner 1231. Rank: Not Recorded, from: HM Ship Cleopatra, Not Recorded.
    Cap: 21 Sep 1813 Not Recorded by Dragon Int: 16 Nov 1813 Dis: 15 Apr 1814.
    Received from HMS Sceptre. Surrendered himself. Diana Transport for Halifax.

Cornett, William   Prisoner 9. Rank: Captain, from: General Blake, Merchant.
    Cap: 09 Jul 1812 near Bermuda by Recruit Int: 28 Aug 1812 Dis: 10 Sep 1812.
    Received from HM Schooner Cuttle. Schooner Hero for N Y.

Cornwall, A   Prisoner 326. Rank: Seaman, from: James, Merchant Ship.
    Cap: 03 Nov 1812 at Sea by HM Ship Tartarus Int: 17 Nov 1812 Dis: 27 Jan 1813.
    Received from HM Ship Tartarus. Bostock Cartel for New York.

Cornwall, Edward   Prisoner 876. Rank: Seaman, from: Christiana, Merchant.
    Cap: 03 Mar 1813 Chesapeake by Marlborough Int: 23 Mar 1813 Dis: 05 May 1813.
    Received from Laurustinus. Prize Ship St. Michael.

Cornwall, Robert   Prisoner 729. Rank: Seaman, from: High Flyer, Privateer.
    Cap: 09 Jan 1813 at Sea by HM Ship Acasta Int: 21 Jan 1813 Dis: 27 Jan 1813.
    Received from HMS Acasta. Bostock Cartel for New York.

Cory, Green   Prisoner 1273. Rank: Seaman, from: United States, Merchant Vessel.
    Cap: 14 Nov 1813 Long Island by HM Brig Borer Int: 19 Dec 1813 Dis: 15 Apr 1814.
    Received from HMS Acasta. Diana for Halifax.

American Prisoners of War Held at Bermuda During the War of 1812

Costin, Thomas   Prisoner 1323. Rank: Seaman, from: Rolla, Privateer.
    Cap: 10 Dec 1813 Block Island by Loire Int: 20 Dec 1813 Dis: 15 Apr 1814.
    Received from San Domingo. HMS Rammillies for Halifax.

Cotterell, Thomas   Prisoner 1537. Rank: Seaman, from: Isabella, Merchant Vessel.
    Cap: 31 Dec 1813 at Sea by Belvidera Int: 24 Jan 1814 Dis: 15 Apr 1814.
    Received from Belvidera. Diana for Halifax.

Cottle, Henry   Prisoner 1971. Rank: Mate, from: Carrol, Merchant Vessel.
    Cap: 21 Aug 1814 off Cape Henry by Fairy Int: 14 Sep 1814 Dis: 17 Mar 1815.
    Received from Goree. Merchant Vessel.

Courtney, Edward   Prisoner 1088. Rank: Boy, from: Langdon Cheves, Merchant.
    Cap: 12 May 1813 at Sea by HM Sloop Atalante Int: 25 May 1813 Dis: 24 Jun 1813.
    Received from HMS Atalante. Magnet Cartel for New York.

Cousens, Benjamin   Prisoner 1314. Rank: Seaman, from: Rolla, Privateer.
    Cap: 10 Dec 1813 Block Island by Loire Int: 20 Dec 1813 Dis: 15 Apr 1814.
    Received from San Domingo. HMS Rammillies for Halifax.

Cousins, John   Prisoner 1884. Rank: Seaman, from: Frolic, U States.
    Cap: Not Recorded by Not Recorded Int: Dis: 28 Mar 1815.
    Clarendon Transport for U States. (Dates of capture and internment not recorded.)

Coutigo, Frederick   Prisoner 1913. Rank: Master, from: Dolphin, Packet.
    Cap: 20 Aug 1814 St. Catherine by Lacedaemonian Int: 09 Sep 1814 Dis: 05 Nov 1814.
    Received from Lacedaemonian. Order Adml Cockburn.

Couts, John   Prisoner 224. Rank: Marine, from: Wasp, Sloop of War.
    Cap: 18 Oct 1812 at Sea by HM Ship Poictiers Int: 26 Oct 1812 Dis: 05 Nov 1812.
    Received from HM Ship Poictiers. Brig Diamond on Parole to new London United States of America.

Covington, John K   Prisoner 684. Rank: Seaman, from: High Flyer, Privateer.
    Cap: 09 Jan 1813 at Sea by HM Ship Acasta Int: 21 Jan 1813 Dis: 27 Jan 1813.
    Received from HMS Acasta. Bostock Cartel for New York.

Coward, Thomas   Prisoner 933. Rank: Master, from: Sidney, Letter of Marque Schooner.
    Cap: 09 Mar 1813 Chesapeake by Marlborough Int: 23 Mar 1813 Escaped: 23 May 1813.
    Received from Laurustinus. Escaped.

Cowell, Ezekiel   Prisoner 2704. Rank: Seaman, from: Sally, Merchant Vessel.
    Cap: 26 Jan 1815 off Block Island by Nimrod Int: 18 Feb 1815 Dis: 28 Mar 1815.
    Received from Nimrod. Clarendon Transport for U States.

Cowens, Andrew   Prisoner 2604. Rank: Seaman, from: Mercury, Merchant Vessel.
    Cap: 30 Dec 1814 off New York by HM Ship Pomone Int: 05 Feb 1815 Dis: 13 Mar 1815.
    Received from HMS Forth. Merchant Service.

Cox, Charles   Prisoner 1658. Rank: Seaman, from: Flash, Letter of Marque.
    Cap: 11 Feb 1814 Off Block Island by Acasta Int: 13 Mar 1814 Dis: 23 Apr 1814.
    Received from Active. HMS Bulwark for Halifax.

Cox, Frisby   Prisoner 2290. Rank: Seaman, from: President, U States Frigate.
    Cap: 15 Jan 1815 Not Recorded by Endymion Int: 30 Jan 1815 Dis: 28 Mar 1815.
    Received from Pomone. Mars Transport for U States.

Cox, James   Prisoner 947. Rank: Passenger, from: Bona, Letter of Marque Schooner.
    Cap: 12 Mar 1813 Chesapeake by Laurustinus Int: 23 Mar 1813 Dis: 24 Jun 1813.
    Received from Laurustinus. Permitted to remain in the Colony per order of Adl Evans

Cox, L G F   Prisoner 1670. Rank: 3 Lieutenant, from: Fieri Facias, Privateer.
    Cap: 26 Feb 1814 at Sea by Ramilies Int: 18 Mar 1814 Dis: 15 Apr 1814.
    Received from Ramilies. Rammilles for Halifax.

Coxson, Thomas   Prisoner 674. Rank: Carpenters Mate, from: High Flyer, Privateer.
    Cap: 09 Jan 1813 at Sea by HM Ship Acasta Int: 21 Jan 1813 Dis: 27 Jan 1813.
    Received from HMS Acasta. Bostock Cartel for New York.

Craft, N W   Prisoner 866. Rank: Supercargo, from: Gustavas, Merchant Brig.
    Cap: 16 Mar 1813 Chesapeake by HM Ship Laurustinus Int: 23 Mar 1813 Dis: 24 Apr 1813.
    Received from Laurustinus. Per Order Commodore Evans Vessel Liberated.

Craft, Nathaniel   Prisoner 21. Rank: Captain, from: Hero, Merchant Schooner.
    Cap: 14 Jul 1812 at Bermuda by Cuttle Int: 28 Aug 1812 Dis: 10 Sep 1812.
    Received from HM Schooner Cuttle. Schooner Hero for N Y.

Crafts, John   Prisoner 1347. Rank: Seaman, from: Rolla, Privateer.
    Cap: 10 Dec 1813 Block Island by Loire Int: 20 Dec 1813 Dis: 15 Apr 1814.
    Received from HM Ship San Domingo. HMS Rammillies for Halifax.

Craig, Ephraim   Prisoner 1647. Rank: Seaman, from: Peggy, Merchant Vessel.
    Cap: 07 Dec 1813 Chesapeake by Dragon Int: 28 Feb 1814 Dis: 23 Apr 1814.
    Received from Active. HMS Bulwark for Halifax.

American Prisoners of War Held at Bermuda During the War of 1812

Craig, William   Prisoner 1240. Rank: Not Recorded, from: Little Belt, Merchant Sloop.
    Cap: 21 Sep 1813 American Coast by Armede Int: 16 Nov 1813 Dis: 15 Apr 1814.
    Received from HMS Sceptre. Diana Transport for Halifax.

Cramer, John   Prisoner 2170. Rank: Boy, from: President, U States Frigate.
    Cap: 15 Jan 1815 Not Recorded by Endymion Int: 30 Jan 1815 Dis: 06 Feb 1815.
    Under age. Received from President. Narcissus to the U States by order of Commadore Evans.

Crammet, Joseph   Prisoner 2394. Rank: Seaman, from: President, U States Frigate.
    Cap: 15 Jan 1815 Not Recorded by HM Ship Endymion Int: 04 Feb 1815 Dis: 28 Mar 1815.
    Received from Endymion. Mars Transport for U States.

Crane, Roger   Prisoner 78. Rank: Passenger, from: Ariel, Merchant Brig.
    Cap: 28 Jul 1812 of Bermuda by Recruit Int: 28 Aug 1812 Dis: 10 Sep 1812.
    Received from HM Schooner Cuttle. Schooner Hero for N Y.

Crannell, William   Prisoner 2181. Rank: Marine, from: President, U States Frigate.
    Cap: 15 Jan 1815 Not Recorded by HMS Endymion Int: 30 Jan 1815 Dis: 28 Mar 1815.
    Received from Pomone. Clarenden Transport for U States.

Crawford, John   Prisoner 1122. Rank: Mate, from: Mary, Merchant.
    Cap: 17 Apr 1813 at Sea by HM Ship Fox Int: 21 Jun 1813 Dis: 24 Jun 1813.
    Received from HMS Ruby. Magnet Cartel for New York.

Crawford, Johnson   Prisoner 189. Rank: Marine, from: Wasp, Sloop of War.
    Cap: 18 Oct 1812 at Sea by HMS Poictiers Int: 26 Oct 1812 Dis: 05 Nov 1812.
    Received from HM Ship Poictiers. Brig Diamond on Parole to new London America.

Creasey, Rubin   Prisoner 1402. Rank: Seaman, from: John & James, Merchant Vessel.
    Cap: 07 Dec 1813 Lat 37 by Loire Int: 21 Dec 1813 Dis: 15 Apr 1814.
    Received from Romulus. Diana Transport for Halifax.

Cribb, John   Prisoner 2496. Rank: Marine, from: President, U States Frigate.
    Cap: 15 Jan 1815 Not Recorded by Endymion Int: 04 Feb 1815 Dis: 28 Mar 1815.
    Received from Endymion. Clarenden Transport for U States.

Cross, Jacob   Prisoner 1601. Rank: Seaman, from: Bird, Merchant Vessel.
    Cap: 21 Nov 1813 Block Island by Albion Int: 14 Feb 1814 Dis: 23 Apr 1814.
    Received from Sceptre. HMS Bulwark for Halifax.

Cross, James   Prisoner 1121. Rank: Mate, from: Enterprize, Merchant.
    Cap: 12 Mar 1813 at Sea by HM Sloop Lyra Int: 21 Jun 1813 Dis: 24 Jun 1813.
    Received from HMS Ruby. Magnet Cartel for New York.

Crown, Frederick   Prisoner 1164. Rank: Seaman, from: Caledonian, Merchant.
    Cap: 20 Jul 1813 at Sea by HM Ship Marlborough Int: 15 Aug 1813 Dis: 03 Oct 1813.
    Received from HM Ship Woolwich. Caledonian Order of Commodore Evans she being Liberated.

Crummett, John   Prisoner 1830. Rank: Passenger, from: Not Recorded, Not Recorded.
    Cap: Not Recorded by Not Recorded Int: 14 Jun 1814 Dis: 15 Jun 1814.
    From St. Bartholomew in the Swedish Schooner Oscar. on Parole per Order Com in Chief to America.
    (Date of capture not recorded.)

Cuff, Abraham   Prisoner 1340. Rank: Seaman, from: Rolla, Privateer.
    Cap: 10 Dec 1813 Block Island by Loire Int: 20 Dec 1813 Dis: 15 Apr 1814.
    Received from HM Ship San Domingo. HMS Rammillies for Halifax.

Cullagen, John H   Prisoner 451. Rank: 1 Lieutenant, from: Teazer, Privateer Schooner.
    Cap: 16 Dec 1812 at Sea by HM Ship St. Domingo Int: 21 Dec 1812 Dis: 27 Jan 1813.
    Received from HM Ship St. Domingo. Bostock Cartel for New York.

Cullerton, Noah   Prisoner 518. Rank: Seaman, from: Nancy, Merchant Ship.
    Cap: 18 Dec 1812 off Bermuda by HMS Goree Int: 30 Dec 1812 Dis: 27 Jan 1813.
    Received from HMS Goree. Bostock Cartel for New York.

Culver, Esau   Prisoner 1545. Rank: Seaman, from: Valiant, Not Recorded.
    Cap: Not Recorded by Not Recorded Int: 04 Feb 1814 Dis: 15 Apr 1814.
    Received from Surprize. Surrendered himself a Prisoner of War from Valiant. Diana for Halifax. (Date of capture not recorded.)

Cummings, Edward   Prisoner 103. Rank: Seaman, from: Gossepuim, detained American.
    Cap: 31 Aug 1812 Bermuda by Not Recorded Int: 31 Aug 1812 Dis: 18 Sep 1812.
    Received from HMS Ruby. detained per order of the Commodore. Order of Commd Evans for England.

Cummings, William   Prisoner 2333. Rank: Seaman, from: President, U States Frigate.
    Cap: 15 Jan 1815 Not Recorded by Endymion Int: 04 Feb 1815 Dis: 28 Mar 1815.
    Received from Endymion. Mars Transport for U States.

Cummins, Christopher   Prisoner 2027. Rank: Seaman, from: Swiftsure, Merchant Vessel.
    Cap: 26 Oct 1814 off Halifax by Armide Int: 07 Nov 1814 Dis: 16 Mar 1815.
    Recaptured. Received from HMS Armide. Merchant Service.

American Prisoners of War Held at Bermuda During the War of 1812

Cunon, James   Prisoner 630. Rank: Mate, from: St. Augustina, Merchant Brig.
    Cap: 19 Dec 1812 at Sea by San Domingo   Int: 14 Jan 1813   Dis: 27 Jan 1813.
    Received from St. Augustina. Bostock Cartel for New York.

Cure, Thomas   Prisoner 972. Rank: Seaman, from: Janett, Merchant Brig.
    Cap: 25 Feb 1813 Chesapeake by HMS Junon   Int: 23 Mar 1813   Dis: 24 Jun 1813.
    Received from HM Ship Laurustinus. Magnet Cartel for New York.

Currant, Nicholas   Prisoner 1589. Rank: Seaman, from: Bordeaux Packet, Letter of Marque.
    Cap: 28 Jan 1814 off Cape Henry by Nieman   Int: 12 Feb 1814   Dis: 15 Apr 1814.
    Received from Nieman. Diana Transport for Halifax.

Currey, John   Prisoner 2397. Rank: Seaman, from: President, U States Frigate.
    Cap: 15 Jan 1815 Not Recorded by HM Ship Endymion   Int: 04 Feb 1815   Dis: 28 Mar 1815.
    Received from Endymion. Mars Transport for U States.

Currie, James   Prisoner 1262. Rank: Master, from: Huntress, Merchant Vessel.
    Cap: 12 Nov 1813 Long Island by HM Brig Borer   Int: 19 Dec 1813   Dis: 15 Apr 1814.
    Received from HMS Acasta. HMS Rammillies for Halifax.

Curtis, Lebe   Prisoner 1591. Rank: Seaman, from: Bordeaux Packet, Letter of Marque.
    Cap: 28 Jan 1814 off Cape Henry by Nieman   Int: 12 Feb 1814   Dis: 15 Apr 1814.
    Received from Nieman. Rammilles for Halifax.

Cushin, Lezer   Prisoner 1060. Rank: Seaman, from: Amason, Merchant.
    Cap: 18 Mar 1813 Chesapeake by HM Ship Victorious   Int: 06 Apr 1813   Dis: 24 Jun 1813.
    Received from HMS Junon. Magnet Cartel for New York.

Cushman, Harvey   Prisoner 1061. Rank: Seaman, from: Amason, Merchant.
    Cap: 18 Mar 1813 Chesapeake by HM Ship Victorious   Int: 06 Apr 1813   Dis: 24 Jun 1813.
    Received from HMS Junon. Magnet Cartel for New York.

Cutler, Thomas   Prisoner 1004. Rank: Seaman, from: Jefferson, Merchant.
    Cap: 18 Mar 1813 at Sea by HM Sloop Atalante   Int: 06 Apr 1813   Dis: 24 Jun 1813.
    Received from HMS Junon. Magnet Cartel for New York.

Dacres, John B   Prisoner 1476. Rank: Passenger, from: Teacher, Merchant Schooner.
    Cap: 10 Dec 1813 Cape Charles by Dragon   Int: 06 Jan 1814   Dis: 15 Apr 1814.
    Received from HM Ship Plantagenet. Rammilles for Halifax.

Dagget, Daniel   Prisoner 2864. Rank: Seaman, from: Limerick, Not Recorded.
    Cap: 06 Mar 1815 Not Recorded by Asia   Int: 28 Mar 1815   Dis: 28 Mar 1815.
    From West Indies. Received from Asia. Clarendon Transport for U States.

Dagget, Preston   Prisoner 2862. Rank: Prize Master, from: Limerick, Not Recorded.
    Cap: 06 Mar 1815 Not Recorded by Asia   Int: 28 Mar 1815   Dis: 28 Mar 1815.
    From West Indies. Received from Asia. Clarendon Transport for U States.

Dale, Richard   Prisoner 2150. Rank: Midshipman, from: President, U States Frigate.
    Cap: 15 Jan 1815 Not Recorded by Endymion   Int: 30 Jan 1815   Died: 23 Feb 1815.
    Received from President. Died. Wounds.

Dalton, Thomas   Prisoner 839. Rank: Seaman, from: Portsmouth, Merchant Ship.
    Cap: 27 Feb 1813 off Bermuda by HM Sloop Martin   Int: 09 Mar 1813   Dis: 27 Mar 1813.
    Received from HM Ship Martin. Per Order Commodore Evans the Vessel being Liberated.

Dame, George   Prisoner 523. Rank: Passenger, from: Gosum, Brig.
    Cap: 24 Dec 1812 at Sea by HM Sloop Sophia   Int: 31 Dec 1812   Dis: 27 Jan 1813.
    Received from Prize Brig Gosum. Bostock Cartel for New York.

Dameron, John   Prisoner 946. Rank: Master, from: Bona, Letter of Marque Schooner.
    Cap: 12 Mar 1813 Chesapeake by Laurustinus   Int: 23 Mar 1813   Dis: 24 Jun 1813.
    Received from Laurustinus. Magnet Cartel for New York.

Damore, Samuel   Prisoner 1378. Rank: Seaman, from: Policy, Merchant Vessel.
    Cap: 04 Dec 1813 Not Recorded by Loire   Int: 20 Dec 1813   Dis: 15 Apr 1814.
    Recaptured. Received from San Domingo. Diana Transport for Halifax.

Daniels, John   Prisoner 1742. Rank: Seaman, from: Yankelass, Privateer.
    Cap: 01 May 1814 L 10-4N, L 33-0W by Severn & Surprise   Int: 06 Jun 1814   Dis: 28 Mar 1815.
    Received from Severn. Mars for U States.

Dansey, Peter   Prisoner 1851. Rank: Seaman, from: Little Catherine, Packet.
    Cap: Not Recorded by Not Recorded   Int: Dis: 24 Nov 1814.
    Recaptured. Ardent SL British Subject. (Dates of capture and internment not recorded.)

Darby, Joseph   Prisoner 1746. Rank: Seaman, from: Yankelass, Privateer.
    Cap: 01 May 1814 L 40-4N, Long 38-0W by Severn & Surprise   Int: 06 Jun 1814   Dis: 12 Aug 1814.
    Received from Severn. Old Age Order Com in Chief.

Darby, Joseph   Prisoner 2033. Rank: Seaman, from: Not Recorded, Not Recorded.
    Cap: 22 Oct 1814 St. Georges by Severn   Int: 16 Nov 1814   Died: 29 Mar 1815.
    per order Commodore Evans. Received from HMS Goree. Died. Consumption.

American Prisoners of War Held at Bermuda During the War of 1812

Darley, Jacob   Prisoner 2541. Rank: Marine, from: President, U States Frigate.
    Cap: 15 Jan 1815 Not Recorded by HM Ship Endymion Int: 04 Feb 1815 Dis: 28 Mar 1815.
    Received from HMS Endymion. Clarenden Transport for U States.

Darrel, John S   Prisoner 1906. Rank: Master, from: Sally Jasper, Merchant Vessel.
    Cap: 14 Aug 1814 St. Catherine by Lacedaemonian Int: 09 Sep 1814 Dis: 21 Feb 1815.
    Received from Lacedaemonian. Paroled to the U States having served 6 months as Carpenter's Mate order of Adl Sir Alex Cockburn.

Davernoux, Nicholas   Prisoner 2545. Rank: Seaman, from: Industry, Merchant Vessel.
    Cap: 13 Dec 1814 off N York by Not Recorded Int: 04 Feb 1815 Dis: 28 Mar 1815.
    Recaptured. Received from HMS Endymion. Clarendon Transport for U States. Retaken (2068 former number). Nicholas Douvernier.

Davey, Hugh   Prisoner 1983. Rank: Captain, from: Pike, Privateer.
    Cap: 25 Aug 1814 off Savannah by Primrose Int: 17 Sep 1814 Dis: 22 Mar 1815.
    Received from Lacedaemonian. Merchant Vessel.

David, Michael   Prisoner 855. Rank: Seaman, from: Bona, Letter of Marque Schooner.
    Cap: 12 Mar 1813 Chesapeake by HM Ship Laurustinus Int: 23 Mar 1813 Dis: 31 May 1813.
    Received from HM Ship Laurustinus. Prince of Wales Transport Order Adml Warren.

Davidson, William   Prisoner 2334. Rank: Seaman, from: President, U States Frigate.
    Cap: 15 Jan 1815 Not Recorded by Endymion Int: 04 Feb 1815 Dis: 28 Mar 1815.
    Received from Endymion. Mars Transport for U States.

Davis, Benjamin   Prisoner 2481. Rank: Seaman, from: President, U States Frigate.
    Cap: 15 Jan 1815 Not Recorded by Endymion Int: 04 Feb 1815 Dis: 28 Mar 1815.
    Received from Endymion. Clarenden Transport for U States.

Davis, George   Prisoner 1512. Rank: Gunner, from: Nonsuch, Letter of Marque.
    Cap: 14 Dec 1813 Latt 38.0 by Doterel Int: 22 Jan 1814 Dis: 15 Apr 1814.
    Received from Surprize. Diana for Halifax.

Davis, Israel   Prisoner 1651. Rank: Seaman, from: Argus, Merchant Vessel.
    Cap: 01 Mar 1814 off Bermuda by San Domingo Int: 28 Feb 1814 Dis:
    Received from Active. (Date of interment before date of capture. Date of discharge not recorded.)

Davis, James   Prisoner 1070. Rank: Seaman, from: Sally, Merchant.
    Cap: 15 Mar 1813 Chesapeake by HM Ship Dragon Int: 06 Apr 1813 Dis: 24 Jun 1813.
    Received from HMS Junon. Magnet Cartel for New York.

Davis, John   Prisoner 468. Rank: Seaman, from: Teazer, Privateer Schooner.
    Cap: 16 Dec 1812 at Sea by HM Ship St. Domingo Int: 21 Dec 1812 Dis: 27 Jan 1813.
    Received from HM Ship St. Domingo. Bostock Cartel for New York.

Davis, John   Prisoner 1195. Rank: Seaman, from: Priscilla, Merchant Ship.
    Cap: 09 Aug 1813 at Sea by HM Sloop Forrester Int: 27 Aug 1813 Dis: 03 Sep 1813.
    Received from HM Sloop Forrester. to the American Ship Leander restored. John Davis (1).

Davis, John   Prisoner 1206. Rank: Seaman, from: Willam & Ann, Merchant Ship.
    Cap: 30 Jul 1813 at Sea by HM Sloop Nimrod Int: 21 Sep 1813 Dis: 23 Sep 1813.
    Returned to Prison from the American Ship Leander. Per Order of Capt Talbot of HMS Victorious + Senior Officer of HM Ship Herald. John Davis (2).

Davis, John   Prisoner 1316. Rank: Seaman, from: Rolla, Privateer.
    Cap: 10 Dec 1813 Block Island by Loire Int: 20 Dec 1813 Dis: 15 Apr 1814.
    Received from San Domingo. HMS Rammillies for Halifax.

Davis, John   Prisoner 1810. Rank: Passenger, from: Not Recorded, Not Recorded.
    Cap: Not Recorded by Not Recorded Int: 14 Jun 1814 Dis: 15 Jun 1814.
    From St. Bartholomew in the Swedish Schooner Oscar. on Parole per Order Com in Chief to America. (Date of capture not recorded.)

Davis, John   Prisoner 1967. Rank: Seaman, from: Pike, Privateer.
    Cap: 25 Aug 1814 off Savannah by Primrose Int: 09 Sep 1814 Dis: 05 Dec 1814.
    Received from Lacedaemonian. Ardent S L as a British Subject.

Davis, John   Prisoner 1990. Rank: Seaman, from: Eclipse, Merchant Vessel.
    Cap: 29 Sep 1814 Bermuda by Copark Int: 05 Oct 1814 Dis: 28 Mar 1815.
    Recaptured. Received from Goree. Clarendon Transport for U States.

Davis, John   Prisoner 2209. Rank: Seaman, from: President, U States Frigate.
    Cap: 15 Jan 1815 Not Recorded by Endymion Int: 30 Jan 1815 Dis: 28 Mar 1815.
    Received from Pomone. Mars Transport for U States.

Davis, John   Prisoner 2622. Rank: Mate, from: William, Merchant Vessel.
    Cap: 12 Jan 1815 Cape Hatterus by HMS Telegraph Int: 05 Feb 1815 Dis: 28 Mar 1815.
    Received from HMS Telegraph. Clarendon Transport for U States.

American Prisoners of War Held at Bermuda During the War of 1812

Davis, Josiah   Prisoner 1898. Rank: Seaman, from: Emily, Merchant Vessel.
    Cap: 11 Aug 1814 Tapella Sound by Not Recorded Int: 09 Sep 1814 Dis: 28 Mar 1815.
    Received from Lacedaemonian. Clarendon Transport for U States.

Davis, Michael   Prisoner 116. Rank: Seaman, from: Lydia, Merchant.
    Cap: 03 Sep 1812 Near Bermuda by HMS Orpheus Int: 08 Sep 1812 Dis: 18 Sep 1812.
    Received from HMS Orpheus. Order of Commd Evans England.

Davis, Pascari   Prisoner 1919. Rank: Seaman, from: Dolphin, Packet.
    Cap: 20 Aug 1814 St. Catherine by Lacedaemonian Int: 09 Sep 1814 Dis: 28 Mar 1815.
    Received from Lacedaemonian. Clarendon Transport for U States.

Davis, Peter   Prisoner 1156. Rank: Seaman, from: Acricoake, Merchant.
    Cap: 22 Jul 1813 at Sea by HM Sloop Conflict Int: 13 Aug 1813 Dis: 13 Aug 1813.
    Received from HM Ship Woolwich. American Ship Rolla per Order Governor Strong.

Davis, Samuel   Prisoner 1891. Rank: Seaman, from: Achilles, Merchant Vessel.
    Cap: Not Recorded by Not Recorded Int: Dis: 28 Mar 1815.
    Clarendon Transport for U States. (Dates of capture and internment not recorded.)

Davis, Samuel   Prisoner 2527. Rank: Seaman, from: President, U States Frigate.
    Cap: 15 Jan 1815 Not Recorded by Endymion Int: 04 Feb 1815 Dis: 28 Mar 1815.
    Received from HMS Endymion. Clarenden Transport for U States.

Davis, Thomas   Prisoner 2553. Rank: Seaman, from: President, US Frigate.
    Cap: 15 Jan 1815 off N York by HMS Endymion Int: 05 Feb 1815 Dis: 28 Mar 1815.
    Received from President. Clarenden Transport for U States.

Davis, Thomas   Prisoner 2635. Rank: Seaman, from: Superb, Merchant Vessel.
    Cap: 23 Nov 1814 off Delaware by Spencer Int: 06 Feb 1815 Dis: 13 Mar 1815.
    Received from HMS Telegraph. Merchant Service.

Davis, William   Prisoner 1936. Rank: Seaman, from: Pike, Privateer.
    Cap: 25 Aug 1814 off Savannah by Primrose Int: 09 Sep 1814 Dis: 20 Mar 1815.
    Received from Lacedaemonian. Merchant Vessel.

Davison, William   Prisoner 2491. Rank: Marine, from: President, U States Frigate.
    Cap: 15 Jan 1815 Not Recorded by Endymion Int: 04 Feb 1815 Dis: 28 Mar 1815.
    Received from Endymion. Clarenden Transport for U States.

Dawson, Charles   Prisoner 2668. Rank: Seaman, from: Enterprise, Merchant Vessel.
    Cap: 12 Aug 1814 off New York by Childers Int: 14 Feb 1815 Dis: 25 Mar 1815.
    from N. Providence. Received from Childers. Merchant Vessel.

Dawson, Christopher   Prisoner 1941. Rank: Seaman, from: Pike, Privateer.
    Cap: 25 Aug 1814 off Savannah by Primrose Int: 09 Sep 1814 Dis: 07 Nov 1814.
    Received from Lacedaemonian. Order Adl Cockburn.

Day, William   Prisoner 95. Rank: detained American, from: Gossepuim, Merchant.
    Cap: 16 Aug 1812 of Bermuda by Not Recorded Int: 28 Aug 1812 Dis: 06 Sep 1812.
    Received from HM Schooner Cuttle. detained per order of the President. Sloop Sally for New York.

Day, William   Prisoner 1324. Rank: Seaman, from: Rolla, Privateer.
    Cap: 10 Dec 1813 Block Island by Loire Int: 20 Dec 1813 Dis: 15 Apr 1814.
    Received from San Domingo. HMS Rammillies for Halifax.

De Casta, James   Prisoner 2215. Rank: Seaman, from: President, U States Frigate.
    Cap: 15 Jan 1815 Not Recorded by Endymion Int: 30 Jan 1815 Dis: 28 Mar 1815.
    Received from Pomone. Mars Transport for U States.

De Shitts, Matthew   Prisoner 1159. Rank: Seaman, from: Caledonian, Merchant.
    Cap: 20 Jul 1813 at Sea by HM Ship Marlborough Int: 15 Aug 1813 Dis: 03 Oct 1813.
    Received from HM Ship Woolwich. Caledonian Order of Commodore Evans she being Liberated.

de Valli, Louis   Prisoner 2868. Rank: Seaman, from: Limerick, Not Recorded.
    Cap: 06 Mar 1815 Not Recorded by Asia Int: 29 Mar 1815 Dis: 28 Mar 1815.
    From West Indies. Received from La Brune. Clarendon Transport for U States. (Date of discharge before date of internment.)

De Witch, Samuel   Prisoner 1051. Rank: Seaman, from: Massoil, Merchant.
    Cap: 18 Mar 1813 Chesapeake by HMS Dragon Int: 06 Apr 1813 Dis: 24 Jun 1813.
    Received from HMS Junon. Magnet Cartel for New York.

Deacon, John   Prisoner 328. Rank: Passenger, from: James, Merchant Ship.
    Cap: 03 Nov 1812 at Sea by HM Ship Tartarus Int: 17 Nov 1812 Dis: 12 Dec 1812.
    Received from HM Ship Tartarus. To the United States of America.

Deainson, J   Prisoner 1840. Rank: Seaman, from: Antelope, Merchant Sloop.
    Cap: 30 May 1814 between Cape Roman and Cape Fear by Doteral & Morgiana Int: 30 Jun 1814 Dis:
    Received from HMS Doterel. (Alias J Gillianson. Date of discharge not recorded.)

American Prisoners of War Held at Bermuda During the War of 1812

Decateur, Stephen   Prisoner 2133. Rank: Commander, from: President, U States Frigate.
    Cap: 15 Jan 1815 Not Recorded by Endymion Int: 30 Jan 1815 Dis: 06 Feb 1815.
    Received from President. Narcissus to the U States by the orders of Commadore Evans.

Defield, Jesse   Prisoner 409. Rank: Boatswain, from: Snapper, Privateer Schooner.
    Cap: 16 Nov 1812 at Sea by HM Ship Galus Int: 22 Nov 1812 Dis: 27 Jan 1813.
    Received from HM Ship Galus. Bostock Cartel for New York.

DeForrest, John   Prisoner 2064. Rank: Seaman, from: Industry, Merchant Vessel.
    Cap: 01 Dec 1814 off Cape Henry by HMS Niemen Int: 15 Dec 1814 Dis: 28 Mar 1815.
    Recaptured. Belong to Carolina Privateer. Received from HMS Niemen.
    Clarendon Transport for U States.

Deherty, Dennis   Prisoner 595. Rank: Marine, from: Wasp, Sloop of War.
    Cap: Not Recorded by Not Recorded Int: Dis: 17 Jun 1813.
    (Dates of capture and internment not recorded.) Halifax Order of Adl Sir JB Warren supports to be an Englishman.

Dekoven, Henry L   Prisoner 508. Rank: Passenger, from: St. Augustina, Merchant Brig.
    Cap: 16 Dec 1812 at Sea by HM Ship San Domingo Int: 28 Dec 1812 Dis: 15 Jan 1813.
    Received from the Prize Brig St. Augustina. New York by Order Ad Cockburn.

Delano, Harper   Prisoner 880. Rank: Mate, from: George, Merchant Sloop.
    Cap: 05 Feb 1813 Chesapeake by HM Ship Dragon Int: 23 Mar 1813 Dis: 24 Jun 1813.
    Received from Laurustinus. Magnet Cartel for New York.

Delano, William   Prisoner 2780. Rank: Supercargo, from: Ann Maria, Not Recorded.
    Cap: 30 Jan 1815 Savannah by Severn Int: 03 Mar 1815 Dis: 17 Mar 1815.
    Received from Hebrus. Clarendon Transport for U States.

Delany, Francis   Prisoner 1702. Rank: Seaman, from: Grecian, Letter of Marque.
    Cap: 02 May 1814 Chesapeake by Jansur Int: 26 May 1814 Dis:
    Received from Lacedaemonian. (Date of discharge not recorded.)

Delapp, William   Prisoner 2381. Rank: Seaman, from: President, U States Frigate.
    Cap: 15 Jan 1815 Not Recorded by HMS Endymion Int: 04 Feb 1815 Dis: 28 Mar 1815.
    Received from Endymion. Mars Transport for U States.

Deligall, William   Prisoner 1641. Rank: Mate, from: Mary Ann, Merchant Vessel.
    Cap: 06 Jan 1814 off Charlestown by Recruit Int: 21 Feb 1814 Dis: 13 Apr 1814.
    Received from Recruit. Permitted to reside in Bermuda.

Demers, William   Prisoner 1902. Rank: Master, from: Polly & Sally, Merchant Vessel.
    Cap: 13 Aug 1814 St. Catherine by Lacedaemonian Int: 09 Sep 1814 Died: 25 Dec 1814.
    Received from Lacedaemonian. Died. Fever. Or William Dennis.

Dennett, Thomas   Prisoner 2619. Rank: Mate, from: Attempt, Merchant Vessel.
    Cap: 12 Jan 1815 Cape Hatterus by HMS Telegraph Int: 05 Feb 1815 Dis: 28 Mar 1815.
    Received from HMS Telegraph. Clarendon Transport for U States.

Dennis, James   Prisoner 1877. Rank: Seaman, from: Levant, Merchant Vessel.
    Cap: Not Recorded by Not Recorded Int: Dis: 28 Mar 1815.
    Clarendon Transport for U States. (Dates of capture and internment not recorded.)

Dennis, John   Prisoner 2462. Rank: Seaman, from: President, U States Frigate.
    Cap: 15 Jan 1815 Not Recorded by Endymion Int: 04 Feb 1815 Dis: 28 Mar 1815.
    Received from Endymion. Clarenden Transport for U States.

Dennis, Joseph   Prisoner 687. Rank: Seaman, from: High Flyer, Privateer.
    Cap: 09 Jan 1813 at Sea by HMS Acasta Int: 21 Jan 1813 Dis: 27 Jan 1813.
    Received from HMS Acasta. Bostock Cartel for New York.

Dennis, Thomas   Prisoner 126. Rank: Boy, from: William of Baltimore, Merchant.
    Cap: 31 Aug 1812 Lat 37 by HM Ship Recruit Int: 14 Sep 1812 Dis: 18 Sep 1812.
    Received from Recruit. Order of Commd Evans for England.

Dennison, Isaac   Prisoner 1010. Rank: Mate, from: Nymble, Merchant.
    Cap: 19 Mar 1813 off the Chesapeake by HM Ship San Domingo Int: 06 Apr 1813 Dis: 24 Jun 1813.
    Received from HMS Junon. Magnet Cartel for New York.

Deurege, John   Prisoner 1546. Rank: Mate, from: Dove, Merchant Vessel.
    Cap: 04 Jan 1814 Block Island by Albian Int: 04 Feb 1814 Dis: 15 Apr 1814.
    Received from Surprize, Rammilles for Halifax.

Devall, Pardon   Prisoner 2700. Rank: Seaman, from: Experiment, Merchant Vessel.
    Cap: 19 Jan 1815 off Block Island by Nimrod Int: 18 Feb 1815 Dis: 17 Mar 1815.
    Received from Nimrod. Merchant Vessel.

Deveine, Charles   Prisoner 363. Rank: Seaman, from: Snapper, Privateer Schooner.
    Cap: 16 Nov 1812 at Sea by HM Ship Galus Int: 22 Nov 1812 Dis: 27 Jan 1813.
    Received from HM Ship Galus. Bostock Cartel for New York.

American Prisoners of War Held at Bermuda During the War of 1812

Devereux, Robert   Prisoner 1120. Rank: Master, from: Enterprize, Merchant.
    Cap: 12 Mar 1813 at Sea by HM Sloop Lyra Int: 21 Jun 1813 Dis: 24 Jun 1813.
    Received from HMS Ruby. Magnet Cartel for New York.

Dew, Edward   Prisoner 1974. Rank: Prize Master, from: Antelope, Merchant Vessel.
    Cap: 21 Aug 1814 Western Island by Whiting Int: 17 Sep 1814 Dis: 18 Mar 1815.
    Recaptured. Received from Goree. Merchant Vessel.

Dexter, Dennis   Prisoner 873. Rank: Seaman, from: Christiana, Merchant.
    Cap: 03 Mar 1813 Chesapeake by Marlborough Int: 23 Mar 1813 Dis: 24 Jun 1813.
    Received from Laurustinus. Magnet Cartel for New York.

Dickenfield, William   Prisoner 2648. Rank: Seaman, from: Dash, Merchant Vessel.
    Cap: 19 Jan 1815 Bahamas by HMS Statira Int: 06 Feb 1815 Dis: 25 Mar 1815.
    Received from HMS Statira. Merchant Vessel.

Dickenson, Henry   Prisoner 1894. Rank: Mate, from: Lound Abrona, Merchant Vessel.
    Cap: 13 Aug 1814 St. Catherine by Lacedaemonian Int: 02 Sep 1814 Dis: 17 Mar 1814.
    Received from Goree. Merchant Ship. (Date of discharge before date of capture - should be 1815.)

Dickenson, James   Prisoner 340. Rank: Seaman, from: Snapper, Privateer Schooner.
    Cap: 16 Nov 1812 at Sea by HMS Galus Int: 22 Nov 1812 Dis: 27 Jan 1813.
    Received from HM Ship Galus. Bostock Cartel for New York.

Dickinson, Samuel   Prisoner 503. Rank: Seaman, from: Ann, Merchant Sloop.
    Cap: 19 Dec 1812 at Sea by HMS Sophia Int: 27 Dec 1812 Dis: 27 Jan 1813.
    Received from Sophia. Bostock Cartel for New York.

Dill, Isaiah   Prisoner 1073. Rank: Seaman, from: Ring Dove, Merchant.
    Cap: 31 Mar 1813 Chesapeake by HMS Junon Int: 06 Apr 1813 Dis: 24 Jun 1813.
    Received from HMS Junon. Magnet Cartel for New York.

Dill, Stephen   Prisoner 205. Rank: Seaman, from: Wasp, Sloop of War.
    Cap: 18 Oct 1812 at Sea by HM Ship Poictiers Int: 26 Oct 1812 Dis: 05 Nov 1812.
    Received from HM Ship Poictiers. Brig Diamond on Parole to new London United States of America.

Dill, William   Prisoner 1618. Rank: Seaman, from: Brookhaven, Merchant Vessel.
    Cap: 09 Dec 1813 Block Island by Abion Int: 14 Feb 1814 Dis: 23 Apr 1814.
    Received from Sceptre. HMS Bulwark for Halifax.

Dimond, John   Prisoner 1845. Rank: Passenger, from: Hibernia, Merchant Vessel.
    Cap: Not Recorded by Not Recorded Int: Dis: 21 Feb 1815.
    (Dates of capture and internment not recorded.)

Dischodt, Frederick   Prisoner 2522. Rank: Seaman, from: President, U States Frigate.
    Cap: 15 Jan 1815 Not Recorded by Endymion Int: 04 Feb 1815 Dis: 28 Mar 1815.
    Received from HMS Endymion. Clarenden Transport for U States.

Dix, John   Prisoner 2160. Rank: Surgeons Mate, from: President, U States Frigate.
    Cap: 15 Jan 1815 Not Recorded by Endymion Int: 30 Jan 1815 Dis: 28 Mar 1815.
    Received from President. Clarenden Transport for U States.

Dix, Robert   Prisoner 1695. Rank: Seaman, from: Grecian, Letter of Marque.
    Cap: 02 May 1814 Chesapeake by Jansur Int: 26 May 1814 Dis: 28 Mar 1815.
    Received from Lacedaemonian. Mars Transport for U States.

Dixon, Archibald   Prisoner 1594. Rank: Seaman, from: Hornby, Merchant Vessel.
    Cap: 05 Feb 1814 Latt 39.0 by Sceptre Int: 13 Feb 1814 Dis: 15 Apr 1814.
    Recaptured. Received from Sceptre. Rammilles for Halifax.

Dixon, Closs   Prisoner 72. Rank: Seaman, from: Canaway, Merchant Ship.
    Cap: 08 Aug 1812 of Bermuda by Recruit Int: 28 Aug 1812 Dis: 17 Sep 1812.
    Received from M Schooner Cuttle. Prussian per Order C. Evans.

Dixon, Daniel   Prisoner 246. Rank: Marine, from: Wasp, Sloop of War.
    Cap: 18 Oct 1812 at Sea by HM Ship Poictiers Int: 26 Oct 1812 Dis: 05 Nov 1812.
    Received from HM Ship Poictiers. Brig Diamond on Parole to new London United States of America.

Dixon, John   Prisoner 1365. Rank: Seaman, from: Rolla, Privateer.
    Cap: 10 Dec 1813 Block Island by Loire Int: 20 Dec 1813 Dis: 15 Apr 1814.
    Received from San Domingo. HMS Rammillies for Halifax.

Dixon, M   Prisoner 1415. Rank: Supercargo, from: Nonsuch, Letter of Marque.
    Cap: 14 Dec 1813 Lat 32 by Doterel Int: 25 Dec 1813 Dis: 21 Jan 1814.
    Received from HM Brig Doterel. Without Exchange being a Noncombatant.

Dixon, Richard   Prisoner 718. Rank: Seaman, from: High Flyer, Privateer.
    Cap: 09 Jan 1813 at Sea by HM Ship Acasta Int: 21 Jan 1813 Dis: 27 Jan 1813.
    Received from HMS Acasta. Bostock Cartel for New York.

Dixon, Samuel   Prisoner 2455. Rank: Seaman, from: President, U States Frigate.
    Cap: 15 Jan 1815 Not Recorded by Endymion Int: 04 Feb 1815 Dis: 28 Mar 1815.
    Received from Endymion. Clarenden Transport for U States.

American Prisoners of War Held at Bermuda During the War of 1812

Dixon, William   Prisoner 2498. Rank: Seaman, from: President, U States Frigate.
    Cap: 15 Jan 1815 Not Recorded by Endymion Int: 04 Feb 1815 Dis: 28 Mar 1815.
    Received from Endymion. Clarenden Transport for U States.

Doak, Nathaniel   Prisoner 1791. Rank: Prize Master, from: Yankelass, Privateer.
    Cap: 01 May 1814 Latt 40-4N, Long 38-0W by Severn & Surprise Int: 07 Jun 1814 Dis: 28 Mar 1815.
    Received from Surprise. Mars Transport for U States.

Dobrix, Martin   Prisoner 2657. Rank: Seaman, from: Falcon, Merchant Vessel.
    Cap: 22 Jan 1815 Delaware by Forth Int: 13 Feb 1815 Dis: 17 Feb 1815.
    Received from Goree. Harriot M Vessel order of Commadore Evans.

Dodd, Thomas   Prisoner 1953. Rank: Seaman, from: Pike, Privateer.
    Cap: 25 Aug 1814 off Savannah by Primrose Int: 09 Sep 1814 Dis: 28 Mar 1815.
    Received from Lacedaemonian. Clarendon Transport for U States.

Dodge, Andrew   Prisoner 2478. Rank: Seaman, from: President, U States Frigate.
    Cap: 15 Jan 1815 Not Recorded by Endymion Int: 04 Feb 1815 Dis: 28 Mar 1815.
    Received from Endymion. Clarenden Transport for U States.

Doherty, Dennis   Prisoner 306. Rank: Marine, from: Wasp, Sloop of War.
    Cap: 18 Oct 1812 at Sea by HMS Poictiers Int: 05 Nov 1812 Dis: 17 Jun 1813.
    Received from HM Ship Poictiers. Halifax Order of the Commander in Chief supports to be an Englishman.

Dollman, John   Prisoner 2372. Rank: Seaman, from: President, U States Frigate.
    Cap: 15 Jan 1815 Not Recorded by HMS Endymion Int: 04 Feb 1815 Dis: 28 Mar 1815.
    Received from Endymion. Mars Transport for U States.

Dolphin, Edward   Prisoner 2776. Rank: Seaman, from: Hope, Not Recorded.
    Cap: 21 Feb 1815 off St Augustine by Hebrus Int: 03 Mar 1815 Dis: 28 Mar 1815.
    Received from Hebrus. Clarendon Transport for U States.

Domenick, Caper   Prisoner 2852. Rank: Seaman, from: Limerick, Not Recorded.
    Cap: 15 Mar 1815 Not Recorded by Asia Int: 25 Mar 1815 Dis:
    From Depot at Jamaica. Received from Asia. (Date of discharge not recorded.)

Dominga, N   Prisoner 941. Rank: Seaman, from: Salley, Merchant Sloop.
    Cap: 10 Mar 1813 Chesapeake by HMS Fantome Int: 23 Mar 1813 Dis: 06 Apr 1813.
    Received from Laurustinus. Per Order Commodore Evans a Portuguese.

Dominque, Joseph   Prisoner 2438. Rank: Seaman, from: President, U States Frigate.
    Cap: 15 Jan 1815 Not Recorded by Endymion Int: 04 Feb 1815 Dis: 28 Mar 1815.
    Received from Endymion. Mars Transport for U States.

Donagan, James   Prisoner 2755. Rank: Passenger, from: Speedwell, Not Recorded.
    Cap: 21 Jan 1815 St Augustine by Severn Int: 03 Mar 1815 Dis: 09 Mar 1815.
    Received from Hebrus. Merchant Service.

Donaldson, Benjamin   Prisoner 2351. Rank: Seaman, from: President, U States Frigate.
    Cap: 15 Jan 1815 Not Recorded by HMS Endymion Int: 04 Feb 1815 Dis: 28 Mar 1815.
    Received from Endymion. Mars Transport for U States.

Donavan, Benjamin   Prisoner 1149. Rank: Seaman, from: Acricoake, Merchant.
    Cap: 22 Jul 1813 at Sea by HM Sloop Conflict Int: 13 Aug 1813 Dis: 13 Aug 1813.
    Received from HM Ship Woolwich. Per Order Commr Evans Governor Strong.

Donnelly, Joseph   Prisoner 2050. Rank: Seaman, from: Mary, Merchant Schooner.
    Cap: 26 Nov 1814 off Cape Delaware by Telegraph Int: 05 Dec 1814 Dis: 28 Mar 1815.
    Received from HMS Goree. Clarendon Transport for U States.

Dore, Daniel   Prisoner 2081. Rank: Seaman, from: Trim, Merchant Vessel.
    Cap: 28 Dec 1814 Lat 34, Long 68 by HMS Telegraph Int: 04 Jan 1815 Dis: 24 Mar 1815.
    Received from HMS Goree. Merchant Vessel.

Dorington, Charles   Prisoner 1842. Rank: Seaman, from: Hibernia, Merchant Vessel.
    Cap: Not Recorded by Not Recorded Int: Dis: 24 Mar 1815.
    Merchant Vessel. (Dates of capture and internment not recorded.)

Dormain, John   Prisoner 361. Rank: Seaman, from: Snapper, Privateer Schooner.
    Cap: 16 Nov 1812 at Sea by HM Ship Galus Int: 22 Nov 1812 Dis: 27 Jan 1813.
    Received from HM Ship Galus. Bostock Cartel for New York.

Dormaine, George   Prisoner 481. Rank: Seaman, from: Teazer, Privateer Schooner.
    Cap: 16 Dec 1812 at Sea by HM Ship St. Domingo Int: 21 Dec 1812 Dis: 27 Jan 1813.
    Received from HM Ship St. Domingo. Bostock Cartel for New York.

Doughty, Russell   Prisoner 1875. Rank: Seaman, from: Mary, Merchant Vessel.
    Cap: Not Recorded by Not Recorded Int: Dis: 28 Mar 1815.
    Clarendon Transport for U States. (Dates of capture and internment not recorded.)

American Prisoners of War Held at Bermuda During the War of 1812

Douglas, Josiah   Prisoner 96. Rank: detained American, from: Gossepuim, Merchant.
    Cap: 16 Aug 1812 of Bermuda by Not Recorded Int: 28 Aug 1812 Dis: 06 Sep 1812.
    Received from HM Schooner Cuttle. detained per order of the President. Sloop Sally for New York.

Douglas, William   Prisoner 2316. Rank: Seaman, from: President, U States Frigate.
    Cap: 15 Jan 1815 Not Recorded by Endymion Int: 04 Feb 1815 Dis: 28 Mar 1815.
    Received from Endymion. Mars Transport for U States.

Douglass, Aquilla   Prisoner 1639. Rank: Seaman, from: Not Recorded, Not Recorded.
    Cap: 05 Feb 1814 Not Recorded by Sceptre Int: 14 Feb 1814 Escaped: 24 Nov 1814.
    Received from Sceptre. Run.

Douglass, Robert   Prisoner 1499. Rank: Master, from: Yankee, Merchant Sloop.
    Cap: 16 Dec 1813 Latt by Poictiers Int: 17 Jan 1814 Dis: 15 Apr 1814.
    Received from Poictiers. Released per Com in Chief. (Latitude number not recorded.)

Douglass, Simon   Prisoner 1405. Rank: Seaman, from: John & James, Merchant Vessel.
    Cap: 07 Dec 1813 Lat 37 by Loire Int: 21 Dec 1813 Dis: 15 Apr 1814.
    Received from Romulus. Diana Transport for Halifax.

Douvernier, Nicholas   Prisoner 2068. Rank: Seaman, from: Industry, Merchant Vessel.
    Cap: 01 Dec 1814 off Cape Henry by HMS Niemen Int: 15 Dec 1814 Dis: 25 Jan 1815.
    Recaptured. Belong to Carolina Privateer. Received from HMS Niemen. Bridges Transport being Subject to Friendly power Order Com Evans.

Dove, Samuel   Prisoner 1952. Rank: Seaman, from: Pike, Privateer.
    Cap: 25 Aug 1814 off Savannah by Primrose Int: 09 Sep 1814 Dis: 28 Mar 1815.
    Received from Lacedaemonian. Clarendon Transport for U States.

Doverell, Thomas   Prisoner 2710. Rank: Seaman, from: South Boston, Merchant Vessel.
    Cap: 13 Feb 1815 off Charleston by Pandora Int: 02 Mar 1815 Dis: 28 Mar 1815.
    Received from Pandora. Clarendon Transport for U States.

Dow, Timothy   Prisoner 780. Rank: Seaman, from: Governor Ankerheim, Merchant.
    Cap: 24 Jan 1813 at Sea by HM Ship Ramiles Int: 04 Feb 1813 Dis: 13 Mar 1813.
    Received from HMS Ramilies. Per Order Sir John Warren the Vessel being Liberated.

Dowling, Peter   Prisoner 101. Rank: detained American, from: Gossepuim, Merchant.
    Cap: 16 Aug 1812 of Bermuda by Not Recorded Int: 31 Aug 1812 Dis: 18 Sep 1812.
    Received from HMS Ruby. detained per order of the Commodore. Order of Commd Evans for England.

Down, John   Prisoner 1503. Rank: Master, from: Jackall, Merchant Vessel.
    Cap: 23 Dec 1813 off the Delaware by Belvidera Int: 18 Jan 1814 Dis: 01 Feb 1814.
    Received from Belvidera. Released per Order of the Commander in Chief.

Downing, George   Prisoner 1721. Rank: 1 Mate, from: Grecian, Letter of Marque.
    Cap: 02 May 1814 Chesapeake by Jansur Int: 26 May 1814 Dis:
    Received from Lacedaemonian. (Date of discharge not recorded.)

Downing, James   Prisoner 2459. Rank: Marine, from: President, U States Frigate.
    Cap: 15 Jan 1815 Not Recorded by Endymion Int: 04 Feb 1815 Dis: 28 Mar 1815.
    Received from Endymion. Clarenden Transport for U States.

Downridge, Stephen   Prisoner 898. Rank: Seaman, from: Princessa, Merchant Brig.
    Cap: 07 Feb 1813 Chesapeake by HMS Marlborough Int: 23 Mar 1813 Dis: 24 Jun 1813.
    Received from HM Ship Laurustinus. Magnet Cartel for New York.

Downs, Jeremiah   Prisoner 237. Rank: Seaman, from: Wasp, Sloop of War.
    Cap: 18 Oct 1812 at Sea by HM Ship Poictiers Int: 26 Oct 1812 Dis: 05 Nov 1812.
    Received from HM Ship Poictiers. Brig Diamond on Parole to new London United States of America.

Downs, Nasa   Prisoner 618. Rank: Seaman, from: HM Schooner Elizabeth, Not Recorded.
    Cap: Not Recorded by Not Recorded Int: 12 Jan 1813 Dis: 27 Jan 1813.
    Received from HMS Belvidera. Bostock Cartel for New York. formally serving on Board HM Schooner Elizabeth. (Date of capture not recorded.)

Doyle, Lewis   Prisoner 301. Rank: Seaman, from: Symmetry, Merchant Ship.
    Cap: 05 Jul 1812 at Sea by HM Ship Rattler Int: 02 Nov 1812 Dis: 04 Nov 1812.
    Received from HMS Poictiers. Brig Diamond on Parole to new London United States of America.

Drake, Harrison   Prisoner 1627. Rank: Seaman, from: Perseferanda, Merchant Vessel.
    Cap: 03 Jan 1814 Block Island by Albion Int: 14 Feb 1814 Dis: 23 Apr 1814.
    Received from Sceptre. HMS Bulwark for Halifax.

Drew, Benjamin   Prisoner 1717. Rank: Seaman, from: Olive Branch, Merchant Vessel.
    Cap: 16 Apr 1814 Chesapeake by Acasta Int: 26 May 1814 Dis: 24 Mar 1815.
    Received from Lacedaemonian. Merchant Vessel.

Drew, Ezekiel   Prisoner 1160. Rank: Seaman, from: Caledonian, Merchant.
    Cap: 20 Jul 1813 at Sea by HM Ship Marlborough Int: 15 Aug 1813 Dis: 03 Oct 1813.
    Received from HM Ship Woolwich. Caledonian Order of Commodore Evans she being Liberated.

American Prisoners of War Held at Bermuda During the War of 1812

Dryden, John   Prisoner 1309. Rank: Seaman, from: Rolla, Privateer.
    Cap: 10 Dec 1813 Block Island by Loire Int: 20 Dec 1813 Dis: 15 Apr 1814.
    Received from San Domingo. HMS Rammillies for Halifax.

Dubbin, R   Prisoner 2715. Rank: Seaman, from: American Gun Boat, Not Recorded.
    Cap: 06 Feb 1815 off Charleston by Tonnant Int: 02 Mar 1815 Dis: 28 Mar 1815.
    Received from Armede. Clarendon Transport for U States.

Duffie, David   Prisoner 287. Rank: Seaman, from: Wasp, Sloop of War.
    Cap: 18 Oct 1812 at Sea by HMS Poictiers Int: 02 Nov 1812 Dis: 04 Nov 1812.
    Received from HMS Poictiers. Brig Diamond on Parole to new London United States of America.

Dugden, Gilbert   Prisoner 2567. Rank: Seaman, from: Funchall, Merchant Vessel.
    Cap: 15 Jan 1815 off New York by HMS Pomone Int: 05 Feb 1815 Dis: 13 Mar 1815.
    Received from HMS Forth. Merchant Service.

Dumatee, M   Prisoner 2713. Rank: Seaman, from: American Gun Boat, Not Recorded.
    Cap: 06 Feb 1815 off Charleston by Tonnant Int: 02 Mar 1815 Dis: 28 Mar 1815.
    Received from Armede. Clarendon Transport for U States.

Dumkley, Isaac   Prisoner 463. Rank: Seaman, from: Teazer, Privateer Schooner.
    Cap: 16 Dec 1812 at Sea by HM Ship St. Domingo Int: 21 Dec 1812 Dis: 27 Jan 1813.
    Received from HM Ship St. Domingo. Bostock Cartel for New York.

Duncan, Mathew   Prisoner 721. Rank: Seaman, from: High Flyer, Privateer.
    Cap: 09 Jan 1813 at Sea by HM Ship Acasta Int: 21 Jan 1813 Dis: 27 Jan 1813.
    Received from HMS Acasta. Bostock Cartel for New York.

Dunkan, Henrick   Prisoner 113. Rank: Mate, from: Lydia, Merchant.
    Cap: 03 Sep 1812 Near Bermuda by HMS Orpheus Int: 08 Sep 1812 Dis: 10 Sep 1812.
    Received from HMS Orpheus. a Sweed per Order Cmd Evans.

Dunkley, Isaac   Prisoner 281. Rank: Seaman, from: Little William, Merchant Brig.
    Cap: 18 Oct 1812 at Sea by HM Ship Poictiers Int: 30 Oct 1812 Dis: 05 Nov 1812.
    Received from HM Ship Poictiers. Brig Diamond on Parole to new London United States of America.

Dunn, James   Prisoner 2173. Rank: Seaman, from: President, U States Frigate.
    Cap: 15 Jan 1815 Not Recorded by HMS Endymion Int: 30 Jan 1815 Dis: 28 Mar 1815.
    Received from President. Mars Transport for U States.

Dunsenberg, D   Prisoner 2803. Rank: Seaman, from: Limerick, Not Recorded.
    Cap: 04 Mar 1815 Not Recorded by Asia Int: 25 Mar 1815 Dis:
    From Depot at Jamaica. Received from Asia. (Date of discharge not recorded.)

Dunton, G   Prisoner 1414. Rank: Captain, from: Nonsuch, Letter of Marque.
    Cap: 14 Dec 1813 Lat 32 by Doterel Int: 25 Dec 1813 Dis: 15 Apr 1814.
    Received from HM Brig Doterel. Rammilles for Halifax.

Dunton, Robert   Prisoner 1247. Rank: Not Recorded, from: Fox, Merchant Schooner.
    Cap: 13 Oct 1813 Chesapeake by Sophie Int: 02 Dec 1813 Dis: 24 Mar 1814.
    Received from HMS Sceptre. Boy under Age per Order of Commander in Chief.

Dunton, Thomas   Prisoner 1245. Rank: Not Recorded, from: Fox, Merchant Schooner.
    Cap: 13 Oct 1813 Chesapeake by Sophie Int: 02 Dec 1813 Died: 19 Feb 1814.
    Received from HMS Sceptre. Died. Dysentery.

Dunton, Thomas   Prisoner 1246. Rank: Not Recorded, from: Fox, Merchant Schooner.
    Cap: 13 Oct 1813 Chesapeake by Sophie Int: 02 Dec 1813 Dis: 24 Mar 1814.
    Received from HMS Sceptre. Boy under Age per Order of Commander in Chief.

Dupecy, John   Prisoner 2110. Rank: Boy, from: Rufus King, Merchant Vessel.
    Cap: 01 Jan 1815 off Bermuda by Peruvian Int: 19 Jan 1815 Dis: 25 Jan 1815.
    Received from HMS Peruvian. Bridges Transport Subject to friendly power Order Commadore Evans.
    2y Vic List 28 March 1815.

Duplantes, Eugene   Prisoner 678. Rank: Seaman, from: High Flyer, Privateer.
    Cap: 09 Jan 1813 at Sea by HM Ship Acasta Int: 21 Jan 1813 Dis: 27 Jan 1813.
    Received from HMS Acasta. Bostock Cartel for New York.

Dupree, John   Prisoner 2546. Rank: Seaman, from: Rufus King, Seaman.
    Cap: 13 Dec 1814 off N York by Not Recorded Int: 04 Feb 1815 Dis: 28 Mar 1815.
    Recaptured. Received from HMS Endymion. Into Merchamt Service. Retaken (2110 former number).
    John Dupesy.

Duram, Peter   Prisoner 1704. Rank: Seaman, from: Grecian, Letter of Marque.
    Cap: 02 May 1814 Chesapeake by Jansur Int: 26 May 1814 Dis:
    Received from Lacedaemonian. (Date of discharge not recorded.)

Durant, John   Prisoner 53. Rank: Seaman, from: Ariel, Merchant Brig.
    Cap: 28 Jul 1812 of Bermuda by Recruit Int: 28 Aug 1812 Dis: 18 Sep 1812.
    Received from M Schooner Cuttle. Order of Commd Evans for England.

American Prisoners of War Held at Bermuda During the War of 1812

Durvin, Gerrald   Prisoner 781. Rank: Seaman, from: Governor Ankerheim, Merchant.
    Cap: 24 Jan 1813 at Sea by HM Ship Ramiles Int: 04 Feb 1813 Dis: 13 Mar 1813.
    Received from HMS Ramilies. Per Order Sir John Warren the Vessel being Liberated.

Dustaine, Peter   Prisoner 337. Rank: Seaman, from: Snapper, Privateer Schooner.
    Cap: 16 Nov 1812 at Sea by HMS Galus Int: 22 Nov 1812 Dis: 27 Jan 1813.
    Received from HM Ship Galus. Bostock Cartel for New York.

Dutch, Esra T   Prisoner 143. Rank: Master, from: Factor of Salem, Merchant Brig.
    Cap: 30 Sep 1812 Lat 35, Long 65 W by HMS Tartarus Int: 13 Oct 1812 Dis: 24 Oct 1812.
    Received from HMS Tartarus. Brig Diamond on Parole to New London United States of America.

Dutch, Nathaniel   Prisoner 1107. Rank: Seaman, from: Apollo, Merchant Vessel.
    Cap: 15 May 1813 at Sea by HM Ship Success Int: 27 May 1813 Dis: 24 Jun 1813.
    Received from HMS Success. Magnet Cartel for New York.

Dutton, Nathan   Prisoner 2251. Rank: Seaman, from: President, U States Frigate.
    Cap: 15 Jan 1815 Not Recorded by Endymion Int: 30 Jan 1815 Dis: 28 Mar 1815.
    Received from Pomone. Mars Transport for U States.

Dyer, Ezekial   Prisoner 107. Rank: Seaman, from: Gossepuim, detained American.
    Cap: 02 Sep 1812 Bermuda by Not Recorded Int: 02 Sep 1812 Dis: 18 Sep 1812.
    Received from HMS Ruby. detained per order of the President. Order of Commd Evans for England.

Dyer, John   Prisoner 672. Rank: Boatswains Mate, from: High Flyer, Privateer.
    Cap: 09 Jan 1813 at Sea by HM Ship Acasta Int: 21 Jan 1813 Dis: 27 Jan 1813.
    Received from HMS Acasta. Bostock Cartel for New York.

Eagles, John   Prisoner 296. Rank: Seaman, from: Symmetry, Merchant Ship.
    Cap: 05 Jul 1812 at Sea by HM Ship Rattler Int: 02 Nov 1812 Dis: 04 Nov 1812.
    Received from HMS Poictiers. Brig Diamond on Parole to new London United States of America.

Earp, Aquilla   Prisoner 2663. Rank: Seaman, from: President, U States Frigate.
    Cap: 15 Jan 1815 off New York by Endymion Int: 14 Feb 1815 Dis: 28 Mar 1815.
    Received from Goree. Clarenden Transport for U States.

Easton, Isaac   Prisoner 157. Rank: Seaman, from: Ranger, Merchant Ship.
    Cap: 02 Oct 1812 Lat 32, Long 65 W by HM Ship Goree Int: 13 Oct 1812 Dis: 24 Oct 1812.
    Received from HMS Goree. Brig Diamond on Parole to new London United States of America.

Eaton, Andrew   Prisoner 428. Rank: Seaman, from: Eliza, Merchant Ship.
    Cap: 25 Nov 1812 Lat 37.00, Long 65.46 by HM Ship Tartarus Int: 03 Dec 1812 Dis: 27 Jan 1813.
    Received from HM Ship Tartarus. Bostock Cartel for New York.

Eaton, Israel   Prisoner 22. Rank: Mate, from: Hero, Merchant Schooner.
    Cap: 14 Jul 1812 at Bermuda by Cuttle Int: 28 Aug 1812 Dis: 10 Sep 1812.
    Received from HM Schooner Cuttle. Schooner Hero for N Y.

Eaton, James   Prisoner 2712. Rank: Seaman, from: American Gun Boat, Not Recorded.
    Cap: 06 Feb 1815 off Charleston by Tonnant Int: 02 Mar 1815 Dis: 28 Mar 1815.
    Received from Armede. Clarendon Transport for U States.

Eddy, Edward   Prisoner 2805. Rank: Seaman, from: Limerick, Not Recorded.
    Cap: 04 Mar 1815 Not Recorded by Asia Int: 25 Mar 1815 Dis:
    From Depot at Jamaica. Received from Asia. (Date of discharge not recorded.)

Edes, Benjamin   Prisoner 1452. Rank: Seaman, from: Vixen, Man of War.
    Cap: 25 Dec 1813 Lat 38.0 by Belvidera Int: 05 Jan 1814 Dis: 15 Apr 1814.
    U States Schooner. Received from HMS Belvidera. Diana Transport for Halifax.

Edgehill, Washington   Prisoner 2555. Rank: Seaman, from: President, US Frigate.
    Cap: 15 Jan 1815 off N York by HMS Endymion Int: 05 Feb 1815 Dis: 28 Mar 1815.
    Received from President. Clarenden Transport for U States.

Edinburgh, Peter   Prisoner 2842. Rank: Seaman, from: Limerick, Not Recorded.
    Cap: 15 Mar 1815 Not Recorded by Asia Int: 25 Mar 1815 Dis:
    From Depot at Jamaica. Received from Asia. (Date of discharge not recorded.)

Edmonds, Thomas   Prisoner 894. Rank: Seaman, from: Hannah, Merchant Schooner.
    Cap: 24 Feb 1813 Chesapeake by HMS Marlborough Int: 23 Mar 1813 Dis: 24 Jun 1813.
    Received from HM Ship Laurustinus. Magnet Cartel for New York.

Edred, Benjamin   Prisoner 2608. Rank: Seaman, from: Edward, Merchant Vessel.
    Cap: 30 Dec 1814 Sandy Hook by HM Ship Pomone Int: 05 Feb 1815 Dis: 28 Mar 1815.
    Received from HMS Forth. Clarendon Transport for U States.

Edward, Simon   Prisoner 1938. Rank: Seaman, from: Pike, Privateer.
    Cap: 25 Aug 1814 off Savannah by Primrose Int: 09 Sep 1814 Dis: 28 Mar 1815.
    Received from Lacedaemonian. Clarendon Transport for U States.

Edwards, Benjamin   Prisoner 2008. Rank: Seaman, from: Bridges, Merchant Vessel.
    Cap: 25 Oct 1814 off Halifax by Armide Int: 07 Nov 1814 Dis: 28 Mar 1815.
    Recaptured. Received from HMS Armide. Clarendon Transport for U States.

American Prisoners of War Held at Bermuda During the War of 1812

Edwards, George Thomas   Prisoner 294. Rank: Seaman, from: Symmetry, Merchant Ship.
    Cap: 05 Jul 1812 at Sea by HM Ship Rattler Int: 02 Nov 1812 Dis: 04 Nov 1812.
    Received from HMS Poictiers. Brig Diamond on Parole to new London United States of America.

Edwards, John   Prisoner 471. Rank: Seaman, from: Teazer, Privateer Schooner.
    Cap: 16 Dec 1812 at Sea by HM Ship St. Domingo Int: 21 Dec 1812 Dis: 27 Jan 1813.
    Received from HM Ship St. Domingo. Bostock Cartel for New York.

Edwards, John   Prisoner 2277. Rank: Seaman, from: President, U States Frigate.
    Cap: 15 Jan 1815 Not Recorded by Endymion Int: 30 Jan 1815 Dis: 28 Mar 1815.
    Received from Pomone. Mars Transport for U States.

Edwards, Nicholas   Prisoner 1413. Rank: Passenger, from: Industry, Merchant Vessel.
    Cap: 08 Dec 1813 Lat 37.25 by Loire Int: 21 Dec 1813 Dis: 15 Apr 1814.
    Received from Romulus. Diana for Halifax.

Edwards, William   Prisoner 184. Rank: Marine, from: Wasp, Sloop of War.
    Cap: 18 Oct 1812 at Sea by HMS Poictiers Int: 26 Oct 1812 Dis: 05 Nov 1812.
    Received from HM Ship Poictiers. Brig Diamond on Parole to new London America.

Edwards, William   Prisoner 1394. Rank: Seaman, from: Scorpion, Merchant Vessel.
    Cap: 29 Nov 1813 Lat 39 by Loire Int: 21 Dec 1813 Dis: 15 Apr 1814.
    Received from Romulus. Diana for Halifax.

Edwards, William   Prisoner 2157. Rank: Sail Maker, from: President, U States Frigate.
    Cap: 15 Jan 1815 Not Recorded by Endymion Int: 30 Jan 1815 Dis: 28 Mar 1815.
    Received from President. Mars Transport for U States.

Egbert, Frederick   Prisoner 2573. Rank: Seaman, from: Mercury, Merchant Vessel.
    Cap: 30 Dec 1814 off New York by HMS Pomone Int: 05 Feb 1815 Dis: 17 Feb 1815.
    Received from HMS Forth. Harriot M Vessel per order of Commd Evans.

Elbey, James   Prisoner 506. Rank: Seaman, from: Teazer, Privateer Schooner.
    Cap: 16 Dec 1812 at Sea by HM Ship St. Domingo Int: 28 Dec 1812 Dis: 21 Jan 1813.
    Received from San. Domingo. French Prison Halifax per Order Commander in Chief.

Eldridge, David   Prisoner 2096. Rank: Seaman, from: Phaeton, Mechant Vessel.
    Cap: 07 Feb 1815 cast away on Barbary by Forester Int: 19 Jan 1815 Dis: 13 Mar 1815.
    Received from HMS Peruvian. Merchant Service. (Date of internment before date of capture
    - should be 1814.)

Elkin, M   Prisoner 1399. Rank: Seaman, from: John & James, Merchant Vessel.
    Cap: 07 Dec 1813 Lat 37 by Loire Int: 21 Dec 1813 Dis: 05 Jun 1814.
    Received from Romulus. United States on Parole. (First name not legible.)

Elliot, John   Prisoner 1079. Rank: Seaman, from: Not Recorded, Not Recorded.
    Cap: Not Recorded by Not Recorded Int: 23 Apr 1813 Dis: 24 Jun 1813.
    Surrendered them Selves as Prisoners of War. Magnet Cartel for New York.
    (Date of capture not recorded.)

Elliot, Nicholas   Prisoner 916. Rank: Seaman, from: Albert, Merchant Schooner.
    Cap: 05 Mar 1813 Chesapeake by HM Ship Marlborough Int: 23 Mar 1813 Dis: 24 Jun 1813.
    Received from Laurustinus. Magnet Cartel for New York.

Elliot, Robert   Prisoner 1939. Rank: Seaman, from: Pike, Privateer.
    Cap: 25 Aug 1814 off Savannah by Primrose Int: 09 Sep 1814 Dis: 28 Mar 1815.
    Received from Lacedaemonian. Clarendon Transport for U States.

Elliott, John   Prisoner 1234. Rank: Not Recorded, from: HM Ship Cleopatra, Not Recorded.
    Cap: 21 Sep 1813 Not Recorded by Dragon Int: 16 Nov 1813 Dis: 15 Apr 1814.
    Received from HMS Sceptre. Surrendered himself. Diana Transport for Halifax.

Elliott, John   Prisoner 2586. Rank: Mate, from: Thestis, Merchant Vessel.
    Cap: 18 Nov 1814 off New York by HM Ship Majestic Int: 05 Feb 1815 Dis: 28 Mar 1815.
    Received from HMS Forth. Clarendon Transport for U States.

Ellis, Aaron   Prisoner 341. Rank: Seaman, from: Snapper, Privateer Schooner.
    Cap: 16 Nov 1812 at Sea by HMS Galus Int: 22 Nov 1812 Dis: 27 Jan 1813.
    Received from HM Ship Galus. Bostock Cartel for New York.

Ellis, William   Prisoner 2679. Rank: Seaman, from: Gunboat 160, U States Man of War.
    Cap: 06 Sep 1814 off New York by Lacedaemonian Int: 14 Feb 1815 Dis: 28 Mar 1815.
    Gun Vessel. Received from Childers. Clarendon Transport for U States.

Ellridge, Henry   Prisoner 1598. Rank: Seaman, from: Dispatch, Merchant Vessel.
    Cap: 26 Oct 1813 Block Island by Narcissus Int: 14 Feb 1814 Dis: 23 Apr 1814.
    Received from Sceptre. HMS Bulwark for Halifax.

Elwell, Francis   Prisoner 2627. Rank: Seaman, from: William, Merchant Vessel.
    Cap: 12 Jan 1815 Cape Hatterus by HMS Telegraph Int: 05 Feb 1815 Dis: 28 Mar 1815.
    Received from HMS Telegraph. Clarendon Transport for U States.

American Prisoners of War Held at Bermuda During the War of 1812

Emerson, Andrew   Prisoner 1153. Rank: Seaman, from: Acricoake, Merchant.
    Cap: 22 Jul 1813 at Sea by HM Sloop Conflict Int: 13 Aug 1813 Dis: 13 Aug 1813.
    Received from HM Ship Woolwich. American Ship Rolla per Order Governor Strong.

Emerson, John   Prisoner 2871. Rank: Seaman, from: Limerick, Not Recorded.
    Cap: 06 Mar 1815 Not Recorded by Asia Int: 29 Mar 1815 Dis: 28 Mar 1815.
    From West Indies. Received from La Brune. Clarendon Transport for U States. (Date of discharge before date of internment.)

Emerus, John   Prisoner 131. Rank: 1 Lieutenant, from: James Maddison, Man of War.
    Cap: 22 Aug 1812 Lat 31 by HMS Barbados Int: 14 Sep 1812 Dis: 24 Oct 1812.
    Received from HMS Barbados. Brig Diamond on Parole to new London United States of America.

Emmet, C T   Prisoner 2148. Rank: Midshipman, from: President, U States Frigate.
    Cap: 15 Jan 1815 Not Recorded by Endymion Int: 30 Jan 1815 Dis: 28 Mar 1815.
    Received from President. Mars Transport for U States.

Emory, Samuel   Prisoner 1904. Rank: Seaman, from: Polly & Sally, Merchant Vessel.
    Cap: 13 Aug 1814 St. Catherine by Lacedaemonian Int: 09 Sep 1814 Dis: 28 Mar 1814.
    Received from Lacedaemonian. Clarendon Transport for U States.

Ennis, Lewis   Prisoner 235. Rank: Seaman, from: Wasp, Sloop of War.
    Cap: 18 Oct 1812 at Sea by HM Ship Poictiers Int: 26 Oct 1812 Dis: 05 Nov 1812.
    Received from HM Ship Poictiers. Brig Diamond on Parole to new London United States of America.

Eroundy, Francis   Prisoner 1151. Rank: Seaman, from: Acricoake, Merchant.
    Cap: 22 Jul 1813 at Sea by HM Sloop Conflict Int: 13 Aug 1813 Dis: 13 Aug 1813.
    Received from HM Ship Woolwich. American Ship Rolla per Order Governor Strong.

Ervin, Charles   Prisoner 449. Rank: Master, from: Famers Fancy, Merchant.
    Cap: 11 Dec 1812 at Sea by HMS Acasta Int: 20 Dec 1812 Dis: 27 Jan 1813.
    Received from Farmers Fancy. Bostock Cartel for New York.

Ervin, John   Prisoner 549. Rank: Seaman, from: Herald, Letter of Marque Brig.
    Cap: 25 Dec 1812 at Sea by HM Ship Maidstone Int: 05 Jan 1813 Dis: 27 Jan 1813.
    Received from HM Ship Maidstone. Bostock Cartel for New York.

Ervin, John   Prisoner 1127. Rank: Seaman, from: Mary, Merchant.
    Cap: 17 Apr 1813 at Sea by HM Ship Fox Int: 21 Jun 1813 Dis: 24 Jun 1813.
    Received from HM Ship Ruby. Magnet Cartel for New York.

Esbourn, Francis   Prisoner 2572. Rank: Seaman, from: Mercury, Merchant Vessel.
    Cap: 30 Dec 1814 off New York by HMS Pomone Int: 05 Feb 1815 Dis: 24 Mar 1815.
    Received from HMS Forth. Merchant Vessel.

Estes, J H T   Prisoner 854. Rank: Master, from: Bona, Letter of Marque Schooner.
    Cap: 12 Mar 1813 Chesapeake by HM Ship Laurustinus Int: 23 Mar 1813 Escaped: 21 Apr 1813.
    Received from HM Ship Laurustinus. Escaped.

Evans, Benjamin   Prisoner 1451. Rank: Masters Mate, from: Vixen, Man of War.
    Cap: 25 Dec 1813 Lat 38.0 by Belvidera Int: 05 Jan 1814 Dis: 15 Apr 1814.
    U States Schooner. Received from HMS Belvidera. Rammilles for Halifax.

Evans, Jerry   Prisoner 336. Rank: Seaman, from: Snapper, Privateer Schooner.
    Cap: 16 Nov 1812 at Sea by HMS Galus Int: 22 Nov 1812 Dis: 27 Jan 1813.
    Received from HM Ship Galus. Bostock Cartel for New York.

Evans, John   Prisoner 1799. Rank: Steward, from: Yankelass, Privateer.
    Cap: 01 May 1814 L 40-4P, Long 30-11W by Severn & Surprise Int: 07 Jun 1814 Dis: 24 Mar 1815.
    Yankee lass. Received from Surprise. Merchant Vessel.

Evans, John   Prisoner 2195. Rank: Seaman, from: President, U States Frigate.
    Cap: 15 Jan 1815 Not Recorded by HMS Endymion Int: 30 Jan 1815 Dis: 28 Mar 1815.
    Received from Pomone. Mars Transport for U States.

Evans, Joseph   Prisoner 2339. Rank: Seaman, from: President, U States Frigate.
    Cap: 15 Jan 1815 Not Recorded by Endymion Int: 04 Feb 1815 Dis: 28 Mar 1815.
    Received from Endymion. Mars Transport for U States.

Evans, William   Prisoner 1694. Rank: Seaman, from: Grecian, Letter of Marque.
    Cap: 02 May 1814 Chesapeake by Jansur Int: 26 May 1814 Dis:
    Received from Lacedaemonian. (Date of discharge not recorded.)

Exley, William   Prisoner 1115. Rank: Supercargo, from: Mary, Merchant.
    Cap: 17 Apr 1813 at Sea by HM Ship Fox Int: 08 Jun 1813 Dis: 24 Jun 1813.
    Received from HMS Success. Magnet Cartel for New York.

Eyre, Jacob   Prisoner 589. Rank: Seaman, from: Lydia, Merchant Ship.
    Cap: 26 Dec 1812 at Sea by HM Ship Maidstone Int: 06 Jan 1813 Dis: 27 Jan 1813.
    Received from HM Ship Maidstone. Bostock Cartel for New York.

American Prisoners of War Held at Bermuda During the War of 1812

Fackson, J W   Prisoner 960. Rank: Seaman, from: Bona, Letter of Marque Schooner.
    Cap: 12 Mar 1813 Chesapeake by Laurustinus Int: 23 Mar 1813 Dis: 24 Jun 1813.
    Received from Laurustinus. Magnet Cartel for New York.

Fair, Samuel   Prisoner 2691. Rank: Seaman, from: Speed, Merchant Vessel.
    Cap: 19 Jan 1815 off Nantucket by Pylades Int: 17 Feb 1815 Dis: 17 Mar 1815.
    Received from Majestic. Merchant Vessel.

Fairbanks, Noah   Prisoner 698. Rank: Seaman, from: High Flyer, Privateer.
    Cap: 09 Jan 1813 at Sea by HMS Acasta Int: 21 Jan 1813 Dis: 27 Jan 1813.
    Received from HMS Acasta. Bostock Cartel for New York.

Fairfield, James M   Prisoner 1666. Rank: 1 Mate, from: Argus, Letter of Marque.
    Cap: 01 Mar 1814 off Bermuda by San Domingo Int: 15 Mar 1814 Dis: 15 Apr 1814.
    Received from Ruby. Rammilles for Halifax.

Falford, William   Prisoner 387. Rank: Seaman, from: Snapper, Privateer Schooner.
    Cap: 16 Nov 1812 at Sea by HM Ship Galus Int: 22 Nov 1812 Dis: 27 Jan 1813.
    Received from HM Ship Galus. Bostock Cartel for New York.

Falk, John   Prisoner 297. Rank: Seaman, from: Symmetry, Merchant Ship.
    Cap: 05 Jul 1812 at Sea by HM Ship Rattler Int: 02 Nov 1812 Dis: 04 Nov 1812.
    Received from HMS Poictiers. Brig Diamond on Parole to new London United States of America.

Fall, Alphun   Prisoner 1933. Rank: Armour, from: Pike, Privateer.
    Cap: 25 Aug 1814 off Savannah by Primrose Int: 09 Sep 1814 Dis: 28 Mar 1815.
    Received from Lacedaemonian. Clarendon Transport for U States. Or Alphun Hall.

Farret, William   Prisoner 371. Rank: Prize Master, from: Snapper, Privateer Schooner.
    Cap: 16 Nov 1812 at Sea by HM Ship Galus Int: 22 Nov 1812 Dis: 27 Jan 1813.
    Received from HM Ship Galus. Bostock Cartel for New York.

Fearine, Isiah   Prisoner 862. Rank: Supercargo, from: Alert, Merchant Sloop.
    Cap: 14 Mar 1813 Chesapeake by HM Ship Laurustinus Int: 23 Mar 1813 Dis: 24 Jun 1813.
    Received from Laurustinus. Magnet Cartel for New York.

Febre, William   Prisoner 1219. Rank: Seaman, from: HMS Sceptre, Not Recorded.
    Cap: 16 Mar 1813 Not Recorded by HMS Sceptre Int: 16 Nov 1813 Dis: 15 Apr 1814.
    Received from HMS Sceptre. HMS Rammillies Halifax.

Fellows, G H   Prisoner 1297. Rank: Captain, from: Rolla, Privateer.
    Cap: 10 Dec 1813 Block Island by Loire Int: 20 Dec 1813 Dis: 15 Apr 1814.
    Received from San Domingo. HMS Rammilies for Halifax.

Fellows, Nathaniel   Prisoner 1299. Rank: Clerk, from: Rolla, Privateer.
    Cap: 10 Dec 1813 Block Island by Loire Int: 20 Dec 1813 Dis: 15 Apr 1814.
    Received from San Domingo. HMS Rammilies for Halifax.

Felt, John   Prisoner 2223. Rank: Seaman, from: President, U States Frigate.
    Cap: 15 Jan 1815 Not Recorded by Endymion Int: 30 Jan 1815 Dis: 28 Mar 1815.
    Received from Pomone. Mars Transport for U States.

Fenderson, Steward   Prisoner 1966. Rank: Seaman, from: Pike, Privateer.
    Cap: 25 Aug 1814 off Savannah by Primrose Int: 09 Sep 1814 Dis: 13 Feb 1815.
    Received from Lacedaemonian. Bellona Transport.

Ferguson, Patrick   Prisoner 2497. Rank: Marine, from: President, U States Frigate.
    Cap: 15 Jan 1815 Not Recorded by Endymion Int: 04 Feb 1815 Dis: 28 Mar 1815.
    Received from Endymion. Clarenden Transport for U States.

Ferguson, Thomas   Prisoner 435. Rank: Seaman, from: Eliza, Merchant Ship.
    Cap: 25 Nov 1812 Lat 37.00, Long 65.46 by HM Ship Tartarus Int: 03 Dec 1812 Dis: 27 Jan 1813.
    Received from HM Ship Tartarus. Bostock Cartel for New York.

Fernand, John   Prisoner 693. Rank: Seaman, from: High Flyer, Privateer.
    Cap: 09 Jan 1813 at Sea by HMS Acasta Int: 21 Jan 1813 Dis: 27 Jan 1813.
    Received from HMS Acasta. Bostock Cartel for New York.

Fernandez, Peter   Prisoner 2793. Rank: Seaman, from: Limerick, Not Recorded.
    Cap: 07 Mar 1815 Lat 30, Long 75.38 W by Asia Int: 25 Mar 1815 Dis:
    Received from Asia. (Date of discharge not recorded.)

Ferrander, Antonio   Prisoner 2066. Rank: Seaman, from: Industry, Merchant Vessel.
    Cap: 01 Dec 1814 off Cape Henry by HMS Niemen Int: 15 Dec 1814 Dis: 22 Dec 1814.
    Recaptured. Belong to Carolina Privateer. Received from HMS Niemen. Rolla Transport Swedish Subject Order of Com Evans.

Ferrat, Charles   Prisoner 356. Rank: Seaman, from: Snapper, Privateer Schooner.
    Cap: 16 Nov 1812 at Sea by HMS Galus Int: 22 Nov 1812 Dis: 27 Jan 1813.
    Received from HM Ship Galus. Bostock Cartel for New York.

American Prisoners of War Held at Bermuda During the War of 1812

Feunce, Bartlet   Prisoner 767. Rank: Seaman, from: Lucy, Merchant Schooner.
    Cap: 28 Dec 1812 Lat 36.45, Long 73.18 by HM Sloop Sylph Int: 26 Jan 1813 Dis: 14 Jun 1813.
    Received from Sloop Sylph. Permitted to return to the United States in the Perseverance Cartel.

Fevion, John   Prisoner 2449. Rank: Seaman, from: President, U States Frigate.
    Cap: 15 Jan 1815 Not Recorded by Endymion Int: 04 Feb 1815 Dis: 28 Mar 1815.
    Received from Endymion. Clarenden Transport for U States.

Fifer, Edward   Prisoner 2448. Rank: Seaman, from: President, U States Frigate.
    Cap: 15 Jan 1815 Not Recorded by Endymion Int: 04 Feb 1815 Dis: 28 Mar 1815.
    Received from Endymion. Clarenden Transport for U States.

Figges, William   Prisoner 1197. Rank: Seaman, from: Mary, Merchant Ship.
    Cap: 30 Jul 1813 at Sea by HM Sloop Nimrod Int: 05 Sep 1813 Dis: 12 Sep 1813.
    Recaptured Sloop. Received from HM Sloop Nimrod. Per Order of Commodore Evans to the American Ship Georgiana restored.

Finch, William   Prisoner 614. Rank: Acting Lieutenant, from: Noetoin, Packet Brig.
    Cap: 05 Jan 1813 at Sea by HMS Belvidera Int: 11 Jan 1813 Dis: 27 Jan 1813.
    Received from HMS Belvidera. Bostock Cartel for New York.

Finis, Peter   Prisoner 1028. Rank: Seaman, from: Dart, Merchant Schooner.
    Cap: 17 Mar 1813 off the Chesapeake by HMS Statira Int: 06 Apr 1813 Dis: 24 Jun 1813.
    Received from HMS Junon. Magnet Cartel for New York.

Finny, Isaac   Prisoner 1682. Rank: Seaman, from: St. Joquin, Merchant Vessel.
    Cap: 26 Mar 1814 Chesapeake by Albion Int: 16 Apr 1814 Dis: 23 Apr 1814.
    Received from Canso. HMS Bulwark for Halifax Order Comm in Chief.

Fish, Allen   Prisoner 856. Rank: Mate, from: Bona, Letter of Marque Schooner.
    Cap: 12 Mar 1813 Chesapeake by HM Ship Laurustinus Int: 23 Mar 1813 Dis: 24 Jun 1813.
    Received from HM Ship Laurustinus. Magnet Cartel for New York.

Fisher, Ephraim   Prisoner 1020. Rank: Seaman, from: Lusiana, Merchant.
    Cap: 20 Mar 1813 off the Chesapeake by HM Ship Rammillies Int: 06 Apr 1813 Dis: 20 May 1813.
    Received from HMS Junon. Vessel being Liberated per Order Commodore Evans.

Fisher, John   Prisoner 1552. Rank: Seaman, from: Bordeaux Packet, Letter of Marque.
    Cap: 28 Jan 1814 off Cape Henry by Nieman Int: 12 Feb 1814 Dis: 06 Apr 1814.
    Received from Nieman. being a Prussian.

Fisher, John W   Prisoner 2083. Rank: Masters Mate, from: Yankey, Privateer.
    Cap: 12 Dec 1814 Not Recorded by Albion Int: 04 Jan 1815 Dis: 28 Mar 1815.
    Received from HMS Goree. Clarendon Transport for U States.

Fisher, John D   Prisoner 2144. Rank: Midshipman, from: President, U States Frigate.
    Cap: 15 Jan 1815 Not Recorded by Endymion Int: 30 Jan 1815 Dis: 22 Mar 1815.
    Received from President. Merchant Vessel.

Fisher, William   Prisoner 1065. Rank: Seaman, from: Amason, Merchant.
    Cap: 18 Mar 1813 Chesapeake by HM Ship Victorious Int: 06 Apr 1813 Dis: 24 Jun 1813.
    Received from HMS Junon. Magnet Cartel for New York.

Fisk, Esra   Prisoner 2690. Rank: Master, from: Speed, Merchant Vessel.
    Cap: 19 Jan 1815 off Nantucket by Pylades Int: 17 Feb 1815 Dis: 17 Mar 1815.
    Received from Majestic. Merchant Vessel.

Fitzgerald, William   Prisoner 590. Rank: Master, from: Lydia, Merchant Ship.
    Cap: 26 Dec 1812 at Sea by HM Ship Maidstone Int: 07 Jan 1813 Dis: 27 Jan 1813.
    Received from Prize Ship Lydia. Bostock Cartel for New York.

Fleek, H F   Prisoner 2234. Rank: Seaman, from: President, U States Frigate.
    Cap: 15 Jan 1815 Not Recorded by Endymion Int: 30 Jan 1815 Dis: 28 Mar 1815.
    Received from Pomone. Mars Transport for U States.

Fletcher, Aron   Prisoner 2795. Rank: Seaman, from: Limerick, Not Recorded.
    Cap: 04 Mar 1815 Not Recorded by Asia Int: 25 Mar 1815 Dis:
    From Depot at Jamaica. Received from Asia. (Date of discharge not recorded.)

Fletcher, F C   Prisoner 2643. Rank: Seaman, from: Dash, Merchant Vessel.
    Cap: 19 Jan 1815 Bahamas by HMS Statira Int: 06 Feb 1815 Dis: 28 Mar 1815.
    Received from HMS Statira. Clarendon Transport for U States.

Flick, John   Prisoner 339. Rank: Seaman, from: Snapper, Privateer Schooner.
    Cap: 16 Nov 1812 at Sea by HMS Galus Int: 22 Nov 1812 Dis: 27 Jan 1813.
    Received from HM Ship Galus. Bostock Cartel for New York.

Flinn, Pierre   Prisoner 405. Rank: Seaman, from: Snapper, Privateer Schooner.
    Cap: 16 Nov 1812 at Sea by HM Ship Galus Int: 22 Nov 1812 Dis: 27 Jan 1813.
    Received from HM Ship Galus. Bostock Cartel for New York.

American Prisoners of War Held at Bermuda During the War of 1812

Flora, Peter   Prisoner 2049. Rank: Seaman, from: Mary, Merchant Schooner.
  Cap: 26 Nov 1814 off Cape Delaware by Telegraph Int: 05 Dec 1814 Dis: 13 Dec 1814.
  Received from HMS Goree. Jublilee Transport Spanish Subject Order of Commadore Evans.

Floyd, Thomas   Prisoner 1201. Rank: Seaman, from: Willam & Ann, Merchant Ship.
  Cap: 30 Jul 1813 at Sea by HM Sloop Nimrod Int: 05 Sep 1813 Dis: 12 Sep 1813.
  Received from HM Sloop Nimrod. Per Order of Commodore Evans to the American Ship Georgiana restored.

Fodder, Francis   Prisoner 1158. Rank: Seaman, from: Acricoake, Merchant.
  Cap: 22 Jul 1813 at Sea by HM Sloop Conflict Int: 13 Aug 1813 Dis: 13 Aug 1813.
  Received from HM Ship Woolwich. American Ship Rolla per Order Governor Strong.

Fonerty, Martin   Prisoner 539. Rank: Seaman, from: Herald, Letter of Marque Brig.
  Cap: 25 Dec 1812 at Sea by HM Ship Maidstone Int: 05 Jan 1813 Dis: 27 Jan 1813.
  Received from HM Ship Maidstone. Bostock Cartel for New York.

Foot, James   Prisoner 2006. Rank: Prize Master, from: Bridges, Merchant Vessel.
  Cap: 25 Oct 1814 off Halifax by Armide Int: 07 Nov 1814 Dis: 17 Mar 1815.
  Recaptured. Received from HMS Armide. Merchant Vessel.

Foot, Jonathan   Prisoner 514. Rank: Boatswain, from: Nancy, Merchant Ship.
  Cap: 18 Dec 1812 off Bermuda by HMS Goree Int: 30 Dec 1812 Dis: 27 Jan 1813.
  Received from HMS Goree. Bostock Cartel for New York.

Forbes, John   Prisoner 1054. Rank: Seaman, from: Massoil, Merchant.
  Cap: 18 Mar 1813 Chesapeake by HMS Dragon Int: 06 Apr 1813 Dis: 24 Jun 1813.
  Received from HMS Junon. Magnet Cartel for New York.

Forbes, Sandy   Prisoner 800. Rank: Seaman, from: Not Recorded, Not Recorded.
  Cap: Not Recorded by Not Recorded Int: 14 Feb 1813 Dis: 24 Jun 1813.
  Received from Narcissus. Surrendered himself as a Prisoner of War. Magnet Cartel for New York. (Date of capture not recorded.)

Ford, John   Prisoner 25. Rank: Seaman, from: Hero, Merchant Schooner.
  Cap: 14 Jul 1812 at Bermuda by Cuttle Int: 28 Aug 1812 Dis: 10 Sep 1812.
  Received from HM Schooner Cuttle. Rattler an Englishman.

Ford, Standi   Prisoner 1582. Rank: Seaman, from: Bordeaux Packet, Letter of Marque.
  Cap: 28 Jan 1814 off Cape Henry by Nieman Int: 12 Feb 1814 Dis: 15 Apr 1814.
  Received from Nieman. Diana Transport for Halifax.

Forger, Joseph   Prisoner 1391. Rank: Seaman, from: Gardner, Merchant Vessel.
  Cap: 02 Dec 1813 Lat 37 by Loire Int: 20 Dec 1813 Dis: 06 Apr 1814.
  Received from San Domingo. being a Portuguese.

Forrest, Abraham   Prisoner 787. Rank: Seaman, from: Gustar Adolph, Merchant.
  Cap: 28 Jan 1813 at Sea by HM Ship Ramilies Int: 04 Feb 1813 Dis: 13 Mar 1813.
  Received from Ramilies. Per Order Sir John Warren the Vessel being Liberated.

Forrest, James   Prisoner 517. Rank: Seaman, from: Nancy, Merchant Ship.
  Cap: 18 Dec 1812 off Bermuda by HMS Goree Int: 30 Dec 1812 Dis: 27 Jan 1813.
  Received from HMS Goree. Bostock Cartel for New York.

Forrest, John   Prisoner 1194. Rank: Seaman, from: Priscilla, Merchant Ship.
  Cap: 09 Aug 1813 at Sea by HM Sloop Forrester Int: 27 Aug 1813 Dis: 03 Sep 1813.
  Received from HM Sloop Forrester. to the American Ship Leander restored.

Forshew, John   Prisoner 1519. Rank: Seaman, from: Flower de Pumainbueo, Merchant Vessel.
  Cap: 19 Jan 1814 St. Georges by Masquerade Int: 22 Jan 1814 Dis: 20 Feb 1814.
  Received from Surprize. Per Order of the Commander in Chief.

Forster, James   Prisoner 1964. Rank: Seaman, from: Pike, Privateer.
  Cap: 25 Aug 1814 off Savannah by Primrose Int: 09 Sep 1814 Dis: 18 Mar 1815.
  Received from Lacedaemonian. Merchant Vessel.

Forster, William   Prisoner 260. Rank: Seaman, from: Wasp, Sloop of War.
  Cap: 18 Oct 1812 at Sea by HM Ship Poictiers Int: 26 Oct 1812 Dis: 05 Nov 1812.
  Received from HM Ship Poictiers. Brig Diamond on Parole to new London United States of America.

Forster, William   Prisoner 2591. Rank: SM, from: Lark, Merchant Vessel.
  Cap: 01 Dec 1814 off New York by HM Ship Majestic Int: 05 Feb 1815 Dis: 28 Mar 1815.
  Recaptured. York Privateer. Received from HMS Forth. Clarendon Transport for U States.

Forsyth, Asa   Prisoner 1037. Rank: Master, from: Revinue, Merchant Sloop.
  Cap: 19 Mar 1813 off the Chesapeake by HMS Statira Int: 06 Apr 1813 Dis: 24 Jun 1813.
  Received from HMS Junon. Magnet Cartel for New York.

Foss, Supply   Prisoner 146. Rank: Mate, from: Hero, Merchant Brig.
  Cap: 25 Sep 1812 Lat 42, Long 63 W by HMS Tartarus Int: 13 Oct 1812 Dis: 24 Oct 1812.
  Received from HMS Tartarus. Brig Diamond on Parole to new London United States of America.

American Prisoners of War Held at Bermuda During the War of 1812

Foster, Charles   Prisoner 1380. Rank: Seaman, from: Policy, Merchant Vessel.
    Cap: 04 Dec 1813 Not Recorded by Loire Int: 20 Dec 1813 Dis: 15 Apr 1814.
    Recaptured. Received from San Domingo. Diana Transport for Halifax.

Foster, James   Prisoner 2856. Rank: Seaman, from: Limerick, Not Recorded.
    Cap: 15 Mar 1815 Not Recorded by Asia Int: 25 Mar 1815 Dis:
    From Depot at Jamaica. Received from Asia. (Date of discharge not recorded.)

Fowle, Josiah C   Prisoner 97. Rank: detained American, from: Gossepuim, Merchant.
    Cap: 16 Aug 1812 of Bermuda by Not Recorded Int: 28 Aug 1812 Dis: 06 Sep 1812.
    Received from HM Schooner Cuttle. detained per order of the President. Sloop Sally for New York.

Fowler, Peter   Prisoner 2473. Rank: Seaman, from: President, U States Frigate.
    Cap: 15 Jan 1815 Not Recorded by Endymion Int: 04 Feb 1815 Dis: 28 Mar 1815.
    Received from Endymion. Clarenden Transport for U States.

Fox, Charles   Prisoner 2222. Rank: Seaman, from: President, U States Frigate.
    Cap: 15 Jan 1815 Not Recorded by Endymion Int: 30 Jan 1815 Dis: 28 Mar 1815.
    Received from Pomone. Mars Transport for U States.

Fox, George   Prisoner 1736. Rank: Seaman, from: Yankelass, Privateer.
    Cap: 01 May 1814 L 10-4N, L 33-0W by Severn & Surprise Int: 06 Jun 1814 Dis: 21 Feb 1815.
    Received from Severn. Paroled to the U States having served six months as Carpenter's Mate order of Adl Sir Alex Cockburn.

Foye, James   Prisoner 635. Rank: Seaman, from: Not Recorded, Not Recorded.
    Cap: Not Recorded by Not Recorded Int: 14 Jan 1813 Dis: 27 Jan 1813.
    Surrendered himself up as an American. Bostock Cartel for New York. (Date of capture not recorded.)

Foyte, Henry   Prisoner 1467. Rank: Seaman, from: Vixen, Man of War.
    Cap: 25 Dec 1813 Lat 38.0 by Belvidera Int: 05 Jan 1814 Dis: 15 Apr 1814.
    U States Schooner. Received from HMS Belvidera. Diana Transport for Halifax.

Fracey, Charles   Prisoner 706. Rank: Seaman, from: High Flyer, Privateer.
    Cap: 09 Jan 1813 at Sea by HMS Acasta Int: 21 Jan 1813 Dis: 27 Jan 1813.
    Received from HMS Acasta. Bostock Cartel for New York.

Frances, Michael   Prisoner 1555. Rank: Seaman, from: Bordeaux Packet, Letter of Marque.
    Cap: 28 Jan 1814 off Cape Henry by Nieman Int: 12 Feb 1814 Dis: 15 Apr 1814.
    Received from Nieman. Diana Transport for Halifax.

Francis, John   Prisoner 1625. Rank: Seaman, from: Perseferanda, Merchant Vessel.
    Cap: 03 Jan 1814 Block Island by Albion Int: 14 Feb 1814 Dis: 23 Apr 1814.
    Received from Sceptre. HMS Bulwark for Halifax.

Francis, Lewis   Prisoner 303. Rank: Seaman, from: Symmetry, Merchant Ship.
    Cap: 05 Jul 1812 at Sea by HM Ship Rattler Int: 02 Nov 1812 Dis: 04 Nov 1812.
    Received from HMS Poictiers. Brig Diamond on Parole to new London United States of America.

Francisco, Antonio   Prisoner 1456. Rank: Seaman, from: Vixen, Man of War.
    Cap: 25 Dec 1813 Lat 38.0 by Belvidera Int: 05 Jan 1814 Dis: 10 Mar 1814.
    U States Schooner. Received from HMS Belvidera. By order of the Com in Chief being a Portuguese.

Francisco, Clias   Prisoner 1455. Rank: Seaman, from: Vixen, Man of War.
    Cap: 25 Dec 1813 Lat 38.0 by Belvidera Int: 05 Jan 1814 Dis:
    U States Schooner. Received from HMS Belvidera. (Date of discharge not recorded.)

Francisco, John Pedro   Prisoner 111. Rank: Seaman, from: Gossepuim, detained American.
    Cap: 07 Sep 1812 Bermuda by Goree Int: 06 Sep 1812 Dis: 15 Sep 1812.
    Received from HMS Ruby. detained per order of the President. a Spaniard per Order C. Evans. (Date of internment before date of capture.)

Frank, John   Prisoner 1624. Rank: Seaman, from: Perseferanda, Merchant Vessel.
    Cap: 03 Jan 1814 Block Island by Albion Int: 14 Feb 1814 Dis: 23 Apr 1814.
    Received from Sceptre. HMS Bulwark for Halifax.

Frankland, Benjamin   Prisoner 1404. Rank: Seaman, from: John & James, Merchant Vessel.
    Cap: 07 Dec 1813 Lat 37 by Loire Int: 21 Dec 1813 Dis: 15 Apr 1814.
    Received from Romulus. Diana Transport for Halifax.

Franklin, John   Prisoner 745. Rank: Seaman, from: Savannah Packet, Merchant Brig.
    Cap: 05 Jan 1813 at Sea by HM Ship Poictiers Int: 21 Jan 1813 Dis: 27 Jan 1813.
    Received from HMS Poictiers. Bostock Cartel for New York.

Frazier, York   Prisoner 2824. Rank: Seaman, from: Limerick, Not Recorded.
    Cap: 15 Mar 1815 Not Recorded by Asia Int: 25 Mar 1815 Dis:
    From Depot at Jamaica. Received from Asia. (Date of discharge not recorded.)

Frederick, John   Prisoner 527. Rank: Seaman, from: Herald, Letter of Marque Brig.
    Cap: 25 Dec 1812 at Sea by HMS Maidstone Int: 05 Jan 1813 Dis: 27 Jan 1813.
    Received from HM Ship Maidstone. Bostock Cartel for New York.

American Prisoners of War Held at Bermuda During the War of 1812

Frederick, John   Prisoner 1237. Rank: Not Recorded, from: Farmer, Merchant Vessel.
    Cap: 23 Sep 1813 Chesapeake by Lacedaemonian Int: 16 Nov 1813 Dis: 15 Apr 1814.
    Received from HMS Sceptre. Diana Transport for Halifax.

Frederick, John   Prisoner 2662. Rank: Seaman, from: Amicus, Merchant Vessel.
    Cap: 10 Jan 1815 Delaware by Forth Int: 14 Feb 1815 Dis: 17 Feb 1815.
    Recaptured. Chapeur Privateer. Received from Goree. Harriot M Vessel order of Commadore Evans.

Frederick, Thomas   Prisoner 921. Rank: Seaman, from: Albert, Merchant Schooner.
    Cap: 05 Mar 1813 Chesapeake by HM Ship Marlborough Int: 23 Mar 1813 Dis: 24 Jun 1813.
    Received from Laurustinus. Magnet Cartel for New York.

Free, James   Prisoner 382. Rank: Seaman, from: Snapper, Privateer Schooner.
    Cap: 16 Nov 1812 at Sea by HM Ship Galus Int: 22 Nov 1812 Dis: 27 Jan 1813.
    Received from HM Ship Galus. Bostock Cartel for New York.

Freeman, A   Prisoner 1494. Rank: Seaman, from: Maresoil, Merchant Brig.
    Cap: 25 Dec 1813 Latt 35.0 by HMS Fox Int: 09 Jan 1814 Dis: 15 Apr 1814.
    Received from Fox. Diana Transport for Halifax.

Freeman, Francis   Prisoner 801. Rank: Seaman, from: Not Recorded, Not Recorded.
    Cap: Not Recorded by Not Recorded Int: 14 Feb 1813 Dis: 24 Jun 1813.
    Received from Narcissus. Surrendered himself as a Prisoner of War. Magnet Cartel for New York.
    (Date of capture not recorded.)

Freeman, Jesse   Prisoner 1075. Rank: Seaman, from: Ring Dove, Merchant.
    Cap: 31 Mar 1813 Chesapeake by HM Ship Junon Int: 06 Apr 1813 Dis: 24 Jun 1813.
    Received from HMS Junon. Magnet Cartel for New York.

Freeman, John   Prisoner 43. Rank: Seaman, from: Trim, Merchant Schooner.
    Cap: 28 Jul 1812 of Bermuda by Cuttle Int: 28 Aug 1812 Dis: 18 Sep 1812.
    Received from HM Schooner Cuttle. Order Commd Evans for England.

Freeman, Nathaniel   Prisoner 999. Rank: Seaman, from: Orion, Merchant.
    Cap: 25 Mar 1813 at Sea by HM Sloop Childers Int: 04 Apr 1813 Dis: 09 Apr 1813.
    Received from HM Sloop Childers. Per Order Commodore Evans Vessel Liberated.

Freeman, Peter   Prisoner 267. Rank: Seaman, from: Wasp, Sloop of War.
    Cap: 18 Oct 1812 at Sea by HM Ship Poictiers Int: 26 Oct 1812 Dis: 05 Nov 1812.
    Received from HM Ship Poictiers. Brig Diamond on Parole to new London United States of America.

French, Calvin   Prisoner 775. Rank: Seaman, from: Trinadada, Merchant Brig.
    Cap: 06 Jan 1813 Lat 37.20, Long 75.00 by HM Sloop Sylph Int: 26 Jan 1813 Dis: 14 Mar 1813.
    Received from Sloop Sylph. Savannah Packet for New York per Order Adl Sir J B Warren.

French, John   Prisoner 2037. Rank: Prize Master, from: James, Merchant Vessel.
    Cap: 31 Oct 1814 off Charlestown by Schooner Whiting Int: 21 Nov 1814 Dis: 28 Mar 1815.
    Recaptured. Received from M Schooner Whiting. Clarendon Transport for U States.

Fresk, John   Prisoner 789. Rank: Seaman, from: Resolution, Merchant Schooner.
    Cap: 26 Jan 1813 at Sea by HM Ship Victorious Int: 04 Feb 1813 Dis: 14 Mar 1813.
    Received from Victorious. Savannah Packet for New York per Order Adl Sir J B Warren.

Frith, William   Prisoner 474. Rank: Seaman, from: Teazer, Privateer Schooner.
    Cap: 16 Dec 1812 at Sea by HM Ship St. Domingo Int: 21 Dec 1812 Dis: 27 Jan 1813.
    Received from HM Ship St. Domingo. Bostock Cartel for New York.

Froes, John   Prisoner 671. Rank: Boatswain, from: High Flyer, Privateer.
    Cap: 09 Jan 1813 at Sea by HM Ship Acasta Int: 21 Jan 1813 Dis: 27 Jan 1813.
    Received from HMS Acasta. Bostock Cartel for New York.

Fuller, Benjamin   Prisoner 791. Rank: Seaman, from: Resolution, Merchant Schooner.
    Cap: 26 Jan 1813 at Sea by HM Ship Victorious Int: 04 Feb 1813 Dis: 14 Jun 1813.
    Received from Victorious. Permitted to return to the United States in the Perseverance Cartel.

Funk, Nathaniel   Prisoner 2602. Rank: Seaman, from: Mercury, Merchant Vessel.
    Cap: 30 Dec 1814 off New York by HMS Pomone Int: 05 Feb 1815 Dis: 16 Mar 1815.
    Received from HMS Forth. Merchant Service.

Funning, David   Prisoner 2510. Rank: Seaman, from: President, U States Frigate.
    Cap: 15 Jan 1815 Not Recorded by Endymion Int: 04 Feb 1815 Dis: 28 Mar 1815.
    Received from HMS Endymion. Clarenden Transport for U States.

Furance, George   Prisoner 1881. Rank: Seaman, from: Levant, Merchant Vessel.
    Cap: Not Recorded by Not Recorded Int: Dis: 28 Mar 1815.
    Clarendon Transport for U States. (Dates of capture and internment not recorded.)

Furber, Theodore P   Prisoner 148. Rank: Boy, from: Hero, Merchant Brig.
    Cap: 25 Sep 1812 Lat 42, Long 63 W by HMS Tartarus Int: 13 Oct 1812 Dis: 24 Oct 1812.
    Received from HMS Tartarus. Brig Diamond on Parole to new London United States of America.

American Prisoners of War Held at Bermuda During the War of 1812

Furnell, Tobias   Prisoner 77. Rank: Seaman, from: White Oak, Merchant.
    Cap: 08 Aug 1812 of Bermuda by Recruit Int: 28 Aug 1812 Dis: 18 Sep 1812.
    Received from M Schooner Cuttle. Order of Commd Evans for England.

Fuster, David   Prisoner 2465. Rank: Seaman, from: President, U States Frigate.
    Cap: 15 Jan 1815 Not Recorded by Endymion Int: 04 Feb 1815 Dis: 28 Mar 1815.
    Received from Endymion. Clarenden Transport for U States.

Fyler, John C   Prisoner 2667. Rank: Seaman, from: President, U States Frigate.
    Cap: 15 Jan 1815 off New York by Endymion Int: 14 Feb 1815 Dis: 28 Mar 1815.
    Received from Childers. Clarenden Transport for U States. (Ship received from should be Goree.)

Gage, William   Prisoner 1036. Rank: Seaman, from: Dart, Merchant Schooner.
    Cap: 17 Mar 1813 off the Chesapeake by HMS Statira Int: 06 Apr 1813 Dis: 24 Jun 1813.
    Received from HMS Junon. Magnet Cartel for New York.

Gage, Zachariah   Prisoner 1505. Rank: Seaman, from: Jackall, Merchant Vessel.
    Cap: 23 Dec 1813 off the Delaware by Belvidera Int: 18 Jan 1814 Dis: 15 Apr 1814.
    Received from Belvidera. Diana Transport for Halifax.

Gaimsley, Thomas   Prisoner 1145. Rank: Boy, from: Asp, Man of War Schooner.
    Cap: 20 Jul 1813 at Sea by HM Ship San Domingo Int: 13 Aug 1813 Dis: 13 Aug 1813.
    Received from HM Ship Woolwich. American Ship Rolla per Order Governor Strong.

Gainer, William   Prisoner 2280. Rank: Marine, from: President, U States Frigate.
    Cap: 15 Jan 1815 Not Recorded by Endymion Int: 30 Jan 1815 Dis: 28 Mar 1815.
    Received from Pomone. Clarenden Transport for U States.

Gale, Thomas   Prisoner 1699. Rank: Seaman, from: Grecian, Letter of Marque.
    Cap: 02 May 1814 Chesapeake by Jansur Int: 26 May 1814 Dis: 28 Mar 1815.
    Received from Lacedaemonian. Mars Transport for U States. Thomas Gale (1).

Gale, Thomas   Prisoner 1711. Rank: Seaman, from: Grecian, Letter of Marque.
    Cap: 02 May 1814 Chesapeake by Jansur Int: 26 May 1814 Dis: 28 Mar 1815.
    Received from Lacedaemonian. Mars Transport for U States. Thomas Gale (2).

Gall, John   Prisoner 1090. Rank: Seaman, from: Langdon Cheves, Merchant.
    Cap: 12 May 1813 at Sea by HM Sloop Atalante Int: 25 May 1813 Dis: 24 Jun 1813.
    Received from HMS Atalante. Magnet Cartel for New York.

Gall, William   Prisoner 2077. Rank: Seaman, from: Banyer, Letter of Marque.
    Cap: 03 Dec 1814 coast of America by HMS Severn Int: 04 Jan 1815 Dis: 24 Mar 1815.
    Subject was of America. Received from HMS Goree. Merchant Vessel.

Gallagher, John   Prisoner 2135. Rank: Lieutenant, from: President, U States Frigate.
    Cap: 15 Jan 1815 Not Recorded by Endymion Int: 30 Jan 1815 Dis: 28 Mar 1815.
    Received from President. Mars Transport for U States.

Gallick, D   Prisoner 2725. Rank: Citizen, from: St Marys, Not Recorded.
    Cap: 18 Feb 1815 St Marys by Primrose Int: 03 Mar 1815 Dis: 28 Mar 1815.
    Received from Hebrus. Clarendon Transport for U States.

Galloway, Michael   Prisoner 1150. Rank: Seaman, from: Acricoake, Merchant.
    Cap: 22 Jul 1813 at Sea by HM Sloop Conflict Int: 13 Aug 1813 Dis: 13 Aug 1813.
    Received from HM Ship Woolwich. American Ship Rolla per Order Commr Evans.

Gambee, Daniel   Prisoner 661. Rank: Seaman, from: Pekin, Merchant Ship.
    Cap: 17 Dec 1812 at Sea by HM Ship Acasta Int: 21 Jan 1813 Dis: 27 Jan 1813.
    Received from Ship Pekin. Bostock Cartel for New York.

Garcia, James   Prisoner 1778. Rank: Seaman, from: Yankelass, Privateer.
    Cap: 01 May 1814 Latt 40-4N, Long 38-0W by Severn & Surprise Int: 07 Jun 1814 Dis:
    Received from Surprise. (Date of discharge not recorded.)

Gardener, Able   Prisoner 151. Rank: Seaman, from: Ranger, Merchant Ship.
    Cap: 02 Oct 1812 Lat 32, Long 65 W by HMS Goree Int: 13 Oct 1812 Dis: 24 Oct 1812.
    Received from HMS Goree. Brig Diamond on Parole to new London United States of America.

Gardner, Anthony   Prisoner 2571. Rank: Seaman, from: Mercury, Merchant Vessel.
    Cap: 30 Dec 1814 off New York by HMS Pomone Int: 05 Feb 1815 Dis: 28 Mar 1815.
    Received from HMS Forth. Clarendon Transport for U States.

Gardner, Galen   Prisoner 2479. Rank: Seaman, from: President, U States Frigate.
    Cap: 15 Jan 1815 Not Recorded by Endymion Int: 04 Feb 1815 Dis: 28 Mar 1815.
    Received from Endymion. Clarenden Transport for U States.

Gardner, Rowland   Prisoner 882. Rank: Seaman, from: George, Merchant Sloop.
    Cap: 05 Feb 1813 Chesapeake by HM Ship Dragon Int: 23 Mar 1813 Dis: 13 Jun 1813.
    Received from Laurustinus. Perseverance Cartel for the United States per Order Adml Sir J B Warren.

Gardner, Timothy   Prisoner 1361. Rank: Seaman, from: Rolla, Privateer.
    Cap: 10 Dec 1813 Block Island by Loire Int: 20 Dec 1813 Dis: 15 Apr 1814.
    Received from San Domingo. HMS Rammillies for Halifax.

American Prisoners of War Held at Bermuda During the War of 1812

Gardner, William   Prisoner 2168. Rank: Servant, from: President, U States Frigate.
    Cap: 15 Jan 1815 Not Recorded by Endymion Int: 30 Jan 1815 Dis: 06 Feb 1815.
    Received from President. Narcissus to the U States by order of Commadore Evans.

Gardner, William   Prisoner 2395. Rank: Seaman, from: President, U States Frigate.
    Cap: 15 Jan 1815 Not Recorded by HM Ship Endymion Int: 04 Feb 1815 Dis: 28 Mar 1815.
    Received from Endymion. Mars Transport for U States.

Garnay, George   Prisoner 2499. Rank: Seaman, from: President, U States Frigate.
    Cap: 15 Jan 1815 Not Recorded by Endymion Int: 04 Feb 1815 Dis: 28 Mar 1815.
    Received from Endymion. Clarenden Transport for U States.

Garrett, Robert   Prisoner 1637. Rank: Seaman, from: Not Recorded, Not Recorded.
    Cap: 05 Feb 1814 Not Recorded by Sceptre Int: 14 Feb 1814 Dis: 15 Apr 1814.
    Received from Sceptre. Rammilles for Halifax.

Garrison, Ephraim   Prisoner 1911. Rank: Seaman, from: Resolution, Merchant Vessel.
    Cap: 20 Aug 1814 St. Catherine by Lacedaemonian Int: 09 Sep 1814 Dis: 28 Mar 1815.
    Received from Lacedaemonian. Clarendon Transport for U States.

Garrison, Joseph   Prisoner 2752. Rank: Seaman, from: Speedwell, Not Recorded.
    Cap: 21 Jan 1815 St Augustine by Severn Int: 03 Mar 1815 Dis: 17 Mar 1815.
    Received from Hebrus. Merchant Vessel,

Gasalo, John   Prisoner 2689. Rank: Seaman, from: Superb, Merchant Vessel.
    Cap: 27 Jan 1815 off Delaware by Sophie Int: 17 Feb 1815 Dis: 25 Feb 1815.
    from a Spanish Brig recaptured. Received from Childers. Mars Transport per order of Commadore Evans.

Gasaway, George   Prisoner 1114. Rank: Seaman, from: Dolphin, Privateer.
    Cap: 03 Apr 1813 at Sea by By the Boats of the Squadron Int: 07 Jun 1813 Dis: 24 Jun 1813.
    Received from Ship Dragon. Magnet Cartel for New York.

Gasper, John   Prisoner 1480. Rank: Seaman, from: Luckey, Merchant Vessel.
    Cap: 19 Dec 1813 off the Delaware by Niemen Int: 07 Jan 1814 Dis: 07 Apr 1814.
    Received from HM Sloop Jaseur. being a Spaniard. (Name of capturing ship not legible, assume to be Nieman.)

Gaunt, Charles   Prisoner 179. Rank: Midshipman, from: Wasp, Sloop of War.
    Cap: 18 Oct 1812 at Sea by HMS Poictiers Int: 26 Oct 1812 Dis: 05 Nov 1812.
    Received from HM Ship Poictiers. Brig Diamond on Parole to new London America.

Geary, Asburn   Prisoner 683. Rank: Seaman, from: High Flyer, Privateer.
    Cap: 09 Jan 1813 at Sea by HM Ship Acasta Int: 21 Jan 1813 Dis: 27 Jan 1813.
    Received from HMS Acasta. Bostock Cartel for New York.

Geer, John   Prisoner 1199. Rank: Seaman, from: Mary, Merchant Ship.
    Cap: 30 Jul 1813 at Sea by HM Sloop Nimrod Int: 05 Sep 1813 Dis: 12 Sep 1813.
    Recaptured Sloop. Received from HM Sloop Nimrod. Per Order of Commodore Evans to the American Ship Georgiana restored.

Geesson, Frederick   Prisoner 650. Rank: Seaman, from: Little William, Merchant Brig.
    Cap: 29 Oct 1812 at Sea by HM Ship Poictiers Int: 19 Jan 1813 Dis: 27 Jan 1813.
    Received from the Prize Brig Little William. Bostock Cartel for New York.

Geiste, George   Prisoner 1286. Rank: Seaman, from: Perry, Merchant Schooner.
    Cap: 03 Dec 1813 Long Island by Indemyion Int: 19 Dec 1813 Dis: 15 Apr 1814.
    Received from Sceptre. Diana Transport for Halifax.

Genn, William   Prisoner 2561. Rank: Seaman, from: Funchall, Merchant Vessel.
    Cap: 15 Jan 1815 off New York by HMS Pomone Int: 05 Feb 1815 Dis: 13 Mar 1815.
    Received from HMS Forth. Merchant Service.

George, Peter   Prisoner 93. Rank: Seaman, from: Gossepuim, Merchant.
    Cap: 16 Aug 1812 of Bermuda by Goree Int: 28 Aug 1812 Dis: 18 Sep 1812.
    Received from HM Schooner Cuttle. Order of Commd Evans for England.

Gerlock, Charles   Prisoner 736. Rank: Surgeon, from: High Flyer, Privateer.
    Cap: 09 Jan 1813 at Sea by HM Ship Acasta Int: 21 Jan 1813 Died: 25 Jan 1813.
    Received from HMS Acasta. Died. Wound.

Gerry, Samuel R   Prisoner 1539. Rank: Master, from: Defiance, Merchant Vessel.
    Cap: 05 Jan 1814 at Sea by Childers Int: 26 Jan 1814 Dis:
    Received from Childers. (Date of discharge not recorded.)

Gibbs, Henry   Prisoner 817. Rank: Seaman, from: Stockholm, Merchant Schooner.
    Cap: 18 Feb 1813 at Sea by HMS Statira Int: 01 Mar 1813 Dis: 14 Apr 1813.
    Received from HMS Statira. Per Order Commodore Evans Vessel Liberated.

Gibbs, J   Prisoner 1381. Rank: Seaman, from: Policy, Merchant Vessel.
    Cap: 04 Dec 1813 Not Recorded by Loire Int: 20 Dec 1813 Dis: 15 Apr 1814.
    Recaptured. Received from San Domingo. Diana Transport for Halifax.

American Prisoners of War Held at Bermuda During the War of 1812

Gibbs, John   Prisoner 1612. Rank: Seaman, from: Brookhaven, Merchant Vessel.
    Cap: 09 Dec 1813 Block Island by Albion Int: 14 Feb 1814 Dis: 23 Apr 1814.
    Received from Sceptre. HMS Bulwark for Halifax.

Gibbs, Moses   Prisoner 1266. Rank: Mate, from: United States, Merchant Vessel.
    Cap: 14 Nov 1813 Long Island by HM Brig Borer Int: 19 Dec 1813 Dis: 15 Apr 1814.
    Received from HMS Acasta. Rammilles for Halifax.

Gibbs, Samuel   Prisoner 1976. Rank: Seaman, from: Antelope, Merchant Vessel.
    Cap: 21 Aug 1814 Western Island by Whiting Int: 17 Sep 1814 Dis: 24 Mar 1815.
    Recaptured. Received from Goree. Merchant Vessel.

Giblet, Bendus   Prisoner 1642. Rank: Boy, from: Mary Ann, Merchant Vessel.
    Cap: 06 Jan 1814 off Charlestown by Recruit Int: 21 Feb 1814 Dis: 23 Apr 1814.
    Received from Recruit. HMS Bulwark for Halifax.

Gibson, James   Prisoner 487. Rank: Seaman, from: Teazer, Privateer Schooner.
    Cap: 16 Dec 1812 at Sea by HM Ship St. Domingo Int: 21 Dec 1812 Dis: 27 Jan 1813.
    Received from HM Ship St. Domingo. Bostock Cartel for New York.

Gibson, Robert   Prisoner 2729. Rank: Passenger, from: Kate, Not Recorded.
    Cap: 10 Nov 1814 Potomac by Dragon Int: 03 Mar 1815 Dis: 28 Mar 1815.
    Received from Hebrus. Clarendon Transport for U States.

Gibson, William   Prisoner 128. Rank: Seaman, from: William of Baltimore, Merchant.
    Cap: 31 Aug 1812 Lat 37 by HM Ship Recruit Int: 14 Sep 1812 Dis: 18 Sep 1812.
    Received from HMS Recruit. Order of Commd Evans for England.

Gibson, William   Prisoner 2232. Rank: Quartermaster, from: President, U States Frigate.
    Cap: 15 Jan 1815 Not Recorded by Endymion Int: 30 Jan 1815 Dis: 28 Mar 1815.
    Received from Pomone. Mars Transport for U States.

Giffigan, Thomas   Prisoner 1734. Rank: Seaman, from: Yankelass, Privateer.
    Cap: 01 May 1814 L 10-4N, L 33-0W by Severn & Surprise Int: 06 Jun 1814 Dis: 28 Mar 1815.
    Received from Severn. Mars for U States.

Gilbert, Benjamin   Prisoner 788. Rank: Seaman, from: Resolution, Merchant Schooner.
    Cap: 26 Jan 1813 at Sea by HM Ship Victorious Int: 04 Feb 1813 Dis: 14 Mar 1813.
    Received from Victorious. Savannah Packet for New York per Order Adl Sir J B Warren.

Giles, Charles   Prisoner 1653. Rank: Seaman, from: Flash, Letter of Marque.
    Cap: 11 Feb 1814 Off Block Island by Acasta Int: 13 Mar 1814 Dis: 23 Apr 1814.
    Received from Active. HMS Bulwark for Halifax.

Giles, Edmund   Prisoner 2611. Rank: Seaman, from: Falcon, Merchant Vessel.
    Cap: 22 Jan 1815 Sandy Hook by HM Ship Pomone Int: 05 Feb 1815 Dis: 28 Mar 1815.
    Received from HMS Forth. Clarendon Transport for U States.

Giles, Robert   Prisoner 2178. Rank: Seaman, from: President, U States Frigate.
    Cap: 15 Jan 1815 Not Recorded by HMS Endymion Int: 30 Jan 1815 Dis: 28 Mar 1815.
    Received from Pomone. Mars Transport for U States.

Gillet, Nathan   Prisoner 414. Rank: 1 Mate, from: Isabella, Merchant Brig.
    Cap: 15 Nov 1812 at Sea by HM Sloop Childers Int: 24 Nov 1812 Dis: 27 Jan 1813.
    Received from HM Ship Childers. Bostock Cartel for New York.

Gillings, Benjamin   Prisoner 1987. Rank: Seaman, from: Eclipse, Merchant Vessel.
    Cap: 29 Sep 1814 Bermuda by Copark Int: 05 Oct 1814 Dis: 28 Mar 1815.
    Recaptured. Received from Goree. Clarendon Transport for U States.

Ginney, Andrew   Prisoner 2575. Rank: Seaman, from: John, Merchant Vessel.
    Cap: 30 Dec 1814 off New York by HMS Pomone Int: 05 Feb 1815 Dis: 16 Mar 1815.
    Received from HMS Forth. Merchant Service.

Given, Francis   Prisoner 2686. Rank: Seaman, from: Superb, Merchant Vessel.
    Cap: 27 Jan 1815 off Delaware by Sophie Int: 17 Feb 1815 Dis: 28 Mar 1815.
    from a Spanish Brig recaptured. Received from Childers. Clarendon Transport for U States.

Gleaves, George   Prisoner 936. Rank: Seaman, from: Sidney, Letter of Marque Schooner.
    Cap: 09 Mar 1813 Chesapeake by Marlborough Int: 23 Mar 1813 Dis: 24 Jun 1813.
    Received from Laurustinus. Magnet Cartel for New York.

Godfrey, John   Prisoner 604. Rank: Seaman, from: Noetoin, Packet Brig.
    Cap: 05 Jan 1813 at Sea by HM Ship Belvidera Int: 10 Jan 1813 Dis: 27 Jan 1813.
    Received from HMS Belvidera. Bostock Cartel for New York.

Godfrey, John   Prisoner 1818. Rank: Passenger, from: Not Recorded, Not Recorded.
    Cap: Not Recorded by Not Recorded Int: 14 Jun 1814 Dis: 15 Jun 1814.
    From St. Bartholomew in the Swedish Schooner Oscar. on Parole per Order Com in Chief to America.
    (Date of capture not recorded.)

American Prisoners of War Held at Bermuda During the War of 1812

Godwin, Isaac   Prisoner 728. Rank: Seaman, from: High Flyer, Privateer.
    Cap: 09 Jan 1813 at Sea by HM Ship Acasta Int: 21 Jan 1813 Dis: 27 Jan 1813.
    Received from HMS Acasta. Bostock Cartel for New York.

Goff, Dina   Prisoner 1782. Rank: Boy, from: Yankelass, Privateer.
    Cap: 01 May 1814 Latt 40-4N, Long 38-0W by Severn & Surprise Int: 07 Jun 1814 Dis: 28 Mar 1815.
    Received from Surprise. Mars Transport for U States.

Gold, Samuel   Prisoner 799. Rank: Seaman, from: Not Recorded, Not Recorded.
    Cap: Not Recorded by Not Recorded Int: 14 Feb 1813 Dis: 24 Jun 1813.
    Received from Narcissus. Surrendered himself as a Prisoner of War. Magnet Cartel for New York.
    (Date of capture not recorded.)

Gold, Thomas   Prisoner 572. Rank: Seaman, from: Peakin, Merchant Ship.
    Cap: 17 Dec 1812 at Sea by HM Ship Acasta Int: 06 Jan 1813 Dis: 27 Jan 1813.
    Received from HM Ship Maidstone. Bostock Cartel for New York.

Golden, Edward   Prisoner 1212. Rank: Seaman, from: Not Recorded, Not Recorded.
    Cap: 25 Jan 1813 Not Recorded by Tender to St. Domingo Int: 06 Nov 1813 Dis: 24 Apr 1814.
    Received from HMS Ruby. HMS Sceptre for England.

Goldtrap, William   Prisoner 359. Rank: Seaman, from: Snapper, Privateer Schooner.
    Cap: 16 Nov 1812 at Sea by HM Ship Galus Int: 22 Nov 1812 Dis: 27 Jan 1813.
    Received from HM Ship Galus. Bostock Cartel for New York.

Golen, Francis   Prisoner 2688. Rank: Seaman, from: Superb, Merchant Vessel.
    Cap: 27 Jan 1815 off Delaware by Sophie Int: 17 Feb 1815. Dis: 28 Mar 1815.
    from a Spanish Brig recaptured. Received from Childers. Clarendon Transport for U States.

Goley, David   Prisoner 2329. Rank: Marine, from: President, U States Frigate.
    Cap: 15 Jan 1815 Not Recorded by Endymion Int: 04 Feb 1815 Dis: 28 Mar 1815.
    Received from Endymion. Clarenden Transport for U States.

Gonsalvos, Joseph   Prisoner 1980. Rank: Seaman, from: Antelope, Merchant Vessel.
    Cap: 21 Aug 1814 Western Island by Whiting Int: 17 Sep 1814 Dis: 07 Nov 1814.
    Recaptured. Received from Goree. Order Adl Cockburn.

Good, Frederick   Prisoner 385. Rank: Seaman, from: Snapper, Privateer Schooner.
    Cap: 16 Nov 1812 at Sea by HM Ship Galus Int: 22 Nov 1812 Dis: 27 Jan 1813.
    Received from HM Ship Galus. Bostock Cartel for New York.

Goodall, William   Prisoner 1140. Rank: Seaman, from: Asp, Man of War Schooner.
    Cap: 20 Jul 1813 at Sea by HM Ship San Domingo Int: 13 Aug 1813 Dis: 13 Aug 1813.
    Received from HM Ship Woolwich. American Ship Rolla per Order Commr Evans.

Goodridge, E   Prisoner 1836. Rank: Passenger, from: Hibernia, Merchant Sloop.
    Cap: 30 May 1814 between Cape Roman and Cape Fear by Doteral & Morgiana Int: 30 Jun 1814 Dis:
    28 Mar 1815. Received from HMS Doterel. Clarendon Transport for U States.

Goodspeed, Joseph   Prisoner 1176. Rank: Seaman, from: Elizabeth, Merchant.
    Cap: 15 Jun 1813 at Sea by HM Ship Marlborough Int: 15 Aug 1813 Dis: 02 Sep 1813.
    Received from HM Ship Woolwich. Per order of Commodore Evans vessel being liberated.

Goodwin, Joseph   Prisoner 627. Rank: Boy, from: Dolphin, Merchant Brig.
    Cap: 30 Dec 1812 at Sea by HM Ship Galus Int: 12 Jan 1813 Dis: 27 Jan 1813.
    Received from Prize Brig Dolphin. Bostock Cartel for New York.

Gorden, William   Prisoner 562. Rank: Seaman, from: Rising Hope, Merchant Brig.
    Cap: 27 Dec 1812 at Sea by HM Sloop Wanderer Int: 05 Jan 1813 Dis: 27 Jan 1813.
    Received from HM Sloop Wanderer. Bostock Cartel for New York.

Gordine, Anthony   Prisoner 1226. Rank: Not Recorded, from: HMS Sloop Calibri, Not Recorded.
    Cap: Aug 1813 Not Recorded by HMS Calibri Int: 16 Nov 1813 Dis: 15 Apr 1814.
    Received from HMS Sceptre. Surrendered himself being a American. Diana Transport for Halifax.

Gordon, Alexander   Prisoner 2518. Rank: Quartermaster, from: President, U States Frigate.
    Cap: 15 Jan 1815 Not Recorded by Endymion Int: 04 Feb 1815 Dis: 28 Mar 1815.
    Received from HMS Endymion. Clarenden Transport for U States.

Gordon, John   Prisoner 1406. Rank: Seaman, from: John & James, Merchant Vessel.
    Cap: 07 Dec 1813 Lat 37 by Loire Int: 21 Dec 1813 Dis: 15 Apr 1814.
    Received from Romulus. Diana Transport for Halifax.

Gordon, William   Prisoner 1559. Rank: Seaman, from: Bordeaux Packet, Letter of Marque.
    Cap: 28 Jan 1814 off Cape Henry by Nieman Int: 12 Feb 1814 Dis: 15 Apr 1814.
    Received from Nieman. Diana Transport for Halifax.

Gore, John   Prisoner 2343. Rank: Seaman, from: President, U States Frigate.
    Cap: 15 Jan 1815 Not Recorded by HMS Endymion Int: 04 Feb 1815 Dis: 28 Mar 1815.
    Received from Endymion. Clarenden Transport for U States.

American Prisoners of War Held at Bermuda During the War of 1812

Gore, Thomas   Prisoner 2559. Rank: Seaman, from: President, U States Frigate.
    Cap: 15 Jan 1815 Not Recorded by HM Ship Endymion Int: 05 Feb 1815 Dis: 28 Mar 1815.
    Received from President. Clarenden Transport for U States.

Goss, Thomas   Prisoner 1660. Rank: Seaman, from: Flash, Letter of Marque.
    Cap: 11 Feb 1814 Off Block Island by Acasta Int: 13 Mar 1814 Dis: 23 Apr 1814.
    Received from Active. HMS Bulwark for Halifax.

Goswilling, David   Prisoner 521. Rank: Mecanic, from: Not Recorded, Not Recorded.
    Cap: Not Recorded by Not Recorded Int: 31 Dec 1812 Dis: 27 Jan 1813.
    Surrendered himself up as an American from HM Dock Yard. Order Com Evans. (Date of capture not recorded.)

Gott, Joseph   Prisoner 2596. Rank: Seaman, from: Lark, Merchant Vessel.
    Cap: 01 Dec 1814 off New York by HM Ship Majestic Int: 05 Feb 1815 Dis: 28 Mar 1815.
    Recaptured. York Privateer. Received from HMS Forth. Clarendon Transport for U States.

Gouchon, John   Prisoner 1921. Rank: Seaman, from: Dolphin, Packet.
    Cap: 20 Aug 1814 St. Catherine by Lacedaemonian Int: 09 Sep 1814 Dis: 28 Mar 1815.
    Received from Lacedaemonian. Clarendon Transport for U States.

Gough, John   Prisoner 2213. Rank: Seaman, from: President, U States Frigate.
    Cap: 15 Jan 1815 Not Recorded by Endymion Int: 30 Jan 1815 Dis: 28 Mar 1815.
    Received from Pomone. Mars Transport for U States.

Gould, Abraham   Prisoner 320. Rank: Seaman, from: James, Merchant Ship.
    Cap: 03 Nov 1812 at Sea by HM Ship Tartarus Int: 17 Nov 1812 Dis: 27 Jan 1813.
    Received from HM Ship Tartarus. Bostock Cartel for New York.

Gould, James   Prisoner 1173. Rank: Seaman, from: Elizabeth, Merchant.
    Cap: 15 Jun 1813 at Sea by HM Ship Marlborough Int: 15 Aug 1813 Dis: 02 Sep 1813.
    Received from HM Ship Woolwich. Per order of Commodore Evans vessel being liberated.

Gould, John   Prisoner 1278. Rank: Seaman, from: Perry, Merchant Schooner.
    Cap: 03 Dec 1813 Long Island by Indemyion Int: 19 Dec 1813 Dis: .
    Received from Sceptre. Diana Transport for Halifax.

Gould, Thomas   Prisoner 1141. Rank: Seaman, from: Asp, Man of War Schooner.
    Cap: 20 Jul 1813 at Sea by HM Ship San Domingo Int: 13 Aug 1813 Dis: 13 Aug 1813.
    Received from HM Ship Woolwich. American Ship Rolla per Order Governor Strong.

Gover, Daniel   Prisoner 464. Rank: Seaman, from: Teazer, Privateer Schooner.
    Cap: 16 Dec 1812 at Sea by HM Ship St. Domingo Int: 21 Dec 1812 Dis: 27 Jan 1813.
    Received from HM Ship St. Domingo. Bostock Cartel for New York.

Graman, John   Prisoner 2855. Rank: Seaman, from: Limerick, Not Recorded.
    Cap: 15 Mar 1815 Not Recorded by Asia Int: 25 Mar 1815 Dis:
    From Depot at Jamaica. Received from Asia. (Date of discharge not recorded.)

Grant, Peter   Prisoner 477. Rank: Seaman, from: Teazer, Privateer Schooner.
    Cap: 16 Dec 1812 at Sea by HM Ship St. Domingo Int: 21 Dec 1812 Dis: 27 Jan 1813.
    Received from HM Ship St. Domingo. Bostock Cartel for New York.

Grant, Thomas   Prisoner 594. Rank: Supercargo, from: Rising Hope, Merchant Brig.
    Cap: 27 Dec 1812 at Sea by HM Ship Maidstone Int: 09 Jan 1813 Dis: 05 Feb 1813.
    Received from Sloop Wanderer. Permitted to return to New York per Order of Adl Cockburn.

Grave, Henry   Prisoner 2777. Rank: Seaman, from: Hope, Not Recorded.
    Cap: 21 Feb 1815 off St Augustine by Hebrus Int: 03 Mar 1815 Dis: 28 Mar 1815.
    Received from Hebrus. Clarendon Transport for U States.

Grave, John   Prisoner 2418. Rank: Seaman, from: President, U States Frigate.
    Cap: 15 Jan 1815 Not Recorded by HM Ship Endymion Int: 04 Feb 1815 Dis: 28 Mar 1815.
    Received from Endymion. Mars Transport for U States.

Graves, John   Prisoner 809. Rank: Seaman, from: Elouisa, Merchant Schooner.
    Cap: 16 Feb 1813 at Sea by HM Sloop Morgiana Int: 25 Feb 1813 Dis: 14 Jun 1813.
    Received from Morgiana. Permitted to return to the United States in the Perseverance Cartel.

Gray, David   Prisoner 2338. Rank: Seaman, from: President, U States Frigate.
    Cap: 15 Jan 1815 Not Recorded by Endymion Int: 04 Feb 1815 Dis: 28 Mar 1815.
    Received from Endymion. Mars Transport for U States.

Gray, Edward   Prisoner 2053. Rank: Seaman, from: Amy, Merchant Brig.
    Cap: 26 Nov 1814 off Cape Delaware by Telegraph Int: 05 Dec 1814 Dis: 25 Jan 1815.
    Received from HMS Goree. Bridges Transport being Subject to Friendly power Order Com Evans.

Gray, Mathew   Prisoner 2539. Rank: Marine, from: President, U States Frigate.
    Cap: 15 Jan 1815 Not Recorded by HM Ship Endymion Int: 04 Feb 1815 Dis: 28 Mar 1815.
    Received from HMS Endymion. Clarenden Transport for U States.

American Prisoners of War Held at Bermuda During the War of 1812

Gray, Nehemiah   Prisoner 1103. Rank: Seaman, from: Apollo, Merchant Vessel.
    Cap: 15 May 1813 at Sea by HM Ship Success Int: 27 May 1813 Dis: 24 Jun 1813.
    Received from HMS Success. Magnet Cartel for New York.

Greason, George   Prisoner 1081. Rank: Seaman, from: Not Recorded, Not Recorded.
    Cap: Not Recorded by Not Recorded Int: 24 Apr 1813 Dis: 24 Jun 1813.
    Received from HMS Barrosa. Surrendered them Selves as Prisoners of War. Magnet Cartel for New York. (Date of capture not recorded.)

Greeman, Edward   Prisoner 2587. Rank: Seaman, from: Thestis, Merchant Vessel.
    Cap: 18 Nov 1814 off New York by HM Ship Majestic Int: 05 Feb 1815 Dis: 28 Mar 1815.
    Received from HMS Forth. Clarendon Transport for U States.

Green, Ezekiel   Prisoner 752. Rank: Mate, from: Delaclea, Merchant Schooner.
    Cap: 17 Dec 1812 Lat 34.31 N, Long 74.44 W by HM Sloop Sylph Int: 26 Jan 1813 Dis: 08 Apr 1813.
    Received from Sloop Sylph. United States per Order Commodore Evans.

Green, James   Prisoner 329. Rank: Captain, from: Snapper, Privateer Schooner.
    Cap: 16 Nov 1812 at Sea by HM Ship Galus Int: 22 Nov 1812 Dis: 27 Jan 1813.
    Received from HM Ship Galus. Bostock Cartel for New York.

Green, James   Prisoner 437. Rank: Cook, from: Logan, Merchant Brig.
    Cap: 20 Nov 1812 Lat 36.20, Long 69.40 by HMS Poictiers Int: 04 Dec 1812 Dis: 27 Jan 1813.
    Received from Prize Brig Logan. Bostock Cartel for New York.

Green, James   Prisoner 2568. Rank: Seaman, from: Funchall, Merchant Vessel.
    Cap: 15 Jan 1815 off New York by HMS Pomone Int: 05 Feb 1815 Dis: 13 Mar 1815.
    Received from HMS Forth. Merchant Service.

Green, Jessy   Prisoner 2257. Rank: Seaman, from: President, U States Frigate.
    Cap: 15 Jan 1815 Not Recorded by Endymion Int: 30 Jan 1815 Dis: 28 Mar 1815.
    Received from Pomone. Mars Transport for U States.

Green, John   Prisoner 1143. Rank: Seaman, from: Asp, Man of War Schooner.
    Cap: 20 Jul 1813 at Sea by HM Ship San Domingo Int: 13 Aug 1813 Dis: 13 Aug 1813.
    Received from HM Ship Woolwich. American Ship Rolla per Order Governor Strong.

Green, John   Prisoner 1421. Rank: Seaman, from: Nonsuch, Letter of Marque.
    Cap: 14 Dec 1813 Lat 32 by Doterel Int: 25 Dec 1813 Dis: 15 Apr 1814.
    Received from HM Brig Doterel. Diana Transport for Halifax.

Green, John   Prisoner 1732. Rank: Seaman, from: Yankelass, Privateer.
    Cap: 01 May 1814 L 10-4N, L 33-0W by Severn & Surprise Int: 06 Jun 1814 Dis:
    Received from Severn. (Date of discharge not recorded.)

Green, John   Prisoner 1750. Rank: Seaman, from: Yankelass, Privateer.
    Cap: 01 May 1814 L 40-4N, Long 38-0W by Severn & Surprise Int: 06 Jun 1814 Dis: 28 Mar 1815.
    Received from Severn. Mars Transport for U States.

Green, John   Prisoner 2800. Rank: Seaman, from: Limerick, Not Recorded.
    Cap: 04 Mar 1815 Not Recorded by Asia Int: 25 Mar 1815 Dis:
    From Depot at Jamaica. Received from Asia. (Date of discharge not recorded.)

Green, Joseph   Prisoner 1858. Rank: Seaman, from: Isa Colly, Merchant Vessel.
    Cap: Not Recorded by Not Recorded Int: Dis: 04 Sep 1814.
    to join these Proper Ships having been delivered up Order Comm Evans. (Dates of capture and internment not recorded.)

Green, Peter   Prisoner 1385. Rank: Seaman, from: Policy, Merchant Vessel.
    Cap: 04 Dec 1813 Not Recorded by Loire Int: 20 Dec 1813 Dis: 15 Apr 1814.
    Recaptured. Received from San Domingo. Diana Transport for Halifax.

Greenfield, Joseph   Prisoner 779. Rank: Seaman, from: Governor Ankerheim, Merchant.
    Cap: 24 Jan 1813 at Sea by HM Ship Ramiles Int: 04 Feb 1813 Dis: 13 Mar 1813.
    Received from HMS Ramilies. Per Order Sir John Warren the Vessel being Liberated.

Gregoris, Dominic   Prisoner 1169. Rank: Seaman, from: Elizabeth, Merchant.
    Cap: 15 Jun 1813 at Sea by HM Ship Marlborough Int: 15 Aug 1813 Dis: 02 Sep 1813.
    Received from HM Ship Woolwich. Per order of Commodore Evans being liberated.

Gregory, John   Prisoner 970. Rank: Seaman, from: Janett, Merchant Brig.
    Cap: 25 Feb 1813 Chesapeake by HMS Junon Int: 23 Mar 1813 Dis: 24 Jun 1813.
    Received from HM Ship Laurustinus. Magnet Cartel for New York.

Gridney, John   Prisoner 268. Rank: Carpenter, from: Wasp, Sloop of War.
    Cap: 18 Oct 1812 at Sea by HM Ship Poictiers Int: 26 Oct 1812 Dis: 05 Nov 1812.
    Received from HM Ship Poictiers. Brig Diamond on Parole to new London United States of America.

Grieves, Whitny   Prisoner 1411. Rank: Seaman, from: Industry, Merchant Vessel.
    Cap: 08 Dec 1813 Lat 37.25 by Loire Int: 21 Dec 1813 Dis: 15 Apr 1814.
    Received from Romulus. Rammilles for Halifax.

American Prisoners of War Held at Bermuda During the War of 1812

Griffin, James Prisoner 760. Rank: Seaman, from: Hazard, Merchant Brig.
    Cap: 28 Dec 1812 Lat 37.35, Long 70.10 by HM Sloop Sylph Int: 26 Jan 1813 Dis: 14 Jun 1813.
    Received from Sloop Sylph. Permitted to return to the United States in the Perseverance Cartel.

Griffin, John Prisoner 2019. Rank: Seaman, from: Bridges, Merchant Vessel.
    Cap: 25 Oct 1814 off Halifax by Armide Int: 07 Nov 1814 Dis: 28 Mar 1815.
    Recaptured. Received from HMS Armide. Clarendon Transport for U States.

Griffin, Stewart Prisoner 2525. Rank: Quartermaster, from: President, U States Frigate.
    Cap: 15 Jan 1815 Not Recorded by Endymion Int: 04 Feb 1815 Dis: 28 Mar 1815.
    Received from HMS Endymion. Clarenden Transport for U States.

Griffith, David Prisoner 526. Rank: Passenger, from: Herald, Letter of Marque Brig.
    Cap: 25 Dec 1812 at Sea by HMS Maidstone Int: 05 Jan 1813 Dis: 27 Jan 1813.
    Received from HM Ship Maidstone. Bostock Cartel for New York.

Grigous, William Prisoner 55. Rank: Seaman, from: Ariel, Merchant Brig.
    Cap: 28 Jul 1812 of Bermuda by Recruit Int: 28 Aug 1812 Dis: 18 Sep 1812.
    Received from M Schooner Cuttle. Order of Commd Evans for England.

Grimes, George Prisoner 1571. Rank: Seaman, from: Bordeaux Packet, Letter of Marque.
    Cap: 28 Jan 1814 off Cape Henry by Nieman Int: 12 Feb 1814 Dis: 15 Apr 1814.
    Received from Nieman. Diana Transport for Halifax.

Grimes, Richard Prisoner 1789. Rank: Prize Master, from: Yankelass, Privateer.
    Cap: 01 May 1814 Latt 40-4N, Long 38-0W by Severn & Surprise Int: 07 Jun 1814 Dis: 16 Mar 1815.
    Received from Surprise. Merchant Service.

Grindell, Henry Prisoner 1354. Rank: Seaman, from: Rolla, Privateer.
    Cap: 10 Dec 1813 Block Island by Loire Int: 20 Dec 1813 Dis: 15 Apr 1814.
    Received from San Domingo. HMS Rammillies for Halifax.

Griswold, Charles Prisoner 591. Rank: Passenger, from: Lydia, Merchant Ship.
    Cap: 26 Dec 1812 at Sea by HM Ship Maidstone Int: 07 Jan 1813 Dis: 15 Jan 1813.
    Received from Prize Ship Lydia. New York per Order Ad Cockburn.

Grush, Philip Prisoner 2617. Rank: Seaman, from: Falcon, Merchant Vessel.
    Cap: 22 Jan 1815 Sandy Hook by HM Ship Pomone Int: 05 Feb 1815 Dis: 09 Mar 1815.
    Received from HMS Forth. Merchant Service.

Gualt, Charles Prisoner 2041. Rank: Prize Master, from: Rising Sun, Merchant Vessel.
    Cap: 20 Nov 1814 off Bermuda by Pandora Int: 28 Nov 1814 Dis: 25 Mar 1815.
    Recaptured. Received from HMS Goree. Merchant Vessel.

Guard, Andrew Prisoner 877. Rank: Seaman, from: Christiana, Merchant.
    Cap: 03 Mar 1813 Chesapeake by Marlborough Int: 23 Mar 1813 Dis: 13 Jun 1813.
    Received from Laurustinus. Perseverance Cartel for the United States per Order Adml Sir J B Warren.

Guest, Edward Prisoner 1992. Rank: Seaman, from: Fairplay, Merchant Vessel.
    Cap: 22 Oct 1814 Lat 31.58 by Dothrel Int: 26 Oct 1814 Dis: 28 Mar 1815.
    Recaptured. Received from Dothrel. Clarendon Transport for U States.

Gum, Jacob Prisoner 261. Rank: Pilot, from: Wasp, Sloop of War.
    Cap: 18 Oct 1812 at Sea by HM Ship Poictiers Int: 26 Oct 1812 Dis: 05 Nov 1812.
    Received from HM Ship Poictiers. Brig Diamond on Parole to new London United States of America.

Gursting, Oliver Prisoner 2016. Rank: Seaman, from: Bridges, Merchant Vessel.
    Cap: 25 Oct 1814 off Halifax by Armide Int: 07 Nov 1814 Dis: 28 Mar 1815.
    Recaptured. Received from HMS Armide. Clarendon Transport for U States.

Gusta, Charles Prisoner 2566. Rank: Seaman, from: Funchall, Merchant Vessel.
    Cap: 15 Jan 1815 off New York by HMS Pomone Int: 05 Feb 1815 Dis: 17 Mar 1815.
    Received from HMS Forth. Harriot M Vessel order of Commadore Evans.

Guswold, Truman Prisoner 1792. Rank: Clerk, from: Yankelass, Privateer.
    Cap: 01 May 1814 Latt 40-4N, Long 38-0W by Severn & Surprise Int: 07 Jun 1814 Dis:
    Received from Surprise. (Date of discharge not recorded.)

Guthwright, James Prisoner 315. Rank: Seaman, from: Wasp, Sloop of War.
    Cap: 18 Oct 1812 at Sea by HMS Poictiers Int: 05 Nov 1812 Dis: 17 Jun 1813.
    Received from HM Ship Poictiers. Halifax Order of the Commander in Chief supports to be an Englishman.

Gutry, James Prisoner 219. Rank: Seaman, from: Wasp, Sloop of War.
    Cap: 18 Oct 1812 at Sea by HM Ship Poictiers Int: 26 Oct 1812 Dis: 05 Nov 1812.
    Received from HM Ship Poictiers. Brig Diamond on Parole to new London United States of America.

Gyles, William Prisoner 564. Rank: Seaman, from: Rising Hope, Merchant Brig.
    Cap: 27 Dec 1812 at Sea by HM Sloop Wanderer Int: 05 Jan 1813 Dis: 27 Jan 1813.
    Received from HM Sloop Wanderer. Bostock Cartel for New York.

American Prisoners of War Held at Bermuda During the War of 1812

Hadley, John   Prisoner 1707. Rank: Seaman, from: Grecian, Letter of Marque.
    Cap: 02 May 1814 Chesapeake by Jansur Int: 26 May 1814 Escaped: 23 Nov 1814.
    Received from Lacedaemonian. Run.

Haggerty, James   Prisoner 2214. Rank: Marine, from: President, U States Frigate.
    Cap: 15 Jan 1815 Not Recorded by Endymion Int: 30 Jan 1815 Dis: 28 Mar 1815.
    Received from Pomone. Clarenden Transport for U States.

Hague, Charles   Prisoner 607. Rank: Seaman, from: Noetoin, Packet Brig.
    Cap: 05 Jan 1813 at Sea by HM Ship Belvidera Int: 10 Jan 1813 Dis: 27 Jan 1813.
    Received from HMS Belvidera. Bostock Cartel for New York.

Hail, Sylvester   Prisoner 819. Rank: Seaman, from: Elove & Unity, Merchant.
    Cap: 07 Mar 1813 at Bermuda by Sandimingo Int: 08 Mar 1813 Dis: 13 Jun 1813.
    Received from Sandimingo. Perseverance Cartel for the United States per Order Adm Sir J B Warren.

Halborn, Thomas   Prisoner 919. Rank: Seaman, from: Albert, Merchant Schooner.
    Cap: 05 Mar 1813 Chesapeake by HM Ship Marlborough Int: 23 Mar 1813 Dis: 24 Jun 1813.
    Received from Laurustinus. Magnet Cartel for New York.

Hales, John   Prisoner 2409. Rank: Seaman, from: President, U States Frigate.
    Cap: 15 Jan 1815 Not Recorded by HM Ship Endymion Int: 04 Feb 1815 Dis: 28 Mar 1815.
    Received from Endymion. Mars Transport for U States.

Haley, John   Prisoner 2415. Rank: Seaman, from: President, U States Frigate.
    Cap: 15 Jan 1815 Not Recorded by HM Ship Endymion Int: 04 Feb 1815 Dis: 28 Mar 1815.
    Received from Endymion. Mars Transport for U States.

Halgreen, Peter   Prisoner 1094. Rank: Seaman, from: Langdon Cheves, Merchant.
    Cap: 12 May 1813 at Sea by HM Sloop Atalante Int: 25 May 1813 Dis: 24 Jun 1813.
    Received from HMS Atalante. Magnet Cartel for New York.

Hall, D   Prisoner 2799. Rank: Seaman, from: Limerick, Not Recorded.
    Cap: 04 Mar 1815 Not Recorded by Asia Int: 25 Mar 1815 Dis:
    From Depot at Jamaica. Received from Asia. (Date of discharge not recorded.)

Hall, Edward   Prisoner 2639. Rank: Seaman, from: Platoff, Merchant Vessel.
    Cap: 16 Jan 1815 off New York by Spencer Int: 06 Feb 1815 Dis: 13 Mar 1815.
    Received from HMS Telegraph. Merchant Service.

Hall, George   Prisoner 51. Rank: Seaman, from: Ariel, Merchant Brig.
    Cap: 28 Jul 1812 of Bermuda by Recruit Int: 28 Aug 1812 Dis: 18 Sep 1812.
    Received from HM Schooner Cuttle. Order Commd Evans for England.

Hall, George   Prisoner 2461. Rank: Captains Crew, from: President, U States Frigate.
    Cap: 15 Jan 1815 Not Recorded by Endymion Int: 04 Feb 1815 Dis: 28 Mar 1815.
    Received from Endymion. Clarenden Transport for U States.

Hall, Henry   Prisoner 1806. Rank: Passenger, from: Not Recorded, Not Recorded.
    Cap: Not Recorded by Not Recorded Int: 14 Jun 1814 Dis: 15 Jun 1814.
    From St. Bartholomew in the Swedish Schooner Oscar. on Parole per Order Com in Chief to America.
    (Date of capture not recorded.)

Hall, Hezekiah   Prisoner 815. Rank: Seaman, from: Stockholm, Merchant Schooner.
    Cap: 18 Feb 1813 at Sea by HMS Statira Int: 01 Mar 1813 Dis: 14 Apr 1813.
    Received from HMS Statira. Per Order Commodore Evans Vessel Liberated.

Hall, Humes   Prisoner 1449. Rank: Sailing Master, from: Vixen, Man of War.
    Cap: 25 Dec 1813 Lat 38.0 by Belvidera Int: 05 Jan 1814 Dis: 15 Apr 1814.
    U States Schooner. Received from HMS Belvidera. Rammilles for Halifax.

Hall, John   Prisoner 1487. Rank: Supercargo, from: Matthews, Merchant Schooner.
    Cap: 24 Dec 1813 Gulph of Mexico by HM Schooner Canew Int: 08 Jan 1814 Dis: 15 Apr 1814.
    Received from HM Schooner Canew. Rammilles for Halifax.

Hall, Robert   Prisoner 44. Rank: Seaman, from: Trim, Merchant Schooner.
    Cap: 28 Jul 1812 of Bermuda by Cuttle Int: 28 Aug 1812 Dis: 18 Sep 1812.
    Received from HM Schooner Cuttle. Order Commd Evans for England.

Hall, Robert   Prisoner 1488. Rank: Boy, from: Matthews, Merchant Schooner.
    Cap: 24 Dec 1813 Gulph of Mexico by HM Schooner Canew Int: 08 Jan 1814 Dis: 15 Apr 1814.
    Received from HM Schooner Canew. Rammilles for Halifax.

Hall, Samuel   Prisoner 239. Rank: Seaman, from: Wasp, Sloop of War.
    Cap: 18 Oct 1812 at Sea by HM Ship Poictiers Int: 26 Oct 1812 Dis: 05 Nov 1812.
    Received from HM Ship Poictiers. Brig Diamond on Parole to new London United States of America.

Hall, William   Prisoner 469. Rank: Seaman, from: Teazer, Privateer Schooner.
    Cap: 16 Dec 1812 at Sea by HM Ship St. Domingo Int: 21 Dec 1812 Dis: 27 Jan 1813.
    Received from HM Ship St. Domingo. Bostock Cartel for New York.

American Prisoners of War Held at Bermuda During the War of 1812

Hall, William   Prisoner 680. Rank: Seaman, from: High Flyer, Privateer.
    Cap: 09 Jan 1813 at Sea by HM Ship Acasta Int: 21 Jan 1813 Dis: 27 Jan 1813.
    Received from HMS Acasta. Bostock Cartel for New York.

Hall, William   Prisoner 875. Rank: Seaman, from: Christiana, Merchant.
    Cap: 03 Mar 1813 Chesapeake by Marlborough Int: 23 Mar 1813 Dis: 13 Jun 1813.
    Received from Laurustinus. Perseverance Cartel for the United States per Order Adml Sir J B Warren.

Hall, William   Prisoner 1489. Rank: Master, from: Matthews, Merchant Schooner.
    Cap: 24 Dec 1813 Gulph of Mexico by HM Schooner Canew Int: 08 Jan 1814 Dis: 15 Apr 1814.
    Received from HM Schooner Canew. Rammilles for Halifax.

Hall, William F   Prisoner 2074. Rank: Seaman, from: May Flower, Merchant Sloop.
    Cap: 22 Dec 1814 Grafy Bay Bermuda by Came in by Stress of Weather Int: 22 Dec 1814 Dis: 11 Jan 1815. Received from American Sloop May Flower. This Vessel was blown off the Coast of America & ran into Bermuda in Distress. To wait for a passage to the United States.

Hallett, James   Prisoner 2683. Rank: Seaman, from: Farmers Branch, Merchant Vessel.
    Cap: 06 Feb 1815 off Delaware by Lacedaemonian Int: 14 Feb 1815 Dis: 28 Mar 1815.
    Received from Childers. Clarendon Transport for U States.

Halsey, John   Prisoner 896. Rank: Mate, from: Princessa, Merchant Brig.
    Cap: 07 Feb 1813 Chesapeake by HMS Marlborough Int: 23 Mar 1813 Dis: 21 Jun 1813.
    Received from HM Ship Laurustinus. Being a Passenger.

Ham, Anthony   Prisoner 2419. Rank: Captains Crew, from: President, U States Frigate.
    Cap: 15 Jan 1815 Not Recorded by HM Ship Endymion Int: 04 Feb 1815 Dis: 28 Mar 1815.
    Received from Endymion. Mars Transport for U States.

Hamburgh, Peter   Prisoner 2778. Rank: Seaman, from: Hope, Not Recorded.
    Cap: 21 Feb 1815 off St Augustine by Hebrus Int: 03 Mar 1815 Dis: 20 Mar 1815.
    Received from Hebrus. Merchant Vessel.

Hammond, Benjamin   Prisoner 566. Rank: Seaman, from: Fly, Merchant.
    Cap: 06 Dec 1812 at Sea by HM Ship Maidstone Int: 06 Jan 1813 Dis: 27 Jan 1813.
    Received from HM Ship Maidstone. Bostock Cartel for New York.

Hammond, J   Prisoner 1441. Rank: Seaman, from: Nonsuch, Letter of Marque.
    Cap: 14 Dec 1813 Lat 32 by Doterel Int: 25 Dec 1813 Dis: 15 Apr 1814.
    Received from HM Brig Doterel. Diana Transport for Halifax.

Hammond, Samuel   Prisoner 1336. Rank: Seaman, from: Rolla, Privateer.
    Cap: 10 Dec 1813 Block Island by Loire Int: 20 Dec 1813 Dis: 15 Apr 1814.
    Received from HM Ship San Domingo. HMS Rammillies for Halifax.

Hammond, Stephen   Prisoner 7. Rank: Seaman, from: Yorick, Merchant Ship.
    Cap: 09 Jul 1812 near Bermuda by Rattler Int: 28 Aug 1812 Dis: 18 Sep 1812.
    Received from HM Schooner Cuttle. Order of Commd Evans for England.

Hammond, Stephen   Prisoner 2550. Rank: Seaman, from: President, US Frigate.
    Cap: 15 Jan 1815 off N York by HMS Endymion Int: 05 Feb 1815 Dis: 28 Mar 1815.
    Received from President. Clarenden Transport for U States.

Hammond, William   Prisoner 1923. Rank: Prize Master, from: Timer, Merchant Vessel.
    Cap: 23 Aug 1814 off Savannah by Lacedaemonian Int: 09 Sep 1814 Dis: 28 Mar 1815.
    Received from Lacedaemonian. Clarendon Transport for U States.

Hancock, James   Prisoner 1157. Rank: Seaman, from: Acricoake, Merchant.
    Cap: 22 Jul 1813 at Sea by HM Sloop Conflict Int: 13 Aug 1813 Dis: 13 Aug 1813.
    Received from HM Ship Woolwich. American Ship Rolla per Order Governor Strong.

Hanfelt, O   Prisoner 1387. Rank: Seaman, from: Policy, Merchant Vessel.
    Cap: 04 Dec 1813 Not Recorded by Loire Int: 20 Dec 1813 Dis: 06 Apr 1814.
    Recaptured. Received from San Domingo. being a Swede.

Hanford, William   Prisoner 2281. Rank: Seaman, from: President, U States Frigate.
    Cap: 15 Jan 1815 Not Recorded by Endymion Int: 30 Jan 1815 Dis: 28 Mar 1815.
    Received from Pomone. Mars Transport for U States.

Hanlow, Alexander   Prisoner 2164. Rank: Captains Clerk, from: President, U States Frigate.
    Cap: 15 Jan 1815 Not Recorded by Endymion Int: 30 Jan 1815 Dis: 06 Feb 1815.
    Received from President. Narcissus to the U States by order of Commadore Evans.

Hanna, Edward   Prisoner 1735. Rank: Seaman, from: Yankelass, Privateer.
    Cap: 01 May 1814 L 10-4N, L 33-0W by Severn & Surprise Int: 06 Jun 1814 Dis: 20 Mar 1815.
    Received from Severn. Merchant Vessel.

Hansey, William   Prisoner 2811. Rank: Seaman, from: Limerick, Not Recorded.
    Cap: 04 Mar 1815 Not Recorded by Asia Int: 25 Mar 1815 Dis:
    From Depot at Jamaica. Received from Asia. (Date of discharge not recorded.)

American Prisoners of War Held at Bermuda During the War of 1812

Hanson, Howe   Prisoner 577. Rank: Seaman, from: Herald, Letter of Marque Brig.
  Cap: 25 Dec 1812 at Sea by HM Ship Maidstone   Int: 06 Jan 1813   Died: 18 Feb 1813.
  Received from HM Ship Maidstone. Died. Fever.

Hanster, John   Prisoner 1738. Rank: Seaman, from: Yankelass, Privateer.
  Cap: 01 May 1814 L 10-4N, L 33-0W by Severn & Surprise   Int: 06 Jun 1814   Dis: 28 Mar 1815.
  Received from Severn. Mars Transport for U States.

Happy, Abraham   Prisoner 2661. Rank: Seaman, from: Amicus, Merchant Vessel.
  Cap: 10 Jan 1815 Delaware by Forth   Int: 14 Feb 1815   Dis: 28 Mar 1815.
  Recaptured. Chapeur Privateer. Received from Goree. Clarendon Transport for U States.

Hardy, Robert   Prisoner 1418. Rank: Seaman, from: Nonsuch, Letter of Marque.
  Cap: 14 Dec 1813 Lat 32 by Doterel   Int: 25 Dec 1813   Dis: 24 Apr 1814.
  Received from HM Brig Doterel. HMS Sceptre for England.

Harford, Thomas   Prisoner 274. Rank: Mate, from: Little William, Merchant Brig.
  Cap: 18 Oct 1812 at Sea by HM Ship Poictiers   Int: 26 Oct 1812   Dis: 05 Nov 1812.
  Received from HM Ship Poictiers. Brig Diamond on Parole to new London United States of America.

Harlow, Benjamin   Prisoner 765. Rank: 1 Mate, from: Lucy, Merchant Schooner.
  Cap: 28 Dec 1812 Lat 36.45, Long 73.18 by HM Sloop Sylph   Int: 26 Jan 1813   Dis: 24 Jun 1813.
  Received from Sloop Sylph. Magnet Cartel for New York.

Harrimond, John   Prisoner 953. Rank: Seaman, from: Bona, Letter of Marque Schooner.
  Cap: 12 Mar 1813 Chesapeake by Laurustinus   Int: 23 Mar 1813   Escaped: 21 Apr 1813.
  Received from Laurustinus. Escaped.

Harrington, Ebenezer   Prisoner 252. Rank: Seaman, from: Wasp, Sloop of War.
  Cap: 18 Oct 1812 at Sea by HM Ship Poictiers   Int: 26 Oct 1812   Dis: 05 Nov 1812.
  Received from HM Ship Poictiers. Brig Diamond on Parole to new London United States of America.

Harrington, Lyman   Prisoner 807. Rank: Seaman, from: Elouisa, Merchant Schooner.
  Cap: 16 Feb 1813 at Sea by HM Sloop Morgiana   Int: 25 Feb 1813   Dis: 14 Jun 1813.
  Received from Morgiana. Permitted to return to the United States in the Perseverance Cartel.

Harrington, Samuel   Prisoner 1249. Rank: Not Recorded, from: Welcome Return, Merchant Vessel.
  Cap: 08 Oct 1813 Chesapeake by Acteon   Int: 02 Dec 1813   Dis: 15 Apr 1814.
  Received from HMS Sceptre. Diana Transport for Halifax.

Harris, Benjamin   Prisoner 538. Rank: Seaman, from: Herald, Letter of Marque Brig.
  Cap: 25 Dec 1812 at Sea by HM Ship Maidstone   Int: 05 Jan 1813   Dis: 27 Jan 1813.
  Received from HM Ship Maidstone. Bostock Cartel for New York.

Harris, Charles   Prisoner 1016. Rank: Seaman, from: Nautalus, Merchant.
  Cap: 20 Mar 1813 off the Chesapeake by HM Ship Rammillies   Int: 06 Apr 1813   Dis: 24 Jun 1813.
  Received from HMS Junon. Magnet Cartel for New York.

Harris, J W   Prisoner 285. Rank: Surgeon, from: Wasp, Sloop of War.
  Cap: 18 Oct 1812 at Sea by HM Ship Poictiers   Int: 01 Nov 1812   Dis: 04 Nov 1812.
  Received from HM Ship Poictiers. Brig Diamond on Parole to new London United States of America.

Harris, James   Prisoner 802. Rank: Seaman, from: Not Recorded, Not Recorded.
  Cap: Not Recorded by Not Recorded   Int: 14 Feb 1813   Dis: 24 Jun 1813.
  Received from Narcissus. Surrendered himself as a Prisoner of War. Magnet Cartel for New York.
  (Date of capture not recorded.)

Harris, John   Prisoner 2104. Rank: Seaman, from: Rufus King, Merchant Vessel.
  Cap: 01 Jan 1815 off Bermuda by Peruvian   Int: 19 Jan 1815   Dis: 17 Feb 1815.
  Received from HMS Peruvian. Bridges Transport per Order of Comm Evans.

Harris, William   Prisoner 1152. Rank: Seaman, from: Acricoake, Merchant.
  Cap: 22 Jul 1813 at Sea by HM Sloop Conflict   Int: 13 Aug 1813   Dis: 13 Aug 1813.
  Received from HM Ship Woolwich. American Ship Rolla per Order Commr Evans.

Harris, William   Prisoner 2526. Rank: Seaman, from: President, U States Frigate.
  Cap: 15 Jan 1815 Not Recorded by Endymion   Int: 04 Feb 1815   Dis: 28 Mar 1815.
  Received from HMS Endymion. Clarenden Transport for U States.

Harrison, Samuel   Prisoner 2812. Rank: Master, from: Limerick, Not Recorded.
  Cap: 04 Mar 1815 Not Recorded by Asia   Int: 25 Mar 1815   Dis:
  From Depot at Jamaica. Received from Asia. (Date of discharge not recorded.)

Harrod, Joseph   Prisoner 966. Rank: Passenger, from: Janett, Merchant Brig.
  Cap: 25 Feb 1813 Chesapeake by HMS Junon   Int: 23 Mar 1813   Dis: 24 Jun 1813.
  Received from HM Ship Laurustinus. Noncombatant permitted to return to the United States.

Harron, William   Prisoner 2216. Rank: Seaman, from: President, U States Frigate.
  Cap: 15 Jan 1815 Not Recorded by Endymion   Int: 30 Jan 1815   Dis: 28 Mar 1815.
  Received from Pomone. Mars Transport for U States.

American Prisoners of War Held at Bermuda During the War of 1812

Hart, Daniel   Prisoner 712. Rank: Seaman, from: High Flyer, Privateer.
    Cap: 09 Jan 1813 at Sea by HM Ship Acasta Int: 21 Jan 1813 Dis: 27 Jan 1813.
    Received from HMS Acasta. Bostock Cartel for New York.

Hart, Robert   Prisoner 793. Rank: Master, from: Sheppard, Merchant Schooner.
    Cap: 04 Jan 1813 at Sea by Narcissus Int: 13 Feb 1813 Dis: 24 Jun 1813.
    Received from Narcissus. Magnet Cartel for New York.

Hartley, Lewis   Prisoner 403. Rank: Seaman, from: Snapper, Privateer Schooner.
    Cap: 16 Nov 1812 at Sea by HM Ship Galus Int: 22 Nov 1812 Dis: 27 Jan 1813.
    Received from HM Ship Galus. Bostock Cartel for New York.

Harvey, Amon   Prisoner 2651. Rank: Seaman, from: President, U States Frigate.
    Cap: 11 Feb 1815 off N York by Endymion Int: 11 Feb 1815 Dis: 28 Mar 1815.
    Received from President. Clarenden Transport for U States. (Date of capture should be January 15, 1815.)

Harvey, John   Prisoner 1383. Rank: Seaman, from: Policy, Merchant Vessel.
    Cap: 04 Dec 1813 Not Recorded by Loire Int: 20 Dec 1813 Dis: 15 Apr 1814.
    Recaptured. Received from San Domingo. Diana Transport for Halifax.

Harvey, John   Prisoner 2389. Rank: (Not legible) Mate, from: President, U States Frigate.
    Cap: 15 Jan 1815 Not Recorded by HM Ship Endymion Int: 04 Feb 1815 Dis: 28 Mar 1815.
    Received from Endymion. Mars Transport for U States.

Harvey, Joseph   Prisoner 92. Rank: Seaman, from: Gossepuim, Merchant.
    Cap: 16 Aug 1812 of Bermuda by Goree Int: 28 Aug 1812 Dis: 18 Sep 1812.
    Received from HM Schooner Cuttle. Order of Commd Evans for England.

Haskell, Joseph   Prisoner 979. Rank: Seaman, from: Betsy Ann, Merchant.
    Cap: 04 Mar 1813 Chesapeake by HM Ship Fantom Int: 23 Mar 1813 Dis: 24 Jun 1813.
    Received from HM Ship Laurustinus. Magnet Cartel for New York.

Hatch, James   Prisoner 685. Rank: Seaman, from: High Flyer, Privateer.
    Cap: 09 Jan 1813 at Sea by HMS Acasta Int: 21 Jan 1813 Dis: 27 Jan 1813.
    Received from HMS Acasta. Bostock Cartel for New York.

Hatch, John   Prisoner 1285. Rank: Seaman, from: Perry, Merchant Schooner.
    Cap: 03 Dec 1813 Long Island by Indemyion Int: 19 Dec 1813 Dis: 15 Apr 1814.
    Received from Sceptre. Diana Transport for Halifax.

Hathaway, Pardon   Prisoner 1119. Rank: Mate, from: Gold Coiner, Merchant.
    Cap: 24 Mar 1813 at Sea by HM Sloop Lyra Int: 21 Jun 1813 Dis: 24 Jun 1813.
    Received from HMS Ruby. Magnet Cartel for New York.

Hatwood, P   Prisoner 1596. Rank: Seaman, from: Dispatch, Merchant Vessel.
    Cap: 26 Oct 1813 Block Island by Narcissus Int: 14 Feb 1814 Dis: 23 Apr 1814.
    Received from Sceptre. HMS Bulwark for Halifax.

Haughtman, John   Prisoner 2295. Rank: 2 Gunner, from: President, U States Frigate.
    Cap: 15 Jan 1815 Not Recorded by Endymion Int: 04 Feb 1815 Dis: 28 Mar 1815.
    Received from Endymion. Mars Transport for U States.

Haughton, William   Prisoner 831. Rank: Seaman, from: Portsmouth, Merchant Ship.
    Cap: 27 Feb 1813 off Bermuda by HM Sloop Martin Int: 09 Mar 1813 Dis: 27 Mar 1813.
    Received from Sloop Martin. Per Order Commodore Evans the Vessel being Liberated.

Havins, William   Prisoner 1293. Rank: Seaman, from: Dolphin, Merchant Sloop.
    Cap: 03 Dec 1813 off Cape Henry by Lacedaemonian Int: 19 Dec 1813 Dis: 15 Apr 1814.
    Received from Sceptre. Diana Transport for Halifax.

Hawkins, William   Prisoner 857. Rank: Seaman, from: Bona, Letter of Marque Schooner.
    Cap: 12 Mar 1813 Chesapeake by HM Ship Laurustinus Int: 23 Mar 1813 Dis: 24 Jun 1813.
    Received from HM Ship Laurustinus. Magnet Cartel for New York.

Haynes, Joseph   Prisoner 2521. Rank: Seaman, from: President, U States Frigate.
    Cap: 15 Jan 1815 Not Recorded by Endymion Int: 04 Feb 1815 Dis: 28 Mar 1815.
    Received from HMS Endymion. Clarenden Transport for U States.

Hays, Abraham   Prisoner 351. Rank: Seaman, from: Snapper, Privateer Schooner.
    Cap: 16 Nov 1812 at Sea by HMS Galus Int: 22 Nov 1812 Dis: 27 Jan 1813.
    Received from HM Ship Galus. Bostock Cartel for New York.

Haywood, John   Prisoner 91. Rank: Seaman, from: Gossepuim, Merchant.
    Cap: 16 Aug 1812 of Bermuda by Goree Int: 28 Aug 1812 Dis: 18 Sep 1812.
    Received from HM Schooner Cuttle. Order of Commd Evans for England.

Hazard, D   Prisoner 1360. Rank: Seaman, from: Rolla, Privateer.
    Cap: 10 Dec 1813 Block Island by Loire Int: 20 Dec 1813 Dis: 15 Apr 1814.
    Received from San Domingo. HMS Rammillies for Halifax.

American Prisoners of War Held at Bermuda During the War of 1812

Hazard, Wanton   Prisoner 851. Rank: Seaman, from: Resolution, Merchant Schooner.
    Cap: 26 Jan 1813 at Sea by Victorious Int: 20 Mar 1813 Dis: 20 Mar 1813.
    Received from HMS Galus. Savannah Packet for New York per Order Adl Sir J B Warren.

Headley, James   Prisoner 2108. Rank: Seaman, from: Rufus King, Merchant Vessel.
    Cap: 01 Jan 1815 off Bermuda by Peruvian Int: 19 Jan 1815 Dis: 16 Mar 1815.
    Received from HMS Peruvian. Merchant Service.

Healey, Edward   Prisoner 1577. Rank: Seaman, from: Bordeaux Packet, Letter of Marque.
    Cap: 28 Jan 1814 off Cape Henry by Nieman Int: 12 Feb 1814 Dis: 15 Apr 1814.
    Received from Nieman. Diana Transport for Halifax.

Heartie, Isaac   Prisoner 1472. Rank: 1 Mate, from: Rapid, Letter of Marque Schooner.
    Cap: 16 Dec 1813 off Sandy Rock by Plantagenet Int: 06 Jan 1814 Dis:
    Received from HM Ship Plantagenet. (Date of discharge not recorded.)

Heath, Durham   Prisoner 666. Rank: Clerk, from: High Flyer, Privateer.
    Cap: 09 Jan 1813 at Sea by HM Ship Acasta Int: 21 Jan 1813 Dis: 27 Jan 1813.
    Received from HMS Acasta. Bostock Cartel for New York.

Heath, William   Prisoner 2578. Rank: Seaman, from: Recovery, Merchant Vessel.
    Cap: 20 Nov 1814 off New York by HMS Majestic Int: 05 Feb 1815 Dis: 28 Mar 1815.
    Received from HMS Forth. Clarendon Transport for U States.

Heddon, John   Prisoner 1567. Rank: Seaman, from: Bordeaux Packet, Letter of Marque.
    Cap: 28 Jan 1814 off Cape Henry by Nieman Int: 12 Feb 1814 Dis: 15 Apr 1814.
    Received from Nieman. Diana Transport for Halifax.

Helsia, William   Prisoner 2565. Rank: Seaman, from: Funchall, Merchant Vessel.
    Cap: 15 Jan 1815 off New York by HMS Pomone Int: 05 Feb 1815 Dis: 13 Mar 1815.
    Received from HMS Forth. Merchant Service.

Henderson, Francis   Prisoner 1358. Rank: Seaman, from: Rolla, Privateer.
    Cap: 10 Dec 1813 Block Island by Loire Int: 20 Dec 1813 Dis: 15 Apr 1814.
    Received from San Domingo. HMS Rammillies for Halifax.

Henderson, Hans   Prisoner 2342. Rank: Seaman, from: President, U States Frigate.
    Cap: 15 Jan 1815 Not Recorded by HMS Endymion Int: 04 Feb 1815 Dis: 28 Mar 1815.
    Received from Endymion. Mars Transport for U States.

Henderson, Henry   Prisoner 348. Rank: Seaman, from: Snapper, Privateer Schooner.
    Cap: 16 Nov 1812 at Sea by HMS Galus Int: 22 Nov 1812 Dis: 27 Jan 1813.
    Received from HM Ship Galus. Bostock Cartel for New York.

Hendree, John   Prisoner 118. Rank: Surgeon, from: James Maddison, Man of War.
    Cap: 22 Aug 1812 Lat 31 by HMS Barbados Int: 10 Sep 1812 Dis: 10 Sep 1812.
    Received from HMS Barbados. Schooner Hero for New Y.

Hendrick, Hugh   Prisoner 136. Rank: Seaman, from: Citzen, Merchant Schooner.
    Cap: 10 Sep 1812 Lat 37 by HMS Belvidera Int: 26 Sep 1812 Died: 18 Oct 1812.
    Received from HMS Belvidera. Died. Fever.

Hendrickson, John   Prisoner 1569. Rank: Seaman, from: Bordeaux Packet, Letter of Marque.
    Cap: 28 Jan 1814 off Cape Henry by Nieman Int: 12 Feb 1814 Dis: 15 Apr 1814.
    Received from Nieman. Diana Transport for Halifax.

Henfield, Thomas   Prisoner 212. Rank: Seaman, from: Wasp, Sloop of War.
    Cap: 18 Oct 1812 at Sea by HM Ship Poictiers Int: 26 Oct 1812 Dis: 05 Nov 1812.
    Received from HM Ship Poictiers. Brig Diamond on Parole to new London United States of America.

Henley, George   Prisoner 2192. Rank: Seaman, from: President, U States Frigate.
    Cap: 15 Jan 1815 Not Recorded by HMS Endymion Int: 30 Jan 1815 Dis: 28 Mar 1815.
    Received from Pomone. Mars Transport for U States.

Henman, Richard   Prisoner 1801. Rank: Seaman, from: Yankelass, Privateer.
    Cap: 01 May 1814 L 40-4P, Long 30-11W by Severn & Surprise Int: 07 Jun 1814 Dis: 28 Mar 1815.
    Yankee lass. Received from Surprise. Clarendon Transport for U States.

Hennee, John D   Prisoner 122. Rank: Seaman, from: William of Baltimore, Merchant.
    Cap: 31 Aug 1812 Lat 37 by HM Ship Recruit Int: 14 Sep 1812 Dis: 18 Sep 1812.
    Received from Recruit. Order of Commd Evans for England.

Henry, James   Prisoner 2314. Rank: Seaman, from: President, U States Frigate.
    Cap: 15 Jan 1815 Not Recorded by Endymion Int: 04 Feb 1815 Dis: 28 Mar 1815.
    Received from Endymion. Mars Transport for U States.

Henry, James   Prisoner 2797. Rank: Seaman, from: Limerick, Not Recorded.
    Cap: 04 Mar 1815 Not Recorded by Asia Int: 25 Mar 1815 Dis:
    From Depot at Jamaica. Received from Asia. (Date of discharge not recorded.)

Henry, Lewis   Prisoner 2172. Rank: Seaman, from: President, U States Frigate.
    Cap: 15 Jan 1815 Not Recorded by HMS Endymion Int: 30 Jan 1815 Dis: 28 Mar 1815.
    Received from President. Mars Transport for U States.

American Prisoners of War Held at Bermuda During the War of 1812

Henry, Robert   Prisoner 2267. Rank: Marine, from: President, U States Frigate.
    Cap: 15 Jan 1815 Not Recorded by Endymion Int: 30 Jan 1815 Dis: 28 Mar 1815.
    Received from Pomone. Clarenden Transport for U States.

Henry, Samuel   Prisoner 1860. Rank: Seaman, from: Sally, Merchant Vessel.
    Cap: Not Recorded by Not Recorded Int: Died: 19 Jan 1815.
    Died. Fever. (Dates of capture and internment not recorded.)

Henry, William   Prisoner 1982. Rank: Seaman, from: Antelope, Merchant Vessel.
    Cap: 21 Aug 1814 Western Island by Whiting Int: 17 Sep 1814 Dis: 28 Mar 1815.
    Recaptured. Received from Goree. Clarendon Transport for U States.

Hensworth, Log   Prisoner 2585. Rank: Boy, from: Advocate, Merchant Vessel.
    Cap: 16 Nov 1814 off New York by HM Ship Majestic Int: 05 Feb 1815 Dis: 28 Mar 1815.
    Received from HMS Forth. Clarendon Transport for U States.

Henthorn, William   Prisoner 2674. Rank: Seaman, from: Gunboat 160, U States Man of War.
    Cap: 06 Sep 1814 off New York by Lacedaemonian Int: 14 Feb 1815 Dis: 28 Mar 1815.
    Gun Vessel. Received from Childers. Clarendon Transport for U States.

Henyon, James   Prisoner 2292. Rank: Marine, from: President, U States Frigate.
    Cap: 15 Jan 1815 Not Recorded by Endymion Int: 30 Jan 1815 Dis: 28 Mar 1815.
    Received from Pomone. Clarenden Transport for U States.

Hepburn, John   Prisoner 1165. Rank: Seaman, from: Caledonian, Merchant.
    Cap: 20 Jul 1813 at Sea by HM Ship Marlborough Int: 15 Aug 1813 Dis: 03 Oct 1813.
    Received from HM Ship Woolwich. Caledonian Order of Commodore Evans she being Liberated.

Hepp, James   Prisoner 1257. Rank: Mate, from: Hero, Merchant Schooner.
    Cap: 14 Nov 1813 Delaware by Belvidera Int: 06 Dec 1813 Dis: 15 Apr 1814.
    Received from HMS Sceptre. HMS Ramillies for Halifax.

Herbert, John   Prisoner 2211. Rank: Seaman, from: President, U States Frigate.
    Cap: 15 Jan 1815 Not Recorded by Endymion Int: 30 Jan 1815 Dis: 28 Mar 1815.
    Received from Pomone. Mars Transport for U States.

Hernetha, F   Prisoner 2741. Rank: Seaman, from: Cataline, Not Recorded.
    Cap: 13 Jan 1815 St Marys by Dragon Int: 03 Mar 1815 Dis: 13 Mar 1815.
    Received from Hebrus. Merchant Service.

Hero, John   Prisoner 1566. Rank: Seaman, from: Bordeaux Packet, Letter of Marque.
    Cap: 28 Jan 1814 off Cape Henry by Nieman Int: 12 Feb 1814 Dis: 15 Apr 1814.
    Received from Nieman. Diana Transport for Halifax.

Hersey, Thomas   Prisoner 2152. Rank: Masters Mate, from: President, U States Frigate.
    Cap: 15 Jan 1815 Not Recorded by Endymion Int: 30 Jan 1815 Dis: 18 Mar 1815.
    Received from President. Merchant Vessel.

Heth, John   Prisoner 2145. Rank: Midshipman, from: President, U States Frigate.
    Cap: 15 Jan 1815 Not Recorded by Endymion Int: 30 Jan 1815 Dis: 18 Mar 1815.
    Received from President. Merchant Vessel.

Hewston, J   Prisoner 1448. Rank: Passenger, from: Betsey, Merchant Sloop.
    Cap: 15 Dec 1813 Lat 32 by Doterel Int: 25 Dec 1813 Dis: 21 Jan 1814.
    Received from Doterel. Without Exchange being a Noncombatant.

Heyle, Philip   Prisoner 2061. Rank: Supercargo, from: Mary, Merchant Schooner.
    Cap: 26 Nov 1814 off Cape Delaware by Telegraph Int: 11 Dec 1814 Dis: 21 Feb 1815.
    Received from HMS Goree. Paroled to U States order of Sir Alex Cockburn.

Hibbets, John   Prisoner 186. Rank: Seaman, from: Wasp, Sloop of War.
    Cap: 18 Oct 1812 at Sea by HMS Poictiers Int: 26 Oct 1812 Dis: 05 Nov 1812.
    Received from HM Ship Poictiers. Brig Diamond on Parole to new London America.

Hickman, George   Prisoner 2226. Rank: Seaman, from: President, U States Frigate.
    Cap: 15 Jan 1815 Not Recorded by Endymion Int: 30 Jan 1815 Dis: 28 Mar 1815.
    Received from Pomone. Mars Transport for U States.

Hicks, John   Prisoner 1520. Rank: Seaman, from: Lukey, Merchant Vessel.
    Cap: 19 Dec 1813 off the Delaware by Nieman Int: 22 Jan 1814 Dis: 15 Apr 1814.
    Received from Jaseur. Diana Transport for Halifax.

Hicks, Samuel   Prisoner 908. Rank: Seaman, from: Elizabeth, Merchant Brig.
    Cap: 26 Feb 1813 Chesapeake by HMS Marlborough Int: 23 Mar 1813 Dis: 24 Jun 1813.
    Received from HM Ship Laurustinus. Magnet Cartel for New York.

Higgenbottom, William   Prisoner 1549. Rank: Mate, from: Bordeaux Packet, Letter of Marque.
    Cap: 28 Jan 1814 off Cape Henry by Nieman Int: 12 Feb 1814 Dis: 15 Apr 1814.
    Received from Nieman. Rammilles for Halifax.

Higgins, Joseph   Prisoner 2014. Rank: Seaman, from: Bridges, Merchant Vessel.
    Cap: 25 Oct 1814 off Halifax by Armide Int: 07 Nov 1814 Dis: 28 Mar 1815.
    Recaptured. Received from HMS Armide. Clarendon Transport for U States.

American Prisoners of War Held at Bermuda During the War of 1812

Hight, Temple   Prisoner 2299. Rank: Quartermaster, from: President, U States Frigate.
  Cap: 15 Jan 1815 Not Recorded by Endymion Int: 04 Feb 1815 Dis: 28 Mar 1815.
  Received from Endymion. Mars Transport for U States.

Hilbert, Samuel   Prisoner 1034. Rank: Seaman, from: Dart, Merchant Schooner.
  Cap: 17 Mar 1813 off the Chesapeake by HMS Statira Int: 06 Apr 1813 Dis: 24 Jun 1813.
  Received from HMS Junon. Magnet Cartel for New York.

Hill, Hugh   Prisoner 2693. Rank: Seaman, from: Speed, Merchant Vessel.
  Cap: 19 Jan 1815 off Nantucket by Pylades Int: 17 Feb 1815 Dis: 28 Mar 1815.
  Received from Majestic. Clarendon Transport for U States.

Hill, Jeremiah   Prisoner 641. Rank: Mate, from: Dolphin, Merchant Brig.
  Cap: 30 Dec 1812 at Sea by HM Ship Galus Int: 17 Jan 1813 Dis: 27 Jan 1813.
  Received from HM Ship Galus. Bostock Cartel for New York.

Hill, John   Prisoner 1109. Rank: Seaman, from: Revenge, Privateer Brig.
  Cap: 25 May 1813 at Sea by Narcissus Int: 27 May 1813 Dis: 24 Jun 1813.
  Received from HM Ship San Domingo. Magnet Cartel for New York.

Hill, Joseph   Prisoner 2103. Rank: Seaman, from: Rufus King, Merchant Vessel.
  Cap: 01 Jan 1815 off Bermuda by Peruvian Int: 19 Jan 1815 Dis: 19 Mar 1815.
  Received from HMS Peruvian. Merchant Service.

Hill, Pompey   Prisoner 1373. Rank: Seaman, from: Rolla, Privateer.
  Cap: 10 Dec 1813 Block Island by Loire Int: 20 Dec 1813 Dis: 15 Apr 1814.
  Received from San Domingo. HMS Rammillies for Halifax.

Hill, Thomas   Prisoner 2337. Rank: Seaman, from: President, U States Frigate.
  Cap: 15 Jan 1815 Not Recorded by Endymion Int: 04 Feb 1815 Dis: 28 Mar 1815.
  Received from Endymion. Mars Transport for U States.

Hill, William   Prisoner 2547. Rank: Seaman, from: President, US Frigate.
  Cap: 15 Jan 1815 off N York by HMS Endymion Int: 05 Feb 1815 Dis: 28 Mar 1815.
  Received from President. Clarenden Transport for U States.

Hiller, George   Prisoner 2592. Rank: Seaman, from: Lark, Merchant Vessel.
  Cap: 01 Dec 1814 off New York by HM Ship Majestic Int: 05 Feb 1815 Dis: 28 Mar 1815.
  Recaptured. York Privateer. Received from HMS Forth. Clarendon Transport for U States.

Hiller, George   Prisoner 2875. Rank: Seaman, from: His Majesty's Ship Goree, Not Recorded.
  Cap: Not Recorded by Not Recorded Int: 29 Mar 1815 Dis: 28 Mar 1815.
  Received from Goree. an American Subject. Clarendon Transport for U States. (Date of capture not recorded. Date of discharge before date of internment.)

Hillman, Jonathan   Prisoner 2699. Rank: Master, from: Experiment, Merchant Vessel.
  Cap: 19 Jan 1815 off Block Island by Nimrod Int: 18 Feb 1815 Dis: 01 Mar 1815.
  Received from Nimrod. on Parole to the U States.

Hinley, Joseph   Prisoner 2003. Rank: Seaman, from: Dry Farbourn, Merchant Vessel.
  Cap: 21 Oct 1814 off Bermuda by Pandora Int: 27 Oct 1814 Dis: 16 Mar 1815.
  Dry Farborn. Recaptured. Received from Goree. Merchant Vessel.

Hippencott, Caleb   Prisoner 1691. Rank: Seaman, from: Lark, Merchant Vessel.
  Cap: 06 Apr 1814 L 29.0 by Recruit Int: 11 May 1814 Dis: 28 Mar 1815.
  Recaptured. Received from Recruit. Mars Transport for U States.

Hippeny, Anthony   Prisoner 1592. Rank: Seaman, from: Bordeaux Packet, Letter of Marque.
  Cap: 28 Jan 1814 off Cape Henry by Nieman Int: 12 Feb 1814 Dis: 23 Apr 1814.
  Received from Nieman. HMS Bulwark for Halifax.

Hitton, William   Prisoner 2562. Rank: Seaman, from: Funchall, Merchant Vessel.
  Cap: 15 Jan 1815 off New York by HMS Pomone Int: 05 Feb 1815 Dis: 25 Mar 1815.
  Received from HMS Forth. Merchant Vessel.

Hobey, John   Prisoner 2293. Rank: Seaman, from: President, U States Frigate.
  Cap: 15 Jan 1815 Not Recorded by Endymion Int: 04 Feb 1815 Dis: 28 Mar 1815.
  Received from Endymion. Mars Transport for U States.

Hodges, Gabriel   Prisoner 144. Rank: Mate, from: Factor of Salem, Merchant Brig.
  Cap: 30 Sep 1812 Lat 35, Long 65 W by HMS Tartarus Int: 13 Oct 1812 Dis: 24 Oct 1812.
  Received from HMS Tartarus. Brig Diamond on Parole to New London United States of America.

Hodges, Gamiel   Prisoner 1392. Rank: Captain, from: Scorpion, Merchant Vessel.
  Cap: 29 Nov 1813 Lat 39 by Loire Int: 21 Dec 1813 Dis: 15 Apr 1814.
  Received from Romulus. Rammilles for Halifax.

Hodgkin, Nathaniel   Prisoner 1824. Rank: Passenger, from: Not Recorded, Not Recorded.
  Cap: Not Recorded by Not Recorded Int: 14 Jun 1814 Dis: 15 Jun 1814.
  From St. Bartholomew in the Swedish Schooner Oscar. on Parole per Order Com in Chief to America. (Date of capture not recorded.)

American Prisoners of War Held at Bermuda During the War of 1812

Hoffman, Henry   Prisoner 2362. Rank: Cooper, from: President, U States Frigate.
    Cap: 15 Jan 1815 Not Recorded by HMS Endymion Int: 04 Feb 1815 Dis: 28 Mar 1815.
    Received from Endymion. Mars Transport for U States.

Hoffman, Ogden   Prisoner 2141. Rank: Midshipman, from: President, U States Frigate.
    Cap: 15 Jan 1815 Not Recorded by Endymion Int: 30 Jan 1815 Dis: 28 Mar 1815.
    Received from President. Mars Transport for U States.

Hogan, Norman A   Prisoner 1780. Rank: Gunner, from: Yankelass, Privateer.
    Cap: 01 May 1814 Latt 40-4N, Long 38-0W by Severn & Surprise Int: 07 Jun 1814 Dis: 21 Feb 1815.
    Received from Surprise. Paroled to the U States having served six months as Carpenter's Mate order of Adl Sir Alex Cockburn.

Holbrock, Richard   Prisoner 634. Rank: Seaman, from: Not Recorded, Not Recorded.
    Cap: Not Recorded by Not Recorded Int: 14 Jan 1813 Dis: 27 Jan 1813.
    Surrendered himself up as an American. Bostock Cartel for New York. (Date of capture not recorded.)

Holcomb, John C   Prisoner 176. Rank: Midshipman, from: Wasp, Sloop of War.
    Cap: 18 Oct 1812 at Sea by HMS Poictiers Int: 26 Oct 1812 Dis: 05 Nov 1812.
    Received from HM Ship Poictiers. on Parole Brig Diamond to new London America.

Holden, James   Prisoner 1313. Rank: Seaman, from: Rolla, Privateer.
    Cap: 10 Dec 1813 Block Island by Loire Int: 20 Dec 1813 Dis: 15 Apr 1814.
    Received from San Domingo. HMS Rammillies for Halifax.

Holder, Jeremiah   Prisoner 1124. Rank: Seaman, from: Mary, Merchant.
    Cap: 17 Apr 1813 at Sea by HM Ship Fox Int: 21 Jun 1813 Dis: 24 Jun 1813.
    Received from HMS Ruby. Magnet Cartel for New York.

Holding, Ebenezer   Prisoner 2598. Rank: Seaman, from: John, Merchant Vessel.
    Cap: 18 Dec 1814 off New York by HMS Pomone Int: 05 Feb 1815 Dis: 16 Mar 1815.
    Received from HMS Forth. Merchant Service.

Holesley, John   Prisoner 1214. Rank: Seaman, from: Portuguese Bark, Merchant.
    Cap: 19 Feb 1813 Cape Hatterus by San Domingo Int: 06 Nov 1813 Dis: 24 Apr 1814.
    Received from HMS Ruby. HMS Sceptre for England.

Holland, J H   Prisoner 1303. Rank: Prize Master, from: Rolla, Privateer.
    Cap: 10 Dec 1813 Block Island by Loire Int: 20 Dec 1813 Dis: 15 Apr 1814.
    Received from San Domingo. HMS Rammillies for Halifax.

Holland, John   Prisoner 1643. Rank: Seaman, from: Seaflower, Merchant Vessel.
    Cap: 13 Dec 1813 Chesapeake by Active Int: 28 Feb 1814 Dis: 23 Apr 1814.
    Received from Active. HMS Bulwark for Halifax.

Holland, Rons   Prisoner 500. Rank: Seaman, from: Ann, Merchant Sloop.
    Cap: 19 Dec 1812 at Sea by HMS Sophia Int: 27 Dec 1812 Dis: 27 Jan 1813.
    Received from Sophia. Bostock Cartel for New York.

Holland, William   Prisoner 2410. Rank: Seaman, from: President, U States Frigate.
    Cap: 15 Jan 1815 Not Recorded by HM Ship Endymion Int: 04 Feb 1815 Dis: 28 Mar 1815.
    Received from Endymion. Clarenden Transport for U States.

Hollingsworth, William   Prisoner 2727. Rank: Citizen, from: St Marys, Not Recorded.
    Cap: 18 Feb 1815 St Marys by Primrose Int: 03 Mar 1815 Dis: 28 Mar 1815.
    Received from Hebrus. Clarendon Transport for U States.

Hollins, George N   Prisoner 2147. Rank: Midshipman, from: President, U States Frigate.
    Cap: 15 Jan 1815 Not Recorded by Endymion Int: 30 Jan 1815 Dis: 24 Feb 1815.
    Received from President. United States for Exchange.

Holman, William   Prisoner 2035. Rank: Seaman, from: James, Merchant Vessel.
    Cap: 31 Oct 1814 off Charlestown by Schooner Whiting Int: 21 Nov 1814 Dis: 28 Mar 1815.
    Recaptured. Received from M Schooner Whiting. Clarendon Transport for U States.

Holmer, Robert   Prisoner 1972. Rank: Seaman, from: Carrol, Merchant Vessel.
    Cap: 21 Aug 1814 off Cape Henry by Fairy Int: 14 Sep 1814 Dis: 28 Mar 1815.
    Received from Goree. Clarendon Transport for U States.

Holmes, C K   Prisoner 561. Rank: Seaman, from: Rising Hope, Merchant Brig.
    Cap: 27 Dec 1812 at Sea by HM Sloop Wanderer Int: 05 Jan 1813 Dis: 27 Jan 1813.
    Received from HM Sloop Wanderer. Bostock Cartel for New York.

Holmes, Jahiel   Prisoner 480. Rank: Seaman, from: Teazer, Privateer Schooner.
    Cap: 16 Dec 1812 at Sea by HM Ship St. Domingo Int: 21 Dec 1812 Dis: 27 Jan 1813.
    Received from HM Ship St. Domingo. Bostock Cartel for New York.

Holmes, James   Prisoner 2503. Rank: Seaman, from: President, U States Frigate.
    Cap: 15 Jan 1815 Not Recorded by Endymion Int: 04 Feb 1815 Dis: 28 Mar 1815.
    Received from Endymion. Clarenden Transport for U States.

American Prisoners of War Held at Bermuda During the War of 1812

Holmes, John   Prisoner 1513. Rank: Seaman, from: Nonsuch, Letter of Marque.
    Cap: 14 Dec 1813 Latt 38.0 by Doterel Int: 22 Jan 1814 Dis: 15 Apr 1814.
    Received from Surprize. Diana for Halifax.

Holshem, Andrew   Prisoner 1095. Rank: Seaman, from: Langdon Cheves, Merchant.
    Cap: 12 May 1813 at Sea by HM Sloop Atalante Int: 25 May 1813 Dis: 24 Jun 1813.
    Received from HMS Atalante. Magnet Cartel for New York.

Holt, William   Prisoner 1013. Rank: Mate, from: Nautalus, Merchant.
    Cap: 20 Mar 1813 off the Chesapeake by HM Ship Rammillies Int: 06 Apr 1813 Dis: 24 Jun 1813.
    Received from HMS Junon. Magnet Cartel for New York.

Homan, John   Prisoner 2018. Rank: Seaman, from: Bridges, Merchant Vessel.
    Cap: 25 Oct 1814 off Halifax by Armide Int: 07 Nov 1814 Dis: 28 Mar 1815.
    Recaptured. Received from HMS Armide. Clarendon Transport for U States.

Homan, Peter   Prisoner 1504. Rank: Mate, from: Jackall, Merchant Vessel.
    Cap: 23 Dec 1813 off the Delaware by Belvidera Int: 18 Jan 1814 Dis: 15 Apr 1814.
    Received from Belvidera. HMS Rammillies for Halifax.

Honest, John   Prisoner 932. Rank: Seaman, from: Ulissus, Merchant Schooner.
    Cap: 03 Mar 1813 Chesapeake by HMS Narcissus Int: 23 Mar 1813 Dis: 24 Jun 1813.
    Received from Laurustinus. Magnet Cartel for New York.

Honquest, Peter   Prisoner 1479. Rank: Seaman, from: Luckey, Merchant Vessel.
    Cap: 19 Dec 1813 off the Delaware by Niemen Int: 07 Jan 1814 Dis: 08 Mar 1814.
    Received from HM Sloop Jaseur. Being a Swede per order of Commander in Chief. (Name of capturing ship not legible, assume to be Nieman.)

Hooper, John   Prisoner 599. Rank: Pay Master, from: Windward Planter, Merchant Sloop.
    Cap: 22 Dec 1812 at Sea by HM Ship Belvidera Int: 10 Jan 1813 Dis: 27 Jan 1813.
    Received from HMS Belvidera. Bostock Cartel for New York.

Hooper, John   Prisoner 1675. Rank: Prize Master, from: Martha, Merchant Vessel.
    Cap: 26 Feb 1814 at Sea by Belvidera Int: 18 Mar 1814 Dis: 15 Apr 1814.
    Recaptured. Received from Belvidera. Rammilles for Halifax.

Hooper, Thomas   Prisoner 1542. Rank: Seaman, from: Defiance, Merchant Vessel.
    Cap: 05 Jan 1814 at Sea by Childers Int: 26 Jan 1814 Dis: 15 Apr 1814.
    Received from Childers. Diana for Halifax.

Hopkins, M H   Prisoner 1319. Rank: Seaman, from: Rolla, Privateer.
    Cap: 10 Dec 1813 Block Island by Loire Int: 20 Dec 1813 Escaped: 24 Nov 1814.
    Received from San Domingo. Run.

Hopkins, Samuel   Prisoner 1230. Rank: Not Recorded, from: HM Ship Cleopatra, Not Recorded.
    Cap: 21 Sep 1813 Not Recorded by Dragon Int: 16 Nov 1813 Dis: 15 Apr 1814.
    Received from HMS Sceptre. Surrendered himself. Diana Transport for Halifax.

Hopkins, Stephen   Prisoner 2733. Rank: Mate, from: Matilda, Not Recorded.
    Cap: 01 Dec 1814 Chesapeake by Dragon Int: 03 Mar 1815 Dis: 28 Mar 1815.
    Received from Hebrus. Clarendon Transport for U States.

Horley, John   Prisoner 2384. Rank: Seaman, from: President, U States Frigate.
    Cap: 15 Jan 1815 Not Recorded by HMS Endymion Int: 04 Feb 1815 Dis: 28 Mar 1815.
    Received from Endymion. Mars Transport for U States.

Horsey, William   Prisoner 325. Rank: Seaman, from: James, Merchant Ship.
    Cap: 03 Nov 1812 at Sea by HM Ship Tartarus Int: 17 Nov 1812 Dis: 27 Jan 1813.
    Received from HM Ship Tartarus. Bostock Cartel for New York.

Horton, J H   Prisoner 2772. Rank: Prize Master, from: Hope, Not Recorded.
    Cap: 21 Feb 1815 St Augustine by Hebrus Int: 03 Mar 1815 Dis: 28 Mar 1815.
    Received from Hebrus. Clarendon Transport for U States.

Hoskin, Cato   Prisoner 1352. Rank: Seaman, from: Rolla, Privateer.
    Cap: 10 Dec 1813 Block Island by Loire Int: 20 Dec 1813 Dis: 15 Apr 1814.
    Received from San Domingo. HMS Rammillies for Halifax.

Hossday, William   Prisoner 1375. Rank: Seaman, from: Rolla, Privateer.
    Cap: 10 Dec 1813 Block Island by Loire Int: 20 Dec 1813 Dis: 15 Apr 1814.
    Received from San Domingo. HMS Rammillies for Halifax.

Hoswell, James   Prisoner 358. Rank: Seaman, from: Snapper, Privateer Schooner.
    Cap: 16 Nov 1812 at Sea by HM Ship Galus Int: 22 Nov 1812 Dis: 27 Jan 1813.
    Received from HM Ship Galus. Bostock Cartel for New York.

Houlval, John   Prisoner 321. Rank: Seaman, from: James, Merchant Ship.
    Cap: 03 Nov 1812 at Sea by HM Ship Tartarus Int: 17 Nov 1812 Dis: 27 Jan 1813.
    Received from HM Ship Tartarus. Bostock Cartel for New York.

American Prisoners of War Held at Bermuda During the War of 1812

Houton, William Prisoner 2102. Rank: Seaman, from: Rufus King, Merchant Vessel.
    Cap: 01 Jan 1815 off Bermuda by Peruvian Int: 19 Jan 1815 Dis: 28 Mar 1815.
    Received from HMS Peruvian. Clarendon Transport for U States.

Howard, Benjamin Prisoner 1668. Rank: 1 Lieutenant, from: Fieri Facias, Privateer.
    Cap: 26 Feb 1814 at Sea by Ramilies Int: 18 Mar 1814 Dis: 24 Apr 1814.
    Received from Ramilies. HMS Sceptre for England.

Howard, Eliah Prisoner 2754. Rank: Passenger, from: Speedwell, Not Recorded.
    Cap: 21 Jan 1815 St Augustine by Severn Int: 03 Mar 1815 Dis: 17 Mar 1815.
    Received from Hebrus. Merchant Vessel.

Howard, Henry Prisoner 2111. Rank: Seaman, from: Rufus King, Merchant Vessel.
    Cap: 01 Jan 1815 off Bermuda by Peruvian Int: 19 Jan 1815 Dis: 20 Jan 1815.
    Received from HMS Peruvian. HMS Ardent gave himself up as a British Subject.

Howard, William Prisoner 977. Rank: Seaman, from: Betsy Ann, Merchant.
    Cap: 04 Mar 1813 Chesapeake by HM Ship Fantom Int: 23 Mar 1813 Dis: 19 May 1813.
    Received from HM Ship Laurustinus. United States to Effect their Exchange per Order Commd Evans.

Howe, Edward Prisoner 1677. Rank: Master, from: Argus, Letter of Marque.
    Cap: 01 Mar 1814 off Bermuda by San Domingo Int: 04 Apr 1814 Dis: 15 Apr 1814.
    Received from San Domingo. admitted to Parole. Rammilles for Halifax.

Howell, William Prisoner 2078. Rank: Seaman, from: Banyer, Letter of Marque.
    Cap: 03 Dec 1814 coast of America by HMS Severn Int: 04 Jan 1815 Dis: 28 Mar 1815.
    Subject was of America. Received from HMS Goree. Clarendon Transport for U States.

Howes, George Prisoner 1708. Rank: Seaman, from: Grecian, Letter of Marque.
    Cap: 02 May 1814 Chesapeake by Jansur Int: 26 May 1814 Dis: 28 Mar 1815.
    Received from Lacedaemonian. Mars Transport for U States.

Howland, John Prisoner 1062. Rank: Seaman, from: Amason, Merchant.
    Cap: 18 Mar 1813 Chesapeake by HM Ship Victorious Int: 06 Apr 1813 Dis: 24 Jun 1813.
    Received from HMS Junon. Magnet Cartel for New York.

Howland, Robert Prisoner 1613. Rank: Seaman, from: Brookhaven, Merchant Vessel.
    Cap: 09 Dec 1813 Block Island by Albion Int: 14 Feb 1814 Escaped: 24 Nov 1814.
    Received from Sceptre. Run.

Howlen, Barney Prisoner 2480. Rank: Seaman, from: President, U States Frigate.
    Cap: 15 Jan 1815 Not Recorded by Endymion Int: 04 Feb 1815 Dis: 28 Mar 1815.
    Received from Endymion. Clarenden Transport for U States.

Hoxon, Richard Prisoner 2804. Rank: Seaman, from: Limerick, Not Recorded.
    Cap: 04 Mar 1815 Not Recorded by Asia Int: 25 Mar 1815 Dis:
    From Depot at Jamaica. Received from Asia. (Date of discharge not recorded.)

Hoyt, James M Prisoner 28. Rank: Seaman, from: Survanou, Merchant.
    Cap: 14 Jul 1812 at Bermuda by Recruit Int: 28 Aug 1812 Dis: 18 Sep 1812.
    Received from HM Schooner Cuttle. Order of Commd Evans for England.

Hozier, Samuel Prisoner 955. Rank: Seaman, from: Bona, Letter of Marque Schooner.
    Cap: 12 Mar 1813 Chesapeake by Laurustinus Int: 23 Mar 1813 Dis: 24 Jun 1813.
    Received from Laurustinus. Magnet Cartel for New York.

Hubbard, Jeremiah Prisoner 1828. Rank: Passenger, from: Not Recorded, Not Recorded.
    Cap: Not Recorded by Not Recorded Int: 14 Jun 1814 Dis: 15 Jun 1814.
    From St. Bartholomew in the Swedish Schooner Oscar. on Parole per Order Com in Chief to America. (Date of capture not recorded.)

Hubbard, John Prisoner 611. Rank: Seaman, from: Noetoin, Packet Brig.
    Cap: 05 Jan 1813 at Sea by HMS Belvidera Int: 10 Jan 1813 Dis: 27 Jan 1813.
    Received from HMS Belvidera. Bostock Cartel for New York.

Hubbard, Peter Prisoner 461. Rank: 2 Master, from: Teazer, Privateer Schooner.
    Cap: 16 Dec 1812 at Sea by HM Ship St. Domingo Int: 21 Dec 1812 Dis: 27 Jan 1813.
    Received from HM Ship St. Domingo. Bostock Cartel for New York.

Huckstep, Barnard Prisoner 654. Rank: Seaman, from: Not Recorded, Not Recorded.
    Cap: Not Recorded by Not Recorded Int: 21 Jan 1813 Dis: 27 Jan 1813.
    Received from HMS Ruby. Surrendered them selves as Prisoners of War. Bostock Cartel for New York.

Hughes, John Prisoner 2221. Rank: Seaman, from: President, U States Frigate.
    Cap: 15 Jan 1815 Not Recorded by Endymion Int: 30 Jan 1815 Dis: 28 Mar 1815.
    Received from Pomone. Mars Transport for U States.

Hughes, William Prisoner 1444. Rank: Seaman, from: Nonsuch, Letter of Marque.
    Cap: 14 Dec 1813 Lat 32 by Doterel Int: 25 Dec 1813 Dis: 15 Apr 1814.
    Received from HM Brig Doterel. Diana Transport for Halifax.

American Prisoners of War Held at Bermuda During the War of 1812

Hulitz, Joseph   Prisoner 852. Rank: Master, from: Huckimer, Merchant Schooner.
    Cap: 18 Jan 1813 at Sea by HMS St. Domingo   Int: 20 Mar 1813   Dis: 20 Mar 1813.
    Received from San Domingo. Savannah Packet for New York per Order Adl Sir J B Warren.

Hull, Henry   Prisoner 412. Rank: Supercargo, from: Isabella, Merchant Brig.
    Cap: 15 Nov 1812 at Sea by HM Sloop Childers   Int: 24 Nov 1812   Dis: 05 Feb 1813.
    Received from HM Ship Childers. Permitted to Return to New York per Order Adl Cockburn.

Hull, Peter   Prisoner 2228. Rank: Seaman, from: President, U States Frigate.
    Cap: 15 Jan 1815 Not Recorded by Endymion   Int: 30 Jan 1815   Dis: 28 Mar 1815.
    Received from Pomone. Clarenden Transport for U States.

Hulland, Nathaniel   Prisoner 216. Rank: Seaman, from: Wasp, Sloop of War.
    Cap: 18 Oct 1812 at Sea by HM Ship Poictiers   Int: 26 Oct 1812   Dis: 05 Nov 1812.
    Received from HM Ship Poictiers. Brig Diamond on Parole to new London United States of America.

Hulton, John   Prisoner 2739. Rank: Seaman, from: Not Recorded, Not Recorded.
    Cap: 13 Jan 1815 St Marys by Dragon   Int: 03 Mar 1815   Dis: 13 Mar 1815.
    by Kings Troops. Received from Hebrus. Merchant Service.

Humphrey, James   Prisoner 485. Rank: Seaman, from: Teazer, Privateer Schooner.
    Cap: 16 Dec 1812 at Sea by HM Ship St. Domingo   Int: 21 Dec 1812   Dis: 27 Jan 1813.
    Received from HM Ship St. Domingo. Bostock Cartel for New York.

Humphries, Horiatio   Prisoner 1650. Rank: Seaman, from: Atalanta, Merchant Vessel.
    Cap: 22 Dec 1813 Chesapeake by Dragon   Int: 28 Feb 1814   Dis: 23 Apr 1814.
    Received from Active. HMS Bulwark for Halifax.

Humphries, Thomas   Prisoner 1474. Rank: Master, from: Republican, Merchant Schooner.
    Cap: 06 Dec 1813 Cape Charles by Dragon   Int: 06 Jan 1814   Dis: 15 Apr 1814.
    Received from HM Ship Plantagenet. Rammilles for Halifax.

Humpson, John   Prisoner 1482. Rank: Seaman, from: Luckey, Merchant Vessel.
    Cap: 19 Dec 1813 off the Delaware by Niemen   Int: 07 Jan 1814   Dis: 15 Apr 1814.
    Received from HM Sloop Jaseur. Diana Transport for Halifax. (Name of capturing ship not legible, assume to be Nieman.)

Hunt, Dudley   Prisoner 89. Rank: Seaman, from: Gossepuim, Merchant.
    Cap: 16 Aug 1812 of Bermuda by Goree   Int: 28 Aug 1812   Dis: 18 Sep 1812.
    Received from HM Schooner Cuttle. Order of Commd Evans for England.

Hunt, Edward P   Prisoner 1041. Rank: Passenger, from: Revinue, Merchant Sloop.
    Cap: 19 Mar 1813 off the Chesapeake by HMS Statira   Int: 06 Apr 1813   Dis: 13 Jun 1813.
    Received from HMS Junon. Perseverance Cartel for the United States per Order Adml Sir J B Warren.

Hunt, Isaac A   Prisoner 1730. Rank: Seaman, from: Yankelass, Privateer.
    Cap: 01 May 1814 L 10-4N, L 33-0W by Severn & Surprise   Int: 06 Jun 1814   Dis: 27 Mar 1815.
    Received from Severn. Merchant Vessel.

Hunt, Thomas   Prisoner 2023. Rank: Seaman, from: Swiftsure, Merchant Vessel.
    Cap: 26 Oct 1814 off Halifax by Armide   Int: 07 Nov 1814   Dis: 28 Mar 1815.
    Recaptured. Received from HMS Armide. Clarendon Transport for U States.

Hunter, Samuel   Prisoner 1490. Rank: Mate, from: Maresoil, Merchant Brig.
    Cap: 25 Dec 1813 Latt 35.0 by HMS Fox   Int: 09 Jan 1814   Dis: 15 Apr 1814.
    Received from Fox. Order Com in Chief.

Hunter, William   Prisoner 2472. Rank: Seaman, from: President, U States Frigate.
    Cap: 15 Jan 1815 Not Recorded by Endymion   Int: 04 Feb 1815   Dis: 28 Mar 1815.
    Received from Endymion. Clarenden Transport for U States.

Huntington, E   Prisoner 1372. Rank: Seaman, from: Rolla, Privateer.
    Cap: 10 Dec 1813 Block Island by Loire   Int: 20 Dec 1813   Dis: 15 Apr 1814.
    Received from San Domingo. HMS Rammillies for Halifax.

Huntington, John   Prisoner 1856. Rank: Mate, from: Isa Colly, Merchant Vessel.
    Cap: Not Recorded by Not Recorded   Int: Dis: 04 Sep 1814.
    to join these Proper Ships having been delivered up Order Comm Evans. (Dates of capture and internment not recorded.)

Hupper, Samuel   Prisoner 2501. Rank: Seaman, from: President, U States Frigate.
    Cap: 15 Jan 1815 Not Recorded by Endymion   Int: 04 Feb 1815   Dis: 28 Mar 1815.
    Received from Endymion. Clarenden Transport for U States.

Huring, William   Prisoner 1722. Rank: 2 Mate, from: Grecian, Letter of Marque.
    Cap: 02 May 1814 Chesapeake by Jansur   Int: 26 May 1814   Dis:
    Received from Lacedaemonian. (Date of discharge not recorded.)

Hurth, Charles   Prisoner 1033. Rank: Seaman, from: Dart, Merchant Schooner.
    Cap: 17 Mar 1813 off the Chesapeake by HMS Statira   Int: 06 Apr 1813   Dis: 24 Jun 1813.
    Received from HMS Junon. Magnet Cartel for New York.

American Prisoners of War Held at Bermuda During the War of 1812

Hussey, R   Prisoner 1515. Rank: 1 Mate, from: Mary Ann, Merchant Vessel.
    Cap: 26 Dec 1813 Chesapeake by Sophie Int: 22 Jan 1814 Dis: 15 Apr 1814.
    Received from Surprize. Rammilles for Halifax.

Hussey, Robert   Prisoner 2695. Rank: Seaman, from: Speed, Merchant Vessel.
    Cap: 19 Jan 1815 off Nantucket by Pylades Int: 17 Feb 1815 Dis: 28 Mar 1815.
    Received from Majestic. Clarendon Transport for U States.

Hutchinson, John   Prisoner 1045. Rank: Seaman, from: General Knox, Merchant.
    Cap: 18 Mar 1813 off the Chesapeake by HM Ship Victorious Int: 06 Apr 1813 Dis:
    Received from HMS Junon. (Date of discharge not on roster.)

Hutchinson, Joseph   Prisoner 109. Rank: Captain, from: Gossepuim, detained American.
    Cap: 02 Sep 1812 Bermuda by Not Recorded Int: 02 Sep 1812 Dis: 06 Sep 1812.
    Received from HMS Ruby. detained per order of the President. Sloop Sally for New York.

Hutchison, Henry   Prisoner 560. Rank: Seaman, from: Rising Hope, Merchant Brig.
    Cap: 27 Dec 1812 at Sea by HM Sloop Wanderer Int: 05 Jan 1813 Dis: 27 Jan 1813.
    Received from HM Sloop Wanderer. Bostock Cartel for New York.

Hutson, James   Prisoner 597. Rank: Seaman, from: Windward Planter, Merchant Sloop.
    Cap: 22 Dec 1812 at Sea by HM Ship Belvidera Int: 10 Jan 1813 Dis: 27 Jan 1813.
    Received from HMS Belvidera. Bostock Cartel for New York.

Huver, John   Prisoner 478. Rank: Seaman, from: Teazer, Privateer Schooner.
    Cap: 16 Dec 1812 at Sea by HM Ship St. Domingo Int: 21 Dec 1812 Dis: 27 Jan 1813.
    Received from HM Ship St. Domingo. Bostock Cartel for New York.

Hyatt, Abel   Prisoner 2026. Rank: Seaman, from: Swiftsure, Merchant Vessel.
    Cap: 26 Oct 1814 off Halifax by Armide Int: 07 Nov 1814 Dis: 18 Mar 1815.
    Recaptured. Received from HMS Armide. Merchant Service.

Hyler, Adam   Prisoner 2538. Rank: Marine, from: President, U States Frigate.
    Cap: 15 Jan 1815 Not Recorded by HM Ship Endymion Int: 04 Feb 1815 Dis: 28 Mar 1815.
    Received from HMS Endymion. Clarenden Transport for U States.

Ingersole, James   Prisoner 1282. Rank: Seaman, from: Perry, Merchant Schooner.
    Cap: 03 Dec 1813 Long Island by Indemyion Int: 19 Dec 1813 Dis: 15 Apr 1814.
    Received from Sceptre. Diana Transport for Halifax.

Ingle, George   Prisoner 909. Rank: Seaman, from: Elizabeth, Merchant Brig.
    Cap: 26 Feb 1813 Chesapeake by HMS Marlborough Int: 23 Mar 1813 Dis: 24 Jun 1813.
    Received from HM Ship Laurustinus. Magnet Cartel for New York.

Ingram, George   Prisoner 1501. Rank: Seaman, from: Yankee, Merchant Sloop.
    Cap: 16 Dec 1813 Latt by Poictiers Int: 17 Jan 1814 Dis: 15 Apr 1814.
    Received from Poictiers. Diana Transport for Halifax. (Latitude number not recorded.)

Ingram, Henry   Prisoner 23. Rank: Seaman, from: Hero, Merchant Schooner.
    Cap: 14 Jul 1812 at Bermuda by Cuttle Int: 28 Aug 1812 Dis: 10 Sep 1812.
    Received from HM Schooner Cuttle. Ruby an Englishman.

Ingram, William   Prisoner 33. Rank: Captain, from: Laura, Merchant Sloop.
    Cap: 24 Jul 1812 of Bermuda by Cuttle Int: 28 Aug 1812 Dis: 10 Sep 1812.
    Received from HM Schooner Cuttle. Schooner Hero for N Y.

Ingream, John   Prisoner 730. Rank: Seaman, from: High Flyer, Privateer.
    Cap: 09 Jan 1813 at Sea by HM Ship Acasta Int: 21 Jan 1813 Dis: 27 Jan 1813.
    Received from HMS Acasta. Bostock Cartel for New York.

Innis, Benjamin   Prisoner 881. Rank: Seaman, from: George, Merchant Sloop.
    Cap: 05 Feb 1813 Chesapeake by HM Ship Dragon Int: 23 Mar 1813 Dis: 13 Jun 1813.
    Received from Laurustinus. Perseverance Cartel for the United States per Order Adml Sir J B Warren.

Innis, William   Prisoner 879. Rank: Master, from: George, Merchant Sloop.
    Cap: 05 Feb 1813 Chesapeake by HM Ship Dragon Int: 23 Mar 1813 Dis: 24 Jun 1813.
    Received from Laurustinus. Magnet Cartel for New York.

Ireland, Jacob   Prisoner 559. Rank: Seaman, from: Rising Hope, Merchant Brig.
    Cap: 27 Dec 1812 at Sea by HM Sloop Wanderer Int: 05 Jan 1813 Dis: 27 Jan 1813.
    Received from HM Sloop Wanderer. Bostock Cartel for New York.

Irvin, Charles   Prisoner 2751. Rank: Master, from: Speedwell, Not Recorded.
    Cap: 21 Jan 1815 St Augustine by Severn Int: 03 Mar 1815 Dis: 16 Mar 1815.
    Received from Hebrus. Merchant Service.

Iverson, Peter   Prisoner 2666. Rank: Seaman, from: President, U States Frigate.
    Cap: 15 Jan 1815 off New York by Endymion Int: 14 Feb 1815 Dis: 28 Mar 1815.
    Received from Goree. Clarenden Transport for U States.

Ives, John   Prisoner 2706. Rank: Seaman, from: South Boston, Merchant Vessel.
    Cap: 13 Feb 1815 off Charleston by Pandora Int: 02 Mar 1815 Dis: 16 Mar 1815.
    Received from Pandora. Merchant Service.

American Prisoners of War Held at Bermuda During the War of 1812

Jackay, Joseph   Prisoner 1460. Rank: Seaman, from: Vixen, Man of War.
    Cap: 25 Dec 1813 Lat 38.0 by Belvidera   Int: 05 Jan 1814   Dis: 07 Apr 1814.
    U States Schooner. Received from HMS Belvidera. being a Portugee.

Jackman, Benjamin   Prisoner 2431. Rank: Captain Marines, from: President, U States Frigate.
    Cap: 15 Jan 1815 Not Recorded by HM Ship Endymion   Int: 04 Feb 1815   Dis: 28 Mar 1815.
    Received from Endymion. Clarenden Transport for U States.

Jackson, Benjamin   Prisoner 2850. Rank: Seaman, from: Limerick, Not Recorded.
    Cap: 15 Mar 1815 Not Recorded by Asia   Int: 25 Mar 1815   Dis:
    From Depot at Jamaica. Received from Asia. (Date of discharge not recorded.)

Jackson, George   Prisoner 247. Rank: Gunner, from: Wasp, Sloop of War.
    Cap: 18 Oct 1812 at Sea by HM Ship Poictiers   Int: 26 Oct 1812   Dis: 05 Nov 1812.
    Received from HM Ship Poictiers. Brig Diamond on Parole to new London United States of America.

Jackson, John   Prisoner 241. Rank: Seaman, from: Wasp, Sloop of War.
    Cap: 18 Oct 1812 at Sea by HM Ship Poictiers   Int: 26 Oct 1812   Dis: 05 Nov 1812.
    Received from HM Ship Poictiers. Brig Diamond on Parole to new London United States of America.

Jackson, John   Prisoner 2090. Rank: Masters Mate, from: Gunboat 160, U States Man of War.
    Cap: 05 Oct 1814 coast of America by Lacedaemonian   Int: 19 Jan 1815   Dis: 28 Mar 1815.
    Received from HMS Peruvian. Clarendon Transport for U States.

Jackson, Lewis   Prisoner 1777. Rank: Seaman, from: Yankelass, Privateer.
    Cap: 01 May 1814 Latt 40-4N, Long 38-0W by Severn & Surprise   Int: 07 Jun 1814   Dis: 28 Mar 1815.
    Received from Surprise. Mars Transport for U States.

Jackson, M   Prisoner 937. Rank: Seaman, from: Sidney, Letter of Marque Schooner.
    Cap: 09 Mar 1813 Chesapeake by Marlborough   Int: 23 Mar 1813   Dis: 24 Jun 1813.
    Received from Laurustinus. Magnet Cartel for New York.

Jackson, William   Prisoner 1518. Rank: Seaman, from: Hollowell, Merchant Vessel.
    Cap: 13 Dec 1813 St. Georges Banks by Nieman   Int: 22 Jan 1814   Dis: 15 Apr 1814.
    Received from Surprize. Diana Transport for Halifax.

Jackson, William   Prisoner 1954. Rank: Seaman, from: Pike, Privateer.
    Cap: 25 Aug 1814 off Savannah by Primrose   Int: 09 Sep 1814   Dis: 13 Feb 1815.
    Received from Lacedaemonian. Bridges Transport.

Jackson, William   Prisoner 2130. Rank: Seaman, from: New York, Merchant Vessel.
    Cap: 09 Jan 1815 off Delaware by Dispatch   Int: 27 Jan 1815   Dis: 28 Mar 1815.
    Received from Pictolus. Clarendon Transport for U States.

Jackson, William   Prisoner 2742. Rank: Seaman, from: Aroof, Not Recorded.
    Cap: 16 Jan 1815 St Augustine by Manly   Int: 03 Mar 1815   Dis: 28 Mar 1815.
    Received from Hebrus. Clarendon Transport for U States.

Jacobs, Cupid   Prisoner 1693. Rank: Seaman, from: Lark, Merchant Vessel.
    Cap: 06 Apr 1814 L 29.0 by Recruit   Int: 11 May 1814   Dis: 28 Mar 1815.
    Recaptured. Received from Recruit. Mars Transport for U States.

Jacobs, David   Prisoner 2507. Rank: Seaman, from: President, U States Frigate.
    Cap: 15 Jan 1815 Not Recorded by Endymion   Int: 04 Feb 1815   Dis: 28 Mar 1815.
    Received from Endymion. Clarenden Transport for U States.

Jacobs, Francis   Prisoner 622. Rank: Seaman, from: Enterprize, Merchant Schooner.
    Cap: 15 Dec 1812 at Sea by HMS Tartant   Int: 12 Jan 1813   Dis: 27 Jan 1813.
    Received from Schooner Enterprize. Bostock Cartel for New York.

Jacobs, Peter   Prisoner 2849. Rank: Seaman, from: Limerick, Not Recorded.
    Cap: 15 Mar 1815 Not Recorded by Asia   Int: 25 Mar 1815   Dis:
    From Depot at Jamaica. Received from Asia. (Date of discharge not recorded.)

Jacobs, Samuel   Prisoner 1200. Rank: Seaman, from: Mary, Merchant Ship.
    Cap: 30 Jul 1813 at Sea by HM Sloop Nimrod   Int: 05 Sep 1813   Dis: 12 Sep 1813.
    Recaptured Sloop. Received from HM Sloop Nimrod. Per Order of Commodore Evans to the American Ship Georgiana restored.

Jacobs, William   Prisoner 56. Rank: Seaman, from: Ariel, Merchant Brig.
    Cap: 28 Jul 1812 of Bermuda by Recruit   Int: 28 Aug 1812   Dis: 03 Sep 1812.
    Received from M Schooner Cuttle. Hospital not Victualled until the 5th September.

Jacobs, William   Prisoner 138. Rank: Seaman, from: Ariel, Merchant Brig.
    Cap: 28 Jul 1812 off Bermuda by HMS Recurit   Int: 11 Oct 1812   Dis:
    Received from Hospital. (Date of discharge not on roster.)

Jaimeson, John   Prisoner 195. Rank: Seaman, from: Wasp, Sloop of War.
    Cap: 18 Oct 1812 at Sea by HMS Poictiers   Int: 26 Oct 1812   Dis: 05 Nov 1812.
    Received from HM Ship Poictiers. Brig Diamond on Parole to new London America.
    John Jaimeson (1st).

American Prisoners of War Held at Bermuda During the War of 1812

Jaimeson, John   Prisoner 218. Rank: Seaman, from: Wasp, Sloop of War.
    Cap: 18 Oct 1812 at Sea by HM Ship Poictiers Int: 26 Oct 1812 Dis: 05 Nov 1812.
    Received from HM Ship Poictiers. Brig Diamond on Parole to new London United States of America. John Jaimeson (2).

James, Benjamin   Prisoner 1217. Rank: Seaman, from: HM Sloop Sappho, Not Recorded.
    Cap: 04 Mar 1813 Not Recorded by Not Recorded Int: 06 Nov 1813 Dis: 15 Apr 1814.
    Received from HMS Ruby. HMS Rammillies Halifax.

James, Charles   Prisoner 2106. Rank: Seaman, from: Rufus King, Merchant Vessel.
    Cap: 01 Jan 1815 off Bermuda by Peruvian Int: 19 Jan 1815 Dis: 28 Mar 1815.
    Received from HMS Peruvian. Clarendon Transport for U States.

James, John   Prisoner 82. Rank: Mate, from: Ariel, Merchant Brig.
    Cap: 13 Aug 1812 of Bermuda by Goree Int: 28 Aug 1812 Dis: 10 Sep 1812.
    Received from HM Schooner Cuttle. Schooner Hero for New York.

James, John   Prisoner 1419. Rank: Seaman, from: Nonsuch, Letter of Marque.
    Cap: 14 Dec 1813 Lat 32 by Doterel Int: 25 Dec 1813 Dis: 15 Apr 1814.
    Received from HM Brig Doterel. Diana Transport for Halifax.

James, John   Prisoner 1636. Rank: Seaman, from: Not Recorded, Not Recorded.
    Cap: 05 Feb 1814 Not Recorded by Sceptre Int: 14 Feb 1814 Dis: 15 Apr 1814.
    Received from Sceptre. Rammilles for Halifax.

James, John   Prisoner 2437. Rank: Marine, from: President, U States Frigate.
    Cap: 15 Jan 1815 Not Recorded by Endymion Int: 04 Feb 1815 Dis: 28 Mar 1815.
    Received from Endymion. Clarenden Transport for U States.

James, Reuben   Prisoner 2352. Rank: 2 Gunner, from: President, U States Frigate.
    Cap: 15 Jan 1815 Not Recorded by HMS Endymion Int: 04 Feb 1815 Dis: 28 Mar 1815.
    Received from Endymion. Mars Transport for U States.

James, Sidney   Prisoner 1631. Rank: Seaman, from: Dove, Merchant Vessel.
    Cap: 04 Jan 1814 Block Island by Albion Int: 14 Feb 1814 Dis: 15 Apr 1814.
    Received from Sceptre. Diana Transport for Halifax.

Jarey, John   Prisoner 708. Rank: Seaman, from: High Flyer, Privateer.
    Cap: 09 Jan 1813 at Sea by HMS Acasta Int: 21 Jan 1813 Dis: 27 Jan 1813.
    Received from HMS Acasta. Bostock Cartel for New York.

Javar, William   Prisoner 223. Rank: Seaman, from: Wasp, Sloop of War.
    Cap: 18 Oct 1812 at Sea by HM Ship Poictiers Int: 26 Oct 1812 Dis: 05 Nov 1812.
    Received from HM Ship Poictiers. Brig Diamond on Parole to new London United States of America.

Jay, Bennet   Prisoner 2406. Rank: Seaman, from: President, U States Frigate.
    Cap: 15 Jan 1815 Not Recorded by HM Ship Endymion Int: 04 Feb 1815 Dis: 28 Mar 1815.
    Received from Endymion. Mars Transport for U States.

Jefferson, Isaac   Prisoner 1043. Rank: Seaman, from: General Knox, Merchant.
    Cap: 18 Mar 1813 off the Chesapeake by HM Ship Victorious Int: 06 Apr 1813 Dis:
    Received from HMS Junon. (Date of discharge not on roster.)

Jefferson, Jacob   Prisoner 1554. Rank: Seaman, from: Bordeaux Packet, Letter of Marque.
    Cap: 28 Jan 1814 off Cape Henry by Nieman Int: 12 Feb 1814 Dis: 15 Apr 1814.
    Received from Nieman. Diana Transport for Halifax.

Jeffery, Samuel   Prisoner 372. Rank: Seaman, from: Snapper, Privateer Schooner.
    Cap: 16 Nov 1812 at Sea by HM Ship Galus Int: 22 Nov 1812 Dis: 27 Jan 1813.
    Received from HM Ship Galus. Bostock Cartel for New York.

Jeffreys, Phillip   Prisoner 99. Rank: detained American, from: Gossepuim, Merchant.
    Cap: 16 Aug 1812 of Bermuda by Not Recorded Int: 31 Aug 1812 Dis: 18 Sep 1812.
    Received from HMS Ruby. detained per order of the Commodore. Order of Commd Evans for England.

Jehoff, John   Prisoner 812. Rank: Seaman, from: Elouisa, Merchant Schooner.
    Cap: 16 Feb 1813 at Sea by Morgiana Int: 25 Feb 1813 Dis: 14 Jun 1813.
    Received from HMS Morgiana. Permitted to return to the United States in the Perseverance Cartel.

Jenkins, Ludwick   Prisoner 2434. Rank: Carpenters Mate, from: President, U States Frigate.
    Cap: 15 Jan 1815 Not Recorded by HM Ship Endymion Int: 04 Feb 1815 Dis: 28 Mar 1815.
    Received from Endymion. Mars Transport for U States.

Jenkins, Robert   Prisoner 930. Rank: Seaman, from: Ulissus, Merchant Schooner.
    Cap: 03 Mar 1813 Chesapeake by HMS Narcissus Int: 23 Mar 1813 Dis: 24 Jun 1813.
    Received from Laurustinus. Magnet Cartel for New York.

Jenkins, Robert   Prisoner 2011. Rank: Seaman, from: Bridges, Merchant Vessel.
    Cap: 25 Oct 1814 off Halifax by Armide Int: 07 Nov 1814 Dis: 28 Mar 1815.
    Recaptured. Received from HMS Armide. Clarendon Transport for U States.

American Prisoners of War Held at Bermuda During the War of 1812

Jenkins, Ruben   Prisoner 152. Rank: Seaman, from: Ranger, Merchant Ship.
    Cap: 02 Oct 1812 Lat 32, Long 65 W by HMS Goree Int: 13 Oct 1812 Dis: 24 Oct 1812.
    Received from HMS Goree. Brig Diamond on Parole to new London United States of America.

Jenkins, William   Prisoner 2796. Rank: Seaman, from: Limerick, Not Recorded.
    Cap: 04 Mar 1815 Not Recorded by Asia Int: 25 Mar 1815 Dis:
    From Depot at Jamaica. Received from Asia. (Date of discharge not recorded.)

Jennings, Jacob   Prisoner 431. Rank: Seaman, from: Eliza, Merchant Ship.
    Cap: 25 Nov 1812 Lat 37.00, Long 65.46 by HM Ship Tartarus Int: 03 Dec 1812 Dis: 27 Jan 1813.
    Received from HM Ship Tartarus. Bostock Cartel for New York.

Jermain, Joseph   Prisoner 1225. Rank: Not Recorded, from: HMS Sloop Calibri, Not Recorded.
    Cap: Aug 1813 Not Recorded by HMS Calibri Int: 16 Nov 1813 Dis:
    Received from HMS Sceptre. Surrendered himself being an American. (Date of discharge not recorded.)

Jewet, Theodore F   Prisoner 145. Rank: Master, from: Hero, Merchant Brig.
    Cap: 25 Sep 1812 Lat 42, Long 63 W by HMS Tartarus Int: 13 Oct 1812 Dis: 24 Oct 1812.
    Received from HMS Tartarus. Brig Diamond on Parole to New London United States of America.

Joachina, Josia   Prisoner 899. Rank: Seaman, from: Princessa, Merchant Brig.
    Cap: 07 Feb 1813 Chesapeake by HMS Marlborough Int: 23 Mar 1813 Dis: 06 Apr 1813.
    Received from HM Ship Laurustinus. Order of Commodore Evans a Portuguese.

Johnson, Charles   Prisoner 1611. Rank: Seaman, from: Brookhaven, Merchant Vessel.
    Cap: 09 Dec 1813 Block Island by Albion Int: 14 Feb 1814 Dis: 21 Apr 1814.
    Received from Sceptre. being a Slave belonging to Bermuda.

Johnson, Francis   Prisoner 2036. Rank: Seaman, from: James, Merchant Vessel.
    Cap: 31 Oct 1814 off Charlestown by Schooner Whiting Int: 21 Nov 1814 Dis: 28 Mar 1815.
    Recaptured. Received from M Schooner Whiting. Clarendon Transport for U States.

Johnson, Francis   Prisoner 2360. Rank: Seaman, from: President, U States Frigate.
    Cap: 15 Jan 1815 Not Recorded by HMS Endymion Int: 04 Feb 1815 Dis: 28 Mar 1815.
    Received from Endymion. Mars Transport for U States.

Johnson, Frederick   Prisoner 450. Rank: Captain, from: Teazer, Privateer Schooner.
    Cap: 16 Dec 1812 at Sea by HM Ship St. Domingo Int: 21 Dec 1812 Dis: 27 Jan 1813.
    Received from HM Ship St. Domingo. Bostock Cartel for New York.

Johnson, G   Prisoner 2421. Rank: Seaman, from: President, U States Frigate.
    Cap: 15 Jan 1815 Not Recorded by HM Ship Endymion Int: 04 Feb 1815 Dis: 28 Mar 1815.
    Received from Endymion. Mars Transport for U States.

Johnson, Ham   Prisoner 2676. Rank: Seaman, from: Gunboat 160, U States Man of War.
    Cap: 06 Sep 1814 off New York by Lacedaemonian Int: 14 Feb 1815 Dis: 17 Feb 1815.
    Gun Vessel. Received from Childers. Harriat M Vessel order of Commadore Evans.

Johnson, Henry   Prisoner 838. Rank: Seaman, from: Portsmouth, Merchant Ship.
    Cap: 27 Feb 1813 off Bermuda by HM Sloop Martin Int: 09 Mar 1813 Dis: 27 Mar 1813.
    Received from HM Ship Martin. Per Order Commodore Evans the Vessel being Liberated.

Johnson, Henry   Prisoner 2677. Rank: Seaman, from: Gunboat 160, U States Man of War.
    Cap: 06 Sep 1814 off New York by Lacedaemonian Int: 14 Feb 1815 Dis: 28 Mar 1815.
    Gun Vessel. Received from Childers. Clarendon Transport for U States.

Johnson, Jacob   Prisoner 1564. Rank: Seaman, from: Bordeaux Packet, Letter of Marque.
    Cap: 28 Jan 1814 off Cape Henry by Nieman Int: 12 Feb 1814 Dis: 15 Apr 1814.
    Received from Nieman. Diana Transport for Halifax.

Johnson, James   Prisoner 1350. Rank: Seaman, from: Rolla, Privateer.
    Cap: 10 Dec 1813 Block Island by Loire Int: 20 Dec 1813 Dis: 15 Apr 1814.
    Received from San Domingo. HMS Rammillies for Halifax.

Johnson, James   Prisoner 1674. Rank: Boy, from: Fieri Facias, Privateer.
    Cap: 26 Feb 1814 at Sea by Ramilies Int: 18 Mar 1814 Dis: 15 Apr 1814.
    Received from Ramilies. Rammilles for Halifax.

Johnson, John   Prisoner 829. Rank: Seaman, from: Portsmouth, Merchant Ship.
    Cap: 27 Feb 1813 off Bermuda by HM Sloop Martin Int: 09 Mar 1813 Dis: 27 Mar 1813.
    Received from Sloop Martin. Per Order Commodore Evans the Vessel being Liberated.

Johnson, John   Prisoner 1126. Rank: Seaman, from: Mary, Merchant.
    Cap: 17 Apr 1813 at Sea by HM Ship Fox Int: 21 Jun 1813 Dis: 24 Jun 1813.
    Received from HM Ship Ruby. Magnet Cartel for New York.

Johnson, John   Prisoner 1998. Rank: Seaman, from: Dry Farbourn, Merchant Vessel.
    Cap: 21 Oct 1814 off Bermuda by Pandora Int: 27 Oct 1814 Dis: 05 Nov 1814.
    Recaptured. Received from Goree. Order Adl Cockburn.

American Prisoners of War Held at Bermuda During the War of 1812

Johnson, Jonas   Prisoner 872. Rank: Seaman, from: Gustavas, Merchant Brig.
    Cap: 16 Mar 1813 Chesapeake by HM Ship Laurustinus Int: 23 Mar 1813 Dis: 24 Apr 1813.
    Received from Laurustinus. Per Order Commodore Evans Vessel Liberated.

Johnson, Joseph   Prisoner 1500. Rank: Mate, from: Yankee, Merchant Sloop.
    Cap: 16 Dec 1813 Latt by Poictiers Int: 17 Jan 1814 Dis: 15 Apr 1814.
    Received from Poictiers. Diana Transport for Halifax. (Latitude number not recorded.)

Johnson, Joseph   Prisoner 1922. Rank: Seaman, from: Dolphin, Packet.
    Cap: 20 Aug 1814 St. Catherine by Lacedaemonian Int: 09 Sep 1814 Dis: 28 Mar 1815.
    Received from Lacedaemonian. Clarendon Transport for U States.

Johnson, Loyd   Prisoner 2072. Rank: Seaman, from: Industry, Merchant Vessel.
    Cap: 01 Dec 1814 off Cape Henry by HMS Niemen Int: 15 Dec 1814 Dis: 28 Mar 1815.
    Recaptured. Belong to Carolina Privateer. Received from HMS Niemen. Clarendon Transport for U States.

Johnson, Peter   Prisoner 258. Rank: Seaman, from: Wasp, Sloop of War.
    Cap: 18 Oct 1812 at Sea by HM Ship Poictiers Int: 26 Oct 1812 Dis: 05 Nov 1812.
    Received from HM Ship Poictiers. Brig Diamond on Parole to new London United States of America.

Johnson, Peter   Prisoner 743. Rank: Seaman, from: Savannah Packet, Merchant Brig.
    Cap: 05 Jan 1813 at Sea by HM Ship Poictiers Int: 21 Jan 1813 Dis: 27 Jan 1813.
    Received from HMS Poictiers. Bostock Cartel for New York.

Johnson, Peter   Prisoner 1616. Rank: Seaman, from: Monticello, Merchant Vessel.
    Cap: 09 Dec 1813 Block Island by Abion Int: 14 Apr 1814 Dis: 06 Apr 1814.
    Received from Sceptre. being a Subject of Holland.

Johnson, Peter   Prisoner 1634. Rank: Seaman, from: Not Recorded, Not Recorded.
    Cap: 05 Feb 1814 Not Recorded by Sceptre Int: 14 Feb 1814 Dis: 15 Apr 1814.
    Received from Sceptre. Rammilles for Halifax.

Johnson, R   Prisoner 903. Rank: Mate, from: Elizabeth, Merchant Brig.
    Cap: 26 Feb 1813 Chesapeake by HMS Marlborough Int: 23 Mar 1813 Dis: 24 Apr 1813.
    Received from HM Ship Laurustinus. Vessel Liberated By Order Commodore Evans. (First name not legible.)

Johnson, Richard   Prisoner 844. Rank: Seaman, from: St. Michael, Merchant.
    Cap: 02 Feb 1813 off Bermuda by By the Boat of the Squadron Int: 10 Mar 1813 Dis: 13 Jun 1813.
    Received from St. Michael Prize. Perseverance Cartel for the United States per Order Adml Sir J B Warren.

Johnson, Richard   Prisoner 2319. Rank: Seaman, from: President, U States Frigate.
    Cap: 15 Jan 1815 Not Recorded by Endymion Int: 04 Feb 1815 Dis: 28 Mar 1815.
    Received from Endymion. Mars Transport for U States.

Johnson, Robert   Prisoner 71. Rank: Seaman, from: Canaway, Merchant Ship.
    Cap: 08 Aug 1812 of Bermuda by Recruit Int: 28 Aug 1812 Dis: 18 Sep 1812.
    Received from M Schooner Cuttle. Order of Commd Evans for England.

Johnson, Robert   Prisoner 2101. Rank: Mate, from: Rufus King, Merchant Vessel.
    Cap: 01 Jan 1815 off Bermuda by Peruvian Int: 19 Jan 1815 Dis: 17 Mar 1815.
    Received from HMS Peruvian. Merchant Vessel.

Johnson, Robert   Prisoner 2825. Rank: Seaman, from: Limerick, Not Recorded.
    Cap: 15 Mar 1815 Not Recorded by Asia Int: 25 Mar 1815 Dis:
    From Depot at Jamaica. Received from Asia. (Date of discharge not recorded.)

Johnson, Samuel   Prisoner 1771. Rank: Seaman, from: Yankelass, Privateer.
    Cap: 01 May 1814 Latt 40-4N, Long 38-0W by Severn & Surprise Int: 07 Jun 1814 Dis: 24 Mar 1815.
    Received from Surprise. Merchant Vessel.

Johnson, Thomas   Prisoner 1483. Rank: Seaman, from: Luckey, Merchant Vessel.
    Cap: 19 Dec 1813 off the Delaware by Niemen Int: 07 Jan 1814 Dis: 15 Apr 1814.
    Received from HM Sloop Jaseur. Diana Transport for Halifax. (Name of capturing ship not legible, assume to be Nieman.)

Johnson, Thomas   Prisoner 1731. Rank: Seaman, from: Yankelass, Privateer.
    Cap: 01 May 1814 L 10-4N, L 33-0W by Severn & Surprise Int: 06 Jun 1814 Dis: 28 Mar 1815.
    Received from Severn. Mars Transport for U States.

Johnson, William   Prisoner 530. Rank: Seaman, from: Herald, Letter of Marque Brig.
    Cap: 25 Dec 1812 at Sea by HMS Maidstone Int: 05 Jan 1813 Dis:
    Received from HM Ship Maidstone. (Date of discharge not recorded.)

Johnson, William   Prisoner 917. Rank: Seaman, from: Albert, Merchant Schooner.
    Cap: 05 Mar 1813 Chesapeake by HM Ship Marlborough Int: 23 Mar 1813 Dis: 24 Jun 1813.
    Received from Laurustinus. Magnet Cartel for New York.

American Prisoners of War Held at Bermuda During the War of 1812

Johnson, William   Prisoner 1672. Rank: Purser, from: Fieri Facias, Privateer.
    Cap: 26 Feb 1814 at Sea by Ramilies Int: 18 Mar 1814 Dis: 15 Apr 1814.
    Received from Ramilies. Rammilles for Halifax.

Johnson, William   Prisoner 2774. Rank: Seaman, from: Hope, Not Recorded.
    Cap: 21 Feb 1815 St Augustine by Hebrus Int: 03 Mar 1815 Dis: 28 Mar 1815.
    Received from Hebrus. Clarendon Transport for U States.

Johnston, John   Prisoner 2249. Rank: Seaman, from: President, U States Frigate.
    Cap: 15 Jan 1815 Not Recorded by Endymion Int: 30 Jan 1815 Dis: 28 Mar 1815.
    Received from Pomone. Mars Transport for U States.

Johnston, William   Prisoner 1134. Rank: Seaman, from: Good Intent, Merchant.
    Cap: 02 Aug 1813 at Sea by HM Sloop Rifleman Int: 13 Aug 1813 Dis: 03 Sep 1813.
    Received from HM Sloop Rifleman. Per Order of Comm Evans to the American Ship Leander restored.

Johnston, William   Prisoner 1205. Rank: Seaman, from: Willam & Ann, Merchant Ship.
    Cap: 30 Jul 1813 at Sea by HM Sloop Nimrod Int: 21 Sep 1813 Dis: 15 Apr 1814.
    Returned to Prison from the American Ship Leander. HMS Ramillies for Halifax.

Johnstone, John   Prisoner 1204. Rank: Seaman, from: Willam & Ann, Merchant Ship.
    Cap: 30 Jul 1813 at Sea by HM Sloop Nimrod Int: 21 Sep 1813 Dis: 12 Sep 1813.
    Returned to Prison from the American Ship Leander. Per Order of Commodore Evans to the American Ship Georgiana restored. (Internment date after discharge date.)

Jolly, John   Prisoner 2169. Rank: Cook, from: President, U States Frigate.
    Cap: 15 Jan 1815 Not Recorded by Endymion Int: 30 Jan 1815 Dis: 06 Feb 1815.
    Received from President. Narcissus to the U States by order of Commadore Evans.

Jones, Abraham   Prisoner 1606. Rank: Seaman, from: Monticello, Merchant Vessel.
    Cap: 09 Dec 1813 Block Island by Albion Int: 14 Feb 1814 Dis: 23 Apr 1814.
    Received from Sceptre. HMS Bulwark for Halifax.

Jones, Cato   Prisoner 2821. Rank: Seaman, from: Limerick, Not Recorded.
    Cap: 15 Mar 1815 Not Recorded by Asia Int: 25 Mar 1815 Dis:
    From Depot at Jamaica. Received from Asia. (Date of discharge not recorded.)

Jones, Charles   Prisoner 1517. Rank: Seaman, from: Rising States, Merchant Vessel.
    Cap: 13 Jan 1814 off Cape May by Nieman Int: 22 Jan 1814 Dis: 15 Apr 1814.
    Received from Surprize. Diana Transport for Halifax.

Jones, Daniel   Prisoner 1046. Rank: Seaman, from: General Knox, Merchant.
    Cap: 18 Mar 1813 off the Chesapeake by HM Ship Victorious Int: 06 Apr 1813 Dis:
    Received from HMS Junon. (Date of discharge not on roster.)

Jones, Edward   Prisoner 1310. Rank: Seaman, from: Rolla, Privateer.
    Cap: 10 Dec 1813 Block Island by Loire Int: 20 Dec 1813 Dis: 15 Apr 1814.
    Received from San Domingo. HMS Rammillies for Halifax.

Jones, Henry   Prisoner 232. Rank: Seaman, from: Wasp, Sloop of War.
    Cap: 18 Oct 1812 at Sea by HM Ship Poictiers Int: 26 Oct 1812 Dis: 05 Nov 1812.
    Received from HM Ship Poictiers. Brig Diamond on Parole to new London United States of America.

Jones, Isaac   Prisoner 69. Rank: Captain, from: Canaway, Merchant Ship.
    Cap: 08 Aug 1812 of Bermuda by Recruit Int: 28 Aug 1812 Dis: 10 Sep 1812.
    Received from M Schooner Cuttle. Schooner Hero for N Y.

Jones, Jacob   Prisoner 163. Rank: Captain, from: Wasp, Sloop of War.
    Cap: 18 Oct 1812 at Sea by HMS Poictiers Int: 26 Oct 1812 Dis: 05 Nov 1812.
    Received from HM Ship Poictiers. on Parole Brig Diamond to new London America.

Jones, James   Prisoner 980. Rank: Seaman, from: Betsy Ann, Merchant.
    Cap: 04 Mar 1813 Chesapeake by HM Ship Fantom Int: 23 Mar 1813 Dis: 24 Jun 1813.
    Received from HM Ship Laurustinus. Magnet Cartel for New York.

Jones, John   Prisoner 2116. Rank: Seaman, from: Armistice, Merchant Vessel.
    Cap: 07 Dec 1814 off Delaware by Pictolus Int: 27 Jan 1815 Dis: 28 Mar 1815.
    Received from Pictolus. Clarendon Transport for U States.

Jones, John   Prisoner 2187. Rank: Seaman, from: President, U States Frigate.
    Cap: 15 Jan 1815 Not Recorded by HMS Endymion Int: 30 Jan 1815 Dis: 28 Mar 1815.
    Received from Pomone. Mars Transport for U States.

Jones, Richard   Prisoner 2569. Rank: Seaman, from: Funchall, Merchant Vessel.
    Cap: 15 Jan 1815 off New York by HMS Pomone Int: 05 Feb 1815 Dis: 28 Mar 1815.
    Received from HMS Forth. Clarendon Transport for U States.

Jones, Samuel   Prisoner 1697. Rank: Seaman, from: Grecian, Letter of Marque.
    Cap: 02 May 1814 Chesapeake by Jansur Int: 26 May 1814 Dis: 20 Mar 1815.
    Received from Lacedaemonian. Merchant Vessel.

American Prisoners of War Held at Bermuda During the War of 1812

Jones, Watkins   Prisoner 2368. Rank: Seaman, from: President, U States Frigate.
    Cap: 15 Jan 1815 Not Recorded by HMS Endymion Int: 04 Feb 1815 Dis: 28 Mar 1815.
    Received from Endymion. Mars Transport for U States.

Jones, William   Prisoner 338. Rank: Seaman, from: Snapper, Privateer Schooner.
    Cap: 16 Nov 1812 at Sea by HMS Galus Int: 22 Nov 1812 Dis: 27 Jan 1813.
    Received from HM Ship Galus. Bostock Cartel for New York.

Jones, William   Prisoner 665. Rank: Lieutenant Marines, from: High Flyer, Privateer.
    Cap: 09 Jan 1813 at Sea by HM Ship Acasta Int: 21 Jan 1813 Dis: 27 Jan 1813.
    Received from HMS Acasta. Bostock Cartel for New York.

Jones, William   Prisoner 737. Rank: Seaman, from: High Flyer, Privateer.
    Cap: 09 Jan 1813 at Sea by HM Ship Acasta Int: 21 Jan 1813 Dis: 27 Jan 1813.
    Received from HMS Acasta. Bostock Cartel for New York.

Jordon, Ralph   Prisoner 2399. Rank: Seaman, from: President, U States Frigate.
    Cap: 15 Jan 1815 Not Recorded by HM Ship Endymion Int: 04 Feb 1815 Dis: 28 Mar 1815.
    Received from Endymion. Mars Transport for U States.

Jordon, Simon   Prisoner 18. Rank: Mate, from: Amiable, Merchant Schooner.
    Cap: 14 Jul 1812 at Bermuda by Cuttle Int: 28 Aug 1812 Dis: 10 Sep 1812.
    Received from HM Schooner Cuttle. Schooner Hero for N Y.

Josamana, P   Prisoner 925. Rank: Seaman, from: Albert, Merchant Schooner.
    Cap: 05 Mar 1813 Chesapeake by HM Ship Marlborough Int: 23 Mar 1813 Dis: 24 Mar 1813.
    Received from Laurustinus. St. Michael per Order Adl Sir J B Warren.

Joseph, Anthony   Prisoner 2289. Rank: Seaman, from: President, U States Frigate.
    Cap: 15 Jan 1815 Not Recorded by Endymion Int: 30 Jan 1815 Dis: 28 Mar 1815.
    Received from Pomone. Mars Transport for U States.

Joseph, Charles   Prisoner 354. Rank: Seaman, from: Snapper, Privateer Schooner.
    Cap: 16 Nov 1812 at Sea by HMS Galus Int: 22 Nov 1812 Dis: 27 Jan 1813.
    Received from HM Ship Galus. Bostock Cartel for New York.

Joseph, Fortunata   Prisoner 1459. Rank: Seaman, from: Vixen, Man of War.
    Cap: 25 Dec 1813 Lat 38.0 by Belvidera Int: 05 Jan 1814 Dis: 10 Mar 1814.
    U States Schooner. Received from HMS Belvidera. By order of the Com in Chief being a Portuguese.

Joseph, Francis   Prisoner 2508. Rank: Seaman, from: President, U States Frigate.
    Cap: 15 Jan 1815 Not Recorded by Endymion Int: 04 Feb 1815 Dis: 28 Mar 1815.
    Received from HMS Endymion. Clarenden Transport for U States.

Joseph, Francis   Prisoner 2658. Rank: Seaman, from: Falcon, Merchant Vessel.
    Cap: 22 Jan 1815 Delaware by Forth Int: 13 Feb 1815 Dis: 17 Feb 1815.
    Received from Goree. Harriot M Vessel order of Commadore Evans.

Joseph, Howard   Prisoner 534. Rank: Seaman, from: Herald, Letter of Marque Brig.
    Cap: 25 Dec 1812 at Sea by HM Ship Maidstone Int: 05 Jan 1813 Dis: 27 Jan 1813.
    Received from HM Ship Maidstone. Bostock Cartel for New York.

Joseph, John   Prisoner 531. Rank: Seaman, from: Herald, Letter of Marque Brig.
    Cap: 25 Dec 1812 at Sea by HMS Maidstone Int: 05 Jan 1813 Dis: 27 Jan 1813.
    Received from HM Ship Maidstone. Bostock Cartel New York.

Joseph, John   Prisoner 759. Rank: Seaman, from: Hazard, Merchant Brig.
    Cap: 28 Dec 1812 Lat 37.35, Long 70.10 by HM Sloop Sylph Int: 26 Jan 1813 Dis: 14 Jun 1813.
    Received from Sloop Sylph. Permitted to return to the United States in the Perseverance.

Joseph, John   Prisoner 1772. Rank: Seaman, from: Yankelass, Privateer.
    Cap: 01 May 1814 Latt 40-4N, Long 38-0W by Severn & Surprise Int: 07 Jun 1814 Died:
    26 Feb 1815. Received from Surprise. Died. Fever.

Joseph, Louis   Prisoner 2417. Rank: Seaman, from: President, U States Frigate.
    Cap: 15 Jan 1815 Not Recorded by HM Ship Endymion Int: 04 Feb 1815 Dis: 28 Mar 1815.
    Received from Endymion. Mars Transport for U States.

Josey, Jack   Prisoner 897. Rank: Seaman, from: Princessa, Merchant Brig.
    Cap: 07 Feb 1813 Chesapeake by HMS Marlborough Int: 23 Mar 1813 Dis: 24 Mar 1813.
    Received from HM Ship Laurustinus. St. Michael per Order Adl Sir J B Warren.

Josif, Antinio   Prisoner 1737. Rank: Seaman, from: Yankelass, Privateer.
    Cap: 01 May 1814 L 10-4N, L 33-0W by Severn & Surprise Int: 06 Jun 1814 Dis:
    Received from Severn. (Date of discharge not recorded.)

Joy, David   Prisoner 962. Rank: Seaman, from: Bona, Letter of Marque Schooner.
    Cap: 12 Mar 1813 Chesapeake by Laurustinus Int: 23 Mar 1813 Dis: 24 Jun 1813.
    Received from Laurustinus. Magnet Cartel for New York.

Joy, William   Prisoner 141. Rank: Master, from: Ranger of Nantucket, Merchant Ship.
    Cap: 02 Oct 1812 Lat 32, Long 65 by HMS Goree Int: 11 Oct 1812 Dis: 24 Oct 1812.
    Received from HMS Goree. Brig Diamond on Parole to New London United States of America.

American Prisoners of War Held at Bermuda During the War of 1812

Joyce, John   Prisoner 1059. Rank: Seaman, from: Amason, Merchant.
    Cap: 18 Mar 1813 Chesapeake by HM Ship Victorious Int: 06 Apr 1813 Dis: 24 Jun 1813.
    Received from HMS Junon. Magnet Cartel for New York.

Juan, Francis   Prisoner 928. Rank: Seaman, from: Albert, Merchant Schooner.
    Cap: 05 Mar 1813 Chesapeake by HM Ship Marlborough Int: 23 Mar 1813 Dis: 24 Mar 1813.
    Received from Laurustinus. St. Michael per Order Adl Sir J B Warren.

Judkins, Charles   Prisoner 2735. Rank: Soldier, from: Not Recorded, Not Recorded.
    Cap: 13 Jan 1815 St Marys by Dragon Int: 03 Mar 1815 Dis: 28 Mar 1815.
    by Kings Troops. Received from Hebrus. Clarendon Transport for U States.

Judy, Joseph   Prisoner 277. Rank: Seaman, from: Little William, Merchant Brig.
    Cap: 18 Oct 1812 at Sea by HM Ship Poictiers Int: 26 Oct 1812 Dis: 05 Nov 1812.
    Received from HM Ship Poictiers. Brig Diamond on Parole to new London United States of America.

Justin, William   Prisoner 1351. Rank: Seaman, from: Rolla, Privateer.
    Cap: 10 Dec 1813 Block Island by Loire Int: 20 Dec 1813 Dis: 15 Apr 1814.
    Received from San Domingo. HMS Rammillies for Halifax.

Kainsford, Josiah   Prisoner 2166. Rank: Pursers (Not legible), from: President, U States Frigate.
    Cap: 15 Jan 1815 Not Recorded by Endymion Int: 30 Jan 1815 Dis: 28 Mar 1815.
    Received from President. Mars Transport for U States.

Kane, William   Prisoner 2748. Rank: Seaman, from: Fair American, Not Recorded.
    Cap: 10 Dec 1814 St Augustine by Dragon Int: 03 Mar 1815 Dis: 28 Mar 1815.
    Received from Hebrus. Clarendon Transport for U States.

Keir, John   Prisoner 1116. Rank: Seaman, from: Not Recorded, Not Recorded.
    Cap: Not Recorded by Not Recorded Int: 08 Jun 1813 Dis: 24 Jun 1813.
    Received from HMS Dragon. Surrendered Him Self a Prisoner of War. Magnet Cartel for New York.
    (Date of capture not recorded.)

Keith, James   Prisoner 2291. Rank: Seaman, from: President, U States Frigate.
    Cap: 15 Jan 1815 Not Recorded by Endymion Int: 30 Jan 1815 Dis: 28 Mar 1815.
    Received from Pomone. Mars Transport for U States.

Keith, John   Prisoner 2254. Rank: Seaman, from: President, U States Frigate.
    Cap: 15 Jan 1815 Not Recorded by Endymion Int: 30 Jan 1815 Dis: 28 Mar 1815.
    Received from Pomone. Mars Transport for U States.

Keith, William   Prisoner 2570. Rank: Mate, from: Mercury, Merchant Vessel.
    Cap: 30 Dec 1814 off New York by HMS Pomone Int: 05 Feb 1815 Dis: 28 Mar 1815.
    Received from HMS Forth. Clarendon Transport for U States.

Kellegan, James   Prisoner 1508. Rank: Seaman, from: Plantagenet, Not Recorded.
    Cap: Not Recorded by Not Recorded Int: 19 Jan 1814 Dis: 15 Apr 1814.
    Received from Plantagenet. being an American. Diana Transport for Halifax.
    (Date of capture not recorded.)

Keller, Anthony   Prisoner 2470. Rank: Marine, from: President, U States Frigate.
    Cap: 15 Jan 1815 Not Recorded by Endymion Int: 04 Feb 1815 Dis: 28 Mar 1815.
    Received from Endymion. Clarenden Transport for U States.

Kellog, Junior, Samuel   Prisoner 32. Rank: Supercargo, from: Laura, Merchant Sloop.
    Cap: 24 Jul 1812 of Bermuda by Cuttle Int: 28 Aug 1812 Dis: 10 Sep 1812.
    Received from HM Schooner Cuttle. Schooner Hero for N Y.

Kelly, Henry   Prisoner 75. Rank: Seaman, from: White Oak, Merchant.
    Cap: 08 Aug 1812 of Bermuda by Recruit Int: 28 Aug 1812 Dis: 18 Sep 1812.
    Received from M Schooner Cuttle. Order of Commd Evans for England.

Kelly, John   Prisoner 761. Rank: Seaman, from: Hazard, Merchant Brig.
    Cap: 28 Dec 1812 Lat 37.35, Long 70.10 by HM Sloop Sylph Int: 26 Jan 1813 Dis: 14 Jun 1813.
    Received from Sloop Sylph. Permitted to return to the United States in the Perseverance Cartel.

Kelly, John   Prisoner 1689. Rank: Seaman, from: Lark, Merchant Vessel.
    Cap: 06 Apr 1814 L 29.0 by Recruit Int: 11 May 1814 Dis: 28 Mar 1815.
    Recaptured. Received from Recruit. Mars Transport for U States.

Kelly, John   Prisoner 2411. Rank: Marine, from: President, U States Frigate.
    Cap: 15 Jan 1815 Not Recorded by HM Ship Endymion Int: 04 Feb 1815 Dis: 28 Mar 1815.
    Received from Endymion. Clarenden Transport for U States.

Kelly, Joshua   Prisoner 836. Rank: Seaman, from: Portsmouth, Merchant Ship.
    Cap: 27 Feb 1813 off Bermuda by HM Sloop Martin Int: 09 Mar 1813 Dis: 27 Mar 1813.
    Received from HM Ship Martin. Per Order Commodore Evans the Vessel being Liberated.

Kelly, Thomas   Prisoner 806. Rank: Seaman, from: Viper, Sloop of War.
    Cap: 17 Jan 1813 at Sea by Narcissus Int: 16 Feb 1813 Dis: 13 Jun 1813.
    Received from Narcissus. Perseverance Cartel for the United States per Order Adm Sir J B Warren.

American Prisoners of War Held at Bermuda During the War of 1812

Kelly, Thomas   Prisoner 2556. Rank: Seaman, from: President, U States Frigate.
    Cap: 15 Jan 1815 Not Recorded by HM Ship Endymion Int: 05 Feb 1815 Dis: 28 Mar 1815.
    Received from President. Clarenden Transport for U States.

Kelso, George   Prisoner 912. Rank: Master, from: Allisses, Merchant Schooner.
    Cap: 03 Mar 1813 Chesapeake by HM Ship Narcissus Int: 23 Mar 1813 Dis: 13 Jun 1813.
    Received from HM Ship Laurustinus. Perseverance Cartel for the United States per Order Adml Sir J B Warren.

Kelso, John   Prisoner 2632. Rank: Mate, from: Superb, Merchant Vessel.
    Cap: 23 Nov 1814 off Delaware by Spencer Int: 06 Feb 1815 Dis: 16 Mar 1815.
    Received from HMS Telegraph. Merchant Service.

Kemp, John   Prisoner 557. Rank: 1 Mate, from: Rising Hope, Merchant Brig.
    Cap: 27 Dec 1812 at Sea by HM Sloop Wanderer Int: 05 Jan 1813 Dis: 27 Jan 1813.
    Received from HM Sloop Wanderer. Bostock Cartel for New York.

Kempenfield, William   Prisoner 1035. Rank: Seaman, from: Dart, Merchant Schooner.
    Cap: 17 Mar 1813 off the Chesapeake by HMS Statira Int: 06 Apr 1813 Dis: 24 Jun 1813.
    Received from HMS Junon. Magnet Cartel for New York.

Kempton, Noah S   Prisoner 2038. Rank: Mate, from: Live, Merchant Sloop.
    Cap: 26 Oct 1814 off Delaware by St. Laurence Int: 21 Nov 1814 Dis: 28 Mar 1815.
    Received from M Schooner Whiting. Clarendon Transport for U States.

Kendel, Henry   Prisoner 563. Rank: Seaman, from: Rising Hope, Merchant Brig.
    Cap: 27 Dec 1812 at Sea by HM Sloop Wanderer Int: 05 Jan 1813 Dis: 27 Jan 1813.
    Received from HM Sloop Wanderer. Bostock Cartel for New York.

Kene, Davis   Prisoner 1580. Rank: Seaman, from: Bordeaux Packet, Letter of Marque.
    Cap: 28 Jan 1814 off Cape Henry by Nieman Int: 12 Feb 1814 Dis: 15 Apr 1814.
    Received from Nieman. Diana Transport for Halifax.

Kennedy, Dennis   Prisoner 324. Rank: Seaman, from: James, Merchant Ship.
    Cap: 03 Nov 1812 at Sea by HM Ship Tartarus Int: 17 Nov 1812 Dis: 27 Jan 1813.
    Received from HM Ship Tartarus. Bostock Cartel for New York.

Kennedy, James   Prisoner 441. Rank: Master, from: Rebecca, Merchant Ship.
    Cap: 26 Nov 1812 off the Cape of Virginia by HM Ship Poictiers Int: 16 Dec 1812 Dis: 08 Feb 1813.
    Received from Prize Ship Rebecca. Permitted to Remain in the Colony by Order of the Governor.

Kennedy, Peter   Prisoner 747. Rank: Master, from: Rhode, Merchant Schooner.
    Cap: 07 Jan 1813 at Sea by HM Ship Poictiers Int: 21 Jan 1813 Dis: 27 Jan 1813.
    Received from HMS Poictiers. Bostock Cartel for New York.

Kent, Obediah   Prisoner 1015. Rank: Seaman, from: Nautalus, Merchant.
    Cap: 20 Mar 1813 off the Chesapeake by HM Ship Rammillies Int: 06 Apr 1813 Dis: 24 Jun 1813.
    Received from HMS Junon. Magnet Cartel for New York.

Kern, Nicholas   Prisoner 771. Rank: Seaman, from: Trinadada, Merchant Brig.
    Cap: 06 Jan 1813 Lat 37.20, Long 75.00 by HM Sloop Sylph Int: 26 Jan 1813 Dis: 14 Jun 1813.
    Received from Sloop Sylph. Permitted to return to the United States in the Perseverance.

Kerns, George   Prisoner 370. Rank: Clerk, from: Snapper, Privateer Schooner.
    Cap: 16 Nov 1812 at Sea by HM Ship Galus Int: 22 Nov 1812 Dis: 27 Jan 1813.
    Received from HM Ship Galus. Bostock Cartel for New York.

Kerr, Adam   Prisoner 2427. Rank: Seaman, from: President, U States Frigate.
    Cap: 15 Jan 1815 Not Recorded by HM Ship Endymion Int: 04 Feb 1815 Dis: 28 Mar 1815.
    Received from Endymion. Mars Transport for U States.

Kershaw, Newman   Prisoner 2088. Rank: Passenger, from: Fox, Packet Boat.
    Cap: 04 Oct 1814 coast of America by Lacedaemonian Int: 19 Jan 1815 Dis: 21 Feb 1815.
    Received from HMS Peruvian. Paroled to U States per order of Sir Alex Cochrane.

Kerson, George   Prisoner 1111. Rank: Seaman, from: Revenge, Privateer Brig.
    Cap: 25 May 1813 at Sea by Narcissus Int: 27 May 1813 Dis: 24 Jun 1813.
    Received from HM Ship San Domingo. Magnet Cartel for New York.

Kettletas, Benjamin   Prisoner 2237. Rank: Seaman, from: President, U States Frigate.
    Cap: 15 Jan 1815 Not Recorded by Endymion Int: 30 Jan 1815 Dis: 28 Mar 1815.
    Received from Pomone. Mars Transport for U States.

Key, John   Prisoner 2858. Rank: Seaman, from: Limerick, Not Recorded.
    Cap: 15 Mar 1815 Not Recorded by Asia Int: 25 Mar 1815 Dis:
    From Depot at Jamaica. Received from Asia. (Date of discharge not recorded.)

Keys, William   Prisoner 2653. Rank: Seaman, from: President, U States Frigate.
    Cap: 11 Feb 1815 off N York by Endymion Int: 11 Feb 1815 Dis: 28 Mar 1815.
    Received from President. Clarenden Transport for U States.
    (Date of capture should be January 15, 1815.)

American Prisoners of War Held at Bermuda During the War of 1812

Kidmore, Joseph   Prisoner 1957. Rank: Seaman, from: Pike, Privateer.
    Cap: 25 Aug 1814 off Savannah by Primrose Int: 09 Sep 1814 Dis: 28 Mar 1815.
    Received from Lacedaemonian. Clarendon Transport for U States.

Kids, R F   Prisoner 1847. Rank: Seaman, from: Little Catherine, Merchant Vessel.
    Cap: Not Recorded by Not Recorded Int: Not Recorded Escaped: 26 Aug 1814.
    Recaptured. Run from Naval Hospital. (Dates of capture and internment not recorded.)

Kielsey, Henry   Prisoner 1502. Rank: Seaman, from: Yankee, Merchant Sloop.
    Cap: 16 Dec 1813 Latt by Poictiers Int: 17 Jan 1814 Dis: 15 Apr 1814.
    Received from Poictiers. Diana Transport for Halifax. (Latitude number not recorded.)

Kimbury, John   Prisoner 1703. Rank: Seaman, from: Grecian, Letter of Marque.
    Cap: 02 May 1814 Chesapeake by Jansur Int: 26 May 1814 Dis:
    Received from Lacedaemonian. (Date of discharge not recorded.)

King, William   Prisoner 139. Rank: Seaman, from: Yorick, Merchant Ship.
    Cap: 09 Jul 1812 off Bermuda by Rattler Int: 11 Oct 1812 Dis: 24 Oct 1812.
    Received from Hospital. Brig Diamond on Parole to New London United States of America.

Kings, Thomas   Prisoner 1395. Rank: Seaman, from: Scorpion, Merchant Vessel.
    Cap: 29 Nov 1813 Lat 39 by Loire Int: 21 Dec 1813 Dis: 15 Apr 1814.
    Received from Romulus. Diana for Halifax.

Knap, Samuel   Prisoner 1101. Rank: Seaman, from: Apollo, Merchant Vessel.
    Cap: 15 May 1813 at Sea by HM Ship Success Int: 27 May 1813 Dis: 24 Jun 1813.
    Received from HMS Success. Magnet Cartel for New York.

Knapp, Samuel   Prisoner 2012. Rank: Seaman, from: Bridges, Merchant Vessel.
    Cap: 25 Oct 1814 off Halifax by Armide Int: 07 Nov 1814 Dis: 28 Mar 1815.
    Recaptured. Received from HMS Armide. Clarendon Transport for U States.

Knapp, Thomas   Prisoner 1720. Rank: Master, from: Grecian, Letter of Marque.
    Cap: 02 May 1814 Chesapeake by Jansur Int: 26 May 1814 Dis: 19 Jun 1814.
    Received from Lacedaemonian. United States for Parole.

Kneeland, Edward M   Prisoner 2124. Rank: Seaman, from: Post Boy, Merchant Vessel.
    Cap: 09 Dec 1814 off Delaware by HMS Pictolus Int: 27 Jan 1815 Dis: 28 Mar 1815.
    Received from Pictolus. Clarendon Transport for U States.

Kneese, James   Prisoner 2408. Rank: Seaman, from: President, U States Frigate.
    Cap: 15 Jan 1815 Not Recorded by HM Ship Endymion Int: 04 Feb 1815 Dis: 28 Mar 1815.
    Received from Endymion. Mars Transport for U States.

Knight, Charles   Prisoner 1086. Rank: Seaman, from: Fanny, Merchant.
    Cap: 22 Apr 1813 off Block Island by Ramillies Int: 07 May 1813 Dis: 24 Jun 1813.
    Received from Prize Fanny. Magnet Cartel for New York.

Knight, John   Prisoner 226. Rank: Seaman, from: Wasp, Sloop of War.
    Cap: 18 Oct 1812 at Sea by HM Ship Poictiers Int: 26 Oct 1812 Dis: 05 Nov 1812.
    Received from HM Ship Poictiers. Brig Diamond on Parole to new London United States of America.

Knight, William   Prisoner 168. Rank: Master, from: Wasp, Sloop of War.
    Cap: 18 Oct 1812 at Sea by HMS Poictiers Int: 26 Oct 1812 Dis: 05 Nov 1812.
    Received from HM Ship Poictiers. on Parole Brig Diamond to new London America.

Knipmire, George   Prisoner 722. Rank: Seaman, from: High Flyer, Privateer.
    Cap: 09 Jan 1813 at Sea by HM Ship Acasta Int: 21 Jan 1813 Dis: 27 Jan 1813.
    Received from HMS Acasta. Bostock Cartel for New York.

Knowles, Thorpolin   Prisoner 1072. Rank: Seaman, from: Ring Dove, Merchant.
    Cap: 31 Mar 1813 Chesapeake by HMS Junon Int: 06 Apr 1813 Dis: 24 Jun 1813.
    Received from HMS Junon. Magnet Cartel for New York.

Kregoe, Martin   Prisoner 2065. Rank: Seaman, from: Industry, Merchant Vessel.
    Cap: 01 Dec 1814 off Cape Henry by HMS Niemen Int: 15 Dec 1814 Dis: 22 Dec 1814.
    Recaptured. Belong to Carolina Privateer. Received from HMS Niemen. Rolla Transport Swedish Subject Order of Com Evans.

Krutson, John   Prisoner 2255. Rank: Seaman, from: President, U States Frigate.
    Cap: 15 Jan 1815 Not Recorded by Endymion Int: 30 Jan 1815 Dis: 17 Feb 1815.
    Received from Pomone. Bridges Transport per Order of Com Evans. 2 Y Vid List 28 March 1815 Mars Transport for U States.

Kussleu, Moses   Prisoner 384. Rank: Seaman, from: Snapper, Privateer Schooner.
    Cap: 16 Nov 1812 at Sea by HM Ship Galus Int: 22 Nov 1812 Dis: 27 Jan 1813.
    Received from HM Ship Galus. Bostock Cartel for New York.

La Mour, John   Prisoner 8. Rank: Seaman, from: Yorick, Merchant Ship.
    Cap: 09 Jul 1812 near Bermuda by Rattler Int: 28 Aug 1812 Dis: 18 Sep 1812.
    Received from HM Schooner Cuttle. Order of Commd Evans for England.

American Prisoners of War Held at Bermuda During the War of 1812

La Vie, Antonia   Prisoner 352. Rank: Seaman, from: Snapper, Privateer Schooner.
    Cap: 16 Nov 1812 at Sea by HMS Galus Int: 22 Nov 1812 Dis: 27 Jan 1813.
    Received from HM Ship Galus. Bostock Cartel for New York.

Label, Antonia   Prisoner 400. Rank: Seaman, from: Snapper, Privateer Schooner.
    Cap: 16 Nov 1812 at Sea by HM Ship Galus Int: 22 Nov 1812 Dis: 14 Dec 1812.
    Received from HM Ship Galus. per Order Commodore Evans.

Lacha, Lewis   Prisoner 2783. Rank: Seaman, from: Limerick, Not Recorded.
    Cap: 07 Mar 1815 Lat 30, Long 75.38 W by Asia Int: 25 Mar 1815 Dis:
    Received from Asia. (Date of discharge not recorded.)

Lackley, Joseph   Prisoner 1989. Rank: Seaman, from: Eclipse, Merchant Vessel.
    Cap: 29 Sep 1814 Bermuda by Copark Int: 05 Oct 1814 Dis: 28 Mar 1815.
    Recaptured. Received from Goree. Clarendon Transport for U States.

Lafebui, Bartin   Prisoner 1221. Rank: Seaman, from: Flavoriott, Merchant Schooner.
    Cap: Aug 1813 off Charlestown by HMS Calibri Int: 16 Nov 1813 Dis: 15 Apr 1814.
    Received from HMS Sceptre. Diana Transport for Halifax.

Lake, Benjamin   Prisoner 1382. Rank: Mate, from: Policy, Merchant Vessel.
    Cap: 04 Dec 1813 Not Recorded by Loire Int: 20 Dec 1813 Dis: 15 Apr 1814.
    Recaptured. Received from San Domingo. Diana Transport for Halifax.

Lake, Levin   Prisoner 10. Rank: Mate, from: General Blake, Merchant.
    Cap: 09 Jul 1812 near Bermuda by Recruit Int: 28 Aug 1812 Dis: 10 Sep 1812.
    Received from HM Schooner Cuttle. Schooner Hero for N Y.

Lamber, David   Prisoner 705. Rank: Seaman, from: High Flyer, Privateer.
    Cap: 09 Jan 1813 at Sea by HMS Acasta Int: 21 Jan 1813 Dis: 27 Jan 1813.
    Received from HMS Acasta. Bostock Cartel for New York.

Lamberg, John   Prisoner 1270. Rank: Seaman, from: United States, Merchant Vessel.
    Cap: 14 Nov 1813 Long Island by HM Brig Borer Int: 19 Dec 1813 Dis: 15 Apr 1814.
    Received from HMS Acasta. Diana for Halifax.

Lambert, James   Prisoner 1673. Rank: Master, from: Fieri Facias, Privateer.
    Cap: 26 Feb 1814 at Sea by Ramilies Int: 18 Mar 1814 Dis: 15 Apr 1814.
    Received from Ramilies. Rammilles for Halifax.

Lampher, Clamlin   Prisoner 2514. Rank: Seaman, from: President, U States Frigate.
    Cap: 15 Jan 1815 Not Recorded by Endymion Int: 04 Feb 1815 Dis: 28 Mar 1815.
    Received from HMS Endymion. Clarenden Transport for U States.

Lanboon, Andrew   Prisoner 234. Rank: Seaman, from: Wasp, Sloop of War.
    Cap: 18 Oct 1812 at Sea by HM Ship Poictiers Int: 26 Oct 1812 Dis: 05 Nov 1812.
    Received from HM Ship Poictiers. Brig Diamond on Parole to new London United States of America.

Lands, John   Prisoner 1893. Rank: Seaman, from: Pylader, Not Recorded.
    Cap: Not Recorded by Not Recorded Int: 12 Aug 1814 Dis: 24 Nov 1814.
    Received from Pylader. delivered himself up as an American Subject. Dryharbour MV order Com Evans. (Date of capture not recorded.)

Lane, Alexander   Prisoner 2092. Rank: Passenger, from: Factor, Merchant Vessel.
    Cap: 06 Dec 1814 Coast of America by Lacedaemonian Int: 19 Jan 1815 Dis:
    Received from HMS Peruvian. (Date of discharge not recorded.)

Lane, Horice   Prisoner 484. Rank: Seaman, from: Teazer, Privateer Schooner.
    Cap: 16 Dec 1812 at Sea by HM Ship St. Domingo Int: 21 Dec 1812 Dis: 27 Jan 1813.
    Received from HM Ship St. Domingo. Bostock Cartel for New York.

Lane, John   Prisoner 408. Rank: Seaman, from: Snapper, Privateer Schooner.
    Cap: 16 Nov 1812 at Sea by HM Ship Galus Int: 22 Nov 1812 Dis: 15 Dec 1812.
    Received from HM Ship Galus. Entered on Board HMS Goree.

Lane, John   Prisoner 995. Rank: Seaman, from: Snapper, Privateer.
    Cap: 16 Nov 1812 at Sea by HMS Ship Galus Int: 03 Apr 1813 Dis: 05 May 1813.
    Received from HMS Goree. Prize Ship St. Michael.

Lane, Timothy   Prisoner 206. Rank: Seaman, from: Wasp, Sloop of War.
    Cap: 18 Oct 1812 at Sea by HM Ship Poictiers Int: 26 Oct 1812 Dis: 05 Nov 1812.
    Received from HM Ship Poictiers. Brig Diamond on Parole to new London United States of America.

Lang, James   Prisoner 2268. Rank: Marine, from: President, U States Frigate.
    Cap: 15 Jan 1815 Not Recorded by Endymion Int: 30 Jan 1815 Dis: 28 Mar 1815.
    Received from Pomone. Clarenden Transport for U States.

Lang, John   Prisoner 187. Rank: Seaman, from: Wasp, Sloop of War.
    Cap: 18 Oct 1812 at Sea by HMS Poictiers Int: 26 Oct 1812 Dis: 05 Nov 1812.
    Received from HM Ship Poictiers. Brig Diamond on Parole to new London America.

American Prisoners of War Held at Bermuda During the War of 1812

Lang, R   Prisoner 1604. Rank: Seaman, from: Monticello, Merchant Vessel.
   Cap: 09 Dec 1813 Block Island by Albion Int: 14 Feb 1814 Dis: 23 Apr 1814.
   Received from Sceptre. HMS Bulwark for Halifax.

Langreen, Andrew   Prisoner 65. Rank: Seaman, from: Mary, Merchant Brig.
   Cap: 08 Aug 1812 of Bermuda by Cuttle Int: 28 Aug 1812 Dis: 18 Sep 1812.
   Received from M Schooner Cuttle. Order of Commd Evans for England.

Langshore, Richard   Prisoner 2802. Rank: Seaman, from: Limerick, Not Recorded.
   Cap: 04 Mar 1815 Not Recorded by Asia Int: 25 Mar 1815 Dis:
   From Depot at Jamaica. Received from Asia. (Date of discharge not recorded.)

Langueth, Matthew   Prisoner 2818. Rank: Seaman, from: Limerick, Not Recorded.
   Cap: 15 Mar 1815 Not Recorded by Asia Int: 25 Mar 1815 Dis:
   From Depot at Jamaica. Received from Asia. (Date of discharge not recorded.)

Lansing, E A   Prisoner 2146. Rank: Midshipman, from: President, U States Frigate.
   Cap: 15 Jan 1815 Not Recorded by Endymion Int: 30 Jan 1815 Dis: 28 Mar 1815.
   Received from President. Mars Transport for U States.

Lapee, Silvester   Prisoner 1091. Rank: Seaman, from: Langdon Cheves, Merchant.
   Cap: 12 May 1813 at Sea by HM Sloop Atalante Int: 25 May 1813 Dis: 24 Jun 1813.
   Received from HMS Atalante. Magnet Cartel for New York.

Larke, James R   Prisoner 934. Rank: Mate, from: Sidney, Letter of Marque Schooner.
   Cap: 09 Mar 1813 Chesapeake by Marlborough Int: 23 Mar 1813 Dis: 24 Jun 1813.
   Received from Laurustinus. Magnet Cartel for New York.

Larkin, Lewis   Prisoner 1331. Rank: Seaman, from: Rolla, Privateer.
   Cap: 10 Dec 1813 Block Island by Loire Int: 20 Dec 1813 Dis: 23 Apr 1814.
   Received from HM Ship San Domingo. Discharged from the Hospital to the Bulwark for Halifax.

Larkin, Peter   Prisoner 2422. Rank: Seaman, from: President, U States Frigate.
   Cap: 15 Jan 1815 Not Recorded by HM Ship Endymion Int: 04 Feb 1815 Dis: 28 Mar 1815.
   Received from Endymion. Mars Transport for U States.

Larraby, Joseph   Prisoner 2233. Rank: Seaman, from: President, U States Frigate.
   Cap: 15 Jan 1815 Not Recorded by Endymion Int: 30 Jan 1815 Dis: 28 Mar 1815.
   Received from Pomone. Mars Transport for U States.

Lary, Peter   Prisoner 2365. Rank: Seaman, from: President, U States Frigate.
   Cap: 15 Jan 1815 Not Recorded by HMS Endymion Int: 04 Feb 1815 Dis: 28 Mar 1815.
   Received from Endymion. Mars Transport for U States.

Lascell, William   Prisoner 751. Rank: Seaman, from: Rhode, Merchant Schooner.
   Cap: 07 Jan 1813 at Sea by HM Ship Poictiers Int: 21 Jan 1813 Dis: 27 Jan 1813.
   Received from HMS Poictiers. Bostock Cartel for New York.

Lasky, George   Prisoner 536. Rank: Seaman, from: Herald, Letter of Marque Brig.
   Cap: 25 Dec 1812 at Sea by HM Ship Maidstone Int: 05 Jan 1813 Dis: 27 Jan 1813.
   Received from HM Ship Maidstone. Bostock Cartel for New York.

Latham, A B   Prisoner 1298. Rank: Lieutenant, from: Rolla, Privateer.
   Cap: 10 Dec 1813 Block Island by Loire Int: 20 Dec 1813 Dis: 15 Apr 1814.
   Received from San Domingo. HMS Rammillies for Halifax.

Latham, Giles   Prisoner 1688. Rank: Prize Master, from: Lark, Merchant Vessel.
   Cap: 06 Apr 1814 L 29.0 by Recruit Int: 11 May 1814 Dis:
   Recaptured. Received from Recruit. (Date of discharge not recorded.)

Lathan, Thomas   Prisoner 402. Rank: Seaman, from: Snapper, Privateer Schooner.
   Cap: 16 Nov 1812 at Sea by HM Ship Galus Int: 22 Nov 1812 Dis: 27 Jan 1813.
   Received from HM Ship Galus. Bostock Cartel for New York.

Lattimore, C N   Prisoner 1678. Rank: Seaman, from: Saragosa, Merchant Vessel.
   Cap: 16 Feb 1814 off Charlestown by Morgiana Int: 10 Apr 1814 Dis: 23 Apr 1814.
   Received from Morgiana. HMS Bulwark for Halifax Order Comm in Chief.

Lattimore, James   Prisoner 20. Rank: Captain, from: Amiable, Merchant Schooner.
   Cap: 14 Jul 1812 at Bermuda by Cuttle Int: 28 Aug 1812 Dis: 26 Sep 1812.
   Received from HM Schooner Cuttle. Permitted to remain in the Colony.

Laughton, Otis   Prisoner 104. Rank: Seaman, from: Gossepuim, detained American.
   Cap: 31 Aug 1812 Bermuda by Not Recorded Int: 31 Aug 1812 Dis: 18 Sep 1812.
   Received from HMS Ruby. detained per order of the Commodore. Order of Commd Evans for England.

Laurence, Adam   Prisoner 1377. Rank: Seaman, from: Policy, Merchant Vessel.
   Cap: 04 Dec 1813 Not Recorded by Loire Int: 20 Dec 1813 Dis: 15 Apr 1814.
   Recaptured. Received from San Domingo. Diana Transport for Halifax.

American Prisoners of War Held at Bermuda During the War of 1812

Laurence, William   Prisoner 1665. Rank: Seaman, from: Mary Ann, Merchant Vessel.
    Cap: 26 Dec 1813 Chesapeake by Sophie   Int: 13 Mar 1814   Dis: 23 Apr 1814.
    Received from Active. HMS Bulwark for Halifax.

Law, Thomas   Prisoner 1583. Rank: Seaman, from: Bordeaux Packet, Letter of Marque.
    Cap: 28 Jan 1814 off Cape Henry by Nieman   Int: 12 Feb 1814   Dis: 15 Apr 1814.
    Received from Nieman. Diana Transport for Halifax.

Lawrence, John   Prisoner 197. Rank: Seaman, from: Wasp, Sloop of War.
    Cap: 18 Oct 1812 at Sea by HMS Poictiers   Int: 26 Oct 1812   Dis: 05 Nov 1812.
    Received from HM Ship Poictiers. Brig Diamond on Parole to new London America.

Lawrence, Peter   Prisoner 2634. Rank: Seaman, from: Superb, Merchant Vessel.
    Cap: 23 Nov 1814 off Delaware by Spencer   Int: 06 Feb 1815   Dis: 28 Mar 1815.
    Received from HMS Telegraph. Clarendon Transport for U States.

Lawson, James   Prisoner 2240. Rank: Seaman, from: President, U States Frigate.
    Cap: 15 Jan 1815 Not Recorded by Endymion   Int: 30 Jan 1815   Dis: 28 Mar 1815.
    Received from Pomone. Lord Collingwood.

Lawson, William   Prisoner 2073. Rank: Master, from: May Flower, Merchant Sloop.
    Cap: 22 Dec 1814 Grafy Bay Bermuda by Came in by Stress of Weather   Int: 22 Dec 1814   Dis: 11 Jan 1815. Received from American Sloop May Flower. This Vessel was blown off the Coast of America & ran into Bermuda in Distress. To wait for a passage to the United States.

Lawton, G   Prisoner 1447. Rank: Master, from: Betsey, Merchant Sloop.
    Cap: 15 Dec 1813 Lat 32 by Doterel   Int: 25 Dec 1813   Dis: 15 Apr 1814.
    Received from Doterel. Rammilles for Halifax.

Laxes, Peter   Prisoner 12. Rank: Seaman, from: General Blake, Merchant.
    Cap: 09 Jul 1812 near Bermuda by Recruit   Int: 28 Aug 1812   Dis: 18 Sep 1812.
    Received from HM Schooner Cuttle. Order of Commd Evans for England.

Layfield, William   Prisoner 1030. Rank: Seaman, from: Dart, Merchant Schooner.
    Cap: 17 Mar 1813 off the Chesapeake by HMS Statira   Int: 06 Apr 1813   Dis: 24 Jun 1813.
    Received from HMS Junon. Magnet Cartel for New York.

Le Count, Philip   Prisoner 859. Rank: Boy, from: Bona, Letter of Marque Schooner.
    Cap: 12 Mar 1813 Chesapeake by HM Ship Laurustinus   Int: 23 Mar 1813   Dis: 20 Apr 1813.
    Received from HM Ship Laurustinus. being Under Age per Order Commodore Evans.

Le Fause, Cade   Prisoner 366. Rank: Seaman, from: Snapper, Privateer Schooner.
    Cap: 16 Nov 1812 at Sea by HM Ship Galus   Int: 22 Nov 1812   Dis: 27 Jan 1813.
    Received from HM Ship Galus. Bostock Cartel for New York.

Le Porte, Archibald   Prisoner 976. Rank: Seaman, from: Janett, Merchant Brig.
    Cap: 25 Feb 1813 Chesapeake by HMS Junon   Int: 23 Mar 1813   Dis: 13 Jun 1813.
    Received from HM Ship Laurustinus. Perseverance Cartel for the United States per Order Adml Sir J B Warren.

Leadworth, Michael   Prisoner 610. Rank: Seaman, from: Noetoin, Packet Brig.
    Cap: 05 Jan 1813 at Sea by HMS Belvidera   Int: 10 Jan 1813   Dis: 27 Jan 1813.
    Received from HMS Belvidera. Bostock Cartel for New York.

Leary, John   Prisoner 2184. Rank: Seaman, from: President, U States Frigate.
    Cap: 15 Jan 1815 Not Recorded by HMS Endymion   Int: 30 Jan 1815   Dis: 28 Mar 1815.
    Received from Pomone. Mars Transport for U States.

Leathan, Thomas   Prisoner 1425. Rank: Seaman, from: Nonsuch, Letter of Marque.
    Cap: 14 Dec 1813 Lat 32 by Doterel   Int: 25 Dec 1813   Dis: 15 Apr 1814.
    Received from HM Brig Doterel. Diana Transport for Halifax.

Lee, David   Prisoner 386. Rank: Seaman, from: Snapper, Privateer Schooner.
    Cap: 16 Nov 1812 at Sea by HM Ship Galus   Int: 22 Nov 1812   Dis: 27 Jan 1813.
    Received from HM Ship Galus. Bostock Cartel for New York.

Lee, George   Prisoner 1548. Rank: Master, from: Bordeaux Packet, Letter of Marque.
    Cap: 28 Jan 1814 off Cape Henry by Nieman   Int: 12 Feb 1814   Dis: 15 Apr 1814.
    Received from Nieman. Rammilles for Halifax.

Lee, Hezekiah I   Prisoner 1808. Rank: Passenger, from: Not Recorded, Not Recorded.
    Cap: Not Recorded by Not Recorded   Int: 14 Jun 1814   Dis: 15 Jun 1814.
    From St. Bartholomew in the Swedish Schooner Oscar. on Parole per Order Com in Chief to America. (Date of capture not recorded.)

Lee, John   Prisoner 1776. Rank: Seaman, from: Yankelass, Privateer.
    Cap: 01 May 1814 Latt 40-4N, Long 38-0W by Severn & Surprise   Int: 07 Jun 1814   Dis: 10 Nov 1814.
    Received from Surprise. Joseph MV order Rear Adm Cockburn.

Lee, Samuel   Prisoner 1321. Rank: Seaman, from: Rolla, Privateer.
    Cap: 10 Dec 1813 Block Island by Loire   Int: 20 Dec 1813   Dis: 15 Apr 1814.
    Received from San Domingo. HMS Rammillies for Halifax.

American Prisoners of War Held at Bermuda During the War of 1812

Lee, W R   Prisoner 1229. Rank: Not Recorded, from: HM Ship Cleopatra, Not Recorded.
    Cap: 21 Sep 1813 Not Recorded by Dragon Int: 16 Nov 1813 Dis: 15 Apr 1814.
    Received from HMS Sceptre. Surrendered himself. Diana Transport for Halifax.

Leech, Nathaniel   Prisoner 392. Rank: Seaman, from: Snapper, Privateer Schooner.
    Cap: 16 Nov 1812 at Sea by HM Ship Galus Int: 22 Nov 1812 Dis: 27 Jan 1813.
    Received from HM Ship Galus. Bostock Cartel for New York.

Leger, Daniel   Prisoner 1276. Rank: Mate, from: Perry, Merchant Schooner.
    Cap: 03 Dec 1813 Long Island by Indemyion Int: 19 Dec 1813 Dis: 15 Apr 1814.
    Received from Sceptre. HMS Rammillies for Halifax.

Leggar, Daniel   Prisoner 578. Rank: 1 Mate, from: Lydia, Merchant Ship.
    Cap: 25 Dec 1812 at Sea by HM Ship Maidstone Int: 06 Jan 1813 Dis: 27 Jan 1813.
    Received from HM Ship Maidstone. Bostock Cartel for New York.

Lemer, John   Prisoner 688. Rank: Seaman, from: High Flyer, Privateer.
    Cap: 09 Jan 1813 at Sea by HMS Acasta Int: 21 Jan 1813 Dis: 27 Jan 1813.
    Received from HMS Acasta. Bostock Cartel for New York.

Lent, Benjamin   Prisoner 476. Rank: Seaman, from: Teazer, Privateer Schooner.
    Cap: 16 Dec 1812 at Sea by HM Ship St. Domingo Int: 21 Dec 1812 Dis: 27 Jan 1813.
    Received from HM Ship St. Domingo. Bostock Cartel for New York.

Leonard, Robert   Prisoner 2460. Rank: Quartermaster, from: President, U States Frigate.
    Cap: 15 Jan 1815 Not Recorded by Endymion Int: 04 Feb 1815 Dis: 28 Mar 1815.
    Received from Endymion. Clarenden Transport for U States.

Leters, Charles   Prisoner 1166. Rank: Seaman, from: Caledonian, Merchant.
    Cap: 20 Jul 1813 at Sea by HM Ship Marlborough Int: 15 Aug 1813 Dis: 03 Oct 1813.
    Received from HM Ship Woolwich. Caledonian Order of Commodore Evans she being Liberated.

Levina, Lewis   Prisoner 2167. Rank: Captains Steward, from: President, U States Frigate.
    Cap: 15 Jan 1815 Not Recorded by Endymion Int: 30 Jan 1815 Dis: 06 Feb 1815.
    Received from President. Narcissus to the U States by order of Commadore Evans.

Lewis, Charles   Prisoner 2660. Rank: Seaman, from: Amicus, Merchant Vessel.
    Cap: 10 Jan 1815 Delaware by Forth Int: 14 Feb 1815 Dis: 17 Feb 1815.
    Recaptured. Chapeur Privateer. Received from Goree. Harriot M Vessel order of Commadore Evans.

Lewis, D   Prisoner 1364. Rank: Seaman, from: Rolla, Privateer.
    Cap: 10 Dec 1813 Block Island by Loire Int: 20 Dec 1813 Dis: 15 Apr 1814.
    Received from San Domingo. HMS Rammillies for Halifax.

Lewis, Henry   Prisoner 763. Rank: Seaman, from: Hazard, Merchant Brig.
    Cap: 28 Dec 1812 Lat 37.35, Long 70.10 by HM Sloop Sylph Int: 26 Jan 1813 Dis: 14 Jun 1813.
    Received from Sloop Sylph. Permitted to return to the United States in the Perseverance Cartel.

Lewis, James   Prisoner 1657. Rank: Seaman, from: Flash, Letter of Marque.
    Cap: 11 Feb 1814 Off Block Island by Acasta Int: 13 Mar 1814 Dis: 23 Apr 1814.
    Received from Active. HMS Bulwark for Halifax.

Lewis, John   Prisoner 580. Rank: Cook, from: Lydia, Merchant Ship.
    Cap: 25 Dec 1812 at Sea by HM Ship Maidstone Int: 06 Jan 1813 Dis: 27 Jan 1813.
    Received from HM Ship Maidstone. Bostock Cartel for New York.

Lewis, Michael   Prisoner 1676. Rank: Passenger, from: Vixen, Man of War.
    Cap: 25 Dec 1813 Latt 38.0 by Belvidera Int: 18 Mar 1814 Dis: 15 Apr 1814.
    MS Schooner. Received from Hospital. Rammilles for Halifax.

Lewis, Roswelling   Prisoner 810. Rank: Seaman, from: Elouisa, Merchant Schooner.
    Cap: 16 Feb 1813 at Sea by HM Sloop Morgiana Int: 25 Feb 1813 Dis: 14 Jun 1813.
    Received from Morgiana. Permitted to return to the United States in the Perseverance Cartel.

Lewis, S H B   Prisoner 997. Rank: Seaman, from: Orion, Merchant.
    Cap: 25 Mar 1813 at Sea by HM Sloop Childers Int: 04 Apr 1813 Dis: 09 Apr 1813.
    Received from HM Sloop Childers. Per Order Commodore Evans Vessel Liberated.

Lewis, Sol   Prisoner 1255. Rank: Not Recorded, from: Circe, Merchant Vessel.
    Cap: 08 Oct 1813 Chesapeake by Lacedaemonian Int: 02 Dec 1813 Dis: 15 Apr 1814.
    Received from HMS Sceptre. Diana Transport for Halifax.

Lewis, William   Prisoner 278. Rank: Seaman, from: Little William, Merchant Brig.
    Cap: 18 Oct 1812 at Sea by HM Ship Poictiers Int: 26 Oct 1812 Dis: 05 Nov 1812.
    Received from HM Ship Poictiers. Brig Diamond on Parole to new London United States of America.

Lewis, William   Prisoner 1988. Rank: Seaman, from: Eclipse, Merchant Vessel.
    Cap: 29 Sep 1814 Bermuda by Copark Int: 05 Oct 1814 Dis: 28 Mar 1815.
    Recaptured. Received from Goree. Clarendon Transport for U States.

Lewy, Frederick   Prisoner 496. Rank: Seaman, from: Teazer, Privateer Schooner.
    Cap: 16 Dec 1812 at Sea by HM Ship St. Domingo Int: 21 Dec 1812 Dis: 27 Jan 1813.
    Received from HM Ship St. Domingo. Bostock Cartel for New York.

American Prisoners of War Held at Bermuda During the War of 1812

Libbey, Richard   Prisoner 939. Rank: Mate, from: Alert, Merchant Sloop.
    Cap: 13 Mar 1813 Chesapeake by Laurustinus Int: 23 Mar 1813 Dis: 24 Jun 1813.
    Received from Laurustinus. Magnet Cartel for New York.

Liffler, Henry   Prisoner 1984. Rank: Prize Master, from: Eclipse, Merchant Vessel.
    Cap: 29 Sep 1814 Bermuda by Copark Int: 05 Oct 1814 Dis: 05 Nov 1814.
    Recaptured. Received from Goree. Order Adl Cockburn.

Lincoln, Charles   Prisoner 735. Rank: Mate, from: Fernando, Merchant Brig.
    Cap: 09 Jan 1813 at Sea by HM Ship Acasta Int: 21 Jan 1813 Dis: 27 Jan 1813.
    Received from HMS Acasta. Bostock Cartel for New York.

Lincoln, Nicholas   Prisoner 438. Rank: Master, from: Experience, Merchant Brig.
    Cap: 25 Nov 1812 at Sea by HM Sloop Sophia Int: 11 Dec 1812 Dis: 27 Jan 1813.
    Received from Prize Brig Enterprise. Bostock Cartel for New York.

Lindsey, Joseph   Prisoner 1117. Rank: Seaman, from: Not Recorded, Not Recorded.
    Cap: Not Recorded by Not Recorded Int: 08 Jun 1813 Dis: 24 Jun 1813.
    Received from HM Sloop Moselle. Surrendered Him Self a Prisoner of War. Magnet Cartel for New York. (Date of capture not recorded.)

Linnell, Jonathan   Prisoner 87. Rank: Seaman, from: Gossepuim, Merchant.
    Cap: 16 Aug 1812 of Bermuda by Goree Int: 28 Aug 1812 Dis: 18 Sep 1812.
    Received from HM Schooner Cuttle. Order of Commd Evans for England.

Linnot, Morgan   Prisoner 420. Rank: Cook, from: Isabella, Merchant Brig.
    Cap: 15 Nov 1812 at Sea by HM Sloop Childers Int: 24 Nov 1812 Dis: 27 Jan 1813.
    Received from HM Ship Childers. Bostock Cartel for New York.

Linscott, John   Prisoner 2529. Rank: Seaman, from: President, U States Frigate.
    Cap: 15 Jan 1815 Not Recorded by Endymion Int: 04 Feb 1815 Dis: 28 Mar 1815.
    Received from HMS Endymion. Clarenden Transport for U States.

Lint, John   Prisoner 2833. Rank: Seaman, from: Limerick, Not Recorded.
    Cap: 15 Mar 1815 Not Recorded by Asia Int: 25 Mar 1815 Dis:
    From Depot at Jamaica. Received from Asia. (Date of discharge not recorded.)

Litchfield, John   Prisoner 2328. Rank: Seaman, from: President, U States Frigate.
    Cap: 15 Jan 1815 Not Recorded by Endymion Int: 04 Feb 1815 Dis: 28 Mar 1815.
    Received from Endymion. Mars Transport for U States.

Little, William   Prisoner 229. Rank: Seaman, from: Wasp, Sloop of War.
    Cap: 18 Oct 1812 at Sea by HM Ship Poictiers Int: 26 Oct 1812 Dis: 05 Nov 1812.
    Received from HM Ship Poictiers. Brig Diamond on Parole to new London United States of America.

Little, William   Prisoner 1371. Rank: Seaman, from: Rolla, Privateer.
    Cap: 10 Dec 1813 Block Island by Loire Int: 20 Dec 1813 Dis: 15 Apr 1814.
    Received from San Domingo. HMS Rammillies for Halifax.

Littlefield, John   Prisoner 2433. Rank: Seaman, from: President, U States Frigate.
    Cap: 15 Jan 1815 Not Recorded by HM Ship Endymion Int: 04 Feb 1815 Dis: 28 Mar 1815.
    Received from Endymion. Mars Transport for U States.

Littlefield, Lyman   Prisoner 984. Rank: Seaman, from: Mary, Merchant.
    Cap: 10 Mar 1813 Chesapeake by HMS Maidstone Int: 23 Mar 1813 Dis: 24 Jun 1813.
    Received from HM Ship Laurustinus. Magnet Cartel for New York.

Littlefield, N   Prisoner 1209. Rank: Seaman, from: Ambition, Merchant Sloop.
    Cap: 26 Sep 1813 at Sea by HM Brig Acteon Int: 16 Nov 1813 Dis: 15 Apr 1814.
    Received from the Custody of Lieut Bacon. HMS Ramillies for Halifax.

Lock, Nathaniel   Prisoner 105. Rank: Seaman, from: Gossepuim, detained American.
    Cap: 02 Sep 1812 Bermuda by Not Recorded Int: 02 Sep 1812 Dis: 18 Sep 1812.
    Received from HMS Ruby. detained per order of the President. Order of Commd Evans for England.

Locket, Agnetu   Prisoner 1714. Rank: Master, from: Olive Branch, Merchant Vessel.
    Cap: 16 Apr 1814 Chesapeake by Acasta Int: 26 May 1814 Dis: 14 Jun 1814.
    Received from Lacedaemonian. United States on Parole.

Lolly, William   Prisoner 1924. Rank: Seaman, from: Timer, Merchant Vessel.
    Cap: 23 Aug 1814 off Savannah by Lacedaemonian Int: 09 Sep 1814 Dis: 28 Mar 1815.
    Received from Lacedaemonian. Clarendon Transport for U States.

Long, John   Prisoner 2056. Rank: Seaman, from: Amy, Merchant Schooner.
    Cap: 26 Nov 1814 off Cape Delaware by Telegraph Int: 05 Dec 1814 Dis: 16 Mar 1815.
    Received from HMS Goree. Merchant Vessel.

Long, Robert   Prisoner 1961. Rank: Seaman, from: Pike, Privateer.
    Cap: 25 Aug 1814 off Savannah by Primrose Int: 09 Sep 1814 Dis: 28 Mar 1815.
    Received from Lacedaemonian. Clarendon Transport for U States.

American Prisoners of War Held at Bermuda During the War of 1812

Longel, Matthew   Prisoner 191. Rank: Seaman, from: Wasp, Sloop of War.
    Cap: 18 Oct 1812 at Sea by HMS Poictiers Int: 26 Oct 1812 Dis: 05 Nov 1812.
    Received from HM Ship Poictiers. Brig Diamond on Parole to new London America.

Longford, Samuel   Prisoner 588. Rank: Seaman, from: Lydia, Merchant Ship.
    Cap: 26 Dec 1812 at Sea by HM Ship Maidstone Int: 06 Jan 1813 Dis: 27 Jan 1813.
    Received from HM Ship Maidstone. Bostock Cartel for New York.

Longshore, Thomas   Prisoner 1833. Rank: Passenger, from: Not Recorded, Not Recorded.
    Cap: Not Recorded by Not Recorded Int: 14 Jun 1814 Dis: 15 Jun 1814.
    From St. Bartholomew in the Swedish Schooner Oscar. on Parole per Order Com in Chief to America.
    (Date of capture not recorded.)

Look, John   Prisoner 1050. Rank: Mate, from: Massoil, Merchant.
    Cap: 18 Mar 1813 Chesapeake by HMS Dragon Int: 06 Apr 1813 Dis: 24 Jun 1813.
    Received from HMS Junon. Magnet Cartel for New York.

Lord, Jonas   Prisoner 2435. Rank: Seaman, from: President, U States Frigate.
    Cap: 15 Jan 1815 Not Recorded by HM Ship Endymion Int: 04 Feb 1815 Dis: 28 Mar 1815.
    Received from Endymion. Mars Transport for U States.

Lorgeunt, Samuel   Prisoner 2302. Rank: Captains Crew, from: President, U States Frigate.
    Cap: 15 Jan 1815 Not Recorded by Endymion Int: 04 Feb 1815 Dis: 28 Mar 1815.
    Received from Endymion. Mars Transport for U States.

Lorin, George   Prisoner 1363. Rank: Seaman, from: Rolla, Privateer.
    Cap: 10 Dec 1813 Block Island by Loire Int: 20 Dec 1813 Dis: 15 Apr 1814.
    Received from San Domingo. HMS Rammillies for Halifax.

Loring, Almond   Prisoner 755. Rank: Seaman, from: Delaclea, Merchant Schooner.
    Cap: 17 Dec 1812 Lat 34.31 N, Long 74.44 W by HM Sloop Sylph Int: 26 Jan 1812 Dis: 14 Apr 1813.
    Received from Sloop Sylph. Per Order Commodore Evans Vessel Liberated.

Lourey, James   Prisoner 2321. Rank: Marine, from: President, U States Frigate.
    Cap: 15 Jan 1815 Not Recorded by Endymion Int: 04 Feb 1815 Dis: 28 Mar 1815.
    Received from Endymion. Clarenden Transport for U States.

Lovett, William   Prisoner 1178. Rank: Seaman, from: Calmer, Merchant.
    Cap: 15 Jun 1813 at Sea by HM Ship Marlborough Int: 15 Aug 1813 Dis: 21 Aug 1813.
    Received from HM Ship Woolwich. Per Order Commodore Evans.

Loviet, Joseph   Prisoner 2610. Rank: Seaman, from: Falcon, Merchant Vessel.
    Cap: 22 Jan 1815 Sandy Hook by HM Ship Pomone Int: 05 Feb 1815 Dis: 28 Mar 1815.
    Received from HMS Forth. Clarendon Transport for U States.

Low, John   Prisoner 2197. Rank: Seaman, from: President, U States Frigate.
    Cap: 15 Jan 1815 Not Recorded by Endymion Int: 30 Jan 1815 Dis: 28 Mar 1815.
    Received from Pomone. Mars Transport for U States.

Lowe, John   Prisoner 626. Rank: Seaman, from: Dolphin, Merchant Brig.
    Cap: 30 Dec 1812 at Sea by HM Ship Galus Int: 12 Jan 1813 Dis: 27 Jan 1813.
    Received from Prize Brig Dolphin. Bostock Cartel for New York.

Lowe, John   Prisoner 2623. Rank: Seaman, from: William, Merchant Vessel.
    Cap: 12 Jan 1815 Cape Hatterus by HMS Telegraph Int: 05 Feb 1815 Dis: 28 Mar 1815.
    Received from HMS Telegraph. Clarendon Transport for U States.

Lowry, William   Prisoner 2446. Rank: Seaman, from: President, U States Frigate.
    Cap: 15 Jan 1815 Not Recorded by Endymion Int: 04 Feb 1815 Dis: 28 Mar 1815.
    Received from Endymion. Clarenden Transport for U States.

Lucas, William   Prisoner 133. Rank: Lieutenant, from: James Maddison, Man of War.
    Cap: 22 Aug 1812 Lat 31 by HMS Barbados Int: 14 Sep 1812 Dis: 24 Oct 1812.
    Received from HMS Barbados. Brig Diamond on Parole to new London United States of America.

Lucas, William   Prisoner 2021. Rank: Seaman, from: Swiftsure, Merchant Vessel.
    Cap: 26 Oct 1814 off Halifax by Armide Int: 07 Nov 1814 Dis: 24 Mar 1815.
    Recaptured. Received from HMS Armide. Merchant Vessel.

Ludlow, William   Prisoner 870. Rank: Seaman, from: Gustavas, Merchant Brig.
    Cap: 16 Mar 1813 Chesapeake by HM Ship Laurustinus Int: 23 Mar 1813 Dis: 24 Apr 1813.
    Received from Laurustinus. Per Order Commodore Evans Vessel Liberated.

Luke, Clarke   Prisoner 883. Rank: Boy, from: George, Merchant Sloop.
    Cap: 05 Feb 1813 Chesapeake by HM Ship Dragon Int: 23 Mar 1813 Dis: 27 Apr 1813.
    Received from Laurustinus. being Under Age per Order Commodore Evans.

Luky, Jacob   Prisoner 381. Rank: Seaman, from: Snapper, Privateer Schooner.
    Cap: 16 Nov 1812 at Sea by HM Ship Galus Int: 22 Nov 1812 Dis: 27 Jan 1813.
    Received from HM Ship Galus. Bostock Cartel for New York.

American Prisoners of War Held at Bermuda During the War of 1812

Luther, Nathaniel   Prisoner 820. Rank: Seaman, from: Elove & Unity, Merchant.
    Cap: 07 Mar 1813 at Bermuda by Sandimingo Int: 08 Mar 1813 Dis: 13 Jun 1813.
    Received from Sandimingo. Perseverance Cartel for the United States per Order Adm Sir J B Warren.

Luthers, Jeremiah   Prisoner 2524. Rank: Seaman, from: President, U States Frigate.
    Cap: 15 Jan 1815 Not Recorded by Endymion Int: 04 Feb 1815 Dis: 28 Mar 1815.
    Received from HMS Endymion. Subject of Holland.

Lyceet, John   Prisoner 238. Rank: Seaman, from: Wasp, Sloop of War.
    Cap: 18 Oct 1812 at Sea by HM Ship Poictiers Int: 26 Oct 1812 Dis: 05 Nov 1812.
    Received from HM Ship Poictiers. Brig Diamond on Parole to new London United States of America.

Lyn, John   Prisoner 1155. Rank: Seaman, from: Acricoake, Merchant.
    Cap: 22 Jul 1813 at Sea by HM Sloop Conflict Int: 13 Aug 1813 Dis: 13 Aug 1813.
    Received from HM Ship Woolwich. American Ship Rolla per Order Governor Strong.

Lyons, Henry G   Prisoner 1595. Rank: Seaman, from: Hornby, Merchant Vessel.
    Cap: 05 Feb 1814 Latt 39.0 by Sceptre Int: 13 Feb 1814 Dis: 15 Apr 1814.
    Recaptured. Received from Sceptre. Rammilles for Halifax.

Lyons, Henry   Prisoner 2870. Rank: Seaman, from: Limerick, Not Recorded.
    Cap: 06 Mar 1815 Not Recorded by Asia Int: 29 Mar 1815 Dis: 28 Mar 1815.
    From West Indies. Received from La Brune. Clarendon Transport for U States. (Date of discharge before date of internment.)

Lyons, John   Prisoner 2323. Rank: 2 Gunner, from: President, U States Frigate.
    Cap: 15 Jan 1815 Not Recorded by Endymion Int: 04 Feb 1815 Dis: 28 Mar 1815.
    Received from Endymion. Mars Transport for U States.

Macamber, Samuel   Prisoner 568. Rank: Seaman, from: Fly, Merchant.
    Cap: 06 Dec 1812 at Sea by HM Ship Maidstone Int: 06 Jan 1813 Dis: 27 Jan 1813.
    Received from HM Ship Maidstone. Bostock Cartel for New York.

Mace, Henry   Prisoner 2594. Rank: Boy, from: Lark, Merchant Vessel.
    Cap: 01 Dec 1814 off New York by HM Ship Majestic Int: 05 Feb 1815 Dis: 16 Mar 1815.
    Recaptured. York Privateer. Received from HMS Forth. Merchant Service.

Macey, F G   Prisoner 1530. Rank: Master, from: Romp, Merchant Vessel.
    Cap: 02 Jan 1814 Latt 22.0 by Prometheus Int: 23 Jan 1814 Dis: 15 Apr 1814.
    Received from Prometheus. Rammilles for Halifax.

Mack, Charles   Prisoner 739. Rank: Seaman, from: Fanny, Merchant Schooner.
    Cap: 04 Jan 1813 at Sea by HM Ship Poictiers Int: 21 Jan 1813 Dis: 27 Jan 1813.
    Received from HMS Poictiers. Bostock Cartel for New York.

Mack, William   Prisoner 738. Rank: Seaman, from: Fanny, Merchant Schooner.
    Cap: 04 Jan 1813 at Sea by HM Ship Poictiers Int: 21 Jan 1813 Dis: 27 Jan 1813.
    Received from HMS Acasta. Bostock Cartel for New York.

Mackay, James F   Prisoner 1275. Rank: Master, from: Perry, Merchant Schooner.
    Cap: 03 Dec 1813 Long Island by Indemyion Int: 19 Dec 1813 Dis: 15 Apr 1814.
    Received from Sceptre. HMS Rammillies for Halifax.

Maclever, Francis   Prisoner 1770. Rank: Seaman, from: Yankelass, Privateer.
    Cap: 01 May 1814 L 40-4N, Long 38-0W by Severn & Surprise Int: 07 Jun 1814 Dis: 28 Mar 1815.
    Received from Surprise. Mars Transport for U States.

Madden, Laurence   Prisoner 2595. Rank: SM, from: Lark, Merchant Vessel.
    Cap: 01 Dec 1814 off New York by HM Ship Majestic Int: 05 Feb 1815 Dis: 28 Mar 1815.
    Recaptured. York Privateer. Received from HMS Forth. Clarendon Transport for U States.

Madden, Michael   Prisoner 2511. Rank: Seaman, from: President, U States Frigate.
    Cap: 15 Jan 1815 Not Recorded by Endymion Int: 04 Feb 1815 Dis: 28 Mar 1815.
    Received from HMS Endymion. Clarenden Transport for U States.

Maddox, Samuel   Prisoner 707. Rank: Seaman, from: High Flyer, Privateer.
    Cap: 09 Jan 1813 at Sea by HMS Acasta Int: 21 Jan 1813 Dis: 27 Jan 1813.
    Received from HMS Acasta. Bostock Cartel for New York.

Madison, Andrew   Prisoner 1543. Rank: Boy, from: Defiance, Merchant Vessel.
    Cap: 05 Jan 1814 at Sea by Childers Int: 26 Jan 1814 Dis: 15 Apr 1814.
    Received from Childers. Diana for Halifax.

Magruder, Thomas W   Prisoner 565. Rank: Midshipman, from: Fly, Merchant.
    Cap: 06 Dec 1812 at Sea by HM Ship Maidstone Int: 06 Jan 1813 Dis: 27 Jan 1813.
    Received from HM Ship Maidstone. Bostock Cartel for New York.

Mailer, Charles   Prisoner 375. Rank: Seaman, from: Snapper, Privateer Schooner.
    Cap: 16 Nov 1812 at Sea by HM Ship Galus Int: 22 Nov 1812 Dis: 27 Jan 1813.
    Received from HM Ship Galus. Bostock Cartel for New York.

American Prisoners of War Held at Bermuda During the War of 1812

Mallet, John   Prisoner 1242. Rank: Not Recorded, from: Julia, Schooner.
    Cap: 10 Aug 1813 Lake Ontario by Wolf Int: 30 Nov 1813 Dis: 15 Apr 1814.
    Received from HM Ship Goliah. Diana Transport for Halifax.

Malstom, James   Prisoner 723. Rank: Seaman, from: High Flyer, Privateer.
    Cap: 09 Jan 1813 at Sea by HM Ship Acasta Int: 21 Jan 1813 Dis: 27 Jan 1813.
    Received from HMS Acasta. Bostock Cartel for New York.

Mandell, John   Prisoner 676. Rank: Seaman, from: High Flyer, Privateer.
    Cap: 09 Jan 1813 at Sea by HM Ship Acasta Int: 21 Jan 1813 Dis: 27 Jan 1813.
    Received from HMS Acasta. Bostock Cartel for New York.

Manley, Samuel   Prisoner 605. Rank: Seaman, from: Noetoin, Packet Brig.
    Cap: 05 Jan 1813 at Sea by HM Ship Belvidera Int: 10 Jan 1813 Dis: 27 Jan 1813.
    Received from HMS Belvidera. Bostock Cartel for New York.

Mann, John   Prisoner 668. Rank: Carpenters Mate, from: High Flyer, Privateer.
    Cap: 09 Jan 1813 at Sea by HM Ship Acasta Int: 21 Jan 1813 Dis: 27 Jan 1813.
    Received from HMS Acasta. Bostock Cartel for New York.

Mann, Thomas   Prisoner 1179. Rank: Seaman, from: Calmer, Merchant.
    Cap: 15 Jun 1813 at Sea by HM Ship Marlborough Int: 15 Aug 1813 Dis: 21 Aug 1813.
    Received from HM Ship Woolwich. Per Order Commodore Evans.

Manston, David   Prisoner 973. Rank: Seaman, from: Janett, Merchant Brig.
    Cap: 25 Feb 1813 Chesapeake by HMS Junon Int: 23 Mar 1813 Dis: 24 Jun 1813.
    Received from HM Ship Laurustinus. Magnet Cartel for New York.

Marble, Benjamin   Prisoner 2628. Rank: Boy, from: William, Merchant Vessel.
    Cap: 19 Jan 1815 off Cape Hatterus by HMS Telegraph Int: 05 Feb 1815 Dis: 28 Mar 1815.
    Received from HMS Telegraph. Clarendon Transport for U States. (Rest of crew has date of capture January 12, 1815.)

March, Charles   Prisoner 2681. Rank: Mate, from: Farmers Branch, Merchant Vessel.
    Cap: 06 Feb 1815 off Delaware by Lacedaemonian Int: 14 Feb 1815 Dis: 28 Mar 1815.
    Received from Childers. Merchant Vessel.

Marina, Nicholas   Prisoner 61. Rank: Seaman, from: Mary, Merchant Brig.
    Cap: 08 Aug 1812 of Bermuda by Cuttle Int: 28 Aug 1812 Dis: 15 Sep 1812.
    Received from M Schooner Cuttle. being Spaniard C. Evans.

Mariner, Joseph   Prisoner 2317. Rank: Seaman, from: President, U States Frigate.
    Cap: 15 Jan 1815 Not Recorded by Endymion Int: 04 Feb 1815 Dis: 28 Mar 1815.
    Received from Endymion. Mars Transport for U States.

Mark, John   Prisoner 1640. Rank: Master, from: Mary Ann, Merchant Vessel.
    Cap: 06 Jan 1814 off Charlestown by Recruit Int: 21 Feb 1814 Dis:
    Received from Recruit. (Date of discharge not recorded.)

Marlin, William   Prisoner 847. Rank: Seaman, from: Polly Maria, Merchant.
    Cap: 03 Feb 1813 at Sea by HMS Sophia Int: 17 Mar 1813 Dis: 13 Jun 1813.
    Received from HMS Sophia. Perseverance Cartel for the United States per Order Adml Sir J B Warren.

Marsden, William   Prisoner 827. Rank: Seaman, from: Portsmouth, Merchant Ship.
    Cap: 27 Feb 1813 off Bermuda by HM Sloop Martin Int: 09 Mar 1813 Dis: 27 Mar 1813.
    Received from Sloop Martin. Per Order Commodore Evans the Vessel being Liberated.

Marsden, William   Prisoner 2301. Rank: Seaman, from: President, U States Frigate.
    Cap: 15 Jan 1815 Not Recorded by Endymion Int: 04 Feb 1815 Dis: 28 Mar 1815.
    Received from Endymion. Mars Transport for U States.

Marsdon, George   Prisoner 1916. Rank: Seaman, from: Dolphin, Packet.
    Cap: 20 Aug 1814 St. Catherine by Lacedaemonian Int: 09 Sep 1814 Dis: 28 Mar 1815.
    Received from Lacedaemonian. Clarendon Transport for U States.

Marsh, Lubilen   Prisoner 2354. Rank: Seaman, from: President, U States Frigate.
    Cap: 15 Jan 1815 Not Recorded by HMS Endymion Int: 04 Feb 1815 Dis: 28 Mar 1815.
    Received from Endymion. Mars Transport for U States.

Marshall, David   Prisoner 1926. Rank: 1 Lieutenant, from: Pike, Privateer.
    Cap: 25 Aug 1814 off Savannah by Primrose Int: 09 Sep 1814 Dis: 28 Mar 1815.
    Received from Lacedaemonian. Clarendon Transport for U States.

Marshall, G   Prisoner 1426. Rank: Seaman, from: Nonsuch, Letter of Marque.
    Cap: 14 Dec 1813 Lat 32 by Doterel Int: 25 Dec 1813 Dis: 15 Apr 1814.
    Received from HM Brig Doterel. Diana Transport for Halifax.

Marshall, John   Prisoner 1186. Rank: Seaman, from: Caledonian, Merchant.
    Cap: 20 Jul 1813 at Sea by HM Ship Marlborough Int: 18 Aug 1813 Dis: 03 Oct 1813.
    Received from HM Ship Woolwich. Caledonian per Order of Commodore Evans she being Liberated.

American Prisoners of War Held at Bermuda During the War of 1812

Marshall, Thomas   Prisoner 2308. Rank: Seaman, from: President, U States Frigate.
    Cap: 15 Jan 1815 Not Recorded by Endymion Int: 04 Feb 1815 Dis: 28 Mar 1815.
    Received from Endymion. Mars Transport for U States.

Marson, Peter   Prisoner 2489. Rank: Seaman, from: President, U States Frigate.
    Cap: 15 Jan 1815 Not Recorded by Endymion Int: 04 Feb 1815 Dis: 28 Mar 1815.
    Received from Endymion. Clarenden Transport for U States.

Marta, S P   Prisoner 323. Rank: Seaman, from: James, Merchant Ship.
    Cap: 03 Nov 1812 at Sea by HM Ship Tartarus Int: 17 Nov 1812 Dis: 27 Jan 1813.
    Received from HM Ship Tartarus. Bostock Cartel for New York.

Martin, Charles   Prisoner 1942. Rank: Seaman, from: Pike, Privateer.
    Cap: 25 Aug 1814 off Savannah by Primrose Int: 09 Sep 1814 Dis: 28 Mar 1815.
    Received from Lacedaemonian. Clarendon Transport for U States.

Martin, George   Prisoner 2207. Rank: Seaman, from: President, U States Frigate.
    Cap: 15 Jan 1815 Not Recorded by Endymion Int: 30 Jan 1815 Dis: 28 Mar 1815.
    Received from Pomone. Mars Transport for U States.

Martin, Henry   Prisoner 369. Rank: Prize Master, from: Snapper, Privateer Schooner.
    Cap: 16 Nov 1812 at Sea by HM Ship Galus Int: 22 Nov 1812 Dis: 27 Jan 1813.
    Received from HM Ship Galus. Bostock Cartel for New York.

Martin, Isaac   Prisoner 2085. Rank: Not legible, from: Erin, Merchant Vessel.
    Cap: 20 Dec 1814 off Charleston by Portia Int: 06 Jan 1815 Dis: 27 Mar 1815.
    Received from HMS Portia. Lord Collingwood.

Martin, John   Prisoner 307. Rank: Seaman, from: Wasp, Sloop of War.
    Cap: 18 Oct 1812 at Sea by HMS Poictiers Int: 05 Nov 1812 Dis: 17 Jun 1813.
    Received from HM Ship Poictiers. Halifax Order of the Commander in Chief supports to be an Englishman.

Martin, Samuel   Prisoner 1367. Rank: Seaman, from: Rolla, Privateer.
    Cap: 10 Dec 1813 Block Island by Loire Int: 20 Dec 1813 Dis: 15 Apr 1814.
    Received from San Domingo. HMS Rammillies for Halifax.

Martin, Thomas   Prisoner 2771. Rank: Seaman, from: Brant, Not Recorded.
    Cap: 05 Feb 1815 St Augustine by Severn Int: 03 Mar 1815 Dis: 28 Mar 1815.
    Received from Hebrus. Clarendon Transport for U States.

Martin, William   Prisoner 2208. Rank: Seaman, from: President, U States Frigate.
    Cap: 15 Jan 1815 Not Recorded by Endymion Int: 30 Jan 1815 Dis: 28 Mar 1815.
    Received from Pomone. Mars Transport for U States.

Martins, Michael   Prisoner 2276. Rank: Marine, from: President, U States Frigate.
    Cap: 15 Jan 1815 Not Recorded by Endymion Int: 30 Jan 1815 Dis: 28 Mar 1815.
    Received from Pomone. Clarenden Transport for U States.

Mason, Francis   Prisoner 1572. Rank: Seaman, from: Bordeaux Packet, Letter of Marque.
    Cap: 28 Jan 1814 off Cape Henry by Nieman Int: 12 Feb 1814 Dis: 15 Apr 1814.
    Received from Nieman. Diana Transport for Halifax.

Mason, Joel   Prisoner 2387. Rank: Seaman, from: President, U States Frigate.
    Cap: 15 Jan 1815 Not Recorded by HMS Endymion Int: 04 Feb 1815 Dis: 28 Mar 1815.
    Received from Endymion. Mars Transport for U States.

Mason, John   Prisoner 2488. Rank: Seaman, from: President, U States Frigate.
    Cap: 15 Jan 1815 Not Recorded by Endymion Int: 04 Feb 1815 Dis: 28 Mar 1815.
    Received from Endymion. Clarenden Transport for U States.

Mason, Manuel   Prisoner 1190. Rank: Seaman, from: Elizabeth, Merchant.
    Cap: 15 Jun 1813 at Sea by HM Ship Marlborough Int: 18 Aug 1813 Dis: 02 Sep 1813.
    Received from HM Ship Woolwich. Per order of Commodore Evans vessel being liberated.

Mason, Samuel   Prisoner 2722. Rank: Seaman, from: American Gun Boat, Not Recorded.
    Cap: 06 Feb 1815 off Charleston by Tonnant Int: 02 Mar 1815 Dis:
    Received from Armede. (Date of discharge not recorded.)

Mason, Thomas   Prisoner 1066. Rank: Seaman, from: Amason, Merchant.
    Cap: 18 Mar 1813 Chesapeake by HM Ship Victorious Int: 06 Apr 1813 Dis: 24 Jun 1813.
    Received from HMS Junon. Magnet Cartel for New York.

Mass, Moses   Prisoner 1182. Rank: Seaman, from: Calmer, Merchant.
    Cap: 15 Jun 1813 at Sea by HM Ship Marlborough Int: 15 Aug 1813 Dis: 21 Aug 1813.
    Received from HM Ship Woolwich. Per Order Commodore Evans.

Masselin, Horace F   Prisoner 1997. Rank: Prize Master, from: Dry Farbourn, Merchant Vessel.
    Cap: 21 Oct 1814 off Bermuda by Pandora Int: 27 Oct 1814 Dis: 28 Mar 1815.
    Recaptured. Received from Goree. Clarendon Transport for U States.

American Prisoners of War Held at Bermuda During the War of 1812

Masta, Antonia   Prisoner 364. Rank: Seaman, from: Snapper, Privateer Schooner.
    Cap: 16 Nov 1812 at Sea by HM Ship Galus Int: 22 Nov 1812 Dis: 14 Dec 1812.
    Received from HM Ship Galus. per Order of Commd Evans.

Matheu, John   Prisoner 1920. Rank: Seaman, from: Dolphin, Packet.
    Cap: 20 Aug 1814 St. Catherine by Lacedaemonian Int: 09 Sep 1814 Dis: 28 Mar 1815.
    Received from Lacedaemonian. Clarendon Transport for U States.

Mathews, David   Prisoner 2523. Rank: Seaman, from: President, U States Frigate.
    Cap: 15 Jan 1815 Not Recorded by Endymion Int: 04 Feb 1815 Dis: 28 Mar 1815.
    Received from HMS Endymion. Clarenden Transport for U States.

Mathews, Henry   Prisoner 1463. Rank: Seaman, from: Vixen, Man of War.
    Cap: 25 Dec 1813 Lat 38.0 by Belvidera Int: 05 Jan 1814 Dis: 15 Apr 1814.
    U States Schooner. Received from HMS Belvidera. Diana Transport for Halifax.

Matthews, Edward   Prisoner 971. Rank: Seaman, from: Janett, Merchant Brig.
    Cap: 25 Feb 1813 Chesapeake by HMS Junon Int: 23 Mar 1813 Dis: 24 Jun 1813.
    Received from HM Ship Laurustinus. Magnet Cartel for New York.

Mauney, John   Prisoner 1700. Rank: Seaman, from: Grecian, Letter of Marque.
    Cap: 02 May 1814 Chesapeake by Jansur Int: 26 May 1814 Dis: 20 Mar 1815.
    Received from Lacedaemonian. Merchant Vessel.

Mavington, William   Prisoner 670. Rank: Gunners Mate, from: High Flyer, Privateer.
    Cap: 09 Jan 1813 at Sea by HM Ship Acasta Int: 21 Jan 1813 Dis: 27 Jan 1813.
    Received from HMS Acasta. Bostock Cartel for New York.

Mawn, Mathias   Prisoner 1526. Rank: Seaman, from: Matchless, Merchant Vessel.
    Cap: 02 Jan 1814 Latt 22.0 by Prometheus Int: 23 Jan 1814 Dis: 15 Apr 1814.
    Received from Prometheus. Diana for Halifax.

Maxworth, Mathew   Prisoner 1203. Rank: Seaman, from: Willam & Ann, Merchant Ship.
    Cap: 30 Jul 1813 at Sea by HM Sloop Nimrod Int: 05 Sep 1813 Dis: 12 Sep 1813.
    Received from HM Sloop Nimrod. Per Order of Commodore Evans to the American Ship Georgiana restored.

May, William   Prisoner 1208. Rank: Seaman, from: Ambition, Merchant Sloop.
    Cap: 26 Sep 1813 at Sea by HM Brig Acteon Int: 06 Nov 1813 Dis: 17 Nov 1813.
    Received from the Custody of Lieut Bacon. United States per Order of Rear Adml Cockburn.

McAfferty, William   Prisoner 304. Rank: Seaman, from: HMS Elizabeth, Not Recorded.
    Cap: Not Recorded by Not Recorded Int: 04 Nov 1812 Dis: 04 Nov 1812.
    Received from HM Schooner Elizabeth. formally serving on Board HMS Elizabeth. Brig Diamond on Parole to new London United States of America. (Date of capture not recorded.)

McCall, Thomas William   Prisoner 1973. Rank: Midshipman, from: Tamer, Merchant Vessel.
    Cap: 23 Aug 1814 St. Catherine by Lacedaemonian Int: 14 Sep 1814 Dis:
    Recaptured. Received from Goree. (Date of discharge not recorded.)

McCannon, Isaac   Prisoner 1758. Rank: Seaman, from: Yankelass, Privateer.
    Cap: 01 May 1814 L 40-4N, Long 38-0W by Severn & Surprise Int: 06 Jun 1814 Dis: 28 Mar 1815.
    Received from Severn. Mars Transport for U States.

McCarthy, James   Prisoner 1713. Rank: Seaman, from: Grecian, Letter of Marque.
    Cap: 02 May 1814 Chesapeake by Jansur Int: 26 May 1814 Dis: 16 Mar 1815.
    Received from Lacedaemonian. Merchant Service.

McCaun, John   Prisoner 1012. Rank: Seaman, from: Nymble, Merchant.
    Cap: 19 Mar 1813 off the Chesapeake by HM Ship San Domingo Int: 06 Apr 1813 Dis: 24 Jun 1813.
    Received from HMS Junon. Magnet Cartel for New York.

McChusney, William   Prisoner 1450. Rank: Midshipman, from: Vixen, Man of War.
    Cap: 25 Dec 1813 Lat 38.0 by Belvidera Int: 05 Jan 1814 Dis: 15 Apr 1814.
    U States Schooner. Received from HMS Belvidera. Rammilles for Halifax.

McCloud, John   Prisoner 312. Rank: Boatswain, from: Wasp, Sloop of War.
    Cap: 18 Oct 1812 at Sea by HMS Poictiers Int: 05 Nov 1812 Dis: 17 Jun 1813.
    Received from HM Ship Poictiers. Halifax Order of the Commander in Chief supports to be an Englishman.

McCloud, John   Prisoner 422. Rank: Seaman, from: Wasp, Sloop of War.
    Cap: Not Recorded by Not Recorded Int: Dis: 17 Jun 1813.
    Halifax Order of the Commander in Chief supports to be an Englishman. (Dates of capture and interment not recorded. Apparent duplicate of prisoner # 312.)

McClure, James   Prisoner 2490. Rank: Marine, from: President, U States Frigate.
    Cap: 15 Jan 1815 Not Recorded by Endymion Int: 04 Feb 1815 Dis: 28 Mar 1815.
    Received from Endymion. Clarenden Transport for U States.

American Prisoners of War Held at Bermuda During the War of 1812

McCollock, Robert   Prisoner 1461. Rank: Seaman, from: Vixen, Man of War.
    Cap: 25 Dec 1813 Lat 38.0 by Belvidera Int: 05 Jan 1814 Dis: 15 Apr 1814.
    U States Schooner. Received from HMS Belvidera. Diana Transport for Halifax.

McCoy, John   Prisoner 554. Rank: Seaman, from: Herald, Letter of Marque Brig.
    Cap: 25 Dec 1812 at Sea by HM Ship Maidstone Int: 05 Jan 1813 Dis: 27 Jan 1813.
    Received from HM Ship Maidstone. Bostock Cartel for New York.

McDermott, James   Prisoner 505. Rank: Seaman, from: Teazer, Privateer Schooner.
    Cap: 16 Dec 1812 at Sea by HM Ship St. Domingo Int: 28 Dec 1812 Dis: 17 Jun 1813.
    Received from San. Domingo. Halifax Order of the Commander in Chief supports to be an Englishman.

McDonald, Alexander   Prisoner 1290. Rank: Seaman, from: Perry, Merchant Schooner.
    Cap: 03 Dec 1813 Long Island by Indemyion Int: 19 Dec 1813 Dis: 15 Apr 1814.
    Received from Sceptre. Diana Transport for Halifax.

McDonald, David   Prisoner 2069. Rank: Seaman, from: Industry, Merchant Vessel.
    Cap: 01 Dec 1814 off Cape Henry by HMS Niemen Int: 15 Dec 1814 Dis: 28 Mar 1815.
    Recaptured. Belong to Carolina Privateer. Received from HMS Niemen. Clarendon Transport for U States.

McDonald, Ebenezer   Prisoner 2363. Rank: Seaman, from: President, U States Frigate.
    Cap: 15 Jan 1815 Not Recorded by HMS Endymion Int: 04 Feb 1815 Dis: 28 Mar 1815.
    Received from Endymion. Mars Transport for U States.

McDonald, James   Prisoner 2760. Rank: Passenger, from: Mayflower, Not Recorded.
    Cap: 20 Jan 1815 St Augustine by Severn Int: 03 Mar 1815 Dis: 17 Mar 1815.
    Received from Hebrus. Merchant Vessel.

McEldry, Hugh   Prisoner 633. Rank: 2 Mate, from: Herald, Letter of Marque Brig.
    Cap: 25 Dec 1812 at Sea by HMS Maidstone Int: 14 Jan 1813 Dis: 27 Jan 1813.
    Received from HMS Maidstone. Bostock Cartel for New York.

McFeadon, John   Prisoner 1565. Rank: Seaman, from: Bordeaux Packet, Letter of Marque.
    Cap: 28 Jan 1814 off Cape Henry by Nieman Int: 12 Feb 1814 Dis: 15 Apr 1814.
    Received from Nieman. Diana Transport for Halifax.

McGee, John   Prisoner 1334. Rank: Seaman, from: Rolla, Privateer.
    Cap: 10 Dec 1813 Block Island by Loire Int: 20 Dec 1813 Dis: 15 Apr 1814.
    Received from HM Ship San Domingo. HMS Rammillies for Halifax.

McGill, Mathew   Prisoner 2467. Rank: Seaman, from: President, U States Frigate.
    Cap: 15 Jan 1815 Not Recorded by Endymion Int: 04 Feb 1815 Dis: 28 Mar 1815.
    Received from Endymion. Clarenden Transport for U States.

McIntire, Abraham   Prisoner 1632. Rank: Prize Master, from: Not Recorded, Not Recorded.
    Cap: 05 Feb 1814 Not Recorded by Sceptre Int: 14 Feb 1814 Dis: 24 Apr 1814.
    Received from Sceptre. HMS Sceptre for England.

McIntire, J L   Prisoner 1889. Rank: Passenger, from: Sally, Merchant Vessel.
    Cap: Not Recorded by Not Recorded Int: Dis: 28 Mar 1815.
    Clarendon Transport for U States. (Dates of capture and internment not recorded.)

McKenny, Nathan   Prisoner 446. Rank: Seaman, from: Adventure, Merchant Brig.
    Cap: 15 Dec 1812 off Bermuda by HM Sloop Childers Int: 17 Dec 1812 Dis: 27 Jan 1813.
    Received from HM Sloop Childers. Bostock Cartel for New York.

McKenzie, Daniel   Prisoner 490. Rank: Seaman, from: Teazer, Privateer Schooner.
    Cap: 16 Dec 1812 at Sea by HM Ship St. Domingo Int: 21 Dec 1812 Dis: 27 Jan 1813.
    Received from HM Ship St. Domingo. Bostock Cartel for New York.

McKenzie, Thomas   Prisoner 1027. Rank: Seaman, from: Dart, Merchant Schooner.
    Cap: 17 Mar 1813 off the Chesapeake by HMS Statira Int: 06 Apr 1813 Escaped: 21 Apr 1813.
    Received from HMS Junon. Escaped.

McKey, James   Prisoner 2731. Rank: Master, from: Kate, Not Recorded.
    Cap: 10 Nov 1814 Potomac by Dragon Int: 03 Mar 1815 Dis: 16 Mar 1815.
    Received from Hebrus. Merchant Service.

McKinley, Alexander   Prisoner 389. Rank: Seaman, from: Snapper, Privateer Schooner.
    Cap: 16 Nov 1812 at Sea by HM Ship Galus Int: 22 Nov 1812 Dis: 27 Jan 1813.
    Received from HM Ship Galus. Bostock Cartel for New York.

McKowen, Alex   Prisoner 221. Rank: Seaman, from: Wasp, Sloop of War.
    Cap: 18 Oct 1812 at Sea by HM Ship Poictiers Int: 26 Oct 1812 Dis: 05 Nov 1812.
    Received from HM Ship Poictiers. Brig Diamond on Parole to new London United States of America.

McKurlee, Alexander   Prisoner 663. Rank: 2 Lieutenant, from: High Flyer, Privateer.
    Cap: 09 Jan 1813 at Sea by HM Ship Acasta Int: 21 Jan 1813 Dis: 27 Jan 1813.
    Received from HMS Acasta. Bostock Cartel for New York.

American Prisoners of War Held at Bermuda During the War of 1812

McLuney, William   Prisoner 178. Rank: Midshipman, from: Wasp, Sloop of War.
    Cap: 18 Oct 1812 at Sea by HMS Poictiers Int: 26 Oct 1812 Dis: 05 Nov 1812.
    Received from HM Ship Poictiers. Brig Diamond on Parole to new London America.

McNatley, Michael   Prisoner 2476. Rank: Marine, from: President, U States Frigate.
    Cap: 15 Jan 1815 Not Recorded by Endymion Int: 04 Feb 1815 Dis: 28 Mar 1815.
    Received from Endymion. Clarenden Transport for U States.

McPherson, William   Prisoner 2201. Rank: Boatswains Mate, from: President, U States Frigate.
    Cap: 15 Jan 1815 Not Recorded by Endymion Int: 30 Jan 1815 Dis: 28 Mar 1815.
    Received from Pomone. Mars Transport for U States.

McPrelvey, Thomas   Prisoner 1123. Rank: Seaman, from: Mary, Merchant.
    Cap: 17 Apr 1813 at Sea by HM Ship Fox Int: 21 Jun 1813 Dis: 24 Jun 1813.
    Received from HMS Ruby. Magnet Cartel for New York.

McRea, John   Prisoner 430. Rank: Seaman, from: Eliza, Merchant Ship.
    Cap: 25 Nov 1812 Lat 37.00, Long 65.46 by HM Ship Tartarus Int: 03 Dec 1812 Dis: 27 Jan 1813.
    Received from HM Ship Tartarus. Bostock Cartel for New York.

Meany, Cornelius   Prisoner 2377. Rank: Seaman, from: President, U States Frigate.
    Cap: 15 Jan 1815 Not Recorded by HMS Endymion Int: 04 Feb 1815 Dis: 28 Mar 1815.
    Received from Endymion. Mars Transport for U States.

Mears, William   Prisoner 2822. Rank: Seaman, from: Limerick, Not Recorded.
    Cap: 15 Mar 1815 Not Recorded by Asia Int: 25 Mar 1815 Dis:
    From Depot at Jamaica. Received from Asia. (Date of discharge not recorded.)

Mecanger, Michael   Prisoner 2032. Rank: Passenger, from: Not Recorded, Not Recorded.
    Cap: 25 Jul 1814 of Cape Blass by Sophie Int: 11 Nov 1814 Dis: 24 Nov 1814.
    Received from HMS Wolverine. Dryharbor MV French Subject.

Medad, Emos   Prisoner 1128. Rank: Seaman, from: Mary, Merchant.
    Cap: 17 Apr 1813 at Sea by HM Ship Fox Int: 21 Jun 1813 Dis: 24 Jun 1813.
    Received from HM Ship Ruby. Magnet Cartel for New York.

Meek, John   Prisoner 1106. Rank: Seaman, from: Apollo, Merchant Vessel.
    Cap: 15 May 1813 at Sea by HM Ship Success Int: 27 May 1813 Dis: 24 Jun 1813.
    Received from HMS Success. Magnet Cartel for New York.

Meensey, Daniel   Prisoner 1588. Rank: Seaman, from: Bordeaux Packet, Letter of Marque.
    Cap: 28 Jan 1814 off Cape Henry by Nieman Int: 12 Feb 1814 Dis: 15 Apr 1814.
    Received from Nieman. Diana Transport for Halifax.

Mellville, John   Prisoner 2650. Rank: Seaman, from: President, U States Frigate.
    Cap: 11 Feb 1815 off N York by Endymion Int: 11 Feb 1815 Dis:
    Received from President. (Date of discharge not recorded. Date of capture should be January 15, 1815.)

Melna, Joseph   Prisoner 1681. Rank: Seaman, from: St. Joquin, Merchant Vessel.
    Cap: 26 Mar 1814 Chesapeake by Albion Int: 16 Apr 1814 Dis: 23 Apr 1814.
    Received from Canso. HMS Bulwark for Halifax Order Comm in Chief.

Memenbery, Jacob   Prisoner 2371. Rank: (Not legible) Mate, from: President, U States Frigate.
    Cap: 15 Jan 1815 Not Recorded by HMS Endymion Int: 04 Feb 1815 Dis: 28 Mar 1815.
    Received from Endymion. Mars Transport for U States.

Mennett, Thomas   Prisoner 2393. Rank: Marine, from: President, U States Frigate.
    Cap: 15 Jan 1815 Not Recorded by HM Ship Endymion Int: 04 Feb 1815 Dis: 28 Mar 1815.
    Received from Endymion. Clarenden Transport for U States.

Merchant, Abram   Prisoner 153. Rank: Seaman, from: Ranger, Merchant Ship.
    Cap: 02 Oct 1812 Lat 32, Long 65 W by HM Ship Goree Int: 13 Oct 1812 Dis: 24 Oct 1812.
    Received from HMS Goree. Brig Diamond on Parole to new London United States of America.

Merchant, Peter B   Prisoner 2584. Rank: Seaman, from: Advocate, Merchant Vessel.
    Cap: 16 Nov 1814 off New York by HM Ship Majestic Int: 05 Feb 1815 Dis: 16 Mar 1815.
    Received from HMS Forth. Merchant Service.

Merig, John   Prisoner 1083. Rank: Seaman, from: Maria Louisa, Merchant.
    Cap: 10 Apr 1813 off Sandy Hook by HMS Acasta Int: 03 May 1813 Dis: 24 Jun 1813.
    Received from HMS Acasta. Magnet Cartel for New York.

Merrick, Ebenezer   Prisoner 2039. Rank: Seaman, from: Live, Merchant Sloop.
    Cap: 26 Oct 1814 off Delaware by St. Laurence Int: 21 Nov 1814 Dis: 25 Mar 1815.
    Received from M Schooner Whiting. Merchant Vessel.

Merrick, John F   Prisoner 1905. Rank: Seaman, from: Polly & Sally, Merchant Vessel.
    Cap: 13 Aug 1814 St. Catherine by Lacedaemonian Int: 09 Sep 1814 Dis: 16 Mar 1815.
    Received from Lacedaemonian. Merchant Service.

Merrill, Elias   Prisoner 79. Rank: Captain, from: Ariel, Merchant Brig.
    Cap: 28 Jul 1812 of Bermuda by Recruit Int: 28 Aug 1812 Dis: 24 Oct 1812.
    Received from HM Schooner Cuttle. on Parole to New London US of America, Diamond Brig.

American Prisoners of War Held at Bermuda During the War of 1812

Merry, William   Prisoner 1082. Rank: Seaman, from: Not Recorded, Not Recorded.
    Cap: Not Recorded by Not Recorded Int: 01 May 1813 Dis: 24 Jun 1813.
    Received from HM Packet Speay. Surrendered him Self a Prisoner of War. Magnet Cartel for New York. (Date of capture not recorded.)

Messavy, Philip   Prisoner 240. Rank: Seaman, from: Wasp, Sloop of War.
    Cap: 18 Oct 1812 at Sea by HM Ship Poictiers Int: 26 Oct 1812 Dis: 05 Nov 1812.
    Received from HM Ship Poictiers. Brig Diamond on Parole to new London United States of America.

Metler, Leonard   Prisoner 694. Rank: Seaman, from: High Flyer, Privateer.
    Cap: 09 Jan 1813 at Sea by HMS Acasta Int: 21 Jan 1813 Dis: 27 Jan 1813.
    Received from HMS Acasta. Bostock Cartel for New York.

Metrash, Ezekial   Prisoner 125. Rank: Seaman, from: William of Baltimore, Merchant.
    Cap: 31 Aug 1812 Lat 37 by HM Ship Recruit Int: 14 Sep 1812 Dis: 18 Sep 1812.
    Received from Recruit. Order of Commd Evans for England.

Metrois, John   Prisoner 541. Rank: Seaman, from: Herald, Letter of Marque Brig.
    Cap: 25 Dec 1812 at Sea by HM Ship Maidstone Int: 05 Jan 1813 Dis: 27 Jan 1813.
    Received from HM Ship Maidstone. Bostock Cartel for New York.

Metzger, C D   Prisoner 1329. Rank: Seaman, from: Rolla, Privateer.
    Cap: 10 Dec 1813 Block Island by Loire Int: 20 Dec 1813 Dis: 15 Apr 1814.
    Received from HM Ship San Domingo. HMS Rammillies for Halifax.

Metzger, John   Prisoner 2093. Rank: Passenger, from: Factor, Merchant Vessel.
    Cap: 27 Nov 1814 coast of America by Primrose Int: 19 Jan 1815 Dis:
    Received from HMS Peruvian. (Date of discharge not recorded.)

Meyers, John   Prisoner 2782. Rank: Seaman, from: Limerick, Not Recorded.
    Cap: 07 Mar 1815 Lat 30, Long 75.38 W by Asia Int: 25 Mar 1815 Dis:
    Received from Asia. (Date of discharge not recorded.)

Mezarux, Ephraim   Prisoner 1014. Rank: Seaman, from: Nautalus, Merchant.
    Cap: 20 Mar 1813 off the Chesapeake by HM Ship Rammillies Int: 06 Apr 1813 Dis: 24 Jun 1813.
    Received from HMS Junon. Magnet Cartel for New York.

Michael, John   Prisoner 2675. Rank: Seaman, from: Gunboat 160, U States Man of War.
    Cap: 06 Sep 1814 off New York by Lacedaemonian Int: 14 Feb 1815 Dis: 16 Mar 1815.
    Gun Vessel. Received from Childers. Merchant Serice.

Micklins, John   Prisoner 892. Rank: Seaman, from: Hannah, Merchant Schooner.
    Cap: 24 Feb 1813 Chesapeake by HMS Marlborough Int: 23 Mar 1813 Dis: 13 Jun 1813.
    Received from HM Ship Laurustinus. Perseverance Cartel for the United States per Order Admiral Sir J B Warren.

Miers, Edward   Prisoner 1241. Rank: Not Recorded, from: Julia, Schooner.
    Cap: 10 Aug 1813 Lake Ontario by Wolf Int: 30 Nov 1813 Dis: 15 Apr 1814.
    Received from HM Ship Goliah. Diana Transport for Halifax.

Miggs, John   Prisoner 2549. Rank: Seaman, from: President, US Frigate.
    Cap: 15 Jan 1815 off N York by HMS Endymion Int: 05 Feb 1815 Dis: 28 Mar 1815.
    Received from President. Clarenden Transport for U States.

Miles, David   Prisoner 667. Rank: Carpenter, from: High Flyer, Privateer.
    Cap: 09 Jan 1813 at Sea by HM Ship Acasta Int: 21 Jan 1813 Dis: 27 Jan 1813.
    Received from HMS Acasta. Bostock Cartel for New York.

Millehus, Frederick   Prisoner 842. Rank: Seaman, from: Portsmouth, Merchant Ship.
    Cap: 27 Feb 1813 off Bermuda by HM Sloop Martin Int: 09 Mar 1813 Dis: 27 Mar 1813.
    Received from HM Ship Martin. Per Order Commodore Evans the Vessel being Liberated.

Miller, David   Prisoner 225. Rank: Seaman, from: Wasp, Sloop of War.
    Cap: 18 Oct 1812 at Sea by HM Ship Poictiers Int: 26 Oct 1812 Dis: 05 Nov 1812.
    Received from HM Ship Poictiers. Brig Diamond on Parole to new London United States of America.

Miller, Ezekial   Prisoner 15. Rank: Seaman, from: General Blake, Merchant.
    Cap: 09 Jul 1812 near Bermuda by Recruit Int: 28 Aug 1812 Dis: 18 Sep 1812.
    Received from HM Schooner Cuttle. Order of Commd Evans for England.

Miller, George   Prisoner 39. Rank: Boy, from: Laura, Merchant Sloop.
    Cap: 24 Jul 1812 of Bermuda by Cuttle Int: 28 Aug 1812 Dis: 28 Aug 1812.
    Received from HM Schooner Cuttle. under Age.

Miller, James   Prisoner 2396. Rank: Seaman, from: President, U States Frigate.
    Cap: 15 Jan 1815 Not Recorded by HM Ship Endymion Int: 04 Feb 1815 Dis: 28 Mar 1815.
    Received from Endymion. Mars Transport for U States.

Miller, John   Prisoner 748. Rank: Mate, from: Rhode, Merchant Schooner.
    Cap: 07 Jan 1813 at Sea by HM Ship Poictiers Int: 21 Jan 1813 Dis: 27 Jan 1813.
    Received from HMS Poictiers. Bostock Cartel for New York.

American Prisoners of War Held at Bermuda During the War of 1812

Miller, Martin   Prisoner 996. Rank: Seaman, from: Orion, Merchant.
   Cap: 25 Mar 1813 at Sea by HM Sloop Childers Int: 04 Apr 1813 Dis: 09 Apr 1813.
   Received from HM Sloop Childers. Per Order Commodore Evans Vessel Liberated.
Miller, Petter   Prisoner 1528. Rank: Seaman, from: Matchless, Merchant Vessel.
   Cap: 02 Jan 1814 Latt 22.0 by Prometheus Int: 23 Jan 1814 Dis: 15 Apr 1814.
   Received from Prometheus. Diana for Halifax.
Miller, Thomas   Prisoner 1558. Rank: Seaman, from: Bordeaux Packet, Letter of Marque.
   Cap: 28 Jan 1814 off Cape Henry by Nieman Int: 12 Feb 1814 Dis: 15 Apr 1814.
   Received from Nieman. Diana Transport for Halifax.
Miller, William   Prisoner 1253. Rank: Not Recorded, from: Circe, Merchant Vessel.
   Cap: 23 Oct 1813 Cape Hatterus by Acteon Int: 02 Dec 1813 Dis: 15 Apr 1814.
   Received from HMS Sceptre. Diana Transport for Halifax.
Millington, F   Prisoner 1443. Rank: Seaman, from: Nonsuch, Letter of Marque.
   Cap: 14 Dec 1813 Lat 32 by Doterel Int: 25 Dec 1813 Dis: 15 Apr 1814.
   Received from HM Brig Doterel. Diana Transport for Halifax.
Millington, Robert   Prisoner 379. Rank: Seaman, from: Snapper, Privateer Schooner.
   Cap: 16 Nov 1812 at Sea by HM Ship Galus Int: 22 Nov 1812 Dis: 27 Jan 1813.
   Received from HM Ship Galus. Bostock Cartel for New York.
Millis, John   Prisoner 343. Rank: Seaman, from: Snapper, Privateer Schooner.
   Cap: 16 Nov 1812 at Sea by HMS Galus Int: 22 Nov 1812 Dis: 27 Jan 1813.
   Received from HM Ship Galus. Bostock Cartel for New York.
Mills, James   Prisoner 2484. Rank: Seaman, from: President, U States Frigate.
   Cap: 15 Jan 1815 Not Recorded by Endymion Int: 04 Feb 1815 Dis: 28 Mar 1815.
   Received from Endymion. Clarenden Transport for U States.
Miln, Michael   Prisoner 1009. Rank: Seaman, from: Ohio, Merchant.
   Cap: 20 Mar 1813 off the Chesapeake by HM Sloop Atalante Int: 06 Apr 1813 Dis: 24 Jun 1813.
   Received from HMS Junon. Magnet Cartel for New York.
Mingle, William   Prisoner 648. Rank: Seaman, from: Eliza, Merchant Ship.
   Cap: 24 Nov 1812 at Sea by HM Ship Marlborough Int: 18 Jan 1813 Dis: 27 Jan 1813.
   Received from HM Ship Marlborough. Bostock Cartel for New York. Ship Eliza (2).
Mitchel, Chester   Prisoner 1032. Rank: Seaman, from: Dart, Merchant Schooner.
   Cap: 17 Mar 1813 off the Chesapeake by HMS Statira Int: 06 Apr 1813 Dis: 24 Jun 1813.
   Received from HMS Junon. Magnet Cartel for New York.
Mitchell, Chester   Prisoner 1527. Rank: Seaman, from: Matchless, Merchant Vessel.
   Cap: 02 Jan 1814 Latt 22.0 by Prometheus Int: 23 Jan 1814 Dis: 15 Apr 1814.
   Received from Prometheus. Diana for Halifax.
Mitchell, Henry   Prisoner 254. Rank: Seaman, from: Wasp, Sloop of War.
   Cap: 18 Oct 1812 at Sea by HM Ship Poictiers Int: 26 Oct 1812 Dis: 05 Nov 1812.
   Received from HM Ship Poictiers. Brig Diamond on Parole to new London United States of America.
Mitchell, Jonah   Prisoner 1747. Rank: Seaman, from: Yankelass, Privateer.
   Cap: 01 May 1814 L 40-4N, Long 38-0W by Severn & Surprise Int: 06 Jun 1814 Dis:
   Received from Severn. (Date of discharge not recorded.)
Mitchell, Lewis   Prisoner 1154. Rank: Seaman, from: Acricoake, Merchant.
   Cap: 22 Jul 1813 at Sea by HM Sloop Conflict Int: 13 Aug 1813 Dis: 13 Aug 1813.
   Received from HM Ship Woolwich. American Ship Rolla per Order Commr Evans.
Mitchell, Lloyd   Prisoner 2528. Rank: Seaman, from: President, U States Frigate.
   Cap: 15 Jan 1815 Not Recorded by Endymion Int: 04 Feb 1815 Dis: 28 Mar 1815.
   Received from HMS Endymion. Clarenden Transport for U States.
Mitchell, William   Prisoner 313. Rank: Seaman, from: Wasp, Sloop of War.
   Cap: 18 Oct 1812 at Sea by HMS Poictiers Int: 05 Nov 1812 Dis: 17 Jun 1813.
   Received from HM Ship Poictiers. Halifax Order of the Commander in Chief supports to be an Englishman.
Mitchell, William   Prisoner 2495. Rank: Seaman, from: President, U States Frigate.
   Cap: 15 Jan 1815 Not Recorded by Endymion Int: 04 Feb 1815 Dis: 28 Mar 1815.
   Received from Endymion. Clarenden Transport for U States.
Mitret, Onies   Prisoner 551. Rank: Seaman, from: Herald, Letter of Marque Brig.
   Cap: 25 Dec 1812 at Sea by HM Ship Maidstone Int: 05 Jan 1813 Dis: 27 Jan 1813.
   Received from HM Ship Maidstone. Bostock Cartel for New York.
Miure, William   Prisoner 1716. Rank: Seaman, from: Olive Branch, Merchant Vessel.
   Cap: 16 Apr 1814 Chesapeake by Acasta Int: 26 May 1814 Dis: 13 Feb 1815.
   Received from Lacedaemonian. Bellonair Transport per order Comm Evans.

American Prisoners of War Held at Bermuda During the War of 1812

Moat, James   Prisoner 823. Rank: 2 Mate, from: Portsmouth, Merchant Ship.
    Cap: 27 Feb 1813 off Bermuda by Sandimingo Int: 09 Mar 1813 Dis: 27 Mar 1813.
    Received from Sloop Martin. Per Order Commodore Evans the Vessel being Liberated.

Moat, William   Prisoner 2834. Rank: Seaman, from: Limerick, Not Recorded.
    Cap: 15 Mar 1815 Not Recorded by Asia Int: 25 Mar 1815 Dis:
    From Depot at Jamaica. Received from Asia. (Date of discharge not recorded.)

Modun, James   Prisoner 2848. Rank: Seaman, from: Limerick, Not Recorded.
    Cap: 15 Mar 1815 Not Recorded by Asia Int: 25 Mar 1815 Dis:
    From Depot at Jamaica. Received from Asia. (Date of discharge not recorded.)

Moffatt, John   Prisoner 1951. Rank: Seaman, from: Pike, Privateer.
    Cap: 25 Aug 1814 off Savannah by Primrose Int: 09 Sep 1814 Dis: 28 Mar 1815.
    Received from Lacedaemonian. Clarendon Transport for U States.

Mofford, Gardner   Prisoner 1752. Rank: Seaman, from: Yankelass, Privateer.
    Cap: 01 May 1814 L 40-4N, Long 38-0W by Severn & Surprise Int: 06 Jun 1814 Dis: 21 Feb 1815.
    Received from Severn. U States having served 6 months as Carpenter's M order of Adl Sir Alex Cockburn.

Moffott, Hugh   Prisoner 432. Rank: Seaman, from: Eliza, Merchant Ship.
    Cap: 25 Nov 1812 Lat 37.00, Long 65.46 by HM Ship Tartarus Int: 03 Dec 1812 Dis: 27 Jan 1813.
    Received from HM Ship Tartarus. Bostock Cartel for New York.

Moffunire, Henry   Prisoner 1760. Rank: Seaman, from: Yankelass, Privateer.
    Cap: 01 May 1814 L 40-4N, Long 38-0W by Severn & Surprise Int: 06 Jun 1814 Dis:
    Received from Severn. (Date of discharge not recorded.)

Molton, C P   Prisoner 1311. Rank: Seaman, from: Rolla, Privateer.
    Cap: 10 Dec 1813 Block Island by Loire Int: 20 Dec 1813 Dis: 15 Apr 1814.
    Received from San Domingo. HMS Rammillies for Halifax.

Monger, William   Prisoner 1963. Rank: Seaman, from: Pike, Privateer.
    Cap: 25 Aug 1814 off Savannah by Primrose Int: 09 Sep 1814 Dis: 20 Feb 1814.
    Received from Lacedaemonian. Alexander Order of Comm Evans.

Montaque, James   Prisoner 2607. Rank: Seaman, from: Edward, Merchant Vessel.
    Cap: 30 Dec 1814 Sandy Hook by HM Ship Pomone Int: 05 Feb 1815 Dis: 16 Mar 1815.
    Received from HMS Forth. Merchant Service.

Montgomery, Robert   Prisoner 4. Rank: Mate, from: Yorick, Merchant Ship.
    Cap: 09 Jul 1812 near Bermuda by Rattler Int: 28 Aug 1812 Dis: 10 Sep 1812.
    Received from HM Schooner Cuttle. Schooner Hero for N Y.

Montsele, John   Prisoner 360. Rank: Seaman, from: Snapper, Privateer Schooner.
    Cap: 16 Nov 1812 at Sea by HM Ship Galus Int: 22 Nov 1812 Dis: 18 Jan 1813.
    Received from HM Ship Galus. being a Spaniard per Order of Adl Evans.

Moody, Sea   Prisoner 699. Rank: Seaman, from: High Flyer, Privateer.
    Cap: 09 Jan 1813 at Sea by HMS Acasta Int: 21 Jan 1813 Dis: 27 Jan 1813.
    Received from HMS Acasta. Bostock Cartel for New York.

Moon, John   Prisoner 1857. Rank: Seaman, from: Isa Colly, Merchant Vessel.
    Cap: Not Recorded by Not Recorded Int: Dis: 04 Sep 1814.
    to join these Proper Ships having been delivered up Order Comm Evans. (Dates of capture and internment not recorded.)

Moordie, John   Prisoner 1868. Rank: Seaman, from: Sally, Merchant Vessel.
    Cap: Not Recorded by Not Recorded Int: Dis: 24 Mar 1815.
    Merchant Vessel. (Dates of capture and internment not recorded.)

Moore, Abraham   Prisoner 373. Rank: Seaman, from: Snapper, Privateer Schooner.
    Cap: 16 Nov 1812 at Sea by HM Ship Galus Int: 22 Nov 1812 Dis: 27 Jan 1813.
    Received from HM Ship Galus. Bostock Cartel for New York.

Moore, Isaac   Prisoner 495. Rank: Seaman, from: Teazer, Privateer Schooner.
    Cap: 16 Dec 1812 at Sea by HM Ship St. Domingo Int: 21 Dec 1812 Dis: 27 Jan 1813.
    Received from HM Ship St. Domingo. Bostock Cartel for New York.

Moore, John   Prisoner 840. Rank: Seaman, from: Portsmouth, Merchant Ship.
    Cap: 27 Feb 1813 off Bermuda by HM Sloop Martin Int: 09 Mar 1813 Dis: 27 Mar 1813.
    Received from HM Ship Martin. Per Order Commodore Evans the Vessel being Liberated.

Moore, Marus   Prisoner 249. Rank: Seaman, from: Wasp, Sloop of War.
    Cap: 18 Oct 1812 at Sea by HM Ship Poictiers Int: 26 Oct 1812 Dis: 05 Nov 1812.
    Received from HM Ship Poictiers. Brig Diamond on Parole to new London United States of America.

Moore, Prince   Prisoner 1622. Rank: Seaman, from: Perseferanda, Merchant Vessel.
    Cap: 03 Jan 1814 Block Island by Albion Int: 14 Feb 1814 Dis: 23 Apr 1814.
    Received from Sceptre. HMS Bulwark for Halifax.

American Prisoners of War Held at Bermuda During the War of 1812

Moore, Robert   Prisoner 1048. Rank: 2 Mate, from: General Knox, Merchant.
    Cap: 18 Mar 1813 Chesapeake by HM Ship Victorious Int: 06 Apr 1813 Dis:
    Received from HMS Junon. (Date of discharge not on roster.)

Moore, William   Prisoner 1130. Rank: Seaman, from: Good Intent, Merchant.
    Cap: 02 Aug 1813 at Sea by HM Sloop Rifleman Int: 13 Aug 1813 Dis: 03 Sep 1813.
    Received from HM Sloop Rifleman. Per Order of Comm Evans to the American Ship Leander restored.

Moore, William   Prisoner 1931. Rank: Boatswain, from: Pike, Privateer.
    Cap: 25 Aug 1814 off Savannah by Primrose Int: 09 Sep 1814 Dis: 24 Mar 1815.
    Received from Lacedaemonian. Merchant Vessel.

Morgan, Alexander   Prisoner 322. Rank: Seaman, from: James, Merchant Ship.
    Cap: 03 Nov 1812 at Sea by HM Ship Tartarus Int: 17 Nov 1812 Dis: 27 Jan 1813.
    Received from HM Ship Tartarus. Bostock Cartel for New York.

Morgan, John   Prisoner 2118. Rank: Seaman, from: Armistice, Merchant Vessel.
    Cap: 07 Dec 1814 off Delaware by Pictolus Int: 27 Jan 1815 Dis: 13 Mar 1815.
    Received from Pictolus. Merchant Service.

Morgan, Littleton T   Prisoner 41. Rank: Captain, from: Trim, Merchant Schooner.
    Cap: 28 Jul 1812 of Bermuda by Cuttle Int: 28 Aug 1812 Dis: 10 Sep 1812.
    Received from HM Schooner Cuttle. Schooner Hero for N Y.

Morgan, William   Prisoner 2326. Rank: Seaman, from: President, U States Frigate.
    Cap: 15 Jan 1815 Not Recorded by Endymion Int: 04 Feb 1815 Dis: 28 Mar 1815.
    Received from Endymion. Mars Transport for U States.

Morgan, William   Prisoner 2471. Rank: Seaman, from: President, U States Frigate.
    Cap: 15 Jan 1815 Not Recorded by Endymion Int: 04 Feb 1815 Dis: 28 Mar 1815.
    Received from Endymion. Clarenden Transport for U States.

Morians, Joshua   Prisoner 353. Rank: Seaman, from: Snapper, Privateer Schooner.
    Cap: 16 Nov 1812 at Sea by HMS Galus Int: 22 Nov 1812 Dis: 27 Jan 1813.
    Received from HM Ship Galus. Bostock Cartel for New York.

Morice, Marcus   Prisoner 1739. Rank: Seaman, from: Yankelass, Privateer.
    Cap: 01 May 1814 L 10-4N, L 33-0W by Severn & Surprise Int: 06 Jun 1814 Dis: 24 Mar 1815.
    Received from Severn. Merchant Vessel.

Morrill, Charles   Prisoner 2114. Rank: Seaman, from: Armistice, Merchant Vessel.
    Cap: 07 Dec 1814 off Delaware by Pictolus Int: 27 Jan 1815 Dis: 15 Mar 1815.
    Received from Pictolus. Merchant Service.

Morrin, John   Prisoner 2519. Rank: Seaman, from: President, U States Frigate.
    Cap: 15 Jan 1815 Not Recorded by Endymion Int: 04 Feb 1815 Dis: 28 Mar 1815.
    Received from HMS Endymion. Clarenden Transport for U States.

Morris, Andrew   Prisoner 200. Rank: Marine, from: Wasp, Sloop of War.
    Cap: 18 Oct 1812 at Sea by HMS Poictiers Int: 26 Oct 1812 Dis: 05 Nov 1812.
    Received from HM Ship Poictiers. Brig Diamond on Parole to new London America.

Morris, Charles   Prisoner 397. Rank: Seaman, from: Snapper, Privateer Schooner.
    Cap: 16 Nov 1812 at Sea by HM Ship Galus Int: 22 Nov 1812 Dis: 27 Jan 1813.
    Received from HM Ship Galus. Bostock Cartel for New York.

Morris, Emanuel   Prisoner 73. Rank: Captain, from: White Oak, Merchant.
    Cap: 08 Aug 1812 of Bermuda by Recruit Int: 28 Aug 1812 Dis: 10 Sep 1812.
    Received from M Schooner Cuttle. Schooner Hero for New York.

Morris, Frank   Prisoner 1137. Rank: Seaman, from: Asp, Man of War Schooner.
    Cap: 20 Jul 1813 at Sea by HM Ship San Domingo Int: 13 Aug 1813 Dis: 13 Aug 1813.
    Received from HM Ship Woolwich. American Ship Rolla per Order Governor Strong.

Morris, James   Prisoner 2841. Rank: Seaman, from: Limerick, Not Recorded.
    Cap: 15 Mar 1815 Not Recorded by Asia Int: 25 Mar 1815 Dis:
    From Depot at Jamaica. Received from Asia. (Date of discharge not recorded.)

Morris, John   Prisoner 1950. Rank: Seaman, from: Pike, Privateer.
    Cap: 25 Aug 1814 off Savannah by Primrose Int: 09 Sep 1814 Dis: 27 Mar 1815.
    Received from Lacedaemonian. Merchant Vessel.

Morris, John   Prisoner 2001. Rank: Seaman, from: Dry Farbourn, Merchant Vessel.
    Cap: 21 Oct 1814 off Bermuda by Pandora Int: 27 Oct 1814 Dis: 07 Nov 1814.
    Dry Farborn. Recaptured. Received from Goree. Order Adl Cockburn.

Morris, Josiah   Prisoner 609. Rank: Seaman, from: Noetoin, Packet Brig.
    Cap: 05 Jan 1813 at Sea by HMS Belvidera Int: 10 Jan 1813 Dis: 27 Jan 1813.
    Received from HMS Belvidera. Bostock Cartel for New York.

Morrison, Samuel   Prisoner 1167. Rank: Master, from: Elizabeth, Merchant.
    Cap: 15 Jun 1813 at Sea by HM Ship Marlborough Int: 15 Aug 1813 Dis: 02 Sep 1813.
    Received from HM Ship Woolwich. Per order of Commodore Evans being liberated.

American Prisoners of War Held at Bermuda During the War of 1812

Morrison, William   Prisoner 401. Rank: Seaman, from: Snapper, Privateer Schooner.
     Cap: 16 Nov 1812 at Sea by HM Ship Galus   Int: 22 Nov 1812   Dis: 27 Jan 1813.
     Received from HM Ship Galus. Bostock Cartel for New York.

Morse, T   Prisoner 2131. Rank: Seaman, from: New York, Merchant Vessel.
     Cap: 09 Jan 1815 off Delaware by Dispatch   Int: 27 Jan 1815   Dis: 28 Mar 1815.
     Received from Pictolus. Clarendon Transport for U States.

Morson, Joseph   Prisoner 1999. Rank: Seaman, from: Dry Farbourn, Merchant Vessel.
     Cap: 21 Oct 1814 off Bermuda by Pandora   Int: 27 Oct 1814   Dis: 07 Nov 1814.
     Recaptured. Received from Goree. Diadem for a Passage to England.

Morton, Abraham   Prisoner 961. Rank: Seaman, from: Bona, Letter of Marque Schooner.
     Cap: 12 Mar 1813 Chesapeake by Laurustinus   Int: 23 Mar 1813   Dis: 24 Jun 1813.
     Received from Laurustinus. Magnet Cartel for New York.

Morton, Thomas   Prisoner 1. Rank: Captain, from: Symmetry, Merchant Ship.
     Cap: 05 Jul 1812 Not Recorded by Rattler   Int: 28 Aug 1812   Dis: 10 Sep 1812.
     Received from HM Schooner Cuttle. Schooner Hero for N York per order Commd Evans.

Mott, Charles   Prisoner 624. Rank: Cook, from: Betsey, Merchant Schooner.
     Cap: 11 Dec 1812 at Sea by HM Ship Maidstone   Int: 12 Jan 1813   Dis: 27 Jan 1813.
     Received from Schooner Betsey. Bostock Cartel for New York.

Mott, John   Prisoner 740. Rank: Mate, from: Savannah Packet, Merchant Brig.
     Cap: 05 Jan 1813 at Sea by HM Ship Poictiers   Int: 21 Jan 1813   Dis: 27 Jan 1813.
     Received from HMS Poictiers. Bostock Cartel for New York.

Mottley, Alexander   Prisoner 2296. Rank: Seaman, from: President, U States Frigate.
     Cap: 15 Jan 1815 Not Recorded by Endymion   Int: 04 Feb 1815   Dis: 28 Mar 1815.
     Received from Endymion. Mars Transport for U States.

Moulton, William   Prisoner 2344. Rank: Seaman, from: President, U States Frigate.
     Cap: 15 Jan 1815 Not Recorded by HMS Endymion   Int: 04 Feb 1815   Dis: 28 Mar 1815.
     Received from Endymion. Mars Transport for U States.

Mounteam, Henry   Prisoner 1638. Rank: Seaman, from: Not Recorded, Not Recorded.
     Cap: 05 Feb 1814 Not Recorded by Sceptre   Int: 14 Feb 1814   Dis: 15 Apr 1814.
     Received from Sceptre. Rammilles for Halifax.

Mourice, Joseph   Prisoner 1575. Rank: Seaman, from: Bordeaux Packet, Letter of Marque.
     Cap: 28 Jan 1814 off Cape Henry by Nieman   Int: 12 Feb 1814   Dis: 15 Apr 1814.
     Received from Nieman. Diana Transport for Halifax.

Mowton, George   Prisoner 1133. Rank: Seaman, from: Good Intent, Merchant.
     Cap: 02 Aug 1813 at Sea by HM Sloop Rifleman   Int: 13 Aug 1813   Dis: 20 Aug 1813.
     Received from HM Sloop Rifleman. HM Sloop Rifleman.

Mucker, Herim   Prisoner 2709. Rank: Seaman, from: South Boston, Merchant Vessel.
     Cap: 13 Feb 1815 off Charleston by Pandora   Int: 02 Mar 1815   Dis: 25 Mar 1815.
     Received from Pandora. Merchant Vessel.

Multy, James   Prisoner 2854. Rank: Seaman, from: Limerick, Not Recorded.
     Cap: 15 Mar 1815 Not Recorded by Asia   Int: 25 Mar 1815   Dis:
     From Depot at Jamaica. Received from Asia. (Date of discharge not recorded.)

Mumford, James   Prisoner 2644. Rank: Seaman, from: Dash, Merchant Vessel.
     Cap: 19 Jan 1815 Bahamas by HMS Statira   Int: 06 Feb 1815   Dis: 28 Mar 1815.
     Received from HMS Statira. Clarendon Transport for U States.

Mun, George   Prisoner 2874. Rank: Seaman, from: Limerick, Not Recorded.
     Cap: 06 Mar 1815 Not Recorded by Asia   Int: 29 Mar 1815   Dis: 28 Mar 1815.
     From West Indies. Received from La Brune. Clarendon Transport for U States. (Date of discharge before date of internment.)

Mure, D W   Prisoner 918. Rank: Seaman, from: Albert, Merchant Schooner.
     Cap: 05 Mar 1813 Chesapeake by HM Ship Marlborough   Int: 23 Mar 1813   Dis: 24 Jun 1813.
     Received from Laurustinus. Magnet Cartel for New York.

Murphey, Daniel   Prisoner 845. Rank: Cook, from: Lottery, Merchant Schooner.
     Cap: 08 Feb 1813 at Sea by HMS Statira   Int: 13 Mar 1813   Dis: 13 Jun 1813.
     Received from HMS Statira. Perseverance Cartel for the United States per Order Adml Sir J B Warren.

Murphey, John   Prisoner 1162. Rank: Seaman, from: Caledonian, Merchant.
     Cap: 20 Jul 1813 at Sea by HM Ship Marlborough   Int: 15 Aug 1813   Dis: 03 Oct 1813.
     Received from HM Ship Woolwich. Caledonian Order of Commodore Evans she being Liberated.

Murphey, John   Prisoner 1748. Rank: Seaman, from: Yankelass, Privateer.
     Cap: 01 May 1814 L 40-4N, Long 38-0W by Severn & Surprise   Int: 06 Jun 1814   Dis: 28 Mar 1815.
     Received from Severn. Mars Transport for U States.

American Prisoners of War Held at Bermuda During the War of 1812

Murphey, William   Prisoner 292. Rank: Sail Maker, from: Wasp, Sloop of War.
  Cap: 18 Oct 1812 at Sea by HMS Poictiers Int: 02 Nov 1812 Dis: 04 Nov 1812.
  Received from HMS Poictiers. Brig Diamond on Parole to new London United States of America.

Murray, Alexander   Prisoner 2665. Rank: Seaman, from: President, U States Frigate.
  Cap: 15 Jan 1815 off New York by Endymion Int: 14 Feb 1815 Dis: 28 Mar 1815.
  Received from Goree. Clarenden Transport for U States.

Murray, David   Prisoner 2245. Rank: Seaman, from: President, U States Frigate.
  Cap: 15 Jan 1815 Not Recorded by Endymion Int: 30 Jan 1815 Dis: 28 Mar 1815.
  Received from Pomone. Mars Transport for U States.

Muskett, William   Prisoner 2045. Rank: Seaman, from: Rising Sun, Merchant Vessel.
  Cap: 20 Nov 1814 off Bermuda by Pandora Int: 28 Nov 1814 Dis: 28 Mar 1815.
  Recaptured. Received from HMS Goree. Clarendon Transport for U States.

Myers, George   Prisoner 467. Rank: Seaman, from: Teazer, Privateer Schooner.
  Cap: 16 Dec 1812 at Sea by HM Ship St. Domingo Int: 21 Dec 1812 Dis: 27 Jan 1813.
  Received from HM Ship St. Domingo. Bostock Cartel for New York.

Myres, Charles   Prisoner 2287. Rank: Seaman, from: President, U States Frigate.
  Cap: 15 Jan 1815 Not Recorded by Endymion Int: 30 Jan 1815 Dis: 28 Mar 1815.
  Received from Pomone. Mars Transport for U States. 2 Y Vic List 28 March 1815 Merchant Vessel.

Naire, Joseph Lee   Prisoner 214. Rank: Marine, from: Wasp, Sloop of War.
  Cap: 18 Oct 1812 at Sea by HM Ship Poictiers Int: 26 Oct 1812 Dis: 05 Nov 1812.
  Received from HM Ship Poictiers. Brig Diamond on Parole to new London United States of America.

Napier, William   Prisoner 2231. Rank: Marine, from: President, U States Frigate.
  Cap: 15 Jan 1815 Not Recorded by Endymion Int: 30 Jan 1815 Dis: 28 Mar 1815.
  Received from Pomone. Clarenden Transport for U States.

Nason, Aaron   Prisoner 2017. Rank: Seaman, from: Bridges, Merchant Vessel.
  Cap: 25 Oct 1814 off Halifax by Armide Int: 07 Nov 1814 Dis: 28 Mar 1815.
  Recaptured. Received from HMS Armide. Clarendon Transport for U States.

Nathans, David   Prisoner 368. Rank: Prize Master, from: Snapper, Privateer Schooner.
  Cap: 16 Nov 1812 at Sea by HM Ship Galus Int: 22 Nov 1812 Dis: 27 Jan 1813.
  Received from HM Ship Galus. Bostock Cartel for New York.

Naus, Littleton   Prisoner 861. Rank: Mate, from: Ann, Merchant.
  Cap: 10 Mar 1813 Chesapeake by HM Ship Laurustinus Int: 23 Mar 1813 Dis: 24 Jun 1813.
  Received from HM Ship Laurustinus. Magnet Cartel for New York.

Neaves, Samuel   Prisoner 1822. Rank: Passenger, from: Not Recorded, Not Recorded.
  Cap: Not Recorded by Not Recorded Int: 14 Jun 1814 Dis: 15 Jun 1814.
  From St. Bartholomew in the Swedish Schooner Oscar. on Parole per Order Com in Chief to America.
  (Date of capture not recorded.)

Nellands, Adam   Prisoner 532. Rank: Seaman, from: Herald, Letter of Marque Brig.
  Cap: 25 Dec 1812 at Sea by HM Ship Maidstone Int: 05 Jan 1813 Dis: 27 Jan 1813.
  Received from HM Ship Maidstone. Bostock Cartel for New York.

Nelson, Andrew   Prisoner 2364. Rank: Seaman, from: President, U States Frigate.
  Cap: 15 Jan 1815 Not Recorded by HMS Endymion Int: 04 Feb 1815 Dis: 28 Mar 1815.
  Received from Endymion. Mars Transport for U States.

Nelson, John   Prisoner 545. Rank: Seaman, from: Herald, Letter of Marque Brig.
  Cap: 25 Dec 1812 at Sea by HM Ship Maidstone Int: 05 Jan 1813 Dis:
  Received from HM Ship Maidstone. (Date of discharge not recorded.)

Nelson, T W   Prisoner 958. Rank: Seaman, from: Bona, Letter of Marque Schooner.
  Cap: 12 Mar 1813 Chesapeake by Laurustinus Int: 23 Mar 1813 Escaped: 21 Apr 1813.
  Received from Laurustinus. Escaped.

Nemo, Henry   Prisoner 2588. Rank: Seaman, from: Thestis, Merchant Vessel.
  Cap: 18 Nov 1814 off New York by HM Ship Majestic Int: 05 Feb 1815 Dis: 28 Mar 1815.
  Received from HMS Forth. Clarendon Transport for U States.

Nevill, James   Prisoner 458. Rank: Mate, from: Teazer, Privateer Schooner.
  Cap: 16 Dec 1812 at Sea by HM Ship St. Domingo Int: 21 Dec 1812 Dis: 27 Jan 1813.
  Received from HM Ship St. Domingo. Bostock Cartel for New York.

New, Walter W   Prisoner 169. Rank: Assistant Surgeon, from: Wasp, Sloop of War.
  Cap: 18 Oct 1812 at Sea by HMS Poictiers Int: 26 Oct 1812 Dis: 05 Nov 1812.
  Received from HM Ship Poictiers. on Parole Brig Diamond to new London America.

Newman, Robert   Prisoner 522. Rank: Master, from: Logan, Merchant Brig.
  Cap: 20 Nov 1812 Lat 36.20, Long 69.40 by HMS Poictiers Int: 31 Dec 1812 Dis: 27 Jan 1813.
  Received from Prize Brig Logan. Bostock Cartel for New York.

American Prisoners of War Held at Bermuda During the War of 1812

Newman, W D   Prisoner 2149. Rank: Midshipman, from: President, U States Frigate.
    Cap: 15 Jan 1815 Not Recorded by Endymion Int: 30 Jan 1815 Dis: 28 Mar 1815.
    Received from President. Clarendon Transport for U States.

Newton, George   Prisoner 2746. Rank: Seaman, from: Aroof, Not Recorded.
    Cap: 16 Jan 1815 St Augustine by Manly Int: 03 Mar 1815 Dis: 28 Mar 1815.
    Received from Hebrus. Clarendon Transport for U States.

Nicholas, John   Prisoner 2687. Rank: Seaman, from: Superb, Merchant Vessel.
    Cap: 27 Jan 1815 off Delaware by Sophie Int: 17 Feb 1815 Dis: 28 Mar 1815.
    from a Spanish Brig recaptured. Received from Childers. Clarendon Transport for U States.

Nicholson, James   Prisoner 2557. Rank: Seaman, from: President, U States Frigate.
    Cap: 15 Jan 1815 Not Recorded by HM Ship Endymion Int: 05 Feb 1815 Dis: 28 Mar 1815.
    Received from President. Clarenden Transport for U States.

Nicholson, Joseph   Prisoner 2743. Rank: Seaman, from: Aroof, Not Recorded.
    Cap: 16 Jan 1815 St Augustine by Manly Int: 03 Mar 1815 Dis: 28 Mar 1815.
    Received from Hebrus. Clarendon Transport for U States.

Nicholson, Martin   Prisoner 1525. Rank: Seaman, from: Matchless, Merchant Vessel.
    Cap: 02 Jan 1814 Latt 22.0 by Prometheus Int: 23 Jan 1814 Dis: 15 Apr 1814.
    Received from Prometheus. Diana for Halifax.

Nicholson, William   Prisoner 1470. Rank: Seaman, from: Vixen, Man of War.
    Cap: 25 Dec 1813 Lat 38.0 by Belvidera Int: 05 Jan 1814 Dis: 15 Apr 1814.
    U States Schooner. Received from HMS Belvidera. Diana Transport for Halifax.

Nickerson, James C   Prisoner 2517. Rank: Seaman, from: President, U States Frigate.
    Cap: 15 Jan 1815 Not Recorded by Endymion Int: 04 Feb 1815 Dis: 28 Mar 1815.
    Received from HMS Endymion. Clarenden Transport for U States.

Nicklos, William   Prisoner 1017. Rank: Seaman, from: Nautalus, Merchant.
    Cap: 20 Mar 1813 off the Chesapeake by HM Ship Rammillies Int: 06 Apr 1813 Dis: 24 Jun 1813.
    Received from HMS Junon. Magnet Cartel for New York.

Nicklye, John L   Prisoner 985. Rank: Passenger, from: Sally, Merchant Sloop.
    Cap: 10 Mar 1813 Chesapeake by HMS Fantome Int: 23 Mar 1813 Dis: 08 Jun 1813.
    Received from HM Ship Laurustinus. Permitted to remain in the Colony per order of RA J B Warren.

Nickson, Robert   Prisoner 344. Rank: Seaman, from: Snapper, Privateer Schooner.
    Cap: 16 Nov 1812 at Sea by HMS Galus Int: 22 Nov 1812 Dis: 27 Jan 1813.
    Received from HM Ship Galus. Bostock Cartel for New York.

Nightingale, Joseph   Prisoner 1729. Rank: Seaman, from: Yankelass, Privateer.
    Cap: 01 May 1814 L 10-4N, L 33-0W by Severn & Surprise Int: 06 Jun 1814 Dis: 25 Mar 1815.
    Received from Severn. Merchant Vessel.

Nisbett, William   Prisoner 2558. Rank: Seaman, from: President, U States Frigate.
    Cap: 15 Jan 1815 Not Recorded by HM Ship Endymion Int: 05 Feb 1815 Dis: 28 Mar 1815.
    Received from President. Clarenden Transport for U States.

Noble, Andrew   Prisoner 1507. Rank: Seaman, from: Vixen, Man of War.
    Cap: 25 Dec 1813 Latt 38.0 by Belvidera Int: 18 Jan 1814 Dis: 15 Apr 1814.
    US Schooner. Received from Belvidera. Diana Transport for Halifax.

Noble, Daniel   Prisoner 750. Rank: Seaman, from: Rhode, Merchant Schooner.
    Cap: 07 Jan 1813 at Sea by HM Ship Poictiers Int: 21 Jan 1813 Dis: 27 Jan 1813.
    Received from HMS Poictiers. Bostock Cartel for New York.

Nollins, Thomas   Prisoner 2816. Rank: Mate, from: Limerick, Not Recorded.
    Cap: 04 Mar 1815 Not Recorded by Asia Int: 25 Mar 1815 Dis:
    From Depot at Jamaica. Received from Asia. (Date of discharge not recorded.)

Norbury, Charles   Prisoner 1944. Rank: Seaman, from: Pike, Privateer.
    Cap: 25 Aug 1814 off Savannah by Primrose Int: 09 Sep 1814 Dis: 05 Nov 1814.
    Received from Lacedaemonian. Order Adl Cockburn.

Norkott, Dennis   Prisoner 2250. Rank: Seaman, from: President, U States Frigate.
    Cap: 15 Jan 1815 Not Recorded by Endymion Int: 30 Jan 1815 Dis: 28 Mar 1815.
    Received from Pomone. Mars Transport for U States.

North, John N   Prisoner 1655. Rank: Seaman, from: Flash, Letter of Marque.
    Cap: 11 Feb 1814 Off Block Island by Acasta Int: 13 Mar 1814 Dis: 15 Apr 1814.
    Received from Active. Diana Transport for Halifax.

Northorp, Alexander   Prisoner 1521. Rank: Seaman, from: Lukey, Merchant Vessel.
    Cap: 19 Dec 1813 off the Delaware by Nieman Int: 22 Jan 1814 Escaped: 24 Nov 1814.
    Received from Jaseur. Run.

Norton, Joseph   Prisoner 2785. Rank: Seaman, from: Limerick, Not Recorded.
    Cap: 07 Mar 1815 Lat 30, Long 75.38 W by Asia Int: 25 Mar 1815 Dis:
    Received from Asia. (Date of discharge not recorded.)

American Prisoners of War Held at Bermuda During the War of 1812

Noss, Henry   Prisoner 1431. Rank: Seaman, from: Nonsuch, Letter of Marque.
    Cap: 14 Dec 1813 Lat 32 by Doterel Int: 25 Dec 1813 Dis: 06 Apr 1814.
    Received from HM Brig Doterel. being a Swede.

Nostend, Daniel   Prisoner 2442. Rank: Marine, from: President, U States Frigate.
    Cap: 15 Jan 1815 Not Recorded by Endymion Int: 04 Feb 1815 Dis: 28 Mar 1815.
    Received from Endymion. Clarenden Transport for U States.

Noyce, Nathaniel   Prisoner 1049. Rank: Master, from: Massoil, Merchant.
    Cap: 18 Mar 1813 Chesapeake by HMS Dragon Int: 06 Apr 1813 Dis: 24 Jun 1813.
    Received from HMS Junon. Permitted to remain in the Colony order of Ad Evans.

Nulty, Thomas   Prisoner 2076. Rank: Seaman, from: Not Recorded, Not Recorded.
    Cap: Not Recorded by HMS Surprise Int: 25 Dec 1814 Dis:
    Received from HMS Surprise. Gave himself up as a American Subject. (Dates of capture and discharge not recorded.)

Nye, Stephen   Prisoner 2506. Rank: Seaman, from: President, U States Frigate.
    Cap: 15 Jan 1815 Not Recorded by Endymion Int: 04 Feb 1815 Dis: 28 Mar 1815.
    Received from Endymion. Clarenden Transport for U States.

O'Brian, James   Prisoner 792. Rank: Master, from: Bellona, Merchant Schooner.
    Cap: 25 Jan 1813 at Sea by Sloop Colbrie Int: 10 Feb 1813 Dis: 20 Mar 1813.
    Received from Sloop Colbrie. Savannah Packet for New York per Order Adl Sir J B Warren.

Odnell, Samuel   Prisoner 1874. Rank: Seaman, from: Lion, Merchant Vessel.
    Cap: Not Recorded by Not Recorded Int: Dis: 28 Mar 1815.
    Clarendon Transport for U States. (Dates of capture and internment not recorded.)

Oliver, Antonia   Prisoner 327. Rank: Seaman, from: James, Merchant Ship.
    Cap: 03 Nov 1812 at Sea by HM Ship Tartarus Int: 17 Nov 1812 Dis: 27 Jan 1813.
    Received from HM Ship Tartarus. Bostock Cartel for New York.

Oliver, John   Prisoner 2649. Rank: Seaman, from: HMS Bacchant, Not Recorded.
    Cap: Not Recorded by Not Recorded Int: 08 Feb 1815 Dis: 16 Mar 1815.
    Received from HMS Bacchant. American Subject. Merchant Service. (Date of capture not recorded.)

Oliver, Joseph   Prisoner 2440. Rank: Marine, from: President, U States Frigate.
    Cap: 15 Jan 1815 Not Recorded by Endymion Int: 04 Feb 1815 Dis: 28 Mar 1815.
    Received from Endymion. Clarenden Transport for U States.

Oliver, Samuel   Prisoner 2445. Rank: Sergeant Marines, from: President, U States Frigate.
    Cap: 15 Jan 1815 Not Recorded by Endymion Int: 04 Feb 1815 Dis: 28 Mar 1815.
    Received from Endymion. Clarenden Transport for U States.

Oliver, Thomas   Prisoner 537. Rank: Seaman, from: Herald, Letter of Marque Brig.
    Cap: 25 Dec 1812 at Sea by HM Ship Maidstone Int: 05 Jan 1813 Dis: 27 Jan 1813.
    Received from HM Ship Maidstone. Bostock Cartel for New York.

O'Neal, Robert   Prisoner 2413. Rank: Seaman, from: President, U States Frigate.
    Cap: 15 Jan 1815 Not Recorded by HM Ship Endymion Int: 04 Feb 1815 Dis: 28 Mar 1815.
    Received from Endymion. Mars Transport for U States.

Orrioto, Dominica   Prisoner 524. Rank: Passenger, from: Herald, Letter of Marque Brig.
    Cap: 25 Dec 1812 at Sea by HMS Maidstone Int: 05 Jan 1813 Dis: 27 Jan 1813.
    Received from HM Ship Maidstone. Bostock Cartel for New York.

Osmondo, Anthony   Prisoner 2740. Rank: Seaman, from: Cataline, Not Recorded.
    Cap: 13 Jan 1815 St Marys by Dragon Int: 03 Mar 1815 Dis: 28 Mar 1815.
    Received from Hebrus. Clarendon Transport for U States.

Ostler, George   Prisoner 248. Rank: Seaman, from: Wasp, Sloop of War.
    Cap: 18 Oct 1812 at Sea by HM Ship Poictiers Int: 26 Oct 1812 Dis: 05 Nov 1812.
    Received from HM Ship Poictiers. Brig Diamond on Parole to new London United States of America.

Owens, William   Prisoner 2246. Rank: Seaman, from: President, U States Frigate.
    Cap: 15 Jan 1815 Not Recorded by Endymion Int: 30 Jan 1815 Dis: 28 Mar 1815.
    Received from Pomone. Mars Transport for U States.

Owlin, George   Prisoner 2155. Rank: Gunner, from: President, U States Frigate.
    Cap: 15 Jan 1815 Not Recorded by Endymion Int: 30 Jan 1815 Dis: 28 Mar 1815.
    Received from President. Mars Transport for U States.

Oxand, Michael   Prisoner 1994. Rank: Seaman, from: Fairplay, Merchant Vessel.
    Cap: 22 Oct 1814 Lat 31.58 by Dothrel Int: 26 Oct 1814 Dis: 05 Nov 1815.
    Recaptured. Received from Dothrel. Order Adml Cockburn.

Oxford, James   Prisoner 64. Rank: Seaman, from: Mary, Merchant Brig.
    Cap: 08 Aug 1812 of Bermuda by Cuttle Int: 28 Aug 1812 Dis: 18 Sep 1812.
    Received from M Schooner Cuttle. Order of Commd Evans for England.

American Prisoners of War Held at Bermuda During the War of 1812

Pack, Anthony   Prisoner 2312. Rank: Seaman, from: President, U States Frigate.
    Cap: 15 Jan 1815 Not Recorded by Endymion Int: 04 Feb 1815 Dis: 28 Mar 1815.
    Received from Endymion. Mars Transport for U States.

Page, Cato   Prisoner 653. Rank: Seaman, from: HM Sloop Sophia, Not Recorded.
    Cap: Not Recorded by Not Recorded Int: 20 Jan 1813 Dis: 27 Jan 1813.
    Received from the Prize Little Arnold. HM Sloop Sophia Surrendered himself. Bostock Cartel for New York. (Date of capture not recorded.)

Page, Jonkins   Prisoner 832. Rank: Seaman, from: Portsmouth, Merchant Ship.
    Cap: 27 Feb 1813 off Bermuda by HM Sloop Martin Int: 09 Mar 1813 Dis: 27 Mar 1813.
    Received from Sloop Martin. Per Order Commodore Evans the Vessel being Liberated.

Paine, William   Prisoner 1514. Rank: 1 Officer, from: Taalia, Merchant Vessel.
    Cap: 18 Dec 1813 of the Delware by Narcissus Int: 22 Jan 1814 Dis: 15 Apr 1814.
    Received from Surprize. Rammilles for Halifax.

Palmer, Benjamin   Prisoner 1306. Rank: Prize Master, from: Rolla, Privateer.
    Cap: 10 Dec 1813 Block Island by Loire Int: 20 Dec 1813 Dis: 15 Apr 1814.
    Received from San Domingo. HMS Rammillies for Halifax.

Palmer, John   Prisoner 533. Rank: Seaman, from: Herald, Letter of Marque Brig.
    Cap: 25 Dec 1812 at Sea by HM Ship Maidstone Int: 05 Jan 1813 Dis: 27 Jan 1813.
    Received from HM Ship Maidstone. Bostock Cartel for New York.

Palmer, John   Prisoner 907. Rank: Seaman, from: Elizabeth, Merchant Brig.
    Cap: 26 Feb 1813 Chesapeake by HMS Marlborough Int: 23 Mar 1813 Dis: 24 Apr 1813.
    Received from HM Ship Laurustinus. Vessel Liberated By Order Commodore Evans.

Palmer, Justice   Prisoner 486. Rank: Seaman, from: Teazer, Privateer Schooner.
    Cap: 16 Dec 1812 at Sea by HM Ship St. Domingo Int: 21 Dec 1812 Dis: 27 Jan 1813.
    Received from HM Ship St. Domingo. Bostock Cartel for New York.

Palmer, Robert   Prisoner 1590. Rank: Seaman, from: Bordeaux Packet, Letter of Marque.
    Cap: 28 Jan 1814 off Cape Henry by Nieman Int: 12 Feb 1814 Dis: 15 Apr 1814.
    Received from Nieman. Rammilles for Halifax.

Palmer, William   Prisoner 757. Rank: Mate, from: Hazard, Merchant Brig.
    Cap: 28 Dec 1812 Lat 37.35, Long 70.10 by HM Sloop Sylph Int: 26 Jan 1813 Dis: 24 Jun 1813.
    Received from Sloop Sylph. Magnet Cartel for New York.

Palmer, William F   Prisoner 2230. Rank: Quartermaster, from: President, U States Frigate.
    Cap: 15 Jan 1815 Not Recorded by Endymion Int: 30 Jan 1815 Dis: 28 Mar 1815.
    Received from Pomone. Mars Transport for U States.

Parker, B   Prisoner 2761. Rank: Seaman, from: Mayflower, Not Recorded.
    Cap: 20 Jan 1815 St Augustine by Severn Int: 03 Mar 1815 Dis: 09 Mar 1815.
    Received from Hebrus. Merchant Service.

Parker, Benjamin   Prisoner 2217. Rank: Seaman, from: President, U States Frigate.
    Cap: 15 Jan 1815 Not Recorded by Endymion Int: 30 Jan 1815 Dis: 28 Mar 1815.
    Received from Pomone. Mars Transport for U States.

Parker, James B   Prisoner 332. Rank: 2 Lieutenant, from: Snapper, Privateer Schooner.
    Cap: 16 Nov 1812 at Sea by HMS Galus Int: 22 Nov 1812 Dis: 27 Jan 1813.
    Received from HM Ship Galus. Bostock Cartel for New York.

Parker, John   Prisoner 499. Rank: Prize Master, from: Ann, Merchant Sloop.
    Cap: 19 Dec 1812 at Sea by HMS Sophia Int: 27 Dec 1812 Dis: 27 Jan 1813.
    Received from Sophia. Bostock Cartel for New York.

Parker, John   Prisoner 1254. Rank: Not Recorded, from: Circe, Merchant Vessel.
    Cap: 08 Oct 1813 Chesapeake by Lacedaemonian Int: 02 Dec 1813 Dis: 15 Apr 1814.
    Received from HMS Sceptre. Diana Transport for Halifax.

Parker, Joseph   Prisoner 1509. Rank: Seaman, from: Plantagenet, Not Recorded.
    Cap: Not Recorded by Not Recorded Int: 19 Jan 1814 Dis: 15 Apr 1814.
    Received from Plantagenet. being an American. Diana Transport for Halifax.
    (Date of capture not recorded.)

Parker, Redman   Prisoner 824. Rank: Seaman, from: Portsmouth, Merchant Ship.
    Cap: 27 Feb 1813 off Bermuda by HM Sloop Martin Int: 09 Mar 1813 Dis: 27 Mar 1813.
    Received from Sloop Martin. Per Order Commodore Evans the Vessel being Liberated.

Parker, Robert   Prisoner 2151. Rank: Masters Mate, from: President, U States Frigate.
    Cap: 15 Jan 1815 Not Recorded by Endymion Int: 30 Jan 1815 Dis: 18 Mar 1815.
    Received from President. Merchant Vessel.

Parker, S G   Prisoner 874. Rank: Seaman, from: Christiana, Merchant.
    Cap: 03 Mar 1813 Chesapeake by Marlborough Int: 23 Mar 1813 Escaped: 21 Apr 1813.
    Received from Laurustinus. Escaped.

American Prisoners of War Held at Bermuda During the War of 1812

Parker, William   Prisoner 1453. Rank: Seaman, from: Vixen, Man of War.
    Cap: 25 Dec 1813 Lat 38.0 by Belvidera Int: 05 Jan 1814 Dis: 15 Apr 1814.
    U States Schooner. Received from HMS Belvidera. Diana Transport for Halifax.

Parr, James   Prisoner 1213. Rank: Seaman, from: Portuguese Bark, Merchant.
    Cap: 19 Feb 1813 Cape Hatterus by San Domingo Int: 06 Nov 1813 Dis: 24 Apr 1814.
    Received from HMS Ruby. HMS Sceptre for England.

Parrey, John   Prisoner 129. Rank: Seaman, from: William of Baltimore, Merchant.
    Cap: 31 Aug 1812 Lat 37 by HM Ship Recruit Int: 14 Sep 1812 Dis: 18 Sep 1812.
    Received from HMS Recruit. Order of Commd Evans for England.

Parrish, Gideon M   Prisoner 415. Rank: 2 Mate, from: Isabella, Merchant Brig.
    Cap: 15 Nov 1812 at Sea by HM Sloop Childers Int: 24 Nov 1812 Dis: 27 Jan 1813.
    Received from HM Ship Childers. Bostock Cartel for New York.

Parrish, Samuel   Prisoner 516. Rank: Seaman, from: Nancy, Merchant Ship.
    Cap: 18 Dec 1812 off Bermuda by HMS Goree Int: 30 Dec 1812 Dis: 27 Jan 1813.
    Received from HMS Goree. Bostock Cartel for New York.

Parsons, Andrew   Prisoner 2265. Rank: Seaman, from: President, U States Frigate.
    Cap: 15 Jan 1815 Not Recorded by Endymion Int: 30 Jan 1815 Dis: 28 Mar 1815.
    Received from Pomone. Mars Transport for U States.

Partorioat, A Aben   Prisoner 2865. Rank: Prize Master, from: Limerick, Not Recorded.
    Cap: 06 Mar 1815 Not Recorded by Asia Int: 29 Mar 1815 Dis: 28 Mar 1815.
    From West Indies. Received from La Brune. Clarendon Transport for U States. (Date of discharge before date of internment.)

Parvlin, William   Prisoner 1198. Rank: Seaman, from: Mary, Merchant Ship.
    Cap: 30 Jul 1813 at Sea by HM Sloop Nimrod Int: 05 Sep 1813 Dis: 12 Sep 1813.
    Recaptured Sloop. Received from HM Sloop Nimrod. Per Order of Commodore Evans to the American Ship Georgiana restored.

Patch, Joseph   Prisoner 1007. Rank: Seaman, from: Ohio, Merchant.
    Cap: 20 Mar 1813 off the Chesapeake by HM Sloop Atalante Int: 06 Apr 1813 Dis: 24 Jun 1813.
    Received from HMS Junon. Magnet Cartel for New York.

Paterson, John   Prisoner 1188. Rank: Seaman, from: Elizabeth, Merchant.
    Cap: 15 Jun 1813 at Sea by HM Ship Marlborough Int: 18 Aug 1813 Dis: 02 Sep 1813.
    Received from HM Ship Woolwich. Per order of Commodore Evans vessel being liberated.

Patrick, George   Prisoner 1227. Rank: Not Recorded, from: HM Ship Cleopatra, Not Recorded.
    Cap: Aug 1813 Not Recorded by HM Ship Cleopatra Int: 16 Nov 1813 Dis: 15 Apr 1814.
    Received from HMS Sceptre. Surrendered himself. Diana Transport for Halifax.

Patterson, Alexander   Prisoner 215. Rank: Seaman, from: Wasp, Sloop of War.
    Cap: 18 Oct 1812 at Sea by HM Ship Poictiers Int: 26 Oct 1812 Dis: 05 Nov 1812.
    Received from HM Ship Poictiers. Brig Diamond on Parole to new London United States of America.

Patterson, John   Prisoner 217. Rank: Seaman, from: Wasp, Sloop of War.
    Cap: 18 Oct 1812 at Sea by HM Ship Poictiers Int: 26 Oct 1812 Dis: 05 Nov 1812.
    Received from HM Ship Poictiers. Brig Diamond on Parole to new London United States of America.

Patterson, Thomas   Prisoner 493. Rank: Seaman, from: Teazer, Privateer Schooner.
    Cap: 16 Dec 1812 at Sea by HM Ship St. Domingo Int: 21 Dec 1812 Dis: 27 Jan 1813.
    Received from HM Ship St. Domingo. Bostock Cartel for New York.

Paul, John   Prisoner 1148. Rank: Seaman, from: Acricoake, Merchant.
    Cap: 22 Jul 1813 at Sea by HM Sloop Conflict Int: 13 Aug 1813 Dis: 13 Aug 1813.
    Received from HM Ship Woolwich. American Ship Rolla per Order Commr Evans.

Pausland, John   Prisoner 1008. Rank: Seaman, from: Ohio, Merchant.
    Cap: 20 Mar 1813 off the Chesapeake by HM Sloop Atalante Int: 06 Apr 1813 Dis: 24 Jun 1813.
    Received from HMS Junon. Magnet Cartel for New York.

Pawn, Peter   Prisoner 2765. Rank: Seaman, from: Maria, Not Recorded.
    Cap: 16 Feb 1815 St Augustine by Severn Int: 03 Mar 1815 Dis: 28 Mar 1815.
    Received from Hebrus. Clarendon Transport for U States.

Pearce, George   Prisoner 2283. Rank: Seaman, from: President, U States Frigate.
    Cap: 15 Jan 1815 Not Recorded by Endymion Int: 30 Jan 1815 Dis: 28 Mar 1815.
    Received from Pomone. Mars Transport for U States.

Pearce, Henry   Prisoner 2640. Rank: Seaman, from: Platoff, Merchant Vessel.
    Cap: 16 Jan 1815 off New York by Spencer Int: 06 Feb 1815 Dis: 28 Mar 1815.
    Received from HMS Telegraph. Clarendon Transport for U States.

Pearson, William   Prisoner 1110. Rank: Seaman, from: Revenge, Privateer Brig.
    Cap: 25 May 1813 at Sea by Narcissus Int: 27 May 1813 Dis: 24 Jun 1813.
    Received from HM Ship San Domingo. Magnet Cartel for New York.

American Prisoners of War Held at Bermuda During the War of 1812

Peddock, William   Prisoner 149. Rank: Seaman, from: Ranger, Merchant Ship.
    Cap: 02 Oct 1812 Lat 32, Long 65 W by HMS Goree Int: 13 Oct 1812 Dis: 24 Oct 1812.
    Received from HMS Goree. Brig Diamond on Parole to new London United States of America.

Pedrick, George   Prisoner 2391. Rank: Seaman, from: President, U States Frigate.
    Cap: 15 Jan 1815 Not Recorded by HM Ship Endymion Int: 04 Feb 1815 Dis: 28 Mar 1815.
    Received from Endymion. Mars Transport for U States.

Pembroke, John   Prisoner 825. Rank: Seaman, from: Portsmouth, Merchant Ship.
    Cap: 27 Feb 1813 off Bermuda by HM Sloop Martin Int: 09 Mar 1813 Dis: 27 Mar 1813.
    Received from Sloop Martin. Per Order Commodore Evans the Vessel being Liberated.

Pendleton, Daniel   Prisoner 2332. Rank: Seaman, from: President, U States Frigate.
    Cap: 15 Jan 1815 Not Recorded by Endymion Int: 04 Feb 1815 Dis: 28 Mar 1815.
    Received from Endymion. Mars Transport for U States.

Pendleton, Robert   Prisoner 982. Rank: Seaman, from: Mary, Merchant.
    Cap: 10 Mar 1813 Chesapeake by HMS Maidstone Int: 23 Mar 1813 Dis: 24 Jun 1813.
    Received from HM Ship Laurustinus. Magnet Cartel for New York.

Penny, P B   Prisoner 413. Rank: Passenger, from: Isabella, Merchant Brig.
    Cap: 15 Nov 1812 at Sea by HM Sloop Childers Int: 24 Nov 1812 Dis: 18 Jan 1813.
    Received from HM Ship Childers. New York per Order A Cockburn.

Perk, George   Prisoner 2262. Rank: Seaman, from: President, U States Frigate.
    Cap: 15 Jan 1815 Not Recorded by Endymion Int: 30 Jan 1815 Dis: 28 Mar 1815.
    Received from Pomone. Mars Transport for U States.

Perkins, Thomas   Prisoner 2659. Rank: Seaman, from: Falcon, Merchant Vessel.
    Cap: 22 Jan 1815 Delaware by Forth Int: 13 Feb 1815 Dis: 28 Mar 1815.
    Received from Goree. Clarendon Transport for U States.

Perriotte, Louis   Prisoner 1765. Rank: Seaman, from: Yankelass, Privateer.
    Cap: 01 May 1814 L 40-4N, Long 38-0W by Severn & Surprise Int: 07 Jun 1814 Dis:
    Received from Surprise. (Date of discharge not recorded.)

Perruall, Hugh   Prisoner 1568. Rank: Seaman, from: Bordeaux Packet, Letter of Marque.
    Cap: 28 Jan 1814 off Cape Henry by Nieman Int: 12 Feb 1814 Dis: 15 Apr 1814.
    Received from Nieman. Diana Transport for Halifax.

Perry, Henry   Prisoner 1547. Rank: Mate, from: Pacifiranda, Merchant Vessel.
    Cap: 03 Jan 1814 Block Island by Albian Int: 04 Feb 1814 Dis: 15 Apr 1814.
    Received from Surprize, Rammilles for Halifax.

Perry, John   Prisoner 1536. Rank: Seaman, from: Isabella, Merchant Vessel.
    Cap: 31 Dec 1813 at Sea by Belvidera Int: 24 Jan 1814 Dis: 15 Apr 1814.
    Received from Belvidera. Diana for Halifax.

Perry, John   Prisoner 2533. Rank: Seaman, from: President, U States Frigate.
    Cap: 15 Jan 1815 Not Recorded by HM Ship Endymion Int: 04 Feb 1815 Dis: 28 Mar 1815.
    Received from HMS Endymion. Clarenden Transport for U States.

Perry, Liberty   Prisoner 1005. Rank: Mate, from: Ohio, Merchant.
    Cap: 20 Mar 1813 off the Chesapeake by HM Sloop Atalante Int: 06 Apr 1813 Dis: 24 Jun 1813.
    Received from HMS Junon. Magnet Cartel for New York.

Perslaw, Joseph   Prisoner 2678. Rank: Seaman, from: Gunboat 160, U States Man of War.
    Cap: 06 Sep 1814 off New York by Lacedaemonian Int: 14 Feb 1815 Dis: 28 Mar 1815.
    Gun Vessel. Received from Childers. Clarendon Transport for U States.

Pervis, William   Prisoner 1026. Rank: Seaman, from: Dart, Merchant Schooner.
    Cap: 17 Mar 1813 off the Chesapeake by HMS Statira Int: 06 Apr 1813 Dis: 24 Jun 1813.
    Received from HMS Junon. Magnet Cartel for New York.

Pester, James   Prisoner 2452. Rank: Seaman, from: President, U States Frigate.
    Cap: 15 Jan 1815 Not Recorded by Endymion Int: 04 Feb 1815 Dis: 28 Mar 1815.
    Received from Endymion. Clarenden Transport for U States.

Peter, Robert   Prisoner 778. Rank: Seaman, from: Governor Ankerheim, Merchant.
    Cap: 24 Jan 1813 at Sea by HM Ship Ramiles Int: 04 Feb 1813 Dis: 13 Mar 1813.
    Received from HMS Ramilies. Per Order Sir John Warren the Vessel being Liberated.

Petero, John   Prisoner 1529. Rank: Seaman, from: Matchless, Merchant Vessel.
    Cap: 02 Jan 1814 Latt 22.0 by Prometheus Int: 23 Jan 1814 Dis: 15 Apr 1814.
    Received from Prometheus. Diana for Halifax.

Peters, John   Prisoner 127. Rank: Seaman, from: William of Baltimore, Merchant.
    Cap: 31 Aug 1812 Lat 37 by HM Ship Recruit Int: 14 Sep 1812 Dis: 18 Sep 1812.
    Received from HMS Recruit. Order of Commd Evans for England.

Peters, John   Prisoner 1288. Rank: Seaman, from: Perry, Merchant Schooner.
    Cap: 03 Dec 1813 Long Island by Indemyion Int: 19 Dec 1813 Dis: 15 Apr 1814.
    Received from Sceptre. Diana Transport for Halifax. John Peters (1).

American Prisoners of War Held at Bermuda During the War of 1812

Peterson, Jacob   Prisoner 923. Rank: Seaman, from: Albert, Merchant Schooner.
    Cap: 05 Mar 1813 Chesapeake by HM Ship Marlborough Int: 23 Mar 1813 Dis: 05 May 1813.
    Received from Laurustinus. Prize Ship St. Michael.

Peterson, James   Prisoner 1432. Rank: Seaman, from: Nonsuch, Letter of Marque.
    Cap: 14 Dec 1813 Lat 32 by Doterel Int: 25 Dec 1813 Dis: 15 Apr 1814.
    Received from HM Brig Doterel. Diana Transport for Halifax.

Peterson, John   Prisoner 1433. Rank: Seaman, from: Nonsuch, Letter of Marque.
    Cap: 14 Dec 1813 Lat 32 by Doterel Int: 25 Dec 1813 Dis: 17 Mar 1814.
    Received from HM Brig Doterel. Terpscicore Prize Frigate for a passage to England per order of Commander in Chief.

Peterson, John   Prisoner 2530. Rank: Seaman, from: President, U States Frigate.
    Cap: 15 Jan 1815 Not Recorded by Endymion Int: 04 Feb 1815 Dis: 28 Mar 1815.
    Received from HMS Endymion. Clarenden Transport for U States.

Peterson, Lawrence   Prisoner 1437. Rank: Seaman, from: Nonsuch, Letter of Marque.
    Cap: 14 Dec 1813 Lat 32 by Doterel Int: 25 Dec 1813 Dis: 15 Apr 1814.
    Received from HM Brig Doterel. Diana Transport for Halifax.

Peterson, P   Prisoner 1420. Rank: 3 Officer, from: Nonsuch, Letter of Marque.
    Cap: 14 Dec 1813 Lat 32 by Doterel Int: 25 Dec 1813 Dis: 15 Apr 1814.
    Received from HM Brig Doterel. Rammilles for Halifax.

Peterson, Thomas   Prisoner 784. Rank: Seaman, from: Gustar Adolph, Merchant.
    Cap: 24 Jan 1813 at Sea by HM Ship Ramiles Int: 04 Feb 1813 Dis: 13 Mar 1813.
    Received from HMS Ramilies. Per Order Sir John Warren the Vessel being Liberated.

Peterson, Thomas   Prisoner 952. Rank: Seaman, from: Bona, Letter of Marque Schooner.
    Cap: 12 Mar 1813 Chesapeake by Laurustinus Int: 23 Mar 1813 Dis: 05 May 1813.
    Received from Laurustinus. Prize Ship St. Michael.

Petman, Richard   Prisoner 584. Rank: Seaman, from: Lydia, Merchant Ship.
    Cap: 26 Dec 1812 at Sea by HM Ship Maidstone Int: 06 Jan 1813 Dis: 27 Jan 1813.
    Received from HM Ship Maidstone. Bostock Cartel for New York.

Pew, Doliver   Prisoner 2625. Rank: Seaman, from: William, Merchant Vessel.
    Cap: 12 Jan 1815 Cape Hatterus by HMS Telegraph Int: 05 Feb 1815 Dis: 25 Mar 1815.
    Received from HMS Telegraph. Merchant Vessel.

Peyton, James   Prisoner 992. Rank: Seaman, from: Theresa, Merchant.
    Cap: 25 Feb 1813 at Sea by HMS Narcissus Int: 24 Mar 1813 Dis: 17 Jun 1813.
    Received from Theresa Prize. Halifax Order of the Commander in Chief supports to be an Englishman.

Phelps, Elijah   Prisoner 1308. Rank: Master at Arms, from: Rolla, Privateer.
    Cap: 10 Dec 1813 Block Island by Loire Int: 20 Dec 1813 Dis: 15 Apr 1814.
    Received from San Domingo. HMS Rammillies for Halifax.

Philips, John   Prisoner 140. Rank: Seaman, from: Yorick, Merchant Ship.
    Cap: 09 Jul 1812 off Bermuda by Rattler Int: 11 Oct 1812 Dis: 24 Oct 1812.
    Received from Hospital. Brig Diamond on Parole to New London United States of America.

Philips, Thomas   Prisoner 310. Rank: Seaman, from: Wasp, Sloop of War.
    Cap: 18 Oct 1812 at Sea by HMS Poictiers Int: 05 Nov 1812 Dis: 17 Jun 1813.
    Received from HM Ship Poictiers. Halifax Order of the Commander in Chief supports to be an Englishman.

Phillips, Henry   Prisoner 2817. Rank: Seaman, from: Limerick, Not Recorded.
    Cap: 15 Mar 1815 Not Recorded by Asia Int: 25 Mar 1815 Dis: 25 Mar 1815.
    From Depot at Jamaica. Received from Asia. Merchant Vessel.

Phillips, John   Prisoner 1814. Rank: Passenger, from: Not Recorded, Not Recorded.
    Cap: Not Recorded by Not Recorded Int: 14 Jun 1814 Dis: 15 Jun 1814.
    From St. Bartholomew in the Swedish Schooner Oscar. on Parole per Order Com in Chief to America. (Date of capture not recorded.)

Phillips, John   Prisoner 2773. Rank: Mate, from: Hope, Not Recorded.
    Cap: 21 Feb 1815 St Augustine by Hebrus Int: 03 Mar 1815 Dis: 16 Mar 1815.
    Received from Hebrus. Merchant Service.

Phillips, R W   Prisoner 2806. Rank: Seaman, from: Limerick, Not Recorded.
    Cap: 04 Mar 1815 Not Recorded by Asia Int: 25 Mar 1815 Dis:
    From Depot at Jamaica. Received from Asia. (Date of discharge not recorded.)

Pickens, Samuel   Prisoner 1741. Rank: Seaman, from: Yankelass, Privateer.
    Cap: 01 May 1814 L 10-4N, L 33-0W by Severn & Surprise Int: 06 Jun 1814 Dis: 20 Mar 1815.
    Received from Severn. Merchant Vessel.

Piedmont, Thomas   Prisoner 1093. Rank: Seaman, from: Langdon Cheves, Merchant.
    Cap: 12 May 1813 at Sea by HM Sloop Atalante Int: 25 May 1813 Dis: 24 Jun 1813.
    Received from HMS Atalante. Magnet Cartel for New York.

American Prisoners of War Held at Bermuda During the War of 1812

Pierce, John C   Prisoner 616. Rank: Master, from: Morning Star, Merchant Schooner.
    Cap: 17 Dec 1812 at Sea by HM Ship Tartarus Int: 12 Jan 1813 Dis: 05 Feb 1813.
    Received from HMS Belvidera. Permitted to return to New York per Order of Adl Cockburn.

Pierce, Nathaniel   Prisoner 6. Rank: Seaman, from: Yorick, Merchant Ship.
    Cap: 09 Jul 1812 near Bermuda by Rattler Int: 28 Aug 1812 Dis: 18 Sep 1812.
    Received from HM Schooner Cuttle. Order of Commd Evans for England.

Pike, John   Prisoner 1785. Rank: Seaman, from: Yankelass, Privateer.
    Cap: 01 May 1814 Latt 40-4N, Long 38-0W by Severn & Surprise Int: 07 Jun 1814 Dis: 28 Mar 1815.
    Received from Surprise. Mars Transport for U States.

Pinshaw, Joseph   Prisoner 1654. Rank: Seaman, from: Flash, Letter of Marque.
    Cap: 11 Feb 1814 Off Block Island by Acasta Int: 13 Mar 1814 Dis: 23 Apr 1814.
    Received from Active. HMS Bulwark for Halifax.

Pitee, James   Prisoner 679. Rank: Seaman, from: High Flyer, Privateer.
    Cap: 09 Jan 1813 at Sea by HM Ship Acasta Int: 21 Jan 1813 Dis: 27 Jan 1813.
    Received from HMS Acasta. Bostock Cartel for New York.

Pitts, Peter   Prisoner 2744. Rank: Seaman, from: Aroof, Not Recorded.
    Cap: 16 Jan 1815 St Augustine by Manly Int: 03 Mar 1815 Dis: 28 Mar 1815.
    Received from Hebrus. Clarendon Transport for U States.

Pitts, Samuel   Prisoner 1764. Rank: Seaman, from: Yankelass, Privateer.
    Cap: 01 May 1814 L 40-4N, Long 38-0W by Severn & Surprise Int: 07 Jun 1814 Dis: 15 Jun 1814.
    Received from Surprise. per order Com in Chief.

Planter, John   Prisoner 194. Rank: Seaman, from: Wasp, Sloop of War.
    Cap: 18 Oct 1812 at Sea by HMS Poictiers Int: 26 Oct 1812 Dis: 05 Nov 1812.
    Received from HM Ship Poictiers. Brig Diamond on Parole to new London America.

Plier, Ezekiel   Prisoner 2564. Rank: Seaman, from: Funchall, Merchant Vessel.
    Cap: 15 Jan 1815 off New York by HMS Pomone Int: 05 Feb 1815 Dis: 16 Mar 1815.
    Received from HMS Forth. Merchant Service.

Plumely, John   Prisoner 1790. Rank: Prize Master, from: Yankelass, Privateer.
    Cap: 01 May 1814 Latt 40-4N, Long 38-0W by Severn & Surprise Int: 07 Jun 1814 Dis: 26 Oct 1814.
    Received from Surprise. Order R Adm Cockburn.

Plummer, Isaac L   Prisoner 1733. Rank: Seaman, from: Yankelass, Privateer.
    Cap: 01 May 1814 L 10-4N, L 33-0W by Severn & Surprise Int: 06 Jun 1814 Dis: 28 Mar 1815.
    Received from Severn. Mars for U States.

Plummer, Joseph   Prisoner 2327. Rank: Cooper, from: President, U States Frigate.
    Cap: 15 Jan 1815 Not Recorded by Endymion Int: 04 Feb 1815 Dis: 28 Mar 1815.
    Received from Endymion. Mars Transport for U States.

Pointer, James   Prisoner 442. Rank: Master, from: Adventure, Merchant Brig.
    Cap: 15 Dec 1812 off Bermuda by HM Sloop Childers Int: 17 Dec 1812 Dis: 27 Jan 1813.
    Received from HM Sloop Childers. Bostock Cartel for New York.

Poland, Oliver   Prisoner 2719. Rank: Seaman, from: American Gun Boat, Not Recorded.
    Cap: 06 Feb 1815 off Charleston by Tonnant Int: 02 Mar 1815 Dis:
    Received from Armede. (Date of discharge not recorded.)

Polk, Samuel   Prisoner 1025. Rank: Seaman, from: Dart, Merchant Schooner.
    Cap: 17 Mar 1813 off the Chesapeake by HMS Statira Int: 06 Apr 1813 Dis: 24 Jun 1813.
    Received from HMS Junon. Magnet Cartel for New York.

Pollard, George   Prisoner 664. Rank: Sailing Master, from: High Flyer, Privateer.
    Cap: 09 Jan 1813 at Sea by HM Ship Acasta Int: 21 Jan 1813 Dis: 27 Jan 1813.
    Received from HMS Acasta. Bostock Cartel for New York.

Pollard, William   Prisoner 1279. Rank: Seaman, from: Perry, Merchant Schooner.
    Cap: 03 Dec 1813 Long Island by Indemyion Int: 19 Dec 1813 Dis: 15 Apr 1814.
    Received from Sceptre. Diana Transport for Halifax.

Pool, Richard   Prisoner 519. Rank: Seaman, from: Nancy, Merchant Ship.
    Cap: 18 Dec 1812 off Bermuda by HMS Goree Int: 30 Dec 1812 Dis: 27 Jan 1813.
    Received from HMS Goree. Bostock Cartel for New York.

Poop, Elijah   Prisoner 956. Rank: Seaman, from: Bona, Letter of Marque Schooner.
    Cap: 12 Mar 1813 Chesapeake by Laurustinus Int: 23 Mar 1813 Dis: 24 Jun 1813.
    Received from Laurustinus. Magnet Cartel for New York.

Poore, David   Prisoner 2721. Rank: Seaman, from: American Gun Boat, Not Recorded.
    Cap: 06 Feb 1815 off Charleston by Tonnant Int: 02 Mar 1815 Dis:
    Received from Armede. (Date of discharge not recorded.)

Poore, Isaac   Prisoner 2720. Rank: Seaman, from: American Gun Boat, Not Recorded.
    Cap: 06 Feb 1815 off Charleston by Tonnant Int: 02 Mar 1815 Dis:
    Received from Armede. (Date of discharge not recorded.)

American Prisoners of War Held at Bermuda During the War of 1812

Poore, Thomas   Prisoner 2007. Rank: Seaman, from: Bridges, Merchant Vessel.
    Cap: 25 Oct 1814 off Halifax by Armide Int: 07 Nov 1814 Dis: 28 Mar 1815.
    Recaptured. Received from HMS Armide. Clarendon Transport for U States.

Porter, Ezra   Prisoner 2860. Rank: Seaman, from: Limerick, Not Recorded.
    Cap: 15 Mar 1815 Not Recorded by Asia Int: 27 Mar 1815 Dis: 28 Mar 1815.
    From Depot at Jamaica. Received from Goree. Clarendon Transport for U States.

Porter, J C   Prisoner 602. Rank: Seaman, from: Noetoin, Packet Brig.
    Cap: 05 Jan 1813 at Sea by HM Ship Belvidera Int: 10 Jan 1813 Dis: 27 Jan 1813.
    Received from HMS Belvidera. Bostock Cartel for New York.

Porter, John C   Prisoner 2239. Rank: Seaman, from: President, U States Frigate.
    Cap: 15 Jan 1815 Not Recorded by Endymion Int: 30 Jan 1815 Dis: 28 Mar 1815.
    Received from Pomone. Mars Transport for U States.

Porter, Joshua   Prisoner 425. Rank: 2 Mate, from: Eliza, Merchant Ship.
    Cap: 25 Nov 1812 Lat 37.00, Long 65.46 by HM Ship Tartarus Int: 03 Dec 1812 Dis: 27 Jan 1813.
    Received from HM Ship Tartarus. Bostock Cartel for New York.

Porter, Levi   Prisoner 208. Rank: Marine, from: Wasp, Sloop of War.
    Cap: 18 Oct 1812 at Sea by HM Ship Poictiers Int: 26 Oct 1812 Dis: 05 Nov 1812.
    Received from HM Ship Poictiers. Brig Diamond on Parole to new London United States of America.

Porter, William   Prisoner 67. Rank: Supercargo, from: Canaway, Merchant Ship.
    Cap: 08 Aug 1812 of Bermuda by Recruit Int: 28 Aug 1812 Dis: 06 Sep 1812.
    Received from M Schooner Cuttle. Sloop Sally for New York.

Post, Anthony   Prisoner 2121. Rank: Seaman, from: Armistice, Merchant Vessel.
    Cap: 07 Dec 1814 off Delaware by Pictolus Int: 27 Jan 1815 Dis: 28 Mar 1815.
    Received from Pictolus. Clarendon Transport for U States.

Potter, Joseph   Prisoner 2516. Rank: Seaman, from: President, U States Frigate.
    Cap: 15 Jan 1815 Not Recorded by Endymion Int: 04 Feb 1815 Dis: 28 Mar 1815.
    Received from HMS Endymion. Clarenden Transport for U States.

Poulson, Alex   Prisoner 1846. Rank: Passenger, from: Hibernia, Merchant Vessel.
    Cap: Not Recorded by Not Recorded Int: Dis: 28 Mar 1815.
    Clarendon Transport for U States. (Dates of capture and internment not recorded.)

Pouree, Stephen   Prisoner 172. Rank: Masters Mate, from: Wasp, Sloop of War.
    Cap: 18 Oct 1812 at Sea by HMS Poictiers Int: 26 Oct 1812 Dis: 05 Nov 1812.
    Received from HM Ship Poictiers. on Parole Brig Diamond to new London America.

Powell, Elisha   Prisoner 1698. Rank: Seaman, from: Grecian, Letter of Marque.
    Cap: 02 May 1814 Chesapeake by Jansur Int: 26 May 1814 Dis: 28 Mar 1815.
    Received from Lacedaemonian. Mars Transport for U States.

Powell, John   Prisoner 2247. Rank: Seaman, from: President, U States Frigate.
    Cap: 15 Jan 1815 Not Recorded by Endymion Int: 30 Jan 1815 Dis: 28 Mar 1815.
    Received from Pomone. Mars Transport for U States.

Powell, William   Prisoner 134. Rank: Seaman, from: William of Baltimore, Merchant.
    Cap: 31 Aug 1812 Lat 37 by Recruit Int: 17 Sep 1812 Dis: 18 Sep 1812.
    Received from Recruit. Order of Commd Evans for England.

Powell, William   Prisoner 2814. Rank: Seaman, from: Limerick, Not Recorded.
    Cap: 04 Mar 1815 Not Recorded by Asia Int: 25 Mar 1815 Dis:
    From Depot at Jamaica. Received from Asia. (Date of discharge not recorded.)

Powers, John   Prisoner 1113. Rank: Quartermaster, from: Dolphin, Privateer.
    Cap: 03 Apr 1813 at Sea by By the Boats of the Squadron Int: 07 Jun 1813 Dis: 24 Jun 1813.
    Received from Ship Dragon. Magnet Cartel for New York.

Powers, John   Prisoner 1550. Rank: Mate, from: Bordeaux Packet, Letter of Marque.
    Cap: 28 Jan 1814 off Cape Henry by Nieman Int: 12 Feb 1814 Dis: 15 Apr 1814.
    Received from Nieman. Rammilles for Halifax.

Powers, John   Prisoner 2853. Rank: Seaman, from: Limerick, Not Recorded.
    Cap: 15 Mar 1815 Not Recorded by Asia Int: 25 Mar 1815 Dis:
    From Depot at Jamaica. Received from Asia. (Date of discharge not recorded.)

Powers, Richard   Prisoner 2414. Rank: Seaman, from: President, U States Frigate.
    Cap: 15 Jan 1815 Not Recorded by HM Ship Endymion Int: 04 Feb 1815 Dis: 28 Mar 1815.
    Received from Endymion. Mars Transport for U States.

Prader, Manuel   Prisoner 901. Rank: Seaman, from: Princessa, Merchant Brig.
    Cap: 07 Feb 1813 Chesapeake by HMS Marlborough Int: 23 Mar 1813 Dis: 24 Mar 1813.
    Received from HM Ship Laurustinus. St. Michael per Order Adl Sir J B Warren.

Prassur, John   Prisoner 2428. Rank: Seaman, from: President, U States Frigate.
    Cap: 15 Jan 1815 Not Recorded by HM Ship Endymion Int: 04 Feb 1815 Dis: 28 Mar 1815.
    Received from Endymion. Mars Transport for U States.

American Prisoners of War Held at Bermuda During the War of 1812

Pratt, Anza   Prisoner 1274. Rank: Seaman, from: Laura, Merchant Vessel.
    Cap: 15 Oct 1813 Long Island by HM Brig Borer Int: 19 Dec 1813 Dis: 15 Apr 1814.
    Received from HMS Acasta. Diana for Halifax.

Pratt, John   Prisoner 783. Rank: Seaman, from: Governor Ankerheim, Merchant.
    Cap: 24 Jan 1813 at Sea by HM Ship Ramiles Int: 04 Feb 1813 Dis: 13 Mar 1813.
    Received from HMS Ramilies. Per Order Sir John Warren the Vessel being Liberated.

Pratt, Samuel   Prisoner 1765. Rank: Seaman, from: Yankelass, Privateer.
    Cap: 01 May 1814 L 40-4N, Long 38-0W by Severn & Surprise Int: 06 Jun 1814 Dis: 28 Mar 1815.
    Received from Severn. Mars Transport for U States.

Pray, Caterwick   Prisoner 1724. Rank: Prize Master, from: Revinue, Merchant Vessel.
    Cap: 15 May 1814 at Sea by Lacedaemonian Int: 30 May 1814 Dis: 28 Mar 1815.
    Received from Asia. Mars Transport for U States.

Pready, Marshall   Prisoner 2554. Rank: Seaman, from: President, US Frigate.
    Cap: 15 Jan 1815 off N York by HMS Endymion Int: 05 Feb 1815 Dis: 28 Mar 1815.
    Received from President. Clarenden Transport for U States.

Price, Charles   Prisoner 1635. Rank: Seaman, from: Not Recorded, Not Recorded.
    Cap: 05 Feb 1814 Not Recorded by Sceptre Int: 14 Feb 1814 Dis: 15 Apr 1814.
    Received from Sceptre. Rammilles for Halifax.

Price, Edward   Prisoner 2140. Rank: Midshipman, from: President, U States Frigate.
    Cap: 15 Jan 1815 Not Recorded by Endymion Int: 30 Jan 1815 Dis: 28 Mar 1815.
    Received from President. Clarenden Transport for U States.

Priest, Stephen   Prisoner 659. Rank: Seaman, from: Pekin, Merchant Ship.
    Cap: 17 Dec 1812 at Sea by HM Ship Acasta Int: 21 Jan 1813 Dis: 27 Jan 1813.
    Received from Ship Pekin. Bostock Cartel for New York.

Prindale, S   Prisoner 1422. Rank: Seaman, from: Nonsuch, Letter of Marque.
    Cap: 14 Dec 1813 Lat 32 by Doterel Int: 25 Dec 1813 Dis: 15 Apr 1814.
    Received from HM Brig Doterel. Diana Transport for Halifax.

Pritchard, Charles   Prisoner 965. Rank: Boy, from: Janett, Merchant Brig.
    Cap: 25 Feb 1813 Chesapeake by HMS Junon Int: 23 Mar 1813 Dis: 08 Apr 1813.
    Received from Laurustinus. Per Order Commodore Evans being under Age.

Pritchard, John   Prisoner 967. Rank: Master, from: Janett, Merchant Brig.
    Cap: 25 Feb 1813 Chesapeake by HMS Junon Int: 23 Mar 1813 Dis:
    Received from HM Ship Laurustinus. (Date of discharge not recorded.)

Pritchard, William   Prisoner 2186. Rank: Seaman, from: President, U States Frigate.
    Cap: 15 Jan 1815 Not Recorded by HMS Endymion Int: 30 Jan 1815 Dis: 28 Mar 1815.
    Received from Pomone. Mars Transport for U States.

Prout, Jacob   Prisoner 444. Rank: Cook, from: Adventure, Merchant Brig.
    Cap: 15 Dec 1812 off Bermuda by HM Sloop Childers Int: 17 Dec 1812 Dis: 27 Jan 1813.
    Received from HM Sloop Childers. Bostock Cartel for New York.

Providence, Thomas   Prisoner 2750. Rank: Seaman, from: Speedwell, Not Recorded.
    Cap: 21 Jan 1815 St Augustine by Severn Int: 03 Mar 1815 Dis: 28 Mar 1815.
    Received from Hebrus. Clarendon Transport for U States.

Prowe, Tudar   Prisoner 1751. Rank: Seaman, from: Yankelass, Privateer.
    Cap: 01 May 1814 L 40-4N, Long 38-0W by Severn & Surprise Int: 06 Jun 1814 Dis: 10 Nov 1814.
    Received from Severn. Joseph MV Rear Adm Cockburn.

Pullock, Joseph   Prisoner 703. Rank: Seaman, from: High Flyer, Privateer.
    Cap: 09 Jan 1813 at Sea by HMS Acasta Int: 21 Jan 1813 Dis: 27 Jan 1813.
    Received from HMS Acasta. Bostock Cartel for New York.

Quenon, Augustus   Prisoner 709. Rank: Seaman, from: High Flyer, Privateer.
    Cap: 09 Jan 1813 at Sea by HMS Acasta Int: 21 Jan 1813 Dis: 27 Jan 1813.
    Received from HMS Acasta. Bostock Cartel for New York.

Quin, Francis   Prisoner 543. Rank: Seaman, from: Herald, Letter of Marque Brig.
    Cap: 25 Dec 1812 at Sea by HM Ship Maidstone Int: 05 Jan 1813 Dis: 27 Jan 1813.
    Received from HM Ship Maidstone. Bostock Cartel for New York.

Quin, Michael   Prisoner 2441. Rank: Marine, from: President, U States Frigate.
    Cap: 15 Jan 1815 Not Recorded by Endymion Int: 04 Feb 1815 Dis: 28 Mar 1815.
    Received from Endymion. Clarenden Transport for U States.

Quinolis, Frederick   Prisoner 399. Rank: Seaman, from: Snapper, Privateer Schooner.
    Cap: 16 Nov 1812 at Sea by HM Ship Galus Int: 22 Nov 1812 Dis: 14 Dec 1812.
    Received from HM Ship Galus. per Order Commodore Evans.

Randall, Cater   Prisoner 1599. Rank: Seaman, from: Dispatch, Merchant Vessel.
    Cap: 26 Oct 1813 Block Island by Narcissus Int: 14 Feb 1814 Dis: 23 Apr 1814.
    Received from Sceptre. HMS Bulwark for Halifax.

American Prisoners of War Held at Bermuda During the War of 1812

Randall, Oates   Prisoner 1686. Rank: Seaman, from: Dispatch, Merchant Vessel.
    Cap: 26 Oct 1813 Block Island by Narcissus Int: 06 May 1814 Dis: 20 Mar 1815.
    Received from Hospital. Merchant Vessel.

Randall, William   Prisoner 2203. Rank: Seaman, from: President, U States Frigate.
    Cap: 15 Jan 1815 Not Recorded by Endymion Int: 30 Jan 1815 Dis: 28 Mar 1815.
    Received from Pomone. Mars Transport for U States.

Randell, Stephen   Prisoner 669. Rank: Gunner, from: High Flyer, Privateer.
    Cap: 09 Jan 1813 at Sea by HM Ship Acasta Int: 21 Jan 1813 Dis: 27 Jan 1813.
    Received from HMS Acasta. Bostock Cartel for New York.

Randolph, R B   Prisoner 2138. Rank: Midshipman, from: President, U States Frigate.
    Cap: 15 Jan 1815 Not Recorded by Endymion Int: 30 Jan 1815 Dis: 18 Mar 1815.
    Received from President. Merchant Vessel.

Ranes, Zachariah   Prisoner 725. Rank: Seaman, from: High Flyer, Privateer.
    Cap: 09 Jan 1813 at Sea by HM Ship Acasta Int: 21 Jan 1813 Dis: 27 Jan 1813.
    Received from HMS Acasta. Bostock Cartel for New York.

Rapp, Henry B   Prisoner 167. Rank: Midshipman, from: Wasp, Sloop of War.
    Cap: 18 Oct 1812 at Sea by HMS Poictiers Int: 26 Oct 1812 Dis: 05 Nov 1812.
    Received from HM Ship Poictiers. on Parole Brig Diamond to new London America.

Rawson, Jonathan   Prisoner 319. Rank: Mate, from: James, Merchant Ship.
    Cap: 03 Nov 1812 at Sea by HM Ship Tartarus Int: 17 Nov 1812 Dis: 27 Jan 1813.
    Received from HM Ship Tartarus. Bostock Cartel for New York.

Ray, R   Prisoner 1602. Rank: Seaman, from: Monticello, Merchant Vessel.
    Cap: 09 Dec 1813 Block Island by Albion Int: 14 Feb 1814 Dis: 23 Apr 1814.
    Received from Sceptre. HMS Bulwark for Halifax.

Ray, Thomas   Prisoner 2259. Rank: Marine, from: President, U States Frigate.
    Cap: 15 Jan 1815 Not Recorded by Endymion Int: 30 Jan 1815 Dis: 28 Mar 1815.
    Received from Pomone. Clarenden Transport for U States.

Ray, Thomas   Prisoner 2485. Rank: Seaman, from: President, U States Frigate.
    Cap: 15 Jan 1815 Not Recorded by Endymion Int: 04 Feb 1815 Dis: 28 Mar 1815.
    Received from Endymion. Clarenden Transport for U States.

Raymond, William   Prisoner 1506. Rank: Seaman, from: Jackall, Merchant Vessel.
    Cap: 23 Dec 1813 off the Delaware by Belvidera Int: 18 Jan 1814 Dis: 15 Apr 1814.
    Received from Belvidera. Diana Transport for Halifax.

Raynolds, John H   Prisoner 2285. Rank: Seaman, from: President, U States Frigate.
    Cap: 15 Jan 1815 Not Recorded by Endymion Int: 30 Jan 1815 Dis: 28 Mar 1815.
    Received from Pomone. Mars Transport for U States.

Raynolds, William L   Prisoner 2288. Rank: Seaman, from: President, U States Frigate.
    Cap: 15 Jan 1815 Not Recorded by Endymion Int: 30 Jan 1815 Dis: 28 Mar 1815.
    Received from Pomone. Mars Transport for U States.

Rea, John   Prisoner 288. Rank: Seaman, from: Wasp, Sloop of War.
    Cap: 18 Oct 1812 at Sea by HMS Poictiers Int: 02 Nov 1812 Dis: 04 Nov 1812.
    Received from HMS Poictiers. Brig Diamond on Parole to new London United States of America.

Reane, John   Prisoner 227. Rank: Seaman, from: Wasp, Sloop of War.
    Cap: 18 Oct 1812 at Sea by HM Ship Poictiers Int: 26 Oct 1812 Dis: 05 Nov 1812.
    Received from HM Ship Poictiers. Brig Diamond on Parole to new London United States of America.

Redman, James   Prisoner 2827. Rank: Seaman, from: Limerick, Not Recorded.
    Cap: 15 Mar 1815 Not Recorded by Asia Int: 25 Mar 1815 Dis:
    From Depot at Jamaica. Received from Asia. (Date of discharge not recorded.)

Reed, George   Prisoner 305. Rank: Seaman, from: Wasp, Sloop of War.
    Cap: 18 Oct 1812 at Sea by HMS Poictiers Int: 05 Nov 1812 Dis: 17 Jun 1813.
    Received from HM Ship Poictiers. Halifax Order of the Commander in Chief supports to be an Englishman.

Reed, Perry   Prisoner 342. Rank: Seaman, from: Snapper, Privateer Schooner.
    Cap: 16 Nov 1812 at Sea by HMS Galus Int: 22 Nov 1812 Dis: 27 Jan 1813.
    Received from HM Ship Galus. Bostock Cartel for New York.

Reed, Richard   Prisoner 515. Rank: Seaman, from: Nancy, Merchant Ship.
    Cap: 18 Dec 1812 off Bermuda by HMS Goree Int: 30 Dec 1812 Dis: 27 Jan 1813.
    Received from HMS Goree. Bostock Cartel for New York.

Reed, Robert   Prisoner 520. Rank: Seaman, from: Nancy, Merchant Ship.
    Cap: 18 Dec 1812 off Bermuda by HMS Goree Int: 30 Dec 1812 Dis: 27 Jan 1813.
    Received from HMS Goree. Bostock Cartel for New York.

American Prisoners of War Held at Bermuda During the War of 1812

Reeves, Joseph   Prisoner 2345. Rank: Seaman, from: President, U States Frigate.
    Cap: 15 Jan 1815 Not Recorded by HMS Endymion Int: 04 Feb 1815 Dis: 28 Mar 1815.
    Received from Endymion. Mars Transport for U States.

Regan, John   Prisoner 2548. Rank: Seaman, from: President, US Frigate.
    Cap: 15 Jan 1815 off N York by HMS Endymion Int: 05 Feb 1815 Dis: 28 Mar 1815.
    Received from President. Clarenden Transport for U States.

Reid, Luke   Prisoner 108. Rank: Merchant, from: Gossepuim, detained American.
    Cap: 02 Sep 1812 Bermuda by Not Recorded Int: 02 Sep 1812 Dis: 26 Sep 1812.
    Received from HMS Ruby. detained per order of the President. Permitted to remain in the Colony per order of the Commodore.

Renney, Comfort S   Prisoner 112. Rank: Captain, from: Lydia, Merchant.
    Cap: 03 Sep 1812 Near Bermuda by HMS Orpheus Int: 08 Sep 1812 Dis: 10 Sep 1812.
    Received from HMS Orpheus. a Sweed per Order Cmd Evans.

Retman, Richard   Prisoner 636. Rank: Seaman, from: Lydia, Merchant Ship.
    Cap: Not Recorded by Not Recorded Int: Dis: 27 Jan 1813.
    Bostock Cartel for New York. (Dates of capture and internment not recorded.)

Reybold, George   Prisoner 1959. Rank: Seaman, from: Pike, Privateer.
    Cap: 25 Aug 1814 off Savannah by Primrose Int: 09 Sep 1814 Dis: 05 Nov 1814.
    Received from Lacedaemonian. Order Adml Cockburn.

Reynolds, James   Prisoner 452. Rank: 2 Lieutenant, from: Teazer, Privateer Schooner.
    Cap: 16 Dec 1812 at Sea by HM Ship St. Domingo Int: 21 Dec 1812 Dis: 27 Jan 1813.
    Received from HM Ship St. Domingo. Bostock Cartel for New York.

Reynolds, John   Prisoner 331. Rank: 1 Lieutenant, from: Snapper, Privateer Schooner.
    Cap: 16 Nov 1812 at Sea by HMS Galus Int: 22 Nov 1812 Dis: 27 Jan 1813.
    Received from HM Ship Galus. Bostock Cartel for New York.

Rhodes, Charles   Prisoner 429. Rank: Seaman, from: Eliza, Merchant Ship.
    Cap: 25 Nov 1812 Lat 37.00, Long 65.46 by HM Ship Tartarus Int: 03 Dec 1812 Dis: 27 Jan 1813.
    Received from HM Ship Tartarus. Bostock Cartel for New York.

Rhodes, Daniel   Prisoner 732. Rank: Seaman, from: Fernando, Merchant Brig.
    Cap: 09 Jan 1813 at Sea by HM Ship Acasta Int: 21 Jan 1813 Dis: 27 Jan 1813.
    Received from HMS Acasta. Bostock Cartel for New York.

Rhodes, Pomp   Prisoner 640. Rank: Seaman, from: Crown Prince, Merchant Schooner.
    Cap: 19 Dec 1812 at Sea by HM Ship Galus Int: 17 Jan 1813 Dis: 27 Jan 1813.
    Received from HM Ship Galus. Bostock Cartel for New York.

Rhodes, Romanto   Prisoner 2520. Rank: Seaman, from: President, U States Frigate.
    Cap: 15 Jan 1815 Not Recorded by Endymion Int: 04 Feb 1815 Dis: 28 Mar 1815.
    Received from HMS Endymion. Clarenden Transport for U States.

Rice, John   Prisoner 1271. Rank: Seaman, from: United States, Merchant Vessel.
    Cap: 14 Nov 1813 Long Island by HM Brig Borer Int: 19 Dec 1813 Dis: 15 Apr 1814.
    Received from HMS Acasta. Diana for Halifax.

Richards, A   Prisoner 2829. Rank: Seaman, from: Limerick, Not Recorded.
    Cap: 15 Mar 1815 Not Recorded by Asia Int: 25 Mar 1815 Dis:
    From Depot at Jamaica. Received from Asia. (Date of discharge not recorded.)

Richards, Guy   Prisoner 1811. Rank: Passenger, from: Not Recorded, Not Recorded.
    Cap: Not Recorded by Not Recorded Int: 14 Jun 1814 Dis: 15 Jun 1814.
    From St. Bartholomew in the Swedish Schooner Oscar. on Parole per Order Com in Chief to America. (Date of capture not recorded.)

Richards, John   Prisoner 1039. Rank: Seaman, from: Revinue, Merchant Sloop.
    Cap: 19 Mar 1813 off the Chesapeake by HMS Statira Int: 06 Apr 1813 Dis: 24 Jun 1813.
    Received from HMS Junon. Magnet Cartel for New York.

Richards, Rocy   Prisoner 731. Rank: Seaman, from: High Flyer, Privateer.
    Cap: 09 Jan 1813 at Sea by HM Ship Acasta Int: 21 Jan 1813 Dis: 27 Jan 1813.
    Received from HMS Acasta. Bostock Cartel for New York.

Richards, Steven   Prisoner 1825. Rank: Passenger, from: Not Recorded, Not Recorded.
    Cap: Not Recorded by Not Recorded Int: 14 Jun 1814 Dis: 15 Jun 1814.
    From St. Bartholomew in the Swedish Schooner Oscar. on Parole per Order Com in Chief to America. (Date of capture not recorded.)

Richards, Toby   Prisoner 1907. Rank: Seaman, from: Sally Jasper, Merchant Vessel.
    Cap: 14 Aug 1814 St. Catherine by Lacedaemonian Int: 09 Sep 1814 Dis: 28 Mar 1815.
    Received from Lacedaemonian. Clarendon Transport for U States.

Richards, William   Prisoner 416. Rank: Seaman, from: Isabella, Merchant Brig.
    Cap: 15 Nov 1812 at Sea by HM Sloop Childers Int: 24 Nov 1812 Dis: 27 Jan 1813.
    Received from HM Ship Childers. Bostock Cartel for New York.

American Prisoners of War Held at Bermuda During the War of 1812

Richards, William   Prisoner 975. Rank: Seaman, from: Janett, Merchant Brig.
    Cap: 25 Feb 1813 Chesapeake by HMS Junon Int: 23 Mar 1813 Dis: 17 Jun 1813.
    Received from HM Ship Laurustinus. Halifax Order of the Commander in Chief supports to be an Englishman.

Richardson, James   Prisoner 1690. Rank: Seaman, from: Lark, Merchant Vessel.
    Cap: 06 Apr 1814 L 29.0 by Recruit Int: 11 May 1814 Dis: 17 Mar 1815.
    Recaptured. Received from Recruit. Merchant Vessel.

Richardson, James   Prisoner 1855. Rank: Owner, from: Isa Colly, Merchant Vessel.
    Cap: Not Recorded by Not Recorded Int: Dis: 04 Sep 1814.
    to join these Proper Ships having been delivered up Order Comm Evans. (Dates of capture and internment not recorded.)

Richardson, Joseph   Prisoner 1965. Rank: Seaman, from: Pike, Privateer.
    Cap: 25 Aug 1814 off Savannah by Primrose Int: 09 Sep 1814 Dis: 28 Mar 1815.
    Received from Lacedaemonian. Clarendon Transport for U States.

Richardson, Perry   Prisoner 1320. Rank: Seaman, from: Rolla, Privateer.
    Cap: 10 Dec 1813 Block Island by Loire Int: 20 Dec 1813 Dis: 15 Apr 1814.
    Received from San Domingo. HMS Rammillies for Halifax.

Richardson, Randolph   Prisoner 42. Rank: Seaman, from: Trim, Merchant Schooner.
    Cap: 28 Jul 1812 of Bermuda by Cuttle Int: 28 Aug 1812 Dis: 18 Sep 1812.
    Received from HM Schooner Cuttle. Order Commd Evans for England.

Richardson, Thomas   Prisoner 2210. Rank: Marine, from: President, U States Frigate.
    Cap: 15 Jan 1815 Not Recorded by Endymion Int: 30 Jan 1815 Dis: 28 Mar 1815.
    Received from Pomone. Clarenden Transport for U States.

Richardson, William   Prisoner 482. Rank: Seaman, from: Teazer, Privateer Schooner.
    Cap: 16 Dec 1812 at Sea by HM Ship St. Domingo Int: 21 Dec 1812 Dis: 27 Jan 1813.
    Received from HM Ship St. Domingo. Bostock Cartel for New York.

Richardson, William   Prisoner 2303. Rank: Marine, from: President, U States Frigate.
    Cap: 15 Jan 1815 Not Recorded by Endymion Int: 04 Feb 1815 Dis: 28 Mar 1815.
    Received from Endymion. Clarendon Transport for U States.

Ricker, Edward   Prisoner 2380. Rank: Seaman, from: President, U States Frigate.
    Cap: 15 Jan 1815 Not Recorded by HMS Endymion Int: 04 Feb 1815 Dis: 28 Mar 1815.
    Received from Endymion. Mars Transport for U States.

Rifley, George   Prisoner 1495. Rank: Seaman, from: Santo Cateno Venturuso, Merchant.
    Cap: 28 Dec 1813 Latt 34.0 by HMS Fox Int: 09 Jan 1814 Dis: 15 Apr 1814.
    Received from Fox. Diana Transport for Halifax.

Riley, William   Prisoner 2046. Rank: Seaman, from: Rising Sun, Merchant Vessel.
    Cap: 20 Nov 1814 off Bermuda by Pandora Int: 28 Nov 1814 Dis: 14 Dec 1814.
    Recaptured. Received from HMS Goree. Ruby gave himself up as a British Subject.

Ritchen, Robert   Prisoner 1560. Rank: Seaman, from: Bordeaux Packet, Letter of Marque.
    Cap: 28 Jan 1814 off Cape Henry by Nieman Int: 12 Feb 1814 Dis: 15 Apr 1814.
    Received from Nieman. Diana Transport for Halifax.

Ritter, Michael   Prisoner 1975. Rank: Seaman, from: Antelope, Merchant Vessel.
    Cap: 21 Aug 1814 Western Island by Whiting Int: 17 Sep 1814 Dis: 28 Mar 1815.
    Recaptured. Received from Goree. Clarendon Transport for U States.

Roach, John   Prisoner 2603. Rank: Seaman, from: Mercury, Merchant Vessel.
    Cap: 30 Dec 1814 off New York by HMS Pomone Int: 05 Feb 1815 Dis: 13 Mar 1815.
    Received from HMS Forth. Merchant Service.

Roach, William   Prisoner 1768. Rank: Seaman, from: Yankelass, Privateer.
    Cap: 01 May 1814 L 40-4N, Long 38-0W by Severn & Surprise Int: 07 Jun 1814 Dis: 28 Mar 1815.
    Received from Surprise. Mars Transport for U States.

Roberts, A   Prisoner 2400. Rank: Seaman, from: President, U States Frigate.
    Cap: 15 Jan 1815 Not Recorded by HM Ship Endymion Int: 04 Feb 1815 Dis: 28 Mar 1815.
    Received from Endymion. Mars Transport for U States. (First name not legible.)

Roberts, Charles   Prisoner 1663. Rank: Seaman, from: Tram, Merchant Vessel.
    Cap: 20 Feb 1814 Chesapeake by Dragon Int: 13 Mar 1814 Dis: 23 Apr 1814.
    Received from Active. HMS Bulwark for Halifax.

Roberts, John   Prisoner 298. Rank: Seaman, from: Symmetry, Merchant Ship.
    Cap: 05 Jul 1812 at Sea by HM Ship Rattler Int: 02 Nov 1812 Dis: 04 Nov 1812.
    Received from HMS Poictiers. Brig Diamond on Parole to new London United States of America.

Roberts, Nicholas   Prisoner 50. Rank: Seaman, from: Ariel, Merchant Brig.
    Cap: 28 Jul 1812 of Bermuda by Recruit Int: 28 Aug 1812 Dis: 18 Sep 1812.
    Received from HM Schooner Cuttle. Order Commd Evans for England.

American Prisoners of War Held at Bermuda During the War of 1812

Roberts, Samuel   Prisoner 2054. Rank: Seaman, from: Amy, Merchant Schooner.
    Cap: 26 Nov 1814 off Cape Delaware by Telegraph Int: 05 Dec 1814 Dis: 28 Mar 1815.
    Received from HMS Goree. Clarendon Transport for U States.

Roberts, Samuel   Prisoner 2775. Rank: Seaman, from: Hope, Not Recorded.
    Cap: 21 Feb 1815 off St Augustine by Hebrus Int: 03 Mar 1815 Dis: 24 Mar 1815.
    Received from Hebrus. Merchant Vessel.

Roberts, William D   Prisoner 513. Rank: Mate, from: Nancy, Merchant Ship.
    Cap: 18 Dec 1812 off Bermuda by HMS Goree Int: 30 Dec 1812 Dis: 27 Jan 1813.
    Received from HMS Goree. Bostock Cartel for New York.

Roberts, William   Prisoner 2376. Rank: Seaman, from: President, U States Frigate.
    Cap: 15 Jan 1815 Not Recorded by HMS Endymion Int: 04 Feb 1815 Dis: 28 Mar 1815.
    Received from Endymion. Mars Transport for U States.

Robertson, David   Prisoner 1705. Rank: Seaman, from: Grecian, Letter of Marque.
    Cap: 02 May 1814 Chesapeake by Jansur Int: 26 May 1814 Dis: 28 Mar 1815.
    Received from Lacedaemonian. Mars Transport for U States.

Robertson, James   Prisoner 1781. Rank: Seaman, from: Yankelass, Privateer.
    Cap: 01 May 1814 Latt 40-4N, Long 38-0W by Severn & Surprise Int: 07 Jun 1814 Dis: 28 Mar 1815.
    Received from Surprise. Mars Transport for U States.

Robertson, James   Prisoner 2236. Rank: Seaman, from: President, U States Frigate.
    Cap: 15 Jan 1815 Not Recorded by Endymion Int: 30 Jan 1815 Dis: 28 Mar 1815.
    Received from Pomone. Mars Transport for U States.

Robins, Henry   Prisoner 2444. Rank: Seaman, from: President, U States Frigate.
    Cap: 15 Jan 1815 Not Recorded by Endymion Int: 04 Feb 1815 Dis: 28 Mar 1815.
    Received from Endymion. Mars Transport for U States.

Robinson, George   Prisoner 1696. Rank: Seaman, from: Grecian, Letter of Marque.
    Cap: 02 May 1814 Chesapeake by Jansur Int: 26 May 1814 Dis: 20 Feb 1815.
    Received from Lacedaemonian. Mars per Order of Comm Evans.

Robinson, Henry   Prisoner 2162. Rank: Chaplin, from: President, U States Frigate.
    Cap: 15 Jan 1815 Not Recorded by Endymion Int: 30 Jan 1815 Dis: 06 Feb 1815.
    Received from President. Narcissus to the U States by order of Commadore Evans.

Robinson, John   Prisoner 1744. Rank: Seaman, from: Yankelass, Privateer.
    Cap: 01 May 1814 L 10-4N, L 33-0W by Severn & Surprise Int: 06 Jun 1814 Dis: 28 Mar 1815.
    Received from Severn. Mars for United States.

Robinson, Nathan   Prisoner 2707. Rank: Seaman, from: South Boston, Merchant Vessel.
    Cap: 13 Feb 1815 off Charleston by Pandora Int: 02 Mar 1815 Dis: 28 Mar 1815.
    Received from Pandora. Clarendon Transport for U States.

Robinson, Robert   Prisoner 1283. Rank: Seaman, from: Perry, Merchant Schooner.
    Cap: 03 Dec 1813 Long Island by Indemyion Int: 19 Dec 1813 Dis: 15 Apr 1814.
    Received from Sceptre. Diana Transport for Halifax.

Robinson, Thomas   Prisoner 1900. Rank: Seaman, from: Dusty Miller, Merchant Vessel.
    Cap: 11 Aug 1814 Tapella Sound by Not Recorded Int: 09 Sep 1814 Dis:
    Received from Lacedaemonian. (Date of discharge not recorded.)

Robinson, Thomas   Prisoner 2756. Rank: Seaman, from: Mayflower, Not Recorded.
    Cap: 20 Jan 1815 St Augustine by Severn Int: 03 Mar 1815 Dis: 28 Mar 1815.
    Received from Hebrus. Clarendon Transport for U States.

Robson, John   Prisoner 2062. Rank: Prize Master, from: Industry, Merchant Vessel.
    Cap: 01 Dec 1814 off Cape Henry by HMS Niemen Int: 15 Dec 1814 Dis: 28 Mar 1815.
    Recaptured. Belong to Carolina Privateer. Received from HMS Niemen.
    Clarendon Transport for U States.

Rockhill, James   Prisoner 1570. Rank: Seaman, from: Bordeaux Packet, Letter of Marque.
    Cap: 28 Jan 1814 off Cape Henry by Nieman Int: 12 Feb 1814 Dis: 15 Apr 1814.
    Received from Nieman. Diana Transport for Halifax.

Rockwell, Merritt   Prisoner 2583. Rank: Seaman, from: Advocate, Merchant Vessel.
    Cap: 16 Nov 1814 off New York by HM Ship Majestic Int: 05 Feb 1815 Dis: 16 Mar 1815.
    Received from HMS Forth. Merchant Service.

Roderique, John   Prisoner 902. Rank: Seaman, from: Princessa, Merchant Brig.
    Cap: 07 Feb 1813 Chesapeake by HMS Marlborough Int: 23 Mar 1813 Dis: 06 Apr 1813.
    Received from HM Ship Laurustinus. By Order Commodore Evans a Portuguese.

Rodgers, Smith   Prisoner 1832. Rank: Passenger, from: Not Recorded, Not Recorded.
    Cap: Not Recorded by Not Recorded Int: 14 Jun 1814 Dis: 15 Jun 1814.
    From St. Bartholomew in the Swedish Schooner Oscar. on Parole per Order Com in Chief to America.
    (Date of capture not recorded.)

American Prisoners of War Held at Bermuda During the War of 1812

Rogers, Errin   Prisoner 950. Rank: Seaman, from: Bona, Letter of Marque Schooner.
    Cap: 12 Mar 1813 Chesapeake by Laurustinus Int: 23 Mar 1813 Dis: 24 Jun 1813.
    Received from Laurustinus. Magnet Cartel for New York.

Rogers, Francis   Prisoner 2535. Rank: Seaman, from: President, U States Frigate.
    Cap: 15 Jan 1815 Not Recorded by HM Ship Endymion Int: 04 Feb 1815 Dis: 28 Mar 1815.
    Received from HMS Endymion. Clarenden Transport for U States.

Rogers, G W   Prisoner 164. Rank: 1 Lieutenant, from: Wasp, Sloop of War.
    Cap: 18 Oct 1812 at Sea by HMS Poictiers Int: 26 Oct 1812 Dis: 05 Nov 1812.
    Received from HM Ship Poictiers. on Parole Brig Diamond to new London America.

Rogers, Henry   Prisoner 1581. Rank: Seaman, from: Bordeaux Packet, Letter of Marque.
    Cap: 28 Jan 1814 off Cape Henry by Nieman Int: 12 Feb 1814 Dis: 15 Apr 1814.
    Received from Nieman. Diana Transport for Halifax.

Rogers, James   Prisoner 45. Rank: Seaman, from: Trim, Merchant Schooner.
    Cap: 28 Jul 1812 of Bermuda by Cuttle Int: 28 Aug 1812 Dis: 18 Sep 1812.
    Received from HM Schooner Cuttle. Order Commd Evans for England.

Rogers, James M   Prisoner 58. Rank: Supercargo, from: Mary, Merchant Brig.
    Cap: 08 Aug 1812 of Bermuda by Cuttle Int: 28 Aug 1812 Dis: 06 Sep 1812.
    Received from M Schooner Cuttle. Sloop Sally for New York.

Rogers, James   Prisoner 2136. Rank: Master, from: President, U States Frigate.
    Cap: 15 Jan 1815 Not Recorded by Endymion Int: 30 Jan 1815 Dis: 18 Mar 1815.
    Received from President. Merchant Vessel.

Rogers, John   Prisoner 1135. Rank: Seaman, from: Good Intent, Merchant.
    Cap: 02 Aug 1813 at Sea by HM Sloop Rifleman Int: 13 Aug 1813 Dis: 03 Sep 1813.
    Received from HM Sloop Rifleman. Per Order of Comm Evans to the American Ship Leander restored.

Rogers, John   Prisoner 1207. Rank: Seaman, from: Willam & Ann, Merchant Ship.
    Cap: 30 Jul 1813 at Sea by HM Sloop Nimrod Int: 21 Sep 1813 Dis: 14 Nov 1813.
    Returned to Prison from the American Ship Leander. HM Store Ship Dolphin Rear Adm Cockburn.

Rogers, John   Prisoner 2132. Rank: Passenger, from: Rufus King, Merchant Vessel.
    Cap: 01 Jan 1815 off Bermuda by Peruvian Int: 30 Jan 1815 Dis:
    Received from Peruvian. (Date of discharge not recorded.)

Rogers, Thomas   Prisoner 768. Rank: Seaman, from: Lucy, Merchant Schooner.
    Cap: 28 Dec 1812 Lat 36.45, Long 73.18 by HM Sloop Sylph Int: 26 Jan 1813 Dis: 14 Jun 1813.
    Received from Sloop Sylph. Permitted to return to the United States in the Perseverance Cartel.

Rogers, William   Prisoner 473. Rank: Seaman, from: Teazer, Privateer Schooner.
    Cap: 16 Dec 1812 at Sea by HM Ship St. Domingo Int: 21 Dec 1812 Dis: 27 Jan 1813.
    Received from HM Ship St. Domingo. Bostock Cartel for New York.

Rogers, William   Prisoner 2551. Rank: Seaman, from: President, US Frigate.
    Cap: 15 Jan 1815 off N York by HMS Endymion Int: 05 Feb 1815 Dis: 28 Mar 1815.
    Received from President. Clarenden Transport for U States.

Rollins, John   Prisoner 291. Rank: Seaman, from: Wasp, Sloop of War.
    Cap: 18 Oct 1812 at Sea by HMS Poictiers Int: 02 Nov 1812 Dis: 04 Nov 1812.
    Received from HMS Poictiers. Brig Diamond on Parole to new London United States of America.

Rose, James   Prisoner 1958. Rank: Seaman, from: Pike, Privateer.
    Cap: 25 Aug 1814 off Savannah by Primrose Int: 09 Sep 1814 Dis: 05 Nov 1814.
    Received from Lacedaemonian. Order Adml Cockburn.

Rose, John   Prisoner 316. Rank: Seaman, from: Wasp, Sloop of War.
    Cap: 18 Oct 1812 at Sea by HMS Poictiers Int: 05 Nov 1812 Died: 06 Dec 1812.
    Received from HM Ship Poictiers. Died. Wound.

Rose, Perry   Prisoner 569. Rank: Master, from: Betsey, Merchant Schooner.
    Cap: 06 Dec 1812 at Sea by HM Ship Maidstone Int: 06 Jan 1813 Dis: 27 Jan 1813.
    Received from HM Ship Maidstone. Bostock Cartel for New York.

Ross, Alexander   Prisoner 2599. Rank: Seaman, from: John, Merchant Vessel.
    Cap: 18 Dec 1814 off New York by HMS Pomone Int: 05 Feb 1815 Dis: 16 Mar 1815.
    Received from HMS Forth. Merchant Service.

Rossan, Aman   Prisoner 1184. Rank: Passenger, from: Caledonian, Merchant.
    Cap: 20 Jul 1813 at Sea by HM Ship Marlborough Int: 18 Aug 1813 Dis: 03 Oct 1813.
    Received from HM Ship Woolwich. Caledonian per Order of Commodore Evans she being Liberated.

Rosseau, Peter   Prisoner 355. Rank: Seaman, from: Snapper, Privateer Schooner.
    Cap: 16 Nov 1812 at Sea by HMS Galus Int: 22 Nov 1812 Dis: 27 Jan 1813.
    Received from HM Ship Galus. Bostock Cartel for New York.

Rousseau, Laurence   Prisoner 794. Rank: 1 Lieutenant, from: Viper, Sloop of War.
    Cap: 17 Jan 1813 at Sea by Narcissus Int: 13 Feb 1813 Dis: 13 Jun 1813.
    Received from Narcissus. Perseverance Cartel for the United States per Order Admiral Sir J B Warren.

American Prisoners of War Held at Bermuda During the War of 1812

Rovada, Antony   Prisoner 926. Rank: Seaman, from: Albert, Merchant Schooner.
    Cap: 05 Mar 1813 Chesapeake by HM Ship Marlborough Int: 23 Mar 1813 Dis: 24 Mar 1813.
    Received from Laurustinus. St. Michael per Order Adl Sir J B Warren.

Row, Joseph   Prisoner 686. Rank: Seaman, from: High Flyer, Privateer.
    Cap: 09 Jan 1813 at Sea by HMS Acasta Int: 21 Jan 1813 Dis: 27 Jan 1813.
    Received from HMS Acasta. Bostock Cartel for New York.

Rowlins, Joshua   Prisoner 596. Rank: Seaman, from: Windward Planter, Merchant Sloop.
    Cap: 22 Dec 1812 at Sea by HM Ship Belvidera Int: 10 Jan 1813 Dis: 27 Jan 1813.
    Received from HMS Belvidera. Bostock Cartel for New York.

Rozier, Francis   Prisoner 266. Rank: Seaman, from: Wasp, Sloop of War.
    Cap: 18 Oct 1812 at Sea by HM Ship Poictiers Int: 26 Oct 1812 Dis: 05 Nov 1812.
    Received from HM Ship Poictiers. Brig Diamond on Parole to new London United States of America.

Rud, George   Prisoner 2779. Rank: Seaman, from: Hope, Not Recorded.
    Cap: 21 Feb 1815 off St Augustine by Hebrus Int: 03 Mar 1815 Dis: 16 Mar 1815.
    Received from Hebrus. Merchant Service.

Russel, Simon   Prisoner 5. Rank: Seaman, from: Yorick, Merchant Ship.
    Cap: 09 Jul 1812 near Bermuda by Rattler Int: 28 Aug 1812 Dis: 10 Sep 1812.
    Received from HM Schooner Cuttle. Schooner Hero for N Y.

Russell, Peter   Prisoner 2264. Rank: Seaman, from: President, U States Frigate.
    Cap: 15 Jan 1815 Not Recorded by Endymion Int: 30 Jan 1815 Dis: 28 Mar 1815.
    Received from Pomone. Mars Transport for U States.

Russell, Samuel   Prisoner 2423. Rank: Seaman, from: President, U States Frigate.
    Cap: 15 Jan 1815 Not Recorded by HM Ship Endymion Int: 04 Feb 1815 Dis: 28 Mar 1815.
    Received from Endymion. Mars Transport for U States.

Russell, Thomas   Prisoner 1793. Rank: Sailing Master, from: Yankelass, Privateer.
    Cap: 01 May 1814 Latt 40-4N, Long 38-0W by Severn & Surprise Int: 07 Jun 1814 Dis:
    Received from Surprise. (Date of discharge not recorded.)

Rust, John   Prisoner 115. Rank: Seaman, from: Lydia, Merchant.
    Cap: 03 Sep 1812 Near Bermuda by HMS Orpheus Int: 08 Sep 1812 Dis: 18 Sep 1812.
    Received from HMS Orpheus. Order of Commd Evans England.

Rutter, Samuel   Prisoner 211. Rank: Marine, from: Wasp, Sloop of War.
    Cap: 18 Oct 1812 at Sea by HM Ship Poictiers Int: 26 Oct 1812 Dis: 05 Nov 1812.
    Received from HM Ship Poictiers. Brig Diamond on Parole to new London United States of America.

Ryan, John   Prisoner 2512. Rank: Seaman, from: President, U States Frigate.
    Cap: 15 Jan 1815 Not Recorded by Endymion Int: 04 Feb 1815 Dis: 28 Mar 1815.
    Received from HMS Endymion. Clarenden Transport for U States.

Ryan, Patrick   Prisoner 1996. Rank: Seaman, from: Fairplay, Merchant Vessel.
    Cap: 22 Oct 1814 Lat 31.58 by Dothrel Int: 26 Oct 1814 Died: 09 Feb 1815.
    Recaptured. Received from Dothrel. Died. Fever.

Ryan, William   Prisoner 2286. Rank: Seaman, from: President, U States Frigate.
    Cap: 15 Jan 1815 Not Recorded by Endymion Int: 30 Jan 1815 Dis: 28 Mar 1815.
    Received from Pomone. Mars Transport for U States.

Ryley, William   Prisoner 290. Rank: Seaman, from: Wasp, Sloop of War.
    Cap: 18 Oct 1812 at Sea by HMS Poictiers Int: 02 Nov 1812 Dis: 04 Nov 1812.
    Received from HMS Poictiers. Brig Diamond on Parole to new London United States of America.

Sabins, John   Prisoner 1823. Rank: Passenger, from: Not Recorded, Not Recorded.
    Cap: Not Recorded by Not Recorded Int: 14 Jun 1814 Dis: 15 Jun 1814.
    From St. Bartholomew in the Swedish Schooner Oscar. on Parole per Order Com in Chief to America.
    (Date of capture not recorded.)

Sage, John   Prisoner 1096. Rank: Prize Master, from: Apollo, Merchant Vessel.
    Cap: 15 May 1813 at Sea by Success Int: 27 May 1813 Dis: 24 Jun 1813.
    Received from HMS Atalante. Magnet Cartel for New York.

Sailor, William   Prisoner 2753. Rank: Seaman, from: Speedwell, Not Recorded.
    Cap: 21 Jan 1815 St Augustine by Severn Int: 03 Mar 1815 Dis: 28 Mar 1815.
    Received from Hebrus. Clarendon Transport for U States.

Sailsbury, John   Prisoner 154. Rank: Seaman, from: Ranger, Merchant Ship.
    Cap: 02 Oct 1812 Lat 32, Long 65 W by HM Ship Goree Int: 13 Oct 1812 Dis: 24 Oct 1812.
    Received from HMS Goree. Brig Diamond on Parole to new London United States of America.

Salbory, John M   Prisoner 717. Rank: Seaman, from: High Flyer, Privateer.
    Cap: 09 Jan 1813 at Sea by HM Ship Acasta Int: 21 Jan 1813 Dis: 27 Jan 1813.
    Received from HMS Acasta. Bostock Cartel for New York.

American Prisoners of War Held at Bermuda During the War of 1812

Salinder, John   Prisoner 2361. Rank: Cooper, from: President, U States Frigate.
   Cap: 15 Jan 1815 Not Recorded by HMS Endymion Int: 04 Feb 1815 Dis: 28 Mar 1815.
   Received from Endymion. Mars Transport for U States.

Salsburg, William   Prisoner 1272. Rank: Seaman, from: United States, Merchant Vessel.
   Cap: 14 Nov 1813 Long Island by HM Brig Borer Int: 19 Dec 1813 Dis: 15 Apr 1814.
   Received from HMS Acasta. Diana for Halifax.

Sambo, Joseph   Prisoner 1798. Rank: Seaman, from: Yankelass, Privateer.
   Cap: 01 May 1814 L 40-4P, Long 30-11W by Severn & Surprise Int: 07 Jun 1814 Dis: 28 Mar 1815.
   Yankee lass. Received from Surprise. Clarendon Transport for U States.

Samborn, Joseph   Prisoner 198. Rank: Seaman, from: Wasp, Sloop of War.
   Cap: 18 Oct 1812 at Sea by HMS Poictiers Int: 26 Oct 1812 Dis: 05 Nov 1812.
   Received from HM Ship Poictiers. Brig Diamond on Parole to new London America.

Samoe, David   Prisoner 2100. Rank: Seaman, from: Amelia, Merchant Vessel.
   Cap: 24 Jun 1813 Charleston by Sophie Int: 19 Jan 1815 Dis: 25 Jan 1815.
   Received from HMS Peruvian. Bridges Transport being Subject to Friendly power Order Com Evans.

Sampson, George   Prisoner 362. Rank: Seaman, from: Snapper, Privateer Schooner.
   Cap: 16 Nov 1812 at Sea by HM Ship Galus Int: 22 Nov 1812 Dis: 27 Jan 1813.
   Received from HM Ship Galus. Bostock Cartel for New York.

Sampson, Samuel   Prisoner 2764. Rank: Seaman, from: Maria, Not Recorded.
   Cap: 16 Feb 1815 St Augustine by Severn Int: 03 Mar 1815 Dis: 28 Mar 1815.
   Received from Hebrus. Clarendon Transport for U States.

Sancho, Antonio   Prisoner 2580. Rank: Seaman, from: Recovery, Merchant Vessel.
   Cap: 20 Nov 1814 off New York by HM Ship Majestic Int: 05 Feb 1815 Dis: 25 Feb 1815.
   Received from HMS Forth. Mars Transport per order of Commadore Evans.

Sandbug, Charles   Prisoner 841. Rank: Seaman, from: Portsmouth, Merchant Ship.
   Cap: 27 Feb 1813 off Bermuda by HM Sloop Martin Int: 09 Mar 1813 Dis: 27 Mar 1813.
   Received from HM Ship Martin. Per Order Commodore Evans the Vessel being Liberated.

Sanders, Job   Prisoner 959. Rank: Seaman, from: Bona, Letter of Marque Schooner.
   Cap: 12 Mar 1813 Chesapeake by Laurustinus Int: 23 Mar 1813 Dis: 24 Jun 1813.
   Received from Laurustinus. Magnet Cartel for New York.

Sanderson, Francis   Prisoner 911. Rank: Seaman, from: Elizabeth, Merchant Brig.
   Cap: 26 Feb 1813 Chesapeake by HMS Marlborough Int: 23 Mar 1813 Dis: 24 Jun 1813.
   Received from HM Ship Laurustinus. Magnet Cartel for New York.

Sandford, Daniel   Prisoner 773. Rank: Seaman, from: Trinadada, Merchant Brig.
   Cap: 06 Jan 1813 Lat 37.20, Long 75.00 by HM Sloop Sylph Int: 26 Jan 1813 Dis: 14 Mar 1813.
   Received from Sloop Sylph. Savannah Packet for New York per Order Adl Sir J B Warren.

Sandford, Giles   Prisoner 1067. Rank: Master, from: Mary Barrett, Merchant.
   Cap: 04 Mar 1813 Chesapeake by HM Ship San Domingo Int: 06 Apr 1813 Dis: 24 Jun 1813.
   Received from HMS Junon. Magnet Cartel for New York.

Sandford, Royal   Prisoner 774. Rank: Seaman, from: Trinadada, Merchant Brig.
   Cap: 06 Jan 1813 Lat 37.20, Long 75.00 by HM Sloop Sylph Int: 26 Jan 1813 Dis: 14 Jun 1813.
   Received from Sloop Sylph. Permitted to return to the United States in the Perseverance.

Sandford, Samuel   Prisoner 2048. Rank: Seaman, from: Mary, Merchant Schooner.
   Cap: 26 Nov 1814 off Cape Delaware by Telegraph Int: 05 Dec 1814 Dis: 28 Mar 1815.
   Received from HMS Goree. Clarendon Transport for U States.

Sansum, Philip   Prisoner 1852. Rank: Seaman, from: Little Catherine, Packet.
   Cap: Not Recorded by Not Recorded Int: Dis: 28 Mar 1815.
   Recaptured. Clarendon Transport for U States. (Dates of capture and internment not recorded.)

Sarose, Belling   Prisoner 606. Rank: Seaman, from: Noetoin, Packet Brig.
   Cap: 05 Jan 1813 at Sea by HM Ship Belvidera Int: 10 Jan 1813 Dis: 24 Jun 1813.
   Received from HMS Belvidera. Magnet Cartel for New York.

Satchell, Jonathan   Prisoner 1328. Rank: Seaman, from: Rolla, Privateer.
   Cap: 10 Dec 1813 Block Island by Loire Int: 20 Dec 1813 Dis: 15 Apr 1814.
   Received from HM Ship San Domingo. HMS Rammillies for Halifax.

Sauls, John   Prisoner 2346. Rank: Seaman, from: President, U States Frigate.
   Cap: 15 Jan 1815 Not Recorded by HMS Endymion Int: 04 Feb 1815 Dis: 28 Mar 1815.
   Received from Endymion. Mars Transport for U States.

Saunder, James L   Prisoner 1929. Rank: Surgeon, from: Pike, Privateer.
   Cap: 25 Aug 1814 off Savannah by Primrose Int: 09 Sep 1814 Dis: 21 Sep 1814.
   Received from Lacedaemonian. as a Noncombatant Order Commodore Evans.

Saunder, William   Prisoner 1947. Rank: Seaman, from: Pike, Privateer.
   Cap: 25 Aug 1814 off Savannah by Primrose Int: 09 Sep 1814 Dis: 28 Mar 1815.
   Received from Lacedaemonian. Clarendon Transport for U States.

American Prisoners of War Held at Bermuda During the War of 1812

Saunders, Joseph   Prisoner 52. Rank: Seaman, from: Ariel, Merchant Brig.
    Cap: 28 Jul 1812 of Bermuda by Recruit Int: 28 Aug 1812 Dis: 18 Sep 1812.
    Received from M Schooner Cuttle. Order of Commd Evans for England.

Saunders, Priest   Prisoner 535. Rank: Seaman, from: Herald, Letter of Marque Brig.
    Cap: 25 Dec 1812 at Sea by HM Ship Maidstone Int: 05 Jan 1813 Dis: 27 Jan 1813.
    Received from HM Ship Maidstone. Bostock Cartel for New York.

Saunders, Thomas   Prisoner 2696. Rank: Seaman, from: Speed, Merchant Vessel.
    Cap: 19 Jan 1815 off Nantucket by Pylades Int: 17 Feb 1815 Dis: 28 Mar 1815.
    Received from Majestic. Clarendon Transport for U States.

Saunders, William   Prisoner 2642. Rank: Master, from: Dash, Merchant Vessel.
    Cap: 19 Jan 1815 Bahamas by HMS Statira Int: 06 Feb 1815 Dis: 17 Mar 1815.
    Received from HMS Statira. Merchant Vessel.

Savage, Absolam   Prisoner 1803. Rank: Passenger, from: Not Recorded, Not Recorded.
    Cap: Not Recorded by Not Recorded Int: 14 Jun 1814 Dis: 15 Jun 1814.
    From St. Bartholomew in the Swedish Schooner Oscar. on Parole per Order Com in Chief to America.
    (Date of capture not recorded.)

Savage, Timothy   Prisoner 1802. Rank: Passenger, from: Not Recorded, Not Recorded.
    Cap: Not Recorded by Not Recorded Int: 14 Jun 1814 Dis: 15 Jun 1814.
    From St. Bartholomew in the Swedish Schooner Oscar. on Parole per Order Com in Chief to America.
    (Date of capture not recorded.)

Savil, Francis O   Prisoner 1498. Rank: Seaman, from: Santo Cateno Venturuso, Merchant.
    Cap: 28 Dec 1813 Latt 34.00 by HMS Fox Int: 09 Jan 1814 Dis: 19 Jan 1814.
    Received from HM Ship Fox. Order Commander in Chief being a Spaniard.

Sawyer, Nathaniel   Prisoner 998. Rank: Seaman, from: Orion, Merchant.
    Cap: 25 Mar 1813 at Sea by HM Sloop Childers Int: 04 Apr 1813 Dis: 09 Apr 1813.
    Received from HM Sloop Childers. Per Order Commodore Evans Vessel Liberated.

Sawyer, Robert   Prisoner 2626. Rank: Seaman, from: William, Merchant Vessel.
    Cap: 12 Jan 1815 Cape Hatterus by HMS Telegraph Int: 05 Feb 1815 Dis: 28 Mar 1815.
    Received from HMS Telegraph. Clarendon Transport for U States.

Scandlings, Peter   Prisoner 2248. Rank: Marine, from: President, U States Frigate.
    Cap: 15 Jan 1815 Not Recorded by Endymion Int: 30 Jan 1815 Dis: 28 Mar 1815.
    Received from Pomone. Clarenden Transport for U States.

Scank, Samuel   Prisoner 318. Rank: Seaman, from: Gangee, Merchant Ship.
    Cap: Not Recorded by Not Recorded Int: Dis: 27 Jan 1813.
    Bostock Cartel for New York. (Dates of capture and interment not recorded.)

Scantling, Owen   Prisoner 2542. Rank: Marine, from: President, U States Frigate.
    Cap: 15 Jan 1815 Not Recorded by HM Ship Endymion Int: 04 Feb 1815 Dis: 28 Mar 1815.
    Received from HMS Endymion. Clarenden Transport for U States.

Scapina, Mathias   Prisoner 68. Rank: Seaman, from: Canaway, Merchant Ship.
    Cap: 08 Aug 1812 of Bermuda by Recruit Int: 28 Aug 1812 Dis: 15 Sep 1812.
    Received from M Schooner Cuttle. a Spaniard Order Comd Evans.

Schasser, John W   Prisoner 714. Rank: Seaman, from: High Flyer, Privateer.
    Cap: 09 Jan 1813 at Sea by HM Ship Acasta Int: 21 Jan 1813 Dis: 27 Jan 1813.
    Received from HMS Acasta. Bostock Cartel for New York.

Schrothn, David   Prisoner 2000. Rank: Seaman, from: Dry Farbourn, Merchant Vessel.
    Cap: 21 Oct 1814 off Bermuda by Pandora Int: 27 Oct 1814 Dis: 05 Nov 1814.
    Recaptured. Received from Goree. Diadem for a Passage to England.

Schutte, Harms   Prisoner 1092. Rank: Seaman, from: Langdon Cheves, Merchant.
    Cap: 12 May 1813 at Sea by HM Sloop Atalante Int: 25 May 1813 Dis: 24 Jun 1813.
    Received from HMS Atalante. Magnet Cartel for New York.

Scofield, Isaac   Prisoner 629. Rank: Seaman, from: Isabella, Merchant Brig.
    Cap: 29 Nov 1812 at Sea by Letter of Marque Bastain Int: 14 Jan 1813 Dis: 27 Jan 1813.
    Received from Brig Isabella. Bostock Cartel for New York. Brig Isabella (2).

Scott, Francis   Prisoner 2188. Rank: Seaman, from: President, U States Frigate.
    Cap: 15 Jan 1815 Not Recorded by HMS Endymion Int: 30 Jan 1815 Dis: 28 Mar 1815.
    Received from Pomone. Mars Transport for U States.

Scott, George   Prisoner 2115. Rank: Seaman, from: Armistice, Merchant Vessel.
    Cap: 07 Dec 1814 off Delaware by Pictolus Int: 27 Jan 1815 Dis: 28 Mar 1815.
    Received from Pictolus. Clarendon Transport for U States.

Scott, Joshua   Prisoner 2185. Rank: Seaman, from: President, U States Frigate.
    Cap: 15 Jan 1815 Not Recorded by HMS Endymion Int: 30 Jan 1815 Dis: 28 Mar 1815.
    Received from Pomone. Mars Transport for U States.

American Prisoners of War Held at Bermuda During the War of 1812

Scott, Pleasant   Prisoner 1064. Rank: Seaman, from: Amason, Merchant.
    Cap: 18 Mar 1813 Chesapeake by HM Ship Victorious Int: 06 Apr 1813 Escaped: 21 Apr 1813.
    Received from HMS Junon. Escaped.

Seaman, Isaac   Prisoner 853. Rank: Seaman, from: American Eagle, Merchant Schooner.
    Cap: 01 Feb 1813 at Sea by HMS St. Domingo Int: 20 Mar 1813 Dis: 20 Mar 1813.
    Received from San Domingo. Savannah Packet for New York per Order Adl Sir J B Warren.

Sebor, William   Prisoner 507. Rank: Mate, from: St. Augustina, Merchant Brig.
    Cap: 16 Dec 1812 at Sea by HM Ship San Domingo Int: 28 Dec 1812 Dis: 27 Jan 1813.
    Received from the Prize Brig St. Augustina. Bostock Cartel for New York.

Sebvea, Andrew   Prisoner 460. Rank: Mate, from: Teazer, Privateer Schooner.
    Cap: 16 Dec 1812 at Sea by HM Ship St. Domingo Int: 21 Dec 1812 Dis: 27 Jan 1813.
    Received from HM Ship St. Domingo. Bostock Cartel for New York.

Segoss, Ezekiel   Prisoner 1864. Rank: Seaman, from: Yankelass, Merchant Vessel.
    Cap: Not Recorded by Not Recorded Int: Dis: 20 Mar 1815.
    Yankey Lass. Merchant Vessel. (Dates of capture and internment not recorded.)

Selles, Hamilton   Prisoner 662. Rank: 1 Lieutenant, from: High Flyer, Privateer.
    Cap: 09 Jan 1813 at Sea by HM Ship Acasta Int: 21 Jan 1813 Dis: 27 Jan 1813.
    Received from HMS Acasta. Bostock Cartel for New York.

Selolom, John   Prisoner 2194. Rank: Seaman, from: President, U States Frigate.
    Cap: 15 Jan 1815 Not Recorded by HMS Endymion Int: 30 Jan 1815 Dis: 28 Mar 1815.
    Received from Pomone. Mars Transport for U States.

Sephey, Peter   Prisoner 2057. Rank: Seaman, from: Amy, Merchant Schooner.
    Cap: 26 Nov 1814 off Cape Delaware by Telegraph Int: 05 Dec 1814 Dis: 28 Mar 1815.
    Received from HMS Goree. Clarendon Transport for U States.

Serman, Robert   Prisoner 2305. Rank: Seaman, from: President, U States Frigate.
    Cap: 15 Jan 1815 Not Recorded by Endymion Int: 04 Feb 1815 Dis: 28 Mar 1815.
    Received from Endymion. Mars Transport for U States.

Seward, Henry   Prisoner 250. Rank: Seaman, from: Wasp, Sloop of War.
    Cap: 18 Oct 1812 at Sea by HM Ship Poictiers Int: 26 Oct 1812 Dis: 05 Nov 1812.
    Received from HM Ship Poictiers. Brig Diamond on Parole to new London United States of America.

Seward, Theodore   Prisoner 1850. Rank: Seaman, from: Little Catherine, Packet.
    Cap: Not Recorded by Not Recorded Int: Dis: 28 Mar 1815.
    Recaptured. Clarendon Transport for U States. (Dates of capture and internment not recorded.)

Sewen, Henry   Prisoner 625. Rank: Mate, from: Herald, Letter of Marque Brig.
    Cap: 25 Dec 1812 at Sea by HM Ship Maidstone Int: 12 Jan 1813 Dis: 27 Jan 1813.
    Received from Brig Herald. Bostock Cartel for New York.

Sexton, James   Prisoner 2052. Rank: Seaman, from: Mary, Merchant Schooner.
    Cap: 26 Nov 1814 off Cape Delaware by Telegraph Int: 05 Dec 1814 Dis: 13 Mar 1815.
    Received from HMS Goree. Merchant Service.

Shaddock, Anthony   Prisoner 1908. Rank: Master, from: Factor, Merchant Vessel.
    Cap: 20 Aug 1814 St. Catherine by Lacedaemonian Int: 09 Sep 1814 Dis: 26 Feb 1815.
    Received from Lacedaemonian. Ruby Transport.

Shadell, James   Prisoner 2424. Rank: Marine, from: President, U States Frigate.
    Cap: 15 Jan 1815 Not Recorded by HM Ship Endymion Int: 04 Feb 1815 Dis: 28 Mar 1815.
    Received from Endymion. Clarenden Transport for U States.

Shallon, Egbert   Prisoner 511. Rank: Seaman, from: St. Augustina, Merchant Brig.
    Cap: 19 Dec 1812 at Sea by HM Ship San Domingo Int: 29 Dec 1812 Dis: 27 Jan 1813.
    Received from HM Ship San Domingo. Bostock Cartel for New York.

Shannon, Henry   Prisoner 228. Rank: Seaman, from: Wasp, Sloop of War.
    Cap: 18 Oct 1812 at Sea by HM Ship Poictiers Int: 26 Oct 1812 Dis: 05 Nov 1812.
    Received from HM Ship Poictiers. Brig Diamond on Parole to new London United States of America.

Shapper, William   Prisoner 1044. Rank: Seaman, from: General Knox, Merchant.
    Cap: 18 Mar 1813 off the Chesapeake by HM Ship Victorious Int: 06 Apr 1813 Dis:
    Received from HMS Junon. (Date of discharge not on roster.)

Sharp, Peter   Prisoner 54. Rank: Seaman, from: Ariel, Merchant Brig.
    Cap: 28 Jul 1812 of Bermuda by Recruit Int: 28 Aug 1812 Dis: 18 Sep 1812.
    Received from M Schooner Cuttle. Order of Commd Evans for England.

Shaw, Benjamin   Prisoner 884. Rank: Master, from: Hannah, Merchant Schooner.
    Cap: 24 Feb 1813 Chesapeake by Marlborough Int: 23 Mar 1813 Dis: 21 May 1813.
    Received from Laurustinus. Per Order Commodore Evans the Vessel being Liberated.

Shaw, Joseph   Prisoner 1307. Rank: Prize Master, from: Rolla, Privateer.
    Cap: 10 Dec 1813 Block Island by Loire Int: 20 Dec 1813 Dis: 15 Apr 1814.
    Received from San Domingo. HMS Rammillies for Halifax.

American Prisoners of War Held at Bermuda During the War of 1812

Shaw, Robert   Prisoner 1374. Rank: Seaman, from: Rolla, Privateer.
    Cap: 10 Dec 1813 Block Island by Loire Int: 20 Dec 1813 Dis: 15 Apr 1814.
    Received from San Domingo. HMS Rammillies for Halifax.

Shaw, Samuel   Prisoner 885. Rank: Mate, from: Hannah, Merchant Schooner.
    Cap: 24 Feb 1813 Chesapeake by Marlborough Int: 23 Mar 1813 Dis: 21 May 1813.
    Received from Laurustinus. Per Order Commodore Evans the Vessel being Liberated.

Shaw, William   Prisoner 2847. Rank: Seaman, from: Limerick, Not Recorded.
    Cap: 15 Mar 1815 Not Recorded by Asia Int: 25 Mar 1815 Dis:
    From Depot at Jamaica. Received from Asia. (Date of discharge not recorded.)

Shawe, Daniel   Prisoner 406. Rank: Seaman, from: Snapper, Privateer Schooner.
    Cap: 16 Nov 1812 at Sea by HM Ship Galus Int: 22 Nov 1812 Dis: 27 Jan 1813.
    Received from HM Ship Galus. Bostock Cartel for New York.

Shawe, Edgebert   Prisoner 244. Rank: Seaman, from: Wasp, Sloop of War.
    Cap: 18 Oct 1812 at Sea by HM Ship Poictiers Int: 26 Oct 1812 Dis: 05 Nov 1812.
    Received from HM Ship Poictiers. Brig Diamond on Parole to new London United States of America.

Sheffield, A   Prisoner 2128. Rank: Mate, from: New York, Merchant Vessel.
    Cap: 09 Jan 1815 off Delaware by Dispatch Int: 27 Jan 1815 Dis: 28 Mar 1815.
    Received from Pictolus. Clarendon Transport for U States.

Sheffield, William   Prisoner 1168. Rank: Mate, from: Elizabeth, Merchant.
    Cap: 15 Jun 1813 at Sea by HM Ship Marlborough Int: 15 Aug 1813 Dis: 02 Sep 1813.
    Received from HM Ship Woolwich. Per order of Commodore Evans being liberated.

Sheldon, Job   Prisoner 2726. Rank: Citizen, from: St Marys, Not Recorded.
    Cap: 18 Feb 1815 St Marys by Primrose Int: 03 Mar 1815 Dis: 28 Mar 1815.
    Received from Hebrus. Clarendon Transport for U States.

Shellebar, George   Prisoner 1600. Rank: Seaman, from: Bird, Merchant Vessel.
    Cap: 21 Nov 1813 Block Island by Albion Int: 14 Feb 1814 Dis: 23 Apr 1814.
    Received from Sceptre. HMS Bulwark for Halifax.

Sheppard, John   Prisoner 631. Rank: Mate, from: Freeman, Merchant Brig.
    Cap: 21 Jul 1812 at Sea by HMS Liberty Int: 14 Jan 1813 Dis: 27 Jan 1813.
    Received from Brig Freeman. Bostock Cartel for New York.

Shepperd, John   Prisoner 576. Rank: Seaman, from: Herald, Letter of Marque Brig.
    Cap: 25 Dec 1812 at Sea by HM Ship Maidstone Int: 06 Jan 1813 Dis: 27 Jan 1813.
    Received from HM Ship Maidstone. Bostock Cartel for New York.

Sherlock, Samuel   Prisoner 957. Rank: Seaman, from: Bona, Letter of Marque Schooner.
    Cap: 12 Mar 1813 Chesapeake by Laurustinus Int: 23 Mar 1813 Dis: 24 Jun 1813.
    Received from Laurustinus. Magnet Cartel for New York.

Sherwood, Ralph   Prisoner 1991. Rank: Prize Master, from: Fairplay, Merchant Vessel.
    Cap: 22 Oct 1814 Lat 31.58 by Dothrel Int: 26 Oct 1814 Dis: 28 Mar 1815.
    Recaptured. Received from Dothrel. Clarendon Transport for U States.

Sheverick, Elijah   Prisoner 2702. Rank: Seaman, from: Sally, Merchant Vessel.
    Cap: 26 Jan 1815 off Block Island by Nimrod Int: 18 Feb 1815 Dis: 28 Mar 1815.
    Received from Nimrod. Clarendon Transport for U States.

Shooter, Charles   Prisoner 1019. Rank: Seaman, from: Lusiana, Merchant.
    Cap: 20 Mar 1813 off the Chesapeake by HM Ship Rammillies Int: 06 Apr 1813 Dis: 20 May 1813.
    Received from HMS Junon. Vessel being Liberated per Order Commodore Evans.

Short, Moses   Prisoner 931. Rank: Seaman, from: Ulissus, Merchant Schooner.
    Cap: 03 Mar 1813 Chesapeake by HMS Narcissus Int: 23 Mar 1813 Dis: 24 Jun 1813.
    Received from Laurustinus. Magnet Cartel for New York.

Shorter, Jesse   Prisoner 990. Rank: Seaman, from: Nancy, Merchant.
    Cap: 04 Mar 1813 Chesapeake by Narcissus Int: 23 Mar 1813 Dis: 24 Jun 1813.
    Received from HM Ship Laurustinus. Magnet Cartel for New York.

Shorter, Roger   Prisoner 1236. Rank: Not Recorded, from: Lively John, Merchant Schooner.
    Cap: 21 Sep 1813 Chesapeake by Lacedaemonian Int: 16 Nov 1813 Dis: 15 Apr 1814.
    Received from HMS Sceptre. Diana Transport for Halifax.

Shubick, Irvine   Prisoner 2143. Rank: Midshipman, from: President, U States Frigate.
    Cap: 15 Jan 1815 Not Recorded by Endymion Int: 30 Jan 1815 Dis: 22 Mar 1815.
    Received from President. Merchant Vessel.

Shubruk, John   Prisoner 2134. Rank: Lieutenant, from: President, U States Frigate.
    Cap: 15 Jan 1815 Not Recorded by Endymion Int: 30 Jan 1815 Dis: 06 Feb 1815.
    Received from President. Narcissus to the U States by the orders of Commadore Evans.

Shuffield, Joseph   Prisoner 1493. Rank: Seaman, from: Maresoil, Merchant Brig.
    Cap: 25 Dec 1813 Latt 35.0 by HMS Fox Int: 09 Jan 1814 Dis: 15 Apr 1814.
    Received from Fox. Diana Transport for Halifax.

American Prisoners of War Held at Bermuda During the War of 1812

Shustliff, John   Prisoner 1338. Rank: Seaman, from: Rolla, Privateer.
    Cap: 10 Dec 1813 Block Island by Loire Int: 20 Dec 1813 Dis: 15 Apr 1814.
    Received from HM Ship San Domingo. HMS Rammillies for Halifax.

Sidney, Edward   Prisoner 887. Rank: Seaman, from: Hannah, Merchant Schooner.
    Cap: 24 Feb 1813 Chesapeake by Marlborough Int: 23 Mar 1813 Dis: 21 May 1813.
    Received from Laurustinus. Per Order Commodore Evans the Vessel being Liberated.

Sillsby, Benjamin   Prisoner 2122. Rank: Mate, from: Post Boy, Merchant Vessel.
    Cap: 09 Dec 1814 off Delaware by Pictolus Int: 27 Jan 1815 Dis: 17 Mar 1815.
    Received from Pictolus. Merchant Vessel.

Silsbee, Benjamin   Prisoner 1191. Rank: Seaman, from: Priscilla, Merchant Ship.
    Cap: 09 Aug 1813 at Sea by HM Sloop Forrester Int: 27 Aug 1813 Dis: 03 Sep 1813.
    Received from HM Sloop Forrester. to the American Ship Leander restored.

Silsbee, J W   Prisoner 1192. Rank: Seaman, from: Priscilla, Merchant Ship.
    Cap: 09 Aug 1813 at Sea by HM Sloop Forrester Int: 27 Aug 1813 Dis: 03 Sep 1813.
    Received from HM Sloop Forrester. to the American Ship Leander restored.

Silsby, John W   Prisoner 1098. Rank: Seaman, from: Apollo, Merchant Vessel.
    Cap: 15 May 1813 at Sea by Success Int: 27 May 1813 Dis: 24 Jun 1813.
    Received from HMS Atalante. Magnet Cartel for New York.

Silvarus, John   Prisoner 1386. Rank: Seaman, from: Policy, Merchant Vessel.
    Cap: 04 Dec 1813 Not Recorded by Loire Int: 20 Dec 1813 Dis: 15 Apr 1814.
    Recaptured. Received from San Domingo. Diana Transport for Halifax.

Silvester, Emis   Prisoner 1424. Rank: Seaman, from: Nonsuch, Letter of Marque.
    Cap: 14 Dec 1813 Lat 32 by Doterel Int: 25 Dec 1813 Dis: 15 Apr 1814.
    Received from HM Brig Doterel. Diana Transport for Halifax.

Simmonds, George   Prisoner 346. Rank: Seaman, from: Snapper, Privateer Schooner.
    Cap: 16 Nov 1812 at Sea by HMS Galus Int: 22 Nov 1812 Dis: 27 Jan 1813.
    Received from HM Ship Galus. Bostock Cartel for New York.

Simmonds, Isaac   Prisoner 388. Rank: Seaman, from: Snapper, Privateer Schooner.
    Cap: 16 Nov 1812 at Sea by HM Ship Galus Int: 22 Nov 1812 Dis: 27 Jan 1813.
    Received from HM Ship Galus. Bostock Cartel for New York.

Simmonds, Jacob   Prisoner 2457. Rank: Seaman, from: President, U States Frigate.
    Cap: 15 Jan 1815 Not Recorded by Endymion Int: 04 Feb 1815 Dis: 28 Mar 1815.
    Received from Endymion. Clarenden Transport for U States.

Simmonds, John   Prisoner 2430. Rank: Seaman, from: President, U States Frigate.
    Cap: 15 Jan 1815 Not Recorded by HM Ship Endymion Int: 04 Feb 1815 Dis: 28 Mar 1815.
    Received from Endymion. Mars Transport for U States.

Simonds, Andrew   Prisoner 2698. Rank: Cook, from: Speed, Merchant Vessel.
    Cap: 19 Jan 1815 off Nantucket by Pylades Int: 17 Feb 1815 Dis: 28 Mar 1815.
    Received from Majestic. Clarendon Transport for U States.

Simons, Evan   Prisoner 1761. Rank: Seaman, from: Yankelass, Privateer.
    Cap: 01 May 1814 L 40-4N, Long 38-0W by Severn & Surprise Int: 06 Jun 1814 Dis: 28 Mar 1815.
    Received from Severn. Mars Transport for U States.

Simons, John   Prisoner 2325. Rank: Boatswains Mate, from: President, U States Frigate.
    Cap: 15 Jan 1815 Not Recorded by Endymion Int: 04 Feb 1815 Dis: 28 Mar 1815.
    Received from Endymion. Mars Transport for U States.

Simpson, John   Prisoner 1345. Rank: Seaman, from: Rolla, Privateer.
    Cap: 10 Dec 1813 Block Island by Loire Int: 20 Dec 1813 Dis: 15 Apr 1814.
    Received from HM Ship San Domingo. HMS Rammillies for Halifax.

Simpson, William   Prisoner 295. Rank: Seaman, from: Symmetry, Merchant Ship.
    Cap: 05 Jul 1812 at Sea by HM Ship Rattler Int: 02 Nov 1812 Dis: 04 Nov 1812.
    Received from HMS Poictiers. Brig Diamond on Parole to new London United States of America.

Sinclair, William   Prisoner 612. Rank: Seaman, from: Noetoin, Packet Brig.
    Cap: 05 Jan 1813 at Sea by HMS Belvidera Int: 10 Jan 1813 Dis: 27 Jan 1813.
    Received from HMS Belvidera. Bostock Cartel for New York.

Sinnett, James   Prisoner 2225. Rank: Seaman, from: President, U States Frigate.
    Cap: 15 Jan 1815 Not Recorded by Endymion Int: 30 Jan 1815 Dis: 28 Mar 1815.
    Received from Pomone. Mars Transport for U States.

Skank, Samuel   Prisoner 155. Rank: Seaman, from: Ranger, Merchant Ship.
    Cap: 02 Oct 1812 Lat 32, Long 65 W by HM Ship Goree Int: 13 Oct 1812 Dis: 24 Oct 1812.
    Received from HMS Goree. Brig Diamond on Parole to new London United States of America.

Skank, Samuel   Prisoner 286. Rank: Seaman, from: Ranger, Merchant Ship.
    Cap: 02 Oct 1812 at Sea by HM Ship Goree Int: 02 Nov 1812 Dis: 02 Nov 1812.
    Hospital Victualled the day Discharged. Brig Diamond Cartel.

American Prisoners of War Held at Bermuda During the War of 1812

Skant, John Prisoner 2300. Rank: Marine, from: President, U States Frigate.
    Cap: 15 Jan 1815 Not Recorded by Endymion Int: 04 Feb 1815 Dis: 28 Mar 1815.
    Received from Endymion. Clarenden Transport for U States.

Skinner, Joseph Prisoner 2861. Rank: Seaman, from: Limerick, Not Recorded.
    Cap: 15 Mar 1815 Not Recorded by Asia Int: 27 Mar 1815 Dis: 28 Mar 1815.
    From Depot at Jamaica. Received from Goree. Clarendon Transport for U States.

Sloan, Henry Prisoner 1038. Rank: Seaman, from: Revinue, Merchant Sloop.
    Cap: 19 Mar 1813 off the Chesapeake by HMS Statira Int: 06 Apr 1813 Dis: 24 Jun 1813.
    Received from HMS Junon. Magnet Cartel for New York.

Sloan, James Prisoner 2537. Rank: Seaman, from: President, U States Frigate.
    Cap: 15 Jan 1815 Not Recorded by HM Ship Endymion Int: 04 Feb 1815 Dis: 28 Mar 1815.
    Received from HMS Endymion. Clarenden Transport for U States.

Sloane, William Prisoner 2839. Rank: Seaman, from: Limerick, Not Recorded.
    Cap: 15 Mar 1815 Not Recorded by Asia Int: 25 Mar 1815 Dis:
    From Depot at Jamaica. Received from Asia. (Date of discharge not recorded.)

Slocolm, John Prisoner 772. Rank: Seaman, from: Trinadada, Merchant Brig.
    Cap: 06 Jan 1813 Lat 37.20, Long 75.00 by HM Sloop Sylph Int: 26 Jan 1813 Dis: 14 Mar 1813.
    Received from Sloop Sylph. Savannah Packet for New York per Order Adl Sir J B Warren.

Slocum, George Prisoner 1018. Rank: Mate, from: Lusiana, Merchant.
    Cap: 20 Mar 1813 off the Chesapeake by HM Ship Rammillies Int: 06 Apr 1813 Dis: 20 May 1813.
    Received from HMS Junon. Vessel being Liberated per Order Commodore Evans.

Slowbridge, Benjamin Prisoner 394. Rank: Seaman, from: Snapper, Privateer Schooner.
    Cap: 16 Nov 1812 at Sea by HM Ship Galus Int: 22 Nov 1812 Dis: 27 Jan 1813.
    Received from HM Ship Galus. Bostock Cartel for New York.

Small, Benjamin Prisoner 1757. Rank: Seaman, from: Yankelass, Privateer.
    Cap: 01 May 1814 L 40-4N, Long 38-0W by Severn & Surprise Int: 06 Jun 1814 Dis: 28 Mar 1815.
    Received from Severn. Mars Transport for U States.

Small, Elisha Prisoner 2127. Rank: Seaman, from: Post Boy, Merchant Vessel.
    Cap: 09 Dec 1814 off Delaware by HMS Pictolus Int: 27 Jan 1815 Dis: 13 Mar 1815.
    Received from Pictolus. Merchant Service.

Smell, Charles Prisoner 2671. Rank: Masters Mate, from: Gunboat 160, U States Man of War.
    Cap: 06 Sep 1814 off New York by Lacedaemonian Int: 14 Feb 1815 Dis: 22 Mar 1815.
    Gun Vessel. Received from Childers. Merchant Vessel.

Smith, Charles Prisoner 300. Rank: Seaman, from: Symmetry, Merchant Ship.
    Cap: 05 Jul 1812 at Sea by HM Ship Rattler Int: 02 Nov 1812 Dis: 04 Nov 1812.
    Received from HMS Poictiers. Brig Diamond on Parole to new London United States of America.

Smith, Charles Prisoner 2582. Rank: Mate, from: Advocate, Merchant Vessel.
    Cap: 16 Nov 1814 off New York by HM Ship Majestic Int: 05 Feb 1815 Dis: 17 Mar 1815.
    Received from HMS Forth. Merchant Vessel.

Smith, Chester Prisoner 570. Rank: Mate, from: Eliza, Merchant.
    Cap: 18 Nov 1812 at Sea by HM Ship Maidstone Int: 06 Jan 1813 Dis: 27 Jan 1813.
    Received from HM Ship Maidstone. Bostock Cartel for New York.

Smith, Christopher Prisoner 2370. Rank: Boatswains Mate, from: President, U States Frigate.
    Cap: 15 Jan 1815 Not Recorded by HMS Endymion Int: 04 Feb 1815 Dis: 28 Mar 1815.
    Received from Endymion. Mars Transport for U States.

Smith, Daniel Prisoner 494. Rank: Seaman, from: Teazer, Privateer Schooner.
    Cap: 16 Dec 1812 at Sea by HM Ship St. Domingo Int: 21 Dec 1812 Dis: 27 Jan 1813.
    Received from HM Ship St. Domingo. Bostock Cartel for New York.

Smith, David Prisoner 585. Rank: Seaman, from: Lydia, Merchant Ship.
    Cap: 26 Dec 1812 at Sea by HM Ship Maidstone Int: 06 Jan 1813 Dis: 27 Jan 1813.
    Received from HM Ship Maidstone. Bostock Cartel for New York.

Smith, Deliverance Prisoner 2103. Rank: Seaman, from: Rufus King, Merchant Vessel.
    Cap: 01 Jan 1815 off Bermuda by Peruvian Int: 19 Jan 1815 Dis: 13 Mar 1815.
    Received from HMS Peruvian. Clarendon Transport for U States.

Smith, E Prisoner 1867. Rank: Seaman, from: Viper, Merchant Vessel.
    Cap: Not Recorded by Not Recorded Int: Dis: 28 Mar 1815.
    Clarendon Transport for U States. (Dates of capture and internment not recorded.)

Smith, Ebenezer Prisoner 2123. Rank: Seaman, from: Post Boy, Merchant Vessel.
    Cap: 09 Dec 1814 off Delaware by Pictolus Int: 27 Jan 1815 Dis: 28 Mar 1815.
    Received from Pictolus. Clarendon Transport for U States.

Smith, Edward Prisoner 2463. Rank: Seaman, from: President, U States Frigate.
    Cap: 15 Jan 1815 Not Recorded by Endymion Int: 04 Feb 1815 Dis: 28 Mar 1815.
    Received from Endymion. Clarenden Transport for U States.

American Prisoners of War Held at Bermuda During the War of 1812

Smith, Elias   Prisoner 1679. Rank: Seaman, from: St. Joquin, Merchant Vessel.
    Cap: 26 Mar 1814 Chesapeake by Albion Int: 16 Apr 1814 Dis: 23 Apr 1814.
    Received from Canso. HMS Bulwark for Halifax Order Comm in Chief.

Smith, Frederick William   Prisoner 795. Rank: 2 Lieutenant, from: Viper, Sloop of War.
    Cap: 17 Jan 1813 at Sea by Narcissus Int: 13 Feb 1813 Dis: 13 Jun 1813.
    Received from Narcissus. Perseverance Cartel for the United States per Order Admiral Sir J B Warren.

Smith, Gorham   Prisoner 2654. Rank: Mate, from: Edward, Merchant Vessel.
    Cap: 30 Dec 1814 off New York by Pomone Int: 13 Feb 1815 Dis: 09 Mar 1815.
    Received from HMS Forth. Merchant Serice.

Smith, Ichabod   Prisoner 1812. Rank: Passenger, from: Not Recorded, Not Recorded.
    Cap: Not Recorded by Not Recorded Int: 14 Jun 1814 Dis: 15 Jun 1814.
    From St. Bartholomew in the Swedish Schooner Oscar. on Parole per Order Com in Chief to America.
    (Date of capture not recorded.)

Smith, Jacob   Prisoner 850. Rank: Master, from: Resolution, Merchant Schooner.
    Cap: 26 Jan 1813 at Sea by Victorious Int: 20 Mar 1813 Dis: 20 Mar 1813.
    Received from HMS Galus. Savannah Packet for New York per Order Adl Sir J B Warren.

Smith, Jacob   Prisoner 1610. Rank: Seaman, from: Brookhaven, Merchant Vessel.
    Cap: 09 Dec 1813 Block Island by Albion Int: 14 Feb 1814 Dis: 23 Apr 1814.
    Received from Sceptre. HMS Bulwark for Halifax.

Smith, James   Prisoner 715. Rank: Seaman, from: High Flyer, Privateer.
    Cap: 09 Jan 1813 at Sea by HM Ship Acasta Int: 21 Jan 1813 Dis: 27 Jan 1813.
    Received from HMS Acasta. Bostock Cartel for New York.

Smith, James   Prisoner 762. Rank: Seaman, from: Hazard, Merchant Brig.
    Cap: 28 Dec 1812 Lat 37.35, Long 70.10 by HM Sloop Sylph Int: 26 Jan 1813 Dis: 14 Jun 1813.
    Received from Sloop Sylph. Permitted to return to the United States in the Perseverance Cartel.

Smith, James   Prisoner 1701. Rank: Seaman, from: Grecian, Letter of Marque.
    Cap: 02 May 1814 Chesapeake by Jansur Int: 26 May 1814 Dis: 28 Mar 1815.
    Received from Lacedaemonian. Mars Transport for U States. James Smith (1).

Smith, James   Prisoner 1709. Rank: Seaman, from: Grecian, Letter of Marque.
    Cap: 02 May 1814 Chesapeake by Jansur Int: 26 May 1814 Dis: 28 Mar 1815.
    Received from Lacedaemonian. Mars Transport for U States. James Smith (2).

Smith, James   Prisoner 1854. Rank: Seaman, from: Little Catherine, Merchant Vessel.
    Cap: Not Recorded by Not Recorded Int: Not Recorded Escaped: 26 Aug 1814.
    Run from Naval Hospital. (Dates of capture and internment not recorded.)

Smith, James   Prisoner 1945. Rank: Seaman, from: Pike, Privateer.
    Cap: 25 Aug 1814 off Savannah by Primrose Int: 09 Sep 1814 Dis: 28 Mar 1815.
    Received from Lacedaemonian. Clarendon Transport for U States.

Smith, James   Prisoner 2349. Rank: Seaman, from: President, U States Frigate.
    Cap: 15 Jan 1815 Not Recorded by HMS Endymion Int: 04 Feb 1815 Dis: 28 Mar 1815.
    Received from Endymion. Mars Transport for U States.

Smith, John   Prisoner 29. Rank: Seaman, from: Survanou, Merchant.
    Cap: 14 Jul 1812 at Bermuda by Recruit Int: 28 Aug 1812 Dis: 18 Sep 1812.
    Received from HM Schooner Cuttle. Order of Commd Evans for England.

Smith, John   Prisoner 623. Rank: Master, from: Independence, Merchant.
    Cap: 31 Dec 1812 at Sea by HMS Tartant Int: 12 Jan 1813 Dis: 05 Feb 1813.
    Received from the Prize Independence. Permitted to return to New York per Order of Adl Cockburn.

Smith, John   Prisoner 1102. Rank: Seaman, from: Apollo, Merchant Vessel.
    Cap: 15 May 1813 at Sea by HM Ship Success Int: 27 May 1813 Dis: 24 Jun 1813.
    Received from HMS Success. Magnet Cartel for New York.

Smith, John   Prisoner 1146. Rank: Seaman, from: Acricoake, Merchant.
    Cap: 22 Jul 1813 at Sea by HM Sloop Conflict Int: 13 Aug 1813 Dis: 13 Aug 1813.
    Received from HM Ship Woolwich. American Ship Rolla per Order Commr Evans.

Smith, John   Prisoner 1341. Rank: Seaman, from: Rolla, Privateer.
    Cap: 10 Dec 1813 Block Island by Loire Int: 20 Dec 1813 Dis: 15 Apr 1814.
    Received from HM Ship San Domingo. HMS Rammillies for Halifax.

Smith, John   Prisoner 1353. Rank: Seaman, from: Rolla, Privateer.
    Cap: 10 Dec 1813 Block Island by Loire Int: 20 Dec 1813 Dis:
    Received from San Domingo. John Smith (2). (date of discharge not recorded.)

Smith, John   Prisoner 1593. Rank: Seaman, from: Bordeaux Packet, Letter of Marque.
    Cap: 28 Jan 1814 off Cape Henry by Nieman Int: 12 Feb 1814 Dis: 23 Apr 1814.
    Received from Nieman. HMS Bulwark for Halifax. John Smith (3d).

American Prisoners of War Held at Bermuda During the War of 1812

Smith, John   Prisoner 1892. Rank: Prize Master, from: Little Catherine, Merchant Vessel.
    Cap: Not Recorded by Not Recorded Int: Dis: 29 Aug 1814.
    Commodore Evans Order. (Dates of capture and internment not recorded.)

Smith, John   Prisoner 2198. Rank: Seaman, from: President, U States Frigate.
    Cap: 15 Jan 1815 Not Recorded by Endymion Int: 30 Jan 1815 Dis: 28 Mar 1815.
    Received from Pomone. Mars Transport for U States.

Smith, John   Prisoner 2258. Rank: Seaman, from: President, U States Frigate.
    Cap: 15 Jan 1815 Not Recorded by Endymion Int: 30 Jan 1815 Dis: 28 Mar 1815.
    Received from Pomone. Mars Transport for U States.

Smith, John   Prisoner 2385. Rank: Seaman, from: President, U States Frigate.
    Cap: 15 Jan 1815 Not Recorded by HMS Endymion Int: 04 Feb 1815 Dis:
    Received from Endymion. (Date of discharge not recorded.)

Smith, John   Prisoner 2436. Rank: Quartermaster, from: President, U States Frigate.
    Cap: 15 Jan 1815 Not Recorded by Endymion Int: 04 Feb 1815 Dis: 28 Mar 1815.
    Received from Endymion. Mars Transport for U States.

Smith, Joseph   Prisoner 753. Rank: Seaman, from: Delaclea, Merchant Schooner.
    Cap: 17 Dec 1812 Lat 34.31 N, Long 74.44 W by HM Sloop Sylph Int: 26 Jan 1813 Dis: 14 Jun 1813.
    Received from Sloop Sylph. Permitted to return to the United States in Perseverance. 2y 13 June 1813.

Smith, Joseph   Prisoner 1914. Rank: Seaman, from: Dolphin, Packet.
    Cap: 20 Aug 1814 St. Catherine by Lacedaemonian Int: 09 Sep 1814 Dis: 02 Mar 1814.
    Received from Lacedaemonian. US without exchange.

Smith, Joseph F   Prisoner 1927. Rank: 2 Lieutenant, from: Pike, Privateer.
    Cap: 25 Aug 1814 off Savannah by Primrose Int: 09 Sep 1814 Dis: 28 Mar 1815.
    Received from Lacedaemonian. Clarendon Transport for U States.

Smith, Lawrence   Prisoner 2738. Rank: Seaman, from: Not Recorded, Not Recorded.
    Cap: 13 Jan 1815 St Marys by Dragon Int: 03 Mar 1815 Dis: 28 Mar 1815.
    by Kings Troops. Received from Hebrus. Clarendon Transport for U States.

Smith, Major   Prisoner 863. Rank: Master, from: Alert, Merchant Sloop.
    Cap: 14 Mar 1813 Chesapeake by HM Ship Laurustinus Int: 23 Mar 1813 Dis: 24 Jun 1813.
    Received from Laurustinus. Magnet Cartel for New York.

Smith, Moses   Prisoner 2768. Rank: Seaman, from: Brant, Not Recorded.
    Cap: 05 Feb 1815 St Augustine by Severn Int: 03 Mar 1815 Dis: 17 Mar 1815.
    Received from Hebrus. Merchant Vessel.

Smith, Nathaniel   Prisoner 2615. Rank: Seaman, from: Falcon, Merchant Vessel.
    Cap: 22 Jan 1815 Sandy Hook by HM Ship Pomone Int: 05 Feb 1815 Dis: 28 Mar 1815.
    Received from HMS Forth. Clarendon Transport for U States.

Smith, Ralph   Prisoner 2532. Rank: Seaman, from: President, U States Frigate.
    Cap: 15 Jan 1815 Not Recorded by HM Ship Endymion Int: 04 Feb 1815 Dis: 28 Mar 1815.
    Received from HMS Endymion. Clarenden Transport for U States.

Smith, Thomas R   Prisoner 121. Rank: Seaman, from: William of Baltimore, Merchant.
    Cap: 31 Aug 1812 Lat 37 by HM Ship Recruit Int: 14 Sep 1812 Dis: 18 Sep 1812.
    Received from Recruit. Order of Commd Evans for England.

Smith, Thomas   Prisoner 639. Rank: Seaman, from: Crown Prince, Merchant Schooner.
    Cap: 19 Dec 1812 at Sea by HM Ship Galus Int: 17 Jan 1813 Dis: 27 Jan 1813.
    Received from HM Ship Galus. Bostock Cartel for New York.

Smith, Thomas   Prisoner 1289. Rank: Seaman, from: Perry, Merchant Schooner.
    Cap: 03 Dec 1813 Long Island by Indemyion Int: 19 Dec 1813 Dis: 15 Apr 1814.
    Received from Sceptre. Diana Transport for Halifax.

Smith, Weston   Prisoner 864. Rank: Seaman, from: Alert, Merchant Sloop.
    Cap: 14 Mar 1813 Chesapeake by HM Ship Laurustinus Int: 23 Mar 1813 Dis: 13 Jun 1813.
    Received from Laurustinus. Perseverance Cartel for the United States per Order Adml Sir J B Warren.

Smith, William   Prisoner 88. Rank: Seaman, from: Gossepuim, Merchant.
    Cap: 16 Aug 1812 of Bermuda by Goree Int: 28 Aug 1812 Dis: 18 Sep 1812.
    Received from HM Schooner Cuttle. Order of Commd Evans for England.

Smith, William   Prisoner 720. Rank: Seaman, from: High Flyer, Privateer.
    Cap: 09 Jan 1813 at Sea by HM Ship Acasta Int: 21 Jan 1813 Dis: 27 Jan 1813.
    Received from HMS Acasta. Bostock Cartel for New York.

Smith, William   Prisoner 1935. Rank: Seaman, from: Pike, Privateer.
    Cap: 25 Aug 1814 off Savannah by Primrose Int: 09 Sep 1814 Dis: 28 Mar 1815.
    Received from Lacedaemonian. Clarendon Transport for U States.

Smith, William   Prisoner 2341. Rank: Seaman, from: President, U States Frigate.
    Cap: 15 Jan 1815 Not Recorded by HMS Endymion Int: 04 Feb 1815 Dis: 28 Mar 1815.
    Received from Endymion. Mars Transport for U States.

American Prisoners of War Held at Bermuda During the War of 1812

Smith, William   Prisoner 2844. Rank: Seaman, from: Limerick, Not Recorded.
    Cap: 15 Mar 1815 Not Recorded by Asia Int: 25 Mar 1815 Dis:
    From Depot at Jamaica. Received from Asia. (Date of discharge not recorded.)

Snail, Robert   Prisoner 293. Rank: Seaman, from: Symmetry, Merchant Ship.
    Cap: 05 Jul 1812 at Sea by HM Ship Rattler Int: 02 Nov 1812 Dis:
    Received from HMS Poictiers. Permitted to remain on Board the Symmetry per Order Commd Evans. (Date of discharge not on roster.)

Snow, James   Prisoner 2789. Rank: Seaman, from: Limerick, Not Recorded.
    Cap: 07 Mar 1815 Lat 30, Long 75.38 W by Asia Int: 25 Mar 1815 Dis:
    Received from Asia. (Date of discharge not recorded.)

Snow, Joseph   Prisoner 1076. Rank: Seaman, from: Ring Dove, Merchant.
    Cap: 31 Mar 1813 Chesapeake by HM Ship Junon Int: 06 Apr 1813 Dis: 24 Jun 1813.
    Received from HMS Junon. Magnet Cartel for New York.

Snow, William   Prisoner 2474. Rank: Seaman, from: President, U States Frigate.
    Cap: 15 Jan 1815 Not Recorded by Endymion Int: 04 Feb 1815 Dis: 28 Mar 1815.
    Received from Endymion. Clarenden Transport for U States.

Soalby, Nathaniel   Prisoner 1099. Rank: Boy, from: Apollo, Merchant Vessel.
    Cap: 15 May 1813 at Sea by Success Int: 27 May 1813 Dis: 24 Jun 1813.
    Received from HMS Atalante. Magnet Cartel for New York.

Solaris, Francis   Prisoner 1078. Rank: Seaman, from: Not Recorded, Not Recorded.
    Cap: Not Recorded by Not Recorded Int: 08 Apr 1813 Dis: 24 Jun 1813.
    Received from HMS Ruby. Surrendered them Selves as Prisoners of War. Magnet Cartel for New York. (Date of capture not recorded.)

Somerdyke, Joseph   Prisoner 24. Rank: Seaman, from: Hero, Merchant Schooner.
    Cap: 14 Jul 1812 at Bermuda by Cuttle Int: 28 Aug 1812 Dis: 18 Sep 1812.
    Received from HM Schooner Cuttle. Order of Commd Evans for England.

Sommers, Frederick   Prisoner 1949. Rank: Seaman, from: Pike, Privateer.
    Cap: 25 Aug 1814 off Savannah by Primrose Int: 09 Sep 1814 Dis: 20 Mar 1815.
    Received from Lacedaemonian. Merchant Vessel.

Sooty, Darooke   Prisoner 544. Rank: Seaman, from: Herald, Letter of Marque Brig.
    Cap: 25 Dec 1812 at Sea by HM Ship Maidstone Int: 05 Jan 1813 Dis: 27 Jan 1813.
    Received from HM Ship Maidstone. Bostock Cartel for New York.

Southworth, George   Prisoner 35. Rank: Seaman, from: Laura, Merchant Sloop.
    Cap: 24 Jul 1812 of Bermuda by Cuttle Int: 28 Aug 1812 Dis: 03 Sep 1812.
    Received from HM Schooner Cuttle. Hospital not Victualed until the 5th September.

Southworth, George   Prisoner 137. Rank: Seaman, from: Laura, Merchant Sloop.
    Cap: 24 Jul 1812 off Bermuda by Schooner Cuttle Int: 11 Oct 1812 Dis: 24 Oct 1812.
    Received from Hospital. Brig Diamond on Parole to the United States of America.

Southworth, John   Prisoner 1056. Rank: Master, from: Amason, Merchant.
    Cap: 18 Mar 1813 Chesapeake by HM Ship Victorious Int: 06 Apr 1813 Dis: 24 Jun 1813.
    Received from HMS Junon. Magnet Cartel for New York.

Southworth, Justice   Prisoner 34. Rank: Mate, from: Laura, Merchant Sloop.
    Cap: 24 Jul 1812 of Bermuda by Cuttle Int: 28 Aug 1812 Dis: 10 Sep 1812.
    Received from HM Schooner Cuttle. Schooner Hero for N Y.

Sowle, Peley   Prisoner 455. Rank: Prize Master, from: Teazer, Privateer Schooner.
    Cap: 16 Dec 1812 at Sea by HM Ship St. Domingo Int: 21 Dec 1812 Dis: 27 Jan 1813.
    Received from HM Ship St. Domingo. Bostock Cartel for New York.

Spanger, Edward   Prisoner 1063. Rank: Seaman, from: Amason, Merchant.
    Cap: 18 Mar 1813 Chesapeake by HM Ship Victorious Int: 06 Apr 1813 Dis: 24 Jun 1813.
    Received from HMS Junon. Magnet Cartel for New York.

Spaniola, John   Prisoner 1466. Rank: Seaman, from: Vixen, Man of War.
    Cap: 25 Dec 1813 Lat 38.0 by Belvidera Int: 05 Jan 1814 Dis: 15 Apr 1814.
    U States Schooner. Received from HMS Belvidera. Diana Transport for Halifax.

Sparkanork, John   Prisoner 2692. Rank: Seaman, from: Speed, Merchant Vessel.
    Cap: 19 Jan 1815 off Nantucket by Pylades Int: 17 Feb 1815 Dis: 28 Mar 1815.
    Received from Majestic. Clarendon Transport for U States.

Spear, William   Prisoner 696. Rank: Seaman, from: High Flyer, Privateer.
    Cap: 09 Jan 1813 at Sea by HMS Acasta Int: 21 Jan 1813 Dis: 27 Jan 1813.
    Received from HMS Acasta. Bostock Cartel for New York.

Spencer, Job F   Prisoner 1743. Rank: Seaman, from: Yankelass, Privateer.
    Cap: 01 May 1814 L 10-4N, L 33-0W by Severn & Surprise Int: 06 Jun 1814 Dis: 21 Feb 1815.
    Received from Severn. Paroled to the U States having served six months as Carpenter's Mate order of Adl Sir Alex Cockburn.

American Prisoners of War Held at Bermuda During the War of 1812

Spencer, Robert   Prisoner 2235. Rank: Seaman, from: President, U States Frigate.
   Cap: 15 Jan 1815 Not Recorded by Endymion Int: 30 Jan 1815 Dis: 28 Mar 1815.
   Received from Pomone. Mars Transport for U States.

Spencer, S   Prisoner 2766. Rank: Seaman, from: Maria, Not Recorded.
   Cap: 16 Feb 1815 St Augustine by Severn Int: 03 Mar 1815 Dis: 28 Mar 1815.
   Received from Hebrus. Clarendon Transport for U States.

Spincker, Gerard   Prisoner 660. Rank: Seaman, from: Pekin, Merchant Ship.
   Cap: 17 Dec 1812 at Sea by HM Ship Acasta Int: 21 Jan 1813 Dis: 27 Jan 1813.
   Received from Ship Pekin. Bostock Cartel for New York.

Sportfield, Collin   Prisoner 1917. Rank: Seaman, from: Dolphin, Packet.
   Cap: 20 Aug 1814 St. Catherine by Lacedaemonian Int: 09 Sep 1814 Dis: 28 Mar 1815.
   Received from Lacedaemonian. Clarendon Transport for U States.

Spring, Daniel   Prisoner 1478. Rank: Seaman, from: Luckey, Merchant Vessel.
   Cap: 19 Dec 1813 off the Delaware by Niemen Int: 07 Jan 1814 Dis: 15 Apr 1814.
   Received from HM Sloop Jaseur. Diana for Halifax. (Name of capturing ship not legible, assume to be Nieman.)

Spurn, Elias   Prisoner 574. Rank: Seaman, from: Peakin, Merchant Ship.
   Cap: 17 Dec 1812 at Sea by HM Ship Acasta Int: 06 Jan 1813 Dis: 27 Jan 1813.
   Received from HM Ship Maidstone. Bostock Cartel for New York.

Squires, Samuel C   Prisoner 1250. Rank: Not Recorded, from: Circe, Merchant Vessel.
   Cap: 22 Oct 1813 Cape Hatterus by Acteon Int: 02 Dec 1813 Dis: 15 Apr 1814.
   Received from HMS Sceptre. Diana Transport for Halifax.

Stacey, R S   Prisoner 1909. Rank: Master, from: Resolution, Merchant Vessel.
   Cap: 20 Aug 1814 St. Catherine by Lacedaemonian Int: 09 Sep 1814 Dis: 28 Mar 1815.
   Received from Lacedaemonian. Clarendon Transport for U States.

Stage, Abraham   Prisoner 2673. Rank: Seaman, from: Gunboat 160, U States Man of War.
   Cap: 06 Sep 1814 off New York by Lacedaemonian Int: 14 Feb 1815 Dis: 28 Mar 1815.
   Gun Vessel. Received from Childers. Clarendon Transport for U States.

Stamford, William   Prisoner 2786. Rank: Seaman, from: Limerick, Not Recorded.
   Cap: 07 Mar 1815 Lat 30, Long 75.38 W by Asia Int: 25 Mar 1815 Dis: 25 Mar 1815.
   Received from Asia. Merchant Vessel.

Stamphouse, Henry   Prisoner 66. Rank: Seaman, from: Mary, Merchant Brig.
   Cap: 08 Aug 1812 of Bermuda by Cuttle Int: 28 Aug 1812 Dis: 17 Sep 1812.
   Received from M Schooner Cuttle. being a German Order C. Evans.

Standly, Timothy   Prisoner 1878. Rank: Seaman, from: Levant, Merchant Vessel.
   Cap: Not Recorded by Not Recorded Int: Dis: 13 Mar 1815.
   Merchant Service. (Dates of capture and internment not recorded.)

Stanford, James   Prisoner 2191. Rank: Seaman, from: President, U States Frigate.
   Cap: 15 Jan 1815 Not Recorded by HMS Endymion Int: 30 Jan 1815 Dis: 28 Mar 1815.
   Received from Pomone. Mars Transport for U States.

Stanhour, Francis   Prisoner 1416. Rank: 1 Officer, from: Nonsuch, Letter of Marque.
   Cap: 14 Dec 1813 Lat 32 by Doterel Int: 25 Dec 1813 Dis: 15 Apr 1814.
   Received from HM Brig Doterel. Rammilles for Halifax.

Stanley, Benjamin   Prisoner 2614. Rank: Seaman, from: Falcon, Merchant Vessel.
   Cap: 22 Jan 1815 Sandy Hook by HM Ship Pomone Int: 05 Feb 1815 Dis: 28 Mar 1815.
   Received from HMS Forth. Clarendon Transport for U States.

Stanley, Peter   Prisoner 76. Rank: Seaman, from: White Oak, Merchant.
   Cap: 08 Aug 1812 of Bermuda by Recruit Int: 28 Aug 1812 Dis: 18 Sep 1812.
   Received from M Schooner Cuttle. Order of Commd Evans for England.

Stantos, Andrew D   Prisoner 2450. Rank: Seaman, from: President, U States Frigate.
   Cap: 15 Jan 1815 Not Recorded by Endymion Int: 04 Feb 1815 Dis: 28 Mar 1815.
   Received from Endymion. Clarenden Transport for U States.

Stapford, D F   Prisoner 1532. Rank: Seaman, from: Romp, Merchant Vessel.
   Cap: 02 Jan 1814 Latt 22.0 by Prometheus Int: 23 Jan 1814 Dis: 15 Apr 1814.
   Received from Prometheus. Diana for Halifax.

Staple, Thomas   Prisoner 1202. Rank: Seaman, from: Willam & Ann, Merchant Ship.
   Cap: 30 Jul 1813 at Sea by HM Sloop Nimrod Int: 05 Sep 1813 Dis: 12 Sep 1813.
   Received from HM Sloop Nimrod. Per Order of Commodore Evans to the American Ship Georgiana restored.

Starr, John   Prisoner 1040. Rank: Passenger, from: Revinue, Merchant Sloop.
   Cap: 19 Mar 1813 off the Chesapeake by HMS Statira Int: 06 Apr 1813 Dis: 24 Jun 1813.
   Received from HMS Junon. Magnet Cartel for New York.

American Prisoners of War Held at Bermuda During the War of 1812

Steady, James   Prisoner 182. Rank: Seaman, from: Wasp, Sloop of War.
    Cap: 18 Oct 1812 at Sea by HMS Poictiers Int: 26 Oct 1812 Dis: 05 Nov 1812.
    Received from HM Ship Poictiers. Brig Diamond on Parole to new London America.

Stephen, G   Prisoner 2843. Rank: Seaman, from: Limerick, Not Recorded.
    Cap: 15 Mar 1815 Not Recorded by Asia Int: 25 Mar 1815 Dis:
    From Depot at Jamaica. Received from Asia. (Date of discharge not recorded.)

Stephens, David   Prisoner 347. Rank: Seaman, from: Snapper, Privateer Schooner.
    Cap: 16 Nov 1812 at Sea by HMS Galus Int: 22 Nov 1812 Dis: 27 Jan 1813.
    Received from HM Ship Galus. Bostock Cartel for New York.

Stephens, Henry   Prisoner 457. Rank: Mate, from: Teazer, Privateer Schooner.
    Cap: 16 Dec 1812 at Sea by HM Ship St. Domingo Int: 21 Dec 1812 Dis: 27 Jan 1813.
    Received from HM Ship St. Domingo. Bostock Cartel for New York.

Stephens, James   Prisoner 954. Rank: Seaman, from: Bona, Letter of Marque Schooner.
    Cap: 12 Mar 1813 Chesapeake by Laurustinus Int: 23 Mar 1813 Dis: 24 Jun 1813.
    Received from Laurustinus. Magnet Cartel for New York.

Stephens, James   Prisoner 1215. Rank: Seaman, from: Rebecca, Merchant Ship.
    Cap: 19 Jan 1813 off Philadelphia by Poictiers Int: 06 Nov 1813 Dis: 24 Apr 1814.
    Received from HMS Ruby. HMS Sceptre for England.

Stephens, John   Prisoner 311. Rank: Seaman, from: Wasp, Sloop of War.
    Cap: 18 Oct 1812 at Sea by HMS Poictiers Int: 05 Nov 1812 Died: 01 Feb 1813.
    Received from HM Ship Poictiers. Died. Fever.

Stephens, Levi   Prisoner 181. Rank: Seaman, from: Wasp, Sloop of War.
    Cap: 18 Oct 1812 at Sea by HMS Poictiers Int: 26 Oct 1812 Dis: 05 Nov 1812.
    Received from HM Ship Poictiers. Brig Diamond on Parole to new London America.

Stephens, Loyd   Prisoner 333. Rank: Seaman, from: Snapper, Privateer Schooner.
    Cap: 16 Nov 1812 at Sea by HMS Galus Int: 22 Nov 1812 Dis: 27 Jan 1813.
    Received from HM Ship Galus. Bostock Cartel for New York.

Stephenson, David   Prisoner 948. Rank: Seaman, from: Bona, Letter of Marque Schooner.
    Cap: 12 Mar 1813 Chesapeake by Laurustinus Int: 23 Mar 1813 Dis: 24 Jun 1813.
    Received from Laurustinus. Magnet Cartel for New York.

Stephenson, John   Prisoner 1218. Rank: Seaman, from: HM Ship Nieman, Not Recorded.
    Cap: 12 Mar 1813 Not Recorded by Nieman Int: 13 Nov 1813 Dis: 15 Apr 1814.
    Received from HMS Nieman. HMS Rammillies Halifax.

Stephenson, Thomas   Prisoner 2513. Rank: Seaman, from: President, U States Frigate.
    Cap: 15 Jan 1815 Not Recorded by Endymion Int: 04 Feb 1815 Dis: 28 Mar 1815.
    Received from HMS Endymion. Clarenden Transport for U States.

Sterns, David   Prisoner 263. Rank: Seaman, from: Wasp, Sloop of War.
    Cap: 18 Oct 1812 at Sea by HM Ship Poictiers Int: 26 Oct 1812 Dis: 05 Nov 1812.
    Received from HM Ship Poictiers. Brig Diamond on Parole to new London United States of America.

Stetson, Smith   Prisoner 558. Rank: 2 Mate, from: Rising Hope, Merchant Brig.
    Cap: 27 Dec 1812 at Sea by HM Sloop Wanderer Int: 05 Jan 1813 Dis: 27 Jan 1813.
    Received from HM Sloop Wanderer. Bostock Cartel for New York.

Stevens, L   Prisoner 2350. Rank: Seaman, from: President, U States Frigate.
    Cap: 15 Jan 1815 Not Recorded by HMS Endymion Int: 04 Feb 1815 Dis: 28 Mar 1815.
    Received from Endymion. Mars Transport for U States.

Steward, Alexander   Prisoner 2641. Rank: Seaman, from: Platoff, Merchant Vessel.
    Cap: 16 Jan 1815 off New York by Spencer Int: 06 Feb 1815 Dis: 28 Mar 1815.
    Received from HMS Telegraph. Clarendon Transport for U States.

Steward, John   Prisoner 1816. Rank: Passenger, from: Not Recorded, Not Recorded.
    Cap: Not Recorded by Not Recorded Int: 14 Jun 1814 Dis: 15 Jun 1814.
    From St. Bartholomew in the Swedish Schooner Oscar. on Parole per Order Com in Chief to America.
    (Date of capture not recorded.)

Steward, Joseph   Prisoner 2109. Rank: Seaman, from: Rufus King, Merchant Vessel.
    Cap: 01 Jan 1815 off Bermuda by Peruvian Int: 19 Jan 1815 Dis: 28 Mar 1815.
    Received from HMS Peruvian. Clarendon Transport for U States.

Steward, Samuel   Prisoner 1646. Rank: Seaman, from: Mary Ann, Merchant Vessel.
    Cap: 26 Dec 1813 off Cape Henry by Sophie Int: 28 Feb 1814 Dis: 23 Apr 1814.
    Received from Active. HMS Bulwark for Halifax.

Stewart, James   Prisoner 620. Rank: Boy, from: Experience, Merchant Brig.
    Cap: 25 Nov 1812 at Sea by HMS Sophia Int: 12 Jan 1813 Dis: 27 Jan 1813.
    Received from HMS Belvidera. Bostock Cartel for New York.

American Prisoners of War Held at Bermuda During the War of 1812

Stewart, John P   Prisoner 470. Rank: Seaman, from: Teazer, Privateer Schooner.
    Cap: 16 Dec 1812 at Sea by HM Ship St. Domingo Int: 21 Dec 1812 Dis: 27 Jan 1813.
    Received from HM Ship St. Domingo. Bostock Cartel for New York.

Stime, Wallis   Prisoner 2320. Rank: Seaman, from: President, U States Frigate.
    Cap: 15 Jan 1815 Not Recorded by Endymion Int: 04 Feb 1815 Dis: 28 Mar 1815.
    Received from Endymion. Mars Transport for U States.

Stocking, William   Prisoner 2832. Rank: Seaman, from: Limerick, Not Recorded.
    Cap: 15 Mar 1815 Not Recorded by Asia Int: 25 Mar 1815 Dis:
    From Depot at Jamaica. Received from Asia. (Date of discharge not recorded.)

Stoddart, Isaac   Prisoner 1359. Rank: Seaman, from: Rolla, Privateer.
    Cap: 10 Dec 1813 Block Island by Loire Int: 20 Dec 1813 Dis: 15 Apr 1814.
    Received from San Domingo. HMS Rammillies for Halifax.

Stoddien, Warren   Prisoner 1022. Rank: Seaman, from: Lusiana, Merchant.
    Cap: 20 Mar 1813 off the Chesapeake by HM Ship Rammillies Int: 06 Apr 1813 Dis: 20 May 1813.
    Received from HMS Junon. Vessel being Liberated per Order Commodore Evans.

Stodson, Benjamin   Prisoner 573. Rank: Seaman, from: Peakin, Merchant Ship.
    Cap: 17 Dec 1812 at Sea by HM Ship Acasta Int: 06 Jan 1813 Dis: 27 Jan 1813.
    Received from HM Ship Maidstone. Bostock Cartel for New York.

Stoel, Peter   Prisoner 2199. Rank: Seaman, from: President, U States Frigate.
    Cap: 15 Jan 1815 Not Recorded by Endymion Int: 30 Jan 1815 Dis: 28 Mar 1815.
    Received from Pomone. Mars Transport for U States.

Stokely, John   Prisoner 2826. Rank: Seaman, from: Limerick, Not Recorded.
    Cap: 15 Mar 1815 Not Recorded by Asia Int: 25 Mar 1815 Dis:
    From Depot at Jamaica. Received from Asia. (Date of discharge not recorded.)

Stone, James   Prisoner 1880. Rank: Seaman, from: Levant, Merchant Vessel.
    Cap: Not Recorded by Not Recorded Int: Dis: 28 Mar 1815.
    Clarendon Transport for U States. (Dates of capture and internment not recorded.)

Stone, Samuel   Prisoner 489. Rank: Seaman, from: Teazer, Privateer Schooner.
    Cap: 16 Dec 1812 at Sea by HM Ship St. Domingo Int: 21 Dec 1812 Dis: 27 Jan 1813.
    Received from HM Ship St. Domingo. Bostock Cartel for New York.

Stone, Zachariah   Prisoner 2718. Rank: Mate, from: American Gun Boat, Not Recorded.
    Cap: 06 Feb 1815 off Charleston by Tonnant Int: 02 Mar 1815 Dis:
    Received from Armede. (Date of discharge not recorded.)

Storey, Abel   Prisoner 2838. Rank: Seaman, from: Limerick, Not Recorded.
    Cap: 15 Mar 1815 Not Recorded by Asia Int: 25 Mar 1815 Dis:
    From Depot at Jamaica. Received from Asia. (Date of discharge not recorded.)

Storey, Peter   Prisoner 904. Rank: Seaman, from: Elizabeth, Merchant Brig.
    Cap: 26 Feb 1813 Chesapeake by HMS Marlborough Int: 23 Mar 1813 Dis: 24 Apr 1813.
    Received from HM Ship Laurustinus. Vessel Liberated By Order Commodore Evans.

Storme, Daniel   Prisoner 466. Rank: Seaman, from: Teazer, Privateer Schooner.
    Cap: 16 Dec 1812 at Sea by HM Ship St. Domingo Int: 21 Dec 1812 Dis: 27 Jan 1813.
    Received from HM Ship St. Domingo. Bostock Cartel for New York.

Stout, Scuder   Prisoner 63. Rank: Seaman, from: Mary, Merchant Brig.
    Cap: 08 Aug 1812 of Bermuda by Cuttle Int: 28 Aug 1812 Dis: 18 Sep 1812.
    Received from M Schooner Cuttle. Order of Commd Evans for England.

Stover, David   Prisoner 643. Rank: Seaman, from: Dolphin, Merchant Brig.
    Cap: 30 Dec 1812 at Sea by HM Ship Galus Int: 17 Jan 1813 Dis: 27 Jan 1813.
    Received from HM Ship Galus. Bostock Cartel for New York.

Stover, Samuel   Prisoner 2621. Rank: Seaman, from: Attempt, Merchant Vessel.
    Cap: 12 Jan 1815 Cape Hatterus by HMS Telegraph Int: 05 Feb 1815 Dis: 28 Mar 1815.
    Received from HMS Telegraph. Clarendon Transport for U States.

Stover, William   Prisoner 644. Rank: Seaman, from: Dolphin, Merchant Brig.
    Cap: 30 Dec 1812 at Sea by HM Ship Galus Int: 17 Jan 1813 Dis: 27 Jan 1813.
    Received from HM Ship Galus. Bostock Cartel for New York.

Stowe, John   Prisoner 1827. Rank: Passenger, from: Not Recorded, Not Recorded.
    Cap: Not Recorded by Not Recorded Int: 14 Jun 1814 Dis: 15 Jun 1814.
    From St. Bartholomew in the Swedish Schooner Oscar. on Parole per Order Com in Chief to America.
    (Date of capture not recorded.)

Stringer, Isaac   Prisoner 1269. Rank: Seaman, from: United States, Merchant Vessel.
    Cap: 14 Nov 1813 Long Island by HM Brig Borer Int: 19 Dec 1813 Dis: 15 Apr 1814.
    Received from HMS Acasta. Diana for Halifax.

American Prisoners of War Held at Bermuda During the War of 1812

Stringer, Thomas   Prisoner 1239. Rank: Not Recorded, from: Ambition, Merchant Vessel.
    Cap: 21 Sep 1813 Cape Hatterus by Acteon Int: 16 Nov 1813 Dis: 15 Apr 1814.
    Received from HMS Sceptre. Diana Transport for Halifax.

Stringer, William   Prisoner 1216. Rank: Seaman, from: HM Sloop Sappho, Not Recorded.
    Cap: 04 Mar 1813 Not Recorded by Not Recorded Int: 06 Nov 1813 Dis: 23 Apr 1814.
    Received from HMS Ruby. Discharged from the Hospital to the Butwork for Halifax.

Strong, Ceres   Prisoner 1774. Rank: Seaman, from: Yankelass, Privateer.
    Cap: 01 May 1814 Latt 40-4N, Long 38-0W by Severn & Surprise Int: 07 Jun 1814 Dis: 03 Dec 1814.
    Received from Surprise. Ardent SL as British Subject.

Strong, Robert   Prisoner 1807. Rank: Passenger, from: Not Recorded, Not Recorded.
    Cap: Not Recorded by Not Recorded Int: 14 Jun 1814 Dis: 15 Jun 1814.
    From St. Bartholomew in the Swedish Schooner Oscar. on Parole per Order Com in Chief to America.
    (Date of capture not recorded.)

Strumbell, Abraham   Prisoner 2504. Rank: Seaman, from: President, U States Frigate.
    Cap: 15 Jan 1815 Not Recorded by Endymion Int: 04 Feb 1815 Dis: 28 Mar 1815.
    Received from Endymion. Clarenden Transport for U States.

Strut, James   Prisoner 2620. Rank: Seaman, from: Limerick, Not Recorded.
    Cap: 15 Mar 1815 Not Recorded by Asia Int: 25 Mar 1815 Dis:
    From Depot at Jamaica. Received from Asia. (Date of discharge not recorded.)

Studson, D   Prisoner 2763. Rank: Seaman, from: Maria, Not Recorded.
    Cap: 16 Feb 1815 St Augustine by Severn Int: 03 Mar 1815 Dis: 28 Mar 1815.
    Received from Hebrus. Clarendon Transport for U States.

Studson, Daniel   Prisoner 540. Rank: Seaman, from: Herald, Letter of Marque Brig.
    Cap: 25 Dec 1812 at Sea by HM Ship Maidstone Int: 05 Jan 1813 Dis: 27 Jan 1813.
    Received from HM Ship Maidstone. Bostock Cartel for New York.

Stuges, John   Prisoner 701. Rank: Seaman, from: High Flyer, Privateer.
    Cap: 09 Jan 1813 at Sea by HMS Acasta Int: 21 Jan 1813 Dis: 27 Jan 1813.
    Received from HMS Acasta. Bostock Cartel for New York.

Sturtevant, Nehemiah   Prisoner 1644. Rank: Seaman, from: Pheobe, Merchant Vessel.
    Cap: 13 Dec 1813 Chesapeake by Active Int: 28 Feb 1814 Dis: 23 Apr 1814.
    Received from Active. HMS Bulwark for Halifax.

Styles, John   Prisoner 567. Rank: Seaman, from: Fly, Merchant.
    Cap: 06 Dec 1812 at Sea by HM Ship Maidstone Int: 06 Jan 1813 Dis: 27 Jan 1813.
    Received from HM Ship Maidstone. Bostock Cartel for New York.

Sulivan, James   Prisoner 1112. Rank: Captains Clerk, from: Dolphin, Privateer.
    Cap: 03 Apr 1813 at Sea by By the Boats of the Squadron Int: 07 Jun 1813 Dis: 24 Jun 1813.
    Received from Ship Dragon. Magnet Cartel for New York.

Sullingell, William F   Prisoner 492. Rank: Seaman, from: Teazer, Privateer Schooner.
    Cap: 16 Dec 1812 at Sea by HM Ship St. Domingo Int: 21 Dec 1812 Dis: 27 Jan 1813.
    Received from HM Ship St. Domingo. Bostock Cartel for New York.

Sullivan, Daniel   Prisoner 2487. Rank: Seaman, from: President, U States Frigate.
    Cap: 15 Jan 1815 Not Recorded by Endymion Int: 04 Feb 1815 Dis: 28 Mar 1815.
    Received from Endymion. Clarenden Transport for U States.

Sullivan, John   Prisoner 1510. Rank: Midshipman, from: Not Recorded, Not Recorded.
    Cap: Not Recorded by Belvidera Int: 19 Jan 1814 Dis: 15 Apr 1814.
    Received from Bermuda Hospital. Rammilles for Halifax. (Date of capture not recorded.)

Sullivan, Richard   Prisoner 1379. Rank: Seaman, from: Policy, Merchant Vessel.
    Cap: 04 Dec 1813 Not Recorded by Loire Int: 20 Dec 1813 Dis: 15 Apr 1814.
    Recaptured. Received from San Domingo. Diana Transport for Halifax.

Sullivan, Samuel   Prisoner 1587. Rank: Seaman, from: Bordeaux Packet, Letter of Marque.
    Cap: 28 Jan 1814 off Cape Henry by Nieman Int: 12 Feb 1814 Dis: 15 Apr 1814.
    Received from Nieman. Diana Transport for Halifax.

Sumers, Langford   Prisoner 2494. Rank: Marine, from: President, U States Frigate.
    Cap: 15 Jan 1815 Not Recorded by Endymion Int: 04 Feb 1815 Dis: 28 Mar 1815.
    Received from Endymion. Clarenden Transport for U States.

Summers, Anthony   Prisoner 2304. Rank: Seaman, from: President, U States Frigate.
    Cap: 15 Jan 1815 Not Recorded by Endymion Int: 04 Feb 1815 Dis: 28 Mar 1815.
    Received from Endymion. Mars Transport for U States.

Sumner, Charles   Prisoner 2757. Rank: Seaman, from: Mayflower, Not Recorded.
    Cap: 20 Jan 1815 St Augustine by Severn Int: 03 Mar 1815 Dis: 28 Mar 1815.
    Received from Hebrus. Clarendon Transport for U States.

American Prisoners of War Held at Bermuda During the War of 1812

Sungrain, Oliver   Prisoner 1029. Rank: Seaman, from: Dart, Merchant Schooner.
    Cap: 17 Mar 1813 off the Chesapeake by HMS Statira Int: 06 Apr 1813 Dis: 05 May 1813.
    Received from HMS Junon. Prize Ship St. Michael.

Surgor, John F   Prisoner 1003. Rank: Seaman, from: Jefferson, Merchant.
    Cap: 18 Mar 1813 at Sea by HM Sloop Atalante Int: 06 Apr 1813 Dis: 24 Jun 1813.
    Received from HMS Junon. Magnet Cartel for New York.

Sutherland, John   Prisoner 1584. Rank: Seaman, from: Bordeaux Packet, Letter of Marque.
    Cap: 28 Jan 1814 off Cape Henry by Nieman Int: 12 Feb 1814 Dis: 15 Apr 1814.
    Received from Nieman. Diana Transport for Halifax.

Sutlet, William   Prisoner 2112. Rank: Passenger, from: Fox, Merchant Vessel.
    Cap: 06 Sep 1814 off Amelia by Lacedaemonian Int: 19 Jan 1815 Dis: 21 Feb 1815.
    Received from HMS Peruvian. United States.

Sutton, Nathan   Prisoner 1457. Rank: Seaman, from: Vixen, Man of War.
    Cap: 25 Dec 1813 Lat 38.0 by Belvidera Int: 05 Jan 1814 Dis: 15 Apr 1814.
    U States Schooner. Received from HMS Belvidera. Diana Transport for Halifax.

Swain, John   Prisoner 1400. Rank: Seaman, from: John & James, Merchant Vessel.
    Cap: 07 Dec 1813 Lat 37 by Loire Int: 21 Dec 1813 Dis: 15 Apr 1814.
    Received from Romulus. Diana Transport for Halifax.

Swain, Joseph   Prisoner 716. Rank: Seaman, from: High Flyer, Privateer.
    Cap: 09 Jan 1813 at Sea by HM Ship Acasta Int: 21 Jan 1813 Dis: 27 Jan 1813.
    Received from HMS Acasta. Bostock Cartel for New York.

Swaine, William   Prisoner 1605. Rank: Seaman, from: Monticello, Merchant Vessel.
    Cap: 09 Dec 1813 Block Island by Albion Int: 14 Feb 1814 Dis: 23 Apr 1814.
    Received from Sceptre. HMS Bulwark for Halifax.

Swanson, Andrew   Prisoner 646. Rank: Seaman, from: Eliza, Merchant Ship.
    Cap: 24 Nov 1812 at Sea by HM Ship Marlborough Int: 18 Jan 1813 Dis: 27 Jan 1813.
    Received from HM Ship Marlborough. Bostock Cartel for New York. Ship Eliza (2).

Swanson, Jacob   Prisoner 1819. Rank: Passenger, from: Not Recorded, Not Recorded.
    Cap: Not Recorded by Not Recorded Int: 14 Jun 1814 Dis: 15 Jun 1814.
    From St. Bartholomew in the Swedish Schooner Oscar. on Parole per Order Com in Chief to America. (Date of capture not recorded.)

Swanson, Peter   Prisoner 1940. Rank: Seaman, from: Pike, Privateer.
    Cap: 25 Aug 1814 off Savannah by Primrose Int: 09 Sep 1814 Dis: 05 Nov 1814.
    Received from Lacedaemonian. Order Adl Cockburn.

Swarts, Joshua   Prisoner 404. Rank: Seaman, from: Snapper, Privateer Schooner.
    Cap: 16 Nov 1812 at Sea by HM Ship Galus Int: 22 Nov 1812 Dis: 27 Jan 1813.
    Received from HM Ship Galus. Bostock Cartel for New York.

Swatt, Christian   Prisoner 1645. Rank: Seaman, from: George, Merchant Vessel.
    Cap: 22 Dec 1813 Chesapeake by Active Int: 28 Feb 1814 Dis: 06 Apr 1814.
    Received from Active. being a Prussian.

Sweedy, P   Prisoner 1608. Rank: Seaman, from: Monticello, Merchant Vessel.
    Cap: 09 Dec 1813 Block Island by Albion Int: 14 Feb 1814 Dis: 23 Apr 1814.
    Received from Sceptre. HMS Bulwark for Halifax.

Sweet, Moses   Prisoner 106. Rank: Seaman, from: Gossepuim, detained American.
    Cap: 02 Sep 1812 Bermuda by Not Recorded Int: 02 Sep 1812 Dis: 18 Sep 1812.
    Received from HMS Ruby. detained per order of the President. Order of Commd Evans for England.

Sweet, Stephen   Prisoner 1849. Rank: Seaman, from: Little Catherine, Merchant Vessel.
    Cap: Not Recorded by Not Recorded Int: Dis: 20 Mar 1815.
    Recaptured. Merchant Vessel. (Dates of capture and internment not recorded.)

Sweney, Hugh   Prisoner 171. Rank: Masters Mate, from: Wasp, Sloop of War.
    Cap: 18 Oct 1812 at Sea by HMS Poictiers Int: 26 Oct 1812 Dis: 05 Nov 1812.
    Received from HM Ship Poictiers. on Parole Brig Diamond to new London America.

Swensen, Hans   Prisoner 1534. Rank: Seaman, from: Romp, Merchant Vessel.
    Cap: 02 Jan 1814 Latt 22.0 by Prometheus Int: 23 Jan 1814 Dis: 06 Apr 1814.
    Received from Prometheus. being a Norwegian.

Swiney, Alexander   Prisoner 2297. Rank: Seaman, from: President, U States Frigate.
    Cap: 15 Jan 1815 Not Recorded by Endymion Int: 04 Feb 1815 Dis: 28 Mar 1815.
    Received from Endymion. Mars Transport for U States.

Swinney, Benjamin   Prisoner 1312. Rank: Seaman, from: Rolla, Privateer.
    Cap: 10 Dec 1813 Block Island by Loire Int: 20 Dec 1813 Dis: 15 Apr 1814.
    Received from San Domingo. HMS Rammillies for Halifax.

American Prisoners of War Held at Bermuda During the War of 1812

Taber, Humphrey   Prisoner 119. Rank: Master, from: William of Baltimore, Merchant.
    Cap: 31 Aug 1812 Lat 37 by HM Ship Recruit Int: 14 Sep 1812 Dis: 08 Feb 1813.
    Received from Recruit. Permitted to remain in the Colony per order of the Governor.

Taber, Isaac   Prisoner 156. Rank: Seaman, from: Ranger, Merchant Ship.
    Cap: 02 Oct 1812 Lat 32, Long 65 W by HM Ship Goree Int: 13 Oct 1812 Dis: 24 Oct 1812.
    Received from HMS Goree. Brig Diamond on Parole to new London United States of America.

Taber, Rubin   Prisoner 1797. Rank: Steward, from: Yankelass, Privateer.
    Cap: 01 May 1814 Latt 40-4N, Long 38-0W by Severn & Surprise Int: 07 Jun 1814 Dis: 28 Mar 1815.
    Received from Surprise. Clarendon Transport for U States.

Taber, William M   Prisoner 2040. Rank: Boy, from: Live, Merchant Sloop.
    Cap: 26 Oct 1814 off Delaware by St. Laurence Int: 21 Nov 1814 Dis: 28 Mar 1815.
    Received from M Schooner Whiting. Clarendon Transport for U States.

Tabor, Daniel   Prisoner 1977. Rank: Seaman, from: Antelope, Merchant Vessel.
    Cap: 21 Aug 1814 Western Island by Whiting Int: 17 Sep 1814 Dis: 20 Mar 1815.
    Recaptured. Received from Goree. Merchant Vessel.

Talman, Joseph   Prisoner 1579. Rank: Seaman, from: Bordeaux Packet, Letter of Marque.
    Cap: 28 Jan 1814 off Cape Henry by Nieman Int: 12 Feb 1814 Dis: 15 Apr 1814.
    Received from Nieman. Diana Transport for Halifax.

Talpee, John   Prisoner 642. Rank: Seaman, from: Dolphin, Merchant Brig.
    Cap: 30 Dec 1812 at Sea by HM Ship Galus Int: 17 Jan 1813 Dis: 27 Jan 1813.
    Received from HM Ship Galus. Bostock Cartel for New York.

Talton, Thomas P   Prisoner 147. Rank: Seaman, from: Hero, Merchant Brig.
    Cap: 25 Sep 1812 Lat 42, Long 63 W by HMS Tartarus Int: 13 Oct 1812 Dis: 24 Oct 1812.
    Received from HMS Tartarus. Brig Diamond on Parole to new London United States of America.

Tamley, John   Prisoner 2685. Rank: Seaman, from: Superb, Merchant Vessel.
    Cap: 27 Jan 1815 off Delaware by Sophie Int: 17 Feb 1815 Dis:
    from a Spanish Brig recaptured. Received from Childers. (Date of discharge not recorded.)

Taros, Vecentia   Prisoner 2020. Rank: Seaman, from: Swiftsure, Merchant Vessel.
    Cap: 26 Oct 1814 off Halifax by Armide Int: 07 Nov 1814 Dis: 10 Nov 1814.
    Recaptured. Received from HMS Armide. Joseph MV order Cockburne.

Taylor, Charles   Prisoner 746. Rank: Seaman, from: Savannah Packet, Merchant Brig.
    Cap: 05 Jan 1813 at Sea by HM Ship Poictiers Int: 21 Jan 1813 Dis: 27 Jan 1813.
    Received from HMS Poictiers. Bostock Cartel for New York.

Taylor, Charles   Prisoner 2670. Rank: Seaman, from: Gunboat 160, U States Man of War.
    Cap: 06 Sep 1814 off New York by Lacedaemonian Int: 14 Feb 1815 Dis: 28 Mar 1815.
    Gun Vessel. Received from Childers. Clarendon Transport for U States.

Taylor, Dugomier   Prisoner 929. Rank: Midshipman, from: Ulissus, Merchant Schooner.
    Cap: 03 Mar 1813 Chesapeake by HMS Narcissus Int: 23 Mar 1813 Dis: 13 Jun 1813.
    Received from Laurustinus. Perseverance Cartel for the United States per Order Adml Sir J B Warren.

Taylor, James D   Prisoner 2042. Rank: Seaman, from: Rising Sun, Merchant Vessel.
    Cap: 20 Nov 1814 off Bermuda by Pandora Int: 28 Nov 1814 Dis:
    Recaptured. Received from HMS Goree. (Date of discharge not recorded.)

Taylor, James   Prisoner 2071. Rank: Seaman, from: Industry, Merchant Vessel.
    Cap: 01 Dec 1814 off Cape Henry by HMS Niemen Int: 15 Dec 1814 Dis: 28 Mar 1815.
    Recaptured. Belong to Carolina Privateer. Received from HMS Niemen.
    Clarendon Transport for U States.

Taylor, James   Prisoner 2190. Rank: Seaman, from: President, U States Frigate.
    Cap: 15 Jan 1815 Not Recorded by HMS Endymion Int: 30 Jan 1815 Dis: 28 Mar 1815.
    Received from Pomone. Mars Transport for U States.

Taylor, John   Prisoner 1937. Rank: Seaman, from: Pike, Privateer.
    Cap: 25 Aug 1814 off Savannah by Primrose Int: 09 Sep 1814 Dis: 28 Mar 1815.
    Received from Lacedaemonian. Clarendon Transport for U States.

Taylor, Thomas   Prisoner 1023. Rank: 1 Mate, from: Dart, Merchant Schooner.
    Cap: 17 Mar 1813 off the Chesapeake by HMS Statira Int: 06 Apr 1813 Dis: 24 Jun 1813.
    Received from HMS Junon. Magnet Cartel for New York.

Teaser, James   Prisoner 1471. Rank: Master, from: Rapid, Letter of Marque Schooner.
    Cap: 16 Dec 1813 off Sandy Rock by Plantagenet Int: 06 Jan 1814 Dis: 15 Apr 1814.
    Received from HM Ship Plantagenet. Rammilles for Halifax.

Temple, Joseph   Prisoner 334. Rank: Seaman, from: Snapper, Privateer Schooner.
    Cap: 16 Nov 1812 at Sea by HMS Galus Int: 22 Nov 1812 Dis: 27 Jan 1813.
    Received from HM Ship Galus. Bostock Cartel for New York.

American Prisoners of War Held at Bermuda During the War of 1812

Templing, Henry   Prisoner 395. Rank: Seaman, from: Snapper, Privateer Schooner.
    Cap: 16 Nov 1812 at Sea by HM Ship Galus Int: 22 Nov 1812 Dis: 27 Jan 1813.
    Received from HM Ship Galus. Bostock Cartel for New York.

Ten Eck, Abram S   Prisoner 174. Rank: Midshipman, from: Wasp, Sloop of War.
    Cap: 18 Oct 1812 at Sea by HMS Poictiers Int: 26 Oct 1812 Dis: 05 Nov 1812.
    Received from HM Ship Poictiers. on Parole Brig Diamond to new London America.

Tennis, Benjamin   Prisoner 2466. Rank: Captains Crew, from: President, U States Frigate.
    Cap: 15 Jan 1815 Not Recorded by Endymion Int: 04 Feb 1815 Dis: 28 Mar 1815.
    Received from Endymion. Clarenden Transport for U States.

Terron, James   Prisoner 2544. Rank: Seaman, from: Packet, Merchant Vessel.
    Cap: 13 Dec 1814 off N York by Tenedos Int: 04 Feb 1815 Dis: 28 Mar 1815.
    Received from HMS Endymion. Clarendon Transport for U States.

Terry, Thomas C   Prisoner 1835. Rank: Passenger, from: Hibernia, Merchant Sloop.
    Cap: 30 May 1814 between Cape Roman and Cape Fear by Doteral & Morgiana Int: 30 Jun 1814 Dis:
    26 Feb 1815. Received from HMS Doterel. Paroled to the U States having served 6 months as
    Carpenter's Mate order of Adl Sir Alex Cockburn.

Thaitis, John   Prisoner 1557. Rank: Seaman, from: Bordeaux Packet, Letter of Marque.
    Cap: 28 Jan 1814 off Cape Henry by Nieman Int: 12 Feb 1814 Dis: 15 Apr 1814.
    Received from Nieman. Diana Transport for Halifax.

Thatcher, John   Prisoner 846. Rank: Mate, from: Polly Maria, Merchant.
    Cap: 03 Feb 1813 at Sea by HMS Sophia Int: 17 Mar 1813 Dis: 24 Jun 1813.
    Received from HMS Sophia. Magnet Cartel for New York.

Thatcher, Stephen   Prisoner 418. Rank: Seaman, from: Isabella, Merchant Brig.
    Cap: 15 Nov 1812 at Sea by HM Sloop Childers Int: 24 Nov 1812 Dis: 27 Jan 1813.
    Received from HM Ship Childers. Bostock Cartel for New York.

Thayre, Elijah   Prisoner 2182. Rank: Seaman, from: President, U States Frigate.
    Cap: 15 Jan 1815 Not Recorded by HMS Endymion Int: 30 Jan 1815 Dis: 28 Mar 1815.
    Received from Pomone. Mars Transport for U States.

Theafe, William   Prisoner 886. Rank: Seaman, from: Hannah, Merchant Schooner.
    Cap: 24 Feb 1813 Chesapeake by Marlborough Int: 23 Mar 1813 Dis: 21 May 1813.
    Received from Laurustinus. Per Order Commodore Evans the Vessel being Liberated.

Theodore, Joseph   Prisoner 2404. Rank: Seaman, from: President, U States Frigate.
    Cap: 15 Jan 1815 Not Recorded by HM Ship Endymion Int: 04 Feb 1815 Dis: 28 Mar 1815.
    Received from Endymion. Mars Transport for U States.

Theyer, J H   Prisoner 1837. Rank: Passenger, from: Hibernia, Merchant Sloop.
    Cap: 30 May 1814 between Cape Roman and Cape Fear by Doteral & Morgiana Int: 30 Jun 1814 Dis:
    17 Mar 1815. Received from HMS Doterel. Merchant Vessel.

Thicket, Elliot   Prisoner 1053. Rank: Seaman, from: Massoil, Merchant.
    Cap: 18 Mar 1813 Chesapeake by HMS Dragon Int: 06 Apr 1813 Dis: 24 Jun 1813.
    Received from HMS Junon. Magnet Cartel for New York.

Thomas, Corbet   Prisoner 1861. Rank: Seaman, from: Sally, Merchant Vessel.
    Cap: Not Recorded by Not Recorded Int: Dis: 24 Mar 1815.
    Merchant Vessel. (Dates of capture and internment not recorded.)

Thomas, David   Prisoner 2202. Rank: Seaman, from: President, U States Frigate.
    Cap: 15 Jan 1815 Not Recorded by Endymion Int: 30 Jan 1815 Dis: 28 Mar 1815.
    Received from Pomone. Mars Transport for U States.

Thomas, Francis   Prisoner 1084. Rank: Seaman, from: Maria Louisa, Merchant.
    Cap: 10 Apr 1813 off Sandy Hook by HMS Acasta Int: 03 May 1813 Dis: 24 Jun 1813.
    Received from HMS Acasta. Magnet Cartel for New York.

Thomas, Isaac   Prisoner 488. Rank: Seaman, from: Teazer, Privateer Schooner.
    Cap: 16 Dec 1812 at Sea by HM Ship St. Domingo Int: 21 Dec 1812 Dis: 27 Jan 1813.
    Received from HM Ship St. Domingo. Bostock Cartel for New York.

Thomas, James   Prisoner 1787. Rank: Prize Master, from: Yankelass, Privateer.
    Cap: 01 May 1814 Latt 40-4N, Long 38-0W by Severn & Surprise Int: 07 Jun 1814 Dis:
    Received from Surprise. (Date of discharge not recorded.)

Thomas, John   Prisoner 677. Rank: Seaman, from: High Flyer, Privateer.
    Cap: 09 Jan 1813 at Sea by HM Ship Acasta Int: 21 Jan 1813 Dis: 27 Jan 1813.
    Received from HMS Acasta. Bostock Cartel for New York.

Thomas, John   Prisoner 1177. Rank: Seaman, from: Calmer, Merchant.
    Cap: 15 Jun 1813 at Sea by HM Ship Marlborough Int: 15 Aug 1813 Dis: 21 Aug 1813.
    Received from HM Ship Woolwich. Per Order Commodore Evans.

American Prisoners of War Held at Bermuda During the War of 1812

Thomas, John   Prisoner 1563. Rank: Seaman, from: Bordeaux Packet, Letter of Marque.
    Cap: 28 Jan 1814 off Cape Henry by Nieman Int: 12 Feb 1814 Dis: 15 Apr 1814.
    Received from Nieman. Diana Transport for Halifax.

Thomas, Moses   Prisoner 2836. Rank: Seaman, from: Limerick, Not Recorded.
    Cap: 15 Mar 1815 Not Recorded by Asia Int: 25 Mar 1815 Dis:
    From Depot at Jamaica. Received from Asia. (Date of discharge not recorded.)

Thomas, William   Prisoner 1362. Rank: Seaman, from: Rolla, Privateer.
    Cap: 10 Dec 1813 Block Island by Loire Int: 20 Dec 1813 Dis: 15 Apr 1814.
    Received from San Domingo. HMS Rammillies for Halifax.

Thompson, Benjamin   Prisoner 1820. Rank: Passenger, from: Not Recorded, Not Recorded.
    Cap: Not Recorded by Not Recorded Int: 14 Jun 1814 Dis: 15 Jun 1814.
    From St. Bartholomew in the Swedish Schooner Oscar. on Parole per Order Com in Chief to America.
    (Date of capture not recorded.)

Thompson, Charles   Prisoner 2086. Rank: Seaman, from: Erin, Merchant Vessel.
    Cap: 20 Dec 1814 off Charleston by Portia Int: 06 Jan 1815 Dis: 24 Mar 1815.
    Received from HMS Portia. Merchant Vessel.

Thompson, George   Prisoner 2405. Rank: Seaman, from: President, U States Frigate.
    Cap: 15 Jan 1815 Not Recorded by HM Ship Endymion Int: 04 Feb 1815 Dis: 28 Mar 1815.
    Received from Endymion. Mars Transport for U States.

Thompson, James   Prisoner 1649. Rank: Seaman, from: Michael & Eliza, Merchant Vessel.
    Cap: 22 Dec 1813 Chesapeake by Dragon Int: 28 Feb 1814 Dis: 23 Apr 1814.
    Received from Active. HMS Bulwark for Halifax.

Thompson, James   Prisoner 1685. Rank: Seaman, from: Michael & Eliza, Merchant Vessel.
    Cap: 22 Dec 1813 Chesapeake by Dragon Int: 06 May 1814 Dis: 20 Mar 1815.
    Received from Hospital. Merchant Vessel.

Thompson, James   Prisoner 1995. Rank: Seaman, from: Fairplay, Merchant Vessel.
    Cap: 22 Oct 1814 Lat 31.58 by Dothrel Int: 26 Oct 1814 Escaped: 07 Feb 1815.
    Recaptured. Received from Dothrel. Run.

Thompson, James   Prisoner 2098. Rank: Seaman, from: Frolic, Man of War.
    Cap: 18 Apr 1814 off Havanna by Orpheus Int: 19 Jan 1815 Dis: 28 Mar 1815.
    US Sloop of War. Received from HMS Peruvian. Clarendon Transport for U States.

Thompson, James   Prisoner 2196. Rank: Seaman, from: President, U States Frigate.
    Cap: 15 Jan 1815 Not Recorded by Endymion Int: 30 Jan 1815 Dis: 28 Mar 1815.
    Received from Pomone. Mars Transport for U States.

Thompson, Jesse   Prisoner 443. Rank: Supercargo, from: Adventure, Merchant Brig.
    Cap: 15 Dec 1812 off Bermuda by HM Sloop Childers Int: 17 Dec 1812 Dis: 08 Feb 1813.
    Received from HM Sloop Childers. Permitted to Remain in the Colony by Order of the Governor.

Thompson, John   Prisoner 804. Rank: Seaman, from: Sheppard, Merchant Schooner.
    Cap: 04 Jan 1813 at Sea by Sheppard Int: 16 Feb 1813 Dis: 24 Jun 1813.
    Received from Narcissus. Magnet Cartel for New York.

Thompson, John   Prisoner 2379. Rank: Seaman, from: President, U States Frigate.
    Cap: 15 Jan 1815 Not Recorded by HMS Endymion Int: 04 Feb 1815 Dis: 28 Mar 1815.
    Received from Endymion. Mars Transport for U States.

Thompson, Simon   Prisoner 38. Rank: Seaman, from: Laura, Merchant Sloop.
    Cap: 24 Jul 1812 of Bermuda by Cuttle Int: 28 Aug 1812 Dis: 18 Sep 1812.
    Received from HM Schooner Cuttle. Order of Commd Evans for England.

Thompson, William   Prisoner 1087. Rank: Seaman, from: Langdon Cheves, Merchant.
    Cap: 12 May 1813 at Sea by HM Sloop Atalante Int: 25 May 1813 Dis: 24 Jun 1813.
    Received from HMS Atalante. Magnet Cartel for New York.

Thompson, William   Prisoner 2307. Rank: Seaman, from: President, U States Frigate.
    Cap: 15 Jan 1815 Not Recorded by Endymion Int: 04 Feb 1815 Dis: 28 Mar 1815.
    Received from Endymion. Mars Transport for U States.

Thorp, George   Prisoner 1719. Rank: Passenger, from: Revinue, Merchant Vessel.
    Cap: 15 May 1814 at Sea by Lacedaemonian Int: 26 May 1814 Dis: 21 Feb 1815.
    Received from Lacedaemonian. U States.

Thorpe, William   Prisoner 2176. Rank: Seaman, from: President, U States Frigate.
    Cap: 15 Jan 1815 Not Recorded by HMS Endymion Int: 30 Jan 1815 Dis: 28 Mar 1815.
    Received from Pomone. Mars Transport for U States.

Thoxter, Leavitt   Prisoner 571. Rank: 2 Mate, from: Peakin, Merchant Ship.
    Cap: 17 Dec 1812 at Sea by HM Ship Acasta Int: 06 Jan 1813 Dis: 27 Jan 1813.
    Received from HM Ship Maidstone. Bostock Cartel for New York.

American Prisoners of War Held at Bermuda During the War of 1812

Throughgood, William   Prisoner 895. Rank: Seaman, from: Hannah, Merchant Schooner.
    Cap: 24 Feb 1813 Chesapeake by HMS Marlborough Int: 23 Mar 1813 Dis: 24 Jun 1813.
    Received from HM Ship Laurustinus. Magnet Cartel for New York.

Tibbets, James   Prisoner 317. Rank: Master, from: James, Merchant Ship.
    Cap: 03 Nov 1812 at Sea by HM Ship Tartarus Int: 17 Nov 1812 Dis: 12 Dec 1812.
    Received from HM Ship Tartarus. To United States America.

Tickle, John   Prisoner 2204. Rank: Seaman, from: President, U States Frigate.
    Cap: 15 Jan 1815 Not Recorded by Endymion Int: 30 Jan 1815 Dis: 28 Mar 1815.
    Received from Pomone. Mars Transport for U States.

Tilbots, Benjamin   Prisoner 1800. Rank: Seaman, from: Yankelass, Privateer.
    Cap: 01 May 1814 L 40-4P, Long 30-11W by Severn & Surprise Int: 07 Jun 1814 Dis: 18 Mar 1815.
    Yankee lass. Received from Surprise. Merchant Vessel.

Tiler, Christian   Prisoner 1769. Rank: Seaman, from: Yankelass, Privateer.
    Cap: 01 May 1814 L 40-4N, Long 38-0W by Severn & Surprise Int: 07 Jun 1814 Dis: 28 Mar 1815.
    Received from Surprise. Mars Transport for U States.

Timberlake, J B   Prisoner 2161. Rank: Purser, from: President, U States Frigate.
    Cap: 15 Jan 1815 Not Recorded by Endymion Int: 30 Jan 1815 Dis: 28 Mar 1815.
    Received from President. Mars Transport for U States.

Tinney, Nathaniel   Prisoner 2601. Rank: Passenger, from: John, Merchant Vessel.
    Cap: 28 Dec 1814 off New York by HMS Pomone Int: 05 Feb 1815 Dis: 17 Mar 1815.
    Received from HMS Forth. Merchant Vessel.

Tipereal, Andrew   Prisoner 2034. Rank: Seaman, from: Not Recorded, Not Recorded.
    Cap: 01 Oct 1814 Not Recorded by Ganymede Int: 20 Nov 1814 Dis: 25 Mar 1815.
    Received from Ganymede. gave himself up as a American Subject. Merchant Vessel.

Tisdale, Sterling   Prisoner 2030. Rank: Seaman, from: Innocentia, Merchant Vessel.
    Cap: 15 Nov 1813 off New Providence by Ringdove Int: 11 Nov 1814 Dis: 17 Mar 1815.
    Received from HMS Wolverine. Merchant Vessel.

Toddy, William   Prisoner 1597. Rank: Seaman, from: Dispatch, Merchant Vessel.
    Cap: 26 Oct 1813 Block Island by Narcissus Int: 14 Feb 1814 Dis: 23 Apr 1814.
    Received from Sceptre. HMS Bulwark for Halifax.

Tolman, Artemus   Prisoner 2425. Rank: Seaman, from: President, U States Frigate.
    Cap: 15 Jan 1815 Not Recorded by HM Ship Endymion Int: 04 Feb 1815 Dis: 28 Mar 1815.
    Received from Endymion. Mars Transport for U States.

Tomlin, Samuel   Prisoner 1189. Rank: Seaman, from: Elizabeth, Merchant.
    Cap: 15 Jun 1813 at Sea by HM Ship Marlborough Int: 18 Aug 1813 Dis: 03 Oct 1813.
    Received from HM Ship Woolwich. Caledonian per Order of Commodore Evans she being Liberated.

Tompkins, James   Prisoner 345. Rank: Seaman, from: Snapper, Privateer Schooner.
    Cap: 16 Nov 1812 at Sea by HMS Galus Int: 22 Nov 1812 Dis: 27 Jan 1813.
    Received from HM Ship Galus. Bostock Cartel for New York.

Tone, William P   Prisoner 1475. Rank: Passenger, from: Republican, Merchant Schooner.
    Cap: 06 Dec 1813 Cape Charles by Dragon Int: 06 Jan 1814 Dis: 15 Apr 1814.
    Received from HM Ship Plantagenet. Rammilles for Halifax.

Toney, E   Prisoner 2810. Rank: Seaman, from: Limerick, Not Recorded.
    Cap: 04 Mar 1815 Not Recorded by Asia Int: 25 Mar 1815 Dis:
    From Depot at Jamaica. Received from Asia. (Date of discharge not recorded.)

Tooling, Francoi   Prisoner 1985. Rank: Seaman, from: Eclipse, Merchant Vessel.
    Cap: 29 Sep 1814 Bermuda by Copark Int: 05 Oct 1814 Dis: 07 Nov 1814.
    Recaptured. Received from Goree. Diadem for a Passage to England.

Toppin, John P   Prisoner 860. Rank: Master, from: Ann, Merchant.
    Cap: 10 Mar 1813 Chesapeake by HM Ship Laurustinus Int: 23 Mar 1813 Dis: 24 Jun 1813.
    Received from HM Ship Laurustinus. Magnet Cartel for New York.

Townsend, G   Prisoner 2840. Rank: Seaman, from: Limerick, Not Recorded.
    Cap: 15 Mar 1815 Not Recorded by Asia Int: 25 Mar 1815 Dis:
    From Depot at Jamaica. Received from Asia. (Date of discharge not recorded.)

Trader, William   Prisoner 2815. Rank: Seaman, from: Limerick, Not Recorded.
    Cap: 04 Mar 1815 Not Recorded by Asia Int: 25 Mar 1815 Dis:
    From Depot at Jamaica. Received from Asia. (Date of discharge not recorded.)

Traquave, John   Prisoner 920. Rank: Seaman, from: Albert, Merchant Schooner.
    Cap: 05 Mar 1813 Chesapeake by HM Ship Marlborough Int: 23 Mar 1813 Dis: 24 Mar 1813.
    Received from Laurustinus. St. Michael per Order Adl Sir J B Warren.

Travers, Jiffy   Prisoner 2219. Rank: Seaman, from: President, U States Frigate.
    Cap: 15 Jan 1815 Not Recorded by Endymion Int: 30 Jan 1815 Dis: 28 Mar 1815.
    Received from Pomone. Mars Transport for U States.

American Prisoners of War Held at Bermuda During the War of 1812

Traverse, Henry   Prisoner 695. Rank: Seaman, from: High Flyer, Privateer.
    Cap: 09 Jan 1813 at Sea by HMS Acasta Int: 21 Jan 1813 Dis: 27 Jan 1813.
    Received from HMS Acasta. Bostock Cartel for New York.

Trevett, Samuel R   Prisoner 2158. Rank: Surgeon, from: President, U States Frigate.
    Cap: 15 Jan 1815 Not Recorded by Endymion Int: 30 Jan 1815 Dis: 18 Mar 1815.
    Received from President. Merchant Vessel.

Tridwell, Alpheus   Prisoner 90. Rank: Seaman, from: Gossepuim, Merchant.
    Cap: 16 Aug 1812 of Bermuda by Goree Int: 28 Aug 1812 Dis: 18 Sep 1812.
    Received from HM Schooner Cuttle. Order of Commd Evans for England.

Trigony, Peter   Prisoner 1174. Rank: Seaman, from: Elizabeth, Merchant.
    Cap: 15 Jun 1813 at Sea by HM Ship Marlborough Int: 15 Aug 1813 Dis: 02 Sep 1813.
    Received from HM Ship Woolwich. Per order of Commodore Evans vessel being liberated.

Tronmonger, Edward   Prisoner 943. Rank: Passenger, from: Mary, Merchant Schooner.
    Cap: 10 Mar 1813 Chesapeake by HMS Maidstone Int: 23 Mar 1813 Dis: 24 Jun 1813.
    Received from Laurustinus. Magnet Cartel for New York.

Troop, C   Prisoner 2600. Rank: Passenger, from: Funchall, Merchant Vessel.
    Cap: 18 Dec 1814 off New York by HMS Pomone Int: 05 Feb 1815 Dis: 13 Feb 1815.
    Received from HMS Forth. Ruby gave himself up as a British Subject.

Trout, Nathaniel   Prisoner 1585. Rank: Seaman, from: Bordeaux Packet, Letter of Marque.
    Cap: 28 Jan 1814 off Cape Henry by Nieman Int: 12 Feb 1814 Dis: 15 Apr 1814.
    Received from Nieman. Diana Transport for Halifax.

Trowbridge, William   Prisoner 814. Rank: Seaman, from: Stockholm, Merchant Schooner.
    Cap: 18 Feb 1813 at Sea by HMS Statira Int: 01 Mar 1813 Dis: 14 Apr 1813.
    Received from HMS Statira. Per Order Commodore Evans Vessel Liberated.

Trueman, Job   Prisoner 2769. Rank: Seaman, from: Brant, Not Recorded.
    Cap: 05 Feb 1815 St Augustine by Severn Int: 03 Mar 1815 Dis: 28 Mar 1815.
    Received from Hebrus. Clarendon Transport for U States.

Truman, William   Prisoner 2788. Rank: Seaman, from: Limerick, Not Recorded.
    Cap: 07 Mar 1815 Lat 30, Long 75.38 W by Asia Int: 25 Mar 1815 Dis:
    Received from Asia. (Date of discharge not recorded.)

Tsdale, James   Prisoner 649. Rank: Seaman, from: Eliza, Merchant Ship.
    Cap: 24 Nov 1812 at Sea by HM Ship Marlborough Int: 18 Jan 1813 Dis: 27 Jan 1813.
    Received from HM Ship Marlborough. Bostock Cartel for New York. Ship Eliza (2).

Tubeter, James   Prisoner 491. Rank: Seaman, from: Teazer, Privateer Schooner.
    Cap: 16 Dec 1812 at Sea by HM Ship St. Domingo Int: 21 Dec 1812 Dis: 27 Jan 1813.
    Received from HM Ship St. Domingo. Bostock Cartel for New York.

Tuck, John   Prisoner 2543. Rank: Seaman, from: Packet, Merchant Vessel.
    Cap: 13 Dec 1814 off N York by Tenedos Int: 04 Feb 1815 Dis: 28 Mar 1815.
    Received from HMS Endymion. Clarendon Transport for U States. Or John Guck.

Tuck, Joseph   Prisoner 2500. Rank: Seaman, from: President, U States Frigate.
    Cap: 15 Jan 1815 Not Recorded by Endymion Int: 04 Feb 1815 Dis: 28 Mar 1815.
    Received from Endymion. Clarenden Transport for U States.

Tucker, D F   Prisoner 1876. Rank: Seaman, from: Levant, Merchant Vessel.
    Cap: Not Recorded by Not Recorded Int: Dis: 20 Mar 1815.
    Merchant Vessel. (Dates of capture and internment not recorded.)

Tucker, D A   Prisoner 2828. Rank: Seaman, from: Limerick, Not Recorded.
    Cap: 15 Mar 1815 Not Recorded by Asia Int: 25 Mar 1815 Dis:
    From Depot at Jamaica. Received from Asia. (Date of discharge not recorded.)

Tucker, James B   Prisoner 2099. Rank: Seaman, from: Frolic, Man of War.
    Cap: 18 Apr 1814 off Havanna by Orpheus Int: 19 Jan 1815 Dis: 28 Mar 1815.
    US Sloop of War. Received from HMS Peruvian. Clarendon Transport for U States.

Tucker, John   Prisoner 270. Rank: Seaman, from: Wasp, Sloop of War.
    Cap: 18 Oct 1812 at Sea by HM Ship Poictiers Int: 26 Oct 1812 Dis: 05 Nov 1812.
    Received from HM Ship Poictiers. Brig Diamond on Parole to new London United States of America.

Tuger, Henry   Prisoner 2794. Rank: Master, from: Limerick, Not Recorded.
    Cap: 04 Mar 1815 Not Recorded by Asia Int: 25 Mar 1815 Dis:
    From Depot at Jamaica. Received from Asia. (Date of discharge not recorded.)

Tunis, John   Prisoner 938. Rank: Seaman, from: Sidney, Letter of Marque Schooner.
    Cap: 09 Mar 1813 Chesapeake by Marlborough Int: 23 Mar 1813 Dis: 24 Jun 1813.
    Received from Laurustinus. Magnet Cartel for New York.

Tunisdale, William   Prisoner 2857. Rank: Seaman, from: Limerick, Not Recorded.
    Cap: 15 Mar 1815 Not Recorded by Asia Int: 25 Mar 1815 Dis:
    From Depot at Jamaica. Received from Asia. (Date of discharge not recorded.)

American Prisoners of War Held at Bermuda During the War of 1812

Tupp, John   Prisoner 1465. Rank: Seaman, from: Vixen, Man of War.
    Cap: 25 Dec 1813 Lat 38.0 by Belvidera Int: 05 Jan 1814 Dis: 15 Apr 1814.
    U States Schooner. Received from HMS Belvidera. Diana Transport for Halifax.

Turley, Enoch   Prisoner 2091. Rank: Master, from: Aurora, Merchant Vessel.
    Cap: 02 Oct 1814 near New Providence by Cockchafer Int: 19 Jan 1815 Dis: 18 Mar 1815.
    Received from HMS Peruvian. Merchant Vessel.

Turner, Daniel   Prisoner 758. Rank: Seaman, from: Hazard, Merchant Brig.
    Cap: 28 Dec 1812 Lat 37.35, Long 70.10 by HM Sloop Sylph Int: 26 Jan 1813 Dis: 14 Jun 1813.
    Received from Sloop Sylph. Permitted to return to the United States in the Perseverance.

Turner, Henry B   Prisoner 31. Rank: Seaman, from: Survanou, Merchant.
    Cap: 14 Jul 1812 at Bermuda by Recruit Int: 28 Aug 1812 Dis: 18 Sep 1812.
    Received from HM Schooner Cuttle. Order of Commd Evans for England.

Turner, Samuel   Prisoner 2536. Rank: Seaman, from: President, U States Frigate.
    Cap: 15 Jan 1815 Not Recorded by HM Ship Endymion Int: 04 Feb 1815 Dis: 28 Mar 1815.
    Received from HMS Endymion. Clarenden Transport for U States.

Turner, William   Prisoner 407. Rank: Seaman, from: Snapper, Privateer Schooner.
    Cap: 16 Nov 1812 at Sea by HM Ship Galus Int: 22 Nov 1812 Dis: 27 Jan 1813.
    Received from HM Ship Galus. Bostock Cartel for New York.

Turner, William   Prisoner 1718. Rank: Seaman, from: Revinue, Merchant Vessel.
    Cap: 15 May 1814 at Sea by Lacedaemonian Int: 26 May 1814 Dis: 16 Mar 1815.
    Received from Lacedaemonian. Merchant Service.

Turney, George   Prisoner 2244. Rank: Seaman, from: President, U States Frigate.
    Cap: 15 Jan 1815 Not Recorded by Endymion Int: 30 Jan 1815 Dis: 28 Mar 1815.
    Received from Pomone. Mars Transport for U States.

Tutton, Joseph   Prisoner 2403. Rank: Seaman, from: President, U States Frigate.
    Cap: 15 Jan 1815 Not Recorded by HM Ship Endymion Int: 04 Feb 1815 Dis: 28 Mar 1815.
    Received from Endymion. Mars Transport for U States.

Twigds, Levi   Prisoner 2137. Rank: Lieutenant Marine, from: President, U States Frigate.
    Cap: 15 Jan 1815 Not Recorded by Endymion Int: 30 Jan 1815 Dis: 28 Mar 1815.
    Received from President. Clarenden Transport for U States.

Tyler, Daniel   Prisoner 1317. Rank: Seaman, from: Rolla, Privateer.
    Cap: 10 Dec 1813 Block Island by Loire Int: 20 Dec 1813 Dis: 15 Apr 1814.
    Received from San Domingo. HMS Rammillies for Halifax.

Tyler, William   Prisoner 231. Rank: Seaman, from: Wasp, Sloop of War.
    Cap: 18 Oct 1812 at Sea by HM Ship Poictiers Int: 26 Oct 1812 Dis: 05 Nov 1812.
    Received from HM Ship Poictiers. Brig Diamond on Parole to new London United States of America.

Unewell, John   Prisoner 1332. Rank: Seaman, from: Rolla, Privateer.
    Cap: 10 Dec 1813 Block Island by Loire Int: 20 Dec 1813 Dis: 15 Apr 1814.
    Received from HM Ship San Domingo. HMS Rammillies for Halifax.

Updike, Richard   Prisoner 2174. Rank: Boy, from: President, U States Frigate.
    Cap: 15 Jan 1815 Not Recorded by HMS Endymion Int: 30 Jan 1815 Dis: 28 Mar 1815.
    Received from President. Mars Transport for U States.

Usher, Robert   Prisoner 713. Rank: Seaman, from: High Flyer, Privateer.
    Cap: 09 Jan 1813 at Sea by HM Ship Acasta Int: 21 Jan 1813 Dis: 27 Jan 1813.
    Received from HMS Acasta. Bostock Cartel for New York.

Uzzielphant, Uriah   Prisoner 2872. Rank: Seaman, from: Limerick, Not Recorded.
    Cap: 06 Mar 1815 Not Recorded by Asia Int: 29 Mar 1815 Dis: 28 Mar 1815.
    From West Indies. Received from La Brune. Clarendon Transport for U States. (Date of discharge before date of internment.)

Valentine, Cata   Prisoner 1859. Rank: Seaman, from: Isa Colly, Merchant Vessel.
    Cap: Not Recorded by Not Recorded Int: Dis: 04 Sep 1814.
    to join these Proper Ships having been delivered up Order Comm Evans. (Dates of capture and internment not recorded.)

Van Cleave, G W   Prisoner 173. Rank: Midshipman, from: Wasp, Sloop of War.
    Cap: 18 Oct 1812 at Sea by HMS Poictiers Int: 26 Oct 1812 Dis: 05 Nov 1812.
    Received from HM Ship Poictiers. on Parole Brig Diamond to new London America.

Van Kleek, John   Prisoner 60. Rank: Mate, from: Mary, Merchant Brig.
    Cap: 08 Aug 1812 of Bermuda by Cuttle Int: 28 Aug 1812 Dis: 10 Sep 1812.
    Received from M Schooner Cuttle. Schooner Hero for New York.

Van Tassell, Barney   Prisoner 2579. Rank: Seaman, from: Recovery, Merchant Vessel.
    Cap: 20 Nov 1814 off New York by HMS Majestic Int: 05 Feb 1815 Dis: 28 Mar 1815.
    Received from HMS Forth. Clarendon Transport for U States.

American Prisoners of War Held at Bermuda During the War of 1812

Van Vorous, Robert   Prisoner 2560. Rank: Mate, from: Funchall, Merchant Vessel.
    Cap: 15 Jan 1815 off New York by HMS Pomone Int: 05 Feb 1815 Dis: 09 Mar 1815.
    Received from HMS Forth. Merchant Service.

Vantz, John   Prisoner 726. Rank: Seaman, from: High Flyer, Privateer.
    Cap: 09 Jan 1813 at Sea by HM Ship Acasta Int: 21 Jan 1813 Dis: 27 Jan 1813.
    Received from HMS Acasta. Bostock Cartel for New York.

Vaun, Samuel   Prisoner 2348. Rank: Seaman, from: President, U States Frigate.
    Cap: 15 Jan 1815 Not Recorded by HMS Endymion Int: 04 Feb 1815 Dis: 28 Mar 1815.
    Received from Endymion. Mars Transport for U States.

Vere, Jean   Prisoner 1993. Rank: Seaman, from: Fairplay, Merchant Vessel.
    Cap: 22 Oct 1814 Lat 31.58 by Dothrel Int: 26 Oct 1814 Dis: 28 Mar 1815.
    Recaptured. Received from Dothrel. Clarendon Transport for U States.

Vickery, C   Prisoner 1865. Rank: Seaman, from: Viper, Merchant Vessel.
    Cap: Not Recorded by Not Recorded Int: Dis: 20 Mar 1815.
    Merchant Vessel. (Dates of capture and internment not recorded.)

Victor, William   Prisoner 1185. Rank: Seaman, from: Caledonian, Merchant.
    Cap: 20 Jul 1813 at Sea by HM Ship Marlborough Int: 18 Aug 1813 Dis: 03 Oct 1813.
    Received from HM Ship Woolwich. Caledonian per Order of Commodore Evans she being Liberated.

Vinghew, Francis   Prisoner 2647. Rank: Seaman, from: Dash, Merchant Vessel.
    Cap: 19 Jan 1815 Bahamas by HMS Statira Int: 06 Feb 1815 Dis: 25 Feb 1815.
    Received from HMS Statira. Mars Transport per order of Commadore Evans.

Voorhes, Ralph   Prisoner 2139. Rank: Midshipman, from: President, U States Frigate.
    Cap: 15 Jan 1815 Not Recorded by Endymion Int: 30 Jan 1815 Dis: 28 Mar 1815.
    Received from President. Clarenden Transport for U States.

Vorris, Philip   Prisoner 1562. Rank: Seaman, from: Bordeaux Packet, Letter of Marque.
    Cap: 28 Jan 1814 off Cape Henry by Nieman Int: 12 Feb 1814 Dis: 15 Apr 1814.
    Received from Nieman. Diana Transport for Halifax.

Vose, Avery   Prisoner 1492. Rank: Seaman, from: Maresoil, Merchant Brig.
    Cap: 25 Dec 1813 Latt 35.0 by HMS Fox Int: 09 Jan 1814 Dis: 15 Apr 1814.
    Received from Fox. Diana Transport for Halifax.

Vowsland, John   Prisoner 2613. Rank: Seaman, from: Falcon, Merchant Vessel.
    Cap: 22 Jan 1815 Sandy Hook by HM Ship Pomone Int: 05 Feb 1815 Dis: 28 Mar 1815.
    Received from HMS Forth. Clarendon Transport for U States.

Vowsland, William   Prisoner 2612. Rank: Seaman, from: Falcon, Merchant Vessel.
    Cap: 22 Jan 1815 Sandy Hook by HM Ship Pomone Int: 05 Feb 1815 Dis: 28 Mar 1815.
    Received from HMS Forth. Clarendon Transport for U States.

Wade, Alfred   Prisoner 2165. Rank: Pursers Clerk, from: President, U States Frigate.
    Cap: 15 Jan 1815 Not Recorded by Endymion Int: 30 Jan 1815 Dis: 28 Mar 1815.
    Received from President. Mars Transport for U States.

Wade, Robert   Prisoner 2084. Rank: Mate, from: Erin, Merchant Vessel.
    Cap: 20 Dec 1814 off Charleston by Portia Int: 06 Jan 1815 Dis: 17 Mar 1815.
    Received from HMS Portia. Merchant Vessel.

Wagner, Christian   Prisoner 2356. Rank: Seaman, from: President, U States Frigate.
    Cap: 15 Jan 1815 Not Recorded by HMS Endymion Int: 04 Feb 1815 Dis: 28 Mar 1815.
    Received from Endymion. Mars Transport for U States.

Walden, Samuel   Prisoner 940. Rank: Mate, from: Salley, Merchant Sloop.
    Cap: 10 Mar 1813 Chesapeake by HMS Fantome Int: 23 Mar 1813 Dis: 08 Jun 1813.
    Received from Laurustinus. Permitted to remain in the Colony per order of Ad J B Warren.

Walford, Thomas   Prisoner 419. Rank: Seaman, from: Isabella, Merchant Brig.
    Cap: 15 Nov 1812 at Sea by HM Sloop Childers Int: 24 Nov 1812 Dis: 27 Jan 1813.
    Received from HM Ship Childers. Bostock Cartel for New York.

Walker, Aron   Prisoner 2866. Rank: Seaman, from: Limerick, Not Recorded.
    Cap: 06 Mar 1815 Not Recorded by Asia Int: 29 Mar 1815 Dis: 28 Mar 1815.
    From West Indies. Received from La Brune. Clarendon Transport for U States. (Date of discharge before date of internment.)

Walker, Benjamin   Prisoner 1057. Rank: Mate, from: Amason, Merchant.
    Cap: 18 Mar 1813 Chesapeake by HM Ship Victorious Int: 06 Apr 1813 Dis: 24 Jun 1813.
    Received from HMS Junon. Magnet Cartel for New York.

Walker, David   Prisoner 1683. Rank: Seaman, from: St. Joquin, Merchant Vessel.
    Cap: 26 Mar 1814 Chesapeake by Albion Int: 16 Apr 1814 Dis: 23 Apr 1814.
    Received from Canso. HMS Bulwark for Halifax Order Comm in Chief.

American Prisoners of War Held at Bermuda During the War of 1812

Walker, John   Prisoner 426. Rank: Seaman, from: Eliza, Merchant Ship.
    Cap: 25 Nov 1812 Lat 37.00, Long 65.46 by HM Ship Tartarus Int: 03 Dec 1812 Dis: 27 Jan 1813.
    Received from HM Ship Tartarus. Bostock Cartel for New York.

Walker, Thomas   Prisoner 2378. Rank: Seaman, from: President, U States Frigate.
    Cap: 15 Jan 1815 Not Recorded by HMS Endymion Int: 04 Feb 1815 Dis: 28 Mar 1815.
    Received from Endymion. Mars Transport for U States.

Wallace, Andrew   Prisoner 702. Rank: Seaman, from: High Flyer, Privateer.
    Cap: 09 Jan 1813 at Sea by HMS Acasta Int: 21 Jan 1813 Dis: 27 Jan 1813.
    Received from HMS Acasta. Bostock Cartel for New York.

Wallace, Matthew   Prisoner 945. Rank: Seaman, from: Mary, Merchant Schooner.
    Cap: 10 Mar 1813 Chesapeake by HMS Maidstone Int: 23 Mar 1813 Dis: 24 Jun 1813.
    Received from Laurustinus. Magnet Cartel for New York.

Wallace, Peter   Prisoner 944. Rank: Seaman, from: Mary, Merchant Schooner.
    Cap: 10 Mar 1813 Chesapeake by HMS Maidstone Int: 23 Mar 1813 Dis: 24 Jun 1813.
    Received from Laurustinus. Magnet Cartel for New York.

Wallace, Thomas   Prisoner 742. Rank: Seaman, from: Savannah Packet, Merchant Brig.
    Cap: 05 Jan 1813 at Sea by HM Ship Poictiers Int: 21 Jan 1813 Dis: 27 Jan 1813.
    Received from HMS Poictiers. Bostock Cartel for New York.

Wallis, Newport   Prisoner 2792. Rank: Seaman, from: Limerick, Not Recorded.
    Cap: 07 Mar 1815 Lat 30, Long 75.38 W by Asia Int: 25 Mar 1815 Dis:
    Received from Asia. (Date of discharge not recorded.)

Walter, Nathaniel   Prisoner 542. Rank: Seaman, from: Herald, Letter of Marque Brig.
    Cap: 25 Dec 1812 at Sea by HM Ship Maidstone Int: 05 Jan 1813 Dis: 27 Jan 1813.
    Received from HM Ship Maidstone. Bostock Cartel for New York.

Ward, James   Prisoner 256. Rank: Seaman, from: Wasp, Sloop of War.
    Cap: 18 Oct 1812 at Sea by HM Ship Poictiers Int: 26 Oct 1812 Dis: 05 Nov 1812.
    Received from HM Ship Poictiers. Brig Diamond on Parole to new London United States of America.

Warden, Appleton   Prisoner 2781. Rank: Seaman, from: Limerick, Not Recorded.
    Cap: 07 Mar 1815 Lat 30, Long 75.38 W by Asia Int: 25 Mar 1815 Dis:
    Received from Asia. (Date of discharge not recorded.)

Warden, John   Prisoner 427. Rank: Seaman, from: Eliza, Merchant Ship.
    Cap: 25 Nov 1812 Lat 37.00, Long 65.46 by HM Ship Tartarus Int: 03 Dec 1812 Dis: 27 Jan 1813.
    Received from HM Ship Tartarus. Bostock Cartel for New York.

Wardnell, Solomon   Prisoner 1870. Rank: Seaman, from: Lion, Merchant Vessel.
    Cap: Not Recorded by Not Recorded Int: Dis: 28 Mar 1815.
    Clarendon Transport for U States. (Dates of capture and internment not recorded.)

Wards, William   Prisoner 2383. Rank: Seaman, from: President, U States Frigate.
    Cap: 15 Jan 1815 Not Recorded by HMS Endymion Int: 04 Feb 1815 Dis: 28 Mar 1815.
    Received from Endymion. Mars Transport for U States.

Ware, John   Prisoner 1333. Rank: Seaman, from: Rolla, Privateer.
    Cap: 10 Dec 1813 Block Island by Loire Int: 20 Dec 1813 Dis: 15 Apr 1814.
    Received from HM Ship San Domingo. HMS Rammillies for Halifax.

Warner, Samuel   Prisoner 2113. Rank: Passenger, from: Armistice, Merchant Vessel.
    Cap: 07 Dec 1814 off Delaware by Pictolus Int: 27 Jan 1815 Dis:
    Received from Pictolus. (Date of discharge not recorded.)

Warren, Clark   Prisoner 2294. Rank: 2 Gunner, from: President, U States Frigate.
    Cap: 15 Jan 1815 Not Recorded by Endymion Int: 04 Feb 1815 Dis: 28 Mar 1815.
    Received from Endymion. Mars Transport for U States.

Warren, Cyrus   Prisoner 2705. Rank: Mate, from: South Boston, Merchant Vessel.
    Cap: 13 Feb 1815 off Charleston by Pandora Int: 02 Mar 1815 Dis: 17 Mar 1815.
    Received from Pandora. Merchant Vessel.

Warren, John   Prisoner 963. Rank: Seaman, from: Bona, Letter of Marque Schooner.
    Cap: 12 Mar 1813 Chesapeake by Laurustinus Int: 23 Mar 1813 Dis: 24 Jun 1813.
    Received from Laurustinus. Magnet Cartel for New York.

Warren, Thomas   Prisoner 689. Rank: Seaman, from: High Flyer, Privateer.
    Cap: 09 Jan 1813 at Sea by HMS Acasta Int: 21 Jan 1813 Dis: 27 Jan 1813.
    Received from HMS Acasta. Bostock Cartel for New York.

Washington, John   Prisoner 1330. Rank: Seaman, from: Rolla, Privateer.
    Cap: 10 Dec 1813 Block Island by Loire Int: 20 Dec 1813 Dis: 15 Apr 1814.
    Received from HM Ship San Domingo. HMS Rammillies for Halifax.

Waterhouse, John   Prisoner 1181. Rank: Seaman, from: Calmer, Merchant.
    Cap: 15 Jun 1813 at Sea by HM Ship Marlborough Int: 15 Aug 1813 Dis: 21 Aug 1813.
    Received from HM Ship Woolwich. Per Order Commodore Evans.

American Prisoners of War Held at Bermuda During the War of 1812

Waters, Richard   Prisoner 2263. Rank: Seaman, from: President, U States Frigate.
    Cap: 15 Jan 1815 Not Recorded by Endymion Int: 30 Jan 1815 Dis: 28 Mar 1815.
    Received from Pomone. Mars Transport for U States.

Watkin, William   Prisoner 1429. Rank: Seaman, from: Nonsuch, Letter of Marque.
    Cap: 14 Dec 1813 Lat 32 by Doterel Int: 25 Dec 1813 Dis: 15 Apr 1814.
    Received from HM Brig Doterel. Diana Transport for Halifax.

Watson, George   Prisoner 2624. Rank: Seaman, from: William, Merchant Vessel.
    Cap: 12 Jan 1815 Cape Hatterus by HMS Telegraph Int: 05 Feb 1815 Dis: 16 Mar 1815.
    Received from HMS Telegraph. Merchant Service.

Watson, John   Prisoner 2708. Rank: Seaman, from: South Boston, Merchant Vessel.
    Cap: 13 Feb 1815 off Charleston by Pandora Int: 02 Mar 1815 Dis: 28 Mar 1815.
    Received from Pandora. Clarendon Transport for U States.

Watson, T   Prisoner 1626. Rank: Seaman, from: Perseferanda, Merchant Vessel.
    Cap: 03 Jan 1814 Block Island by Albion Int: 14 Feb 1814 Dis: 23 Apr 1814.
    Received from Sceptre. HMS Bulwark for Halifax.

Watson, William   Prisoner 1712. Rank: Seaman, from: Grecian, Letter of Marque.
    Cap: 02 May 1814 Chesapeake by Jansur Int: 26 May 1814 Dis: 28 Mar 1815.
    Received from Lacedaemonian. Mars Transport for U States.

Watson, William   Prisoner 2004. Rank: Seaman, from: Not Recorded, Not Recorded.
    Cap: Alexandria by Atetior Int: 29 Oct 1814 Dis: 14 Dec 1814.
    Ruby gave himself up as a British Subject. (Date of capture not recorded.)

Watson, William   Prisoner 2736. Rank: Soldier, from: Not Recorded, Not Recorded.
    Cap: 13 Jan 1815 St Marys by Dragon Int: 03 Mar 1815 Dis: 28 Mar 1815.
    by Kings Troops. Received from Hebrus. Clarendon Transport for U States.

Watt, John   Prisoner 1728. Rank: Seaman, from: Yankelass, Privateer.
    Cap: 01 May 1814 L 10-4N, L 33-0W by Severn & Surprise Int: 06 Jun 1814 Dis: 10 Nov 1814.
    Received from Severn. Joseph Merchant V by Order Rear Adm Cockburn.

Watts, John   Prisoner 1656. Rank: Seaman, from: Flash, Letter of Marque.
    Cap: 11 Feb 1814 Off Block Island by Acasta Int: 13 Mar 1814 Dis: 23 Apr 1814.
    Received from Active. HMS Bulwark for Halifax.

Waymore, John   Prisoner 1349. Rank: Seaman, from: Rolla, Privateer.
    Cap: 10 Dec 1813 Block Island by Loire Int: 20 Dec 1813 Dis: 15 Apr 1814.
    Received from HM Ship San Domingo. HMS Rammillies for Halifax.

Weaver, Nicholas   Prisoner 1576. Rank: Seaman, from: Bordeaux Packet, Letter of Marque.
    Cap: 28 Jan 1814 off Cape Henry by Nieman Int: 12 Feb 1814 Dis: 15 Apr 1814.
    Received from Nieman. Diana Transport for Halifax.

Webb, T B   Prisoner 2694. Rank: Seaman, from: Speed. Merchant Vessel.
    Cap: 19 Jan 1815 off Nantucket by Pylades Int: 17 Feb 1815 Dis: 28 Mar 1815.
    Received from Majestic. Clarendon Transport for U States.

Webber, Daniel   Prisoner 2022. Rank: Seaman, from: Swiftsure, Merchant Vessel.
    Cap: 26 Oct 1814 off Halifax by Armide Int: 07 Nov 1814 Dis: 28 Mar 1815.
    Recaptured. Received from HMS Armide. Clarendon Transport for U States.

Webber, William   Prisoner 878. Rank: Seaman, from: Christiana, Merchant.
    Cap: 03 Mar 1813 Chesapeake by Marlborough Int: 23 Mar 1813 Dis: 13 Jun 1813.
    Received from Laurustinus. Perseverance Cartel for the United States per Order Adml Sir J B Warren.

Webster, William H   Prisoner 2031. Rank: Actor, from: Not Recorded, Not Recorded.
    Cap: 13 Aug 1814 Not Recorded by Not Recorded Int: 11 Nov 1814 Dis: 24 Nov 1814.
    Received from HMS Wolverine. Ardent SL British Subject.

Wedder, Anthony H   Prisoner 456. Rank: Prize Master, from: Teazer, Privateer Schooner.
    Cap: 16 Dec 1812 at Sea by HM Ship St. Domingo Int: 21 Dec 1812 Dis: 27 Jan 1813.
    Received from HM Ship St. Domingo. Bostock Cartel for New York.

Weed, James   Prisoner 704. Rank: Seaman, from: High Flyer, Privateer.
    Cap: 09 Jan 1813 at Sea by HMS Acasta Int: 21 Jan 1813 Dis: 27 Jan 1813.
    Received from HMS Acasta. Bostock Cartel for New York.

Weeks, Henry   Prisoner 2851. Rank: Seaman, from: Limerick, Not Recorded.
    Cap: 15 Mar 1815 Not Recorded by Asia Int: 25 Mar 1815 Dis:
    From Depot at Jamaica. Received from Asia. (Date of discharge not recorded.)

Weeks, John   Prisoner 2620. Rank: Seaman, from: Attempt, Merchant Vessel.
    Cap: 12 Jan 1815 Cape Hatterus by HMS Telegraph Int: 05 Feb 1815 Dis: 16 Mar 1815.
    Received from HMS Telegraph. Merchant Service.

Weeks, Joseph   Prisoner 1468. Rank: Seaman, from: Vixen, Man of War.
    Cap: 25 Dec 1813 Lat 38.0 by Belvidera Int: 05 Jan 1814 Dis: 15 Apr 1814.
    U States Schooner. Received from HMS Belvidera. Diana Transport for Halifax.

American Prisoners of War Held at Bermuda During the War of 1812

Weeks, Josiah   Prisoner 2097. Rank: Seaman, from: Phaeton, Mechant Vessel.
    Cap: 07 Feb 1815 cast away on Barbary by Forester Int: 19 Jan 1815 Dis: 28 Mar 1815.
    Received from HMS Peruvian. Clarendon Transport for U States. (Date of internment before date of capture - should be 1814.)

Weeks, William   Prisoner 733. Rank: Seaman, from: Fernando, Merchant Brig.
    Cap: 09 Jan 1813 at Sea by HM Ship Acasta Int: 21 Jan 1813 Dis: 27 Jan 1813.
    Received from HMS Acasta. Bostock Cartel for New York.

Welch, James   Prisoner 2306. Rank: Captains Crew, from: President, U States Frigate.
    Cap: 15 Jan 1815 Not Recorded by Endymion Int: 04 Feb 1815 Dis: 28 Mar 1815.
    Received from Endymion. Mars Transport for U States.

Welch, Thomas   Prisoner 1388. Rank: Seaman, from: Policy, Merchant Vessel.
    Cap: 04 Dec 1813 Not Recorded by Loire Int: 20 Dec 1813 Dis: 15 Apr 1814.
    Recaptured. Received from San Domingo. Diana Transport for Halifax.

Welch, Thomas   Prisoner 1439. Rank: Seaman, from: Nonsuch, Letter of Marque.
    Cap: 14 Dec 1813 Lat 32 by Doterel Int: 25 Dec 1813 Dis: 15 Apr 1814.
    Received from HM Brig Doterel. Diana Transport for Halifax.

Wellman, Timothy   Prisoner 1882. Rank: Seaman, from: Levant, Merchant Vessel.
    Cap: Not Recorded by Not Recorded Int: Dis: 28 Mar 1815.
    Clarendon Transport for U States. (Dates of capture and internment not recorded.)

Wells, George   Prisoner 1759. Rank: Seaman, from: Yankelass, Privateer.
    Cap: 01 May 1814 L 40-4N, Long 38-0W by Severn & Surprise Int: 06 Jun 1814 Dis: 28 Mar 1815.
    Received from Severn. Mars Transport for U States.

Wells, Thomas   Prisoner 987. Rank: Mate, from: Nancy, Merchant.
    Cap: 04 Mar 1813 Chesapeake by Narcissus Int: 23 Mar 1813 Dis: 24 Jun 1813.
    Received from HM Ship Laurustinus. Magnet Cartel for New York.

Wells, Thomas   Prisoner 2059. Rank: Master, from: Mary, Merchant Schooner.
    Cap: 26 Nov 1814 off Cape Delaware by Telegraph Int: 11 Dec 1814 Dis: 18 Mar 1815.
    Received from HMS Goree. Merchant Vessel.

Wendall, Abraham   Prisoner 1872. Rank: Seaman, from: Lion, Merchant Vessel.
    Cap: Not Recorded by Not Recorded Int: Dis: 28 Mar 1815.
    Clarendon Transport for U States. (Dates of capture and internment not recorded.)

Wentsworth, Paul   Prisoner 2375. Rank: Seaman, from: President, U States Frigate.
    Cap: 15 Jan 1815 Not Recorded by HMS Endymion Int: 04 Feb 1815 Dis: 28 Mar 1815.
    Received from Endymion. Mars Transport for U States.

Wentworth, Alexander   Prisoner 40. Rank: Supercargo, from: Trim, Merchant Schooner.
    Cap: 28 Jul 1812 of Bermuda by Cuttle Int: 28 Aug 1812 Dis: 10 Sep 1812.
    Received from HM Schooner Cuttle. Schooner Hero for N Y.

Wentworth, Paul   Prisoner 619. Rank: Seaman, from: HM Schooner Elizabeth, Not Recorded.
    Cap: Not Recorded by Not Recorded Int: 12 Jan 1813 Dis: 27 Jan 1813.
    Received from HMS Belvidera. Bostock Cartel for New York. formally serving on Board HM Schooner Elizabeth. (Date of capture not recorded.)

Wentworth, Richard   Prisoner 434. Rank: Seaman, from: Eliza, Merchant Ship.
    Cap: 25 Nov 1812 Lat 37.00, Long 65.46 by HM Ship Tartarus Int: 03 Dec 1812 Dis: 27 Jan 1813.
    Received from HM Ship Tartarus. Bostock Cartel for New York.

West, Francis   Prisoner 1723. Rank: Master, from: Revinue, Merchant Vessel.
    Cap: 15 May 1814 at Sea by Lacedaemonian Int: 26 May 1814 Dis: 05 Jun 1814.
    Received from Lacedaemonian. United States for Parole.

West, James   Prisoner 1614. Rank: Seaman, from: Brookhaven, Merchant Vessel.
    Cap: 09 Dec 1813 Block Island by Albion Int: 14 Feb 1814 Dis: 23 Apr 1814.
    Received from Sceptre. HMS Bulwark for Halifax.

West, John   Prisoner 993. Rank: Seaman, from: Jacob Gettig, Merchant.
    Cap: 18 Feb 1813 at Sea by HM Ship Galus Int: 25 Mar 1813 Dis: 24 Jun 1813.
    Received from HMS Galus. Magnet Cartel for New York.

Weston, George   Prisoner 785. Rank: Seaman, from: Governor Ankerheim, Merchant.
    Cap: 28 Jan 1813 at Sea by HM Ship Ramilies Int: 04 Feb 1813 Dis: 13 Mar 1813.
    Received from HMS Ramilies. Per Order Sir John Warren the Vessel being Liberated.

Westurick, William   Prisoner 2200. Rank: Seaman, from: President, U States Frigate.
    Cap: 15 Jan 1815 Not Recorded by Endymion Int: 30 Jan 1815 Dis: 28 Mar 1815.
    Received from Pomone. Mars Transport for U States.

Westwick, William   Prisoner 233. Rank: Seaman, from: Wasp, Sloop of War.
    Cap: 18 Oct 1812 at Sea by HM Ship Poictiers Int: 26 Oct 1812 Dis: 05 Nov 1812.
    Received from HM Ship Poictiers. Brig Diamond on Parole to new London United States of America.

American Prisoners of War Held at Bermuda During the War of 1812

Weyman, Charles   Prisoner 2340. Rank: Seaman, from: President, U States Frigate.
　　Cap: 15 Jan 1815 Not Recorded by HMS Endymion Int: 04 Feb 1815 Dis: 28 Mar 1815.
　　Received from Endymion. Mars Transport for U States.

Wheeler, Andrew   Prisoner 2205. Rank: Seaman, from: President, U States Frigate.
　　Cap: 15 Jan 1815 Not Recorded by Endymion Int: 30 Jan 1815 Dis: 28 Mar 1815.
　　Received from Pomone. Mars Transport for U States.

Wheeler, David   Prisoner 1629. Rank: Seaman, from: Dove, Merchant Vessel.
　　Cap: 04 Jan 1814 Block Island by Albion Int: 14 Feb 1814 Dis: 23 Apr 1814.
　　Received from Sceptre. HMS Bulwark for Halifax.

Wheelwright, Joseph   Prisoner 2453. Rank: Seaman, from: President, U States Frigate.
　　Cap: 15 Jan 1815 Not Recorded by Endymion Int: 04 Feb 1815 Dis: 28 Mar 1815.
　　Received from Endymion. Clarenden Transport for U States.

Whigs, George   Prisoner 2577. Rank: Seaman, from: Recovery, Merchant Vessel.
　　Cap: 20 Nov 1814 off New York by HMS Majestic Int: 05 Feb 1815 Dis: 28 Mar 1815.
　　Received from HMS Forth. Clarendon Transport for U States.

Whippey, W C   Prisoner 1538. Rank: Mate, from: Romp, Merchant Vessel.
　　Cap: 02 Jan 1814 Latt 22.0 by Prometheus Int: 25 Jan 1814 Dis: 15 Apr 1814.
　　Received from Surprize. Rammilles for Halifax.

Whipple, John   Prisoner 741. Rank: Seaman, from: Savannah Packet, Merchant Brig.
　　Cap: 05 Jan 1813 at Sea by HM Ship Poictiers Int: 21 Jan 1813 Dis: 27 Jan 1813.
　　Received from HMS Poictiers. Bostock Cartel for New York.

Whitaker, Manly   Prisoner 1796. Rank: Armourer, from: Yankelass, Privateer.
　　Cap: 01 May 1814 Latt 40-4N, Long 38-0W by Severn & Surprise Int: 07 Jun 1814 Dis: 28 Mar 1815.
　　Received from Surprise. Clarendon Transport for U States.

White, Cornelius   Prisoner 756. Rank: Passenger, from: Hazard, Merchant Brig.
　　Cap: 28 Dec 1812 Lat 37.35, Long 70.10 by HM Sloop Sylph Int: 26 Jan 1813 Dis: 08 Feb 1813.
　　Received from Sloop Sylph. Permitted to return to the United States per Order Adl Cockburn.

White, Edward   Prisoner 377. Rank: Seaman, from: Snapper, Privateer Schooner.
　　Cap: 16 Nov 1812 at Sea by HM Ship Galus Int: 22 Nov 1812 Dis: 27 Jan 1813.
　　Received from HM Ship Galus. Bostock Cartel for New York.

White, Henry C   Prisoner 1671. Rank: Surgeon, from: Fieri Facias, Privateer.
　　Cap: 26 Feb 1814 at Sea by Ramilies Int: 18 Mar 1814 Dis: 31 Mar 1814.
　　Received from Ramilies. Non Combatant per Commander in Chief.

White, Isaac   Prisoner 1284. Rank: Seaman, from: Perry, Merchant Schooner.
　　Cap: 03 Dec 1813 Long Island by Indemyion Int: 19 Dec 1813 Dis: 15 Apr 1814.
　　Received from Sceptre. Diana Transport for Halifax.

White, Isaac   Prisoner 1809. Rank: Passenger, from: Not Recorded, Not Recorded.
　　Cap: Not Recorded by Not Recorded Int: 14 Jun 1814 Dis: 15 Jun 1814.
　　From St. Bartholomew in the Swedish Schooner Oscar. on Parole per Order Com in Chief to America.
　　(Date of capture not recorded.)

White, James   Prisoner 262. Rank: Seaman, from: Wasp, Sloop of War.
　　Cap: 18 Oct 1812 at Sea by HM Ship Poictiers Int: 26 Oct 1812 Dis: 05 Nov 1812.
　　Received from HM Ship Poictiers. Brig Diamond on Parole to new London United States of America.

White, James   Prisoner 2253. Rank: Seaman, from: President, U States Frigate.
　　Cap: 15 Jan 1815 Not Recorded by Endymion Int: 30 Jan 1815 Dis: 28 Mar 1815.
　　Received from Pomone. Mars Transport for U States.

White, John   Prisoner 2260. Rank: Seaman, from: President, U States Frigate.
　　Cap: 15 Jan 1815 Not Recorded by Endymion Int: 30 Jan 1815 Dis: 28 Mar 1815.
　　Received from Pomone. Mars Transport for U States.

White, John   Prisoner 2367. Rank: Seaman, from: President, U States Frigate.
　　Cap: 15 Jan 1815 Not Recorded by HMS Endymion Int: 04 Feb 1815 Dis: 28 Mar 1815.
　　Received from Endymion. Mars Transport for U States.

White, John   Prisoner 2382. Rank: Seaman, from: President, U States Frigate.
　　Cap: 15 Jan 1815 Not Recorded by HMS Endymion Int: 04 Feb 1815 Dis: 28 Mar 1815.
　　Received from Endymion. Mars Transport for U States.

White, John   Prisoner 2758. Rank: Seaman, from: Mayflower, Not Recorded.
　　Cap: 20 Jan 1815 St Augustine by Severn Int: 03 Mar 1815 Dis: 28 Mar 1815.
　　Received from Hebrus. Clarendon Transport for U States.

White, Joseph   Prisoner 2080. Rank: Mate, from: Trim, Merchant Vessel.
　　Cap: 28 Dec 1814 Lat 34, Long 68 by HMS Telegraph Int: 04 Jan 1815 Dis: 18 Mar 1815.
　　Received from HMS Goree. Merchant Vessel.

American Prisoners of War Held at Bermuda During the War of 1812

White, N   Prisoner 2714. Rank: Seaman, from: American Gun Boat, Not Recorded.
    Cap: 06 Feb 1815 off Charleston by Tonnant Int: 02 Mar 1815 Dis: 28 Mar 1815.
    Received from Armede. Clarendon Transport for U States.

White, Obediah   Prisoner 724. Rank: Seaman, from: High Flyer, Privateer.
    Cap: 09 Jan 1813 at Sea by HM Ship Acasta Int: 21 Jan 1813 Dis: 27 Jan 1813.
    Received from HMS Acasta. Bostock Cartel for New York.

White, Philip   Prisoner 2275. Rank: Seaman, from: President, U States Frigate.
    Cap: 15 Jan 1815 Not Recorded by Endymion Int: 30 Jan 1815 Dis: 28 Mar 1815.
    Received from Pomone. Mars Transport for U States.

White, Ramsay   Prisoner 608. Rank: Seaman, from: Noetoin, Packet Brig.
    Cap: 05 Jan 1813 at Sea by HM Ship Belvidera Int: 10 Jan 1813 Dis: 27 Jan 1813.
    Received from HMS Belvidera. Bostock Cartel for New York.

White, Ramsey   Prisoner 2347. Rank: Seaman, from: President, U States Frigate.
    Cap: 15 Jan 1815 Not Recorded by HMS Endymion Int: 04 Feb 1815 Dis: 28 Mar 1815.
    Received from Endymion. Mars Transport for U States.

White, Robert   Prisoner 2079. Rank: Master, from: Trim, Merchant Vessel.
    Cap: 28 Dec 1814 Lat 34, Long 68 by HMS Telegraph Int: 04 Jan 1815 Dis: 17 Mar 1815.
    Received from HMS Goree. Merchant Vessel.

White, Thomas   Prisoner 433. Rank: Seaman, from: Eliza, Merchant Ship.
    Cap: 25 Nov 1812 Lat 37.00, Long 65.46 by HM Ship Tartarus Int: 03 Dec 1812 Dis: 27 Jan 1813.
    Received from HM Ship Tartarus. Bostock Cartel for New York.

White, William   Prisoner 552. Rank: Seaman, from: Herald, Letter of Marque Brig.
    Cap: 25 Dec 1812 at Sea by HM Ship Maidstone Int: 05 Jan 1813 Dis: 27 Jan 1813.
    Received from HM Ship Maidstone. Bostock Cartel for New York.

White, William   Prisoner 786. Rank: Seaman, from: Gustar Adolph, Merchant.
    Cap: 28 Jan 1813 at Sea by HM Ship Ramilies Int: 04 Feb 1813 Dis: 13 Mar 1813.
    Received from Ramilies. Per Order Sir John Warren the Vessel being Liberated.

White, William   Prisoner 2402. Rank: Seaman, from: President, U States Frigate.
    Cap: 15 Jan 1815 Not Recorded by HM Ship Endymion Int: 04 Feb 1815 Dis: 28 Mar 1815.
    Received from Endymion. Mars Transport for U States.

Whitman, John   Prisoner 2759. Rank: Passenger, from: Mayflower, Not Recorded.
    Cap: 20 Jan 1815 St Augustine by Severn Int: 03 Mar 1815 Dis: 17 Mar 1815.
    Received from Hebrus. Merchant Vessel.

Whitmarsh, Z   Prisoner 988. Rank: Seaman, from: Nancy, Merchant.
    Cap: 04 Mar 1813 Chesapeake by Narcissus Int: 23 Mar 1813 Dis: 24 Jun 1813.
    Received from HM Ship Laurustinus. Magnet Cartel for New York.

Whitney, James   Prisoner 1136. Rank: Seaman, from: Asp, Man of War Schooner.
    Cap: 20 Jul 1813 at Sea by HM Ship San Domingo Int: 13 Aug 1813 Dis: 13 Aug 1813.
    Received from HM Ship Woolwich. American Ship Rolla per Order Commr Evans.

Whitten, Joseph   Prisoner 821. Rank: Seaman, from: Elove & Unity, Merchant.
    Cap: 07 Mar 1813 at Bermuda by Sandimingo Int: 08 Mar 1813 Dis: 13 Jun 1813.
    Received from Sandimingo. Perseverance Cartel for the United States per Order Adm Sir J B Warren.

Whittetson, P   Prisoner 2809. Rank: Seaman, from: Limerick, Not Recorded.
    Cap: 04 Mar 1815 Not Recorded by Asia Int: 25 Mar 1815 Dis:
    From Depot at Jamaica. Received from Asia. (Date of discharge not recorded.)

Whyley, Philip   Prisoner 2359. Rank: Seaman, from: President, U States Frigate.
    Cap: 15 Jan 1815 Not Recorded by HMS Endymion Int: 04 Feb 1815 Dis: 28 Mar 1815.
    Received from Endymion. Mars Transport for U States.

Wickes, J D   Prisoner 2159. Rank: Surgeons Mate, from: President, U States Frigate.
    Cap: 15 Jan 1815 Not Recorded by Endymion Int: 30 Jan 1815 Dis: 28 Mar 1815.
    Received from President. Mars Transport for U States.

Wickes, Samuel   Prisoner 1438. Rank: Seaman, from: Nonsuch, Letter of Marque.
    Cap: 14 Dec 1813 Lat 32 by Doterel Int: 25 Dec 1813 Dis: 24 Apr 1814.
    Received from HM Brig Doterel. HMS Sceptre for England.

Wickman, Andrew   Prisoner 1144. Rank: Boy, from: Asp, Man of War Schooner.
    Cap: 20 Jul 1813 at Sea by HM Ship San Domingo Int: 13 Aug 1813 Dis: 13 Aug 1813.
    Received from HM Ship Woolwich. American Ship Rolla per Order Commr Evans.

Widget, Abrea   Prisoner 1369. Rank: Seaman, from: Rolla, Privateer.
    Cap: 10 Dec 1813 Block Island by Loire Int: 20 Dec 1813 Dis: 15 Apr 1814.
    Received from San Domingo. HMS Rammillies for Halifax.

Wiggs, Benjamin   Prisoner 592. Rank: Seaman, from: Rising Hope, Merchant Brig.
    Cap: 27 Dec 1812 at Sea by HM Ship Maidstone Int: 09 Jan 1813 Dis: 27 Jan 1813.
    Received from Sloop Wanderer. Bostock Cartel for New York.

American Prisoners of War Held at Bermuda During the War of 1812

Wilcocks, William   Prisoner 1243. Rank: Not Recorded, from: Julia, Schooner.
    Cap: 10 Aug 1813 Lake Ontario by Wolf Int: 30 Nov 1813 Dis: 15 Apr 1814.
    Received from HM Ship Goliah. Diana Transport for Halifax.

Wilcox, Pelic   Prisoner 983. Rank: Seaman, from: Mary, Merchant.
    Cap: 10 Mar 1813 Chesapeake by HMS Maidstone Int: 23 Mar 1813 Dis: 24 Jun 1813.
    Received from HM Ship Laurustinus. Magnet Cartel for New York.

Wiley, Jonathan   Prisoner 826. Rank: Seaman, from: Portsmouth, Merchant Ship.
    Cap: 27 Feb 1813 off Bermuda by HM Sloop Martin Int: 09 Mar 1813 Dis: 27 Mar 1813.
    Received from Sloop Martin. Per Order Commodore Evans the Vessel being Liberated.

Wilkes, Joseph   Prisoner 2284. Rank: Marine, from: President, U States Frigate.
    Cap: 15 Jan 1815 Not Recorded by Endymion Int: 30 Jan 1815 Dis: 28 Mar 1815.
    Received from Pomone. Clarenden Transport for U States.

Wilkinson, Francis   Prisoner 1925. Rank: Seaman, from: Timer, Merchant Vessel.
    Cap: 23 Aug 1814 off Savannah by Lacedaemonian Int: 09 Sep 1814 Dis: 28 Mar 1815.
    Received from Lacedaemonian. Clarendon Transport for U States.

Wilkinson, Thomas   Prisoner 2745. Rank: Seaman, from: Aroof, Not Recorded.
    Cap: 16 Jan 1815 St Augustine by Manly Int: 03 Mar 1815 Dis: 28 Mar 1815.
    Received from Hebrus. Clarendon Transport for U States.

Wilkinson, William   Prisoner 2366. Rank: Seaman, from: President, U States Frigate.
    Cap: 15 Jan 1815 Not Recorded by HMS Endymion Int: 04 Feb 1815 Dis: 28 Mar 1815.
    Received from Endymion. Mars Transport for U States.

Willams, John   Prisoner 601. Rank: Seaman, from: Noetoin, Packet Brig.
    Cap: 05 Jan 1813 at Sea by HM Ship Belvidera Int: 10 Jan 1813 Dis: 27 Jan 1813.
    Received from HMS Belvidera. Bostock Cartel for New York.

Willard, Benjamin S   Prisoner 396. Rank: Seaman, from: Snapper, Privateer Schooner.
    Cap: 16 Nov 1812 at Sea by HM Ship Galus Int: 22 Nov 1812 Dis: 27 Jan 1813.
    Received from HM Ship Galus. Bostock Cartel for New York.

Willard, John   Prisoner 1052. Rank: Seaman, from: Massoil, Merchant.
    Cap: 18 Mar 1813 Chesapeake by HMS Dragon Int: 06 Apr 1813 Dis: 24 Jun 1813.
    Received from HMS Junon. Magnet Cartel for New York.

Willberger, Joseph S   Prisoner 1979. Rank: Seaman, from: Antelope, Merchant Vessel.
    Cap: 21 Aug 1814 Western Island by Whiting Int: 17 Sep 1814 Dis: 28 Mar 1815.
    Recaptured. Received from Goree. Clarendon Transport for U States.

Willden, Charles   Prisoner 2483. Rank: Seaman, from: President, U States Frigate.
    Cap: 15 Jan 1815 Not Recorded by Endymion Int: 04 Feb 1815 Dis: 28 Mar 1815.
    Received from Endymion. Clarenden Transport for U States.

Williams, Charles   Prisoner 2279. Rank: Marine, from: President, U States Frigate.
    Cap: 15 Jan 1815 Not Recorded by Endymion Int: 30 Jan 1815 Dis: 28 Mar 1815.
    Received from Pomone. Clarenden Transport for U States.

Williams, Daniel   Prisoner 210. Rank: Marine, from: Wasp, Sloop of War.
    Cap: 18 Oct 1812 at Sea by HM Ship Poictiers Int: 26 Oct 1812 Dis: 05 Nov 1812.
    Received from HM Ship Poictiers. Brig Diamond on Parole to new London United States of America.

Williams, Daniel   Prisoner 1740. Rank: Seaman, from: Yankelass, Privateer.
    Cap: 01 May 1814 L 10-4N, L 33-0W by Severn & Surprise Int: 06 Jun 1814 Dis: 28 Mar 1815.
    Received from Severn. Mars Transport for U States.

Williams, Daniel   Prisoner 2401. Rank: Seaman, from: President, U States Frigate.
    Cap: 15 Jan 1815 Not Recorded by HM Ship Endymion Int: 04 Feb 1815 Dis: 28 Mar 1815.
    Received from Endymion. Mars Transport for U States.

Williams, Dennis   Prisoner 102. Rank: Seaman, from: Gossepuim, Merchant.
    Cap: 16 Aug 1812 of Bermuda by Not Recorded Int: 31 Aug 1812 Dis: 18 Sep 1812.
    Received from HMS Ruby. detained per order of the Commodore. Order of Commd Evans for England.

Williams, Jacob   Prisoner 2581. Rank: Seaman, from: Recovery, Merchant Vessel.
    Cap: 20 Nov 1814 off New York by HM Ship Majestic Int: 05 Feb 1815 Dis: 28 Mar 1815.
    Received from HMS Forth. Clarendon Transport for U States.

Williams, John   Prisoner 436. Rank: Seaman, from: HMS Childers, Not Recorded.
    Cap: Not Recorded by Not Recorded Int: 04 Dec 1812 Dis: 27 Jan 1813.
    Received from HMS Childers. formally serving on board HMS Childers. Bostock Cartel for New York. (Date of capture not recorded.)

Williams, John   Prisoner 475. Rank: Seaman, from: Teazer, Privateer Schooner.
    Cap: 16 Dec 1812 at Sea by HM Ship St. Domingo Int: 21 Dec 1812 Dis: 27 Jan 1813.
    Received from HM Ship St. Domingo. Bostock Cartel for New York. John Williams (1st).

American Prisoners of War Held at Bermuda During the War of 1812

Williams, John   Prisoner 479. Rank: Seaman, from: Teazer, Privateer Schooner.
    Cap: 16 Dec 1812 at Sea by HM Ship St. Domingo Int: 21 Dec 1812 Dis: 27 Jan 1813.
    Received from HM Ship St. Domingo. Bostock Cartel for New York. John Williams (2nd).

Williams, John   Prisoner 798. Rank: Seaman, from: Not Recorded, Not Recorded.
    Cap: Not Recorded by Not Recorded Int: 14 Feb 1813 Dis: 24 Jun 1813.
    Received from Narcissus. Surrendered himself as a Prisoner of War. Magnet Cartel for New York. (Date of capture not recorded.)

Williams, John   Prisoner 1464. Rank: Seaman, from: Vixen, Man of War.
    Cap: 25 Dec 1813 Lat 38.0 by Belvidera Int: 05 Jan 1814 Dis: 15 Apr 1814.
    U States Schooner. Received from HMS Belvidera. Diana Transport for Halifax.

Williams, John   Prisoner 1946. Rank: Seaman, from: Pike, Privateer.
    Cap: 25 Aug 1814 off Savannah by Primrose Int: 09 Sep 1814 Dis: 07 Nov 1814.
    Received from Lacedaemonian. Order Adl Cockburn.

Williams, John   Prisoner 2107. Rank: Seaman, from: Rufus King, Merchant Vessel.
    Cap: 01 Jan 1815 off Bermuda by Peruvian Int: 19 Jan 1815 Dis: 13 Mar 1815.
    Received from HMS Peruvian. Merchant Service.

Williams, John   Prisoner 2278. Rank: Seaman, from: President, U States Frigate.
    Cap: 15 Jan 1815 Not Recorded by Endymion Int: 30 Jan 1815 Dis: 28 Mar 1815.
    Received from Pomone. Mars Transport for U States.

Williams, John   Prisoner 2458. Rank: Seaman, from: President, U States Frigate.
    Cap: 15 Jan 1815 Not Recorded by Endymion Int: 04 Feb 1815 Dis: 28 Mar 1815.
    Received from Endymion. Clarenden Transport for U States.

Williams, Joshua   Prisoner 647. Rank: Seaman, from: Eliza, Merchant Ship.
    Cap: 24 Nov 1812 at Sea by HM Ship Marlborough Int: 18 Jan 1813 Dis: 27 Jan 1813.
    Received from HM Ship Marlborough. Bostock Cartel for New York. Ship Eliza (2).

Williams, Lloyd   Prisoner 1910. Rank: Seaman, from: Resolution, Merchant Vessel.
    Cap: 20 Aug 1814 St. Catherine by Lacedaemonian Int: 09 Sep 1814 Dis: 10 Nov 1814.
    Received from Lacedaemonian. Joseph MV Order Rear Adm Cockburn.

Williams, Nicholas   Prisoner 1766. Rank: Seaman, from: Yankelass, Privateer.
    Cap: 01 May 1814 L 40-4N, Long 38-0W by Severn & Surprise Int: 07 Jun 1814 Dis:
    Received from Surprise. (Date of discharge not recorded.)

Williams, Samuel   Prisoner 1804. Rank: Passenger, from: Not Recorded, Not Recorded.
    Cap: Not Recorded by Not Recorded Int: 14 Jun 1814 Dis: 15 Jun 1814.
    From St. Bartholomew in the Swedish Schooner Oscar. on Parole per Order Com in Chief to America. (Date of capture not recorded.)

Williams, Samuel   Prisoner 1886. Rank: Seaman, from: Sally, Merchant Vessel.
    Cap: Not Recorded by Not Recorded Int: Dis: 26 Oct 1814.
    R A Cockburn. (Dates of capture and internment not recorded.)

Williams, Tatem   Prisoner 282. Rank: Seaman, from: Little William, Merchant Brig.
    Cap: 18 Oct 1812 at Sea by HM Ship Poictiers Int: 30 Oct 1812 Dis: 05 Nov 1812.
    Received from HM Ship Poictiers. Brig Diamond on Parole to new London United States of America.

Williams, William   Prisoner 1077. Rank: Seaman, from: Not Recorded, Not Recorded.
    Cap: Not Recorded by Not Recorded Int: 08 Apr 1813 Dis: 24 Jun 1813.
    Received from HMS Ruby. Surrendered them Selves as Prisoners of War. Magnet Cartel for New York. (Date of capture not recorded.)

Williams, William   Prisoner 1829. Rank: Passenger, from: Not Recorded, Not Recorded.
    Cap: Not Recorded by Not Recorded Int: 14 Jun 1814 Dis: 15 Jun 1814.
    From St. Bartholomew in the Swedish Schooner Oscar. on Parole per Order Com in Chief to America. (Date of capture not recorded.)

Williams, William   Prisoner 1843. Rank: Passenger, from: Hibernia, Merchant Vessel.
    Cap: Not Recorded by Not Recorded Int: Dis: 21 Feb 1815.
    Paroled to the U States having served 6 months as Carpenter's Mate order of Adl Sir Alex Cockburn. (Dates of capture and internment not recorded.)

Williams, William   Prisoner 2432. Rank: Seaman, from: President, U States Frigate.
    Cap: 15 Jan 1815 Not Recorded by HM Ship Endymion Int: 04 Feb 1815 Dis:
    Received from Endymion. (Date of discharge not recorded.)

Williams, Williams   Prisoner 393. Rank: Seaman, from: Snapper, Privateer Schooner.
    Cap: 16 Nov 1812 at Sea by HM Ship Galus Int: 22 Nov 1812 Dis: 27 Jan 1813.
    Received from HM Ship Galus. Bostock Cartel for New York.

Williamson, Charles   Prisoner 2509. Rank: Seaman, from: President, U States Frigate.
    Cap: 15 Jan 1815 Not Recorded by Endymion Int: 04 Feb 1815 Dis: 28 Mar 1815.
    Received from HMS Endymion. Clarenden Transport for U States.

American Prisoners of War Held at Bermuda During the War of 1812

Williamson, Thomas   Prisoner 2180. Rank: Seaman, from: President, U States Frigate.
    Cap: 15 Jan 1815 Not Recorded by HMS Endymion Int: 30 Jan 1815 Dis: 28 Mar 1815.
    Received from Pomone. Mars Transport for U States.

Willis, J   Prisoner 1524. Rank: Master, from: Matchless, Merchant Vessel.
    Cap: 02 Jan 1814 Latt 22.0 by Prometheus Int: 23 Jan 1814 Dis: 15 Apr 1814.
    Received from Prometheus. Rammilles for Halifax.

Willock, Henry   Prisoner 357. Rank: Seaman, from: Snapper, Privateer Schooner.
    Cap: 16 Nov 1812 at Sea by HM Ship Galus Int: 22 Nov 1812 Dis: 27 Jan 1813.
    Received from HM Ship Galus. Bostock Cartel for New York.

Wills, Philip   Prisoner 1132. Rank: Seaman, from: Good Intent, Merchant.
    Cap: 02 Aug 1813 at Sea by HM Sloop Rifleman Int: 13 Aug 1813 Dis: 03 Sep 1813.
    Received from HM Sloop Rifleman. Per Order of Comm Evans to the American Ship Leander restored.

Willson, Andrew   Prisoner 1630. Rank: Seaman, from: Dove, Merchant Vessel.
    Cap: 04 Jan 1814 Block Island by Albion Int: 14 Feb 1814 Dis: 23 Apr 1814.
    Received from Sceptre. HMS Bulwark for Halifax.

Willson, George   Prisoner 1745. Rank: Seaman, from: Yankelass, Privateer.
    Cap: 01 May 1814 L 40-4N, Long 38-0W by Severn & Surprise Int: 06 Jun 1814 Dis:
    Received from Severn. (Date of discharge not recorded.)

Willum, William   Prisoner 1692. Rank: Seaman, from: Lark, Merchant Vessel.
    Cap: 06 Apr 1814 L 29.0 by Recruit Int: 11 May 1814 Dis: 28 Mar 1815.
    Recaptured. Received from Recruit. Mars Transport for U States.

Wilson, Caesar R   Prisoner 180. Rank: Captains Clerk, from: Wasp, Sloop of War.
    Cap: 18 Oct 1812 at Sea by HMS Poictiers Int: 26 Oct 1812 Dis: 05 Nov 1812.
    Received from HM Ship Poictiers. Brig Diamond on Parole to new London America.

Wilson, Sidney   Prisoner 2044. Rank: Seaman, from: Rising Sun, Merchant Vessel.
    Cap: 20 Nov 1814 off Bermuda by Pandora Int: 28 Nov 1814 Dis: 28 Mar 1815.
    Recaptured. Received from HMS Goree. Clarendon Transport for U States.

Wilson, William   Prisoner 13. Rank: Seaman, from: General Blake, Merchant.
    Cap: 09 Jul 1812 near Bermuda by Recruit Int: 28 Aug 1812 Dis: 18 Sep 1812.
    Received from HM Schooner Cuttle. Order of Commd Evans for England.

Wilson, William   Prisoner 245. Rank: Seaman, from: Wasp, Sloop of War.
    Cap: 18 Oct 1812 at Sea by HM Ship Poictiers Int: 26 Oct 1812 Dis: 05 Nov 1812.
    Received from HM Ship Poictiers. Brig Diamond on Parole to new London United States of America.

Windwood, William   Prisoner 1344. Rank: Seaman, from: Rolla, Privateer.
    Cap: 10 Dec 1813 Block Island by Loire Int: 20 Dec 1813 Dis: 15 Apr 1814.
    Received from HM Ship San Domingo. HMS Rammillies for Halifax.

Winer, Elijah   Prisoner 1410. Rank: Captain, from: Industry, Merchant Vessel.
    Cap: 08 Dec 1813 Lat 37.25 by Loire Int: 21 Dec 1813 Dis: 15 Apr 1814.
    Received from Romulus. Rammilles for Halifax.

Wing, George   Prisoner 2094. Rank: Passenger, from: George & Joseph, Merchant Vessel.
    Cap: 06 Dec 1814 coast of America by Lacedaemonian Int: 19 Jan 1815 Dis: 25 Feb 1815.
    Received from HMS Peruvian. United States per order Sir Alex Cochrane.

Wing, Paul   Prisoner 1068. Rank: Mate, from: Sally, Merchant.
    Cap: 15 Mar 1813 Chesapeake by HM Ship Dragon Int: 06 Apr 1813 Dis: 24 Jun 1813.
    Received from HMS Junon. Magnet Cartel for New York.

Wing, Philip   Prisoner 1069. Rank: Master, from: Sally, Merchant.
    Cap: 15 Mar 1813 Chesapeake by HM Ship Dragon Int: 06 Apr 1813 Dis: 26 Jul 1813.
    Received from HMS Junon. New Bedford United States.

Winner, Joseph   Prisoner 283. Rank: Seaman, from: Little William, Merchant Brig.
    Cap: 18 Oct 1812 at Sea by HM Ship Poictiers Int: 30 Oct 1812 Dis: 05 Nov 1812.
    Received from HM Ship Poictiers. Brig Diamond on Parole to new London United States of America.

Winsley, William   Prisoner 1496. Rank: Seaman, from: Santo Cateno Venturuso, Merchant.
    Cap: 28 Dec 1813 Latt 34.0 by HMS Fox Int: 09 Jan 1814 Dis: 15 Apr 1814.
    Received from HM Ship Fox. Diana Transport for Halifax.

Winslow, Oliver   Prisoner 1477. Rank: Seaman, from: Luckey, Merchant Vessel.
    Cap: 19 Dec 1813 off the Delaware by Niemen Int: 07 Jan 1814 Dis: 15 Apr 1814.
    Received from HM Sloop Jaseur. Diana for Halifax. (Name of capturing ship not legible, assume to be Nieman.)

Wisbec, Caleb   Prisoner 1481. Rank: Seaman, from: Luckey, Merchant Vessel.
    Cap: 19 Dec 1813 off the Delaware by Niemen Int: 07 Jan 1814 Dis: 15 Apr 1814.
    Received from HM Sloop Jaseur. Diana Transport for Halifax. (Name of capturing ship not legible, assume to be Nieman.)

American Prisoners of War Held at Bermuda During the War of 1812

Wise, George   Prisoner 269. Rank: Purser, from: Wasp, Sloop of War.
    Cap: 18 Oct 1812 at Sea by HM Ship Poictiers Int: 26 Oct 1812 Dis: 05 Nov 1812.
    Received from HM Ship Poictiers. Brig Diamond on Parole to new London United States of America.

Wise, Joseph   Prisoner 1753. Rank: Seaman, from: Yankelass, Privateer.
    Cap: 01 May 1814 L 40-4N, Long 38-0W by Severn & Surprise Int: 06 Jun 1814 Dis: 28 Mar 1815.
    Received from Severn. Mars Transport for U States.

Witherall, William   Prisoner 593. Rank: Master, from: Rising Hope, Merchant Brig.
    Cap: 27 Dec 1812 at Sea by HM Ship Maidstone Int: 09 Jan 1813 Dis: 05 Feb 1813.
    Received from Sloop Wanderer. Permitted to return to New York per Order of Adl Cockburn.

Witten, Elijah   Prisoner 257. Rank: Seaman, from: Wasp, Sloop of War.
    Cap: 18 Oct 1812 at Sea by HM Ship Poictiers Int: 26 Oct 1812 Dis: 05 Nov 1812.
    Received from HM Ship Poictiers. Brig Diamond on Parole to new London United States of America.

Woats, John   Prisoner 2315. Rank: Marine, from: President, U States Frigate.
    Cap: 15 Jan 1815 Not Recorded by Endymion Int: 04 Feb 1815 Dis: 28 Mar 1815.
    Received from Endymion. Clarenden Transport for U States.

Wolf, Henry   Prisoner 830. Rank: Seaman, from: Portsmouth, Merchant Ship.
    Cap: 27 Feb 1813 off Bermuda by HM Sloop Martin Int: 09 Mar 1813 Dis: 27 Mar 1813.
    Received from Sloop Martin. Per Order Commodore Evans the Vessel being Liberated.

Wolf, Henry   Prisoner 1281. Rank: Seaman, from: Perry, Merchant Schooner.
    Cap: 03 Dec 1813 Long Island by Indemyion Int: 19 Dec 1813 Dis: 15 Apr 1814.
    Received from Sceptre. Diana Transport for Halifax.

Wolfe, William   Prisoner 251. Rank: Seaman, from: Wasp, Sloop of War.
    Cap: 18 Oct 1812 at Sea by HM Ship Poictiers Int: 26 Oct 1812 Dis: 05 Nov 1812.
    Received from HM Ship Poictiers. Brig Diamond on Parole to new London United States of America.

Womack, John   Prisoner 2386. Rank: Seaman, from: President, U States Frigate.
    Cap: 15 Jan 1815 Not Recorded by HMS Endymion Int: 04 Feb 1815 Dis: 28 Mar 1815.
    Received from Endymion. Mars Transport for U States.

Wood, Bill   Prisoner 1831. Rank: Passenger, from: Not Recorded, Not Recorded.
    Cap: Not Recorded by Not Recorded Int: 14 Jun 1814 Dis: 15 Jun 1814.
    From St. Bartholomew in the Swedish Schooner Oscar. on Parole per Order Com in Chief to America.
    (Date of capture not recorded.)

Wood, James   Prisoner 85. Rank: Captain, from: Gossepuim, Merchant.
    Cap: 16 Aug 1812 of Bermuda by Goree Int: 28 Aug 1812 Dis: 06 Sep 1812.
    Received from HM Schooner Cuttle. Sloop Sally for New York.

Wood, John   Prisoner 19. Rank: Seaman, from: Amiable, Merchant Schooner.
    Cap: 14 Jul 1812 at Bermuda by Cuttle Int: 28 Aug 1812 Dis: 18 Sep 1812.
    Received from HM Schooner Cuttle. Order of Commd Evans for England.

Wood, John   Prisoner 1968. Rank: Seaman, from: Pike, Privateer.
    Cap: 25 Aug 1814 off Savannah by Primrose Int: 09 Sep 1814 Dis: 22 Nov 1814.
    Received from Lacedaemonian. Ardent S L British Subject.

Wood, John   Prisoner 2784. Rank: Seaman, from: Limerick, Not Recorded.
    Cap: 07 Mar 1815 Lat 30, Long 75.38 W by Asia Int: 25 Mar 1815 Dis:
    Received from Asia. (Date of discharge not recorded.)

Woodburn, Edward   Prisoner 330. Rank: Surgeon, from: Snapper, Privateer Schooner.
    Cap: 16 Nov 1812 at Sea by HM Ship Galus Int: 22 Nov 1812 Dis: 27 Jan 1813.
    Received from HM Ship Galus. Bostock Cartel for New York.

Woodburst, Benjamin   Prisoner 598. Rank: Seaman, from: Windward Planter, Merchant Sloop.
    Cap: 22 Dec 1812 at Sea by HM Ship Belvidera Int: 10 Jan 1813 Dis: 27 Jan 1813.
    Received from HMS Belvidera. Bostock Cartel for New York.

Woodbury, Thomas   Prisoner 1000. Rank: Master, from: Nautalus, Merchant.
    Cap: 20 Mar 1813 at Sea by HM Ship Rammillies Int: 05 Apr 1813 Dis: 10 Apr 1813.
    Received from Prize Nautalus. United States per Order Commodore Evans.

Woodbury, William   Prisoner 1006. Rank: Seaman, from: Ohio, Merchant.
    Cap: 20 Mar 1813 off the Chesapeake by HM Sloop Atalante Int: 06 Apr 1813 Dis: 24 Jun 1813.
    Received from HMS Junon. Magnet Cartel for New York.

Woodman, Constant   Prisoner 2047. Rank: Mate, from: Mary, Merchant Schooner.
    Cap: 26 Nov 1814 off Cape Delaware by Telegraph Int: 05 Dec 1814 Dis: 28 Mar 1815.
    Received from HMS Goree. Clarendon Transport for U States.

Woodman, Rufus   Prisoner 734. Rank: Seaman, from: Fernando, Merchant Brig.
    Cap: 09 Jan 1813 at Sea by HM Ship Acasta Int: 21 Jan 1813 Dis: 27 Jan 1813.
    Received from HMS Acasta. Bostock Cartel for New York.

American Prisoners of War Held at Bermuda During the War of 1812

Woodruff, John   Prisoner 2426. Rank: Seaman, from: President, U States Frigate.
    Cap: 15 Jan 1815 Not Recorded by HM Ship Endymion Int: 04 Feb 1815 Dis: 28 Mar 1815.
    Received from Endymion. Mars Transport for U States.

Woodward, Richard   Prisoner 2682. Rank: Seaman, from: Farmers Branch, Merchant Vessel.
    Cap: 06 Feb 1815 off Delaware by Lacedaemonian Int: 14 Feb 1815 Dis: 28 Mar 1815.
    Received from Childers. Clarendon Transport for U States.

Worth, John   Prisoner 1268. Rank: Seaman, from: United States, Merchant Vessel.
    Cap: 14 Nov 1813 Long Island by HM Brig Borer Int: 19 Dec 1813 Dis: 15 Apr 1814.
    Received from HMS Acasta. Diana for Halifax.

Woxin, Joseph   Prisoner 84. Rank: Seaman, from: Ariel, Merchant Brig.
    Cap: 13 Aug 1812 of Bermuda by Goree Int: 28 Aug 1812 Dis: 24 Oct 1812.
    Received from HM Schooner Cuttle. Brig Diamond on Parole to new London America.

Wragg, Erasmus R   Prisoner 2089. Rank: Passenger, from: Fox, Packet Boat.
    Cap: 04 Oct 1814 coast of America by Lacedaemonian Int: 19 Jan 1815 Dis: 21 Feb 1815.
    Received from HMS Peruvian. Paroled to U States per order of Sir Alex Cochrane.

Wright, James   Prisoner 843. Rank: 1 Mate, from: Portsmouth, Merchant Ship.
    Cap: 27 Feb 1813 off Bermuda by HM Sloop Martin Int: 09 Mar 1813 Dis: 27 Mar 1813.
    Received from HM Ship Martin. Per Order Commodore Evans the Vessel being Liberated.

Wright, James   Prisoner 1883. Rank: Seaman, from: Robert, Merchant Vessel.
    Cap: Not Recorded by Not Recorded Int: Dis: 28 Mar 1815.
    Recaptured. Clarendon Transport for U States. (Dates of capture and internment not recorded.)

Wright, James   Prisoner 2636. Rank: Seaman, from: Superb, Merchant Vessel.
    Cap: 23 Nov 1814 off Delaware by Spencer Int: 06 Feb 1815 Dis: 24 Mar 1815.
    Received from HMS Telegraph. Merchant Vessel.

Wright, John   Prisoner 314. Rank: Seaman, from: Wasp, Sloop of War.
    Cap: 18 Oct 1812 at Sea by HMS Poictiers Int: 05 Nov 1812 Dis: 17 Jun 1813.
    Received from HM Ship Poictiers. Halifax Order of the Commander in Chief supports to be an Englishman.

Wright, John   Prisoner 1131. Rank: Seaman, from: Good Intent, Merchant.
    Cap: 02 Aug 1813 at Sea by HM Sloop Rifleman Int: 13 Aug 1813 Dis: 03 Sep 1813.
    Received from HM Sloop Rifleman. Per Order of Comm Evans to the American Ship Leander restored.

Wright, John   Prisoner 2505. Rank: Seaman, from: President, U States Frigate.
    Cap: 15 Jan 1815 Not Recorded by Endymion Int: 04 Feb 1815 Dis: 28 Mar 1815.
    Received from Endymion. Clarenden Transport for U States.

Wright, Samuel   Prisoner 805. Rank: Seaman, from: Viper, Sloop of War.
    Cap: 17 Jan 1813 at Sea by Narcissus Int: 16 Feb 1813 Escaped: 21 Apr 1813.
    Received from Narcissus. Escaped.

Wright, William   Prisoner 2454. Rank: Seaman, from: President, U States Frigate.
    Cap: 15 Jan 1815 Not Recorded by Endymion Int: 04 Feb 1815 Dis: 28 Mar 1815.
    Received from Endymion. Clarenden Transport for U States.

Wright, Yorick   Prisoner 2747. Rank: Seaman, from: Aroof, Not Recorded.
    Cap: 16 Jan 1815 St Augustine by Manly Int: 03 Mar 1815 Dis: 28 Mar 1815.
    Received from Hebrus. Clarendon Transport for U States.

Wyer, Joseph   Prisoner 888. Rank: Seaman, from: Hannah, Merchant Schooner.
    Cap: 24 Feb 1813 Chesapeake by HMS Marlborough Int: 23 Mar 1813 Dis: 21 May 1813.
    Received from HM Ship Laurustinus. Per Order Commodore Evans the Vessel being Liberated.

Wyland, Christian   Prisoner 70. Rank: Seaman, from: Canaway, Merchant Ship.
    Cap: 08 Aug 1812 of Bermuda by Recruit Int: 28 Aug 1812 Dis: 17 Sep 1812.
    Received from M Schooner Cuttle. a Prussian per Order C. Evans.

Wyley, Nathaniel   Prisoner 273. Rank: Master, from: Little William, Merchant Brig.
    Cap: 18 Oct 1812 at Sea by HM Ship Poictiers Int: 26 Oct 1812 Dis: 05 Nov 1812.
    Received from HM Ship Poictiers. Brig Diamond on Parole to new London United States of America.

Yarnell, William   Prisoner 1428. Rank: Seaman, from: Nonsuch, Letter of Marque.
    Cap: 14 Dec 1813 Lat 32 by Doterel Int: 25 Dec 1813 Dis: 15 Apr 1814.
    Received from HM Brig Doterel. Diana Transport for Halifax.

Yeoman, John   Prisoner 1578. Rank: Seaman, from: Bordeaux Packet, Letter of Marque.
    Cap: 28 Jan 1814 off Cape Henry by Nieman Int: 12 Feb 1814 Dis: 15 Apr 1814.
    Received from Nieman. Diana Transport for Halifax.

Yong, Bill   Prisoner 1222. Rank: Seaman, from: Flavoriott, Merchant Schooner.
    Cap: Aug 1813 off Charlestown by HMS Calibri Int: 16 Nov 1813 Dis: 15 Apr 1814.
    Received from HMS Sceptre. Diana Transport for Halifax.

American Prisoners of War Held at Bermuda During the War of 1812

Young, David   Prisoner 483. Rank: Seaman, from: Teazer, Privateer Schooner.
    Cap: 16 Dec 1812 at Sea by HM Ship St. Domingo Int: 21 Dec 1812 Dis: 27 Jan 1813.
    Received from HM Ship St. Domingo. Bostock Cartel for New York.

Young, James   Prisoner 80. Rank: Mate, from: Ariel, Merchant Brig.
    Cap: 28 Jul 1812 of Bermuda by Goree Int: 28 Aug 1812 Dis: 28 Oct 1812.
    Received from HM Schooner Cuttle. on Parole to New London United States of America, Diamond Brig.

Young, James W   Prisoner 1390. Rank: Mate, from: West Indian Schooner, Merchant Vessel.
    Cap: 06 Dec 1813 Cape Philadelphia by Loire Int: 20 Dec 1813 Dis: 15 Apr 1814.
    Received from San Domingo. HMS Rammillies for Halifax.

Young, James   Prisoner 2863. Rank: Mate, from: Limerick, Not Recorded.
    Cap: 06 Mar 1815 Not Recorded by Asia Int: 28 Mar 1815 Dis: 28 Mar 1815.
    From West Indies. Received from Asia. Clarendon Transport for U States.

Young, John   Prisoner 587. Rank: Seaman, from: Lydia, Merchant Ship.
    Cap: 26 Dec 1812 at Sea by HM Ship Maidstone Int: 06 Jan 1813 Dis: 27 Jan 1813.
    Received from HM Ship Maidstone. Bostock Cartel for New York.

Young, John   Prisoner 1838. Rank: Passenger, from: Hibernia, Merchant Sloop.
    Cap: 30 May 1814 between Cape Roman and Cape Fear by Doteral & Morgiana Int: 30 Jun 1814 Dis: 28 Mar 1815. Received from HMS Doterel. Clarendon Transport for U States.

Young, Joshua   Prisoner 848. Rank: Seaman, from: Caroline, Merchant Brig.
    Cap: 10 Feb 1813 off Charlestown by HMS Galus Int: 18 Mar 1813 Dis: 13 Jun 1813.
    Received from HMS Galus. Perseverance Cartel for the United States per Order Adml Sir J B Warren.

Young, Martin   Prisoner 135. Rank: Seaman, from: Citzen, Merchant Schooner.
    Cap: 10 Sep 1812 Lat 37 by HMS Belvidera Int: 26 Sep 1812 Dis:
    Received from HMS Belvidera. (Date of discharge not on roster.)

Young, Moses   Prisoner 110. Rank: Seaman, from: Gossepuim, detained American.
    Cap: 06 Sep 1812 Bermuda by Goree Int: 05 Sep 1812 Dis: 18 Sep 1812.
    Received from HMS Ruby. detained per order of the President. Order of Commd Evans for England. (Date of internment before date of capture.)

Young, Richard   Prisoner 1783. Rank: Seaman, from: Yankelass, Privateer.
    Cap: 01 May 1814 Latt 40-4N, Long 38-0W by Severn & Surprise Int: 07 Jun 1814 Dis:
    Received from Surprise. (Date of discharge not recorded.)

Young, Richard   Prisoner 1934. Rank: Seaman, from: Pike, Privateer.
    Cap: 25 Aug 1814 off Savannah by Primrose Int: 09 Sep 1814 Dis: 28 Mar 1815.
    Received from Lacedaemonian. Clarendon Transport for U States.

Young, Robert   Prisoner 2024. Rank: Seaman, from: Swiftsure, Merchant Vessel.
    Cap: 26 Oct 1814 off Halifax by Armide Int: 07 Nov 1814 Dis: 13 Dec 1814.
    Recaptured. Received from HMS Armide. Hyana Store Ship Subject of Sandwich Islands in lieu of Chief Mate Order of Com Evans.

Young, Samuel   Prisoner 2798. Rank: Seaman, from: Limerick, Not Recorded.
    Cap: 04 Mar 1815 Not Recorded by Asia Int: 25 Mar 1815 Dis:
    From Depot at Jamaica. Received from Asia. (Date of discharge not recorded.)

Young, William   Prisoner 1664. Rank: Seaman, from: Tram, Merchant Vessel.
    Cap: 20 Feb 1814 Chesapeake by Dragon Int: 13 Mar 1814 Dis: 23 Mar 1814.
    Received from Active. Being a Negro Slave belonging to Bermuda.

Zeizell, John O   Prisoner 1805. Rank: Passenger, from: Not Recorded, Not Recorded.
    Cap: Not Recorded by Not Recorded Int: 14 Jun 1814 Dis: 15 Jun 1814.
    From St. Bartholomew in the Swedish Schooner Oscar. on Parole per Order Com in Chief to America. (Date of capture not recorded.)

American Prisoners of War Held at Bermuda During the War of 1812

Numeric listing by prison number

1	Morton, Thomas	70	Wyland, Christian
2	Bakeman, John	71	Johnson, Robert
3	Cole, John	72	Dixon, Closs
4	Montgomery, Robert	73	Morris, Emanuel
5	Russel, Simon	74	Basden, John
6	Pierce, Nathaniel	75	Kelly, Henry
7	Hammond, Stephen	76	Stanley, Peter
8	La Mour, John	77	Furnell, Tobias
9	Cornett, William	78	Crane, Roger
10	Lake, Levin	79	Merrill, Elias
11	Bennett, Albeno	80	Young, James
12	Laxes, Peter	81	Butters, Benjamin
13	Wilson, William	82	James, John
14	Blackburn, William	83	Abrahams, G D
15	Miller, Ezekial	84	Woxin, Joseph
16	Burke, John	85	Wood, James
17	Clark, Obea	86	Coffin, Thaddias
18	Jordon, Simon	87	Linnell, Jonathan
19	Wood, John	88	Smith, William
20	Lattimore, James	89	Hunt, Dudley
21	Craft, Nathaniel	90	Tridwell, Alpheus
22	Eaton, Israel	91	Haywood, John
23	Ingram, Henry	92	Harvey, Joseph
24	Somerdyke, Joseph	93	George, Peter
25	Ford, John	94	Brooks, Edward
26	Clark, John	95	Day, William
27	Contee, Augustus	96	Douglas, Josiah
28	Hoyt, James M	97	Fowle, Josiah C
29	Smith, John	98	Congdon, Henry
30	Barber, Henry	99	Jeffreys, Phillip
31	Turner, Henry B	100	Cer, Levi
32	Kellog, Junior, Samuel	101	Dowling, Peter
33	Ingram, William	102	Williams, Dennis
34	Southworth, Justice	103	Cummings, Edward
35	Southworth, George	104	Laughton, Otis
36	Allen, David	105	Lock, Nathaniel
37	Bradbury, Nathaniel	106	Sweet, Moses
38	Thompson, Simon	107	Dyer, Ezekial
39	Miller, George	108	Reid, Luke
40	Wentworth, Alexander	109	Hutchinson, Joseph
41	Morgan, Littleton T	110	Young, Moses
42	Richardson, Randolph	111	Francisco, John Pedro
43	Freeman, John	112	Renney, Comfort S
44	Hall, Robert	113	Dunkan, Henrick
45	Rogers, James	114	Clark, Erren
46	Caston, John	115	Rust, John
47	Buttler, Lephnik	116	Davis, Michael
48	Combes, Peter	117	Antonia, Joseph
49	Barnes, Isaac	118	Hendree, John
50	Roberts, Nicholas	119	Taber, Humphrey
51	Hall, George	120	Butler, John
52	Saunders, Joseph	121	Smith, Thomas R
53	Durant, John	122	Hennee, John D
54	Sharp, Peter	123	Childsey, Abraham
55	Grigous, William	124	Cooper, John
56	Jacobs, William	125	Metrash, Ezekial
57	Beard, James	126	Dennis, Thomas
58	Rogers, James M	127	Peters, John
59	Carland, Edward	128	Gibson, William
60	Van Kleek, John	129	Parrey, John
61	Marina, Nicholas	130	Brooks, George
62	Bowmen, John	131	Emerus, John
63	Stout, Scuder	132	Cole, Richard
64	Oxford, James	133	Lucas, William
65	Langreen, Andrew	134	Powell, William
66	Stamphouse, Henry	135	Young, Martin
67	Porter, William	136	Hendrick, Hugh
68	Scapina, Mathias	137	Southworth, George
69	Jones, Isaac	138	Jacobs, William

American Prisoners of War Held at Bermuda During the War of 1812

139	King, William	210	Williams, Daniel
140	Philips, John	211	Rutter, Samuel
141	Joy, William	212	Henfield, Thomas
142	Coffin, Obediah	213	Burrett, John
143	Dutch, Esra T	214	Naire, Joseph Lee
144	Hodges, Gabriel	215	Patterson, Alexander
145	Jewet, Theodore F	216	Hulland, Nathaniel
146	Foss, Supply	217	Patterson, John
147	Talton, Thomas P	218	Jaimeson, John
148	Furber, Theodore P	219	Gutry, James
149	Peddock, William	220	Barret, Alexander
150	Chase, Peter	221	McKowen, Alex
151	Gardener, Able	222	Bennedick, George
152	Jenkins, Ruben	223	Javar, William
153	Merchant, Abram	224	Couts, John
154	Sailsbury, John	225	Miller, David
155	Skank, Samuel	226	Knight, John
156	Taber, Isaac	227	Reane, John
157	Easton, Isaac	228	Shannon, Henry
158	Coleman, Robert	229	Little, William
159	Coffin, Edward	230	Brown, Joshua
160	Barret, Samuel	231	Tyler, William
161	Calder, Thomas	232	Jones, Henry
162	Coffin, Barna	233	Westwick, William
163	Jones, Jacob	234	Lanboon, Andrew
164	Rogers, G W	235	Ennis, Lewis
165	Biddle, James	236	Castaway, Antonia
166	Booth, Benjamin W	237	Downs, Jeremiah
167	Rapp, Henry B	238	Lyceet, John
168	Knight, William	239	Hall, Samuel
169	New, Walter W	240	Messavy, Philip
170	Conner, James	241	Jackson, John
171	Sweney, Hugh	242	Clerk, Perry
172	Pouree, Stephen	243	Abbeson, John
173	Van Cleave, G W	244	Shawe, Edgebert
174	Ten Eck, Abram S	245	Wilson, William
175	Baker, John C	246	Dixon, Daniel
176	Holcomb, John C	247	Jackson, George
177	Brashears, Richard	248	Ostler, George
178	McLuney, William	249	Moore, Marus
179	Gaunt, Charles	250	Seward, Henry
180	Wilson, Caesar R	251	Wolfe, William
181	Stephens, Levi	252	Harrington, Ebenezer
182	Steady, James	253	Brown, John
183	Cooper, Thomas	254	Mitchell, Henry
184	Edwards, William	255	Berris, John
185	Beeby, Joseph	256	Ward, James
186	Hibbets, John	257	Witten, Elijah
187	Lang, John	258	Johnson, Peter
188	Baldis, Anthony	259	Barber, John
189	Crawford, Johnson	260	Forster, William
190	Coleman, Samuel	261	Gum, Jacob
191	Longel, Matthew	262	White, James
192	Ambruster, Peter	263	Sterns, David
193	Brown, John	264	Beats, John
194	Planter, John	265	Barlow, Joseph
195	Jaimeson, John	266	Rozier, Francis
196	Bowdel, William	267	Freeman, Peter
197	Lawrence, John	268	Gridney, John
198	Samborn, Joseph	269	Wise, George
199	Catley, William	270	Tucker, John
200	Morris, Andrew	271	Cairns, Thomas
201	Cole, John	272	Bradt, Francis
202	Adams, John	273	Wyley, Nathaniel
203	Atkinson, John	274	Harford, Thomas
204	Bostwick, John	275	Allen, Richard
205	Dill, Stephen	276	Branch, Cyrus
206	Lane, Timothy	277	Judy, Joseph
207	Bowring, Jesse	278	Lewis, William
208	Porter, Levi	279	Apthy, Robert
209	Burns, Daniel	280	Bernard, James

American Prisoners of War Held at Bermuda During the War of 1812

281	Dunkley, Isaac		352	La Vie, Antonia
282	Williams, Tatem		353	Morians, Joshua
283	Winner, Joseph		354	Joseph, Charles
284	Claxton, Alexander		355	Rosseau, Peter
285	Harris, J W		356	Ferrat, Charles
286	Skank, Samuel		357	Willock, Henry
287	Duffie, David		358	Hoswell, James
288	Rea, John		359	Goldtrap, William
289	Briggs, John		360	Montsele, John
290	Ryley, William		361	Dormain, John
291	Rollins, John		362	Sampson, George
292	Murphey, William		363	Deveine, Charles
293	Snail, Robert		364	Masta, Antonia
294	Edwards, George Thomas		365	Casora, Amanuel
295	Simpson, William		366	Le Fause, Cade
296	Eagles, John		367	Bruster, William
297	Falk, John		368	Nathans, David
298	Roberts, John		369	Martin, Henry
299	Barrett, James		370	Kerns, George
300	Smith, Charles		371	Farret, William
301	Doyle, Lewis		372	Jeffery, Samuel
302	Clinton, James		373	Moore, Abraham
303	Francis, Lewis		374	Boyd, Thomas
304	McAfferty, William		375	Mailer, Charles
305	Reed, George		376	Carter, William
306	Doherty, Dennis		377	White, Edward
307	Martin, John		378	Antonis, Frederick
308	Burn, Peter		379	Millington, Robert
309	Conner, John		380	Burch, Robert
310	Philips, Thomas		381	Luky, Jacob
311	Stephens, John		382	Free, James
312	McCloud, John		383	Antonia, Peter
313	Mitchell, William		384	Kussleu, Moses
314	Wright, John		385	Good, Frederick
315	Guthwright, James		386	Lee, David
316	Rose, John		387	Falford, William
317	Tibbets, James		388	Simmonds, Isaac
318	Scank, Samuel		389	McKinley, Alexander
319	Rawson, Jonathan		390	Bayton, John
320	Gould, Abraham		391	Brown, John
321	Houlval, John		392	Leech, Nathaniel
322	Morgan, Alexander		393	Williams, Williams
323	Marta, S P		394	Slowbridge, Benjamin
324	Kennedy, Dennis		395	Templing, Henry
325	Horsey, William		396	Willard, Benjamin S
326	Cornwall, A		397	Morris, Charles
327	Oliver, Antonia		398	Connor, Edward
328	Deacon, John		399	Quinolis, Frederick
329	Green, James		400	Label, Antonia
330	Woodburn, Edward		401	Morrison, William
331	Reynolds, John		402	Lathan, Thomas
332	Parker, James B		403	Hartley, Lewis
333	Stephens, Loyd		404	Swarts, Joshua
334	Temple, Joseph		405	Flinn, Pierre
335	Brown, Charles		406	Shawe, Daniel
336	Evans, Jerry		407	Turner, William
337	Dustaine, Peter		408	Lane, John
338	Jones, William		409	Defield, Jesse
339	Flick, John		410	Casora, Samuel
340	Dickenson, James		411	Bassett, Freeman C
341	Ellis, Aaron		412	Hull, Henry
342	Reed, Perry		413	Penny, P B
343	Millis, John		414	Gillet, Nathan
344	Nickson, Robert		415	Parrish, Gideon M
345	Tompkins, James		416	Richards, William
346	Simmonds, George		417	Brigden, John
347	Stephens, David		418	Thatcher, Stephen
348	Henderson, Henry		419	Walford, Thomas
349	Connor, John		420	Linnot, Morgan
350	Arnon, Peter		421	Barker, Charles
351	Hays, Abraham		422	McCloud, John

American Prisoners of War Held at Bermuda During the War of 1812

423	Bowditch, Joseph		494	Smith, Daniel
424	Abbot, George		495	Moore, Isaac
425	Porter, Joshua		496	Lewy, Frederick
426	Walker, John		497	Collet, Peter
427	Warden, John		498	Connor, John
428	Eaton, Andrew		499	Parker, John
429	Rhodes, Charles		500	Holland, Rons
430	McRea, John		501	Carpenter, James
431	Jennings, Jacob		502	Bowling, Garrett
432	Moffott, Hugh		503	Dickinson, Samuel
433	White, Thomas		504	Clyde, Bartin
434	Wentworth, Richard		505	McDermott, James
435	Ferguson, Thomas		506	Elbey, James
436	Williams, John		507	Sebor, William
437	Green, James		508	Dekoven, Henry L
438	Lincoln, Nicholas		509	Baker, George C
439			510	Britt, Thomas
440			511	Shallon, Egbert
441	Kennedy, James		512	Andrews, Hercules
442	Pointer, James		513	Roberts, William D
443	Thompson, Jesse		514	Foot, Jonathan
444	Prout, Jacob		515	Reed, Richard
445	Boston, Daniel		516	Parrish, Samuel
446	McKenny, Nathan		517	Forrest, James
447	Brown, James		518	Cullerton, Noah
448	---, Nathan		519	Pool, Richard
449	Ervin, Charles		520	Reed, Robert
450	Johnson, Frederick		521	Goswilling, David
451	Cullagen, John H		522	Newman, Robert
452	Reynolds, James		523	Dame, George
453	Bartoph, Abber S		524	Orrioto, Dominica
454	Brager, Abner K		525	Brauphau, Romain
455	Sowle, Peley		526	Griffith, David
456	Wedder, Anthony H		527	Frederick, John
457	Stephens, Henry		528	Alliston, John
458	Nevill, James		529	Anthony, Peter
459	Collins, John		530	Johnson, William
460	Sebvea, Andrew		531	Joseph, John
461	Hubbard, Peter		532	Nellands, Adam
462	Cook, Justice		533	Palmer, John
463	Dumkley, Isaac		534	Joseph, Howard
464	Gover, Daniel		535	Saunders, Priest
465	Burridge, James		536	Lasky, George
466	Storme, Daniel		537	Oliver, Thomas
467	Myers, George		538	Harris, Benjamin
468	Davis, John		539	Fonerty, Martin
469	Hall, William		540	Studson, Daniel
470	Stewart, John P		541	Metrois, John
471	Edwards, John		542	Walter, Nathaniel
472	Cartey, John		543	Quin, Francis
473	Rogers, William		544	Sooty, Darooke
474	Frith, William		545	Nelson, John
475	Williams, John		546	Clarey, John
476	Lent, Benjamin		547	Clop, Abner
477	Grant, Peter		548	Clatt, George
478	Huver, John		549	Ervin, John
479	Williams, John		550	Bayer, Abner
480	Holmes, Jahiel		551	Mitret, Onies
481	Dormaine, George		552	White, William
482	Richardson, William		553	Coole, Nathaniel
483	Young, David		554	McCoy, John
484	Lane, Horice		555	Barlie, Aron
485	Humphrey, James		556	Boyen, James
486	Palmer, Justice		557	Kemp, John
487	Gibson, James		558	Stetson, Smith
488	Thomas, Isaac		559	Ireland, Jacob
489	Stone, Samuel		560	Hutchison, Henry
490	McKenzie, Daniel		561	Holmes, C K
491	Tubeter, James		562	Gorden, William
492	Sullingell, William F		563	Kendel, Henry
493	Patterson, Thomas		564	Gyles, William

American Prisoners of War Held at Bermuda During the War of 1812

565	Magruder, Thomas W	636	Retman, Richard
566	Hammond, Benjamin	637	Clifton, Thomas
567	Styles, John	638	Bosman, Henry
568	Macamber, Samuel	639	Smith, Thomas
569	Rose, Perry	640	Rhodes, Pomp
570	Smith, Chester	641	Hill, Jeremiah
571	Thoxter, Leavitt	642	Talpee, John
572	Gold, Thomas	643	Stover, David
573	Stodson, Benjamin	644	Stover, William
574	Spurn, Elias	645	Bradbury, George
575	Briggs, Barb	646	Swanson, Andrew
576	Shepperd, John	647	Williams, Joshua
577	Hanson, Howe	648	Mingle, William
578	Leggar, Daniel	649	Tsdale, James
579	Brock, Thomas	650	Geesson, Frederick
580	Lewis, John	651	Barnes, Timothy W
581	Blue, George	652	Barnes, William
582	Bunker, Nathaniel	653	Page, Cato
583	Butler, Thomas	654	Huckstep, Barnard
584	Petman, Richard	655	Baty, William
585	Smith, David	657	Carson, John
586	Badger, Peter	658	Casey, Henry
587	Young, John	658	Coole, David
588	Longford, Samuel	659	Priest, Stephen
589	Eyre, Jacob	660	Spincker, Gerard
590	Fitzgerald, William	661	Gambee, Daniel
591	Griswold, Charles	662	Selles, Hamilton
592	Wiggs, Benjamin	663	McKurlee, Alexander
593	Witherall, William	664	Pollard, George
594	Grant, Thomas	665	Jones, William
595	Deherty, Dennis	666	Heath, Durham
596	Rowlins, Joshua	667	Miles, David
597	Hutson, James	668	Mann, John
598	Woodburst, Benjamin	669	Randell, Stephen
599	Hooper, John	670	Mavington, William
600	Berry, Daniel	671	Froes, John
601	Willams, John	672	Dyer, John
602	Porter, J C	673	Beatty, Joshua
603	Bussell, William	674	Coxson, Thomas
604	Godfrey, John	675	Barney, Samuel
605	Manley, Samuel	676	Mandell, John
606	Sarose, Belling	677	Thomas, John
607	Hague, Charles	678	Duplantes, Eugene
608	White, Ramsay	679	Pitee, James
609	Morris, Josiah	680	Hall, William
610	Leadworth, Michael	681	Berryman, John
611	Hubbard, John	682	Cole, Edward
612	Sinclair, William	683	Geary, Asburn
613	Cleary, William	684	Covington, John K
614	Finch, William	685	Hatch, James
615	Conover, Thomas A	686	Row, Joseph
616	Pierce, John C	687	Dennis, Joseph
617	Barns, Lincoln	688	Lemer, John
618	Downs, Nasa	689	Warren, Thomas
619	Wentworth, Paul	690	Brown, John
620	Stewart, James	691	Austin, Joseph
621	Barber, George	692	Bensham, William
622	Jacobs, Francis	693	Fernand, John
623	Smith, John	694	Metler, Leonard
624	Mott, Charles	695	Traverse, Henry
625	Sewen, Henry	696	Spear, William
626	Lowe, John	697	Ashcroft, Hugh
627	Goodwin, Joseph	698	Fairbanks, Noah
628	Clerk, Andrew	699	Moody, Sea
629	Scofield, Isaac	700	Bearans, George
630	Cunon, James	701	Stuges, John
631	Sheppard, John	702	Wallace, Andrew
632	Britt, William K	703	Pullock, Joseph
633	McEldry, Hugh	704	Weed, James
634	Holbrock, Richard	705	Lamber, David
635	Foye, James	706	Fracey, Charles

American Prisoners of War Held at Bermuda During the War of 1812

707	Maddox, Samuel	778	Peter, Robert
708	Jarey, John	779	Greenfield, Joseph
709	Quenon, Augustus	780	Dow, Timothy
710	Cole, Nathaniel	781	Durvin, Gerrald
711	Burk, Greenbury	782	Connor, Charles
712	Hart, Daniel	783	Pratt, John
713	Usher, Robert	784	Peterson, Thomas
714	Schasser, John W	785	Weston, George
715	Smith, James	786	White, William
716	Swain, Joseph	787	Forrest, Abraham
717	Salbory, John M	788	Gilbert, Benjamin
718	Dixon, Richard	789	Fresk, John
719	Adier, Simon	790	Claxton, Philip
720	Smith, William	791	Fuller, Benjamin
721	Duncan, Mathew	792	O'Brian, James
722	Knipmire, George	793	Hart, Robert
723	Malstom, James	794	Rousseau, Laurence
724	White, Obediah	795	Smith, Frederick William
725	Ranes, Zachariah	796	Cane, James
726	Vantz, John	797	Black, David
727	Carter, Benjamin	798	Williams, John
728	Godwin, Isaac	799	Gold, Samuel
729	Cornwall, Robert	800	Forbes, Sandy
730	Ingream, John	801	Freeman, Francis
731	Richards, Rocy	802	Harris, James
732	Rhodes, Daniel	803	Allender, William
733	Weeks, William	804	Thompson, John
734	Woodman, Rufus	805	Wright, Samuel
735	Lincoln, Charles	806	Kelly, Thomas
736	Gerlock, Charles	807	Harrington, Lyman
737	Jones, William	808	Basler, Amos
738	Mack, William	809	Graves, John
739	Mack, Charles	810	Lewis, Roswelling
740	Mott, John	811	Cilley, Cutting
741	Whipple, John	812	Jehoff, John
742	Wallace, Thomas	813	Belding, Emos
743	Johnson, Peter	814	Trowbridge, William
744	Buckland, John	815	Hall, Hezekiah
745	Franklin, John	816	Atwater, Levi
746	Taylor, Charles	817	Gibbs, Henry
747	Kennedy, Peter	818	Claxton, Robert
748	Miller, John	819	Hail, Sylvester
749	Cole, David	820	Luther, Nathaniel
750	Noble, Daniel	821	Whitten, Joseph
751	Lascell, William	822	Brown, Soloman
752	Green, Ezekiel	823	Moat, James
753	Smith, Joseph	824	Parker, Redman
754	Bagley, Daniel	825	Pembroke, John
755	Loring, Almond	826	Wiley, Jonathan
756	White, Cornelius	827	Marsden, William
757	Palmer, William	828	Bocock, Matthew
758	Turner, Daniel	829	Johnson, John
759	Joseph, John	830	Wolf, Henry
760	Griffin, James	831	Haughton, William
761	Kelly, John	832	Page, Jonkins
762	Smith, James	833	Brown, John
763	Lewis, Henry	834	Ball, Isaac
764	---, Paulsow	835	Chuseman, John
765	Harlow, Benjamin	836	Kelly, Joshua
766	Bagnell, Joseph	837	Beach, John
767	Feunce, Bartlet	838	Johnson, Henry
768	Rogers, Thomas	839	Dalton, Thomas
769	Batt, James	840	Moore, John
770	Carter, Benjamin	841	Sandbug, Charles
771	Kern, Nicholas	842	Millehus, Frederick
772	Slocolm, John	843	Wright, James
773	Sandford, Daniel	844	Johnson, Richard
774	Sandford, Royal	845	Murphey, Daniel
775	French, Calvin	846	Thatcher, John
776	Burnell, Thomas	847	Marlin, William
777	Brooks, Thomas	848	Young, Joshua

American Prisoners of War Held at Bermuda During the War of 1812

849	Bringham, John William	920	Traquave, John
850	Smith, Jacob	921	Frederick, Thomas
851	Hazard, Wanton	922	Bond, Robert
852	Hulitz, Joseph	923	Peterson, Jacob
853	Seaman, Isaac	924	Coote, Thomas O
854	Estes, J H T	925	Josamana, P
855	David, Michael	926	Rovada, Antony
856	Fish, Allen	927	Benitt, Juan
857	Hawkins, William	928	Juan, Francis
858	Bennison, Lenord	929	Taylor, Dugomier
859	Le Count, Philip	930	Jenkins, Robert
860	Toppin, John P	931	Short, Moses
861	Naus, Littleton	932	Honest, John
862	Fearine, Isiah	933	Coward, Thomas
863	Smith, Major	934	Larke, James R
864	Smith, Weston	935	Cavines, John
865	Clark, Charles	936	Gleaves, George
866	Craft, N W	937	Jackson, M
867	Brown, Jonas	938	Tunis, John
868	Beers, Oliver	939	Libbey, Richard
869	Appleturit, Charles	940	Walden, Samuel
870	Ludlow, William	941	Dominga, N
871	Abreeve, Pirzanno	942	Berry, Lyman
872	Johnson, Jonas	943	Tronmonger, Edward
873	Dexter, Dennis	944	Wallace, Peter
874	Parker, S G	945	Wallace, Matthew
875	Hall, William	946	Dameron, John
876	Cornwall, Edward	947	Cox, James
877	Guard, Andrew	948	Stephenson, David
878	Webber, William	949	Blayer, Robert
879	Innis, William	950	Rogers, Errin
880	Delano, Harper	951	Binghouse, William
881	Innis, Benjamin	952	Peterson, Thomas
882	Gardner, Rowland	953	Harrimond, John
883	Luke, Clarke	954	Stephens, James
884	Shaw, Benjamin	955	Hozier, Samuel
885	Shaw, Samuel	956	Poop, Elijah
886	Theafe, William	957	Sherlock, Samuel
887	Sidney, Edward	958	Nelson, T W
888	Wyer, Joseph	959	Sanders, Job
889	Anderson, John	960	Fackson, J W
890	Cloeth, John	961	Morton, Abraham
891	Clarke, James	962	Joy, David
892	Micklins, John	963	Warren, John
893	Brown, Daniel	964	Barton, John
894	Edmonds, Thomas	965	Pritchard, Charles
895	Throughgood, William	966	Harrod, Joseph
896	Halsey, John	967	Pritchard, John
897	Josey, Jack	968	Browel, William
898	Downridge, Stephen	969	Bottings, Carter
899	Joachina, Josia	970	Gregory, John
900	Caton, Joseph	971	Matthews, Edward
901	Prader, Manuel	972	Cure, Thomas
902	Roderique, John	973	Manston, David
903	Johnson, R	974	Bowman, William
904	Storey, Peter	975	Richards, William
905	Bradley, Philip	976	Le Porte, Archibald
906	Bartholomew, Herain	977	Howard, William
907	Palmer, John	978	Brockway, John
908	Hicks, Samuel	979	Haskell, Joseph
909	Ingle, George	980	Jones, James
910	Callahan, Joshua	981	Berry, Gordon
911	Sanderson, Francis	982	Pendleton, Robert
912	Kelso, George	983	Wilcox, Pelic
913	Brown, John	984	Littlefield, Lyman
914	Alden, Benjamin	985	Nicklye, John L
915	Anderson, Jacob	986	Brown, Stephen
916	Elliot, Nicholas	987	Wells, Thomas
917	Johnson, William	988	Whitmarsh, Z
918	Mure, D W	989	Brown, Parker
919	Halborn, Thomas	990	Shorter, Jesse

American Prisoners of War Held at Bermuda During the War of 1812

991	Bailie, Joseph		1062	Howland, John
992	Peyton, James		1063	Spanger, Edward
993	West, John		1064	Scott, Pleasant
994	Barns, James		1065	Fisher, William
995	Lane, John		1066	Mason, Thomas
996	Miller, Martin		1067	Sandford, Giles
997	Lewis, S H B		1068	Wing, Paul
998	Sawyer, Nathaniel		1069	Wing, Philip
999	Freeman, Nathaniel		1070	Davis, James
1000	Woodbury, Thomas		1071	Atwood, Isaac
1001	Childs, Adam		1072	Knowles, Thorpolin
1002	Buckin, Bartholomew		1073	Dill, Isaiah
1003	Surgor, John F		1074	Archer, Thomas
1004	Cutler, Thomas		1075	Freeman, Jesse
1005	Perry, Liberty		1076	Snow, Joseph
1006	Woodbury, William		1077	Williams, William
1007	Patch, Joseph		1078	Solaris, Francis
1008	Pausland, John		1079	Elliot, John
1009	Miln, Michael		1080	Anderson, Peter
1010	Dennison, Isaac		1081	Greason, George
1011	Bennett, George		1082	Merry, William
1012	McCaun, John		1083	Merig, John
1013	Holt, William		1084	Thomas, Francis
1014	Mezarux, Ephraim		1085	Cartwright, Alexander
1015	Kent, Obediah		1086	Knight, Charles
1016	Harris, Charles		1087	Thompson, William
1017	Nicklos, William		1088	Courtney, Edward
1018	Slocum, George		1089	Bell, James
1019	Shooter, Charles		1090	Gall, John
1020	Fisher, Ephraim		1091	Lapee, Silvester
1021	Coalman, Joseph		1092	Schutte, Harms
1022	Stoddien, Warren		1093	Piedmont, Thomas
1023	Taylor, Thomas		1094	Halgreen, Peter
1024	Allen, John		1095	Holshem, Andrew
1025	Polk, Samuel		1096	Sage, John
1026	Pervis, William		1097	Buckford, Andrew
1027	McKenzie, Thomas		1098	Silsby, John W
1028	Finis, Peter		1099	Soalby, Nathaniel
1029	Sungrain, Oliver		1100	Collins, John
1030	Layfield, William		1101	Knap, Samuel
1031	Bray, Henry		1102	Smith, John
1032	Mitchel, Chester		1103	Gray, Nehemiah
1033	Hurth, Charles		1104	Clemons, Henry
1034	Hilbert, Samuel		1105	Appleton, John
1035	Kempenfield, William		1106	Meek, John
1036	Gage, William		1107	Dutch, Nathaniel
1037	Forsyth, Asa		1108	Baxter, John
1038	Sloan, Henry		1109	Hill, John
1039	Richards, John		1110	Pearson, William
1040	Starr, John		1111	Kerson, George
1041	Hunt, Edward P		1112	Sulivan, James
1042	Bensley, William		1113	Powers, John
1043	Jefferson, Isaac		1114	Gasaway, George
1044	Shapper, William		1115	Exley, William
1045	Hutchinson, John		1116	Keir, John
1046	Jones, Daniel		1117	Lindsey, Joseph
1047	Allen, Truman		1118	Brown, Webster
1048	Moore, Robert		1119	Hathaway, Pardon
1049	Noyce, Nathaniel		1120	Devereux, Robert
1050	Look, John		1121	Cross, James
1051	De Witch, Samuel		1122	Crawford, John
1052	Willard, John		1123	McPrelvey, Thomas
1053	Thicket, Elliot		1124	Holder, Jeremiah
1054	Forbes, John		1125	Corbett, John
1055	Bruce, James		1126	Johnson, John
1056	Southworth, John		1127	Ervin, John
1057	Walker, Benjamin		1128	Medad, Emos
1058	Cole, Henry		1129	Brown, Liberty
1059	Joyce, John		1130	Moore, William
1060	Cushin, Lezer		1131	Wright, John
1061	Cushman, Harvey		1132	Wills, Philip

American Prisoners of War Held at Bermuda During the War of 1812

1133	Mowton, George	1204	Johnstone, John
1134	Johnston, William	1205	Johnston, William
1135	Rogers, John	1206	Davis, John
1136	Whitney, James	1207	Rogers, John
1137	Morris, Frank	1208	May, William
1138	Anderson, Edward	1209	Littlefield, N
1139	Barton, William	1210	Bradford, John
1140	Goodall, William	1211	Cill, John F
1141	Gould, Thomas	1212	Golden, Edward
1142	Brown, Alexander	1213	Parr, James
1143	Green, John	1214	Holesley, John
1144	Wickman, Andrew	1215	Stephens, James
1145	Gaimsley, Thomas	1216	Stringer, William
1146	Smith, John	1217	James, Benjamin
1147	Anderson, William	1218	Stephenson, John
1148	Paul, John	1219	Febre, William
1149	Donavan, Benjamin	1220	---, George
1150	Galloway, Michael	1221	Lafebui, Bartin
1151	Eroundy, Francis	1222	Yong, Bill
1152	Harris, William	1223	---, Sayler
1153	Emerson, Andrew	1224	---, Tom
1154	Mitchell, Lewis	1225	Jermain, Joseph
1155	Lyn, John	1226	Gordine, Anthony
1156	Davis, Peter	1227	Patrick, George
1157	Hancock, James	1228	Bowman, Thaddus
1158	Fodder, Francis	1229	Lee, W R
1159	De Shitts, Matthew	1230	Hopkins, Samuel
1160	Drew, Ezekiel	1231	Corkes, Dan
1161	Collins, James	1232	Brett, James
1162	Murphey, John	1233	Boyd, Thomas D
1163	---, Poitless Moe	1234	Elliott, John
1164	Crown, Frederick	1235	Callam, John
1165	Hepburn, John	1236	Shorter, Roger
1166	Leters, Charles	1237	Frederick, John
1167	Morrison, Samuel	1238	Callam, Theop
1168	Sheffield, William	1239	Stringer, Thomas
1169	Gregoris, Dominic	1240	Craig, William
1170	Allison, William	1241	Miers, Edward
1171	Corie, John	1242	Mallet, John
1172	Alexander, Hector	1243	Wilcocks, William
1173	Gould, James	1244	Barnet, John
1174	Trigony, Peter	1245	Dunton, Thomas
1175	Benedick, John	1246	Dunton, Thomas
1176	Goodspeed, Joseph	1247	Dunton, Robert
1177	Thomas, John	1248	Ardrey, Alexander
1178	Lovett, William	1249	Harrington, Samuel
1179	Mann, Thomas	1250	Squires, Samuel C
1180	Allock, Elijah	1251	Bladen, Thomas
1181	Waterhouse, John	1252	Blair, John R
1182	Mass, Moses	1253	Miller, William
1183	Allen, Henry	1254	Parker, John
1184	Rossan, Aman	1255	Lewis, Sol
1185	Victor, William	1256	Augh, James Henry
1186	Marshall, John	1257	Hepp, James
1187	Bernard, John	1258	Carven, Thomas
1188	Paterson, John	1259	Briggs, Silvinus
1189	Tomlin, Samuel	1260	Bradbury, John H
1190	Mason, Manuel	1261	Bailey, Cyral
1191	Silsbee, Benjamin	1262	Currie, James
1192	Silsbee, J W	1263	Arnold, William
1193	Collins, Samuel	1264	Bacon, Silvester
1194	Forrest, John	1265	Bulter, Richard
1195	Davis, John	1266	Gibbs, Moses
1196	Clark, William	1267	Baker, Samuel
1197	Figges, William	1268	Worth, John
1198	Parvlin, William	1269	Stringer, Isaac
1199	Geer, John	1270	Lamberg, John
1200	Jacobs, Samuel	1271	Rice, John
1201	Floyd, Thomas	1272	Salsburg, William
1202	Staple, Thomas	1273	Cory, Green
1203	Maxworth, Mathew	1274	Pratt, Anza

American Prisoners of War Held at Bermuda During the War of 1812

1275	Mackay, James F		1346	Bert, Thomas
1276	Leger, Daniel		1347	Crafts, John
1277	Baker, Robert		1348	Castignet, John
1278	Gould, John		1349	Waymore, John
1279	Pollard, William		1350	Johnson, James
1280	Berry, Jessy		1351	Justin, William
1281	Wolf, Henry		1352	Hoskin, Cato
1282	Ingersole, James		1353	Smith, John
1283	Robinson, Robert		1354	Grindell, Henry
1284	White, Isaac		1355	Anderson, Andrew
1285	Hatch, John		1356	Beard, James
1286	Geiste, George		1357	Beard, Martin
1287	Batis, John		1358	Henderson, Francis
1288	Peters, John		1359	Stoddart, Isaac
1289	Smith, Thomas		1360	Hazard, D
1290	McDonald, Alexander		1361	Gardner, Timothy
1291	Bogardus, J B		1362	Thomas, William
1292	Beach, John		1363	Lorin, George
1293	Havins, William		1364	Lewis, D
1294	Campbell, Charles		1365	Dixon, John
1295	Bloom, John		1366	Clark, John
1296	Belfeur, James		1367	Martin, Samuel
1297	Fellows, G H		1368	Brown, Willliam
1298	Latham, A B		1369	Widget, Abrea
1299	Fellows, Nathaniel		1370	Allison, B C
1300	Burrows, A H		1371	Little, William
1301	Borrswell, Paul		1372	Huntington, E
1302	Coil, R M		1373	Hill, Pompey
1303	Holland, J H		1374	Shaw, Robert
1304	Cook, Dennis		1375	Hossday, William
1305	Boss, Joseph		1376	Coffen, G B
1306	Palmer, Benjamin		1377	Laurence, Adam
1307	Shaw, Joseph		1378	Damore, Samuel
1308	Phelps, Elijah		1379	Sullivan, Richard
1309	Dryden, John		1380	Foster, Charles
1310	Jones, Edward		1381	Gibbs, J
1311	Molton, C P		1382	Lake, Benjamin
1312	Swinney, Benjamin		1383	Harvey, John
1313	Holden, James		1384	Collins, John
1314	Cousens, Benjamin		1385	Green, Peter
1315	Bennet, Abua		1386	Silvarus, John
1316	Davis, John		1387	Hanfelt, O
1317	Tyler, Daniel		1388	Welch, Thomas
1318	Batis, John		1389	Barles, Frederick
1319	Hopkins, M H		1390	Young, James W
1320	Richardson, Perry		1391	Forger, Joseph
1321	Lee, Samuel		1392	Hodges, Gamiel
1322	Bushnam, James		1393	Clough, William
1323	Costin, Thomas		1394	Edwards, William
1324	Day, William		1395	Kings, Thomas
1325	Burns, James		1396	Brown, Francis
1326	Briggs, B		1397	Bonker, Daniel
1327	Brown, George		1398	Brook, Peley
1328	Satchell, Jonathan		1399	Elkin, M
1329	Metzger, C D		1400	Swain, John
1330	Washington, John		1401	Chan, Frederick
1331	Larkin, Lewis		1402	Creasey, Rubin
1332	Unewell, John		1403	Butill, Dennis
1333	Ware, John		1404	Frankland, Benjamin
1334	McGee, John		1405	Douglass, Simon
1335	Boon, James		1406	Gordon, John
1336	Hammond, Samuel		1407	Cole, John
1337	Cooper, Lad		1408	Coone, William
1338	Shustliff, John		1409	Bacchus, A
1339	Cole, Nathaniel		1410	Winer, Elijah
1340	Cuff, Abraham		1411	Grieves, Whitny
1341	Smith, John		1412	Avery, Daniel
1342	Bayley, Warren		1413	Edwards, Nicholas
1343	Barber, J H		1414	Dunton, G
1344	Windwood, William		1415	Dixon, M
1345	Simpson, John		1416	Stanhour, Francis

American Prisoners of War Held at Bermuda During the War of 1812

1417	Bennett, Peley	1488	Hall, Robert
1418	Hardy, Robert	1489	Hall, William
1419	James, John	1490	Hunter, Samuel
1420	Peterson, P	1491	Blackwell, William
1421	Green, John	1492	Vose, Avery
1422	Prindale, S	1493	Shuffield, Joseph
1423	Blakely, M	1494	Freeman, A
1424	Silvester, Emis	1495	Rifley, George
1425	Leathan, Thomas	1496	Winsley, William
1426	Marshall, G	1497	Boyles, James
1427	Coles, Charles	1498	Savil, Francis O
1428	Yarnell, William	1499	Douglass, Robert
1429	Watkin, William	1500	Johnson, Joseph
1430	Blocke, Edmond	1501	Ingram, George
1431	Noss, Henry	1502	Kielsey, Henry
1432	Peterson, James	1503	Down, John
1433	Peterson, John	1504	Homan, Peter
1434	Bush, George	1505	Gage, Zachariah
1435	Clasker, C	1506	Raymond, William
1436	Brown, James	1507	Noble, Andrew
1437	Peterson, Lawrence	1508	Kellegan, James
1438	Wickes, Samuel	1509	Parker, Joseph
1439	Welch, Thomas	1510	Sullivan, John
1440	Bankson, W C	1511	Bernard, William
1441	Hammond, J	1512	Davis, George
1442	Canshard, T R	1513	Holmes, John
1443	Millington, F	1514	Paine, William
1444	Hughes, William	1515	Hussey, R
1445	Butler, Robert	1516	Basset, Samuel
1446	Buchan, Benjamin	1517	Jones, Charles
1447	Lawton, G	1518	Jackson, William
1448	Hewston, J	1519	Forshew, John
1449	Hall, Humes	1520	Hicks, John
1450	McChusney, William	1521	Northorp, Alexander
1451	Evans, Benjamin	1522	Catehart, Robert
1452	Edes, Benjamin	1523	Bughton, James
1453	Parker, William	1524	Willis, J
1454	Coles, Thomas	1525	Nicholson, Martin
1455	Francisco, Clias	1526	Mawn, Mathias
1456	Francisco, Antonio	1527	Mitchell, Chester
1457	Sutton, Nathan	1528	Miller, Petter
1458	Carpenter, Nathaniel	1529	Petero, John
1459	Joseph, Fortunata	1530	Macey, F G
1460	Jackay, Joseph	1531	Alexand, John
1461	McCollock, Robert	1532	Stapford, D F
1462	Brown, John L	1533	Coffin, Linzey
1463	Mathews, Henry	1534	Swensen, Hans
1464	Williams, John	1535	Allen, Joseph
1465	Tupp, John	1536	Perry, John
1466	Spaniola, John	1537	Cotterell, Thomas
1467	Foyte, Henry	1538	Whippey, W C
1468	Weeks, Joseph	1539	Gerry, Samuel R
1469	Brooks, Thomas	1540	Blackler, Henry
1470	Nicholson, William	1541	Broughton, Nicholas
1471	Teaser, James	1542	Hooper, Thomas
1472	Heartie, Isaac	1543	Madison, Andrew
1473	Butler, John	1544	,
1474	Humphries, Thomas	1545	Culver, Esau
1475	Tone, William P	1546	Deurege, John
1476	Dacres, John B	1547	Perry, Henry
1477	Winslow, Oliver	1548	Lee, George
1478	Spring, Daniel	1549	Higgenbottom, William
1479	Honquest, Peter	1550	Powers, John
1480	Gasper, John	1551	Apenny, William
1481	Wisbec, Caleb	1552	Fisher, John
1482	Humpson, John	1553	Bennett, Thomas
1483	Johnson, Thomas	1554	Jefferson, Jacob
1484	Coffin, William	1555	Frances, Michael
1485	Catehard, Charles	1556	Childs, Adam
1486	Bunquar, Obsolou	1557	Thaitis, John
1487	Hall, John	1558	Miller, Thomas

American Prisoners of War Held at Bermuda During the War of 1812

1559	Gordon, William		1630	Willson, Andrew
1560	Ritchen, Robert		1631	James, Sidney
1561	Briddon, Thomas		1632	McIntire, Abraham
1562	Vorris, Philip		1633	Clark, Peleg
1563	Thomas, John		1634	Johnson, Peter
1564	Johnson, Jacob		1635	Price, Charles
1565	McFeadon, John		1636	James, John
1566	Hero, John		1637	Garrett, Robert
1567	Heddon, John		1638	Mounteam, Henry
1568	Perruall, Hugh		1639	Douglass, Aquilla
1569	Hendrickson, John		1640	Mark, John
1570	Rockhill, James		1641	Deligall, William
1571	Grimes, George		1642	Giblet, Bendus
1572	Mason, Francis		1643	Holland, John
1573	Burnam, Beasson		1644	Sturtevant, Nehemiah
1574	Barton, Samuel		1645	Swatt, Christian
1575	Mourice, Joseph		1646	Steward, Samuel
1576	Weaver, Nicholas		1647	Craig, Ephraim
1577	Healey, Edward		1648	Colgan, Christian
1578	Yeoman, John		1649	Thompson, James
1579	Talman, Joseph		1650	Humphries, Horiatio
1580	Kene, Davis		1651	Davis, Israel
1581	Rogers, Henry		1652	Collagon, John
1582	Ford, Standi		1653	Giles, Charles
1583	Law, Thomas		1654	Pinshaw, Joseph
1584	Sutherland, John		1655	North, John N
1585	Trout, Nathaniel		1656	Watts, John
1586	Clyne, Lewis		1657	Lewis, James
1587	Sullivan, Samuel		1658	Cox, Charles
1588	Meensey, Daniel		1659	Barrett, Thomas
1589	Currant, Nicholas		1660	Goss, Thomas
1590	Palmer, Robert		1661	Clark, James
1591	Curtis, Lebe		1662	Carpenter, Vincent
1592	Hippeny, Anthony		1663	Roberts, Charles
1593	Smith, John		1664	Young, William
1594	Dixon, Archibald		1665	Laurence, William
1595	Lyons, Henry G		1666	Fairfield, James M
1596	Hatwood, P		1667	Bartholomew, Joseph
1597	Toddy, William		1668	Howard, Benjamin
1598	Ellridge, Henry		1669	Barker, A L
1599	Randall, Cater		1670	Cox, L G F
1600	Shellebar, George		1671	White, Henry C
1601	Cross, Jacob		1672	Johnson, William
1602	Ray, R		1673	Lambert, James
1603	Coffin, Alexander		1674	Johnson, James
1604	Lang, R		1675	Hooper, John
1605	Swaine, William		1676	Lewis, Michael
1606	Jones, Abraham		1677	Howe, Edward
1607	Coleman, William		1678	Lattimore, C N
1608	Sweedy, P		1679	Smith, Elias
1609	Burke, Humphrey		1680	Chidry, Abraham
1610	Smith, Jacob		1681	Melna, Joseph
1611	Johnson, Charles		1682	Finny, Isaac
1612	Gibbs, John		1683	Walker, David
1613	Howland, Robert		1684	Butler, Joseph
1614	West, James		1685	Thompson, James
1615	Cole, H A		1686	Randall, Oates
1616	Johnson, Peter		1687	Chester, William
1617	Barnet, George		1688	Latham, Giles
1618	Dill, William		1689	Kelly, John
1619	Amos, Samuel		1690	Richardson, James
1620	Brailey, Elisha		1691	Hippencott, Caleb
1621	Chester, William		1692	Willum, William
1622	Moore, Prince		1693	Jacobs, Cupid
1623	Bunkar, Isa		1694	Evans, William
1624	Frank, John		1695	Dix, Robert
1625	Francis, John		1696	Robinson, George
1626	Watson, T		1697	Jones, Samuel
1627	Drake, Harrison		1698	Powell, Elisha
1628	Brown, P F		1699	Gale, Thomas
1629	Wheeler, David		1700	Mauney, John

American Prisoners of War Held at Bermuda During the War of 1812

1701	Smith, James	1772	Joseph, John
1702	Delany, Francis	1773	Burding, Joseph
1703	Kimbury, John	1774	Strong, Ceres
1704	Duram, Peter	1775	Bowen, Nathaniel
1705	Robertson, David	1776	Lee, John
1706	Carter, Thomas	1777	Jackson, Lewis
1707	Hadley, John	1778	Garcia, James
1708	Howes, George	1779	Cole, Lutha
1709	Smith, James	1780	Hogan, Norman A
1710	Bashford, William	1781	Robertson, James
1711	Gale, Thomas	1782	Goff, Dina
1712	Watson, William	1783	Young, Richard
1713	McCarthy, James	1784	Campbell, John
1714	Locket, Agnetu	1785	Pike, John
1715	Adams, Isaac	1786	Aspenell, Elijah
1716	Miure, William	1787	Thomas, James
1717	Drew, Benjamin	1788	Barrett, William S
1718	Turner, William	1789	Grimes, Richard
1719	Thorp, George	1790	Plumely, John
1720	Knapp, Thomas	1791	Doak, Nathaniel
1721	Downing, George	1792	Guswold, Truman
1722	Huring, William	1793	Russell, Thomas
1723	West, Francis	1794	Barton, Lette
1724	Pray, Caterwick	1795	Burr, William
1725	Cankling, Thomas C	1796	Whitaker, Manly
1726	Churchill, Benjamin	1797	Taber, Rubin
1727	Cook, Dennis	1798	Sambo, Joseph
1728	Watt, John	1799	Evans, John
1729	Nightingale, Joseph	1800	Tilbots, Benjamin
1730	Hunt, Isaac A	1801	Henman, Richard
1731	Johnson, Thomas	1802	Savage, Timothy
1732	Green, John	1803	Savage, Absolam
1733	Plummer, Isaac L	1804	Williams, Samuel
1734	Giffigan, Thomas	1805	Zeizell, John O
1735	Hanna, Edward	1806	Hall, Henry
1736	Fox, George	1807	Strong, Robert
1737	Josif, Antinio	1808	Lee, Hezekiah I
1738	Hanster, John	1809	White, Isaac
1739	Morice, Marcus	1810	Davis, John
1740	Williams, Daniel	1811	Richards, Guy
1741	Pickens, Samuel	1812	Smith, Ichabod
1742	Daniels, John	1813	Bell, William
1743	Spencer, Job F	1814	Phillips, John
1744	Robinson, John	1815	Brown, Richard
1745	Willson, George	1816	Steward, John
1746	Darby, Joseph	1817	Butler, George
1747	Mitchell, Jonah	1818	Godfrey, John
1748	Murphey, John	1819	Swanson, Jacob
1749	Brown, James	1820	Thompson, Benjamin
1750	Green, John	1821	Bourne, Esra
1751	Prowe, Tudar	1822	Neaves, Samuel
1752	Mofford, Gardner	1823	Sabins, John
1753	Wise, Joseph	1824	Hodgkin, Nathaniel
1754	Bruce, Jonathan	1825	Richards, Steven
1755	Catan, William	1826	Catlin, Othello
1765	Pratt, Samuel	1827	Stowe, John
1757	Small, Benjamin	1828	Hubbard, Jeremiah
1758	McCannon, Isaac	1829	Williams, William
1759	Wells, George	1830	Crummett, John
1760	Moffunire, Henry	1831	Wood, Bill
1761	Simons, Evan	1832	Rodgers, Smith
1762	Collins, Thomas	1833	Longshore, Thomas
1763	Astor, Doroty	1834	Brockitt, William
1764	Pitts, Samuel	1835	Terry, Thomas C
1765	Perriotte, Louis	1836	Goodridge, E
1766	Williams, Nicholas	1837	Theyer, J H
1767	Appleton, John	1838	Young, John
1768	Roach, William	1839	Blass, J G
1769	Tiler, Christian	1840	Deainson, J
1770	Maclever, Francis	1841	
1771	Johnson, Samuel	1842	Dorington, Charles

American Prisoners of War Held at Bermuda During the War of 1812

1843	Williams, William	1914	Smith, Joseph
1844		1915	Bablisto, John
1845	Dimond, John	1916	Marsdon, George
1846	Poulson, Alex	1917	Sportfield, Collin
1847	Kids, R F	1918	Bella, John
1848	Bertram, John	1919	Davis, Pascari
1849	Sweet, Stephen	1920	Matheu, John
1850	Seward, Theodore	1921	Gouchon, John
1851	Dansey, Peter	1922	Johnson, Joseph
1852	Sansum, Philip	1923	Hammond, William
1853		1924	Lolly, William
1854	Smith, James	1925	Wilkinson, Francis
1855	Richardson, James	1926	Marshall, David
1856	Huntington, John	1927	Smith, Joseph F
1857	Moon, John	1928	Brook, Calvin
1858	Green, Joseph	1929	Saunder, James L
1859	Valentine, Cata	1930	Bonwell, Garland
1860	Henry, Samuel	1931	Moore, William
1861	Thomas, Corbet	1932	Clark, Thomas
1862	Andrews, John	1933	Fall, Alphun
1863	Bryan, Fagalte	1934	Young, Richard
1864	Segoss, Ezekiel	1935	Smith, William
1865	Vickery, C	1936	Davis, William
1866	Brown, R	1937	Taylor, John
1867	Smith, E	1938	Edward, Simon
1868	Moordie, John	1939	Elliot, Robert
1869		1940	Swanson, Peter
1870	Wardnell, Solomon	1941	Dawson, Christopher
1871	Brazier, William	1942	Martin, Charles
1872	Wendall, Abraham	1943	Brown, William
1873	Bondleau, Thomas	1944	Norbury, Charles
1874	Odnell, Samuel	1945	Smith, James
1875	Doughty, Russell	1946	Williams, John
1876	Tucker, D F	1947	Saunder, William
1877	Dennis, James	1948	Allen, Peter
1878	Standly, Timothy	1949	Sommers, Frederick
1879	Bradshaw, John	1950	Morris, John
1880	Stone, James	1951	Moffatt, John
1881	Furance, George	1952	Dove, Samuel
1882	Wellman, Timothy	1953	Dodd, Thomas
1883	Wright, James	1954	Jackson, William
1884	Cousins, John	1955	Blyden, John
1885	Cleareyd, James	1956	Cooper, John
1886	Williams, Samuel	1957	Kidmore, Joseph
1887		1958	Rose, James
1888	Bray, Robert	1959	Reybold, George
1889	McIntire, J L	1960	Cawdrick, Samuel
1890	Clement, Joseph	1961	Long, Robert
1891	Davis, Samuel	1962	Cooper, James
1892	Smith, John	1963	Monger, William
1893	Lands, John	1964	Forster, James
1894	Dickenson, Henry	1965	Richardson, Joseph
1895	Bythwood, John	1966	Fenderson, Steward
1896	Cook, Samuel	1967	Davis, John
1897	Campbell, Daniel	1968	Wood, John
1898	Davis, Josiah	1969	Clicy, Peter
1899	---, Hard Times	1970	Cook, Alexander
1900	Robinson, Thomas	1971	Cottle, Henry
1901	---, Pinkey	1972	Holmer, Robert
1902	Demers, William	1973	McCall, Thomas William
1903	Cloutman, Abaneza	1974	Dew, Edward
1904	Emory, Samuel	1975	Ritter, Michael
1905	Merrick, John F	1976	Gibbs, Samuel
1906	Darrel, John S	1977	Tabor, Daniel
1907	Richards, Toby	1978	Beatty, Henry
1908	Shaddock, Anthony	1979	Willberger, Joseph S
1909	Stacey, R S	1980	Gonsalvos, Joseph
1910	Williams, Lloyd	1981	Brown, John F
1911	Garrison, Ephraim	1982	Henry, William
1912	Broughton, Elijah	1983	Davey, Hugh
1913	Coutigo, Frederick	1984	Liffler, Henry

American Prisoners of War Held at Bermuda During the War of 1812

1985	Tooling, Francoi	2056	Long, John
1986	Barsabella, Julian	2057	Sephey, Peter
1987	Gillings, Benjamin	2058	Brown, Hans
1988	Lewis, William	2059	Wells, Thomas
1989	Lackley, Joseph	2060	Anderson, Charles
1990	Davis, John	2061	Heyle, Philip
1991	Sherwood, Ralph	2062	Robson, John
1992	Guest, Edward	2063	Beatey, James
1993	Vere, Jean	2064	DeForrest, John
1994	Oxand, Michael	2065	Kregoe, Martin
1995	Thompson, James	2066	Ferrander, Antonio
1996	Ryan, Patrick	2067	Cherriers, Beattie
1997	Masselin, Horace F	2068	Douvernier, Nicholas
1998	Johnson, John	2069	McDonald, David
1999	Morson, Joseph	2070	Caffsky, John
2000	Schrothn, David	2071	Taylor, James
2001	Morris, John	2072	Johnson, Loyd
2002	Brill, Christopher	2073	Lawson, William
2003	Hinley, Joseph	2074	Hall, William F
2004	Watson, William	2075	Bayley, Joseph
2005	Chavers, Sidney	2076	Nulty, Thomas
2006	Foot, James	2077	Gall, William
2007	Poore, Thomas	2078	Howell, William
2008	Edwards, Benjamin	2079	White, Robert
2009	Carlisle, William	2080	White, Joseph
2010	Butler, John	2081	Dore, Daniel
2011	Jenkins, Robert	2082	Card, John
2012	Knapp, Samuel	2083	Fisher, John W
2013	Bradbury, William	2084	Wade, Robert
2014	Higgins, Joseph	2085	Martin, Isaac
2015	Bragdon, Joseph	2086	Thompson, Charles
2016	Gursting, Oliver	2087	Carrolan, James
2017	Nason, Aaron	2088	Kershaw, Newman
2018	Homan, John	2089	Wragg, Erasmus R
2019	Griffin, John	2090	Jackson, John
2020	Taros, Vecentia	2091	Turley, Enoch
2021	Lucas, William	2092	Lane, Alexander
2022	Webber, Daniel	2093	Metzger, John
2023	Hunt, Thomas	2094	Wing, George
2024	Young, Robert	2095	Butler, John
2025	Barr, Robert	2096	Eldridge, David
2026	Hyatt, Abel	2097	Weeks, Josiah
2027	Cummins, Christopher	2098	Thompson, James
2028	Allen, Duffy	2099	Tucker, James B
2029	Baylee, George	2100	Samoe, David
2030	Tisdale, Sterling	2101	Johnson, Robert
2031	Webster, William H	2102	Houton, William
2032	Mecanger, Michael	2103	Smith, Deliverance
2033	Darby, Joseph	2103	Hill, Joseph
2034	Tipereal, Andrew	2104	Harris, John
2035	Holman, William	2106	James, Charles
2036	Johnson, Francis	2107	Williams, John
2037	French, John	2108	Headley, James
2038	Kempton, Noah S	2109	Steward, Joseph
2039	Merrick, Ebenezer	2110	Dupecy, John
2040	Taber, William M	2111	Howard, Henry
2041	Gualt, Charles	2112	Sutlet, William
2042	Taylor, James D	2113	Warner, Samuel
2043	Afferil, Charles	2114	Morrill, Charles
2044	Wilson, Sidney	2115	Scott, George
2045	Muskett, William	2116	Jones, John
2046	Riley, William	2117	Chessnutt, Adam
2047	Woodman, Constant	2118	Morgan, John
2048	Sandford, Samuel	2119	Barkam, Thomas
2049	Flora, Peter	2120	Atkins, George
2050	Donnelly, Joseph	2121	Post, Anthony
2051	Armstrong, Nicholas C	2122	Sillsby, Benjamin
2052	Sexton, James	2123	Smith, Ebenezer
2053	Gray, Edward	2124	Kneeland, Edward M
2054	Roberts, Samuel	2125	Blanchard, Ebenezer
2055	Antonio, Manuel	2126	Butterfield, Richard

American Prisoners of War Held at Bermuda During the War of 1812

2127	Small, Elisha		2198	Smith, John
2128	Sheffield, A		2199	Stoel, Peter
2129	Coleman, B		2200	Westurick, William
2130	Jackson, William		2201	McPherson, William
2131	Morse, T		2202	Thomas, David
2132	Rogers, John		2203	Randall, William
2133	Decateur, Stephen		2204	Tickle, John
2134	Shubruk, John		2205	Wheeler, Andrew
2135	Gallagher, John		2206	Benson, William
2136	Rogers, James		2207	Martin, George
2137	Twigds, Levi		2208	Martin, William
2138	Randolph, R B		2209	Davis, John
2139	Voorhes, Ralph		2210	Richardson, Thomas
2140	Price, Edward		2211	Herbert, John
2141	Hoffman, Ogden		2212	Bennett, John
2142	Brewster, Benjamin		2213	Gough, John
2143	Shubick, Irvine		2214	Haggerty, James
2144	Fisher, John D		2215	De Casta, James
2145	Heth, John		2216	Harron, William
2146	Lansing, E A		2217	Parker, Benjamin
2147	Hollins, George N		2218	Butler, John
2148	Emmet, C T		2219	Travers, Jiffy
2149	Newman, W D		2220	Bray, Josh E
2150	Dale, Richard		2221	Hughes, John
2151	Parker, Robert		2222	Fox, Charles
2152	Hersey, Thomas		2223	Felt, John
2153	Bell, Samuel		2224	Coleman, James
2154	Banks, James		2225	Sinnett, James
2155	Owlin, George		2226	Hickman, George
2156	Brown, Samuel		2227	Barthoff, Nicholas
2157	Edwards, William		2228	Hull, Peter
2158	Trevett, Samuel R		2229	Caulson, Uriah
2159	Wickes, J D		2230	Palmer, William F
2160	Dix, John		2231	Napier, William
2161	Timberlake, J B		2232	Gibson, William
2162	Robinson, Henry		2233	Larraby, Joseph
2163	Bowre, Henry		2234	Fleek, H F
2164	Hanlow, Alexander		2235	Spencer, Robert
2165	Wade, Alfred		2236	Robertson, James
2166	Kainsford, Josiah		2237	Kettletas, Benjamin
2167	Levina, Lewis		2238	Carter, William
2168	Gardner, William		2239	Porter, John C
2169	Jolly, John		2240	Lawson, James
2170	Cramer, John		2241	Armstrong, William
2171	Caustin, Nicholas		2242	Bird, Henry
2172	Henry, Lewis		2243	Carroll, Carn
2173	Dunn, James		2244	Turney, George
2174	Updike, Richard		2245	Murray, David
2175	Carsay, Richard		2246	Owens, William
2176	Thorpe, William		2247	Powell, John
2177	Bennett, John		2248	Scandlings, Peter
2178	Giles, Robert		2249	Johnston, John
2179	Brown, William		2250	Norkott, Dennis
2180	Williamson, Thomas		2251	Dutton, Nathan
2181	Crannell, William		2252	Closs, Peter
2182	Thayre, Elijah		2253	White, James
2183	Adams, John		2254	Keith, John
2184	Leary, John		2255	Krutson, John
2185	Scott, Joshua		2256	Bramhold, Charles
2186	Pritchard, William		2257	Green, Jessy
2187	Jones, John		2258	Smith, John
2188	Scott, Francis		2259	Ray, Thomas
2189	Barritt, William		2260	White, John
2190	Taylor, James		2261	Burfield, Charles
2191	Stanford, James		2262	Perk, George
2192	Henley, George		2263	Waters, Richard
2193	Brown, Peter		2264	Russell, Peter
2194	Selolom, John		2265	Parsons, Andrew
2195	Evans, John		2266	Brown, John
2196	Thompson, James		2267	Henry, Robert
2197	Low, John		2268	Lang, James

American Prisoners of War Held at Bermuda During the War of 1812

2269	Brant, Solomon	2340	Weyman, Charles
2270	Beckwith, Henry	2341	Smith, William
2271	Bowman, William	2342	Henderson, Hans
2272	Benson, George	2343	Gore, John
2273	Brown, William	2344	Moulton, William
2274	Brown, Samuel	2345	Reeves, Joseph
2275	White, Philip	2346	Sauls, John
2276	Martins, Michael	2347	White, Ramsey
2277	Edwards, John	2348	Vaun, Samuel
2278	Williams, John	2349	Smith, James
2279	Williams, Charles	2350	Stevens, L
2280	Gainer, William	2351	Donaldson, Benjamin
2281	Hanford, William	2352	James, Reuben
2282	Brown, Joseph	2353	Brickman, John
2283	Pearce, George	2354	Marsh, Lubilen
2284	Wilkes, Joseph	2355	Andrews, A
2285	Raynolds, John H	2356	Wagner, Christian
2286	Ryan, William	2357	Carter, John
2287	Myres, Charles	2358	Besson, Joseph
2288	Raynolds, William L	2359	Whyley, Philip
2289	Joseph, Anthony	2360	Johnson, Francis
2290	Cox, Frisby	2361	Salinder, John
2291	Keith, James	2362	Hoffman, Henry
2292	Henyon, James	2363	McDonald, Ebenezer
2293	Hobey, John	2364	Nelson, Andrew
2294	Warren, Clark	2365	Lary, Peter
2295	Haughtman, John	2366	Wilkinson, William
2296	Mottley, Alexander	2367	White, John
2297	Swiney, Alexander	2368	Jones, Watkins
2298	Carton, Joseph	2369	Bryant, James
2299	Hight, Temple	2370	Smith, Christopher
2300	Skant, John	2371	Memenbery, Jacob
2301	Marsden, William	2372	Dollman, John
2302	Lorgeunt, Samuel	2373	Anderson, George
2303	Richardson, William	2374	Bowden, Stephen
2304	Summers, Anthony	2375	Wentsworth, Paul
2305	Serman, Robert	2376	Roberts, William
2306	Welch, James	2377	Meany, Cornelius
2307	Thompson, William	2378	Walker, Thomas
2308	Marshall, Thomas	2379	Thompson, John
2309	Bell, David	2380	Ricker, Edward
2310	Carrans, Joseph	2381	Delapp, William
2311	Axford, Thomas	2382	White, John
2312	Pack, Anthony	2383	Wards, William
2313	Burgess, William	2384	Horley, John
2314	Henry, James	2385	Smith, John
2315	Woats, John	2386	Womack, John
2316	Douglas, William	2387	Mason, Joel
2317	Mariner, Joseph	2388	Brown, Thomas
2318	Bull, Francis	2389	Harvey, John
2319	Johnson, Richard	2390	Adrica, Peter
2320	Stime, Wallis	2391	Pedrick, George
2321	Lourey, James	2392	Beek, James
2322	Anthony, Joseph	2393	Mennett, Thomas
2323	Lyons, John	2394	Crammet, Joseph
2324	Cayton, John	2395	Gardner, William
2325	Simons, John	2396	Miller, James
2326	Morgan, William	2397	Currey, John
2327	Plummer, Joseph	2398	Carroll, Michael
2328	Litchfield, John	2399	Jordon, Ralph
2329	Goley, David	2400	Roberts, A
2330	Clarke, John	2401	Williams, Daniel
2331	Coney, Thomas	2402	White, William
2332	Pendleton, Daniel	2403	Tutton, Joseph
2333	Cummings, William	2404	Theodore, Joseph
2334	Davidson, William	2405	Thompson, George
2335	Coleman, George	2406	Jay, Bennet
2336	Carroll, Thomas	2407	Blosdale, Jacob
2337	Hill, Thomas	2408	Kneese, James
2338	Gray, David	2409	Hales, John
2339	Evans, Joseph	2410	Holland, William

American Prisoners of War Held at Bermuda During the War of 1812

2411	Kelly, John		2482	Blake, Perry
2412	Carnes, Charles		2483	Willden, Charles
2413	O'Neal, Robert		2484	Mills, James
2414	Powers, Richard		2485	Ray, Thomas
2415	Haley, John		2486	Beont, John
2416	Armstrong, John		2487	Sullivan, Daniel
2417	Joseph, Louis		2488	Mason, John
2418	Grave, John		2489	Marson, Peter
2419	Ham, Anthony		2490	McClure, James
2420	Armstrong, James		2491	Davison, William
2421	Johnson, G		2492	Brown, Thomas
2422	Larkin, Peter		2493	Campbell, Thomas
2423	Russell, Samuel		2494	Sumers, Langford
2424	Shadell, James		2495	Mitchell, William
2425	Tolman, Artemus		2496	Cribb, John
2426	Woodruff, John		2497	Ferguson, Patrick
2427	Kerr, Adam		2498	Dixon, William
2428	Prassur, John		2499	Garnay, George
2429	Alderson, Jeremiah		2500	Tuck, Joseph
2430	Simmonds, John		2501	Hupper, Samuel
2431	Jackman, Benjamin		2502	Bemous, Abraham
2432	Williams, William		2503	Holmes, James
2433	Littlefield, John		2504	Strumbell, Abraham
2434	Jenkins, Ludwick		2505	Wright, John
2435	Lord, Jonas		2506	Nye, Stephen
2436	Smith, John		2507	Jacobs, David
2437	James, John		2508	Joseph, Francis
2438	Dominque, Joseph		2509	Williamson, Charles
2439	Bennett, Peter		2510	Funning, David
2440	Oliver, Joseph		2511	Madden, Michael
2441	Quin, Michael		2512	Ryan, John
2442	Nostend, Daniel		2513	Stephenson, Thomas
2443	Carney, Charles		2514	Lampher, Clamlin
2444	Robins, Henry		2515	Adams, William
2445	Oliver, Samuel		2516	Potter, Joseph
2446	Lowry, William		2517	Nickerson, James C
2447	Allen, Samuel		2518	Gordon, Alexander
2448	Fifer, Edward		2519	Morrin, John
2449	Fevion, John		2520	Rhodes, Romanto
2450	Stantos, Andrew D		2521	Haynes, Joseph
2451	Bolt, James		2522	Dischodt, Frederick
2452	Pester, James		2523	Mathews, David
2453	Wheelwright, Joseph		2524	Luthers, Jeremiah
2454	Wright, William		2525	Griffin, Stewart
2455	Dixon, Samuel		2526	Harris, William
2456	Banatt, John		2527	Davis, Samuel
2457	Simmonds, Jacob		2528	Mitchell, Lloyd
2458	Williams, John		2529	Linscott, John
2459	Downing, James		2530	Peterson, John
2460	Leonard, Robert		2531	Chont, Robert
2461	Hall, George		2532	Smith, Ralph
2462	Dennis, John		2533	Perry, John
2463	Smith, Edward		2534	Barnes, Nathaniel
2464	Butler, George		2535	Rogers, Francis
2465	Fuster, David		2536	Turner, Samuel
2466	Tennis, Benjamin		2537	Sloan, James
2467	McGill, Mathew		2538	Hyler, Adam
2468	Callow, Stephen		2539	Gray, Mathew
2469	Awner, Charles		2540	Colloden, Patrick
2470	Keller, Anthony		2541	Darley, Jacob
2471	Morgan, William		2542	Scantling, Owen
2472	Hunter, William		2543	Tuck, John
2473	Fowler, Peter		2544	Terron, James
2474	Snow, William		2545	Davernoux, Nicholas
2475	Caswell, Samuel		2546	Dupree, John
2476	McNatley, Michael		2547	Hill, William
2477	Bell, George		2548	Regan, John
2478	Dodge, Andrew		2549	Miggs, John
2479	Gardner, Galen		2550	Hammond, Stephen
2480	Howlen, Barney		2551	Rogers, William
2481	Davis, Benjamin		2552	Ashbourn, Ralph

American Prisoners of War Held at Bermuda During the War of 1812

2553	Davis, Thomas	2624	Watson, George
2554	Pready, Marshall	2625	Pew, Doliver
2555	Edgehill, Washington	2626	Sawyer, Robert
2556	Kelly, Thomas	2627	Elwell, Francis
2557	Nicholson, James	2628	Marble, Benjamin
2558	Nisbett, William	2629	Bolt, Charles
2559	Gore, Thomas	2630	Adams, Charles
2560	Van Vorous, Robert	2631	Baymanth, Lander
2561	Genn, William	2632	Kelso, John
2562	Hitton, William	2633	Barney, Olpha
2563	Barber, John	2634	Lawrence, Peter
2564	Plier, Ezekiel	2635	Davis, Thomas
2565	Helsia, William	2636	Wright, James
2566	Gusta, Charles	2637	Anderson, Nathaniel
2567	Dugden, Gilbert	2638	Barker, Benjamin
2568	Green, James	2639	Hall, Edward
2569	Jones, Richard	2640	Pearce, Henry
2570	Keith, William	2641	Steward, Alexander
2571	Gardner, Anthony	2642	Saunders, William
2572	Esbourn, Francis	2643	Fletcher, F C
2573	Egbert, Frederick	2644	Mumford, James
2574	Blosom, Joseph	2645	Antonio, John
2575	Ginney, Andrew	2646	Baptiste, John
2576	Cooper, James	2647	Vinghew, Francis
2577	Whigs, George	2648	Dickenfield, William
2578	Heath, William	2649	Oliver, John
2579	Van Tassell, Barney	2650	Mellville, John
2580	Sancho, Antonio	2651	Harvey, Amon
2581	Williams, Jacob	2652	Blether, Nathaniel
2582	Smith, Charles	2653	Keys, William
2583	Rockwell, Merritt	2654	Smith, Gorham
2584	Merchant, Peter B	2655	Burke, Thomas
2585	Hensworth, Log	2656	Adams, Daniel
2586	Elliott, John	2657	Dobrix, Martin
2587	Greeman, Edward	2658	Joseph, Francis
2588	Nemo, Henry	2659	Perkins, Thomas
2589	Bullock, Joseph	2660	Lewis, Charles
2590	Alcock, John	2661	Happy, Abraham
2591	Forster, William	2662	Frederick, John
2592	Hiller, George	2663	Earp, Aquilla
2593	Brooking, John	2664	Baptiste, John
2594	Mace, Henry	2665	Murray, Alexander
2595	Madden, Laurence	2666	Iverson, Peter
2596	Gott, Joseph	2667	Fyler, John C
2597	Cass, Caleb	2668	Dawson, Charles
2598	Holding, Ebenezer	2669	Chaves, M
2599	Ross, Alexander	2670	Taylor, Charles
2600	Troop, C	2671	Smell, Charles
2601	Tinney, Nathaniel	2672	Baptiste, John
2602	Funk, Nathaniel	2673	Stage, Abraham
2603	Roach, John	2674	Henthorn, William
2604	Cowens, Andrew	2675	Michael, John
2605	Barber, Henry	2676	Johnson, Ham
2606	Anderson, William	2677	Johnson, Henry
2607	Montaque, James	2678	Perslaw, Joseph
2608	Edred, Benjamin	2679	Ellis, William
2609	Benson, Samuel	2680	Bowden, Thomas
2610	Loviet, Joseph	2681	March, Charles
2611	Giles, Edmund	2682	Woodward, Richard
2612	Vowsland, William	2683	Hallett, James
2613	Vowsland, John	2684	Bradfort, Cuffy
2614	Stanley, Benjamin	2685	Tamley, John
2615	Smith, Nathaniel	2686	Given, Francis
2616	Carrico, James	2687	Nicholas, John
2617	Grush, Philip	2688	Golen, Francis
2618	Chew, Henry	2689	Gasalo, John
2619	Dennett, Thomas	2690	Fisk, Esra
2620	Weeks, John	2691	Fair, Samuel
2621	Stover, Samuel	2692	Sparkanork, John
2622	Davis, John	2693	Hill, Hugh
2623	Lowe, John	2694	Webb, T B

American Prisoners of War Held at Bermuda During the War of 1812

2695	Hussey, Robert	2766	Spencer, S
2696	Saunders, Thomas	2767	Chinik, G
2697	Archer, John	2768	Smith, Moses
2698	Simonds, Andrew	2769	Trueman, Job
2699	Hillman, Jonathan	2770	Brown, John
2700	Devall, Pardon	2771	Martin, Thomas
2701	Bradford, Carn	2772	Horton, J H
2702	Sheverick, Elijah	2773	Phillips, John
2703	Burgess, Isaah	2774	Johnson, William
2704	Cowell, Ezekiel	2775	Roberts, Samuel
2705	Warren, Cyrus	2776	Dolphin, Edward
2706	Ives, John	2777	Grave, Henry
2707	Robinson, Nathan	2778	Hamburgh, Peter
2708	Watson, John	2779	Rud, George
2709	Mucker, Herim	2780	Delano, William
2710	Doverell, Thomas	2781	Warden, Appleton
2711	Clough, John	2782	Meyers, John
2712	Eaton, James	2783	Lacha, Lewis
2713	Dumatee, M	2784	Wood, John
2714	White, N	2785	Norton, Joseph
2715	Dubbin, R	2786	Stamford, William
2716	---, Francisco	2787	Chiddell, Daniel
2717	Bewditch, Thomas	2788	Truman, William
2718	Stone, Zachariah	2789	Snow, James
2719	Poland, Oliver	2790	Anthony, Joseph
2720	Poore, Isaac	2791	Butler, Joseph
2721	Poore, David	2792	Wallis, Newport
2722	Mason, Samuel	2793	Fernandez, Peter
2723	Brown, James	2794	Tuger, Henry
2724	Coats, Humphrey	2795	Fletcher, Aron
2725	Gallick, D	2796	Jenkins, William
2726	Sheldon, Job	2797	Henry, James
2727	Hollingsworth, William	2798	Young, Samuel
2728	Best, Samuel	2799	Hall, D
2729	Gibson, Robert	2800	Green, John
2730	Boverham, Abraham	2801	Carey, Allen
2731	McKey, James	2802	Langshore, Richard
2732	Bohom, John	2803	Dunsenberg, D
2733	Hopkins, Stephen	2804	Hoxon, Richard
2734	Connell, G	2805	Eddy, Edward
2735	Judkins, Charles	2806	Phillips, R W
2736	Watson, William	2807	Cleveland, H C
2737	Cook, W F	2808	Budgeron, William
2738	Smith, Lawrence	2809	Whittetson, P
2739	Hulton, John	2810	Toney, E
2740	Osmondo, Anthony	2811	Hansey, William
2741	Hernetha, F	2812	Harrison, Samuel
2742	Jackson, William	2813	Boyles, Charles
2743	Nicholson, Joseph	2814	Powell, William
2744	Pitts, Peter	2815	Trader, William
2745	Wilkinson, Thomas	2816	Nollins, Thomas
2746	Newton, George	2817	Phillips, Henry
2747	Wright, Yorick	2818	Langueth, Matthew
2748	Kane, William	2819	Barr, F M
2749	Bohoni, Cazer	2620	Strut, James
2750	Providence, Thomas	2821	Jones, Cato
2751	Irvin, Charles	2822	Mears, William
2752	Garrison, Joseph	2823	Bond, Thomas
2753	Sailor, William	2824	Frazier, York
2754	Howard, Eliah	2825	Johnson, Robert
2755	Donagan, James	2826	Stokely, John
2756	Robinson, Thomas	2827	Redman, James
2757	Sumner, Charles	2828	Tucker, D A
2758	White, John	2829	Richards, A
2759	Whitman, John	2830	Clark, John
2760	McDonald, James	2831	Bartlett, H G
2761	Parker, B	2832	Stocking, William
2762	Atkins, Lemuel	2833	Lint, John
2763	Studson, D	2834	Moat, William
2764	Sampson, Samuel	2835	Barlow, Rodney
2765	Pawn, Peter	2836	Thomas, Moses

American Prisoners of War Held at Bermuda During the War of 1812

2837	Barrett, Peter	2858	Key, John
2838	Storey, Abel	2859	Carpenter, Joseph
2839	Sloane, William	2860	Porter, Ezra
2840	Townsend, G	2861	Skinner, Joseph
2841	Morris, James	2862	Dagget, Preston
2842	Edinburgh, Peter	2863	Young, James
2843	Stephen, G	2864	Dagget, Daniel
2844	Smith, William	2865	Partorioat, A Aben
2845	Boothe, Thomas	2866	Walker, Aron
2846	Bluck, B W	2867	Anderson, William
2847	Shaw, William	2868	de Valli, Louis
2848	Modun, James	2869	Ballast, Samuel
2849	Jacobs, Peter	2870	Lyons, Henry
2850	Jackson, Benjamin	2871	Emerson, John
2851	Weeks, Henry	2872	Uzzielphant, Uriah
2852	Domenick, Caper	2873	Brown, Zacheus
2853	Powers, John	2874	Mun, George
2854	Multy, James	2875	Hiller, George
2855	Graman, John		
2856	Foster, James		
2857	Tunisdale, William		

American Prisoners of War Held at Bermuda During the War of 1812

Crew listing by ship

Achilles
   Clement, Joseph
   Davis, Samuel

Acricoake
   Anderson, William
   Davis, Peter
   Donavan, Benjamin
   Emerson, Andrew
   Eroundy, Francis
   Fodder, Francis
   Galloway, Michael
   Hancock, James
   Harris, William
   Lyn, John
   Mitchell, Lewis
   Paul, John
   Smith, John

Adventure
   ---, Nathan
   Boston, Daniel
   Brown, James
   McKenny, Nathan
   Pointer, James
   Prout, Jacob
   Thompson, Jesse

Advocate
   Hensworth, Log
   Merchant, Peter B
   Rockwell, Merritt
   Smith, Charles

Albert
   Alden, Benjamin
   Anderson, Jacob
   Benitt, Juan
   Bond, Robert
   Coote, Thomas O
   Elliot, Nicholas
   Frederick, Thomas
   Halborn, Thomas
   Johnson, William
   Josamana, P
   Juan, Francis
   Mure, D W
   Peterson, Jacob
   Rovada, Antony
   Traquave, John

Alert
   Clark, Charles
   Fearine, Isiah
   Libbey, Richard
   Smith, Major
   Smith, Weston

Allisses
   Kelso, George

Amason
   Cole, Henry
   Cushin, Lezer
   Cushman, Harvey
   Fisher, William
   Howland, John
   Joyce, John
   Mason, Thomas
   Scott, Pleasant
   Southworth, John
   Spanger, Edward
   Walker, Benjamin

Ambition
   Bradford, John
   Cill, John F
   Littlefield, N
   May, William
   Stringer, Thomas

Amelia
   Samoe, David

American Eagle
   Seaman, Isaac

American Gun Boat
   ---, Francisco
   Bewditch, Thomas
   Brown, James
   Coats, Humphrey
   Dubbin, R
   Dumatee, M
   Eaton, James
   Mason, Samuel
   Poland, Oliver
   Poore, David
   Poore, Isaac
   Stone, Zachariah
   White, N

Amiable
   Jordon, Simon
   Lattimore, James
   Wood, John

Amicus
   Frederick, John
   Happy, Abraham
   Lewis, Charles

Amy
   Antonio, Manuel
   Brown, Hans
   Gray, Edward
   Long, John
   Roberts, Samuel
   Sephey, Peter

Ann
   Bowling, Garrett
   Bryan, Fagalte
   Carpenter, James
   Dickinson, Samuel
   Holland, Rons
   Naus, Littleton
   Parker, John
   Toppin, John P

Ann Maria
   Delano, William

Antelope
   Beatty, Henry
   Blass, J G
   Brown, John F
   Deainson, J
   Dew, Edward
   Gibbs, Samuel
   Gonsalvos, Joseph
   Henry, William
   Ritter, Michael
   Tabor, Daniel
   Willberger, Joseph S

Apollo
   Appleton, John
   Buckford, Andrew
   Clemons, Henry
   Collins, John
   Dutch, Nathaniel
   Gray, Nehemiah
   Knap, Samuel
   Meek, John
   Sage, John
   Silsby, John W
   Smith, John

American Prisoners of War Held at Bermuda During the War of 1812

Soalby, Nathaniel

Argus
- Davis, Israel
- Fairfield, James M
- Howe, Edward

Ariel
- Abrahams, G D
- Barnes, Isaac
- Beard, James
- Butters, Benjamin
- Buttler, Lephnik
- Combes, Peter
- Crane, Roger
- Durant, John
- Grigous, William
- Hall, George
- Jacobs, William
- Jacobs, William
- James, John
- Merrill, Elias
- Roberts, Nicholas
- Saunders, Joseph
- Sharp, Peter
- Woxin, Joseph
- Young, James

Armistice
- Atkins, George
- Barkam, Thomas
- Chessnutt, Adam
- Jones, John
- Morgan, John
- Morrill, Charles
- Post, Anthony
- Scott, George
- Warner, Samuel

Aroof
- Jackson, William
- Newton, George
- Nicholson, Joseph
- Pitts, Peter
- Wilkinson, Thomas
- Wright, Yorick

Asp
- Anderson, Edward
- Barton, William
- Brown, Alexander
- Gaimsley, Thomas
- Goodall, William
- Gould, Thomas
- Green, John
- Morris, Frank
- Whitney, James
- Wickman, Andrew

Atalanta
- Humphries, Horiatio

Attempt
- Dennett, Thomas
- Stover, Samuel
- Weeks, John

Aurora
- Turley, Enoch

Banyer
- Gall, William
- Howell, William

Bellona
- O'Brian, James

Betsey
- Hewston, J
- Lawton, G
- Mott, Charles
- Rose, Perry

Betsy Ann
- Brockway, John
- Haskell, Joseph
- Howard, William
- Jones, James

Bird
- Cross, Jacob
- Shellebar, George

Bona
- Bennison, Lenord
- Binghouse, William
- Blayer, Robert
- Cox, James
- Dameron, John
- David, Michael
- Estes, J H T
- Fackson, J W
- Fish, Allen
- Harrimond, John
- Hawkins, William
- Hozier, Samuel
- Joy, David
- Le Count, Philip
- Morton, Abraham
- Nelson, T W
- Peterson, Thomas
- Poop, Elijah
- Rogers, Errin
- Sanders, Job
- Sherlock, Samuel
- Stephens, James
- Stephenson, David
- Warren, John

Bordeaux Packet
- Apenny, William
- Barton, Samuel
- Bennett, Thomas
- Briddon, Thomas
- Burnam, Beasson
- Childs, Adam
- Clyne, Lewis
- Currant, Nicholas
- Curtis, Lebe
- Fisher, John
- Ford, Standi
- Frances, Michael
- Gordon, William
- Grimes, George
- Healey, Edward
- Heddon, John
- Hendrickson, John
- Hero, John
- Higgenbottom, William
- Hippeny, Anthony
- Jefferson, Jacob
- Johnson, Jacob
- Kene, Davis
- Law, Thomas
- Lee, George
- Mason, Francis
- McFeadon, John
- Meensey, Daniel
- Miller, Thomas
- Mourice, Joseph
- Palmer, Robert
- Perruall, Hugh
- Powers, John
- Ritchen, Robert
- Rockhill, James
- Rogers, Henry
- Smith, John

American Prisoners of War Held at Bermuda During the War of 1812

    Sullivan, Samuel
    Sutherland, John
    Talman, Joseph
    Thaitis, John
    Thomas, John
    Trout, Nathaniel
    Vorris, Philip
    Weaver, Nicholas
    Yeoman, John

Brant
    Brown, John
    Martin, Thomas
    Smith, Moses
    Trueman, Job

Bridges
    Bradbury, William
    Bragdon, Joseph
    Butler, John
    Carlisle, William
    Edwards, Benjamin
    Foot, James
    Griffin, John
    Gursting, Oliver
    Higgins, Joseph
    Homan, John
    Jenkins, Robert
    Knapp, Samuel
    Nason, Aaron
    Poore, Thomas

Brookhaven
    Amos, Samuel
    Dill, William
    Gibbs, John
    Howland, Robert
    Johnson, Charles
    Smith, Jacob
    West, James

Caledonian
    ---, Poitless Moe
    Allen, Henry
    Bernard, John
    Collins, James
    Crown, Frederick
    De Shitts, Matthew
    Drew, Ezekiel
    Hepburn, John
    Leters, Charles
    Marshall, John
    Murphey, John
    Rossan, Aman
    Victor, William

Calmer
    Allock, Elijah
    Lovett, William
    Mann, Thomas
    Mass, Moses
    Thomas, John
    Waterhouse, John

Camelia
    Cartwright, Alexander

Canaway
    Dixon, Closs
    Johnson, Robert
    Jones, Isaac
    Porter, William
    Scapina, Mathias
    Wyland, Christian

Caroline
    Young, Joshua

Carrol
    Cottle, Henry

    Holmer, Robert

Cataline
    Hernetha, F
    Osmondo, Anthony

Christiana
    Cornwall, Edward
    Dexter, Dennis
    Guard, Andrew
    Hall, William
    Parker, S G
    Webber, William

Circe
    Blair, John R
    Lewis, Sol
    Miller, William
    Parker, John
    Squires, Samuel C

Citzen
    Hendrick, Hugh
    Young, Martin

Crown Prince
    Bosman, Henry
    Britt, Thomas
    Britt, William K
    Clifton, Thomas
    Rhodes, Pomp
    Smith, Thomas

Dart
    Allen, John
    Bray, Henry
    Finis, Peter
    Gage, William
    Hilbert, Samuel
    Hurth, Charles
    Kempenfield, William
    Layfield, William
    McKenzie, Thomas
    Mitchel, Chester
    Pervis, William
    Polk, Samuel
    Sungrain, Oliver
    Taylor, Thomas

Dash
    Antonio, John
    Baptiste, John
    Dickenfield, William
    Fletcher, F C
    Mumford, James
    Saunders, William
    Vinghew, Francis

Defiance
    Blackler, Henry
    Broughton, Nicholas
    Gerry, Samuel R
    Hooper, Thomas
    Madison, Andrew

Delaclea
    Bagley, Daniel
    Green, Ezekiel
    Loring, Almond
    Smith, Joseph

Dispatch
    Ellridge, Henry
    Hatwood, P
    Randall, Cater
    Randall, Oates
    Toddy, William

Dolphin
    Bablisto, John
    Beach, John
    Bella, John

American Prisoners of War Held at Bermuda During the War of 1812

    Bladen, Thomas
    Bloom, John
    Bogardus, J B
    Bradbury, George
    Campbell, Charles
    Clerk, Andrew
    Coutigo, Frederick
    Davis, Pascari
    Gasaway, George
    Goodwin, Joseph
    Gouchon, John
    Havins, William
    Hill, Jeremiah
    Johnson, Joseph
    Lowe, John
    Marsdon, George
    Matheu, John
    Powers, John
    Smith, Joseph
    Sportfield, Collin
    Stover, David
    Stover, William
    Sulivan, James
    Talpee, John

Dove
    Chavers, Sidney
    Deurege, John
    James, Sidney
    Wheeler, David
    Willson, Andrew

Dragon
    Belfeur, James

Dry Farbourn
    Brill, Christopher
    Hinley, Joseph
    Johnson, John
    Masselin, Horace F
    Morris, John
    Morson, Joseph
    Schrothn, David

Dusty Miller
    ---, Pinkey
    Robinson, Thomas

Eagle
    Baker, George C

Eclipse
    Barsabella, Julian
    Davis, John
    Gillings, Benjamin
    Lackley, Joseph
    Lewis, William
    Liffler, Henry
    Tooling, Francoi

Edward
    Anderson, William
    Barber, Henry
    Edred, Benjamin
    Montaque, James
    Smith, Gorham

Eliza
    Abbot, George
    Bowditch, Joseph
    Eaton, Andrew
    Ferguson, Thomas
    Jennings, Jacob
    McRea, John
    Mingle, William
    Moffott, Hugh
    Porter, Joshua
    Rhodes, Charles
    Smith, Chester
    Swanson, Andrew
    Tsdale, James
    Walker, John
    Warden, John
    Wentworth, Richard
    White, Thomas
    Williams, Joshua

Eliza & Mary
    Bythwood, John

Eliza & Susan
    Ardrey, Alexander

Elizabeth
    Alexander, Hector
    Allison, William
    Bartholomew, Herain
    Benedick, John
    Bradley, Philip
    Callahan, Joshua
    Corie, John
    Goodspeed, Joseph
    Gould, James
    Gregoris, Dominic
    Hicks, Samuel
    Ingle, George
    Johnson, R
    Mason, Manuel
    Morrison, Samuel
    Palmer, John
    Paterson, John
    Sanderson, Francis
    Sheffield, William
    Storey, Peter
    Tomlin, Samuel
    Trigony, Peter

Elouisa
    Basler, Amos
    Cilley, Cutting
    Graves, John
    Harrington, Lyman
    Jehoff, John
    Lewis, Roswelling

Elove & Unity
    Brown, Soloman
    Hail, Sylvester
    Luther, Nathaniel
    Whitten, Joseph

Emily
    ---, Hard Times
    Campbell, Daniel
    Cook, Samuel
    Davis, Josiah

Enterprise
    Chaves, M
    Dawson, Charles

Enterprize
    Barber, George
    Cross, James
    Devereux, Robert
    Jacobs, Francis

Erin
    Carrolan, James
    Martin, Isaac
    Thompson, Charles
    Wade, Robert

Experience
    Lincoln, Nicholas
    Stewart, James

Experiment
    Bradford, Carn
    Devall, Pardon
    Hillman, Jonathan

American Prisoners of War Held at Bermuda During the War of 1812

Factor
- Lane, Alexander
- Metzger, John
- Shaddock, Anthony

Factor of Salem
- Dutch, Esra T
- Hodges, Gabriel

Fair American
- Bohoni, Cazer
- Kane, William

Fairplay
- Guest, Edward
- Oxand, Michael
- Ryan, Patrick
- Sherwood, Ralph
- Thompson, James
- Vere, Jean

Falcon
- Adams, Daniel
- Benson, Samuel
- Burke, Thomas
- Carrico, James
- Chew, Henry
- Dobrix, Martin
- Giles, Edmund
- Grush, Philip
- Joseph, Francis
- Loviet, Joseph
- Perkins, Thomas
- Smith, Nathaniel
- Stanley, Benjamin
- Vowsland, John
- Vowsland, William

Famers Fancy
- Ervin, Charles

Fanny
- Knight, Charles
- Mack, Charles
- Mack, William

Farmer
- Callam, Theop
- Frederick, John

Farmers Branch
- Bradfort, Cuffy
- Hallett, James
- March, Charles
- Woodward, Richard

Federal Jack
- Bringham, John William

Fernando
- Lincoln, Charles
- Rhodes, Daniel
- Weeks, William
- Woodman, Rufus

Fieri Facias
- Barker, A L
- Bartholomew, Joseph
- Cox, L G F
- Howard, Benjamin
- Johnson, James
- Johnson, William
- Lambert, James
- White, Henry C

Flash
- Barrett, Thomas
- Collagon, John
- Cox, Charles
- Giles, Charles
- Goss, Thomas
- Lewis, James
- North, John N
- Pinshaw, Joseph
- Watts, John

Flavoriott
- ---, George
- ---, Sayler
- ---, Tom
- Lafebui, Bartin
- Yong, Bill

Flower de Pumainbueo
- Forshew, John

Fly
- Hammond, Benjamin
- Macamber, Samuel
- Magruder, Thomas W
- Styles, John

Fox
- Dunton, Robert
- Dunton, Thomas
- Dunton, Thomas
- Kershaw, Newman
- Sutlet, William
- Wragg, Erasmus R

Freeman
- Sheppard, John

Frolic
- Cleareyd, James
- Cousins, John
- Thompson, James
- Tucker, James B

Funchall
- Barber, John
- Dugden, Gilbert
- Genn, William
- Green, James
- Gusta, Charles
- Helsia, William
- Hitton, William
- Jones, Richard
- Plier, Ezekiel
- Troop, C
- Van Vorous, Robert

Gangee
- Scank, Samuel

Gardner
- Forger, Joseph

General Blake
- Bennett, Albeno
- Blackburn, William
- Cornett, William
- Lake, Levin
- Laxes, Peter
- Miller, Ezekial
- Wilson, William

General Knox
- Allen, Truman
- Hutchinson, John
- Jefferson, Isaac
- Jones, Daniel
- Moore, Robert
- Shapper, William

George
- Colgan, Christian
- Delano, Harper
- Gardner, Rowland
- Innis, Benjamin
- Innis, William
- Luke, Clarke
- Swatt, Christian

George & Joseph
- Wing, George

Gold Coiner

American Prisoners of War Held at Bermuda During the War of 1812

    Brown, Webster
    Hathaway, Pardon

Good Intent
    Johnston, William
    Moore, William
    Mowton, George
    Rogers, John
    Wills, Philip
    Wright, John

Gossepuim
    Brooks, Edward
    Cer, Levi
    Coffin, Thaddias
    Congdon, Henry
    Cummings, Edward
    Day, William
    Douglas, Josiah
    Dowling, Peter
    Dyer, Ezekial
    Fowle, Josiah C
    Francisco, John Pedro
    George, Peter
    Harvey, Joseph
    Haywood, John
    Hunt, Dudley
    Hutchinson, Joseph
    Jeffreys, Phillip
    Laughton, Otis
    Linnell, Jonathan
    Lock, Nathaniel
    Reid, Luke
    Smith, William
    Sweet, Moses
    Tridwell, Alpheus
    Williams, Dennis
    Wood, James
    Young, Moses

Gosum
    Dame, George

Governor Ankerheim
    Connor, Charles
    Dow, Timothy
    Durvin, Gerrald
    Greenfield, Joseph
    Peter, Robert
    Pratt, John
    Weston, George

Grecian
    Bashford, William
    Carter, Thomas
    Delany, Francis
    Dix, Robert
    Downing, George
    Duram, Peter
    Evans, William
    Gale, Thomas
    Gale, Thomas
    Hadley, John
    Howes, George
    Huring, William
    Jones, Samuel
    Kimbury, John
    Knapp, Thomas
    Mauney, John
    McCarthy, James
    Powell, Elisha
    Robertson, David
    Robinson, George
    Smith, James
    Smith, James
    Watson, William

Gunboat 160
    Baptiste, John
    Ellis, William
    Henthorn, William
    Jackson, John
    Johnson, Ham
    Johnson, Henry
    Michael, John
    Perslaw, Joseph
    Smell, Charles
    Stage, Abraham
    Taylor, Charles

Gustar Adolph
    Forrest, Abraham
    Peterson, Thomas
    White, William

Gustavas
    Abreeve, Pirzanno
    Appleturit, Charles
    Beers, Oliver
    Brown, Jonas
    Craft, N W
    Johnson, Jonas
    Ludlow, William

Hannah
    Anderson, John
    Brown, Daniel
    Clarke, James
    Cloeth, John
    Edmonds, Thomas
    Micklins, John
    Shaw, Benjamin
    Shaw, Samuel
    Sidney, Edward
    Theafe, William
    Throughgood, William
    Wyer, Joseph

Harmony
    Brown, John

Hazard
    ---, Paulsow
    Griffin, James
    Joseph, John
    Kelly, John
    Lewis, Henry
    Palmer, William
    Smith, James
    Turner, Daniel
    White, Cornelius

Herald
    Alliston, John
    Anthony, Peter
    Barlie, Aron
    Bayer, Abner
    Boyen, James
    Brauphau, Romain
    Clarey, John
    Clatt, George
    Clop, Abner
    Coole, Nathaniel
    Ervin, John
    Fonerty, Martin
    Frederick, John
    Griffith, David
    Hanson, Howe
    Harris, Benjamin
    Johnson, William
    Joseph, Howard
    Joseph, John
    Lasky, George
    McCoy, John

American Prisoners of War Held at Bermuda During the War of 1812

McEldry, Hugh
Metrois, John
Mitret, Onies
Nellands, Adam
Nelson, John
Oliver, Thomas
Orrioto, Dominica
Palmer, John
Quin, Francis
Saunders, Priest
Sewen, Henry
Shepperd, John
Sooty, Darooke
Studson, Daniel
Walter, Nathaniel
White, William

Hero
    Augh, James Henry
    Briggs, Silvinus
    Carven, Thomas
    Clark, John
    Craft, Nathaniel
    Eaton, Israel
    Ford, John
    Foss, Supply
    Furber, Theodore P
    Hepp, James
    Ingram, Henry
    Jewet, Theodore F
    Somerdyke, Joseph
    Talton, Thomas P

Hibernia
    Dimond, John
    Dorington, Charles
    Goodridge, E
    Poulson, Alex
    Terry, Thomas C
    Theyer, J H
    Williams, William
    Young, John

High Flyer
    Adier, Simon
    Ashcroft, Hugh
    Austin, Joseph
    Barney, Samuel
    Bearans, George
    Beatty, Joshua
    Bensham, William
    Berryman, John
    Brown, John
    Burk, Greenbury
    Carter, Benjamin
    Cole, Edward
    Cole, Nathaniel
    Cornwall, Robert
    Covington, John K
    Coxson, Thomas
    Dennis, Joseph
    Dixon, Richard
    Duncan, Mathew
    Duplantes, Eugene
    Dyer, John
    Fairbanks, Noah
    Fernand, John
    Fracey, Charles
    Froes, John
    Geary, Asburn
    Gerlock, Charles
    Godwin, Isaac
    Hall, William
    Hart, Daniel
    Hatch, James
    Heath, Durham
    Ingream, John
    Jarey, John
    Jones, William
    Jones, William
    Knipmire, George
    Lamber, David
    Lemer, John
    Maddox, Samuel
    Malstom, James
    Mandell, John
    Mann, John
    Mavington, William
    McKurlee, Alexander
    Metler, Leonard
    Miles, David
    Moody, Sea
    Pitee, James
    Pollard, George
    Pullock, Joseph
    Quenon, Augustus
    Randell, Stephen
    Ranes, Zachariah
    Richards, Rocy
    Row, Joseph
    Salbory, John M
    Schasser, John W
    Selles, Hamilton
    Smith, James
    Smith, William
    Spear, William
    Stuges, John
    Swain, Joseph
    Thomas, John
    Traverse, Henry
    Usher, Robert
    Vantz, John
    Wallace, Andrew
    Warren, Thomas
    Weed, James
    White, Obediah
    Stephenson, John

Hollowell
    Jackson, William

Hope
    Dolphin, Edward
    Grave, Henry
    Hamburgh, Peter
    Horton, J H
    Johnson, William
    Phillips, John
    Roberts, Samuel
    Rud, George

Hornby
    Dixon, Archibald
    Lyons, Henry G

Hound
    Cankling, Thomas C

Huckimer
    Hulitz, Joseph

Huntress
    Arnold, William
    Bacon, Silvester
    Bulter, Richard
    Currie, James

Independence
    Smith, John

Industry
    Avery, Daniel
    Beatey, James

American Prisoners of War Held at Bermuda During the War of 1812

    Caffsky, John
    Cherriers, Beattie
    Davernoux, Nicholas
    DeForrest, John
    Douvernier, Nicholas
    Edwards, Nicholas
    Ferrander, Antonio
    Grieves, Whitny
    Johnson, Loyd
    Kregoe, Martin
    McDonald, David
    Robson, John
    Taylor, James
    Winer, Elijah

<u>Innocentia</u>
    Tisdale, Sterling

<u>Isa Colly</u>
    Green, Joseph
    Huntington, John
    Moon, John
    Richardson, James
    Valentine, Cata

<u>Isabella</u>
    Barker, Charles
    Bassett, Freeman C
    Brigden, John
    Cotterell, Thomas
    Gillet, Nathan
    Hull, Henry
    Linnot, Morgan
    Parrish, Gideon M
    Penny, P B
    Perry, John
    Richards, William
    Scofield, Isaac
    Thatcher, Stephen
    Walford, Thomas

<u>Jackall</u>
    Down, John
    Gage, Zachariah
    Homan, Peter
    Raymond, William

<u>Jacob Gettig</u>
    West, John

<u>James</u>
    Cornwall, A
    Deacon, John
    French, John
    Gould, Abraham
    Holman, William
    Horsey, William
    Houlval, John
    Johnson, Francis
    Kennedy, Dennis
    Marta, S P
    Morgan, Alexander
    Oliver, Antonia
    Rawson, Jonathan
    Tibbets, James

<u>James Maddison</u>
    Brooks, George
    Cole, Richard
    Emerus, John
    Hendree, John
    Lucas, William

<u>Janett</u>
    Barton, John
    Bottings, Carter
    Bowman, William
    Browel, William
    Cure, Thomas
    Gregory, John
    Harrod, Joseph
    Le Porte, Archibald
    Manston, David
    Matthews, Edward
    Pritchard, Charles
    Pritchard, John
    Richards, William

<u>Jefferson</u>
    Barns, James
    Buckin, Bartholomew
    Childs, Adam
    Cutler, Thomas
    Surgor, John F

<u>John</u>
    Blosom, Joseph
    Cass, Caleb
    Ginney, Andrew
    Holding, Ebenezer
    Ross, Alexander
    Tinney, Nathaniel

<u>John & James</u>
    Bacchus, A
    Bonker, Daniel
    Brook, Peley
    Butill, Dennis
    Chan, Frederick
    Cole, John
    Coone, William
    Creasey, Rubin
    Douglass, Simon
    Elkin, M
    Frankland, Benjamin
    Gordon, John
    Swain, John

<u>Julia</u>
    Barnet, John
    Mallet, John
    Miers, Edward
    Wilcocks, William

<u>Kate</u>
    Boverham, Abraham
    Gibson, Robert
    McKey, James

<u>Langdon Cheves</u>
    Bell, James
    Courtney, Edward
    Gall, John
    Halgreen, Peter
    Holshem, Andrew

<u>Langdon Cheves</u>
    Lapee, Silvester
    Piedmont, Thomas
    Schutte, Harms
    Thompson, William

<u>Lark</u>
    Alcock, John
    Brooking, John
    Forster, William
    Gott, Joseph
    Hiller, George
    Hippencott, Caleb
    Jacobs, Cupid
    Kelly, John
    Latham, Giles
    Mace, Henry
    Madden, Laurence
    Richardson, James
    Willum, William

<u>Laura</u>
    Allen, David

American Prisoners of War Held at Bermuda During the War of 1812

    Bradbury, Nathaniel
    Ingram, William
    Kellog, Junior, Samuel
    Miller, George
    Pratt, Anza
    Southworth, George
    Southworth, George
    Southworth, Justice
    Thompson, Simon

Levant
    Bradshaw, John
    Butler, John
    Dennis, James
    Furance, George
    Standly, Timothy
    Stone, James
    Tucker, D F
    Wellman, Timothy

Limerick
    Anderson, William
    Anthony, Joseph
    Ballast, Samuel
    Barlow, Rodney
    Barr, F M
    Barrett, Peter
    Bartlett, H G
    Bluck, B W
    Bond, Thomas
    Boothe, Thomas
    Boyles, Charles
    Brown, Zacheus
    Budgeron, William
    Butler, Joseph
    Carey, Allen
    Carpenter, Joseph
    Chiddell, Daniel
    Clark, John
    Cleveland, H C
    Dagget, Daniel
    Dagget, Preston
    de Valli, Louis
    Domenick, Caper
    Dunsenberg, D
    Eddy, Edward
    Edinburgh, Peter
    Emerson, John
    Fernandez, Peter
    Fletcher, Aron
    Foster, James
    Frazier, York
    Graman, John
    Green, John
    Hall, D
    Hansey, William
    Harrison, Samuel
    Henry, James
    Hoxon, Richard
    Jackson, Benjamin
    Jacobs, Peter
    Jenkins, William
    Johnson, Robert
    Jones, Cato
    Key, John
    Lacha, Lewis
    Langshore, Richard
    Langueth, Matthew
    Lint, John
    Lyons, Henry
    Mears, William
    Meyers, John
    Moat, William
    Modun, James
    Morris, James
    Multy, James
    Mun, George
    Nollins, Thomas
    Norton, Joseph
    Partorioat, A Aben
    Phillips, Henry
    Phillips, R W
    Porter, Ezra
    Powell, William
    Powers, John
    Redman, James
    Richards, A
    Shaw, William
    Skinner, Joseph
    Sloane, William
    Smith, William
    Snow, James
    Stamford, William
    Stephen, G
    Stocking, William
    Stokely, John
    Storey, Abel
    Strut, James
    Thomas, Moses
    Toney, E
    Townsend, G
    Trader, William
    Truman, William
    Tucker, D A
    Tuger, Henry
    Tunisdale, William
    Uzzielphant, Uriah
    Walker, Aron
    Wallis, Newport
    Warden, Appleton
    Weeks, Henry
    Whittetson, P
    Wood, John
    Young, James
    Young, Samuel

Lion
    Bondleau, Thomas
    Brazier, William
    Odnell, Samuel
    Wardnell, Solomon
    Wendall, Abraham

Little Belt
    Craig, William

Little Catherine
    Bertram, John
    Dansey, Peter
    Kids, R F
    Sansum, Philip
    Seward, Theodore
    Smith, James
    Smith, John
    Sweet, Stephen

Little William
    Allen, Richard
    Apthy, Robert
    Bernard, James
    Branch, Cyrus
    Dunkley, Isaac
    Geesson, Frederick
    Harford, Thomas
    Judy, Joseph
    Lewis, William
    Williams, Tatem
    Winner, Joseph

American Prisoners of War Held at Bermuda During the War of 1812

  Wyley, Nathaniel
Livce
  Bughton, James
Live
  Kempton, Noah S
  Merrick, Ebenezer
  Taber, William M
Lively John
  Shorter, Roger
Logan
  Green, James
  Newman, Robert
Lottery
  Murphey, Daniel
Lound Abrona
  Dickenson, Henry
Luckey
  Bunquar, Obsolou
  Catehard, Charles
  Coffin, William
  Gasper, John
  Honquest, Peter
  Humpson, John
  Johnson, Thomas
  Spring, Daniel
  Winslow, Oliver
  Wisbec, Caleb
Lucy
  Bagnell, Joseph
  Feunce, Bartlet
  Harlow, Benjamin
  Rogers, Thomas
Lukey
  Catehart, Robert
  Hicks, John
  Northorp, Alexander
Lusiana
  Coalman, Joseph
  Fisher, Ephraim
  Shooter, Charles
  Slocum, George
  Stoddien, Warren
Lydia
  Antonia, Joseph
  Badger, Peter
  Blue, George
  Brock, Thomas
  Bunker, Nathaniel
  Butler, Thomas
  Clark, Erren
  Davis, Michael
  Dunkan, Henrick
  Eyre, Jacob
  Fitzgerald, William
  Griswold, Charles
  Leggar, Daniel
  Lewis, John
  Longford, Samuel
  Petman, Richard
  Renney, Comfort S
  Retman, Richard
  Rust, John
  Smith, David
  Young, John
Maresoil
  Blackwell, William
  Freeman, A
  Hunter, Samuel
  Shuffield, Joseph
  Vose, Avery
Maria

  Atkins, Lemuel
  Chinik, G
  Pawn, Peter
  Sampson, Samuel
  Spencer, S
  Studson, D
Maria Louisa
  Merig, John
  Thomas, Francis
Martha
  Hooper, John
Mary
  Anderson, Charles
  Armstrong, Nicholas C
  Berry, Gordon
  Berry, Lyman
  Bowmen, John
  Brown, Liberty
  Carland, Edward
  Corbett, John
  Crawford, John
  Donnelly, Joseph
  Doughty, Russell
  Ervin, John
  Exley, William
  Figges, William
  Flora, Peter
  Geer, John
  Heyle, Philip
  Holder, Jeremiah
  Jacobs, Samuel
  Johnson, John
  Langreen, Andrew
  Littlefield, Lyman
  Marina, Nicholas
  McPrelvey, Thomas
  Medad, Emos
  Oxford, James
  Parvlin, William
  Pendleton, Robert
  Rogers, James M
  Sandford, Samuel
  Sexton, James
  Stamphouse, Henry
  Stout, Scuder
  Tronmonger, Edward
  Van Kleek, John
  Wallace, Matthew
  Wallace, Peter
  Wells, Thomas
  Wilcox, Pelic
  Woodman, Constant
Mary Ann
  Deligall, William
  Giblet, Bendus
  Hussey, R
  Laurence, William
  Mark, John
  Steward, Samuel
Mary Barrett
  Sandford, Giles
Massoil
  Bruce, James
  De Witch, Samuel
  Forbes, John
  Look, John
  Noyce, Nathaniel
  Thicket, Elliot
  Willard, John
Matchless
  Basset, Samuel

American Prisoners of War Held at Bermuda During the War of 1812

    Mawn, Mathias
    Miller, Petter
    Mitchell, Chester
    Nicholson, Martin
    Petero, John
    Willis, J

Matilda
    Hopkins, Stephen

Matthews
    Hall, John
    Hall, Robert
    Hall, William

May Flower
    Bayley, Joseph
    Hall, William F
    Lawson, William

Mayflower
    McDonald, James
    Parker, B
    Robinson, Thomas
    Sumner, Charles
    White, John
    Whitman, John

Mercury
    Cowens, Andrew
    Egbert, Frederick
    Esbourn, Francis
    Funk, Nathaniel
    Gardner, Anthony
    Keith, William
    Roach, John

Michael & Eliza
    Thompson, James
    Thompson, James

Monticello
    Barnet, George
    Burke, Humphrey
    Coffin, Alexander
    Coleman, William
    Johnson, Peter
    Jones, Abraham
    Lang, R
    Ray, R
    Swaine, William
    Sweedy, P

Moreau
    Adams, Charles
    Baymanth, Lander
    Bolt, Charles

Morning Star
    Barns, Lincoln
    Pierce, John C

Nancy
    Bailie, Joseph
    Brown, Parker
    Brown, Stephen
    Cullerton, Noah
    Foot, Jonathan
    Forrest, James
    Parrish, Samuel
    Pool, Richard
    Reed, Richard
    Reed, Robert
    Roberts, William D
    Shorter, Jesse
    Wells, Thomas
    Whitmarsh, Z

Nautalus
    Harris, Charles
    Holt, William
    Kent, Obediah
    Mezarux, Ephraim
    Nicklos, William
    Woodbury, Thomas

New York
    Coleman, B
    Jackson, William
    Morse, T
    Sheffield, A

Noetoin
    Bussell, William
    Cleary, William
    Conover, Thomas A
    Finch, William
    Godfrey, John
    Hague, Charles
    Hubbard, John
    Leadworth, Michael
    Manley, Samuel
    Morris, Josiah
    Porter, J C
    Sarose, Belling
    Sinclair, William
    White, Ramsay
    Willams, John

Nonsuch
    Bankson, W C
    Bennett, Peley
    Bernard, William
    Blakely, M
    Blocke, Edmond
    Brown, James
    Buchan, Benjamin
    Bush, George
    Butler, Robert
    Canshard, T R
    Clasker, C
    Coles, Charles
    Davis, George
    Dixon, M
    Dunton, G
    Green, John
    Hammond, J
    Hardy, Robert
    Holmes, John
    Hughes, William
    James, John
    Leathan, Thomas
    Marshall, G
    Millington, F
    Noss, Henry
    Peterson, James
    Peterson, John
    Peterson, Lawrence
    Peterson, P
    Prindale, S
    Silvester, Emis
    Stanhour, Francis
    Watkin, William
    Welch, Thomas
    Wickes, Samuel
    Yarnell, William

Nymble
    Bennett, George
    Dennison, Isaac
    McCaun, John

Ohio
    Miln, Michael
    Patch, Joseph
    Pausland, John
    Perry, Liberty
    Woodbury, William

American Prisoners of War Held at Bermuda During the War of 1812

Olive Branch
    Adams, Isaac
    Drew, Benjamin
    Locket, Agnetu
    Miure, William

Orion
    Freeman, Nathaniel
    Lewis, S H B
    Miller, Martin
    Sawyer, Nathaniel

Pacifiranda
    Chester, William
    Perry, Henry

Packet
    Terron, James
    Tuck, John

Peakin
    Briggs, Barb
    Gold, Thomas
    Spurn, Elias
    Stodson, Benjamin
    Thoxter, Leavitt

Peggy
    Craig, Ephraim

Pekin
    Gambee, Daniel
    Priest, Stephen
    Spincker, Gerard

Perry
    Baker, Robert
    Batis, John
    Berry, Jessy
    Geiste, George
    Gould, John
    Hatch, John
    Ingersole, James
    Leger, Daniel
    Mackay, James F
    McDonald, Alexander
    Peters, John
    Pollard, William
    Robinson, Robert
    Smith, Thomas
    White, Isaac
    Wolf, Henry

Perseferanda
    Brailey, Elisha
    Brown, P F
    Bunkar, Isa
    Chester, William
    Drake, Harrison
    Francis, John
    Frank, John
    Moore, Prince
    Watson, T

Phaeton
    Eldridge, David
    Weeks, Josiah

Pheobe
    Sturtevant, Nehemiah

Pike
    Allen, Peter
    Blyden, John
    Bonwell, Garland
    Brook, Calvin
    Brown, William
    Cawdrick, Samuel
    Clark, Thomas
    Clicy, Peter
    Cook, Alexander
    Cooper, James
    Cooper, John
    Davey, Hugh
    Davis, John
    Davis, William
    Dawson, Christopher
    Dodd, Thomas
    Dove, Samuel
    Edward, Simon
    Elliot, Robert
    Fall, Alphun
    Fenderson, Steward
    Forster, James
    Jackson, William
    Kidmore, Joseph
    Long, Robert
    Marshall, David
    Martin, Charles
    Moffatt, John
    Monger, William
    Moore, William
    Morris, John
    Norbury, Charles
    Reybold, George
    Richardson, Joseph
    Rose, James
    Saunder, James L
    Saunder, William
    Smith, James
    Smith, Joseph F
    Smith, William
    Sommers, Frederick
    Swanson, Peter
    Taylor, John
    Williams, John
    Wood, John
    Young, Richard

Plantagenet
    Kellegan, James
    Parker, Joseph

Platoff
    Barker, Benjamin
    Hall, Edward
    Pearce, Henry
    Steward, Alexander

Policy
    Barles, Frederick
    Coffen, G B
    Collins, John
    Damore, Samuel
    Foster, Charles
    Gibbs, J
    Green, Peter
    Hanfelt, O
    Harvey, John
    Lake, Benjamin
    Laurence, Adam
    Silvarus, John
    Sullivan, Richard
    Welch, Thomas

Polly & Sally
    Cloutman, Abaneza
    Demers, William
    Emory, Samuel
    Merrick, John F

Polly Maria
    Marlin, William
    Thatcher, John

Portsmouth
    Ball, Isaac
    Beach, John
    Bocock, Matthew

American Prisoners of War Held at Bermuda During the War of 1812

Brown, John
Chuseman, John
Dalton, Thomas
Haughton, William
Johnson, Henry
Johnson, John
Kelly, Joshua
Marsden, William
Millehus, Frederick
Moat, James
Moore, John
Page, Jonkins
Parker, Redman
Pembroke, John
Sandbug, Charles
Wiley, Jonathan
Wolf, Henry
Wright, James

Portuguese Bark
Holesley, John
Parr, James

Post Boy
Blanchard, Ebenezer
Butterfield, Richard
Kneeland, Edward M
Sillsby, Benjamin
Small, Elisha
Smith, Ebenezer

President
Adams, John
Adams, William
Adrica, Peter
Alderson, Jeremiah
Allen, Samuel
Anderson, George
Andrews, A
Anthony, Joseph
Armstrong, James
Armstrong, John
Armstrong, William
Ashbourn, Ralph
Awner, Charles
Axford, Thomas
Banatt, John
Banks, James
Baptiste, John
Barnes, Nathaniel
Barritt, William
Barthoff, Nicholas
Beckwith, Henry
Beek, James
Bell, David
Bell, George
Bell, Samuel
Bemous, Abraham
Bennett, John
Bennett, John
Bennett, Peter
Benson, George
Benson, William
Beont, John
Besson, Joseph
Bird, Henry
Blake, Perry
Blether, Nathaniel
Blosdale, Jacob
Bolt, James
Bowden, Stephen
Bowman, William
Bowre, Henry
Bramhold, Charles

Brant, Solomon
Bray, Josh E
Brewster, Benjamin
Brickman, John
Brown, John
Brown, Joseph
Brown, Peter
Brown, Samuel
Brown, Samuel
Brown, Thomas
Brown, Thomas
Brown, William
Brown, William
Bryant, James
Bull, Francis
Burfield, Charles
Burgess, William
Butler, George
Butler, John
Callow, Stephen
Campbell, Thomas
Carnes, Charles
Carney, Charles
Carrans, Joseph
Carroll, Carn
Carroll, Michael
Carroll, Thomas
Carsay, Richard
Carter, John
Carter, William
Carton, Joseph
Caswell, Samuel
Caulson, Uriah
Caustin, Nicholas
Cayton, John
Chont, Robert
Clarke, John
Closs, Peter
Coleman, George
Coleman, James
Colloden, Patrick
Coney, Thomas
Cox, Frisby
Cramer, John
Crammet, Joseph
Crannell, William
Cribb, John
Cummings, William
Currey, John
Dale, Richard
Darley, Jacob
Davidson, William
Davis, Benjamin
Davis, John
Davis, Samuel
Davis, Thomas
Davison, William
De Casta, James
Decateur, Stephen
Delapp, William
Dennis, John
Dischodt, Frederick
Dix, John
Dixon, Samuel
Dixon, William
Dodge, Andrew
Dollman, John
Dominque, Joseph
Donaldson, Benjamin
Douglas, William
Downing, James

American Prisoners of War Held at Bermuda During the War of 1812

Dunn, James
Dutton, Nathan
Earp, Aquilla
Edgehill, Washington
Edwards, John
Edwards, William
Emmet, C T
Evans, John
Evans, Joseph
Felt, John
Ferguson, Patrick
Fevion, John
Fifer, Edward
Fisher, John D
Fleek, H F
Fowler, Peter
Fox, Charles
Funning, David
Fuster, David
Fyler, John C
Gainer, William
Gallagher, John
Gardner, Galen
Gardner, William
Gardner, William
Garnay, George
Gibson, William
Giles, Robert
Goley, David
Gordon, Alexander
Gore, John
Gore, Thomas
Gough, John
Grave, John
Gray, David
Gray, Mathew
Green, Jessy
Griffin, Stewart
Haggerty, James
Hales, John
Haley, John
Hall, George
Ham, Anthony
Hammond, Stephen
Hanford, William
Hanlow, Alexander
Harris, William
Harron, William
Harvey, Amon
Harvey, John
Haughtman, John
Haynes, Joseph
Henderson, Hans
Henley, George
Henry, James
Henry, Lewis
Henry, Robert
Henyon, James
Herbert, John
Hersey, Thomas
Heth, John
Hickman, George
Hight, Temple
Hill, Thomas
Hill, William
Hobey, John
Hoffman, Henry
Hoffman, Ogden
Holland, William
Hollins, George N
Holmes, James
Horley, John
Howlen, Barney
Hughes, John
Hull, Peter
Hunter, William
Hupper, Samuel
Hyler, Adam
Iverson, Peter
Jackman, Benjamin
Jacobs, David
James, John
James, Reuben
Jay, Bennet
Jenkins, Ludwick
Johnson, Francis
Johnson, G
Johnson, Richard
Johnston, John
Jolly, John
Jones, John
Jones, Watkins
Jordon, Ralph
Joseph, Anthony
Joseph, Francis
Joseph, Louis
Kainsford, Josiah
Keith, James
Keith, John
Keller, Anthony
Kelly, John
Kelly, Thomas
Kerr, Adam
Kettletas, Benjamin
Keys, William
Kneese, James
Krutson, John
Lampher, Clamlin
Lang, James
Lansing, E A
Larkin, Peter
Larraby, Joseph
Lary, Peter
Lawson, James
Leary, John
Leonard, Robert
Levina, Lewis
Linscott, John
Litchfield, John
Littlefield, John
Lord, Jonas
Lorgeunt, Samuel
Lourey, James
Low, John
Lowry, William
Luthers, Jeremiah
Lyons, John
Madden, Michael
Mariner, Joseph
Marsden, William
Marsh, Lubilen
Marshall, Thomas
Marson, Peter
Martin, George
Martin, William
Martins, Michael
Mason, Joel
Mason, John
Mathews, David
McClure, James
McDonald, Ebenezer
McGill, Mathew

American Prisoners of War Held at Bermuda During the War of 1812

McNatley, Michael
McPherson, William
Meany, Cornelius
Mellville, John
Memenbery, Jacob
Mennett, Thomas
Miggs, John
Miller, James
Mills, James
Mitchell, Lloyd
Mitchell, William
Morgan, William
Morgan, William
Morrin, John
Mottley, Alexander
Moulton, William
Murray, Alexander
Murray, David
Myres, Charles
Napier, William
Nelson, Andrew
Newman, W D
Nicholson, James
Nickerson, James C
Nisbett, William
Norkott, Dennis
Nostend, Daniel
Nye, Stephen
Oliver, Joseph
Oliver, Samuel
O'Neal, Robert
Owens, William
Owlin, George
Pack, Anthony
Palmer, William F
Parker, Benjamin
Parker, Robert
Parsons, Andrew
Pearce, George
Pedrick, George
Pendleton, Daniel
Perk, George
Perry, John
Pester, James
Peterson, John
Plummer, Joseph
Porter, John C
Potter, Joseph
Powell, John
Powers, Richard
Prassur, John
Pready, Marshall
Price, Edward
Pritchard, William
Quin, Michael
Randall, William
Randolph, R B
Ray, Thomas
Ray, Thomas
Raynolds, John H
Raynolds, William L
Reeves, Joseph
Regan, John
Rhodes, Romanto
Richardson, Thomas
Richardson, William
Ricker, Edward
Roberts, A
Roberts, William
Robertson, James
Robins, Henry

Robinson, Henry
Rogers, Francis
Rogers, James
Rogers, William
Russell, Peter
Russell, Samuel
Ryan, John
Ryan, William
Salinder, John
Sauls, John
Scandlings, Peter
Scantling, Owen
Scott, Francis
Scott, Joshua
Selolom, John
Serman, Robert
Shadell, James
Shubick, Irvine
Shubruk, John
Simmonds, Jacob
Simmonds, John
Simons, John
Sinnett, James
Skant, John
Sloan, James
Smith, Christopher
Smith, Edward
Smith, James
Smith, John
Smith, John
Smith, John
Smith, John
Smith, Ralph
Smith, William
Snow, William
Spencer, Robert
Stanford, James
Stantos, Andrew D
Stephenson, Thomas
Stevens, L
Stime, Wallis
Stoel, Peter
Strumbell, Abraham
Sullivan, Daniel
Sumers, Langford
Summers, Anthony
Swiney, Alexander
Taylor, James
Tennis, Benjamin
Thayre, Elijah
Theodore, Joseph
Thomas, David
Thompson, George
Thompson, James
Thompson, John
Thompson, William
Thorpe, William
Tickle, John
Timberlake, J B
Tolman, Artemus
Travers, Jiffy
Trevett, Samuel R
Tuck, Joseph
Turner, Samuel
Turney, George
Tutton, Joseph
Twigds, Levi
Updike, Richard
Vaun, Samuel
Voorhes, Ralph
Wade, Alfred

American Prisoners of War Held at Bermuda During the War of 1812

Wagner, Christian
Walker, Thomas
Wards, William
Warren, Clark
Waters, Richard
Welch, James
Wentsworth, Paul
Westurick, William
Weyman, Charles
Wheeler, Andrew
Wheelwright, Joseph
White, James
White, John
White, John
White, John
White, Philip
White, Ramsey
White, William
Whyley, Philip
Wickes, J D
Wilkes, Joseph
Wilkinson, William
Willden, Charles
Williams, Charles
Williams, Daniel
Williams, John
Williams, John
Williams, William
Williamson, Charles
Williamson, Thomas
Woats, John
Womack, John
Woodruff, John
Wright, John
Wright, William

Princessa
    Caton, Joseph
    Downridge, Stephen
    Halsey, John
    Joachina, Josia
    Josey, Jack
    Prader, Manuel
    Roderique, John

Priscilla
    Collins, Samuel
    Davis, John
    Forrest, John
    Silsbee, Benjamin
    Silsbee, J W

Pylader
    Lands, John

Ranger
    Barret, Samuel
    Calder, Thomas
    Chase, Peter
    Coffin, Barna
    Coffin, Edward
    Coleman, Robert
    Easton, Isaac
    Gardener, Able
    Jenkins, Ruben
    Merchant, Abram
    Peddock, William
    Sailsbury, John
    Skank, Samuel
    Skank, Samuel
    Taber, Isaac

Ranger of Nantucket
    Coffin, Obediah
    Joy, William

Rapid
    Butler, John
    Heartie, Isaac
    Teaser, James

Rebecca
    Kennedy, James
    Stephens, James

Recovery
    Cooper, James
    Heath, William
    Sancho, Antonio
    Van Tassell, Barney
    Whigs, George
    Williams, Jacob

Republican
    Humphries, Thomas
    Tone, William P

Resolution
    Broughton, Elijah
    Claxton, Philip
    Claxton, Robert
    Fresk, John
    Fuller, Benjamin
    Garrison, Ephraim
    Gilbert, Benjamin
    Hazard, Wanton
    Smith, Jacob
    Stacey, R S
    Williams, Lloyd

Revenge
    Baxter, John
    Hill, John
    Kerson, George
    Pearson, William

Revinue
    Bensley, William
    Forsyth, Asa
    Hunt, Edward P
    Pray, Caterwick
    Richards, John
    Sloan, Henry
    Starr, John
    Thorp, George
    Turner, William
    West, Francis

Rhode
    Cole, David
    Kennedy, Peter
    Lascell, William
    Miller, John
    Noble, Daniel

Ring Dove
    Archer, Thomas
    Atwood, Isaac
    Dill, Isaiah
    Freeman, Jesse
    Knowles, Thorpolin
    Snow, Joseph

Rising Hope
    Gorden, William
    Grant, Thomas
    Gyles, William
    Holmes, C K
    Hutchison, Henry
    Ireland, Jacob
    Kemp, John
    Kendel, Henry
    Stetson, Smith
    Wiggs, Benjamin
    Witherall, William

Rising States
    Jones, Charles

American Prisoners of War Held at Bermuda During the War of 1812

Rising Sun
    Afferil, Charles
    Brown, Francis
    Gualt, Charles
    Muskett, William
    Riley, William
    Taylor, James D
    Wilson, Sidney
Robert
    Wright, James
Rolla
    Allison, B C
    Anderson, Andrew
    Barber, J H
    Batis, John
    Bayley, Warren
    Beard, James
    Beard, Martin
    Bennet, Abua
    Bert, Thomas
    Boon, James
    Borrswell, Paul
    Boss, Joseph
    Briggs, B
    Brown, George
    Brown, Willliam
    Burns, James
    Burrows, A H
    Bushnam, James
    Castignet, John
    Clark, John
    Coil, R M
    Cole, Nathaniel
    Cook, Dennis
    Cooper, Lad
    Costin, Thomas
    Cousens, Benjamin
    Crafts, John
    Cuff, Abraham
    Davis, John
    Day, William
    Dixon, John
    Dryden, John
    Fellows, G H
    Fellows, Nathaniel
    Gardner, Timothy
    Grindell, Henry
    Hammond, Samuel
    Hazard, D
    Henderson, Francis
    Hill, Pompey
    Holden, James
    Holland, J H
    Hopkins, M H
    Hoskin, Cato
    Hossday, William
    Huntington, E
    Johnson, James
    Jones, Edward
    Justin, William
    Larkin, Lewis
    Latham, A B
    Lee, Samuel
    Lewis, D
    Little, William
    Lorin, George
    Martin, Samuel
    McGee, John
    Metzger, C D
    Molton, C P
    Palmer, Benjamin
    Phelps, Elijah
    Richardson, Perry
    Satchell, Jonathan
    Shaw, Joseph
    Shaw, Robert
    Shustliff, John
    Simpson, John
    Smith, John
    Smith, John
    Stoddart, Isaac
    Swinney, Benjamin
    Thomas, William
    Tyler, Daniel
    Unewell, John
    Ware, John
    Washington, John
    Waymore, John
    Widget, Abrea
    Windwood, William
Romp
    Alexand, John
    Coffin, Linzey
    Macey, F G
    Stapford, D F
    Swensen, Hans
    Whippey, W C
Ruby
    Bowden, Thomas
Rufus King
    Dupecy, John
    Dupree, John
    Harris, John
    Headley, James
    Hill, Joseph
    Houton, William
    Howard, Henry
    James, Charles
    Johnson, Robert
    Rogers, John
    Smith, Deliverance
    Steward, Joseph
    Williams, John
Salley
    Dominga, N
    Walden, Samuel
Sally
    Andrews, John
    Bray, Robert
    Burgess, Isaah
    Burke, John
    Clark, Obea
    Cowell, Ezekiel
    Davis, James
    Henry, Samuel
    McIntire, J L
    Moordie, John
    Nicklye, John L
    Sheverick, Elijah
    Thomas, Corbet
    Williams, Samuel
    Wing, Paul
    Wing, Philip
Sally Jasper
    Darrel, John S
    Richards, Toby
Santo Cateno Venturuso
    Boyles, James
    Rifley, George
    Savil, Francis O
    Winsley, William
Saragosa

American Prisoners of War Held at Bermuda During the War of 1812

      Lattimore, C N

Savannah Packet
- Buckland, John
- Franklin, John
- Johnson, Peter
- Mott, John
- Taylor, Charles
- Wallace, Thomas
- Whipple, John

Scorpion
- Clough, William
- Edwards, William
- Hodges, Gamiel
- Kings, Thomas

Seaflower
- Holland, John

Sheppard
- Allender, William
- Hart, Robert
- Thompson, John

Sidney
- Cavines, John
- Coward, Thomas
- Gleaves, George
- Jackson, M
- Larke, James R
- Tunis, John

Snapper
- Antonia, Peter
- Antonis, Frederick
- Arnon, Peter
- Bayton, John
- Boyd, Thomas
- Brown, Charles
- Brown, John
- Bruster, William
- Burch, Robert
- Carter, William
- Casora, Amanuel
- Casora, Samuel
- Connor, Edward
- Connor, John
- Defield, Jesse
- Deveine, Charles
- Dickenson, James
- Dormain, John
- Dustaine, Peter
- Ellis, Aaron
- Evans, Jerry
- Falford, William
- Farret, William
- Ferrat, Charles
- Flick, John
- Flinn, Pierre
- Free, James
- Goldtrap, William
- Good, Frederick
- Green, James
- Hartley, Lewis
- Hays, Abraham
- Henderson, Henry
- Hoswell, James
- Jeffery, Samuel
- Jones, William
- Joseph, Charles
- Kerns, George
- Kussleu, Moses
- La Vie, Antonia
- Label, Antonia
- Lane, John
- Lane, John
- Lathan, Thomas
- Le Fause, Cade
- Lee, David
- Leech, Nathaniel
- Luky, Jacob
- Mailer, Charles
- Martin, Henry
- Masta, Antonia
- McKinley, Alexander
- Millington, Robert
- Millis, John
- Montsele, John
- Moore, Abraham
- Morians, Joshua
- Morris, Charles
- Morrison, William
- Nathans, David
- Nickson, Robert
- Parker, James B
- Quinolis, Frederick
- Reed, Perry
- Reynolds, John
- Rosseau, Peter
- Sampson, George
- Shawe, Daniel
- Simmonds, George
- Simmonds, Isaac
- Slowbridge, Benjamin
- Stephens, David
- Stephens, Loyd
- Swarts, Joshua
- Temple, Joseph
- Templing, Henry
- Tompkins, James
- Turner, William
- White, Edward
- Willard, Benjamin S
- Williams, Williams
- Willock, Henry
- Woodburn, Edward

South Boston
- Clough, John
- Doverell, Thomas
- Ives, John
- Mucker, Herim
- Robinson, Nathan
- Warren, Cyrus
- Watson, John

Speed
- Archer, John
- Fair, Samuel
- Fisk, Esra
- Hill, Hugh
- Hussey, Robert
- Saunders, Thomas
- Simonds, Andrew
- Sparkanork, John
- Webb, T B

Speedwell
- Donagan, James
- Garrison, Joseph
- Howard, Eliah
- Irvin, Charles
- Providence, Thomas
- Sailor, William

St Marys
- Best, Samuel
- Gallick, D
- Hollingsworth, William
- Sheldon, Job

St. Augustina

American Prisoners of War Held at Bermuda During the War of 1812

    Andrews, Hercules
    Cunon, James
    Dekoven, Henry L
    Sebor, William
    Shallon, Egbert

St. Joquin
    Butler, Joseph
    Chidry, Abraham
    Finny, Isaac
    Melna, Joseph
    Smith, Elias
    Walker, David

St. Michael
    Johnson, Richard

Stockholm
    Atwater, Levi
    Belding, Emos
    Gibbs, Henry
    Hall, Hezekiah
    Trowbridge, William

Superb
    Anderson, Nathaniel
    Barney, Olpha
    Davis, Thomas
    Gasalo, John
    Given, Francis
    Golen, Francis
    Kelso, John
    Lawrence, Peter
    Nicholas, John
    Tamley, John
    Wright, James

Surprize
    Allen, Joseph

Survanou
    Barber, Henry
    Contee, Augustus
    Hoyt, James M
    Smith, John
    Turner, Henry B

Swiftsure
    Allen, Duffy
    Barr, Robert
    Baylee, George
    Cummins, Christopher
    Hunt, Thomas
    Hyatt, Abel
    Lucas, William
    Taros, Vecentia
    Webber, Daniel
    Young, Robert

Symmetry
    Bakeman, John
    Barrett, James
    Clinton, James
    Doyle, Lewis
    Eagles, John
    Edwards, George Thomas
    Falk, John
    Francis, Lewis
    Morton, Thomas
    Roberts, John
    Simpson, William
    Smith, Charles
    Snail, Robert

Taalia
    Paine, William

Tamer
    McCall, Thomas William

Teacher
    Dacres, John B

Teazer
    Bartoph, Abber S
    Brager, Abner K
    Burridge, James
    Cartey, John
    Clyde, Bartin
    Collet, Peter
    Collins, John
    Connor, John
    Cook, Justice
    Cullagen, John H
    Davis, John
    Dormaine, George
    Dumkley, Isaac
    Edwards, John
    Elbey, James
    Frith, William
    Gibson, James
    Gover, Daniel
    Grant, Peter
    Hall, William
    Holmes, Jahiel
    Hubbard, Peter
    Humphrey, James
    Huver, John
    Johnson, Frederick
    Lane, Horice
    Lent, Benjamin
    Lewy, Frederick
    McDermott, James
    McKenzie, Daniel
    Moore, Isaac
    Myers, George
    Nevill, James
    Palmer, Justice
    Patterson, Thomas
    Reynolds, James
    Richardson, William
    Rogers, William
    Sebvea, Andrew
    Smith, Daniel
    Sowle, Peley
    Stephens, Henry
    Stewart, John P
    Stone, Samuel
    Storme, Daniel
    Sullingell, William F
    Thomas, Isaac
    Tubeter, James
    Wedder, Anthony H
    Williams, John
    Williams, John
    Young, David

Telamachur
    Cole, H A

Theresa
    Peyton, James

Thestis
    Bullock, Joseph
    Elliott, John
    Greeman, Edward
    Nemo, Henry

Timer
    Hammond, William
    Lolly, William
    Wilkinson, Francis

Tram
    Carpenter, Vincent
    Clark, James
    Roberts, Charles
    Young, William

American Prisoners of War Held at Bermuda During the War of 1812

Trim
    Card, John
    Caston, John
    Dore, Daniel
    Freeman, John
    Hall, Robert
    Morgan, Littleton T
    Richardson, Randolph
    Rogers, James
    Wentworth, Alexander
    White, Joseph
    White, Robert

Trinadada
    Batt, James
    Carter, Benjamin
    French, Calvin
    Kern, Nicholas
    Sandford, Daniel
    Sandford, Royal
    Slocolm, John

True American
    Bohom, John

Ulissus
    Honest, John
    Jenkins, Robert
    Short, Moses
    Taylor, Dugomier

United States
    Baker, Samuel
    Cory, Green
    Gibbs, Moses
    Lamberg, John
    Rice, John
    Salsburg, William
    Stringer, Isaac
    Worth, John

Valiant
    Culver, Esau

Viper
    Brown, R
    Kelly, Thomas
    Rousseau, Laurence
    Smith, E
    Smith, Frederick William
    Vickery, C
    Wright, Samuel

Vixen
    Brooks, Thomas
    Brown, John L
    Carpenter, Nathaniel
    Coles, Thomas
    Edes, Benjamin
    Evans, Benjamin
    Foyte, Henry
    Francisco, Antonio
    Francisco, Clias
    Hall, Humes
    Jackay, Joseph
    Joseph, Fortunata
    Lewis, Michael
    Mathews, Henry
    McChusney, William
    McCollock, Robert
    Nicholson, William
    Noble, Andrew
    Parker, William
    Spaniola, John
    Sutton, Nathan
    Tupp, John
    Weeks, Joseph
    Williams, John

Wasp
    Abbeson, John
    Adams, John
    Ambruster, Peter
    Atkinson, John
    Baker, John C
    Baldis, Anthony
    Barber, John
    Barlow, Joseph
    Barret, Alexander
    Beats, John
    Beeby, Joseph
    Bennedick, George
    Berris, John
    Biddle, James
    Booth, Benjamin W
    Bostwick, John
    Bowdel, William
    Bowring, Jesse
    Bradt, Francis
    Brashears, Richard
    Briggs, John
    Brown, John
    Brown, John
    Brown, Joshua
    Burn, Peter
    Burns, Daniel
    Burrett, John
    Cairns, Thomas
    Castaway, Antonia
    Catley, William
    Claxton, Alexander
    Clerk, Perry
    Cole, John
    Coleman, Samuel
    Conner, James
    Conner, John
    Cooper, Thomas
    Couts, John
    Crawford, Johnson
    Deherty, Dennis
    Dill, Stephen
    Dixon, Daniel
    Doherty, Dennis
    Downs, Jeremiah
    Duffie, David
    Edwards, William
    Ennis, Lewis
    Forster, William
    Freeman, Peter
    Gaunt, Charles
    Gridney, John
    Gum, Jacob
    Guthwright, James
    Gutry, James
    Hall, Samuel
    Harrington, Ebenezer
    Harris, J W
    Henfield, Thomas
    Hibbets, John
    Holcomb, John C
    Hulland, Nathaniel
    Jackson, George
    Jackson, John
    Jaimeson, John
    Jaimeson, John
    Javar, William
    Johnson, Peter
    Jones, Henry
    Jones, Jacob
    Knight, John

American Prisoners of War Held at Bermuda During the War of 1812

Knight, William
Lanboon, Andrew
Lane, Timothy
Lang, John
Lawrence, John
Little, William
Longel, Matthew
Lyceet, John
Martin, John
McCloud, John
McCloud, John
McKowen, Alex
McLuney, William
Messavy, Philip
Miller, David
Mitchell, Henry
Mitchell, William
Moore, Marus
Morris, Andrew
Murphey, William
Naire, Joseph Lee
New, Walter W
Ostler, George
Patterson, Alexander
Patterson, John
Philips, Thomas
Planter, John
Porter, Levi
Pouree, Stephen
Rapp, Henry B
Rea, John
Reane, John
Reed, George
Rogers, G W
Rollins, John
Rose, John
Rozier, Francis
Rutter, Samuel
Ryley, William
Samborn, Joseph
Seward, Henry
Shannon, Henry
Shawe, Edgebert
Steady, James
Stephens, John
Stephens, Levi
Sterns, David
Sweney, Hugh
Ten Eck, Abram S
Tucker, John
Tyler, William
Van Cleave, G W
Ward, James
Westwick, William
White, James
Williams, Daniel
Wilson, Caesar R
Wilson, William
Wise, George
Witten, Elijah
Wolfe, William
Wright, John

Welcome Return
   Harrington, Samuel

West Indian Schooner
   Young, James W

White Oak
   Basden, John
   Furnell, Tobias
   Kelly, Henry
   Morris, Emanuel
   Stanley, Peter

Willam & Ann
   Davis, John
   Floyd, Thomas
   Johnston, William
   Johnstone, John
   Maxworth, Mathew
   Rogers, John
   Staple, Thomas

William
   Davis, John
   Elwell, Francis
   Lowe, John
   Marble, Benjamin
   Pew, Doliver
   Sawyer, Robert
   Watson, George

William of Baltimore
   Butler, John
   Childsey, Abraham
   Cooper, John
   Dennis, Thomas
   Gibson, William
   Hennee, John D
   Metrash, Ezekial
   Parrey, John
   Peters, John
   Powell, William
   Smith, Thomas R
   Taber, Humphrey

Windward Planter
   Berry, Daniel
   Hooper, John
   Hutson, James
   Rowlins, Joshua
   Woodburst, Benjamin

Yankee
   Douglass, Robert
   Ingram, George
   Johnson, Joseph
   Kielsey, Henry

Yankelass
   Appleton, John
   Aspenell, Elijah
   Astor, Doroty
   Barrett, William S
   Barton, Lette
   Bowen, Nathaniel
   Brown, James
   Bruce, Jonathan
   Burding, Joseph
   Burr, William
   Campbell, John
   Catan, William
   Churchill, Benjamin
   Cole, Lutha
   Collins, Thomas
   Cook, Dennis
   Daniels, John
   Darby, Joseph
   Doak, Nathaniel
   Evans, John
   Fox, George
   Garcia, James
   Giffigan, Thomas
   Goff, Dina
   Green, John
   Green, John
   Grimes, Richard
   Guswold, Truman
   Hanna, Edward

American Prisoners of War Held at Bermuda During the War of 1812

Hanster, John
Henman, Richard
Hogan, Norman A
Hunt, Isaac A
Jackson, Lewis
Johnson, Samuel
Johnson, Thomas
Joseph, John
Josif, Antinio
Lee, John
Maclever, Francis
McCannon, Isaac
Mitchell, Jonah
Mofford, Gardner
Moffunire, Henry
Morice, Marcus
Murphey, John
Nightingale, Joseph
Perriotte, Louis
Pickens, Samuel
Pike, John
Pitts, Samuel
Plumely, John
Plummer, Isaac L
Pratt, Samuel
Prowe, Tudar
Roach, William
Robertson, James
Robinson, John
Russell, Thomas
Sambo, Joseph

Segoss, Ezekiel
Simons, Evan
Small, Benjamin
Spencer, Job F
Strong, Ceres
Taber, Rubin
Thomas, James
Tilbots, Benjamin
Tiler, Christian
Watt, John
Wells, George
Whitaker, Manly
Williams, Daniel
Williams, Nicholas
Willson, George
Wise, Joseph
Young, Richard

<u>Yankey</u>
Fisher, John W

<u>Yorick</u>
Cole, John
Hammond, Stephen
King, William
La Mour, John
Montgomery, Robert
Philips, John
Pierce, Nathaniel
Russel, Simon

Americans on British ships

Allen, Joseph
Bailey, Cyral
Barnes, Timothy W
Barnes, William
Baty, William
Belfeur, James
Bowman, Thaddus
Boyd, Thomas D
Bradbury, John H
Brett, James
Callam, John
Carson, John
Casey, Henry
Clark, William
Coole, David
Corkes, Dan
Culver, Esau
Downs, Nasa
Elliott, John
Febre, William
Gordine, Anthony
Goswilling, David
Hiller, George
Hopkins, Samuel
Huckstep, Barnard
James, Benjamin
Jermain, Joseph
Kellegan, James
Lands, John
Lee, W R
McAfferty, William
Oliver, John
Page, Cato
Parker, Joseph
Patrick, George
Stephenson, John
Stringer, William
Wentworth, Paul

American Prisoners of War Held at Bermuda During the War of 1812

Service affiliation not known

Anderson, Peter
Bell, William
Black, David
Bourne, Esra
Brockitt, William
Brooks, Thomas
Brown, Richard
Burnell, Thomas
Butler, George
Cane, James
Catlin, Othello
Clark, Peleg
Connell, G
Cook, W F
Crummett, John
Darby, Joseph
Davis, John
Douglass, Aquilla
Elliot, John
Forbes, Sandy
Foye, James
Freeman, Francis
Garrett, Robert
Godfrey, John
Gold, Samuel
Golden, Edward
Greason, George
Hall, Henry
Harris, James
Hodgkin, Nathaniel
Holbrock, Richard
Hubbard, Jeremiah
Hulton, John
James, John
Johnson, Peter
Judkins, Charles
Keir, John
Lee, Hezekiah I
Lindsey, Joseph
Longshore, Thomas
McIntire, Abraham
Mecanger, Michael
Merry, William
Mounteam, Henry
Neaves, Samuel
Nulty, Thomas
Phillips, John
Price, Charles
Richards, Guy
Richards, Steven
Rodgers, Smith
Sabins, John
Savage, Absolam
Savage, Timothy
Smith, Ichabod
Smith, Lawrence
Solaris, Francis
Steward, John
Stowe, John
Strong, Robert
Sullivan, John
Swanson, Jacob
Thompson, Benjamin
Tipereal, Andrew
Watson, William
Watson, William
Webster, William H
White, Isaac
Williams, John
Williams, Samuel
Williams, William
Williams, William
Wood, Bill
Zeizell, John O

American Prisoners of War Held at Bermuda During the War of 1812

United States Marines

Allen, Samuel
Ambruster, Peter
Bennett, Peter
Bostwick, John
Bowdel, William
Bowring, Jesse
Bradt, Francis
Brown, Thomas
Burfield, Charles
Burns, Daniel
Carnes, Charles
Coleman, James
Coleman, Samuel
Colloden, Patrick
Couts, John
Crannell, William
Crawford, Johnson
Cribb, John
Darley, Jacob
Davison, William
Deherty, Dennis
Dixon, Daniel
Doherty, Dennis
Downing, James
Edwards, William
Ferguson, Patrick
Gainer, William
Goley, David
Gray, Mathew
Haggerty, James
Henry, Robert
Henyon, James
Hyler, Adam
Jackman, Benjamin
James, John
Jones, William
Keller, Anthony
Kelly, John
Lang, James
Lourey, James
Martins, Michael
McClure, James
McNatley, Michael
Mennett, Thomas
Morris, Andrew
Naire, Joseph Lee
Napier, William
Nostend, Daniel
Oliver, Joseph
Oliver, Samuel
Porter, Levi
Quin, Michael
Ray, Thomas
Richardson, Thomas
Richardson, William
Rutter, Samuel
Scandlings, Peter
Scantling, Owen
Shadell, James
Skant, John
Sumers, Langford
Twigds, Levi
Wilkes, Joseph
Williams, Charles
Williams, Daniel
Woats, John

American Prisoners of War at Cape of Good Hope During the War of 1812

---, Maplino   Prisoner 84. Rank: Seaman, from: Rose, Merchant Vessel.
    Cap: Not Recorded by HM Ships Harpy & Primrose Int: 05 Mar 1813 Dis: 13 Aug 1813.
    Received from HMS Harpy. per Order Rear Adl Tyler. (Date and place of capture 'not mentioned'. Last name not recorded.)

---, Mariano   Prisoner 83. Rank: Seaman, from: Rose, Merchant Vessel.
    Cap: Not Recorded by HM Ships Harpy & Primrose Int: 05 Mar 1813 Dis: 13 Aug 1813.
    Received from HMS Harpy. per Order Rear Adl Tyler. (Date and place of capture 'not mentioned'. Last name not recorded.)

Adams, John   Prisoner 69. Rank: Seaman, from: Rambler, Merchant Vessel.
    Cap: Not Recorded by HMS Harpy Int: 28 Feb 1813 Dis: 10 Feb 1814.
    Received from Morley Transport. For a Passage to England. (Date of capture not recorded.)

Adams, John   Prisoner 119. Rank: Seaman, from: Not Recorded, Not Recorded.
    Cap: Not Recorded by Not Recorded Int: 09 Jul 1813 Dis: 12 Aug 1814.
    Received from HMS Lion. HMS Dannemark order Adl Tayler. (Date of capture not recorded.)

Adams, Nathaniel   Prisoner 167. Rank: Masters Mate, from: Syren, Man of War Brig.
    Cap: 12 Jul 1814 at Sea by HMS Medway Int: 19 Aug 1814 Dis: 06 Apr 1815.
    Received from HMS Medway. HMS Cumberland per Order Vice Adl Sir Charles Tyler.

Allen, John   Prisoner 105. Rank: Seaman, from: Not Recorded, Not Recorded.
    Cap: Not Recorded by Not Recorded Int: 13 Apr 1813 Dis: 12 Aug 1814.
    Received from HMS Astraea being an American. HMS Stag per Order V Adl Tyler. John Allen (2). (Date and place of capture 'not mentioned'.)

Allen, John   Prisoner 140. Rank: Seaman, from: William Penn, Merchant Vessel.
    Cap: 27 Oct 1813 at Sea by HMS Acorn Int: 04 Dec 1813 Dis: 10 Aug 1814.
    Received from HMS Acorn. Exiter Indiaman for England.

Alplin, Joseph   Prisoner 225. Rank: Quartermaster, from: Syren, Man of War Brig.
    Cap: 12 Jul 1814 at Sea by HMS Medway Int: 19 Aug 1814 Dis: 06 Apr 1815.
    Received from HMS Medway. HMS Cumberland per Order VA Sir Charles Tyler.

Andrews, Joseph   Prisoner 230. Rank: Quartermaster, from: Syren, Man of War Brig.
    Cap: 12 Jul 1814 at Sea by HMS Medway Int: 19 Aug 1814 Dis: 06 Apr 1815.
    Received from HMS Medway. HMS Cumberland per Order of VA Sir Charles Tyler.

Andrews, Samuel   Prisoner 175. Rank: Ordinary Seaman, from: Syren, Man of War Brig.
    Cap: 12 Jul 1814 at Sea by HM Ship Medway Int: 19 Aug 1814 Dis: 30 Nov 1814.
    Received from HMS Medway. To HM Ship Desere per order of Vice Adml Tyler.

Arnold, Thomas   Prisoner 10. Rank: Passenger, from: Valentine, Merchant Service.
    Cap: 16 Nov 1812 Table Bay by Minden Int: 07 Jan 1813 Dis:
    Received from Valentine. (Date of discharge not recorded.)

Arnold, Thomas   Prisoner 32. Rank: Passenger, from: Valentine, Not Recorded.
    Cap: Not Recorded by Not Recorded Int: Dis: 10 Feb 1814.
    For a Passage to England. (Dates of capture and internment not recorded. Apparent duplicate of prisoner # 10.)

Arnold, Welcome   Prisoner 11. Rank: 1 Mate, from: Valentine, Merchant Service.
    Cap: 16 Nov 1812 Table Bay by Minden Int: 07 Jan 1813 Dis: 10 Feb 1814.
    Received from Valentine. For a Passage to England HMS Leon.

Atkinson, Charles   Prisoner 65. Rank: Seaman, from: Rambler, Merchant Vessel.
    Cap: Not Recorded by HMS Harpy Int: 28 Feb 1813 Dis: 30 Apr 1814.
    Received from Morley Transport. William Pitt Indiaman London. (Date of capture not recorded.)

Banen, John   Prisoner 237. Rank: Seaman, from: Syren, Man of War Brig.
    Cap: 12 Jul 1814 at Sea by HMS Medway Int: 19 Aug 1814 Dis: 06 Apr 1815.
    Received from HMS Medway. HMS Cumberland per Order of VA Sir Charles Tyler.

Barns, Jacob   Prisoner 208. Rank: Seaman, from: Syren, Man of War Brig.
    Cap: 12 Jul 1814 at Sea by HMS Medway Int: 19 Aug 1814 Dis: 06 Apr 1815.
    Received from HMS Medway. To His Majestys Ship Malacca per Order of Vice Adml Sir Charles Tyler.

Bartlet, Samuel   Prisoner 158. Rank: Seaman, from: Mary, Merchant Vessel.
    Cap: Saldauha Bay by Not Recorded Int: 26 Jul 1814 Dis: 12 Aug 1814.
    Recaptured Ship. Hyair Alley American Privateer. HMS Dannemark order Vice Adl Taylor. (Date of capture not recorded.)

Bassinger, Robert   Prisoner 128. Rank: Seaman, from: Not Recorded, Not Recorded.
    Cap: Not Recorded by Not Recorded Int: 25 Sep 1813 Dis: 12 Aug 1814.
    Received from HMS Semiramis. HMS Dannemark order Vice Adml Taylor. (Date of capture not recorded.)

American Prisoners of War at Cape of Good Hope During the War of 1812

Bennett, Robert   Prisoner 81. Rank: Seaman, from: Rose, Merchant Vessel.
    Cap: Not Recorded by HM Ships Harpy & Primrose Int: 05 Mar 1813 Dis: 30 Apr 1814.
    Received from HMS Harpy. William Pitt Indiaman for London. (Date and place of capture 'not mentioned'.)

Bilt, J J   Prisoner 254. Rank: Midshipman, from: Syren, Man of War Brig.
    Cap: 12 Jul 1814 at Sea by HMS Medway Int: 19 Aug 1814 Dis: 06 Apr 1815.
    Received from HMS Medway. HMS Cumberland per Order VA Sir Charles Tyler.

Bisbey, Isaac   Prisoner 182. Rank: Ordinary Seaman, from: Syren, Man of War Brig.
    Cap: 12 Jul 1814 at Sea by HM Ship Medway Int: 19 Aug 1814 Dis: 06 Apr 1815.
    Received from HMS Medway. To HMS Malacca per Order of Vice Adml Sir Charles Tyler.

Blackford, John   Prisoner 201. Rank: Ordinary Seaman, from: Syren, Man of War Brig.
    Cap: 12 Jul 1814 at Sea by HMS Medway Int: 19 Aug 1814 Dis: 30 Nov 1814.
    Received from HMS Medway. Asia East India Man to assist in navigating her England.

Blair, Samuel   Prisoner 272. Rank: Ordinary Seaman, from: Syren, Man of War Brig.
    Cap: 12 Jul 1814 at Sea by HMS Medway Int: 19 Aug 1814 Dis: 06 Apr 1815.
    Received from HMS Medway. HMS Cumberland per Order of VA Sir Charles Tyler.

Blakey, Charles   Prisoner 259. Rank: Boy, from: Syren, Man of War Brig.
    Cap: 12 Jul 1814 at Sea by HMS Medway Int: 19 Aug 1814 Dis: 06 Apr 1815.
    Received from HMS Medway. HMS Cumberland per Order VA Sir Charles Taylor.

Booder, Joseph   Prisoner 270. Rank: Ordinary Seaman, from: Syren, Man of War Brig.
    Cap: 12 Jul 1814 at Sea by HMS Medway Int: 19 Aug 1814 Dis: 06 Apr 1815.
    Received from HMS Medway. HMS Cumberland per Order VA Sir Charles Taylor.

Bray, George   Prisoner 267. Rank: Seaman, from: Syren, Man of War Brig.
    Cap: 12 Jul 1814 at Sea by HMS Medway Int: 19 Aug 1814 Dis: 06 Apr 1815.
    Received from HMS Medway. HMS Cumberland per Order VA Sir Charles Taylor.

Brevett, Abraham   Prisoner 290. Rank: Private, from: Syren, Man of War Brig.
    Cap: 12 Jul 1814 at Sea by HMS Medway Int: 19 Aug 1814 Dis: 06 Apr 1815.
    Received from HMS Medway. HMS Cumberland per Order VA Sir Charles Tyler.

Briant, Thomas   Prisoner 196. Rank: Boy, from: Syren, Man of War Brig.
    Cap: 12 Jul 1814 at Sea by HM Ship Medway Int: 19 Aug 1814 Dis: 06 Apr 1815.
    Received from HMS Medway. To HMS Malacca per Order of Vice Adml Sir Charles Tyler.

Brooking, Samuel   Prisoner 207. Rank: Ordinary Seaman, from: Syren, Man of War Brig.
    Cap: 12 Jul 1814 at Sea by HMS Medway Int: 19 Aug 1814 Dis: 06 Apr 1815.
    Received from HMS Medway. To His Majestys Ship Malacca per Order of Vice Adml Sir Charles Tyler.

Brooks, John   Prisoner 75. Rank: Seaman, from: Rambler, Merchant Vessel.
    Cap: Not Recorded by HMS Harpy Int: 28 Feb 1813 Dis: 12 Aug 1814.
    Received from Morley Transport. HMS Dannemark order Adl Tyler. (Date of capture not recorded.)

Brown, George   Prisoner 110. Rank: Not Recorded, from: Not Recorded, Not Recorded.
    Cap: Not Recorded by Not Recorded Int: Dis: 12 Aug 1814.
    Received from Town Prison, HMS Stag per Order R Adl Tyler. (Dates of capture and internment not recorded.)

Brown, James   Prisoner 221. Rank: Seaman, from: Syren, Man of War Brig.
    Cap: 12 Jul 1814 at Sea by HMS Medway Int: 19 Aug 1814 Dis: 06 Apr 1815.
    Received from HMS Medway. To His Majestys Ship Malacca per Order of Vice Adml Sir Charles Tyler.

Brown, James   Prisoner 275. Rank: 2 Gunner, from: Syren, Man of War Brig.
    Cap: 12 Jul 1814 at Sea by HMS Medway Int: 19 Aug 1814 Dis: 06 Apr 1815.
    Received from HMS Medway. HMS Cumberland per Order of VA Sir Charles Tyler. James Brown (2).

Bryant, Timothy   Prisoner 57. Rank: Supercargo, from: James, Merchant Vessel.
    Cap: 18 Dec 1812 at Sea by HMS Harpy Int: 28 Feb 1813 Dis: 02 Mar 1814.
    Received from Morley Transport. To the Metcalf.

Bubier, John   Prisoner 271. Rank: Midshipman, from: Syren, Man of War Brig.
    Cap: 12 Jul 1814 at Sea by HMS Medway Int: 19 Aug 1814 Dis: 06 Apr 1815.
    Received from HMS Medway. HMS Cumberland per Order of VA Sir Charles Tyler.

Bucknell, Charles   Prisoner 200. Rank: Ordinary Seaman, from: Syren, Man of War Brig.
    Cap: 12 Jul 1814 at Sea by HM Ship Medway Int: 19 Aug 1814 Dis: 30 Nov 1814.
    Received from HMS Medway. Asia East India Man to assist in navigating her to England.

Bunker, Frederick   Prisoner 80. Rank: Seaman, from: Rose, Merchant Vessel.
    Cap: Not Recorded by HM Ships Harpy & Primrose Int: 05 Mar 1813 Died: 10 Oct 1813.
    Received from HMS Harpy. Died. Fever. (Date and place of capture 'not mentioned'.)

American Prisoners of War at Cape of Good Hope During the War of 1812

Bush, Mathew M Prisoner 37. Rank: Passenger, from: James, Merchant Vessel.
    Cap: 18 Dec 1812 at Sea by HMS Harpy Int: 28 Jan 1813 Dis: 10 Feb 1814.
    Received from James. For a Passage to England.

Butler, John Prisoner 117. Rank: Seaman, from: Not Recorded, Not Recorded.
    Cap: Not Recorded by Not Recorded Int: 09 Jul 1813 Dis: 12 Aug 1814.
    Received from HMS Lion. HMS Dannemark per order Vice Adml Taylor. (Date of capture not recorded.)

Cannor, Edward Prisoner 123. Rank: Seaman, from: Not Recorded, Not Recorded.
    Cap: Not Recorded by Not Recorded Int: 18 Aug 1813 Dis: 12 Aug 1814.
    Received from HMS Lion. To HMS Stag Order V Adl Tyler. (Date of capture not recorded. Duplicate prison # - Lewis Reeay.)

Carns, Thomas Prisoner 138. Rank: Seaman, from: William Penn, Merchant Vessel.
    Cap: 27 Oct 1813 at Sea by HMS Acorn Int: 04 Dec 1813 Dis: 10 Aug 1814.
    Received from HMS Acorn. Exiter Indiaman for England.

Carpenter, Jacon Prisoner 247. Rank: (Not legible) Yeoman, from: Syren, Man of War Brig.
    Cap: 12 Jul 1814 at Sea by HMS Medway Int: 19 Aug 1814 Dis: 06 Apr 1815.
    Received from HMS Medway. HMS Cumberland per Order of VA Sir Charles Tyler.

Carpenter, William Prisoner 260. Rank: Seaman, from: Syren, Man of War Brig.
    Cap: 12 Jul 1814 at Sea by HMS Medway Int: 19 Aug 1814 Dis: 06 Apr 1815.
    Received from HMS Medway. HMS Cumberland per Order VA Sir Charles Taylor.

Cary, C Prisoner 77. Rank: 1 Mate, from: Rose, Merchant Vessel.
    Cap: Not Recorded by HM Ships Harpy & Primrose Int: 05 Mar 1813 Dis: 10 Feb 1814.
    Received from HMS Harpy. for England. (Date and place of capture 'not mentioned'.)

Casper, William Prisoner 184. Rank: Boy, from: Syren, Man of War Brig.
    Cap: 12 Jul 1814 at Sea by HM Ship Medway Int: 19 Aug 1814 Dis: 30 Nov 1814.
    Received from HMS Medway. HM Ship Desere order of R Adl Tyler.

Cavedon, Luke Prisoner 177. Rank: Boy, from: Syren, Man of War Brig.
    Cap: 12 Jul 1814 at Sea by HM Ship Medway Int: 19 Aug 1814 Dis: 06 Apr 1815.
    Received from HMS Medway. To HMS Malacca per Order of Vice Adml Sir Charles Tyler.

Chadwick, John Prisoner 8. Rank: Mate, from: Monticello, Merchant Service.
    Cap: 12 Nov 1812 Table Bay by Racehorse Int: 07 Jan 1813 Dis: .
    Received from Monticello. (Date of discharge not recorded.)

Chapons, Thomas Prisoner 88. Rank: Seaman, from: Rose, Merchant Vessel.
    Cap: Not Recorded by HM Ships Harpy & Primrose Int: 05 Mar 1813 Dis: 10 Aug 1813.
    Received from HMS Harpy. Bahavia Indiaman for England. (Date and place of capture 'not mentioned'.)

Chase, George W Prisoner 141. Rank: Seaman, from: William Penn, Merchant Vessel.
    Cap: 27 Oct 1813 at Sea by HMS Acorn Int: 04 Dec 1813 Dis: 10 Aug 1814.
    Received from HMS Acorn. Exiter Indiaman for England.

Chase, Stephen B Prisoner 9. Rank: Mate, from: Valentine, Merchant Service.
    Cap: 16 Nov 1812 Table Bay by Minden Int: 07 Jan 1813 Dis: 10 Feb 1814.
    Received from Valentine. To the Rose for a passage to England.

Chick, Mons Prisoner 173. Rank: Seaman, from: Syren, Man of War Brig.
    Cap: 12 Jul 1814 at Sea by HMS Medway Int: 19 Aug 1814 Dis: 30 Nov 1814.
    Received from HMS Medway. To HM Ship Desere per order of Vice Adml Tyler.

Clide, John J Prisoner 183. Rank: 2 Gunner, from: Syren, Man of War Brig.
    Cap: 12 Jul 1814 at Sea by HM Ship Medway Int: 19 Aug 1814 Dis: 30 Nov 1814.
    Received from HMS Medway. HM Ship Desere order of R Adl Tyler.

Clinn, George Prisoner 103. Rank: Seaman, from: Not Recorded, Not Recorded.
    Cap: Not Recorded by Not Recorded Int: 13 Apr 1813 Dis: 12 Aug 1814.
    Received from HMS Astraea being an American. HMS Stag per Order V Adl Tyler. (Date and place of capture 'not mentioned'.)

Clohnan, Ephraim Prisoner 174. Rank: Seaman, from: Syren, Man of War Brig.
    Cap: 12 Jul 1814 at Sea by HMS Medway Int: 19 Aug 1814 Dis: 30 Nov 1814.
    Received from HMS Medway. To HM Ship Desere per order of Vice Adml Tyler.

Coats, Russel Prisoner 157. Rank: Seaman, from: Mary, Merchant Vessel.
    Cap: Saldauha Bay by Not Recorded Int: 26 Jul 1814 Dis: 12 Aug 1814.
    Recaptured Ship. Hyair Alley American Privateer. To HMS Stag per Order V Adl Tyler. (Date of capture not recorded.)

Coats, Samuel M Prisoner 180. Rank: Boatswain, from: Syren, Man of War Brig.
    Cap: 12 Jul 1814 at Sea by HM Ship Medway Int: 19 Aug 1814 Dis: 30 Nov 1814.
    Received from HMS Medway. HM Ship Desere order of R Adl Tyler.

American Prisoners of War at Cape of Good Hope During the War of 1812

Coffin, Absolem   Prisoner 23. Rank: Master, from: Ocean, Merchant Service.
    Cap: 17 Nov 1812 at Sea by Atalanta Transport Int: 07 Jan 1813 Dis: 26 Oct 1813.
    Received from Ocean. Ship Ann for England.

Coffin, Josiah P   Prisoner 113. Rank: 3 Mate, from: Rose, Merchant Vessel.
    Cap: 04 Jan 1813 Not Recorded by HMS Harpy Int: 29 Jun 1813 Dis: 27 Apr 1814.
    Received from HMS Racehorse. Baring for London.

Coffin, Valentine   Prisoner 26. Rank: Seaman, from: Ocean, Merchant Vessel.
    Cap: 17 Nov 1812 at Sea by Atalanta Transport Int: 07 Jan 1813 Dis: 10 Feb 1814.
    Received from Ocean. For a Passage to England.

Coffin, Zemie   Prisoner 24. Rank: 1 Mate, from: Ocean, Merchant Service.
    Cap: 17 Nov 1812 at Sea by Atalanta Transport Int: 07 Jan 1813 Dis: 10 Feb 1814.
    Received from Ocean. For a Passage to England.

Colcord, John L   Prisoner 232. Rank: Ordinary Seaman, from: Syren, Man of War Brig.
    Cap: 12 Jul 1814 at Sea by HMS Medway Int: 19 Aug 1814 Dis: 06 Apr 1815.
    Received from HMS Medway. HMS Cumberland per Order of VA Sir Charles Tyler.

Coleman, James   Prisoner 109. Rank: Seaman, from: Not Recorded, Not Recorded.
    Cap: Not Recorded by Not Recorded Int: 13 Apr 1813 Dis: 12 Aug 1814.
    Received from HMS Astraea being an American. HMS Stag per Order V Adl Tyler. (Date and place of capture 'not mentioned'.)

Coleman, John   Prisoner 25. Rank: Seaman, from: Ocean, Merchant Service.
    Cap: 17 Nov 1812 at Sea by Atalanta Transport Int: 07 Jan 1813 Dis: 23 Jan 1813.
    Received from Ocean. To the Hercules English Whaler Order Adml Stafford.

Collins, William   Prisoner 6. Rank: Seaman, from: Monticello, Merchant Service.
    Cap: 12 Nov 1812 Table Bay by Racehorse Int: 07 Jan 1813 Dis: 03 Apr 1813.
    Received from Monticello. Order of Adm Tyler on board the Tyger Merchant Vessel.

Connor, Peter   Prisoner 150. Rank: Seaman, from: William Penn, Merchant Vessel.
    Cap: 27 Oct 1813 at Sea by HMS Acorn Int: 04 Dec 1813 Dis: .
    Received from HMS Acorn. Exiter Indiaman for England. (Date of discharge not recorded.)

Cooper, Greeville   Prisoner 222. Rank: Boy, from: Syren, Man of War Brig.
    Cap: 12 Jul 1814 at Sea by HMS Medway Int: 19 Aug 1814 Dis: 06 Apr 1815.
    Received from HMS Medway. To His Majestys Ship Malacca per Order of Vice Adml Sir Charles Tyler.

Cooper, Thomas   Prisoner 111. Rank: Late Boatswain, from: Not Recorded, Not Recorded.
    Cap: Not Recorded by Not Recorded Int: 08 Jun 1813 Dis: 15 Jun 1813.
    Received from HMS Nisus. HMS Lion per Order Rear Adml Tyler. (Date of capture not recorded.)

Coville, Edmund   Prisoner 126. Rank: Seaman, from: Not Recorded, Not Recorded.
    Cap: Not Recorded by Not Recorded Int: 25 Sep 1813 Dis: 12 Aug 1814.
    Received from HMS Semiramis. To HMS Stag Order V Adl Tyler. (Date of capture not recorded.)

Cowen, William   Prisoner 121. Rank: Seaman, from: Not Recorded, Not Recorded.
    Cap: Not Recorded by Not Recorded Int: 14 Aug 1813 Dis: 30 Apr 1814.
    Received from the Indefatigable China Ship per order of R Ad Tyler. William Pitt for London. (Date of capture not recorded.)

Crapon, George   Prisoner 17. Rank: Seaman, from: Valentine, Merchant Service.
    Cap: 16 Nov 1812 Table Bay by Minden Int: 07 Jan 1813 Dis: 10 Feb 1814.
    Received from Valentine. For a Passage to England HMS Leon.

Crawford, John   Prisoner 40. Rank: Seaman, from: James, Merchant Vessel.
    Cap: 18 Dec 1812 at Sea by HMS Harpy Int: 30 Jan 1813 Dis: 10 Aug 1814.
    Received from Oxford Transport. Union Indiaman for England.

Dalliver, William   Prisoner 251. Rank: Boy, from: Syren, Man of War Brig.
    Cap: 12 Jul 1814 at Sea by HMS Medway Int: 19 Aug 1814 Dis: 06 Apr 1815.
    Received from HMS Medway. HMS Cumberland per Order of VA Sir Charles Tyler.

Damon, Thomas   Prisoner 198. Rank: Ordinary Seaman, from: Syren, Man of War Brig.
    Cap: 12 Jul 1814 at Sea by HM Ship Medway Int: 19 Aug 1814 Dis: 30 Nov 1814.
    Received from HMS Medway. Asia East India Man to assist in navigating her to England.

Daniels, Henry   Prisoner 185. Rank: Seaman, from: Syren, Man of War Brig.
    Cap: 12 Jul 1814 at Sea by HM Ship Medway Int: 19 Aug 1814 Dis: 30 Nov 1814.
    Received from HMS Medway. HM Ship Desere order of R Adl Tyler.

Davies, Thomas   Prisoner 197. Rank: Mate, from: Syren, Man of War Brig.
    Cap: 12 Jul 1814 at Sea by HM Ship Medway Int: 19 Aug 1814 Dis: 30 Nov 1814.
    Received from HMS Medway. Asia East India Man to assist in navigating her to England.

Davis, Henry   Prisoner 13. Rank: Seaman, from: Valentine, Merchant Service.
    Cap: 16 Nov 1812 Table Bay by Minden Int: 07 Jan 1813 Dis: 10 Feb 1814.
    Received from Valentine. For a Passage to England HMS Leon.

American Prisoners of War at Cape of Good Hope During the War of 1812

Deal, Lewis   Prisoner 233. Rank: Quartermaster, from: Syren, Man of War Brig.
    Cap: 12 Jul 1814 at Sea by HMS Medway Int: 19 Aug 1814 Dis: 06 Apr 1815.
    Received from HMS Medway. HMS Cumberland per Order of VA Sir Charles Tyler.

Decruz, N   Prisoner 31. Rank: Cook, from: Valentine, Not Recorded.
    Cap: Not Recorded by Not Recorded Int: Dis: 25 Apr 1813.
    per Order of Re Adml Tyler the Hercules Transport. (Dates of capture and internment not recorded.)

Dessmore, Abraham   Prisoner 58. Rank: 1 Mate, from: James, Merchant Vessel.
    Cap: 18 Dec 1812 at Sea by HMS Harpy Int: 28 Feb 1813 Dis: 29 Apr 1814.
    Received from Morley Transport. Dundea for London.

Dexter, Charles   Prisoner 92. Rank: 1 Mate, from: Derby, Merchant Vessel.
    Cap: 04 Feb 1813 at Sea by HMS Nisus Int: 02 Apr 1813 Dis: 05 Apr 1814.
    Received from HMS Nisus. Ceres for London.

Dexter, George W   Prisoner 94. Rank: Passenger, from: Derby, Merchant Vessel.
    Cap: 04 Feb 1813 at Sea by HMS Nisus Int: 02 Apr 1813 Dis: 05 Apr 1814.
    Received from HMS Nisus. Ceres for London.

Deysey, Wolsten   Prisoner 101. Rank: Seaman, from: Derby, Merchant Vessel.
    Cap: 04 Feb 1813 at Sea by HMS Nisus Int: 02 Apr 1813 Dis: 30 Apr 1814.
    Received from HMS Nisus. Northumberland Indiaman for London.

Downes, Shubart   Prisoner 166. Rank: Master, from: Syren, Man of War Brig.
    Cap: 12 Jul 1814 at Sea by HMS Medway Int: 19 Aug 1814 Dis: 06 Apr 1815.
    Received from HMS Medway. HMS Cumberland per Order Vice Adl Sir Charles Tyler.

Doyer, Thomas   Prisoner 95. Rank: Seaman, from: Derby, Merchant Vessel.
    Cap: 04 Feb 1813 at Sea by HMS Nisus Int: 02 Apr 1813 Dis: 30 Apr 1814.
    Received from HMS Nisus. Sir William Poltney Indiaman for London.

Drew, William   Prisoner 90. Rank: Seaman, from: Rose, Merchant Vessel.
    Cap: Not Recorded by HM Ships Harpy & Primrose Int: 05 Mar 1813 Dis: 11 May 1815.
    Received from HMS Harpy. per Order Vice Admiral Sir Charles Taylor KCB. (Date and place of capture 'not mentioned'.)

Dublet, John   Prisoner 217. Rank: Seaman, from: Syren, Man of War Brig.
    Cap: 12 Jul 1814 at Sea by HMS Medway Int: 19 Aug 1814 Dis: 06 Apr 1815.
    Received from HMS Medway. To His Majestys Ship Malacca per Order of Vice Adml Sir Charles Tyler.

Durham, William   Prisoner 176. Rank: Ordinary Seaman, from: Syren, Man of War Brig.
    Cap: 12 Jul 1814 at Sea by HM Ship Medway Int: 19 Aug 1814 Dis: 30 Nov 1814.
    Received from HMS Medway. To HM Ship Desere per order of Vice Adml Tyler.

Dyke, James   Prisoner 213. Rank: Seaman, from: Syren, Man of War Brig.
    Cap: 12 Jul 1814 at Sea by HMS Medway Int: 19 Aug 1814 Dis: 06 Apr 1815.
    Received from HMS Medway. To His Majestys Ship Malacca per Order of Vice Adml Sir Charles Tyler.

Earl, Joseph   Prisoner 133. Rank: Passenger, from: William Penn, Merchant Vessel.
    Cap: 27 Oct 1813 at Sea by HMS Acorn Int: 04 Dec 1813 Dis: 12 Aug 1814.
    Received from HMS Acorn. HMS Dannemark order Vice Adml Taylor.

Eastor, Peter   Prisoner 115. Rank: Seaman, from: Rose, Merchant Vessel.
    Cap: 04 Jan 1813 Not Recorded by HMS Harpy Int: 29 Jun 1813 Dis: 12 Aug 1814.
    Received from HMS Racehorse. HMS Dannemark per order Vice Adml Taylor.

Ebby, Samuel   Prisoner 144. Rank: Seaman, from: William Penn, Merchant Vessel.
    Cap: 27 Oct 1813 at Sea by HMS Acorn Int: 04 Dec 1813 Dis: 10 Aug 1814.
    Received from HMS Acorn. Hercules MS for England.

Elbert, Hugh   Prisoner 82. Rank: Seaman, from: Rose, Merchant Vessel.
    Cap: Not Recorded by HM Ships Harpy & Primrose Int: 05 Mar 1813 Dis: 11 May 1815.
    Received from HMS Harpy. per Order of Vice Adml Sir Charles Tyler KCB. (Date and place of capture 'not mentioned'.)

Ellis, George   Prisoner 122. Rank: Seaman, from: Not Recorded, Not Recorded.
    Cap: Not Recorded by Not Recorded Int: 14 Aug 1813 Dis: 10 Aug 1814.
    Received from the Indefatigable China Ship per order of R Ad Tyler. Ranger M Ship for England. (Date of capture not recorded.)

Evans, Barah M   Prisoner 215. Rank: Carpenter, from: Syren, Man of War Brig.
    Cap: 12 Jul 1814 at Sea by HMS Medway Int: 19 Aug 1814 Dis: 06 Apr 1815.
    Received from HMS Medway. To His Majestys Ship Malacca per Order of Vice Adml Sir Charles Tyler.

Evans, William   Prisoner 45. Rank: Seaman, from: James, Merchant Vessel.
    Cap: 18 Dec 1812 at Sea by HMS Harpy Int: 30 Jan 1813 Dis: 30 Apr 1814.
    Received from Oxford Transport. Sir William Poltney Indiaman for London.

American Prisoners of War at Cape of Good Hope During the War of 1812

Fales, Charles   Prisoner 219. Rank: Ordinary Seaman, from: Syren, Man of War Brig.
    Cap: 12 Jul 1814 at Sea by HMS Medway Int: 19 Aug 1814 Dis: 06 Apr 1815.
    Received from HMS Medway. To His Majestys Ship Malacca per Order of Vice Adml Sir Charles Tyler.

Falmond, John   Prisoner 54. Rank: Seaman, from: James, Merchant Vessel.
    Cap: 18 Dec 1812 at Sea by HMS Harpy Int: 24 Feb 1813 Dis: 12 Feb 1814.
    Received from Morley Transport. Carmarthen for England.

Felt, George   Prisoner 59. Rank: 2 Mate, from: James, Merchant Vessel.
    Cap: 18 Dec 1812 at Sea by HMS Harpy Int: 28 Feb 1813 Dis: 02 Mar 1814.
    Received from Morley Transport. To the Metcalf.

Fenier, Drury   Prisoner 279. Rank: Seaman, from: Syren, Man of War Brig.
    Cap: 12 Jul 1814 at Sea by HMS Medway Int: 19 Aug 1814 Dis: 06 Apr 1815.
    Received from HMS Medway. HMS Cumberland per Order of VA Sir Charles Tyler.

Fenton, James   Prisoner 216. Rank: Seaman, from: Syren, Man of War Brig.
    Cap: 12 Jul 1814 at Sea by HMS Medway Int: 19 Aug 1814 Dis: 06 Apr 1815.
    Received from HMS Medway. To His Majestys Ship Malacca per Order of Vice Adml Sir Charles Tyler.

Ferguson, Stephen   Prisoner 104. Rank: Seaman, from: Not Recorded, Not Recorded.
    Cap: Not Recorded by Not Recorded Int: 13 Apr 1813 Dis: 12 Aug 1814.
    Received from HMS Astraea being an American. HMS Stag per Order V Adl Tyler. (Date and place of capture 'not mentioned'.)

Field, David   Prisoner 47. Rank: Seaman, from: James, Merchant Vessel.
    Cap: 18 Dec 1812 at Sea by HMS Harpy Int: 30 Jan 1813 Dis: 10 Aug 1814.
    Received from Oxford Transport. Ranger M Ship for England.

Fife, Thomas   Prisoner 46. Rank: Seaman, from: James, Merchant Vessel.
    Cap: 18 Dec 1812 at Sea by HMS Harpy Int: 30 Jan 1813 Dis: 30 Apr 1814.
    Received from Oxford Transport. William Pitt Indiaman for London.

Files, Felice   Prisoner 70. Rank: Seaman, from: Rambler, Merchant Vessel.
    Cap: Not Recorded by HMS Harpy Int: 28 Feb 1813 Dis: 09 Mar 1814.
    Received from Morley Transport. Sir Godfrey Webster for a Passage to England. (Date of capture not recorded.)

Fletcher, Peter   Prisoner 129. Rank: Seaman, from: Not Recorded, Not Recorded.
    Cap: Not Recorded by Not Recorded Int: 25 Sep 1813 Dis: 12 Aug 1814.
    Received from HMS Semiramis. HMS Dannemark order Vice Adml Taylor. (Date of capture not recorded.)

Fountain, Nicholas   Prisoner 273. Rank: Seaman, from: Syren, Man of War Brig.
    Cap: 12 Jul 1814 at Sea by HMS Medway Int: 19 Aug 1814 Dis: 06 Apr 1815.
    Received from HMS Medway. HMS Cumberland per Order of VA Sir Charles Tyler.

Freelern, John   Prisoner 143. Rank: Seaman, from: William Penn, Merchant Vessel.
    Cap: 27 Oct 1813 at Sea by HMS Acorn Int: 04 Dec 1813 Dis: 10 Aug 1814.
    Received from HMS Acorn. Exiter Indiaman for England. Or John Freeman.

Gammell, Joseph   Prisoner 236. Rank: Seaman, from: Syren, Man of War Brig.
    Cap: 12 Jul 1814 at Sea by HMS Medway Int: 19 Aug 1814 Dis: 06 Apr 1815.
    Received from HMS Medway. HMS Cumberland per Order of VA Sir Charles Tyler.

Gardner, George M   Prisoner 130. Rank: Master, from: William Penn, Merchant Vessel.
    Cap: 27 Oct 1813 at Sea by HMS Acorn Int: 04 Dec 1813 Dis: 01 Nov 1814.
    Received from HMS Acorn. To assist in navigating her to England.

Gardner, Nathaniel   Prisoner 91. Rank: Seaman, from: Rose, Merchant Vessel.
    Cap: Not Recorded by HM Ships Harpy & Primrose Int: 05 Mar 1813 Dis: 10 Feb 1814.
    Received from HMS Harpy. Passage to England. (Date and place of capture 'not mentioned'.)

Gardner, Rowland   Prisoner 76. Rank: Master, from: Rose, Merchant Vessel.
    Cap: Not Recorded by HM Ships Harpy & Primrose Int: 05 Mar 1813 Dis: 22 Nov 1813.
    Received from HMS Harpy. To the Countess of London on Parole per order Rear Admiral Tyler on acct of bad health. (Date and place of capture 'not mentioned'.)

Geer, John   Prisoner 68. Rank: Seaman, from: Rambler, Merchant Vessel.
    Cap: Not Recorded by HMS Harpy Int: 28 Feb 1813 Dis: 12 Aug 1814.
    Received from Morley Transport. HMS Dannemark order Adl Tyler. (Date of capture not recorded.)

Genesey, Joseph   Prisoner 7. Rank: Passenger, from: Monticello, Merchant Service.
    Cap: 12 Nov 1812 Table Bay by Racehorse Int: 07 Jan 1813 Dis: .
    Received from Monticello. (Date of discharge not recorded.)

German, Lewis   Prisoner 162. Rank: Lieutenant, from: Syren, Man of War Brig.
    Cap: 12 Jul 1814 at Sea by HMS Medway Int: 19 Aug 1814 Dis: 06 Apr 1815.
    Received from HMS Medway. HMS Cumberland per Order V Adl Sir Charles Tyler.

American Prisoners of War at Cape of Good Hope During the War of 1812

Gerry, Joseph   Prisoner 226. Rank: Seaman, from: Syren, Man of War Brig.
    Cap: 12 Jul 1814 at Sea by HMS Medway Int: 19 Aug 1814 Dis: 06 Apr 1815.
    Received from HMS Medway. HMS Cumberland per Order VA Sir Charles Tyler.

Ginish, Samuel   Prisoner 257. Rank: Seaman, from: Syren, Man of War Brig.
    Cap: 12 Jul 1814 at Sea by HMS Medway Int: 19 Aug 1814 Dis: 06 Apr 1815.
    Received from HMS Medway. HMS Cumberland per Order VA Sir Charles Taylor.

Gitcher, Samuel   Prisoner 295. Rank: Private, from: Syren, Man of War Brig.
    Cap: 12 Jul 1814 at Sea by HMS Medway Int: 19 Aug 1814 Dis: 06 Apr 1815.
    Received from HMS Medway. HMS Cumberland per Order VA Sir Charles Tyler.

Glee, Andrew   Prisoner 52. Rank: Seaman, from: James, Merchant Vessel.
    Cap: 18 Dec 1812 at Sea by HMS Harpy Int: 24 Feb 1813 Dis: .
    Received from Morley Transport. (Date of discharge not recorded.)

Goldsmith, Thomas   Prisoner 72. Rank: Seaman, from: Rambler, Merchant Vessel.
    Cap: Not Recorded by HMS Harpy Int: 28 Feb 1813 Dis: 12 Aug 1814.
    Received from Morley Transport. HMS Dannemark order Adl Tyler. (Date of capture not recorded.)

Gordon, W L   Prisoner 163. Rank: Lieutenant, from: Syren, Man of War Brig.
    Cap: 12 Jul 1814 at Sea by HMS Medway Int: 19 Aug 1814 Dis: 06 Apr 1815.
    Received from HMS Medway. HMS Cumberland per Order V Adl Sir Charles Tyler.

Gorman, Joseph   Prisoner 41. Rank: Seaman, from: James, Merchant Vessel.
    Cap: 18 Dec 1812 at Sea by HMS Harpy Int: 30 Jan 1813 Died: 18 Dec 1812.
    Received from Oxford Transport. Died. Fever. (Date of death before date of internment.)

Gould, Thomas   Prisoner 220. Rank: Seaman, from: Syren, Man of War Brig.
    Cap: 12 Jul 1814 at Sea by HMS Medway Int: 19 Aug 1814 Dis: 06 Apr 1815.
    Received from HMS Medway. To His Majestys Ship Malacca per Order of Vice Adml Sir Charles Tyler.

Greenland, Stephen   Prisoner 3. Rank: 2 Mate, from: Monticello, Merchant Service.
    Cap: 12 Nov 1812 Table Bay by Racehorse Int: 07 Jan 1813 Dis: 10 Feb 1814.
    Received from Monticello. for a Passage to England HMS Leon.

Groverman, Fred C   Prisoner 202. Rank: Ordinary Seaman, from: Syren, Man of War Brig.
    Cap: 12 Jul 1814 at Sea by HMS Medway Int: 19 Aug 1814 Dis: 30 Nov 1814.
    Received from HMS Medway. Asia East India Man to assist in navigating her England.

Hadley, Andrew   Prisoner 289. Rank: Private, from: Syren, Man of War Brig.
    Cap: 12 Jul 1814 at Sea by HMS Medway Int: 19 Aug 1814 Dis: 06 Apr 1815.
    Received from HMS Medway. HMS Cumberland per Order VA Sir Charles Tyler.

Hall, Joseph   Prisoner 127. Rank: Seaman, from: Not Recorded, Not Recorded.
    Cap: Not Recorded by Not Recorded Int: 25 Sep 1813 Dis: 12 Aug 1814.
    Received from HMS Semiramis. HMS Dannemark order Vice Adml Taylor. (Date of capture not recorded.)

Hanson, Cornelius   Prisoner 18. Rank: Seaman, from: Valentine, Merchant Service.
    Cap: 16 Nov 1812 Table Bay by Minden Int: 07 Jan 1813 Dis: 13 Aug 1813.
    Received from Valentine. per Order Rear Adl Tyler.

Harding, Joseph   Prisoner 282. Rank: Ordinary Seaman, from: Syren, Man of War Brig.
    Cap: 12 Jul 1814 at Sea by HMS Medway Int: 19 Aug 1814 Dis: 06 Apr 1815.
    Received from HMS Medway. HMS Cumberland per Order VA Sir Charles Tyler.

Harris, George   Prisoner 137. Rank: Seaman, from: William Penn, Merchant Vessel.
    Cap: 27 Oct 1813 at Sea by HMS Acorn Int: 04 Dec 1813 Dis: 02 May 1814.
    Received from HMS Acorn. Albion Whaler for England.

Harris, Moses   Prisoner 132. Rank: 2 Mate, from: William Penn, Merchant Vessel.
    Cap: 27 Oct 1813 at Sea by HMS Acorn Int: 04 Dec 1813 Dis: 12 Aug 1814.
    Received from HMS Acorn. HMS Dannemark order Vice Adml Taylor.

Hart, Emius   Prisoner 148. Rank: Seaman, from: William Penn, Merchant Vessel.
    Cap: 27 Oct 1813 at Sea by HMS Acorn Int: 04 Dec 1813 Dis: 12 Aug 1814.
    Received from HMS Acorn. HMS Dannemark order Vice Adl Tayler.

Hartford, William   Prisoner 44. Rank: Seaman, from: James, Merchant Vessel.
    Cap: 18 Dec 1812 at Sea by HMS Harpy Int: 30 Jan 1813 Dis: 28 Apr 1814.
    Received from Oxford Transport. Hope for London.

Harwood, James   Prisoner 212. Rank: Cooper, from: Syren, Man of War Brig.
    Cap: 12 Jul 1814 at Sea by HMS Medway Int: 19 Aug 1814 Dis: 06 Apr 1815.
    Received from HMS Medway. To His Majestys Ship Malacca per Order of Vice Adml Sir Charles Tyler.

Haycock, Joseph   Prisoner 188. Rank: 2 Gunner, from: Syren, Man of War Brig.
    Cap: 12 Jul 1814 at Sea by HM Ship Medway Int: 19 Aug 1814 Dis: 30 Nov 1814.
    Received from HMS Medway. HM Ship Desere order of R Adl Tyler.

American Prisoners of War at Cape of Good Hope During the War of 1812

Helen, John P   Prisoner 16. Rank: Seaman, from: Valentine, Merchant Service.
    Cap: 16 Nov 1812 Table Bay by Minden Int: 07 Jan 1813 Dis: 10 Feb 1814.
    Received from Valentine. For a Passage to England HMS Leon.

Henderson, Benjamin   Prisoner 33. Rank: Master, from: James, Merchant Vessel.
    Cap: 18 Dec 1812 at Sea by HMS Harpy Int: 28 Jan 1813 Dis: 10 Feb 1814.
    Received from James. For a Passage to England.

Henrie, Daniel M   Prisoner 136. Rank: Seaman, from: William Penn, Merchant Vessel.
    Cap: 27 Oct 1813 at Sea by HMS Acorn Int: 04 Dec 1813 Dis: 10 Aug 1814.
    Received from HMS Acorn. Exiter Indiaman for England.

Hild, George   Prisoner 263. Rank: Seaman, from: Syren, Man of War Brig.
    Cap: 12 Jul 1814 at Sea by HMS Medway Int: 19 Aug 1814 Dis: 06 Apr 1815.
    Received from HMS Medway. HMS Cumberland per Order VA Sir Charles Taylor.

Hinchman, Lewis   Prisoner 168. Rank: Masters Mate, from: Syren, Man of War Brig.
    Cap: 12 Jul 1814 at Sea by HMS Medway Int: 19 Aug 1814 Dis: 06 Apr 1815.
    Received from HMS Medway. HMS Cumberland per Order Vice Adl Sir Charles Tyler.

Hodge, Edward   Prisoner 206. Rank: Ordinary Seaman, from: Syren, Man of War Brig.
    Cap: 12 Jul 1814 at Sea by HMS Medway Int: 19 Aug 1814 Dis: 30 Nov 1814.
    Received from HMS Medway. To HM Ship Desere per order of Vice Adml Tyler.

Holdbrook, Abrica   Prisoner 98. Rank: Seaman, from: Derby, Merchant Vessel.
    Cap: 04 Feb 1813 at Sea by HMS Nisus Int: 02 Apr 1813 Dis: 10 Aug 1814.
    Received from HMS Nisus. Exiter Indiaman for England.

Holmes, Jedekiah   Prisoner 78. Rank: Seaman, from: Rose, Merchant Vessel.
    Cap: Not Recorded by HM Ships Harpy & Primrose Int: 05 Mar 1813 Dis: 11 May 1815.
    Received from HMS Harpy. per Order of Vice Adml Sir Charles Tyler KCB. (Date and place of capture 'not mentioned'.)

Hood, Daniel   Prisoner 266. Rank: Seaman, from: Syren, Man of War Brig.
    Cap: 12 Jul 1814 at Sea by HMS Medway Int: 19 Aug 1814 Dis: 06 Apr 1815.
    Received from HMS Medway. HMS Cumberland per Order VA Sir Charles Taylor.

Horner, James   Prisoner 239. Rank: Ordinary Seaman, from: Syren, Man of War Brig.
    Cap: 12 Jul 1814 at Sea by HMS Medway Int: 19 Aug 1814 Dis: 06 Apr 1815.
    Received from HMS Medway. HMS Cumberland per Order of VA Sir Charles Tyler.

Hubley, John   Prisoner 285. Rank: Sergeant Marines, from: Syren, Man of War Brig.
    Cap: 12 Jul 1814 at Sea by HMS Medway Int: 19 Aug 1814 Dis: 06 Apr 1815.
    Received from HMS Medway. HMS Cumberland per Order VA Sir Charles Tyler.

Hudson, Joseph   Prisoner 51. Rank: Seaman, from: James, Merchant Vessel.
    Cap: 18 Dec 1812 at Sea by HMS Harpy Int: 24 Feb 1813 Died: 09 Jan 1814.
    Received from Morley Transport. Died. Apoplexy.

Hussey, Joseph   Prisoner 146. Rank: Seaman, from: William Penn, Merchant Vessel.
    Cap: 27 Oct 1813 at Sea by HMS Acorn Int: 04 Dec 1813 Dis: 10 Aug 1814.
    Received from HMS Acorn. Exiter Indiaman for England.

Hutchens, William   Prisoner 281. Rank: Seaman, from: Syren, Man of War Brig.
    Cap: 12 Jul 1814 at Sea by HMS Medway Int: 19 Aug 1814 Dis: 06 Apr 1815.
    Received from HMS Medway. HMS Cumberland per Order VA Sir Charles Tyler.

Ide, John H   Prisoner 36. Rank: Supercargo, from: James, Merchant Vessel.
    Cap: 18 Dec 1812 at Sea by HMS Harpy Int: 28 Jan 1813 Dis: 10 Feb 1814.
    Received from James. For a Passage to England.

Johnson, James   Prisoner 19. Rank: Seaman, from: Valentine, Merchant Service.
    Cap: 16 Nov 1812 Table Bay by Minden Int: 07 Jan 1813 Dis: 10 Feb 1814.
    Received from Valentine. For a Passage to England HMS Leon.

Johnson, Moses   Prisoner 296. Rank: Ordinary Seaman, from: Syren, Man of War Brig.
    Cap: 12 Jul 1814 at Sea by HMS Medway Int: 19 Aug 1814 Dis: 06 Apr 1815.
    Received from HMS Medway. HMS Cumberland per Order VA Sir Charles Tyler.

Johnson, Samuel   Prisoner 246. Rank: Ordinary Seaman, from: Syren, Man of War Brig.
    Cap: 12 Jul 1814 at Sea by HMS Medway Int: 19 Aug 1814 Dis: 06 Apr 1815.
    Received from HMS Medway. HMS Cumberland per Order of VA Sir Charles Tyler.

Johnson, William   Prisoner 265. Rank: Boy, from: Syren, Man of War Brig.
    Cap: 12 Jul 1814 at Sea by HMS Medway Int: 19 Aug 1814 Dis: 06 Apr 1815.
    Received from HMS Medway. HMS Cumberland per Order VA Sir Charles Taylor.

Jones, Ezekiel   Prisoner 280. Rank: Seaman, from: Syren, Man of War Brig.
    Cap: 12 Jul 1814 at Sea by HMS Medway Int: 19 Aug 1814 Dis: 06 Apr 1815.
    Received from HMS Medway. HMS Cumberland per Order VA Sir Charles Tyler.

American Prisoners of War at Cape of Good Hope During the War of 1812

Jones, Samuel B   Prisoner 22. Rank: Seaman, from: Valentine, Merchant Service.
    Cap: 16 Nov 1812 Table Bay by Minden Int: 07 Jan 1813 Dis: 10 Feb 1814.
    Received from Valentine. For a Passage to England HMS Leon.

Kellie, Stephen   Prisoner 204. Rank: Seaman, from: Syren, Man of War Brig.
    Cap: 12 Jul 1814 at Sea by HMS Medway Int: 19 Aug 1814 Dis: 30 Nov 1814.
    Received from HMS Medway. Asia East India Man to assist in navigating her England.

Kimble, John   Prisoner 66. Rank: Seaman, from: Rambler, Merchant Vessel.
    Cap: Not Recorded by HMS Harpy Int: 28 Feb 1813 Dis: 30 Apr 1814.
    Received from Morley Transport. Catherine for London. (Date of capture not recorded.)

Kimble, Samuel   Prisoner 120. Rank: Seaman, from: Not Recorded, Not Recorded.
    Cap: Not Recorded by Not Recorded Int: 14 Aug 1813 Dis: 12 Feb 1814.
    Received from the Indefatigable China Ship per order of R Ad Tyler. Carmarthen for England. (Date of capture not recorded.)

King, William   Prisoner 209. Rank: Gunners Mate, from: Syren, Man of War Brig.
    Cap: 12 Jul 1814 at Sea by HMS Medway Int: 19 Aug 1814 Dis: 06 Apr 1815.
    Received from HMS Medway. To His Majestys Ship Malacca per Order of Vice Adml Sir Charles Tyler.

Kirkby, Robert   Prisoner 189. Rank: Boy, from: Syren, Man of War Brig.
    Cap: 12 Jul 1814 at Sea by HM Ship Medway Int: 19 Aug 1814 Dis: 30 Nov 1814.
    Received from HMS Medway. HM Ship Desere order of R Adl Tyler.

Kitchen, George   Prisoner 187. Rank: Seaman, from: Syren, Man of War Brig.
    Cap: 12 Jul 1814 at Sea by HM Ship Medway Int: 19 Aug 1814 Dis: 30 Nov 1814.
    Received from HMS Medway. HM Ship Desere order of R Adl Tyler.

Lambert, John   Prisoner 262. Rank: Seaman, from: Syren, Man of War Brig.
    Cap: 12 Jul 1814 at Sea by HMS Medway Int: 19 Aug 1814 Dis: 06 Apr 1815.
    Received from HMS Medway. HMS Cumberland per Order VA Sir Charles Taylor.

Leach, Samuel   Prisoner 231. Rank: Boy, from: Syren, Man of War Brig.
    Cap: 12 Jul 1814 at Sea by HMS Medway Int: 19 Aug 1814 Dis: 06 Apr 1815.
    Received from HMS Medway. HMS Cumberland per Order of VA Sir Charles Tyler.

Lee, John   Prisoner 43. Rank: Seaman, from: James, Merchant Vessel.
    Cap: 18 Dec 1812 at Sea by HMS Harpy Int: 30 Jan 1813 Dis: 10 Feb 1814.
    Received from Oxford Transport. For a Passage to England.

Lewis, John   Prisoner 152. Rank: Seaman, from: La Ceres, French Frigate.
    Cap: 06 Jan 1814 off the Cape De be J Island by HMS Nizer Int: 25 Mar 1814 Dis: 10 Aug 1814.
    Received from HMS Laurie. Union Indiaman for England.

Lewis, Raymond   Prisoner 235. Rank: Seaman, from: Syren, Man of War Brig.
    Cap: 12 Jul 1814 at Sea by HMS Medway Int: 19 Aug 1814 Dis: 06 Apr 1815.
    Received from HMS Medway. HMS Cumberland per Order of VA Sir Charles Tyler.

Lewis, Winslow   Prisoner 191. Rank: Seaman, from: Syren, Man of War Brig.
    Cap: 12 Jul 1814 at Sea by HM Ship Medway Int: 19 Aug 1814 Dis: 30 Nov 1814.
    Received from HMS Medway. HM Ship Desere order of R Adl Tyler.

Lincoln, Ruben   Prisoner 242. Rank: Seaman, from: Syren, Man of War Brig.
    Cap: 12 Jul 1814 at Sea by HMS Medway Int: 19 Aug 1814 Dis: 06 Apr 1815.
    Received from HMS Medway. HMS Cumberland per Order of VA Sir Charles Tyler.

Lindon, John   Prisoner 211. Rank: Seaman, from: Syren, Man of War Brig.
    Cap: 12 Jul 1814 at Sea by HMS Medway Int: 19 Aug 1814 Dis: 06 Apr 1815.
    Received from HMS Medway. To His Majestys Ship Malacca per Order of Vice Adml Sir Charles Tyler.

Lockwood, Benoni   Prisoner 15. Rank: Seaman, from: Valentine, Merchant Service.
    Cap: 16 Nov 1812 Table Bay by Minden Int: 07 Jan 1813 Dis: 10 Feb 1814.
    Received from Valentine. For a Passage to England HMS Leon.

Long, David   Prisoner 135. Rank: Seaman, from: William Penn, Merchant Vessel.
    Cap: 27 Oct 1813 at Sea by HMS Acorn Int: 04 Dec 1813 Dis: 12 Aug 1814.
    Received from HMS Acorn. HMS Dannemark per order Vice Adl Taylor.

Luther, Cromwell   Prisoner 21. Rank: Carpenter, from: Valentine, Merchant Service.
    Cap: 16 Nov 1812 Table Bay by Minden Int: 07 Jan 1813 Dis: 10 Feb 1814.
    Received from Valentine. For a Passage to England HMS Leon.

Manuel, Joseph   Prisoner 264. Rank: Seaman, from: Syren, Man of War Brig.
    Cap: 12 Jul 1814 at Sea by HMS Medway Int: 19 Aug 1814 Dis: 06 Apr 1815.
    Received from HMS Medway. HMS Cumberland per Order VA Sir Charles Taylor.

Manuel, Paul   Prisoner 27. Rank: Seaman, from: Ocean, Merchant Vessel.
    Cap: 17 Nov 1812 at Sea by Atalanta Transport Int: 07 Jan 1813 Dis: 30 Jan 1813.
    Received from Ocean. the Favorite English Whaler per Order Adl Stafford.

American Prisoners of War at Cape of Good Hope During the War of 1812

Marshall, Benjamin   Prisoner 89. Rank: Seaman, from: Rose, Merchant Vessel.
    Cap: Not Recorded by HM Ships Harpy & Primrose Int: 05 Mar 1813 Dis: 12 Aug 1814.
    Received from HMS Harpy. HMS Dannemark per order Adl Taylor. (Date and place of capture 'not mentioned'.)

Martin, James   Prisoner 153. Rank: Seaman, from: Not Recorded, Not Recorded.
    Cap: Not Recorded by Not Recorded Int: 12 Apr 1814 Dis: .
    Received from HMS Medway. (Dates of capture and discharge not recorded.)

McCalley, John   Prisoner 292. Rank: Private, from: Syren, Man of War Brig.
    Cap: 12 Jul 1814 at Sea by HMS Medway Int: 19 Aug 1814 Dis: 06 Apr 1815.
    Received from HMS Medway. HMS Cumberland per Order VA Sir Charles Tyler.

Memory, James   Prisoner 203. Rank: Seaman, from: Syren, Man of War Brig.
    Cap: 12 Jul 1814 at Sea by HMS Medway Int: 19 Aug 1814 Dis: 30 Nov 1814.
    Received from HMS Medway. Asia East India Man to assist in navigating her England.

Mergfand, William   Prisoner 71. Rank: Seaman, from: Rambler, Merchant Vessel.
    Cap: Not Recorded by HMS Harpy Int: 28 Feb 1813 Dis: 12 Aug 1814.
    Received from Morley Transport. HMS Dannemark order Adl Tyler. (Date of capture not recorded.)

Miffin, Richard   Prisoner 5. Rank: Seaman, from: Monticello, Merchant Service.
    Cap: 12 Nov 1812 Table Bay by Racehorse Int: 07 Jan 1813 Dis: 12 Aug 1814.
    Received from Monticello. HMS Dannemark order Adm Tyler.

Millar, Francis   Prisoner 55. Rank: Seaman, from: James, Merchant Vessel.
    Cap: 18 Dec 1812 at Sea by HMS Harpy Int: 24 Feb 1813 Dis: 10 Aug 1814.
    Received from Morley Transport. Union Transport for England.

Millar, Samuel   Prisoner 268. Rank: 2 Gunner, from: Syren, Man of War Brig.
    Cap: 12 Jul 1814 at Sea by HMS Medway Int: 19 Aug 1814 Dis: 06 Apr 1815.
    Received from HMS Medway. HMS Cumberland per Order VA Sir Charles Taylor.

Millow, John   Prisoner 186. Rank: Seaman, from: Syren, Man of War Brig.
    Cap: 12 Jul 1814 at Sea by HM Ship Medway Int: 19 Aug 1814 Dis: 30 Nov 1814.
    Received from HMS Medway. HM Ship Desere order of R Adl Tyler.

Mitchell, Jonathan   Prisoner 86. Rank: Seaman, from: Rose, Merchant Vessel.
    Cap: Not Recorded by HM Ships Harpy & Primrose Int: 05 Mar 1813 Dis: 11 May 1815.
    Received from HMS Harpy. per Order of Vice Adml Sir Charles Tyler KCB. (Date and place of capture 'not mentioned'.)

Monk, Joseph   Prisoner 48. Rank: Seaman, from: James, Merchant Vessel.
    Cap: 18 Dec 1812 at Sea by HMS Harpy Int: 30 Jan 1813 Dis: 12 Feb 1814.
    Received from Oxford Transport. Carmarthen for England.

Morris, John   Prisoner 171. Rank: (Not legible) Mate, from: Syren, Man of War Brig.
    Cap: 12 Jul 1814 at Sea by HMS Medway Int: 19 Aug 1814 Dis: 30 Nov 1814.
    Received from HMS Medway. To HM Ship Desere per order of Vice Adml Tyler.

Morrison, Dep   Prisoner 107. Rank: Seaman, from: Not Recorded, Not Recorded.
    Cap: Not Recorded by Not Recorded Int: 13 Apr 1813 Dis: 12 Aug 1814.
    Received from HMS Astraea being an American. HMS Stag per Order V Adl Tyler. (Date and place of capture 'not mentioned'.)

Moses, John   Prisoner 283. Rank: Ordinary Seaman, from: Syren, Man of War Brig.
    Cap: 12 Jul 1814 at Sea by HMS Medway Int: 19 Aug 1814 Dis: 06 Apr 1815.
    Received from HMS Medway. HMS Cumberland per Order VA Sir Charles Tyler.

Murey, Oliver   Prisoner 156. Rank: Seaman, from: Mary, Merchant Vessel.
    Cap: Saldauha Bay by Not Recorded Int: 26 Jul 1814 Dis: 10 Aug 1814.
    Recaptured Ship. Hyair Alley American Privateer. Hercules MS for England. (Date of capture not recorded.)

Murray, Nathaniel   Prisoner 38. Rank: Seaman, from: James, Merchant Vessel.
    Cap: 18 Dec 1812 at Sea by HMS Harpy Int: 28 Jan 1813 Dis: 10 Feb 1814.
    Received from James. For a Passage to England.

Nicholas, Jacob   Prisoner 192. Rank: Seaman, from: Syren, Man of War Brig.
    Cap: 12 Jul 1814 at Sea by HM Ship Medway Int: 19 Aug 1814 Dis: 30 Nov 1814.
    Received from HMS Medway. Asia East India Man to assist in navigating her to England.

Nicholes, Henry   Prisoner 60. Rank: Clerk, from: James, Merchant Vessel.
    Cap: 18 Dec 1812 at Sea by HMS Harpy Int: 28 Feb 1813 Dis: 02 Mar 1814.
    Received from Morley Transport. To the Metcalf.

Norcot, George   Prisoner 30. Rank: Seaman, from: Ocean, Merchant Vessel.
    Cap: 17 Nov 1812 at Sea by Atalanta Transport Int: 07 Jan 1813 Dis: 18 Jan 1813.
    Received from Ocean. Hercules Transport per Order Vice Adl Stafford.

American Prisoners of War at Cape of Good Hope During the War of 1812

Norgrave, Jeremiah Prisoner 34. Rank: 1 Mate, from: James, Merchant Vessel.
    Cap: 18 Dec 1812 at Sea by HMS Harpy Int: 28 Jan 1813 Dis: 10 Feb 1814.
    Received from James. For a Passage to England.

North, Charles Prisoner 131. Rank: 1 Mate, from: William Penn, Merchant Vessel.
    Cap: 27 Oct 1813 at Sea by HMS Acorn Int: 04 Dec 1813 Dis: 01 Nov 1814.
    Received from HMS Acorn. To assist in navigating them to England.

Odey, Thomas Prisoner 53. Rank: Seaman, from: James, Merchant Vessel.
    Cap: 18 Dec 1812 at Sea by HMS Harpy Int: 24 Feb 1813 Dis: 10 Aug 1814.
    Received from Morley Transport. Exiter Indiaman for England.

Ody, George Prisoner 63. Rank: Seaman, from: James, Merchant Vessel.
    Cap: 18 Dec 1812 at Sea by HMS Harpy Int: 28 Feb 1813 Dis: 05 Mar 1814.
    Received from Morley Transport. Ceres Schooner for England.

Olding, Elisha Prisoner 96. Rank: Seaman, from: Derby, Merchant Vessel.
    Cap: 04 Feb 1813 at Sea by HMS Nisus Int: 02 Apr 1813 Dis: 10 Aug 1814.
    Received from HMS Nisus. Hercules MV for England.

Owen, Thomas Prisoner 291. Rank: Private, from: Syren, Man of War Brig.
    Cap: 12 Jul 1814 at Sea by HMS Medway Int: 19 Aug 1814 Dis: 06 Apr 1815.
    Received from HMS Medway. HMS Cumberland per Order VA Sir Charles Tyler.

Parker, John Prisoner 218. Rank: Ordinary Seaman, from: Syren, Man of War Brig.
    Cap: 12 Jul 1814 at Sea by HMS Medway Int: 19 Aug 1814 Dis: 06 Apr 1815.
    Received from HMS Medway. To His Majestys Ship Malacca per Order of Vice Adml Sir Charles Tyler.

Parker, William Prisoner 100. Rank: Seaman, from: Derby, Merchant Vessel.
    Cap: 04 Feb 1813 at Sea by HMS Nisus Int: 02 Apr 1813 Dis: 30 Apr 1814.
    Received from HMS Nisus. Northumberland Indiaman for London.

Parsons, Samuel Prisoner 210. Rank: Seaman, from: Syren, Man of War Brig.
    Cap: 12 Jul 1814 at Sea by HMS Medway Int: 19 Aug 1814 Dis: 06 Apr 1815.
    Received from HMS Medway. To His Majestys Ship Malacca per Order of Vice Adml Sir Charles Tyler.

Pedro, Joseph Prisoner 159. Rank: Seaman, from: Mary, Merchant Vessel.
    Cap: Saldauha Bay by Not Recorded Int: 26 Jul 1814 Dis: 28 Jul 1814.
    Recaptured Ship. Hyair Alley American Privateer. To Malenta Transport per Order R Adl Tyler being Native of Canada. (Date of capture not recorded.)

Peeper, Nathaniel Prisoner 288. Rank: Private, from: Syren, Man of War Brig.
    Cap: 12 Jul 1814 at Sea by HMS Medway Int: 19 Aug 1814 Dis: 06 Apr 1815.
    Received from HMS Medway. HMS Cumberland per Order VA Sir Charles Tyler.

Pen, William Prisoner 287. Rank: Private, from: Syren, Man of War Brig.
    Cap: 12 Jul 1814 at Sea by HMS Medway Int: 19 Aug 1814 Dis: 06 Apr 1815.
    Received from HMS Medway. HMS Cumberland per Order VA Sir Charles Tyler.

Perry, Nathaniel Prisoner 155. Rank: 2 Mate, from: Mary, Merchant Vessel.
    Cap: Saldauha Bay by Not Recorded Int: 26 Jul 1814 Dis: 06 Apr 1815.
    Recaptured Ship. Hyair Alley American Privateer. His M Ship Cumberland. (Date of capture not recorded.)

Peters, John Prisoner 87. Rank: Seaman, from: Rose, Merchant Vessel.
    Cap: Not Recorded by HM Ships Harpy & Primrose Int: 05 Mar 1813 Dis: 31 Aug 1813.
    Received from HMS Harpy. To the James Mer Ship by order of R Adl Tyler being a native of the Isl of France. (Date and place of capture 'not mentioned'.)

Peyster, Afde Prisoner 1. Rank: Master, from: Monticello, Merchant Service.
    Cap: 12 Nov 1812 Table Bay by Racehorse Int: 07 Jan 1813 Dis: 12 Aug 1813.
    Received from Monticello. per Order Rear Adm Tayler.

Philips, George Prisoner 62. Rank: Seaman, from: James, Merchant Vessel.
    Cap: 18 Dec 1812 at Sea by HMS Harpy Int: 28 Feb 1813 Dis: 12 Feb 1814.
    Received from Morley Transport. Carmarthen for England.

Phillips, Nathaniel Prisoner 229. Rank: Steward, from: Syren, Man of War Brig.
    Cap: 12 Jul 1814 at Sea by HMS Medway Int: 19 Aug 1814 Dis: 06 Apr 1815.
    Received from HMS Medway. HMS Cumberland per Order of VA Sir Charles Tyler.

Pickering, Abraham Prisoner 223. Rank: Seaman, from: Syren, Man of War Brig.
    Cap: 12 Jul 1814 at Sea by HMS Medway Int: 19 Aug 1814 Dis: 06 Apr 1815.
    Received from HMS Medway. To His Majestys Ship Malacca per Order of Vice Adml Sir Charles Tyler.

Pierce, John Prisoner 240. Rank: Seaman, from: Syren, Man of War Brig.
    Cap: 12 Jul 1814 at Sea by HMS Medway Int: 19 Aug 1814 Dis: 06 Apr 1815.
    Received from HMS Medway. HMS Cumberland per Order of VA Sir Charles Tyler.

American Prisoners of War at Cape of Good Hope During the War of 1812

Pope, Oliver   Prisoner 190. Rank: Ordinary Seaman, from: Syren, Man of War Brig.
    Cap: 12 Jul 1814 at Sea by HM Ship Medway Int: 19 Aug 1814 Dis: 30 Nov 1814.
    Received from HMS Medway. HM Ship Desere order of R Adl Tyler.

Porter, Frederick   Prisoner 118. Rank: Seaman, from: Not Recorded, Not Recorded.
    Cap: Not Recorded by Not Recorded Int: 09 Jul 1813 Dis: 12 Aug 1814.
    Received from HMS Lion. HMS Stag per Order V Adl Tyler. (Date of capture not recorded.)

Potter, Richard H   Prisoner 12. Rank: 2 Mate, from: Valentine, Merchant Service.
    Cap: 16 Nov 1812 Table Bay by Minden Int: 07 Jan 1813 Dis: 10 Feb 1814.
    Received from Valentine. For a Passage to England HMS Leon.

Prentiss, John E   Prisoner 255. Rank: Midshipman, from: Syren, Man of War Brig.
    Cap: 12 Jul 1814 at Sea by HMS Medway Int: 19 Aug 1814 Dis: 06 Apr 1815.
    Received from HMS Medway. To HMS Malacca per Order of Vice Adml Sir Charles Tyler.

Prout, Henry   Prisoner 172. Rank: Seaman, from: Syren, Man of War Brig.
    Cap: 12 Jul 1814 at Sea by HMS Medway Int: 19 Aug 1814 Dis: 30 Nov 1814.
    Received from HMS Medway. To HM Ship Desere per order of Vice Adml Tyler.

Putnam, Joseph   Prisoner 269. Rank: Seaman, from: Syren, Man of War Brig.
    Cap: 12 Jul 1814 at Sea by HMS Medway Int: 19 Aug 1814 Dis: 06 Apr 1815.
    Received from HMS Medway. HMS Cumberland per Order VA Sir Charles Taylor.

Quaque, Samuel   Prisoner 284. Rank: Ordinary Seaman, from: Syren, Man of War Brig.
    Cap: 12 Jul 1814 at Sea by HMS Medway Int: 19 Aug 1814 Dis: 06 Apr 1815.
    Received from HMS Medway. HMS Cumberland per Order VA Sir Charles Tyler.

Quenn, Patrick   Prisoner 274. Rank: Seaman, from: Syren, Man of War Brig.
    Cap: 12 Jul 1814 at Sea by HMS Medway Int: 19 Aug 1814 Dis: 06 Apr 1815.
    Received from HMS Medway. HMS Cumberland per Order of VA Sir Charles Tyler.

Randall, Henry   Prisoner 261. Rank: Seaman, from: Syren, Man of War Brig.
    Cap: 12 Jul 1814 at Sea by HMS Medway Int: 19 Aug 1814 Dis: 06 Apr 1815.
    Received from HMS Medway. HMS Cumberland per Order VA Sir Charles Taylor. Henry Randall (2).

Randolp, Samuel   Prisoner 245. Rank: Ordinary Seaman, from: Syren, Man of War Brig.
    Cap: 12 Jul 1814 at Sea by HMS Medway Int: 19 Aug 1814 Dis: 06 Apr 1815.
    Received from HMS Medway. HMS Cumberland per Order VA Sir Charles Tyler.

Rankins, William   Prisoner 248. Rank: Seaman, from: Syren, Man of War Brig.
    Cap: 12 Jul 1814 at Sea by HMS Medway Int: 19 Aug 1814 Dis: 06 Apr 1815.
    Received from HMS Medway. HMS Cumberland per Order of VA Sir Charles Tyler.

Ransom, John   Prisoner 74. Rank: Seaman, from: Rambler, Merchant Vessel.
    Cap: Not Recorded by HMS Harpy Int: 28 Feb 1813 Dis: 11 May 1815.
    Received from Morley Transport. per Order of Vice Admiral Sir Charles Tyler KCB. (Date of capture not recorded.)

Ray, William   Prisoner 29. Rank: Seaman, from: Ocean, Merchant Vessel.
    Cap: 17 Nov 1812 at Sea by Atalanta Transport Int: 07 Jan 1813 Dis: 10 Feb 1814.
    Received from Ocean. For a Passage to England.

Raymond, William   Prisoner 114. Rank: Carpenter, from: Rose, Merchant Vessel.
    Cap: 04 Jan 1813 Not Recorded by HMS Harpy Int: 29 Jun 1813 Dis: 11 May 1815.
    Received from HMS Racehorse. per Order Vice Adml Sir Charles Tyler KCB.

Reeay, Lewis   Prisoner 123. Rank: Seaman, from: Not Recorded, Not Recorded.
    Cap: Not Recorded by Not Recorded Int: 18 Aug 1813 Dis: 12 Aug 1814.
    Received from HMS Lion. To HMS Stag Order V Adl Tyler. (Date of capture not recorded. Duplicate prison # - Edward Cannor.)

Rhoades, Charles H   Prisoner 258. Rank: Seaman, from: Syren, Man of War Brig.
    Cap: 12 Jul 1814 at Sea by HMS Medway Int: 19 Aug 1814 Dis: 06 Apr 1815.
    Received from HMS Medway. HMS Cumberland per Order VA Sir Charles Taylor.

Rice, John   Prisoner 35. Rank: 2 Mate, from: James, Merchant Vessel.
    Cap: 18 Dec 1812 at Sea by HMS Harpy Int: 28 Jan 1813 Dis: 10 Feb 1814.
    Received from James. For a Passage to England.

Rice, Samuel   Prisoner 139. Rank: Seaman, from: William Penn, Merchant Vessel.
    Cap: 27 Oct 1813 at Sea by HMS Acorn Int: 04 Dec 1813 Dis: 10 Aug 1814.
    Received from HMS Acorn. Exiter Indiaman for England.

Rich, Francis   Prisoner 151. Rank: Seaman, from: La Ceres, French Frigate.
    Cap: 06 Jan 1814 off the Cape De be J Island by HMS Nizer Int: 25 Mar 1814 Dis: 10 Aug 1814.
    Received from HMS Laurie. Exiter Indiaman for England.

Richards, Lawrence   Prisoner 125. Rank: Seaman, from: Not Recorded, Not Recorded.
    Cap: Not Recorded by Not Recorded Int: 25 Sep 1813 Dis: 12 Aug 1814.
    Received from HMS Semiramis. To HMS Stag Order V Adl Tyler. (Date of capture not recorded.)

American Prisoners of War at Cape of Good Hope During the War of 1812

Richards, Thomas   Prisoner 102. Rank: Seaman, from: Not Recorded, Not Recorded.
    Cap: Not Recorded by Not Recorded Int: 04 Apr 1813 Dis: 12 Aug 1814.
    Received from HMS Harpy being an American. HMS Stag per Order V Adl Tyler. (Date and place of capture 'not mentioned'.)

Richardson, Nathaniel   Prisoner 161. Rank: Lieutenant Commander, from: Syren, Man of War Brig.
    Cap: 12 Jul 1814 at Sea by HMS Medway Int: 19 Aug 1814 Dis: 06 Apr 1815.
    Received from HMS Medway. HMS Cumberland per Order V Adl Sir Charles Tyler.

Rideway, Ebenezer   Prisoner 169. Rank: Midshipman, from: Syren, Man of War Brig.
    Cap: 12 Jul 1814 at Sea by HMS Medway Int: 19 Aug 1814 Dis: 06 Apr 1815.
    Received from HMS Medway. HMS Cumberland per Order Vice Adl Sir Charles Tyler.

Roberts, William   Prisoner 97. Rank: Seaman, from: Derby, Merchant Vessel.
    Cap: 04 Feb 1813 at Sea by HMS Nisus Int: 02 Apr 1813 Dis: 29 Apr 1814.
    Received from HMS Nisus. Emma Transport London.

Robertson, Gardner   Prisoner 147. Rank: Seaman, from: William Penn, Merchant Vessel.
    Cap: 27 Oct 1813 at Sea by HMS Acorn Int: 04 Dec 1813 Dis: 10 Aug 1814.
    Received from HMS Acorn. Exiter Indiaman for England.

Robertson, William   Prisoner 4. Rank: Seaman, from: Monticello, Merchant Service.
    Cap: 12 Nov 1812 Table Bay by Racehorse Int: 07 Jan 1813 Dis: 11 May 1815.
    Received from Monticello. per Order of Vice Admiral Sir Charles Tyler KCB.

Rogers, Samuel   Prisoner 170. Rank: Midshipman, from: Syren, Man of War Brig.
    Cap: 12 Jul 1814 at Sea by HMS Medway Int: 19 Aug 1814 Dis: 06 Apr 1815.
    Received from HMS Medway. To HMS Malacca per Order of Vice Adml Sir Charles Tyler.

Ropes, William   Prisoner 73. Rank: Seaman, from: Rambler, Merchant Vessel.
    Cap: Not Recorded by HMS Harpy Int: 28 Feb 1813 Dis: 10 Aug 1814.
    Received from Morley Transport. Union Indiaman for England. (Date of capture not recorded.)

Roundy, John   Prisoner 252. Rank: Seaman, from: Syren, Man of War Brig.
    Cap: 12 Jul 1814 at Sea by HMS Medway Int: 19 Aug 1814 Dis: 06 Apr 1815.
    Received from HMS Medway. HMS Cumberland per Order of VA Sir Charles Tyler.

Russels, David   Prisoner 67. Rank: Seaman, from: Rambler, Merchant Vessel.
    Cap: Not Recorded by HMS Harpy Int: 28 Feb 1813 Dis: .
    Received from Morley Transport. (Dates of capture and discharge not recorded.)

Rust, Zebulon   Prisoner 195. Rank: Seaman, from: Syren, Man of War Brig.
    Cap: 12 Jul 1814 at Sea by HM Ship Medway Int: 19 Aug 1814 Dis: 30 Nov 1814.
    Received from HMS Medway. Asia East India Man to assist in navigating her to England.

Sawley, Lewis   Prisoner 244. Rank: Seaman, from: Syren, Man of War Brig.
    Cap: 12 Jul 1814 at Sea by HMS Medway Int: 19 Aug 1814 Dis: 06 Apr 1815.
    Received from HMS Medway. HMS Cumberland per Order of VA Sir Charles Tyler.

Shaw, Cesar   Prisoner 149. Rank: Seaman, from: William Penn, Merchant Vessel.
    Cap: 27 Oct 1813 at Sea by HMS Acorn Int: 04 Dec 1813 Dis: 10 Aug 1814.
    Received from HMS Acorn. Exiter Indiaman for England.

Sheperd, John   Prisoner 243. Rank: Seaman, from: Syren, Man of War Brig.
    Cap: 12 Jul 1814 at Sea by HMS Medway Int: 19 Aug 1814 Dis: 06 Apr 1815.
    Received from HMS Medway. HMS Cumberland per Order of VA Sir Charles Tyler.

Shephard, Henry   Prisoner 49. Rank: Seaman, from: James, Merchant Vessel.
    Cap: 18 Dec 1812 at Sea by HMS Harpy Int: 24 Feb 1813 Dis: 28 Apr 1814.
    Received from Morley Transport. Hope for London.

Short, Clem   Prisoner 39. Rank: Seaman, from: James, Merchant Vessel.
    Cap: 18 Dec 1812 at Sea by HMS Harpy Int: 28 Jan 1813 Dis: 10 Feb 1814.
    Received from James. For a Passage to England.

Silbey, John   Prisoner 142. Rank: Seaman, from: William Penn, Merchant Vessel.
    Cap: 27 Oct 1813 at Sea by HMS Acorn Int: 04 Dec 1813 Dis: 02 May 1814.
    Received from HMS Acorn. Albion Whaler for England.

Smith, Gerward   Prisoner 106. Rank: Seaman, from: Not Recorded, Not Recorded.
    Cap: Not Recorded by Not Recorded Int: 13 Apr 1813 Dis: 12 Aug 1814.
    Received from HMS Astraea being an American. HMS Stag per Order V Adl Tyler. (Date and place of capture 'not mentioned'.)

Smith, Kirby   Prisoner 93. Rank: 2 Mate, from: Derby, Merchant Vessel.
    Cap: 04 Feb 1813 at Sea by HMS Nisus Int: 02 Apr 1813 Dis: 05 Apr 1814.
    Received from HMS Nisus. Ceres for London.

Snell, Davy   Prisoner 2. Rank: 1 Mate, from: Monticello, Merchant Service.
    Cap: 12 Nov 1812 Table Bay by Racehorse Int: 07 Jan 1813 Dis: 10 Feb 1814.
    Received from Monticello. for a Passage to England HMS Leon.

American Prisoners of War at Cape of Good Hope During the War of 1812

Snider, Enos   Prisoner 256. Rank: Seaman, from: Syren, Man of War Brig.
    Cap: 12 Jul 1814 at Sea by HMS Medway Int: 19 Aug 1814 Dis: 06 Apr 1815.
    Received from HMS Medway. HMS Cumberland per Order VA Sir Charles Taylor.

Sparks, John   Prisoner 179. Rank: Gunner, from: Syren, Man of War Brig.
    Cap: 12 Jul 1814 at Sea by HM Ship Medway Int: 19 Aug 1814 Dis: 30 Nov 1814.
    Received from HMS Medway. HM Ship Desere order of R Adl Tyler.

Sparks, Peter   Prisoner 85. Rank: Seaman, from: Rose, Merchant Vessel.
    Cap: Not Recorded by HM Ships Harpy & Primrose Int: 05 Mar 1813 Dis: 06 Jan 1814.
    Received from HMS Harpy. To the Morley Transport. (Date and place of capture 'not mentioned'.)

Spear, Joseph   Prisoner 199. Rank: Ordinary Seaman, from: Syren, Man of War Brig.
    Cap: 12 Jul 1814 at Sea by HM Ship Medway Int: 19 Aug 1814 Dis: 30 Nov 1814.
    Received from HMS Medway. Asia East India Man to assist in navigating her to England.

Speares, Joseph   Prisoner 160. Rank: Seaman, from: Mary, Merchant Vessel.
    Cap: Saldauha Bay by Not Recorded Int: 26 Jul 1814 Dis: 28 Jul 1814.
    Recaptured Ship. Hyair Alley American Privateer. To Malenta Transport per Order R Adl Tyler being Native of Canada.   (Date of capture not recorded.)

Spouarts, James   Prisoner 250. Rank: Ordinary Seaman, from: Syren, Man of War Brig.
    Cap: 12 Jul 1814 at Sea by HMS Medway Int: 19 Aug 1814 Dis: 06 Apr 1815.
    Received from HMS Medway. HMS Cumberland per Order of VA Sir Charles Tyler.

Stephens, John   Prisoner 205. Rank: Seaman, from: Syren, Man of War Brig.
    Cap: 12 Jul 1814 at Sea by HMS Medway Int: 19 Aug 1814 Dis: 30 Nov 1814.
    Received from HMS Medway. Asia East India Man to assist in navigating her England.

Stone, John   Prisoner 193. Rank: Seaman, from: Syren, Man of War Brig.
    Cap: 12 Jul 1814 at Sea by HM Ship Medway Int: 19 Aug 1814 Dis: 30 Nov 1814.
    Received from HMS Medway. Asia East India Man to assist in navigating her to England.

Sunner, William   Prisoner 224. Rank: Quartermaster, from: Syren, Man of War Brig.
    Cap: 12 Jul 1814 at Sea by HMS Medway Int: 19 Aug 1814 Dis: 06 Apr 1815.
    Received from HMS Medway. HMS Cumberland per Order VA Sir Charles Tyler.

Swain, Obed   Prisoner 134. Rank: Seaman, from: William Penn, Merchant Vessel.
    Cap: 27 Oct 1813 at Sea by HMS Acorn Int: 04 Dec 1813 Dis: 30 Apr 1814.
    Received from HMS Acorn. William Pitt Indiaman for London.

Swift, William   Prisoner 165. Rank: Surgeon, from: Syren, Man of War Brig.
    Cap: 12 Jul 1814 at Sea by HMS Medway Int: 19 Aug 1814 Dis: 06 Apr 1815.
    Received from HMS Medway. HMS Cumberland per Order Vice Adl Sir Charles Tyler.

Taylor, John   Prisoner 276. Rank: Seaman, from: Syren, Man of War Brig.
    Cap: 12 Jul 1814 at Sea by HMS Medway Int: 19 Aug 1814 Dis: 06 Apr 1815.
    Received from HMS Medway. HMS Cumberland per Order of VA Sir Charles Tyler.

Thomas, George   Prisoner 14. Rank: Seaman, from: Valentine, Merchant Service.
    Cap: 16 Nov 1812 Table Bay by Minden Int: 07 Jan 1813 Dis: 10 Aug 1814.
    Received from Valentine. Union Indiaman for England.

Thomas, John   Prisoner 181. Rank: Master at Arms, from: Syren, Man of War Brig.
    Cap: 12 Jul 1814 at Sea by HM Ship Medway Int: 19 Aug 1814 Dis: 30 Nov 1814.
    Received from HMS Medway. HM Ship Desere order of R Adl Tyler.

Tinker, James   Prisoner 154. Rank: Not Recorded, from: Not Recorded, Not Recorded.
    Cap: Not Recorded by Not Recorded Int: Dis: 12 Aug 1814.
    Received from Town Prison. To HMS Dannemark order Vice Adl Taylor. (Dates of capture and internment not recorded.)

Tonkin, Richard   Prisoner 124. Rank: Seaman, from: Not Recorded, Not Recorded.
    Cap: Not Recorded by Not Recorded Int: 18 Aug 1813 Dis: 12 Aug 1814.
    Received from HMS Lion. To HMS Stag Order V Adl Tyler. (Date of capture not recorded.)

Townly, Joshua H   Prisoner 234. Rank: Ordinary Seaman, from: Syren, Man of War Brig.
    Cap: 12 Jul 1814 at Sea by HMS Medway Int: 19 Aug 1814 Dis: 06 Apr 1815.
    Received from HMS Medway. HMS Cumberland per Order of VA Sir Charles Tyler.

Tunison, Tunis   Prisoner 56. Rank: Captain, from: James, Merchant Vessel.
    Cap: 18 Dec 1812 at Sea by HMS Harpy Int: 28 Feb 1813 Dis: 22 Apr 1814.
    Received from Morley Transport. Baring Transport for London.

Tunnell, Henry   Prisoner 238. Rank: Seaman, from: Syren, Man of War Brig.
    Cap: 12 Jul 1814 at Sea by HMS Medway Int: 19 Aug 1814 Dis: 06 Apr 1815.
    Received from HMS Medway. HMS Cumberland per Order of VA Sir Charles Tyler.

Turner, Davis T   Prisoner 99. Rank: Seaman, from: Derby, Merchant Vessel.
    Cap: 04 Feb 1813 at Sea by HMS Nisus Int: 02 Apr 1813 Dis: 30 Apr 1814.
    Received from HMS Nisus. William Pitt Indiaman London.

American Prisoners of War at Cape of Good Hope During the War of 1812

Turner, Gardner   Prisoner 20. Rank: Seaman, from: Valentine, Merchant Service.
    Cap: 16 Nov 1812 Table Bay by Minden Int: 07 Jan 1813 Dis: 10 Feb 1814.
    Received from Valentine. For a Passage to England HMS Leon.

Vandenberg, Ruben   Prisoner 28. Rank: Seaman, from: Ocean, Merchant Vessel.
    Cap: 17 Nov 1812 at Sea by Atalanta Transport Int: 07 Jan 1813 Dis: 18 Jan 1813.
    Received from Ocean. Hercules Transport per Order Vice Adl Stafford.

Wadley, William   Prisoner 294. Rank: Private, from: Syren, Man of War Brig.
    Cap: 12 Jul 1814 at Sea by HMS Medway Int: 19 Aug 1814 Dis: 06 Apr 1815.
    Received from HMS Medway. HMS Cumberland per Order VA Sir Charles Tyler.

Waine, Thomas   Prisoner 164. Rank: Purser, from: Syren, Man of War Brig.
    Cap: 12 Jul 1814 at Sea by HMS Medway Int: 19 Aug 1814 Dis: 06 Apr 1815.
    Received from HMS Medway. per Order of Vice Adl Sir Charles Tyler.

Ward, William   Prisoner 249. Rank: Seaman, from: Syren, Man of War Brig.
    Cap: 12 Jul 1814 at Sea by HMS Medway Int: 19 Aug 1814 Dis: 06 Apr 1815.
    Received from HMS Medway. HMS Cumberland per Order of VA Sir Charles Tyler.

Warrington, William   Prisoner 64. Rank: Seaman, from: Rambler, Merchant Vessel.
    Cap: Not Recorded by HMS Harpy Int: 28 Feb 1813 Dis: 11 Mar 1815.
    Received from Morley Transport. per Order of Vice Adml Sir Charles Tyler KCB. (Date of capture not recorded.)

Watson, George   Prisoner 277. Rank: Seaman, from: Syren, Man of War Brig.
    Cap: 12 Jul 1814 at Sea by HMS Medway Int: 19 Aug 1814 Dis: 06 Apr 1815.
    Received from HMS Medway. HMS Cumberland per Order of VA Sir Charles Tyler.

Watson, William   Prisoner 227. Rank: Seaman, from: Syren, Man of War Brig.
    Cap: 12 Jul 1814 at Sea by HMS Medway Int: 19 Aug 1814 Dis: 06 Apr 1815.
    Received from HMS Medway. HMS Cumberland per Order VA Sir Charles Tyler.

Weaver, William A   Prisoner 253. Rank: Midshipman, from: Syren, Man of War Brig.
    Cap: 12 Jul 1814 at Sea by HMS Medway Int: 19 Aug 1814 Dis: 06 Apr 1815.
    Received from HMS Medway. HMS Cumberland per Order VA Sir Charles Tyler.

Webb, Thomas   Prisoner 61. Rank: Seaman, from: James, Merchant Vessel.
    Cap: 18 Dec 1812 at Sea by HMS Harpy Int: 28 Feb 1813 Dis: 12 Aug 1814.
    Received from Morley Transport. HMS Dannemark order Adm Tyler.

West, Jacob   Prisoner 178. Rank: Seaman, from: Syren, Man of War Brig.
    Cap: 12 Jul 1814 at Sea by HM Ship Medway Int: 19 Aug 1814 Dis: 30 Nov 1814.
    Received from HMS Medway. HM Ship Desere order of R Adl Tyler.

West, James   Prisoner 145. Rank: Seaman, from: William Penn, Merchant Vessel.
    Cap: 27 Oct 1813 at Sea by HMS Acorn Int: 04 Dec 1813 Dis: 10 Aug 1814.
    Received from HMS Acorn. Union Indiaman for England. Or James White.

Wheeler, John J   Prisoner 194. Rank: Boy, from: Syren, Man of War Brig.
    Cap: 12 Jul 1814 at Sea by HM Ship Medway Int: 19 Aug 1814 Dis: 30 Nov 1814.
    Received from HMS Medway. The Trowbridge Country Ship to assist in navigating her to England.

White, William   Prisoner 278. Rank: Seaman, from: Syren, Man of War Brig.
    Cap: 12 Jul 1814 at Sea by HMS Medway Int: 19 Aug 1814 Dis: 06 Apr 1815.
    Received from HMS Medway. HMS Cumberland per Order of VA Sir Charles Tyler.

Whitiny, Samuel   Prisoner 286. Rank: Corporal, from: Syren, Man of War Brig.
    Cap: 12 Jul 1814 at Sea by HMS Medway Int: 19 Aug 1814 Dis: 06 Apr 1815.
    Received from HMS Medway. HMS Cumberland per Order VA Sir Charles Tyler.

Wiemyer, G W   Prisoner 214. Rank: Seaman, from: Syren, Man of War Brig.
    Cap: 12 Jul 1814 at Sea by HMS Medway Int: 19 Aug 1814 Dis: 06 Apr 1815.
    Received from HMS Medway. To His Majestys Ship Malacca per Order of Vice Adml Sir Charles Tyler.

Wiggins, Samuel   Prisoner 112. Rank: 2 Mate, from: Rose, Merchant Vessel.
    Cap: 04 Jan 1813 Not Recorded by HMS Harpy Int: 29 Jun 1813 Dis: 28 Apr 1814.
    Received from HMS Racehorse. The Hope for London.

Wilber, John   Prisoner 79. Rank: Seaman, from: Rose, Merchant Vessel.
    Cap: Not Recorded by HM Ships Harpy & Primrose Int: 05 Mar 1813 Dis: 12 Aug 1814.
    Received from HMS Harpy. HMS Dannemark order Adl Tyler. (Date and place of capture 'not mentioned'.)

Williams, George   Prisoner 116. Rank: Seaman, from: Not Recorded, Not Recorded.
    Cap: Not Recorded by Not Recorded Int: 09 Jul 1813 Dis: 12 Aug 1814.
    Received from HMS Lion. HMS Dannemark per order Vice Adml Taylor. (Date of capture not recorded.)

American Prisoners of War at Cape of Good Hope During the War of 1812

Williams, John   Prisoner 50. Rank: Seaman, from: James, Merchant Vessel.
    Cap: 18 Dec 1812 at Sea by HMS Harpy Int: 24 Feb 1813 Dis: .
    Received from Morley Transport. (Date of discharge not recorded.)

Williams, Joseph   Prisoner 108. Rank: Seaman, from: Not Recorded, Not Recorded.
    Cap: Not Recorded by Not Recorded Int: 13 Apr 1813 Dis: 12 Aug 1814.
    Received from HMS Astraea being an American. HMS Stag per Order V Adl Tyler. (Date and place of capture 'not mentioned'.)

Williams, William   Prisoner 42. Rank: Seaman, from: James, Merchant Vessel.
    Cap: 18 Dec 1812 at Sea by HMS Harpy Int: 30 Jan 1813 Dis: 28 Apr 1814.
    Received from Oxford Transport. Hope for London.

Willig, Frederick   Prisoner 293. Rank: Private, from: Syren, Man of War Brig.
    Cap: 12 Jul 1814 at Sea by HMS Medway Int: 19 Aug 1814 Dis: 06 Apr 1815.
    Received from HMS Medway. HMS Cumberland per Order VA Sir Charles Tyler.

Woodford, Joseph   Prisoner 241. Rank: Seaman, from: Syren, Man of War Brig.
    Cap: 12 Jul 1814 at Sea by HMS Medway Int: 19 Aug 1814 Dis: 06 Apr 1815.
    Received from HMS Medway. HMS Cumberland per Order of VA Sir Charles Tyler.

Young, William   Prisoner 228. Rank: Seaman, from: Syren, Man of War Brig.
    Cap: 12 Jul 1814 at Sea by HMS Medway Int: 19 Aug 1814 Dis: 06 Apr 1815.
    Received from HMS Medway. HMS Cumberland per Order of VA Sir Charles Tyler.

American Prisoners of War at Cape of Good Hope During the War of 1812

Numeric listing by prison number

1	Peyster, Afde	69	Adams, John
2	Snell, Davy	70	Files, Felice
3	Greenland, Stephen	71	Mergfand, William
4	Robertson, William	72	Goldsmith, Thomas
5	Miffin, Richard	73	Ropes, William
6	Collins, William	74	Ransom, John
7	Genesey, Joseph	75	Brooks, John
8	Chadwick, John	76	Gardner, Rowland
9	Chase, Stephen B	77	Cary, C
10	Arnold, Thomas	78	Holmes, Jedekiah
11	Arnold, Welcome	79	Wilber, John
12	Potter, Richard H	80	Bunker, Frederick
13	Davis, Henry	81	Bennett, Robert
14	Thomas, George	82	Elbert, Hugh
15	Lockwood, Benoni	83	---, Mariano
16	Helen, John P	84	---, Maplino
17	Crapon, George	85	Sparks, Peter
18	Hanson, Cornelius	86	Mitchell, Jonathan
19	Johnson, James	87	Peters, John
20	Turner, Gardner	88	Chapons, Thomas
21	Luther, Cromwell	89	Marshall, Benjamin
22	Jones, Samuel B	90	Drew, William
23	Coffin, Absolem	91	Gardner, Nathaniel
24	Coffin, Zemie	92	Dexter, Charles
25	Coleman, John	93	Smith, Kirby
26	Coffin, Valentine	94	Dexter, George W
27	Manuel, Paul	95	Doyer, Thomas
28	Vandenberg, Ruben	96	Olding, Elisha
29	Ray, William	97	Roberts, William
30	Norcot, George	98	Holdbrook, Abrica
31	Decruz, N	99	Turner, Davis T
32	Arnold, Thomas	100	Parker, William
33	Henderson, Benjamin	101	Deysey, Wolsten
34	Norgrave, Jeremiah	102	Richards, Thomas
35	Rice, John	103	Clinn, George
36	Ide, John H	104	Ferguson, Stephen
37	Bush, Mathew M	105	Allen, John
38	Murray, Nathaniel	106	Smith, Gerward
39	Short, Clem	107	Morrison, Dep
40	Crawford, John	108	Williams, Joseph
41	Gorman, Joseph	109	Coleman, James
42	Williams, William	110	Brown, George
43	Lee, John	111	Cooper, Thomas
44	Hartford, William	112	Wiggins, Samuel
45	Evans, William	113	Coffin, Josiah P
46	Fife, Thomas	114	Raymond, William
47	Field, David	115	Eastor, Peter
48	Monk, Joseph	116	Williams, George
49	Shephard, Henry	117	Butler, John
50	Williams, John	118	Porter, Frederick
51	Hudson, Joseph	119	Adams, John
52	Glee, Andrew	120	Kimble, Samuel
53	Odey, Thomas	121	Cowen, William
54	Falmond, John	122	Ellis, George
55	Millar, Francis	123	Cannor, Edward
56	Tunison, Tunis	123	Reeay, Lewis
57	Bryant, Timothy	124	Tonkin, Richard
58	Dessmore, Abraham	125	Richards, Lawrence
59	Felt, George	126	Coville, Edmund
60	Nicholes, Henry	127	Hall, Joseph
61	Webb, Thomas	128	Bassinger, Robert
62	Philips, George	129	Fletcher, Peter
63	Ody, George	130	Gardner, George M
64	Warrington, William	131	North, Charles
65	Atkinson, Charles	132	Harris, Moses
66	Kimble, John	133	Earl, Joseph
67	Russels, David	134	Swain, Obed
68	Geer, John	135	Long, David

American Prisoners of War at Cape of Good Hope During the War of 1812

136	Henrie, Daniel M		207	Brooking, Samuel
137	Harris, George		208	Barns, Jacob
138	Carns, Thomas		209	King, William
139	Rice, Samuel		210	Parsons, Samuel
140	Allen, John		211	Lindon, John
141	Chase, George W		212	Harwood, James
142	Silbey, John		213	Dyke, James
143	Freelern, John		214	Wiemyer, G W
144	Ebby, Samuel		215	Evans, Barah M
145	West, James		216	Fenton, James
146	Hussey, Joseph		217	Dublet, John
147	Robertson, Gardner		218	Parker, John
148	Hart, Emius		219	Fales, Charles
149	Shaw, Cesar		220	Gould, Thomas
150	Connor, Peter		221	Brown, James
151	Rich, Francis		222	Cooper, Greeville
152	Lewis, John		223	Pickering, Abraham
153	Martin, James		224	Sunner, William
154	Tinker, James		225	Alplin, Joseph
155	Perry, Nathaniel		226	Gerry, Joseph
156	Murey, Oliver		227	Watson, William
157	Coats, Russel		228	Young, William
158	Bartlet, Samuel		229	Phillips, Nathaniel
159	Pedro, Joseph		230	Andrews, Joseph
160	Speares, Joseph		231	Leach, Samuel
161	Richardson, Nathaniel		232	Colcord, John L
162	German, Lewis		233	Deal, Lewis
163	Gordon, W L		234	Townly, Joshua H
164	Waine, Thomas		235	Lewis, Raymond
165	Swift, William		236	Gammell, Joseph
166	Downes, Shubart		237	Banen, John
167	Adams, Nathaniel		238	Tunnell, Henry
168	Hinchman, Lewis		239	Horner, James
169	Rideway, Ebenezer		240	Pierce, John
170	Rogers, Samuel		241	Woodford, Joseph
171	Morris, John		242	Lincoln, Ruben
172	Prout, Henry		243	Sheperd, John
173	Chick, Mons		244	Sawley, Lewis
174	Clohnan, Ephraim		245	Randolp, Samuel
175	Andrews, Samuel		246	Johnson, Samuel
176	Durham, William		247	Carpenter, Jacon
177	Cavedon, Luke		248	Rankins, William
178	West, Jacob		249	Ward, William
179	Sparks, John		250	Spouarts, James
180	Coats, Samuel M		251	Dalliver, William
181	Thomas, John		252	Roundy, John
182	Bisbey, Isaac		253	Weaver, William A
183	Clide, John J		254	Bilt, J J
184	Casper, William		255	Prentiss, John E
185	Daniels, Henry		256	Snider, Enos
186	Millow, John		257	Ginish, Samuel
187	Kitchen, George		258	Rhoades, Charles H
188	Haycock, Joseph		259	Blakey, Charles
189	Kirkby, Robert		260	Carpenter, William
190	Pope, Oliver		261	Randall, Henry
191	Lewis, Winslow		262	Lambert, John
192	Nicholas, Jacob		263	Hild, George
193	Stone, John		264	Manuel, Joseph
194	Wheeler, John J		265	Johnson, William
195	Rust, Zebulon		266	Hood, Daniel
196	Briant, Thomas		267	Bray, George
197	Davies, Thomas		268	Millar, Samuel
198	Damon, Thomas		269	Putnam, Joseph
199	Spear, Joseph		270	Booder, Joseph
200	Bucknell, Charles		271	Bubier, John
201	Blackford, John		272	Blair, Samuel
202	Groverman, Fred C		273	Fountain, Nicholas
203	Memory, James		274	Quenn, Patrick
204	Kellie, Stephen		275	Brown, James
205	Stephens, John		276	Taylor, John
206	Hodge, Edward		277	Watson, George

American Prisoners of War at Cape of Good Hope During the War of 1812

278	White, William		289	Hadley, Andrew
279	Fenier, Drury		290	Brevett, Abraham
280	Jones, Ezekiel		291	Owen, Thomas
281	Hutchens, William		292	McCalley, John
282	Harding, Joseph		293	Willig, Frederick
283	Moses, John		294	Wadley, William
284	Quaque, Samuel		295	Gitcher, Samuel
285	Hubley, John		296	Johnson, Moses
286	Whitiny, Samuel			
287	Pen, William			
288	Peeper, Nathaniel			

American Prisoners of War at Cape of Good Hope During the War of 1812

Crew listing by ship

Derby
- Dexter, Charles
- Dexter, George W
- Deysey, Wolsten
- Doyer, Thomas
- Holdbrook, Abrica
- Olding, Elisha
- Parker, William
- Roberts, William
- Smith, Kirby
- Turner, Davis T

James
- Bryant, Timothy
- Bush, Mathew M
- Crawford, John
- Dessmore, Abraham
- Evans, William
- Falmond, John
- Felt, George
- Field, David
- Fife, Thomas
- Glee, Andrew
- Gorman, Joseph
- Hartford, William
- Henderson, Benjamin
- Hudson, Joseph
- Ide, John H
- Lee, John
- Millar, Francis
- Monk, Joseph
- Murray, Nathaniel
- Nicholes, Henry
- Norgrave, Jeremiah
- Odey, Thomas
- Ody, George
- Philips, George
- Rice, John
- Shephard, Henry
- Short, Clem
- Tunison, Tunis
- Webb, Thomas
- Williams, John
- Williams, William

La Ceres
- Lewis, John
- Rich, Francis

Mary
- Bartlet, Samuel
- Coats, Russel
- Murey, Oliver
- Pedro, Joseph
- Perry, Nathaniel
- Speares, Joseph

Monticello
- Chadwick, John
- Collins, William
- Genesey, Joseph
- Greenland, Stephen
- Miffin, Richard
- Peyster, Afde
- Robertson, William
- Snell, Davy

Ocean
- Coffin, Absolem
- Coffin, Valentine
- Coffin, Zemie
- Coleman, John
- Manuel, Paul
- Norcot, George
- Ray, William
- Vandenberg, Ruben

Rambler
- Adams, John
- Atkinson, Charles
- Brooks, John
- Files, Felice
- Geer, John
- Goldsmith, Thomas
- Kimble, John
- Mergfand, William
- Ransom, John
- Ropes, William
- Russels, David
- Warrington, William

Rose
- ---, Maplino
- ---, Mariano
- Bennett, Robert
- Bunker, Frederick
- Cary, C
- Chapons, Thomas
- Coffin, Josiah P
- Drew, William
- Eastor, Peter
- Elbert, Hugh
- Gardner, Nathaniel
- Gardner, Rowland
- Holmes, Jedekiah
- Marshall, Benjamin
- Mitchell, Jonathan
- Peters, John
- Raymond, William
- Sparks, Peter
- Wiggins, Samuel
- Wilber, John

Syren
- Adams, Nathaniel
- Alplin, Joseph
- Andrews, Joseph
- Andrews, Samuel
- Banen, John
- Barns, Jacob
- Bilt, J J
- Bisbey, Isaac
- Blackford, John
- Blair, Samuel
- Blakey, Charles
- Booder, Joseph
- Bray, George
- Brevett, Abraham
- Briant, Thomas
- Brooking, Samuel
- Brown, James
- Brown, James
- Bubier, John
- Bucknell, Charles
- Carpenter, Jacon
- Carpenter, William
- Casper, William
- Cavedon, Luke
- Chick, Mons
- Clide, John J
- Clohnan, Ephraim
- Coats, Samuel M
- Colcord, John L
- Cooper, Greeville
- Dalliver, William
- Damon, Thomas

American Prisoners of War at Cape of Good Hope During the War of 1812

Daniels, Henry
Davies, Thomas
Deal, Lewis
Downes, Shubart
Dublet, John
Durham, William
Dyke, James
Evans, Barah M
Fales, Charles
Fenier, Drury
Fenton, James
Fountain, Nicholas
Gammell, Joseph
German, Lewis
Gerry, Joseph
Ginish, Samuel
Gitcher, Samuel
Gordon, W L
Gould, Thomas
Groverman, Fred C
Hadley, Andrew
Harding, Joseph
Harwood, James
Haycock, Joseph
Hild, George
Hinchman, Lewis
Hodge, Edward
Hood, Daniel
Horner, James
Hubley, John
Hutchens, William
Johnson, Moses
Johnson, Samuel
Johnson, William
Jones, Ezekiel
Kellie, Stephen
King, William
Kirkby, Robert
Kitchen, George
Lambert, John
Leach, Samuel
Lewis, Raymond
Lewis, Winslow
Lincoln, Ruben
Lindon, John
Manuel, Joseph
McCalley, John
Memory, James
Millar, Samuel
Millow, John
Morris, John
Moses, John
Nicholas, Jacob
Owen, Thomas
Parker, John
Parsons, Samuel
Peeper, Nathaniel
Pen, William
Phillips, Nathaniel
Pickering, Abraham
Pierce, John
Pope, Oliver
Prentiss, John E
Prout, Henry
Putnam, Joseph
Quaque, Samuel
Quenn, Patrick
Randall, Henry
Randolp, Samuel
Rankins, William
Rhoades, Charles H
Richardson, Nathaniel

Rideway, Ebenezer
Rogers, Samuel
Roundy, John
Rust, Zebulon
Sawley, Lewis
Sheperd, John
Snider, Enos
Sparks, John
Spear, Joseph
Spouarts, James
Stephens, John
Stone, John
Sunner, William
Swift, William
Taylor, John
Thomas, John
Townly, Joshua H
Tunnell, Henry
Wadley, William
Waine, Thomas
Ward, William
Watson, George
Watson, William
Weaver, William A
West, Jacob
Wheeler, John J
White, William
Whitiny, Samuel
Wiemyer, G W
Willig, Frederick
Woodford, Joseph
Young, William

Valentine
Arnold, Thomas
Arnold, Thomas
Arnold, Welcome
Chase, Stephen B
Crapon, George
Davis, Henry
Decruz, N
Hanson, Cornelius
Helen, John P
Johnson, James
Jones, Samuel B
Lockwood, Benoni
Luther, Cromwell
Potter, Richard H
Thomas, George
Turner, Gardner

William Penn
Allen, John
Carns, Thomas
Chase, George W
Connor, Peter
Earl, Joseph
Ebby, Samuel
Freelern, John
Gardner, George M
Harris, George
Harris, Moses
Hart, Emius
Henrie, Daniel M
Hussey, Joseph
Long, David
North, Charles
Rice, Samuel
Robertson, Gardner
Shaw, Cesar
Silbey, John
Swain, Obed
West, James

American Prisoners of War Held at Jamaica During the War of 1812

Americans on British ships

Allen, John
Clinn, George
Coleman, James
Ferguson, Stephen
Morrison, Dep
Richards, Thomas
Smith, Gerward
Williams, Joseph

American Prisoners of War Held at Jamaica During the War of 1812

Service affiliation not known

Adams, John
Bassinger, Robert
Brown, George
Butler, John
Cannor, Edward
Cooper, Thomas
Coville, Edmund
Cowen, William
Ellis, George
Fletcher, Peter
Hall, Joseph
Kimble, Samuel
Martin, James
Porter, Frederick
Reeay, Lewis
Richards, Lawrence
Tinker, James
Tonkin, Richard
Williams, George

American Prisoners of War Held at Jamaica During the War of 1812

United States Marines

Brevett, Abraham
Gitcher, Samuel
Hadley, Andrew
Hubley, John
McCalley, John
Owen, Thomas
Peeper, Nathaniel
Pen, William
Wadley, William
Whitiny, Samuel
Willig, Frederick

American Prisoners of War Held at Jamaica During the War of 1812

---, --- Prisoner 780. Rank: Seaman, from: San Francisco de Paula, Privateer.
    Cap: 02 Oct 1813 at Sea by Forrester Int: 07 Oct 1813 Dis:
    Received from Forrester. (Name and date of discharge not recorded.)

---, Antonio Prisoner 837. Rank: Seaman, from: Enterprize, Privateer.
    Cap: 15 Nov 1813 at Sea by Argo Int: 19 Nov 1813 Escaped: 12 May 1814.
    A Carthagenaian. Received from Argo. Escaped. (Last name not recorded.)

---, Autouel Prisoner 910. Rank: Seaman, from: San Francisco Navier, Brig.
    Cap: 05 Dec 1813 at Sea by Sappho Int: 15 Dec 1813 Dis: 08 Aug 1814.
    Taken in the Recaptured Spanish Brig. Prize to the Carthagenaian Privateer Carthagenaian. Received from Sappho. Board's Order. (Last name not recorded.)

---, Bechariah Prisoner 809. Rank: Seaman, from: Enterprize, Privateer.
    Cap: 15 Nov 1813 at Sea by Argo Int: 19 Nov 1813 Dis: 23 Aug 1814.
    A Carthagenaian. Received from Argo. Board's Order. (Last name not recorded.)

---, Bentogomery Prisoner 1173. Rank: Seaman, from: Decatur, Privateer.
    Cap: 05 Jun 1814 at Sea by HM Ship Rhin Int: 20 Jun 1814 Dis: 12 Aug 1814.
    Received from HM Ship Rhin. Board's Order. (Last name not recorded.)

---, Boudon Prisoner 1054. Rank: Seaman, from: Casada el Narino, Privateer.
    Cap: 29 May 1814 at Sea by HM Ship Rhin Int: 04 Jun 1814 Dis: 10 Aug 1814.
    Carthagenaian. Received from North Star. Board's Order. (Last name not recorded.)

---, Boungault Prisoner 1046. Rank: 1 Mate, from: Casada el Narino, Privateer.
    Cap: 29 May 1814 at Sea by HM Ship Rhin Int: 04 Jun 1814 Dis: 21 Aug 1814.
    Carthagenaian. Received from North Star. Board's Order. (Last name not recorded.)

---, Celestier Prisoner 774. Rank: Boy, from: San Francisco de Paula, Privateer.
    Cap: 02 Oct 1813 at Sea by Forrester Int: 07 Oct 1813 Dis: 11 Jan 1814.
    Received from Forrester. per order. (Last name not recorded.)

---, Chripo Prisoner 826. Rank: Seaman, from: Enterprize, Privateer.
    Cap: 15 Nov 1813 at Sea by Argo Int: 19 Nov 1813 Died: 14 May 1814.
    A Carthagenaian. Received from Argo. Killed by the Guard. (Last name not recorded.)

---, Comasin Prisoner 1087. Rank: Seaman, from: Casada el Narino, Privateer.
    Cap: 29 May 1814 at Sea by HM Ship Rhin Int: 04 Jun 1814 Dis: 18 Aug 1814.
    Carthagenaian. Received from North Star. Board's Order. (Last name not recorded.)

---, Deudoit Prisoner 1071. Rank: Seaman, from: Casada el Narino, Privateer.
    Cap: 29 May 1814 at Sea by HM Ship Rhin Int: 04 Jun 1814 Dis: 01 Aug 1814.
    Carthagenaian. Received from North Star. Board's Order. (Last name not recorded.)

---, Duchazrell Prisoner 1174. Rank: Seaman, from: Decatur, Privateer.
    Cap: 05 Jun 1814 at Sea by HM Ship Rhin Int: 20 Jun 1814 Dis: 29 Jul 1814.
    Received from HM Ship Rhin. Board's Order. (Last name not recorded.)

---, Dupre Prisoner 1191. Rank: Seaman, from: Decatur, Privateer.
    Cap: 05 Jun 1814 at Sea by HM Ship Rhin Int: 20 Jun 1814 Dis: 29 Jul 1814.
    Received from HM Ship Rhin. Board's Order. (Last name not recorded.)

---, Felis Prisoner 783. Rank: Boy, from: San Francisco de Paula, Privateer.
    Cap: 02 Oct 1813 at Sea by Forrester Int: 07 Oct 1813 Dis: 21 Jul 1814.
    Received from Forrester. Board's Order. (Last name not recorded.)

---, Francisco Prisoner 758. Rank: Seaman, from: San Francisco de Paula, Privateer.
    Cap: 02 Oct 1813 at Sea by Forrester Int: 07 Oct 1813 Escaped: 30 Dec 1813.
    Received from Forrester. Escaped. (Last name not recorded.)

---, Francisco Prisoner 833. Rank: Seaman, from: Enterprize, Privateer.
    Cap: 15 Nov 1813 at Sea by Argo Int: 19 Nov 1813 Escaped: 30 Dec 1813.
    A Carthagenaian. Received from Argo. Escaped. (Last name not recorded.)

---, Gasparo Prisoner 1052. Rank: Seaman, from: Casada el Narino, Privateer.
    Cap: 29 May 1814 at Sea by HM Ship Rhin Int: 04 Jun 1814 Dis: 30 Jul 1814.
    Carthagenaian. Received from North Star. Board's Order. (Last name not recorded.)

---, Georges Prisoner 827. Rank: Seaman, from: Enterprize, Privateer.
    Cap: 15 Nov 1813 at Sea by Argo Int: 19 Nov 1813 Dis: 16 Aug 1814.
    A Carthagenaian. Received from Argo. Board's Order. (Last name not recorded.)

---, Gout Prisoner 1149. Rank: Seaman, from: Decatur, Privateer.
    Cap: 05 Jun 1814 at Sea by HM Ship Rhin Int: 20 Jun 1814 Dis: 08 Aug 1814.
    Received from HM Ship Rhin. Board's Order. (Last name not recorded.)

---, Hermon Prisoner 600. Rank: Boy, from: Le Ventura, Privateer.
    Cap: 13 Mar 1813 at Sea by Cossac Int: 18 Mar 1813 Dis: 22 Jul 1814.
    Received from Cossac. Board's Order. (Last name not recorded.)

American Prisoners of War Held at Jamaica During the War of 1812

---, Isaac   Prisoner 1062. Rank: Seaman, from: Casada el Narino, Privateer.
    Cap: 29 May 1814 at Sea by HM Ship Rhin Int: 04 Jun 1814 Dis: 18 Aug 1814.
    Carthagenaian. Received from North Star. Board's Order. (Last name not recorded.)

---, Joseph   Prisoner 829. Rank: Seaman, from: Enterprize, Privateer.
    Cap: 15 Nov 1813 at Sea by Argo Int: 19 Nov 1813 Dis: 12 Aug 1814.
    A Carthagenaian. Received from Argo. Board's Order. (Last name not recorded.)

---, Lefarque   Prisoner 1178. Rank: Seaman, from: Decatur, Privateer.
    Cap: 05 Jun 1814 at Sea by HM Ship Rhin Int: 20 Jun 1814 Dis: 08 Aug 1814.
    Received from HM Ship Rhin. Board's Order. (Last name not recorded.)

---, Lefure   Prisoner 1127. Rank: Captain Arms, from: Decatur, Privateer.
    Cap: 05 Jun 1814 at Sea by HM Ship Rhin Int: 20 Jun 1814 Dis: 21 Jul 1814.
    Received from HM Ship Rhin. Board's Order. (Last name not recorded.)

---, Leverien   Prisoner 1049. Rank: Seaman, from: Casada el Narino, Privateer.
    Cap: 29 May 1814 at Sea by HM Ship Rhin Int: 04 Jun 1814 Dis: 29 Jul 1814.
    Carthagenaian. Received from North Star. Board's Order. (Last name not recorded.)

---, Luidoff   Prisoner 624. Rank: Seaman, from: Mary Ann, Privateer.
    Cap: 05 May 1813 at Sea by Sapphire Int: 07 May 1813 Dis: 21 Jul 1814.
    Received from Sapphire. Board's Order. (Last name not recorded.)

---, Manuel   Prisoner 834. Rank: Seaman, from: Enterprize, Privateer.
    Cap: 15 Nov 1813 at Sea by Argo Int: 19 Nov 1813 Dis: 18 Aug 1814.
    A Carthagenaian. Received from Argo. Board's Order. (Last name not recorded.)

---, Martin   Prisoner 803. Rank: Seaman, from: Enterprize, Privateer.
    Cap: 15 Nov 1813 at Sea by Argo Int: 19 Nov 1813 Dis: 11 Jan 1813.
    A Carthagenaian. Received from Argo. per order. (Date of discharge should be January 11, 1814. Last name not recorded.)

---, Oseana   Prisoner 807. Rank: Seaman, from: Enterprize, Privateer.
    Cap: 15 Nov 1813 at Sea by Argo Int: 19 Nov 1813 Dis: 11 Jan 1814.
    A Carthagenaian. Received from Argo. per order. (Last name not recorded.)

---, Pick a Pick   Prisoner 1172. Rank: Seaman, from: Decatur, Privateer.
    Cap: 05 Jun 1814 at Sea by HM Ship Rhin Int: 20 Jun 1814 Dis: 08 Aug 1814.
    Received from HM Ship Rhin. Board's Order. (Last name not recorded.)

---, Piudtel   Prisoner 907. Rank: Seaman, from: San Francisco Navier, Brig.
    Cap: 05 Dec 1813 at Sea by Sappho Int: 15 Dec 1813 Dis: 08 Aug 1814.
    Taken in the Recaptured Spanish Brig. Prize to the Carthagenaian Privateer Carthagenaian. Received from Sappho. Board's Order. (Last name not recorded.)

---, Sequnda   Prisoner 1235. Rank: Not Legible, from: La Union, Spanish Brig.
    Cap: 03 Aug 1814 at Sea by Variable Int: 06 Aug 1814 Dis: 23 Aug 1814.
    Recaptured from the Carthagenaian Privateer White Horse. Received from Variable. Board's Order. (Last name not recorded.)

---, Velario   Prisoner 769. Rank: Seaman, from: San Francisco de Paula, Privateer.
    Cap: 02 Oct 1813 at Sea by Forrester Int: 07 Oct 1813 Dis: 11 Jan 1814.
    Received from Forrester. per order. (Last name not recorded.)

---, Ventura   Prisoner 772. Rank: Seaman, from: San Francisco de Paula, Privateer.
    Cap: 02 Oct 1813 at Sea by Forrester Int: 07 Oct 1813 Dis: 01 Aug 1814.
    Received from Forrester. Board's Order. (Last name not recorded.)

Adair, Samuel   Prisoner 1493. Rank: Boy, from: Not Recorded, Not Recorded.
    Cap: 20 Dec 1814 at Sea by Lacedaemonian Int: 04 Feb 1815 Dis: 08 Feb 1815.
    Taken for Passage to Jamaica Depot. Received from Rota. per order of Sir TM Hardy as a Non-Combatant.

Adams, Cornelius   Prisoner 172. Rank: Mate, from: Hamilton, Merchant Vessel.
    Cap: 28 Sep 1812 at Sea by Southampton Int: 07 Oct 1812 Dis: 09 May 1813.
    Received from Southampton. To America for Exchange.

Adams, Joseph C   Prisoner 1467. Rank: Seaman, from: Not Recorded, Not Recorded.
    Cap: 21 Dec 1814 at Sea by Severn Int: 04 Feb 1815 Dis: 11 Feb 1815.
    Taken for Passage to Jamaica Depot. Received from Rota. Into HMS Ramillies per order of Sir T M Hardy.

Adrie, Domingo   Prisoner 1158. Rank: at Sea, from: Decatur, Privateer.
    Cap: 05 Jun 1814 at Sea by HM Ship Rhin Int: 20 Jun 1814 Dis: 22 Jul 1814.
    Received from HM Ship Rhin. Board's Order.

Akenford, John   Prisoner 1545. Rank: Passenger, from: Le Expedecion, Merchant Vessel.
    Cap: at Sea by HMS Drake Int: 09 Mar 1815 Dis: 16 Mar 1815.
    Received from HMS Rinaldo. being Non-Combatants. (Date of capture not recorded.)

American Prisoners of War Held at Jamaica During the War of 1812

Albarets, Alanasta   Prisoner 1255. Rank: Captain, from: Grauosa, Merchant Vessel.
    Cap: 29 Jun 1814 at Sea by HM Ship Onyx Int: 30 Aug 1814 Dis: 10 Nov 1814.
    Recaptured from the Carethagenians. Received from Shark. Board's Order. (Prisoner numbers 1249 - 1256 all have recorded rank of Captain.)

Albertman, John   Prisoner 596. Rank: Seaman, from: Le Ventura, Privateer.
    Cap: 13 Mar 1813 at Sea by Cossac Int: 18 Mar 1813 Dis: 21 Jul 1814.
    Received from Cossac. Board's Order.

Alexander, James   Prisoner 351. Rank: Seaman, from: Vixen, Man of War.
    Cap: 22 Nov 1812 at Sea by Rhodian late of HM Brig Vixen Int: 14 Dec 1812 Dis: 09 May 1813.
    Received from Rhodian. To America for Exchange.

Alexander, Lewis   Prisoner 1287. Rank: Passenger, from: Dolores, Merchant Schooner.
    Cap: at Sea by HM Sloop Anaconda Int: 07 Oct 1814 Dis: 29 Oct 1814.
    Received from HM Sloop Anaconda. Board's Order. (Date of capture not recorded.)

Alexander, Luis   Prisoner 1084. Rank: Seaman, from: Casada el Narino, Privateer.
    Cap: 29 May 1814 at Sea by HM Ship Rhin Int: 04 Jun 1814 Dis: 14 Jul 1814.
    Carthagenaian. Received from North Star. Per order, being a French Subject.

Alexander, Samuel   Prisoner 663. Rank: Seaman, from: Lovely Lass, Privateer.
    Cap: 21 May 1813 at Sea by Circe Int: 23 May 1813 Dis: 01 Aug 1814.
    Received from Forrester. To American Cartel Brig Aualostaw.

Allen, Asa   Prisoner 427. Rank: Private, from: Vixen, Man of War.
    Cap: 22 Nov 1812 at Sea by Rhodian Int: 14 Dec 1812 Dis: 09 May 1813.
    Received from Brazier. To America for Exchange.

Allen, Bernard   Prisoner 944. Rank: Seaman, from: Coquelle, Merchant Vessel.
    Cap: 24 Dec 1813 at Sea by Sapphire Int: 02 Jan 1814 Dis: 01 Aug 1814.
    Received from Sapphire. To American Cartel Brig Aualostaw.

Allen, Ebenezer   Prisoner 59. Rank: Seaman, from: Not Recorded, Not Recorded.
    Cap: 20 Aug 1812 Not Recorded by Not Recorded Int: 03 Sep 1812 Dis: 09 May 1813.
    Prison Ship at New Providence. Received from HM Schooner Decouverte. to America for Exchange.

Allen, Francis   Prisoner 842. Rank: Seaman, from: Maria, An American Merchant Schooner.
    Cap: 15 Nov 1813 at Sea by Argo Int: 19 Nov 1813 Dis: 21 Jul 1814.
    Received from Argo. Board's Order.

Allen, Henry   Prisoner 488. Rank: Seaman, from: Philip, Merchant Vessel.
    Cap: 28 Jan 1813 at Sea by Morgiana Int: 30 Jan 1813 Dis: 04 Apr 1813.
    Recaptured. Received from Morgiana. To America for Exchange.

Allen, James W   Prisoner 50. Rank: Lieutenant, from: Assaw, Merchant Vessel.
    Cap: 28 Jul 1812 at Sea by HM Ship Garland Int: 27 Aug 1812 Dis: 28 Aug 1812.
    Recapt from Paul Jones Privateer. Received from HM Ship Herald. To Parole.

Allen, John   Prisoner 521. Rank: 2 Lieutenant, from: Defiance, Privateer.
    Cap: 15 Mar 1813 at Sea by Nimrod Int: 17 Mar 1813 Dis: 09 May 1813.
    Received from Nimrod. To America for Exchange.

Allen, Joseph   Prisoner 123. Rank: Seaman, from: Morning Star, Merchant Vessel.
    Cap: 08 Sep 1812 at Sea by HMS Cyane Int: 07 Oct 1812 Dis: 24 Jul 1813.
    Received from Cyane. To American Cartel Brig Aualostaw.

Ambrosia, John   Prisoner 812. Rank: Seaman, from: Enterprize, Privateer.
    Cap: 15 Nov 1813 at Sea by Argo Int: 19 Nov 1813 Dis: 28 Jul 1814.
    A Carthagenaian. Received from Argo. Board's Order.

Ammors, John   Prisoner 421. Rank: Private, from: Vixen, Man of War.
    Cap: 22 Nov 1812 at Sea by Rhodian Int: 14 Dec 1812 Dis: 09 May 1813.
    Received from Brazier. To America for Exchange.

Amontage, Louis   Prisoner 1153. Rank: Seaman, from: Decatur, Privateer.
    Cap: 05 Jun 1814 at Sea by HM Ship Rhin Int: 20 Jun 1814 Dis: 22 Jul 1814.
    Received from HM Ship Rhin. Board's Order.

Anderson, John   Prisoner 1362. Rank: Seaman, from: American Gunboats, Not Recorded.
    Cap: 05 Jan 1815 near New Orleans by Plantagenet Int: 27 Jan 1815 Dis: 05 Feb 1815.
    Taken in the American Gun Boats near New Orleans. Received from Ramilies. Into HM Ship Diomede per order of Sir TM Hardy Baronet.

Andre, Antonie   Prisoner 1326. Rank: Seaman, from: Not Recorded, Not Recorded.
    Cap: at Sea by HMS Shark Int: 07 Jan 1815 Dis: 10 Jan 1815.
    Ship 'Name Unknown'. Received from HMS Shark. Board's Order. (Date of capture not recorded.)

Anquin, Anthony   Prisoner 605. Rank: Lieutenant, from: Hazard, Privateer.
    Cap: 12 Mar 1813 Providence by Moselle Int: 29 Mar 1813 Dis: 24 Jul 1813.
    Received from Moselle. To American Cartel Brig Aualostaw.

American Prisoners of War Held at Jamaica During the War of 1812

Anthony, Francisco   Prisoner 578. Rank: Boatswain, from: Le Ventura, Privateer.
    Cap: 13 Mar 1813 at Sea by Cossac Int: 18 Mar 1813 Dis: 16 Aug 1814.
    Received from Cossac. Board's Order.

Anthony, Juan   Prisoner 584. Rank: Seaman, from: Le Ventura, Privateer.
    Cap: 13 Mar 1813 at Sea by Cossac Int: 18 Mar 1813 Dis: 12 Aug 1814.
    Received from Cossac. Board's Order.

Antonia, Joseph   Prisoner 1442. Rank: Seaman, from: American Gunboats, Not Recorded.
    Cap: 05 Jan 1815 near New Orleans by Plantagenet Int: 27 Jan 1815 Dis: 05 Feb 1815.
    Taken in the American Gun Boats near New Orleans. Received from Ramilies. Into HM Ship Diomede per order of Sir TM Hardy Baronet.

Antonio, Jean   Prisoner 588. Rank: Seaman, from: Le Ventura, Privateer.
    Cap: 13 Mar 1813 at Sea by Cossac Int: 18 Mar 1813 Dis: 08 Aug 1814.
    Received from Cossac. Board's Order.

Antonio, Jose   Prisoner 1325. Rank: Seaman, from: Not Recorded, Not Recorded.
    Cap: at Sea by HMS Shark Int: 07 Jan 1815 Dis: 10 Jan 1815.
    Ship 'Name Unknown'. Received from HMS Shark. Board's Order. (Date of capture not recorded.)

Antonio, Joseph   Prisoner 997. Rank: Seaman, from: Farmer's Daughter, Merchant Vessel.
    Cap: 30 Mar 1814 at Sea by Leviathan Int: 03 Apr 1814 Dis: 21 Jul 1814.
    Received from Leviathan. Board's Order.

Antonio, Joseph   Prisoner 1108. Rank: Seaman, from: Romano & Adamante, Merchant Brig.
    Cap: 31 May 1814 at Sea by Leviathan Int: 17 Jun 1814 Dis: 04 Sep 1814.
    Received from Leviathan. Board's Order.

Antonio, Juan P   Prisoner 1105. Rank: Seaman, from: Romano & Adamante, Merchant Brig.
    Cap: 31 May 1814 at Sea by Leviathan Int: 17 Jun 1814 Dis: 18 Aug 1814.
    Received from Leviathan. Board's Order.

Antonio, Manuel   Prisoner 1189. Rank: Seaman, from: Decatur, Privateer.
    Cap: 05 Jun 1814 at Sea by HM Ship Rhin Int: 20 Jun 1814 Dis: 12 Aug 1814.
    Received from HM Ship Rhin. Board's Order.

Anwiste, Hugh   Prisoner 161. Rank: Seaman, from: Rebecca Sims, Merchant Vessel.
    Cap: 12 Sep 1812 at Sea by Southampton Int: 07 Oct 1812 Escaped: 09 May 1813.
    Received from Southampton. Escaped.

Apt, James   Prisoner 321. Rank: Seaman, from: Pirtshire, English Merchant Ship.
    Cap: Nov 1812 at Sea by Fawn Int: 06 Dec 1812 Dis: 09 May 1813.
    Recaptured. Eagle Privateer. Received from Fawn. To America for Exchange. (Day of capture not recorded.)

Aquilar, Lorenzo   Prisoner 1223. Rank: Seaman, from: La Union, Spanish Brig.
    Cap: 03 Aug 1814 at Sea by Variable Int: 06 Aug 1814 Dis: 21 Aug 1814.
    Recaptured from the Carthagenaian Privateer White Horse. Received from Variable. Board's Order.

Aquilar, Pedro Jose   Prisoner 1067. Rank: Seaman, from: Casada el Narino, Privateer.
    Cap: 29 May 1814 at Sea by HM Ship Rhin Int: 04 Jun 1814 Dis: 18 Aug 1814.
    Carthagenaian. Received from North Star. Board's Order.

Aquilaro, J   Prisoner 1088. Rank: Seaman, from: Casada el Narino, Privateer.
    Cap: 29 May 1814 at Sea by HM Ship Rhin Int: 04 Jun 1814 Dis: 18 Aug 1814.
    Carthagenaian. Received from North Star. Board's Order. (First name not legible.)

Aquire, Bernardo   Prisoner 851. Rank: Seaman, from: Le Galzo, Spanish Brig.
    Cap: 17 Nov 1813 at Sea by Variable Int: 28 Nov 1813 Dis: 08 Aug 1814.
    Recaptured from the Carthagenaian Privateer Le Legislateur. Received from Variable. Board's Order.

Arbona, John   Prisoner 651. Rank: Surgeon, from: Lovely Lass, Privateer.
    Cap: 21 May 1813 at Sea by Circe Int: 23 May 1813 Dis: 24 Jul 1813.
    Received from Forrester. To American Cartel Brig Aualostaw.

Armstrong, Charles   Prisoner 1012. Rank: 2 Mate, from: Chance, Privateer.
    Cap: 01 Apr 1814 at Sea by Statira Int: 20 Apr 1814 Dis: 02 Jan 1815.
    Received from Statira. Into HM Ship Sultan per order of Captain John West.

Army, Lewis   Prisoner 697. Rank: Seaman, from: Lovely Lass, Privateer.
    Cap: 15 May 1813 at Sea by Circe Int: 29 May 1813 Dis: 28 Jul 1814.
    Received from Circe. Board's Order.

Arrickson, D   Prisoner 407. Rank: Seaman, from: Vixen, Man of War.
    Cap: 22 Nov 1812 at Sea by Rhodian late of US Brig Vixen Int: 14 Dec 1812 Dis: 09 May 1813.
    Received from Rhodian. To America for Exchange.

Arrvis, Jose   Prisoner 927. Rank: Seaman, from: Cartagenaian, Privateer.
    Cap: 05 Dec 1813 at Sea by Sappho Int: 15 Dec 1813 Dis: 23 Aug 1814.
    Belonging to the Carthagenaian Privateer Carthagenaian. Received from Sappho. Board's Order.

American Prisoners of War Held at Jamaica During the War of 1812

Artego, John   Prisoner 1143. Rank: Seaman, from: Decatur, Privateer.
  Cap: 05 Jun 1814 at Sea by HM Ship Rhin Int: 20 Jun 1814 Dis: 18 Aug 1814.
  Received from HM Ship Rhin. Board's Order.
Askew, James   Prisoner 939. Rank: Seaman, from: Coquelle, Merchant Vessel.
  Cap: 24 Dec 1813 at Sea by Sapphire Int: 02 Jan 1814 Dis: 01 Aug 1814.
  Received from Sapphire. To American Cartel Brig Aualostaw.
Aucruen, John   Prisoner 1186. Rank: Seaman, from: Decatur, Privateer.
  Cap: 05 Jun 1814 at Sea by HM Ship Rhin Int: 20 Jun 1814 Dis: 02 Jan 1815.
  Received from HM Ship Rhin. Into HM Ship Sultan per order of Captain John West.
Augustine, Cadet   Prisoner 753. Rank: Clerk, from: San Francisco de Paula, Privateer.
  Cap: 02 Oct 1813 at Sea by Forrester Int: 07 Oct 1813 Dis: 12 Aug 1813.
  Received from Forrester. Board's Order. (Prisoner numbers 750 - 755 all have recorded rank of clerk.)
Aurry, Lewis   Prisoner 747. Rank: Commander, from: San Francisco de Paula, Privateer.
  Cap: 02 Oct 1813 at Sea by Forrester Int: 07 Oct 1813 Escaped: 30 Jan 1814.
  Received from Forrester. Escaped.
Bachindoz, Enock   Prisoner 980. Rank: Seaman, from: Suspense, Merchant Vessel.
  Cap: 20 Feb 1814 at Sea by Leviathan Int: 26 Mar 1814 Dis: 01 Aug 1814.
  Received from Mohawk. To American Cartel Brig Aualostaw.
Baco, F   Prisoner 1091. Rank: Seaman, from: Casada el Narino, Privateer.
  Cap: 29 May 1814 at Sea by HM Ship Rhin Int: 04 Jun 1814 Dis: 21 Aug 1814.
  Carthagenaian. Received from North Star. Board's Order. (First name not legible.)
Bailey, Joseph   Prisoner 104. Rank: Seaman, from: Poor Sailor, Privateer.
  Cap: 13 Sep 1812 at Sea by Garland Int: 18 Sep 1812 Dis: 24 Jul 1813.
  Received from Garland. To American Cartel Brig Aualostaw.
Bailey, Samuel   Prisoner 1293. Rank: Passenger, from: Dolores, Merchant Schooner.
  Cap: at Sea by HM Sloop Anaconda Int: 07 Oct 1814 Dis: 02 Jan 1815.
  Received from HM Sloop Anaconda. Into HM Ship Sultan per order of Captain John West. (Date of capture not recorded.)
Baker, James   Prisoner 491. Rank: Seaman, from: Philip, Merchant Vessel.
  Cap: 28 Jan 1813 at Sea by Morgiana Int: 30 Jan 1813 Dis: 24 Jul 1813.
  Recaptured. Received from Morgiana. To American Cartel Brig Aualostaw.
Baker, Peter   Prisoner 722. Rank: Seaman, from: Mount Vernon, Merchant Man.
  Cap: at Sea by Argo Int: 27 Jun 1813 Dis: 02 Jul 1813.
  Received from Mount Vernon. To Mount Vernon per order of Adml Brown this date. (Date of capture not recorded.)
Baker, Thomas   Prisoner 1307. Rank: Master, from: Nettervitte, Merchant Schooner.
  Cap: Not Recorded by HM Sloop Onyx Int: 01 Jan 1815 Dis: 02 Jan 1815.
  Received from HM Sloop Onyx. Into HM Ship Sultan per order of Captain John West. (Date of capture not recorded.)
Baker, William   Prisoner 551. Rank: Seaman, from: Defiance, Privateer.
  Cap: 15 Mar 1813 at Sea by Nimrod Int: 17 Mar 1813 Escaped: 28 Jun 1813.
  Received from Nimrod. Escaped.
Bakers, G D   Prisoner 1393. Rank: Seaman, from: American Gunboats, Not Recorded.
  Cap: 05 Jan 1815 near New Orleans by Plantagenet Int: 27 Jan 1815 Dis: 05 Feb 1815.
  Taken in the American Gun Boats near New Orleans. Received from Ramilies. Into HM Ship Diomede per order of Sir TM Hardy Baronet.
Balard, Peter   Prisoner 629. Rank: Seaman, from: Mary Ann, Privateer.
  Cap: 05 May 1813 at Sea by Sapphire Int: 07 May 1813 Dis: 27 Jul 1814.
  Received from Sapphire. Board's Order.
Baldwin, Pearson   Prisoner 484. Rank: Prize Master, from: Philip, Merchant Vessel.
  Cap: 28 Jan 1813 at Sea by Morgiana Int: 30 Jan 1813 Dis: 04 Apr 1813.
  Recaptured. Received from Morgiana. To America for Exchange.
Baldwin, Theophilus   Prisoner 1321. Rank: Seaman, from: Triton, Merchant Ship.
  Cap: Not Recorded by Not Recorded Int: 30 Dec 1814 Dis: 02 Jan 1815.
  These men were sent from the Triton Merchant Ship for Notorious behavior, had previously shipped in her as Englishmen. Received from HM Ship Suttan. Into HM Ship Sultan per order of Captain John West. (Date capture not recorded.)
Baley, Oliver   Prisoner 631. Rank: Seaman, from: Mary Ann, Privateer.
  Cap: 05 May 1813 at Sea by Sapphire Int: 07 May 1813 Dis: 01 Aug 1814.
  Received from Sapphire. To American Cartel Brig Aualostaw.
Ball, E   Prisoner 800. Rank: Seaman, from: Enterprize, Privateer.
  Cap: 15 Nov 1813 at Sea by Argo Int: 19 Nov 1813 Died: 30 Dec 1813.
  A Carthagenaian. Received from Argo. Killed by the Guard.

American Prisoners of War Held at Jamaica During the War of 1812

Ballabergen, Peter   Prisoner 1458. Rank: Seaman, from: Not Recorded, Not Recorded.
    Cap: 21 Dec 1814 at Sea by Severn Int: 04 Feb 1815 Dis: 08 Feb 1815.
    Taken for Passage to Jamaica Depot. Received from Rota. per order of Sir TM Hardy as a Non-Combatant.

Ballow, William   Prisoner 2. Rank: Seaman, from: Assaw, Merchant Vessel.
    Cap: 28 Jul 1812 at Sea by Garland Int: 22 Aug 1812 Dis: 04 Apr 1813.
    Recaptured having been taken by the American Privateer the Paul Jones. Received from Garland. to America for Exchange.

Banks, William   Prisoner 165. Rank: Seaman, from: Rebecca Sims, Merchant Vessel.
    Cap: 12 Sep 1812 at Sea by Southampton Int: 07 Oct 1812 Dis: 01 Mar 1813.
    Received from Southampton. per Order of Admiral Stirling.

Bantista, Juan   Prisoner 1073. Rank: Seaman, from: Casada el Narino, Privateer.
    Cap: 29 May 1814 at Sea by HM Ship Rhin Int: 04 Jun 1814 Dis: 23 Aug 1814.
    Carthagenaian. Received from North Star. Board's Order.

Baptist, John   Prisoner 14. Rank: Seaman, from: Superb, Merchant Vessel.
    Cap: 02 Aug 1812 at Sea by Garland Int: 22 Aug 1812 Escaped: 24 Apr 1813.
    Received from Garland. Escaped.

Baptist, Joseph   Prisoner 534. Rank: Seaman, from: Defiance, Privateer.
    Cap: 15 Mar 1813 at Sea by Nimrod Int: 17 Mar 1813 Dis: 24 Jul 1813.
    Received from Nimrod. To American Cartel Brig Aualostaw.

Baptista, Antonio   Prisoner 765. Rank: Seaman, from: San Francisco de Paula, Privateer.
    Cap: 02 Oct 1813 at Sea by Forrester Int: 07 Oct 1813 Dis: 11 Jan 1814.
    Received from Forrester. per order.

Baptista, Juan   Prisoner 1106. Rank: Seaman, from: Romano & Adamante, Merchant Brig.
    Cap: 31 May 1814 at Sea by Leviathan Int: 17 Jun 1814 Dis: 18 Aug 1814.
    Received from Leviathan. Board's Order.

Baptiste, John   Prisoner 1312. Rank: Seaman, from: Nettervitte, Merchant Schooner.
    Cap: Not Recorded by HM Sloop Onyx Int: 30 Dec 1814 Dis: 02 Jan 1815.
    Received from HM Sloop Onyx. Into HM Ship Sultan per order of Captain John West. (Date of capture not recorded.)

Baque, Jean   Prisoner 1281. Rank: Passenger, from: Dolores, Merchant Schooner.
    Cap: at Sea by HM Sloop Anaconda Int: 07 Oct 1814 Dis: 29 Oct 1814.
    Received from HM Sloop Anaconda. Board's Order. (Date of capture not recorded.)

Barchela, Andres   Prisoner 911. Rank: Seaman, from: San Francisco Navier, Brig.
    Cap: 05 Dec 1813 at Sea by Sappho Int: 15 Dec 1813 Dis: 22 Jul 1814.
    Taken in the Recaptured Spanish Brig. Prize to the Carthagenaian Privateer Carthagenaian. Received from Sappho. Board's Order.

Barderse, Josse   Prisoner 595. Rank: Seaman, from: Le Ventura, Privateer.
    Cap: 13 Mar 1813 at Sea by Cossac Int: 18 Mar 1813 Dis: 12 Aug 1814.
    Received from Cossac. Board's Order.

Barker, Abraham   Prisoner 1370. Rank: Seaman, from: American Gunboats, Not Recorded.
    Cap: 05 Jan 1815 near New Orleans by Plantagenet Int: 27 Jan 1815 Dis: 05 Feb 1815.
    Taken in the American Gun Boats near New Orleans. Received from Ramilies. Into HM Ship Diomede per order of Sir TM Hardy Baronet.

Barlez, Juan   Prisoner 577. Rank: Gunner, from: Le Ventura, Privateer.
    Cap: 13 Mar 1813 at Sea by Cossac Int: 18 Mar 1813 Escaped: 28 Jun 1813.
    Received from Cossac. Escaped.

Barlow, Aroa   Prisoner 654. Rank: Seaman, from: Lovely Lass, Privateer.
    Cap: 21 May 1813 at Sea by Circe Int: 23 May 1813 Dis: 01 Aug 1814.
    Received from Forrester. To American Cartel Brig Aualostaw.

Barlow, John   Prisoner 821. Rank: Seaman, from: Enterprize, Privateer.
    Cap: 15 Nov 1813 at Sea by Argo Int: 19 Nov 1813 Dis: 11 Jan 1814.
    A Carthagenaian. Received from Argo. per order.

Barlow, Rodney   Prisoner 1479. Rank: Seaman, from: Not Recorded, Not Recorded.
    Cap: 21 Dec 1814 at Sea by Severn Int: 04 Feb 1815 Dis: 11 Feb 1815.
    Taken for Passage to Jamaica Depot. Received from Rota. Into HMS Ramillies per order of Sir T M Hardy.

Barnes, John   Prisoner 694. Rank: Seaman, from: Lovely Lass, Privateer.
    Cap: 15 May 1813 at Sea by Circe Int: 29 May 1813 Dis: 21 Jul 1814.
    Received from Circe. Board's Order.

Barr, Benjamin   Prisoner 277. Rank: Seaman, from: Joseph & Mary, Privateer.
    Cap: 24 Nov 1812 at Sea by Narcissus Int: 26 Nov 1812 Dis: 24 Jul 1813.
    Received from Narcissus. To American Cartel Brig Aualostaw.

American Prisoners of War Held at Jamaica During the War of 1812

Barrel, Juan   Prisoner 917. Rank: Seaman, from: San Francisco Navier, Brig.
    Cap: 05 Dec 1813 at Sea by Sappho Int: 15 Dec 1813 Dis: 01 Aug 1814.
    Taken in the Recaptured Spanish Brig. Prize to the Carthagenaian Privateer Carthagenaian. Received from Sappho. Board's Order.

Barrett, Peter   Prisoner 1481. Rank: Seaman, from: Not Recorded, Not Recorded.
    Cap: 21 Dec 1814 at Sea by Severn Int: 04 Feb 1815 Dis: 11 Feb 1815.
    Taken for Passage to Jamaica Depot. Received from Rota. Into HMS Ramillies per order of Sir T M Hardy.

Barritt, Roman   Prisoner 748. Rank: Lieutenant, from: San Francisco de Paula, Privateer.
    Cap: 02 Oct 1813 at Sea by Forrester Int: 07 Oct 1813 Dis: 11 Jan 1814.
    Received from Forrester. per order.

Barry, John   Prisoner 1454. Rank: Captain, from: Not Recorded, Not Recorded.
    Cap: 21 Dec 1814 at Sea by Severn Int: 04 Feb 1815 Dis: 08 Feb 1815.
    Taken for Passage to Jamaica Depot. Received from Rota. per order of Sir TM Hardy as a Non-Combatant.

Bartire, John   Prisoner 810. Rank: Seaman, from: Enterprize, Privateer.
    Cap: 15 Nov 1813 at Sea by Argo Int: 19 Nov 1813 Dis: 29 Jul 1814.
    A Carthagenaian. Received from Argo. Board's Order.

Bartlett, H G   Prisoner 1473. Rank: Seaman, from: Not Recorded, Not Recorded.
    Cap: 21 Dec 1814 at Sea by Severn Int: 04 Feb 1815 Dis: 11 Feb 1815.
    Taken for Passage to Jamaica Depot. Received from Rota. Into HMS Ramillies per order of Sir T M Hardy.

Basante, Jose   Prisoner 779. Rank: Seaman, from: San Francisco de Paula, Privateer.
    Cap: 02 Oct 1813 at Sea by Forrester Int: 07 Oct 1813 Dis: 11 Jan 1814.
    Received from Forrester. per order.

Bata, Peter   Prisoner 627. Rank: Seaman, from: Mary Ann, Privateer.
    Cap: 05 May 1813 at Sea by Sapphire Int: 07 May 1813 Dis: 21 Jul 1814.
    Received from Sapphire. Board's Order.

Bateiers, Platricia   Prisoner 1276. Rank: Seaman, from: Dolores, Merchant Schooner.
    Cap: at Sea by HM Sloop Anaconda Int: 07 Oct 1814 Dis: 10 Nov 1814.
    Received from HM Sloop Anaconda. Board's Order. (Date of capture not recorded.)

Batista, Luis   Prisoner 918. Rank: Seaman, from: San Francisco Navier, Brig.
    Cap: 05 Dec 1813 at Sea by Sappho Int: 15 Dec 1813 Dis: 29 Jul 1814.
    Taken in the Recaptured Spanish Brig. Prize to the Carthagenaian Privateer Carthagenaian. Received from Sappho. Board's Order.

Batiste, John   Prisoner 1016. Rank: Seaman, from: Chance, Privateer.
    Cap: 01 Apr 1814 at Sea by Statira Int: 20 Apr 1814 Dis: 21 Jul 1814.
    Received from Statira. Board's Order.

Battle, Joseph   Prisoner 1263. Rank: Seaman, from: Not Recorded, Not Recorded.
    Cap: Kingston by Not Recorded Int: 08 Sep 1814 Dis: 02 Jan 1815.
    Seized at Kingston last night being Americans. Received from Talbot. Into HM Ship Sultan per order of Captain John West. (Date of capture assumed to be September 7, 1814.)

Bayley, Frederick   Prisoner 430. Rank: Private, from: Vixen, Man of War.
    Cap: 22 Nov 1812 at Sea by Rhodian Int: 14 Dec 1812 Dis: 09 May 1813.
    Received from Brazier. To America for Exchange.

Bayley, Gardner   Prisoner 274. Rank: Corporal, from: Joseph & Mary, Privateer.
    Cap: 24 Nov 1812 at Sea by Narcissus Int: 26 Nov 1812 Dis: 24 Jul 1813.
    Received from Narcissus. To American Cartel Brig Aualostaw.

Baylis, Charles   Prisoner 1496. Rank: Mate, from: Not Recorded, Not Recorded.
    Cap: 20 Dec 1814 at Sea by Lacedaemonian Int: 04 Feb 1815 Dis: 11 Feb 1815.
    Taken for Passage to Jamaica Depot. Received from Rota. Into HMS Ramillies per order of Sir T M Hardy.

Bayne, John   Prisoner 1535. Rank: Pilot, from: William & Mary, Merchant Vessel.
    Cap: 12 Feb 1815 at Sea by HM Sloop Carnation Int: 23 Feb 1815 Dis: 30 Mar 1815.
    Received from HM Sloop Carnation. In consequence of Peace with America.

Beard, Andrew   Prisoner 260. Rank: Seaman, from: Joseph & Mary, Privateer.
    Cap: 24 Nov 1812 at Sea by Narcissus Int: 26 Nov 1812 Dis: 24 Jul 1813.
    Received from Narcissus. To American Cartel Brig Aualostaw.

Beari, Samuel   Prisoner 955. Rank: Mate, from: Swift, Merchant Vessel.
    Cap: at Sea by Leonidas Int: 25 Jan 1814 Dis: 01 Aug 1814.
    Received from Leonidas. To American Cartel Brig Aualostaw. (Date of capture not recorded. Prisoner numbers 951 - 956 all have recorded rank of mate.)

American Prisoners of War Held at Jamaica During the War of 1812

Beck, Francisco   Prisoner 1184. Rank: Seaman, from: Decatur, Privateer.
    Cap: 05 Jun 1814 at Sea by HM Ship Rhin Int: 20 Jun 1814 Dis: 02 Jan 1815.
    Received from HM Ship Rhin. Into HM Ship Sultan per order of Captain John West.

Beck, Michael   Prisoner 1549. Rank: Master, from: John, Merchant Vessel.
    Cap: at Sea by HMS Talbot Int: 20 Mar 1815 Dis: 30 Mar 1815.
    Received from HMS Talbot. In consequence of Peace with America. (Date of capture not recorded.)

Befay, Samuel   Prisoner 460. Rank: Seaman, from: Saratoga, Merchant Vessel.
    Cap: 1813 at Sea by Fawn Int: 13 Jan 1813 Dis: 04 Apr 1813.
    Received from Sapphire. To America for Exchange. (Day and month of capture not recorded.)

Begotte, Juan   Prisoner 764. Rank: Seaman, from: San Francisco de Paula, Privateer.
    Cap: 02 Oct 1813 at Sea by Forrester Int: 07 Oct 1813 Escaped: 30 Dec 1813.
    Received from Forrester. Escaped.

Bell, John   Prisoner 205. Rank: Seaman, from: Blandie, Merchant Vessel.
    Cap: 21 Oct 1812 at Sea by Not Recorded Int: 25 Oct 1812 Dis: 24 Jul 1813.
    Recaptured. Taken from the Recapd Schooner Blandie, belonging to the American Privateer Schooner Comet. Received from Sappho. To American Cartel Brig Aualostaw.

Belor, Miguel   Prisoner 1230. Rank: Seaman, from: La Union, Spanish Brig.
    Cap: 03 Aug 1814 at Sea by Variable Int: 06 Aug 1814 Dis: 23 Aug 1814.
    Recaptured from the Carthagenaian Privateer White Horse. Received from Variable. Board's Order.

Belt, James   Prisoner 25. Rank: Passenger, from: Madisonia, Merchant Vessel.
    Cap: 03 Aug 1812 at Sea by Garland Int: 22 Aug 1812 Dis: 11 Nov 1812.
    Received from Garland. Medosa American Flag of Truce per order of VA Stirling.

Beltram, Martin   Prisoner 1219. Rank: Seaman, from: La Union, Spanish Brig.
    Cap: 03 Aug 1814 at Sea by Variable Int: 06 Aug 1814 Dis: 23 Aug 1814.
    Recaptured from the Carthagenaian Privateer White Horse. Received from Variable. Board's Order.

Bennett, James   Prisoner 883. Rank: Seaman, from: Lapwing, Packet.
    Cap: 08 Dec 1813 at Sea by Barrosa Int: 10 Dec 1813 Dis: 21 Jul 1814.
    Recaptured. Received from Barrosa. Board's Order.

Bennett, William   Prisoner 1407. Rank: Seaman, from: American Gunboats, Not Recorded.
    Cap: 05 Jan 1815 near New Orleans by Plantagenet Int: 27 Jan 1815 Dis: 05 Feb 1815.
    Taken in the American Gun Boats near New Orleans. Received from Ramilies. Into HM Ship Diomede per order of Sir TM Hardy Baronet.

Benson, John   Prisoner 125. Rank: Seaman, from: Morning Star, Merchant Vessel.
    Cap: 08 Sep 1812 at Sea by HMS Cyane Int: 07 Oct 1812 Dis: 24 Jul 1813.
    Received from Cyane. To American Cartel Brig Aualostaw.

Benton, Samuel   Prisoner 994. Rank: Seaman, from: Farmer's Daughter, Merchant Vessel.
    Cap: 30 Mar 1814 at Sea by Leviathan Int: 03 Apr 1814 Dis: 02 Jan 1815.
    Received from Leviathan. Into HM Ship Sultan per order of Captain John West.

Berios, Samoa   Prisoner 1331. Rank: Seaman, from: Not Recorded, Not Recorded.
    Cap: at Sea by HMS Shark Int: 07 Jan 1815 Dis: 10 Jan 1815.
    Ship 'Name Unknown'. Received from HMS Shark. Board's Order. (Date of capture not recorded.)

Berlack, William   Prisoner 609. Rank: Seaman, from: Fly, Merchant Schooner.
    Cap: 15 Apr 1813 at Sea by Argo Int: 18 Apr 1813 Dis: 09 May 1813.
    Received from Argo. To America for Exchange.

Bernard, Leonard   Prisoner 580. Rank: Seaman, from: Le Ventura, Privateer.
    Cap: 13 Mar 1813 at Sea by Cossac Int: 18 Mar 1813 Dis: 12 Aug 1814.
    Received from Cossac. Board's Order.

Bernard, Peter   Prisoner 1277. Rank: Seaman, from: Dolores, Merchant Schooner.
    Cap: at Sea by HM Sloop Anaconda Int: 07 Oct 1814 Dis: 10 Nov 1814.
    Received from HM Sloop Anaconda. Board's Order. (Date of capture not recorded.)

Berry, Gorton   Prisoner 933. Rank: Captain, from: Milly, Schooner.
    Cap: 29 Nov 1813 at Sea by Decouverte Int: 29 Nov 1813 Dis: 01 Jan 1814.
    Taken out of the American Schooner Milly. Received from Decouverte. To Parole. (Dates of capture and internment the same.)

Berry, James   Prisoner 291. Rank: Seaman, from: Mary, Merchant Vessel.
    Cap: 26 Nov 1812 at Sea by Sappho Int: 30 Nov 1812 Dis: 24 Jul 1813.
    Received from Sappho. To American Cartel Brig Aualostaw.

Berto, John   Prisoner 538. Rank: Seaman, from: Defiance, Privateer.
    Cap: 15 Mar 1813 at Sea by Nimrod Int: 17 Mar 1813 Dis: 24 Jul 1813.
    Received from Nimrod. To American Cartel Brig Aualostaw.

American Prisoners of War Held at Jamaica During the War of 1812

Bertrand, Jean   Prisoner 1256. Rank: Captain, from: Grauosa, Merchant Vessel.
    Cap: 29 Jun 1814 at Sea by HM Ship Onyx Int: 30 Aug 1814 Dis: 10 Nov 1814.
    Recaptured from the Carethagenians. Received from Shark. Board's Order. (Prisoner numbers 1249 - 1256 all have recorded rank of Captain.)

Betagh, James   Prisoner 1244. Rank: Passenger but Seaman, from: John, Merchant Vessel.
    Cap: 11 Aug 1814 at Sea by Variable Int: 15 Aug 1814 Dis: 02 Jan 1815.
    Received from Variable. Into HM Ship Sultan per order of Captain John West.

Betincourt, Lewis   Prisoner 417. Rank: Private, from: Vixen, Man of War.
    Cap: 22 Nov 1812 at Sea by Rhodian Int: 14 Dec 1812 Dis: 09 May 1813.
    Received from Brazier. To America for Exchange.

Betincourt, Nathaniel A   Prisoner 425. Rank: Private, from: Vixen, Man of War.
    Cap: 22 Nov 1812 at Sea by Rhodian Int: 14 Dec 1812 Dis: 22 Apr 1814.
    Received from Brazier. Per Order of Rear Adml Brown into the Spanish Vessel Cupida.

Betrange, Pedro   Prisoner 1201. Rank: Seaman, from: Neustra Cantado, Merchant Vessel.
    Cap: 01 Jun 1814 at Sea by HM Ship Argo Int: 27 Jun 1814 Dis: 30 Jul 1814.
    Retaken in the Spanish Ship Neustra Cantado. Received from HM Ship Argo. Board's Order.

Bettys, Henry   Prisoner 266. Rank: Seaman, from: Joseph & Mary, Privateer.
    Cap: 24 Nov 1812 at Sea by Narcissus Int: 26 Nov 1812 Dis: 09 May 1813.
    Received from Narcissus. To America for Exchange.

Bezzett, Robert   Prisoner 818. Rank: Seaman, from: Enterprize, Privateer.
    Cap: 15 Nov 1813 at Sea by Argo Int: 19 Nov 1813 Dis: 02 Jan 1815.
    A Carthagenaian. Received from Argo. Into HM Ship Sultan per order of Captain John West.

Bilot, Pierre   Prisoner 1282. Rank: Passenger, from: Dolores, Merchant Schooner.
    Cap: at Sea by HM Sloop Anaconda Int: 07 Oct 1814 Dis: 29 Oct 1814.
    Received from HM Sloop Anaconda. Board's Order. (Date of capture not recorded.)

Bilot, Pierre An   Prisoner 1283. Rank: Passenger, from: Dolores, Merchant Schooner.
    Cap: at Sea by HM Sloop Anaconda Int: 07 Oct 1814 Dis: 29 Oct 1814.
    Received from HM Sloop Anaconda. Board's Order. (Date of capture not recorded.)

Bisar, Julian   Prisoner 1074. Rank: Seaman, from: Casada el Narino, Privateer.
    Cap: 29 May 1814 at Sea by HM Ship Rhin Int: 04 Jun 1814 Dis: 10 Aug 1814.
    Carthagenaian. Received from North Star. Board's Order.

Bisong, Juba   Prisoner 674. Rank: Seaman, from: Lovely Lass, Privateer.
    Cap: 21 May 1813 at Sea by Circe Int: 23 May 1813 Dis: 21 Jul 1814.
    Received from Forrester. Board's Order.

Blace, James   Prisoner 445. Rank: Midshipman, from: Vixen, Man of War.
    Cap: 24 Dec 1812 at Sea by Rhodian Int: 24 Dec 1812 Dis: 24 Dec 1812.
    Received from Rhodian. To Parole. (Dates of capture, interment and discharge the same.)

Black, Britain Ham   Prisoner 1492. Rank: Seaman, from: Not Recorded, Not Recorded.
    Cap: 20 Dec 1814 at Sea by Lacedaemonian Int: 04 Feb 1815 Dis: 11 Feb 1815.
    Taken for Passage to Jamaica Depot. Received from Rota. Into HMS Ramillies per order of Sir T M Hardy.

Black, Joseph   Prisoner 1269. Rank: Mate, from: Fanny, Merchant Vessel.
    Cap: 02 Sep 1814 at Sea by Jalouse Int: 10 Sep 1814 Dis: 26 Sep 1814.
    Swedish Schooner. Received from Jalouse. Board's Order.

Black, William   Prisoner 1351. Rank: Seaman, from: Ellena, Mechant Vessel.
    Cap: at Sea by Thracian Int: 13 Jan 1815 Dis: 04 Feb 1815.
    Received from Thracian. Board's Order. (Date of capture not recorded.)

Blackford, John   Prisoner 547. Rank: Seaman, from: Defiance, Privateer.
    Cap: 15 Mar 1813 at Sea by Nimrod Int: 17 Mar 1813 Dis: 24 Jul 1813.
    Received from Nimrod. To American Cartel Brig Aualostaw.

Blain, David   Prisoner 639. Rank: Seaman, from: Mary Ann, Privateer.
    Cap: 05 May 1813 at Sea by Sapphire Int: 07 May 1813 Dis: 01 Aug 1814.
    Received from Sapphire. To American Cartel Brig Aualostaw.

Blair, John K   Prisoner 113. Rank: 2 Prize Master, from: Poor Sailor, Privateer.
    Cap: 13 Sep 1812 at Sea by Garland Int: 18 Sep 1812 Dis: 09 May 1813.
    Received from Garland. To America for Exchange.

Blair, Thomas   Prisoner 990. Rank: Seaman, from: Young Eagle, Merchant Vessel.
    Cap: 28 Feb 1814 at Sea by Ringdove Int: 27 Mar 1814 Dis: 03 Aug 1814.
    Received from Ringdove. To American Cartel Brig Aualostaw.

Blakely, Sinclair   Prisoner 528. Rank: Seaman, from: Defiance, Privateer.
    Cap: 15 Mar 1813 at Sea by Nimrod Int: 17 Mar 1813 Dis: 24 Jul 1813.
    Received from Nimrod. To American Cartel Brig Aualostaw.

American Prisoners of War Held at Jamaica During the War of 1812

Blanco, Carlo Prisoner 906. Rank: Carpenter, from: San Francisco Navier, Brig.
    Cap: 05 Dec 1813 at Sea by Sappho Int: 15 Dec 1813 Dis: 08 Aug 1814.
    Taken in the Recaptured Spanish Brig. Prize to the Carthagenaian Privateer Carthagenaian. Received from Sappho. Board's Order.

Blenny, William Prisoner 116. Rank: 3 Prize Master, from: Poor Sailor, Privateer.
    Cap: 13 Sep 1812 at Sea by Garland Int: 18 Sep 1812 Escaped: 15 Nov 1812.
    Received from Garland. Escaped.

Bloham, Behrand Prisoner 1181. Rank: Seaman, from: Decatur, Privateer.
    Cap: 05 Jun 1814 at Sea by HM Ship Rhin Int: 20 Jun 1814 Dis: 16 Aug 1814.
    Received from HM Ship Rhin. Board's Order.

Boale, Jose Prisoner 761. Rank: Seaman, from: San Francisco de Paula, Privateer.
    Cap: 02 Oct 1813 at Sea by Forrester Int: 07 Oct 1813 Dis: 11 Jan 1814.
    Received from Forrester. per order.

Bodeye, Michael Prisoner 1275. Rank: Mate, from: Dolores, Merchant Schooner.
    Cap: at Sea by HM Sloop Anaconda Int: 07 Oct 1814 Dis: 22 Oct 1814.
    Received from HM Sloop Anaconda. To Parole. (Date of capture not recorded.)

Body, John Prisoner 4. Rank: Seaman, from: Assaw, Merchant Vessel.
    Cap: 28 Jul 1812 at Sea by Garland Int: 22 Aug 1812 Dis: 09 May 1813.
    Recaptured having been taken by the American Privateer the Paul Jones. Received from Garland. to America for Exchange.

Bolston, Jacob Prisoner 79. Rank: Seaman, from: Poor Sailor, Privateer.
    Cap: 13 Sep 1812 at Sea by Garland Int: 18 Sep 1812 Escaped: 15 Nov 1812.
    Received from Garland. Escaped.

Bommell, Andre Prisoner 1324. Rank: Seaman, from: Not Recorded, Not Recorded.
    Cap: at Sea by HMS Shark Int: 07 Jan 1815 Dis: 10 Jan 1815.
    Ship 'Name Unknown'. Received from HMS Shark. Board's Order. (Date of capture not recorded.)

Bond, Abraham Prisoner 254. Rank: Seaman, from: Joseph & Mary, Privateer.
    Cap: 24 Nov 1812 at Sea by Narcissus Int: 26 Nov 1812 Dis: 24 Jul 1813.
    Received from Narcissus. To American Cartel Brig Aualostaw.

Bond, Thomas Prisoner 1459. Rank: Seaman, from: Not Recorded, Not Recorded.
    Cap: 21 Dec 1814 at Sea by Severn Int: 04 Feb 1815 Dis: 11 Feb 1815.
    Taken for Passage to Jamaica Depot. Received from Rota. Into HMS Ramillies per order of Sir T M Hardy.

Borely, David Prisoner 1294. Rank: Passenger, from: Cora, Letter of Marque.
    Cap: 31 Jul 1814 at Sea by Rota Int: 06 Nov 1814 Dis: 21 Nov 1814.
    Received from Rota. Board's Order.

Borrison, John Prisoner 406. Rank: Seaman, from: Vixen, Man of War.
    Cap: 22 Nov 1812 at Sea by Rhodian late of US Brig Vixen Int: 14 Dec 1812 Dis: 09 May 1813.
    Received from Rhodian. To America for Exchange.

Bortiense, Jacques Prisoner 1342. Rank: Seaman, from: Not Recorded, Not Recorded.
    Cap: at Sea by HMS Shark Int: 07 Jan 1815 Dis: 10 Jan 1815.
    Ship 'Name Unknown'. Received from HMS Shark. Board's Order. (Date of capture not recorded.)

Bosque, Pierre Prisoner 1345. Rank: Seaman, from: Not Recorded, Not Recorded.
    Cap: at Sea by HMS Shark Int: 07 Jan 1815 Dis: 10 Jan 1815.
    Ship 'Name Unknown'. Received from HMS Shark. Board's Order. (Date of capture not recorded.)

Boss, Jacob Prisoner 1436. Rank: Seaman, from: American Gunboats, Not Recorded.
    Cap: 05 Jan 1815 near New Orleans by Plantagenet Int: 27 Jan 1815 Dis: 05 Feb 1815.
    Taken in the American Gun Boats near New Orleans. Received from Ramilies. Into HM Ship Diomede per order of Sir TM Hardy Baronet.

Both, Thomas Prisoner 1491. Rank: Seaman, from: Not Recorded, Not Recorded.
    Cap: 20 Dec 1814 at Sea by Lacedaemonian Int: 04 Feb 1815 Dis: 11 Feb 1815.
    Taken for Passage to Jamaica Depot. Received from Rota. Into HMS Ramillies per order of Sir T M Hardy.

Bouche, John Prisoner 1335. Rank: Seaman, from: Not Recorded, Not Recorded.
    Cap: at Sea by HMS Shark Int: 07 Jan 1815 Dis: 10 Jan 1815.
    Ship 'Name Unknown'. Received from HMS Shark. Board's Order. (Date of capture not recorded.)

Boudmon, Andrew Prisoner 628. Rank: Seaman, from: Mary Ann, Privateer.
    Cap: 05 May 1813 at Sea by Sapphire Int: 07 May 1813 Dis: 27 Jul 1814.
    Received from Sapphire. Board's Order.

Bouepou, Antonie Prisoner 1116. Rank: 2 Lieutenant, from: Decatur, Privateer.
    Cap: 05 Jun 1814 at Sea by HM Ship Rhin Int: 20 Jun 1814 Dis: 02 Jan 1815.
    Received from HM Ship Rhin. Into HM Ship Sultan per order of Captain John West.

American Prisoners of War Held at Jamaica During the War of 1812

Boughon, Miguel   Prisoner 1102. Rank: Seaman, from: Romano & Adamante, Merchant Brig.
    Cap: 31 May 1814 at Sea by Leviathan Int: 17 Jun 1814 Dis: 22 Jul 1814.
    Received from Leviathan. Board's Order.

Bourn, Charles   Prisoner 1543. Rank: Master, from: Le Expedecion, Merchant Vessel.
    Cap: at Sea by HMS Drake Int: 09 Mar 1815 Dis: 29 Mar 1815.
    Received from HMS Rinaldo. To Parole. (Date of capture not recorded.)

Boutel, Isaac   Prisoner 1150. Rank: Seaman, from: Decatur, Privateer.
    Cap: 05 Jun 1814 at Sea by HM Ship Rhin Int: 20 Jun 1814 Dis: 10 Aug 1814.
    Received from HM Ship Rhin. Board's Order.

Bowen, John   Prisoner 1205. Rank: Seaman, from: Not Recorded, Not Recorded.
    Cap: 26 May 1814 Bay of Honduras by HM Sloop Talbot Int: 29 Jun 1814 Dis: 02 Jan 1815.
    Given up as American. Received from HM Sloop Talbot. Into HM Ship Sultan per order of Captain John West.

Bowlin, John   Prisoner 881. Rank: Seaman, from: Lapwing, Packet.
    Cap: 08 Dec 1813 at Sea by Barrosa Int: 10 Dec 1813 Dis: 01 Aug 1814.
    Recaptured. Received from Barrosa. To American Cartel Brig Aualostaw.

Boyd, Pannilson   Prisoner 1416. Rank: Seaman, from: American Gunboats, Not Recorded.
    Cap: 05 Jan 1815 near New Orleans by Plantagenet Int: 27 Jan 1815 Dis: 05 Feb 1815.
    Taken in the American Gun Boats near New Orleans. Received from Ramilies. Into HM Ship Diomede per order of Sir TM Hardy Baronet.

Boyia, Thomas   Prisoner 820. Rank: Seaman, from: Enterprize, Privateer.
    Cap: 15 Nov 1813 at Sea by Argo Int: 19 Nov 1813 Died: 28 Jan 1814.
    A Carthagenaian. Received from Argo. Died.

Brackston, William   Prisoner 1315. Rank: Seaman, from: Nettervitte, Merchant Schooner.
    Cap: Not Recorded by HM Sloop Onyx Int: 30 Dec 1814 Dis: 02 Jan 1815.
    Received from HM Sloop Onyx. Into HM Ship Sultan per order of Captain John West. (Date of capture not recorded.)

Bradford, John   Prisoner 1475. Rank: Seaman, from: Not Recorded, Not Recorded.
    Cap: 21 Dec 1814 at Sea by Severn Int: 04 Feb 1815 Dis: 11 Feb 1815.
    Taken for Passage to Jamaica Depot. Received from Rota. Into HMS Ramillies per order of Sir T M Hardy.

Bradley, Abraham   Prisoner 354. Rank: Seaman, from: Vixen, Man of War.
    Cap: 22 Nov 1812 at Sea by Rhodian late of HM Brig Vixen Int: 14 Dec 1812 Dis: 09 May 1813.
    Received from Rhodian. To America for Exchange.

Bramore, Christopher   Prisoner 77. Rank: Seaman, from: Poor Sailor, Privateer.
    Cap: 13 Sep 1812 at Sea by Garland Int: 18 Sep 1812 Escaped: 15 Nov 1812.
    Received from Garland. Escaped.

Branson, C J   Prisoner 685. Rank: Seaman, from: Arethusa, Man of War.
    Cap: 18 Apr 1813 Not Recorded by Variable Int: 26 May 1813 Dis: 15 Oct 1813.
    Received from Variable. per Order of W Brown Rear Adml being a Hanoverian.

Branson, M   Prisoner 195. Rank: Master, from: Hamilton, Merchant Vessel.
    Cap: 28 Sep 1812 at Sea by Southampton Int: 10 Oct 1812 Dis: 16 Oct 1812.
    Received from Shark. On Parole.

Bremfield, George   Prisoner 249. Rank: Seaman, from: Joseph & Mary, Privateer.
    Cap: 24 Nov 1812 at Sea by Narcissus Int: 26 Nov 1812 Dis: 24 Jul 1813.
    Received from Narcissus. To American Cartel Brig Aualostaw.

Brewton, M   Prisoner 198. Rank: Master, from: Rebecca Sims, Merchant Vessel.
    Cap: 28 Sep 1812 at Sea by Southampton Int: 19 Oct 1812 Dis: 19 Oct 1812.
    Received from Southampton. On Parole.

Brewton, William   Prisoner 184. Rank: Mate, from: Rebecca Sims, Merchant Vessel.
    Cap: 12 Sep 1812 at Sea by Southampton Int: 09 Oct 1812 Dis: 22 Oct 1812.
    Received from Southampton. On Parole.

Brian, Peter   Prisoner 559. Rank: Seaman, from: Defiance, Privateer.
    Cap: 15 Mar 1813 at Sea by Nimrod Int: 17 Mar 1813 Dis: 09 May 1813.
    Received from Nimrod. To America for Exchange.

Bridges, Edward   Prisoner 376. Rank: Seaman, from: Vixen, Man of War.
    Cap: 22 Nov 1812 at Sea by Rhodian late of US Brig Vixen Int: 14 Dec 1812 Dis: 09 May 1813.
    Received from Rhodian. To America for Exchange.

Britain, John   Prisoner 94. Rank: Seaman, from: Poor Sailor, Privateer.
    Cap: 13 Sep 1812 at Sea by Garland Int: 18 Sep 1812 Dis: 24 Jul 1813.
    Received from Garland. To American Cartel Brig Aualostaw.

American Prisoners of War Held at Jamaica During the War of 1812

Broadbew, William   Prisoner 18. Rank: Seaman, from: Dal, Merchant Vessel.
    Cap: 03 Aug 1812 at Sea by Garland Int: 22 Aug 1812 Dis: 09 May 1813.
    Received from Garland. to America for Exchange.

Brown, Daniel   Prisoner 171. Rank: Mate, from: Hamilton, Merchant Vessel.
    Cap: 28 Sep 1812 at Sea by Southampton Int: 07 Oct 1812 Dis: 04 Apr 1813.
    Received from Southampton. To America for Exchange.

Brown, James   Prisoner 132. Rank: Seaman, from: Whim, Merchant Vessel.
    Cap: 18 Sep 1812 at Sea by HMS Cyane Int: 07 Oct 1812 Dis: 09 May 1813.
    Received from Cyane. To America for Exchange.

Brown, James   Prisoner 292. Rank: Seaman, from: Mary, Merchant Vessel.
    Cap: 26 Nov 1812 at Sea by Sappho Int: 30 Nov 1812 Dis: 09 May 1813.
    Received from Sappho. To America for Exchange.

Brown, James   Prisoner 1365. Rank: Seaman, from: American Gunboats, Not Recorded.
    Cap: 05 Jan 1815 near New Orleans by Plantagenet Int: 27 Jan 1815 Dis: 05 Feb 1815.
    Taken in the American Gun Boats near New Orleans. Received from Ramilies. Into HM Ship Diomede per order of Sir TM Hardy Baronet.

Brown, James A   Prisoner 1401. Rank: Seaman, from: American Gunboats, Not Recorded.
    Cap: 05 Jan 1815 near New Orleans by Plantagenet Int: 27 Jan 1815 Dis: 05 Feb 1815.
    Taken in the American Gun Boats near New Orleans. Received from Ramilies. Into HM Ship Diomede per order of Sir TM Hardy Baronet.

Brown, John   Prisoner 105. Rank: Seaman, from: Poor Sailor, Privateer.
    Cap: 13 Sep 1812 at Sea by Garland Int: 18 Sep 1812 Dis: 24 Jul 1813.
    Received from Garland. To American Cartel Brig Aualostaw.

Brown, John   Prisoner 880. Rank: Seaman, from: Lapwing, Packet.
    Cap: 08 Dec 1813 at Sea by Barrosa Int: 10 Dec 1813 Dis: 01 Aug 1814.
    Recaptured. Received from Barrosa. To American Cartel Brig Aualostaw.

Brown, John   Prisoner 889. Rank: Seaman, from: Milly, Schooner.
    Cap: 25 Nov 1813 at Sea by Decouverte Int: 10 Dec 1813 Dis: 01 Aug 1814.
    Taken out of the American Schooner Milly. Received from Decouverte. To American Cartel Brig Aualostaw.

Brown, John   Prisoner 991. Rank: Seaman, from: Young Eagle, Merchant Vessel.
    Cap: 28 Feb 1814 at Sea by Ringdove Int: 27 Mar 1814 Dis: 03 Aug 1814.
    Received from Ringdove. To American Cartel Brig Aualostaw.

Brown, John   Prisoner 1162. Rank: Seaman, from: Decatur, Privateer.
    Cap: 05 Jun 1814 at Sea by HM Ship Rhin Int: 20 Jun 1814 Dis: 22 Jul 1814.
    Received from HM Ship Rhin. Board's Order.

Brown, John   Prisoner 1262. Rank: Seaman, from: Not Recorded, Not Recorded.
    Cap: Kingston by Not Recorded Int: 08 Sep 1814 Escaped: 18 Dec 1814.
    Seized at Kingston last night being Americans. Received from Talbot. Escaped. (Date of capture assumed to be September 7, 1814.)

Brown, Joseph   Prisoner 212. Rank: Mate, from: Dominicana, Merchant Vessel.
    Cap: 21 Oct 1812 at Sea by HM Ship Liberty Int: 25 Oct 1812 Dis: 11 Nov 1812.
    Taken out of Brigantine Dominicana by HM Ship Liberty and brot into Port Royal. Received from Decouverte. American Flag of Truce Medosa per order of Vice Adml Stirling.

Brown, Obadiah   Prisoner 404. Rank: Seaman, from: Vixen, Man of War.
    Cap: 22 Nov 1812 at Sea by Rhodian late of US Brig Vixen Int: 14 Dec 1812 Dis: 09 May 1813.
    Received from Rhodian. To America for Exchange.

Brown, Peter   Prisoner 84. Rank: Seaman, from: Poor Sailor, Privateer.
    Cap: 13 Sep 1812 at Sea by Garland Int: 18 Sep 1812 Dis: 24 Jul 1813.
    Received from Garland. To American Cartel Brig Aualostaw.

Brown, Philip   Prisoner 391. Rank: Seaman, from: Vixen, Man of War.
    Cap: 22 Nov 1812 at Sea by Rhodian late of US Brig Vixen Int: 14 Dec 1812 Dis: 09 May 1813.
    Received from Rhodian. To America for Exchange.

Brown, Thomas   Prisoner 494. Rank: Seaman, from: Philip, Merchant Vessel.
    Cap: 28 Jan 1813 at Sea by Morgiana Int: 30 Jan 1813 Dis: 09 May 1813.
    Recaptured. Received from Morgiana. To America for Exchange.

Brown, William D   Prisoner 91. Rank: Gunner, from: Poor Sailor, Privateer.
    Cap: 13 Sep 1812 at Sea by Garland Int: 18 Sep 1812 Escaped: 15 Nov 1812.
    Received from Garland. Escaped.

Brown, William   Prisoner 608. Rank: Seaman, from: Fly, Merchant Schooner.
    Cap: 15 Apr 1813 at Sea by Argo Int: 18 Apr 1813 Dis: 09 May 1813.
    Received from Argo. To America for Exchange.

American Prisoners of War Held at Jamaica During the War of 1812

Brown, William   Prisoner 843. Rank: Seaman, from: Maria, An American Merchant Schooner.
    Cap: 15 Nov 1813 at Sea by Argo Int: 19 Nov 1813 Dis: 01 Aug 1814.
    Received from Argo. To American Cartel Brig Aualostaw.

Brown, William   Prisoner 1215. Rank: Seaman, from: Mary, Merchant Schooner.
    Cap: 17 Jun 1814 at Sea by Sapphire Int: 10 Jul 1814 Dis: 02 Jan 1815.
    Recaptured. Received from Sapphire. Into HM Ship Suttan per order of Captain John West.

Bryan, George   Prisoner 203. Rank: Second Officer, from: Blandie, Merchant Vessel.
    Cap: 21 Oct 1812 at Sea by Not Recorded Int: 25 Oct 1812 Escaped: 06 Jan 1813.
    Recaptured. Taken from the Recapd Schooner Blandie, belonging to the American Privateer Schooner Comet. Received from Sappho. Escaped.

Brydges, Culpeper   Prisoner 501. Rank: Supercargo, from: Three Friends, Merchant Vessel.
    Cap: 03 Dec 1812 at Sea by Circe Int: Dis: 29 Jan 1813.
    Received from Circe. To Parole. (Date of internment not recorded.)

Brydges, Culpeper   Prisoner 505. Rank: Not Recorded, from: Not Recorded, Not Recorded.
    Cap: Not Recorded by Not Recorded Int: Dis:
    (Entry crossed out. Prisoner number 501.)

Bryne, Thomas   Prisoner 9. Rank: Seaman, from: Assaw, Merchant Vessel.
    Cap: 28 Jul 1812 at Sea by Garland Int: 22 Aug 1812 Dis: 04 Apr 1813.
    Recaptured having been taken by the American Privateer the Paul Jones. Received from Garland. to America for Exchange.

Buch, Josuah   Prisoner 311. Rank: Seaman, from: Joseph & Mary, Privateer.
    Cap: 24 Nov 1812 at Sea by Narcissus Int: 05 Dec 1812 Dis: 24 Jul 1813.
    Received from Narcissus. To American Cartel Brig Aualostaw.

Buck, Balthazar   Prisoner 948. Rank: Mate, from: Ann, Merchant Vessel.
    Cap: 01 Jan 1814 at Sea by Sappho Int: 19 Jan 1814 Dis: 18 Mar 1814.
    Received from Sappho. To Parole.

Buckley, Walter   Prisoner 1217. Rank: Prize Master, from: Mary, Merchant Schooner.
    Cap: 17 Jun 1814 at Sea by Sapphire Int: 10 Jul 1814 Dis: 02 Jan 1815.
    Recaptured. Received from Sapphire. Into HM Ship Suttan per order of Captain John West.

Bucklin, Warren   Prisoner 290. Rank: Seaman, from: Flora, Merchant Vessel.
    Cap: 13 Nov 1812 at Sea by Sappho Int: 30 Nov 1812 Dis: 24 Jul 1813.
    Received from Sappho. To American Cartel Brig Aualostaw.

Budgeron, W   Prisoner 1524. Rank: Seaman, from: Not Recorded, Not Recorded.
    Cap: 08 Dec 1814 at Sea by Albion Int: 04 Feb 1815 Dis: 11 Feb 1815.
    Taken for Passage to Jamaica Depot. Received from Rota. Into HM Ship Rota per order of Sir TM Hardy.

Budie, Andrew   Prisoner 36. Rank: Seaman, from: Not Recorded, Not Recorded.
    Cap: Not Recorded by Not Recorded Int: 22 Aug 1812 Dis: 09 May 1813.
    Given themselves up as American and refused to serve. Received from Garland. to America for Exchange. (Date of capture not recorded.)

Bunnell, Charles   Prisoner 1415. Rank: Seaman, from: American Gunboats, Not Recorded.
    Cap: 05 Jan 1815 near New Orleans by Plantagenet Int: 27 Jan 1815 Dis: 05 Feb 1815.
    Taken in the American Gun Boats near New Orleans. Received from Ramilies. Into HM Ship Diomede per order of Sir TM Hardy Baronet.

Buntly, Isom   Prisoner 964. Rank: Seaman, from: Active, Merchant Vessel.
    Cap: at Sea by Leonidas Int: 25 Jan 1814 Dis: 01 Aug 1814.
    Received from Leonidas. To American Cartel Brig Aualostaw. (Date of capture not recorded.)

Burdeck, Enos   Prisoner 506. Rank: Seaman, from: Not Recorded, Not Recorded.
    Cap: 10 Feb 1813 at Lucea by Not Recorded Int: 26 Feb 1813 Escaped: 10 May 1813.
    Retaken. Received from Sea Horse. Escaped. (Enos Burdett. Prisoner number 106.)

Burdett, Enos   Prisoner 106. Rank: Seaman, from: Poor Sailor, Privateer.
    Cap: 13 Sep 1812 at Sea by Garland Int: 18 Sep 1812 Escaped: 30 Jan 1813.
    Received from Garland. Escaped.

Burke, Thomas   Prisoner 602. Rank: Seaman, from: Not Recorded, Not Recorded.
    Cap: Not Recorded by Not Recorded Int: 24 Mar 1813 Dis: 04 Apr 1813.
    an American refusing to serve. Received from Shark. To America for Exchange. (Date of capture not recorded.)

Burnham, William   Prisoner 979. Rank: Seaman, from: Suspense, Merchant Vessel.
    Cap: 20 Feb 1814 at Sea by Leviathan Int: 26 Mar 1814 Dis: 01 Aug 1814.
    Received from Mohawk. To American Cartel Brig Aualostaw.

American Prisoners of War Held at Jamaica During the War of 1812

Burr, N M   Prisoner 1527. Rank: Seaman, from: Not Recorded, Not Recorded.
    Cap: 08 Dec 1814 at Sea by Albion Int: 04 Feb 1815 Dis: 11 Feb 1815.
    Taken for Passage to Jamaica Depot. Received from Rota. Into HMS Ramillies per order of Sir T M Hardy.

Burrows, Edward   Prisoner 402. Rank: Masters Mate, from: Vixen, Man of War.
    Cap: 22 Nov 1812 at Sea by Rhodian late of US Brig Vixen Int: 14 Dec 1812 Dis: 04 Apr 1813.
    Received from Rhodian. To America for Exchange.

Busher, Lawrence   Prisoner 1020. Rank: Seaman, from: Chance, Privateer.
    Cap: 01 Apr 1814 at Sea by Statira Int: 20 Apr 1814 Dis: 21 Jul 1814.
    Received from Statira. Board's Order.

Butcher, Jacob   Prisoner 819. Rank: Seaman, from: Enterprize, Privateer.
    Cap: 15 Nov 1813 at Sea by Argo Int: 19 Nov 1813 Dis: 02 Jan 1815.
    A Carthagenaian. Received from Argo. Into HM Ship Sultan per order of Captain John West.

Butil, Francis   Prisoner 575. Rank: Captain, from: Le Ventura, Privateer.
    Cap: 13 Mar 1813 at Sea by Cossac Int: 18 Mar 1813 Escaped: 04 Sep 1813.
    Received from Cossac. Escaped.

Butler, David   Prisoner 1014. Rank: Seaman, from: Chance, Privateer.
    Cap: 01 Apr 1814 at Sea by Statira Int: 20 Apr 1814 Dis: 02 Jan 1815.
    Received from Statira. Into HM Ship Sultan per order of Captain John West.

Butler, Henry   Prisoner 1009. Rank: Seaman, from: Not Recorded, Not Recorded.
    Cap: Not Recorded by Variable Int: 16 Apr 1814 Dis: 02 Jan 1815.
    Given up as an American. Received from Variable. Into HM Ship Sultan per order of Captain John West. (Date of capture not recorded.)

Cabais, Pedro   Prisoner 791. Rank: Seaman, from: San Francisco de Paula, Privateer.
    Cap: 02 Oct 1813 at Sea by Forrester Int: 07 Oct 1813 Dis: 16 Aug 1814.
    Received from Forrester. Board's Order.

Cable, Peter   Prisoner 571. Rank: Seaman, from: Defiance, Privateer.
    Cap: 15 Mar 1813 at Sea by Nimrod Int: 17 Mar 1813 Escaped: 28 Jun 1813.
    Received from Nimrod. Escaped.

Caderer, John   Prisoner 537. Rank: Seaman, from: Defiance, Privateer.
    Cap: 15 Mar 1813 at Sea by Nimrod Int: 17 Mar 1813 Dis: 24 Jul 1813.
    Received from Nimrod. To American Cartel Brig Aualostaw.

Cadinetto, Robert   Prisoner 592. Rank: Seaman, from: Le Ventura, Privateer.
    Cap: 13 Mar 1813 at Sea by Cossac Int: 18 Mar 1813 Dis: 08 Aug 1814.
    Received from Cossac. Board's Order.

Cain, William   Prisoner 211. Rank: Seaman, from: Blandie, Merchant Vessel.
    Cap: 21 Oct 1812 at Sea by Not Recorded Int: 25 Oct 1812 Dis: 24 Jul 1813.
    Recaptured. Taken from the Recapd Schooner Blandie, belonging to the American Privateer Schooner Comet. Received from Sappho. To American Cartel Brig Aualostaw.

Calbert, James   Prisoner 214. Rank: Seaman, from: Dominicana, Merchant Vessel.
    Cap: 21 Oct 1812 at Sea by HM Ship Liberty Int: 25 Oct 1812 Dis: 11 Nov 1812.
    Taken out of Brigantine Dominicana by HM Ship Liberty and brot into Port Royal. Received from Decouverte. American Flag of Truce Medosa per order of Vice Adml Stirling.

Call, Benjamin   Prisoner 374. Rank: Seaman, from: Vixen, Man of War.
    Cap: 22 Nov 1812 at Sea by Rhodian late of US Brig Vixen Int: 14 Dec 1812 Dis: 09 May 1813.
    Received from Rhodian. To America for Exchange.

Callerist, Collin   Prisoner 1168. Rank: Cabin Boy, from: Decatur, Privateer.
    Cap: 05 Jun 1814 at Sea by HM Ship Rhin Int: 20 Jun 1814 Dis: .
    Received from HM Ship Rhin. Included in list but never received into custody. (No date of discharge.)

Callerist, Y P   Prisoner 1169. Rank: Seaman, from: Decatur, Privateer.
    Cap: 05 Jun 1814 at Sea by HM Ship Rhin Int: 20 Jun 1814 Dis: 21 Jul 1814.
    Received from HM Ship Rhin. Board's Order.

Calluga, Damasco   Prisoner 1086. Rank: Seaman, from: Casada el Narino, Privateer.
    Cap: 29 May 1814 at Sea by HM Ship Rhin Int: 04 Jun 1814 Dis: 18 Aug 1814.
    Carthagenaian. Received from North Star. Board's Order.

Cambell, Henry   Prisoner 1207. Rank: Seaman, from: Not Recorded, Not Recorded.
    Cap: 26 May 1814 Bay of Honduras by HM Sloop Talbot Int: 29 Jun 1814 Dis: 02 Jan 1815.
    Given up as an American. Received from HM Sloop Talbot. Into HM Ship Sultan per order of Captain John West.

Cameron, America   Prisoner 720. Rank: Seaman, from: Mount Vernon, Merchant Man.
    Cap: at Sea by Argo Int: 27 Jun 1813 Dis: 02 Jul 1813.
    Received from Mount Vernon. To Mount Vernon per order of Adml Brown this date. (Date of capture not recorded.)

American Prisoners of War Held at Jamaica During the War of 1812

Cameron, Eli   Prisoner 723. Rank: Seaman, from: Mount Vernon, Merchant Man.
    Cap: at Sea by Argo Int: 27 Jun 1813 Dis: 02 Jul 1813.
    Received from Mount Vernon. To Mount Vernon per order of Adml Brown this date. (Date of capture not recorded.)

Campbell, E   Prisoner 970. Rank: Not Recorded, from: Packet, Merchant Vessel.
    Cap: 08 Feb 1814 at Sea by Snake Int: 17 Feb 1814 Dis: 01 Aug 1814.
    Received from Snake. To American Cartel Brig Aualostaw.

Canning, Joseph   Prisoner 1417. Rank: Seaman, from: American Gunboats, Not Recorded.
    Cap: 05 Jan 1815 near New Orleans by Plantagenet Int: 27 Jan 1815 Dis: 05 Feb 1815.
    Taken in the American Gun Boats near New Orleans. Received from Ramilies. Into HM Ship Diomede per order of Sir TM Hardy Baronet.

Capura, Nicholas   Prisoner 771. Rank: Seaman, from: San Francisco de Paula, Privateer.
    Cap: 02 Oct 1813 at Sea by Forrester Int: 07 Oct 1813 Dis: 21 Jul 1814.
    Received from Forrester. per order.

Carbon, John   Prisoner 635. Rank: Seaman, from: Mary Ann, Privateer.
    Cap: 05 May 1813 at Sea by Sapphire Int: 07 May 1813 Dis: 21 Jul 1814.
    Received from Sapphire. Escaped but returned a few hours after, being picked up by Corporal Goodhall of the Magazine Ship. Board's Order.

Care, Beatte   Prisoner 1085. Rank: Seaman, from: Casada el Narino, Privateer.
    Cap: 29 May 1814 at Sea by HM Ship Rhin Int: 04 Jun 1814 Dis: 18 Aug 1814.
    Carthagenaian. Received from North Star. Board's Order.

Carier, Pierre   Prisoner 1333. Rank: Seaman, from: Not Recorded, Not Recorded.
    Cap: at Sea by HMS Shark Int: 07 Jan 1815 Dis: 10 Jan 1815.
    Ship 'Name Unknown'. Received from HMS Shark. Board's Order. (Date of capture not recorded.)

Carlo, James   Prisoner 1000. Rank: Seaman, from: Farmer's Daughter, Merchant Vessel.
    Cap: 30 Mar 1814 at Sea by Leviathan Int: 03 Apr 1814 Dis: 02 Jan 1815.
    Received from Leviathan. Into HM Ship Sultan per order of Captain John West.

Carlton, Thomas   Prisoner 861. Rank: Seaman, from: Cato Georgiana, Not Recorded.
    Cap: 28 Nov 1813 at Sea by Barrosa Int: 10 Dec 1813 Dis: 01 Aug 1814.
    Prize to the US Frigate Essex. Received from Barrosa. To American Cartel Brig Aualostaw.

Carnation, Jose   Prisoner 1328. Rank: Seaman, from: Not Recorded, Not Recorded.
    Cap: at Sea by HMS Shark Int: 07 Jan 1815 Dis: 10 Jan 1815.
    Ship 'Name Unknown'. Received from HMS Shark. Board's Order. (Date of capture not recorded.)

Carpenter, Benezer   Prisoner 1371. Rank: Seaman, from: American Gunboats, Not Recorded.
    Cap: 05 Jan 1815 near New Orleans by Plantagenet Int: 27 Jan 1815 Dis: 05 Feb 1815.
    Taken in the American Gun Boats near New Orleans. Received from Ramilies. Into HM Ship Diomede per order of Sir TM Hardy Baronet.

Carpenter, Jeremiah   Prisoner 1530. Rank: Seaman, from: American Gunboats, Not Recorded.
    Cap: 05 Jan 1815 near New Orleans by Plantagenet Int: 05 Feb 1815 Dis: 11 Feb 1815.
    Taken in the American Flotilla near New Orleans. Received from Rota. Into HMS Ramillies per order of Sir T M Hardy.

Carpenter, Lewis   Prisoner 237. Rank: Seaman, from: Joseph & Mary, Privateer.
    Cap: 24 Nov 1812 at Sea by Narcissus Int: 26 Nov 1812 Dis: 09 May 1813.
    Received from Narcissus. To America for Exchange.

Carrol, John   Prisoner 319. Rank: Seaman, from: Pirtshire, English Merchant Ship.
    Cap: Nov 1812 at Sea by Fawn Int: 06 Dec 1812 Dis: 24 Jul 1813.
    Recaptured. Eagle Privateer. Received from Fawn. To American Cartel Brig Aualostaw. (Day of capture not recorded.)

Carrott, William   Prisoner 346. Rank: Seaman, from: Vixen, Man of War.
    Cap: 22 Nov 1812 at Sea by Rhodian late of HM Brig Vixen Int: 14 Dec 1812 Dis: 09 May 1813.
    Received from Rhodian. To America for Exchange.

Carruation, Corui   Prisoner 786. Rank: Seaman, from: San Francisco de Paula, Privateer.
    Cap: 02 Oct 1813 at Sea by Forrester Int: 07 Oct 1813 Dis: 11 Jan 1814.
    Received from Forrester. per order.

Carrura, Josef   Prisoner 932. Rank: Seaman, from: Cartagenaian, Privateer.
    Cap: 05 Dec 1813 at Sea by Sappho Int: 15 Dec 1813 Dis: 16 Aug 1814.
    Belonging to the Carthagenaian Privateer Carthagenaian. Received from Sappho. Board's Order.

Carter, Henry   Prisoner 1403. Rank: Seaman, from: American Gunboats, Not Recorded.
    Cap: 05 Jan 1815 near New Orleans by Plantagenet Int: 27 Jan 1815 Dis: 05 Feb 1815.
    Taken in the American Gun Boats near New Orleans. Received from Ramilies. Into HM Ship Diomede per order of Sir TM Hardy Baronet.

American Prisoners of War Held at Jamaica During the War of 1812

Carter, James   Prisoner 447. Rank: Midshipman, from: Vixen, Man of War.
    Cap: 24 Dec 1812 at Sea by Rhodian Int: 24 Dec 1812 Dis: 11 Feb 1813.
    Received from Rhodian. for Exchange order of VA Stirling. (Dates of capture and interment the same.)
Carter, James   Prisoner 963. Rank: Seaman, from: Active, Merchant Vessel.
    Cap: at Sea by Leonidas Int: 25 Jan 1814 Dis: 01 Aug 1814.
    Received from Leonidas. To American Cartel Brig Aualostaw. (Date of capture not recorded.)
Carter, Joshua   Prisoner 667. Rank: Seaman, from: Lovely Lass, Privateer.
    Cap: 21 May 1813 at Sea by Circe Int: 23 May 1813 Dis: 29 Jul 1814.
    Received from Forrester. Board's Order.
Case, John   Prisoner 562. Rank: Seaman, from: Defiance, Privateer.
    Cap: 15 Mar 1813 at Sea by Nimrod Int: 17 Mar 1813 Dis: 24 Jul 1813.
    Received from Nimrod. To American Cartel Brig Aualostaw.
Casera, Juan   Prisoner 1048. Rank: Seaman, from: Casada el Narino, Privateer.
    Cap: 29 May 1814 at Sea by HM Ship Rhin Int: 04 Jun 1814 Dis: 24 Jul 1814.
    Carthagenaian. Received from North Star. Board's Order.
Cassack, Charles   Prisoner 782. Rank: Seaman, from: San Francisco de Paula, Privateer.
    Cap: 02 Oct 1813 at Sea by Forrester Int: 07 Oct 1813 Dis: 11 Jan 1814.
    Received from Forrester. per order.
Cassaire, John   Prisoner 633. Rank: Seaman, from: Mary Ann, Privateer.
    Cap: 05 May 1813 at Sea by Sapphire Int: 07 May 1813 Dis: 27 Jul 1814.
    Received from Sapphire. Board's Order.
Catalante, Imannual   Prisoner 785. Rank: Seaman, from: San Francisco de Paula, Privateer.
    Cap: 02 Oct 1813 at Sea by Forrester Int: 07 Oct 1813 Dis: 11 Jan 1814.
    Received from Forrester. per order.
Cater, Benjamin   Prisoner 951. Rank: Mate, from: Swift, Merchant Vessel.
    Cap: at Sea by Leonidas Int: 25 Jan 1814 Dis: 01 Aug 1814.
    Received from Leonidas. To American Cartel Brig Aualostaw. (Date of capture not recorded. Prisoner numbers 951 - 956 all have recorded rank of mate.)
Caximo, Josef M   Prisoner 1160. Rank: Seaman, from: Decatur, Privateer.
    Cap: 05 Jun 1814 at Sea by HM Ship Rhin Int: 20 Jun 1814 Dis: 12 Aug 1814.
    Received from HM Ship Rhin. Board's Order.
Cebo, Francisco   Prisoner 1072. Rank: Seaman, from: Casada el Narino, Privateer.
    Cap: 29 May 1814 at Sea by HM Ship Rhin Int: 04 Jun 1814 Dis: 23 Aug 1814.
    Carthagenaian. Received from North Star. Board's Order.
Cezard, J   Prisoner 856. Rank: Seaman, from: Le Galzo, Spanish Brig.
    Cap: 17 Nov 1813 at Sea by Variable Int: 28 Nov 1813 Dis: 12 May 1814.
    Recaptured from the Carthagenaian Privateer Le Legislateur. Received from Variable. Escaped.
Chalmers, David   Prisoner 112. Rank: 1 Prize Master, from: Poor Sailor, Privateer.
    Cap: 13 Sep 1812 at Sea by Garland Int: 18 Sep 1812 Dis: 09 May 1813.
    Received from Garland. To America for Exchange.
Chamberlain, John   Prisoner 867. Rank: Seaman, from: Cato Georgiana, Not Recorded.
    Cap: 28 Nov 1813 at Sea by Barrosa Int: 10 Dec 1813 Dis: 01 Aug 1814.
    Prize to the US Frigate Essex. Received from Barrosa. To American Cartel Brig Aualostaw.
Chambiere, Theodore   Prisoner 853. Rank: Seaman, from: Le Galzo, Spanish Brig.
    Cap: 17 Nov 1813 at Sea by Variable Int: 28 Nov 1813 Escaped: 30 Dec 1813.
    Recaptured from the Carthagenaian Privateer Le Legislateur. Received from Variable. Escaped.
Chambierre, Joseph   Prisoner 852. Rank: Seaman, from: Le Galzo, Spanish Brig.
    Cap: 17 Nov 1813 at Sea by Variable Int: 28 Nov 1813 Dis: 29 Jul 1814.
    Recaptured from the Carthagenaian Privateer Le Legislateur. Received from Variable. Board's Order.
Chamstead, John   Prisoner 942. Rank: Seaman, from: Coquelle, Merchant Vessel.
    Cap: 24 Dec 1813 at Sea by Sapphire Int: 02 Jan 1814 Dis: 01 Aug 1814.
    Received from Sapphire. To American Cartel Brig Aualostaw.
Chapel, John Peter   Prisoner 519. Rank: Captain, from: Defiance, Privateer.
    Cap: 15 Mar 1813 at Sea by Nimrod Int: 17 Mar 1813 Dis: 30 Mar 1813.
    Received from Nimrod. To America for Exchange.
Chapman, J L   Prisoner 458. Rank: Seaman, from: Rachel, Merchant Vessel.
    Cap: 1813 at Sea by Fawn Int: 13 Jan 1813 Dis: 24 Jul 1813.
    Received from Sapphire. To American Cartel Brig Aualostaw. (Day and month of capture not recorded.)
Chariol, Peter   Prisoner 613. Rank: Master, from: Mary Ann, Privateer.
    Cap: 05 May 1813 at Sea by Sapphire Int: 07 May 1813 Dis: 21 Jul 1814.
    Received from Sapphire. Board's Order.

American Prisoners of War Held at Jamaica During the War of 1812

Charles, John   Prisoner 1329. Rank: Seaman, from: Not Recorded, Not Recorded.
    Cap: at Sea by HMS Shark Int: 07 Jan 1815 Dis: 10 Jan 1815.
    Ship 'Name Unknown'. Received from HMS Shark. Board's Order. (Date of capture not recorded.)

Charles, Stephen   Prisoner 1240. Rank: Passenger, from: John, Merchant Vessel.
    Cap: 11 Aug 1814 at Sea by Variable Int: 15 Aug 1814 Dis: 20 Aug 1814.
    Received from Variable. per order Non - Combatant.

Charleston, Joseph   Prisoner 1187. Rank: Seaman, from: Decatur, Privateer.
    Cap: 05 Jun 1814 at Sea by HM Ship Rhin Int: 20 Jun 1814 Dis: 01 Sep 1814.
    Received from HM Ship Rhin. Board's Order.

Charrier, Jean B   Prisoner 850. Rank: Seaman, from: Le Galzo, Spanish Brig.
    Cap: 17 Nov 1813 at Sea by Variable Int: 28 Nov 1813 Escaped: 30 Dec 1813.
    Recaptured from the Carthagenaian Privateer Le Legislateur. Received from Variable. Escaped.

Cherin, Pedro   Prisoner 915. Rank: Seaman, from: San Francisco Navier, Brig.
    Cap: 05 Dec 1813 at Sea by Sappho Int: 15 Dec 1813 Dis: 16 Aug 1814.
    Taken in the Recaptured Spanish Brig. Prize to the Carthagenaian Privateer Carthagenaian. Received from Sappho. Board's Order.

Chessm, George   Prisoner 567. Rank: Seaman, from: Defiance, Privateer.
    Cap: 15 Mar 1813 at Sea by Nimrod Int: 17 Mar 1813 Dis: 24 Jul 1813.
    Received from Nimrod. To American Cartel Brig Aualostaw.

Chine, Peter   Prisoner 623. Rank: Seaman, from: Mary Ann, Privateer.
    Cap: 05 May 1813 at Sea by Sapphire Int: 07 May 1813 Dis: 21 Jul 1814.
    Received from Sapphire. Board's Order.

Chinny, John   Prisoner 1372. Rank: Seaman, from: American Gunboats, Not Recorded.
    Cap: 05 Jan 1815 near New Orleans by Plantagenet Int: 27 Jan 1815 Dis: 05 Feb 1815.
    Taken in the American Gun Boats near New Orleans. Received from Ramilies. Into HM Ship Diomede per order of Sir TM Hardy Baronet.

Christie, William   Prisoner 180. Rank: Chief Mate, from: Philip, Merchant Vessel.
    Cap: 10 Sep 1812 at Sea by Southampton Int: 09 Oct 1812 Dis: 22 Oct 1812.
    Received from Southampton. On Parole.

Clackston, James   Prisoner 328. Rank: Seaman, from: Sauders, Merchant Vessel.
    Cap: Nov 1812 at Sea by Merchant Vessel Monarch Int: 09 Dec 1812 Dis: 24 Jul 1813.
    Received from Monarch. To American Cartel. (Day of capture not recorded.)

Clark, James   Prisoner 1039. Rank: Seaman, from: Jennett, Brig.
    Cap: 29 May 1814 at Sea by HM Ship Rhin Int: 04 Jun 1814 Dis: 02 Jan 1815.
    Taken in the Swedish Brig Jennet. Received from North Star. Into HM Ship Sultan per order of Captain John West.

Clark, John   Prisoner 1471. Rank: Seaman, from: Not Recorded, Not Recorded.
    Cap: 21 Dec 1814 at Sea by Severn Int: 04 Feb 1815 Dis: 11 Feb 1815.
    Taken for Passage to Jamaica Depot. Received from Rota. Into HMS Ramillies per order of Sir T M Hardy.

Clark, Sylvester   Prisoner 611. Rank: Seaman, from: Fly, Merchant Schooner.
    Cap: 15 Apr 1813 at Sea by Argo Int: 18 Apr 1813 Dis: 01 Aug 1814.
    Received from Argo. To American Cartel Brig Aualostaw.

Clarke, Alb   Prisoner 17. Rank: Seaman, from: Dal, Merchant Vessel.
    Cap: 03 Aug 1812 at Sea by Garland Int: 22 Aug 1812 Dis: 09 May 1813.
    Received from Garland. to America for Exchange.

Clarke, Bernard   Prisoner 209. Rank: Seaman, from: Blandie, Merchant Vessel.
    Cap: 21 Oct 1812 at Sea by Not Recorded Int: 25 Oct 1812 Dis: 04 Apr 1813.
    Recaptured. Taken from the Recapd Schooner Blandie, belonging to the American Privateer Schooner Comet. Received from Sappho. To America for Exchange.

Clarke, George   Prisoner 872. Rank: Seaman, from: Lapwing, Packet.
    Cap: 08 Dec 1813 at Sea by Barrosa Int: 10 Dec 1813 Dis: 01 Aug 1814.
    Recaptured. Received from Barrosa. To American Cartel Brig Aualostaw.

Clarke, George   Prisoner 1547. Rank: Seaman, from: Le Expedecion, Merchant Vessel.
    Cap: at Sea by HMS Drake Int: 09 Mar 1815 Dis: 30 Mar 1815.
    Received from HMS Rinaldo. In consequence of Peace with America. (Date of capture not recorded.)

Clarke, John   Prisoner 246. Rank: Seaman, from: Joseph & Mary, Privateer.
    Cap: 24 Nov 1812 at Sea by Narcissus Int: 26 Nov 1812 Escaped: 30 Jan 1813.
    Received from Narcissus. Escaped.

Clarke, John   Prisoner 511. Rank: Seaman, from: Not Recorded, Not Recorded.
    Cap: 11 Feb 1813 at Lucea by Not Recorded Int: 26 Feb 1813 Escaped: 28 Mar 1813.
    Retaken. Received from Sea Horse. Escaped. May 10, 1813. Escaped. (Prisoner number 246.)

American Prisoners of War Held at Jamaica During the War of 1812

Clarke, John   Prisoner 601. Rank: Boy, from: Not Recorded, Not Recorded.
    Cap: Not Recorded by Not Recorded Int: 18 Mar 1813 Escaped: 10 May 1813.
    Retaken. Escaped. (Date of capture not recorded. Prisoner numbers 246 & 511.)

Clarke, John   Prisoner 1290. Rank: Passenger, from: Dolores, Merchant Schooner.
    Cap: at Sea by HM Sloop Anaconda Int: 07 Oct 1814 Dis: 29 Oct 1814.
    Received from HM Sloop Anaconda. Board's Order. (Date of capture not recorded.)

Class, Jean   Prisoner 1165. Rank: Seaman, from: Decatur, Privateer.
    Cap: 05 Jun 1814 at Sea by HM Ship Rhin Int: 20 Jun 1814 Dis: 23 Aug 1814.
    Received from HM Ship Rhin. Board's Order.

Clay, William   Prisoner 1399. Rank: Seaman, from: American Gunboats, Not Recorded.
    Cap: 05 Jan 1815 near New Orleans by Plantagenet Int: 27 Jan 1815 Dis: 05 Feb 1815.
    Taken in the American Gun Boats near New Orleans. Received from Ramilies. Into HM Ship Diomede per order of Sir TM Hardy Baronet.

Cleburn, Francis   Prisoner 463. Rank: Seaman, from: Saratoga, Merchant Vessel.
    Cap: 1813 at Sea by Fawn Int: 13 Jan 1813 Dis: 04 Apr 1813.
    Received from Sapphire. To America for Exchange. (Day and month of capture not recorded.)

Clemon, Pierre   Prisoner 1200. Rank: Seaman, from: Neustra Cantado, Merchant Vessel.
    Cap: 01 Jun 1814 at Sea by HM Ship Argo Int: 27 Jun 1814 Dis: 10 Aug 1814.
    Retaken in the Spanish Ship Neustra Cantado. Received from HM Ship Argo. Board's Order.

Clermont, J B   Prisoner 648. Rank: Seaman, from: Mary Ann, Privateer.
    Cap: 05 May 1813 at Sea by Sapphire Int: 07 May 1813 Dis: 21 Jul 1814.
    Received from Sapphire. Board's Order.

Cleveland, W C   Prisoner 1523. Rank: Seaman, from: Not Recorded, Not Recorded.
    Cap: 08 Dec 1814 at Sea by Albion Int: 04 Feb 1815 Dis: 11 Feb 1815.
    Taken for Passage to Jamaica Depot. Received from Rota. Into HM Ship Rota per order of Sir TM Hardy.

Closcharden, John   Prisoner 416. Rank: Private, from: Vixen, Man of War.
    Cap: 22 Nov 1812 at Sea by Rhodian Int: 14 Dec 1812 Dis: 09 May 1813.
    Received from Brazier. To America for Exchange.

Cloud, Peter   Prisoner 690. Rank: Seaman, from: Lovely Lass, Privateer.
    Cap: 15 May 1813 at Sea by Circe Int: 29 May 1813 Escaped: 27 Sep 1813.
    Received from Circe. Escaped.

Clury, William   Prisoner 364. Rank: Seaman, from: Vixen, Man of War.
    Cap: 22 Nov 1812 at Sea by Rhodian late of US Brig Vixen Int: 14 Dec 1812 Dis: 09 May 1813.
    Received from Rhodian. To America for Exchange.

Cochran, Paunay   Prisoner 102. Rank: Seaman, from: Poor Sailor, Privateer.
    Cap: 13 Sep 1812 at Sea by Garland Int: 18 Sep 1812 Dis: 24 Jul 1813.
    Received from Garland. To American Cartel Brig Aualostaw.

Cocks, John S H   Prisoner 110. Rank: 1 Lieutenant, from: Poor Sailor, Privateer.
    Cap: 13 Sep 1812 at Sea by Garland Int: 18 Sep 1812 Escaped: 06 Jan 1813.
    Received from Garland. Escaped.

Cocks, William   Prisoner 437. Rank: Not Recorded, from: Vixen, Man of War.
    Cap: 22 Nov 1812 at Sea by Rhodian Int: Dis: .
    Received from Rhodian. Entered below. (Entry crossed out. Prisoner # 452, Willam Cox. Dates of interment and discharge not recorded.)

Coit, S   Prisoner 131. Rank: Chief Mate, from: Whim, Merchant Vessel.
    Cap: 18 Sep 1812 at Sea by HMS Cyane Int: 07 Oct 1812 Dis: 22 Oct 1812.
    Received from Cyane. On Parole.

Coleby, John   Prisoner 935. Rank: Seaman, from: Not Recorded, Not Recorded.
    Cap: 24 Dec 1813 at Sea by Minerva Int: 24 Dec 1813 Dis: 01 Aug 1814.
    Given up as An American. Received from Minerva. To American Cartel Brig Aualostaw. (Dates of capture and internment the same.)

Coles, Charles   Prisoner 65. Rank: Not legible, from: Books, Not Recorded.
    Cap: Not Recorded by Not Recorded Int: 06 Sep 1812 Dis: 28 Jul 1813.
    From the Ship Books refusing to serve as American. Received from Moselle. To America Cartel Brig Aualostaw.

Collins, John   Prisoner 1209. Rank: Seaman, from: Not Recorded, Not Recorded.
    Cap: 26 Jun 1814 Not Recorded by HM Sloop Emulous Int: 09 Jul 1814 Escaped: 18 Dec 1814.
    Given up as an American. Received from HM Sloop Emulous. Escaped.

Collum, Robert   Prisoner 1433. Rank: Seaman, from: American Gunboats, Not Recorded.
    Cap: 05 Jan 1815 near New Orleans by Plantagenet Int: 27 Jan 1815 Dis: 05 Feb 1815.
    Taken in the American Gun Boats near New Orleans. Received from Ramilies. Into HM Ship Diomede per order of Sir TM Hardy Baronet.

American Prisoners of War Held at Jamaica During the War of 1812

Colmen, Christian   Prisoner 7. Rank: Seaman, from: Assaw, Merchant Vessel.
    Cap: 28 Jul 1812 at Sea by Garland Int: 22 Aug 1812 Dis: 09 May 1813.
    Recaptured having been taken by the American Privateer the Paul Jones. Received from Garland. to America for Exchange.

Colreto, Joseph   Prisoner 1427. Rank: Seaman, from: American Gunboats, Not Recorded.
    Cap: 05 Jan 1815 near New Orleans by Plantagenet Int: 27 Jan 1815 Dis: 05 Feb 1815.
    Taken in the American Gun Boats near New Orleans. Received from Ramilies. Into HM Ship Diomede per order of Sir TM Hardy Baronet.

Combs, John   Prisoner 1142. Rank: Seaman, from: Decatur, Privateer.
    Cap: 05 Jun 1814 at Sea by HM Ship Rhin Int: 20 Jun 1814 Dis: 02 Jan 1815.
    Received from HM Ship Rhin. Into HM Ship Sultan per order of Captain John West.

Connor, John   Prisoner 1376. Rank: Seaman, from: American Gunboats, Not Recorded.
    Cap: 05 Jan 1815 near New Orleans by Plantagenet Int: 27 Jan 1815 Dis: 05 Feb 1815.
    Taken in the American Gun Boats near New Orleans. Received from Ramilies. Into HM Ship Diomede per order of Sir TM Hardy Baronet.

Connor, William   Prisoner 121. Rank: Seaman, from: Morning Star, Merchant Vessel.
    Cap: 08 Sep 1812 at Sea by HMS Cyane Int: 22 Sep 1812 Dis: 24 Jul 1813.
    Received from Morning Star. To American Cartel Brig Aualostaw.

Cooney, Joseph   Prisoner 1406. Rank: Seaman, from: American Gunboats, Not Recorded.
    Cap: 05 Jan 1815 near New Orleans by Plantagenet Int: 27 Jan 1815 Dis: 05 Feb 1815.
    Taken in the American Gun Boats near New Orleans. Received from Ramilies. Into HM Ship Diomede per order of Sir TM Hardy Baronet.

Cooper, Peter   Prisoner 1316. Rank: Seaman, from: Nettervitte, Merchant Schooner.
    Cap: Not Recorded by HM Sloop Onyx Int: 30 Dec 1814 Dis: 02 Jan 1815.
    Received from HM Sloop Onyx. Into HM Ship Sultan per order of Captain John West. (Date of capture not recorded.)

Cooper, Sylus   Prisoner 93. Rank: Seaman, from: Poor Sailor, Privateer.
    Cap: 13 Sep 1812 at Sea by Garland Int: 18 Sep 1812 Dis: 04 Apr 1813.
    Received from Garland. To America for Exchange.

Cordelia, Nicholas   Prisoner 790. Rank: Seaman, from: San Francisco de Paula, Privateer.
    Cap: 02 Oct 1813 at Sea by Forrester Int: 07 Oct 1813 Dis: 29 Jul 1814.
    Received from Forrester. Board's Order.

Corey, Allen   Prisoner 1517. Rank: Seaman, from: Not Recorded, Not Recorded.
    Cap: 08 Dec 1814 at Sea by Albion Int: 04 Feb 1815 Dis: 11 Feb 1815.
    Taken for Passage to Jamaica Depot. Received from Rota. Into HM Ship Rota per order of Sir TM Hardy.

Corez, Juan Jose   Prisoner 1078. Rank: Seaman, from: Casada el Narino, Privateer.
    Cap: 29 May 1814 at Sea by HM Ship Rhin Int: 04 Jun 1814 Dis: 18 Aug 1814.
    Carthagenaian. Received from North Star. Board's Order.

Cornelius, Peter   Prisoner 1273. Rank: Seaman, from: Wolfe, Not Recorded.
    Cap: at Sea by Jalouse Int: 10 Sep 1814 Dis: 26 Sep 1814.
    American Schooner. Received from Jalouse. Board's Order. (Date of capture not recorded.)

Corral, Philip   Prisoner 882. Rank: Seaman, from: Lapwing, Packet.
    Cap: 08 Dec 1813 at Sea by Barrosa Int: 10 Dec 1813 Dis: 01 Aug 1814.
    Recaptured. Received from Barrosa. To American Cartel Brig Aualostaw.

Corwell, Timothy   Prisoner 1386. Rank: Seaman, from: American Gunboats, Not Recorded.
    Cap: 05 Jan 1815 near New Orleans by Plantagenet Int: 27 Jan 1815 Dis: 05 Feb 1815.
    Taken in the American Gun Boats near New Orleans. Received from Ramilies. Into HM Ship Diomede per order of Sir TM Hardy Baronet.

Cosgrove, J G   Prisoner 228. Rank: Gunner, from: Joseph & Mary, Privateer.
    Cap: 24 Nov 1812 at Sea by Narcissus Int: 26 Nov 1812 Escaped: 08 Mar 1813.
    Received from Narcissus. Escaped.

Cotterell, Thomson   Prisoner 466. Rank: Seaman, from: Saratoga, Merchant Vessel.
    Cap: 1813 at Sea by Fawn Int: 13 Jan 1813 Dis: 24 Jul 1813.
    Received from Sapphire. To American Cartel Brig Aualostaw. (Day and month of capture not recorded.)

Cotton, Ignatius   Prisoner 1414. Rank: Seaman, from: American Gunboats, Not Recorded.
    Cap: 05 Jan 1815 near New Orleans by Plantagenet Int: 27 Jan 1815 Dis: 05 Feb 1815.
    Taken in the American Gun Boats near New Orleans. Received from Ramilies. Into HM Ship Diomede per order of Sir TM Hardy Baronet.

American Prisoners of War Held at Jamaica During the War of 1812

Cotton, Philemon   Prisoner 1462. Rank: Seaman, from: Not Recorded, Not Recorded.
    Cap: 21 Dec 1814 at Sea by Severn Int: 04 Feb 1815 Dis: 11 Feb 1815.
    Taken for Passage to Jamaica Depot. Received from Rota. Into HMS Ramillies per order of Sir T M Hardy.

Cottwell, Rowland   Prisoner 1413. Rank: Seaman, from: American Gunboats, Not Recorded.
    Cap: 05 Jan 1815 near New Orleans by Plantagenet Int: 27 Jan 1815 Dis: 05 Feb 1815.
    Taken in the American Gun Boats near New Orleans. Received from Ramilies. Into HM Ship Diomede per order of Sir TM Hardy Baronet.

Coturel, Juan   Prisoner 909. Rank: Seaman, from: San Francisco Navier, Brig.
    Cap: 05 Dec 1813 at Sea by Sappho Int: 15 Dec 1813 Dis: 08 Aug 1814.
    Taken in the Recaptured Spanish Brig. Prize to the Carthagenaian Privateer Carthagenaian. Received from Sappho. Board's Order.

Courade, Christopher   Prisoner 665. Rank: Seaman, from: Lovely Lass, Privateer.
    Cap: 21 May 1813 at Sea by Circe Int: 23 May 1813 Dis: 22 Jul 1814.
    Received from Forrester. Board's Order.

Course, Peter   Prisoner 478. Rank: Seaman, from: Three Friends, Merchant Schooner.
    Cap: 03 Dec 1812 at Sea by Circe Int: 20 Jan 1813 Dis: 04 Apr 1813.
    Received from Circe. To America for Exchange.

Coursoll, Peter   Prisoner 1238. Rank: Seaman, from: Wolfe, Schooner.
    Cap: Not Recorded by Jalouse Int: 09 Aug 1814 Dis: 18 Aug 1814.
    Board's Order. (Date of capture not recorded.)

Court, John   Prisoner 808. Rank: Seaman, from: Enterprize, Privateer.
    Cap: 15 Nov 1813 at Sea by Argo Int: 19 Nov 1813 Dis: 05 Aug 1814.
    A Carthagenaian. Received from Argo. Board's Order.

Cowan, Jonathan   Prisoner 1412. Rank: Seaman, from: American Gunboats, Not Recorded.
    Cap: 05 Jan 1815 near New Orleans by Plantagenet Int: 27 Jan 1815 Dis: 05 Feb 1815.
    Taken in the American Gun Boats near New Orleans. Received from Ramilies. Into HM Ship Diomede per order of Sir TM Hardy Baronet.

Cowloff, Jacob   Prisoner 465. Rank: Seaman, from: Saratoga, Merchant Vessel.
    Cap: 1813 at Sea by Fawn Int: 13 Jan 1813 Dis: 24 Jul 1813.
    Received from Sapphire. To American Cartel Brig Aualostaw. (Day and month of capture not recorded.)

Cox, William   Prisoner 452. Rank: Seaman, from: Vixen, Man of War.
    Cap: 26 Dec 1812 at Sea by Rhodian Int: 26 Dec 1812 Dis: 04 Apr 1813.
    Received from Rhodian. Out of Custody under 12 years old. (Dates of capture and interment the same. Prisoner # 437, William Cocks.)

Crawford, John   Prisoner 28. Rank: Seaman, from: Madisonia, Merchant Vessel.
    Cap: 03 Aug 1812 at Sea by Garland Int: 22 Aug 1812 Dis: 09 May 1813.
    Received from Garland. to America for Exchange.

Crawford, Robert   Prisoner 388. Rank: Seaman, from: Vixen, Man of War.
    Cap: 22 Nov 1812 at Sea by Rhodian late of US Brig Vixen Int: 14 Dec 1812 Dis: 09 May 1813.
    Received from Rhodian. To America for Exchange.

Cricktus, Henry   Prisoner 1410. Rank: Seaman, from: American Gunboats, Not Recorded.
    Cap: 05 Jan 1815 near New Orleans by Plantagenet Int: 27 Jan 1815 Dis: 05 Feb 1815.
    Taken in the American Gun Boats near New Orleans. Received from Ramilies. Into HM Ship Diomede per order of Sir TM Hardy Baronet.

Crisby, Ransom   Prisoner 24. Rank: 2 Mate, from: Dal, Merchant Vessel.
    Cap: 03 Aug 1812 at Sea by Garland Int: 22 Aug 1812 Dis: 04 Apr 1813.
    Received from Garland. to America for Exchange.

Croft, William   Prisoner 952. Rank: Mate, from: Swift, Merchant Vessel.
    Cap: at Sea by Leonidas Int: 25 Jan 1814 Dis: 01 Aug 1814.
    Received from Leonidas. To American Cartel Brig Aualostaw. (Date of capture not recorded. Prisoner numbers 951 - 956 all have recorded rank of mate.)

Croker, Daul   Prisoner 486. Rank: Seaman, from: Philip, Merchant Vessel.
    Cap: 28 Jan 1813 at Sea by Morgiana Int: 30 Jan 1813 Dis: 24 Jul 1813.
    Recaptured. Received from Morgiana. To American Cartel Brig Aualostaw.

Croker, Lemiel   Prisoner 687. Rank: Seaman, from: Lovely Lass, Privateer.
    Cap: 15 May 1813 at Sea by Circe Int: 29 May 1813 Dis: 01 Aug 1814.
    Received from Circe. To American Cartel Brig Aualostaw.

Cromerty, Vincent   Prisoner 86. Rank: Seaman, from: Poor Sailor, Privateer.
    Cap: 13 Sep 1812 at Sea by Garland Int: 18 Sep 1812 Dis: 09 May 1813.
    Received from Garland. To America for Exchange.

American Prisoners of War Held at Jamaica During the War of 1812

Cromwell, Joseph   Prisoner 224. Rank: Prize Master, from: Joseph & Mary, Privateer.
    Cap: 24 Nov 1812 at Sea by Narcissus Int: 26 Nov 1812 Dis: 09 May 1813.
    Received from Narcissus. To America for Exchange.

Cropper, Isaac   Prisoner 301. Rank: Passenger, from: Mary, Merchant Vessel.
    Cap: 26 Nov 1812 at Sea by Sappho Int: 30 Nov 1812 Dis: 04 Apr 1813.
    Received from Sappho. To America for Exchange.

Crosby, James   Prisoner 1392. Rank: Seaman, from: American Gunboats, Not Recorded.
    Cap: 05 Jan 1815 near New Orleans by Plantagenet Int: 27 Jan 1815 Dis: 05 Feb 1815.
    Taken in the American Gun Boats near New Orleans. Received from Ramilies. Into HM Ship Diomede per order of Sir TM Hardy Baronet.

Crosier, William   Prisoner 729. Rank: Seaman, from: Not Recorded, Not Recorded.
    Cap: Not Recorded by Asia Int: 11 Jul 1813 Dis: 01 Aug 1814.
    An American. Received from Asia. To American Cartel Brig Aualostaw. (Date of capture not recorded.)

Crostinal, Demetreo   Prisoner 1233. Rank: Prize Master, from: La Union, Spanish Brig.
    Cap: 03 Aug 1814 at Sea by Variable Int: 06 Aug 1814 Dis: 23 Aug 1814.
    Recaptured from the Carthagenaian Privateer White Horse. Received from Variable. Board's Order.

Cuffy, Paul   Prisoner 300. Rank: Passenger, from: Mary, Merchant Vessel.
    Cap: 26 Nov 1812 at Sea by Sappho Int: 30 Nov 1812 Dis: 09 May 1813.
    Received from Sappho. To America for Exchange.

Cunningham, Henry   Prisoner 1395. Rank: Seaman, from: American Gunboats, Not Recorded.
    Cap: 05 Jan 1815 near New Orleans by Plantagenet Int: 27 Jan 1815 Dis: 05 Feb 1815.
    Taken in the American Gun Boats near New Orleans. Received from Ramilies. Into HM Ship Diomede per order of Sir TM Hardy Baronet.

Cunningham, James   Prisoner 381. Rank: Seaman, from: Vixen, Man of War.
    Cap: 22 Nov 1812 at Sea by Rhodian late of US Brig Vixen Int: 14 Dec 1812 Dis: 10 Feb 1813.
    Received from Rhodian. To Shark.

Currey, George   Prisoner 529. Rank: Seaman, from: Defiance, Privateer.
    Cap: 15 Mar 1813 at Sea by Nimrod Int: 17 Mar 1813 Dis: 24 Jul 1813.
    Received from Nimrod. To American Cartel Brig Aualostaw.

Curtis, Dennis   Prisoner 468. Rank: Seaman, from: Not Recorded, Merchant Vessel.
    Cap: Not Recorded by Not Recorded Int: 14 Jan 1813 Dis: 24 Jul 1813.
    An American. Received from Sapphire. To American Cartel Brig Aualostaw. (Date of capture not recorded.)

Cute, William   Prisoner 705. Rank: Seaman, from: Lovely Lass, Privateer.
    Cap: 15 May 1813 at Sea by Circe Int: 29 May 1813 Dis: 01 Aug 1814.
    Received from Circe. To American Cartel Brig Aualostaw.

Cuthall, Hoste   Prisoner 225. Rank: Masters Mate, from: Joseph & Mary, Privateer.
    Cap: 24 Nov 1812 at Sea by Narcissus Int: 26 Nov 1812 Dis: 04 Apr 1813.
    Received from Narcissus. To America for Exchange.

Cutter, Abraham   Prisoner 436. Rank: Not Recorded, from: Vixen, Man of War.
    Cap: 22 Nov 1812 at Sea by Rhodian Int: Dis:
    Received from Rhodian. Entered below. (Entry crossed out. Prisoner # 451. Dates of interment and discharge not recorded.)

Cutter, Abraham   Prisoner 451. Rank: Seaman, from: Vixen, Man of War.
    Cap: 26 Dec 1812 at Sea by Rhodian Int: 26 Dec 1812 Dis: 04 Apr 1813.
    Received from Rhodian. To America for Exchange. (Dates of capture and interment the same. Prisoner # 436.)

Daily, William   Prisoner 556. Rank: Seaman, from: Defiance, Privateer.
    Cap: 15 Mar 1813 at Sea by Nimrod Int: 17 Mar 1813 Dis: 24 Jul 1813.
    Received from Nimrod. To American Cartel Brig Aualostaw.

Daimont, Louis   Prisoner 1177. Rank: Seaman, from: Decatur, Privateer.
    Cap: 05 Jun 1814 at Sea by HM Ship Rhin Int: 20 Jun 1814 Dis: 10 Aug 1814.
    Received from HM Ship Rhin. Board's Order.

Dalbrow, Daniel   Prisoner 746. Rank: Seaman, from: Eliza, Merchant Vessel.
    Cap: 17 Jul 1813 at Sea by Sappho Int: 26 Jul 1813 Dis: 01 Aug 1814.
    Received from Sappho. To American Cartel Brig Aualostaw.

Dallew, James   Prisoner 279. Rank: Seaman, from: Joseph & Mary, Privateer.
    Cap: 24 Nov 1812 at Sea by Narcissus Int: 26 Nov 1812 Dis: 24 Jul 1813.
    Received from Narcissus. To American Cartel Brig Aualostaw.

Daly, John   Prisoner 1383. Rank: Seaman, from: American Gunboats, Not Recorded.
    Cap: 05 Jan 1815 near New Orleans by Plantagenet Int: 27 Jan 1815 Dis: 05 Feb 1815.
    Taken in the American Gun Boats near New Orleans. Received from Ramilies. Into HM Ship Diomede per order of Sir TM Hardy Baronet.

American Prisoners of War Held at Jamaica During the War of 1812

Damian, Jose   Prisoner 1228. Rank: Seaman, from: La Union, Spanish Brig.
    Cap: 03 Aug 1814 at Sea by Variable Int: 06 Aug 1814 Dis: 01 Sep 1814.
    Recaptured from the Carthagenaian Privateer White Horse. Received from Variable. Board's Order.

Daniels, John   Prisoner 163. Rank: Seaman, from: Rebecca Sims, Merchant Vessel.
    Cap: 12 Sep 1812 at Sea by Southampton Int: 07 Oct 1812 Dis: 01 Mar 1813.
    Received from Southampton. per Order of Admiral Stirling.

Darssliu, John   Prisoner 553. Rank: Seaman, from: Defiance, Privateer.
    Cap: 15 Mar 1813 at Sea by Nimrod Int: 17 Mar 1813 Dis: 24 Jul 1813.
    Received from Nimrod. To American Cartel Brig Aualostaw.

Dart, Stanton   Prisoner 69. Rank: Seaman, from: Poor Sailor, Privateer.
    Cap: 13 Sep 1812 at Sea by Garland Int: 18 Sep 1812 Dis: 24 Jul 1813.
    Received from Garland. To American Cartel Brig Aualostaw.

Dauast, Nicholas   Prisoner 987. Rank: Master, from: Young Eagle, Merchant Vessel.
    Cap: 28 Feb 1814 at Sea by Ringdove Int: 27 Mar 1814 Dis: 21 Jul 1814.
    Received from Ringdove. Board's Order.

Davenport, William   Prisoner 19. Rank: Seaman, from: Dal, Merchant Vessel.
    Cap: 03 Aug 1812 at Sea by Garland Int: 22 Aug 1812 Escaped: 30 Jan 1813.
    Received from Garland. Escaped.

Davenport, William   Prisoner 513. Rank: Seaman, from: Not Recorded, Not Recorded.
    Cap: 11 Feb 1813 at Lucea by Not Recorded Int: 26 Feb 1813 Dis: 09 May 1813.
    Retaken. Received from Sea Horse. To America for Exchange. (Prisoner number 19.)

David, Charles   Prisoner 355. Rank: Seaman, from: Vixen, Man of War.
    Cap: 22 Nov 1812 at Sea by Rhodian late of HM Brig Vixen Int: 14 Dec 1812 Dis: 09 May 1813.
    Received from Rhodian. To America for Exchange.

Davidson, Robert   Prisoner 1419. Rank: Seaman, from: American Gunboats, Not Recorded.
    Cap: 05 Jan 1815 near New Orleans by Plantagenet Int: 27 Jan 1815 Dis: 05 Feb 1815.
    Taken in the American Gun Boats near New Orleans. Received from Ramilies. Into HM Ship Diomede per order of Sir TM Hardy Baronet.

Davidson, Samuel   Prisoner 264. Rank: Seaman, from: Joseph & Mary, Privateer.
    Cap: 24 Nov 1812 at Sea by Narcissus Int: 26 Nov 1812 Dis: 09 May 1813.
    Received from Narcissus. To America for Exchange.

Davidson, William   Prisoner 1398. Rank: Seaman, from: American Gunboats, Not Recorded.
    Cap: 05 Jan 1815 near New Orleans by Plantagenet Int: 27 Jan 1815 Dis: 05 Feb 1815.
    Taken in the American Gun Boats near New Orleans. Received from Ramilies. Into HM Ship Diomede per order of Sir TM Hardy Baronet.

Davis, Daul   Prisoner 1017. Rank: Seaman, from: Chance, Privateer.
    Cap: 01 Apr 1814 at Sea by Statira Int: 20 Apr 1814 Dis: 11 Feb 1815.
    Received from Statira. per order of Sir T M Hardy Into HMS Ramillies.

Davis, E R   Prisoner 442. Rank: 2 Lieutenant, from: Vixen, Man of War.
    Cap: 24 Dec 1812 at Sea by Rhodian Int: 24 Dec 1812 Dis: 24 Dec 1812.
    Received from Rhodian. To Parole. (Dates of capture, interment and discharge the same.)

Davis, G P   Prisoner 1194. Rank: Prize Master, from: Neustra Cantado, Merchant Vessel.
    Cap: 01 Jun 1814 at Sea by HM Ship Argo Int: 27 Jun 1814 Dis: 29 Jul 1814.
    Retaken in the Spanish Ship Neustra Cantado. Received from HM Ship Argo. Board's Order.

Davis, Henry   Prisoner 1444. Rank: Seaman, from: American Gunboats, Not Recorded.
    Cap: 05 Jan 1815 near New Orleans by Plantagenet Int: 27 Jan 1815 Dis: 05 Feb 1815.
    Taken in the American Gun Boats near New Orleans. Received from Ramilies. Into HM Ship Diomede per order of Sir TM Hardy Baronet.

Davis, John   Prisoner 261. Rank: Seaman, from: Joseph & Mary, Privateer.
    Cap: 24 Nov 1812 at Sea by Narcissus Int: 26 Nov 1812 Dis: 24 Jul 1813.
    Received from Narcissus. To American Cartel Brig Aualostaw.

Davis, John   Prisoner 360. Rank: Seaman, from: Vixen, Man of War.
    Cap: 22 Nov 1812 at Sea by Rhodian late of HM Brig Vixen Int: 14 Dec 1812 Dis: 09 May 1813.
    Received from Rhodian. To America for Exchange. John Davis (1).

Davis, John   Prisoner 398. Rank: Seaman, from: Vixen, Man of War.
    Cap: 22 Nov 1812 at Sea by Rhodian late of US Brig Vixen Int: 14 Dec 1812 Dis: 09 May 1813.
    Received from Rhodian. To America for Exchange. John Davis (2).

Davis, John   Prisoner 650. Rank: Seaman, from: Not Recorded, Not Recorded.
    Cap: 17 May 1813 Not Recorded by Shark Int: 23 May 1813 Dis: 01 Aug 1814.
    An American. Received from Shark. To American Cartel Brig Aualostaw.

Davis, Luther   Prisoner 495. Rank: Seaman, from: Philip, Merchant Vessel.
    Cap: 28 Jan 1813 at Sea by Morgiana Int: 30 Jan 1813 Dis: 24 Jul 1813.
    Recaptured. Received from Morgiana. To American Cartel Brig Aualostaw.

American Prisoners of War Held at Jamaica During the War of 1812

Davis, Richman   Prisoner 1323. Rank: Seaman, from: Triton, Merchant Ship.
    Cap: Not Recorded by Not Recorded Int: 30 Dec 1814 Dis: 02 Jan 1815.
    These men were sent from the Triton Merchant Ship for Notorious behavior, had previously shipped in her as Englishmen. Received from HM Ship Suttan. Into HM Ship Sultan per order of Captain John West. (Date capture not recorded.)

Davis, Wallis   Prisoner 33. Rank: Seaman, from: Madisonia, Merchant Vessel.
    Cap: 03 Aug 1812 at Sea by Garland Int: 22 Aug 1812 Dis: 09 May 1813.
    Received from Garland. to America for Exchange.

Dawson, John   Prisoner 995. Rank: Seaman, from: Farmer's Daughter, Merchant Vessel.
    Cap: 30 Mar 1814 at Sea by Leviathan Int: 03 Apr 1814 Dis: 02 Jan 1815.
    Received from Leviathan. Into HM Ship Sultan per order of Captain John West.

Day, Ephram   Prisoner 959. Rank: Seaman, from: Active, Merchant Vessel.
    Cap: at Sea by Leonidas Int: 25 Jan 1814 Dis: 01 Aug 1814.
    Received from Leonidas. To American Cartel Brig Aualostaw. (Date of capture not recorded.)

Day, S   Prisoner 1137. Rank: Seaman, from: Decatur, Privateer.
    Cap: 05 Jun 1814 at Sea by HM Ship Rhin Int: 20 Jun 1814 Dis: 02 Jan 1815.
    Received from HM Ship Rhin. Into HM Ship Sultan per order of Captain John West.

de Anuila, Peadro   Prisoner 1109. Rank: Seaman, from: Romano & Adamante, Merchant Brig.
    Cap: 31 May 1814 at Sea by Leviathan Int: 17 Jun 1814 Dis: 18 Aug 1814.
    Received from Leviathan. Board's Order.

De Camp, William   Prisoner 239. Rank: Seaman, from: Joseph & Mary, Privateer.
    Cap: 24 Nov 1812 at Sea by Narcissus Int: 26 Nov 1812 Dis: 09 May 1813.
    Received from Narcissus. To America for Exchange.

de Cruz, Juan   Prisoner 762. Rank: Seaman, from: San Francisco de Paula, Privateer.
    Cap: 02 Oct 1813 at Sea by Forrester Int: 07 Oct 1813 Dis: 11 Jan 1814.
    Received from Forrester. per order.

de doVair, Epprough   Prisoner 1040. Rank: Seaman, from: Jennett, Brig.
    Cap: 29 May 1814 at Sea by HM Ship Rhin Int: 04 Jun 1814 Dis: 02 Jan 1815.
    Taken in the Swedish Brig Jennet. Received from North Star. Into HM Ship Sultan per order of Captain John West.

De Fatrime, Jacque   Prisoner 278. Rank: Seaman, from: Joseph & Mary, Privateer.
    Cap: 24 Nov 1812 at Sea by Narcissus Int: 26 Nov 1812 Dis: 21 Jul 1812.
    Received from Narcissus. Board's Order.

de Legran, Juan   Prisoner 913. Rank: Seaman, from: San Francisco Navier, Brig.
    Cap: 05 Dec 1813 at Sea by Sappho Int: 15 Dec 1813 Escaped: 12 May 1814.
    Taken in the Recaptured Spanish Brig. Prize to the Carthagenaian Privateer Carthagenaian. Received from Sappho. Escaped.

de Manuel, Juz   Prisoner 1103. Rank: Boy, from: Romano & Adamante, Merchant Brig.
    Cap: 31 May 1814 at Sea by Leviathan Int: 17 Jun 1814 Dis: 22 Jul 1814.
    Received from Leviathan. Board's Order.

De Maury, Lewis   Prisoner 418. Rank: Private, from: Vixen, Man of War.
    Cap: 22 Nov 1812 at Sea by Rhodian Int: 14 Dec 1812 Dis: 09 May 1813.
    Received from Brazier. To America for Exchange.

De Pena, N   Prisoner 1080. Rank: Seaman, from: Casada el Narino, Privateer.
    Cap: 29 May 1814 at Sea by HM Ship Rhin Int: 04 Jun 1814 Dis: 18 Aug 1814.
    Carthagenaian. Received from North Star. Board's Order.

Deale, William   Prisoner 743. Rank: Seaman, from: Eliza, Merchant Vessel.
    Cap: 17 Jul 1813 at Sea by Sappho Int: 26 Jul 1813 Escaped: 27 Sep 1813.
    Received from Sappho. Escaped.

Deas, Manuel   Prisoner 899. Rank: Lieutenant, from: Cartagenaian, Privateer.
    Cap: 05 Dec 1813 at Sea by Sappho Int: 15 Dec 1813 Dis: 11 Jan 1814.
    Belonging to the Carthagenaian Privateer Carthagenaian. Received from Sappho. per order.

Decossae, Louis   Prisoner 1167. Rank: Seaman, from: Decatur, Privateer.
    Cap: 05 Jun 1814 at Sea by HM Ship Rhin Int: 20 Jun 1814 Dis: 18 Aug 1814.
    Received from HM Ship Rhin. Board's Order.

Deledra, Francisco   Prisoner 1089. Rank: Seaman, from: Casada el Narino, Privateer.
    Cap: 29 May 1814 at Sea by HM Ship Rhin Int: 04 Jun 1814 Dis: 21 Aug 1814.
    Carthagenaian. Received from North Star. Board's Order.

Demon, John   Prisoner 1373. Rank: Seaman, from: American Gunboats, Not Recorded.
    Cap: 05 Jan 1815 near New Orleans by Plantagenet Int: 27 Jan 1815 Dis: 05 Feb 1815.
    Taken in the American Gun Boats near New Orleans. Received from Ramilies. Into HM Ship Diomede per order of Sir TM Hardy Baronet.

American Prisoners of War Held at Jamaica During the War of 1812

Denike, John   Prisoner 324. Rank: Seaman, from: Pirtshire, English Merchant Ship.
    Cap: Nov 1812 at Sea by Fawn Int: 06 Dec 1812 DEscaped: 28 Jun 1813.
    Recaptured. Eagle Privateer. Received from Fawn. Escaped. (Day of capture not recorded.)

Denis, Generio   Prisoner 1179. Rank: Seaman, from: Decatur, Privateer.
    Cap: 05 Jun 1814 at Sea by HM Ship Rhin Int: 20 Jun 1814 Dis: 21 Jul 1814.
    Received from HM Ship Rhin. Board's Order.

Dennet, William   Prisoner 1025. Rank: Seaman, from: Chance, Privateer.
    Cap: 01 Apr 1814 at Sea by Statira Int: 20 Apr 1814 Died: 02 Sep 1814.
    Received from Statira. Died.

Depont, Lewis   Prisoner 75. Rank: Seaman, from: Poor Sailor, Privateer.
    Cap: 13 Sep 1812 at Sea by Garland Int: 18 Sep 1812 Dis: 24 Jul 1813.
    Received from Garland. To American Cartel Brig Aualostaw.

Depot, Henry   Prisoner 525. Rank: Seaman, from: Defiance, Privateer.
    Cap: 15 Mar 1813 at Sea by Nimrod Int: 17 Mar 1813 Escaped: 24 Apr 1813.
    Received from Nimrod. Escaped.

Dequen, Julian   Prisoner 1161. Rank: Seaman, from: Decatur, Privateer.
    Cap: 05 Jun 1814 at Sea by HM Ship Rhin Int: 20 Jun 1814 Dis: 10 Aug 1814.
    Received from HM Ship Rhin. Board's Order.

Derrick, William   Prisoner 1010. Rank: Captain, from: Chance, Privateer.
    Cap: 01 Apr 1814 at Sea by Statira Int: 20 Apr 1814 Dis: 08 May 1814.
    Received from Statira. To Parole.

Destandes, Joseph   Prisoner 1300. Rank: Seaman, from: Dorothea, Merchant Vessel.
    Cap: 06 Dec 1814 off the River Bacascao |Cuba| by North Star Int: 15 Dec 1814 Dis: 02 Jan 1815.
    Received from North Star. Into HM Ship Sultan per order of Captain John West.

Detale, Juan   Prisoner 1159. Rank: Seaman, from: Decatur, Privateer.
    Cap: 05 Jun 1814 at Sea by HM Ship Rhin Int: 20 Jun 1814 Dis: 23 Aug 1814.
    Received from HM Ship Rhin. Board's Order.

Devaril, John   Prisoner 1035. Rank: Seaman, from: Jennett, Brig.
    Cap: 29 May 1814 at Sea by HM Ship Rhin Int: 04 Jun 1814 Dis: 02 Jan 1815.
    Taken in the Swedish Brig Jennet. Received from North Star. Into HM Ship Sultan per order of Captain John West.

Devenero, Francis   Prisoner 530. Rank: Seaman, from: Defiance, Privateer.
    Cap: 15 Mar 1813 at Sea by Nimrod Int: 17 Mar 1813 Died: 14 May 1813.
    Received from Nimrod. Died.

Dewallis, Macklin   Prisoner 527. Rank: Seaman, from: Defiance, Privateer.
    Cap: 15 Mar 1813 at Sea by Nimrod Int: 17 Mar 1813 Dis: 24 Jul 1813.
    Received from Nimrod. To American Cartel Brig Aualostaw.

Dexter, Charles   Prisoner 796. Rank: Lieutenant, from: Enterprize, Privateer.
    Cap: 15 Nov 1813 at Sea by Argo Int: 19 Nov 1813 Died: 30 Dec 1813.
    A Carthagenaian. Received from Argo. Killed by the Guard.

Diamond, John   Prisoner 320. Rank: Seaman, from: Pirtshire, English Merchant Ship.
    Cap: Nov 1812 at Sea by Fawn Int: 06 Dec 1812 Dis: 24 Jul 1813.
    Recaptured. Eagle Privateer. Received from Fawn. To American Cartel Brig Aualostaw. (Day of capture not recorded.)

Diani, Lewis   Prisoner 1330. Rank: Seaman, from: Not Recorded, Not Recorded.
    Cap: at Sea by HMS Shark Int: 07 Jan 1815 Dis: 10 Jan 1815.
    Ship 'Name Unknown'. Received from HMS Shark. Board's Order. (Date of capture not recorded.)

Dias, Andrew   Prisoner 1064. Rank: Seaman, from: Casada el Narino, Privateer.
    Cap: 29 May 1814 at Sea by HM Ship Rhin Int: 04 Jun 1814 Dis: 23 Aug 1814.
    Carthagenaian. Received from North Star. Board's Order.

Dibbett, Charles A   Prisoner 870. Rank: Prize Master, from: Lapwing, Packet.
    Cap: 08 Dec 1813 at Sea by Barrosa Int: 10 Dec 1813 Dis: 22 Jul 1814.
    Recaptured. Received from Barrosa. Board's Order.

Dibwa, John   Prisoner 672. Rank: Seaman, from: Lovely Lass, Privateer.
    Cap: 21 May 1813 at Sea by Circe Int: 23 May 1813 Dis: 21 Jul 1814.
    Received from Forrester. Board's Order.

Dick, David   Prisoner 518. Rank: Seaman, from: Not Recorded, Not Recorded.
    Cap: Not Recorded by Not Recorded Int: 12 Mar 1813 Dis: 24 Jul 1813.
    Received from Cyane. An American refusing to serve. To American Cartel Brig Aualostaw. (Date of capture not recorded.)

Dick, John   Prisoner 662. Rank: Seaman, from: Lovely Lass, Privateer.
    Cap: 21 May 1813 at Sea by Circe Int: 23 May 1813 Escaped: 28 Jun 1813.
    Received from Forrester. Escaped.

American Prisoners of War Held at Jamaica During the War of 1812

Dickey, Robert   Prisoner 392. Rank: Seaman, from: Vixen, Man of War.
    Cap: 22 Nov 1812 at Sea by Rhodian late of US Brig Vixen Int: 14 Dec 1812 Dis: 09 May 1813.
    Received from Rhodian. To America for Exchange.

Dickson, Peter   Prisoner 82. Rank: Seaman, from: Poor Sailor, Privateer.
    Cap: 13 Sep 1812 at Sea by Garland Int: 18 Sep 1812 Escaped: 15 Nov 1812.
    Received from Garland. Escaped.

Disgardins, Louis J   Prisoner 1126. Rank: Gunner, from: Decatur, Privateer.
    Cap: 05 Jun 1814 at Sea by HM Ship Rhin Int: 20 Jun 1814 Dis: 03 Aug 1814.
    Received from HM Ship Rhin. Board's Order.

Diskanskep, Christian   Prisoner 489. Rank: Seaman, from: Philip, Merchant Vessel.
    Cap: 28 Jan 1813 at Sea by Morgiana Int: 30 Jan 1813 Dis: 24 Jul 1813.
    Recaptured. Received from Morgiana. To American Cartel Brig Aualostaw.

Dixon, Dominique   Prisoner 1113. Rank: Captain, from: Decatur, Privateer.
    Cap: 05 Jun 1814 at Sea by HM Ship Rhin Int: 20 Jun 1814 Dis: .
    Received from HM Ship Rhin. Included in list but never received into custody. (No date of discharge.)

Dixon, James   Prisoner 269. Rank: Seaman, from: Joseph & Mary, Privateer.
    Cap: 24 Nov 1812 at Sea by Narcissus Int: 26 Nov 1812 Dis: 09 May 1813.
    Received from Narcissus. To America for Exchange.

Dixon, James   Prisoner 866. Rank: Seaman, from: Cato Georgiana, Not Recorded.
    Cap: 28 Nov 1813 at Sea by Barrosa Int: 10 Dec 1813 Dis: 01 Aug 1814.
    Prize to the US Frigate Essex. Received from Barrosa. To American Cartel Brig Aualostaw.

Dixon, Moses   Prisoner 726. Rank: Seaman, from: Mount Vernon, Merchant Man.
    Cap: at Sea by Argo Int: 27 Jun 1813 Dis: 02 Jul 1813.
    Received from Mount Vernon. To Mount Vernon per order of Adml Brown this date. (Date of capture not recorded.)

Dixon, P   Prisoner 1170. Rank: Seaman, from: Decatur, Privateer.
    Cap: 05 Jun 1814 at Sea by HM Ship Rhin Int: 20 Jun 1814 Dis: 21 Jul 1814.
    Received from HM Ship Rhin. Board's Order.

Dodge, Lewis   Prisoner 61. Rank: Seaman, from: Not Recorded, Not Recorded.
    Cap: 20 Aug 1812 Not Recorded by Not Recorded Int: 03 Sep 1812 Dis: 09 May 1813.
    Prison Ship at New Providence. Received from HM Schooner Decouverte. to America for Exchange.

Doing, D O   Prisoner 799. Rank: Seaman, from: Enterprize, Privateer.
    Cap: 15 Nov 1813 at Sea by Argo Int: 19 Nov 1813 Dis: 02 Jan 1815.
    A Carthagenaian. Received from Argo. Into HM Ship Sultan per order of Captain John West. (First name not legible.)

Dolft, John   Prisoner 63. Rank: Ordinary Seaman, from: Books, Not Recorded.
    Cap: Not Recorded by Not Recorded Int: 06 Sep 1812 Escaped: 15 Nov 1812.
    Received from Moselle. Escaped. (Date of capture not recorded.)

Dolino, Angel   Prisoner 1175. Rank: Seaman, from: Decatur, Privateer.
    Cap: 05 Jun 1814 at Sea by HM Ship Rhin Int: 20 Jun 1814 Dis: 16 Aug 1814.
    Received from HM Ship Rhin. Board's Order.

Dolore, Juan   Prisoner 914. Rank: Seaman, from: San Francisco Navier, Brig.
    Cap: 05 Dec 1813 at Sea by Sappho Int: 15 Dec 1813 Dis: 11 Jan 1814.
    Taken in the Recaptured Spanish Brig. Prize to the Carthagenaian Privateer Carthagenaian. Received from Sappho. per order.

Dolph, Joseph   Prisoner 684. Rank: Seaman, from: Arethusa, Man of War.
    Cap: 18 Apr 1813 Not Recorded by Variable Int: 26 May 1813 Dis: 01 Aug 1814.
    Received from Variable. To American Cartel Brig Aualostaw.

Dominico, John   Prisoner 1027. Rank: Cook, from: Chance, Privateer.
    Cap: 01 Apr 1814 at Sea by Statira Int: 20 Apr 1814 Dis: 02 Jan 1815.
    Received from Statira. Into HM Ship Sultan per order of Captain John West.

Donaldson, Frederick   Prisoner 323. Rank: Seaman, from: Pirtshire, English Merchant Ship.
    Cap: Nov 1812 at Sea by Fawn Int: 06 Dec 1812 Dis: 01 Aug 1814.
    Recaptured. Eagle Privateer. Received from Fawn. To America for Exchange. (Day of capture not recorded.)

Dore, James   Prisoner 395. Rank: Seaman, from: Vixen, Man of War.
    Cap: 22 Nov 1812 at Sea by Rhodian late of US Brig Vixen Int: 14 Dec 1812 Dis: 09 May 1813.
    Received from Rhodian. To America for Exchange.

Dotlaud, Martin   Prisoner 89. Rank: Seaman, from: Poor Sailor, Privateer.
    Cap: 13 Sep 1812 at Sea by Garland Int: 18 Sep 1812 Dis: 24 Jul 1813.
    Received from Garland. To American Cartel Brig Aualostaw.

American Prisoners of War Held at Jamaica During the War of 1812

Dotterside, William   Prisoner 309. Rank: Seaman, from: Joseph & Mary, Privateer.
    Cap: 24 Nov 1812 at Sea by Narcissus Int: 05 Dec 1812 Dis: 04 Apr 1813.
    Received from Narcissus. To America for Exchange.

Douglass, John   Prisoner 971. Rank: Not Recorded, from: Packet, Merchant Vessel.
    Cap: 08 Feb 1814 at Sea by Snake Int: 17 Feb 1814 Dis: 01 Aug 1814.
    Received from Snake. To American Cartel Brig Aualostaw.

Dow, Thomas   Prisoner 954. Rank: Mate, from: Swift, Merchant Vessel.
    Cap: at Sea by Leonidas Int: 25 Jan 1814 Dis: 01 Aug 1814.
    Received from Leonidas. To American Cartel Brig Aualostaw. (Date of capture not recorded. Prisoner numbers 951 - 956 all have recorded rank of mate.)

Drago, Francisco   Prisoner 1176. Rank: Seaman, from: Decatur, Privateer.
    Cap: 05 Jun 1814 at Sea by HM Ship Rhin Int: 20 Jun 1814 Dis: 22 Jul 1814.
    Received from HM Ship Rhin. Board's Order.

Drayton, Glen   Prisoner 441. Rank: 1 Lieutenant, from: Vixen, Man of War.
    Cap: 24 Dec 1812 at Sea by Rhodian Int: 24 Dec 1812 Dis: 24 Dec 1812.
    Received from Rhodian. To Parole. (Dates of capture, interment and discharge the same.)

Dreux, Edmond   Prisoner 1059. Rank: Seaman, from: Casada el Narino, Privateer.
    Cap: 29 May 1814 at Sea by HM Ship Rhin Int: 04 Jun 1814 Dis: 10 Aug 1814.
    Carthagenaian. Received from North Star. Board's Order.

Drew, Edmond   Prisoner 1285. Rank: Passenger, from: Dolores, Merchant Schooner.
    Cap: at Sea by HM Sloop Anaconda Int: 07 Oct 1814 Dis: 29 Oct 1814.
    Received from HM Sloop Anaconda. Board's Order. (Date of capture not recorded.)

Drew, Exra   Prisoner 236. Rank: Quartermaster, from: Joseph & Mary, Privateer.
    Cap: 24 Nov 1812 at Sea by Narcissus Int: 26 Nov 1812 Dis: 04 Apr 1813.
    Received from Narcissus. To America for Exchange.

Drummond, Robert   Prisoner 708. Rank: Mate, from: William, Merchant Man.
    Cap: 17 May 1813 at Sea by Circe Int: 29 May 1813 Dis: 15 Jan 1813.
    Received from Circe. To Parole. (Date of discharge should be January 15, 1814.)

Dunbar, Charles   Prisoner 363. Rank: Seaman, from: Vixen, Man of War.
    Cap: 22 Nov 1812 at Sea by Rhodian late of US Brig Vixen Int: 14 Dec 1812 Dis: 09 May 1813.
    Received from Rhodian. To America for Exchange.

Dupies, Alexander   Prisoner 895. Rank: Seaman, from: San Francisco Navier, Brig.
    Cap: 03 Dec 1813 at Sea by Sappho Int: 15 Dec 1813 Escaped: 12 May 1814.
    Taken in the Recaptured Spanish Brig. Prize to the Carthagenaian Privateer Carthagenaian. Received from Sappho. Escaped.

Duprat, Anthony   Prisoner 615. Rank: Surgeon, from: Mary Ann, Privateer.
    Cap: 05 May 1813 at Sea by Sapphire Int: 07 May 1813 Dis: 24 Jul 1813.
    Received from Sapphire. Board's Order.

Durant, John   Prisoner 544. Rank: Seaman, from: Defiance, Privateer.
    Cap: 15 Mar 1813 at Sea by Nimrod Int: 17 Mar 1813 Escaped: 28 Jun 1813.
    Received from Nimrod. Escaped.

Dursse, Laurence   Prisoner 523. Rank: Captain Marines, from: Defiance, Privateer.
    Cap: 15 Mar 1813 at Sea by Nimrod Int: 17 Mar 1813 Escaped: 28 Jun 1813.
    Received from Nimrod. Escaped.

Dusane, Levi   Prisoner 581. Rank: Seaman, from: Le Ventura, Privateer.
    Cap: 13 Mar 1813 at Sea by Cossac Int: 18 Mar 1813 Dis: 21 Jul 1814.
    Received from Cossac. Board's Order.

Dusenburg, David   Prisoner 1519. Rank: Seaman, from: Not Recorded, Not Recorded.
    Cap: 08 Dec 1814 at Sea by Albion Int: 04 Feb 1815 Dis: 11 Feb 1815.
    Taken for Passage to Jamaica Depot. Received from Rota. Into HM Ship Rota per order of Sir TM Hardy.

Dutuor, John   Prisoner 614. Rank: Lieutenant, from: Mary Ann, Privateer.
    Cap: 05 May 1813 at Sea by Sapphire Int: 07 May 1813 Dis: 21 Jul 1814.
    Received from Sapphire. Board's Order.

Dyer, Charles   Prisoner 1098. Rank: Seaman, from: Jennett, Brig.
    Cap: 29 May 1814 at Sea by HM Ship Rhin Int: 04 Jun 1814 Dis: 02 Jan 1815.
    Taken in the detained Swedish Brig Jennett. Received from North Star. Into HM Ship Sultan per order of Captain John West.

Dyer, John   Prisoner 202. Rank: Boy, from: Whim, Merchant Vessel.
    Cap: 18 Sep 1812 at Sea by Cyane Int: 20 Oct 1812 Dis: 20 Oct 1812.
    Received from Shark. Liberated.

American Prisoners of War Held at Jamaica During the War of 1812

Dyer, Shubald   Prisoner 568. Rank: Seaman, from: Defiance, Privateer.
    Cap: 15 Mar 1813 at Sea by Nimrod Int: 17 Mar 1813 Dis: 24 Jul 1813.
    Received from Nimrod. To American Cartel Brig Aualostaw.

Dyer, Watson   Prisoner 189. Rank: Seaman, from: Hamilton, Merchant Vessel.
    Cap: 28 Sep 1812 at Sea by Southampton Int: 09 Oct 1812 Dis: 09 May 1813.
    Received from Southampton. To America for Exchange.

Dykes, Sol   Prisoner 377. Rank: Seaman, from: Vixen, Man of War.
    Cap: 22 Nov 1812 at Sea by Rhodian late of US Brig Vixen Int: 14 Dec 1812 Dis: 09 May 1813.
    Received from Rhodian. To America for Exchange.

Eagelson, David   Prisoner 958. Rank: Mate, from: Active, Merchant Vessel.
    Cap: at Sea by Leonidas Int: 25 Jan 1814 Dis: 01 Aug 1814.
    Received from Leonidas. To American Cartel Brig Aualostaw. (Date of capture not recorded.)

Eastward, Jack   Prisoner 721. Rank: Seaman, from: Mount Vernon, Merchant Man.
    Cap: at Sea by Argo Int: 27 Jun 1813 Dis: 02 Jul 1813.
    Received from Mount Vernon. To Mount Vernon per order of Adml Brown this date. (Date of capture not recorded.)

Eaton, James   Prisoner 1426. Rank: Seaman, from: American Gunboats, Not Recorded.
    Cap: 05 Jan 1815 near New Orleans by Plantagenet Int: 27 Jan 1815 Dis: 05 Feb 1815.
    Taken in the American Gun Boats near New Orleans. Received from Ramilies. Into HM Ship Diomede per order of Sir TM Hardy Baronet.

Eden, Thomas   Prisoner 692. Rank: Seaman, from: Lovely Lass, Privateer.
    Cap: 15 May 1813 at Sea by Circe Int: 29 May 1813 Dis: 01 Aug 1814.
    Received from Circe. To American Cartel Brig Aualostaw.

Edgerton, Charles   Prisoner 272. Rank: Sergeant Marines, from: Joseph & Mary, Privateer.
    Cap: 24 Nov 1812 at Sea by Narcissus Int: 26 Nov 1812 Dis: 04 Apr 1813.
    Received from Narcissus. On Parole for Exchange.

Edinburgh, Peter   Prisoner 1487. Rank: Seaman, from: Not Recorded, Not Recorded.
    Cap: 20 Dec 1814 at Sea by Lacedaemonian Int: 04 Feb 1815 Dis: 11 Feb 1815.
    Taken for Passage to Jamaica Depot. Received from Rota. Into HMS Ramillies per order of Sir T M Hardy.

Edward, Pierre   Prisoner 855. Rank: Seaman, from: Le Galzo, Spanish Brig.
    Cap: 17 Nov 1813 at Sea by Variable Int: 28 Nov 1813 Dis: 22 Jul 1814.
    Recaptured from the Carthagenaian Privateer Le Legislateur. Received from Variable. Board's Order.

Edwards, William   Prisoner 996. Rank: Seaman, from: Farmer's Daughter, Merchant Vessel.
    Cap: 30 Mar 1814 at Sea by Leviathan Int: 03 Apr 1814 Dis: 02 Jan 1815.
    Received from Leviathan. Into HM Ship Sultan per order of Captain John West.

Edwards, William   Prisoner 1366. Rank: Seaman, from: American Gunboats, Not Recorded.
    Cap: 05 Jan 1815 near New Orleans by Plantagenet Int: 27 Jan 1815 Dis: 05 Feb 1815.
    Taken in the American Gun Boats near New Orleans. Received from Ramilies. Into HM Ship Diomede per order of Sir TM Hardy Baronet.

Edy, Edward   Prisoner 1521. Rank: Seaman, from: Not Recorded, Not Recorded.
    Cap: 08 Dec 1814 at Sea by Albion Int: 04 Feb 1815 Dis: 11 Feb 1815.
    Taken for Passage to Jamaica Depot. Received from Rota. Into HM Ship Rota per order of Sir TM Hardy.

Elberte, Mingo   Prisoner 347. Rank: Seaman, from: Vixen, Man of War.
    Cap: 22 Nov 1812 at Sea by Rhodian late of HM Brig Vixen Int: 14 Dec 1812 Dis: 09 May 1813.
    Received from Rhodian. To America for Exchange.

Elford, Roswell   Prisoner 497. Rank: Seaman, from: Not Recorded, Not Recorded.
    Cap: 29 Jan 1813 Not Recorded by Sapphire Int: 31 Jan 1813 Dis: 04 Apr 1813.
    Impressed American. Received from Sapphire. To America for Exchange.

Elisha, Thomas   Prisoner 177. Rank: Chief Mate, from: William Penn, Merchant Vessel.
    Cap: 08 Sep 1812 at Sea by Southampton Int: 09 Oct 1812 Dis: 22 Oct 1812.
    Received from Southampton. On Parole.

Elleridge, James H   Prisoner 607. Rank: Mate, from: Fly, Merchant Schooner.
    Cap: 15 Apr 1813 at Sea by Argo Int: 18 Apr 1813 Dis: 09 May 1813.
    Received from Argo. To American Cartel Brig Aualostaw.

Elliot, Alexander   Prisoner 96. Rank: Seaman, from: Poor Sailor, Privateer.
    Cap: 13 Sep 1812 at Sea by Garland Int: 18 Sep 1812 Dis: 24 Jul 1813.
    Received from Garland. To American Cartel Brig Aualostaw.

Elms, Robert   Prisoner 384. Rank: Seaman, from: Vixen, Man of War.
    Cap: 22 Nov 1812 at Sea by Rhodian late of US Brig Vixen Int: 14 Dec 1812 Dis: 09 May 1813.
    Received from Rhodian. To America for Exchange.

American Prisoners of War Held at Jamaica During the War of 1812

Emar, Joseph   Prisoner 688. Rank: Seaman, from: Lovely Lass, Privateer.
    Cap: 15 May 1813 at Sea by Circe Int: 29 May 1813 Dis: 27 Jul 1814.
    Received from Circe. Board's Order.

Emery, John   Prisoner 710. Rank: Seaman, from: William, Merchant Man.
    Cap: 17 May 1813 at Sea by Circe Int: 29 May 1813 Dis: 01 Aug 1814.
    Received from Circe. (No entry for discharge date.)

Emmery, David   Prisoner 403. Rank: Seaman, from: Vixen, Man of War.
    Cap: 22 Nov 1812 at Sea by Rhodian late of US Brig Vixen Int: 14 Dec 1812 Dis: 09 May 1813.
    Received from Rhodian. To America for Exchange.

Eperwiere, Jean   Prisoner 1131. Rank: Not Recorded, from: Decatur, Privateer.
    Cap: 05 Jun 1814 at Sea by HM Ship Rhin Int: 20 Jun 1814 Dis: 10 Aug 1814.
    Received from HM Ship Rhin. Board's Order.

Evans, John   Prisoner 446. Rank: Midshipman, from: Vixen, Man of War.
    Cap: 24 Dec 1812 at Sea by Rhodian Int: 24 Dec 1812 Dis: 26 Jan 1813.
    Received from Rhodian. To Parole from Hospital. (Dates of capture and interment the same.)

Everson, Benjamin   Prisoner 283. Rank: Seaman, from: Joseph & Mary, Privateer.
    Cap: 24 Nov 1812 at Sea by Narcissus Int: 26 Nov 1812 Dis: 04 Apr 1813.
    Received from Narcissus. To America for Exchange.

Fairo, James   Prisoner 334. Rank: Seaman, from: Sauders, Merchant Vessel.
    Cap: Nov 1812 at Sea by Merchant Vessel Monarch Int: 09 Dec 1812 Dis: 24 Jul 1813.
    Received from Monarch. To American Cartel Brig Aualostaw. (Day of capture not recorded.)

Falls, Richard   Prisoner 1394. Rank: Seaman, from: American Gunboats, Not Recorded.
    Cap: 05 Jan 1815 near New Orleans by Plantagenet Int: 27 Jan 1815 Dis: 05 Feb 1815.
    Taken in the American Gun Boats near New Orleans. Received from Ramilies. Into HM Ship Diomede per order of Sir TM Hardy Baronet.

Farmer, Robert   Prisoner 732. Rank: Seaman, from: Eliza, Merchant Vessel.
    Cap: 17 Jul 1813 at Sea by Sappho Int: 26 Jul 1813 Dis: 01 Aug 1814.
    Received from Sappho. To American Cartel Brig Aualostaw.

Faulin, Joseph   Prisoner 1286. Rank: Passenger, from: Dolores, Merchant Schooner.
    Cap: at Sea by HM Sloop Anaconda Int: 07 Oct 1814 Dis: 29 Oct 1814.
    Received from HM Sloop Anaconda. Board's Order. (Date of capture not recorded.)

Faviman, Lawrence   Prisoner 100. Rank: Seaman, from: Poor Sailor, Privateer.
    Cap: 13 Sep 1812 at Sea by Garland Int: 18 Sep 1812 Dis: 24 Jul 1813.
    Received from Garland. To American Cartel Brig Aualostaw.

Fawcett, Elles   Prisoner 480. Rank: Seaman, from: Three Friends, Merchant Schooner.
    Cap: 03 Dec 1812 at Sea by Circe Int: 20 Jan 1813 Dis: 04 Apr 1813.
    Received from Circe. To America for Exchange.

Fencho, Eiten   Prisoner 1303. Rank: Seaman, from: Not Recorded, Not Recorded.
    Cap: Not Recorded by HM Sloop Dasher Int: 16 Dec 1814 Dis: 02 Jan 1815.
    Ship 'Name Unknown'. Received from HM Sloop Dasher. Into HM Ship Sultan per order of Captain John West. (Date of capture not recorded.)

Fenhold, David   Prisoner 477. Rank: Seaman, from: Three Friends, Merchant Schooner.
    Cap: 03 Dec 1812 at Sea by Circe Int: 20 Jan 1813 Dis: 04 Apr 1813.
    Received from Circe. To America for Exchange.

Fernandes, Euscbio   Prisoner 750. Rank: Clerk, from: San Francisco de Paula, Privateer.
    Cap: 02 Oct 1813 at Sea by Forrester Int: 07 Oct 1813 Dis: 11 Jan 1814.
    Received from Forrester. per order. (Prisoner numbers 750 - 755 all have recorded rank of clerk.)

Fernandez, Emanuel   Prisoner 1077. Rank: Seaman, from: Casada el Narino, Privateer.
    Cap: 29 May 1814 at Sea by HM Ship Rhin Int: 04 Jun 1814 Dis: 18 Aug 1814.
    Carthagenaian. Received from North Star. Board's Order.

Fernandez, Francisco   Prisoner 1075. Rank: Seaman, from: Casada el Narino, Privateer.
    Cap: 29 May 1814 at Sea by HM Ship Rhin Int: 04 Jun 1814 Dis: 18 Aug 1814.
    Carthagenaian. Received from North Star. Board's Order.

Fertion, J B   Prisoner 1343. Rank: Seaman, from: Not Recorded, Not Recorded.
    Cap: at Sea by HMS Shark Int: 07 Jan 1815 Dis: 10 Jan 1815.
    Ship 'Name Unknown'. Received from HMS Shark. Board's Order. (Date of capture not recorded.)

Fertizon, Rene   Prisoner 1338. Rank: Seaman, from: Not Recorded, Not Recorded.
    Cap: at Sea by HMS Shark Int: 07 Jan 1815 Dis: 10 Jan 1815.
    Ship 'Name Unknown'. Received from HMS Shark. Board's Order. (Date of capture not recorded.)

Field, Henry   Prisoner 645. Rank: Seaman, from: Mary Ann, Privateer.
    Cap: 05 May 1813 at Sea by Sapphire Int: 07 May 1813 Dis: 01 Aug 1814.
    Received from Sapphire. To American Cartel Brig Aualostaw.

American Prisoners of War Held at Jamaica During the War of 1812

Fifer, Jacob   Prisoner 258. Rank: Seaman, from: Joseph & Mary, Privateer.
 Cap: 24 Nov 1812 at Sea by Narcissus Int: 26 Nov 1812 Dis: 24 Jul 1813.
 Received from Narcissus. To American Cartel Brig Aualostaw.

Figuire, G   Prisoner 1050. Rank: Seaman, from: Casada el Narino, Privateer.
 Cap: 29 May 1814 at Sea by HM Ship Rhin Int: 04 Jun 1814 Dis: 05 Aug 1814.
 Carthagenaian. Received from North Star. Board's Order.

Fisher, John   Prisoner 536. Rank: Seaman, from: Defiance, Privateer.
 Cap: 15 Mar 1813 at Sea by Nimrod Int: 17 Mar 1813 Dis: 24 Jul 1813.
 Received from Nimrod. To American Cartel Brig Aualostaw.

Fishwort, William   Prisoner 841. Rank: Seaman, from: Maria, An American Merchant Schooner.
 Cap: 15 Nov 1813 at Sea by Argo Int: 19 Nov 1813 Dis: 01 Aug 1814.
 Received from Argo. To American Cartel Brig Aualostaw.

Fivash, John   Prisoner 1216. Rank: Seaman, from: Mary, Merchant Schooner.
 Cap: 17 Jun 1814 at Sea by Sapphire Int: 10 Jul 1814 Dis: 02 Jan 1815.
 Recaptured. Received from Sapphire. Into HM Ship Suttan per order of Captain John West.

Fletcher, Aaron   Prisoner 1510. Rank: Seaman, from: Not Recorded, Not Recorded.
 Cap: 08 Dec 1814 at Sea by Albion Int: 04 Feb 1815 Dis: 11 Feb 1815.
 Taken for Passage to Jamaica Depot. Received from Rota. Into HM Ship Rota per order of Sir TM Hardy.

Fleury, Joseph   Prisoner 1242. Rank: Seaman, from: John, Merchant Vessel.
 Cap: 11 Aug 1814 at Sea by Variable Int: 15 Aug 1814 Dis: 10 Nov 1814.
 Received from Variable. Board's Order.

Flood, Samuel   Prisoner 151. Rank: Seaman, from: Philip, Merchant Vessel.
 Cap: 10 Sep 1812 at Sea by Southampton Int: 07 Oct 1812 Dis: 01 Mar 1813.
 Received from Southampton. per Order of Adml Stirling to American Ship Philip.

Flurit, Aman   Prisoner 792. Rank: Lieutenant, from: San Francisco de Paula, Privateer.
 Cap: 02 Oct 1813 at Sea by Forrester Int: 07 Oct 1813 Died: 30 Dec 1813.
 Received from Forrester. Killed By the Guard.

Fodham, Charles   Prisoner 1440. Rank: Seaman, from: American Gunboats, Not Recorded.
 Cap: 05 Jan 1815 near New Orleans by Plantagenet Int: 27 Jan 1815 Dis: 05 Feb 1815.
 Taken in the American Gun Boats near New Orleans. Received from Ramilies. Into HM Ship Diomede per order of Sir TM Hardy Baronet.

Fokey, William   Prisoner 348. Rank: Seaman, from: Vixen, Man of War.
 Cap: 22 Nov 1812 at Sea by Rhodian late of HM Brig Vixen Int: 14 Dec 1812 Dis: 09 May 1813.
 Received from Rhodian. To America for Exchange.

Ford, Bapt   Prisoner 29. Rank: Seaman, from: Madisonia, Merchant Vessel.
 Cap: 03 Aug 1812 at Sea by Garland Int: 22 Aug 1812 Dis: 09 May 1813.
 Received from Garland. to America for Exchange.

Ford, Samuel   Prisoner 238. Rank: Seaman, from: Joseph & Mary, Privateer.
 Cap: 24 Nov 1812 at Sea by Narcissus Int: 26 Nov 1812 Dis: 09 May 1813.
 Received from Narcissus. To America for Exchange.

Forewell, George   Prisoner 1368. Rank: Seaman, from: American Gunboats, Not Recorded.
 Cap: 05 Jan 1815 near New Orleans by Plantagenet Int: 27 Jan 1815 Dis: 05 Feb 1815.
 Taken in the American Gun Boats near New Orleans. Received from Ramilies. Into HM Ship Diomede per order of Sir TM Hardy Baronet.

Forkiere, Edward   Prisoner 563. Rank: Seaman, from: Defiance, Privateer.
 Cap: 15 Mar 1813 at Sea by Nimrod Int: 17 Mar 1813 Dis: 24 Jul 1813.
 Received from Nimrod. To American Cartel Brig Aualostaw.

Forne, Barto   Prisoner 754. Rank: Clerk, from: San Francisco de Paula, Privateer.
 Cap: 02 Oct 1813 at Sea by Forrester Int: 07 Oct 1813 Dis: 01 Aug 1814.
 Received from Forrester. Board's Order. (Prisoner numbers 750 - 755 all have recorded rank of clerk.)

Forster, William   Prisoner 281. Rank: Seaman, from: Joseph & Mary, Privateer.
 Cap: 24 Nov 1812 at Sea by Narcissus Int: 26 Nov 1812 Dis: 04 Apr 1813.
 Received from Narcissus. To America for Exchange.

Fortunel, Pedro   Prisoner 1051. Rank: Seaman, from: Casada el Narino, Privateer.
 Cap: 29 May 1814 at Sea by HM Ship Rhin Int: 04 Jun 1814 Dis: 26 Jul 1814.
 Carthagenaian. Received from North Star. Board's Order.

Foster, Jonathan   Prisoner 6. Rank: Seaman, from: Assaw, Merchant Vessel.
 Cap: 28 Jul 1812 at Sea by Garland Int: 22 Aug 1812 Dis: 09 May 1813.
 Recaptured having been taken by the American Privateer the Paul Jones. Received from Garland. to America for Exchange.

American Prisoners of War Held at Jamaica During the War of 1812

Foster, Samuel   Prisoner 499. Rank: Seaman, from: Not Recorded, Not Recorded.
    Cap: 05 Feb 1813 Not Recorded by Sapphire Int: 05 Feb 1813 Dis: 04 Apr 1813.
    Impressed American. Received from Sapphire. To America for Exchange.

Foutnay, Francis   Prisoner 698. Rank: Seaman, from: Lovely Lass, Privateer.
    Cap: 15 May 1813 at Sea by Circe Int: 29 May 1813 Dis: 27 Jul 1814.
    Received from Circe. Board's Order.

Fox, Edward   Prisoner 1298. Rank: Master, from: Not Recorded, Merchant Vessel.
    Cap: Not Recorded by Lacedaemonian Int: 01 Dec 1814 Dis: 02 Jan 1815.
    Broke his Parole at Nassau New Providence and arrived at this Port yesterday in a Merchant Sloop.
    Received from Magnificent. Into HM Ship Sultan per order of Captain John West. (Date of capture not

Foxwill, George   Prisoner 487. Rank: Seaman, from: Philip, Merchant Vessel.
    Cap: 28 Jan 1813 at Sea by Morgiana Int: 30 Jan 1813 Dis: 04 Apr 1813.
    Recaptured. Received from Morgiana. To America for Exchange.

Frances, Henry   Prisoner 186. Rank: Seaman, from: Rebecca Sims, Merchant Vessel.
    Cap: 12 Sep 1812 at Sea by Southampton Int: 09 Oct 1812 Dis: 01 Mar 1813.
    Received from Southampton. per Order of Admiral Stirling.

Francisco, Jose   Prisoner 788. Rank: Seaman, from: San Francisco de Paula, Privateer.
    Cap: 02 Oct 1813 at Sea by Forrester Int: 07 Oct 1813 Dis: 23 Nov 1813.
    Received from Forrester. per order of Rear Adml Brown.

Francisco, Juan   Prisoner 589. Rank: Seaman, from: Le Ventura, Privateer.
    Cap: 13 Mar 1813 at Sea by Cossac Int: 18 Mar 1813 Dis: 01 Aug 1814.
    Received from Cossac. Board's Order.

Francisco, Juan   Prisoner 1232. Rank: Seaman, from: La Union, Spanish Brig.
    Cap: 03 Aug 1814 at Sea by Variable Int: 06 Aug 1814 Dis: 01 Sep 1814.
    Recaptured from the Carthagenaian Privateer White Horse. Received from Variable. Board's Order.

Frank, John   Prisoner 548. Rank: Seaman, from: Defiance, Privateer.
    Cap: 15 Mar 1813 at Sea by Nimrod Int: 17 Mar 1813 Dis: 24 Jul 1813.
    Received from Nimrod. To American Cartel Brig Aualostaw.

Frank, Peter   Prisoner 700. Rank: Seaman, from: Lovely Lass, Privateer.
    Cap: 15 May 1813 at Sea by Circe Int: 29 May 1813 Dis: 01 Aug 1814.
    Received from Circe. To American Cartel Brig Aualostaw.

Franklin, Edward   Prisoner 39. Rank: Seaman, from: Petham, Merchant Vessel.
    Cap: 20 Aug 1812 Port Royal by Tartaus Int: 22 Aug 1812 Dis: 15 Nov 1812.
    Taken from the British Merchant Ship Petham at Port Royal. Received from Tartaus. Escaped. fs Retd
    2 September.

Fraser, John   Prisoner 378. Rank: Seaman, from: Vixen, Man of War.
    Cap: 22 Nov 1812 at Sea by Rhodian late of US Brig Vixen Int: 14 Dec 1812 Dis: 09 May 1813.
    Received from Rhodian. To America for Exchange.

Fraunswell, Lewis   Prisoner 659. Rank: Seaman, from: Lovely Lass, Privateer.
    Cap: 21 May 1813 at Sea by Circe Int: 23 May 1813 Dis: 21 Jul 1814.
    Received from Forrester. Board's Order.

Frazer, Henry   Prisoner 1509. Rank: Master, from: Not Recorded, Not Recorded.
    Cap: 08 Dec 1814 at Sea by Albion Int: 04 Feb 1815 Dis: 11 Feb 1815.
    Taken for Passage to Jamaica Depot. Received from Rota. Into HM Ship Rota per order of Sir TM
    Hardy.

Frazier, York   Prisoner 1460. Rank: Seaman, from: Not Recorded, Not Recorded.
    Cap: 21 Dec 1814 at Sea by Severn Int: 04 Feb 1815 Dis: 11 Feb 1815.
    Taken for Passage to Jamaica Depot. Received from Rota. Into HMS Ramillies per order of Sir T M
    Hardy.

Frederick, John   Prisoner 728. Rank: Seaman, from: Not Recorded, Not Recorded.
    Cap: Not Recorded by Fawn Int: 10 Jul 1813 Dis: 01 Aug 1814.
    An American. Received from Fawn.To American Cartel Brig Aualostaw. (Date of capture not
    recorded.)

Free, George   Prisoner 1183. Rank: Seaman, from: Decatur, Privateer.
    Cap: 05 Jun 1814 at Sea by HM Ship Rhin Int: 20 Jun 1814 Escaped: 18 Dec 1814.
    Received from HM Ship Rhin. Escaped.

Freeman, Maul   Prisoner 81. Rank: Seaman, from: Poor Sailor, Privateer.
    Cap: 13 Sep 1812 at Sea by Garland Int: 18 Sep 1812 Dis: 09 May 1813.
    Received from Garland. To America for Exchange.

Freeman, Thomas   Prisoner 514. Rank: Seaman, from: Not Recorded, Not Recorded.
    Cap: Not Recorded by Not Recorded Int: 05 Mar 1813 Dis: 09 May 1813.
    Received from Algerine. An American refusing to serve. To America for Exchange. (Date of capture
    not recorded.)

American Prisoners of War Held at Jamaica During the War of 1812

French, Abraham   Prisoner 1264. Rank: Seaman, from: Not Recorded, Not Recorded.
    Cap: Kingston by Not Recorded Int: 08 Sep 1814 Dis: 02 Jan 1815.
    Seized at Kingston last night being Americans. Received from Talbot. Into HM Ship Sultan per order of Captain John West. (Date of capture assumed to be September 7, 1814.)

Fuller, Peter   Prisoner 1193. Rank: Seaman, from: Not Recorded, Not Recorded.
    Cap: 01 Feb 1813 Barbados by HM Schooner Elizabeth Int: 25 Jun 1814 Dis: 01 Dec 1814.
    Given up as an American. Received from HM Schooner Elizabeth. Board's Order.

Fuller, Peter   Prisoner 1541. Rank: Seaman, from: Not Recorded, Not Recorded.
    Cap: 04 Jan 1815 at Sea by Thracian Int: 04 Mar 1815 Dis: 30 Mar 1815.
    Impressed. Received from Thracian. In consequence of Peace with America.

Furneau, George   Prisoner 574. Rank: Seaman, from: Defiance, Privateer.
    Cap: 15 Mar 1813 at Sea by Nimrod Int: 17 Mar 1813 Dis: 09 May 1813.
    Received from Nimrod. To America for Exchange.

Furney, John   Prisoner 367. Rank: Seaman, from: Vixen, Man of War.
    Cap: 22 Nov 1812 at Sea by Rhodian late of US Brig Vixen Int: 14 Dec 1812 Dis: 04 Apr 1813.
    Received from Rhodian. To America for Exchange.

Furrall, Thomas   Prisoner 22. Rank: Seaman, from: Dal, Merchant Vessel.
    Cap: 03 Aug 1812 at Sea by Garland Int: 22 Aug 1812 Dis: 09 May 1813.
    Received from Garland. to America for Exchange.

Furrell, John   Prisoner 1246. Rank: Passenger but Seaman, from: John, Merchant Vessel.
    Cap: 11 Aug 1814 at Sea by Variable Int: 15 Aug 1814 Dis: 02 Jan 1815.
    Received from Variable. Into HM Ship Sultan per order of Captain John West.

Gabeirre, John   Prisoner 1134. Rank: Mate, from: Decatur, Privateer.
    Cap: 05 Jun 1814 at Sea by HM Ship Rhin Int: 20 Jun 1814 Dis: 02 Jan 1815.
    Received from HM Ship Rhin. Into HM Ship Sultan per order of Captain John West.

Gabriel, James   Prisoner 977. Rank: Seaman, from: 26th October 1812, Merchant Vessel.
    Cap: 20 Feb 1814 at Sea by Leviathan Int: 06 Mar 1814 Dis: 01 Aug 1814.
    Received from Leviathan. To American Cartel Brig Aualostaw.

Gale, Russel   Prisoner 1024. Rank: Seaman, from: Chance, Privateer.
    Cap: 01 Apr 1814 at Sea by Statira Int: 20 Apr 1814 Dis: 02 Jan 1815.
    Received from Statira. Into HM Ship Sultan per order of Captain John West.

Garbin, John   Prisoner 182. Rank: Chief Mate, from: Rebecca Sims, Merchant Vessel.
    Cap: 12 Sep 1812 at Sea by Southampton Int: 09 Oct 1812 Dis: 22 Mar 1813.
    Received from Southampton. On Parole.

Gardner, Samuel   Prisoner 223. Rank: Master, from: Joseph & Mary, Privateer.
    Cap: 24 Nov 1812 at Sea by Narcissus Int: 26 Nov 1812 Dis: 04 Apr 1813.
    Received from Narcissus. To America for Exchange.

Garland, Robert   Prisoner 138. Rank: Seaman, from: Whim, Merchant Vessel.
    Cap: 04 Oct 1812 at Sea by HM Brig Liberty Int: 07 Oct 1812 Dis: 29 Apr 1813.
    Received from Cyane. To Phanix.

Garner, Robert   Prisoner 1447. Rank: Seaman, from: American Gunboats, Not Recorded.
    Cap: 05 Jan 1815 near New Orleans by Plantagenet Int: 27 Jan 1815 Dis: 05 Feb 1815.
    Taken in the American Gun Boats near New Orleans. Received from Ramilies. Into HM Ship Diomede per order of Sir TM Hardy Baronet.

Gasee, Nicholas   Prisoner 816. Rank: Seaman, from: Enterprize, Privateer.
    Cap: 15 Nov 1813 at Sea by Argo Int: 19 Nov 1813 Dis: 11 Jan 1814.
    A Carthagenaian. Received from Argo. per order.

Gaul, John   Prisoner 217. Rank: Prisoner, from: Not Recorded, Privateer.
    Cap: New Providence by Sappho Int: 28 Oct 1812 Dis: 04 Apr 1813.
    Unknown. Received from Sappho. To America for Exchange. (Date of capture not recorded.)

Gay, Peter   Prisoner 1431. Rank: Seaman, from: American Gunboats, Not Recorded.
    Cap: 05 Jan 1815 near New Orleans by Plantagenet Int: 27 Jan 1815 Dis: 05 Feb 1815.
    Taken in the American Gun Boats near New Orleans. Received from Ramilies. Into HM Ship Diomede per order of Sir TM Hardy Baronet.

Gebeau, Anthony   Prisoner 524. Rank: Prize Master, from: Defiance, Privateer.
    Cap: 15 Mar 1813 at Sea by Nimrod Int: 17 Mar 1813 Dis: 24 Jul 1813.
    Received from Nimrod. To American Cartel Brig Aualostaw.

Gebeau, John   Prisoner 545. Rank: Seaman, from: Defiance, Privateer.
    Cap: 15 Mar 1813 at Sea by Nimrod Int: 17 Mar 1813 Dis: 24 Jul 1813.
    Received from Nimrod. To American Cartel Brig Aualostaw.

Gebson, James   Prisoner 482. Rank: Seaman, from: Ardent, Merchant Vessel.
    Cap: 18 Jan 1813 at Sea by Circe Int: 20 Jan 1813 Dis: 09 May 1813.
    Received from Circe. To America for Exchange.

American Prisoners of War Held at Jamaica During the War of 1812

George, Thomas   Prisoner 625. Rank: Seaman, from: Mary Ann, Privateer.
    Cap: 05 Mar 1813 at Sea by Sapphire Int: 07 May 1813 Dis: 01 Aug 1814.
    Received from Sapphire. To American Cartel Brig Aualostaw.

George, William   Prisoner 330. Rank: Seaman, from: Sauders, Merchant Vessel.
    Cap: Nov 1812 at Sea by Merchant Vessel Monarch Int: 09 Dec 1812 Dis: 24 Jul 1813.
    Received from Monarch. To American Cartel Brig Aualostaw. (Day of capture not recorded.)

Geraldine, Jose   Prisoner 1066. Rank: Seaman, from: Casada el Narino, Privateer.
    Cap: 29 May 1814 at Sea by HM Ship Rhin Int: 04 Jun 1814 Dis: 23 Jul 1814.
    Carthagenaian. Received from North Star. Board's Order.

Gerin, Luis   Prisoner 916. Rank: Seaman, from: San Francisco Navier, Brig.
    Cap: 05 Dec 1813 at Sea by Sappho Int: 15 Dec 1813 Died: 14 May 1814.
    Taken in the Recaptured Spanish Brig. Prize to the Carthagenaian Privateer Carthagenaian. Received from Sappho. Killed by the Guard.

Gerloo, Peter   Prisoner 558. Rank: Seaman, from: Defiance, Privateer.
    Cap: 15 Mar 1813 at Sea by Nimrod Int: 17 Mar 1813 Dis: 09 May 1813.
    Received from Nimrod. To America for Exchange.

Ghado, Maina   Prisoner 1125. Rank: Boatswain, from: Decatur, Privateer.
    Cap: 05 Jun 1814 at Sea by HM Ship Rhin Int: 20 Jun 1814 Dis: 24 Jul 1814.
    Received from HM Ship Rhin. Board's Order.

Ghering, John   Prisoner 695. Rank: Seaman, from: Lovely Lass, Privateer.
    Cap: 15 May 1813 at Sea by Circe Int: 29 May 1813 Dis: 01 Aug 1814.
    Received from Circe. To American Cartel Brig Aualostaw.

Gibbons, John   Prisoner 874. Rank: Seaman, from: Lapwing, Packet.
    Cap: 08 Dec 1813 at Sea by Barrosa Int: 10 Dec 1813 Escaped: 31 Jan 1814.
    Recaptured. Received from Barrosa. Escaped.

Gibson, John   Prisoner 1363. Rank: Seaman, from: American Gunboats, Not Recorded.
    Cap: 05 Jan 1815 near New Orleans by Plantagenet Int: 27 Jan 1815 Dis: 05 Feb 1815.
    Taken in the American Gun Boats near New Orleans. Received from Ramilies. Into HM Ship Diomede per order of Sir TM Hardy Baronet.

Gilbert, Martin   Prisoner 869. Rank: Seaman, from: Cato Georgiana, Not Recorded.
    Cap: 28 Nov 1813 at Sea by Barrosa Int: 10 Dec 1813 Dis: 01 Aug 1814.
    Prize to the US Frigate Essex. Received from Barrosa. To American Cartel Brig Aualostaw.

Gillbert, Antonio   Prisoner 1157. Rank: Seaman, from: Decatur, Privateer.
    Cap: 05 Jun 1814 at Sea by HM Ship Rhin Int: 20 Jun 1814 Dis: 12 Aug 1814.
    Received from HM Ship Rhin. Board's Order.

Gilpin, John   Prisoner 55. Rank: Chief Mate, from: Madisonia, Merchant Vessel.
    Cap: 03 Aug 1812 at Sea by HM Ship Garland Int: 27 Aug 1812 Dis: 28 Aug 1812.
    Received from HM Ship Herald. To Parole.

Gleeves, Jacob   Prisoner 268. Rank: Boy, from: Joseph & Mary, Privateer.
    Cap: 24 Nov 1812 at Sea by Narcissus Int: 26 Nov 1812 Dis: 24 Jul 1813.
    Received from Narcissus. To American Cartel Brig Aualostaw.

Glen, Peter   Prisoner 490. Rank: Seaman, from: Philip, Merchant Vessel.
    Cap: 28 Jan 1813 at Sea by Morgiana Int: 30 Jan 1813 Dis: 24 Jul 1813.
    Recaptured. Received from Morgiana. To American Cartel Brig Aualostaw.

Gluton, M   Prisoner 232. Rank: Carpenters Mate, from: Joseph & Mary, Privateer.
    Cap: 24 Nov 1812 at Sea by Narcissus Int: 26 Nov 1812 Dis: 09 May 1813.
    Received from Narcissus. To America for Exchange. (First name not legible.)

Godfrey, William   Prisoner 149. Rank: Seaman, from: William Penn, Merchant Vessel.
    Cap: 08 Sep 1812 at Sea by Southampton Int: 07 Oct 1812 Escaped: 15 Nov 1812.
    Received from Southampton. Escaped.

Godfrey, William   Prisoner 1357. Rank: Seaman, from: American Gunboats, Not Recorded.
    Cap: 05 Jan 1815 near New Orleans by Plantagenet Int: 27 Jan 1815 Dis: 05 Feb 1815.
    Taken in the American Gun Boats near New Orleans. Received from Ramilies. Into HM Ship Diomede per order of Sir TM Hardy Baronet.

Goding, Joseph   Prisoner 1124. Rank: Surgeon, from: Decatur, Privateer.
    Cap: 05 Jun 1814 at Sea by HM Ship Rhin Int: 20 Jun 1814 Dis: 24 Jun 1814.
    Received from HM Ship Rhin. per order being a Non-Combatant.

Goldrick, William   Prisoner 345. Rank: Seaman, from: Vixen, Man of War.
    Cap: 22 Nov 1812 at Sea by Rhodian late of HM Brig Vixen Int: 14 Dec 1812 Dis: 09 May 1813.
    Received from Rhodian. To America for Exchange.

Gomand, Joseph   Prisoner 1348. Rank: Seaman, from: Not Recorded, Not Recorded.
    Cap: at Sea by HMS Shark Int: 10 Jan 1815 Dis: 10 Jan 1815.
    Ship 'Name Unknown'. Received from HMS Shark. Board's Order. (Date of capture not recorded.)

American Prisoners of War Held at Jamaica During the War of 1812

Gomand, Pierre   Prisoner 1332. Rank: Seaman, from: Not Recorded, Not Recorded.
    Cap: at Sea by HMS Shark Int: 07 Jan 1815 Dis: 10 Jan 1815.
    Ship 'Name Unknown'. Received from HMS Shark. Board's Order. (Date of capture not recorded.)

Gomer, Edward   Prisoner 35. Rank: Seaman, from: Not Recorded, Not Recorded.
    Cap: Not Recorded by Not Recorded Int: 22 Aug 1812 Dis: 09 May 1813.
    Given themselves up as American and refused to serve. Received from Garland. to America for Exchange. (Date of capture not recorded.)

Gomez, Felipe   Prisoner 1053. Rank: Seaman, from: Casada el Narino, Privateer.
    Cap: 29 May 1814 at Sea by HM Ship Rhin Int: 04 Jun 1814 Dis: 21 Jul 1814.
    Carthagenaian. Received from North Star. Board's Order.

Gomie, Andres   Prisoner 904. Rank: Gunner, from: San Francisco Navier, Brig.
    Cap: 05 Dec 1813 at Sea by Sappho Int: 15 Dec 1813 Dis: 11 Jan 1814.
    Taken in the Recaptured Spanish Brig. Prize to the Carthagenaian Privateer Carthagenaian. Received from Sappho. per order.

Gordon, Abaneza   Prisoner 1494. Rank: Boy, from: Not Recorded, Not Recorded.
    Cap: 20 Dec 1814 at Sea by Lacedaemonian Int: 04 Feb 1815 Dis: 08 Feb 1815.
    Taken for Passage to Jamaica Depot. Received from Rota. per order of Sir TM Hardy as a Non-Combatant.

Gordon, Worton   Prisoner 243. Rank: 2 Lieutenant, from: Joseph & Mary, Privateer.
    Cap: 24 Nov 1812 at Sea by Narcissus Int: 26 Nov 1812 Dis: 04 Apr 1813.
    Received from Narcissus. To America for Exchange.

Goreham, John   Prisoner 937. Rank: 1 Mate, from: Coquelle, Merchant Vessel.
    Cap: 24 Dec 1813 at Sea by Sapphire Int: 02 Jan 1814 Dis: 15 Jan 1814.
    Received from Sapphire. To Parole.

Gorgaud, Michael   Prisoner 90. Rank: Seaman, from: Poor Sailor, Privateer.
    Cap: 13 Sep 1812 at Sea by Garland Int: 18 Sep 1812 Dis: 09 May 1813.
    Received from Garland. To America for Exchange.

Gorton, Luis   Prisoner 1090. Rank: Seaman, from: Casada el Narino, Privateer.
    Cap: 29 May 1814 at Sea by HM Ship Rhin Int: 04 Jun 1814 Dis: 08 Aug 1814.
    Carthagenaian. Received from North Star. Board's Order.

Goss, John   Prisoner 716. Rank: Master, from: William, Merchant Man.
    Cap: 17 May 1813 at Sea by Circe Int: 29 May 1813 Dis: 23 Jul 1813.
    Received from Circe. To Parole. Died 14 Nov 1813.

Gough, Moses   Prisoner 603. Rank: Seaman, from: Not Recorded, Not Recorded.
    Cap: Not Recorded by Not Recorded Int: 24 Mar 1813 Dis: 24 Jul 1813.
    an American refusing to serve. Received from Shark. To American Cartel Brig Aualostaw. (Date of capture not recorded.)

Gould, Samuel   Prisoner 42. Rank: Seaman, from: Petham, Merchant Vessel.
    Cap: 20 Aug 1812 Port Royal by Tartaus Int: 22 Aug 1812 Escaped: 22 Mar 1813.
    Taken from the British Merchant Ship Petham at Port Royal. Received from Garland. Escaped.

Gould, Thomas   Prisoner 884. Rank: Boy, from: Lapwing, Packet.
    Cap: 08 Dec 1813 at Sea by Barrosa Int: 10 Dec 1813 Dis: 28 May 1814.
    Recaptured. Received from Barrosa. per order Non-Combatant.

Goumar, J   Prisoner 1082. Rank: Seaman, from: Casada el Narino, Privateer.
    Cap: 29 May 1814 at Sea by HM Ship Rhin Int: 04 Jun 1814 Dis: 18 Aug 1814.
    Carthagenaian. Received from North Star. Board's Order. (First name not legible.)

Goverman, Frederick   Prisoner 242. Rank: Seaman, from: Joseph & Mary, Privateer.
    Cap: 24 Nov 1812 at Sea by Narcissus Int: 26 Nov 1812 Escaped: 30 Jan 1813.
    Received from Narcissus. Escaped.

Goverman, Frederick   Prisoner 507. Rank: Seaman, from: Joseph & Mary, Not Recorded.
    Cap: 10 Feb 1813 at Lucea by Not Recorded Int: 26 Feb 1813 Dis: 24 Jul 1813.
    Retaken. Received from Sea Horse. To American Cartel Brig Aualostaw. (Prisoner number 242.)

Gowdon, F E   Prisoner 618. Rank: Clerk, from: Mary Ann, Privateer.
    Cap: 05 May 1813 at Sea by Sapphire Int: 07 May 1813 Dis: 24 Jul 1813.
    Received from Sapphire. To American Cartel Brig Aualostaw.

Gowner, Joseph   Prisoner 1042. Rank: Seaman, from: Jennett, Brig.
    Cap: 29 May 1814 at Sea by HM Ship Rhin Int: 04 Jun 1814 Dis: 02 Jan 1815.
    Taken in the Swedish Brig Jennet. Received from North Star. Into HM Ship Sultan per order of Captain John West.

Grace, Skinner   Prisoner 1508. Rank: Passenger, from: Not Recorded, Not Recorded.
    Cap: 08 Dec 1814 at Sea by Albion Int: 04 Feb 1815 Dis: 08 Feb 1815.
    Taken for Passage to Jamaica Depot. Received from Rota. per order of Sir TM Hardy as a Non-Combatant.

American Prisoners of War Held at Jamaica During the War of 1812

Gracia, Archibald K   Prisoner 1484. Rank: Prize Master, from: Not Recorded, Not Recorded.
    Cap: 20 Dec 1814 at Sea by Lacedaemonian Int: 04 Feb 1815 Dis: 08 Feb 1815.
    Taken for Passage to Jamaica Depot. Received from Rota. per order of Sir TM Hardy as a Non-Combatant.

Graham, John   Prisoner 276. Rank: Seaman, from: Joseph & Mary, Privateer.
    Cap: 24 Nov 1812 at Sea by Narcissus Int: 26 Nov 1812 Dis: 24 Jul 1813.
    Received from Narcissus. To American Cartel Brig Aualostaw.

Grandy, Poll   Prisoner 966. Rank: Seaman, from: New Granada, Privateer.
    Cap: 03 Feb 1814 at Sea by Ringdove Int: 07 Feb 1814 Died: 14 May 1814.
    Received by Ringdove. Killed by the Guard.

Grant, Israel   Prisoner 475. Rank: Seaman, from: Three Friends, Merchant Schooner.
    Cap: 03 Dec 1812 at Sea by Circe Int: 20 Jan 1813 Dis: 04 Apr 1813.
    Received from Circe. To America for Exchange.

Graperius, John   Prisoner 336. Rank: Seaman, from: Not Recorded, Merchant Vessel.
    Cap: 08 Dec 1812 at Sea by Rhodian late Southampton Int: 14 Dec 1812 Dis: 09 May 1813.
    Unknown. Received from Rhodian. To America for Exchange.

Graves, J   Prisoner 399. Rank: Seaman, from: Vixen, Man of War.
    Cap: 22 Nov 1812 at Sea by Rhodian late of US Brig Vixen Int: 14 Dec 1812 Dis: 09 May 1813.
    Received from Rhodian. To America for Exchange.

Gray, John   Prisoner 247. Rank: Seaman, from: Joseph & Mary, Privateer.
    Cap: 24 Nov 1812 at Sea by Narcissus Int: 26 Nov 1812 Dis: 24 Jul 1813.
    Received from Narcissus. To American Cartel Brig Aualostaw.

Gree, Joseph   Prisoner 617. Rank: Mate, from: Mary Ann, Privateer.
    Cap: 05 May 1813 at Sea by Sapphire Int: 07 May 1813 Escaped: 21 Sep 1813.
    Received from Sapphire. Escaped.

Green, John   Prisoner 471. Rank: Seaman, from: Cyrus, Merchant Vessel.
    Cap: 03 Jan 1813 at Sea by Rhodian Int: 16 Jan 1813 Dis: 04 Apr 1813.
    Received from Rhodian. To America for Exchange.

Green, John   Prisoner 1516. Rank: Seaman, from: Not Recorded, Not Recorded.
    Cap: 08 Dec 1814 at Sea by Albion Int: 04 Feb 1815 Dis: 11 Feb 1815.
    Taken for Passage to Jamaica Depot. Received from Rota. Into HM Ship Rota per order of Sir TM Hardy.

Green, Peter C   Prisoner 1354. Rank: Seaman, from: American Gunboats, Not Recorded.
    Cap: 05 Jan 1815 near New Orleans by Plantagenet Int: 27 Jan 1815 Dis: 05 Feb 1815.
    Taken in the American Gun Boats near New Orleans. Received from Ramilies. Into HM Ship Diomede per order of Sir TM Hardy Baronet.

Gregon, Francis   Prisoner 98. Rank: Seaman, from: Poor Sailor, Privateer.
    Cap: 13 Sep 1812 at Sea by Garland Int: 18 Sep 1812 Dis: 24 Jul 1813.
    Received from Garland. To American Cartel Brig Aualostaw.

Gregorio, Juan   Prisoner 1069. Rank: Seaman, from: Casada el Narino, Privateer.
    Cap: 29 May 1814 at Sea by HM Ship Rhin Int: 04 Jun 1814 Dis: 10 Aug 1814.
    Carthagenaian. Received from North Star. Board's Order.

Gregory, Caspar   Prisoner 141. Rank: Seaman, from: Caroline, Merchant Vessel.
    Cap: 21 Aug 1812 at Sea by Southampton Int: 07 Oct 1812 Escaped: 09 May 1813.
    Received from Southampton. Escaped.

Griffin, Heathcote   Prisoner 1002. Rank: Seaman, from: Farmer's Daughter, Merchant Vessel.
    Cap: 30 Mar 1814 at Sea by Leviathan Int: 03 Apr 1814 Dis: 02 Jan 1815.
    Received from Leviathan. Into HM Ship Sultan per order of Captain John West.

Griffin, Samuel   Prisoner 655. Rank: Seaman, from: Lovely Lass, Privateer.
    Cap: 21 May 1813 at Sea by Circe Int: 23 May 1813 Dis: 01 Aug 1814.
    Received from Forrester. To American Cartel Brig Aualostaw.

Griffin, William B   Prisoner 965. Rank: Seaman, from: Active, Merchant Vessel.
    Cap: at Sea by Leonidas Int: 25 Jan 1814 Dis: 01 Aug 1814.
    Received from Leonidas. To American Cartel Brig Aualostaw. (Date of capture not recorded.)

Griffiths, Edward   Prisoner 715. Rank: Seaman, from: Lovely Lass, Merchant Man.
    Cap: 15 May 1813 at Sea by Circe Int: 29 May 1813 Dis: 01 Aug 1814.
    Received from Circe. (No entry for discharge date. Other entries for vessel show Privateer.)

Guchand, Coco   Prisoner 1092. Rank: Seaman, from: Casada el Narino, Privateer.
    Cap: 29 May 1814 at Sea by HM Ship Rhin Int: 04 Jun 1814 Dis: 18 Aug 1814.
    Carthagenaian. Received from North Star. Board's Order.

American Prisoners of War Held at Jamaica During the War of 1812

Guerd, Joseph   Prisoner 1380. Rank: Seaman, from: American Gunboats, Not Recorded.
    Cap: 05 Jan 1815 near New Orleans by Plantagenet Int: 27 Jan 1815 Dis: 05 Feb 1815.
    Taken in the American Gun Boats near New Orleans. Received from Ramilies. Into HM Ship Diomede per order of Sir TM Hardy Baronet.

Guiterroz, Francisco N   Prisoner 900. Rank: Prize Master, from: Cartagenaian, Privateer.
    Cap: 05 Dec 1813 at Sea by Sappho Int: 15 Dec 1813 Dis: 11 Jan 1814.
    Belonging to the Carthagenaian Privateer Carthagenaian. Received from Sappho. per order.

Guttring, John   Prisoner 164. Rank: Seaman, from: Rebecca Sims, Merchant Vessel.
    Cap: 12 Sep 1812 at Sea by Southampton Int: 07 Oct 1812 Dis: 01 Mar 1813.
    Received from Southampton. per Order of Admiral Stirling.

Guy, Luis   Prisoner 773. Rank: Seaman, from: San Francisco de Paula, Privateer.
    Cap: 02 Oct 1813 at Sea by Forrester Int: 07 Oct 1813 Escaped: 01 Nov 1813.
    Received from Forrester. Escaped.

Haddington, Levi   Prisoner 1531. Rank: Mate, from: William & Mary, Merchant Vessel.
    Cap: 12 Feb 1815 at Sea by HM Sloop Carnation Int: 23 Feb 1815 Dis: 30 Mar 1815.
    Received from HM Sloop Carnation. In consequence of Peace with America.

Hall, Charles   Prisoner 1349. Rank: Master, from: Ellena, Mechant Vessel.
    Cap: at Sea by Thracian Int: 13 Jan 1815 Dis: 04 Feb 1815.
    Received from Thracian. Board's Order. (Date of capture not recorded.)

Hall, D   Prisoner 1514. Rank: Seaman, from: Not Recorded, Not Recorded.
    Cap: 08 Dec 1814 at Sea by Albion Int: 04 Feb 1815 Dis: 11 Feb 1815.
    Taken for Passage to Jamaica Depot. Received from Rota. Into HM Ship Rota per order of Sir TM Hardy.

Hall, Daniel   Prisoner 159. Rank: Seaman, from: Rebecca Sims, Merchant Vessel.
    Cap: 12 Sep 1812 at Sea by Southampton Int: 07 Oct 1812 Dis: 01 Mar 1813.
    Received from Southampton. per Order of Adml Stirling to Rebecca Sims.

Hall, John   Prisoner 197. Rank: Master, from: Philip, Merchant Vessel.
    Cap: 28 Sep 1812 at Sea by Southampton Int: 19 Oct 1812 Dis: 19 Oct 1812.
    Received from Southampton. On Parole.

Haman, John   Prisoner 840. Rank: Seaman, from: Maria, An American Merchant Schooner.
    Cap: 15 Nov 1813 at Sea by Argo Int: 19 Nov 1813 Dis: 01 Aug 1814.
    Received from Argo. To American Cartel Brig Aualostaw.

Hamilton, William   Prisoner 52. Rank: Chief Mate, from: Superb, Merchant Vessel.
    Cap: 02 Aug 1812 at Sea by HM Ship Garland Int: 27 Aug 1812 Dis: 28 Aug 1812.
    Received from HM Ship Herald. To Parole.

Hamlet, Joshua   Prisoner 12. Rank: Seaman, from: Superb, Merchant Vessel.
    Cap: 02 Aug 1812 at Sea by Garland Int: 22 Aug 1812 Dis: 04 Apr 1813.
    Received from Garland. to America for Exchange.

Hamsby, Andrew   Prisoner 140. Rank: Seaman, from: Caroline, Merchant Vessel.
    Cap: 21 Aug 1812 at Sea by Southampton Int: 07 Oct 1812 Dis: 04 Apr 1813.
    Received from Southampton. To America for Exchange.

Hanchett, Charles   Prisoner 1443. Rank: Seaman, from: American Gunboats, Not Recorded.
    Cap: 05 Jan 1815 near New Orleans by Plantagenet Int: 27 Jan 1815 Dis: 05 Feb 1815.
    Taken in the American Gun Boats near New Orleans. Received from Ramilies. Into HM Ship Diomede per order of Sir TM Hardy Baronet.

Hancock, Richard   Prisoner 1542. Rank: Seaman, from: Cora, Merchant Vessel.
    Cap: 02 Feb 1815 at Sea by HMS Rinaldo Int: 09 Mar 1815 Dis: 30 Mar 1815.
    Received from HMS Rinaldo. In consequence of Peace with America.

Handley, William   Prisoner 1384. Rank: Seaman, from: American Gunboats, Not Recorded.
    Cap: 05 Jan 1815 near New Orleans by Plantagenet Int: 27 Jan 1815 Dis: 05 Feb 1815.
    Taken in the American Gun Boats near New Orleans. Received from Ramilies. Into HM Ship Diomede per order of Sir TM Hardy Baronet.

Handy, Joseph   Prisoner 1322. Rank: Seaman, from: Triton, Merchant Ship.
    Cap: Not Recorded by Not Recorded Int: 30 Dec 1814 Dis: 02 Jan 1815.
    These men were sent from the Triton Merchant Ship for Notorious behavior, had previously shipped in her as Englishmen. Received from HM Ship Suttan. Into HM Ship Sultan per order of Captain John West. (Date capture not recorded.)

Hangerford, John   Prisoner 169. Rank: Seaman, from: Rebecca Sims, Merchant Vessel.
    Cap: 12 Sep 1812 at Sea by Southampton Int: 07 Oct 1812 Dis: 01 Mar 1813.
    Received from Southampton. per Order of Admiral Stirling.

American Prisoners of War Held at Jamaica During the War of 1812

Hansey, William   Prisoner 1528. Rank: Seaman, from: Not Recorded, Not Recorded.
    Cap: 08 Dec 1814 at Sea by Albion Int: 04 Feb 1815 Dis: 11 Feb 1815.
    Taken for Passage to Jamaica Depot. Received from Rota. Into HM Ship Rota per order of Sir TM Hardy.

Hanson, Edward   Prisoner 670. Rank: Seaman, from: Lovely Lass, Privateer.
    Cap: 21 May 1813 at Sea by Circe Int: 23 May 1813 Dis: 01 Aug 1814.
    Received from Forrester. To American Cartel Brig Aualostaw.

Harrington, Samuel   Prisoner 734. Rank: Seaman, from: Eliza, Merchant Vessel.
    Cap: 17 Jul 1813 at Sea by Sappho Int: 26 Jul 1813 Dis: 01 Aug 1814.
    Received from Sappho. To American Cartel Brig Aualostaw.

Harris, John Winslow   Prisoner 216. Rank: Seaman, from: Dominicana, Merchant Vessel.
    Cap: 21 Oct 1812 at Sea by HM Ship Liberty Int: 25 Oct 1812 Dis: 09 May 1813.
    Taken out of Brigantine Dominicana by HM Ship Liberty and brot into Port Royal. Received from Decouverte. To America for Exchange.

Harris, John   Prisoner 379. Rank: Seaman, from: Vixen, Man of War.
    Cap: 22 Nov 1812 at Sea by Rhodian late of US Brig Vixen Int: 14 Dec 1812 Dis: 09 May 1813.
    Received from Rhodian. To America for Exchange.

Harris, John   Prisoner 1043. Rank: Seaman, from: Jennett, Brig.
    Cap: 29 May 1814 at Sea by HM Ship Rhin Int: 04 Jun 1814 Dis: 24 Jan 1815.
    Taken in the Swedish Brig Jennet. Received from North Star. Board's Order.

Harris, Robert   Prisoner 1195. Rank: Seaman, from: Neustra Cantado, Merchant Vessel.
    Cap: 01 Jun 1814 at Sea by HM Ship Argo Int: 27 Jun 1814 Dis: 22 Jul 1814.
    Retaken in the Spanish Ship Neustra Cantado. Received from HM Ship Argo. Board's Order.

Harris, William   Prisoner 1259. Rank: Seaman, from: Not Recorded, Not Recorded.
    Cap: 07 Jul 1814 at Sea by HM Ship Onyx Int: 30 Aug 1814 Dis: 25 Nov 1814.
    Ship 'Name Unknown'. Received from Shark. Board's Order.

Harrison, Isaac   Prisoner 70. Rank: Seaman, from: Poor Sailor, Privateer.
    Cap: 13 Sep 1812 at Sea by Garland Int: 18 Sep 1812 Dis: 04 Apr 1813.
    Received from Garland. to America for Exchange.

Harrison, James   Prisoner 455. Rank: Assistant Surgeon, from: Rachel, Merchant Vessel.
    Cap: 1813 at Sea by Fawn Int: 13 Jan 1812 Dis: 11 Feb 1813.
    Received from Sapphire. Non-Combatant per order of VA Stirling. (Day and month of capture not recorded. Year of internment should be 1813.)

Harrison, Samuel   Prisoner 1268. Rank: Captain, from: Fanny, Merchant Vessel.
    Cap: 02 Sep 1814 at Sea by Jalouse Int: 10 Sep 1814 Dis: 02 Oct 1814.
    Swedish Schooner. Received from Jalouse. To Parole.

Harrison, Samuel   Prisoner 1352. Rank: Captain, from: Fanny, Merchant Vessel.
    Cap: 02 Sep 1814 at Sea by Jalouse Int: 24 Jan 1815 Dis: 11 Feb 1815.
    Swedish Schooner. Retaken after having broke his Parole since the 18th (Not legible). Into HM Ship Rota per order of Sir TM Hardy. (Prisoner number 1268.)

Harry, Richard   Prisoner 616. Rank: Prize Master, from: Mary Ann, Privateer.
    Cap: 05 May 1813 at Sea by Sapphire Int: 07 May 1813 Dis: 01 Aug 1814.
    Received from Sapphire. To American Cartel Brig Aualostaw.

Hart, George   Prisoner 183. Rank: Chief Mate, from: Rebecca Sims, Merchant Vessel.
    Cap: 12 Sep 1812 at Sea by Southampton Int: 09 Oct 1812 Escaped: 30 Jan 1813.
    Received from Southampton. Escaped.

Hart, George   Prisoner 509. Rank: Seaman, from: Not Recorded, Not Recorded.
    Cap: 11 Feb 1813 at Lucea by Not Recorded Int: 26 Feb 1813 Dis: 01 Mar 1813.
    Retaken. Received from Sea Horse. per Order of Adml Stirling. (Prisoner number 183.)

Hart, Philip   Prisoner 1388. Rank: Seaman, from: American Gunboats, Not Recorded.
    Cap: 05 Jan 1815 near New Orleans by Plantagenet Int: 27 Jan 1815 Dis: 05 Feb 1815.
    Taken in the American Gun Boats near New Orleans. Received from Ramilies. Into HM Ship Diomede per order of Sir TM Hardy Baronet.

Hartman, John   Prisoner 342. Rank: Seaman, from: Vixen, Man of War.
    Cap: 22 Nov 1812 at Sea by Rhodian late of HM Brig Vixen Int: 14 Dec 1812 Dis: 09 May 1813.
    Received from Rhodian. To America for Exchange.

Harvey, James   Prisoner 380. Rank: Seaman, from: Vixen, Man of War.
    Cap: 22 Nov 1812 at Sea by Rhodian late of US Brig Vixen Int: 14 Dec 1812 Dis: 09 May 1813.
    Received from Rhodian. To America for Exchange.

Harvey, James   Prisoner 1310. Rank: Seaman, from: Nettervitte, Merchant Schooner.
    Cap: Not Recorded by HM Sloop Onyx Int: 30 Dec 1814 Dis: 02 Jan 1815.
    Received from HM Sloop Onyx. Into HM Ship Sultan per order of Captain John West. (Date of capture not recorded.)

American Prisoners of War Held at Jamaica During the War of 1812

Harvey, Michael   Prisoner 349. Rank: Seaman, from: Vixen, Man of War.
    Cap: 22 Nov 1812 at Sea by Rhodian late of HM Brig Vixen Int: 14 Dec 1812 Dis: 09 May 1813.
    Received from Rhodian. To America for Exchange.

Harvey, Peter   Prisoner 619. Rank: Boatswain, from: Mary Ann, Privateer.
    Cap: 05 May 1813 at Sea by Sapphire Int: 07 May 1813 Died: 13 Jul 1814.
    Received from Sapphire. Died.

Hasser, John   Prisoner 95. Rank: Seaman, from: Poor Sailor, Privateer.
    Cap: 13 Sep 1812 at Sea by Garland Int: 18 Sep 1812 Dis: 09 May 1813.
    Received from Garland. To America for Exchange.

Hatch, Walter   Prisoner 135. Rank: Seaman, from: Whim, Merchant Vessel.
    Cap: 04 Oct 1812 at Sea by HM Brig Liberty Int: 07 Oct 1812 Dis: 18 Dec 1812.
    Received from Cyane. Into the Experiment for Passage to England.

Hatcher, Thomas   Prisoner 73. Rank: Seaman, from: Poor Sailor, Privateer.
    Cap: 13 Sep 1812 at Sea by Garland Int: 18 Sep 1812 Dis: 09 May 1813.
    Received from Garland. To America for Exchange.

Hauagan, Peter   Prisoner 385. Rank: Seaman, from: Vixen, Man of War.
    Cap: 22 Nov 1812 at Sea by Rhodian late of US Brig Vixen Int: 14 Dec 1812 Dis: 09 May 1813.
    Received from Rhodian. To America for Exchange.

Hauce, John H   Prisoner 795. Rank: Captain, from: Enterprize, Privateer.
    Cap: 15 Nov 1813 at Sea by Argo Int: 19 Nov 1813 Dis: 28 Jul 1814.
    A Carthagenaian. Received from Argo. Board's Order.

Haufield, Jonathan   Prisoner 863. Rank: Seaman, from: Cato Georgiana, Not Recorded.
    Cap: 28 Nov 1813 at Sea by Barrosa Int: 10 Dec 1813 Dis: 01 Aug 1814.
    Prize to the US Frigate Essex. Received from Barrosa. To American Cartel Brig Aualostaw.

Hauscorn, John   Prisoner 117. Rank: Commander, from: Poor Sailor, Privateer.
    Cap: 13 Sep 1812 at Sea by Garland Int: 18 Sep 1812 Dis: 10 Oct 1812.
    Received from Garland. To Parole.

Hauseir, Peter   Prisoner 1013. Rank: Boatswain, from: Chance, Privateer.
    Cap: 01 Apr 1814 at Sea by Statira Int: 20 Apr 1814 Dis: 02 Jan 1815.
    Received from Statira. Into HM Ship Sultan per order of Captain John West.

Hawthorn, William   Prisoner 794. Rank: Seaman, from: Not Recorded, Not Recorded.
    Cap: 18 Oct 1813 Not Recorded by Forrester Int: 18 Oct 1813 Dis: 01 Aug 1814.
    An American. Received from Forrester. To American Cartel Brig Aualostaw.

Haxon, Richard   Prisoner 1520. Rank: Seaman, from: Not Recorded, Not Recorded.
    Cap: 08 Dec 1814 at Sea by Albion Int: 04 Feb 1815 Dis: 11 Feb 1815.
    Taken for Passage to Jamaica Depot. Received from Rota. Into HM Ship Rota per order of Sir TM Hardy.

Hazel, John   Prisoner 130. Rank: Seaman, from: Peru, Merchant Vessel.
    Cap: 15 Sep 1812 at Sea by HMS Cyane Int: 07 Oct 1812 Escaped: 28 Jun 1813.
    Received from Cyane. Escaped.

Hazledine, John   Prisoner 280. Rank: Seaman, from: Joseph & Mary, Privateer.
    Cap: 24 Nov 1812 at Sea by Narcissus Int: 26 Nov 1812 Dis: 24 Jul 1813.
    Received from Narcissus. To American Cartel Brig Aualostaw.

Header, William   Prisoner 492. Rank: Seaman, from: Philip, Merchant Vessel.
    Cap: 28 Jan 1813 at Sea by Morgiana Int: 30 Jan 1813 Dis: 09 May 1813.
    Recaptured. Received from Morgiana. To America for Exchange.

Heber, Neil   Prisoner 409. Rank: Seaman, from: Vixen, Man of War.
    Cap: 22 Nov 1812 at Sea by Rhodian late of US Brig Vixen Int: 14 Dec 1812 Dis: 09 May 1813.
    Received from Rhodian. To America for Exchange.

Heger, Francisco   Prisoner 586. Rank: Seaman, from: Le Ventura, Privateer.
    Cap: 13 Mar 1813 at Sea by Cossac Int: 18 Mar 1813 Dis: 16 Aug 1814.
    Received from Cossac. Board's Order.

Henderson, Joseph   Prisoner 1243. Rank: Passenger but Seaman, from: John, Merchant Vessel.
    Cap: 11 Aug 1814 at Sea by Variable Int: 15 Aug 1814 Dis: 02 Jan 1815.
    Received from Variable. Into HM Ship Sultan per order of Captain John West.

Hendry, William   Prisoner 1208. Rank: Seaman, from: Not Recorded, Not Recorded.
    Cap: Not Recorded by HM Ship Shark Int: 04 Jul 1814 Dis: 02 Jan 1815.
    Given up as an American. Received from HM Ship Shark. Into HM Ship Sultan per order of Captain John West. (Date of capture not recorded.)

Henry, James   Prisoner 1512. Rank: Seaman, from: Not Recorded, Not Recorded.
    Cap: 08 Dec 1814 at Sea by Albion Int: 04 Feb 1815 Dis: 11 Feb 1815.
    Taken for Passage to Jamaica Depot. Received from Rota. Into HM Ship Rota per order of Sir TM Hardy.

American Prisoners of War Held at Jamaica During the War of 1812

Henry, John   Prisoner 938. Rank: 2 Mate, from: Coquelle, Merchant Vessel.
    Cap: 24 Dec 1813 at Sea by Sapphire Int: 02 Jan 1814 Dis: 01 Aug 1814.
    Received from Sapphire. To American Cartel Brig Aualostaw.

Henry, Thomas   Prisoner 133. Rank: Seaman, from: Whim, Merchant Vessel.
    Cap: 18 Sep 1812 at Sea by HMS Cyane Int: 07 Oct 1812 Dis: 24 Jul 1813.
    Received from Cyane. To American Cartel Brig Aualostaw.

Henry, William   Prisoner 282. Rank: Seaman, from: Joseph & Mary, Privateer.
    Cap: 24 Nov 1812 at Sea by Narcissus Int: 26 Nov 1812 Dis: 24 Jul 1813.
    Received from Narcissus. To American Cartel Brig Aualostaw.

Hernandes, Nicholas   Prisoner 1280. Rank: Seaman, from: Dolores, Merchant Schooner.
    Cap: at Sea by HM Sloop Anaconda Int: 07 Oct 1814 Dis: 10 Nov 1814.
    Received from HM Sloop Anaconda. Board's Order. (Date of capture not recorded.)

Heschaultz, Charles   Prisoner 703. Rank: Seaman, from: Lovely Lass, Privateer.
    Cap: 15 May 1813 at Sea by Circe Int: 29 May 1813 Dis: 22 Jul 1814.
    Received from Circe. Board's Order.

Hibbard, George   Prisoner 1361. Rank: Seaman, from: American Gunboats, Not Recorded.
    Cap: 05 Jan 1815 near New Orleans by Plantagenet Int: 27 Jan 1815 Dis: 05 Feb 1815.
    Taken in the American Gun Boats near New Orleans. Received from Ramilies. Into HM Ship Diomede per order of Sir TM Hardy Baronet.

Hickey, James   Prisoner 158. Rank: Seaman, from: Rebecca Sims, Merchant Vessel.
    Cap: 12 Sep 1812 at Sea by Southampton Int: 07 Oct 1812 Dis: 01 Mar 1813.
    Received from Southampton. per Order of Adml Stirling to Rebecca Sims.

Hicks, Benjamin   Prisoner 1212. Rank: Seaman, from: Mary, Merchant Schooner.
    Cap: 17 Jun 1814 at Sea by Sapphire Int: 10 Jul 1814 Dis: 02 Jan 1815.
    Recaptured. Received from Sapphire. Into HM Ship Suttan per order of Captain John West.

Hields, William   Prisoner 470. Rank: Master, from: Cyrus, Merchant Vessel.
    Cap: 03 Jan 1813 at Sea by Rhodian Int: 16 Jan 1813 Dis: 04 Apr 1813.
    Received from Rhodian. To America for Exchange.

Higgins, Peter   Prisoner 1429. Rank: Seaman, from: American Gunboats, Not Recorded.
    Cap: 05 Jan 1815 near New Orleans by Plantagenet Int: 27 Jan 1815 Dis: 05 Feb 1815.
    Taken in the American Gun Boats near New Orleans. Received from Ramilies. Into HM Ship Diomede per order of Sir TM Hardy Baronet.

Hiley, David   Prisoner 642. Rank: Seaman, from: Mary Ann, Privateer.
    Cap: 05 May 1813 at Sea by Sapphire Int: 07 May 1813 Dis: 01 Aug 1814.
    Received from Sapphire. To American Cartel Brig Aualostaw.

Hill, Ashmel   Prisoner 53. Rank: Chief Mate, from: Dal, Merchant Vessel.
    Cap: 03 Aug 1812 at Sea by HM Ship Garland Int: 27 Aug 1812 Dis: 28 Aug 1812.
    Received from HM Ship Herald. To Parole.

Hill, Francis   Prisoner 1026. Rank: Seaman, from: Chance, Privateer.
    Cap: 01 Apr 1814 at Sea by Statira Int: 20 Apr 1814 Dis: 02 Jan 1815.
    Received from Statira. Into HM Ship Sultan per order of Captain John West.

Hill, John   Prisoner 481. Rank: Seaman, from: Birch, Merchant Vessel.
    Cap: 16 Jan 1813 at Sea by Circe Int: 20 Jan 1813 Dis: 24 Jul 1813.
    Received from Circe. To American Cartel Brig Aualostaw.

Hill, Ross   Prisoner 257. Rank: Seaman, from: Joseph & Mary, Privateer.
    Cap: 24 Nov 1812 at Sea by Narcissus Int: 26 Nov 1812 Dis: 24 Jul 1813.
    Received from Narcissus. To American Cartel Brig Aualostaw.

Hill, William   Prisoner 947. Rank: Boy, from: Coquelle, Merchant Vessel.
    Cap: 24 Dec 1813 at Sea by Sapphire Int: 02 Jan 1814 Dis: 01 Aug 1814.
    Received from Sapphire. To American Cartel Brig Aualostaw.

Hinchman, George   Prisoner 1248. Rank: Captain, from: John, Merchant Vessel.
    Cap: 11 Aug 1814 at Sea by Variable Int: 15 Aug 1814 Dis: 02 Jan 1815.
    Received from Variable. Into HM Ship Sultan per order of Captain John West.

Hindman, John   Prisoner 1311. Rank: Seaman, from: Nettervitte, Merchant Schooner.
    Cap: Not Recorded by HM Sloop Onyx Int: 30 Dec 1814 Dis: 02 Jan 1815.
    Received from HM Sloop Onyx. Into HM Ship Sultan per order of Captain John West. (Date of capture not recorded.)

Hine, Henry   Prisoner 652. Rank: Seaman, from: Lovely Lass, Privateer.
    Cap: 21 May 1813 at Sea by Circe Int: 23 May 1813 Dis: 19 Jul 1814.
    Received from Forrester. Being a Dutchman.

Hirst, Charles   Prisoner 483. Rank: Seaman, from: Three Friends, Merchant Vessel.
    Cap: 03 Dec 1812 at Sea by Circe Int: 23 Jan 1813 Dis: 10 Feb 1813.
    3 Friends. Received from Circe. under 12 years old.

American Prisoners of War Held at Jamaica During the War of 1812

Holmes, Isaac   Prisoner 1038. Rank: Seaman, from: Jennett, Brig.
    Cap: 29 May 1814 at Sea by HM Ship Rhin Int: 04 Jun 1814 Dis: 02 Jan 1815.
    Taken in the Swedish Brig Jennet. Received from North Star. Into HM Ship Sultan per order of Captain John West.

Holmes, William   Prisoner 485. Rank: Seaman, from: Philip, Merchant Vessel.
    Cap: 28 Jan 1813 at Sea by Morgiana Int: 30 Jan 1813 Dis: 24 Jul 1813.
    Recaptured. Received from Morgiana. To American Cartel Brig Aualostaw.

Holston, Isaac   Prisoner 99. Rank: Seaman, from: Poor Sailor, Privateer.
    Cap: 13 Sep 1812 at Sea by Garland Int: 18 Sep 1812 Dis: 04 Apr 1813.
    Received from Garland. To America for Exchange.

Homan, John   Prisoner 1015. Rank: Seaman, from: Chance, Privateer.
    Cap: 01 Apr 1814 at Sea by Statira Int: 20 Apr 1814 Dis: 22 Jul 1814.
    Received from Statira. Board's Order.

Homan, William   Prisoner 539. Rank: Seaman, from: Defiance, Privateer.
    Cap: 15 Mar 1813 at Sea by Nimrod Int: 17 Mar 1813 Escaped: 09 May 1813.
    Received from Nimrod. Escaped.

Homer, Jacob   Prisoner 122. Rank: Chief Mate, from: Morning Star, Merchant Vessel.
    Cap: 08 Sep 1812 at Sea by HMS Cyane Int: 07 Oct 1812 Dis: 22 Oct 1812.
    Received from Cyane. On Parole.

Hopkins, Caleb   Prisoner 30. Rank: Seaman, from: Madisonia, Merchant Vessel.
    Cap: 03 Aug 1812 at Sea by Garland Int: 22 Aug 1812 Dis: 09 May 1813.
    Received from Garland. to America for Exchange.

Horseley, Samuel   Prisoner 438. Rank: Surgeon, from: Vixen, Man of War.
    Cap: 24 Dec 1812 at Sea by Rhodian Int: 24 Dec 1812 Dis: 11 Feb 1813.
    Received from Rhodian. Non-Combatant per order of VA Stirling.

Horton, Richard   Prisoner 1411. Rank: Seaman, from: American Gunboats, Not Recorded.
    Cap: 05 Jan 1815 near New Orleans by Plantagenet Int: 27 Jan 1815 Dis: 05 Feb 1815.
    Taken in the American Gun Boats near New Orleans. Received from Ramilies. Into HM Ship Diomede per order of Sir TM Hardy Baronet.

Howland, Barnalas   Prisoner 307. Rank: Boatswain, from: Joseph & Mary, Privateer.
    Cap: 24 Nov 1812 at Sea by Narcissus Int: 05 Dec 1812 Dis: 24 Jul 1813.
    Received from Narcissus. To American Cartel Brig Aualostaw.

Hubbard, Elijah   Prisoner 498. Rank: Seaman, from: Not Recorded, Not Recorded.
    Cap: 30 Jan 1813 Not Recorded by Sapphire Int: 31 Jan 1813 Dis: 24 Jul 1813.
    Impressed American. Received from Sapphire. To American Cartel Brig Aualostaw.

Hubbard, Robert   Prisoner 1437. Rank: Seaman, from: American Gunboats, Not Recorded.
    Cap: 05 Jan 1815 near New Orleans by Plantagenet Int: 27 Jan 1815 Dis: 05 Feb 1815.
    Taken in the American Gun Boats near New Orleans. Received from Ramilies. Into HM Ship Diomede per order of Sir TM Hardy Baronet.

Hulse, G J   Prisoner 1111. Rank: Seaman, from: Romano & Adamante, Merchant Brig.
    Cap: 31 May 1814 at Sea by Leviathan Int: 17 Jun 1814 Dis: 02 Jan 1815.
    Received from Leviathan. Into HM Ship Sultan per order of Captain John West.

Hunter, Francis   Prisoner 293. Rank: Seaman, from: Mary, Merchant Vessel.
    Cap: 26 Nov 1812 at Sea by Sappho Int: 30 Nov 1812 Dis: 09 May 1813.
    Received from Sappho. To America for Exchange.

Hunter, William M   Prisoner 443. Rank: Master, from: Vixen, Man of War.
    Cap: 24 Dec 1812 at Sea by Rhodian Int: 24 Dec 1812 Dis: 24 Dec 1812.
    Received from Rhodian. To Parole. (Dates of capture, interment and discharge the same.)

Hurst, James   Prisoner 993. Rank: Seaman, from: Farmer's Daughter, Merchant Vessel.
    Cap: 30 Mar 1814 at Sea by Leviathan Int: 03 Apr 1814 Dis: 02 Jan 1815.
    Received from Leviathan. Into HM Ship Sultan per order of Captain John West.

Hutchins, Amos   Prisoner 40. Rank: Seaman, from: Petham, Merchant Vessel.
    Cap: 20 Aug 1812 Port Royal by Tartaus Int: 22 Aug 1812 Dis: 09 May 1813.
    Taken from the British Merchant Ship Petham at Port Royal. Received from Garland. to America for Exchange.

Hutchins, B   Prisoner 303. Rank: Passenger, from: Mary, Merchant Vessel.
    Cap: 26 Nov 1812 at Sea by Sappho Int: 30 Nov 1812 Dis: 24 Dec 1812.
    Received from Sappho. On Parole.

Hutchins, B   Prisoner 502. Rank: Mate, from: Mary, Merchant Vessel.
    Cap: 26 Nov 1812 at Sea by Sappho Int: 23 Jan 1813 Dis: 10 Feb 1813.
    from Parole. for Exchange order of VA Stirling. (Prisoner number 303.)

American Prisoners of War Held at Jamaica During the War of 1812

Hyde, Thomas   Prisoner 1257. Rank: Prize Master, from: Not Recorded, Not Recorded.
    Cap: 07 Jul 1814 at Sea by HM Ship Onyx Int: 30 Aug 1814 Dis: 25 Nov 1814.
    Ship 'Name Unknown'. Received from Shark. Board's Order.

Hyer, Rober   Prisoner 1245. Rank: Passenger but Seaman, from: John, Merchant Vessel.
    Cap: 11 Aug 1814 at Sea by Variable Int: 15 Aug 1814 Dis: 01 Dec 1814.
    Received from Variable. Board's Order.

Iglecia, Juan   Prisoner 1296. Rank: Passenger, from: Cora, Letter of Marque.
    Cap: 31 Jul 1814 at Sea by Rota Int: 06 Nov 1814 Dis: 21 Nov 1814.
    Received from Rota. Board's Order.

Inkley, Thomas   Prisoner 103. Rank: Seaman, from: Poor Sailor, Privateer.
    Cap: 13 Sep 1812 at Sea by Garland Int: 18 Sep 1812 Escaped: 27 Oct 1812.
    Received from Garland. Escaped.

Ioe, Francis   Prisoner 542. Rank: Seaman, from: Defiance, Privateer.
    Cap: 15 Mar 1813 at Sea by Nimrod Int: 17 Mar 1813 Dis: 24 Jul 1813.
    Received from Nimrod. To American Cartel Brig Aualostaw.

Isaacs, George   Prisoner 1537. Rank: Seaman, from: Fortuneatus, Schooner.
    Cap: 15 Jan 1815 at Sea by HMS Jalouse Int: 01 Mar 1815 Dis: 30 Mar 1815.
    The English Schooner Fortuneatus detained by HMS Jalouse this American Prisoner of War found on Board her. Received from HMS Jalouse. In consequence of Peace with America.

Jack, John   Prisoner 532. Rank: Seaman, from: Defiance, Privateer.
    Cap: 15 Mar 1813 at Sea by Nimrod Int: 17 Mar 1813 Escaped: 28 Jun 1813.
    Received from Nimrod. Escaped.

Jack, John   Prisoner 828. Rank: Seaman, from: Enterprize, Privateer.
    Cap: 15 Nov 1813 at Sea by Argo Int: 19 Nov 1813 Dis: 16 Aug 1814.
    A Carthagenaian. Received from Argo. Board's Order.

Jackerman, Count   Prisoner 813. Rank: Seaman, from: Enterprize, Privateer.
    Cap: 15 Nov 1813 at Sea by Argo Int: 19 Nov 1813 Dis: 29 Jul 1814.
    A Carthagenaian. Received from Argo. Board's Order.

Jackson, Benjamin   Prisoner 1501. Rank: Seaman, from: Not Recorded, Not Recorded.
    Cap: 20 Dec 1814 at Sea by Lacedaemonian Int: 04 Feb 1815 Dis: 11 Feb 1815.
    Taken for Passage to Jamaica Depot. Received from Rota. Into HMS Ramillies per order of Sir T M Hardy.

Jackson, George   Prisoner 31. Rank: Seaman, from: Madisonia, Merchant Vessel.
    Cap: 03 Aug 1812 at Sea by Garland Int: 22 Aug 1812 Dis: 18 Dec 1812.
    Received from Garland. Merchant Ship Experiment for Passage to England.

Jackson, George   Prisoner 400. Rank: Seaman, from: Vixen, Man of War.
    Cap: 22 Nov 1812 at Sea by Rhodian late of US Brig Vixen Int: 14 Dec 1812 Dis: 09 May 1813.
    Received from Rhodian. To America for Exchange.

Jackson, Henry   Prisoner 1409. Rank: Seaman, from: American Gunboats, Not Recorded.
    Cap: 05 Jan 1815 near New Orleans by Plantagenet Int: 27 Jan 1815 Dis: 05 Feb 1815.
    Taken in the American Gun Boats near New Orleans. Received from Ramilies. Into HM Ship Diomede per order of Sir TM Hardy Baronet.

Jackson, John   Prisoner 653. Rank: Seaman, from: Lovely Lass, Privateer.
    Cap: 21 May 1813 at Sea by Circe Int: 23 May 1813 Dis: 01 Aug 1814.
    Received from Forrester. To American Cartel Brig Aualostaw.

Jackson, John   Prisoner 836. Rank: Seaman, from: Enterprize, Privateer.
    Cap: 15 Nov 1813 at Sea by Argo Int: 19 Nov 1813 Dis: 02 Jan 1815.
    A Carthagenaian. Received from Argo. Into HM Ship Sultan per order of Captain John West.

Jackson, William   Prisoner 333. Rank: Seaman, from: Sauders, Merchant Vessel.
    Cap: Nov 1812 at Sea by Merchant Vessel Monarch Int: 09 Dec 1812 Dis: 09 May 1813.
    Received from Monarch. To America for Exchange. (Day of capture not recorded.)

Jacob, John   Prisoner 533. Rank: Seaman, from: Defiance, Privateer.
    Cap: 15 Mar 1813 at Sea by Nimrod Int: 17 Mar 1813 Escaped: 21 Apr 1813.
    Received from Nimrod. Escaped.

Jacob, Louis   Prisoner 1249. Rank: Captain, from: Grauosa, Merchant Vessel.
    Cap: 29 Jun 1814 at Sea by HM Ship Onyx Int: 30 Aug 1814 Dis: 10 Nov 1814.
    Recaptured from the Carethagenians. Received from Shark. Board's Order. (Prisoner numbers 1249 - 1256 all have recorded rank of Captain.)

Jacobs, Charles   Prisoner 366. Rank: Seaman, from: Vixen, Man of War.
    Cap: 22 Nov 1812 at Sea by Rhodian late of US Brig Vixen Int: 14 Dec 1812 Dis: 04 Apr 1813.
    Received from Rhodian. To America for Exchange.

American Prisoners of War Held at Jamaica During the War of 1812

Jacobs, Peter   Prisoner 1499. Rank: Mate, from: Not Recorded, Not Recorded.
    Cap: 20 Dec 1814 at Sea by Lacedaemonian Int: 04 Feb 1815 Dis: 11 Feb 1815.
    Taken for Passage to Jamaica Depot. Received from Rota. Into HMS Ramillies per order of Sir T M Hardy.

Jacobson, Frederick   Prisoner 1182. Rank: Seaman, from: Decatur, Privateer.
    Cap: 05 Jun 1814 at Sea by HM Ship Rhin Int: 20 Jun 1814 Dis: 16 Aug 1814.
    Received from HM Ship Rhin. Board's Order.

Jantzue, Lewis   Prisoner 520. Rank: 1 Lieutenant, from: Defiance, Privateer.
    Cap: 15 Mar 1813 at Sea by Nimrod Int: 17 Mar 1813 Dis: 30 Mar 1813.
    Received from Nimrod. To America for Exchange.

Jaque, Jacinta Jean   Prisoner 1252. Rank: Captain, from: Grauosa, Merchant Vessel.
    Cap: 29 Jun 1814 at Sea by HM Ship Onyx Int: 30 Aug 1814 Dis: 10 Nov 1814.
    Recaptured from the Carethagenians. Received from Shark. Board's Order. (Prisoner numbers 1249 - 1256 all have recorded rank of Captain.)

Jarua, Charles   Prisoner 361. Rank: Seaman, from: Vixen, Man of War.
    Cap: 22 Nov 1812 at Sea by Rhodian late of HM Brig Vixen Int: 14 Dec 1812 Dis: 09 May 1813.
    Received from Rhodian. To America for Exchange.

Jarvis, John   Prisoner 1375. Rank: Seaman, from: American Gunboats, Not Recorded.
    Cap: 05 Jan 1815 near New Orleans by Plantagenet Int: 27 Jan 1815 Dis: 05 Feb 1815.
    Taken in the American Gun Boats near New Orleans. Received from Ramilies. Into HM Ship Diomede per order of Sir TM Hardy Baronet.

Jasser, Juan   Prisoner 582. Rank: Seaman, from: Le Ventura, Privateer.
    Cap: 13 Mar 1813 at Sea by Cossac Int: 18 Mar 1813 Died: 05 Sep 1814.
    Received from Cossac. Died.

Jemmison, Charles   Prisoner 864. Rank: Seaman, from: Cato Georgiana, Not Recorded.
    Cap: 28 Nov 1813 at Sea by Barrosa Int: 10 Dec 1813 Dis: 01 Aug 1814.
    Prize to the US Frigate Essex. Received from Barrosa. To American Cartel Brig Aualostaw.

Jenkins, John   Prisoner 396. Rank: Seaman, from: Vixen, Man of War.
    Cap: 22 Nov 1812 at Sea by Rhodian late of US Brig Vixen Int: 14 Dec 1812 Dis: 09 May 1813.
    Received from Rhodian. To America for Exchange.

Jenkins, Luderwick   Prisoner 549. Rank: Seaman, from: Defiance, Privateer.
    Cap: 15 Mar 1813 at Sea by Nimrod Int: 17 Mar 1813 Dis: 24 Jul 1813.
    Received from Nimrod. To American Cartel Brig Aualostaw.

Jenkins, Thomas   Prisoner 1309. Rank: 2 Mate, from: Nettervitte, Merchant Schooner.
    Cap: Not Recorded by HM Sloop Onyx Int: 30 Dec 1814 Dis: 02 Jan 1815.
    Received from HM Sloop Onyx. Into HM Ship Sultan per order of Captain John West. (Date of capture not recorded.)

Jenkins, William   Prisoner 1511. Rank: Seaman, from: Not Recorded, Not Recorded.
    Cap: 08 Dec 1814 at Sea by Albion Int: 04 Feb 1815 Dis: 11 Feb 1815.
    Taken for Passage to Jamaica Depot. Received from Rota. Into HM Ship Rota per order of Sir TM Hardy.

Jennings, Francis   Prisoner 825. Rank: Seaman, from: Enterprize, Privateer.
    Cap: 15 Nov 1813 at Sea by Argo Int: 19 Nov 1813 Dis: 02 Jan 1815.
    A Carthagenaian. Received from Argo. Into HM Ship Sultan per order of Captain John West.

Jennings, Henry   Prisoner 108. Rank: Seaman, from: Poor Sailor, Privateer.
    Cap: 13 Sep 1812 at Sea by Garland Int: 18 Sep 1812 Dis: 24 Jul 1813.
    Received from Garland. To American Cartel Brig Aualostaw.

Jennings, John   Prisoner 879. Rank: Seaman, from: Lapwing, Packet.
    Cap: 08 Dec 1813 at Sea by Barrosa Int: 10 Dec 1813 Dis: 01 Aug 1814.
    Recaptured. Received from Barrosa. To American Cartel Brig Aualostaw.

Jerrard, William   Prisoner 1540. Rank: Seaman, from: Delight, Merchant Sloop.
    Cap: at Sea by Statira Int: 04 Mar 1815 Dis: 30 Mar 1815.
    Received from HM Transport Request. In consequence of Peace with America. (Date of capture not recorded.)

Jerry, Mathias H   Prisoner 873. Rank: Seaman, from: Lapwing, Packet.
    Cap: 08 Dec 1813 at Sea by Barrosa Int: 10 Dec 1813 Dis: 01 Aug 1814.
    Recaptured. Received from Barrosa. To American Cartel Brig Aualostaw.

Jervis, William   Prisoner 27. Rank: Seaman, from: Madisonia, Merchant Vessel.
    Cap: 03 Aug 1812 at Sea by Garland Int: 22 Aug 1812 Dis: 09 May 1813.
    Received from Garland. to America for Exchange.

Joagin, Pedro   Prisoner 1061. Rank: Seaman, from: Casada el Narino, Privateer.
    Cap: 29 May 1814 at Sea by HM Ship Rhin Int: 04 Jun 1814 Dis: 12 Aug 1812.
    Carthagenaian. Received from North Star. Board's Order.

American Prisoners of War Held at Jamaica During the War of 1812

Jocelyn, John   Prisoner 680. Rank: Seaman, from: Teuiriffe, Merchant.
    Cap: 10 May 1813 at Sea by Fawn Int: 25 May 1813 Dis: 01 Aug 1814.
    Received from Fawn. To American Cartel Brig Aualostaw.

John, Cato   Prisoner 331. Rank: Seaman, from: Sauders, Merchant Vessel.
    Cap: Nov 1812 at Sea by Merchant Vessel Monarch Int: 09 Dec 1812 Dis: 24 Jul 1813.
    Received from Monarch. To American Cartel Brig Aualostaw. (Day of capture not recorded.)

John, John   Prisoner 555. Rank: Seaman, from: Defiance, Privateer.
    Cap: 15 Mar 1813 at Sea by Nimrod Int: 17 Mar 1813 Dis: 24 Jul 1813.
    Received from Nimrod. To American Cartel Brig Aualostaw. (First and last name the same.)

John, Peter   Prisoner 424. Rank: Private, from: Vixen, Man of War.
    Cap: 22 Nov 1812 at Sea by Rhodian Int: 14 Dec 1812 Dis: 09 May 1813.
    Received from Brazier. To America for Exchange.

John, Samuel   Prisoner 469. Rank: Seaman, from: Bakerbrooke, Merchant Vessel.
    Cap: at Sea by Herald Int: 15 Jan 1813 Dis: 24 Jul 1813.
    An American. Taken from Bakerbrooke of Halifax. Received from Herald. To American Cartel Brig Aualostaw. (Date of capture not recorded.)

Johnnos, Logan   Prisoner 1320. Rank: Seaman, from: Nettervitte, Merchant Schooner.
    Cap: Not Recorded by HM Sloop Onyx Int: 30 Dec 1814 Dis: 02 Jan 1815.
    Received from HM Sloop Onyx. Into HM Ship Sultan per order of Captain John West. (Date of capture not recorded.)

Johnson, Abraham   Prisoner 372. Rank: Seaman, from: Vixen, Man of War.
    Cap: 22 Nov 1812 at Sea by Rhodian late of US Brig Vixen Int: 14 Dec 1812 Dis: 09 May 1813.
    Received from Rhodian. To America for Exchange.

Johnson, Abraham   Prisoner 1110. Rank: Seaman, from: Romano & Adamante, Merchant Brig.
    Cap: 31 May 1814 at Sea by Leviathan Int: 17 Jun 1814 Dis: 02 Jan 1815.
    Received from Leviathan. Into HM Ship Sultan per order of Captain John West.

Johnson, Charles   Prisoner 686. Rank: Seaman, from: Lovely Lass, Privateer.
    Cap: 15 May 1813 at Sea by Circe Int: 29 May 1813 Dis: 01 Aug 1814.
    Received from Circe. To American Cartel Brig Aualostaw.

Johnson, Charles   Prisoner 1140. Rank: Seaman, from: Decatur, Privateer.
    Cap: 05 Jun 1814 at Sea by HM Ship Rhin Int: 20 Jun 1814 Dis: 02 Jan 1815.
    Received from HM Ship Rhin. Into HM Ship Sultan per order of Captain John West.

Johnson, Dick   Prisoner 724. Rank: Seaman, from: Mount Vernon, Merchant Man.
    Cap: at Sea by Argo Int: 27 Jun 1813 Dis: 02 Jul 1813.
    Received from Mount Vernon. To Mount Vernon per order of Adml Brown this date. (Date of capture not recorded.)

Johnson, James   Prisoner 1397. Rank: Seaman, from: American Gunboats, Not Recorded.
    Cap: 05 Jan 1815 near New Orleans by Plantagenet Int: 27 Jan 1815 Dis: 05 Feb 1815.
    Taken in the American Gun Boats near New Orleans. Received from Ramilies. Into HM Ship Diomede per order of Sir TM Hardy Baronet.

Johnson, Joseph   Prisoner 476. Rank: Seaman, from: Three Friends, Merchant Schooner.
    Cap: 03 Dec 1812 at Sea by Circe Int: 20 Jan 1813 Dis: 04 Apr 1813.
    Received from Circe. To America for Exchange.

Johnson, Matthew   Prisoner 1435. Rank: Seaman, from: American Gunboats, Not Recorded.
    Cap: 05 Jan 1815 near New Orleans by Plantagenet Int: 27 Jan 1815 Dis: 05 Feb 1815.
    Taken in the American Gun Boats near New Orleans. Received from Ramilies. Into HM Ship Diomede per order of Sir TM Hardy Baronet.

Johnson, Robert   Prisoner 1004. Rank: Seaman, from: Henrietta, Merchant Vessel.
    Cap: 20 Feb 1814 at Sea by Carnation Int: 04 Apr 1814 Dis: 01 Aug 1814.
    Received from Rota. Board's Order.

Johnson, Robert   Prisoner 1236. Rank: Seaman, from: Not Recorded, Not Recorded.
    Cap: 04 Aug 1814 Kingston by Variable Int: 07 Aug 1814 Dis: 11 Feb 1815.
    Impressed. Received from Talbot. Into HMS Ramillies per order of T M Hardy.

Johnson, Robert   Prisoner 1464. Rank: Seaman, from: Not Recorded, Not Recorded.
    Cap: 21 Dec 1814 at Sea by Severn Int: 04 Feb 1815 Dis: 11 Feb 1815.
    Taken for Passage to Jamaica Depot. Received from Rota. Into HMS Ramillies per order of Sir T M Hardy.

Johnson, Samuel J   Prisoner 877. Rank: Seaman, from: Lapwing, Packet.
    Cap: 08 Dec 1813 at Sea by Barrosa Int: 10 Dec 1813 Dis: 01 Aug 1814.
    Recaptured. Received from Barrosa. To American Cartel Brig Aualostaw.

Johnson, Thomas   Prisoner 21. Rank: Seaman, from: Dal, Merchant Vessel.
    Cap: 03 Aug 1812 at Sea by Garland Int: 22 Aug 1812 Dis: 09 May 1813.
    Received from Garland. to America for Exchange.

American Prisoners of War Held at Jamaica During the War of 1812

Johnson, Thomas   Prisoner 999. Rank: Seaman, from: Farmer's Daughter, Merchant Vessel.
    Cap: 30 Mar 1814 at Sea by Leviathan Int: 03 Apr 1814 Dis: 02 Jan 1815.
    Received from Leviathan. Into HM Ship Sultan per order of Captain John West.

Johnson, William   Prisoner 1141. Rank: Seaman, from: Decatur, Privateer.
    Cap: 05 Jun 1814 at Sea by HM Ship Rhin Int: 20 Jun 1814 Dis: 02 Jan 1815.
    Received from HM Ship Rhin. Into HM Ship Sultan per order of Captain John West.

Johnston, Benjamin   Prisoner 155. Rank: Seaman, from: Philip, Merchant Vessel.
    Cap: 10 Sep 1812 at Sea by Southampton Int: 07 Oct 1812 Dis: 01 Mar 1813.
    Received from Southampton. per Order of Adml Stirling to American Ship Philip.

Joiner, Benjamin   Prisoner 414. Rank: Private, from: Vixen, Man of War.
    Cap: 22 Nov 1812 at Sea by Rhodian Int: 14 Dec 1812 Dis: 09 May 1813.
    Received from Brazier. To America for Exchange.

Jones, Cato   Prisoner 1305. Rank: Seaman, from: Not Recorded, Not Recorded.
    Cap: Not Recorded by Not Recorded Int: 21 Dec 1814 Dis: 11 Feb 1815.
    Impressed. Received from HM Sloop Carnation. Into HMS Ramillies per order of Sir T M Hardy. (Date of capture not recorded.)

Jones, Henry   Prisoner 156. Rank: Seaman, from: Philip, Merchant Vessel.
    Cap: 10 Sep 1812 at Sea by Southampton Int: 07 Oct 1812 Dis: 01 Mar 1813.
    Received from Southampton. per Order of Adml Stirling to American Ship Philip.

Jones, Henry   Prisoner 1304. Rank: Seaman, from: Not Recorded, Not Recorded.
    Cap: Not Recorded by HM Sloop Dasher Int: 16 Dec 1814 Dis: 02 Jan 1815.
    Ship 'Name Unknown'. Received from HM Sloop Dasher. Into HM Ship Sultan per order of Captain John West. (Date of capture not recorded.)

Jones, Jacob   Prisoner 170. Rank: Seaman, from: Rebecca Sims, Merchant Vessel.
    Cap: 12 Sep 1812 at Sea by Southampton Int: 07 Oct 1812 Dis: 01 Mar 1813.
    Received from Southampton. per Order of Admiral Stirling.

Jones, James   Prisoner 1318. Rank: Seaman, from: Nettervitte, Merchant Schooner.
    Cap: Not Recorded by HM Sloop Onyx Int: 31 Dec 1814 Dis: 02 Jan 1815.
    Received from HM Sloop Onyx. Into HM Ship Sultan per order of Captain John West. (Date of capture not recorded.)

Jones, James   Prisoner 1507. Rank: Owner, from: Not Recorded, Not Recorded.
    Cap: 08 Dec 1814 at Sea by Albion Int: 04 Feb 1815 Dis: 08 Feb 1815.
    Taken for Passage to Jamaica Depot. Received from Rota. per order of Sir TM Hardy as a Non-Combatant.

Jones, John   Prisoner 297. Rank: Passenger, from: Mary, Merchant Vessel.
    Cap: 26 Nov 1812 at Sea by Sappho Int: 30 Nov 1812 Dis: 24 Jul 1813.
    Received from Sappho. To American Cartel Brig Aualostaw.

Jones, John   Prisoner 632. Rank: Seaman, from: Mary Ann, Privateer.
    Cap: 05 May 1813 at Sea by Sapphire Int: 07 May 1813 Dis: 01 Aug 1814.
    Received from Sapphire. To American Cartel Brig Aualostaw.

Jones, Michael   Prisoner 234. Rank: Boatswains Mate, from: Joseph & Mary, Privateer.
    Cap: 24 Nov 1812 at Sea by Narcissus Int: 26 Nov 1812 Dis: 24 Jul 1813.
    Received from Narcissus. To American Cartel Brig Aualostaw.

Jones, Peter   Prisoner 493. Rank: Seaman, from: Philip, Merchant Vessel.
    Cap: 28 Jan 1813 at Sea by Morgiana Int: 30 Jan 1813 Dis: 24 Jul 1813.
    Recaptured. Received from Morgiana. To American Cartel Brig Aualostaw.

Jones, Samuel   Prisoner 640. Rank: Seaman, from: Mary Ann, Privateer.
    Cap: 05 May 1813 at Sea by Sapphire Int: 07 May 1813 Dis: 01 Aug 1814.
    Received from Sapphire. To American Cartel Brig Aualostaw.

Jones, William   Prisoner 1364. Rank: Seaman, from: American Gunboats, Not Recorded.
    Cap: 05 Jan 1815 near New Orleans by Plantagenet Int: 27 Jan 1815 Dis: 05 Feb 1815.
    Taken in the American Gun Boats near New Orleans. Received from Ramilies. Into HM Ship Diomede per order of Sir TM Hardy Baronet.

Jordan, John G   Prisoner 389. Rank: Seaman, from: Vixen, Man of War.
    Cap: 22 Nov 1812 at Sea by Rhodian late of US Brig Vixen Int: 14 Dec 1812 Dis: 09 May 1813.
    Received from Rhodian. To America for Exchange.

Jordon, Benjamin   Prisoner 233. Rank: Boatswains Mate, from: Joseph & Mary, Privateer.
    Cap: 24 Nov 1812 at Sea by Narcissus Int: 26 Nov 1812 Dis: 24 Jul 1813.
    Received from Narcissus. To American Cartel Brig Aualostaw.

Jose, Pedro   Prisoner 922. Rank: Seaman, from: San Francisco Navier, Brig.
    Cap: 05 Dec 1813 at Sea by Sappho Int: 15 Dec 1813 Dis: 18 Aug 1814.
    Taken in the Recaptured Spanish Brig. Prize to the Carthagenaian Privateer Carthagenaian. Received from Sappho. Board's Order.

American Prisoners of War Held at Jamaica During the War of 1812

Jose, Thomas   Prisoner 752. Rank: Clerk, from: San Francisco de Paula, Privateer.
    Cap: 02 Oct 1813 at Sea by Forrester Int: 07 Oct 1813 Dis: 22 Apr 1814.
    Received from Forrester. per order, being a Spanish Subject into the Cupida. (Prisoner numbers 750 - 755 all have recorded rank of clerk.)

Josef, Jean   Prisoner 930. Rank: Seaman, from: Cartagenaian, Privateer.
    Cap: 05 Dec 1813 at Sea by Sappho Int: 15 Dec 1813 Dis: 27 Jan 1814.
    Belonging to the Carthagenaian Privateer Carthagenaian. Received from Sappho. being claimed as a Slave.

Joseph, Anthony   Prisoner 32. Rank: Portuguese Boy, from: Madisonia, Merchant Vessel.
    Cap: 03 Aug 1812 at Sea by Garland Int: 22 Aug 1812 Dis: 25 Aug 1812.
    Received from Garland. HM Ship Herald for Passage to Morant Bay being liberated by order of VA Stirling.

Joseph, John   Prisoner 286. Rank: Seaman, from: Joseph & Mary, Privateer.
    Cap: 24 Nov 1812 at Sea by Narcissus Int: 26 Nov 1812 Escaped: 21 Apr 1813.
    Received from Narcissus. Escaped.

Joseph, John   Prisoner 543. Rank: Seaman, from: Defiance, Privateer.
    Cap: 15 Mar 1813 at Sea by Nimrod Int: 17 Mar 1813 Dis: 24 Jul 1813.
    Received from Nimrod. To American Cartel Brig Aualostaw.

Joseph, John   Prisoner 934. Rank: Seaman, from: Milly, Schooner.
    Cap: 29 Nov 1813 at Sea by Decouverte Int: 29 Nov 1813 Dis: 21 Jul 1814.
    Taken out of the American Schooner Milly. Received from Decouverte. Board's Order. (Dates of capture and internment the same.)

Joseph, Lewis   Prisoner 1439. Rank: Seaman, from: American Gunboats, Not Recorded.
    Cap: 05 Jan 1815 near New Orleans by Plantagenet Int: 27 Jan 1815 Dis: 05 Feb 1815.
    Taken in the American Gun Boats near New Orleans. Received from Ramilies. Into HM Ship Diomede per order of Sir TM Hardy Baronet.

Joseph, Peter   Prisoner 579. Rank: Seaman, from: Le Ventura, Privateer.
    Cap: 13 Mar 1813 at Sea by Cossac Int: 18 Mar 1813 Died: 01 Jul 1813.
    Received from Cossac. Died.

Joseph, William   Prisoner 1135. Rank: Cook, from: Decatur, Privateer.
    Cap: 05 Jun 1814 at Sea by HM Ship Rhin Int: 20 Jun 1814 Dis: 22 Jul 1814.
    Received from HM Ship Rhin. Board's Order.

Juan, Pedro   Prisoner 770. Rank: Seaman, from: San Francisco de Paula, Privateer.
    Cap: 02 Oct 1813 at Sea by Forrester Int: 07 Oct 1813 Escaped: 01 Nov 1813.
    Received from Forrester. Escaped.

Julian, Quitnet   Prisoner 1060. Rank: Seaman, from: Casada el Narino, Privateer.
    Cap: 29 May 1814 at Sea by HM Ship Rhin Int: 04 Jun 1814 Dis: 10 Aug 1814.
    Carthagenaian. Received from North Star. Board's Order.

Kawson, George   Prisoner 387. Rank: Seaman, from: Vixen, Man of War.
    Cap: 22 Nov 1812 at Sea by Rhodian late of US Brig Vixen Int: 14 Dec 1812 Dis: 09 May 1813.
    Received from Rhodian. To America for Exchange.

Keith, Thomas   Prisoner 636. Rank: Seaman, from: Mary Ann, Privateer.
    Cap: 05 May 1813 at Sea by Sapphire Int: 07 May 1813 Dis: 01 Aug 1814.
    Received from Sapphire. To American Cartel Brig Aualostaw.

Kell, Francis   Prisoner 1313. Rank: Seaman, from: Nettervitte, Merchant Schooner.
    Cap: Not Recorded by HM Sloop Onyx Int: 30 Dec 1814 Dis: 02 Jan 1815.
    Received from HM Sloop Onyx. Into HM Ship Sultan per order of Captain John West. (Date of capture not recorded.)

Keller, John   Prisoner 415. Rank: Private, from: Vixen, Man of War.
    Cap: 22 Nov 1812 at Sea by Rhodian Int: 14 Dec 1812 Dis: 09 May 1813.
    Received from Brazier. To America for Exchange.

Kelly, Stephen   Prisoner 946. Rank: Cook, from: Coquelle, Merchant Vessel.
    Cap: 24 Dec 1813 at Sea by Sapphire Int: 02 Jan 1814 Dis: 01 Aug 1814.
    Received from Sapphire. To American Cartel Brig Aualostaw.

Ketchell, George   Prisoner 1213. Rank: Seaman, from: Mary, Merchant Schooner.
    Cap: 17 Jun 1814 at Sea by Sapphire Int: 10 Jul 1814 Dis: 02 Jan 1815.
    Recaptured. Received from Sapphire. Into HM Ship Suttan per order of Captain John West.

Key, John   Prisoner 1097. Rank: Seaman, from: Jennett, Brig.
    Cap: 29 May 1814 at Sea by HM Ship Rhin Int: 04 Jun 1814 Dis: 11 Feb 1815.
    Taken in the detained Swedish Brig Jennett. Received from North Star. Into HMS Ramillies per order of Sir T M Hardy.

American Prisoners of War Held at Jamaica During the War of 1812

Key, Oleanto   Prisoner 1278. Rank: Seaman, from: Dolores, Merchant Schooner.
    Cap: at Sea by HM Sloop Anaconda Int: 07 Oct 1814 Dis: 10 Nov 1814.
    Received from HM Sloop Anaconda. Board's Order. Alias William Butterfied. (Date of capture not recorded.)

King, Thomas   Prisoner 435. Rank: Not Recorded, from: Vixen, Man of War.
    Cap: 22 Nov 1812 at Sea by Rhodian Int: Dis: .
    Received from Rhodian. Entered below. (Entry crossed out. Prisoner # 450. Dates of interment and discharge not recorded.)

King, Thomas   Prisoner 450. Rank: Seaman, from: Vixen, Man of War.
    Cap: 26 Dec 1812 at Sea by Rhodian Int: 26 Dec 1812 Dis: 04 Apr 1813.
    Received from Rhodian. To America for Exchange. (Dates of capture and interment the same. Prisoner # 435.)

Kingdom, John   Prisoner 998. Rank: Seaman, from: Farmer's Daughter, Merchant Vessel.
    Cap: 30 Mar 1814 at Sea by Leviathan Int: 03 Apr 1814 Dis: 02 Jan 1815.
    Received from Leviathan. Into HM Ship Sultan per order of Captain John West.

Kinner, Joseph S   Prisoner 1353. Rank: Seaman, from: Not Recorded, Spainsh Brigdet.
    Cap: Not Recorded by Retaliation Int: 23 Jan 1815 Dis: 11 Feb 1815.
    A Spanish Brigdet by HMS Leviathan. From the Hospital where he had been first sent instead of on board the Prison Ship. Into HMS Ramillies per order of Sir T M Hardy. (Date of capture not recorded.)

Kirby, John   Prisoner 983. Rank: Seaman, from: Suspense, Merchant Vessel.
    Cap: 20 Feb 1814 at Sea by Leviathan Int: 26 Mar 1814 Dis: 01 Aug 1814.
    Received from Mohawk. To American Cartel Brig Aualostaw.

Kitten, Abraham   Prisoner 1314. Rank: Seaman, from: Nettervitte, Merchant Schooner.
    Cap: Not Recorded by HM Sloop Onyx Int: 30 Dec 1814 Dis: 02 Jan 1815.
    Received from HM Sloop Onyx. Into HM Ship Sultan per order of Captain John West. (Date of capture not recorded.)

Knott, John   Prisoner 1449. Rank: Seaman, from: American Gunboats, Not Recorded.
    Cap: 05 Jan 1815 near New Orleans by Plantagenet Int: 27 Jan 1815 Dis: 05 Feb 1815.
    Taken in the American Gun Boats near New Orleans. Received from Ramilies. Into HM Ship Diomede per order of Sir TM Hardy Baronet.

Knowlton, David   Prisoner 394. Rank: Seaman, from: Vixen, Man of War.
    Cap: 22 Nov 1812 at Sea by Rhodian late of US Brig Vixen Int: 14 Dec 1812 Dis: 09 May 1813.
    Received from Rhodian. To America for Exchange.

Knull, Heinrich   Prisoner 371. Rank: 2 Gunner, from: Vixen, Man of War.
    Cap: 22 Nov 1812 at Sea by Rhodian late of US Brig Vixen Int: 14 Dec 1812 Dis: 04 Apr 1813.
    Received from Rhodian. To America for Exchange.

Kroger, John   Prisoner 193. Rank: Seaman, from: Morning Star, Merchant Vessel.
    Cap: 08 Sep 1812 at Sea by Cyane Int: 10 Oct 1812 Dis: 24 Jul 1813.
    Received from Cyane. To American Cartel Brig Aualostaw.

Kuntoz, Jacob   Prisoner 1094. Rank: Seaman, from: Jennett, Brig.
    Cap: 29 May 1814 at Sea by HM Ship Rhin Int: 04 Jun 1814 Dis: 02 Jan 1815.
    Taken in the detained Swedish Brig Jennett. Received from North Star. Into HM Ship Sultan per order of Captain John West.

La Cloud, Peter   Prisoner 968. Rank: Seaman, from: New Granada, Privateer.
    Cap: 03 Feb 1814 at Sea by Ringdove Int: 07 Feb 1814 Dis: 22 Jul 1814.
    Received by Ringdove. Board's Order.

La Cruz, Juan   Prisoner 768. Rank: Seaman, from: San Francisco de Paula, Privateer.
    Cap: 02 Oct 1813 at Sea by Forrester Int: 07 Oct 1813 Dis: 11 Jan 1814.
    Received from Forrester. per order.

La Fait, Lewis   Prisoner 572. Rank: Seaman, from: Defiance, Privateer.
    Cap: 15 Mar 1813 at Sea by Nimrod Int: 17 Mar 1813 Escaped: 20 Sep 1813.
    Received from Nimrod. Escaped.

La Lauda, Pedro   Prisoner 776. Rank: Seaman, from: San Francisco de Paula, Privateer.
    Cap: 02 Oct 1813 at Sea by Forrester Int: 07 Oct 1813 Dis: 11 Jan 1814.
    Received from Forrester. per order.

La Place, Peter   Prisoner 849. Rank: Seaman, from: Le Galzo, Spanish Brig.
    Cap: 17 Nov 1813 at Sea by Variable Int: 28 Nov 1813 Dis: 24 Jul 1814.
    Recaptured from the Carthagenaian Privateer Le Legislateur. Received from Variable. Board's Order.

Lacette, John   Prisoner 541. Rank: Seaman, from: Defiance, Privateer.
    Cap: 15 Mar 1813 at Sea by Nimrod Int: 17 Mar 1813 Dis: 24 Jul 1813.
    Received from Nimrod. To American Cartel Brig Aualostaw.

American Prisoners of War Held at Jamaica During the War of 1812

Lacey, James   Prisoner 1546. Rank: Seaman, from: Le Expedecion, Merchant Vessel.
    Cap: at Sea by HMS Drake Int: 09 Mar 1815 Dis: 30 Mar 1815.
    Received from HMS Rinaldo. In consequence of Peace with America. (Date of capture not recorded.)

Lacroyde, Houore   Prisoner 924. Rank: Seaman, from: San Francisco Navier, Brig.
    Cap: 05 Dec 1813 at Sea by Sappho Int: 15 Dec 1813 Dis: 08 Aug 1814.
    Taken in the Recaptured Spanish Brig. Prize to the Carthagenaian Privateer Carthagenaian. Received from Sappho. Board's Order.

Lactie, John   Prisoner 630. Rank: Seaman, from: Mary Ann, Privateer.
    Cap: 05 May 1813 at Sea by Sapphire Int: 07 May 1813 Dis: 21 Jul 1814.
    Received from Sapphire. Board's Order.

Lacurries, Juan Batista   Prisoner 749. Rank: Surgeon, from: San Francisco de Paula, Privateer.
    Cap: 02 Oct 1813 at Sea by Forrester Int: 07 Oct 1813 Dis: 11 Jan 1814.
    Received from Forrester. per order.

Lagoardett, Pedro   Prisoner 1128. Rank: Sergeant Arms, from: Decatur, Privateer.
    Cap: 05 Jun 1814 at Sea by HM Ship Rhin Int: 20 Jun 1814 Dis: 02 Aug 1814.
    Received from HM Ship Rhin. Into HM Ship Suttan per order of Captain John West.

Laman, William   Prisoner 166. Rank: Seaman, from: Rebecca Sims, Merchant Vessel.
    Cap: 12 Sep 1812 at Sea by Southampton Int: 07 Oct 1812 Dis: 01 Mar 1813.
    Received from Southampton. per Order of Admiral Stirling.

Lamber, Pier   Prisoner 576. Rank: 2 Captain, from: Le Ventura, Privateer.
    Cap: 13 Mar 1813 at Sea by Cossac Int: 18 Mar 1813 Escaped: 12 May 1814.
    Received from Cossac. Escaped.

Lamel, Louis   Prisoner 1152. Rank: Seaman, from: Decatur, Privateer.
    Cap: 05 Jun 1814 at Sea by HM Ship Rhin Int: 20 Jun 1814 Dis: .
    Received from HM Ship Rhin. Included in list but never received into custody. (No date of discharge.)

Lane, John   Prisoner 1350. Rank: Mate, from: Ellena, Mechant Vessel.
    Cap: at Sea by Thracian Int: 13 Jan 1815 Dis: 04 Feb 1815.
    Received from Thracian. Board's Order. (Date of capture not recorded.)

Lane, Thomas   Prisoner 838. Rank: Captain, from: Maria, An American Merchant Schooner.
    Cap: 15 Nov 1813 at Sea by Argo Int: 19 Nov 1813 Dis: 12 Apr 1814.
    Received from Argo. To Parole.

Lang, John   Prisoner 1551. Rank: Seaman, from: John, Merchant Vessel.
    Cap: at Sea by HMS Talbot Int: 20 Mar 1815 Dis: 30 Mar 1815.
    Received from HMS Talbot. In consequence of Peace with America. (Date of capture not recorded.)

Lang, Jose   Prisoner 1047. Rank: 2 Mate, from: Casada el Narino, Privateer.
    Cap: 29 May 1814 at Sea by HM Ship Rhin Int: 04 Jun 1814 Dis: 22 Jul 1814.
    Carthagenaian. Received from North Star. Board's Order.

Laniba, Michael   Prisoner 814. Rank: Seaman, from: Enterprize, Privateer.
    Cap: 15 Nov 1813 at Sea by Argo Int: 19 Nov 1813 Dis: 29 Jul 1814.
    A Carthagenaian. Received from Argo. Board's Order.

Laory, Josh   Prisoner 1123. Rank: Pilot, from: Decatur, Privateer.
    Cap: 05 Jun 1814 at Sea by HM Ship Rhin Int: 20 Jun 1814 Dis: 02 Jan 1815.
    Received from HM Ship Rhin. Into HM Ship Sultan per order of Captain John West.

Lapongau, Chery   Prisoner 1288. Rank: Passenger, from: Dolores, Merchant Schooner.
    Cap: at Sea by HM Sloop Anaconda Int: 07 Oct 1814 Dis: 29 Oct 1814.
    Received from HM Sloop Anaconda. Board's Order. (Date of capture not recorded.)

Larkins, John   Prisoner 423. Rank: Private, from: Vixen, Man of War.
    Cap: 22 Nov 1812 at Sea by Rhodian Int: 14 Dec 1812 Dis: 09 May 1813.
    Received from Brazier. To America for Exchange.

Lassetto, Joseph   Prisoner 1250. Rank: Captain, from: Grauosa, Merchant Vessel.
    Cap: 29 Jun 1814 at Sea by HM Ship Onyx Int: 30 Aug 1814 Dis: 10 Nov 1814.
    Recaptured from the Carethagenians. Received from Shark. Board's Order. (Prisoner numbers 1249 - 1256 all have recorded rank of Captain.)

Latham, Jerry   Prisoner 646. Rank: Seaman, from: Mary Ann, Privateer.
    Cap: 05 May 1813 at Sea by Sapphire Int: 07 May 1813 Dis: 01 Aug 1814.
    Received from Sapphire. To American Cartel Brig Aualostaw.

Laurence, Francis   Prisoner 1299. Rank: Seaman, from: Dorothea, Merchant Vessel.
    Cap: 06 Dec 1814 off the River Bacascao |Cuba| by North Star Int: 15 Dec 1814 Dis: 02 Jan 1815.
    Received from North Star. Into HM Ship Sultan per order of Captain John West.

Laurence, Francis   Prisoner 1474. Rank: Seaman, from: Not Recorded, Not Recorded.
    Cap: 21 Dec 1814 at Sea by Severn Int: 04 Feb 1815 Dis: 11 Feb 1815.
    Taken for Passage to Jamaica Depot. Received from Rota. Into HMS Ramillies per order of Sir T M Hardy.

American Prisoners of War Held at Jamaica During the War of 1812

Layton, N G   Prisoner 192. Rank: Seaman, from: Books, Not Recorded.
    Cap: Not Recorded by Not Recorded   Int: 10 Oct 1812   Dis: 04 Apr 1813.
    Received from Cyane. To America for Exchange. (Date of capture not recorded.)

Layton, N G   Prisoner 194. Rank: Seaman, from: Books, Not Recorded.
    Cap: Not Recorded by Not Recorded   Int: 10 Oct 1812   Dis: .
    Received from Cyane. Entered before. No. 192. (Entry crossed out.)

Le Grand, Louis   Prisoner 1346. Rank: Seaman, from: Not Recorded, Not Recorded.
    Cap: at Sea by HMS Shark   Int: 07 Jan 1815   Dis: 10 Jan 1815.
    Ship 'Name Unknown'. Received from HMS Shark. Board's Order. (Date of capture not recorded.)

Le Jea, Artimus   Prisoner 317. Rank: Seaman, from: Pirtshire, English Merchant Ship.
    Cap: Nov 1812 at Sea by Fawn   Int: 06 Dec 1812   Dis: 24 Jul 1813.
    Recaptured. Eagle Privateer. Received from Fawn. To American Cartel Brig Aualostaw. (Day of capture not recorded.)

Le Rose, Ramoin   Prisoner 967. Rank: Seaman, from: New Granada, Privateer.
    Cap: 03 Feb 1814 at Sea by Ringdove   Int: 07 Feb 1814   Dis: 23 Aug 1814.
    Received by Ringdove. Board's Order.

Le Roux, Mare   Prisoner 1344. Rank: Seaman, from: Not Recorded, Not Recorded.
    Cap: at Sea by HMS Shark   Int: 07 Jan 1815   Dis: 10 Jan 1815.
    Ship 'Name Unknown'. Received from HMS Shark. Board's Order. (Date of capture not recorded.)

Leatherby, Joseph   Prisoner 644. Rank: Seaman, from: Mary Ann, Privateer.
    Cap: 05 May 1813 at Sea by Sapphire   Int: 07 May 1813   Dis: 01 Aug 1814.
    Received from Sapphire. To American Cartel Brig Aualostaw.

Leceux, Augustine   Prisoner 1065. Rank: Seaman, from: Casada el Narino, Privateer.
    Cap: 29 May 1814 at Sea by HM Ship Rhin   Int: 04 Jun 1814   Dis: 22 Jul 1814.
    Carthagenaian. Received from North Star. Board's Order.

Lee, Henry   Prisoner 255. Rank: Seaman, from: Joseph & Mary, Privateer.
    Cap: 24 Nov 1812 at Sea by Narcissus   Int: 26 Nov 1812   Dis: 24 Jul 1813.
    Received from Narcissus. To American Cartel Brig Aualostaw.

Lee, John Roger   Prisoner 181. Rank: Seaman, from: Philip, Merchant Vessel.
    Cap: 10 Sep 1812 at Sea by Southampton   Int: 09 Oct 1812   Dis: 01 Mar 1813.
    Received from Southampton. per Order of Admiral Stirling.

Lee, William   Prisoner 953. Rank: Mate, from: Swift, Merchant Vessel.
    Cap: at Sea by Leonidas   Int: 25 Jan 1814   Dis: 01 Aug 1814.
    Received from Leonidas. To American Cartel Brig Aualostaw. (Date of capture not recorded. Prisoner numbers 951 - 956 all have recorded rank of mate.)

Legal, Juan   Prisoner 1056. Rank: Seaman, from: Casada el Narino, Privateer.
    Cap: 29 May 1814 at Sea by HM Ship Rhin   Int: 04 Jun 1814   Dis: 10 Aug 1814.
    Carthagenaian. Received from North Star. Board's Order.

Leggett, George   Prisoner 373. Rank: Seaman, from: Vixen, Man of War.
    Cap: 22 Nov 1812 at Sea by Rhodian late of US Brig Vixen   Int: 14 Dec 1812   Dis: 09 May 1813.
    Received from Rhodian. To America for Exchange.

Legre, Juan   Prisoner 755. Rank: Clerk, from: San Francisco de Paula, Privateer.
    Cap: 02 Oct 1813 at Sea by Forrester   Int: 07 Oct 1813   Dis: 11 Jan 1814.
    Received from Forrester. per order. (Prisoner numbers 750 - 755 all have recorded rank of clerk.)

Leneel, Francis   Prisoner 1063. Rank: Seaman, from: Casada el Narino, Privateer.
    Cap: 29 May 1814 at Sea by HM Ship Rhin   Int: 04 Jun 1814   Dis: 10 Aug 1814.
    Carthagenaian. Received from North Star. Board's Order.

Lenquish, Mathew   Prisoner 1241. Rank: Passenger but Seaman, from: John, Merchant Vessel.
    Cap: 11 Aug 1814 at Sea by Variable   Int: 15 Aug 1814   Dis: 11 Feb 1815.
    Received from Variable. Into HMS Ramillies per order of Sir T M Hardy.

Leof, Unis   Prisoner 375. Rank: Seaman, from: Vixen, Man of War.
    Cap: 22 Nov 1812 at Sea by Rhodian late of US Brig Vixen   Int: 14 Dec 1812   Died: 26 Apr 1813.
    Received from Rhodian. Died.

Leon, Anthony   Prisoner 8. Rank: Seaman, from: Assaw, Merchant Vessel.
    Cap: 28 Jul 1812 at Sea by Garland   Int: 22 Aug 1812   Escaped: 30 Jan 1813.
    Recaptured having been taken by the American Privateer the Paul Jones. Received from Garland. Escaped.

Leon, Anthony   Prisoner 510. Rank: Seaman, from: Not Recorded, Not Recorded.
    Cap: 11 Feb 1813 at Lucea by Not Recorded   Int: 26 Feb 1813   Dis: 09 May 1813.
    Retaken. Received from Sea Horse. To America for Exchange. (Prisoner number 8.)

Lespioult, Francis   Prisoner 1289. Rank: Passenger, from: Dolores, Merchant Schooner.
    Cap: at Sea by HM Sloop Anaconda   Int: 07 Oct 1814   Dis: 29 Oct 1814.
    Received from HM Sloop Anaconda. Board's Order. (Date of capture not recorded.)

Leuox, John   Prisoner 273. Rank: Sergeant, from: Joseph & Mary, Privateer.
    Cap: 24 Nov 1812 at Sea by Narcissus Int: 26 Nov 1812 Dis: 09 May 1813.
    Received from Narcissus. To America for Exchange.

Leut, William   Prisoner 702. Rank: Seaman, from: Lovely Lass, Privateer.
    Cap: 15 May 1813 at Sea by Circe Int: 29 May 1813 Escaped: 13 Oct 1813.
    Received from Circe. Escaped.

Lewis, Augustus   Prisoner 1292. Rank: Passenger, from: Dolores, Merchant Schooner.
    Cap: at Sea by HM Sloop Anaconda Int: 07 Oct 1814 Dis: 29 Oct 1814.
    Received from HM Sloop Anaconda. Board's Order. (Date of capture not recorded.)

Lewis, Daniel   Prisoner 1430. Rank: Seaman, from: American Gunboats, Not Recorded.
    Cap: 05 Jan 1815 near New Orleans by Plantagenet Int: 27 Jan 1815 Dis: 05 Feb 1815.
    Taken in the American Gun Boats near New Orleans. Received from Ramilies. Into HM Ship Diomede per order of Sir TM Hardy Baronet.

Lewis, Eben A   Prisoner 454. Rank: Prize Mate, from: Rachel, Merchant Vessel.
    Cap: 1813 at Sea by Fawn Int: 13 Jan 1812 Dis: 04 Apr 1813.
    Received from Sapphire. To America for Exchange. (Day and month of capture not recorded. Year of internment should be 1813.)

Lewis, Francis   Prisoner 88. Rank: Seaman, from: Poor Sailor, Privateer.
    Cap: 13 Sep 1812 at Sea by Garland Int: 18 Sep 1812 Dis: 24 Jul 1813.
    Received from Garland. To American Cartel Brig Aualostaw.

Lewis, James H   Prisoner 973. Rank: Prize Master, from: 26th October 1812, Merchant Vessel.
    Cap: 20 Feb 1814 at Sea by Ringdove Int: 20 Feb 1814 Dis: 01 Aug 1814.
    Received from Ringdove. To American Cartel Brig Aualostaw.

Lewis, John   Prisoner 554. Rank: Seaman, from: Defiance, Privateer.
    Cap: 15 Mar 1813 at Sea by Nimrod Int: 17 Mar 1813 Escaped: 28 Jun 1813.
    Received from Nimrod. Escaped.

Lewis, John   Prisoner 725. Rank: Seaman, from: Mount Vernon, Merchant Man.
    Cap: at Sea by Argo Int: 27 Jun 1813 Dis: 02 Jul 1813.
    Received from Mount Vernon. To Mount Vernon per order of Adml Brown this date. (Date of capture not recorded.)

Lewis, Peter   Prisoner 846. Rank: Seaman, from: Maria, An American Merchant Schooner.
    Cap: 15 Nov 1813 at Sea by Argo Int: 19 Nov 1813 Dis: 01 Aug 1814.
    Received from Argo. To American Cartel Brig Aualostaw.

Lewis, Valentine   Prisoner 1185. Rank: Seaman, from: Decatur, Privateer.
    Cap: 05 Jun 1814 at Sea by HM Ship Rhin Int: 20 Jun 1814 Dis: 02 Aug 1814.
    Received from HM Ship Rhin. Board's Order.

Lewis, Winslow   Prisoner 251. Rank: Seaman, from: Joseph & Mary, Privateer.
    Cap: 24 Nov 1812 at Sea by Narcissus Int: 26 Nov 1812 Dis: 24 Jul 1813.
    Received from Narcissus. To American Cartel Brig Aualostaw.

Libbett, Richard   Prisoner 1478. Rank: Seaman, from: Not Recorded, Not Recorded.
    Cap: 21 Dec 1814 at Sea by Severn Int: 04 Feb 1815 Dis: 11 Feb 1815.
    Taken for Passage to Jamaica Depot. Received from Rota. Into HMS Ramillies per order of Sir T M Hardy.

Liberal, August   Prisoner 1274. Rank: Master, from: Dolores, Merchant Schooner.
    Cap: at Sea by HM Sloop Anaconda Int: 07 Oct 1814 Dis: 11 Oct 1814.
    Received from HM Sloop Anaconda. To Parole. (Date of capture not recorded.)

Lindoff, John   Prisoner 1423. Rank: Seaman, from: American Gunboats, Not Recorded.
    Cap: 05 Jan 1815 near New Orleans by Plantagenet Int: 27 Jan 1815 Dis: 05 Feb 1815.
    Taken in the American Gun Boats near New Orleans. Received from Ramilies. Into HM Ship Diomede per order of Sir TM Hardy Baronet.

Lint, John   Prisoner 1477. Rank: Seaman, from: Not Recorded, Not Recorded.
    Cap: 21 Dec 1814 at Sea by Severn Int: 04 Feb 1815 Dis: 11 Feb 1815.
    Taken for Passage to Jamaica Depot. Received from Rota. Into HMS Ramillies per order of Sir T M Hardy.

Lirour, Peter   Prisoner 634. Rank: Seaman, from: Mary Ann, Privateer.
    Cap: 05 May 1813 at Sea by Sapphire Int: 07 May 1813 Dis: 21 Jul 1814.
    Received from Sapphire. Board's Order.

List, Moses   Prisoner 1258. Rank: Seaman, from: Not Recorded, Not Recorded.
    Cap: 07 Jul 1814 at Sea by HM Ship Onyx Int: 30 Aug 1814 Dis: 25 Nov 1814.
    Ship 'Name Unknown'. Received from Shark. Board's Order.

American Prisoners of War Held at Jamaica During the War of 1812

Little, Charles   Prisoner 1306. Rank: Seaman, from: Not Recorded, Not Recorded.
    Cap: at Sea by HM Ship Rinaldo Int: 16 Dec 1814 Dis: 02 Jan 1815.
    Ship 'Name Unknown'. Received from HM Ship Rinaldo. Into HM Ship Sultan per order of Captain John West. (Date of capture not recorded.)

Little, Peter   Prisoner 564. Rank: Seaman, from: Defiance, Privateer.
    Cap: 15 Mar 1813 at Sea by Nimrod Int: 17 Mar 1813 Dis: 24 Jul 1813.
    Received from Nimrod. To American Cartel Brig Aualostaw.

Little, William   Prisoner 1018. Rank: Seaman, from: Chance, Privateer.
    Cap: 01 Apr 1814 at Sea by Statira Int: 20 Apr 1814 Dis: 02 Jan 1815.
    Received from Statira. Into HM Ship Sultan per order of Captain John West.

Littlefield, Erick   Prisoner 550. Rank: Seaman, from: Defiance, Privateer.
    Cap: 15 Mar 1813 at Sea by Nimrod Int: 17 Mar 1813 Dis: 24 Jul 1813.
    Received from Nimrod. To American Cartel Brig Aualostaw.

Lloyd, Robert   Prisoner 733. Rank: Seaman, from: Eliza, Merchant Vessel.
    Cap: 17 Jul 1813 at Sea by Sappho Int: 26 Jul 1813 Dis: 01 Aug 1814.
    Received from Sappho. To American Cartel Brig Aualostaw.

Lock, N   Prisoner 847. Rank: Seaman, from: Maria, An American Merchant Schooner.
    Cap: 15 Nov 1813 at Sea by Argo Int: 19 Nov 1813 Dis: 01 Aug 1814.
    Received from Argo. To American Cartel Brig Aualostaw.

Logine, Zamie   Prisoner 599. Rank: Seaman, from: Le Ventura, Privateer.
    Cap: 13 Mar 1813 at Sea by Cossac Int: 18 Mar 1813 Escaped: 15 Oct 1813.
    Received from Cossac. Escaped.

Lombard, Ephrim   Prisoner 60. Rank: Seaman, from: Not Recorded, Not Recorded.
    Cap: 20 Aug 1812 Not Recorded by Not Recorded Int: 03 Sep 1812 Dis: 09 May 1813.
    Prison Ship at New Providence. Received from HM Schooner Decouverte. to America for Exchange.

Long, Nathaniel   Prisoner 244. Rank: Seaman, from: Joseph & Mary, Privateer.
    Cap: 24 Nov 1812 at Sea by Narcissus Int: 26 Nov 1812 Dis: 24 Jul 1813.
    Received from Narcissus. To American Cartel Brig Aualostaw.

Longshore, Richard   Prisoner 1518. Rank: Seaman, from: Not Recorded, Not Recorded.
    Cap: 08 Dec 1814 at Sea by Albion Int: 04 Feb 1815 Dis: 11 Feb 1815.
    Taken for Passage to Jamaica Depot. Received from Rota. Into HM Ship Rota per order of Sir TM Hardy.

Lopes, Victorino   Prisoner 1227. Rank: Seaman, from: La Union, Spanish Brig.
    Cap: 03 Aug 1814 at Sea by Variable Int: 06 Aug 1814 Dis: 01 Sep 1814.
    Recaptured from the Carthagenaian Privateer White Horse. Received from Variable. Board's Order.

Lopez, Francis   Prisoner 637. Rank: Seaman, from: Mary Ann, Privateer.
    Cap: 05 May 1813 at Sea by Sapphire Int: 07 May 1813 Died: 10 Dec 1813.
    Received from Sapphire. Died.

Loring, Elephet   Prisoner 250. Rank: Seaman, from: Joseph & Mary, Privateer.
    Cap: 24 Nov 1812 at Sea by Narcissus Int: 26 Nov 1812 Dis: 04 Apr 1813.
    Received from Narcissus. To America for Exchange.

Loring, Shibbard   Prisoner 1538. Rank: Captain, from: Delight, Merchant Sloop.
    Cap: at Sea by Statira Int: 04 Mar 1815 Dis: 07 Mar 1815.
    Received from HM Transport Request. To Parole. (Date of capture not recorded.)

Lorique, G   Prisoner 1154. Rank: Seaman, from: Decatur, Privateer.
    Cap: 05 Jun 1814 at Sea by HM Ship Rhin Int: 20 Jun 1814 Dis: 10 Aug 1814.
    Received from HM Ship Rhin. Board's Order. (First name not legible.)

Lott, John   Prisoner 660. Rank: Seaman, from: Lovely Lass, Privateer.
    Cap: 21 May 1813 at Sea by Circe Int: 23 May 1813 Escaped: 28 Jun 1813.
    Received from Forrester. Escaped.

Louis, Pierre   Prisoner 1339. Rank: Seaman, from: Not Recorded, Not Recorded.
    Cap: at Sea by HMS Shark Int: 07 Jan 1815 Dis: 10 Jan 1815.
    Ship 'Name Unknown'. Received from HMS Shark. Board's Order. (Date of capture not recorded.)

Lounsby, Frederick   Prisoner 1214. Rank: Seaman, from: Mary, Merchant Schooner.
    Cap: 17 Jun 1814 at Sea by Sapphire Int: 10 Jul 1814 Dis: 02 Jan 1815.
    Recaptured. Received from Sapphire. Into HM Ship Suttan per order of Captain John West.

Lour, John   Prisoner 1445. Rank: Seaman, from: American Gunboats, Not Recorded.
    Cap: 05 Jan 1815 near New Orleans by Plantagenet Int: 27 Jan 1815 Dis: 05 Feb 1815.
    Taken in the American Gun Boats near New Orleans. Received from Ramilies. Into HM Ship Diomede per order of Sir TM Hardy Baronet.

Lowrie, Joseph   Prisoner 669. Rank: Seaman, from: Lovely Lass, Privateer.
    Cap: 21 May 1813 at Sea by Circe Int: 23 May 1813 Dis: 21 Jul 1814.
    Received from Forrester. Board's Order.

American Prisoners of War Held at Jamaica During the War of 1812

Luero, Pedro   Prisoner 778. Rank: Seaman, from: San Francisco de Paula, Privateer.
    Cap: 02 Oct 1813 at Sea by Forrester Int: 07 Oct 1813 Dis: 30 Mar 1814.
    Received from Forrester. per order.

Lugh, Wright   Prisoner 139. Rank: Seaman, from: Whim, Merchant Vessel.
    Cap: 18 Sep 1812 at Sea by HM Brig Liberty Int: 07 Oct 1812 Escaped: 15 Nov 1812.
    Received from Cyane. Escaped.

Luis, Juan   Prisoner 1070. Rank: Seaman, from: Casada el Narino, Privateer.
    Cap: 29 May 1814 at Sea by HM Ship Rhin Int: 04 Jun 1814 Dis: 18 Aug 1814.
    Carthagenaian. Received from North Star. Board's Order.

Luis, Pedro   Prisoner 763. Rank: Seaman, from: San Francisco de Paula, Privateer.
    Cap: 02 Oct 1813 at Sea by Forrester Int: 07 Oct 1813 Dis: 30 Mar 1814.
    Received from Forrester. per order.

Lund, Oliver   Prisoner 68. Rank: Seaman, from: Poor Sailor, Privateer.
    Cap: 13 Sep 1812 at Sea by Garland Int: 18 Sep 1812 Dis: 04 Apr 1813.
    Received from Garland. to America for Exchange.

Lynn, John   Prisoner 302. Rank: Passenger, from: Mary, Merchant Vessel.
    Cap: 26 Nov 1812 at Sea by Sappho Int: 30 Nov 1812 Dis: 24 Jul 1813.
    Received from Sappho. To American Cartel Brig Aualostaw.

MaCarty, Frederick   Prisoner 739. Rank: Seaman, from: Eliza, Merchant Vessel.
    Cap: 17 Jul 1813 at Sea by Sappho Int: 26 Jul 1813 Dis: 01 Aug 1814.
    Received from Sappho. To American Cartel Brig Aualostaw.

Maceman, Thomas   Prisoner 1022. Rank: Seaman, from: Chance, Privateer.
    Cap: 01 Apr 1814 at Sea by Statira Int: 20 Apr 1814 Dis: 02 Jan 1815.
    Received from Statira. Into HM Ship Sultan per order of Captain John West.

Mackboy, John   Prisoner 1036. Rank: Seaman, from: Jennett, Brig.
    Cap: 29 May 1814 at Sea by HM Ship Rhin Int: 04 Jun 1814 Dis: 01 Dec 1814.
    Taken in the Swedish Brig Jennet. Received from North Star. Board's Order.

Mackey, John   Prisoner 981. Rank: Masters Mate, from: Suspense, Merchant Vessel.
    Cap: 20 Feb 1814 at Sea by Leviathan Int: 26 Mar 1814 Dis: 01 Aug 1814.
    Received from Mohawk. To American Cartel Brig Aualostaw.

Mackey, Michael   Prisoner 401. Rank: Seaman, from: Vixen, Man of War.
    Cap: 22 Nov 1812 at Sea by Rhodian late of US Brig Vixen Int: 14 Dec 1812 Dis: 09 May 1813.
    Received from Rhodian. To America for Exchange.

Macklin, John   Prisoner 1023. Rank: Seaman, from: Chance, Privateer.
    Cap: 01 Apr 1814 at Sea by Statira Int: 20 Apr 1814 Dis: 02 Jan 1815.
    Received from Statira. Into HM Ship Sultan per order of Captain John West.

Madding, John   Prisoner 1317. Rank: Seaman, from: Nettervitte, Merchant Schooner.
    Cap: Not Recorded by HM Sloop Onyx Int: 30 Dec 1814 Dis: 02 Jan 1815.
    Received from HM Sloop Onyx. Into HM Ship Sultan per order of Captain John West.
    (Date of capture not recorded.)

Maddison, Charless   Prisoner 701. Rank: Seaman, from: Lovely Lass, Privateer.
    Cap: 15 May 1813 at Sea by Circe Int: 29 May 1813 Dis: 01 Aug 1814.
    Received from Circe. To American Cartel Brig Aualostaw.

Maddison, Samuel   Prisoner 1260. Rank: Seaman, from: Not Recorded, Not Recorded.
    Cap: 07 Jul 1814 at Sea by HM Ship Onyx Int: 30 Aug 1814 Dis: 25 Nov 1814.
    Ship 'Name Unknown'. Received from Shark. Board's Order.

Madura, Francisco   Prisoner 531. Rank: Seaman, from: Defiance, Privateer.
    Cap: 15 Mar 1813 at Sea by Nimrod Int: 17 Mar 1813 Escaped: 28 Jun 1813.
    Received from Nimrod. Escaped.

Maltes, Francisco   Prisoner 923. Rank: Seaman, from: San Francisco Navier, Brig.
    Cap: 05 Dec 1813 at Sea by Sappho Int: 15 Dec 1813 Dis: 12 Aug 1814.
    Taken in the Recaptured Spanish Brig. Prize to the Carthagenaian Privateer Carthagenaian. Received from Sappho. Board's Order.

Malther, William   Prisoner 44. Rank: Seaman, from: Prest, Merchant Vessel.
    Cap: 22 Aug 1812 at Kingston by Tartaus Int: 22 Aug 1812 Dis: 09 May 1813.
    to America for Exchange.

Mancell, John   Prisoner 1144. Rank: Seaman, from: Decatur, Privateer.
    Cap: 05 Jun 1814 at Sea by HM Ship Rhin Int: 20 Jun 1814 Dis: 10 Aug 1814.
    Received from HM Ship Rhin. Board's Order.

Manger, Gear   Prisoner 1147. Rank: Seaman, from: Decatur, Privateer.
    Cap: 05 Jun 1814 at Sea by HM Ship Rhin Int: 20 Jun 1814 Dis: 10 Aug 1814.
    Received from HM Ship Rhin. Board's Order.

American Prisoners of War Held at Jamaica During the War of 1812

Mann, Charles   Prisoner 64. Rank: Not legible, from: Books, Not Recorded.
    Cap: Not Recorded by Not Recorded Int: 06 Sep 1812 Dis: 09 May 1813.
    Received from Moselle. to America for Exchange. (Date of capture not recorded.)

Mansfield, James   Prisoner 420. Rank: Private, from: Vixen, Man of War.
    Cap: 22 Nov 1812 at Sea by Rhodian Int: 14 Dec 1812 Dis: 09 May 1813.
    Received from Brazier. To America for Exchange.

Manuel, J   Prisoner 1104. Rank: Seaman, from: Romano & Adamante, Merchant Brig.
    Cap: 31 May 1814 at Sea by Leviathan Int: 17 Jun 1814 Dis: 19 Aug 1814.
    Received from Leviathan. Board's Order. (First name not legible.)

Manusa, Osa   Prisoner 1196. Rank: Seaman, from: Neustra Cantado, Merchant Vessel.
    Cap: 01 Jun 1814 at Sea by HM Ship Argo Int: 27 Jun 1814 Dis: 18 Aug 1814.
    Retaken in the Spanish Ship Neustra Cantado. Received from HM Ship Argo. Board's Order.

Manwell, Antonio   Prisoner 1197. Rank: Seaman, from: Neustra Cantado, Merchant Vessel.
    Cap: 01 Jun 1814 at Sea by HM Ship Argo Int: 27 Jun 1814 Dis: 22 Jul 1814.
    Retaken in the Spanish Ship Neustra Cantado. Received from HM Ship Argo. Board's Order.

Manyard, John   Prisoner 535. Rank: Seaman, from: Defiance, Privateer.
    Cap: 15 Mar 1813 at Sea by Nimrod Int: 17 Mar 1813 Dis: 30 Mar 1813.
    Received from Nimrod. Boy under 12 years old.

Marciar, Juan   Prisoner 902. Rank: Boatswain, from: San Francisco Navier, Brig.
    Cap: 05 Dec 1813 at Sea by Sappho Int: 15 Dec 1813 Dis: 11 Jan 1814.
    Taken in the Recaptured Spanish Brig. Prize to the Carthagenaian Privateer Carthagenaian. Received from Sappho. per order.

Maria, Jon   Prisoner 1202. Rank: Seaman, from: Neustra Cantado, Merchant Vessel.
    Cap: 01 Jun 1814 at Sea by HM Ship Argo Int: 27 Jun 1814 Dis: 12 Aug 1814.
    Retaken in the Spanish Ship Neustra Cantado. Received from HM Ship Argo. Board's Order.

Maria, Joseph   Prisoner 1334. Rank: Seaman, from: Not Recorded, Not Recorded.
    Cap: at Sea by HMS Shark Int: 07 Jan 1815 Dis: 10 Jan 1815.
    Ship 'Name Unknown'. Received from HMS Shark. Board's Order. (Date of capture not recorded.)

Marie, John   Prisoner 325. Rank: Seaman, from: Pirtshire, English Merchant Ship.
    Cap: Nov 1812 at Sea by Fawn Int: 06 Dec 1812 Dis: 24 Jul 1813.
    Recaptured. Eagle Privateer. Received from Fawn. To American Cartel. (Day of capture not recorded.)

Marine, Daniel   Prisoner 815. Rank: Seaman, from: Enterprize, Privateer.
    Cap: 15 Nov 1813 at Sea by Argo Int: 19 Nov 1813 Dis: 11 Jan 1814.
    A Carthagenaian. Received from Argo. per order.

Maris, William   Prisoner 1457. Rank: Seaman, from: Not Recorded, Not Recorded.
    Cap: 21 Dec 1814 at Sea by Severn Int: 04 Feb 1815 Dis: 11 Feb 1815.
    Taken for Passage to Jamaica Depot. Received from Rota. Into HMS Ramillies per order of Sir T M Hardy.

Market, John   Prisoner 176. Rank: Mate, from: William Penn, Merchant Vessel.
    Cap: 08 Sep 1812 at Sea by Southampton Int: 09 Oct 1812 Dis: 01 Mar 1813.
    Received from Southampton. per Order of Admiral Stirling.

Marley, John   Prisoner 210. Rank: Seaman, from: Blandie, Merchant Vessel.
    Cap: 21 Oct 1812 at Sea by Not Recorded Int: 25 Oct 1812 Dis: 04 Apr 1813.
    Recaptured. Taken from the Recapd Schooner Blandie, belonging to the American Privateer Schooner Comet. Received from Sappho. To America for Exchange.

Marque, Antonio   Prisoner 1340. Rank: Seaman, from: Not Recorded, Not Recorded.
    Cap: at Sea by HMS Shark Int: 07 Jan 1815 Dis: 29 Jan 1815.
    Ship 'Name Unknown'. Received from HMS Shark. Board's Order. (Date of capture not recorded.)

Marsback, John F   Prisoner 681. Rank: Seaman, from: Teuiriffe, Merchant.
    Cap: 10 May 1813 at Sea by Fawn Int: 25 May 1813 Dis: 01 Aug 1814.
    Received from Fawn. To American Cartel Brig Aualostaw.

Marshall, D F   Prisoner 612. Rank: Seaman, from: Not Recorded, Not Recorded.
    Cap: Not Recorded by Not Recorded Int: 21 Apr 1813 Dis: 01 Aug 1814.
    An American. Received from Pekican. To American Cartel Brig Aualostaw. (Date of capture not recorded.)

Marta, Pedro   Prisoner 1199. Rank: Seaman, from: Neustra Cantado, Merchant Vessel.
    Cap: 01 Jun 1814 at Sea by HM Ship Argo Int: 27 Jun 1814 Dis: 18 Aug 1814.
    Retaken in the Spanish Ship Neustra Cantado. Received from HM Ship Argo. Board's Order.

Martel, Pedro   Prisoner 1221. Rank: Seaman, from: La Union, Spanish Brig.
    Cap: 03 Aug 1814 at Sea by Variable Int: 06 Aug 1814 Dis: 01 Sep 1814.
    Recaptured from the Carthagenaian Privateer White Horse. Received from Variable. Board's Order.

American Prisoners of War Held at Jamaica During the War of 1812

Martin, Francis   Prisoner 620. Rank: Gunner, from: Mary Ann, Privateer.
    Cap: 05 May 1813 at Sea by Sapphire Int: 07 May 1813 Dis: 21 Jul 1814.
    Received from Sapphire. Board's Order.

Martin, George   Prisoner 1472. Rank: Seaman, from: Not Recorded, Not Recorded.
    Cap: 21 Dec 1814 at Sea by Severn Int: 04 Feb 1815 Dis: 11 Feb 1815.
    Taken for Passage to Jamaica Depot. Received from Rota. Into HMS Ramillies per order of Sir T M Hardy.

Martin, J W   Prisoner 76. Rank: Seaman, from: Poor Sailor, Privateer.
    Cap: 13 Sep 1812 at Sea by Garland Int: 18 Sep 1812 Dis: 09 May 1813.
    Received from Garland. To America for Exchange.

Martin, John   Prisoner 231. Rank: Carpenters Mate, from: Joseph & Mary, Privateer.
    Cap: 24 Nov 1812 at Sea by Narcissus Int: 26 Nov 1812 Dis: 24 Jul 1813.
    Received from Narcissus. To American Cartel Brig Aualostaw.

Martin, John   Prisoner 479. Rank: Seaman, from: Three Friends, Merchant Schooner.
    Cap: 03 Dec 1812 at Sea by Circe Int: 20 Jan 1813 Dis: 04 Apr 1813.
    Received from Circe. To America for Exchange.

Martin, John   Prisoner 943. Rank: Seaman, from: Coquelle, Merchant Vessel.
    Cap: 24 Dec 1813 at Sea by Sapphire Int: 02 Jan 1814 Dis: 01 Aug 1814.
    Received from Sapphire. To American Cartel Brig Aualostaw.

Martin, Juan   Prisoner 760. Rank: Seaman, from: San Francisco de Paula, Privateer.
    Cap: 02 Oct 1813 at Sea by Forrester Int: 07 Oct 1813 Dis: 11 Jan 1814.
    Received from Forrester. per order.

Martin, Louis   Prisoner 1163. Rank: Seaman, from: Decatur, Privateer.
    Cap: 05 Jun 1814 at Sea by HM Ship Rhin Int: 20 Jun 1814 Dis: 18 Aug 1814.
    Received from HM Ship Rhin. Board's Order.

Martin, Luther   Prisoner 679. Rank: Seaman, from: Teuiriffe, Merchant.
    Cap: 10 May 1813 at Sea by Fawn Int: 25 May 1813 Dis: 01 Aug 1814.
    Received from Fawn. To American Cartel Brig Aualostaw.

Martin, Peter   Prisoner 1428. Rank: Seaman, from: American Gunboats, Not Recorded.
    Cap: 05 Jan 1815 near New Orleans by Plantagenet Int: 27 Jan 1815 Dis: 05 Feb 1815.
    Taken in the American Gun Boats near New Orleans. Received from Ramilies. Into HM Ship Diomede per order of Sir TM Hardy Baronet.

Martin, Richard   Prisoner 1291. Rank: Passenger, from: Dolores, Merchant Schooner.
    Cap: at Sea by HM Sloop Anaconda Int: 07 Oct 1814 Dis: 29 Oct 1814.
    Received from HM Sloop Anaconda. Board's Order. (Date of capture not recorded.)

Martin, William   Prisoner 1008. Rank: Mate, from: Farmer's Daughter, Merchant Vessel.
    Cap: 30 Mar 1814 at Sea by Leviathan Int: 06 Apr 1814 Dis: 27 Apr 1814.
    Received from Leviathan. To Parole.

Martini, Alberto   Prisoner 1253. Rank: Captain, from: Grauosa, Merchant Vessel.
    Cap: 29 Jun 1814 at Sea by HM Ship Onyx Int: 30 Aug 1814 Dis: 10 Nov 1814.
    Recaptured from the Carethagenians. Received from Shark. Board's Order. (Prisoner numbers 1249 - 1256 all have recorded rank of Captain.)

Masse, Juan M   Prisoner 901. Rank: Clerk, from: San Francisco Navier, Brig.
    Cap: 05 Dec 1813 at Sea by Sappho Int: 15 Dec 1813 Dis: 11 Jan 1814.
    Taken in the Recaptured Spanish Brig. Prize to the Carthagenaian Privateer Carthagenaian. Received from Sappho. per order.

Mattolland, William   Prisoner 344. Rank: Seaman, from: Vixen, Man of War.
    Cap: 22 Nov 1812 at Sea by Rhodian late of HM Brig Vixen Int: 14 Dec 1812 Dis: 09 May 1813.
    Received from Rhodian. To America for Exchange.

Mauwi, Juan   Prisoner 585. Rank: Seaman, from: Le Ventura, Privateer.
    Cap: 13 Mar 1813 at Sea by Cossac Int: 18 Mar 1813 Dis: 22 Apr 1814.
    Received from Cossac. per Order of R Adml Brown into the Cupida being a Spanish subject.

Maxey, Elias   Prisoner 20. Rank: Seaman, from: Dal, Merchant Vessel.
    Cap: 03 Aug 1812 at Sea by Garland Int: 22 Aug 1812 Dis: 09 May 1813.
    Received from Garland. to America for Exchange.

Maxwell, William   Prisoner 657. Rank: Seaman, from: Lovely Lass, Privateer.
    Cap: 21 May 1813 at Sea by Circe Int: 23 May 1813 Dis: 01 Aug 1814.
    Received from Forrester. To American Cartel Brig Aualostaw.

May, Nicholas   Prisoner 289. Rank: Seaman, from: Mary, Merchant Vessel.
    Cap: 26 Nov 1812 at Sea by Sappho Int: 29 Nov 1812 Dis: 24 Jul 1813.
    Received from Sappho. To American Cartel Brig Aualostaw.

American Prisoners of War Held at Jamaica During the War of 1812

Mazire, Francis   Prisoner 854. Rank: Seaman, from: Le Galzo, Spanish Brig.
    Cap: 17 Nov 1813 at Sea by Variable Int: 28 Nov 1813 Escaped: 12 May 1814.
    Recaptured from the Carthagenaian Privateer Le Legislateur. Received from Variable. Escaped.

McBride, James   Prisoner 522. Rank: Surgeon, from: Defiance, Privateer.
    Cap: 15 Mar 1813 at Sea by Nimrod Int: 17 Mar 1813 Dis: 30 Mar 1813.
    Received from Nimrod. To America for Exchange.

McCabe, Levi   Prisoner 353. Rank: Seaman, from: Vixen, Man of War.
    Cap: 22 Nov 1812 at Sea by Rhodian late of HM Brig Vixen Int: 14 Dec 1812 Dis: 04 Apr 1813.
    Received from Rhodian. To America for Exchange.

McCarthy, Samuel   Prisoner 1302. Rank: Seaman, from: Not Recorded, Not Recorded.
    Cap: Not Recorded by HM Sloop Dasher Int: 16 Dec 1814 Dis: 02 Jan 1815.
    Ship 'Name Unknown'. Received from HM Sloop Dasher. Into HM Ship Sultan per order of Captain John West. (Date of capture not recorded.)

McChrystal, Edward   Prisoner 1381. Rank: Seaman, from: American Gunboats, Not Recorded.
    Cap: 05 Jan 1815 near New Orleans by Plantagenet Int: 27 Jan 1815 Dis: 05 Feb 1815.
    Taken in the American Gun Boats near New Orleans. Received from Ramilies. Into HM Ship Diomede per order of Sir TM Hardy Baronet.

McClintock, William   Prisoner 713. Rank: Seaman, from: William, Merchant Man.
    Cap: 17 May 1813 at Sea by Circe Int: 29 May 1813 Dis: 01 Aug 1814.
    Received from Circe. (No entry for discharge date.)

McCormick, James   Prisoner 339. Rank: Seaman, from: Not Recorded, Merchant Vessel.
    Cap: 08 Dec 1812 at Sea by Rhodian late Southampton Int: 14 Dec 1812 Dis: 04 Apr 1813.
    Unknown. Received from Rhodian. To America for Exchange.

McCormick, James   Prisoner 1032. Rank: Seaman, from: Not Recorded, Not Recorded.
    Cap: Not Recorded by Mohawk Int: 09 May 1814 Dis: 02 Jan 1815.
    Given up as an American. Received from Mohawk. Into HM Ship Sultan per order of Captain John West. (Date of capture not recorded.)

McCulloch, Alexander   Prisoner 706. Rank: Seaman, from: Lovely Lass, Privateer.
    Cap: 15 May 1813 at Sea by Circe Int: 29 May 1813 Dis: 01 Aug 1814.
    Received from Circe. To American Cartel Brig Aualostaw.

McCullum, Joseph   Prisoner 1448. Rank: Seaman, from: American Gunboats, Not Recorded.
    Cap: 05 Jan 1815 near New Orleans by Plantagenet Int: 27 Jan 1815 Dis: 05 Feb 1815.
    Taken in the American Gun Boats near New Orleans. Received from Ramilies. Into HM Ship Diomede per order of Sir TM Hardy Baronet.

McDonald, Daniel   Prisoner 744. Rank: Seaman, from: Eliza, Merchant Vessel.
    Cap: 17 Jul 1813 at Sea by Sappho Int: 26 Jul 1813 Dis: 01 Aug 1814.
    Received from Sappho. To American Cartel Brig Aualostaw.

McFart, John   Prisoner 433. Rank: Boastwain, from: Vixen, Man of War.
    Cap: 22 Nov 1812 at Sea by Rhodian Int: 23 Dec 1812 Dis: 04 Apr 1813.
    Received from Brazier. To America for Exchange.

McGlachan, Turner   Prisoner 208. Rank: Seaman, from: Blandie, Merchant Vessel.
    Cap: 21 Oct 1812 at Sea by Not Recorded Int: 25 Oct 1812 Dis: 04 Apr 1813.
    Recaptured. Taken from the Recapd Schooner Blandie, belonging to the American Privateer Schooner Comet. Received from Sappho. To America for Exchange.

McKeel, James   Prisoner 1548. Rank: Seaman, from: Le Expedecion, Merchant Vessel.
    Cap: at Sea by HMS Drake Int: 09 Mar 1815 Dis: 30 Mar 1815.
    Received from HMS Rinaldo. In consequence of Peace with America. (Date of capture not recorded.)

McKinnee, James   Prisoner 337. Rank: Seaman, from: Not Recorded, Merchant Vessel.
    Cap: 08 Dec 1812 at Sea by Rhodian late Southampton Int: 14 Dec 1812 Dis: 24 Jul 1813.
    Unknown. Received from Rhodian. To American Cartel Brig Aualostaw. Alias James McKinlay.

McLaughlin, Edward   Prisoner 62. Rank: Seaman, from: Decouverte, Not Recorded.
    Cap: Not Recorded by Not Recorded Int: 03 Sep 1812 Dis: 09 May 1813.
    Received from HM Schooner Decouverte. to America for Exchange. (Date of capture not recorded.)

McLaughlin, P   Prisoner 109. Rank: Commander, from: Poor Sailor, Privateer.
    Cap: 13 Sep 1812 at Sea by Garland Int: 18 Sep 1812 Dis: .
    Received from Garland. Discharged Maude's time, date of order (not legible) unknown.

McLear, Francis   Prisoner 327. Rank: Seaman, from: Pirtshire, English Merchant Ship.
    Cap: Nov 1812 at Sea by Fawn Int: 06 Dec 1812 Dis: 24 Jul 1813.
    Recaptured. Eagle Privateer. Received from Fawn. To American Cartel. (Day of capture not recorded.)

McNeil, Archibald   Prisoner 448. Rank: Midshipman, from: Vixen, Man of War.
    Cap: 24 Dec 1812 at Sea by Rhodian Int: 24 Dec 1812 Dis: 24 Dec 1812.
    Received from Rhodian. To Parole. (Dates of capture, interment and discharge the same.)

American Prisoners of War Held at Jamaica During the War of 1812

McNeil, Daniel   Prisoner 656. Rank: Seaman, from: Lovely Lass, Privateer.
    Cap: 21 May 1813 at Sea by Circe Int: 23 May 1813 Escaped: 13 Oct 1813.
    Received from Forrester. Escaped.

McNeil, Daniel   Prisoner 1120. Rank: Prize Master, from: Decatur, Privateer.
    Cap: 05 Jun 1814 at Sea by HM Ship Rhin Int: 20 Jun 1814 Dis: 02 Jan 1815.
    Received from HM Ship Rhin. Into HM Ship Sultan per order of Captain John West.

McPhid, Reynold   Prisoner 1367. Rank: Seaman, from: American Gunboats, Not Recorded.
    Cap: 05 Jan 1815 near New Orleans by Plantagenet Int: 27 Jan 1815 Dis: 05 Feb 1815.
    Taken in the American Gun Boats near New Orleans. Received from Ramilies. Into HM Ship Diomede per order of Sir TM Hardy Baronet.

Mealo, Vinzente   Prisoner 1218. Rank: Seaman, from: La Union, Spanish Brig.
    Cap: 03 Aug 1814 at Sea by Variable Int: 06 Aug 1814 Dis: 10 Sep 1814.
    Recaptured from the Carthagenaian Privateer White Horse. Received from Variable. Board's Order.

Means, Robert   Prisoner 200. Rank: Master, from: Peru, Merchant Vessel.
    Cap: 08 Sep 1812 at Sea by Cyane Int: 20 Oct 1812 Dis: 20 Oct 1812.
    Received from Shark. On Parole.

Meleache, Jean   Prisoner 641. Rank: Seaman, from: Mary Ann, Privateer.
    Cap: 05 May 1813 at Sea by Sapphire Int: 07 May 1813 Dis: 21 Jul 1814.
    Received from Sapphire. Board's Order.

Mememey, James   Prisoner 1356. Rank: Seaman, from: American Gunboats, Not Recorded.
    Cap: 05 Jan 1815 near New Orleans by Plantagenet Int: 27 Jan 1815 Dis: 05 Feb 1815.
    Taken in the American Gun Boats near New Orleans. Received from Ramilies. Into HM Ship Diomede per order of Sir TM Hardy Baronet.

Merit, Isaac   Prisoner 508. Rank: Seaman, from: Not Recorded, Not Recorded.
    Cap: 11 Feb 1813 at Lucea by Not Recorded Int: 26 Feb 1813 Dis: 04 Apr 1813.
    Retaken. Received from Sea Horse. To America for Exchange. (Isaac Mirrack. Prisoner number 10.)

Merrhew, Joseph   Prisoner 606. Rank: Master, from: Fly, Merchant Schooner.
    Cap: 15 Apr 1813 at Sea by Argo Int: 18 Apr 1813 Dis: 09 May 1813.
    Received from Argo. To American Cartel Brig Aualostaw.

Merritt, Erek   Prisoner 383. Rank: Quartermaster, from: Vixen, Man of War.
    Cap: 22 Nov 1812 at Sea by Rhodian late of US Brig Vixen Int: 14 Dec 1812 Dis: 04 Apr 1813.
    Received from Rhodian. To America for Exchange.

Merritt, Samuel   Prisoner 1239. Rank: Surgeon & Passenger, from: John, Merchant Vessel.
    Cap: 11 Aug 1814 at Sea by Variable Int: 15 Aug 1814 Dis: 26 Sep 1814.
    Received from Variable. per order Non - Combatant.

Mery, Pedro   Prisoner 928. Rank: Seaman, from: Cartagenaian, Privateer.
    Cap: 05 Dec 1813 at Sea by Sappho Int: 15 Dec 1813 Dis: 08 Aug 1814.
    Belonging to the Carthagenaian Privateer Carthagenaian. Received from Sappho. Board's Order.

Metz, George   Prisoner 262. Rank: Seaman, from: Joseph & Mary, Privateer.
    Cap: 24 Nov 1812 at Sea by Narcissus Int: 26 Nov 1812 Dis: 24 Jul 1813.
    Received from Narcissus. To American Cartel Brig Aualostaw.

Michel, Chouran   Prisoner 1133. Rank: Corporal, from: Decatur, Privateer.
    Cap: 05 Jun 1814 at Sea by HM Ship Rhin Int: 20 Jun 1814 Dis: 10 Aug 1814.
    Received from HM Ship Rhin. Board's Order.

Michell, Jean Batista   Prisoner 1132. Rank: 2 Gunner, from: Decatur, Privateer.
    Cap: 05 Jun 1814 at Sea by HM Ship Rhin Int: 20 Jun 1814 Dis: 02 Aug 1814.
    Received from HM Ship Rhin. Board's Order.

Micridales, Joseph   Prisoner 893. Rank: Seaman, from: San Francisco Navier, Brig.
    Cap: 03 Dec 1813 at Sea by Sappho Int: 15 Dec 1813 Dis: 11 Jan 1814.
    Taken in the Recaptured Spanish Brig. Prize to the Carthagenaian Privateer Carthagenaian. Received from Sappho. per order.

Middleton, Thomas   Prisoner 683. Rank: Seaman, from: Not Recorded, Man of War.
    Cap: 18 May 1813 from Providence by Variable Int: 26 May 1813 Dis: 01 Aug 1814.
    impressed. Received from Variable. To American Cartel Brig Aualostaw.

Mile, John   Prisoner 1438. Rank: Seaman, from: American Gunboats, Not Recorded.
    Cap: 05 Jan 1815 near New Orleans by Plantagenet Int: 27 Jan 1815 Dis: 05 Feb 1815.
    Taken in the American Gun Boats near New Orleans. Received from Ramilies. Into HM Ship Diomede per order of Sir TM Hardy Baronet.

Miles, Robert   Prisoner 878. Rank: Seaman, from: Lapwing, Packet.
    Cap: 08 Dec 1813 at Sea by Barrosa Int: 10 Dec 1813 Dis: 01 Aug 1814.
    Recaptured. Received from Barrosa. To American Cartel Brig Aualostaw.

American Prisoners of War Held at Jamaica During the War of 1812

Millega, Gilbert   Prisoner 411. Rank: Private, from: Vixen, Man of War.
    Cap: 22 Nov 1812 at Sea by Rhodian Int: 14 Dec 1812 Dis: 09 May 1813.
    Received from Brazier. To America for Exchange.

Miller, Christian   Prisoner 316. Rank: Seaman, from: Pirtshire, English Merchant Ship.
    Cap: Nov 1812 at Sea by Fawn Int: 06 Dec 1812 Dis: 24 Jul 1813.
    Recaptured. Eagle Privateer. Received from Fawn. To American Cartel Brig Aualostaw. (Day of capture not recorded.)

Miller, James   Prisoner 985. Rank: Seaman, from: Suspense, Merchant Vessel.
    Cap: 20 Feb 1814 at Sea by Leviathan Int: 26 Mar 1814 Dis: 01 Aug 1814.
    Received from Mohawk. To American Cartel Brig Aualostaw.

Miller, John   Prisoner 134. Rank: Seaman, from: Whim, Merchant Vessel.
    Cap: 18 Sep 1812 at Sea by HMS Cyane Int: 07 Oct 1812 Dis: 24 Jul 1813.
    Received from Cyane. To American Cartel Brig Aualostaw.

Miller, Oliver   Prisoner 709. Rank: Seaman, from: William, Merchant Man.
    Cap: 17 May 1813 at Sea by Circe Int: 29 May 1813 Dis: 01 Aug 1814.
    Received from Circe. (No entry for discharge date.)

Miller, Thomas   Prisoner 719. Rank: Seaman, from: Not Recorded, Not Recorded.
    Cap: 23 Oct 1812 Salvador by Dotrel Int: 20 Jun 1813 Dis: 01 Aug 1814.
    impressed. Received from Dotrel. To American Cartel Brig Aualostaw.

Millet, Andrew   Prisoner 956. Rank: Mate, from: Swift, Merchant Vessel.
    Cap: at Sea by Leonidas Int: 25 Jan 1814 Dis: 01 Aug 1814.
    Received from Leonidas. To American Cartel Brig Aualostaw. (Date of capture not recorded. Prisoner numbers 951 - 956 all have recorded rank of mate.)

Mills, George   Prisoner 1553. Rank: Seaman, from: John, Merchant Vessel.
    Cap: at Sea by HMS Talbot Int: 20 Mar 1815 Dis: 30 Mar 1815.
    Received from HMS Talbot. In consequence of Peace with America. (Date of capture not recorded.)

Mills, James   Prisoner 136. Rank: Seaman, from: Whim, Merchant Vessel.
    Cap: 04 Oct 1812 at Sea by HM Brig Liberty Int: 07 Oct 1812 Dis: 24 Jul 1813.
    Received from Cyane. To American Cartel Brig Aualostaw.

Mirack, Isaac   Prisoner 10. Rank: Seaman, from: Superb, Merchant Vessel.
    Cap: 02 Aug 1812 at Sea by Garland Int: 22 Aug 1812 Escaped: 30 Jan 1813.
    Received from Garland. Escaped.

Mitchell, Elisha   Prisoner 712. Rank: Seaman, from: William, Merchant Man.
    Cap: 17 May 1813 at Sea by Circe Int: 29 May 1813 Dis: 01 Aug 1814.
    Received from Circe. (No entry for discharge date.)

Mitchell, James   Prisoner 745. Rank: Seaman, from: Eliza, Merchant Vessel.
    Cap: 17 Jul 1813 at Sea by Sappho Int: 26 Jul 1813 Dis: 01 Aug 1814.
    Received from Sappho. To American Cartel Brig Aualostaw.

Moderen, James   Prisoner 1498. Rank: Master, from: Not Recorded, Not Recorded.
    Cap: 20 Dec 1814 at Sea by Lacedaemonian Int: 04 Feb 1815 Dis: 11 Feb 1815.
    Taken for Passage to Jamaica Depot. Received from Rota. Into HMS Ramillies per order of Sir T M Hardy.

Molaneir, Pedro   Prisoner 802. Rank: Seaman, from: Enterprize, Privateer.
    Cap: 15 Nov 1813 at Sea by Argo Int: 19 Nov 1813 Dis: 29 Jul 1814.
    A Carthagenaian. Received from Argo. Board's Order.

Mollin, Charles   Prisoner 1434. Rank: Seaman, from: American Gunboats, Not Recorded.
    Cap: 05 Jan 1815 near New Orleans by Plantagenet Int: 27 Jan 1815 Dis: 05 Feb 1815.
    Taken in the American Gun Boats near New Orleans. Received from Ramilies. Into HM Ship Diomede per order of Sir TM Hardy Baronet.

Montati, Antonio   Prisoner 890. Rank: Prize Master, from: San Francisco Navier, Brig.
    Cap: 03 Dec 1813 at Sea by Sappho Int: 15 Dec 1813 Dis: 26 Jul 1814.
    Taken in the Recaptured Spanish Brig. Prize to the Carthagenaian Privateer Carthagenaian. Received from Sappho. Board's Order.

Monteque, Caleb   Prisoner 428. Rank: Private, from: Vixen, Man of War.
    Cap: 22 Nov 1812 at Sea by Rhodian Int: 14 Dec 1812 Dis: 04 Apr 1813.
    Received from Brazier. To America for Exchange.

Montgomery, G   Prisoner 118. Rank: Passenger, from: Bernardo, Merchant Vessel.
    Cap: 14 Sep 1812 at Sea by Garland Int: 18 Sep 1812 Dis: 25 Sep 1812.
    Schooner under Spanish Colors. Received from Garland. Liberated.

Montgomery, R   Prisoner 338. Rank: Seaman, from: Not Recorded, Merchant Vessel.
    Cap: 08 Dec 1812 at Sea by Rhodian late Southampton Int: 14 Dec 1812 Dis: 09 May 1813.
    Unknown. Received from Rhodian. To America for Exchange.

American Prisoners of War Held at Jamaica During the War of 1812

Montgomery, Thomas   Prisoner 677. Rank: Seaman, from: Lovely Lass, Privateer.
    Cap: 21 May 1813 at Sea by Circe Int: 23 May 1813 Dis: 01 Aug 1814.
    Received from Forrester. To American Cartel Brig Aualostaw.

Moon, Isaac   Prisoner 1360. Rank: Seaman, from: American Gunboats, Not Recorded.
    Cap: 05 Jan 1815 near New Orleans by Plantagenet Int: 27 Jan 1815 Dis: 05 Feb 1815.
    Taken in the American Gun Boats near New Orleans. Received from Ramilies. Into HM Ship Diomede per order of Sir TM Hardy Baronet.

Moore, Jonathan   Prisoner 691. Rank: Seaman, from: Lovely Lass, Privateer.
    Cap: 15 May 1813 at Sea by Circe Int: 29 May 1813 Dis: 01 Aug 1814.
    Received from Circe. To American Cartel Brig Aualostaw.

Moore, Thomas   Prisoner 308. Rank: Seaman, from: Joseph & Mary, Privateer.
    Cap: 24 Nov 1812 at Sea by Narcissus Int: 05 Dec 1812 Dis: 24 Jul 1813.
    Received from Narcissus. To American Cartel Brig Aualostaw.

Moore, William   Prisoner 74. Rank: Seaman, from: Poor Sailor, Privateer.
    Cap: 13 Sep 1812 at Sea by Garland Int: 18 Sep 1812 Dis: 09 May 1813.
    Received from Garland. To America for Exchange.

Moore, William   Prisoner 305. Rank: Mate, from: Flora, Merchant Vessel.
    Cap: 26 Nov 1812 at Sea by Sappho Int: 03 Dec 1812 Dis: 24 Dec 1812.
    Received from Sappho. To America Cartel Brig Aualostaw. (Date of discharge should be July 24, 1813.)

Moore, William   Prisoner 1211. Rank: Seaman, from: Mary, Merchant Schooner.
    Cap: 17 Jun 1814 at Sea by Sapphire Int: 10 Jul 1814 Dis: 02 Jan 1815.
    Recaptured. Received from Sapphire. Into HM Ship Suttan per order of Captain John West.

Morando, Domingo   Prisoner 797. Rank: Seaman, from: Enterprize, Privateer.
    Cap: 15 Nov 1813 at Sea by Argo Int: 19 Nov 1813 Dis: 29 Jul 1814.
    A Carthagenaian. Received from Argo. Board's Order.

Morean, Guettend   Prisoner 1337. Rank: Seaman, from: Not Recorded, Not Recorded.
    Cap: at Sea by HMS Shark Int: 07 Jan 1815 Dis: 10 Jan 1815.
    Ship 'Name Unknown'. Received from HMS Shark. Board's Order. (Date of capture not recorded.)

Morris, Benjamin   Prisoner 737. Rank: Seaman, from: Eliza, Merchant Vessel.
    Cap: 17 Jul 1813 at Sea by Sappho Int: 26 Jul 1813 Dis: 01 Aug 1814.
    Received from Sappho. To American Cartel Brig Aualostaw.

Morris, George   Prisoner 1374. Rank: Seaman, from: American Gunboats, Not Recorded.
    Cap: 05 Jan 1815 near New Orleans by Plantagenet Int: 27 Jan 1815 Dis: 05 Feb 1815.
    Taken in the American Gun Boats near New Orleans. Received from Ramilies. Into HM Ship Diomede per order of Sir TM Hardy Baronet.

Morris, Jacob   Prisoner 167. Rank: Seaman, from: Rebecca Sims, Merchant Vessel.
    Cap: 12 Sep 1812 at Sea by Southampton Int: 07 Oct 1812 Dis: 01 Mar 1813.
    Received from Southampton. per Order of Admiral Stirling.

Morris, James   Prisoner 1486. Rank: Seaman, from: Not Recorded, Not Recorded.
    Cap: 20 Dec 1814 at Sea by Lacedaemonian Int: 04 Feb 1815 Dis: 11 Feb 1815.
    Taken for Passage to Jamaica Depot. Received from Rota. Into HMS Ramillies per order of Sir T M Hardy.

Morris, James   Prisoner 1532. Rank: Seaman, from: William & Mary, Merchant Vessel.
    Cap: 12 Feb 1815 at Sea by HM Sloop Carnation Int: 23 Feb 1815 Dis: 30 Mar 1815.
    Received from HM Sloop Carnation. In consequence of Peace with America.

Morterae, John   Prisoner 565. Rank: Seaman, from: Defiance, Privateer.
    Cap: 15 Mar 1813 at Sea by Nimrod Int: 17 Mar 1813 Dis: 24 Jul 1813.
    Received from Nimrod. To American Cartel Brig Aualostaw.

Moservy, Daniel J   Prisoner 11. Rank: Seaman, from: Superb, Merchant Vessel.
    Cap: 02 Aug 1812 at Sea by Garland Int: 22 Aug 1812 Escaped: 15 Nov 1812.
    Received from Garland. Escaped.

Mosquera, Jose   Prisoner 1226. Rank: Seaman, from: La Union, Spanish Brig.
    Cap: 03 Aug 1814 at Sea by Variable Int: 06 Aug 1814 Dis: 01 Sep 1814.
    Recaptured from the Carthagenaian Privateer White Horse. Received from Variable. Board's Order.

Moss, Elijah   Prisoner 143. Rank: Seaman, from: William Penn, Merchant Vessel.
    Cap: 08 Sep 1812 at Sea by Southampton Int: 07 Oct 1812 Died: 29 Nov 1812.
    Received from Southampton. Died.

Moucrieff, James   Prisoner 453. Rank: Prize Master, from: Rachel, Merchant Vessel.
    Cap: 26 Nov 1812 at Sea by Fawn Int: 13 Jan 1812 Died: 30 Jan 1813.
    Received from Sapphire. Died. (Year of internment should be 1813.)

American Prisoners of War Held at Jamaica During the War of 1812

Murdock, Archibald   Prisoner 742. Rank: Seaman, from: Eliza, Merchant Vessel.
    Cap: 17 Jul 1813 at Sea by Sappho Int: 26 Jul 1813 Dis: 01 Aug 1814.
    Received from Sappho. To American Cartel Brig Aualostaw.

Murtien, Charles   Prisoner 675. Rank: Seaman, from: Lovely Lass, Privateer.
    Cap: 21 May 1813 at Sea by Circe Int: 23 May 1813 Dis: 27 Jul 1814.
    Received from Forrester. Board's Order.

Nachidon, Francis   Prisoner 318. Rank: Seaman, from: Pirtshire, English Merchant Ship.
    Cap: Nov 1812 at Sea by Fawn Int: 06 Dec 1812 Dis: 24 Jul 1813.
    Recaptured. Eagle Privateer. Received from Fawn. To American Cartel Brig Aualostaw. (Day of capture not recorded.)

Napo, Casar   Prisoner 1222. Rank: Seaman, from: La Union, Spanish Brig.
    Cap: 03 Aug 1814 at Sea by Variable Int: 06 Aug 1814 Dis: 23 Aug 1814.
    Recaptured from the Carthagenaian Privateer White Horse. Received from Variable. Board's Order.

Natal, Juan   Prisoner 1327. Rank: Seaman, from: Not Recorded, Not Recorded.
    Cap: at Sea by HMS Shark Int: 07 Jan 1815 Dis: 10 Jan 1815.
    Ship 'Name Unknown'. Received from HMS Shark. Board's Order. (Date of capture not recorded.)

Navallo, Diego   Prisoner 1341. Rank: Seaman, from: Not Recorded, Not Recorded.
    Cap: at Sea by HMS Shark Int: 07 Jan 1815 Dis: 10 Jan 1815.
    Ship 'Name Unknown'. Received from HMS Shark. Board's Order. (Date of capture not recorded.)

Neal, Francis   Prisoner 459. Rank: Seaman, from: Saratoga, Merchant Vessel.
    Cap: 1813 at Sea by Fawn Int: 13 Jan 1813 Dis: 24 Jul 1813.
    Received from Sapphire. To American Cartel Brig Aualostaw. (Day and month of capture not recorded.)

Neil, Jeremiah   Prisoner 661. Rank: Seaman, from: Lovely Lass, Privateer.
    Cap: 21 May 1813 at Sea by Circe Int: 23 May 1813 Dis: 01 Aug 1814.
    Received from Forrester. To American Cartel Brig Aualostaw.

Nelson, Bristol   Prisoner 1502. Rank: Seaman, from: Not Recorded, Not Recorded.
    Cap: 20 Dec 1814 at Sea by Lacedaemonian Int: 04 Feb 1815 Dis: 08 Feb 1815.
    Taken for Passage to Jamaica Depot. Received from Rota. per order of Sir TM Hardy as a Non-Combatant.

Nelson, Christopher   Prisoner 1500. Rank: Passenger, from: Not Recorded, Not Recorded.
    Cap: 20 Dec 1814 at Sea by Lacedaemonian Int: 04 Feb 1815 Dis: 08 Feb 1815.
    Taken for Passage to Jamaica Depot. Received from Rota. per order of Sir TM Hardy as a Non-Combatant.

Nelson, James   Prisoner 887. Rank: Seaman, from: Milly, Schooner.
    Cap: 25 Nov 1813 at Sea by Decouverte Int: 10 Dec 1813 Dis: 01 Aug 1814.
    Taken out of the American Schooner Milly. Received from Decouverte. To American Cartel Brig Aualostaw.

Nelson, Jean   Prisoner 591. Rank: Seaman, from: Le Ventura, Privateer.
    Cap: 13 Mar 1813 at Sea by Cossac Int: 18 Mar 1813 Dis: 16 Aug 1814.
    Received from Cossac. Board's Order.

Nelson, John   Prisoner 241. Rank: Seaman, from: Joseph & Mary, Privateer.
    Cap: 24 Nov 1812 at Sea by Narcissus Int: 26 Nov 1812 Dis: 24 Jul 1813.
    Received from Narcissus. To American Cartel Brig Aualostaw.

Nelson, Piere   Prisoner 593. Rank: Seaman, from: Le Ventura, Privateer.
    Cap: 13 Mar 1813 at Sea by Cossac Int: 18 Mar 1813 Dis: 10 Aug 1814.
    Received from Cossac. Board's Order.

Neo, Juan   Prisoner 1231. Rank: Seaman, from: La Union, Spanish Brig.
    Cap: 03 Aug 1814 at Sea by Variable Int: 06 Aug 1814 Dis: 01 Sep 1814.
    Recaptured from the Carthagenaian Privateer White Horse. Received from Variable. Board's Order.

Newham, Thomas   Prisoner 1539. Rank: Seaman, from: Delight, Merchant Sloop.
    Cap: at Sea by Statira Int: 04 Mar 1815 Dis: 30 Mar 1815.
    Received from HM Transport Request. In consequence of Peace with America. (Date of capture not recorded.)

Nichols, Jacob   Prisoner 473. Rank: Seaman, from: Cyrus, Merchant Vessel.
    Cap: 03 Jan 1813 at Sea by Rhodian Int: 16 Jan 1813 Dis: 24 Jul 1813.
    Received from Rhodian. To American Cartel Brig Aualostaw.

Nicholson, George   Prisoner 78. Rank: Seaman, from: Poor Sailor, Privateer.
    Cap: 13 Sep 1812 at Sea by Garland Int: 18 Sep 1812 Escaped: 15 Nov 1812.
    Received from Garland. Escaped.

American Prisoners of War Held at Jamaica During the War of 1812

Nicholson, Jesse   Prisoner 34. Rank: Seaman, from: Not Recorded, Not Recorded.
    Cap: Not Recorded by Not Recorded Int: 22 Aug 1812 Dis: 09 May 1813.
    Given themselves up as American and refused to serve. Received from Garland. to America for Exchange. (Date of capture not recorded.)

Nicholson, John   Prisoner 43. Rank: Seaman, from: Petham, Merchant Vessel.
    Cap: 20 Aug 1812 Port Royal by Tartaus Int: 22 Aug 1812 Dis: 09 May 1813.
    Taken from the British Merchant Ship Petham at Port Royal. Received from Garland. to America for Exchange.

Niel, Herrea   Prisoner 1297. Rank: Passenger, from: Cora, Letter of Marque.
    Cap: 31 Jul 1814 at Sea by Rota Int: 06 Nov 1814 Dis: 21 Nov 1814.
    Received from Rota. Board's Order.

Nixon, Lewis   Prisoner 666. Rank: Seaman, from: Lovely Lass, Privateer.
    Cap: 21 May 1813 at Sea by Circe Int: 23 May 1813 Dis: 01 Aug 1814.
    Received from Forrester. To American Cartel Brig Aualostaw.

Noche, Juan   Prisoner 756. Rank: Seaman, from: San Francisco de Paula, Privateer.
    Cap: 02 Oct 1813 at Sea by Forrester Int: 07 Oct 1813 Escaped: 28 Dec 1813.
    Received from Forrester. Escaped.

Nolt, Paul   Prisoner 1155. Rank: Seaman, from: Decatur, Privateer.
    Cap: 05 Jun 1814 at Sea by HM Ship Rhin Int: 20 Jun 1814 Dis: 08 Aug 1814.
    Received from HM Ship Rhin. Board's Order.

Norins, William   Prisoner 1139. Rank: Seaman, from: Decatur, Privateer.
    Cap: 05 Jun 1814 at Sea by HM Ship Rhin Int: 20 Jun 1814 Escaped: 18 Dec 1814.
    Received from HM Ship Rhin. Escaped.

Norris, Gilles   Prisoner 638. Rank: Seaman, from: Mary Ann, Privateer.
    Cap: 05 May 1813 at Sea by Sapphire Int: 07 May 1813 Dis: 01 Aug 1814.
    Received from Sapphire. To American Cartel Brig Aualostaw.

Norris, Samuel   Prisoner 332. Rank: Seaman, from: Sauders, Merchant Vessel.
    Cap: Nov 1812 at Sea by Merchant Vessel Monarch Int: 09 Dec 1812 Dis: 04 Apr 1813.
    Received from Monarch. To America for Exchange. (Day of capture not recorded.)

Nowland, James   Prisoner 1396. Rank: Seaman, from: American Gunboats, Not Recorded.
    Cap: 05 Jan 1815 near New Orleans by Plantagenet Int: 27 Jan 1815 Dis: 05 Feb 1815.
    Taken in the American Gun Boats near New Orleans. Received from Ramilies. Into HM Ship Diomede per order of Sir TM Hardy Baronet.

Nowland, John   Prisoner 886. Rank: Seaman, from: Milly, Schooner.
    Cap: 25 Nov 1813 at Sea by Decouverte Int: 10 Dec 1813 Dis: 01 Aug 1814.
    Taken out of the American Schooner Milly. Received from Decouverte. To American Cartel Brig Aualostaw.

Nutter, George   Prisoner 397. Rank: Seaman, from: Vixen, Man of War.
    Cap: 22 Nov 1812 at Sea by Rhodian late of US Brig Vixen Int: 14 Dec 1812 Dis: 09 May 1813.
    Received from Rhodian. To America for Exchange.

Nyon, Francis   Prisoner 552. Rank: Seaman, from: Defiance, Privateer.
    Cap: 15 Mar 1813 at Sea by Nimrod Int: 17 Mar 1813 Dis: 24 Jul 1813.
    Received from Nimrod. To American Cartel Brig Aualostaw.

Ogdon, Thomas   Prisoner 717. Rank: Seaman, from: Not Recorded, Not Recorded.
    Cap: 05 Jun 1813 Kingston by Circe Int: 05 Jun 1813 Dis: 01 Aug 1814.
    impressed. Received from Circe. To American Cartel Brig Aualostaw.

Oldner, George   Prisoner 988. Rank: Seaman, from: Young Eagle, Merchant Vessel.
    Cap: 28 Feb 1814 at Sea by Ringdove Int: 27 Mar 1814 Dis: 03 Aug 1814.
    Received from Ringdove. To American Cartel Brig Aualostaw.

Oliney, Samuel   Prisoner 56. Rank: Seaman, from: Not Recorded, Not Recorded.
    Cap: 20 Aug 1812 Not Recorded by Not Recorded Int: 03 Sep 1812 Dis: 09 May 1813.
    Prison Ship at New Providence. Received from HM Schooner Decouverte. to America for Exchange.

Olmer, Joseph   Prisoner 888. Rank: Seaman, from: Milly, Schooner.
    Cap: 25 Nov 1813 at Sea by Decouverte Int: 10 Dec 1813 Dis: 01 Aug 1814.
    Taken out of the American Schooner Milly. Received from Decouverte. To American Cartel Brig Aualostaw.

Olson, John   Prisoner 1452. Rank: Seaman, from: American Gunboats, Not Recorded.
    Cap: 05 Jan 1815 near New Orleans by Plantagenet Int: 27 Jan 1815 Dis: 05 Feb 1815.
    Taken in the American Gun Boats near New Orleans. Received from Ramilies. Into HM Ship Diomede per order of Sir TM Hardy Baronet.

O'Neal, Andrew   Prisoner 422. Rank: Private, from: Vixen, Man of War.
    Cap: 22 Nov 1812 at Sea by Rhodian Int: 14 Dec 1812 Dis: 09 May 1813.
    Received from Brazier. To America for Exchange.

American Prisoners of War Held at Jamaica During the War of 1812

O'Neil, Edward   Prisoner 865. Rank: Seaman, from: Cato Georgiana, Not Recorded.
    Cap: 28 Nov 1813 at Sea by Barrosa Int: 10 Dec 1813 Dis: 01 Aug 1814.
    Prize to the US Frigate Essex. Received from Barrosa. To American Cartel Brig Aualostaw.

Onil, Henry   Prisoner 984. Rank: Seaman, from: Suspense, Merchant Vessel.
    Cap: 20 Feb 1814 at Sea by Leviathan Int: 26 Mar 1814 Dis: 01 Aug 1814.
    Received from Mohawk. To American Cartel Brig Aualostaw.

Ordet, Tal   Prisoner 905. Rank: 2 Gunner, from: San Francisco Navier, Brig.
    Cap: 05 Dec 1813 at Sea by Sappho Int: 15 Dec 1813 Dis: 08 Aug 1814.
    Taken in the Recaptured Spanish Brig. Prize to the Carthagenaian Privateer Carthagenaian. Received from Sappho. Board's Order.

Orick, John   Prisoner 839. Rank: Mate, from: Maria, An American Merchant Schooner.
    Cap: 15 Nov 1813 at Sea by Argo Int: 19 Nov 1813 Dis: 12 Apr 1814.
    Received from Argo. To Parole.

Orne, Julian   Prisoner 735. Rank: Seaman, from: Eliza, Merchant Vessel.
    Cap: 17 Jul 1813 at Sea by Sappho Int: 26 Jul 1813 Dis: 01 Aug 1814.
    Received from Sappho. To American Cartel Brig Aualostaw.

Orno, John   Prisoner 358. Rank: Seaman, from: Vixen, Man of War.
    Cap: 22 Nov 1812 at Sea by Rhodian late of HM Brig Vixen Int: 14 Dec 1812 Dis: 09 May 1813.
    Received from Rhodian. To America for Exchange.

Osbourn, Thomas   Prisoner 45. Rank: Sail Maker, from: Books, Not Recorded.
    Cap: Not Recorded by HMS Herald Int: 22 Aug 1812 Dis: 04 Apr 1813.
    From the Ship Books refusing to serve being an American. Received from HM Ship Herald. to America for Exchange. (Date of capture not recorded.)

Otto, Nicholas   Prisoner 941. Rank: Seaman, from: Coquelle, Merchant Vessel.
    Cap: 24 Dec 1813 at Sea by Sapphire Int: 02 Jan 1814 Dis: 01 Aug 1814.
    Received from Sapphire. To American Cartel Brig Aualostaw.

Oure, Constant   Prisoner 805. Rank: Seaman, from: Enterprize, Privateer.
    Cap: 15 Nov 1813 at Sea by Argo Int: 19 Nov 1813 Dis: 22 Jul 1814.
    A Carthagenaian.

Owen, Francis   Prisoner 610. Rank: Seaman, from: Fly, Merchant Schooner.
    Cap: 15 Apr 1813 at Sea by Argo Int: 18 Apr 1813 Dis: 09 May 1813.
    Received from Argo. To America for Exchange.

Owens, James   Prisoner 1418. Rank: Seaman, from: American Gunboats, Not Recorded.
    Cap: 05 Jan 1815 near New Orleans by Plantagenet Int: 27 Jan 1815 Dis: 05 Feb 1815.
    Taken in the American Gun Boats near New Orleans. Received from Ramilies. Into HM Ship Diomede per order of Sir TM Hardy Baronet.

Padelia, F   Prisoner 1076. Rank: Seaman, from: Casada el Narino, Privateer.
    Cap: 29 May 1814 at Sea by HM Ship Rhin Int: 04 Jun 1814 Dis: 18 Aug 1814.
    Carthagenaian. Received from North Star. Board's Order. (First name not legible.)

Paillet, Peter Noel   Prisoner 1261. Rank: Master, from: Cora, Merchant Vessel.
    Cap: Not Recorded by Rota Int: 05 Sep 1814 Dis: 07 Sep 1814.
    Received from Rota. To Parole. (Date of capture not recorded.)

Pairer, Francis   Prisoner 1204. Rank: Seaman, from: Neustra Cantado, Merchant Vessel.
    Cap: 01 Jun 1814 at Sea by HM Ship Argo Int: 27 Jun 1814 Dis: 10 Aug 1814.
    Retaken in the Spanish Ship Neustra Cantado. Received from HM Ship Argo. Board's Order.

Pane, Cheny   Prisoner 583. Rank: Seaman, from: Le Ventura, Privateer.
    Cap: 13 Mar 1813 at Sea by Cossac Int: 18 Mar 1813 Died: 29 Nov 1813.
    Received from Cossac. Died.

Papil, Sauteaga   Prisoner 751. Rank: Clerk, from: San Francisco de Paula, Privateer.
    Cap: 02 Oct 1813 at Sea by Forrester Int: 07 Oct 1813 Dis: 29 Jul 1814.
    Received from Forrester. Board's Order. (Prisoner numbers 750 - 755 all have recorded rank of clerk.)

Paptist, John   Prisoner 570. Rank: Seaman, from: Defiance, Privateer.
    Cap: 15 Mar 1813 at Sea by Nimrod Int: 17 Mar 1813 Dis: 24 Jul 1813.
    Received from Nimrod. To American Cartel Brig Aualostaw.

Paree, S W   Prisoner 153. Rank: Seaman, from: Philip, Merchant Vessel.
    Cap: 10 Sep 1812 at Sea by Southampton Int: 07 Oct 1812 Dis: 01 Mar 1813.
    Received from Southampton. per Order of Adml Stirling to American Ship Philip.

Parish, John   Prisoner 58. Rank: Seaman, from: Not Recorded, Not Recorded.
    Cap: 20 Aug 1812 Not Recorded by Not Recorded Int: 03 Sep 1812 Dis: 09 May 1813.
    Prison Ship at New Providence. Received from HM Schooner Decouverte. to America for Exchange.

Parker, Joseph   Prisoner 310. Rank: Seaman, from: Joseph & Mary, Privateer.
    Cap: 24 Nov 1812 at Sea by Narcissus Int: 05 Dec 1812 Dis: 09 May 1813.
    Received from Narcissus. To America for Exchange.

American Prisoners of War Held at Jamaica During the War of 1812

Parleman, William   Prisoner 1382. Rank: Seaman, from: American Gunboats, Not Recorded.
    Cap: 05 Jan 1815 near New Orleans by Plantagenet Int: 27 Jan 1815 Dis: 05 Feb 1815.
    Taken in the American Gun Boats near New Orleans. Received from Ramilies. Into HM Ship Diomede per order of Sir TM Hardy Baronet.

Parrote, Daniel   Prisoner 1497. Rank: Passenger, from: Not Recorded, Not Recorded.
    Cap: 20 Dec 1814 at Sea by Lacedaemonian Int: 04 Feb 1815 Dis: 08 Feb 1815.
    Taken for Passage to Jamaica Depot. Received from Rota. per order of Sir TM Hardy as a Non-Combatant.

Parsons, George   Prisoner 962. Rank: Seaman, from: Active, Merchant Vessel.
    Cap: at Sea by Leonidas Int: 25 Jan 1814 Dis: 01 Aug 1814.
    Received from Leonidas. To American Cartel Brig Aualostaw. (Date of capture not recorded.)

Parsons, Isaac   Prisoner 960. Rank: Seaman, from: Active, Merchant Vessel.
    Cap: at Sea by Leonidas Int: 25 Jan 1814 Dis: 01 Aug 1814.
    Received from Leonidas. To American Cartel Brig Aualostaw. (Date of capture not recorded.)

Parsons, James   Prisoner 1265. Rank: Seaman, from: Not Recorded, Not Recorded.
    Cap: Kingston by Not Recorded Int: 08 Sep 1814 Dis: 02 Jan 1815.
    Seized at Kingston last night being Americans. Received from Talbot. Into HM Ship Sultan per order of Captain John West. (Date of capture assumed to be September 7, 1814.)

Parsons, William   Prisoner 957. Rank: Captain, from: Active, Merchant Vessel.
    Cap: at Sea by Leonidas Int: 25 Jan 1814 Dis: 17 Feb 1814.
    Received from Leonidas. To Parole. (Date of capture not recorded.)

Pascal, Antonio   Prisoner 649. Rank: Lieutenant Marines, from: Mary Ann, Privateer.
    Cap: 05 Mar 1813 at Sea by Sapphire Int: 07 Mar 1813 Dis: 27 Jul 1814.
    Received from Sapphire. Board's Order.

Patterson, John   Prisoner 343. Rank: Seaman, from: Vixen, Man of War.
    Cap: 22 Nov 1812 at Sea by Rhodian late of HM Brig Vixen Int: 14 Dec 1812 Dis: 09 May 1813.
    Received from Rhodian. To America for Exchange.

Patterson, M   Prisoner 188. Rank: Seaman, from: Hamilton, Merchant Vessel.
    Cap: 28 Sep 1812 at Sea by Southampton Int: 09 Oct 1812 Dis: 09 May 1813.
    Received from Southampton. To America for Exchange.

Patterson, N   Prisoner 178. Rank: Seaman, from: William Penn, Merchant Vessel.
    Cap: 08 Sep 1812 at Sea by Southampton Int: 09 Oct 1812 Dis: 01 Mar 1813.
    Received from Southampton. per Order of Admiral Stirling.

Patton, Edward   Prisoner 271. Rank: Seaman, from: Joseph & Mary, Privateer.
    Cap: 24 Nov 1812 at Sea by Narcissus Int: 26 Nov 1812 Dis: 09 May 1813.
    Received from Narcissus. under 12 years old.

Peabody, John   Prisoner 950. Rank: Captain, from: Swift, Merchant Vessel.
    Cap: at Sea by Leonidas Int: 25 Jan 1814 Dis: 01 Aug 1814.
    Received from Leonidas. To American Cartel Brig Aualostaw. (Date of capture not recorded.)

Pearce, David   Prisoner 731. Rank: Seaman, from: Eliza, Merchant Vessel.
    Cap: 17 Jul 1813 at Sea by Sappho Int: 26 Jul 1813 Escaped: 18 Feb 1814.
    Received from Sappho. Escaped.

Peck, Salisbury   Prisoner 1237. Rank: Seaman, from: Not Recorded, Not Recorded.
    Cap: 04 Aug 1814 Kingston by Talbot Int: 07 Aug 1814 Escaped: 18 Dec 1814.
    Impressed. Received from Talbot. Escaped.

Pedro, John   Prisoner 831. Rank: Seaman, from: Enterprize, Privateer.
    Cap: 15 Nov 1813 at Sea by Argo Int: 19 Nov 1813 Dis: 12 Aug 1814.
    A Carthagenaian. Received from Argo. Board's Order. (Date of discharge changed from August 23, 1814.)

Pedro, John   Prisoner 835. Rank: Seaman, from: Enterprize, Privateer.
    Cap: 15 Nov 1813 at Sea by Argo Int: 19 Nov 1813 Dis: 11 Jan 1814.
    A Carthagenaian. Received from Argo. per order. John Pedro (2).

Pedro, Juan   Prisoner 787. Rank: Seaman, from: San Francisco de Paula, Privateer.
    Cap: 02 Oct 1813 at Sea by Forrester Int: 07 Oct 1813 Dis: 11 Jan 1814.
    Received from Forrester. per order.

Pedro, Juan   Prisoner 1234. Rank: Seaman, from: La Union, Spanish Brig.
    Cap: 03 Aug 1814 at Sea by Variable Int: 06 Aug 1814 Dis: 23 Aug 1814.
    Recaptured from the Carthagenaian Privateer White Horse. Received from Variable. Board's Order.

Pedro, Manuel   Prisoner 824. Rank: Seaman, from: Enterprize, Privateer.
    Cap: 15 Nov 1813 at Sea by Argo Int: 19 Nov 1813 Dis: 11 Jan 1814.
    A Carthagenaian. Received from Argo. per order.

American Prisoners of War Held at Jamaica During the War of 1812

Peek, Darius   Prisoner 248. Rank: Seaman, from: Joseph & Mary, Privateer.
    Cap: 24 Nov 1812 at Sea by Narcissus Int: 26 Nov 1812 Died: 10 Dec 1812.
    Received from Narcissus. Died.

Peland, Louis Marie   Prisoner 1180. Rank: Seaman, from: Decatur, Privateer.
    Cap: 05 Jun 1814 at Sea by HM Ship Rhin Int: 20 Jun 1814 Dis: 23 Aug 1814.
    Received from HM Ship Rhin. Board's Order.

Peliou, Jose   Prisoner 908. Rank: Seaman, from: San Francisco Navier, Brig.
    Cap: 05 Dec 1813 at Sea by Sappho Int: 15 Dec 1813 Dis: 11 Jan 1814.
    Taken in the Recaptured Spanish Brig. Prize to the Carthagenaian Privateer Carthagenaian. Received from Sappho. per order.

Penn, William   Prisoner 51. Rank: Master, from: Superb, Merchant Vessel.
    Cap: 02 Aug 1812 at Sea by HM Ship Garland Int: 27 Aug 1812 Dis: 28 Aug 1812.
    Received from HM Ship Herald. To Parole.

Pepper, Martin   Prisoner 1272. Rank: Seaman, from: Wolfe, Not Recorded.
    Cap: at Sea by Jalouse Int: 10 Sep 1814 Dis: 26 Sep 1814.
    American Schooner. Received from Jalouse. Board's Order. (Date of capture not recorded.)

Peres, Domingo   Prisoner 1224. Rank: Seaman, from: La Union, Spanish Brig.
    Cap: 03 Aug 1814 at Sea by Variable Int: 06 Aug 1814 Dis: 01 Sep 1814.
    Recaptured from the Carthagenaian Privateer White Horse. Received from Variable. Board's Order.

Peres, Juan Francisco   Prisoner 898. Rank: 2 Captain, from: Cartagenaian, Privateer.
    Cap: 05 Dec 1813 at Sea by Sappho Int: 15 Dec 1813 Dis: 21 Jul 1814.
    Belonging to the Carthagenaian Privateer Carthagenaian. Received from Sappho. Board's Order.

Perez, M Antonio   Prisoner 1229. Rank: Seaman, from: La Union, Spanish Brig.
    Cap: 03 Aug 1814 at Sea by Variable Int: 06 Aug 1814 Dis: 01 Sep 1814.
    Recaptured from the Carthagenaian Privateer White Horse. Received from Variable. Board's Order.

Perkins, Joseph   Prisoner 144. Rank: Seaman, from: William Penn, Merchant Vessel.
    Cap: 08 Sep 1812 at Sea by Southampton Int: 07 Oct 1812 Dis: 01 Mar 1813.
    Received from Southampton. per Order of Admiral Stirling.

Perkins, Seth   Prisoner 142. Rank: Seaman, from: William Penn, Merchant Vessel.
    Cap: 08 Sep 1812 at Sea by Southampton Int: 07 Oct 1812 Dis: 01 Mar 1813.
    Received from Southampton. per Order of Admiral Stirling.

Perkins, Simon   Prisoner 47. Rank: Seaman, from: Not Recorded, Not Recorded.
    Cap: 24 Aug 1812 Kingston by Garland Int: 23 Aug 1812 Dis: 24 Jul 1813.
    apprehended on Shore. Received from Garland. to American Cartel Brig Aualostaw. (Date of capture after date of internment.)

Perry, John   Prisoner 1355. Rank: Seaman, from: American Gunboats, Not Recorded.
    Cap: 05 Jan 1815 near New Orleans by Plantagenet Int: 27 Jan 1815 Dis: 05 Feb 1815.
    Taken in the American Gun Boats near New Orleans. Received from Ramilies. Into HM Ship Diomede per order of Sir TM Hardy Baronet.

Perry, William   Prisoner 1347. Rank: Seaman, from: Not Recorded, Not Recorded.
    Cap: at Sea by HMS Shark Int: 07 Jan 1815 Dis: 04 Feb 1815.
    Ship 'Name Unknown'. Received from HMS Shark. Board's Order. (Date of capture not recorded.)

Peter, Juan   Prisoner 587. Rank: Seaman, from: Le Ventura, Privateer.
    Cap: 13 Mar 1813 at Sea by Cossac Int: 18 Mar 1813 Escaped: 12 May 1814.
    Received from Cossac. Escaped.

Peter, Mathias   Prisoner 1203. Rank: Seaman, from: Neustra Cantado, Merchant Vessel.
    Cap: 01 Jun 1814 at Sea by HM Ship Argo Int: 27 Jun 1814 Dis: 18 Aug 1814.
    Retaken in the Spanish Ship Neustra Cantado. Received from HM Ship Argo. Board's Order.

Peter, Solomon   Prisoner 359. Rank: Seaman, from: Vixen, Man of War.
    Cap: 22 Nov 1812 at Sea by Rhodian late of HM Brig Vixen Int: 14 Dec 1812 Dis: 09 May 1813.
    Received from Rhodian. To America for Exchange.

Peters, George   Prisoner 1171. Rank: Seaman, from: Decatur, Privateer.
    Cap: 05 Jun 1814 at Sea by HM Ship Rhin Int: 20 Jun 1814 Dis: 02 Aug 1814.
    Received from HM Ship Rhin. Board's Order.

Peters, John   Prisoner 173. Rank: Mate, from: Hamilton, Merchant Vessel.
    Cap: 28 Sep 1812 at Sea by Southampton Int: 07 Oct 1812 Escaped: 28 Jun 1813.
    Received from Southampton. Escaped.

Peters, John   Prisoner 218. Rank: Cook, from: Philip, Merchant Vessel.
    Cap: 10 Sep 1812 at Sea by Southampton Int: 11 Nov 1812 Dis: 01 Mar 1813.
    Received from Philip. per Order of Adml Stirling.

Peters, John   Prisoner 370. Rank: Seaman, from: Vixen, Man of War.
    Cap: 22 Nov 1812 at Sea by Rhodian late of US Brig Vixen Int: 14 Dec 1812 Dis: 09 May 1813.
    Received from Rhodian. To America for Exchange.

American Prisoners of War Held at Jamaica During the War of 1812

Peterson, Lewis   Prisoner 1463. Rank: Seaman, from: Not Recorded, Not Recorded.
    Cap: 21 Dec 1814 at Sea by Severn Int: 04 Feb 1815 Dis: 11 Feb 1815.
    Taken for Passage to Jamaica Depot. Received from Rota. Into HMS Ramillies per order of Sir T M Hardy.

Peterson, William   Prisoner 1421. Rank: Seaman, from: American Gunboats, Not Recorded.
    Cap: 05 Jan 1815 near New Orleans by Plantagenet Int: 27 Jan 1815 Dis: 05 Feb 1815.
    Taken in the American Gun Boats near New Orleans. Received from Ramilies. Into HM Ship Diomede per order of Sir TM Hardy Baronet.

Petet, Jean   Prisoner 929. Rank: Seaman, from: Cartagenaian, Privateer.
    Cap: 05 Dec 1813 at Sea by Sappho Int: 15 Dec 1813 Dis: 08 Aug 1814.
    Belonging to the Carthagenaian Privateer Carthagenaian. Received from Sappho. Board's Order.

Pettigrew, Thomas   Prisoner 449. Rank: Midshipman, from: Vixen, Man of War.
    Cap: 24 Dec 1812 at Sea by Rhodian Int: 24 Dec 1812 Dis: 24 Dec 1812.
    Received from Rhodian. To Parole. (Dates of capture, interment and discharge the same.)

Peurice, Thomas   Prisoner 936. Rank: Master, from: Coquelle, Merchant Vessel.
    Cap: 24 Dec 1813 at Sea by Sapphire Int: 02 Jan 1814 Dis: 15 Jan 1814.
    Received from Sapphire. To Parole.

Phdiger, John   Prisoner 1156. Rank: Seaman, from: Decatur, Privateer.
    Cap: 05 Jun 1814 at Sea by HM Ship Rhin Int: 20 Jun 1814 Dis: 10 Aug 1814.
    Received from HM Ship Rhin. Board's Order.

Phelps, A Y   Prisoner 1455. Rank: Mate, from: Not Recorded, Not Recorded.
    Cap: 21 Dec 1814 at Sea by Severn Int: 04 Feb 1815 Dis: 11 Feb 1815.
    Taken for Passage to Jamaica Depot. Received from Rota. Into HMS Ramillies per order of Sir T M Hardy.

Philips, John   Prisoner 1206. Rank: Seaman, from: Not Recorded, Not Recorded.
    Cap: 26 May 1814 Bay of Honduras by HM Sloop Talbot Int: 29 Jun 1814 Dis: 02 Jan 1815.
    Given up as an American. Received from HM Sloop Talbot. Into HM Ship Sultan per order of Captain John West.

Phillips, Bertram   Prisoner 789. Rank: Seaman, from: San Francisco de Paula, Privateer.
    Cap: 02 Oct 1813 at Sea by Forrester Int: 07 Oct 1813 Dis: 23 Nov 1813.
    Received from Forrester. per order of Rear Adml Brown.

Phillips, John   Prisoner 740. Rank: Seaman, from: Eliza, Merchant Vessel.
    Cap: 17 Jul 1813 at Sea by Sappho Int: 26 Jul 1813 Escaped: 23 Oct 1813.
    Received from Sappho. Escaped.

Phillips, John   Prisoner 1192. Rank: Seaman, from: Decatur, Privateer.
    Cap: 05 Jun 1814 at Sea by HM Ship Rhin Int: 20 Jun 1814 Dis: 03 Aug 1814.
    Received from HM Ship Rhin. Board's Order.

Phillips, R W   Prisoner 1522. Rank: Seaman, from: Not Recorded, Not Recorded.
    Cap: 08 Dec 1814 at Sea by Albion Int: 04 Feb 1815 Dis: 11 Feb 1815.
    Taken for Passage to Jamaica Depot. Received from Rota. Into HM Ship Rota per order of Sir TM Hardy.

Phillips, William   Prisoner 1121. Rank: Pilot, from: Decatur, Privateer.
    Cap: 05 Jun 1814 at Sea by HM Ship Rhin Int: 20 Jun 1814 Dis: 02 Jan 1815.
    Received from HM Ship Rhin. Into HM Ship Sultan per order of Captain John West.

Phyning, Josiah   Prisoner 1122. Rank: Pilot, from: Decatur, Privateer.
    Cap: 05 Jun 1814 at Sea by HM Ship Rhin Int: 20 Jun 1814 Dis: 02 Jan 1815.
    Received from HM Ship Rhin. Into HM Ship Sultan per order of Captain John West.

Pickens, Thomas   Prisoner 1095. Rank: Seaman, from: Jennett, Brig.
    Cap: 29 May 1814 at Sea by HM Ship Rhin Int: 04 Jun 1814 Dis: 02 Jan 1815.
    Taken in the detained Swedish Brig Jennett. Received from North Star. Into HM Ship Sultan per order of Captain John West.

Piere, Jean   Prisoner 598. Rank: Seaman, from: Le Ventura, Privateer.
    Cap: 13 Mar 1813 at Sea by Cossac Int: 18 Mar 1813 Dis: 16 Aug 1814.
    Received from Cossac. Board's Order.

Pierre, John   Prisoner 832. Rank: Seaman, from: Enterprize, Privateer.
    Cap: 15 Nov 1813 at Sea by Argo Int: 19 Nov 1813 Dis: 23 Aug 1814.
    A Carthagenaian. Received from Argo. Board's Order. John Pierre (1).

Pierro, Jean   Prisoner 1130. Rank: Quartermaster, from: Decatur, Privateer.
    Cap: 05 Jun 1814 at Sea by HM Ship Rhin Int: 20 Jun 1814 Dis: 03 Aug 1814.
    Received from HM Ship Rhin. Board's Order.

Piper, Henry   Prisoner 860. Rank: Seaman, from: Cato Georgiana, Not Recorded.
    Cap: 28 Nov 1813 at Sea by Barrosa Int: 10 Dec 1813 Dis: 01 Aug 1814.
    Prize to the US Frigate Essex. Received from Barrosa. To American Cartel Brig Aualostaw.

American Prisoners of War Held at Jamaica During the War of 1812

Pitner, Aaron   Prisoner 294. Rank: Passenger, from: Mary, Merchant Vessel.
    Cap: 26 Nov 1812 at Sea by Sappho Int: 30 Nov 1812 Dis: 24 Dec 1812.
    Received from Sappho. On Parole.

Pitt, Gabes   Prisoner 221. Rank: Prize Master, from: Joseph & Mary, Privateer.
    Cap: 24 Nov 1812 at Sea by Narcissus Int: 26 Nov 1812 Escaped: 06 Jan 1813.
    Received from Narcissus. Escaped.

Pluck, Mike   Prisoner 515. Rank: Seaman, from: Not Recorded, Not Recorded.
    Cap: Not Recorded by Not Recorded Int: 13 Mar 1813 Dis: 24 Jul 1813.
    Received from Shark. An American refusing to serve. To American Cartel Brig Aualostaw. (Date of capture not recorded.)

Pockmet, Zackuess   Prisoner 1034. Rank: Seaman, from: Jennett, Brig.
    Cap: 29 May 1814 at Sea by HM Ship Rhin Int: 04 Jun 1814 Dis: 02 Jan 1815.
    Taken in the Swedish Brig Jennet. Received from North Star. Into HM Ship Slttan per order of Captain John West.

Pole, Juan   Prisoner 590. Rank: Seaman, from: Le Ventura, Privateer.
    Cap: 13 Mar 1813 at Sea by Cossac Int: 18 Mar 1813 Dis: 16 Aug 1814.
    Received from Cossac. Board's Order.

Porrn, Joseph   Prisoner 626. Rank: Seaman, from: Mary Ann, Privateer.
    Cap: 05 May 1813 at Sea by Sapphire Int: 07 May 1813 Escaped: 13 Oct 1813.
    Received from Sapphire. Escaped.

Porter, Hans   Prisoner 1005. Rank: Seaman, from: Henrietta, Merchant Vessel.
    Cap: 20 Feb 1814 at Sea by Carnation Int: 04 Apr 1814 Dis: 11 Feb 1815.
    Received from Rota. per order of Sir T M Hardy Into HMS Ramillies.

Porter, William   Prisoner 1267. Rank: Seaman, from: Cora, Merchant Vessel.
    Cap: Not Recorded by Decouverte Int: 10 Sep 1814 Dis: 02 Jan 1815.
    Received from Decouverte. Into HM Ship Sultan per order of Captain John West. (Date of capture not recorded.)

Porto, Juan   Prisoner 757. Rank: Seaman, from: San Francisco de Paula, Privateer.
    Cap: 02 Oct 1813 at Sea by Forrester Int: 07 Oct 1813 Dis: 12 Aug 1814.
    Received from Forrester. Board's Order.

Poteron, Julian   Prisoner 1151. Rank: Seaman, from: Decatur, Privateer.
    Cap: 05 Jun 1814 at Sea by HM Ship Rhin Int: 20 Jun 1814 Dis: 10 Aug 1814.
    Received from HM Ship Rhin. Board's Order.

Potts, Samuel   Prisoner 718. Rank: Seaman, from: Not Recorded, Not Recorded.
    Cap: 05 Jun 1813 Kingston by Circe Int: 05 Jun 1813 Dis: 01 Aug 1814.
    impressed. Received from Circe. To American Cartel Brig Aualostaw.

Pouch, John   Prisoner 87. Rank: Seaman, from: Poor Sailor, Privateer.
    Cap: 13 Sep 1812 at Sea by Garland Int: 18 Sep 1812 Dis: 24 Jul 1813.
    Received from Garland. To American Cartel Brig Aualostaw.

Powell, John   Prisoner 569. Rank: Seaman, from: Defiance, Privateer.
    Cap: 15 Mar 1813 at Sea by Nimrod Int: 17 Mar 1813 Dis: 24 Jul 1813.
    Received from Nimrod. To American Cartel Brig Aualostaw.

Powell, Juan   Prisoner 784. Rank: Seaman, from: San Francisco de Paula, Privateer.
    Cap: 02 Oct 1813 at Sea by Forrester Int: 07 Oct 1813 Died: 30 Dec 1814.
    Received from Forrester. Killed by the Guard.

Powell, William   Prisoner 1503. Rank: Seaman, from: Not Recorded, Not Recorded.
    Cap: 20 Dec 1814 at Sea by Lacedaemonian Int: 04 Feb 1815 Dis: 11 Feb 1815.
    Taken for Passage to Jamaica Depot. Received from Rota. Into HM Ship Rota per order of Sir TM Hardy.

Pratt, Allen   Prisoner 312. Rank: 2 Lieutenant, from: Pirtshire, English Merchant Ship.
    Cap: Nov 1812 at Sea by Fawn Int: 06 Dec 1812 Escaped: 06 Jan 1813.
    Recaptured. Received from Fawn. Escaped. (Day of capture not recorded.)

Pratt, George S   Prisoner 974. Rank: Passenger, from: 26th October 1812, Merchant Vessel.
    Cap: 20 Feb 1814 at Sea by Ringdove Int: 20 Feb 1814 Dis: 12 Apr 1814.
    Received from Ringdove. To Parole.

Price, Charles   Prisoner 1379. Rank: Seaman, from: American Gunboats, Not Recorded.
    Cap: 05 Jan 1815 near New Orleans by Plantagenet Int: 27 Jan 1815 Dis: 05 Feb 1815.
    Taken in the American Gun Boats near New Orleans. Received from Ramilies. Into HM Ship Diomede per order of Sir TM Hardy Baronet.

Prior, John   Prisoner 561. Rank: Seaman, from: Defiance, Privateer.
    Cap: 15 Mar 1813 at Sea by Nimrod Int: 17 Mar 1813 Dis: 24 Jul 1813.
    Received from Nimrod. To American Cartel Brig Aualostaw.

American Prisoners of War Held at Jamaica During the War of 1812

Pujne, Dominique   Prisoner 1254. Rank: Captain, from: Grauosa, Merchant Vessel.
    Cap: 29 Jun 1814 at Sea by HM Ship Onyx Int: 30 Aug 1814 Dis: 10 Nov 1814.
    Recaptured from the Carethagenians. Received from Shark. Board's Order. (Prisoner numbers 1249 - 1256 all have recorded rank of Captain.)

Puosa, Joseph   Prisoner 817. Rank: Seaman, from: Enterprize, Privateer.
    Cap: 15 Nov 1813 at Sea by Argo Int: 19 Nov 1813 Dis: 01 Aug 1814.
    A Carthagenaian. Received from Argo. Board's Order.

Purdew, Joseph   Prisoner 284. Rank: Seaman, from: Joseph & Mary, Privateer.
    Cap: 24 Nov 1812 at Sea by Narcissus Int: 26 Nov 1812 Dis: 24 Jul 1813.
    Received from Narcissus. To American Cartel Brig Aualostaw.

Puritan, Themat   Prisoner 1146. Rank: Seaman, from: Decatur, Privateer.
    Cap: 05 Jun 1814 at Sea by HM Ship Rhin Int: 20 Jun 1814 Dis: 22 Jul 1814.
    Received from HM Ship Rhin. Board's Order.

Quick, George   Prisoner 357. Rank: Seaman, from: Vixen, Man of War.
    Cap: 22 Nov 1812 at Sea by Rhodian late of HM Brig Vixen Int: 14 Dec 1812 Dis: 04 Apr 1813.
    Received from Rhodian. To America for Exchange.

Quigley, Matthew   Prisoner 413. Rank: Private, from: Vixen, Man of War.
    Cap: 22 Nov 1812 at Sea by Rhodian Int: 14 Dec 1812 Dis: 09 May 1813.
    Received from Brazier. To America for Exchange.

Rabuirero, Nicolas   Prisoner 1225. Rank: Seaman, from: La Union, Spanish Brig.
    Cap: 03 Aug 1814 at Sea by Variable Int: 06 Aug 1814 Dis: 01 Sep 1814.
    Recaptured from the Carthagenaian Privateer White Horse. Received from Variable. Board's Order.

Ram, Thomas   Prisoner 356. Rank: Seaman, from: Vixen, Man of War.
    Cap: 22 Nov 1812 at Sea by Rhodian late of HM Brig Vixen Int: 14 Dec 1812 Dis: 09 May 1813.
    Received from Rhodian. To America for Exchange.

Ramsdell, Charles   Prisoner 1301. Rank: Seaman, from: Not Recorded, Not Recorded.
    Cap: Not Recorded by HM Sloop Dasher Int: 16 Dec 1814 Dis: 02 Jan 1815.
    Ship 'Name Unknown'. Received from HM Sloop Dasher. Into HM Ship Sultan per order of Captain John West. (Date of capture not recorded.)

Randales, Thomas   Prisoner 798. Rank: Seaman, from: Enterprize, Privateer.
    Cap: 15 Nov 1813 at Sea by Argo Int: 19 Nov 1813 Dis: 02 Jan 1815.
    A Carthagenaian. Received from Argo. Into HM Ship Sultan per order of Captain John West.

Randell, Benjamin   Prisoner 1550. Rank: Mate, from: John, Merchant Vessel.
    Cap: at Sea by HMS Talbot Int: 20 Mar 1815 Dis: 30 Mar 1815.
    Received from HMS Talbot. In consequence of Peace with America. (Date of capture not recorded.)

Randell, Edward   Prisoner 71. Rank: Seaman, from: Poor Sailor, Privateer.
    Cap: 13 Sep 1812 at Sea by Garland Int: 18 Sep 1812 Dis: 09 May 1813.
    Received from Garland. to America for Exchange.

Rawlings, Thomas   Prisoner 1456. Rank: Seaman, from: Not Recorded, Not Recorded.
    Cap: 21 Dec 1814 at Sea by Severn Int: 04 Feb 1815 Dis: 11 Feb 1815.
    Taken for Passage to Jamaica Depot. Received from Rota. Into HMS Ramillies per order of Sir T M Hardy.

Ray, John   Prisoner 540. Rank: Seaman, from: Defiance, Privateer.
    Cap: 15 Mar 1813 at Sea by Nimrod Int: 17 Mar 1813 Dis: 24 Jul 1813.
    Received from Nimrod. To American Cartel Brig Aualostaw.

Ray, Moses   Prisoner 119. Rank: Passenger, from: Bernardo, Merchant Vessel.
    Cap: 14 Sep 1812 at Sea by Garland Int: 18 Sep 1812 Dis: 20 Oct 1812.
    Schooner under Spanish Colors. Received from Garland. Liberated.

Raymond, Nathaniel   Prisoner 1506. Rank: Passenger, from: Not Recorded, Not Recorded.
    Cap: 08 Dec 1814 at Sea by Albion Int: 04 Feb 1815 Dis: 08 Feb 1815.
    Taken for Passage to Jamaica Depot. Received from Rota. per order of Sir TM Hardy as a Non-Combatant.

Raysan, Pedro   Prisoner 1045. Rank: 2 Captain, from: Casada el Narino, Privateer.
    Cap: 29 May 1814 at Sea by HM Ship Rhin Int: 04 Jun 1814 Dis: 22 Jul 1814.
    Cartagenaian. Received from North Star. Board's Order.

Read, Charles   Prisoner 1451. Rank: Seaman, from: American Gunboats, Not Recorded.
    Cap: 05 Jan 1815 near New Orleans by Plantagenet Int: 27 Jan 1815 Dis: 05 Feb 1815.
    Taken in the American Gun Boats near New Orleans. Received from Ramilies. Into HM Ship Diomede per order of Sir TM Hardy Baronet.

Redman, James   Prisoner 1468. Rank: Seaman, from: Not Recorded, Not Recorded.
    Cap: 21 Dec 1814 at Sea by Severn Int: 04 Feb 1815 Dis: 11 Feb 1815.
    Taken for Passage to Jamaica Depot. Received from Rota. Into HMS Ramillies per order of Sir T M Hardy.

American Prisoners of War Held at Jamaica During the War of 1812

Reed, G W   Prisoner 440. Rank: Commander, from: Vixen, Man of War.
    Cap: 24 Dec 1812 at Sea by Rhodian Int: 24 Dec 1812 Dis: 04 Jan 1813.
    Received from Rhodian. (No entry for discharge date.)

Reed, John   Prisoner 1. Rank: Seaman, from: Assaw, Merchant Vessel.
    Cap: 28 Jul 1812 at Sea by Garland Int: 22 Aug 1812 Escaped: 15 Nov 1812.
    Recaptured having been taken by the American Privateer the Paul Jones. Received from Garland. Escaped.

Reick, Nicholas   Prisoner 315. Rank: Seaman, from: Pirtshire, English Merchant Ship.
    Cap: Nov 1812 at Sea by Fawn Int: 06 Dec 1812 Dis: 24 Jul 1813.
    Recaptured. Eagle Privateer. Received from Fawn. To American Cartel Brig Aualostaw. (Day of capture not recorded.)

Reid, Robert   Prisoner 126. Rank: Chief Mate, from: Peru, Merchant Vessel.
    Cap: 15 Sep 1812 at Sea by HMS Cyane Int: 07 Oct 1812 Dis: 22 Oct 1812.
    Received from Cyane. On Parole.

Renard, Jean   Prisoner 1148. Rank: Seaman, from: Decatur, Privateer.
    Cap: 05 Jun 1814 at Sea by HM Ship Rhin Int: 20 Jun 1814 Dis: 18 Aug 1814.
    Received from HM Ship Rhin. Board's Order.

Renneck, Isaac   Prisoner 496. Rank: Seaman, from: Philip, Merchant Vessel.
    Cap: 28 Jan 1813 at Sea by Morgiana Int: 30 Jan 1813 Dis: 24 Jul 1813.
    Recaptured. Received from Morgiana. To American Cartel Brig Aualostaw.

Reuon, Santiago   Prisoner 857. Rank: Seaman, from: Le Galzo, Spanish Brig.
    Cap: 17 Nov 1813 at Sea by Variable Int: 28 Nov 1813 Dis: 29 Jul 1814.
    Recaptured from the Carthagenaian Privateer Le Legislateur. Received from Variable. Board's Order.

Reynolds, Christian   Prisoner 313. Rank: Prize Master, from: Pirtshire, English Merchant Ship.
    Cap: Nov 1812 at Sea by Fawn Int: 06 Dec 1812 Died: 10 Apr 1813.
    Recaptured. Received from Fawn. Died. (Day of capture not recorded.)

Reynolds, James   Prisoner 1378. Rank: Seaman, from: American Gunboats, Not Recorded.
    Cap: 05 Jan 1815 near New Orleans by Plantagenet Int: 27 Jan 1815 Dis: 05 Feb 1815.
    Taken in the American Gun Boats near New Orleans. Received from Ramilies. Into HM Ship Diomede per order of Sir TM Hardy Baronet.

Ribe, Francis   Prisoner 676. Rank: Seaman, from: Lovely Lass, Privateer.
    Cap: 21 May 1813 at Sea by Circe Int: 23 May 1813 Dis: 28 Jul 1814.
    Received from Forrester. Board's Order.

Rice, Samuel   Prisoner 368. Rank: Seaman, from: Vixen, Man of War.
    Cap: 22 Nov 1812 at Sea by Rhodian late of US Brig Vixen Int: 14 Dec 1812 Dis: 09 May 1813.
    Received from Rhodian. To America for Exchange.

Richards, Augustus   Prisoner 1470. Rank: Seaman, from: Not Recorded, Not Recorded.
    Cap: 21 Dec 1814 at Sea by Severn Int: 04 Feb 1815 Dis: 11 Feb 1815.
    Taken for Passage to Jamaica Depot. Received from Rota. Into HMS Ramillies per order of Sir T M Hardy.

Richards, Thomas   Prisoner 175. Rank: Mate, from: Books, Not Recorded.
    Cap: Not Recorded by Not Recorded Int: 07 Oct 1812 Dis: 09 May 1813.
    Received from Southampton. To America for Exchange.

Richardson, William   Prisoner 245. Rank: Seaman, from: Joseph & Mary, Privateer.
    Cap: 24 Nov 1812 at Sea by Narcissus Int: 26 Nov 1812 Dis: 24 Jul 1813.
    Received from Narcissus. To American Cartel Brig Aualostaw.

Richmond, William   Prisoner 969. Rank: Not Recorded, from: Packet, Merchant Vessel.
    Cap: 08 Feb 1814 at Sea by Snake Int: 17 Feb 1814 Dis: 01 Aug 1814.
    Received from Snake. To American Cartel Brig Aualostaw.

Rionaine, Jean   Prisoner 1164. Rank: Seaman, from: Decatur, Privateer.
    Cap: 05 Jun 1814 at Sea by HM Ship Rhin Int: 20 Jun 1814 Dis: 21 Jul 1814.
    Received from HM Ship Rhin. Board's Order.

Robb, Charles   Prisoner 730. Rank: Seaman, from: Eliza, Merchant Vessel.
    Cap: 17 Jul 1813 at Sea by Sappho Int: 26 Jul 1813 Dis: 01 Aug 1814.
    Received from Sappho. To American Cartel Brig Aualostaw.

Robert, Pedro   Prisoner 1055. Rank: Seaman, from: Casada el Narino, Privateer.
    Cap: 29 May 1814 at Sea by HM Ship Rhin Int: 04 Jun 1814 Dis: 08 Aug 1814.
    Carthagenaian. Received from North Star. Board's Order.

Roberts, Christopher   Prisoner 1536. Rank: Master, from: William & Mary, Merchant Vessel.
    Cap: 12 Feb 1815 at Sea by HM Sloop Carnation Int: 23 Feb 1815 Dis: 05 Mar 1815.
    Received from HM Sloop Carnation. To Parole.

American Prisoners of War Held at Jamaica During the War of 1812

Roberts, G R   Prisoner 219. Rank: Seaman, from: Not Recorded, Privateer.
    Cap: 04 Nov 1812 at Sea by Cyane Int: 22 Nov 1812 Dis: 09 May 1813.
    An American Schooner. Received from Cyane. To America for Exchange.

Roberts, Michael   Prisoner 696. Rank: Seaman, from: Lovely Lass, Privateer.
    Cap: 15 May 1813 at Sea by Circe Int: 29 May 1813 Dis: 21 Jul 1814.
    Received from Circe. Board's Order.

Roberts, Samuel   Prisoner 259. Rank: Seaman, from: Joseph & Mary, Privateer.
    Cap: 24 Nov 1812 at Sea by Narcissus Int: 26 Nov 1812 Dis: 24 Jul 1813.
    Received from Narcissus. To American Cartel Brig Aualostaw.

Robien, John   Prisoner 823. Rank: Seaman, from: Enterprize, Privateer.
    Cap: 15 Nov 1813 at Sea by Argo Int: 19 Nov 1813 Died: 16 Jan 1814.
    A Carthagenaian. Received from Argo. Died.

Robins, Thomas   Prisoner 546. Rank: Seaman, from: Defiance, Privateer.
    Cap: 15 Mar 1813 at Sea by Nimrod Int: 17 Mar 1813 Dis: 24 Jul 1813.
    Received from Nimrod. To American Cartel Brig Aualostaw.

Robinson, James   Prisoner 643. Rank: Seaman, from: Mary Ann, Privateer.
    Cap: 05 May 1813 at Sea by Sapphire Int: 07 May 1813 Dis: 01 Aug 1814.
    Received from Sapphire. To American Cartel Brig Aualostaw.

Robinson, Richard   Prisoner 736. Rank: Seaman, from: Eliza, Merchant Vessel.
    Cap: 17 Jul 1813 at Sea by Sappho Int: 26 Jul 1813 Dis: 01 Aug 1814.
    Received from Sappho. To American Cartel Brig Aualostaw.

Robinson, Thomas   Prisoner 154. Rank: Seaman, from: Philip, Merchant Vessel.
    Cap: 10 Sep 1812 at Sea by Southampton Int: 07 Oct 1812 Dis: 01 Mar 1813.
    Received from Southampton. per Order of Adml Stirling to American Ship Philip.

Robisa, Victor   Prisoner 1031. Rank: Seaman, from: Not Recorded, Not Recorded.
    Cap: at Sea by Not Recorded Int: 24 Apr 1814 Dis: 10 Aug 1814.
    Retaken in a Dragger. Belonging to the Saucy Jack. Received from Kingston Barracks.
    (Date of capture not recorded.)

Roco, Thomas   Prisoner 1058. Rank: Seaman, from: Casada el Narino, Privateer.
    Cap: 29 May 1814 at Sea by HM Ship Rhin Int: 04 Jun 1814 Dis: 10 Aug 1814.
    Carthagenaian. Received from North Star. Board's Order.

Roderick, Anthony   Prisoner 1003. Rank: Seaman, from: Henrietta, Merchant Vessel.
    Cap: 20 Feb 1814 at Sea by Carnation Int: 04 Apr 1814 Dis: 22 Apr 1814.
    Received from Rota. per Order of Rear Brown into the Spanish Vessel Cupida.

Rodrigo, Andrew   Prisoner 822. Rank: Seaman, from: Enterprize, Privateer.
    Cap: 15 Nov 1813 at Sea by Argo Int: 19 Nov 1813 Dis: 12 Aug 1814.
    A Carthagenaian. Received from Argo. Board's Order.

Rodrigues, Manuel   Prisoner 949. Rank: Seaman, from: Ann, Merchant Vessel.
    Cap: 01 Jan 1814 at Sea by Sappho Int: 19 Jan 1814 Dis: 28 Jul 1814.
    Received from Sappho. Board's Order.

Rodriguez, Antonio   Prisoner 775. Rank: Seaman, from: San Francisco de Paula, Privateer.
    Cap: 02 Oct 1813 at Sea by Forrester Int: 07 Oct 1813 Escaped: 30 Dec 1813.
    Received from Forrester. Escaped.

Rodriguez, Manuel   Prisoner 891. Rank: Seaman, from: San Francisco Navier, Brig.
    Cap: 03 Dec 1813 at Sea by Sappho Int: 15 Dec 1813 Dis: 11 Jan 1814.
    Taken in the Recaptured Spanish Brig. Prize to the Carthagenaian Privateer Carthagenaian. Received
    from Sappho. per order.

Rodriguez, Oza   Prisoner 1198. Rank: Seaman, from: Neustra Cantado, Merchant Vessel.
    Cap: 01 Jun 1814 at Sea by HM Ship Argo Int: 27 Jun 1814 Dis: 01 Sep 1814.
    Retaken in the Spanish Ship Neustra Cantado. Received from HM Ship Argo. Board's Order.

Rodriques, Luis   Prisoner 931. Rank: Seaman, from: Cartagenaian, Privateer.
    Cap: 05 Dec 1813 at Sea by Sappho Int: 15 Dec 1813 Dis: 11 Jan 1814.
    Belonging to the Carthagenaian Privateer Carthagenaian. Received from Sappho. per order.

Roe, Cornwel   Prisoner 5. Rank: Seaman, from: Assaw, Merchant Vessel.
    Cap: 28 Jul 1812 at Sea by Garland Int: 22 Aug 1812 Dis: 04 Apr 1813.
    Recaptured having been taken by the American Privateer the Paul Jones. Received from Garland. to
    America for Exchange.

Roe, John   Prisoner 267. Rank: Boy, from: Joseph & Mary, Privateer.
    Cap: 24 Nov 1812 at Sea by Narcissus Int: 26 Nov 1812 Dis: 04 Apr 1813.
    Received from Narcissus. To America, under 12 years old.

American Prisoners of War Held at Jamaica During the War of 1812

Rogers, Thomas   Prisoner 517. Rank: Seaman, from: Not Recorded, Not Recorded.
    Cap: Not Recorded by Not Recorded Int: 12 Mar 1813 Dis: 24 Jul 1813.
    Received from Cyane. An American refusing to serve. To American Cartel Brig Aualostaw.
    (Date of capture not recorded.)

Rolston, Leven   Prisoner 296. Rank: Passenger, from: Mary, Merchant Vessel.
    Cap: 26 Nov 1812 at Sea by Sappho Int: 30 Nov 1812 Dis: 24 Jul 1813.
    Received from Sappho. To American Cartel Brig Aualostaw.

Romero, Ignacio   Prisoner 1279. Rank: Seaman, from: Dolores, Merchant Schooner.
    Cap: at Sea by HM Sloop Anaconda Int: 07 Oct 1814 Dis: 10 Nov 1814.
    Received from HM Sloop Anaconda. Board's Order. (Date of capture not recorded.)

Roper, John   Prisoner 597. Rank: Seaman, from: Le Ventura, Privateer.
    Cap: 13 Mar 1813 at Sea by Cossac Int: 18 Mar 1813 Dis: 21 Jul 1814.
    Received from Cossac. Board's Order.

Rosario, Francisco   Prisoner 920. Rank: Seaman, from: San Francisco Navier, Brig.
    Cap: 05 Dec 1813 at Sea by Sappho Int: 15 Dec 1813 Dis: 05 Aug 1814.
    Taken in the Recaptured Spanish Brig. Prize to the Carthagenaian Privateer Carthagenaian. Received from Sappho. Board's Order.

Rosemond, William   Prisoner 682. Rank: Seaman, from: Arethusa, Man of War.
    Cap: 03 Feb 1813 Not Recorded by Variable Int: 26 May 1813 Dis: 01 Aug 1814.
    Received from Variable. To American Cartel Brig Aualostaw.

Roshin, Dominique   Prisoner 1190. Rank: Seaman, from: Decatur, Privateer.
    Cap: 05 Jun 1814 at Sea by HM Ship Rhin Int: 20 Jun 1814 Dis: 10 Aug 1814.
    Received from HM Ship Rhin. Board's Order.

Rosiere, Celestian   Prisoner 1251. Rank: Captain, from: Grauosa, Merchant Vessel.
    Cap: 29 Jun 1814 at Sea by HM Ship Onyx Int: 30 Aug 1814 Dis: 10 Nov 1814.
    Recaptured from the Carethagenians. Received from Shark. Board's Order. (Prisoner numbers 1249 - 1256 all have recorded rank of Captain.)

Rosin, John   Prisoner 179. Rank: Seaman, from: Philip, Merchant Vessel.
    Cap: 10 Sep 1812 at Sea by Southampton Int: 09 Oct 1812 Dis: 01 Mar 1813.
    Received from Southampton. per Order of Admiral Stirling.

Rosinloof, Thomas   Prisoner 97. Rank: Seaman, from: Poor Sailor, Privateer.
    Cap: 13 Sep 1812 at Sea by Garland Int: 18 Sep 1812 Dis: 18 Dec 1812.
    Received from Garland. Merchant Ship Experiment for Passage to England.

Rosse, Henri   Prisoner 896. Rank: Seaman, from: San Francisco Navier, Brig.
    Cap: 03 Dec 1813 at Sea by Sappho Int: 15 Dec 1813 Dis: 01 Aug 1814.
    Taken in the Recaptured Spanish Brig. Prize to the Carthagenaian Privateer Carthagenaian. Received from Sappho. Board's Order.

Roteu, Peter   Prisoner 940. Rank: Seaman, from: Coquelle, Merchant Vessel.
    Cap: 24 Dec 1813 at Sea by Sapphire Int: 02 Jan 1814 Dis: 01 Aug 1814.
    Received from Sapphire. To American Cartel Brig Aualostaw.

Rough, Daniel   Prisoner 806. Rank: Seaman, from: Enterprize, Privateer.
    Cap: 15 Nov 1813 at Sea by Argo Int: 19 Nov 1813 Dis: 21 Jul 1814.
    A Carthagenaian. Received from Argo. Board's Order.

Round, William   Prisoner 419. Rank: Private, from: Vixen, Man of War.
    Cap: 22 Nov 1812 at Sea by Rhodian Int: 14 Dec 1812 Dis: 09 May 1813.
    Received from Brazier. To America for Exchange.

Rousseau, Juan   Prisoner 926. Rank: Seaman, from: Cartagenaian, Privateer.
    Cap: 05 Dec 1813 at Sea by Sappho Int: 15 Dec 1813 Dis: 12 Aug 1814.
    Belonging to the Carthagenaian Privateer Carthagenaian. Received from Sappho. Board's Order.

Rowley, Isaac   Prisoner 1400. Rank: Seaman, from: American Gunboats, Not Recorded.
    Cap: 05 Jan 1815 near New Orleans by Plantagenet Int: 27 Jan 1815 Dis: 05 Feb 1815.
    Taken in the American Gun Boats near New Orleans. Received from Ramilies. Into HM Ship Diomede per order of Sir TM Hardy Baronet.

Roysdon, Joseph   Prisoner 594. Rank: Seaman, from: Le Ventura, Privateer.
    Cap: 13 Mar 1813 at Sea by Cossac Int: 18 Mar 1813 Dis: 08 Aug 1814.
    Received from Cossac. Board's Order.

Rushs, Springer   Prisoner 1515. Rank: Prize Master, from: Not Recorded, Not Recorded.
    Cap: 08 Dec 1814 at Sea by Albion Int: 04 Feb 1815 Dis: 08 Feb 1815.
    Taken for Passage to Jamaica Depot. Received from Rota. per order of Sir TM Hardy as a Non-Combatant.

Russell, James   Prisoner 107. Rank: Seaman, from: Poor Sailor, Privateer.
    Cap: 13 Sep 1812 at Sea by Garland Int: 18 Sep 1812 Escaped: 15 Nov 1812.
    Received from Garland. Escaped.

American Prisoners of War Held at Jamaica During the War of 1812

Rutter, William   Prisoner 263. Rank: Seaman, from: Joseph & Mary, Privateer.
    Cap: 24 Nov 1812 at Sea by Narcissus Int: 26 Nov 1812 Dis: 24 Jul 1813.
    Received from Narcissus. To American Cartel Brig Aualostaw.

Sadler, William   Prisoner 1369. Rank: Seaman, from: American Gunboats, Not Recorded.
    Cap: 05 Jan 1815 near New Orleans by Plantagenet Int: 27 Jan 1815 Dis: 05 Feb 1815.
    Taken in the American Gun Boats near New Orleans. Received from Ramilies. Into HM Ship Diomede per order of Sir TM Hardy Baronet.

Saffarque, Andrew   Prisoner 1166. Rank: Seaman, from: Decatur, Privateer.
    Cap: 05 Jun 1814 at Sea by HM Ship Rhin Int: 20 Jun 1814 Dis: 03 Aug 1814.
    Received from HM Ship Rhin. Board's Order.

Saladin, Carlos   Prisoner 759. Rank: Seaman, from: San Francisco de Paula, Privateer.
    Cap: 02 Oct 1813 at Sea by Forrester Int: 07 Oct 1813 Dis: 11 Jan 1814.
    Received from Forrester. per order.

Sales, Samuel   Prisoner 410. Rank: Sergeant, from: Vixen, Man of War.
    Cap: 22 Nov 1812 at Sea by Rhodian Int: 14 Dec 1812 Dis: 09 May 1813.
    Received from Brazier. To America for Exchange.

Salisbury, Jose   Prisoner 1033. Rank: Seaman, from: Jennett, Brig.
    Cap: 29 May 1814 at Sea by HM Ship Rhin Int: 04 Jun 1814 Dis: 02 Jan 1815.
    Taken in the Swedish Brig Jennet. Received from North Star. Into HM Ship Sultan per order of Captain John West.

Samson, Pure   Prisoner 604. Rank: Captain, from: Hazard, Privateer.
    Cap: 12 Mar 1813 Providence by Moselle Int: 29 Mar 1813 Dis: 04 Apr 1813.
    Received from Moselle. To America for Exchange.

Sanchez, Simon   Prisoner 1079. Rank: Seaman, from: Casada el Narino, Privateer.
    Cap: 29 May 1814 at Sea by HM Ship Rhin Int: 04 Jun 1814 Dis: 18 Aug 1814.
    Carthagenaian. Received from North Star. Board's Order.

Sandford, Abraham   Prisoner 49. Rank: Seaman, from: Not Recorded, Not Recorded.
    Cap: 24 Aug 1812 Kingston by HM Ship Garland Int: 23 Aug 1812 Escaped: 30 Jan 1813.
    apprehended on Shore. Received from HM Ship Garland. Escaped. (Date of capture after date of internment.)

Sandford, Abraham   Prisoner 512. Rank: Seaman, from: Not Recorded, Not Recorded.
    Cap: 11 Feb 1813 at Lucea by Not Recorded Int: 26 Feb 1813 Dis: 04 Apr 1813.
    Retaken. Received from Sea Horse. To America for Exchange. (Prisoner number 49.)

Sarasin, Fifi   Prisoner 921. Rank: Seaman, from: San Francisco Navier, Brig.
    Cap: 05 Dec 1813 at Sea by Sappho Int: 15 Dec 1813 Dis: 23 Aug 1814.
    Taken in the Recaptured Spanish Brig. Prize to the Carthagenaian Privateer Carthagenaian. Received from Sappho. Board's Order.

Sario, Juan   Prisoner 777. Rank: Seaman, from: San Francisco de Paula, Privateer.
    Cap: 02 Oct 1813 at Sea by Forrester Int: 07 Oct 1813 Escaped: 30 Dec 1813.
    Received from Forrester. Escaped.

Sasky, John   Prisoner 668. Rank: Seaman, from: Lovely Lass, Privateer.
    Cap: 21 May 1813 at Sea by Circe Int: 23 May 1813 Dis: 27 Jul 1814.
    Received from Forrester. Board's Order.

Satchell, Thomas   Prisoner 256. Rank: Seaman, from: Joseph & Mary, Privateer.
    Cap: 24 Nov 1812 at Sea by Narcissus Int: 26 Nov 1812 Dis: 24 Jul 1813.
    Received from Narcissus. To American Cartel Brig Aualostaw.

Satterwhite, Edwin   Prisoner 439. Rank: Purser, from: Vixen, Man of War.
    Cap: 24 Dec 1812 at Sea by Rhodian Int: 24 Dec 1812 Dis: 11 Feb 1813.
    Received from Rhodian. Non-Combatant per order of VA Stirling.

Saue, Aaron   Prisoner 975. Rank: Seaman, from: 26th October 1812, Merchant Vessel.
    Cap: 20 Feb 1814 at Sea by Ringdove Int: 20 Feb 1814 Dis: 01 Aug 1814.
    Received from Ringdove. To American Cartel Brig Aualostaw.

Saumon, Pier   Prisoner 699. Rank: Seaman, from: Lovely Lass, Privateer.
    Cap: 15 May 1813 at Sea by Circe Int: 29 May 1813 Dis: 27 Jul 1814.
    Received from Circe. Board's Order.

Savanel, Jean G   Prisoner 1284. Rank: Passenger, from: Dolores, Merchant Schooner.
    Cap: at Sea by HM Sloop Anaconda Int: 07 Oct 1814 Dis: 29 Oct 1814.
    Received from HM Sloop Anaconda. Board's Order. (Date of capture not recorded.)

Scott, Eleazer   Prisoner 557. Rank: Seaman, from: Defiance, Privateer.
    Cap: 15 Mar 1813 at Sea by Nimrod Int: 17 Mar 1813 Dis: 09 May 1813.
    Received from Nimrod. To America for Exchange.

American Prisoners of War Held at Jamaica During the War of 1812

Scott, John   Prisoner 859. Rank: Seaman, from: Cato Georgiana, Not Recorded.
    Cap: 28 Nov 1813 at Sea by Barrosa Int: 10 Dec 1813 Dis: 01 Aug 1814.
    Prize to the US Frigate Essex. Received from Barrosa. To American Cartel Brig Aualostaw.

Seagrave, Jean   Prisoner 1145. Rank: Seaman, from: Decatur, Privateer.
    Cap: 05 Jun 1814 at Sea by HM Ship Rhin Int: 20 Jun 1814 Dis: 21 Jul 1814.
    Received from HM Ship Rhin. Board's Order.

Seale, Charles   Prisoner 191. Rank: Seaman, from: Hamilton, Merchant Vessel.
    Cap: 28 Sep 1812 at Sea by Southampton Int: 09 Oct 1812 Dis: 08 Nov 1812.
    Received from Southampton. liberated.

Sears, Zebrua   Prisoner 711. Rank: Seaman, from: William, Merchant Man.
    Cap: 17 May 1813 at Sea by Circe Int: 29 May 1813 Dis: 01 Aug 1814.
    Received from Circe. (No entry for discharge date.)

Seburia, Thomas   Prisoner 326. Rank: Seaman, from: Pirtshire, English Merchant Ship.
    Cap: Nov 1812 at Sea by Fawn Int: 06 Dec 1812 Dis: 24 Jul 1813.
    Recaptured. Eagle Privateer. Received from Fawn. To American Cartel. (Day of capture not recorded.)

Secan, St Yago   Prisoner 1044. Rank: 1 Captain, from: Casada el Narino, Privateer.
    Cap: 29 May 1814 at Sea by HM Ship Rhin Int: 04 Jun 1814 Dis: 24 Jul 1814.
    Cartagenaian. Received from North Star. Board's Order.

Selby, Joseph   Prisoner 350. Rank: Seaman, from: Vixen, Man of War.
    Cap: 22 Nov 1812 at Sea by Rhodian late of HM Brig Vixen Int: 14 Dec 1812 Died: 10 Mar 1812.
    Received from Rhodian. Died.

Selby, Miles   Prisoner 185. Rank: Boy, from: Rebecca Sims, Merchant Vessel.
    Cap: 12 Sep 1812 at Sea by Southampton Int: 09 Oct 1812 Dis: 20 Oct 1812.
    Received from Southampton. liberated being under 12 years Old.

Seldon, John   Prisoner 560. Rank: Seaman, from: Defiance, Privateer.
    Cap: 15 Mar 1813 at Sea by Nimrod Int: 17 Mar 1813 Dis: 24 Jul 1813.
    Received from Nimrod. To American Cartel Brig Aualostaw.

Seprast, John   Prisoner 114. Rank: Surgeon, from: Poor Sailor, Privateer.
    Cap: 13 Sep 1812 at Sea by Garland Int: 18 Sep 1812 Dis: 24 Sep 1812.
    Received from Garland. To Parole.

Serin, John   Prisoner 982. Rank: Seaman, from: Suspense, Merchant Vessel.
    Cap: 20 Feb 1814 at Sea by Leviathan Int: 26 Mar 1814 Dis: 01 Aug 1814.
    Received from Mohawk. To American Cartel Brig Aualostaw.

Settle, Ellis   Prisoner 124. Rank: Seaman, from: Morning Star, Merchant Vessel.
    Cap: 08 Sep 1812 at Sea by HMS Cyane Int: 07 Oct 1812 Escaped: 15 Nov 1812.
    Received from Cyane. Escaped.

Seutimand, Alexander   Prisoner 689. Rank: Seaman, from: Lovely Lass, Privateer.
    Cap: 15 May 1813 at Sea by Circe Int: 29 May 1813 Dis: 27 Jul 1814.
    Received from Circe. Board's Order.

Sewell, George   Prisoner 467. Rank: Seaman, from: Not Recorded, Merchant Vessel.
    Cap: Not Recorded by Not Recorded Int: 14 Jan 1813 Dis: 24 Jul 1813.
    An American. Received from Sapphire. To American Cartel Brig Aualostaw. (Date of capture not recorded.)

Shamberk, Henry   Prisoner 1390. Rank: Seaman, from: American Gunboats, Not Recorded.
    Cap: 05 Jan 1815 near New Orleans by Plantagenet Int: 27 Jan 1815 Dis: 05 Feb 1815.
    Taken in the American Gun Boats near New Orleans. Received from Ramilies. Into HM Ship Diomede per order of Sir TM Hardy Baronet.

Shaw, Francis   Prisoner 15. Rank: Seaman, from: Superb, Merchant Vessel.
    Cap: 02 Aug 1812 at Sea by Garland Int: 22 Aug 1812 Dis: 09 May 1813.
    Received from Garland. to America for Exchange.

Shaw, William   Prisoner 1495. Rank: Master, from: Not Recorded, Not Recorded.
    Cap: 20 Dec 1814 at Sea by Lacedaemonian Int: 04 Feb 1815 Dis: 11 Feb 1815.
    Taken for Passage to Jamaica Depot. Received from Rota. Into HMS Ramillies per order of Sir T M Hardy.

Shephard, Joseph   Prisoner 432. Rank: Gunner, from: Vixen, Man of War.
    Cap: 22 Nov 1812 at Sea by Rhodian Int: 23 Dec 1812 Dis: 04 Apr 1813.
    Received from Brazier. To America for Exchange.

Shepheard, John   Prisoner 222. Rank: Prize Master, from: Joseph & Mary, Privateer.
    Cap: 24 Nov 1812 at Sea by Narcissus Int: 26 Nov 1812 Dis: 04 Apr 1813.
    Received from Narcissus. To America for Exchange.

American Prisoners of War Held at Jamaica During the War of 1812

Shiddell, John   Prisoner 1529. Rank: Supercargo, from: Not Recorded, Not Recorded.
    Cap: 20 Dec 1814 at Sea by Sevrin Int: 07 Feb 1815 Dis: 08 Feb 1815.
    Taken for Passage to Jamaica Depot. Received from Rota. per order of Sir TM Hardy as a Non-Combatant.

Shields, William   Prisoner 444. Rank: Midshipman, from: Vixen, Man of War.
    Cap: 24 Dec 1812 at Sea by Rhodian Int: 24 Dec 1812 Dis: 24 Dec 1812.
    Received from Rhodian. To Parole. (Dates of capture, interment and discharge the same.)

Shitcatt, Richard   Prisoner 1387. Rank: Seaman, from: American Gunboats, Not Recorded.
    Cap: 05 Jan 1815 near New Orleans by Plantagenet Int: 27 Jan 1815 Dis: 05 Feb 1815.
    Taken in the American Gun Boats near New Orleans. Received from Ramilies. Into HM Ship Diomede per order of Sir TM Hardy Baronet.

Sidawire, Julian   Prisoner 622. Rank: Seaman, from: Mary Ann, Privateer.
    Cap: 05 May 1813 at Sea by Sapphire Int: 07 May 1813 Dis: 27 Jul 1814.
    Received from Sapphire. Board's Order.

Silotic, Antonio   Prisoner 903. Rank: 2 Boatswain, from: San Francisco Navier, Brig.
    Cap: 05 Dec 1813 at Sea by Sappho Int: 15 Dec 1813 Dis: 29 Jul 1814.
    Taken in the Recaptured Spanish Brig. Prize to the Carthagenaian Privateer Carthagenaian. Received from Sappho. Board's Order.

Silver, John   Prisoner 1422. Rank: Seaman, from: American Gunboats, Not Recorded.
    Cap: 05 Jan 1815 near New Orleans by Plantagenet Int: 27 Jan 1815 Dis: 05 Feb 1815.
    Taken in the American Gun Boats near New Orleans. Received from Ramilies. Into HM Ship Diomede per order of Sir TM Hardy Baronet.

Simmonds, William   Prisoner 1552. Rank: Seaman, from: John, Merchant Vessel.
    Cap: at Sea by HMS Talbot Int: 20 Mar 1815 Dis: 01 Apr 1815.
    Received from HMS Talbot. In consequence of Peace with America. (Date of capture not recorded.)

Simmons, James   Prisoner 1404. Rank: Seaman, from: American Gunboats, Not Recorded.
    Cap: 05 Jan 1815 near New Orleans by Plantagenet Int: 27 Jan 1815 Dis: 05 Feb 1815.
    Taken in the American Gun Boats near New Orleans. Received from Ramilies. Into HM Ship Diomede per order of Sir TM Hardy Baronet.

Simon, Jerome   Prisoner 335. Rank: Seaman, from: Not Recorded, Merchant Vessel.
    Cap: 08 Dec 1812 at Sea by Rhodian late Southampton Int: 14 Dec 1812 Dis: 24 Jul 1813.
    Unknown. Received from Rhodian. To American Cartel Brig Aualostaw.

Simon, Joseph   Prisoner 526. Rank: Seaman, from: Defiance, Privateer.
    Cap: 15 Mar 1813 at Sea by Nimrod Int: 17 Mar 1813 Dis: 24 Jul 1813.
    Received from Nimrod. To American Cartel Brig Aualostaw.

Simpson, James   Prisoner 148. Rank: Seaman, from: William Penn, Merchant Vessel.
    Cap: 08 Sep 1812 at Sea by Southampton Int: 07 Oct 1812 Dis: 01 Mar 1813.
    Received from Southampton. per Order of Adml Stirling to American Ship William Penn.

Simpson, James   Prisoner 664. Rank: Seaman, from: Lovely Lass, Privateer.
    Cap: 21 May 1813 at Sea by Circe Int: 23 May 1813 Dis: 01 Aug 1814.
    Received from Forrester. To American Cartel Brig Aualostaw.

Simpson, Thomas   Prisoner 1425. Rank: Seaman, from: American Gunboats, Not Recorded.
    Cap: 05 Jan 1815 near New Orleans by Plantagenet Int: 27 Jan 1815 Dis: 05 Feb 1815.
    Taken in the American Gun Boats near New Orleans. Received from Ramilies. Into HM Ship Diomede per order of Sir TM Hardy Baronet.

Sinpire, Pedro   Prisoner 925. Rank: Seaman, from: Cartagenaian, Privateer.
    Cap: 05 Dec 1813 at Sea by Sappho Int: 15 Dec 1813 Escaped: 30 Dec 1813.
    Belonging to the Carthagenaian Privateer Carthagenaian. Received from Sappho. Escaped.

Skakelton, Roger   Prisoner 162. Rank: Seaman, from: Rebecca Sims, Merchant Vessel.
    Cap: 12 Sep 1812 at Sea by Southampton Int: 07 Oct 1812 Dis: 21 Oct 1812.
    Received from Southampton. being an Englishman.

Skinner, Lewis   Prisoner 741. Rank: Seaman, from: Eliza, Merchant Vessel.
    Cap: 17 Jul 1813 at Sea by Sappho Int: 26 Jul 1813 Dis: 01 Aug 1814.
    Received from Sappho. To American Cartel Brig Aualostaw.

Skipper, John   Prisoner 1041. Rank: Seaman, from: Jennett, Brig.
    Cap: 29 May 1814 at Sea by HM Ship Rhin Int: 04 Jun 1814 Dis: 02 Jan 1815.
    Taken in the Swedish Brig Jennet. Received from North Star. Into HM Ship Sultan per order of Captain John West.

Slippy, William   Prisoner 270. Rank: Seaman, from: Joseph & Mary, Privateer.
    Cap: 24 Nov 1812 at Sea by Narcissus Int: 26 Nov 1812 Dis: 04 Apr 1813.
    Received from Narcissus. To America, under 12 years old.

American Prisoners of War Held at Jamaica During the War of 1812

Sloane, William   Prisoner 1483. Rank: Prize Master, from: Not Recorded, Not Recorded.
    Cap: 20 Dec 1814 at Sea by Lacedaemonian Int: 04 Feb 1815 Dis: 11 Feb 1815.
    Taken for Passage to Jamaica Depot. Received from Rota. Into HMS Ramillies per order of Sir T M Hardy.

Small, Jacob   Prisoner 285. Rank: Surgeon, from: Joseph & Mary, Privateer.
    Cap: 24 Nov 1812 at Sea by Narcissus Int: 26 Nov 1812 Dis: 24 Dec 1812.
    Received from Narcissus. On Parole.

Small, William   Prisoner 1544. Rank: Passenger, from: Le Expedecion, Merchant Vessel.
    Cap: at Sea by HMS Drake Int: 09 Mar 1815 Dis: 16 Mar 1815.
    Received from HMS Rinaldo. being Non-Combatants. (Date of capture not recorded.)

Smart, David   Prisoner 111. Rank: 2 Lieutenant, from: Poor Sailor, Privateer.
    Cap: 13 Sep 1812 at Sea by Garland Int: 18 Sep 1812 Dis: 18 Sep 1813.
    Received from Garland. per Order of the Admiral.

Smith, Benjamin   Prisoner 227. Rank: Masters Mate, from: Joseph & Mary, Privateer.
    Cap: 24 Nov 1812 at Sea by Narcissus Int: 26 Nov 1812 Dis: 04 Apr 1813.
    Received from Narcissus. To America for Exchange.

Smith, Benjamin   Prisoner 1021. Rank: Seaman, from: Chance, Privateer.
    Cap: 01 Apr 1814 at Sea by Statira Int: 20 Apr 1814 Dis: 02 Jan 1815.
    Received from Statira. Into HM Ship Sultan per order of Captain John West.

Smith, Charles   Prisoner 240. Rank: Seaman, from: Joseph & Mary, Privateer.
    Cap: 24 Nov 1812 at Sea by Narcissus Int: 26 Nov 1812 Dis: 09 May 1813.
    Received from Narcissus. To America for Exchange.

Smith, Charles   Prisoner 1210. Rank: Seaman, from: Not Recorded, Not Recorded.
    Cap: 26 Jun 1814 Not Recorded by HM Sloop Emulous Int: 09 Jul 1814 Escaped: 18 Dec 1814.
    Given up as an American. Received from HM Sloop Emulous. Escaped.

Smith, David   Prisoner 678. Rank: Prize Master, from: Teuiriffe, Merchant.
    Cap: 10 May 1813 at Sea by Fawn Int: 25 May 1813 Dis: 01 Aug 1814.
    Rosamond Privateer. Received from Fawn. To American Cartel Brig Aualostaw.

Smith, James   Prisoner 714. Rank: Commander, from: Lovely Lass, Merchant Man.
    Cap: 15 May 1813 at Sea by Circe Int: 29 May 1813 Dis: 01 Aug 1814.
    Received from Circe. (No entry for discharge date. Other entries for vessel show Privateer.)

Smith, James   Prisoner 1424. Rank: Seaman, from: American Gunboats, Not Recorded.
    Cap: 05 Jan 1815 near New Orleans by Plantagenet Int: 27 Jan 1815 Dis: 05 Feb 1815.
    Taken in the American Gun Boats near New Orleans. Received from Ramilies. Into HM Ship Diomede per order of Sir TM Hardy Baronet.

Smith, John   Prisoner 190. Rank: Seaman, from: Hamilton, Merchant Vessel.
    Cap: 28 Sep 1812 at Sea by Southampton Int: 09 Oct 1812 Dis: 04 Apr 1813.
    Received from Southampton. To America for Exchange.

Smith, John   Prisoner 369. Rank: Seaman, from: Vixen, Man of War.
    Cap: 22 Nov 1812 at Sea by Rhodian late of US Brig Vixen Int: 14 Dec 1812 Dis: 09 May 1813.
    Received from Rhodian. To America for Exchange.

Smith, John   Prisoner 848. Rank: Seaman, from: Not Recorded, Not Recorded.
    Cap: 23 Nov 1813 Not Recorded by Moselle Int: 26 Nov 1813 Dis: 01 Aug 1814.
    An American, Received from Moselle. To American Cartel Brig Aualostaw.

Smith, John   Prisoner 1007. Rank: Passenger, from: Farmer's Daughter, Merchant Vessel.
    Cap: 30 Mar 1814 at Sea by Leviathan Int: 06 Apr 1814 Dis: 27 Apr 1814.
    Received from Leviathan. Being a Non-Combatant.

Smith, John   Prisoner 1030. Rank: Seaman, from: Not Recorded, Not Recorded.
    Cap: at Sea by Not Recorded Int: 24 Apr 1814 Dis: 02 Jan 1815.
    Retaken in a Dragger. Belonging to the Saucy Jack. Received from Kingston Barracks. Into HM Ship Sultan per order of Captain John West. (Date of capture not recorded.)

Smith, John   Prisoner 1377. Rank: Seaman, from: American Gunboats, Not Recorded.
    Cap: 05 Jan 1815 near New Orleans by Plantagenet Int: 27 Jan 1815 Dis: 05 Feb 1815.
    Taken in the American Gun Boats near New Orleans. Received from Ramilies. Into HM Ship Diomede per order of Sir TM Hardy Baronet.

Smith, Joseph   Prisoner 673. Rank: Seaman, from: Lovely Lass, Privateer.
    Cap: 21 May 1813 at Sea by Circe Int: 23 May 1813 Dis: 01 Aug 1814.
    Received from Forrester. To American Cartel Brig Aualostaw.

Smith, Robert   Prisoner 252. Rank: Seaman, from: Joseph & Mary, Privateer.
    Cap: 24 Nov 1812 at Sea by Narcissus Int: 26 Nov 1812 Dis: 24 Jul 1813.
    Received from Narcissus. To American Cartel Brig Aualostaw.

American Prisoners of War Held at Jamaica During the War of 1812

Smith, Robert   Prisoner 945. Rank: Seaman, from: Coquelle, Merchant Vessel.
    Cap: 24 Dec 1813 at Sea by Sapphire Int: 02 Jan 1814 Dis: 01 Aug 1814.
    Received from Sapphire. To American Cartel Brig Aualostaw.

Smith, Robert   Prisoner 1006. Rank: Master, from: Farmer's Daughter, Merchant Vessel.
    Cap: 30 Mar 1814 at Sea by Leviathan Int: 06 Apr 1814 Dis: 27 Apr 1814.
    Received from Leviathan. Board's Order.

Smith, Thomas   Prisoner 1465. Rank: Seaman, from: Not Recorded, Not Recorded.
    Cap: 21 Dec 1814 at Sea by Severn Int: 04 Feb 1815 Dis: 11 Feb 1815.
    Taken for Passage to Jamaica Depot. Received from Rota. Into HMS Ramillies per order of Sir T M Hardy.

Smith, Timothy   Prisoner 408. Rank: Seaman, from: Vixen, Man of War.
    Cap: 22 Nov 1812 at Sea by Rhodian late of US Brig Vixen Int: 14 Dec 1812 Dis: 09 May 1813.
    Received from Rhodian. To America for Exchange.

Smith, William   Prisoner 1490. Rank: Seaman, from: Not Recorded, Not Recorded.
    Cap: 20 Dec 1814 at Sea by Lacedaemonian Int: 04 Feb 1815 Dis: 11 Feb 1815.
    Taken for Passage to Jamaica Depot. Received from Rota. Into HMS Ramillies per order of Sir T M Hardy.

Snow, Samuel   Prisoner 986. Rank: Lieutenant, from: Suspense, Merchant Vessel.
    Cap: 20 Feb 1814 at Sea by Leviathan Int: 26 Mar 1814 Dis: 01 Aug 1814.
    Received from Mohawk. To American Cartel Brig Aualostaw.

Sole, Jordan   Prisoner 871. Rank: Seaman, from: Lapwing, Packet.
    Cap: 08 Dec 1813 at Sea by Barrosa Int: 10 Dec 1813 Dis: 01 Aug 1814.
    Recaptured. Received from Barrosa. To American Cartel Brig Aualostaw.

Southcombe, Peter   Prisoner 1308. Rank: 1 Mate, from: Nettervitte, Merchant Schooner.
    Cap: Not Recorded by HM Sloop Onyx Int: 30 Dec 1814 Dis: 02 Jan 1815.
    Received from HM Sloop Onyx. Into HM Ship Sultan per order of Captain John West. (Date of capture not recorded.)

Spalding, Reeves   Prisoner 220. Rank: 1 Lieutenant, from: Joseph & Mary, Privateer.
    Cap: 24 Nov 1812 at Sea by Narcissus Int: 26 Nov 1812 Escaped: 06 Jan 1813.
    Received from Narcissus. Escaped.

Speries, Thomas   Prisoner 1107. Rank: Seaman, from: Romano & Adamante, Merchant Brig.
    Cap: 31 May 1814 at Sea by Leviathan Int: 17 Jun 1814 Dis: 18 Aug 1814.
    Received from Leviathan. Board's Order.

Spragge, Archibald   Prisoner 503. Rank: Seaman, from: Not Recorded, Not Recorded.
    Cap: 02 Feb 1813 Not Recorded by Not Recorded Int: 02 Feb 1813 Dis: 09 May 1813.
    Retaken. To America for Exchange. (Prisoner number 213.)

Spreggs, Archibald   Prisoner 213. Rank: Seaman, from: Dominicana, Merchant Vessel.
    Cap: 21 Oct 1812 at Sea by HM Ship Liberty Int: 25 Oct 1812 Escaped: 31 Jan 1813.
    Taken out of Brigantine Dominicana by HM Ship Liberty and brot into Port Royal. Received from Decouverte. Escaped.

Springer, William   Prisoner 1534. Rank: Seaman, from: William & Mary, Merchant Vessel.
    Cap: 12 Feb 1815 at Sea by HM Sloop Carnation Int: 23 Feb 1815 Died: 27 Mar 1815.
    Received from HM Sloop Carnation. Died.

Squibb, Silas   Prisoner 461. Rank: Seaman, from: Saratoga, Merchant Vessel.
    Cap: 1813 at Sea by Fawn Int: 13 Jan 1813 Dis: 24 Jul 1813.
    Received from Sapphire. To American Cartel Brig Aualostaw. (Day and month of capture not recorded.)

St. Clair, Robert   Prisoner 885. Rank: Mate, from: Milly, Schooner.
    Cap: 25 Nov 1813 at Sea by Decouverte Int: 10 Dec 1813 Dis: 04 Mar 1814.
    Taken out of the American Schooner Milly. Received from Decouverte. To Parole.

St. George, George   Prisoner 101. Rank: Seaman, from: Poor Sailor, Privateer.
    Cap: 13 Sep 1812 at Sea by Garland Int: 18 Sep 1812 Dis: 24 Jul 1813.
    Received from Garland. To American Cartel Brig Aualostaw.

Staggs, Thomas   Prisoner 341. Rank: Seaman, from: Vixen, Man of War.
    Cap: 22 Nov 1812 at Sea by Rhodian late of HM Brig Vixen Int: 14 Dec 1812 Dis: 09 May 1813.
    Received from Rhodian. To America for Exchange.

Stan, Pedro   Prisoner 811. Rank: Seaman, from: Enterprize, Privateer.
    Cap: 15 Nov 1813 at Sea by Argo Int: 19 Nov 1813 Dis: 29 Jul 1814.
    A Carthagenaian. Received from Argo. Board's Order.

Stanley, Simon   Prisoner 1100. Rank: Seaman, from: Jennett, Brig.
    Cap: 29 May 1814 at Sea by HM Ship Rhin Int: 04 Jun 1814 Died: 10 Jun 1814.
    Taken in the detained Swedish Brig Jennett. Received from North Star. Died.

American Prisoners of War Held at Jamaica During the War of 1812

Steel, John   Prisoner 1118. Rank: Prize Master, from: Decatur, Privateer.
    Cap: 05 Jun 1814 at Sea by HM Ship Rhin Int: 20 Jun 1814 Dis: 02 Jan 1815.
    Received from HM Ship Rhin. Into HM Ship Sultan per order of Captain John West.

Stephen, George   Prisoner 1488. Rank: Seaman, from: Not Recorded, Not Recorded.
    Cap: 20 Dec 1814 at Sea by Lacedaemonian Int: 04 Feb 1815 Dis: 11 Feb 1815.
    Taken for Passage to Jamaica Depot. Received from Rota. Into HMS Ramillies per order of Sir T M Hardy.

Stevens, Francis   Prisoner 1402. Rank: Seaman, from: American Gunboats, Not Recorded.
    Cap: 05 Jan 1815 near New Orleans by Plantagenet Int: 27 Jan 1815 Dis: 05 Feb 1815.
    Taken in the American Gun Boats near New Orleans. Received from Ramilies. Into HM Ship Diomede per order of Sir TM Hardy Baronet.

Stevens, James   Prisoner 434. Rank: Carpenter, from: Vixen, Man of War.
    Cap: 22 Nov 1812 at Sea by Rhodian Int: 23 Nov 1812 Dis: 04 Apr 1813.
    Received from Rhodian. To America for Exchange. (Month of internment should be December.)

Stevens, Leverett   Prisoner 201. Rank: Master, from: Whim, Merchant Vessel.
    Cap: 18 Sep 1812 at Sea by Cyane Int: 20 Oct 1812 Dis: 20 Oct 1812.
    Received from Shark. On Parole.

Stevens, Russel   Prisoner 304. Rank: Master, from: Flora, Merchant Vessel.
    Cap: 26 Nov 1812 at Sea by Sappho Int: 03 Dec 1812 Dis: 24 Dec 1812.
    Received from Sappho. On Parole.

Stevenson, David   Prisoner 83. Rank: Seaman, from: Poor Sailor, Privateer.
    Cap: 13 Sep 1812 at Sea by Garland Int: 18 Sep 1812 Escaped: 15 Nov 1812.
    Received from Garland. Escaped.

Stevenson, George   Prisoner 287. Rank: Seaman, from: Joseph & Mary, Privateer.
    Cap: 24 Nov 1812 at Sea by Narcissus Int: 26 Nov 1812 Dis: 04 Apr 1813.
    Received from Narcissus. To America, under 12 years old.

Stevoine, John   Prisoner 1420. Rank: Seaman, from: American Gunboats, Not Recorded.
    Cap: 05 Jan 1815 near New Orleans by Plantagenet Int: 27 Jan 1815 Dis: 05 Feb 1815.
    Taken in the American Gun Boats near New Orleans. Received from Ramilies. Into HM Ship Diomede per order of Sir TM Hardy Baronet.

Stewart, Charles   Prisoner 1408. Rank: Seaman, from: American Gunboats, Not Recorded.
    Cap: 05 Jan 1815 near New Orleans by Plantagenet Int: 27 Jan 1815 Dis: 05 Feb 1815.
    Taken in the American Gun Boats near New Orleans. Received from Ramilies. Into HM Ship Diomede per order of Sir TM Hardy Baronet.

Stewart, Henry   Prisoner 67. Rank: Seaman, from: Elizabeth, Merchant Vessel.
    Cap: 07 Sep 1812 Port Royal by HM Sloop Shark Int: 17 Sep 1812 Dis: 24 Jul 1813.
    from the English Merchant Brig Elizabeth. Received from Shark. To American Cartel Brig Aualostaw.

Stewart, James W   Prisoner 868. Rank: Seaman, from: Cato Georgiana, Not Recorded.
    Cap: 28 Nov 1813 at Sea by Barrosa Int: 10 Dec 1813 Dis: 01 Aug 1814.
    Prize to the US Frigate Essex. Received from Barrosa. To American Cartel Brig Aualostaw.

Stocking, William   Prisoner 1476. Rank: Seaman, from: Not Recorded, Not Recorded.
    Cap: 21 Dec 1814 at Sea by Severn Int: 04 Feb 1815 Dis: 11 Feb 1815.
    Taken for Passage to Jamaica Depot. Received from Rota. Into HMS Ramillies per order of Sir T M Hardy.

Stokeley, J   Prisoner 1466. Rank: Seaman, from: Not Recorded, Not Recorded.
    Cap: 21 Dec 1814 at Sea by Severn Int: 04 Feb 1815 Dis: 11 Feb 1815.
    Taken for Passage to Jamaica Depot. Received from Rota. Into HMS Ramillies per order of Sir T M Hardy.

Stokes, John   Prisoner 386. Rank: Seaman, from: Vixen, Man of War.
    Cap: 22 Nov 1812 at Sea by Rhodian late of US Brig Vixen Int: 14 Dec 1812 Dis: 09 May 1813.
    Received from Rhodian. To America for Exchange.

Stolesby, Anthony   Prisoner 168. Rank: Seaman, from: Rebecca Sims, Merchant Vessel.
    Cap: 12 Sep 1812 at Sea by Southampton Int: 07 Oct 1812 Dis: 01 Mar 1813.
    Received from Southampton. per Order of Admiral Stirling.

Stone, Samuel   Prisoner 128. Rank: Seaman, from: Peru, Merchant Vessel.
    Cap: 15 Sep 1812 at Sea by HMS Cyane Int: 07 Oct 1812 Dis: 24 Jul 1813.
    Received from Cyane. To American Cartel Brig Aualostaw.

Storey, John   Prisoner 229. Rank: Carpenter, from: Joseph & Mary, Privateer.
    Cap: 24 Nov 1812 at Sea by Narcissus Int: 26 Nov 1812 Dis: 04 Apr 1813.
    Received from Narcissus. To America for Exchange.

American Prisoners of War Held at Jamaica During the War of 1812

Story, Abiel   Prisoner 1482. Rank: Prize Master, from: Not Recorded, Not Recorded.
    Cap: 20 Dec 1814 at Sea by Lacedaemonian Int: 04 Feb 1815 Dis: 11 Feb 1815.
    Taken for Passage to Jamaica Depot. Received from Rota. Into HMS Ramillies per order of Sir T M Hardy.

Street, James   Prisoner 1138. Rank: Seaman, from: Decatur, Privateer.
    Cap: 05 Jun 1814 at Sea by HM Ship Rhin Int: 20 Jun 1814 Dis: 11 Feb 1815.
    Received from HM Ship Rhin. Into HMS Ramillies per order of Sir T M Hardy.

Strong, Selvister   Prisoner 295. Rank: Passenger, from: Mary, Merchant Vessel.
    Cap: 26 Nov 1812 at Sea by Sappho Int: 30 Nov 1813 Died: 24 Jan 1813.
    Received from Sappho. Died.

Stuart, Charles   Prisoner 160. Rank: Seaman, from: Rebecca Sims, Merchant Vessel.
    Cap: 12 Sep 1812 at Sea by Southampton Int: 07 Oct 1812 Escaped: 15 Nov 1812.
    Received from Southampton. Escaped.

Sturges, E P   Prisoner 54. Rank: Master, from: Madisonia, Merchant Vessel.
    Cap: 03 Aug 1812 at Sea by HM Ship Garland Int: 27 Aug 1812 Dis: 28 Aug 1812.
    Received from HM Ship Herald. To Parole.

Sturko, P   Prisoner 671. Rank: Seaman, from: Lovely Lass, Privateer.
    Cap: 21 May 1813 at Sea by Circe Int: 23 May 1813 Escaped: 02 Oct 1813.
    Received from Forrester. Escaped.

Sullen, Peter   Prisoner 152. Rank: Seaman, from: Philip, Merchant Vessel.
    Cap: 10 Sep 1812 at Sea by Southampton Int: 07 Oct 1812 Dis: 01 Mar 1813.
    Received from Southampton. per Order of Adml Stirling to American Ship Philip.

Sullender, C   Prisoner 431. Rank: Private, from: Vixen, Man of War.
    Cap: 22 Nov 1812 at Sea by Rhodian Int: 14 Dec 1812 Dis: 04 Apr 1813.
    Received from Brazier. To America for Exchange.

Sullivan, Daniel   Prisoner 235. Rank: Quartermaster, from: Joseph & Mary, Privateer.
    Cap: 24 Nov 1812 at Sea by Narcissus Int: 26 Nov 1812 Dis: 24 Jul 1813.
    Received from Narcissus. To American Cartel Brig Aualostaw.

Summer, John   Prisoner 393. Rank: Seaman, from: Vixen, Man of War.
    Cap: 22 Nov 1812 at Sea by Rhodian late of US Brig Vixen Int: 14 Dec 1812 Dis: 09 May 1813.
    Received from Rhodian. To America for Exchange.

Summers, Philip   Prisoner 226. Rank: Masters Mate, from: Joseph & Mary, Privateer.
    Cap: 24 Nov 1812 at Sea by Narcissus Int: 26 Nov 1812 Dis: 09 May 1813.
    Received from Narcissus. To America for Exchange.

Swain, Luke   Prisoner 115. Rank: Sailing Master, from: Poor Sailor, Privateer.
    Cap: 13 Sep 1812 at Sea by Garland Int: 18 Sep 1812 Dis: 24 Jul 1813.
    Received from Garland. To American Cartel Brig Aualostaw.

Swatoz, Chuspere   Prisoner 1270. Rank: Seaman, from: Wolfe, Not Recorded.
    Cap: at Sea by Jalouse Int: 10 Sep 1814 Dis: 26 Sep 1814.
    American Schooner. Received from Jalouse. Board's Order. (Date of capture not recorded.)

Tagers, Anthony   Prisoner 299. Rank: Passenger, from: Mary, Merchant Vessel.
    Cap: 26 Nov 1812 at Sea by Sappho Int: 30 Nov 1812 Dis: 24 Jul 1813.
    Received from Sappho. To American Cartel Brig Aualostaw.

Talon, Francisco   Prisoner 894. Rank: Seaman, from: San Francisco Navier, Brig.
    Cap: 03 Dec 1813 at Sea by Sappho Int: 15 Dec 1813 Escaped: 30 Dec 1813.
    Taken in the Recaptured Spanish Brig. Prize to the Carthagenaian Privateer Carthagenaian. Received from Sappho. Escaped.

Tapp, George   Prisoner 37. Rank: Seaman, from: Not Recorded, Not Recorded.
    Cap: Not Recorded by Not Recorded Int: 22 Aug 1812 Dis: 09 May 1813.
    Given themselves up as American and refused to serve. Received from Garland. to America for Exchange. (Date of capture not recorded.)

Taylor, Alexander   Prisoner 516. Rank: Seaman, from: Not Recorded, Not Recorded.
    Cap: Not Recorded by Not Recorded Int: 13 Mar 1813 Dis: 24 Jul 1813.
    Received from Shark. An American refusing to serve. To American Cartel Brig Aualostaw. (Date of capture not recorded.)

Taylor, John   Prisoner 1385. Rank: Seaman, from: American Gunboats, Not Recorded.
    Cap: 05 Jan 1815 near New Orleans by Plantagenet Int: 27 Jan 1815 Dis: 05 Feb 1815.
    Taken in the American Gun Boats near New Orleans. Received from Ramilies. Into HM Ship Diomede per order of Sir TM Hardy Baronet.

Taylor, William   Prisoner 1119. Rank: Prize Master, from: Decatur, Privateer.
    Cap: 05 Jun 1814 at Sea by HM Ship Rhin Int: 20 Jun 1814 Dis: 02 Jan 1815.
    Received from HM Ship Rhin. Into HM Ship Sultan per order of Captain John West.

American Prisoners of War Held at Jamaica During the War of 1812

Tebez, Martin   Prisoner 919. Rank: Seaman, from: San Francisco Navier, Brig.
    Cap: 05 Dec 1813 at Sea by Sappho Int: 15 Dec 1813 Dis: 01 Aug 1814.
    Taken in the Recaptured Spanish Brig. Prize to the Carthagenaian Privateer Carthagenaian. Received from Sappho. Board's Order.

Tebot, Pedro   Prisoner 912. Rank: Seaman, from: San Francisco Navier, Brig.
    Cap: 05 Dec 1813 at Sea by Sappho Int: 15 Dec 1813 Dis: 11 Jan 1814.
    Taken in the Recaptured Spanish Brig. Prize to the Carthagenaian Privateer Carthagenaian. Received from Sappho. per order.

Tequin, William   Prisoner 92. Rank: Seaman, from: Poor Sailor, Privateer.
    Cap: 13 Sep 1812 at Sea by Garland Int: 18 Sep 1812 Dis: 09 May 1813.
    Received from Garland. To America for Exchange.

Tesser, Sean   Prisoner 1115. Rank: 1 Lieutenant, from: Decatur, Privateer.
    Cap: 05 Jun 1814 at Sea by HM Ship Rhin Int: 20 Jun 1814 Dis: 24 Jul 1814.
    Received from HM Ship Rhin. Board's Order.

Theobald, Charles   Prisoner 992. Rank: Seaman, from: Sophia, Merchant Vessel.
    Cap: at Sea by Not Recorded Int: 27 Mar 1814 Dis: 03 Aug 1814.
    Received from Ringdove. To American Cartel Brig Aualostaw. (Date of capture not recorded.)

Thomas, Francisco   Prisoner 1083. Rank: Seaman, from: Casada el Narino, Privateer.
    Cap: 29 May 1814 at Sea by HM Ship Rhin Int: 04 Jun 1814 Dis: 14 Jul 1814.
    Carthagenaian. Received from North Star. Per order, being a French Subject.

Thomas, John   Prisoner 85. Rank: Seaman, from: Poor Sailor, Privateer.
    Cap: 13 Sep 1812 at Sea by Garland Int: 18 Sep 1812 Dis: 09 May 1813.
    Received from Garland. To America for Exchange.

Thomas, John   Prisoner 989. Rank: Seaman, from: Young Eagle, Merchant Vessel.
    Cap: 28 Feb 1814 at Sea by Ringdove Int: 27 Mar 1814 Dis: 03 Aug 1814.
    Received from Ringdove. To American Cartel Brig Aualostaw.

Thomas, Joseph   Prisoner 405. Rank: Seaman, from: Vixen, Man of War.
    Cap: 22 Nov 1812 at Sea by Rhodian late of US Brig Vixen Int: 14 Dec 1812 Dis: 09 May 1813.
    Received from Rhodian. To America for Exchange.

Thomas, Moses   Prisoner 1480. Rank: Seaman, from: Not Recorded, Not Recorded.
    Cap: 21 Dec 1814 at Sea by Severn Int: 04 Feb 1815 Dis: 11 Feb 1815.
    Taken for Passage to Jamaica Depot. Received from Rota. Into HMS Ramillies per order of Sir T M Hardy.

Thomas, Timothy   Prisoner 16. Rank: Seaman, from: Dal, Merchant Vessel.
    Cap: 03 Aug 1812 at Sea by Garland Int: 22 Aug 1812 Dis: 09 May 1813.
    Received from Garland. to America for Exchange.

Thompson, Charles A   Prisoner 365. Rank: Seaman, from: Vixen, Man of War.
    Cap: 22 Nov 1812 at Sea by Rhodian late of US Brig Vixen Int: 14 Dec 1812 Dis: 04 Apr 1813.
    Received from Rhodian. To America for Exchange.

Thompson, George   Prisoner 1485. Rank: Seaman, from: Not Recorded, Not Recorded.
    Cap: 20 Dec 1814 at Sea by Lacedaemonian Int: 04 Feb 1815 Dis: 11 Feb 1815.
    Taken for Passage to Jamaica Depot. Received from Rota. Into HMS Ramillies per order of Sir T M Hardy.

Thompson, James   Prisoner 1453. Rank: Seaman, from: American Gunboats, Not Recorded.
    Cap: 14 Dec 1814 off New Orleans by Boats of the Squadron Int: 30 Jan 1815 Dis: 13 Feb 1815.
    Taken in the American Gun Boats near New Orleans. Received from Ramilies. Into HMS Ramillies per order of Sir T M Hardy.

Thompson, John   Prisoner 352. Rank: Seaman, from: Vixen, Man of War.
    Cap: 22 Nov 1812 at Sea by Rhodian late of HM Brig Vixen Int: 14 Dec 1812 Dis: 09 May 1813.
    Received from Rhodian. To America for Exchange.

Thompson, Joseph   Prisoner 573. Rank: Seaman, from: Defiance, Privateer.
    Cap: 15 Mar 1813 at Sea by Nimrod Int: 17 Mar 1813 Dis: 09 May 1813.
    Received from Nimrod. To America for Exchange.

Thompson, Philip   Prisoner 80. Rank: Seaman, from: Poor Sailor, Privateer.
    Cap: 13 Sep 1812 at Sea by Garland Int: 18 Sep 1812 Died: 12 Dec 1812.
    Received from Garland. Died.

Thompson, Thomas   Prisoner 804. Rank: Seaman, from: Enterprize, Privateer.
    Cap: 15 Nov 1813 at Sea by Argo Int: 19 Nov 1813 Dis: 21 Jul 1814.
    A Carthagenaian. Received from Argo. Board's Order.

Thornton, Walter   Prisoner 204. Rank: Seaman, from: Blandie, Merchant Vessel.
    Cap: 21 Oct 1812 at Sea by Not Recorded Int: 25 Oct 1812 Dis: 24 Jul 1813.
    Recaptured. Taken from the Recapd Schooner Blandie, belonging to the American Privateer Schooner Comet. Received from Sappho. To American Cartel Brig Aualostaw.

American Prisoners of War Held at Jamaica During the War of 1812

Thurston, Troy   Prisoner 174. Rank: Mate, from: Hamilton, Merchant Vessel.
    Cap: 28 Sep 1812 at Sea by Southampton Int: 07 Oct 1812 Dis: 24 Jul 1813.
    Received from Southampton. To American Cartel Brig Aualostaw.

Tier, Albioa   Prisoner 120. Rank: American Pilot, from: Bernardo, Merchant Vessel.
    Cap: 14 Sep 1812 at Sea by Garland Int: 18 Sep 1812 Dis: 11 Nov 1812.
    Schooner under Spanish Colors. Received from Garland. Medosa American Flag of Truce from US bound to Philadelphia.

Tieu, John   Prisoner 845. Rank: Seaman, from: Maria, An American Merchant Schooner.
    Cap: 15 Nov 1813 at Sea by Argo Int: 19 Nov 1813 Died: 08 May 1814.
    Received from Argo. Died at the Hospital.

Tomkins, Joseph   Prisoner 426. Rank: Private, from: Vixen, Man of War.
    Cap: 22 Nov 1812 at Sea by Rhodian Int: 14 Dec 1812 Dis: 09 May 1813.
    Received from Brazier. To America for Exchange.

Tooker, D A   Prisoner 1469. Rank: Seaman, from: Not Recorded, Not Recorded.
    Cap: 21 Dec 1814 at Sea by Severn Int: 04 Feb 1815 Dis: 11 Feb 1815.
    Taken for Passage to Jamaica Depot. Received from Rota. Into HMS Ramillies per order of Sir T M Hardy.

Topoy, Pedro   Prisoner 1068. Rank: Seaman, from: Casada el Narino, Privateer.
    Cap: 29 May 1814 at Sea by HM Ship Rhin Int: 04 Jun 1814 Dis: 10 Aug 1814.
    Carthagenaian. Received from North Star. Board's Order.

Toucy, E   Prisoner 1526. Rank: Seaman, from: Not Recorded, Not Recorded.
    Cap: 08 Dec 1814 at Sea by Albion Int: 04 Feb 1815 Dis: 11 Feb 1815.
    Taken for Passage to Jamaica Depot. Received from Rota. Into HM Ship Rota per order of Sir TM Hardy.

Towley, Henry   Prisoner 48. Rank: Seaman, from: Not Recorded, Not Recorded.
    Cap: 24 Aug 1812 Kingston by Garland Int: 23 Aug 1812 Dis: 09 May 1813.
    apprehended on Shore. Received from Garland. to America for Exchange. (Date of capture after date of internment.)

Towner, Benjamin   Prisoner 1011. Rank: Mate, from: Chance, Privateer.
    Cap: 01 Apr 1814 at Sea by Statira Int: 20 Apr 1814 Dis: 08 May 1814.
    Received from Statira. To Parole.

Townson, George   Prisoner 1266. Rank: Seaman, from: Cora, Merchant Vessel.
    Cap: Not Recorded by Decouverte Int: 10 Sep 1814 Escaped: 18 Dec 1814.
    Received from Decouverte. Escaped. (Date of capture not recorded.)

Trader, William   Prisoner 1504. Rank: Seaman, from: Not Recorded, Not Recorded.
    Cap: 08 Dec 1814 at Sea by Albion Int: 04 Feb 1815 Dis: 11 Feb 1815.
    Taken for Passage to Jamaica Depot. Received from Rota. Into HM Ship Rota per order of Sir TM Hardy.

Travis, James   Prisoner 314. Rank: Seaman, from: Pirtshire, English Merchant Ship.
    Cap: Nov 1812 at Sea by Fawn Int: 06 Dec 1812 Dis: 06 Apr 1813.
    Recaptured. Eagle Privateer. Received from Fawn. To America Cartel Brig Aualostaw. (Day of capture not recorded. Date of discharge associated with To America for Exchange.)

Trout, Nathaniel   Prisoner 322. Rank: Seaman, from: Pirtshire, English Merchant Ship.
    Cap: Nov 1812 at Sea by Fawn Int: 06 Dec 1812 Dis: 24 Jul 1813.
    Recaptured. Eagle Privateer. Received from Fawn. To American Cartel Brig Aualostaw. (Day of capture not recorded.)

Trust, Elijah   Prisoner 145. Rank: Seaman, from: William Penn, Merchant Vessel.
    Cap: 08 Sep 1812 at Sea by Southampton Int: 07 Oct 1812 Dis: 01 Mar 1813.
    Received from Southampton. per Order of Adml Stirling to American Ship William Penn.

Turk, Richard   Prisoner 801. Rank: Surgeon, from: Enterprize, Privateer.
    Cap: 15 Nov 1813 at Sea by Argo Int: 19 Nov 1813 Died: 30 Dec 1813.
    A Carthagenaian. Received from Argo. Killed by the Guard.

Turner, Henry   Prisoner 658. Rank: Seaman, from: Lovely Lass, Privateer.
    Cap: 21 May 1813 at Sea by Circe Int: 23 May 1813 Dis: 01 Aug 1814.
    Received from Forrester. To American Cartel Brig Aualostaw.

Turner, James   Prisoner 206. Rank: Seaman, from: Blandie, Merchant Vessel.
    Cap: 21 Oct 1812 at Sea by Not Recorded Int: 25 Oct 1812 Dis: 24 Jul 1813.
    Recaptured. Taken from the Recapd Schooner Blandie, belonging to the American Privateer Schooner Comet. Received from Sappho. To American Cartel Brig Aualostaw.

Turner, James   Prisoner 961. Rank: Seaman, from: Active, Merchant Vessel.
    Cap: at Sea by Leonidas Int: 25 Jan 1814 Dis: 01 Aug 1814.
    Received from Leonidas. To American Cartel Brig Aualostaw. (Date of capture not recorded.)

American Prisoners of War Held at Jamaica During the War of 1812

Turner, Joshua   Prisoner 1099. Rank: Seaman, from: Jennett, Brig.
    Cap: 29 May 1814 at Sea by HM Ship Rhin Int: 04 Jun 1814 Dis: 02 Jan 1815.
    Taken in the detained Swedish Brig Jennett. Received from North Star. Into HM Ship Sultan per order of Captain John West.

Turner, Michael   Prisoner 362. Rank: Seaman, from: Vixen, Man of War.
    Cap: 22 Nov 1812 at Sea by Rhodian late of US Brig Vixen Int: 14 Dec 1812 Dis: 09 May 1813.
    Received from Rhodian. To America for Exchange.

Turpin, Jacques   Prisoner 978. Rank: Prize Master, from: Suspense, Merchant Vessel.
    Cap: 20 Feb 1814 at Sea by Leviathan Int: 26 Mar 1814 Dis: 21 Jul 1814.
    Received from Mohawk. Board's Order.

Tynes, John   Prisoner 704. Rank: Seaman, from: Lovely Lass, Privateer.
    Cap: 15 May 1813 at Sea by Circe Int: 29 May 1813 Dis: 22 Apr 1814.
    Received from Circe. per Order of R A Brown into the Cupida being a Spanish subject.

Uerin, Julian   Prisoner 1220. Rank: Seaman, from: La Union, Spanish Brig.
    Cap: 03 Aug 1814 at Sea by Variable Int: 06 Aug 1814 Dis: 16 Aug 1814.
    Recaptured from the Carthagenaian Privateer White Horse. Received from Variable. Board's Order.

Underhill, Elijah   Prisoner 738. Rank: Seaman, from: Eliza, Merchant Vessel.
    Cap: 17 Jul 1813 at Sea by Sappho Int: 26 Jul 1813 Dis: 01 Aug 1814.
    Received from Sappho. To American Cartel Brig Aualostaw.

Underhill, Isaac   Prisoner 1358. Rank: Seaman, from: American Gunboats, Not Recorded.
    Cap: 05 Jan 1815 near New Orleans by Plantagenet Int: 27 Jan 1815 Dis: 05 Feb 1815.
    Taken in the American Gun Boats near New Orleans. Received from Ramilies. Into HM Ship Diomede per order of Sir TM Hardy Baronet.

Vack, Pedro   Prisoner 781. Rank: Seaman, from: San Francisco de Paula, Privateer.
    Cap: 02 Oct 1813 at Sea by Forrester Int: 07 Oct 1813 Dis: 11 Jan 1814.
    Received from Forrester. per order.

Van Faivan, Thomas   Prisoner 147. Rank: Seaman, from: William Penn, Merchant Vessel.
    Cap: 08 Sep 1812 at Sea by Southampton Int: 07 Oct 1812 Dis: 01 Mar 1813.
    Received from Southampton. per Order of Adml Stirling to American Ship William Penn.

Vance, Thomas   Prisoner 972. Rank: Not Recorded, from: Packet, Merchant Vessel.
    Cap: 08 Feb 1814 at Sea by Snake Int: 17 Feb 1814 Dis: 01 Aug 1814.
    Received from Snake. To American Cartel Brig Aualostaw.

Vandirson, Samuel   Prisoner 3. Rank: Seaman, from: Assaw, Merchant Vessel.
    Cap: 28 Jul 1812 at Sea by Garland Int: 22 Aug 1812 Dis: 04 Apr 1813.
    Recaptured having been taken by the American Privateer the Paul Jones. Received from Garland. to America for Exchange.

Vanwick, Thomas   Prisoner 457. Rank: Seaman, from: Rachel, Merchant Vessel.
    Cap: 1813 at Sea by Fawn Int: 13 Jan 1812 Died: 30 Jan 1813.
    Received from Sapphire. Died. (Day and month of capture not recorded. Year of internment should be 1813.)

Vasques, Thomas   Prisoner 892. Rank: Seaman, from: San Francisco Navier, Brig.
    Cap: 03 Dec 1813 at Sea by Sappho Int: 15 Dec 1813 Dis: 11 Jan 1814.
    Taken in the Recaptured Spanish Brig. Prize to the Carthagenaian Privateer Carthagenaian. Received from Sappho. per order.

Veitte, Etanne   Prisoner 1129. Rank: Not legible, from: Decatur, Privateer.
    Cap: 05 Jun 1814 at Sea by HM Ship Rhin Int: 20 Jun 1814 Dis: 24 Jun 1814.
    Received from HM Ship Rhin. per order being a Non-Combatant.

Venar, Juan   Prisoner 766. Rank: Seaman, from: San Francisco de Paula, Privateer.
    Cap: 02 Oct 1813 at Sea by Forrester Int: 07 Oct 1813 Dis: 11 Jan 1814.
    Received from Forrester. per order.

Venian, Charles   Prisoner 1336. Rank: Seaman, from: Not Recorded, Not Recorded.
    Cap: at Sea by HMS Shark Int: 07 Jan 1815 Dis: 10 Jan 1815.
    Ship 'Name Unknown'. Received from HMS Shark. Board's Order. (Date of capture not recorded.)

Vincent, David   Prisoner 707. Rank: Seaman, from: Lovely Lass, Privateer.
    Cap: 15 May 1813 at Sea by Circe Int: 29 May 1813 Dis: 28 Jul 1814.
    Received from Circe. Board's Order.

Volapy, Frafan   Prisoner 1081. Rank: Seaman, from: Casada el Narino, Privateer.
    Cap: 29 May 1814 at Sea by HM Ship Rhin Int: 04 Jun 1814 Dis: 18 Aug 1814.
    Carthagenaian. Received from North Star. Board's Order.

Volt, Peter   Prisoner 390. Rank: Seaman, from: Vixen, Man of War.
    Cap: 22 Nov 1812 at Sea by Rhodian late of US Brig Vixen Int: 14 Dec 1812 Dis: 09 May 1813.
    Received from Rhodian. To America for Exchange.

American Prisoners of War Held at Jamaica During the War of 1812

Voss, Matthew   Prisoner 57. Rank: Seaman, from: Not Recorded, Not Recorded.
    Cap: 20 Aug 1812 Not Recorded by Not Recorded   Int: 03 Sep 1812   Dis: 09 May 1813.
    Prison Ship at New Providence. Received from HM Schooner Decouverte. to America for Exchange.

Voudover, Lawrence   Prisoner 1101. Rank: Seaman, from: Romano & Adamante, Merchant Brig.
    Cap: 31 May 1814 at Sea by Leviathan   Int: 17 Jun 1814   Dis: 22 Jul 1814.
    Received from Leviathan. Board's Order.

Wade, Squire R   Prisoner 72. Rank: Seaman, from: Poor Sailor, Privateer.
    Cap: 13 Sep 1812 at Sea by Garland   Int: 18 Sep 1812   Dis: 04 Apr 1813.
    Received from Garland. To America for Exchange.

Waistcoat, Rufus   Prisoner 127. Rank: Seaman, from: Peru, Merchant Vessel.
    Cap: 15 Sep 1812 at Sea by HMS Cyane   Int: 07 Oct 1812   Dis: 24 Jul 1813.
    Received from Cyane. To American Cartel Brig Aualostaw.

Walgrove, Charles   Prisoner 412. Rank: Private, from: Vixen, Man of War.
    Cap: 22 Nov 1812 at Sea by Rhodian   Int: 14 Dec 1812   Dis: 09 May 1813.
    Received from Brazier. To America for Exchange.

Walker, Daniel   Prisoner 1037. Rank: Seaman, from: Jennett, Brig.
    Cap: 29 May 1814 at Sea by HM Ship Rhin   Int: 04 Jun 1814   Dis: 02 Jan 1815.
    Taken in the Swedish Brig Jennet. Received from North Star. Into HM Ship Sultan per order of Captain John West.

Walker, Thomas   Prisoner 1505. Rank: Passenger, from: Not Recorded, Not Recorded.
    Cap: 08 Dec 1814 at Sea by Albion   Int: 04 Feb 1815   Dis: 08 Feb 1815.
    Taken for Passage to Jamaica Depot. Received from Rota. per order of Sir TM Hardy as a Non-Combatant.

Wall, William   Prisoner 1533. Rank: Cook, from: William & Mary, Merchant Vessel.
    Cap: 12 Feb 1815 at Sea by HM Sloop Carnation   Int: 23 Feb 1815   Dis: 30 Mar 1815.
    Received from HM Sloop Carnation. In consequence of Peace with America.

Wallace, John   Prisoner 500. Rank: Master, from: Three Friends, Merchant Vessel.
    Cap: 03 Dec 1812 at Sea by Circe   Int: 10 Feb 1813   Dis: 10 Feb 1813.
    Received from Circe. for Exchange order of VA Stirling.

Walt, Samuel   Prisoner 1319. Rank: Seaman, from: Nettervitte, Merchant Schooner.
    Cap: Not Recorded by HM Sloop Onyx   Int: 30 Dec 1814   Dis: 02 Jan 1815.
    Received from HM Sloop Onyx. Into HM Ship Sultan per order of Captain John West. (Date of capture not recorded.)

Waltham, Charles   Prisoner 275. Rank: Corporal, from: Joseph & Mary, Privateer.
    Cap: 24 Nov 1812 at Sea by Narcissus   Int: 26 Nov 1812   Dis: 24 Jul 1813.
    Received from Narcissus. To American Cartel Brig Aualostaw.

Walton, John   Prisoner 456. Rank: Seaman, from: Rachel, Merchant Vessel.
    Cap: 1813 at Sea by Fawn   Int: 13 Jan 1812   Escaped: 28 Jun 1813.
    Received from Sapphire. Escaped. (Day and month of capture not recorded. Year of internment should be 1813.)

Warden, James   Prisoner 66. Rank: Seaman, from: Elizabeth, Merchant Vessel.
    Cap: 07 Sep 1812 Port Royal by HM Sloop Shark   Int: 17 Sep 1812   Escaped: 01 Feb 1813.
    from the English Merchant Brig Elizabeth. Received from Shark. Escaped. on P Ship 17th.

Warden, James   Prisoner 504. Rank: Seaman, from: Not Recorded, Not Recorded.
    Cap: 03 Feb 1813 Not Recorded by Not Recorded   Int: 03 Feb 1813   Dis: 09 May 1813.
    Retaken. To America for Exchange. (Prisoner number 66.)

Warden, Stephen   Prisoner 1432. Rank: Seaman, from: American Gunboats, Not Recorded.
    Cap: 05 Jan 1815 near New Orleans by Plantagenet   Int: 27 Jan 1815   Dis: 05 Feb 1815.
    Taken in the American Gun Boats near New Orleans. Received from Ramilies. Into HM Ship Diomede per order of Sir TM Hardy Baronet.

Warner, Vincent   Prisoner 1489. Rank: Seaman, from: Not Recorded, Not Recorded.
    Cap: 20 Dec 1814 at Sea by Lacedaemonian   Int: 04 Feb 1815   Dis: 11 Feb 1815.
    Taken for Passage to Jamaica Depot. Received from Rota. Into HMS Ramillies per order of Sir T M Hardy.

Warren, Series   Prisoner 621. Rank: Carpenter, from: Mary Ann, Privateer.
    Cap: 05 May 1813 at Sea by Sapphire   Int: 07 May 1813   Dis: 01 Aug 1814.
    Received from Sapphire. To American Cartel Brig Aualostaw.

Washington, Z   Prisoner 429. Rank: Private, from: Vixen, Man of War.
    Cap: 22 Nov 1812 at Sea by Rhodian   Int: 14 Dec 1812   Dis: 11 Feb 1813.
    Received from Brazier. under 12 years old.

Waters, Louis   Prisoner 1028. Rank: Steward, from: Chance, Privateer.
    Cap: 01 Apr 1814 at Sea by Statira   Int: 20 Apr 1814   Dis: 02 Jan 1815.
    Received from Statira. Into HM Ship Sultan per order of Captain John West.

American Prisoners of War Held at Jamaica During the War of 1812

Watson, Benjamin   Prisoner 137. Rank: Seaman, from: Whim, Merchant Vessel.
    Cap: 04 Oct 1812 at Sea by HM Brig Liberty Int: 07 Oct 1812 Dis: 24 Jul 1813.
    Received from Cyane. To American Cartel Brig Aualostaw.

Watson, William   Prisoner 146. Rank: Seaman, from: William Penn, Merchant Vessel.
    Cap: 08 Sep 1812 at Sea by Southampton Int: 07 Oct 1812 Dis: 01 Mar 1813.
    Received from Southampton. per Order of Adml Stirling to American Ship William Penn.

Webb, James   Prisoner 329. Rank: Seaman, from: Sauders, Merchant Vessel.
    Cap: Nov 1812 at Sea by Merchant Vessel Monarch Int: 09 Dec 1812 Escaped: 01 Feb 1813.
    Received from Monarch. Escaped. (Day of capture not recorded.)

Webster, Michael   Prisoner 1001. Rank: Seaman, from: Farmer's Daughter, Merchant Vessel.
    Cap: 30 Mar 1814 at Sea by Leviathan Int: 03 Apr 1814 Dis: 02 Jan 1815.
    Received from Leviathan. Into HM Ship Sultan per order of Captain John West.

Welaro, Pedro   Prisoner 1057. Rank: Seaman, from: Casada el Narino, Privateer.
    Cap: 29 May 1814 at Sea by HM Ship Rhin Int: 04 Jun 1814 Dis: 18 Aug 1814.
    Carthagenaian. Received from North Star. Board's Order.

Welch, P   Prisoner 1136. Rank: Seaman, from: Decatur, Privateer.
    Cap: 05 Jun 1814 at Sea by HM Ship Rhin Int: 20 Jun 1814 Dis: 02 Jan 1815.
    Received from HM Ship Rhin. Into HM Ship Sultan per order of Captain John West.

Welcott, A   Prisoner 23. Rank: Seaman, from: Dal, Merchant Vessel.
    Cap: 03 Aug 1812 at Sea by Garland Int: 22 Aug 1812 Dis: 03 May 1813.
    Received from Garland. to America for Exchange. (First name not legible.)

Welliston, P   Prisoner 1525. Rank: Seaman, from: Not Recorded, Not Recorded.
    Cap: 08 Dec 1814 at Sea by Albion Int: 04 Feb 1815 Dis: 11 Feb 1815.
    Taken for Passage to Jamaica Depot. Received from Rota. Into HM Ship Rota per order of Sir TM Hardy.

Wells, Anthony   Prisoner 298. Rank: Passenger, from: Mary, Merchant Vessel.
    Cap: 26 Nov 1812 at Sea by Sappho Int: 30 Nov 1812 Dis: 24 Jul 1813.
    Received from Sappho. To American Cartel Brig Aualostaw.

Welsh, John   Prisoner 875. Rank: Seaman, from: Lapwing, Packet.
    Cap: 08 Dec 1813 at Sea by Barrosa Int: 10 Dec 1813 Dis: 01 Aug 1814.
    Recaptured. Received from Barrosa. To American Cartel Brig Aualostaw.

Welsh, William   Prisoner 13. Rank: Seaman, from: Superb, Merchant Vessel.
    Cap: 02 Aug 1812 at Sea by Garland Int: 22 Aug 1812 Dis: 09 May 1813.
    Received from Garland. to America for Exchange.

Wescott, William   Prisoner 1114. Rank: 1 Lieutenant, from: Decatur, Privateer.
    Cap: 05 Jun 1814 at Sea by HM Ship Rhin Int: 20 Jun 1814 Dis: 02 Jan 1815.
    Received from HM Ship Rhin. Into HM Ship Sultan per order of Captain John West.

West, James   Prisoner 1405. Rank: Seaman, from: American Gunboats, Not Recorded.
    Cap: 05 Jan 1815 near New Orleans by Plantagenet Int: 27 Jan 1815 Dis: 05 Feb 1815.
    Taken in the American Gun Boats near New Orleans. Received from Ramilies. Into HM Ship Diomede per order of Sir TM Hardy Baronet.

West, William   Prisoner 474. Rank: Chief Mate, from: Three Friends, Merchant Schooner.
    Cap: 03 Dec 1812 at Sea by Circe Int: 20 Jan 1813 Dis: 10 Feb 1813.
    Received from Circe. for Exchange order of VA Stirling.

Westcott, William   Prisoner 306. Rank: Captain, from: Joseph & Mary, Privateer.
    Cap: 24 Nov 1812 at Sea by Narcissus Int: 05 Dec 1812 Dis: 04 Apr 1813.
    Received from Narcissus. To America for Exchange.

Whedber, Joseph   Prisoner 1117. Rank: Prize Master, from: Decatur, Privateer.
    Cap: 05 Jun 1814 at Sea by HM Ship Rhin Int: 20 Jun 1814 Dis: 02 Jan 1815.
    Received from HM Ship Rhin. Into HM Ship Sultan per order of Captain John West.

Whipple, John   Prisoner 1019. Rank: Seaman, from: Chance, Privateer.
    Cap: 01 Apr 1814 at Sea by Statira Int: 20 Apr 1814 Dis: 02 Jan 1815.
    Received from Statira. Into HM Ship Sultan per order of Captain John West.

White, James   Prisoner 1247. Rank: Passenger but Seaman, from: John, Merchant Vessel.
    Cap: 11 Aug 1814 at Sea by Variable Int: 15 Aug 1814 Dis: 02 Jan 1815.
    Received from Variable. Into HM Ship Sultan per order of Captain John West.

White, Joseph   Prisoner 464. Rank: Seaman, from: Saratoga, Merchant Vessel.
    Cap: 1813 at Sea by Fawn Int: 13 Jan 1813 Dis: 24 Jul 1813.
    Received from Sapphire. To American Cartel Brig Aualostaw. (Day and month of capture not recorded.)

American Prisoners of War Held at Jamaica During the War of 1812

Whitehead, John   Prisoner 1029. Rank: Seaman, from: Not Recorded, Not Recorded.
    Cap: at Sea by Not Recorded Int: 24 Apr 1814 Dis: 02 Jan 1815.
    Retaken in a Dragger. Belonging to the Saucy Jack. Received from Kingston Barracks. Into HM Ship Sultan per order of Captain John West. (Date of capture not recorded.)

Whitman, Henry   Prisoner 288. Rank: Seaman, from: Mary, Merchant Vessel.
    Cap: 26 Nov 1812 at Sea by Sappho Int: 29 Nov 1812 Dis: 09 May 1813.
    Recaptured from Nonsuch Privateer. Received from Sappho. To America for Exchange.

Whitney, William   Prisoner 1093. Rank: Seaman, from: Jennett, Brig.
    Cap: 29 May 1814 at Sea by HM Ship Rhin Int: 04 Jun 1814 Dis: 02 Jan 1815.
    Taken in the detained Swedish Brig Jennett. Received from North Star. Into HM Ship Sultan per order of Captain John West.

Wilboury, David   Prisoner 1096. Rank: Seaman, from: Jennett, Brig.
    Cap: 29 May 1814 at Sea by HM Ship Rhin Int: 04 Jun 1814 Dis: 02 Jan 1815.
    Taken in the detained Swedish Brig Jennett. Received from North Star. Into HM Ship Sultan per order of Captain John West.

Wilkinson, Thomas   Prisoner 1112. Rank: Seaman, from: Romano & Adamante, Merchant Brig.
    Cap: 31 May 1814 at Sea by Leviathan Int: 17 Jun 1814 Dis: 01 Aug 1814.
    Received from Leviathan. Board's Order.

Willey, Andrew   Prisoner 793. Rank: Seaman, from: Not Recorded, Not Recorded.
    Cap: 15 Oct 1813 Not Recorded by Sapphire Int: 15 Oct 1813 Escaped: 04 Feb 1814.
    An American. Received from Sapphire. Escaped.

William, Daniel   Prisoner 150. Rank: Seaman, from: Philip, Merchant Vessel.
    Cap: 10 Sep 1812 at Sea by Southampton Int: 07 Oct 1812 Dis: 01 Mar 1813.
    Received from Southampton. per Order of Adml Stirling to American Ship Philip.

William, Thomas   Prisoner 1450. Rank: Seaman, from: American Gunboats, Not Recorded.
    Cap: 05 Jan 1815 near New Orleans by Plantagenet Int: 27 Jan 1815 Dis: 05 Feb 1815.
    Taken in the American Gun Boats near New Orleans. Received from Ramilies. Into HM Ship Diomede per order of Sir TM Hardy Baronet.

Williams, John   Prisoner 38. Rank: Seaman, from: Petham, Merchant Vessel.
    Cap: 20 Aug 1812 Port Royal by Tartaus Int: 22 Aug 1812 Dis: 09 May 1813.
    Taken from the British Merchant Ship Petham at Port Royal. Received from Tartaus. to America for Exchange.

Williams, John   Prisoner 129. Rank: Seaman, from: Peru, Merchant Vessel.
    Cap: 15 Sep 1812 at Sea by HMS Cyane Int: 07 Oct 1812 Escaped: 28 Jun 1813.
    Received from Cyane. Escaped.

Williams, John   Prisoner 566. Rank: Seaman, from: Defiance, Privateer.
    Cap: 15 Mar 1813 at Sea by Nimrod Int: 17 Mar 1813 Dis: 24 Jul 1813.
    Received from Nimrod. To American Cartel Brig Aualostaw.

Williams, John   Prisoner 693. Rank: Seaman, from: Lovely Lass, Privateer.
    Cap: 15 May 1813 at Sea by Circe Int: 29 May 1813 Dis: 01 Aug 1814.
    Received from Circe. To American Cartel Brig Aualostaw.

Williams, John   Prisoner 976. Rank: Seaman, from: 26th October 1812, Merchant Vessel.
    Cap: 20 Feb 1814 at Sea by Ringdove Int: 20 Feb 1814 Dis: 01 Aug 1814.
    Received from Ringdove. To American Cartel Brig Aualostaw.

Williams, John   Prisoner 1188. Rank: Seaman, from: Decatur, Privateer.
    Cap: 05 Jun 1814 at Sea by HM Ship Rhin Int: 20 Jun 1814 Dis: 02 Jan 1815.
    Received from HM Ship Rhin. Into HM Ship Sultan per order of Captain John West.

Williams, John   Prisoner 1271. Rank: Seaman, from: Wolfe, Not Recorded.
    Cap: at Sea by Jalouse Int: 10 Sep 1814 Dis: 02 Jan 1815.
    American Schooner. Received from Jalouse. Into HM Ship Sultan per order of Captain John West. (Date of capture not recorded.)

Williams, Jordon   Prisoner 862. Rank: Seaman, from: Cato Georgiana, Not Recorded.
    Cap: 28 Nov 1813 at Sea by Barrosa Int: 10 Dec 1813 Dis: 01 Aug 1814.
    Prize to the US Frigate Essex. Received from Barrosa. To American Cartel Brig Aualostaw.

Williams, Joseph   Prisoner 472. Rank: Seaman, from: Cyrus, Merchant Vessel.
    Cap: 03 Jan 1813 at Sea by Rhodian Int: 16 Jan 1813 Dis: 04 Apr 1813.
    Received from Rhodian. To America for Exchange.

Williams, Joseph   Prisoner 647. Rank: Seaman, from: Mary Ann, Privateer.
    Cap: 05 May 1813 at Sea by Sapphire Int: 07 May 1813 Dis: 01 Aug 1814.
    Received from Sapphire. To American Cartel Brig Aualostaw.

Williams, Juan   Prisoner 767. Rank: Seaman, from: San Francisco de Paula, Privateer.
    Cap: 02 Oct 1813 at Sea by Forrester Int: 07 Oct 1813 Dis: 11 Jan 1814.
    Received from Forrester. per order.

American Prisoners of War Held at Jamaica During the War of 1812

Williams, M   Prisoner 230. Rank: Gunners Mate, from: Joseph & Mary, Privateer.
    Cap: 24 Nov 1812 at Sea by Narcissus Int: 26 Nov 1812 Dis: 18 Dec 1812.
    Received from Narcissus. Merchant Ship Experiment for Passage to England.

Williams, William   Prisoner 876. Rank: Seaman, from: Lapwing, Packet.
    Cap: 08 Dec 1813 at Sea by Barrosa Int: 10 Dec 1813 Escaped: 04 Feb 1814.
    Recaptured. Received from Barrosa. Escaped.

Williamson, George   Prisoner 382. Rank: Seaman, from: Vixen, Man of War.
    Cap: 22 Nov 1812 at Sea by Rhodian late of US Brig Vixen Int: 14 Dec 1812 Dis: 04 Apr 1813.
    Received from Rhodian. To America for Exchange.

Williamson, J   Prisoner 1461. Rank: Seaman, from: Not Recorded, Not Recorded.
    Cap: 21 Dec 1814 at Sea by Severn Int: 04 Feb 1815 Dis: 11 Feb 1815.
    Taken for Passage to Jamaica Depot. Received from Rota. Into HMS Ramillies per order of Sir T M Hardy.

Williamson, John   Prisoner 26. Rank: Seaman, from: Madisonia, Merchant Vessel.
    Cap: 03 Aug 1812 at Sea by Garland Int: 22 Aug 1812 Escaped: 15 Nov 1812.
    Received from Garland. Escaped.

Williamson, Richard   Prisoner 727. Rank: Seaman, from: Not Recorded, Not Recorded.
    Cap: Not Recorded by Asia Int: 06 Jul 1813 Dis: 01 Aug 1814.
    An American. Received from Asia. To American Cartel Brig Aualostaw. (Date of capture not recorded.)

Willies, John   Prisoner 1441. Rank: Seaman, from: American Gunboats, Not Recorded.
    Cap: 05 Jan 1815 near New Orleans by Plantagenet Int: 27 Jan 1815 Dis: 05 Feb 1815.
    Taken in the American Gun Boats near New Orleans. Received from Ramilies. Into HM Ship Diomede per order of Sir TM Hardy Baronet.

Willson, Thomas   Prisoner 1446. Rank: Seaman, from: American Gunboats, Not Recorded.
    Cap: 05 Jan 1815 near New Orleans by Plantagenet Int: 27 Jan 1815 Dis: 05 Feb 1815.
    Taken in the American Gun Boats near New Orleans. Received from Ramilies. Into HM Ship Diomede per order of Sir TM Hardy Baronet.

Wilson, A   Prisoner 1389. Rank: Seaman, from: American Gunboats, Not Recorded.
    Cap: 05 Jan 1815 near New Orleans by Plantagenet Int: 27 Jan 1815 Dis: 05 Feb 1815.
    Taken in the American Gun Boats near New Orleans. Received from Ramilies. Into HM Ship Diomede per order of Sir TM Hardy Baronet.

Wilson, Charles   Prisoner 46. Rank: Seaman, from: Not Recorded, Not Recorded.
    Cap: 24 Aug 1812 Kingston by Garland Int: 23 Aug 1812 Dis: 24 Jul 1813.
    apprehended on Shore. Received from Garland. to American Cartel Brig Aualostaw. (Date of capture after date of internment.)

Wilson, Cornelius   Prisoner 462. Rank: Seaman, from: Saratoga, Merchant Vessel.
    Cap: 1813 at Sea by Fawn Int: 13 Jan 1813 Dis: 24 Jul 1813.
    Received from Sapphire. To American Cartel Brig Aualostaw. (Day and month of capture not recorded.)

Wilson, James   Prisoner 858. Rank: Lieutenant, from: Cato Georgiana, Not Recorded.
    Cap: 28 Nov 1813 at Sea by Barrosa Int: 10 Dec 1813 Died: 30 Dec 1813.
    Prize to the US Frigate Essex. Received from Barrosa. Died.

Wilson, John   Prisoner 1359. Rank: Seaman, from: American Gunboats, Not Recorded.
    Cap: 05 Jan 1815 near New Orleans by Plantagenet Int: 27 Jan 1815 Dis: 05 Feb 1815.
    Taken in the American Gun Boats near New Orleans. Received from Ramilies. Into HM Ship Diomede per order of Sir TM Hardy Baronet.

Windfinde, William   Prisoner 844. Rank: Seaman, from: Maria, An American Merchant Schooner.
    Cap: 15 Nov 1813 at Sea by Argo Int: 19 Nov 1813 Dis: 01 Aug 1814.
    Received from Argo. To American Cartel Brig Aualostaw.

Winston, Thomas S   Prisoner 199. Rank: Master, from: Morning Star, Merchant Vessel.
    Cap: 08 Sep 1812 at Sea by Cyane Int: 20 Oct 1812 Dis: 20 Oct 1812.
    Received from Shark. On Parole.

Winter, William   Prisoner 187. Rank: Seaman, from: Rebecca Sims, Merchant Vessel.
    Cap: 12 Sep 1812 at Sea by Southampton Int: 09 Oct 1812 Dis: 01 Mar 1813.
    Received from Southampton. per Order of Admiral Stirling.

Witman, Henry   Prisoner 157. Rank: Seaman, from: Rebecca Sims, Merchant Vessel.
    Cap: 12 Sep 1812 at Sea by Southampton Int: 07 Oct 1812 Dis: 09 May 1813.
    Received from Southampton. per Order of Adml Stirling to William Penn.

Wood, Jacob   Prisoner 340. Rank: Seaman, from: Vixen, Man of War.
    Cap: 22 Nov 1812 at Sea by Rhodian late of HM Brig Vixen Int: 14 Dec 1812 Dis: 04 Apr 1813.
    Received from Rhodian. To America for Exchange.

American Prisoners of War Held at Jamaica During the War of 1812

Wrenenui, Joseph   Prisoner 1295. Rank: Passenger, from: Cora, Letter of Marque.
    Cap: 31 Jul 1814 at Sea by Rota Int: 06 Nov 1814 Dis: 21 Nov 1814.
    Received from Rota. Board's Order.

Wulfurtz, Abraham   Prisoner 265. Rank: Seaman, from: Joseph & Mary, Privateer.
    Cap: 24 Nov 1812 at Sea by Narcissus Int: 26 Nov 1812 Dis: 24 Jul 1813.
    Received from Narcissus. To American Cartel Brig Aualostaw.

Wyatt, Benjamin   Prisoner 215. Rank: Seaman, from: Dominicana, Merchant Vessel.
    Cap: 21 Oct 1812 at Sea by HM Ship Liberty Int: 25 Oct 1812 Dis: 24 Jul 1813.
    Taken out of Brigantine Dominicana by HM Ship Liberty and brot into Port Royal. Received from Decouverte. To American Cartel Brig Aualostaw.

Wynn, John   Prisoner 207. Rank: Seaman, from: Blandie, Merchant Vessel.
    Cap: 21 Oct 1812 at Sea by Not Recorded Int: 25 Oct 1812 Dis: 24 Jul 1813.
    Recaptured. Taken from the Recapd Schooner Blandie, belonging to the American Privateer Schooner Comet. Received from Sappho. To American Cartel Brig Aualostaw.

Wysman, E C   Prisoner 196. Rank: Master, from: William Penn, Merchant Vessel.
    Cap: 28 Sep 1812 at Sea by Southampton Int: 19 Oct 1812 Dis: 19 Oct 1812.
    Received from Southampton. On Parole.

Yohet, Pedro   Prisoner 897. Rank: Captain, from: Cartagenaian, Privateer.
    Cap: 05 Dec 1813 at Sea by Sappho Int: 15 Dec 1813 Died: 30 Dec 1813.
    Belonging to the Carthagenaian Privateer Carthagenaian. Received from Sappho. Killed by the Guard.

Young, Joseph   Prisoner 41. Rank: Seaman, from: Petham, Merchant Vessel.
    Cap: 20 Aug 1812 Port Royal by Tartaus Int: 22 Aug 1812 Escaped: 15 Nov 1812.
    Taken from the British Merchant Ship Petham at Port Royal. Received from Garland. Escaped.

Young, Sampson   Prisoner 1513. Rank: Seaman, from: Not Recorded, Not Recorded.
    Cap: 08 Dec 1814 at Sea by Albion Int: 04 Feb 1815 Dis: 11 Feb 1815.
    Taken for Passage to Jamaica Depot. Received from Rota. Into HM Ship Rota per order of Sir TM Hardy.

Young, Truman   Prisoner 1391. Rank: Seaman, from: American Gunboats, Not Recorded.
    Cap: 05 Jan 1815 near New Orleans by Plantagenet Int: 27 Jan 1815 Dis: 05 Feb 1815.
    Taken in the American Gun Boats near New Orleans. Received from Ramilies. Into HM Ship Diomede per order of Sir TM Hardy Baronet.

Young, William   Prisoner 253. Rank: Seaman, from: Joseph & Mary, Privateer.
    Cap: 24 Nov 1812 at Sea by Narcissus Int: 26 Nov 1812 Dis: 24 Jul 1813.
    Received from Narcissus. To American Cartel Brig Aualostaw.

American Prisoners of War Held at Jamaica During the War of 1812

Numeric listing by prison number

1	Reed, John	71	Randell, Edward
2	Ballow, William	72	Wade, Squire R
3	Vandirson, Samuel	73	Hatcher, Thomas
4	Body, John	74	Moore, William
5	Roe, Cornwel	75	Depont, Lewis
6	Foster, Jonathan	76	Martin, J W
7	Colmen, Christian	77	Bramore, Christopher
8	Leon, Anthony	78	Nicholson, George
9	Bryne, Thomas	79	Bolston, Jacob
10	Mirack, Isaac	80	Thompson, Philip
11	Moservy, Daniel J	81	Freeman, Maul
12	Hamlet, Joshua	82	Dickson, Peter
13	Welsh, William	83	Stevenson, David
14	Baptist, John	84	Brown, Peter
15	Shaw, Francis	85	Thomas, John
16	Thomas, Timothy	86	Cromerty, Vincent
17	Clarke, Alb	87	Pouch, John
18	Broadbew, William	88	Lewis, Francis
19	Davenport, William	89	Dotlaud, Martin
20	Maxey, Elias	90	Gorgaud, Michael
21	Johnson, Thomas	91	Brown, William D
22	Furrall, Thomas	92	Tequin, William
23	Welcott, A	93	Cooper, Sylus
24	Crisby, Ransom	94	Britain, John
25	Belt, James	95	Hasser, John
26	Williamson, John	96	Elliot, Alexander
27	Jervis, William	97	Rosinloof, Thomas
28	Crawford, John	98	Gregon, Francis
29	Ford, Bapt	99	Holston, Isaac
30	Hopkins, Caleb	100	Faviman, Lawrence
31	Jackson, George	101	St. George, George
32	Joseph, Anthony	102	Cochran, Paunay
33	Davis, Wallis	103	Inkley, Thomas
34	Nicholson, Jesse	104	Bailey, Joseph
35	Gomer, Edward	105	Brown, John
36	Budie, Andrew	106	Burdett, Enos
37	Tapp, George	107	Russell, James
38	Williams, John	108	Jennings, Henry
39	Franklin, Edward	109	McLaughlin, P
40	Hutchins, Amos	110	Cocks, John S H
41	Young, Joseph	111	Smart, David
42	Gould, Samuel	112	Chalmers, David
43	Nicholson, John	113	Blair, John K
44	Malther, William	114	Seprast, John
45	Osbourn, Thomas	115	Swain, Luke
46	Wilson, Charles	116	Blenny, William
47	Perkins, Simon	117	Hauscorn, John
48	Towley, Henry	118	Montgomery, G
49	Sandford, Abraham	119	Ray, Moses
50	Allen, James W	120	Tier, Albioa
51	Penn, William	121	Connor, William
52	Hamilton, William	122	Homer, Jacob
53	Hill, Ashmel	123	Allen, Joseph
54	Sturges, E P	124	Settle, Ellis
55	Gilpin, John	125	Benson, John
56	Oliney, Samuel	126	Reid, Robert
57	Voss, Matthew	127	Waistcoat, Rufus
58	Parish, John	128	Stone, Samuel
59	Allen, Ebenezer	129	Williams, John
60	Lombard, Ephrim	130	Hazel, John
61	Dodge, Lewis	131	Coit, S
62	McLaughlin, Edward	132	Brown, James
63	Dolft, John	133	Henry, Thomas
64	Mann, Charles	134	Miller, John
65	Coles, Charles	135	Hatch, Walter
66	Warden, James	136	Mills, James
67	Stewart, Henry	137	Watson, Benjamin
68	Lund, Oliver	138	Garland, Robert
69	Dart, Stanton	139	Lugh, Wright
70	Harrison, Isaac	140	Hamsby, Andrew

American Prisoners of War Held at Jamaica During the War of 1812

141	Gregory, Caspar	212	Brown, Joseph
142	Perkins, Seth	213	Spreggs, Archibald
143	Moss, Elijah	214	Calbert, James
144	Perkins, Joseph	215	Wyatt, Benjamin
145	Trust, Elijah	216	Harris, John Winslow
146	Watson, William	217	Gaul, John
147	Van Faivan, Thomas	218	Peters, John
148	Simpson, James	219	Roberts, G R
149	Godfrey, William	220	Spalding, Reeves
150	William, Daniel	221	Pitt, Gabes
151	Flood, Samuel	222	Shepheard, John
152	Sullen, Peter	223	Gardner, Samuel
153	Paree, S W	224	Cromwell, Joseph
154	Robinson, Thomas	225	Cuthall, Hoste
155	Johnston, Benjamin	226	Summers, Philip
156	Jones, Henry	227	Smith, Benjamin
157	Witman, Henry	228	Cosgrove, J G
158	Hickey, James	229	Storey, John
159	Hall, Daniel	230	Williams, M
160	Stuart, Charles	231	Martin, John
161	Anwiste, Hugh	232	Gluton, M
162	Skakelton, Roger	233	Jordon, Benjamin
163	Daniels, John	234	Jones, Michael
164	Guttring, John	235	Sullivan, Daniel
165	Banks, William	236	Drew, Exra
166	Laman, William	237	Carpenter, Lewis
167	Morris, Jacob	238	Ford, Samuel
168	Stolesby, Anthony	239	De Camp, William
169	Hangerford, John	240	Smith, Charles
170	Jones, Jacob	241	Nelson, John
171	Brown, Daniel	242	Goverman, Frederick
172	Adams, Cornelius	243	Gordon, Worton
173	Peters, John	244	Long, Nathaniel
174	Thurston, Troy	245	Richardson, William
175	Richards, Thomas	246	Clarke, John
176	Market, John	247	Gray, John
177	Elisha, Thomas	248	Peek, Darius
178	Patterson, N	249	Bremfield, George
179	Rosin, John	250	Loring, Elephet
180	Christie, William	251	Lewis, Winslow
181	Lee, John Roger	252	Smith, Robert
182	Garbin, John	253	Young, William
183	Hart, George	254	Bond, Abraham
184	Brewton, William	255	Lee, Henry
185	Selby, Miles	256	Satchell, Thomas
186	Frances, Henry	257	Hill, Ross
187	Winter, William	258	Fifer, Jacob
188	Patterson, M	259	Roberts, Samuel
189	Dyer, Watson	260	Beard, Andrew
190	Smith, John	261	Davis, John
191	Seale, Charles	262	Metz, George
192	Layton, N G	263	Rutter, William
193	Kroger, John	264	Davidson, Samuel
194	Layton, N G	265	Wulfurtz, Abraham
195	Branson, M	266	Bettys, Henry
196	Wysman, E C	267	Roe, John
197	Hall, John	268	Gleeves, Jacob
198	Brewton, M	269	Dixon, James
199	Winston, Thomas S	270	Slippy, William
200	Means, Robert	271	Patton, Edward
201	Stevens, Leverett	272	Edgerton, Charles
202	Dyer, John	273	Leuox, John
203	Bryan, George	274	Bayley, Gardner
204	Thornton, Walter	275	Waltham, Charles
205	Bell, John	276	Graham, John
206	Turner, James	277	Barr, Benjamin
207	Wynn, John	278	De Fatrime, Jacque
208	McGlachan, Turner	279	Dallew, James
209	Clarke, Bernard	280	Hazledine, John
210	Marley, John	281	Forster, William
211	Cain, William	282	Henry, William

American Prisoners of War Held at Jamaica During the War of 1812

283	Everson, Benjamin	354	Bradley, Abraham
284	Purdew, Joseph	355	David, Charles
285	Small, Jacob	356	Ram, Thomas
286	Joseph, John	357	Quick, George
287	Stevenson, George	358	Orno, John
288	Whitman, Henry	359	Peter, Solomon
289	May, Nicholas	360	Davis, John
290	Bucklin, Warren	361	Jarua, Charles
291	Berry, James	362	Turner, Michael
292	Brown, James	363	Dunbar, Charles
293	Hunter, Francis	364	Clury, William
294	Pitner, Aaron	365	Thompson, Charles A
295	Strong, Selvister	366	Jacobs, Charles
296	Rolston, Leven	367	Furney, John
297	Jones, John	368	Rice, Samuel
298	Wells, Anthony	369	Smith, John
299	Tagers, Anthony	370	Peters, John
300	Cuffy, Paul	371	Knull, Heinrich
301	Cropper, Isaac	372	Johnson, Abraham
302	Lynn, John	373	Leggett, George
303	Hutchins, B	374	Call, Benjamin
304	Stevens, Russel	375	Leof, Unis
305	Moore, William	376	Bridges, Edward
306	Westcott, William	377	Dykes, Sol
307	Howland, Barnalas	378	Fraser, John
308	Moore, Thomas	379	Harris, John
309	Dotterside, William	380	Harvey, James
310	Parker, Joseph	381	Cunningham, James
311	Buch, Josuah	382	Williamson, George
312	Pratt, Allen	383	Merritt, Erek
313	Reynolds, Christian	384	Elms, Robert
314	Travis, James	385	Hauagan, Peter
315	Reick, Nicholas	386	Stokes, John
316	Miller, Christian	387	Kawson, George
317	Le Jea, Artimus	388	Crawford, Robert
318	Nachidon, Francis	389	Jordan, John G
319	Carrol, John	390	Volt, Peter
320	Diamond, John	391	Brown, Philip
321	Apt, James	392	Dickey, Robert
322	Trout, Nathaniel	393	Summer, John
323	Donaldson, Frederick	394	Knowlton, David
324	Denike, John	395	Dore, James
325	Marie, John	396	Jenkins, John
326	Seburia, Thomas	397	Nutter, George
327	McLear, Francis	398	Davis, John
328	Clackston, James	399	Graves, J
329	Webb, James	400	Jackson, George
330	George, William	401	Mackey, Michael
331	John, Cato	402	Burrows, Edward
332	Norris, Samuel	403	Emmery, David
333	Jackson, William	404	Brown, Obadiah
334	Fairo, James	405	Thomas, Joseph
335	Simon, Jerome	406	Borrison, John
336	Graperius, John	407	Arrickson, D
337	McKinnee, James	408	Smith, Timothy
338	Montgomery, R	409	Heber, Neil
339	McCormick, James	410	Sales, Samuel
340	Wood, Jacob	411	Millega, Gilbert
341	Staggs, Thomas	412	Walgrove, Charles
342	Hartman, John	413	Quigley, Matthew
343	Patterson, John	414	Joiner, Benjamin
344	Mattolland, William	415	Keller, John
345	Goldrick, William	416	Closcharden, John
346	Carrott, William	417	Betincourt, Lewis
347	Elberte, Mingo	418	De Maury, Lewis
348	Fokey, William	419	Round, William
349	Harvey, Michael	420	Mansfield, James
350	Selby, Joseph	421	Ammors, John
351	Alexander, James	422	O'Neal, Andrew
352	Thompson, John	423	Larkins, John
353	McCabe, Levi	424	John, Peter

American Prisoners of War Held at Jamaica During the War of 1812

425	Betincourt, Nathaniel A		496	Renneck, Isaac
426	Tomkins, Joseph		497	Elford, Roswell
427	Allen, Asa		498	Hubbard, Elijah
428	Monteque, Caleb		499	Foster, Samuel
429	Washington, Z		500	Wallace, John
430	Bayley, Frederick		501	Brydges, Culpeper
431	Sullender, C		502	Hutchins, B
432	Shephard, Joseph		503	Spragge, Archibald
433	McFart, John		504	Warden, James
434	Stevens, James		505	Brydges, Culpeper
435	King, Thomas		506	Burdeck, Enos
436	Cutter, Abraham		507	Goverman, Frederick
437	Cocks, William		508	Merit, Isaac
438	Horseley, Samuel		509	Hart, George
439	Satterwhite, Edwin		510	Leon, Anthony
440	Reed, G W		511	Clarke, John
441	Drayton, Glen		512	Sandford, Abraham
442	Davis, E R		513	Davenport, William
443	Hunter, William M		514	Freeman, Thomas
444	Shields, William		515	Pluck, Mike
445	Blace, James		516	Taylor, Alexander
446	Evans, John		517	Rogers, Thomas
447	Carter, James		518	Dick, David
448	McNeil, Archibald		519	Chapel, John Peter
449	Pettigrew, Thomas		520	Jantzue, Lewis
450	King, Thomas		521	Allen, John
451	Cutter, Abraham		522	McBride, James
452	Cox, William		523	Dursse, Laurence
453	Moucrieff, James		524	Gebeau, Anthony
454	Lewis, Eben A		525	Depot, Henry
455	Harrison, James		526	Simon, Joseph
456	Walton, John		527	Dewallis, Macklin
457	Vanwick, Thomas		528	Blakely, Sinclair
458	Chapman, J L		529	Currey, George
459	Neal, Francis		530	Devenero, Francis
460	Befay, Samuel		531	Madura, Francisco
461	Squibb, Silas		532	Jack, John
462	Wilson, Cornelius		533	Jacob, John
463	Cleburn, Francis		534	Baptist, Joseph
464	White, Joseph		535	Manyard, John
465	Cowloff, Jacob		536	Fisher, John
466	Cotterell, Thomson		537	Caderer, John
467	Sewell, George		538	Berto, John
468	Curtis, Dennis		539	Homan, William
469	John, Samuel		540	Ray, John
470	Hields, William		541	Lacette, John
471	Green, John		542	Ioe, Francis
472	Williams, Joseph		543	Joseph, John
473	Nichols, Jacob		544	Durant, John
474	West, William		545	Gebeau, John
475	Grant, Israel		546	Robins, Thomas
476	Johnson, Joseph		547	Blackford, John
477	Fenhold, David		548	Frank, John
478	Course, Peter		549	Jenkins, Luderwick
479	Martin, John		550	Littlefield, Erick
480	Fawcett, Elles		551	Baker, William
481	Hill, John		552	Nyon, Francis
482	Gebson, James		553	Darssliu, John
483	Hirst, Charles		554	Lewis, John
484	Baldwin, Pearson		555	John, John
485	Holmes, William		556	Daily, William
486	Croker, Daul		557	Scott, Eleazer
487	Foxwill, George		558	Gerloo, Peter
488	Allen, Henry		559	Brian, Peter
489	Diskanskep, Christian		560	Seldon, John
490	Glen, Peter		561	Prior, John
491	Baker, James		562	Case, John
492	Header, William		563	Forkiere, Edward
493	Jones, Peter		564	Little, Peter
494	Brown, Thomas		565	Morterae, John
495	Davis, Luther		566	Williams, John

American Prisoners of War Held at Jamaica During the War of 1812

567	Chessm, George		638	Norris, Gilles
568	Dyer, Shubald		639	Blain, David
569	Powell, John		640	Jones, Samuel
570	Paptist, John		641	Meleache, Jean
571	Cable, Peter		642	Hiley, David
572	La Fait, Lewis		643	Robinson, James
573	Thompson, Joseph		644	Leatherby, Joseph
574	Furneau, George		645	Field, Henry
575	Butil, Francis		646	Latham, Jerry
576	Lamber, Pier		647	Williams, Joseph
577	Barlez, Juan		648	Clermont, J B
578	Anthony, Francisco		649	Pascal, Antonio
579	Joseph, Peter		650	Davis, John
580	Bernard, Leonard		651	Arbona, John
581	Dusane, Levi		652	Hine, Henry
582	Jasser, Juan		653	Jackson, John
583	Pane, Cheny		654	Barlow, Aroa
584	Anthony, Juan		655	Griffin, Samuel
585	Mauwi, Juan		656	McNeil, Daniel
586	Heger, Francisco		657	Maxwell, William
587	Peter, Juan		658	Turner, Henry
588	Antonio, Jean		659	Fraunswell, Lewis
589	Francisco, Juan		660	Lott, John
590	Pole, Juan		661	Neil, Jeremiah
591	Nelson, Jean		662	Dick, John
592	Cadinetto, Robert		663	Alexander, Samuel
593	Nelson, Piere		664	Simpson, James
594	Roysdon, Joseph		665	Courade, Christopher
595	Barderse, Josse		666	Nixon, Lewis
596	Albertman, John		667	Carter, Joshua
597	Roper, John		668	Sasky, John
598	Piere, Jean		669	Lowrie, Joseph
599	Logine, Zamie		670	Hanson, Edward
600	---, Hermon		671	Sturko, P
601	Clarke, John		672	Dibwa, John
602	Burke, Thomas		673	Smith, Joseph
603	Gough, Moses		674	Bisong, Juba
604	Samson, Pure		675	Murtien, Charles
605	Anquin, Anthony		676	Ribe, Francis
606	Merrhew, Joseph		677	Montgomery, Thomas
607	Elleridge, James H		678	Smith, David
608	Brown, William		679	Martin, Luther
609	Berlack, William		680	Jocelyn, John
610	Owen, Francis		681	Marsback, John F
611	Clark, Sylvester		682	Rosemond, William
612	Marshall, D F		683	Middleton, Thomas
613	Chariol, Peter		684	Dolph, Joseph
614	Dutuor, John		685	Branson, C J
615	Duprat, Anthony		686	Johnson, Charles
616	Harry, Richard		687	Croker, Lemiel
617	Gree, Joseph		688	Emar, Joseph
618	Gowdon, F E		689	Seutimand, Alexander
619	Harvey, Peter		690	Cloud, Peter
620	Martin, Francis		691	Moore, Jonathan
621	Warren, Series		692	Eden, Thomas
622	Sidawire, Julian		693	Williams, John
623	Chine, Peter		694	Barnes, John
624	---, Luidoff		695	Ghering, John
625	George, Thomas		696	Roberts, Michael
626	Porrn, Joseph		697	Army, Lewis
627	Bata, Peter		698	Foutnay, Francis
628	Boudmon, Andrew		699	Saumon, Pier
629	Balard, Peter		700	Frank, Peter
630	Lactie, John		701	Maddison, Charless
631	Baley, Oliver		702	Leut, William
632	Jones, John		703	Heschaultz, Charles
633	Cassaire, John		704	Tynes, John
634	Lirour, Peter		705	Cute, William
635	Carbon, John		706	McCulloch, Alexander
636	Keith, Thomas		707	Vincent, David
637	Lopez, Francis		708	Drummond, Robert

American Prisoners of War Held at Jamaica During the War of 1812

709	Miller, Oliver	780	---, ---
710	Emery, John	781	Vack, Pedro
711	Sears, Zebrua	782	Cassack, Charles
712	Mitchell, Elisha	783	---, Felis
713	McClintock, William	784	Powell, Juan
714	Smith, James	785	Catalante, Imannual
715	Griffiths, Edward	786	Carruation, Corui
716	Goss, John	787	Pedro, Juan
717	Ogdon, Thomas	788	Francisco, Jose
718	Potts, Samuel	789	Phillips, Bertram
719	Miller, Thomas	790	Cordelia, Nicholas
720	Cameron, America	791	Cabais, Pedro
721	Eastward, Jack	792	Flurit, Aman
722	Baker, Peter	793	Willey, Andrew
723	Cameron, Eli	794	Hawthorn, William
724	Johnson, Dick	795	Hauce, John H
725	Lewis, John	796	Dexter, Charles
726	Dixon, Moses	797	Morando, Domingo
727	Williamson, Richard	798	Randales, Thomas
728	Frederick, John	799	Doing, D O
729	Crosier, William	800	Ball, E
730	Robb, Charles	801	Turk, Richard
731	Pearce, David	802	Molaneir, Pedro
732	Farmer, Robert	803	---, Martin
733	Lloyd, Robert	804	Thompson, Thomas
734	Harrington, Samuel	805	Oure, Constant
735	Orne, Julian	806	Rough, Daniel
736	Robinson, Richard	807	---, Oseana
737	Morris, Benjamin	808	Court, John
738	Underhill, Elijah	809	---, Bechariah
739	MaCarty, Frederick	810	Bartire, John
740	Phillips, John	811	Stan, Pedro
741	Skinner, Lewis	812	Ambrosia, John
742	Murdock, Archibald	813	Jackerman, Count
743	Deale, William	814	Laniba, Michael
744	McDonald, Daniel	815	Marine, Daniel
745	Mitchell, James	816	Gasee, Nicholas
746	Dalbrow, Daniel	817	Puosa, Joseph
747	Aurry, Lewis	818	Bezzett, Robert
748	Barritt, Roman	819	Butcher, Jacob
749	Lacurries, Juan Batista	820	Boyia, Thomas
750	Fernandes, Euscbio	821	Barlow, John
751	Papil, Sauteaga	822	Rodrigo, Andrew
752	Jose, Thomas	823	Robien, John
753	Augustine, Cadet	824	Pedro, Manuel
754	Forne, Barto	825	Jennings, Francis
755	Legre, Juan	826	---, Chripo
756	Noche, Juan	827	---, Georges
757	Porto, Juan	828	Jack, John
758	---, Francisco	829	---, Joseph
759	Saladin, Carlos	830	
760	Martin, Juan	831	Pedro, John
761	Boale, Jose	832	Pierre, John
762	de Cruz, Juan	833	---, Francisco
763	Luis, Pedro	834	---, Manuel
764	Begotte, Juan	835	Pedro, John
765	Baptista, Antonio	836	Jackson, John
766	Venar, Juan	837	---, Antonio
767	Williams, Juan	838	Lane, Thomas
768	La Cruz, Juan	839	Orick, John
769	---, Velario	840	Haman, John
770	Juan, Pedro	841	Fishwort, William
771	Capura, Nicholas	842	Allen, Francis
772	---, Ventura	843	Brown, William
773	Guy, Luis	844	Windfinde, William
774	---, Celestier	845	Tieu, John
775	Rodriguez, Antonio	846	Lewis, Peter
776	La Lauda, Pedro	847	Lock, N
777	Sario, Juan	848	Smith, John
778	Luero, Pedro	849	La Place, Peter
779	Basante, Jose	850	Charrier, Jean B

American Prisoners of War Held at Jamaica During the War of 1812

851	Aquire, Bernardo		922	Jose, Pedro
852	Chambierre, Joseph		923	Maltes, Francisco
853	Chambiere, Theodore		924	Lacroyde, Houore
854	Mazire, Francis		925	Sinpire, Pedro
855	Edward, Pierre		926	Rousseau, Juan
856	Cezard, J		927	Arrvis, Jose
857	Reuon, Santiago		928	Mery, Pedro
858	Wilson, James		929	Petet, Jean
859	Scott, John		930	Josef, Jean
860	Piper, Henry		931	Rodriques, Luis
861	Carlton, Thomas		932	Carrura, Josef
862	Williams, Jordon		933	Berry, Gorton
863	Haufield, Jonathan		934	Joseph, John
864	Jemmison, Charles		935	Coleby, John
865	O'Neil, Edward		936	Peurice, Thomas
866	Dixon, James		937	Goreham, John
867	Chamberlain, John		938	Henry, John
868	Stewart, James W		939	Askew, James
869	Gilbert, Martin		940	Roteu, Peter
870	Dibbett, Charles A		941	Otto, Nicholas
871	Sole, Jordan		942	Chamstead, John
872	Clarke, George		943	Martin, John
873	Jerry, Mathias H		944	Allen, Bernard
874	Gibbons, John		945	Smith, Robert
875	Welsh, John		946	Kelly, Stephen
876	Williams, William		947	Hill, William
877	Johnson, Samuel J		948	Buck, Balthazar
878	Miles, Robert		949	Rodrigues, Manuel
879	Jennings, John		950	Peabody, John
880	Brown, John		951	Cater, Benjamin
881	Bowlin, John		952	Croft, William
882	Corral, Philip		953	Lee, William
883	Bennett, James		954	Dow, Thomas
884	Gould, Thomas		955	Beari, Samuel
885	St. Clair, Robert		956	Millet, Andrew
886	Nowland, John		957	Parsons, William
887	Nelson, James		958	Eagelson, David
888	Olmer, Joseph		959	Day, Ephram
889	Brown, John		960	Parsons, Isaac
890	Montati, Antonio		961	Turner, James
891	Rodriguez, Manuel		962	Parsons, George
892	Vasques, Thomas		963	Carter, James
893	Micridales, Joseph		964	Buntly, Isom
894	Talon, Francisco		965	Griffin, William B
895	Dupies, Alexander		966	Grandy, Poll
896	Rosse, Henri		967	Le Rose, Ramoin
897	Yohet, Pedro		968	La Cloud, Peter
898	Peres, Juan Francisco		969	Richmond, William
899	Deas, Manuel		970	Campbell, E
900	Guiterroz, Francisco N		971	Douglass, John
901	Masse, Juan M		972	Vance, Thomas
902	Marciar, Juan		973	Lewis, James H
903	Silotic, Antonio		974	Pratt, George S
904	Gomie, Andres		975	Saue, Aaron
905	Ordet, Tal		976	Williams, John
906	Blanco, Carlo		977	Gabriel, James
907	---, Piudtel		978	Turpin, Jacques
908	Peliou, Jose		979	Burnham, William
909	Coturel, Juan		980	Bachindoz, Enock
910	---, Autouel		981	Mackey, John
911	Barchela, Andres		982	Serin, John
912	Tebot, Pedro		983	Kirby, John
913	de Legran, Juan		984	Onil, Henry
914	Dolore, Juan		985	Miller, James
915	Cherin, Pedro		986	Snow, Samuel
916	Gerin, Luis		987	Dauast, Nicholas
917	Barrel, Juan		988	Oldner, George
918	Batista, Luis		989	Thomas, John
919	Tebez, Martin		990	Blair, Thomas
920	Rosario, Francisco		991	Brown, John
921	Sarasin, Fifi		992	Theobald, Charles

American Prisoners of War Held at Jamaica During the War of 1812

993	Hurst, James		1064	Dias, Andrew
994	Benton, Samuel		1065	Leceux, Augustine
995	Dawson, John		1066	Geraldine, Jose
996	Edwards, William		1067	Aquilar, Pedro Jose
997	Antonio, Joseph		1068	Topoy, Pedro
998	Kingdom, John		1069	Gregorio, Juan
999	Johnson, Thomas		1070	Luis, Juan
1000	Carlo, James		1071	---, Deudoit
1001	Webster, Michael		1072	Cebo, Francisco
1002	Griffin, Heathcote		1073	Bantista, Juan
1003	Roderick, Anthony		1074	Bisar, Julian
1004	Johnson, Robert		1075	Fernandez, Francisco
1005	Porter, Hans		1076	Padelia, F
1006	Smith, Robert		1077	Fernandez, Emanuel
1007	Smith, John		1078	Corez, Juan Jose
1008	Martin, William		1079	Sanchez, Simon
1009	Butler, Henry		1080	De Pena, N
1010	Derrick, William		1081	Volapy, Frafan
1011	Towner, Benjamin		1082	Goumar, J
1012	Armstrong, Charles		1083	Thomas, Francisco
1013	Hauseir, Peter		1084	Alexander, Luis
1014	Butler, David		1085	Care, Beatte
1015	Homan, John		1086	Calluga, Damasco
1016	Batiste, John		1087	---, Comasin
1017	Davis, Daul		1088	Aquilaro, J
1018	Little, William		1089	Deledra, Francisco
1019	Whipple, John		1090	Gorton, Luis
1020	Busher, Lawrence		1091	Baco, F
1021	Smith, Benjamin		1092	Guchand, Coco
1022	Maceman, Thomas		1093	Whitney, William
1023	Macklin, John		1094	Kuntoz, Jacob
1024	Gale, Russel		1095	Pickens, Thomas
1025	Dennet, William		1096	Wilboury, David
1026	Hill, Francis		1097	Key, John
1027	Dominico, John		1098	Dyer, Charles
1028	Waters, Louis		1099	Turner, Joshua
1029	Whitehead, John		1100	Stanley, Simon
1030	Smith, John		1101	Voudover, Lawrence
1031	Robisa, Victor		1102	Boughon, Miguel
1032	McCormick, James		1103	de Manuel, Juz
1033	Salisbury, Jose		1104	Manuel, J
1034	Pockmet, Zackuess		1105	Antonio, Juan P
1035	Devaril, John		1106	Baptista, Juan
1036	Mackboy, John		1107	Speries, Thomas
1037	Walker, Daniel		1108	Antonio, Joseph
1038	Holmes, Isaac		1109	de Anuila, Peadro
1039	Clark, James		1110	Johnson, Abraham
1040	de doVair, Epprough		1111	Hulse, G J
1041	Skipper, John		1112	Wilkinson, Thomas
1042	Gowner, Joseph		1113	Dixon, Dominique
1043	Harris, John		1114	Wescott, William
1044	Secan, St Yago		1115	Tesser, Sean
1045	Raysan, Pedro		1116	Bouepou, Antonie
1046	---, Boungault		1117	Whedber, Joseph
1047	Lang, Jose		1118	Steel, John
1048	Casera, Juan		1119	Taylor, William
1049	---, Leverien		1120	McNeil, Daniel
1050	Figuire, G		1121	Phillips, William
1051	Fortunel, Pedro		1122	Phyning, Josiah
1052	---, Gasparo		1123	Laory, Josh
1053	Gomez, Felipe		1124	Goding, Joseph
1054	---, Boudon		1125	Ghado, Maina
1055	Robert, Pedro		1126	Disgardins, Louis J
1056	Legal, Juan		1127	---, Lefure
1057	Welaro, Pedro		1128	Lagoardett, Pedro
1058	Roco, Thomas		1129	Veitte, Etanne
1059	Dreux, Edmond		1130	Pierro, Jean
1060	Julian, Quitnet		1131	Eperwiere, Jean
1061	Joagin, Pedro		1132	Michell, Jean Batista
1062	---, Isaac		1133	Michel, Chouran
1063	Leneel, Francis		1134	Gabeirre, John

American Prisoners of War Held at Jamaica During the War of 1812

1135	Joseph, William	1206	Philips, John
1136	Welch, P	1207	Cambell, Henry
1137	Day, S	1208	Hendry, William
1138	Street, James	1209	Collins, John
1139	Norins, William	1210	Smith, Charles
1140	Johnson, Charles	1211	Moore, William
1141	Johnson, William	1212	Hicks, Benjamin
1142	Combs, John	1213	Ketchell, George
1143	Artego, John	1214	Lounsby, Frederick
1144	Mancell, John	1215	Brown, William
1145	Seagrave, Jean	1216	Fivash, John
1146	Puritan, Themat	1217	Buckley, Walter
1147	Manger, Gear	1218	Mealo, Vinzente
1148	Renard, Jean	1219	Beltram, Martin
1149	---, Gout	1220	Uerin, Julian
1150	Boutel, Isaac	1221	Martel, Pedro
1151	Poteron, Julian	1222	Napo, Casar
1152	Lamel, Louis	1223	Aquilar, Lorenzo
1153	Amontage, Louis	1224	Peres, Domingo
1154	Lorique, G	1225	Rabuirero, Nicolas
1155	Nolt, Paul	1226	Mosquera, Jose
1156	Phdiger, John	1227	Lopes, Victorino
1157	Gillbert, Antonio	1228	Damian, Jose
1158	Adrie, Domingo	1229	Perez, M Antonio
1159	Detale, Juan	1230	Belor, Miguel
1160	Caximo, Josef M	1231	Neo, Juan
1161	Dequen, Julian	1232	Francisco, Juan
1162	Brown, John	1233	Crostinal, Demetreo
1163	Martin, Louis	1234	Pedro, Juan
1164	Rionaine, Jean	1235	---, Sequnda
1165	Class, Jean	1236	Johnson, Robert
1166	Saffarque, Andrew	1237	Peck, Salisbury
1167	Decossae, Louis	1238	Coursoll, Peter
1168	Callerist, Collin	1239	Merritt, Samuel
1169	Callerist, Y P	1240	Charles, Stephen
1170	Dixon, P	1241	Lenquish, Mathew
1171	Peters, George	1242	Fleury, Joseph
1172	---, Pick a Pick	1243	Henderson, Joseph
1173	---, Bentogomery	1244	Betagh, James
1174	---, Duchazrell	1245	Hyer, Rober
1175	Dolino, Angel	1246	Furrell, John
1176	Drago, Francisco	1247	White, James
1177	Daimont, Louis	1248	Hinchman, George
1178	---, Lefarque	1249	Jacob, Louis
1179	Denis, Generio	1250	Lassetto, Joseph
1180	Peland, Louis Marie	1251	Rosiere, Celestian
1181	Bloham, Behrand	1252	Jaque, Jacinta Jean
1182	Jacobson, Frederick	1253	Martini, Alberto
1183	Free, George	1254	Pujne, Dominique
1184	Beck, Francisco	1255	Albarets, Alanasta
1185	Lewis, Valentine	1256	Bertrand, Jean
1186	Aucruen, John	1257	Hyde, Thomas
1187	Charleston, Joseph	1258	List, Moses
1188	Williams, John	1259	Harris, William
1189	Antonio, Manuel	1260	Maddison, Samuel
1190	Roshin, Dominique	1261	Paillet, Peter Noel
1191	---, Dupre	1262	Brown, John
1192	Phillips, John	1263	Battle, Joseph
1193	Fuller, Peter	1264	French, Abraham
1194	Davis, G P	1265	Parsons, James
1195	Harris, Robert	1266	Townson, George
1196	Manusa, Osa	1267	Porter, William
1197	Manwell, Antonio	1268	Harrison, Samuel
1198	Rodriguez, Oza	1269	Black, Joseph
1199	Marta, Pedro	1270	Swatoz, Chuspere
1200	Clemon, Pierre	1271	Williams, John
1201	Betrange, Pedro	1272	Pepper, Martin
1202	Maria, Jon	1273	Cornelius, Peter
1203	Peter, Mathias	1274	Liberal, August
1204	Pairer, Francis	1275	Bodeye, Michael
1205	Bowen, John	1276	Bateiers, Platricia

American Prisoners of War Held at Jamaica During the War of 1812

1277	Bernard, Peter		1348	Gomand, Joseph
1278	Key, Oleanto		1349	Hall, Charles
1279	Romero, Ignacio		1350	Lane, John
1280	Hernandes, Nicholas		1351	Black, William
1281	Baque, Jean		1352	Harrison, Samuel
1282	Bilot, Pierre		1353	Kinner, Joseph S
1283	Bilot, Pierre An		1354	Green, Peter C
1284	Savanel, Jean G		1355	Perry, John
1285	Drew, Edmond		1356	Mememey, James
1286	Faulin, Joseph		1357	Godfrey, William
1287	Alexander, Lewis		1358	Underhill, Isaac
1288	Lapongau, Chery		1359	Wilson, John
1289	Lespioult, Francis		1360	Moon, Isaac
1290	Clarke, John		1361	Hibbard, George
1291	Martin, Richard		1362	Anderson, John
1292	Lewis, Augustus		1363	Gibson, John
1293	Bailey, Samuel		1364	Jones, William
1294	Borely, David		1365	Brown, James
1295	Wrenenui, Joseph		1366	Edwards, William
1296	Iglecia, Juan		1367	McPhid, Reynold
1297	Niel, Herrea		1368	Forewell, George
1298	Fox, Edward		1369	Sadler, William
1299	Laurence, Francis		1370	Barker, Abraham
1300	Destandes, Joseph		1371	Carpenter, Benezer
1301	Ramsdell, Charles		1372	Chinny, John
1302	McCarthy, Samuel		1373	Demon, John
1303	Fencho, Eiten		1374	Morris, George
1304	Jones, Henry		1375	Jarvis, John
1305	Jones, Cato		1376	Connor, John
1306	Little, Charles		1377	Smith, John
1307	Baker, Thomas		1378	Reynolds, James
1308	Southcombe, Peter		1379	Price, Charles
1309	Jenkins, Thomas		1380	Guerd, Joseph
1310	Harvey, James		1381	McChrystal, Edward
1311	Hindman, John		1382	Parleman, William
1312	Baptiste, John		1383	Daly, John
1313	Kell, Francis		1384	Handley, William
1314	Kitten, Abraham		1385	Taylor, John
1315	Brackston, William		1386	Corwell, Timothy
1316	Cooper, Peter		1387	Shitcatt, Richard
1317	Madding, John		1388	Hart, Philip
1318	Jones, James		1389	Wilson, A
1319	Walt, Samuel		1390	Shamberk, Henry
1320	Johnnos, Logan		1391	Young, Truman
1321	Baldwin, Theophilus		1392	Crosby, James
1322	Handy, Joseph		1393	Bakers, G D
1323	Davis, Richman		1394	Falls, Richard
1324	Bommell, Andre		1395	Cunningham, Henry
1325	Antonio, Jose		1396	Nowland, James
1326	Andre, Antonie		1397	Johnson, James
1327	Natal, Juan		1398	Davidson, William
1328	Carnation, Jose		1399	Clay, William
1329	Charles, John		1400	Rowley, Isaac
1330	Diani, Lewis		1401	Brown, James A
1331	Berios, Samoa		1402	Stevens, Francis
1332	Gomand, Pierre		1403	Carter, Henry
1333	Carier, Pierre		1404	Simmons, James
1334	Maria, Joseph		1405	West, James
1335	Bouche, John		1406	Cooney, Joseph
1336	Venian, Charles		1407	Bennett, William
1337	Morean, Guettend		1408	Stewart, Charles
1338	Fertizon, Rene		1409	Jackson, Henry
1339	Louis, Pierre		1410	Cricktus, Henry
1340	Marque, Antonio		1411	Horton, Richard
1341	Navallo, Diego		1412	Cowan, Jonathan
1342	Bortiense, Jacques		1413	Cottwell, Rowland
1343	Fertion, J B		1414	Cotton, Ignatius
1344	Le Roux, Mare		1415	Bunnell, Charles
1345	Bosque, Pierre		1416	Boyd, Pannilson
1346	Le Grand, Louis		1417	Canning, Joseph
1347	Perry, William		1418	Owens, James

American Prisoners of War Held at Jamaica During the War of 1812

1419	Davidson, Robert	1488	Stephen, George
1420	Stevoine, John	1489	Warner, Vincent
1421	Peterson, William	1490	Smith, William
1422	Silver, John	1491	Both, Thomas
1423	Lindoff, John	1492	Black, Britain Ham
1424	Smith, James	1493	Adair, Samuel
1425	Simpson, Thomas	1494	Gordon, Abaneza
1426	Eaton, James	1495	Shaw, William
1427	Colreto, Joseph	1496	Baylis, Charles
1428	Martin, Peter	1497	Parrote, Daniel
1429	Higgins, Peter	1498	Moderen, James
1430	Lewis, Daniel	1499	Jacobs, Peter
1431	Gay, Peter	1500	Nelson, Christopher
1432	Warden, Stephen	1501	Jackson, Benjamin
1433	Collum, Robert	1502	Nelson, Bristol
1434	Mollin, Charles	1503	Powell, William
1435	Johnson, Matthew	1504	Trader, William
1436	Boss, Jacob	1505	Walker, Thomas
1437	Hubbard, Robert	1506	Raymond, Nathaniel
1438	Mile, John	1507	Jones, James
1439	Joseph, Lewis	1508	Grace, Skinner
1440	Fodham, Charles	1509	Frazer, Henry
1441	Willies, John	1510	Fletcher, Aaron
1442	Antonia, Joseph	1511	Jenkins, William
1443	Hanchett, Charles	1512	Henry, James
1444	Davis, Henry	1513	Young, Sampson
1445	Lour, John	1514	Hall, D
1446	Willson, Thomas	1515	Rushs, Springer
1447	Garner, Robert	1516	Green, John
1448	McCullum, Joseph	1517	Corey, Allen
1449	Knott, John	1518	Longshore, Richard
1450	William, Thomas	1519	Dusenburg, David
1451	Read, Charles	1520	Haxon, Richard
1452	Olson, John	1521	Edy, Edward
1453	Thompson, James	1522	Phillips, R W
1454	Barry, John	1523	Cleveland, W C
1455	Phelps, A Y	1524	Budgeron, W
1456	Rawlings, Thomas	1525	Welliston, P
1457	Maris, William	1526	Toucy, E
1458	Ballabergen, Peter	1527	Burr, N M
1459	Bond, Thomas	1528	Hansey, William
1460	Frazier, York	1529	Shiddell, John
1461	Williamson, J	1530	Carpenter, Jeremiah
1462	Cotton, Philemon	1531	Haddington, Levi
1463	Peterson, Lewis	1532	Morris, James
1464	Johnson, Robert	1533	Wall, William
1465	Smith, Thomas	1534	Springer, William
1466	Stokeley, J	1535	Bayne, John
1467	Adams, Joseph C	1536	Roberts, Christopher
1468	Redman, James	1537	Isaacs, George
1469	Tooker, D A	1538	Loring, Shibbard
1470	Richards, Augustus	1539	Newham, Thomas
1471	Clark, John	1540	Jerrard, William
1472	Martin, George	1541	Fuller, Peter
1473	Bartlett, H G	1542	Hancock, Richard
1474	Laurence, Francis	1543	Bourn, Charles
1475	Bradford, John	1544	Small, William
1476	Stocking, William	1545	Akenford, John
1477	Lint, John	1546	Lacey, James
1478	Libbett, Richard	1547	Clarke, George
1479	Barlow, Rodney	1548	McKeel, James
1480	Thomas, Moses	1549	Beck, Michael
1481	Barrett, Peter	1550	Randell, Benjamin
1482	Story, Abiel	1551	Lang, John
1483	Sloane, William	1552	Simmonds, William
1484	Gracia, Archibald K	1553	Mills, George
1485	Thompson, George		
1486	Morris, James		
1487	Edinburgh, Peter		

American Prisoners of War Held at Jamaica During the War of 1812

Crew listing by ship

<u>26th October 1812</u>
- Gabriel, James
- Lewis, James H
- Pratt, George S
- Saue, Aaron
- Williams, John

<u>Active</u>
- Buntly, Isom
- Carter, James
- Day, Ephram
- Eagelson, David
- Griffin, William B
- Parsons, George
- Parsons, Isaac
- Parsons, William
- Turner, James

<u>American Gunboats</u>
- Anderson, John
- Antonia, Joseph
- Bakers, G D
- Barker, Abraham
- Bennett, William
- Boss, Jacob
- Boyd, Pannilson
- Brown, James
- Brown, James A
- Bunnell, Charles
- Canning, Joseph
- Carpenter, Benezer
- Carpenter, Jeremiah
- Carter, Henry
- Chinny, John
- Clay, William
- Collum, Robert
- Colreto, Joseph
- Connor, John
- Cooney, Joseph
- Corwell, Timothy
- Cotton, Ignatius
- Cottwell, Rowland
- Cowan, Jonathan
- Cricktus, Henry
- Crosby, James
- Cunningham, Henry
- Daly, John
- Davidson, Robert
- Davidson, William
- Davis, Henry
- Demon, John
- Eaton, James
- Edwards, William
- Falls, Richard
- Fodham, Charles
- Forewell, George
- Garner, Robert
- Gay, Peter
- Gibson, John
- Godfrey, William
- Green, Peter C
- Guerd, Joseph
- Hanchett, Charles
- Handley, William
- Hart, Philip
- Hibbard, George
- Higgins, Peter
- Horton, Richard
- Hubbard, Robert
- Jackson, Henry
- Jarvis, John
- Johnson, James
- Johnson, Matthew
- Jones, William
- Joseph, Lewis
- Knott, John
- Lewis, Daniel
- Lindoff, John
- Lour, John
- Martin, Peter
- McChrystal, Edward
- McCullum, Joseph
- McPhid, Reynold
- Mememey, James
- Mile, John
- Mollin, Charles
- Moon, Isaac
- Morris, George
- Nowland, James
- Olson, John
- Owens, James
- Parleman, William
- Perry, John
- Peterson, William
- Price, Charles
- Read, Charles
- Reynolds, James
- Rowley, Isaac
- Sadler, William
- Shamberk, Henry
- Shitcatt, Richard
- Silver, John
- Simmons, James
- Simpson, Thomas
- Smith, James
- Smith, John
- Stevens, Francis
- Stevoine, John
- Stewart, Charles
- Taylor, John
- Thompson, James
- Underhill, Isaac
- Warden, Stephen
- West, James
- William, Thomas
- Willies, John
- Willson, Thomas
- Wilson, A
- Wilson, John
- Young, Truman

<u>Ann</u>
- Buck, Balthazar
- Rodrigues, Manuel

<u>Ardent</u>
- Gebson, James

<u>Arethusa</u>
- Dolph, Joseph

<u>Assaw</u>
- Allen, James W
- Ballow, William
- Body, John
- Bryne, Thomas
- Colmen, Christian
- Foster, Jonathan
- Leon, Anthony
- Reed, John
- Roe, Cornwel
- Vandirson, Samuel

American Prisoners of War Held at Jamaica During the War of 1812

Bakerbrooke
    John, Samuel
Bernardo
    Montgomery, G
    Ray, Moses
    Tier, Albioa
Birch
    Hill, John
Blandie
    Bell, John
    Bryan, George
    Cain, William
    Clarke, Bernard
    Marley, John
    McGlachan, Turner
    Thornton, Walter
    Turner, James
    Wynn, John
Caroline
    Gregory, Caspar
    Hamsby, Andrew
Cartagenaian
    Arrvis, Jose
    Carrura, Josef
    Deas, Manuel
    Guiterroz, Francisco N
    Josef, Jean
    Mery, Pedro
    Peres, Juan Francisco
    Petet, Jean
    Rodriques, Luis
    Rousseau, Juan
    Sinpire, Pedro
    Yohet, Pedro
Casada el Narino
    ---, Boudon
    ---, Boungault
    ---, Comasin
    ---, Deudoit
    ---, Gasparo
    ---, Isaac
    ---, Leverien
    Alexander, Luis
    Aquilar, Pedro Jose
    Aquilaro, J
    Baco, F
    Bantista, Juan
    Bisar, Julian
    Calluga, Damasco
    Care, Beatte
    Casera, Juan
    Cebo, Francisco
    Corez, Juan Jose
    De Pena, N
    Deledra, Francisco
    Dias, Andrew
    Dreux, Edmond
    Fernandez, Emanuel
Casada el Narino
    Fernandez, Francisco
    Figuire, G
    Fortunel, Pedro
    Geraldine, Jose
    Gomez, Felipe
    Gorton, Luis
    Goumar, J
    Gregorio, Juan
    Guchand, Coco
    Joagin, Pedro
    Julian, Quitnet
    Lang, Jose
    Leceux, Augustine
    Legal, Juan
    Leneel, Francis
    Luis, Juan
    Padelia, F
    Raysan, Pedro
    Robert, Pedro
    Roco, Thomas
    Sanchez, Simon
    Secan, St Yago
    Thomas, Francisco
    Topoy, Pedro
    Volapy, Frafan
    Welaro, Pedro
Cato Georgiana
    Carlton, Thomas
    Chamberlain, John
    Dixon, James
    Gilbert, Martin
    Haufield, Jonathan
    Jemmison, Charles
    O'Neil, Edward
    Piper, Henry
    Scott, John
    Stewart, James W
    Williams, Jordon
    Wilson, James
Chance
    Armstrong, Charles
    Batiste, John
    Busher, Lawrence
    Butler, David
    Davis, Daul
    Dennet, William
    Derrick, William
    Dominico, John
    Gale, Russel
    Hauseir, Peter
    Hill, Francis
    Homan, John
    Little, William
    Maceman, Thomas
    Macklin, John
    Smith, Benjamin
    Towner, Benjamin
    Waters, Louis
    Whipple, John
Coquelle
    Allen, Bernard
    Askew, James
    Chamstead, John
    Goreham, John
    Henry, John
    Hill, William
    Kelly, Stephen
    Martin, John
    Otto, Nicholas
    Peurice, Thomas
    Roteu, Peter
    Smith, Robert
Cora
    Borely, David
    Hancock, Richard
    Iglecia, Juan
    Niel, Herrea
    Paillet, Peter Noel
    Porter, William
    Townson, George
    Wrenenui, Joseph
Cyrus
    Green, John

American Prisoners of War Held at Jamaica During the War of 1812

Dal
- Hields, William
- Nichols, Jacob
- Williams, Joseph

- Broadbew, William
- Clarke, Alb
- Crisby, Ransom
- Davenport, William
- Furrall, Thomas
- Hill, Ashmel
- Johnson, Thomas
- Maxey, Elias
- Thomas, Timothy
- Welcott, A

Decatur
- ---, Bentogomery
- ---, Duchazrell
- ---, Dupre
- ---, Gout
- ---, Lefarque
- ---, Lefure
- ---, Pick a Pick
- Adrie, Domingo
- Amontage, Louis
- Antonio, Manuel
- Artego, John
- Aucruen, John
- Beck, Francisco
- Bloham, Behrand
- Bouepou, Antonie
- Boutel, Isaac
- Brown, John
- Callerist, Collin
- Callerist, Y P
- Caximo, Josef M
- Charleston, Joseph
- Class, Jean
- Combs, John
- Daimont, Louis
- Day, S
- Decossae, Louis
- Denis, Generio
- Dequen, Julian
- Detale, Juan
- Disgardins, Louis J
- Dixon, Dominique
- Dixon, P
- Dolino, Angel
- Drago, Francisco
- Eperwiere, Jean
- Free, George
- Gabeirre, John
- Ghado, Maina
- Gillbert, Antonio
- Goding, Joseph
- Jacobson, Frederick
- Johnson, Charles
- Johnson, William
- Joseph, William
- Lagoardett, Pedro
- Lamel, Louis
- Laory, Josh
- Lewis, Valentine
- Lorique, G
- Mancell, John
- Manger, Gear
- Martin, Louis
- McNeil, Daniel
- Michel, Chouran
- Michell, Jean Batista
- Nolt, Paul

- Norins, William
- Peland, Louis Marie
- Peters, George
- Phdiger, John
- Phillips, John
- Phillips, William
- Phyning, Josiah
- Pierro, Jean
- Poteron, Julian
- Puritan, Themat
- Renard, Jean
- Rionaine, Jean
- Roshin, Dominique
- Saffarque, Andrew
- Seagrave, Jean
- Steel, John
- Street, James
- Taylor, William
- Tesser, Sean
- Veitte, Etanne
- Welch, P
- Wescott, William
- Whedber, Joseph
- Williams, John

Defiance
- Allen, John
- Baker, William
- Baptist, Joseph
- Berto, John
- Blackford, John
- Blakely, Sinclair
- Brian, Peter
- Cable, Peter
- Caderer, John
- Case, John
- Chapel, John Peter
- Chessm, George
- Currey, George
- Daily, William
- Darssliu, John
- Depot, Henry
- Devenero, Francis
- Dewallis, Macklin
- Durant, John
- Dursse, Laurence
- Dyer, Shubald
- Fisher, John
- Forkiere, Edward
- Frank, John
- Furneau, George
- Gebeau, Anthony
- Gebeau, John
- Gerloo, Peter
- Homan, William
- Ioe, Francis
- Jack, John
- Jacob, John
- Jantzue, Lewis
- Jenkins, Luderwick
- John, John
- Joseph, John
- La Fait, Lewis
- Lacette, John
- Lewis, John
- Little, Peter
- Littlefield, Erick
- Madura, Francisco
- Manyard, John
- McBride, James
- Morterae, John
- Nyon, Francis

American Prisoners of War Held at Jamaica During the War of 1812

    Paptist, John
    Powell, John
    Prior, John
    Ray, John
    Robins, Thomas
    Scott, Eleazer
    Seldon, John
    Simon, Joseph
    Thompson, Joseph
    Williams, John

Delight
    Jerrard, William
    Loring, Shibbard
    Newham, Thomas

Dolores
    Alexander, Lewis
    Bailey, Samuel
    Baque, Jean
    Bateiers, Platricia
    Bernard, Peter
    Bilot, Pierre
    Bilot, Pierre An
    Bodeye, Michael
    Clarke, John
    Drew, Edmond
    Faulin, Joseph
    Hernandes, Nicholas
    Key, Oleanto
    Lapongau, Chery
    Lespioult, Francis
    Lewis, Augustus
    Liberal, August
    Martin, Richard
    Romero, Ignacio
    Savanel, Jean G

Dominicana
    Brown, Joseph
    Calbert, James
    Harris, John Winslow
    Spreggs, Archibald
    Wyatt, Benjamin

Dorothea
    Destandes, Joseph
    Laurence, Francis

Eliza
    Dalbrow, Daniel
    Deale, William
    Farmer, Robert
    Harrington, Samuel
    Lloyd, Robert
    MaCarty, Frederick
    McDonald, Daniel
    Mitchell, James
    Morris, Benjamin
    Murdock, Archibald
    Orne, Julian
    Pearce, David
    Phillips, John
    Robb, Charles
    Robinson, Richard
    Skinner, Lewis
    Underhill, Elijah

Elizabeth
    Stewart, Henry
    Warden, James

Ellena
    Black, William
    Hall, Charles
    Lane, John

Enterprize
    ---, Antonio
    ---, Bechariah
    ---, Chripo
    ---, Francisco
    ---, Georges
    ---, Joseph
    ---, Manuel
    ---, Martin
    ---, Oseana
    Ambrosia, John
    Ball, E
    Barlow, John
    Bartire, John
    Bezzett, Robert
    Boyia, Thomas
    Butcher, Jacob
    Court, John
    Dexter, Charles
    Doing, D O
    Gasee, Nicholas
    Hauce, John H
    Jack, John
    Jackerman, Count
    Jackson, John
    Jennings, Francis
    Laniba, Michael
    Marine, Daniel
    Molaneir, Pedro
    Morando, Domingo
    Oure, Constant
    Pedro, John
    Pedro, John
    Pedro, Manuel
    Pierre, John
    Puosa, Joseph
    Randales, Thomas
    Robien, John
    Rodrigo, Andrew
    Rough, Daniel
    Stan, Pedro
    Thompson, Thomas
    Turk, Richard

Fanny
    Black, Joseph
    Harrison, Samuel
    Harrison, Samuel

Farmer's Daughter
    Antonio, Joseph
    Benton, Samuel
    Carlo, James
    Dawson, John
    Edwards, William
    Griffin, Heathcote
    Hurst, James
    Johnson, Thomas
    Kingdom, John
    Martin, William
    Smith, John
    Smith, Robert
    Webster, Michael

Flora
    Bucklin, Warren
    Moore, William
    Stevens, Russel

Fly
    Berlack, William
    Brown, William
    Clark, Sylvester
    Elleridge, James H
    Merrhew, Joseph
    Owen, Francis

Fortuneatus

American Prisoners of War Held at Jamaica During the War of 1812

Isaacs, George

Grauosa
Albarets, Alanasta
Bertrand, Jean
Jacob, Louis
Jaque, Jacinta Jean
Lassetto, Joseph
Martini, Alberto
Pujne, Dominique
Rosiere, Celestian

Hamilton
Adams, Cornelius
Branson, M
Brown, Daniel
Dyer, Watson
Patterson, M
Peters, John
Seale, Charles
Smith, John
Thurston, Troy

Hazard
Anquin, Anthony
Samson, Pure

Henrietta
Johnson, Robert
Porter, Hans
Roderick, Anthony

Jennett
Clark, James
de doVair, Epprough
Devaril, John
Dyer, Charles
Gowner, Joseph
Harris, John
Holmes, Isaac
Key, John
Kuntoz, Jacob
Mackboy, John
Pickens, Thomas
Pockmet, Zackuess
Salisbury, Jose
Skipper, John
Stanley, Simon
Turner, Joshua
Walker, Daniel
Whitney, William
Wilboury, David

John
Beck, Michael
Betagh, James
Charles, Stephen
Fleury, Joseph
Furrell, John
Henderson, Joseph
Hinchman, George
Hyer, Rober
Lang, John
Lenquish, Mathew
Merritt, Samuel
Mills, George
Randell, Benjamin
Simmonds, William
White, James

Joseph & Mary
Barr, Benjamin
Bayley, Gardner
Beard, Andrew
Bettys, Henry
Bond, Abraham
Bremfield, George
Buch, Josuah
Carpenter, Lewis
Clarke, John
Cosgrove, J G
Cromwell, Joseph
Cuthall, Hoste
Dallew, James
Davidson, Samuel
Davis, John
De Camp, William
De Fatrime, Jacque
Dixon, James
Dotterside, William
Drew, Exra
Edgerton, Charles
Everson, Benjamin
Fifer, Jacob
Ford, Samuel
Forster, William
Gardner, Samuel
Gleeves, Jacob
Gluton, M
Gordon, Worton
Goverman, Frederick
Goverman, Frederick
Graham, John
Gray, John
Hazledine, John
Henry, William
Hill, Ross
Howland, Barnalas
Jones, Michael
Jordon, Benjamin
Joseph, John
Lee, Henry
Leuox, John
Lewis, Winslow
Long, Nathaniel
Loring, Elephet
Martin, John
Metz, George
Moore, Thomas
Nelson, John
Parker, Joseph
Patton, Edward
Peek, Darius
Pitt, Gabes
Purdew, Joseph
Richardson, William
Roberts, Samuel
Roe, John
Rutter, William
Satchell, Thomas
Shepheard, John
Slippy, William
Small, Jacob
Smith, Benjamin
Smith, Charles
Smith, Robert
Spalding, Reeves
Stevenson, George
Storey, John
Sullivan, Daniel
Summers, Philip
Waltham, Charles
Westcott, William
Williams, M
Wulfurtz, Abraham
Young, William

La Union
---, Sequnda
Aquilar, Lorenzo

American Prisoners of War Held at Jamaica During the War of 1812

Belor, Miguel
Beltram, Martin
Crostinal, Demetreo
Damian, Jose
Francisco, Juan
Lopes, Victorino
Martel, Pedro
Mealo, Vinzente
Mosquera, Jose
Napo, Casar
Neo, Juan
Pedro, Juan
Peres, Domingo
Perez, M Antonio
Rabuirero, Nicolas
Uerin, Julian

Lapwing
Bennett, James
Bowlin, John
Brown, John
Clarke, George
Corral, Philip
Dibbett, Charles A
Gibbons, John
Gould, Thomas
Jennings, John
Jerry, Mathias H
Johnson, Samuel J
Miles, Robert
Sole, Jordan
Welsh, John
Williams, William

Le Expedecion
Akenford, John
Bourn, Charles
Clarke, George
Lacey, James
McKeel, James
Small, William

Le Galzo
Aquire, Bernardo
Cezard, J
Chambiere, Theodore
Chambierre, Joseph
Charrier, Jean B
Edward, Pierre
La Place, Peter
Mazire, Francis
Reuon, Santiago

Le Ventura
---, Hermon
Albertman, John
Anthony, Francisco
Anthony, Juan
Antonio, Jean
Barderse, Josse
Barlez, Juan
Bernard, Leonard
Butil, Francis
Cadinetto, Robert
Dusane, Levi
Francisco, Juan
Heger, Francisco
Jasser, Juan
Joseph, Peter
Lamber, Pier
Logine, Zamie
Mauwi, Juan
Nelson, Jean
Nelson, Piere
Pane, Cheny

Peter, Juan
Piere, Jean
Pole, Juan
Roper, John
Roysdon, Joseph

Lovely Lass
Alexander, Samuel
Arbona, John
Army, Lewis
Barlow, Aroa
Barnes, John
Bisong, Juba
Carter, Joshua
Cloud, Peter
Courade, Christopher
Croker, Lemiel
Cute, William
Dibwa, John
Dick, John
Eden, Thomas
Emar, Joseph
Foutnay, Francis
Frank, Peter
Fraunswell, Lewis
Ghering, John
Griffin, Samuel
Griffiths, Edward
Hanson, Edward
Heschaultz, Charles
Hine, Henry
Jackson, John
Johnson, Charles
Leut, William
Lott, John
Lowrie, Joseph
Maddison, Charless
Maxwell, William
McCulloch, Alexander
McNeil, Daniel
Montgomery, Thomas
Moore, Jonathan
Murtien, Charles
Neil, Jeremiah
Nixon, Lewis
Ribe, Francis
Roberts, Michael
Sasky, John
Saumon, Pier
Seutimand, Alexander
Simpson, James
Smith, James
Smith, Joseph
Sturko, P
Turner, Henry
Tynes, John
Vincent, David
Williams, John

Madisonia
Belt, James
Crawford, John
Davis, Wallis
Ford, Bapt
Gilpin, John
Hopkins, Caleb
Jackson, George
Jervis, William
Joseph, Anthony
Sturges, E P
Williamson, John

Maria
Allen, Francis

American Prisoners of War Held at Jamaica During the War of 1812

    Brown, William
    Fishwort, William
    Haman, John
    Lane, Thomas
    Lewis, Peter
    Lock, N
    Orick, John
    Tieu, John
    Windfinde, William

<u>Mary</u>
    Berry, James
    Brown, James
    Brown, William
    Buckley, Walter
    Cropper, Isaac
    Cuffy, Paul
    Fivash, John
    Hicks, Benjamin
    Hunter, Francis
    Hutchins, B
    Hutchins, B
    Jones, John
    Ketchell, George
    Lounsby, Frederick
    Lynn, John
    May, Nicholas
    Moore, William
    Pitner, Aaron
    Rolston, Leven
    Strong, Selvister
    Tagers, Anthony
    Wells, Anthony
    Whitman, Henry

<u>Mary Ann</u>
    ---, Luidoff
    Balard, Peter
    Baley, Oliver
    Bata, Peter
    Blain, David
    Boudmon, Andrew
    Carbon, John
    Cassaire, John
    Chariol, Peter
    Chine, Peter
    Clermont, J B
    Duprat, Anthony
    Dutuor, John
    Field, Henry
    George, Thomas
    Gowdon, F E
    Gree, Joseph
    Harry, Richard
    Harvey, Peter
    Hiley, David
    Jones, John
    Jones, Samuel
    Keith, Thomas
    Lactie, John
    Latham, Jerry
    Leatherby, Joseph
    Lirour, Peter
    Lopez, Francis
    Martin, Francis
    Meleache, Jean
    Norris, Gilles
    Pascal, Antonio
    Porrn, Joseph
    Robinson, James
    Sidawire, Julian
    Warren, Series
    Williams, Joseph

<u>Milly</u>
    Berry, Gorton
    Brown, John
    Joseph, John
    Nelson, James
    Nowland, John
    Olmer, Joseph
    St. Clair, Robert

<u>Morning Star</u>
    Allen, Joseph
    Benson, John
    Connor, William
    Homer, Jacob
    Kroger, John
    Settle, Ellis
    Winston, Thomas S

<u>Mount Vernon</u>
    Baker, Peter
    Cameron, America
    Cameron, Eli
    Dixon, Moses
    Eastward, Jack
    Johnson, Dick
    Lewis, John

<u>Nettervitte</u>
    Baker, Thomas
    Baptiste, John
    Brackston, William
    Cooper, Peter
    Harvey, James
    Hindman, John
    Jenkins, Thomas
    Johnnos, Logan
    Jones, James
    Kell, Francis
    Kitten, Abraham
    Madding, John
    Southcombe, Peter
    Walt, Samuel

<u>Neustra Cantado</u>
    Betrange, Pedro
    Clemon, Pierre
    Davis, G P
    Harris, Robert
    Manusa, Osa
    Manwell, Antonio
    Maria, Jon
    Marta, Pedro
    Pairer, Francis
    Peter, Mathias
    Rodriguez, Oza

<u>New Granada</u>
    Grandy, Poll
    La Cloud, Peter
    Le Rose, Ramoin

<u>Packet</u>
    Campbell, E
    Douglass, John
    Richmond, William
    Vance, Thomas

<u>Peru</u>
    Hazel, John
    Means, Robert
    Reid, Robert
    Stone, Samuel
    Waistcoat, Rufus
    Williams, John

<u>Philip</u>
    Allen, Henry
    Baker, James
    Baldwin, Pearson

American Prisoners of War Held at Jamaica During the War of 1812

Brown, Thomas
Christie, William
Croker, Daul
Davis, Luther
Diskanskep, Christian
Flood, Samuel
Foxwill, George
Glen, Peter
Hall, John
Header, William
Holmes, William
Johnston, Benjamin
Jones, Henry
Jones, Peter
Lee, John Roger
Paree, S W
Peters, John
Renneck, Isaac
Robinson, Thomas
Rosin, John
Sullen, Peter
William, Daniel

Pirtshire
Apt, James
Carrol, John
Denike, John
Diamond, John
Donaldson, Frederick
Le Jea, Artimus
Marie, John
McLear, Francis
Miller, Christian
Nachidon, Francis
Pratt, Allen
Reick, Nicholas
Reynolds, Christian
Seburia, Thomas
Travis, James
Trout, Nathaniel

Poor Sailor
Bailey, Joseph
Blair, John K
Blenny, William
Bolston, Jacob
Bramore, Christopher
Britain, John
Brown, John
Brown, Peter
Brown, William D
Burdett, Enos
Chalmers, David
Cochran, Paunay
Cocks, John S H
Cooper, Sylus
Cromerty, Vincent
Dart, Stanton
Depont, Lewis
Dickson, Peter
Dotlaud, Martin
Elliot, Alexander
Faviman, Lawrence
Freeman, Maul
Gorgaud, Michael
Gregon, Francis
Harrison, Isaac
Hasser, John
Hatcher, Thomas
Hauscorn, John
Holston, Isaac
Inkley, Thomas
Jennings, Henry

Lewis, Francis
Lund, Oliver
Martin, J W
McLaughlin, P
Moore, William
Nicholson, George
Pouch, John
Randell, Edward
Rosinloof, Thomas
Russell, James
Seprast, John
Smart, David
St. George, George
Stevenson, David
Swain, Luke
Tequin, William
Thomas, John
Thompson, Philip
Wade, Squire R

Prest
Malther, William

Rachel
Chapman, J L
Harrison, James
Lewis, Eben A
Moucrieff, James
Vanwick, Thomas
Walton, John

Rebecca Sims
Anwiste, Hugh
Banks, William
Brewton, M
Brewton, William
Daniels, John
Frances, Henry
Garbin, John
Guttring, John
Hall, Daniel
Hangerford, John
Hart, George
Hickey, James
Jones, Jacob
Laman, William
Morris, Jacob
Selby, Miles
Skakelton, Roger
Stolesby, Anthony
Stuart, Charles
Winter, William
Witman, Henry

Romano & Adamante
Antonio, Joseph
Antonio, Juan P
Baptista, Juan
Boughon, Miguel
de Anuila, Peadro
de Manuel, Juz
Hulse, G J
Johnson, Abraham
Manuel, J
Speries, Thomas
Voudover, Lawrence
Wilkinson, Thomas

San Francisco de Paula
---, ---
---, Celestier
---, Felis
---, Francisco
---, Velario
---, Ventura
Augustine, Cadet

American Prisoners of War Held at Jamaica During the War of 1812

Aurry, Lewis
Baptista, Antonio
Barritt, Roman
Basante, Jose
Begotte, Juan
Boale, Jose
Cabais, Pedro
Capura, Nicholas
Carruation, Corui
Cassack, Charles
Catalante, Imannual
Cordelia, Nicholas
de Cruz, Juan
Fernandes, Euscbio
Flurit, Aman
Forne, Barto
Francisco, Jose
Guy, Luis
Jose, Thomas
Juan, Pedro
La Cruz, Juan
La Lauda, Pedro
Lacurries, Juan Batista
Legre, Juan
Luero, Pedro
Luis, Pedro
Martin, Juan
Noche, Juan
Papil, Sauteaga
Pedro, Juan
Phillips, Bertram
Porto, Juan
Powell, Juan
Rodriguez, Antonio
Saladin, Carlos
Sario, Juan
Vack, Pedro
Venar, Juan
Williams, Juan

San Francisco Navier
---, Autouel
---, Piudtel
Barchela, Andres
Barrel, Juan
Batista, Luis
Blanco, Carlo
Cherin, Pedro
Coturel, Juan
de Legran, Juan
Dolore, Juan
Dupies, Alexander
Gerin, Luis
Gomie, Andres
Jose, Pedro
Lacroyde, Houore
Maltes, Francisco
Marciar, Juan
Masse, Juan M
Micridales, Joseph
Montati, Antonio
Ordet, Tal
Peliou, Jose
Rodriguez, Manuel
Rosario, Francisco
Rosse, Henri
Sarasin, Fifi
Silotic, Antonio
Talon, Francisco
Tebez, Martin
Tebot, Pedro
Vasques, Thomas

Saratoga
Befay, Samuel
Cleburn, Francis
Cotterell, Thomson
Cowloff, Jacob
Neal, Francis
Squibb, Silas
White, Joseph
Wilson, Cornelius

Sauders
Clackston, James
Fairo, James
George, William
Jackson, William
John, Cato
Norris, Samuel
Webb, James

Sophia
Theobald, Charles

Superb
Baptist, John
Hamilton, William
Hamlet, Joshua
Mirack, Isaac
Moservy, Daniel J
Penn, William
Shaw, Francis
Welsh, William

Suspense
Bachindoz, Enock
Burnham, William
Kirby, John
Mackey, John
Miller, James
Onil, Henry
Serin, John
Snow, Samuel
Turpin, Jacques

Swift
Beari, Samuel
Cater, Benjamin
Croft, William
Dow, Thomas
Lee, William
Millet, Andrew
Peabody, John

Teuiriffe
Jocelyn, John
Marsback, John F
Martin, Luther
Smith, David

Three Friends
Brydges, Culpeper
Course, Peter
Fawcett, Elles
Fenhold, David
Grant, Israel
Hirst, Charles
Johnson, Joseph
Martin, John
Wallace, John
West, William

Vixen
Alexander, James
Allen, Asa
Ammors, John
Arrickson, D
Bayley, Frederick
Betincourt, Lewis
Betincourt, Nathaniel A
Blace, James

American Prisoners of War Held at Jamaica During the War of 1812

Borrison, John
Bradley, Abraham
Bridges, Edward
Brown, Obadiah
Brown, Philip
Burrows, Edward
Call, Benjamin
Carrott, William
Carter, James
Closcharden, John
Clury, William
Cocks, William
Cox, William
Crawford, Robert
Cunningham, James
Cutter, Abraham
Cutter, Abraham
David, Charles
Davis, E R
Davis, John
Davis, John
De Maury, Lewis
Dickey, Robert
Dore, James
Drayton, Glen
Dunbar, Charles
Dykes, Sol
Elberte, Mingo
Elms, Robert
Emmery, David
Evans, John
Fokey, William
Fraser, John
Furney, John
Goldrick, William
Graves, J
Harris, John
Hartman, John
Harvey, James
Harvey, Michael
Hauagan, Peter
Heber, Neil
Horseley, Samuel
Hunter, William M
Jackson, George
Jacobs, Charles
Jarua, Charles
Jenkins, John
John, Peter
Johnson, Abraham
Joiner, Benjamin
Jordan, John G
Kawson, George
Keller, John
King, Thomas
King, Thomas
Knowlton, David
Knull, Heinrich
Larkins, John
Leggett, George
Leof, Unis
Mackey, Michael
Mansfield, James
Mattolland, William
McCabe, Levi
McFart, John
McNeil, Archibald
Merritt, Erek
Millega, Gilbert
Monteque, Caleb
Nutter, George

O'Neal, Andrew
Orno, John
Patterson, John
Peter, Solomon
Peters, John
Pettigrew, Thomas
Quick, George
Quigley, Matthew
Ram, Thomas
Reed, G W
Rice, Samuel
Round, William
Sales, Samuel
Satterwhite, Edwin
Selby, Joseph
Shephard, Joseph
Shields, William
Smith, John
Smith, Timothy
Staggs, Thomas
Stevens, James
Stokes, John
Sullender, C
Summer, John
Thomas, Joseph
Thompson, Charles A
Thompson, John
Tomkins, Joseph
Turner, Michael
Volt, Peter
Walgrove, Charles
Washington, Z
Williamson, George
Wood, Jacob

Whim
Brown, James
Coit, S
Dyer, John
Garland, Robert
Hatch, Walter
Henry, Thomas
Lugh, Wright
Miller, John
Mills, James
Stevens, Leverett
Watson, Benjamin

William
Drummond, Robert
Emery, John
Goss, John
McClintock, William
Miller, Oliver
Mitchell, Elisha
Sears, Zebrua

William & Mary
Bayne, John
Haddington, Levi
Morris, James
Roberts, Christopher
Springer, William
Wall, William

William Penn
Elisha, Thomas
Godfrey, William
Market, John
Moss, Elijah
Patterson, N
Perkins, Joseph
Perkins, Seth
Simpson, James
Trust, Elijah

American Prisoners of War Held at Jamaica During the War of 1812

    Van Faivan, Thomas
    Watson, William
    Wysman, E C

<u>Wolfe</u>

    Cornelius, Peter
    Coursoll, Peter
    Pepper, Martin
    Swatoz, Chuspere
    Williams, John

<u>Young Eagle</u>
    Blair, Thomas
    Brown, John
    Dauast, Nicholas
    Oldner, George
    Thomas, John

American Prisoners of War Held at Jamaica During the War of 1812

Americans on British ships

Baldwin, Theophilus
Bowen, John
Branson, C J
Budie, Andrew
Burke, Thomas
Butler, Henry
Cambell, Henry
Coles, Charles
Collins, John
Crosier, William
Davis, Richman
Dick, David
Dolft, John
Elford, Roswell
Foster, Samuel
Franklin, Edward
Frederick, John
Freeman, Thomas
Fuller, Peter
Gomer, Edward
Gough, Moses
Gould, Samuel
Handy, Joseph
Hawthorn, William
Hendry, William
Hubbard, Elijah
Hutchins, Amos
Johnson, Robert
Jones, Cato
Layton, N G
Mann, Charles
McCormick, James
McLaughlin, Edward
Middleton, Thomas
Miller, Thomas
Nicholson, Jesse
Nicholson, John
Ogdon, Thomas
Osbourn, Thomas
Peck, Salisbury
Philips, John
Pluck, Mike
Potts, Samuel
Richards, Thomas
Rogers, Thomas
Rosemond, William
Smith, Charles
Tapp, George
Taylor, Alexander
Willey, Andrew
Williams, John
Williamson, Richard
Young, Joseph

American Prisoners of War Held at Jamaica During the War of 1812

Service affiliation not known

Adair, Samuel
Adams, Joseph C
Allen, Ebenezer
Andre, Antonie
Antonio, Jose
Ballabergen, Peter
Barlow, Rodney
Barrett, Peter
Barry, John
Bartlett, H G
Battle, Joseph
Baylis, Charles
Berios, Samoa
Black, Britain Ham
Bommell, Andre
Bond, Thomas
Bortiense, Jacques
Bosque, Pierre
Both, Thomas
Bouche, John
Bradford, John
Brown, John
Budgeron, W
Burr, N M
Carier, Pierre
Carnation, Jose
Charles, John
Clark, John
Cleveland, W C
Coleby, John
Corey, Allen
Cotton, Philemon
Curtis, Dennis
Davis, John
Diani, Lewis
Dodge, Lewis
Dusenburg, David
Edinburgh, Peter
Edy, Edward
Fencho, Eiten
Fertion, J B
Fertizon, Rene
Fletcher, Aaron
Fox, Edward
Frazer, Henry
Frazier, York
French, Abraham
Fuller, Peter
Gaul, John
Gomand, Joseph
Gomand, Pierre
Gordon, Abaneza
Grace, Skinner
Gracia, Archibald K
Graperius, John
Green, John
Hall, D
Hansey, William
Harris, William
Haxon, Richard
Henry, James
Hyde, Thomas
Jackson, Benjamin
Jacobs, Peter
Jenkins, William
Johnson, Robert
Jones, Henry
Jones, James
Kinner, Joseph S

Laurence, Francis
Le Grand, Louis
Le Roux, Mare
Libbett, Richard
Lint, John
List, Moses
Little, Charles
Lombard, Ephrim
Longshore, Richard
Louis, Pierre
Maddison, Samuel
Maria, Joseph
Maris, William
Marque, Antonio
Marshall, D F
Martin, George
McCarthy, Samuel
McCormick, James
McKinnee, James
Merit, Isaac
Moderen, James
Montgomery, R
Morean, Guettend
Morris, James
Natal, Juan
Navallo, Diego
Nelson, Bristol
Nelson, Christopher
Oliney, Samuel
Parish, John
Parrote, Daniel
Parsons, James
Perkins, Simon
Perry, William
Peterson, Lewis
Phelps, A Y
Phillips, R W
Powell, William
Ramsdell, Charles
Rawlings, Thomas
Raymond, Nathaniel
Redman, James
Richards, Augustus
Roberts, G R
Robisa, Victor
Rushs, Springer
Sandford, Abraham
Sewell, George
Shaw, William
Shiddell, John
Simon, Jerome
Sloane, William
Smith, John
Smith, John
Smith, Thomas
Smith, William
Stephen, George
Stocking, William
Stokeley, J
Story, Abiel
Thomas, Moses
Thompson, George
Tooker, D A
Toucy, E
Towley, Henry
Trader, William
Venian, Charles
Voss, Matthew
Walker, Thomas

American Prisoners of War Held at Jamaica During the War of 1812

Warner, Vincent
Welliston, P
Whitehead, John
Williamson, J

Wilson, Charles
Young, Sampson

American Prisoners of War Held at Jamaica During the War of 1812

United States Marines

Allen, Asa
Ammors, John
Bayley, Frederick
Bayley, Gardner
Betincourt, Lewis
Betincourt, Nathaniel A
Closcharden, John
De Maury, Lewis
Dursse, Laurence
Edgerton, Charles
John, Peter
Joiner, Benjamin
Keller, John
Larkins, John
Leuox, John
Mansfield, James
Millega, Gilbert
Monteque, Caleb
O'Neal, Andrew
Pascal, Antonio
Quigley, Matthew
Round, William
Sales, Samuel
Tomkins, Joseph
Walgrove, Charles
Waltham, Charles
Washington, Z

www.ingramcontent.com/pod-product-compliance
Lightning Source LLC
Chambersburg PA
CBHW080542230426
43663CB00015B/2682